www.wadsworth.com

wadsworth.com is the World Wide Web site for Wadsworth Publishing Company and is your direct source to dozens of online resources.

At *wadsworth.com* you can find out about supplements, demonstration software, and student resources. You can also send e-mail to many of our authors and preview new publications and exciting new technologies.

wadsworth.com
Changing the way the world learns®

The Lifespan

SIXTH EDITION

Guy R. Lefrançois
University of Alberta

 Wadsworth Publishing Company

I(T)P® An International Thomson Publishing Company

Belmont, CA · Albany, NY · Bonn · Boston · Cincinnati · Detroit · Johannesburg · London
Madrid · Melbourne · Mexico City · New York · Paris · Singapore · Tokyo · Toronto · Washington

Education Editor: Dianne Lindsay
Marketing Manager: Becky Tollerson
Assistant Editor: Valerie Morrison
Project Editor: Jennie Redwitz
Production: Detta Penna, Penna Design and Production
Print Buyer: Barbara Britton
Permissions Editor: Bob Kauser
Designer: Randall Goodall, Seventeenth Street Studios
Art Editor: Peter Penna, Penna Design and Production
Copy Editor: Donald Pharr
Illustrator: Pat Rogondino
Photo Researcher: Susie Friedman
Cover Designer: Stephen Rapley
Cover Illustration: Ferruccio Sardella
Compositor: Thompson Type
Printer: World Color

Printed in the United States of America
2 3 4 5 6 7 8 9 10

For more information, contact Wadsworth Publishing Company,
10 Davis Drive, Belmont, CA 94002, or electronically at
http://www.thomson.com/wadsworth.html

Library of Congress Cataloging-in-Publication Data

Lefrançois, Guy R.
    The lifespan / Guy R. Lefrançois. — 6th ed.
        p.   c.m.
    Includes bibliographical references and index.
    ISBN 0-534-55692-2 (alk. paper)
    1. Developmental psychology.   I. Title.
BF713.L44   1999
155—dc21   98-47232

International Thomson Publishing Europe
Berkshire House 168-173
High Holborn
London, WC1V 7AA, England

International Thomson Editores
Campos Eliseos 385, Piso 7
Col. Polanco
11560 México D.F. México

Thomas Nelson Australia
102 Dodds Street
South Melbourne 3205
Victoria, Australia

International Thomson Publishing Asia
221 Henderson Road
#05-10 Henderson Building
Singapore 0315

Nelson Canada
1120 Birchmount Road
Scarborough, Ontario
Canada M1K 5G4

International Thomson Publishing Japan
Hirakawacho Kyowa Building, 3F
2-2-1 Hirakawacho
Chiyoda-ku, Tokyo 102, Japan

International Thomson Publishing GmbH
Königswinterer Strasse 418
53227 Bonn, Germany

International Thomson Publishing
Southern Africa
Building 18, Constantia Park
240 Old Pretoria Road
Halfway House, 1685 South Africa

DEDICATION

*To my grandparents and all the old people
without whom we would not be here today.*

*To my children and all the young people
without whom we will not be here tomorrow.*

BRIEF CONTENTS

CONTENTS

Know then thyself, presume not God to scan;
The proper study of Mankind is Man.

ALEXANDER POPE
Essays on Man

The dwarf sees farther than the giant, when
he has the giant's shoulders to stand on.

SAMUEL TAYLOR COLERIDGE
The Friend

*Sir Roger told them, with the air of a man who would
not give his judgment rashly, that much might be said
on both sides.*

JOSEPH ADDISON
The Spectator, Vol. 1

*Nature is often hidden, sometimes overcome;
seldom extinguished.*

FRANCES BACON
Of Nature in Man

*I wish either my father or my mother, or indeed
both of them, as they were in duty both equally
bound to it, had minded what they were about
when they begot me.*

LAURENCE STERNE
Tristram Shandy

■ CHAPTER SIX

Social Development: Infancy **155**

Language was not powerful enough to describe the infant phenomenon.

CHARLES DICKENS
Nicholas Nickleby

When the first baby laughed for the first time, the laugh broke into a thousand pieces and they all went skipping about, and that was the beginning of fairies.

JAMES MATTHEW BARRIE
Peter Pan

PART THREE

Early Childhood **181**

■ CHAPTER SEVEN

**Physical and Cognitive Development:
Early Childhood** **183**

Go directly—see what she's doing,
and tell her she mustn't.

Punch, 1872

■ CHAPTER EIGHT

Social Development: Early Childhood 215

More than either, it [England] resembles a family, a rather stuffy Victorian family, with not many black sheep in it but with all its cupboards bursting with skeletons. It has rich relations who have to be kow-towed to and poor relations who are horribly sat upon, and there is a deep conspiracy about the source of the family income. It is a family in which the young are generally thwarted and most of the power is in the hands of irresponsible uncles and bedridden aunts. Still, it is a family.

GEORGE ORWELL
England, Your England

> *Every time a child says "I don't believe in fairies,"*
> *there is a little fairy somewhere that falls down dead.*
>
> JAMES MATTHEW BARRIE
> *Peter Pan*

PART FOUR

Middle Childhood **243**

■ **CHAPTER NINE**

Physical and Cognitive Development:
Middle Childhood **245**

> *"I dare say you haven't had practice," said the Queen.*
> *"When I was your age, I always did it for half an hour*
> *a day. Why, sometimes I've believed as many as six*
> *impossible things before breakfast."*
>
> LEWIS CARROLL
> *Through the Looking-Glass and What Alice Found There*

> *A traveler at Sparta, standing long upon one leg, said to a*
> *Lacedaemonian: "I do not believe you can do as much."*
> *"True," said he, "but every goose can."*
>
> PLUTARCH
> *Laconic Apothegms*

> *See the happy moron, He doesn't give a damn,*
> *I wish I were a moron, My God! Perhaps I am!*
>
> ANONYMOUS
> *Eugenics Review, 1929*

> *Everybody worships me, it's nauseating.*
>
> NOEL COWARD
> *Present Laughter*

*Live as long as you may, the first twenty years
are the longest half of your life.*

ROBERT SOUTHEY
The Doctor

We think so because other people think so,
Or because—or because—after all we do think so,
Or because, we were told so, and think we must think so,
Or because we once thought so, and think we still think so,
Or because having thought so, we think we will think so.

HENRY SIDGWICK
Lines Composed in His Sleep

■ CHAPTER FOURTEEN

Give me chastity and continence, but not yet.

ST. AUGUSTINE
Confessions

I am convinced digestion is the great secret of life.

SYDNEY SMITH
in a letter to Arthur Kinglake

Happiness in marriage is entirely a matter of chance.

JANE AUSTEN
Northanger Abbey

It is always the season for the old to learn.

AESCHYLUS
Fragments

*I keep looking back, as far as I can remember, and I
can't think what it was like to feel young, really young.*

JOHN OSBORNE
Look Back in Anger

So little done, so much to do!

Last words of
CECIL JOHN RHODES

PART NINE
The End 539

And come he slow or come he fast,
It is but Death who comes at last.

SIR WALTER SCOTT
Marmion

Dear Reader,

My grandmother put it very simply: "There's no room for humility in a preface! It's like in advertising. If your preface is going to work, it has to say, 'Listen up, you guys! This is the best dang lifespan textbook you'll ever see!' And then you tell them why. And then you repeat it in case they didn't get it the first time. Then promise them a T-shirt or a mug or something if they buy it."

So listen up, you guys! This is the best. . . .

No, I can't do that. I can't even promise you a mug, although, for a minute there, it seemed like a good idea. And it would have been free with the purchase of two copies of the book. (Hey, you could buy one for your grandmother.) But I'm not a street hawker. So let me just give you only a handful of brief facts about *The Lifespan*.

The purpose of *The Lifespan* is to lay before you, in simple language, the concepts and preoccupations of lifespan developmental psychology, to present clearly and accurately the field's most compelling discoveries, controversies, puzzles, and promises. The substance of *The Lifespan* is contemporary research in human development from conception until death; its sources include psychology, biology, medicine, education, anthropology, philosophy, genetics, history, and demography; its function is to teach.

But teaching is more than just telling. It isn't enough simply to gather and organize the facts of a discipline and squeeze them between two covers. Good teaching also requires motivating, illustrating, explaining, relating, evaluating, reviewing, maybe even inspiring. Good teachers sometimes need to sing and dance and walk on tightropes and juggle flaming brands and stand on their heads. Honest.

The Lifespan tries to be a good teacher. It illustrates and compares; sometimes it wonders; occasionally it is awed or puzzled or even frightened—although mostly it is hopeful. Sometimes it pauses to tell tales about old people or infants, to intrigue with accounts of feral children or the misbehaviors of delinquent adolescents, to alarm with instances of social injustice or environmental atrocity, and puzzle with accounts of life in other cultures. At least once that I can think of, it dances a small jig and even juggles a few things that look a little bit like flaming brands. Another time, it stands on its head.

This sixth edition of *The Lifespan* recognizes more clearly than its predecessors the sometimes enormous demands placed on students' time. Hence, this edition is carefully designed to permit quick review and study. Thus the inclusion of focus questions and outlines at the beginning of each chapter, the use of detailed concept-summarizing tables at the end of every major section (between four and seven per chapter), the provision of brief end-of-chapter summaries in the form of answers for the chapter opening focus questions, the alphabetical listing of important names and terms at the end of every chapter with appropriate page references, and the inclusion of a clear and comprehensive glossary at the end of the book.

In addition, there has been a thorough updating of all topics—with more than 500 new references, the majority of which were published within the last two years. New or significantly expanded topics include sections on the following:

- nutritional needs, obesity, and exercise at all developmental levels

- over-the-counter medication during pregnancy

- update of all demographic data with new U.S. and Canadian statistics

- the rights of the elderly as well as the rights of children

- shaken baby syndrome, elder abuse, child abuse

- male/female differences in aggression

- sociobiology and biophysical development

- rape myths, acquaintance rape, HIV infection

- cloning and other advances in genetic technology

- career preparation and development

- stages of grieving

- poverty among the elderly; palliative care; and so on

The Lifespan deals with all of these concerns, and much more. . . .

ACKNOWLEDGMENTS

Thank You . . .

After six editions, this text is heavily indebted to more people than can easily be listed here: editors from the old days, armies of production people, many dozens of reviewers, legions of students and their professors, squads of sales representatives and marketing people, even my old hunting dog, Zoe, who chewed up parts of an early version before I had learned to hide such things inside a computer. Without all of you, this book wouldn't be what it is. In fact, it would not even be. And so I thank you. Well, maybe not Zoe. . . .

This most recent edition owes an enormous debt to an outstanding publishing team put together by Wadsworth/ITP: Dianne Lindsay, education editor, to whom the ball was passed from many other hands, and for whose enthusiasm and talent I am especially grateful; Valerie Morrison, editorial assistant, who provided welcome continuity through various changes, and whose messages and phone calls were always bright spots on busy days; Detta Penna of Penna Design and Production who put everything together, sometimes to my utter amazement; Peter Penna, also of Penna Design and Production, who had much to do with the attractiveness of the book; Donald Pharr, copy editor; Becky Tollerson, marketing manager; Jennie Redwitz, project editor; Barbara Britton, print buyer; Bob Kauser, permissions editor; Randall Goodall, Seventeenth Street Studios, designer; Pat Rogondino, illustrator; Susie Friedman, photo researcher; Kathy Lee, proofreader; and Thompson Type, compositor. I am also profoundly grateful to reviewers of this and earlier editions, listed below.

There are still dozens of people to thank: Marie, who continues to be so understanding and supportive; the University of Alberta, which is such an excellent place to work and learn; students and professors in many parts of the world; friends and neighbors; my maternal grandmother; the many uncles, aunts, and cousins whose lives inspired some of my stories. To all of you, thank you.

In fact, now that I think of it, there is remarkably little in this book for which I can take complete credit. Unlike other, more generous souls, I am not even willing to say that all the errors, omissions, subtle exaggerations, and blatant stupidities in it are mine. But some of them might be.

■ SIXTH EDITION

Marilyn A. Borges
San Diego State University

Charlotte Callens
Prince George's Community College

Maggie Felton
University of Southern Indiana

Gordon Greenwood
University of Florida, Gainesville

Charles LaBounty
Hamline University

James S. Schork
Elizabethtown Community College

Theresa A. Wozencraft
Midwestern State University

■ PREVIOUS EDITIONS

Christine M. Arco

Michael Bradley

Dan Bellack

David W. Carroll

John Cavanaugh

Sandra Searcy Edwards

Michael G. Green

Robert Kiel

Seth Kunen

Nanette McLain

Karen Nelson

Susan Whitbourne

Ruth Wilson

Mark B. Alcorn, University of Northern Colorado

David Carroll, University of Wisconsin, Superior

Williams R. Fisk, Clemson University

Charles F. Halverson, University of Georgia

Phyllis A. Heath, Central Michigan University

Joan M. Jones, University of Wisconsin, Milwaukee

Lynn Katz, University of Pittsburgh

Suzanne Krinsky, University of Southern Colorado

Joan N. McNeil, Kansas State University

Fayneese Miller, Brown University

Edythe H. Schwartz, California State University, Sacramento

Tony Williams, Marshall University

PART ONE

The Beginning

Things do not change; we change.

HENRY DAVID THOREAU
Walden

hange is what human development is all about—change, yet continuity. First, we are a speck in a mother's womb, microscopic, insignificant; soon, a wailing infant, unfamiliar with the world, helpless, totally dependent; next, a burgeoning child exploring the mysteries of time and space, yet still awed by magic and enchanted by fairies; then, an adolescent practicing newly invented secrets of love and logic, at once sophisticated and naive; now, an adult, vigorous and powerful, but no longer able to see elves and other mystical things; and before we know it, we ease into our last age. ¶ But through all these changes, the essence of who we are, of our *selves,* endures; thus is there continuity in the midst of constant change. ¶ The four chapters in Part One, "The Beginning," are about the things we need to know to understand this change and continuity. The first and second chapters lay out the subject, its methods, its most important theories; the third explores interactions between our genes and our contexts that account for change; and the fourth traces the course of prenatal human development. ¶ There is much to consider if we are to understand how we change.

FOCUS QUESTIONS

1. What is the lifespan perspective of human development?

2. How are growth, maturation, learning, and development related?

3. What are the most basic of children's rights?

4. What questions keep recurring in the study of human development?

5. How do we study lifespan development?

ONE

Studying Human Development

Men fear Death as children fear to go in the dark; and as that natural fear in children is increased with tales, so is the other.

FRANCIS BACON
Essays 2

In this childhood memory, I am only six or seven. I'm lying in bed upstairs with my older brother, Maurice. It's a winter's night, cold and dark as sin up there in northern Saskatchewan, and the chicken-feather comforter hasn't warmed up yet. We have no electricity, and the orange glow from the kerosene lamp downstairs doesn't light any of the corners in our room. ¶ Then "Crowk!" there's another of those groaning noises, and my heart lurches. "They're just nails letting go in the cold," my dad said. But we're not sure, so we listen real hard in case it's something else, which we'll know if it makes a different kind of noise. For a minute, all I can hear is the wind pushing cold against the house. And then, I swear it, I hear a different sound, more like a sigh, and I think, "Oh no, it's a *papoose* this time for sure," which is what we call really bad witches in French. It sounds like it's in the closet, which is where our cousin, Claude, said they hide. "In closets or under beds," he said, "and they'll bloody eat you if they can." ¶ "It's your turn," Maurice says, which I've been hoping he's forgotten, but he hasn't. So, shaking like a leaf, I get out of bed and snake around the wall toward the closet, praying, "Gawd don't let there be one in there this time. Please gawd wait until it's Maurice's turn to look." ¶ "Under the bed," says Maurice. "I heard it under the bed." So now I bend down to peer under the bed, praying desperately, "Please gawd don't put a papoose under the bed tonight. Please gawd wait 'til it's Maurice's turn." ¶

e're almost grown up now, Maurice and I. Our nighttime bedrooms are far quieter than they used to be,* and we've become very familiar with our closets. We no longer need to open their doors and look inside them before we sleep. We know there's nothing in our closets that'll bloody eat us while we sleep, don't we? Children don't always know that; they're less familiar with their closets.

That's a large part of growing up: becoming familiar with what's out there, sorting fact from fancy and magic from reality, discovering what is likely to eat us and what isn't, finding out what's in our closets. Describing how infants, children, adolescents—and even adults—become progressively more familiar with the world is a large part of what *The Lifespan* is about.

The emphasis in this text is on describing and understanding how we change as we develop. When we are 9, how different are we from when we were 6? How will we be different when we are 12? 21? 81? Can we understand the forces that shape what we are becoming? These are the questions of The Lifespan.

The text includes nine parts: The first consists of four introductory chapters (subject and methods of lifespan developmental psychology, main theories, gene–environment interaction, and prenatal development and birth); seven parts deal with physical, intellectual, and social change during infancy, childhood, adolescence, and adulthood; the final part looks at dying.

LIFESPAN DEVELOPMENTAL PSYCHOLOGY

Psychology[†] is a general term for the science that studies behavior and thinking. **Developmental psychology** is concerned specifically with changes that occur over time. Accordingly, **lifespan developmental psychology** is the discipline that studies changes occurring from conception through adulthood and that looks at the processes and influences accounting for these changes.

The Lifespan Perspective

Lifespan developmental psychology is a relatively new area of interest. During the century or so since the beginning of scientific psychology, most studies of human development have focused on infancy, childhood, and, to a lesser extent, adolescence. G. S. Hall, who published a major book on aging in

1922, is sometimes referred to as one of the founders of the study of aging. But even after the publication of Hall's book, the traditional view—one that focuses on the development of children rather than adults—continued to dominate psychological research. This traditional view is dramatically different from the contemporary lifespan view.

The traditional view of human development holds that almost all important developmental changes occur between conception and adolescence. After adulthood is reached, according to this view, little happens that might be of concern to a developmental psychologist. Adulthood is seen as a lengthy period of little change, eventually followed by the declines of old age.

■ DEVELOPMENT IS CONTINUOUS

We now know that the traditional view of development is inaccurate and misleading. The more current lifespan view of

▲ SUMMARY TABLE 1.1
Structure of This Text

PERIOD/PART	APPROXIMATE AGES	CHAPTERS
I. The Beginning	—	1. Studying the Lifespan
		2. Theories of Lifespan Development
		3. Genetics and Context
		4. Prenatal Development and Birth
II. Infancy	Birth to 2 years	5. Physical and Cognitive Development
		6. Social Development
III. Early Childhood	2 to 6–7 years	7. Physical and Cognitive Development
		8. Social Development
IV. Middle Childhood	6–7 to 11–12 years	9. Physical and Cognitive Development
		10. Social Development
V. Adolescence	11–12 to 19–20 years	11. Physical and Cognitive Development
		12. Social Development
VI. Early Adulthood	20 to 40–45 years	13. Physical and Cognitive Development
		14. Social Development
VII. Middle Adulthood	40–45 to 65–70 years	15. Physical and Cognitive Development
		16. Social Development
VIII. Late Adulthood	65–70 years onward	17. Physical and Cognitive Development
		18. Social Development
IX. The End	—	19. Dying and Grieving

---

*"It's your hearing that's shot," said my grandmother, adding meanly, "They're still there, you know."

†Boldfaced terms are defined in the Glossary at the end of the book and are also listed in the Study Terms at the end of each chapter.

development recognizes that important changes occur at all ages throughout the lifespan. In fact, as Lerner and his associates (1992) note, the lifespan view is rooted in the suggestion that the changes that occur in adulthood are similar in magnitude to those of earlier developmental periods. Hence, the single most important characteristic of the lifespan view of human development is the recognition that both children and adults are developing organisms throughout life, that development does not stop with the beginning of adulthood.

MATURITY IS RELATIVE

In its most general sense, *maturity* refers to a state of being fully developed, fully grown, ripe. But because development continues through adulthood, it cannot easily be described in terms of a predetermined final state of maturity. What is important to the developmental psychologist is not the individual's state, which is a constantly changing and evolving thing, so much as the process of change itself. People continually change, moving toward new states of readiness, new competencies. The infant who has just learned to recognize the meaning of the word *mother* is still a long way from a complete understanding of either words or mothers. Similarly, the thirty-year-old who succeeds in resolving an emotional dilemma by finding someone to love may be far from having learned to solve other emotional problems. Thus maturity, like so many other states, is relative: We can be mature in certain areas but not in others. And even as we reach a state of relative maturity, we continue to change.

Change is what human development is about. Emphasis on the ongoing and never-ending processes of change—on the dynamism of the developmental process—is one of the distinguishing characteristics of the contemporary lifespan view of development.

CHILDHOOD IS MORE THAN JUST IMMATURITY

The lifespan view recognizes not only that maturity is relative, but also that *immaturity* is more than an unfinished or incomplete state that will disappear with the advent of maturity. That is, childhood is seen as more than a necessary period of immaturity during which the person can develop the competencies and understanding necessary for adult (that is, *mature*) functioning.

As an illustration of this view, Bjorklund (1997b) points out that a caterpillar is surely an immature form of a butterfly. But scientists also view the caterpillar as an organism with its own integrity, its own organization, its own behaviors—many of which are dramatically different from those of the butterfly. In much the same way, lifespan developmental psychologists view children's thoughts and behaviors not merely as immature precursors to more adult forms of thinking and acting, but as distinct and important in their own right.

DEVELOPMENT OCCURS IN CONTEXT

The lifespan view of human development also recognizes the importance of the individual's context, or what is sometimes termed **ecology.** As a general term, ecology refers to the science that studies the relationship between organisms and their environment (*oikos* is the Greek word for "home"; the suffix *-logy* means "the study of"). As a more specialized term in developmental theory, ecology refers mainly to the social context in which behavior and development occur. Thus, ecological approaches to understanding and explaining development pay a great deal of attention to the individual's social environment and to the changing relationships between the individual and the environment.

DEVELOPMENTAL INFLUENCES ARE BIDIRECTIONAL

"The emphasis in developmental contextualism," write Lerner and associates (1992), "[is] on the bidirectional connections between the individual and the actual settings within which he or she lives" (p. 255). What this means is that developmental psychologists are interested not only in how the person is influenced by social context, but also in how the environment is influenced by the person—that is, they are interested in what is termed the **bidirectionality** of influences. As an illustration, infant Elissa may be profoundly influenced by her mother's behavior, by her mother's singing to her, cradling her, and rocking her as she smiles. However, the fact that her mother sings and smiles may be at least partly due to Elissa's being what psychologists term an "easy" infant—an infant who adjusts easily, cries very little, smiles a great deal, and loves to be cuddled. Were Elissa a more "difficult" infant, would her mother behave in exactly the same way?

As will become increasingly apparent as you progress through this text, these characteristic beliefs of the lifespan view of human development are very important for contemporary lifespan developmental research. Among other things, they are reflected in a shifting of interest from the individual in isolation to the individual as part of a complex social system (ecological orientation). They also are apparent in increased attention to the ways in which the individual affects surrounding social systems as well as the ways in which social systems affect the individual. Finally, they are evident in a shifting of our focus from describing states to investigating processes—that is, a shifting of concern from the static (unchanging) to the dynamic (changing). (See Summary Table 1.2.)

SOME DEFINITIONS IN DEVELOPMENT

Important concepts in the study of the lifespan include growth, maturation, and learning. Put another way, to develop is to grow, to mature, and to learn.

Growth ordinarily refers to physical changes such as increasing height or enlargement of the nose. The changes that define growth are primarily *quantitative;* they involve addition rather than transformation.

THEMES	MEANING
1. Development is continuous.	■ Adults, as well as children, continue to develop and change.
2. Maturity is relative.	■ Because change is continuous, the person never reaches a final state of complete maturity where no further changes occur.
3. Childhood is more than just immaturity.	■ The characteristics of childhood are important in their own right and should not be viewed simply as precursors to more "adult" forms of thinking.
4. Development occurs in context.	■ The individual's changing relationships with the social environment have a great deal to do with outcomes of development.
5. Developmental influences are bidirectional.	■ Not only are individuals profoundly influenced by their social environment, but they in turn affect significant features of that environment.

Psychology	■ The science that studies human thought and behavior.
Developmental Psychology	■ The division of psychology concerned with changes that occur over time, and with the processes and influences that account for these changes.
Development includes:	
Growth	■ Physical changes; primarily quantitative.
Maturation	■ Naturally unfolding changes, relatively independent of the environment (for example, pubescence—the changes of adolescence that lead to sexual maturity).
Learning	■ Relatively permanent changes in behavior that result from experience (rather than from maturation, fatigue, or drugs).

Maturation, as a biological term rather than as a loose, general term, describes changes that are relatively independent of the environment, but that are closely related to heredity—such as the sexual changes of adolescence. In almost all aspects of human development, however, maturation and learning interact. For example, learning to walk requires not only that the child's physical strength and muscular coordination be sufficiently mature but also that there be opportunities to learn the various skills involved.

Learning is defined as relatively permanent changes that result from experiences (experiences like being stung by a bee or going to school) rather than simply from maturation or growth.

In summary, **development** describes the gradual, lifelong process whereby we adapt to our environment. Because we adapt by growing, maturing, and learning, these are the basic aspects of development. (See Summary Table 1.3 for a summary of these definitions.)

HISTORICAL SNAPSHOTS

Lifespan development is a recent area of psychological interest. Its most obvious roots can be found in the study of children. And the scientific study of children, too, is not very old. In fact, most of its development belongs to this century. At least some of the reasons for this long delay in the development of a science of child study have to do with attitudes toward children that appear to have been prevalent throughout much of human history. Some of these attitudes are reflected in the brief historical snapshots that follow.

Note at the outset that these historical snapshots are not always entirely accurate. There are few reliable records of what life might have been like for a child prior to what have sometimes been called the "print" cultures. When Ariès (1962) studied the lives of medieval children, he was forced to put together fragments from a variety of sources—sixteenth- and seventeenth-century paintings, school and university regulations, and Doctor Heroard's description of the upbringing of the French king Louis XIII. The result is a fascinating but not entirely reliable account.

SNAPSHOT 1: CONCEPTS OF CHILDHOOD IN MEDIEVAL EUROPE

In the Middle Ages, Ariès informs us, the idea of childhood as we know it today did not exist. His evidence? Children, he claims, were not seen as innocent creatures in need of nurturing and protection, nor were they provided with clothing or toys designed especially for them. And early paintings often depicted children not with the forms and proportions of children but rather as miniature adults.

But this is not an accurate description, argues Cunningham (1996), claiming that Ariès misinterpreted his evidence and overlooked other contradictory evidence. That there was a clear notion of childhood even in the Middle Ages is evident in the fact that medical writings of that time took pains to describe diseases that were thought to be diseases of childhood rather than of adulthood. Furthermore, many writers described various stages that children were thought to go through as they developed.

However, that the concepts and images of childhood have changed dramatically since the Middle Ages is true, claims Cunningham (1996). One reason for the change is that during the Middle Ages, infant mortality was extremely high compared to what it is today in most of the developed world. As an example, Ariès describes one scene in which a mother has just given birth to her fifth child. She is depressed; there had not been enough food and clothing before. What will it be like now? A neighbor consoles her: "Before they are old enough to bother you," she says, "you will have lost half of them, or perhaps all of them" (quoted in Ariès, 1962, p. 38).

The implication is that the children's dying is somehow preferable to the burden of caring for them. And the inference is that the mother is not strongly attached to the child; hence, there is little need to worry that it might suffer or die. Thus, this snapshot of medieval childhood reflects a cold, callous, unfeeling attitude toward children. We don't know for certain how accurate it is, but we do know that it omits exceptions, and as a result, it exaggerates—as do many historical accounts.

■ SNAPSHOT 2: CHILD ABANDONMENT AND ABUSE: EIGHTEENTH CENTURY

In the eighteenth and nineteenth centuries, written and printed records of childhood became more common as literacy slowly spread through the world. Accordingly, accounts of attitudes toward children are far more reliable than those for earlier periods. Sadly, in some ways they are no less shocking. Laws and courts had not yet begun to grant children any rights or any protection. For example, in 1761 the British courts sentenced Anne Martin to two years in Newgate Prison. Her crime? She habitually poked out the eyes of the children she took begging with her; it increased their success—and hers. Aha, you say, the courts did offer some protection to children! True, but it was skimpy protection indeed. As Pinchbeck and Hewitt (1973) point out, Anne Martin's case

was unusual in that the children whose eyes she removed were somebody else's. Had they been her own, it is likely that no one would have paid any attention. Parents could generally treat their own children in any way they wanted.

The courts were also not above severely punishing children for infractions of laws. Siegel and White (1982) report the case of a seven-year-old girl who stole a petticoat, surely not that terrible a crime. Still, she was brought to trial, convicted, sentenced—and hanged!

Eighteenth-century attitudes toward children are apparent not only in the ways courts treated them but also in the ways parents treated them. In the crowded slums of eighteenth-century European cities, thousands of parents bore children whom they promptly abandoned in the streets or on the doorsteps of churches and orphanages. Foundling homes were established throughout Europe to care for these children, but the majority died in infancy (before the age of two). This was also the case in the United States where, with few exceptions, children in infant homes (asylums) prior to 1915 died before the age of two (Bakwin, 1949). In fact, until the turn of that century, even if a child were not abandoned, the chances of surviving until the age of five were less than one in two (Kessen, 1965). Unfortunately, child abandonment, and even infanticide, are still not entirely uncommon even in industrialized countries such as Britain (Marks, 1996); they are even more common in developing cultures (see "Across Cultures: Piyush Mittal's Sister").

■ SNAPSHOT 3: CHILD LABOR IN THE NINETEENTH CENTURY

The nineteenth century brought some improvement in the status of children and a dramatic reduction in the number of abandonments. Unfortunately, these changes resulted less from increasing love and concern for children than from a perception of their economic value. At that time, for example, children were widely used in British coal mines. Most

Contrasting attitudes toward children are reflected in 18th-century (William Hogarth, above) and 19th-century (Mary Cassatt, right) art.

iyush's sister's story is no different from that of thousands of other infant females born in northern India. It is a very short story. She was born into a proud but poor family of farmers, born into a culture where there is little demand for female labor, where females are not allowed to own property, where the cost of raising daughters is far higher than that of raising sons, and where there is also an intense preference for sons. And so when the newborn's mother saw that there was no appendage between the infant's legs, she shrugged in resignation.

There are different ways of killing an infant. One, quite common in the village of Piyush's parents, is to stuff rice into the newborn's mouth and nose and hold a pillow tight against its face until the struggles stop. In other villages, there is a distaste for violent measures, and the infant is simply "left to die from neglect and want of food" (Miller, 1981, p. 51). Piyush's mother used rice.

"Bury it," she said to Piyush tiredly, "so the dogs don't find it."

In parts of India, female infanticide has apparently long been common, although it became less visible after it was outlawed by the British in 1870. Even today, it is still practiced—as it is also practiced in parts of Japan, Pakistan, Bangladesh, China, and elsewhere. In these countries, says Grant (1992), more than a million female infants die each year simply because they are female. Many are aborted as fetuses following prenatal diagnosis to determine their sex.

There is tremendous discrimination against females in many of the world's less developed countries. "Employment rights, social security rights, legal rights, property rights, and even civil and political liberties," writes Grant (1992), "are all likely to depend upon the one, cruel chromosome" (p. 57). And access to education, too, is far more limited for females than for males.

To Think About

What are the probable implications of granting equal educational opportunity to girls in developing countries? How might this affect the care of children in these countries? Are Piyush's views of life and death, of male and female, likely to resemble yours?

The scientific study of children is a relatively recent undertaking. Where infant mortality is high or where children are highly prized for their economic value, they are perhaps less likely to be loved and studied. Under those circumstances, they are also more likely to be exploited in child labor, as in this early 20th-century cotton mill in Georgia. Note the bare feet dangerously close to the turning spindles, and the completely exposed and unguarded belt and pulley system.

of these mines were underground, and the tunnels that led to them were often no more than about 2 feet in height, poorly ventilated, and sometimes covered with 3 or 4 inches of water. Children were especially valuable in these mines because they were small enough to crawl through the tiny tunnels, dragging baskets loaded with coal behind them using a "girdle and chain."* The Seventh Earl of Shaftesbury (Anthony Ashley Cooper) described the blisters and wounds that resulted from this device, the injuries and diseases children suffered in the mines, the physical and mental abuse, and the beatings. He begged the British House of Commons to pass a bill that would set age thirteen as a minimum for male employment in the coal mines and that would completely prohibit the employment of females underground. Following considerable debate, and in spite of strong opposition, a bill prohibiting females from working underground was passed. But the House was moved by the argument that

---

*This device was a sturdy leather belt that was worn around the waist to serve as a harness. At the front was a metal ring to which was fastened a heavy chain. The chain passed between the legs and was hooked onto the basket behind the child.

Infant Survival

In many parts of the nonindustrialized world, infant death exceeds 100 per 1,000 live births in the first year of life, a figure comparable to that for the United States at the turn of the century. Yet in some countries, such as Finland and Sweden, under-1 infant mortality rates are only 5 per 1,000. Deaths of children under age 5 number about 12.5 million per year, reports Bellamy (1997). More than 60 percent of these can be prevented at a cost of about half of what is spent on cigarettes each year in Europe alone—and about 60 percent of what is spent on business entertainment in Japan or on beer in the United States (Grant, 1993). There is little doubt that education, vaccination, and improved health care could dramatically reduce infant mortality.

FIGURE 1.1

Under-5 mortality rates for selected countries (number of deaths per 1,000 live births for children under age 5). (Based on Bellamy, 1997, pp. 80–81.)

children whose fathers were miners were more likely to profit from an education in the mines than from a "reading" education; boys could continue to work in the mines as long as they had reached the age of ten.

Conditions in North America were, in some instances, not very different from those in some parts of Europe. Large numbers of children were used in factories and cotton mills, in fields and shops. But profound social and economic forces would soon change all that.

◾ SNAPSHOT 4:
THE DEVELOPING WORLD TODAY

The twentieth century also has its share of ignorance, of cruelty, of needless pain and suffering. Some 64 of the world's nations have under-5 mortality rates (abbreviated U5MR) greater than 60 per 1,000 children born alive (Bellamy, 1997). In Niger, for example, almost one of every three infants born alive dies before the age of 5, a rate more than 30 times higher than that of countries such as the United States or Canada (see "At a Glance: Infant Survival"). The United Nations reports that as recently as 1993, in developing countries almost 8 million children under 5 died each year from pneumonia, diarrheal dehydration, or vaccine-preventable diseases such as measles, tetanus, and whooping cough, with starvation adding another 5 or so million to this total (Grant, 1993). That's more than 35,000 children under 5 dying every day, the majority of them from preventable causes (see Figure 1.2).

At a theoretical level, solutions for these social crimes are simple and technically possible: Vaccine-preventable

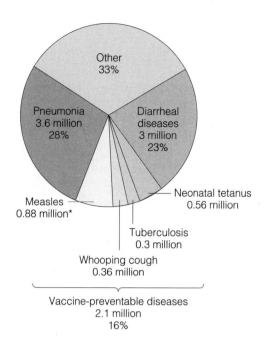

Measles
0.88 million*

Neonatal tetanus
0.56 million

Tuberculosis
0.3 million

Whooping cough
0.36 million

Vaccine-preventable diseases
2.1 million
16%

*Including measles with diarrheal disease
and measles with pneumonia.

FIGURE 1.2

The main causes of the 12.9 million deaths of children under age 5 that occur each year. More than 60 percent are from preventable diseases. (From Grant, 1993, p. 6.)

diseases require immunization; nutrition-related suffering and dying can be alleviated through a redistribution of vast surpluses of food; diarrheal infection can be lessened through sanitation; and the effects of diarrheal infection can be countered through oral rehydration therapy (ORT). (ORT involves an attempt to increase the infected child's fluid intake and to replace essential salts.) And, reassuringly, a concerted drive toward immunization throughout the world has dramatically reduced preventable infant deaths. For example, Bellamy (1996) reports that the proportion of the world's children immunized against measles more than tripled between 1982 and 1995 (from about 25 to more than 75 percent).

Also, infant and child deaths related to vaccine-preventable diseases, diarrheal infection, and poor nutrition can be lessened enormously through something as simple as breastfeeding. Infant survival can also be improved through the education of mothers (Levine, 1987).

■ SNAPSHOT 5:
THE INDUSTRIALIZED WORLD TODAY

Obviously, not all children were murdered in the dark ages that we call antiquity. Nor were all children abandoned during the Middle Ages—or ignored until they died and could be buried in the backyard or in the garden. The children of Europe's eighteenth and nineteenth centuries weren't all beaten into the coal mines, and North America's children weren't all driven into the cotton fields and the textile facto-

ries. Even then, the majority of parents were probably loving and caring. Historical accounts often exaggerate.

In the industrialized world, we no longer abandon children for fear they will prove too much of an economic burden. Nor do we send them into mines and factories. The recognition of childhood as a distinct period, coupled with increasing industrialization and scientific advances, led to organized "child saving" movements, especially in the early twentieth century. "The idea that children have special needs, which sparked the founding of UNICEF 50 years ago," writes Bellamy (1991), "has now given way to the conviction that children have the same spectrum of rights as adults: civil and political, social, cultural and economic" (p. 4). (Children's rights are discussed in more detail later in this chapter.)

This does not mean that all is perfect with the industrialized world's children. Many are still forced to work in sometimes grueling conditions. In fact, some 250 million children throughout the world are employed—and much of this employment is not simply to earn "spending money" (Bellamy, 1997). Nor is child employment restricted only to the poorer, developing regions of the world. For example, a 1992 U.S. Department of Labor survey found more than 11,000 illegal child workers (ILO, 1992). As in many other countries where children are employed, the majority of these children were from ethnic minority groups (employed primarily in agriculture).

Still, the majority of child workers are found in the developing world. Bellamy (1997) estimates that in developing countries, as many as one of every four children between the ages of five and fourteen works. Of these, three-quarters work at least six days a week, and half work more than nine hours a day.

Sadly, working may not be the worst of the possible terrors of childhood: War may be. The nature of war has changed dramatically over the centuries. In medieval times, wars seldom killed anybody other than soldiers. Even as recently as World War One, more than 95 percent of those killed were armed, fighting personnel. This is no longer so as we approach the millennium. Now the world's ongoing wars, which number around forty as of this writing, kill about four civilians for every armed fighter. Not surprisingly, most of those killed are women and children (Grant, 1992; Bellamy, 1996). (See "In the News and on the Net: Children of War.")

Lest this commentary paint too negative a picture of childhood in today's industrialized world, let me hasten to point out that exploitative child labor and children as the victims of war are the exception rather than the rule. The vast majority of children in developed countries lead peaceful, happy, play- and school-filled lives.

■ SNAPSHOT 6: CHILDREN
IN A CHANGING WORLD

Still, the experience of childhood in today's world may be quite different from that of our grandparents. For one thing, there have been dramatic social changes in recent decades, and indications are that many of these changes are still accelerating. For example, the percentage of never married twenty-

IN THE NEWS AND ON THE NET

aujl Davidovich, as he has done so many other times, runs across the open area where, in happier times, the skating rink, *Zetra,* had been. He runs because there are snipers hidden here and there among the bombed and burned buildings that, only 10 years earlier, housed the winter Olympics here in Sarajevo. He is on his way to his grandmother's with whom he now lives because his parents have been killed.

But today, Raujl doesn't make it. Half way across the opening, a bullet tears into his chest, slamming him down hard against the frozen corpse of an old woman. "It doesn't hurt that much," he thinks. It's his last thought.

1. War Crimes. (1994, Feb. 13). *Edmonton Sun,* p. 13.

To Think About

UNICEF estimates that in the past decade alone, wars have killed 2 million children, between 4 and 5 million have been disabled, 12 million have been left homeless, and more than a

million have either been orphaned or separated from their parents. As one political commentator in Rwanda noted, "To kill the big rats, you have to kill the little rats" (quoted in Bellamy, 1996, p. 14). What do you suppose can, or should, be done?

On the Net

For more information, see the UNICEF publication *The State of the World's Children* at

http://www.unicef. org/sowc96pk/ mainmenu.htm

The 1996 issue deals specifically with children in war. For information about a well-known children's aid society, see

http://www.cad. org.uk/Home/ home.htm

---

to twenty-four-year-old women has more than doubled in the past three decades (from 30 in 1960 to 80.1 in 1995: U.S. Bureau of the Census, 1996). In addition, divorce rates have increased dramatically; at present, slightly more than one-quarter of the 70 million or so children under eighteen in the United States live in a one-parent household. In about 82 percent of these families, the mother is the single parent (U.S. Bureau of the Census, 1996). Coupled with this, *demographic* (population) changes have resulted in smaller families, lower birthrates, larger numbers of childless couples, and a greater proportion of young adults (resulting from earlier increases in birthrates) and of elderly people (resulting from medical advances). In addition, note Oberg, Bryant, and Bach (1995), there has been a disproportionate increase in children among the poor, resulting in a higher proportion of children living in poverty. In fact, some surveys indicate that American children are more likely to live in poverty than are children in many other industrialized countries (Taylor, 1996). A 1996 survey reports that about 20 percent of children under age eighteen in the United States live in families whose income is below the poverty level (more than three times higher than France or West Germany: Children's Defense Fund, 1996).

Many of these social and demographic changes, argues Hernandez (1997), may be risk factors for children and may be associated with various developmental and family problems. Among other things, childhood in our times brings

with it a high probability of being looked after by a series of strangers, most likely outside the child's home. It includes, as well, the probability of losing a father or a mother for much of the time of growing up—or at least of losing some of their interest and attention, and perhaps some of their affection as well. Childhood now brings the possibility of major readjustments if one or the other of the parents remarries, particularly if stepsiblings are brought into the family. And it also entails a wide assortment of childhood burdens such as high mortality rate, inadequate educational opportunity, and the hardships of poverty. As Goetting (1994) notes, that many of these possibilities are *preventable* makes one wonder whether Americans really like children.

In fact, says Bullock (1993), childhood may be a terribly lonely and often frightening experience for many. There was a time, not very long ago, when the things that most children feared were highly predictable: pain, death, spinach, darkness, and things that go bump in the night—or that hide in closets or under beds. But, as we saw, recent decades have added some new fears, many of which have to do with unpredictability and instability in the child's life: concerns over whether or not parents will divorce, fears related to being left alone, fears associated with the likelihood of having to make new adjustments, fears associated with poverty.

But the challenges and the changes of current decades don't overwhelm all children and are not always a source of loneliness or despair. For many children, these may be challenges

SUMMARY TABLE 1.4

Snapshots of Historical Trends in Images of Childhood and Treatment of Children*

HISTORICAL PERIOD	SOME INFERRED IMAGES OF CHILDHOOD
1. Medieval Europe	■ Less strong attachment to infants and children partly because of high mortality rates.
2. Eighteenth century	■ Many cases of child abandonment; continuing high mortality rates; little legal protection for children.
3. Nineteenth century	■ Widespread use of young children in mines, factories, and other employment.
4. Twentieth century: the developing world	■ Continued relatively high infant and child mortality rates, often due to preventable causes, and sometimes associated with cultural biases.
5. Twentieth century: the industrialized world	■ Growing recognition of children's rights; some exploitation of children in labor and as victims of war.
6. Children in a changing world	■ Accelerating social changes (increasing divorce rates, declining birthrates, smaller families, an aging population, higher poverty rates for children) may be risk factors sometimes associated with developmental problems.

*Note that although these trends and attitudes are descriptive of some cultures and of some families during the periods in question, they are sometimes not very general. Clearly, although infanticide might once have been acceptable under some circumstances, no society permitted all its infants to be killed. Similarly, even at the height of the period of child labor in the nineteenth century, there were many well-cared-for children who played and went to school and had carefree childhoods in loving homes.

that result in strength rather than in weakness. Keep in mind, too, that these changes have little to do with the lives of many children. (See Summary Table 1.4.)

CHILDREN'S RIGHTS

The brief historical snapshots in the preceding section are included not so that you might be horrified at the inhumanity of your species—or proud of your apparent enlightenment. Rather, they are meant to illustrate how attitudes toward children reflect cultural and historical context—and how context influences development.

Historical Lack of Rights for Children

Today's context—in at least some jurisdictions—emphasizes the rights that children have. It's a context that stands in

A proclamation of the United Nations stipulates that all of the world's children have a right to adequate nutrition, education, affection, love, and protection from abuse and exploitation. And, insists the UN, they have a right to play.

sharp contrast to the medieval era, when one of the sports by which the gentry amused themselves was that of **baby tossing**. Baby tossing was the practice of throwing infants from one gamesman to another, just for the sport of it. One of the unlucky babies used in this game was King Henry IV's infant brother, who was killed when he fell while being tossed from window to window (DeMause, 1974). And in Massachusetts as recently as 1646, parents did not have to put up with unruly offspring. A father whose son wouldn't listen to him, who was making his life miserable, could simply drag him before a magistrate and present his case. As long as the son was sixteen or more, they'd put him to death (Westman, 1991)! That was the law.

Children's Rights Today

By the beginning of the twentieth century, the absolute control that parents and various agencies had over the lives of children had been weakened considerably. Yet it was still possible for parents and teachers to get rid of troublesome children, often by committing them to mental institutions. Until recently, such children had little legal recourse. Now, however, parents no longer have absolute jurisdiction over their children. Increasingly, major court decisions favor children who feel they have been wronged (Roche, 1996). Even in psychotherapy, children cannot simply be brought in by their parents for treatment and subjected to procedures without their "informed" consent (Halasz, 1996). Although both therapists and parents have traditionally assumed they have the right—and the responsibility—to decide such matters for children, there is now an increasing recognition of children's legal and moral right to participate in decisions that affect them directly, including mental health treatment decisions (Hall & Meei-Ju, 1995).

Evidence of increasing concern for the rights of children is apparent not only in court decisions but also in the development of charters of children's rights. Most importantly, a

1990 United Nations World Summit on children resulted in the formulation of an extensive charter of children's rights. This charter has been signed by the vast majority of the world's nations, so more than 90 percent of the world's children now live in jurisdictions where governments are legally bound to protect their rights (Bellamy, 1996).

Children's most important rights, according to this charter, are summarized in Interactive Table 1.5. These are birthrights, says the National Committee for the Rights of the Child: They should apply to all children from all nations (Murphy-Berman, Levesque, & Berman, 1996). Sadly, however, they are not equally available to all children.

Goals for the Millennium

Related to these universal children's rights, the world's nations have also agreed on a number of goals for the year 2000. And considerable progress has already been made toward achieving these goals, which include the following:

- A reduction of the under-5 mortality rate to less than 70 per 1,000 live births. This rate is currently 90 throughout the world, but it ranges from an average of 173 in the least developed countries to 8 in the most highly industrialized (Bellamy, 1997).

- A reduction of *maternal* mortality rates as well as rates of child malnutrition to half of what they were in 1990.

- Ninety percent immunization for children under one, with a view to eradicating polio and reducing measles deaths by 95 percent.

- Fifty percent reduction in child deaths due to diarrheal dehydration.

- Providing basic primary education for at least 80 percent of the world's children, including girls as well as boys.

- Safe water and sanitation for all communities.

- Universal acceptance of the Convention of the Rights of the Child.

- Universal access to family planning information and services.

As Caldwell (1989) notes, the rights of children, which are reflected in the abbreviated list of goals shown in the preceding list, are geared toward providing optimal, growth-fostering conditions for them. In general, they are rights of *protection* rather than rights of *choice*. That is, children need to be protected from the dangers to which their immaturity exposes them, and their access to a growth-fostering environment needs to be safeguarded. Treating children as mini-adults is a misuse of the concept of children's rights, claims Saidla (1992). In many instances, children lack the maturity and the knowledge required for making the best choices in their own lives. Eleven-year-olds have the right to adequate nutrition, medical care, and education, but, understandably, they do not have the right to make all their own nutritional,

educational, and medical choices. Notwithstanding this, as we noted earlier, their right to *informed consent* and their right to participate fully in decisions that affect them are increasingly being recognized.

This does not mean that children have no responsibilities. As Caldwell (1989) points out, society expects its children to assimilate dominant cultural values and eventually foster the continuation of the culture. In addition, society expects that its children will take advantage of the rights and opportunities provided for them—that they will mature and learn.

STUDYING HUMAN DEVELOPMENT

The historical roots of the study of human development are closely linked with profound changes in our attitudes toward children as well as in our recognition that development is a lifelong process. In addition, current demographic changes, especially those associated with the aging of Western industrialized societies (largely as a result of reduced birthrates and increased longevity), have contributed to a shift in focus from the preadult years to the entire lifespan (see "At a Glance: Age Distribution in the United States and Canada"). Now developmental researchers study the old as well as the young. And social activists speak not only of the rights of children, but also of the rights of the aged.

Early Pioneers

Closely associated with the intellectual movements linked to changing attitudes toward children are such individuals as John Locke and Jean-Jacques Rousseau.

t the turn of this century in both Canada and the United States, almost 100 of every 1,000 children died in infancy. But high infant mortality was compensated for by high birthrates, so parents more than replaced themselves. Now, infant mortality has been reduced to about 10 per 1,000, but since 1972, birthrates have been below replacement at between 14 and 16 per 1,000. However, populations continue to grow, largely as a result of increased life expectancy. In 1920, life expectancy in the United States was fifty-four years; in Canada, it was fifty-nine years. It is now about seventy-six in the United States and seventy-eight in Canada (U.S. Bureau of the Census, 1996; *Canada Yearbook*, 1997). Whereas there were once far more young children than old people in North America, in both the United States and Canada there are now about equal numbers of people above age seventy-five as there are under age five.

FIGURE 1.3

U. S. population (in thousands), 1995, by age group and sex. (Based on U.S. Bureau of the Census, 1996, p. 16.)

FIGURE 1.4

Canadian population (in thousands), 1995, by sex and age. (Based on Canada Yearbook, 1997, p. 82.)

LOCKE

John Locke (1699), writing in the late seventeenth century, argued that children are basically rational creatures whose minds are comparable to a blank slate (*tabula rasa*) upon which experience writes messages. Thus, children are passive recipients of knowledge, information, and habits, and they are highly responsive to rewards and punishments.

ROUSSEAU

In contrast, Jean-Jacques Rousseau's child, immortalized in his book *Emile,* is active and inquiring. Furthermore, this child is not a "blank slate," neither good nor bad until the rewards and punishments of experience exert their influence, but innately good—a "noble savage." Rousseau (1911) insists that if children were allowed to develop in their own fashion, untainted by the corruption and evil in the world, they would be undeniably good when grown: "God

makes all things good; man meddles with them and they become evil."

Locke's and Rousseau's ideas have led to fundamentally different conceptions of childhood. Locke's description of the child as a passive creature, molded and shaped by the rewards and punishments of experience, has a close parallel in learning-theory descriptions of development (for example, the work of Skinner and Bandura, described in Chapter 2). Rousseau's view of an active, exploring child purposefully interacting with the environment is illustrated in the work of Jean Piaget (also described in Chapter 2).

Later Pioneers

Although the science of developmental psychology owes much to early "child philosophers" such as Rousseau and Locke, its beginnings are usually attributed to the first systematic observations and written accounts of children. Preyer's detailed observations of his own children are generally considered among the first significant studies in child development (Preyer, 1888/1889), as is Darwin's biography of his son (Darwin, 1877).

■ HALL

Hard on the heels of these two pioneers followed G. Stanley Hall (1891), the first president of the American Psychological Association, who was profoundly influenced by Darwin's theories of evolution. "**Ontogeny** recapitulates **phylogeny,**" Hall informed his colleagues, summarizing in one short sentence his conviction that the development of an individual in a species parallels the evolution of the entire species. As evidence for this theory, Hall described the evolution of children's interests in games, noting how these seem to correspond to the evolution of human occupations and lifestyles. The child is, in sequence, interested in games corresponding to each of the following: tree-dwelling (for example, climbing on chairs and tables); living in caves (crawling into small spaces, making tiny shelters with old blankets); a pastoral existence (playing with animals); an agricultural life (tending flowers and plants); and finally industrialization (playing with vehicles).

Hall pioneered the use of the questionnaire for studying children. Often, he presented his questionnaires to adults, asking them to remember what they had felt and thought as children. And always, he summed, tabulated, averaged, and compared the results of his questionnaires, serving as an important pioneer in the application of scientific procedures in the study of human development.

■ WATSON

Another pioneer of child psychology was John B. Watson, who introduced an experimental, learning-theory-based approach to the study of development. Following his influence, as well as B. F. Skinner's, this model dominated child study through the early part of the twentieth century. It was a model that looked for the causes of developmental change among the rewards and punishments of the environment and viewed the child as the passive recipient of these influences.

Recurring Questions

A handful of important questions have been recurring themes in developmental psychology and have guided much of its research and theorizing. The Locke–Rousseau question is one of them:

> Is it best to view the child as an active, exploring organism, discovering or inventing meaning for the world, as Rousseau argued? Or is it more useful to emphasize, as did Locke, the effects of rewards and punishments on a more passive recipient?

Nowadays, most developmental psychologists don't adhere passionately to one or the other point of view as did Locke and Rousseau. However, the predominant view is of an active,

exploring child (Rousseau's view), while recognizing the importance of reward and punishment.

> What are the relative effects of genes and of environments on the developmental process?

This question has been the source of one of the greatest controversies in psychology: the **nature–nurture controversy.** Extreme points of view maintain either that the environment is solely responsible for whatever we become (nurture) or that genetic background (nature) determines the outcome of development. Although neither of these extreme positions is completely valid, the issue continues to be debated and is discussed in some detail in Chapter 3.

> Is development a continuous, relatively uninterrupted process, or does it consist of separate stages?

As for most of the recurring questions in lifespan development, there is no simple answer; otherwise, the questions would long since have been replaced by their answers. **Stages** in developmental psychology are typically defined as separate, sequential steps in the evolution of abilities, understandings, or competencies, these steps being closely related to age. As we see in the next chapter, many important developmental theories are stage theories (for example, Piaget's or Freud's). But as we also see, it has been difficult to identify abilities or competencies that invariably develop in a fixed, predictable sequence, appearing at a predetermined age. We don't develop like caterpillars: cocoon to butterfly to egg to cocoon to butterfly, each stage undeniably different from the one preceding or following. Nevertheless, stage theories are useful in organizing the facts of human development and in helping us understand and talk about them.

> Is development invariably positive? Does all developmental change represent an improvement in abilities or other characteristics?

The answer seems clear: Age brings some obvious decline in certain physical characteristics such as strength, speed, and stamina, as well as in the functioning of senses such as vision and hearing (even as it brings inevitable death, which, at least in one sense, represents decline). But what is not clear is whether it is also accompanied by inevitable decline in intellectual functions such as remembering or solving problems. And if there is decline in these areas, how bad is it? Can it be avoided or lessened? As is discussed in some detail in Chapter 15, these questions are a source of controversy—not only because some of the answers are not particularly pleasant but also because they sometimes contradict our logic, our research, or our intuition (see Summary Table 1.6).

■ METHODS OF STUDYING THE LIFESPAN

Observers of human development can focus on *natural* events, such as children playing in a park; they may collect information on less naturally occurring events, such as old people being interviewed; or they can collect *experimental* observations. In addition, lifespan research may be *longitudinal* (following the

PIONEERS	IDENTIFYING BELIEF
Locke	■ Children are like empty vessels, passive recipients of the effects of experience.
Rousseau	■ Children are active, inquiring, and basically good unless society corrupts them.
Preyer and Darwin	■ The details of children's development can be clarified through detailed observation and reporting.
Hall	■ Ontogeny (the development of the individual) recapitulates phylogeny (the development of the race).
Watson and Skinner	■ Children are shaped by their environments.

RECURRING QUESTIONS	CAPSULE ANSWERS
1. Is the child best viewed as active or passive?	■ Children are typically seen as actively exploring and learning, but also as influenced by the outcomes of their behavior.
2. What are the relative effects of genes and environments on development?	■ Their interaction is complex; both are critically involved in all facets of development (see Chapter 3).
3. Is development continuous, or does it occur in stages?	■ Although there are no clear breaks between developmental periods, stages are often useful for understanding and summarizing important aspects of human development.
4. Is development invariably positive?	■ Some age-related decline in certain aspects of human functioning seems inevitable. How much decline, in what areas, and the extent to which decline can be delayed, prevented, or reversed are not always clear.

same subjects over a period of time) or *cross-sectional* (using a cross section of different subjects at one point in time). Note that these categories are not mutually exclusive. For example, a lifespan study might be experimental and longitudinal or cross-sectional simultaneously. Each of these approaches is described in the following sections.

Observation

Observation is the basis of all science. The study of the lifespan always begins with either naturalistic or nonnaturalistic observation.

■ NATURALISTIC OBSERVATION

Observations are termed **naturalistic** when people are observed without interference in natural rather than contrived situations—for example, on the playground or in school. Psychologists who observe children and write diary descrip-

tions of their behavior are making use of naturalistic observation. Similarly, those who describe continuous sequences of behavior **(specimen descriptions)**, specific behaviors only **(event sampling)**, or behaviors during specified time intervals **(time sampling)** are using naturalistic observations (Wright, 1960; see also Table 1.7). In each of these naturalistic methods, the hope is that the observation will not affect the subject's behavior. In naturalistic observation, it is important that the investigator be a detached observer.

Time and event sampling are often used together. Time sampling specifies when observations will be made; event sampling specifies what will be observed. For example, if an investigator wanted to determine whether a new approach to teaching encourages student participation, a combination of time and event sampling would be appropriate. During specified intervals over a number of days (time sampling), the investigator would record instances of student participation (event sampling). Subsequently, observed participation before and after introduction of the new teaching method would be compared.

■ NONNATURALISTIC OBSERVATION

In *nonnaturalistic observation,* the investigation affects the subject's behavior. Nonnaturalistic observations are sometimes called *clinical* if they use interviews or questionnaires. If they attempt to manipulate or change the environment, they are termed *experimental.*

Experiments

Science's most powerful tool for gathering useful observations is the **experiment.** An experiment is distinguished from other observations in that it requires deliberately and systematically manipulating some aspect of a situation to detect and measure the effects of doing so. In an experiment, the observer controls certain **variables**—termed **independent**—to investigate their effect on other variables—termed **dependent.** For example, in an experiment designed to investigate the relationship between two teaching methods and the development of language skills, the experimenter can manipulate (control) the variable teaching method by arranging for the use of teaching method A with one group of students and teaching method B with a second group. In addition, if we are to have faith in the results of the experiment, subjects must be randomly assigned to methods A or B to guard against the possibility that students in one group might have some systematic advantage over students in the other.

In this illustration, teaching method is the independent variable; it is under the experimenter's control. Measures of the subjects' language skills are the dependent variable. The experimenter's **hypothesis** (scientific prediction) is that the independent variable (teaching method) will affect the dependent variable (language skills).

Experimental procedures often involve the use of experimental groups and control groups. **Experimental groups** are ordinarily made up of subjects who are treated in some special way. In this case, the goal is usually to discover whether the

TABLE 1.7

Naturalistic Observation in Developmental Research

METHOD	DESCRIPTION	MAIN USES	EXAMPLE
Diary description	Fairly regular (often daily or weekly) descriptions of important events and changes.	Detecting and understanding major changes and developmental sequences.	Investigator keeps detailed, sequential record of child's speech.
Specimen description	Detailed description of sequences of behavior, detailing all aspects of behavior.	Studying individual children in depth; not restricted to only one or two predetermined characteristics.	Investigator videotapes sequences of woman's behavior for later analysis.
Time sampling	Behaviors are recorded intermittently during short but regular periods of time.	Detecting and assessing changes in specific behaviors over time.	Investigator records what prisoner is doing during 30-second spans, once every 30 minutes.
Event sampling	Specific behaviors (events) are recorded during the observational period, and other behaviors are ignored.	Understanding the nature and frequency of specific behaviors (events).	Investigator notes each time child bangs her head on the wall.

Source: Based in part on Wright, 1960.

special treatment (independent variable) has a predictable effect on some outcome (dependent variable). To ensure that any changes in the dependent variable are due to the treatment, it is often necessary to use a second group—the **control group** (also called the *no-treatment* group). This second group must be as similar as possible to the experimental group in all relevant ways. The effect of the special treatment is then assessed by comparing the two groups with respect to some outcome (dependent variable) after the experimental group has been given the treatment.[*]

A careful, well-controlled experiment that can be replicated is science's only reliable method for discovering causes and effects. Experiments that cannot be replicated—that is, experiments that lead to different conclusions on different occasions—tell us nothing about causes and effects. Science pays little attention to things that happen only once.

Unfortunately, there are many situations in psychological research in which a controlled experiment cannot be conducted—or would be highly unethical. For example, although it might be useful to randomly assign children to conditions of poverty (or war, or abuse) in order to determine what the impact of these conditions might be on their development, this can hardly be done. In many such cases, **correlational studies** might be used instead of experiments.

Correlational Studies

Many developmental studies proceed as follows: Researchers decide to investigate the sources (causes) of specific charac-

teristics; people with these characteristics are identified; a comparison group without the same characteristics is found; and an attempt is made to obtain historical information about the people in these two groups (home environment, presence or absence of a father, intelligence, similar characteristics in biological ancestors, and so on). Researchers then compare the two groups with respect to these historical variables. In the end, a relationship (correlation)[*] will be found to exist between specific historical variables and present characteristics, or no relationship will be found.

Through studies such as these, research has established relationships between variables such as poverty and delinquency, and between the personality characteristics of parents and those of children. Many such studies are described in this text. They are sometimes called *retrospective* studies because they try to establish relationships by looking backward at the person's history (*retro* means "backward") to see how factors in the individual's past affect present behavior.

■ THE CORRELATIONAL FALLACY

One caution is very important here. One of the most common errors in the interpretation of research results stems from the apparently logical but false assumption that if two events are related (correlated), one causes the other. This is termed the **correlational fallacy**. For example, some studies have demonstrated that children from disadvantaged homes (low socioeconomic level, low parental education, low academic aspirations, and so on) often do less well in school

---

[*]This is only one of a large variety of experimental designs (arrangements) that are employed in psychological research. For others, see Ray (1993).

---

[*]A correlation is a statistical measure of relationship. It is usually expressed as a number ranging from +1.00 (a perfect *positive* relationship—as one variable increases, so does the other) to −1.00 (a perfect *inverse* relationship—as one variable increases, the other decreases).

than children from more advantaged backgrounds. Does this mean that home background causes low or high achievement? No. At best, correlational studies show relationships or their absence; they do not establish causation. Thus, there is often a high positive correlation between the number of police officers in an area and rates of juvenile delinquency. Does this mean that police officers cause delinquency? No. It is more likely that both are related to a third factor—perhaps something as simple as population. Thus, with higher population there is more crime—and more policing (as well as more churches, more schools, more mothers, and so on). Hence, correlation never establishes that something is necessarily the cause of something else. On the other hand, when two events are causally related, there will be a correlation between them. For this reason, correlational research can be extremely valuable for those who investigate human development, providing that the results of such research are interpreted with caution.

Longitudinal and Cross-Sectional Studies

There are two broad approaches to the study of human development: the longitudinal and the cross-sectional. A **longi-** **tudinal study** observes the *same* subjects over a period of time; a **cross-sectional study** compares *different* subjects at one point in time. For example, there are two ways of investigating changes in the use of game-playing rules by two-year-olds and six-year-olds. One is to observe a group of two-year-olds at play to identify their game rules, and four years later repeat the same procedure with the same children. This is the *longitudinal* approach. The second approach, the *cross-sectional,* might simply look at groups of two- and six-year-old children at one point in time and compare them directly.

For some questions, a longitudinal approach is clearly best. For example, Leiter and Johnsen (1997) asked this question: "Does school performance decline as a function of child abuse and neglect?" The simplest and least time-consuming approach to this question would have been to identify a group of abused or neglected children and to compare their school performance with that of a group of nonabused and nonneglected children. But would this approach actually answer the question? What if the investigators found that the abused children performed less well? Could they now conclude that abuse or neglect leads to poorer school performance?

The answer is no, because a *cross-sectional* approach such as this is insensitive to *intraindividual change.* That is, it cannot reveal that any given individual has changed, but shows

The longitudinal approach to studying human development looks at changes in the same individuals at different points in time. Longitudinal studies sometimes cover very short periods of time, or they might span subjects' entire lives. Shown here are photos of the same individual at different points in his lifespan.

only that this individual (or group of individuals) is different from some other individual(s) at this point in time. And there may well be any number of very plausible explanations for these observed differences. For example, the maltreated children may have been performing less well than others right from the very beginning, perhaps even before they were abused. This, in fact, might be one of the reasons why some of them are maltreated.

Accordingly, to answer the question of whether maltreatment is related to school performance, Leiter and Johnsen (1997) undertook a *longitudinal* investigation. In this study, they studied a sample of 967 maltreated children for whom they had a wealth of data, including information regarding the nature and timing of maltreatment as well as school performance records covering as many as twelve years in some cases. Using this information, they were able to look specifically at the question of whether the school performance of each of these 967 individuals tended to decline following the child's being maltreated (no children who had been maltreated prior to starting school were included in the sample). Their conclusion? A significant relationship exists among child maltreatment and falling grades, school absenteeism, increased behavior problems, school failure, and inclusion in special needs programs. (See Chapter 10 for a more detailed discussion of this study and of the nature, prevalence, and consequences of child maltreatment.)

ADVANTAGES AND DISADVANTAGES

The Leiter and Johnsen (1997) study illustrates the principal advantage of longitudinal research: In contrast with cross-sectional research, the longitudinal approach *is* sensitive to intraindividual change. That is, it allows the investigator to observe change in specific individuals. It is for this reason that longitudinal studies are essential for studying individual development.

Longitudinal research has a number of disadvantages and limitations. Not only can it be very expensive and time-consuming, but there is also the possibility that instruments and methods may become outdated before the research is completed, or that some of the research questions will be answered in some other way. Often, a longitudinal investigation must be designed so that it can go beyond the lifetime of a single investigator (or team of investigators), especially if it is intended to examine most or all of the human lifespan. This is the case with the Terman study of giftedness that began in the early 1920s and continues today (Terman et al., 1925). This kind of longitudinal study encounters an additional problem: loss of subjects either because they die or simply because they drop out of the study. Loss of subjects by death not only reduces the size of samples but may also bias the results. For example, if aggressive people die before those who are not aggressive, a longitudinal study might lead to the conclusion that people become less aggressive as they age.

Loss of subjects because they drop out can also introduce biases. When Janus and Goldberg (1997) looked at subject loss in a longitudinal study of family relationships, they found highly consistent tendencies for families with specific, identifiable characteristics to drop out. As Sullivan and associates (1996) note, the final remaining sample may be clearly nonrepresentative and the conclusions invalid.

Longitudinal research also often suffers from nonrandom sampling. As Bergman (1996) points out, there is a tendency for researchers to select samples that fit certain characteristics: All subjects are in the same school system or the same care facility, they share some important common characteristic, or they are simply willing to be subjects. These sources of bias, coupled with the possibility of further biasing of samples through selective subject attrition, have to be kept in mind when drawing conclusions and generalizing them (Goodman and Blum, 1996).

The cross-sectional approach to studying change through the lifespan compares individuals who are at different developmental stages—sometimes comparing people who represent entirely different generations, of which there are four represented in this photo of a Navajo family from the southwestern United States.

Another limitation of longitudinal studies is that their conclusions often depend on the assumption that currently valid measures will be equally valid later. This problem is illustrated in longitudinal studies of vocabulary growth or intelligence, for example, where rapidly changing cultural conditions may significantly affect the appropriateness of the measures used.

Many of the problems associated with longitudinal research (for example, subject loss, higher cost, greater time requirement, changing contexts in the lives of subjects) apply only to longer-term research. But not all longitudinal research is long-term. For example, longitudinal studies of infant development might span only weeks, or perhaps only days or hours. However, because human development spans a huge spread of years, much of our longitudinal research is necessarily long-term.

The main disadvantage of cross-sectional studies is that they do not tell the researcher anything about changes that occur within individuals. This is so because they do not compare the same children to themselves at different ages. Instead, they compare groups of different children—perhaps of different ages—to each other. Hence, they are useful for providing information about differences among groups but not within individuals.

A second disadvantage of cross-sectional studies is that their conclusions often depend on the validity of the assumption that children at one age level now are comparable to children at that age level at another time. With respect to intelligence, for example, drastic improvements in educational experiences and perhaps in television fare can affect children over time to the extent that measures of intelligence obtained at one time cannot easily be compared with measures obtained earlier.

Sources of Variation: Age, Time, and Cohort

Developmental research looks at how people change as they develop. What researchers are most interested in are changes that are related to age. However, research results are sometimes misleading because changes in human behavior might also be due to one of two other factors. First, there may be influences related to the time of testing. Thus, the same intelligence test given a decade before and decade after the appearance of television might reveal striking differences that are not age-related.

Much more significant for the developmental researcher is the influence of the cohort (Schaie, 1996). A **cohort** is a group of individuals who were born within the same range of time. For example, the cohort of the decade of the 1980s includes all those who were born from the beginning of 1980 to the end of 1989. Therefore, a cohort is of a specific size and composition initially and does not normally increase in size. Instead, it becomes less numerous as members die, until it has completely disappeared. Its composition also changes gradually in important ways. For example, because

men die at younger ages than women, the male:female ratio of a cohort usually changes over time. Similarly, racial composition might also change as a result of different mortality rates.

What is most important for the lifespan psychologist is that members of different cohorts may be subject to very different experiences as they develop. For example, cohort groups such as that of my grandmother date to the turn of this century and include people who were born into a world without radios, automobiles, televisions, or computers. These obvious cohort-related influences might be important in attempting to understand why an eighty-year-old person in 1996 might be quite different from an eighty-year-old in 2026 or in 1946. Less obvious cohort-related influences would also include changes in medical practices (including the general use of a variety of inoculations, for example), nutrition, recreation, work roles, morality, and so on. Because of these influences, cohorts might be very different in some important ways.

SEPARATING THE EFFECTS OF AGE AND COHORT

A serious problem in developmental research is that of separating the effects of age and cohort, which often become confounded in both longitudinal and cross-sectional research. For example, consider the apparently simple task of determining whether performance on intelligence tests changes with age. A cross-sectional approach would require administering intelligence tests to several different groups of subjects— say, one group of twenty-year-olds and one of seventy-year-olds—and comparing their performance. But what would it mean if differences were found among these groups—if, for example, seventy-year-olds scored higher than twenty-year-olds? Would it mean that intelligence increases with age or, at least, that seventy-year-olds are more intelligent than twenty-year-olds?

Perhaps not. The problem is that a cross-sectional design uses samples that, because they are of different ages at the same time, are by definition different cohorts. With a simple cross-sectional design, there is no way to tell whether differences found between groups are related to their different ages, to the distinct experiences that might be associated with different cohorts, or to both.

Would a longitudinal design answer the question more accurately? Suppose that the same subjects were tested when they were twenty and again when they were twenty-five, thirty, and so on. Scores for each individual would then be compared across all age ranges. What if there were differences now? Could we confidently assert that these are related to age and that we have established that intelligence changes in such and such a way as individuals age? Again, perhaps not. One of the problems with longitudinal research is that only one cohort is used throughout the study. As a result, developmental changes identified in such research are not always universal. They might result from something specific to the history of the cohort; they might also be due to the time at which the testing occurred.

Sequential and Time-Lag Designs

One way of overcoming these important research problems is to use **sequential designs** (see Tudge, Shanahan, & Valsiner, 1997). This involves taking sequences of samples at different times of measurement. One well-known sequential design is the **time-lag study**, in which different cohorts are compared at different times. For example, a time-lag study might compare ten-year-olds in 1997 with ten-year-olds in 1999, 2001, and 2003. Because these subjects are the same age when tested but were born in different years, they belong to different cohorts. Consequently, observed differences among the groups might reveal important cohort-related influences.

■ AN ILLUSTRATION

An excellent example of a sequential design is the thirty-five-year longitudinal study conducted by Schaie and associates (see Figure 1.5). The study began in 1956 as a simple cross-sectional investigation of differences in intellectual functioning among groups of individuals ages twenty-five to sixty-seven. Schaie (1996) soon realized that a cross-sectional design would not answer important questions about changes that occur within individuals. Accordingly, seven years later he retested as many of the original samples as he could and also selected a second series of samples ages twenty-five to seventy-four (those who had been sixty-seven in 1956 were now seventy-four). A third group was added seven years later (1970); this group included a sample of eighty-one-year-olds because the oldest samples in the 1956 and 1963 samples were now eighty-one. A fourth sample was added in 1977, a fifth in 1984, and a sixth in 1991. Because samples were selected at seven-year intervals, sub-

jects are grouped by cohort and by age in clusters seven years apart—that is, ages twenty-five, thirty-two, thirty-nine, forty-six, fifty-three, sixty, sixty-seven, seventy-four, eighty-one, eighty-eight, and ninety-five. Results of this study are discussed in Chapter 15.

Which Method?

In practice, the methods used by those who investigate development are determined by the questions they want to answer. Some questions can best be answered with one approach, others with another. And some questions, of course, lend themselves to more than one approach. If you are interested in knowing whether children have more affection for cats than for dogs, you might simply compare the number of children who have dogs with the number who have cats (naturalistic observation). Alternatively, you might ask a sample of children which they like best (interview technique). Or you might arrange for different children, alone and in groups, to meet different cats and dogs—also alone and in groups (experimental approach)—and assess their reactions (through simple visual observation or perhaps by measuring their heart rates and other physiological functions).

Notice that each of these approaches might lead to somewhat different answers for the same questions. Perhaps there are more cats than dogs in the homes of your subjects—many parents think cats are less demanding—but children really like dogs better. And maybe, even if they do like dogs better, more children would be afraid of dogs than of cats because strange dogs are more frightening than strange cats. It's important to keep in mind as you go through the studies described in this text that conclusions are sometimes partly a

FIGURE 1.5

Schematic representation of the sequential design used in the Seattle Longitudinal Study. The years in the table indicate times of measurement. Vertical columns represent possible time-lag studies (different cohorts, different times of measurement, same age); horizontal rows represent longitudinal studies (the same cohort examined at up to five points in time); and diagonals represent cross-sectional studies (as many as nine cohorts examined at a single point in time). (Based on Schaie, 1965; 1983a; 1986; 1996.)

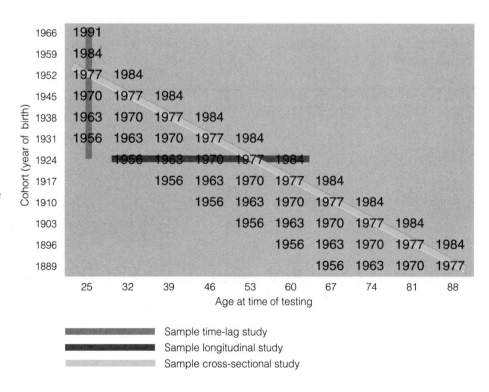

Cohort (year of birth)	25	32	39	46	53	60	67	74	81	88
1966	1991									
1959	1984									
1952	1977	1984								
1945	1970	1977	1984							
1938	1963	1970	1977	1984						
1931	1956	1963	1970	1977	1984					
1924	1956	1963	1970	1977	1984					
1917		1956	1963	1970	1977	1984				
1910			1956	1963	1970	1977	1984			
1903				1956	1963	1970	1977	1984		
1896					1956	1963	1970	1977	1984	
1889						1956	1963	1970	1977	

Age at time of testing

▬▬▬ Sample time-lag study
▬▬▬ Sample longitudinal study
▬▬▬ Sample cross-sectional study

function of research methods; they might have been different had the investigation been conducted differently.

In many cases, the study of the lifespan involves a combination of methods rather than a single method. Experiments typically require observations. Hence, interviews and questionnaires are often part of an experiment. (See Summary Table 1.8.)

CRITERIA FOR EVALUATING LIFESPAN RESEARCH

Truth in psychology, as in most disciplines, is relative rather than absolute. Conclusions derived from research are seldom flatly right or wrong; instead, they are judged in terms of usefulness, clarity, logical consistency, and generalizability. Of all these criteria, perhaps **generalizability** is the most important. The value of conclusions that can't be generalized is highly limited.

Sampling

Researchers in psychology try to reach conclusions that are generalizable to an entire **population**—that is, to entire collections of individuals with similar characteristics. In most cases, the populations that are of interest to the researcher are too large to be investigated in their entirety. What the investigator does, instead, is select a **sample** from this larger population, carefully chosen to represent the entire population. For example, it would be difficult to obtain valid information concerning the moral beliefs and behaviors of American children by observing a sample of subjects from San Francisco or Boston alone. If the results are to be generalized to the entire population, subjects should represent all major geographical areas in the nation. In addition, all nationalities, major religious groups, socioeconomic levels, occupations, and ages should be represented in proportions similar to the entire population. One of the simplest and most effective ways of ensuring that this is the case is to select subjects at random from the population.

Ecological Validity

There is a large body of research that indicates that Japanese students perform better on measures of mathematics achievement than do American students (see, for example, Westbury et al., 1993). Several conclusions can be based on this observation: Japanese students are more intelligent—or at least more capable in mathematics, the Japanese school system is more effective than the American school system, Japanese parents are more demanding than are American parents, or a combination of all three.

Are these conclusions valid? No, says Westbury (1992)—a more careful analysis of the data suggests that the Japanese

▲ **SUMMARY TABLE 1.8**

Methods of Studying Lifespan Development

Observation	■ The basis of all science. Observation is naturalistic when subjects are observed without interference in natural rather than contrived situations. Naturalistic observation may involve time or event sampling, diary descriptions, or specimen descriptions (see Table 1.7). Nonnaturalistic observation may be clinical when it involves structured interviews or questionnaires.
Experiments	■ Science's most powerful means of gathering observations. Experiments involve systematic attempts to manipulate the environment to observe what the effects of specific independent variables are on dependent variables.
Correlational studies	■ Examinations of relationships among two or more variables. A correlation exists when changes in one variable are accompanied by systematic changes in another (for example, during childhood, increasing age is correlated positively with increasing strength). The existence of a correlation is necessary but insufficient for inferring causality.
Longitudinal studies	■ The same subjects are studied at different ages over a period of time **Disadvantages:** Time-consuming; expensive; measures may become invalid before the research is completed; subject loss. Looks at only one cohort; hence, results may not be highly generalizable. **Advantages:** Sensitive to *intraindividual* change, hence essential for studying change in an individual.
Cross-Sectional studies	■ Subjects of different ages are studied at one point in time. **Disadvantages:** Does not detect change within an individual; cannot separate the effects of age from effects of the cohort (period during which subjects were born). **Advantages:** Less time-consuming; less expensive; answers some questions clearly.

mathematics curriculum fits the tests used in the study more closely than does the American curriculum. This gives Japanese students an unfair advantage. When students are compared only on what they have been taught, American students do about as well as Japanese students.*

---

*Not all researchers agree with Westbury's conclusions. Some, like Baker (1993), argue that even when American students are tested only on what they have been taught, they still do more poorly. Considerable controversy exists concerning whether there are real differences between American and Japanese children in mathematics achievement and what the reasons are for any such differences.

When comparing children from different cultures—or even when comparing children within single multicultural nations—we can never be certain that observed differences reflect real differences (in underlying capacities, for example) or whether they result from the influences of different ecologies—different environments. As Bernal, Bonilla, and Bellido (1995) argue, researchers have to be aware of the cultural sensitivity of their approaches and their conclusions. And the consumer of research has to take into consideration the **ecological validity** of scientific findings—that is, the extent to which they are applicable in other contexts.

The fact that people from different cultures often perform differently on various tests and in different situations underlines the importance of asking (1) whether the tests and assessment procedures we're using are suitable for different cultures and (2) what the underlying causes of observed differences might be. Conclusions based on research conducted only with North American samples may not be valid in western Europe or in developing countries. Similarly, research conducted only with white middle-class subjects in North America should not be generalized to the entire North American population. Throughout this text, boxed inserts titled "Across Cultures" are used to emphasize the extent to which we are products of our contexts, as well as the extent to which contexts can vary even within a single culture.

Memory

Studies of the ages at which girls experience their first menstrual period (**menarche**) have often had to rely on the memories of women for whom the event may not be entirely recent; investigations of the ages at which children first walk or talk sometimes base their conclusions on the memories of mothers. Unfortunately, human memory is far from perfect. Not only does it forget, but it also distorts—sometimes in predictable ways, sometimes not.

Honesty

Having to rely on the honesty of subjects is a serious problem with questionnaire and interview data, especially when highly personal areas are being researched. Comparisons of contemporary adolescent sexual behavior with behavior that was characteristic of adolescents several generations ago are typically unreliable mainly for this reason. Given prevailing attitudes toward sexual behavior, it is not unreasonable to suppose that today's adolescent may be more honest about sexual behavior than the adolescent of the 1930s might have been.

Experimenter Bias

Some research indicates that experimenters sometimes inadvertently bias the results of their experiments in the direction of their expectations. One effective way to guard against experimenter bias is the **double-blind procedure.** This requires simply that the experimenters and examiners, as well as subjects, not be aware of the expected outcomes of the research or which subjects are experimental subjects and which are members of the control group.

SUBJECT BIAS

Subject bias may also have an effect on the outcome of an experiment. In a highly publicized experiment, two psychologists compared ways to increase productivity among workers in the Hawthorne plant of the Western Electric Company in Chicago (Roethlisberger & Dickson, 1939). In successive experiments, the workers were subjected to shorter and longer working periods, better and poorer lighting conditions, long and short periods of rest, work incentives such as bonuses, and other conditions. Under most of these conditions, productivity apparently increased. This observation led to the conclusion that if subjects are aware they are members of an experimental group, performance may improve simply because of that fact.

Although the "Hawthorne effect," as it is now called, is usually accepted as fact in social science research, its existence has not been well established—in spite of the experiments just described. Following a careful reexamination of these experiments and interviews with some of the people who were involved at that time, Rice (1982) found little evidence of a Hawthorne effect. He reports that productivity did not increase in many of the experiments but that later reports of the study usually concentrated only on experiments in which there was a marked improvement over the five-year course of the study.[*] It's ironic that the Hawthorne experiments, which were designed to demonstrate subject bias, might instead be an example of experimenter bias.

SOME SPECIAL PROBLEMS

Problems involving inadequate sampling, memory distortions, questionable honesty, and experimenter or subject bias may affect research in all areas of psychology. In addition, lifespan research is faced with a handful of unique problems. One such problem, already mentioned, is that of comparing different cohorts. Many lifespan questions concern important changes that occur with advancing age or that follow major transitions. Identifying and investigating these changes often require the comparison of different cohorts. It is often difficult to determine whether observed differences are due to

---

[*]In this particular experiment, workers (all women) were paid according to the productivity of the entire group. Because there were only seven or eight women in the group, individual productivity would have a noticeable effect on the pay received by each woman. Accordingly, when several of the experimental group members proved to be slower than the average, the other women became unhappy; as a result, the slower workers were dropped from the group. Under these circumstances, is it any wonder that the experimental group's performance should improve?

Those who study lifespan developmental changes are faced with the problem of separating the effects of time from those of the individual's cohort. Because of the vastly different historical periods in which they were born and raised, when the youngest members of this large, extended family have lived as long as the oldest, they might be very different from them.

changes that occur with age or simply reflect different cohort experiences.

A second problem specific to lifespan research is related to difficulties experienced in obtaining large, representative samples. Because most children are in schools for a large part of their childhood and are therefore easily accessible to researchers, this problem applies much less to them than it does to older subjects. In fact, approximately only 5 percent of the "oldest old"* are in retirement homes and other institutions for the aged. Unfortunately, this relatively small number of individuals serves as the subject group for an overwhelming majority of studies of the aged. Accordingly, investigators must be concerned about whether these subjects are actually representative of others not living in institutions. Also, they must always keep in mind that as people become older, they may become less representative. That is, there may be something special that allows ninety-year-olds to live so long. Death does not always select at random.

The use of institutionalized individuals in psychological research poses an additional problem relating to research ethics. First, not all elderly people are capable of informed consent; second, there are sometimes subtle forms of coercion involved in research with those in institutions. Some might feel pressured into participating simply by being members of a group; others might volunteer to please their attendants or to ensure favorable treatment.

The use of children in psychological research also gives rise to ethical issues. These issues are addressed in the American Psychological Association's adoption of ethical prin-

ciples to guide research with children ("Ethical Standards for Research with Children," 1973). These principles recognize that research can be unethical when children are coerced into participating, when they are exposed to stress or other potentially damaging conditions, when their privacy is invaded, and so on. The principles specify not only that permission of parents but also permission of children must be obtained before conducting child research. Furthermore, consent must be "informed" in the sense that all are fully aware of any aspect of the research that might affect their willingness to participate. (See Summary/Interactive Table 1.9 for a checklist for evaluating developmental research.)

THE MYTHICAL AVERAGE

A word of caution is appropriate at this point. This book deals largely with so-called average individuals—with the normal processes of conception, fetal growth, birth, infancy, childhood, adolescence, adulthood, old age, and death. It describes typical behavior and characteristics throughout the lifespan, and it discusses theoretical explanations of normal patterns of development.

There Is No Average Child

But there is no average child, let alone adult! The concept is a convenient invention, a necessary creation if we are to speak coherently of human development. Bear in mind that each person is a unique individual, that each will differ from the average, and that no one theory will account for all behavior. We are incredibly more complex than any description provided by even the most complex of theories. A the-

---

*Although "oldest old" is uncomfortably vague, our studies and theories of aging have not yet provided us with terms that are sufficiently specific and widely understood to discriminate among older age groups in the way that the terms *neonate, infant, child,* and *adolescent* distinguish among those who are younger. In this context, the "very old" are over eighty-five.

ory—and a book—can deal only with the objective details of human behavior, not with its essence.

There Is No Average Context

Just as there is no average child, there is no average environment—no average context. And context is fundamentally important in determining what we become. Being born in a wooden hut in the rain forests of the Amazon basin must surely lead to a very different life than being delivered by a private doctor in a New York City medical center. Being raised in a war-ravaged country or in a peaceful and isolated village must surely shape children's lives in profound ways.

But our world is changing remarkably rapidly. Most of our villages are no longer isolated. Telephones, computers, satellites, television, airplanes, transnational corporations—these bind and shape us in a shrinking global village.

Still, our contexts are different, private. And a psychology that would understand us, that would uncover the mysteries of our lives, must be sensitive to the private mysteries of our worlds.

▲ SUMMARY/INTERACTIVE TABLE 1.9
Checklist for Evaluating Developmental Research

Sampling	■ Is the sample a good representation of the population to which the observations and conclusions are meant to apply?
Ecological validity	■ Is there something special or unique about the social, cultural, or historical context in which observations are made? Do the unique characteristics of the environment reduce the generalizability of the findings?
Memory	■ Does the investigation have to rely on human memories? Has the possibility of systematic or random distortion been taken into account?
Honesty	■ Does the validity of the observations depend on the honesty of subjects? Do they have a reason to distort facts consciously or unconsciously?
Experimenter or subject bias	■ Is there a possibility that experimenter or subject expectations might have influenced observations?
Ethical issues	■ Have the rights of all participants been considered and safeguarded?

Interaction: Analyze an example of lifespan research (for example, a research article), using the preceding checklist as a guide.

▐ FOCUS QUESTIONS: SUMMARY ANSWERS

1. What is the lifespan perspective of human development?

   ■ The contemporary lifespan view of development recognizes that change continues throughout the lifespan, that maturity is a relative and changing state *throughout* the lifespan, that it is important to consider the context (ecology) of human development, and that developmental influences are bidirectional.

2. How are growth, maturation, learning, and development related?

   ■ Development, the total process by which individuals adapt to their environment, includes maturation (genetically programmed unfolding), growth (quantitative changes), and learning (changes due to experience).

3. What are the most basic of children's rights?

   ■ Rights of protection and of access to growth-fostering conditions (rather than the more adult rights of choice). The UN provides a list of specific rights.

4. What questions keep recurring in the study of human development?

   ■ Is the child best seen as active or passive? How do heredity and environment interact? Is development continuous, or does it progress in discrete stages? Is development primarily linear, characterized initially by increments followed by inevitable decline in the later stages of life?

5. How do we study lifespan development?

   ■ Observation (naturalistic or nonnaturalistic) is the basis of all science. Nonnaturalistic observations may be clinical (using questionnaires or interviews) or experimental (deliberately manipulating the environment to investigate cause-and-effect relationships). Longitudinal studies examine the same individuals at different periods in their lives; cross-sectional studies compare different individuals at the same time.

STUDY TERMS

FURTHER READINGS

Ariès provides some fascinating, and sometimes frightening, accounts of how children have been viewed and treated throughout history:

Ariès, P. (1962). *Centuries of childhood: A social history of family life* (R. Baldick, Trans.). New York: Knopf. (Originally published 1960.)

Hwang, Lamb, and Sigel present an unusual approach to uncovering what different cultures and different historical contexts have thought of children and childhood. "Images" of childhood, they argue, are to be found not only in written beliefs about children's nature, their health, their intelligence, and their competence, but also in the myths and proverbs of a culture (as in the Japanese saying "Parents with three children have a happy life" or the Latin saying "Children, drunkards, and fools cannot lie").

Hwang, C. P., Lamb, M. E., & Sigel, I. E. (Eds.). (1996). *Images of childhood.* Mahwah, NJ: Erlbaum.

The following is a short book on science and its methods. It includes a number of useful suggestions for conducting experimental research as well as for writing research articles:

Ray, W. J. (1993). *Methods toward a science of behavior and experience* (4th ed.). Pacific Grove, CA: Brooks/Cole.

A booklet containing all the children's rights articles of the United Nation Convention on the Rights of the Child can be obtained free of charge:

United Nations Children's Fund
UNICEF House, H-9F
United Nations Plaza
New York, NY 10017
(212) 326-7072

An annual UNICEF series of publications titled *The State of the World's Children* presents an up-to-date, international summary of a number of important indicators of the well-being of the world's children. Among other things, these booklets look at child nutrition, mortality rates, education, involvement in war, and child labor:

Bellamy, C. (1997). *The state of the world's children: 1997.* New York: Oxford University Press.

Bellamy, C. (1996). *The state of the world's children: 1996.* New York: Oxford University Press.

FOCUS QUESTIONS

1. What purposes do theories serve?

2. What are the characteristics of a good theory?

3. What are the most basic ideas underlying the theories of Freud? Erikson? Piaget? Havighurst? Skinner? Bandura? Sociobiology? Vygotsky? Bronfenbrenner? Maslow?

TWO

Theories of Lifespan Development

"Now what I want is facts. Teach these boys and girls nothing but Facts. Facts alone are wanted in life. Plant nothing else, and root out everything else. . . . Stick to Facts, Sir!"

CHARLES DICKENS
Hard Times

'm standing on the buying side of the counter in Peltier's store; my dad, Father Paradis, Mr. Peltier, and Ricketts, the local policeman, are on the selling side. ¶ "It wasn't me, honest," I repeat again, like I'm trying to sell them something. But this time I really am innocent. The fact is that it is Sylvia Tremblay who has drowned the three cats in a gunnysack into which she had dropped a cast-iron skillet stolen from Peltier's store. That the gunnysack came from the green shed behind my grandfather's barn is almost the only thing that links me to the crime. ¶ "Maybe it's Sylvia again," says my dad. "Is it Sylvia?" the priest asks me, throwing me into a terrible conflict. To lie to a priest . . . I can almost smell my soul frying. I shrug. It's only half a lie . . . maybe not even half, because what does a shrug mean anyway? ¶ And then Sylvia flounces into the store to buy something, which is bad luck for her because now they point their accusations straight in her direction. "I didn't steal the cats," she insists. "They were just strays." Realizing that she has almost confessed, she quickly adds, "And I didn't drown them neither." But the pockets of her jacket, bulging with unused skillets, shout out her guilt—well, not really *her* jacket because it has just recently come from Marie Boutin's aunt's coat rack. Her boots are from somewhere else. ¶ Because it isn't the first time, they arrest her. Later, she stands in front of a judge and listens while they read a long list of the things she's supposed to have done. Her best friend, Cecile Watrin, stands next to her and holds her hand. Cecile's pockets are full of chocolate bars, which Sylvia gave her. ¶ "These are the facts," says the prosecutor when he finishes reading, smugly, clasping his hands tightly in anticipation. The judge weighs the facts for just a few moments before pronouncing his judgment. "The girl's a kleptomaniac," he says. "That's why she steals things." ¶

This Chapter

The judge was dead wrong. Maybe Sylvia was a kleptomaniac, but that doesn't explain why she stole things. "Kleptomaniac" is just a label, a name. To assume that naming something explains it is a common error called the **nominal fallacy**. To explain behavior, we need more than the labels that the facts suggest.

The *facts* of developmental psychology are the observations we make—the replicable, objective observations that are the basis of the discipline. But isolated facts don't necessarily lead to understanding; they seldom allow us to make predictions or to affect the outcomes of development. We need to go beyond facts; we need to build theories. That's what this chapter is about: theories that lifespan theorists have built to understand and explain their facts. Theories are what allow us to go beyond the facts.

This chapter deals with theories designed to explain normal and abnormal personality development (Freud and Erikson), theories intended to explain how we learn and how we respond to the consequences of our behaviors (conditioning and social-learning theories), theories that look at the development of mental capacities and processes (Piaget's cognitive theory, information-processing theory), theories concerned with the influences of culture and language on development (Vygotsky's sociocultural theories), and theories that look at the influences of biology on behavior (sociobiology and ethology). Each of these theories suggests different explanations for Sylvia Tremblay's behavior, and each might lead to a different kind of understanding.*

PSYCHOLOGICAL THEORIES

A **theory** is essentially a description and explanation of observations. A theory can be so specific and simple, says Kuhn (1970), that it attempts to explain only a single relationship. My grandfather's belief that drinking wild mint tea prevents colds is one such theory. The belief that kleptomaniacs are people whose left-handed mothers got pregnant on the night of a new moon in October is another. These types of beliefs are often labeled **naive theories** (or commonsense theories) (Wellman & Gelman, 1992).

Most of the theories that are important in the study of lifespan development are more general. They consist of collections of statements intended to organize and explain related observations. And most are based on more objective and systematic evidence than are naive theories.

---

*Even my grandmother's beliefs almost find justification in psychological theory. "The apple always falls close to the tree," she says—or "Blood is thicker than water," or "As the twig is bent, so grows the tree." All of these are remarkably good explanations of absolutely nothing at all.

Purposes of Theories

The purpose of theories is to explain. Explanation is important; if we can explain something, we might also be able to make predictions about it, and we might be able to control certain outcomes. If we can explain Sylvia's compulsion to steal, for example, we might be able to predict it before it happens. Or, better yet, we might be able to eradicate this compulsion or change it into something else, like an urge to sing arias from Italian operas.

Not only do theories have a very practical aspect; they are also one of science's primary guides for doing research. In large part, it is a theory—sometimes crude, sometimes elegant and refined—that tells the researcher where to look for a cure for cancer, what the cure will look like when it is found, and how it might be used. In the same way, psychology's theories tell the researcher where and how to look for personality or cognitive change in the lifespan; they also indicate why it might be important to look for that change.

Evaluating Theories

Why, you might ask, must there be a variety of theories if a theory is simply an explanation of facts? One reason is that different theories may be used to explain quite different facts. And even the most general theories of development are not all based on the same observations. Theorists select observations that they think need to be explained. Furthermore, given the same set of observations, not all theorists will arrive at the same explanations. And, finally, fact (or truth) is just as elusive in developmental psychology as it is elsewhere. Our observations are often relative. Their accuracy is affected by the imprecision of our observation (or measurement), they often apply only in specific circumstances and sometimes for specific individuals, and they are colored by our beliefs and expectations.

We cannot easily determine whether a theory is right or wrong, say Wellman and Gelman (1992), but we can evaluate it in terms of its usefulness.

CHARACTERISTICS OF GOOD THEORIES

Thomas (1996) suggests several criteria that might be used to judge a theory. A theory is better, he says, if it (1) accurately reflects the facts, (2) is expressed in a clearly understandable way, (3) is useful for predicting future events as well as explaining past ones, (4) is applicable in a practical sense (that is, has real value for counselors, teachers, pediatricians, and so on), (5) is consistent within itself rather than self-contradictory, and (6) is not based on numerous assumptions (unproven beliefs).

A good theory should also be thought-provoking and should have heuristic value—that is, it should be useful in our quest for knowledge. It should lead to new ideas, new discoveries, or new applications. And it should provide sat-

One of the measures of psychological theories is how useful they are in explaining observations considered important enough to need explaining—even when the observations relate to the thoughts and behaviors of people whose lives and experiences are as different as those of the Indiana Amish and the California surfer pictured here.

SUMMARY TABLE 2.1
Theories of Lifespan Development

Definition	▪ A systematic, organized collection of statements intended to explain important observations.
Purposes	▪ Explanation
	▪ Prediction
	▪ Control
	▪ Guiding further research
Characteristics (of good theories)	▪ Reflect the facts
	▪ Clear and understandable
	▪ Useful for predicting future events and explaining past ones
	▪ Practical in real-life situations
	▪ Logical and consistent
	▪ Thought provoking
	▪ Useful in guiding future research

isfying explanations, says Thomas (1996). (See Summary Table 2.1.)

A PSYCHOANALYTIC APPROACH: FREUD

Among the best known of all psychological theories is the **psychoanalytic** approach advanced by Sigmund Freud. It is labeled psychoanalytic because of Freud's emphasis on analyzing deep-seated, internal (psychic) forces and conflicts.

Sigmund Freud's most basic assumption is that the principal causes of human behavior and personality are unconscious forces within individuals. Freud believed that these forces, because they often lead to conflict between desires and conscience, are at the root of mental disorders. Hence, therapists (psychoanalysts) can help restore mental health, argued Freud, by helping patients understand unconscious drives and resulting conflicts. Among the techniques that he found most useful for this—techniques that soon became part of standard psychoanalytic procedure—were free association; the analysis of dreams and of the unintended use of words and expressions (popularly referred to as Freudian slips), both of which were assumed to reflect unconscious desires or fears; hypnosis; and painstaking analysis of childhood experiences—especially those of a sexual or traumatic (intensely frightening) nature.

Although the principal usefulness of Freudian psychoanalytic theory has been for the treatment of mental disorder, much of the theory is developmental. It's true that the most fundamental beliefs of psychoanalytic theory are no longer an important part of current developmental theories, but they have had a profound influence on the thinking of later theorists. The following sections present an abbreviated account of this complex, sometimes bewildering, but always fascinating view of the development and machinations of human personality.

While going through these brief sections, keep in mind that Freud's theory reflects the Victorian era in which it was developed—an era that, by contemporary standards, was one of extreme sexual repression and masculine domination. These cultural factors greatly influenced Freud's theory and are reflected in the significance he attributed to sexual motives and behaviors and in the masculine orientation of the theory.

Basic Freudian Ideas

Among the most fundamental Freudian ideas is the notion that human behavior and development are motivated by two powerful tendencies: the urge to survive and the urge to procreate. The survival instinct is often of secondary importance because it is not usually endangered by the environment. But because the urge to procreate is often discouraged and even prevented, sexuality is of tremendous importance in Freud's description of human development.

Sexuality is a very broad term in Freud's writings. It includes not only activities clearly associated with sex but also a wide range of other behaviors and feelings—affection and love, as well as actions such as eating, thumb-sucking, and smoking. Sexual urges are so important in Freud's system that they are given a special term—**libido.** The libido is the source of energy for sexual urges; accordingly, the urges themselves are referred to as libidinal urges. In Freud's theory, the satisfaction of sexual impulses need not always involve the sexual regions of the body.

Three Levels of Personality

According to Freud, human development occurs in three broad stages reflected in different aspects (or levels) of personality: *id, ego,* and *superego.*

Freudian theory suggests that this boy will identify with his parents, especially with his father. But the shaving is only a trivial manifestation of identification. Far more important for this lad's development is that he will also adopt many of the values and beliefs of his parents.

ID

The Freudian infant is all instincts and reflexes (unlearned tendencies), a bundle of energy seeking, almost desperately, to satisfy urges that stem from the need to survive and to procreate. These urges, labeled **id,** are a lifetime source of what Freud referred to as psychic energy, the urges and desires that account for behavior. An infant has no idea of what is possible or impossible, no sense of reality, no conscience, no internal moral rules that control behavior. Accordingly, the infant is driven by an almost overwhelming urge to seek *immediate* satisfaction of impulses. A child who is hungry does not wait. Right now is the time for the nipple and the sucking!

EGO

But almost from birth, the child's instinctual urges come into abrupt collision with reality. For example, the hunger urge (linked with survival) can't always be satisfied immediately. The reality of the situation is that the mother is often busy elsewhere and the infant's satisfaction has to be delayed or denied. Similarly, the infant eventually discovers that defecation cannot occur at will, that parental demands sometimes conflict with personal impulses. This constant conflict between the id and reality develops the second level of personality, the **ego.**

In essence, the ego grows out of the infant's gradual realization of what is possible and what is not. It is the rational, intellectual level of human personality. It includes the realization that delaying gratification is often a desirable thing, that long-term goals sometimes require the denial of short-term goals. Although the id wants immediate gratification, the ego channels these desires in the most profitable direction for the individual. Note that the levels of personality represented by the id and the ego are not in opposition. They work together toward the same goal: satisfying the needs and the urges of the individual.

SUPEREGO

In contrast, the third level of personality, the **superego,** sets itself up in opposition to the id and the ego. Like the ego, the superego develops from contact with reality, although it is more concerned with social than physical reality, and relates to the moral aspects of personality (to **conscience**). The development of the superego does not occur until early childhood. Freud assumed that it resulted principally from identifying with (trying to be *like*) parents, particularly the like-sexed parent. To identify in a Freudian sense is to try to adopt the values, beliefs, and behaviors of another person. By identifying with their parents, children learn the religious and cultural rules that govern their parents' behaviors, and these rules then become part of the child's superego. Because many religious rules, as well as many social and cultural rules, oppose the urges of the id, the superego and the id are generally in conflict. Freud assumed that this conflict accounts for much deviant behavior (see Figure 2.1).

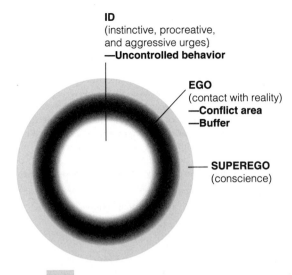

ID
(instinctive, procreative,
and aggressive urges)
—**Uncontrolled behavior**

EGO
(contact with reality)
—**Conflict area**
—**Buffer**

SUPEREGO
(conscience)

FIGURE 2.1

The Freudian conception of the three levels of personality: id, ego, and superego. The id, consisting of instinctual urges, develops first. The ego and the superego (conscience) develop later. In normal personality development, the ego acts as a buffer between the id and superego, which are in conflict with each other. Personality disorders may arise from unrestricted conflict when the ego fails to mediate successfully.

Freud's Psychosexual Stages

Freud's account of the development of the three levels of personality is also a description of **psychosexual development.** In essence, psychosexual development is defined in terms of stages that are distinguished by different objects and activities relating to satisfaction of urges during that stage. Hence, the labels for each stage reflect changes in the areas of sexual satisfaction as the child matures.

ORAL PERIOD

The **oral stage** lasts through infancy (approximately to the age of eighteen months). It is characterized by the infant's preoccupation with the mouth and with sucking. During this first stage, the child's personality consists mainly of id. Children seek constantly to satisfy their urges and are incapable of deliberately delaying gratification. [*]

ANAL PERIOD

Toward the end of the first year, the area of sexual gratification shifts gradually from the oral to the anal region. According to Freud, in the early part of the **anal stage** the child derives pleasure from bowel movements. Later in this stage the child acquires control of sphincter muscles and may then derive considerable pleasure from withholding bowel move-

---

[*] "That's where Robert got stuck," said my grandmother, displaying a remarkable talent for simplifying bizarre and complex things. Freud also believed that development sometimes gets "fixated" at an early stage and that later maladjustments can occasionally be explained in this way.

ments to increase anal sensation. Both of these behaviors oppose the mother's wishes. As a result of these conflicts, the child begins to develop an ego—a sense of reality, an awareness that certain things are possible whereas others are not, coupled with the ability to delay gratification to some extent.

PHALLIC STAGE

The third stage, which lasts roughly from ages two to six, is labeled **phallic,** not only because the zone of sexuality has shifted from the anal to the genital region but also because the phallus (the male genital) is of primary importance in the sexuality of girls as well as boys. Whereas gratification had been obtained earlier by sucking or by expelling or withholding feces, children now often manipulate their genitalia (masturbate).

Normal development now takes the male child through the **Oedipus complex,** when his increasing awareness of the sexual meanings of his genital area leads him to desire his mother (and to wish unconsciously to replace his father). For girls ages four to six, there is the **Electra complex,** in which a girl's sexual feelings for her father lead her to become jealous of her mother.

SEXUAL LATENCY

The resolution of the Oedipus complex marks the transition from the phallic stage to the period of **sexual latency** that follows. The period of latency (ages six to eleven) is marked by a loss of sexual interest and a continued **identification** with the like-sexed parent (attempts to be like the object of identification in terms of beliefs and values). In this way, the child begins to develop a superego.

GENITAL STAGE

Following this lengthy period of sexual neutrality, the child enters the stage of adult sexuality, the genital stage (at around age eleven), and begins to establish the sorts of heterosexual attachments that characterize normal adult sexual relationships. Also during this last developmental stage, the superego (conscience), which has previously been rigid and almost tyrannical, normally becomes progressively more flexible with increasing maturity. (See Summary Table 2.2 for a summary of Freud's stages of psychosexual development. See also Interactive Table 2.3 for a summary of an additional aspect of Freudian theory.)

Freud in Review

Hofer (1981) describes Freud's theory as one of the most comprehensive and influential of all psychological theories. More than anyone else, Freud was responsible for making parents realize how important the experiences of the early years can be. Hence, the theory has had a tremendous impact on our attitudes toward children and on child rearing. In addition, it has also had a profound influence on the development of other theories (for example, those of Erikson and

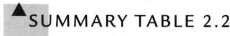

SUMMARY TABLE 2.2
Freud's Stages of Psychosexual Development

STAGE	APPROXIMATE AGES	CHARACTERISTICS
Oral	0–18 months	■ Sources of pleasure include sucking, biting, swallowing, playing with lips. ■ Preoccupation with immediate gratification of impulses. ■ Id is dominant.
Anal	18 months–2 or 3 years	■ Sources of sexual gratification include expelling feces and urination, as well as retaining feces. ■ Id and ego.
Phallic	2 or 3–6 years	■ Child becomes concerned with genitals. ■ Source of sexual pleasure involves manipulating genitals. ■ Period of Oedipus or Electra complex. ■ Id, ego, and superego.
Latency	6–11 years	■ Loss of interest in sexual gratification. ■ Identification with like-sexed parent. ■ Id, ego, and superego.
Genital	11 and older	■ Concern with adult modes of sexual pleasure, barring fixations or regressions.

INTERACTIVE TABLE 2.3

Some Freudian Defense Mechanisms

Defense mechanisms are irrational and sometimes unhealthy methods that many people use to compensate for their inability to satisfy the demands of the id. These mechanisms are invented by the ego as it attempts to establish peace between the id and the superego. Defense mechanisms are particularly important for understanding disturbed personalities, although they are not at all uncommon in the lives of those who have no clearly recognizable disturbances. It is only when people rely on them excessively that defense mechanisms become unhealthy.

Interaction: Can you think of an additional example of each defense mechanism?

MECHANISM	EXAMPLE
Displacement: Undesirable emotions are directed toward a different object.	A man who is angry at his wife kicks his dog.
Reaction formation: Behavior is the opposite of the individual's actual feelings.	A woman loves an unobtainable man and behaves as though she dislikes him.
Intellectualization: Behavior is stripped of its emotional meaning	A mercenary who fears that his enjoyment of his work is unhealthy convinces himself he is moved by duty and not by love of killing.
Projection: People attribute their own undesirable feelings or inclinations to others.	A man who is extremely jealous of a competitor believes it is the competitor who is jealous of him.
Denial: Reality is distorted to make it conform to the individual's wishes.	A heavy smoker is unable to give up the habit and decides that there is no substantial evidence linking nicotine with human diseases.
Repression: Unpleasant experiences are stored deep in the subconscious mind and become inaccessible to waking memory.	A child is sexually abused but remembers nothing of the experience.

Bowlby). However, many of Freud's students and followers have not accepted the theory entirely.

Freud paints a dark and somewhat cynical picture of human nature: In this system, primitive inherited forces over which we have no control drive us relentlessly to try to satisfy our sexual urges and bring us into repeated conflict with reality. Most of Freud's followers present a more optimistic view of human nature. And most give sexual urges a much less prominent role.

Freud's theory is clearly weak from a scientific point of view, based as it is on a limited number of observations collected by a single individual (Freud himself) and not subjected to any rigorous analysis. In addition, it uses difficult and important terms and concepts, such as *unconscious,* in confusing and ambiguous ways; it leads to contradictory predictions; and it places excessive emphasis on sexual and aggressive impulses (Rothstein, 1980). Also, much of what Freud initially thought about development applied primarily to male children, and to females only as a sometimes hasty and incomplete afterthought (Gilligan, 1982).

In spite of these criticisms, Freud's theorizing is an immensely rich basis for understanding human personality. In summarizing the contributions of psychoanalysis, Kegan

(1982) notes that it remains the single most important guide for mental health practitioners in clinics and in hospitals. Ironically, however, its status in academic psychology is relatively minor. In contrast, a theory such as that of Piaget is an ongoing source of debate and research in academic circles, but it continues to have remarkably little influence on the application of psychology in the real world.

A PSYCHOSOCIAL APPROACH: ERIKSON

Of the theories inspired by Freud's psychoanalytic views, perhaps the most important for understanding lifespan human development is that proposed by Erik Erikson (1956, 1959, 1961, 1968). It draws heavily from Freud's work but also departs from it in important ways.

Recall that Freud's primary emphasis was on the role of sexuality (libido) and on the importance of conflicts involving id, ego, and superego in determining personality and mental health. In contrast, Erikson downplays the importance of sexuality and of psychodynamic conflicts. Instead, he emphasizes the importance of the child's social environment. His theory is a theory of **psychosocial** rather than psychosexual development.

A second departure from Freudian theory is Erikson's emphasis on the role of the ego rather than the superego. As a result, the theory is more positively oriented, being concerned with the development of a healthy ego (of **identity**, in Erikson's terms) rather than with the resolution of powerful internal conflicts. Erikson's concern with the healthy personality is a third important difference between his work and that of Freud.

Psychosocial Stages

Erikson describes human development in eight stages, the first five of which span infancy, childhood, and adolescence; the last three describe adulthood. Each of Erikson's stages involves a basic conflict, brought about primarily by a need to adapt to the social environment. Resolution of this conflict results in the development of a sense of competence. Although Erikson's first five stages closely parallel Freud's psychosexual stages in terms of ages, his descriptions and his emphases are quite different. The stages are described briefly here; they are covered in more detail in Chapters 12, 14, 16, and 18.

■ TRUST VERSUS MISTRUST

One of the most basic components of a healthy personality is a sense of trust. This sense of trust toward oneself and toward others develops in the first year of life (Erikson, 1959). The infant is initially faced with a conflict between mistrust of a world about which little is known and an inclination to develop a trusting attitude toward that world—hence **trust versus mistrust.** The most important person in the infant's life at this stage is the primary caregiver—usually the mother. Successful resolution of the conflict between trust and mistrust depends largely on the infant's relationship with this caregiver and on the gradual realization that the world is predictable, safe, and loving. According to Erikson, if the world is unpredictable and the caregiver rejecting, the infant may grow up to be mistrustful and anxious.

■ AUTONOMY VERSUS SHAME AND DOUBT

Initially, infants do not deliberately act upon the world. Instead, they react to it. For example, sucking is not something that the infant deliberately decides to do, but is something that occurs in the face of appropriate stimulation. During this second stage, corresponding to Freud's *anal stage,* children slowly begin to realize that they are the authors of their own actions. As they recognize that they can carry out some of the behaviors they intend, children develop a sense of autonomy. However, this autonomy is threatened by chil-

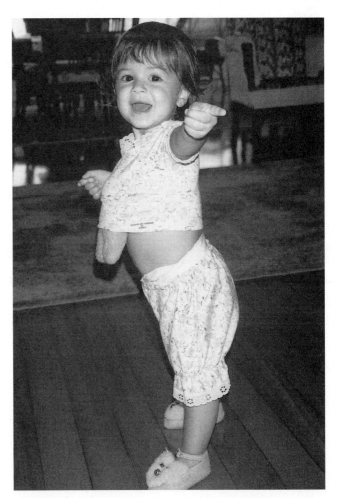

One of the important achievements of the first two or three years, says Erik Erikson, is the development of a sense of autonomy. This achievement is linked with the realization that intentions can be acted out (thus, toys can be gotten by walking over to them—or sometimes just pointing at them) and imitated. (Note the toy the little girl has stuffed inside her shirt. Her mother was pregnant at the time.)

dren's inclination to avoid responsibility for their own actions, to go back to the comfort and security that characterized the first stage—hence the **autonomy versus shame and doubt** conflict. If the child is to successfully resolve this conflict and develop a sense of autonomy, it is important that the parents encourage attempts to explore and provide opportunities for independence. Overprotectiveness can lead to doubt and uncertainty in dealing with the world later.

For Erikson, developmental progress involves resolving important conflicts by acquiring new competencies. In this second stage, children develop a sense of autonomy that surmounts earlier doubts and fears. But here, as in all areas of psychosocial conflict, the resolution is never quite complete. As Baltes and Silverberg (1994) note, the conflict between the need to be autonomous and the urge to remain dependent continues throughout the entire lifespan.

■ INITIATIVE VERSUS GUILT

By the age of four or five, children have resolved the crises of autonomy; in short, they have discovered that they are somebody. During the next stage, they must discover who it is that they are (Erikson, 1959). True to his Freudian orientation, Erikson assumes that children seek to discover who they are by attempting to be like their parents. During this stage, they establish a wider physical environment, made possible by their greater freedom of movement. Their sense of language becomes sufficiently advanced for them to be able to ask many questions and understand some of the answers; it also permits them to imagine all sorts of possibilities about themselves. With their increasing exploration of the environment, children need to develop a sense of initiative with respect to their behaviors. They are autonomous as well as responsible for initiating behavior.

Because the central process involved in resolving the **initiative versus guilt** conflict is one of identification, parents and the family continue to be the most important influences in the child's development. It is important for them to encourage the young child's sense of initiative and to nurture a sense of responsibility, claims Erikson.

■ INDUSTRY VERSUS INFERIORITY

The fourth developmental phase, **industry versus inferiority,** corresponds to Freud's latency period and is marked by the child's increasing need to interact with and be accepted by peers. It now becomes crucial for children to discover that

their selves, their identities, are significant, that they can do things—in short, that they are competent. Children now avail themselves of opportunities to learn things that they think are important to their culture, hoping that by so doing they will become someone. Successful resolution of this stage's conflict depends largely on the responses of significant agencies—especially schools and teachers—to the child's efforts. Recognition and praise are especially important in developing a positive self-concept. If the child's work is continually demeaned, seldom praised, and rarely rewarded, the outcome may well be a lasting sense of inferiority.

■ IDENTITY VERSUS IDENTITY DIFFUSION

Erikson's fifth developmental stage, **identity versus identity diffusion,** covers adolescence and corresponds to the beginning of Freud's genital period. The main developmental task of this period is the development of a sense of identity. Here, Erikson's emphasis on the ego becomes most evident. The development of a strong sense of identity implies the development of a strong ego—hence Erikson's expression *ego identity.*

At a simple level, the formation of an identity appears to involve arriving at a notion not so much of who one is but rather of who one can be. The source of conflict resides in the various possibilities open to the child—possibilities that

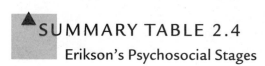

SUMMARY TABLE 2.4
Erikson's Psychosocial Stages

ERIKSON'S PSYCHOSOCIAL STAGES	CORRESPONDING FREUDIAN PSYCHOSEXUAL STAGE	PRINCIPAL DEVELOPMENTAL TASK	IMPORTANT INFLUENCES FOR POSITIVE DEVELOPMENTAL OUTCOME
Trust vs. mistrust	Oral (0–18 months)	Developing sufficient trust in the world to explore it.	Mother; warm, loving interaction.
Autonomy vs. shame and doubt	Anal (18 months–2 or 3 years)	Developing feeling of control over behavior; realizing that intentions can be acted out.	Supportive parents; imitation.
Initiative vs. guilt	Phallic (2 or 3–6 years)	Developing a sense of self through identification with parents and a sense of responsibility for own actions.	Supportive parents; identification.
Industry vs. inferiority	Latency (6–11 years)	Developing a sense of self-worth through interaction with peers.	Schools, teachers; learning and education; encouragement.
Identity vs. identity diffusion	Genital (11 years and older)	Developing a strong sense of identity—of ego (self); selecting among various potential selves.	Peers and role models; social pressure.
Intimacy vs. isolation	Genital (young adulthood)	Developing close relationships with others; achieving the intimacy required for marriage.	Spouse, colleagues, partners, society.
Generativity vs. self-absorption	Genital (adulthood)	Assuming responsible adult roles in the community; contributing; being worthwhile.	Spouse, children, friends, colleagues, community.
Integrity vs. despair	Genital (older adulthood)	Facing death; overcoming potential despair; coming to terms with the meaningfulness of life.	Friends, relatives, children, spouse, community and religious support.

Source: Derived from *Identity and the Life Cycle* by Erik H. Erikson, by permission of W. W. Norton & Company, Inc. Copyright © 1980 by W. W. Norton & Company, Inc. Copyright © 1959 by International Universities Press, Inc.

are magnified by the variety of models in the environment. Conflict and doubt over the choice of identity lead to what Erikson terms *identity diffusion*. It is as though adolescents are torn between early acceptance of a clearly defined self and the dissipation of their energies as they experiment with a variety of roles. The development of identity during adolescence is discussed in Chapter 12.

ADULTHOOD

Erikson's description of development does not end with adolescence but continues through the entire lifespan. He describes three additional psychosocial conflicts that occur during adulthood and old age, and that require new competencies and adjustments. The first of these, *intimacy and solidarity versus isolation,* relates to the need to develop intimate relationships with others (as opposed to being isolated) and is particularly crucial for marital and parental roles. The second, *generativity versus self-absorption,* describes a need to assume social, work, and community responsibilities that will be beneficial to others (that will be generative), rather than remaining absorbed in the self. And the third, *integrity versus despair,* has to do with facing the inevitability of our own ends and realizing that life has meaning—that we should not despair because its end is imminent. The three Eriksonian stages that span adulthood are discussed in greater detail in Chapters 14, 16, and 18. (See Summary Table 2.4.)

Erikson in Review

Erikson describes development in terms of a series of crises through which the individual progresses. Each of these crises involves a conflict between new abilities or attitudes and inclinations that oppose them. Resolution of conflicts results in the development of a sense of competence with respect to a specific capability that is primarily social (hence the label "psychosocial development"). The resolution of conflicts is never perfected during one developmental phase but continues through succeeding stages (hence the label "life cycle"). Perhaps the most crucial crisis involves the development of a strong sense of identity (hence the label "ego psychology").

Although Erikson assigns ages to each psychosocial stage, the ages do little more than indicate a general developmental sequence. This is particularly true during adulthood, when important social, physical, and emotional events such as retirement, children leaving home, illness, and death occur at widely varying ages and sometimes in a totally unpredictable sequence. Some of the important social and physical changes of childhood are far more predictable; hence, ages tied to the psychosocial crises of childhood are more accurate.

Erikson's theory, like Freud's, does not lend itself well to experimental validation. What Erikson's theory provides is a general framework for describing and interpreting some of the major changes that occur in the lifespan. Its usefulness rests largely on the insights that sometimes result from examining the lives of individuals within the context of the theory.

HAVIGHURST'S DEVELOPMENTAL TASKS

Robert Havighurst (1972, 1979) also describes development in terms of a series of developmental tasks that need to be sequentially mastered. Developmental tasks are requirements that are placed on individuals by their societies and by themselves as they progress through life. As Havighurst (1972) put it, "A developmental task is a task which arises at or about a certain period in the life of the individual, successful achievement of which leads to his happiness and to success with later tasks, while failure leads to unhappiness in the individual, disapproval by the society, and difficulty with later tasks" (p. 2).

Developmental tasks begin with the simple and essential requirements of infancy, such as learning to eat, to walk, and to speak. They culminate in the requirements of old age, which include adjusting to changing physical strength and health, and the imminence of death. Thus, developmental tasks provide a rough but sometimes highly useful index of developmental maturity and adjustment within a specific culture. In a sense, they tell us whether a child is ready for school, a young adult for marriage, an older adult for retirement (see Summary Table 2.5).

BEHAVIORISTIC APPROACHES TO DEVELOPMENT

Freud's and Erikson's psychoanalytic approaches have a number of important things in common: (1) They are **developmental theories** in that they are concerned with changes that occur in individuals over time, (2) they are stage theories (development consists of progression through sequential stages), and (3) they make important assumptions concerning the biological (inherited) aspects of behavior and personality.

In contrast, behavioristic approaches (also called *learning-theory* approaches) make few assumptions about biological predispositions (and certainly none about unconscious forces), nor do they describe sequential stages of mounting capabilities and competencies (or, conversely, of declining abilities).

Basic Assumptions of Behavioristic Approaches

As the term implies, **behaviorism** focuses on the person's immediate behavior and on environmental forces that affect behavior. **Behavioristic theory** looks at relationships between experience and behavior and, consequently, makes extensive use of concepts such as reinforcement and punishment, which describe how behavior may be encouraged or discouraged.

Behaviorism reflects two basic assumptions: The most important is that behavior is reducible to responses or behaviors

Havighurst's Developmental Tasks

PERIOD	DEVELOPMENTAL TASKS
Infancy and early childhood (birth through preschool period)	1. Achieving physiological rhythms in sleeping and eating 2. Learning to take solid foods 3. Beginning to relate emotionally to parents and siblings 4. Learning to talk 5. Learning to control elimination of body wastes 6. Learning to walk 7. Learning to distinguish right from wrong 8. Learning sex differences and sexual modesty
Middle childhood (the elementary school period)	1. Learning skills necessary for physical games 2. Building a positive self-concept 3. Adopting an appropriate masculine or feminine role 4. Learning to get along with peers 5. Developing values, a sense of morality, a conscience 6. Becoming personally independent; weakening family ties 7. Developing basic reading, writing, and arithmetic skills 8. Developing an understanding of the self and the world
Adolescence	1. Developing conceptual and problem-solving skills 2. Achieving mature relationships with male and female peers 3. Developing an ethical system to guide behavior 4. Striving toward socially responsible behavior 5. Accepting the changing physique and using the body effectively 6. Preparing for an economically viable career 7. Achieving emotional independence from parents 8. Preparing for marriage and family life
Young adulthood	1. Courting and selecting a mate 2. Learning to live happily with partner 3. Starting a family and assuming parent role 4. Rearing children 5. Assuming home management responsibilities 6. Beginning career or occupation 7. Assuming appropriate civic responsibilities 8. Establishing a social network
Middle adulthood	1. Assisting children in transition from home to world 2. Developing adult leisure activities 3. Relating to spouse as a person 4. Reaching adult social and civic responsibility 5. Maintaining satisfactory career performance 6. Adjusting to physiological changes of middle age 7. Adjusting to aging parents
Old age	1. Adjusting to physical changes 2. Adjusting to retirement and to changes in income 3. Establishing satisfactory living arrangements 4. Learning to live with spouse in retirement 5. Adjusting to death of spouse 6. Forming affiliations with aging peers 7. Adopting flexible social roles

that can be observed, measured, and analyzed, and that can therefore be studied objectively; the second is that responses are affected by consequences such as reinforcement and punishment. Accordingly, one of the main goals of behavioristic theorists is to discover the rules that govern relationships between **stimuli** (conditions that lead to behavior) and **responses**, and to learn how responses can be controlled through the administration of **rewards** and punishments.

■ UNDERLYING MODEL

These are assumptions of what is sometimes labeled the **mechanistic model,** which holds that it is useful to view human beings as though they were a little like machines—that is, passive rather than active, highly responsive to external events such as rewards. If we understand how the machine works, we can predict its actions given sufficient knowledge of immediate circumstances. The goal of the behavioristic theorist is to understand the human machine so well that with sufficient knowledge of past functioning and of immediate circumstances, it might be possible to predict behavior accurately (and perhaps to control it as well). According to this model, the consequences of behavior—especially reinforcements and punishments—are among the most important factors in shaping the course of our development.

■ EARLY PIONEERS

The behavioristic approach was introduced into American psychology through the work of John B. Watson and B. F. Skinner, and led to a dramatic upheaval in psychology. Both theorists believed strongly in the importance of the environment (of context) as the principal force in shaping development, and both believed that development could be understood through an analysis of specific behaviors, the circumstances leading to them, and their consequences. Watson is associated with a learning theory based on a model of **classical conditioning;** Skinner developed a model of **operant conditioning. Conditioning** itself refers to a simple kind of learning whereby certain behaviors are affected by the environment, becoming more or less probable and predictable.

Classical Conditioning

While doing research with dogs, the Russian physiologist Ivan Pavlov (1927) noticed that the more experienced animals in his laboratory began to salivate when they saw their keeper approaching. Because none of the dogs had ever tasted the keeper, Pavlov reasoned that they were salivating not because they expected to eat him but because they had formed an **association** between the sight of the keeper and the presentation of food. This observation led Pavlov to a series of investigations of a simple form of learning called *classical conditioning.* In the best known of these experiments, he paired a tone with food over a number of trials. Eventually, the tone alone brought about salivation.

BASIC ELEMENTS OF CLASSICAL CONDITIONING

Psychology has its own language for the stimuli and responses involved in classical conditioning. The stimulus that is part of the original stimulus–response link is termed the **unconditioned stimulus** (US). Food is a US for Pavlov's dogs; it elicits a response without any new learning taking place. The stimulus that is originally neutral but comes to be effective through repeated pairing with the US is called the conditioning or **conditioned stimulus** (CS). The tone is an example of a CS. Eventually, this CS elicits responses similar to those originally made only for the US. Corresponding responses are termed the **unconditioned response** (UR) or the **conditioned response** (CR), depending on whether they occur in response to the US or the CS. Thus, salivating in response to a buzzer is a CR. (See Figure 2.2.)

A CLASSICAL EXAMPLE: LITTLE ALBERT

One of the best-known studies demonstrating classical conditioning of emotional responses in children is that reported by Watson and Rayner (1920). Watson had reasoned that because infants react with fear to loud noises, it should be possible to make them afraid of any other distinctive stimulus simply by pairing it often enough with a loud noise. In this case, the noise is an unconditioned stimulus because it elicits a fear response without any learning having taken place; the fear responses are unconditioned responses. The conditioning stimulus that Watson and Rayner chose was a white rat. The subject was an eleven-month-old infant named Albert.

At the beginning of the study, Little Albert played with the rat as he sat on his mattress; he wasn't the least bit afraid. But then Watson (or his assistant, Rosalie Rayner—the point is not clear from Watson's notes) pounded on a 3-foot long, 1-inch steel bar just behind Albert. Still, Little Albert didn't cry just yet, reaching instead for the rat again. And once more, someone pounded on the steel bar, this time frightening Albert enough that he began to whimper. "On account of his disturbed condition," wrote Watson (1930), "no further tests were made for one week" (p. 160).

A week later, the procedure was repeated—the loud noise and the rat being paired a total of five more times. And now whenever Little Albert saw the rat, he began to cry and tried to crawl away. "Surely," claimed Watson (1930), "this is proof of the conditioned origin of a fear response. It yields an explanatory principle that will account for the enormous complexity in the emotional behavior of adults" (p. 161).

Although Watson and Rayner's experiment with Albert is more systematic and deliberate than most situations in which we acquire emotional responses, there are numerous examples of conditioned emotional responses in our daily lives. People who react with fear to the sound of a dentist's drill are not fearful because the sound of the drill has been responsible for any pain they have felt in the past. But the sound of the drill is a conditioned stimulus that has previously been associated with pain (an unconditioned response) and has thus acquired the capability of eliciting conditioned emotional reactions (termed CERs) associated with pain. There is considerable evidence that such emotional reactions do transfer from one situation to another.

Operant Conditioning

A classical conditioning model is sometimes useful for explaining the learning of simple behaviors that occur in response to specific stimuli. As Skinner (1953, 1957, 1961) notes, however, many human behaviors or responses are not **elicited** by any obvious stimuli but appear instead to be

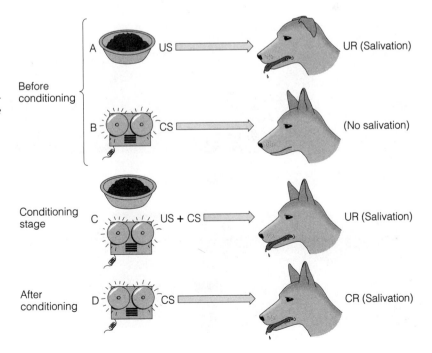

FIGURE 2.2

*Classical conditioning. In **A** an unconditioned stimulus leads to an unconditioned response, whereas in **B** a conditioning stimulus does not lead to the same response. In **C** the unconditioned stimulus is paired with the conditioning stimulus a number of times so that eventually the conditioning stimulus alone elicits the original response, as in **D**.*

emitted by the organism, for whatever reason. In Skinner's terms, an emitted behavior is an **operant**; an elicited response is a **respondent**. Skinner's major work is an attempt to explain how operants are learned.

The simplest explanation of operant conditioning is that the consequences of a response determine how likely it is to be repeated. Behaviors that are reinforced tend to be repeated; those that are not reinforced (or that are punished) are less likely to occur again (see Figure 2.3). This is very different from saying that learning will occur as a function of the pairing of stimuli regardless of consequences. When Little Albert reacted with fear to the rat, it was not because his fear responses led to pleasant consequences but because the rat was paired with some other fear-producing situation.

■ REINFORCEMENT

Whatever increases the probability of a response occurring is reinforcing. A **reinforcer** is the stimulus that reinforces; **reinforcement** is the effect of a reinforcer. Reinforcement can be positive or negative. Both increase the probability that a response will occur. The difference between the two is that **positive reinforcement** results from a reward being added to a situation after the behavior has occurred; **negative reinforcement** results from the removal of an unpleasant stimulus. In simpler terms, positive reinforcement involves a *reward* for behavior; negative reinforcement involves relief from something unpleasant.

Unfortunately, real-life situations are more complicated than this black-and-white terminology suggests. Subjective judgments such as "pleasant" and "unpleasant," although

they make our understanding simpler, are misleading. Reinforcement and punishment have to do with effects rather than perceived pleasantness. Thus, a parent or teacher who keeps "punishing" a child but who observes that the punished behavior becomes more rather than less frequent may well be reinforcing that behavior—or something (someone?) else is. Similarly, on occasion, a teacher's praise of a student's behavior will lead to a drastic reduction of that behavior. Reinforcement? No. By definition, this is **punishment.** The important point is that pleasantness and unpleasantness are subjective. In contrast, reinforcement and punishment are objective phenomena defined in terms of increases or decreases in the frequency of behavior.

■ PUNISHMENT

Both punishment and reinforcement are defined in terms of their effects. Whereas reinforcement, whether positive or negative, serves to make a response more likely, punishment does not.

In the same way as there are two types of reinforcement (positive and negative—or *reward* and *relief*), there are also two distinct kinds of punishment. The kind that we usually think of first involves a clearly unpleasant consequence and is sometimes labeled "punishment I" or, in lay terms, *castigation*. Being beaten with a hickory stick or having one's hair pulled are examples of this kind of punishment.

The second kind of punishment, labeled "punishment II," involves taking away something that is pleasant (in lay terms, a *penalty*). Being prevented from watching television (what psychologists refer to as a *time-out procedure*) and having to

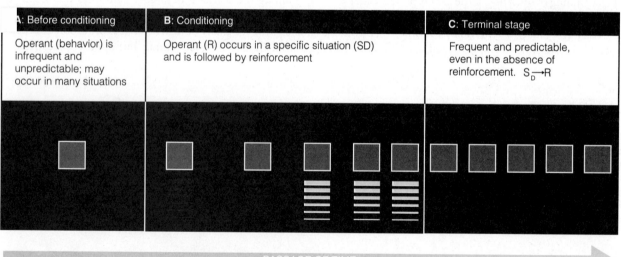

A: Before conditioning	B: Conditioning	C: Terminal stage
Operant (behavior) is infrequent and unpredictable; may occur in many situations	Operant (R) occurs in a specific situation (SD) and is followed by reinforcement	Frequent and predictable, even in the absence of reinforcement. $S_D \rightarrow R$

PASSAGE OF TIME

Key

Operant (R)   Reinforcement

FIGURE 2.3

*Schematic model of operant conditioning. In **A** the operant behavior is not rewarded. In **B** conditioning begins. The operant behavior takes place by chance; it is immediately reinforced. It occurs again, by chance or deliberately, and the reinforcement is repeated. As the timeline chart shows, repetition becomes more and more frequent as the learner catches on. Eventually, the operant behavior continues even without reinforcement at the terminal stage **C**.*

The four alternatives that define punishment and reinforcement, and a fifth where behavior has no apparent consequences, with examples. Were you ever punished or reinforced in these ways? Can you think of specific examples?

	Pleasant consequences	Unpleasant consequences	No consequences
Added to the situation	*Positive reinforcement:* Louella is given a jelly bean for being "good."	*Punishment I:* Louella has her nose tweaked for being "bad."	*Extinction:* Louella's behavior has no apparent effects and is ignored.
Removed from the situation	*Punishment II:* Louella has her jelly beans taken away for being "bad."	*Negative reinforcement:* Louella's nose is released because she says "I'm sorry."	

give up something desirable, such as money or privileges (called *response–cost punishment*), are examples of this kind of punishment.

Another possibility, of course, is that a behavior will have no important consequences and will simply cease to be emitted (will be *extinguished*). Distinctions among the various kinds of reinforcement and punishment are illustrated in Interactive Figure 2.4. As the illustration makes clear, both may involve pleasant or unpleasant stimuli, but whether these stimuli are added to or removed from the situation determines their effect. It is worth repeating that reinforcement and punishment are defined by their effects.

Behavioristic Approaches in Review

Learning-theory explanations for human development emphasize the role of the environment in shaping our personalities and our behaviors. Unlike psychoanalytic approaches, they are not concerned with psychodynamic conflicts and other hidden causes of behavior; and unlike the more cognitive approaches, which we discuss next, they pay relatively little attention to concepts such as *understanding* and *knowing*. Instead, they focus on the role of reinforcement and punishment and on the extent to which behavior can be shaped by its consequences.

One of the main criticisms of these approaches is that they are poorly suited to explain what are referred to as *higher mental processes*—for example, thinking, feeling, analyzing, problem solving, and evaluating. Their emphasis, and their principal usefulness, relates to actual behavior rather than to thinking and feeling.

A second criticism of behavioristic approaches is that to the extent that they emphasize the machinelike qualities of human functioning, they rob us of those capabilities that we consider most human—our ability to think and imagine, and our ability to exercise significant personal control over our own behaviors. In brief, critics have claimed that in its attempts to reduce behavior to a handful of principles governing predictable relationships among stimuli and responses, behaviorism *dehumanizes* us.

Although these criticisms are valid for older, highly rigid interpretations of behaviorism, they are less pertinent for more current positions. For example, Bijou (1989) notes that whereas Watson's theory describes an essentially passive organism, contemporary behaviorism sees the individual "as always being in an interactive relationship with the environment" (p. 68). In his words, the individual is "adjustive" rather than simply reactive. Hence, the environment is given a less important role in determining behavior. The causes of behavior, says Bijou, will be found not in the environment alone, but rather in all the factors that are involved in a person's interactions.

Behavioristic approaches to development are sometimes very useful not only for understanding developmental change, but also for controlling it. The deliberate application of conditioning principles to change behavior (termed **behavior modification**) has proven extremely useful both in the classroom and in psychotherapy. (See Summary Table 2.6.)

SOCIAL-COGNITIVE THEORY

Elements from different theories can sometimes be combined to produce new theories and new insights that go far beyond the original theories. A case in point is Albert Bandura's theorizing, which combines elements of both behaviorism and cognitivism.

At one level, Bandura's work (1977, 1986, 1995) is a behavioristic theory of imitation based on the assumption that much important learning involves models of various kinds that act as social influences on the child. At another level, it is a **cognitive theory** in that it recognizes the importance of our ability to think, to symbolize, to figure out cause-and-effect relationships, to anticipate the outcomes of behavior. There is no doubt, Bandura (1977) assures us, that reinforcement controls much of our behavior. But it does not control us blindly. Its effects depend largely on our awareness of the relationship between our behavior and its outcomes. Because reinforcement often occurs long after the behavior it follows—as happens, for example, when you study for an examination—it isn't reinforcement that is important so much as your ability to anticipate the consequences of behavior.

Behavioristic Approaches
to Lifespan Development

Behavioristic approaches to development look at the relationship between the individual's experiences and behavior, paying special attention to antecedent conditions (stimuli) and to the consequences of behavior (reinforcement or punishment, for example). These approaches are illustrated in classical and operant conditioning.

IMPORTANT TERMS IN BEHAVIORISM	CAPSULE DEFINITIONS
stimulus	any change capable of eliciting a response.
response	a reaction resulting from stimulation.
unconditioned stimulus	stimulus that elicits a response prior to learning.
unconditioned response	response to an unconditioned stimulus.
conditioned stimulus	stimulus that is effective after learning (conditioning).
conditioned response	response to a conditioned stimulus.
reinforcement	an increase in the probability of a behavior; the effect of a reinforcer.
reward	consequence that is reinforcing.
punishment	presentation of an unpleasant stimulus or withdrawal of a pleasant one; has an effect opposite to that of reinforcement.
respondent	behavior *elicited* by a stimulus.
operant	behavior *emitted* by an organism.

CLASSICAL CONDITIONING	OPERANT CONDITIONING
(associated with Watson and Pavlov)	(associated with Skinner)
deals with respondents	deals with operants
that are elicited	that are emitted
by stimuli	by the organism
as reactions *to* the environment	as actions *upon* the environment

We are products of our surroundings—of our contexts. According to Bandura's social-learning theory, much of our behavior is a function of observing the behavior of others. Through observational learning (imitation), we not only learn specific behaviors (such as how to salute) but also acquire complex beliefs about right and wrong (such as notions about honor and duty and patriotism).

Bandura's social-learning theory is a theory of **observational learning** (or **imitation**). It is based on the assumption that a great deal of human learning and behavior is a function of observing and imitating the behavior of models, and that this learning can be explained largely through operant conditioning principles.

Manifestations of Observational Learning

The term **model** may refer to an actual, and perhaps very ordinary, person who does something, and whose behavior serves as a guide or perhaps an inspiration for somebody else. A model might also be symbolic. **Symbolic models** include books, oral or written instructions, pictures, mental images, cartoon or film characters, and television programs.

Learning through imitation is widespread among humans, beginning in infancy (as is discussed in Chapter 5) and continuing into adulthood. And although the result of imitation is often highly positive, resulting in new learning and in socially approved behaviors, that isn't always the case. For example, Wyrwicka (1996) reports how, more than 200 years ago, Johann Wolfgang von Goethe wrote *The Sorrows of Young Werther,* in which he described how a heartbroken Werther killed himself. The book became immensely popular and apparently led to a number of young people committing suicide. It was subsequently banned in Leipzig and in Denmark. And in Milan, city officials went so far as to buy and destroy all copies of the book so that other young people would not be tempted to imitate the unfortunate Young Werther.

Bandura and Walters (1963) describe three different effects of imitation.

■ THE MODELING EFFECT

The **modeling effect** is the learning of novel behavior through imitation. That the rain-forest people of Cameroon speak their own language and not Chippewa is evidence that they model the language that surrounds them. (There is much more to language learning than simply imitation, however; see Chapters 5 and 7.)

■ THE INHIBITORY–DISINHIBITORY EFFECT

The effects of imitation are also found in the **inhibitory effect** (the suppression of deviant behavior) and the **disinhibitory effect** (the appearance of previously suppressed deviant behavior). These effects often result from seeing a model rewarded or punished for engaging in deviant behavior. As an illustration, consider the case of Ray, who is opposed to using drugs but whose friends have begun to use marijuana. The behavior is deviant by Ray's own standards, but *ingapore, Malaysia:* Michael Fay, an American teenager, tore down some street signs and vandalized some cars in Singapore. He was accused of vandalism, tried, convicted, sent to prison for four months, assessed a $2,215 U.S. fine—and given four lashes with a cane. In Singapore, caning is mandatory for offenses such as rape, robbery, vandalism, and illegal immigration; for drug trafficking and armed robbery, the offender is executed (Bramham, 1994). Nor does caning just smart a little. In fact, says Bramham, it is administered by a martial arts expert using a moistened rattan pole. The offender is stripped and folded over a waist-high board with his hands and ankles bound together. The caner rears back and strikes hard enough to knock himself off balance and to split the skin open. The offender often loses consciousness, but the next blow will not come for another 3 minutes. The scarring will be permanent.

Mogadishu, Somalia: Abdulahi Weheliye Omar and his friend, Gelle Omar Ali, both twenty-five, confessed to raping Maryan Hussein Amir, an eighteen-year-old girl. Under Islamic law, Gelle's crime was the least severe because he had never been married. So he was dragged into a public square and, surrounded by several hundred cheering people, was lashed one hundred times

and then dragged off unconscious. "The crowd laughed," writes Watson (1994). "The children laughed loudest, as if they were watching a circus clown" (p. A16).

Abdulahi was not so lucky because he had apparently been married once, although he vigorously denied this. His sentence: stoned to death. About twenty men were allowed to hurl the rocks. His victim asked whether she, too, might throw some rocks, but under the law, only men are allowed to join in. The rocks were about the size of softballs; a few were bigger chunks of concrete. Still, it was a full 20 minutes before Abdulahi died. "No one should feel sorry for Omar," said Sheik Ali Mohamed, "not after what he did" (p. A16).

To Research

In the past several years, Singapore has hanged dozens of criminals (many of them for drug trafficking) and has caned thousands. And in the United States, there have been increasingly insistent demands for tougher punishments, especially of young offenders. Research the proposition that a highly punitive context is less (or more) likely to prevent criminal behavior.

---

the amount of reinforcement (in terms of social prestige, acceptance by the group, and so on) that others appear to get from smoking marijuana may disinhibit drug-using behavior. There is no new learning involved, as there is in modeling, but merely the disinhibition of previously suppressed behavior. If Ray later sees members of his peer group being punished (by law, parents, school authorities, or ill effects of the drug), he might stop using it—an example of the *inhibitory effect.* Again, no new learning is involved, but the change in behavior results from the influence of models (see "Across Cultures: Sticks and Stones").

THE ELICITING EFFECT

The **eliciting effect** occurs when the model's behavior leads to related, but not identical, behavior in the learner—behavior that is neither deviant nor novel. It is as though the model's behavior suggests some related response to observers and therefore elicits that response. For example, a child's being rewarded for doing well in mathematics may motivate other classmates toward achievement-related behaviors in other subjects. (See Summary/Interactive Table 2.7.)

▲ SUMMARY/INTERACTIVE TABLE 2.7
Three Effects of Imitation

EFFECT	DEFINITION
Modeling	■ Acquiring a *new* behavior as a result of observing a model.
Inhibitory-disinhibitory	■ Ceasing or starting some *deviant* behavior as a result of seeing a model punished or rewarded for that behavior.
Eliciting	■ Engaging in behavior *related*—but not identical—to that of a model, where the behavior is neither novel nor deviant.

Interaction: Can you provide specific examples of each of these effects of imitation?

Self-Efficacy

Theories in psychology, as elsewhere, are usually not static, unchanging things—unless the theorist has lost interest, moved on to other issues, or died. But even then, if the theory is at all compelling or important, there will be others who will chew at it, who will try to change its shape to fit new facts and to answer new questions.

Albert Bandura's theorizing is a case in point. His early ideas were based directly on a behavioristic orientation. Thus, his imitation theory of social learning tried to explain the effects of modeling in terms of rewards and punishments. Increasingly, however, as Pajares (1996) notes, Bandura began to pay more attention to the learner's cognitive capacities. As a result, his theorizing gave an increasingly important role to the informative function of models. It is what the observer imagines and anticipates that is fundamentally important in learning through imitation.

Recently, Bandura's research and theorizing have taken yet another turn—one that is even more clearly cognitive and that is often referred to as social cognitivism (Bandura, 1981, 1986; Evans, 1989). It has to do with what is termed **self-referent thought**—thought that relates to our selves, our own mental processes. Among other things, self-referent thought deals with our estimates of our abilities, with our notions about how capable and how effective we are in our dealings with the world and with others. And a very specific term has been coined to describe our estimates of our effectiveness: **self-efficacy.**

DEFINITION OF *SELF-EFFICACY*

In a nutshell, efficacy signifies competence in dealing with the environment. The most efficacious people are those who can most effectively deal with a variety of situations, even when these situations are ambiguous or highly stressful.

As a psychological concept, self-efficacy refers not so much to the skills required for the successful performance of a behavior, but more to the individual's beliefs about personal effectiveness. Self-efficacy refers to the judgments we make about how effective we are likely to be in given situations. Accordingly, self-efficacy is generally assessed by asking individuals about the level and strength of their confidence that they can accomplish a task or be successful in an endeavor (Pajares, 1996).

IMPLICATIONS OF SELF-EFFICACY JUDGMENTS

Among other things, our judgments about our personal effectiveness are extremely important determiners of what we do and don't do. In some situations, in fact, self-efficacy may be a better predictor of behavior than relevant skills are (Bandura, 1993). Under most circumstances, children—and adults—do not seek out and undertake activities in which they expect to perform badly. "Efficacy beliefs," says Bandura, "influence how people feel, think, motivate themselves, and behave" (1993, p. 118).

Judgments of personal efficacy affect not only our choices of activities and settings but also the amount of effort we are willing to expend when faced with difficulties. The stronger an individual's perceptions of efficacy, the more likely the individual is to persist and the greater the effort expended will be. But if notions of self-efficacy are not highly favorable, difficult activities may be abandoned after very little effort and time.

Finally, judgments of self-efficacy influence thoughts and emotions. Those whose estimate of their effectiveness is low are more likely to evaluate their behaviors negatively and to see themselves as being inadequate. Related to this, Cowen and associates (1991) found that children with the most favorable self-efficacy judgments were more resilient, more resistant to stress.

SOURCES OF SELF-EFFICACY JUDGMENTS

Judgments of personal efficacy, Bandura (1986) suggests, stem from several sources. First are the direct effects of behavior. Whether we succeed must surely have some effect on our estimates of how efficacious we are. However, the individual who is mostly successful does not invariably arrive at highly positive judgments of self-efficacy, nor does lack of success always correspond to negative judgments. As Weiner (1980) points out, success—or lack of success—can be attributed to a number of factors. Some of these, such as ability and effort, are under personal control and reflect directly on the efficacy of the individual. Others, such as luck or the difficulty of the task, are not under personal control and do not, therefore, have very direct implications for judgments of self-efficacy. Some individuals are prone to attribute the outcomes of their behaviors to factors over which they have control. Dweck (1975) refers to these people as **mastery-oriented.** Others are more likely to attribute their failures and successes to luck or to the task being too difficult or too easy. They are characterized by **learned helplessness** rather than by a mastery orientation. (See Chapter 10.)

A second influence on judgments of self-efficacy is *vicarious* (secondhand); it comes from observing the performance of others. Even as children, we judge how effective we are partly by comparing ourselves to others. The most informative comparisons we can make are those that involve others whose performance is similar to ours. A twelve-year-old who demolishes his six-year-old brother in a game of skill and intelligence learns very little about his personal effectiveness. Similarly, if he, in turn, is blown away by his father, he may not have learned much more—except, perhaps, a touch of humility.

A third source of influence on self-judgments, Bandura (1986) argues, is *persuasion:* "You can do it. We know you can. Sing for us. We love the way you sing." Persuasion, depending on the characteristics of the persuader and on the relationship between persuader and "persuadee," can sometimes change an individual's judgments of self-efficacy and lead that individual to attempt things that would not otherwise be attempted—or not to attempt them: "They're just flattering you. Please don't sing."

A fourth source of influence on judgments of self-efficacy is the person's arousal level. **Arousal** is a big word with many meanings. In this context, its most important meaning is alertness or intensity of immediate emotional reaction. Whether arousal will have positive or negative effects on the individual's self-judgments may depend largely on experiences the individual has had in situations of high or low arousal. Some people find that moderately high arousal helps their performance; others react in the opposite way. For example, the fear that precedes speaking in public may be seen as helpful by some speakers and as highly negative by others.

In summary, there are four separate sources of influence that can affect the individual's judgments of self-efficacy. Bandura (1986) terms these *enactive* (based on the outcome of the individual's own actions), *vicarious* (based on comparisons between the person's performance and the performance of others), *persuasory* (the result of persuasion), and *emotive* (the result of arousal or emotion).

■ DEVELOPMENT OF SELF-EFFICACY

After watching Superman as a child, did you ever think you could put on a cape and actually fly? Many young children do. They don't have a very good notion of their personal capabilities. Their self-judgment, and their corresponding self-guidance, is less than perfect. As a result, without external controls, they would often be in danger of severely hurting themselves. Instead of imposing on themselves the internal self-judgment "I can't do that," they require the external judgment "You can't do that."

The sense of personal control over behavior that is essential for judgments of personal efficacy begins to develop very early in infancy. Some of its roots lie in the infant's discovery that looking at the mother makes her look back in return, that smiling or crying draws her attention, and that waving a hand makes her smile. Later, as infants start to move around freely, they begin to learn more about the effects of their behaviors—and also more about their effectiveness as "behavers." Language provides them with a means to analyze and think about themselves and a means to symbolize and anticipate the consequences of their behaviors.

In the early stages, Bandura (1986) informs us, the most important source of information for the development of self-referential thought is the family. Soon, however, peers begin to increase in importance. Now the behavior of others, as well as their response to our behavior, is factored into our personal estimates of our efficacy. Eventually, schools also exert their powerful influences. Teachers tell us a great deal about how well—or how badly—we can do things. So, too, do the responses of our classmates—and the responses of our parents to the evidence we bring home of our worthwhileness in school, of our intelligence, of our ability to do the things that teachers require.

And so it continues throughout life. In adolescence, as well as through adulthood and into old age, we continue to face new tasks, new challenges. At every step, these challenges require new competencies and new behaviors—and new judgments of personal effectiveness.

Among the judgments of efficacy that are perhaps most important to us at all stages of life are those that have to do with our ability to capture the attention, the interest, the affection of others. As Kegan (1982) argues, we strive to mean something; we want people to pay attention to us, to like us, to want to be with us, to listen to us, to do things with us. Put another way, we need to feel that we are capable of eliciting these feelings in others—that we are socially effective. Hence the central role of self-efficacy judgments in our lives. And in our happiness.

Social–Cognitive Theory in Review

In some important ways, Bandura's social–cognitive theory bridges the gap between behavioristic theories, which try to explain development entirely in terms of observable, non-mentalistic events such as stimuli and responses, and cognitive positions, which are mainly concerned with mental events. Thus, the theory is based on the notion that certain social behaviors (notably imitative behaviors) are reinforced in various ways, and are therefore more likely to recur. At the same time, it recognizes the power of our ability to imagine the consequences of our actions. It is the child's anticipation of the taste of the ice cream that hurries her to the store, not just a blind reaction to external stimulation.

Bandura's theory is a striking example of how theories need not be static, unchanging things, of how they can change with new information and new beliefs. Thus, his recent writings deal with self-efficacy and are concerned with how what we think, feel, and do is profoundly influenced by our judgments of our personal effectiveness. (See Summary Table 2.8.)

Although the theory provides a useful way of looking at some aspects of development, and especially at social motivation, it is not a comprehensive theory meant to account for most of the important points in human development—unlike the theory of Jean Piaget.

A COGNITIVE APPROACH: PIAGET

Psychoanalytic theorists are concerned primarily with personality development, behavioristic theorists emphasize behavior and its consequences, social-learning theorists are concerned with the influence of culture and experience, and a fourth group of theorists focuses on the intellectual (**cognitive**) development of children.

Cognition is the art or faculty of knowing. Cognitive theorists are concerned with how we know—that is, with how we obtain, process, and use information. The most widely cited and the most influential of all theories of cognitive development is Piaget's (Stanton, 1993), although there are those who suggest that its influence has now begun to wane (for example, Bjorklund, 1997a). Important aspects of his theory are introduced briefly in the following sections. More specific details of the theory, and the contributions of other

SUMMARY TABLE 2.8
Self-Efficacy

Definition	▪ Self-efficacy refers to individuals' private judgments about their effectiveness, their competence, with respect to the demands and challenges they face.
Implications of self-efficacy judgments	▪ Individuals are most likely to seek out, and expend more effort on, tasks at which they expect to be successful (for which they have high estimates of self-efficacy). ▪ Individuals are likely to avoid tasks at which they expect to do badly (for which they have low estimates of self-efficacy). ▪ High judgments of self-efficacy are related to positive self-concepts; low judgments of self-efficacy are associated with more negative judgments of self-worth. ▪ There is a positive relationship between self-efficacy and academic achievement.
Four sources of information related to the development of self-efficacy judgments, with corresponding examples of information that might lead Edna to arrive at positive estimates of her personal efficacy	▪ **Enactive** (based on her own actions): She wins a scholarship to the Northern Alberta Institute of Technology. ▪ **Vicarious** (based on comparisons with others): She learns that Ronald studied hard but wasn't given a scholarship. ▪ **Persuasory** (the result of persuasion): Her teacher tells her she should enroll in the advanced program for gifted learners. ▪ **Emotive** (the result of arousal, or emotion): She was tense before her entrance exam, but felt exhilarated afterward.

approaches to cognitive development, are discussed in subsequent chapters that deal chronologically with intellectual development (Chapters 5, 7, 9, and 11).

Basic Piagetian Ideas

Because Piaget was trained as a biologist rather than a psychologist, it is not surprising that he began his study of children with two of the fundamental questions of biology: (1) What is it that enables organisms to adapt to their environments and survive? and (2) What is the most useful way of classifying living organisms? These biological questions can be rephrased and applied to the development of children: (1) What are the characteristics and capabilities of children that allow them to adapt to their environments? and (2) What is the most useful way of classifying or ordering child development? Piaget's answers for these two questions, developed over an extraordinarily prolific career spanning more than six decades (he died in 1980 at the age of 84), are the basis for his theory. One account indicates that before his

death, he had published 478 articles and 52 books—another five articles and five books were published posthumously—for a total of more than 26,000 pages (Smith, 1993).

ASSIMILATION AND ACCOMMODATION PERMIT ADAPTATION

The newborn infant that Piaget describes is in many ways a helpless little organism, unaware that the world out there is real, with no storehouse of thoughts with which to reason, no capacity for intentional behaviors, no more than a few simple reflexes. But infants are much more than this. They are also remarkable little sensing machines that seem to be naturally predisposed to acquiring and processing a tremendous amount of information. They continually seek out and respond to stimulation. As a result, the sucking, reaching, grasping, and other reflexes that were present at birth become more complex, more coordinated, and, eventually, more purposeful. The process by which this occurs is **adaptation.** And to answer the first of the biology questions as simply as possible, *assimilation* and *accommodation* are the processes that make adaptation possible.

Assimilation involves responding to situations in terms of activities or knowledge that have already been learned or that are present at birth. For example, an infant is born with the capability to suck—with a sucking **scheme**, in Piaget's terms (sometimes called *schema*, pluralized as *schemata*). The sucking scheme allows the infant to assimilate a nipple to the behavior of sucking. Similarly, a child who has learned the rules of addition can assimilate a problem such as 2 + 2 (can respond appropriately in terms of previous learning). Often, however, our understanding of the world is insufficient to deal with the present situation. The newborn's sucking scheme is adequate for ordinary nipples but does not work for fingers and toes; the preschooler's understanding of number is sufficient for keeping track of toys but is inadequate for impressing kindergarten teachers. Changes are required in information and behavior. These changes define **accommodation.** In short, assimilation involves reacting on the basis of previous learning and understanding; accommodation involves a change in understanding. The interplay of assimilation and accommodation leads to adaptation. (See Chapter 5 for further illustration of these concepts.)

DEVELOPMENT CAN BE ORDERED IN STAGES

The second of biology's questions asks what is the most useful way of organizing and classifying child development. Piaget's answer is found in his description of the stages through which each child passes. There are four major stages in this description, each marked by strikingly different perceptions of the world and by different adaptations to it. Each is the product of learning that occurred in earlier stages, and each is a preparation for the next stage.

Note that although Piaget's theory is most easily explained and understood in terms of stages, he nevertheless viewed development as a continuous process of successive changes. Development does not consist of abrupt, clearly recognizable changes like steps on a stairway; it's more like a gradual incline. Although cognitive development moves along relatively smoothly, it's useful, and simpler, to divide it into stages. Doing so allows us to compare behaviors and capabilities that are characteristic of different levels, and sometimes leads to discoveries about the processes underlying change. Note also that the ages Piaget assigned to each stage are simply average ranges reflecting the behaviors of upper-middle-class Swiss children through the middle of the twentieth century. Children from different cultural contexts and with different characteristics sometimes pass through these stages much earlier or much later than Piaget's norms would suggest.

The Stages

Piaget's major stages are summarized very briefly here; they are discussed in more detail in Chapters 5, 7, 9, and 11.

■ SENSORIMOTOR PERIOD

The first two years are labeled the **sensorimotor period** because during this period the child understands the world largely through immediate action and sensation. For the infant, the world exists here and now. It is real only when it is being acted upon and sensed. When the ball is not being chewed, looked at, or touched, it doesn't exist. Only toward the end of the second year do children realize that objects are permanent and have an identity of their own—that they continue to exist when they are out of sight. Also, toward the end of the first two years, the child begins to acquire language and progresses slowly from a sensorimotor to a more cognitive intelligence (see Chapter 5).

■ PREOPERATIONAL THINKING

Following the acquisition of language, the child enters the period of **preoperational thought** (ages two to seven)—a period marked by an excessive reliance on perception rather than logic. For example, in one of Piaget's well-known conservation experiments, children are shown two identical glasses that contain equal amounts of water. The experimenter then pours the contents of one glass into a tall, thin tube—or into a low, flat dish. Do they still have the same amount, or does one now have more than the other? Preoperational children, relying on the appearance of the two containers, almost invariably think that the tall tube has more because it is higher (or less because it is thinner)—or that the flat dish has more because it is "fatter" (or less because it is shorter). Even when they realize that the water could be poured back into the original container so that the two would then be equal, preoperational children continue to rely on perception (on actual appearance) rather than on reasoning (see Chapter 7 for more details).

■ CONCRETE OPERATIONS

The major acquisition of the next period of development is the ability to think operationally (ages seven or eight to eleven or twelve). An **operation** is a thought—what Piaget called an internalized or mental action. Mental actions are governed by certain rules of logic. These rules permit the **concrete-operations** child to laugh at the ridiculous simplicity of a conservation problem. Of course there is the same amount of water in both containers because none has been added or taken away, one misleading dimension is compensated for by the other (it is taller but thinner), and the act of pouring the water from one container to the other can be reversed to prove that nothing has changed. The concrete-operations child is capable of this kind of logic. But it is a logic that is tied to real, concrete objects and events. The child is still unable to reason logically about hypothetical situations or events and cannot go from the real to the merely possible or from the possible to the actual. Thought is bound to the real world, the concrete—hence the label concrete operations (see Chapter 9).

■ FORMAL OPERATIONS

The last stage of cognitive development—**formal operations**—is characterized by the ability to manipulate abstract ideas. During this stage, which begins around age eleven or twelve and ends at fourteen or fifteen, the child's thought has the potential to become as logical as it will ever be. But the emphasis should be on the word *potential*. Many of us remain

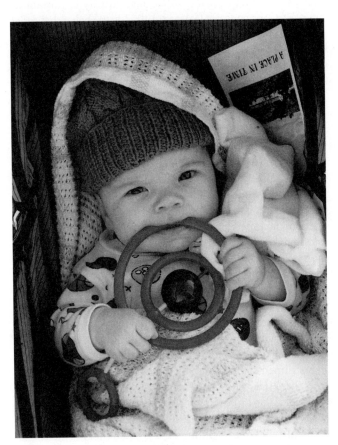

For the sensorimotor infant, says Piaget, the world derives its meaning and its existence from the actions that can be performed on it. Thumbs, fingers, feet, or anything around which the mouth will fit is there to be chewed, sucked, and tasted. These actions, along with touching and looking, are the infant's means of exploring and knowing.

strangers to the deductive logic of formal operations throughout our lives. However, as Ricco (1993) argues, the logic of formal operations is a logic concerned with hypothetical states of affairs; for many of life's problems, other forms of logic—especially those dealing with meaning—are more appropriate. Piaget recognized this, and in some of his latest writings, he discussed a formal operations logic of meanings (see Piaget & Garcia, 1991). (See Summary Table 2.9.)

▲ SUMMARY TABLE 2.9
Piaget's Developmental Theory

Main Ideas	■ Human development is the story of the individual's progressive adaptation to the world through the processes of *assimilation* (the use of previously learned responses in familiar situations) and *accommodation* (the modification of behavior in response to demands of the environment). Infants are predisposed to acquire information as they interact with the world, eventually constructing progressively more logical and useful representations of reality as they develop. Their representations, understanding, and competencies can be described in terms of a series of stages.

STAGE	APPROXIMATE AGE	SOME MAJOR CHARACTERISTICS*
Sensorimotor	0 to 2 years	■ Intelligence in action.
		■ World of the here and now.
		■ No language, no thought, no notion of objective reality at beginning of stage.
Preoperational	2 to 7 years	■ Egocentric thought.
		■ Reason dominated by perception.
		■ Intuitive rather than logical solutions.
		■ Inability to conserve.
Concrete operations	7 to 11 or 12 years	■ Ability to conserve.
		■ Logic of classes and relations.
		■ Understanding of numbers.
		■ Thinking bound to concrete.
		■ Development of reversibility in thought.
Formal operations	11 or 12 to 14 or 15 years	■ Complete generality of thought.
		■ Propositional thinking.
		■ Ability to deal with the hypothetical.
		■ Development of strong idealism.

*Each of these characteristics is detailed in the appropriate sections of Chapters 5, 7, 9, and 11.

Piaget in Review

Development, says Piaget, is best described as the emergence of progressively more logical forms of thought that become increasingly effective in freeing children from the present and allowing them to use powerful symbols to understand and to manipulate the environment. According to the theory, the major characteristics of thinking in each of the four developmental stages influence all aspects of children's understanding of the world, including their notions of space, time, number, reality, causality, and so on. It isn't so much that children discover some ready-made rules of logic that govern their understanding of the world; rather, they invent or construct these rules. Hence the current label **constructivism** to describe theories such as Piaget's (Smith, 1993). Constructivism is an important concept in educational theory and practice, where the teacher's role is often seen as one of aiding students' construction of knowledge (Cobb, 1994). As Driver and associates (1994) put it, "The view that knowledge cannot be transmitted but must be constructed by the mental activity of learners underpins contemporary perspectives" (p. 5).

It's important to note that Piaget's child constructs notions of reality and rules of logic not simply as a result of interaction with real objects and situations. Equally important in Piaget's theory, suggests DeVries (1997), is the belief that *social* interactions are crucial to the child's cognitive development, as well as to the child's moral and emotional development. Hence, both peers and parents play an important role in the child's development.

Because Piaget's theory makes specific predictions about how children function intellectually at different ages, parts of it are relatively easy to evaluate objectively simply by testing the predictions. In general, research that has tried to do this confirms Piaget's initial findings with respect to the order of stages. However, this research also makes it clear that the ages at which different children reach specific stages can vary considerably.

Also, it appears that Piaget vastly underestimated the information-processing capabilities of infants and young children (Wellman & Gelman, 1992). However, this is due less to weaknesses in the theory than to Piaget's lack of instruments and procedures sensitive enough to detect the infant's cognitive capacities. For example, contemporary studies of infant responsiveness often use sophisticated instruments that measure changes in heart and respiration rates, movements of the eyeballs, changes in pupil size, brain-wave activity, and so on—all instruments not available to Piaget in the 1920s and 1930s.

Piaget's theory is also sometimes accused of having overestimated the importance of motor activity in the infant's cognitive development and of underestimating the importance of perception (Bullinger, 1985). Others criticize the theory because it says little about individual differences among children, about the factors that might account for those differences, or about what can be done to promote intellectual development. In addition, the theory's language and concepts are sometimes difficult, and it isn't always clear that terms such as *assimilation* and *accommodation* add significantly to our understanding of human behavior. In spite of these weaknesses, Piagetian theory has been the most dominant cognitive development theory of this century, and it continues to have a profound influence on current research and practice.

BIOLOGICAL APPROACHES: ETHOLOGY AND SOCIOBIOLOGY

Biological approaches to understanding human development stress the importance of innate, predetermined behavior patterns or tendencies. These approaches often stem from research conducted with animals, in which genetic influences are sometimes more readily apparent than they are among humans.

Ethology and Biological Attachment Theory

The importance of biology (of heredity) in determining animal behavior has long been accepted. I accept without question that my English setter is good at sniffing out certain birds precisely because she is an English setter. I would not expect the same behavior of Id, our rather useless but aptly named cat. Even if their early experiences had been identical, I still would not expect Id to enjoy walking at my heels or to drool at the prospect of a cold swim in a duck-filled pond. You see, we know that many of the behaviors and habits characteristic of nonhuman animal species are not acquired solely through experience. A moth does not fly into a flame because it has learned to do so; dead moths don't fly. We can therefore assume that the attraction that light has for a moth, like the

overpowering urge of a goose to go south or a salmon to swim up a specific river, is the result of inherited tendencies.

Are we, in at least some ways, like moths and salmon? If so, what are our flames? Our rivers?

Ethology

Ethologists (scientists whose principal concern is with studying behavior in natural situations) think that yes, we are a little like moths. And although the flames that entice us might be less obvious than those that draw the moth, they are perhaps no less powerful.

Lorenz's (1952) studies of **imprinting** in ducks and geese were among the first to draw parallels between inherited animal behavior and humans. Imprinting is the tendency of newly hatched geese (or chickens, ducks, and related birds) to follow the first moving object they see during a **critical period,** which occurs shortly after hatching. The period is critical because exposure to the same moving object (a **releaser**) before or after this period does not ordinarily result in the appearance of the same imprinted behavior (see Figure 2.5).

Imprinting among newly hatched birds clearly has survival value. The gosling's chances of survival are far better if it, along with all its fellow goslings, follows the mother goose. Of course, the gosling does not follow the mother because it is aware of a genetic relationship between this big bird and itself. It follows its mother simply because she happened to be the first moving object it saw during the critical few hours following hatching. Ethologists have repeatedly demonstrated that if some other object such as a balloon were to replace the mother goose, the young gosling would quite happily follow it instead. When Lorenz substituted himself for the mother goose, the young goslings followed him much as they would have their mother.

The critical period is all-important. Newly hatched geese or chickens that are not exposed to a moving object during this critical period fail to become imprinted and subsequently

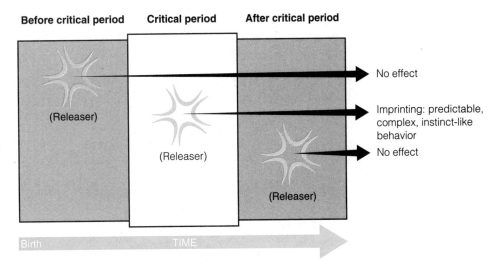

FIGURE 2.5

A model of imprinting. Under appropriate environmental conditions, exposure to a releaser during the critical period leads to imprinting, which is manifested in predictable behaviors in response to specific environmental conditions. Imprinting does not occur if a releaser is not present or if the releaser is presented too early or too late.

will not follow their mothers. Similarly, lambs that are removed from their mothers after birth and not brought back for a week or more do not ordinarily show any evidence of attachment to them. Perhaps even more striking, the mothers themselves do not appear to be attached to their kids under these circumstances and will sometimes butt them out of the way if they insist on coming too close (Thorpe, 1963).

Human Bonding

The search for imprinted behaviors among humans has not led to the discovery of behaviors as obvious as "following" among geese. Still, some theorists, such as John Bowlby (1979, 1980, 1982), believe that there are important links between the findings of ethologists and the development of attachment between mother and infant. Bowlby's research with young infants suggests we have a natural (inherited) tendency to form emotional bonds with our mothers or with some other permanent caregiver, during what Bowlby terms the **sensitive period.** Such bonds, Bowlby argues, would clearly have been important for the infant's survival in a less civilized age. The need for them is evident in the infant's attempts to maintain physical contact, to cling, and to stay in visual contact with the mother (Bowlby, 1969). It is also apparent in the effects of separating mother and infant—effects that are marked by "emotional distress and personality disturbance, including anxiety, anger, depression, and emotional detachment" (Bowlby, 1979, p. 127). (See Chapter 6 for a more detailed review of infant attachment research.)

Biology and Sociobiology

Bowlby is only one of a large number of theorists interested in applying knowledge of biology (and, more specifically, of genetics and evolution) to an understanding of human development and behavior. Some ethologically oriented scientists argue that science has neglected the role of heredity in determining many of the behaviors that we attribute to our environments and upbringing. Sometimes termed *behavioral biologists* or *sociobiologists,* their most striking and controversial belief is that human social behavior is the product of a lengthy evolutionary history—that it is therefore genetically based (Wilson, 1975, 1976). **Sociobiology** is defined as "the systematic study of the biological basis of all social behavior" (Wilson, 1975, p. 4). We are altruistic, sociobiologists argue, because helping others contributes to the group's survival. In much the same way as altruism might be explained by reference to the "selfishness" of genes (it is, after all, genetic material that survives), sociobiological theory can be used to explain maternal love, sexual mores, aggression, spitefulness—indeed, the entire range of human social behaviors.

Ethologists and sociobiologists look for the causes of behavior among genetically determined (or genetically influenced)

The powerful, genetically programmed tendency of young goslings to follow their mother has clear implications for survival. Some researchers think that humans, too, have related genetic tendencies that contribute to survival and adaptation.

tendencies and capabilities. Some theorists argue that the recognition of genetic contributions to behavior, and to human social relationships, is critically important. These contributions, notes D. S. Wilson (1994), have often been ignored by psychology.

Biological Approaches in Review

Biological approaches to human development stress the importance of genetically based biological forces in shaping development. For example, sociobiological theory (also termed behavioral biology) assumes that all social behavior has a genetic basis. Not surprisingly, this assumption has provoked considerable controversy and reaction. Critics have been quick to point out that the theory is highly speculative and is based on a handful of assumptions that cannot easily be tested (Lyne & Howe, 1990). For example, the theory rests on the assumption that behaviors occur because they increase the genetic survival of a group (or the probability that genetic material will survive). How do we know this is so? Because the behavior occurred. Why did the behavior occur? Because it increases average genetic survival. This type of circular reasoning offers no hope of proof. To validate the theory, it would be necessary to establish the presence of "altruistic" genes, for example, by some means unrelated to the behaviors these genes are intended to explain. That has yet to be done.

This does not mean that genetics is therefore irrelevant to understanding human behavior. In fact, as is made clear in Chapter 3, our genes are fundamentally involved in everything we do. What it does mean is that science has not yet succeeded in showing that specific genes, or combinations of genes, directly cause specific individual behaviors. The basic error in interpreting sociobiological theory has to do

Biological Approaches to Human Development

Main emphasis	■ The importance of innate, predetermined tendencies or patterns of behavior.
Representative approaches	■ Bonding theory. ■ Sociobiology.
Important theorists	■ Lorenz (ethology). ■ Bowlby (bonding theory). ■ Wilson (sociobiology).
Principal terms and concepts	■ **Ethology**—science that looks at the behavior of animals in their natural habitats. ■ **Bonding**—biologically based attachment between mother and infant. ■ **Imprinting**—a type of learning involving complex, species-specific behaviors that typically occurs shortly after birth, usually in response to a specific stimulus—for example, "following" in young ducks. ■ **Releaser**—stimulus that elicits (releases) imprinted behavior. ■ **Critical Period**—period during which a releaser must be present for imprinting to occur. ■ **Sensitive Period**—period during which a specific type of learning is most likely to occur, given specific, appropriate experiences. ■ **Sociobiology**—science that studies the biological basis of human behavior. Also termed *behavioral biology*.

with level of explanation. Evolutionary theory, the basis of sociobiology, explains variation at the level of groups with related genetic material (Boyles & Tilman, 1993). It can rarely predict individual behaviors. (See Summary Table 2.10.)

ECOLOGICAL APPROACHES: VYGOTSKY AND BRONFENBRENNER

Ethologists (and sociobiologists) emphasize the importance of biological or genetic contributions to development; in contrast, ecological approaches emphasize the importance of the individual's context—hence the importance of the environment, especially the social environment (or culture) (Bronfenbrenner, 1989). However, the differences between ethological and ecological positions frequently have more to do with different emphases than with different beliefs. Most theorists readily accept that both ecological (cultural or environ-

mental) influences and biological tendencies are intimately involved in determining human development.

Vygotsky's Cultural–Historical Approach

In 1924, at the young age of twenty-eight, the Russian psychologist L. S. Vygotsky was already a major force in Soviet psychology. Sadly, only ten years later, he died of tuberculosis. Still, many of his ideas, old as they may be, have experienced a newfound currency and popularity in today's psychology. Unfortunately, however, these ideas are not always entirely clear. As Nicolopoulou (1993) puts it, "Despite the fact that his writings are full of intuitions and illuminations, they are often sketchy and at times incomplete" (p. 7).

■ VYGOTSKY'S BASIC IDEAS

Vygotsky's clearest and most important ideas provide a strong link between social factors—especially historical and cultural factors—and individual development (Tudge & Winterhoff, 1993). As a result, three basic underlying themes run through Vygotsky's theorizing. One has to do with the centrality of culture in human development, a second deals with the functions of language, and a third relates to the developing child's relationship with the environment—a relationship Vygotsky described as the *zone of proximal development* (Kozulin, 1990).

■ CULTURE

Human development, claimed Vygotsky, is fundamentally different from the development of animals. Why? Because humans can use tools and symbols; as a result, they create cultures. And cultures have a vitality, a life of their own. They grow and change; they exert a very powerful influence on their members. They determine the end result of competent development—the sorts of things that a culture's members have to learn, the ways they should think, the things they are most likely to believe. As Tappan (1997) puts it, culture necessarily shapes human mental functioning. And its most important tool for so doing is language. Or, as Vygotsky (1986) notes, cultures, which are defined largely by language, permit humans to have a history—and perhaps a future as well.

The role of culture in human development is perhaps most evident in the distinction Vygotsky makes between *elementary mental functions* (which both humans and nonhuman animals have in common) and *higher mental functions* (which are exclusively human). Elementary functions are natural, unlearned capacities. They are evident in the newborn's ability to attend to sounds and to discriminate among them. They are apparent in the ability to remember the smell of the mother, or in the capacity to coo and gurgle, to scream and cry. In time, however, these elementary capacities are gradually transformed into higher mental functions—that is, they change from natural, unlearned functions to more sophisticated, learned behaviors and capacities. This transformation,

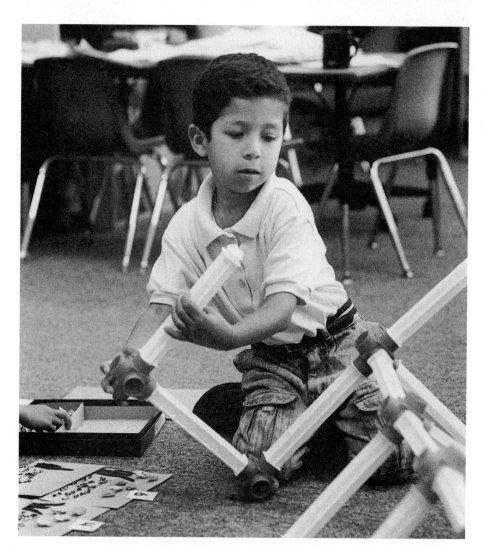

Development (or growth), says Vygotsky, requires that the demands of the environment be at an appropriate level for children—in his words, that they be within the zone of proximal development. Demands that are too trivial can be wasteful; those that are too far beyond a child's capabilities are ineffective.

which is absolutely fundamental to human development, is made possible through language.

■ THE ROLE OF LANGUAGE

Language, after all, is what makes thinking possible, Vygotsky asserts. During the preverbal stage of development, the child's intelligence is much like that of, say, an ape. It is purely natural, purely practical—elementary, in other words. But language changes all that. Language, insists Vygotsky, is absolutely essential for any *conscious* thought of the future. Put quite simply, our *thinking* about the past, the present, and the future is impossible without the form of language that psychologists label **inner speech** (Das, 1995).

Vygotsky describes three forms of language that develop sequentially; each has different functions. The first, **social speech** (also called **external speech**), is common until around the age of three. The most primitive form of speech, its function is largely to control the behavior of others (as in "I want candy!") or to express simple concepts.

Egocentric speech dominates the child's life between ages three and approximately seven. This type of speech is a sort of bridge between the social speech of the preceding period and the more inner speech of the next period. Egocentric

speech often serves to control the child's own behavior, but is frequently spoken out loud. For example, young children may talk to themselves as they are trying to do something: "Push. Okay, now turn. Turn. Turn . . . push. . . ."

Inner speech is our private self-talk—what James (1892) called our stream of consciousness. According to Vygotsky, inner speech is what makes thought possible. It is the basis of all higher mental functioning. Interestingly, by the age of four, children still have very little awareness of inner speech or of verbal thinking. Thus, Flavell and his associates (1997) found that four-year-olds seemed unable to make the inference that people who were reading or counting or doing related "mental" tasks might actually be talking to themselves. In fact, they generally believed that silent, inner speech is not really a possibility. (See Table 2.11.)

■ ZONE OF PROXIMAL DEVELOPMENT

Language, a cultural invention, is one of the most important ways in which the child's environmental context influences and shapes the course of development. For Vygotsky, development is a function of the interaction between culture and the child's basic biological capacities and maturational timetables. But, insisted Vygotsky, it is the environmental

TABLE 2.11

Vygotsky's Description of the Role of Language

STAGE	FUNCTION
Social (external) speech (to age 3)	Controls the behavior of others; expresses simple thoughts and emotions.
Egocentric speech (3 to 7)	Bridge between external and inner speech; serves to control own behavior, but spoken out loud.
Inner speech (7 onwards)	Self-talk; makes possible the direction of our thinking and our behavior; involved in all higher mental functioning.

context (the culture) that is most important—not biological maturation (Valsiner, 1987). Development takes place when environmental opportunities and demands are appropriate for the child. In a sense, the environment instructs the child in the ways of development. But the instruction is effective only if the child's biological maturation and present developmental level are sufficiently advanced. For every child, says Vygotsky, there is a **zone of proximal growth**—a sort of potential for development (Belmont, 1989). Demands that are beyond this zone—in other words, that are beyond the child's capacities—are ineffective in promoting growth. Similarly, demands that are too simple are wasteful.

In summary, Vygotsky's developmental theory underscores the role of culture, especially its most important invention, language. The zone of proximal development—sort of a label for developmental potential—expresses Vygotsky's belief in the interdependence between the processes of child development and the resources that cultures provide. (See Summary Table 2.12.)

Bronfenbrenner's Ecological Systems Theory

Another approach that emphasizes the importance of context–person interaction is Bronfenbrenner's. Like Vygotsky, Bronfenbrenner assigns a centrally important role to culture in determining the processes and outcomes of human development. One of the basic principles of his **ecological systems theory** is that differences in intellectual performance between different groups are a function of interacting with different cultures (or subcultures) that are characterized by different types of cognitive processes. Hence, a person's cognitive competence is always culturally relative. A very intelligent, well-adapted native of the Amazon jungle would not necessarily function very intelligently in downtown Chicago. But then a Chicago lawyer might quickly lose her bearings—and perhaps her marbles—in the Amazon jungle.

Bronfenbrenner refers to psychological, biological, and social systems as **open systems.** What this means is that their existence depends on interaction and that they are constantly subject to change as a function of interaction. The Piagetian

infant, born with a small number of reflexes, adapts and changes as a function of interacting with the environment—in Piaget's terms, as a result of assimilating and accommodating. It is infant–environment interaction that results in the notion that objects are permanent, that symbols represent, that quantities can be added and subtracted, that a fine and elegant logic governs physics and chemistry.

■ HUMAN ECOLOGY

Bronfenbrenner refers to the interaction of the individual with the environment as the *ecology of human development* (also the title of his 1979 book). The cornerstone of his theory is the belief that human development consists of a series of ongoing changes (accommodations) in interactions between the person and the immediate context. Also of fundamental importance are the relationships that exist among different aspects of the contexts in which the individual interacts (Bronfenbrenner, 1989).

Not only are we influenced by our contexts, but we also influence them in turn—a process that Bandura (1995) labels **reciprocal determinism.** If infant Benjamin cries more than is expected, he may change some significant aspects of the environment with which he interacts. His mother may come running sooner than she otherwise would; his nurse might

▲ SUMMARY TABLE 2.12
Vygotsky's Cultural–Historical Theory: Main Concepts

Culture	■ Cultures make us human; without cultures, we would be like animals, relegated to *elementary* mental functions, incapable of *higher* thought.
	■ The most important tool of human cultures is language.
Language	■ Language makes thinking possible; thought is dependent on *inner speech*.
	■ *Inner speech* is self-talk. Developmentally, it appears last. Without inner speech, says Vygotsky, we could not contemplate a future.
	■ *Egocentric speech* bridges internal and external speech, and is common between ages 3 and 7.
	■ *Social speech* is external speech. It is the earliest and most primitive form of speech.
Zone of Proximal Growth	■ Vygotsky's phrase for the child's potential for further development, given appropriate cultural experiences.
	■ In a sense, the *zone* includes the range of tasks of which the individual is capable given appropriate assistance (in the form of suggestions, models, hints, questions, and so on). Tasks *below* this are too simple and of little value; those *above* the zone are too difficult to be very useful.

become more irritable, more impatient; his father might pay more, or less, attention to him; his siblings might openly resent his intrusion in the family; even the dog might be annoyed. And each of these changing aspects of context might, in turn, alter Benjamin's behavior. That his mother runs to soothe his cries might encourage his crying even more. But now, perhaps the mother senses what is happening and comes more slowly, more reluctantly, and again the interaction changes. Thus, the mother's personality and her beliefs about child rearing interact with Benjamin's personality, and his behavior, in a constantly changing, open ecological system. There is always an interplay between the person's characteristics and those of the environment, says Bronfenbrenner: "The one cannot be defined without reference to the other" (1989, p. 225). He also makes the point that some characteristics (termed *developmentally instigative*) are more important than others in influencing contexts. Temperament, size or appearance, age, sex, race, developmental handicaps, and many other factors tend to provoke important reactions—hence changes—in context. These, in turn, affect the individual.

■ DIMENSIONS OF CONTEXT

One of Bronfenbrenner's important contributions to the study of child development lies in his detailed description of the contexts in which development occurs. The ecological system of which he speaks consists of interactions with four different levels of context. From nearest (most proximal) to most remote, these are the microsystem, the mesosystem, the exosystem, and the macrosystem.

- **Microsystem.** Interactions that occur at an immediate, face-to-face level define the microsystem. For the developing child, the most important aspects of the microsystem include patterns of behaviors, roles, and relationships within the home, the school, the peer group, the workplace, the playground, and so on. The interaction of Benjamin's crying with the behaviors of mother, father, siblings, and dog illustrates what is meant by a microsystem. Everybody in a microsystem influences everybody else.

- **Mesosystem.** In turn, microsystems may influence each other in important ways. For example, how Benjamin's mother treats him may be influenced by her interactions with his father. Perhaps she is less likely to be patient with her son if she has just had an argument with her husband. And how Benjamin interacts with his sister may also be negatively affected. Interactions between elements of the microsystem that include the developing person define what is meant by the mesosystem.

- **Exosystem.** All systems are part of other, larger systems. Thus, the home does not exist in isolation, but interacts with school, church, community, and so on. And how parents treat children may be profoundly influenced by schools, teachers, religious leaders, employers, and friends. For example, interactions between Benjamin and his father may be influenced by the father's relationships with his colleagues or his fishing buddies. Inter-

Levels of Context in Bronfenbrenner's Ecological Systems Theory

LEVEL	TYPE OF INTERACTION	EXAMPLE
Microsystem	Child in immediate, face-to-face interaction.	Mother singing to child.
Mesosystem	Relationships between two or more microsystems.	Mother and father interacting.
Exosystem	Linkages and relationships between two or more settings, one of which does not include the child.	Father's relationship with employer.
Macrosystem	The totality of all other systems, evident in the beliefs, the options, the lifestyles, the values, the mores of a culture or subculture.	Society's child-care legislation; expectations and requirements of culture.

actions between an element of the microsystem that ordinarily includes the developing child and an element of the wider context that does not include the child define the exosystem.

- **Macrosystem.** All the interactive systems—micro, meso, and exo—that characterize cultures (or subcultures) define the macrosystem. Macrosystems are describable in terms of beliefs, values, customs, expected behaviors, social roles, status assignments, lifestyles, religions, and so on. In Bronfenbrenner's (1989) words, the macrosystem is "a societal blueprint for a particular culture, subculture, or other broader social context" (p. 228). Macrosystems are identifiable in terms of such things as common beliefs, values, resources, goals, lifestyles, and ambitions.

Changes in macrosystems over time are sometimes very significant for the developing individual. For example, within the last few decades of this century, there have been profound changes in family employment patterns (from one to two wage earners), in family structure (from two- to one-parent families), in child-rearing styles (from home rearing to other child-care options), in age of marriage (from younger to older), in age of childbearing (also from younger to older), in range of expected school attendance. Clearly, many of these macrosystem changes directly affect the microsystems of which the child is a part—the family, the home, the school. (See Summary Table 2.13.)

Cultural and Ecological Approaches in Review

Biological approaches to understanding human development stress the role of genetics; ecological approaches emphasize the role of context. As is made clear in the next chapter, however, both are clearly important in human development. Nor can their influences easily be separated because their effects result from interactions between the two.

A CULTURAL–HISTORICAL APPROACH

Vygotsky's theory underscores the role of culture, especially its most important invention, language. For Vygotsky, the driving force in development is found in the demands and requirements of the culture. As Tudge and Winterhoff (1993) note, Vygotsky believed that development is a social process assisted by adults and more competent peers.

Vygotsky's most important contribution to understanding development is his recognition of the importance of culture in shaping thought and behavior. And although the concepts of culture and language as determiners of development are perhaps too vague to be of immediate practical value to child-care specialists, teachers, or even psychologists, they are absolutely fundamental to our understanding of the complexity and variety of the human experience. In Bruner's (1986) words, Vygotsky serves as an "inspiration"—an inspiration that urges us to see more clearly that the average human beings of which our textbooks speak are always average only in their culture. It is largely to remind ourselves of this that in every chapter of this text, there are boxed inserts dealing with people from different cultures.

ECOLOGICAL SYSTEMS THEORY

Although most contemporary developmental theorists pay lip service to the importance of taking context, person, and interaction into account, many researchers continue to operate within more traditional models. Two such models have dominated much of our thinking and research. One, exemplified in Freud's theories, says that the causes of developmental change are to be found primarily within the individual; the other, evident in behavioristic approaches, insists that the individual's environment is a more important cause of change. It is, of course, the old nature–nurture debate (about which we say more in the next chapter).

The model that underlies our thinking is tremendously important to our research and our conclusions. The first model (Freud, for example) says that if Johnny turns out to be an unmanageable scoundrel, we should look for the cause and the explanation in his temperament and his personality characteristics; the second (behaviorism, for example) says we should look to his environment. Neither of these models says that we should look at how Johnny's characteristics influence his environment, and at how, in turn, his environment influences him. Neither insists that the cause is to be found in the progressive changes in the interactions that take place between Johnny and his alcoholic mother, his overworked and indifferent teachers, his peers (the microsystem). Neither suggests that the aborted love affair between Johnny's mother and his tee-ball coach is of consequence (the mesosystem). Neither is concerned with interactions that might have occurred between Johnny's mother and her employer, leading to a reduction in her pay and chronic disgruntlement (the exosystem). Neither asks the researcher to look at how society's encouragement of the changing structure of the fam-

ily impact on Johnny's well-being (the macrosystem). That they do not ask these questions is a weakness of some of our traditional approaches to understanding child development; that ecological systems theory does pose these questions is among its strengths.

But that is also among its weaknesses. Explanations based on ecological systems theory require careful analysis of an almost infinite number of highly complex interactions. Identifying these interactions, observing and quantifying them, sorting out relationships among them, teasing out reciprocal influences between individuals and their micro-, meso-, and exosystems, and determining how changing cultural values and options impinge on the individual—these are difficult tasks. But perhaps if we chew at them long enough, we may find that they are not impossible. Ecological systems theory at least suggests where we should begin.

HUMANISTIC APPROACHES: MASLOW

Had I spoken of Piaget or Freud, of Skinner or sociology, of ethology or ecology in my grandmother's kitchen, the old lady would have listened politely. She was always polite. But in the end, she would probably have said, "That's just theory. It's all very nice, but what about Frank?" Why Frank? Simply because he was a unique child—as we all were (or are). And although there is little doubt that Freud, Skinner, and Piaget might each have had something very intelligent, and perhaps even useful, to say about Frank's habits of stealing chicken eggs, writing poetry, and dancing little jigs in mudholes, they would have been hard pressed to convince my grandmother that they knew more about Frank than she did. My grandmother was a humanist.

Basic Concepts of Humanism

Humanistic psychologists are concerned with the uniqueness of the individual. A prevalent humanistic notion is that it is impossible to describe the environment, much less a person, in a truly meaningful way because the important features of the environment are particular to each individual. To understand the behavior of others, one must attempt to perceive the world as they see it—from the perspective of their knowledge, experiences, goals, and aspirations (Rogers, 1951). Such an orientation, sometimes labeled **phenomenology,** underscores again that the individual is unique rather than an average.

Because of their emphasis on the uniqueness of the individual, humanistic positions do not lend themselves easily to the formulation of specific theories that are widely applicable. But they do suggest an attitude toward people, and toward the process of developing, that is of tremendous potential value to those concerned with human welfare. Humanistic orientations tend to personalize (that is, to humanize) our attitudes toward others; they restore some of the dynamism of the developmental process that our more static and more very day in war-torn Sudan, helpless and unarmed women and children are hunted down by men mounted on horses—not as an enemy might be hunted, but more as prey. The hunters are slave-traders, mostly Islamic Arabs; the hunted are people of the Dinka, a pacific, agricultural people, predominantly Christian. As slaves, the Dinka command a high price among the wealthy. But wealth is relative; these slaves can be repurchased for the price of three good cows—about $100. The Arab-led government denies the existence of slavery in Sudan. But evidence is that thousands of Dinkas have been enslaved, and thousands more killed. Many of those enslaved have been beaten, tortured, and raped, as Journalist Slobodian discovered when she snuck into Sudan with a small group bent on "redeeming" slaves. Two hun-

dred and ninety four Dinka women and children were purchased on her trip. And set free.

1. Slobodian, L. (1997, Nov. 16). Sudan's ugliest secret. *Edmonton Sun*, Sunday Express, p. 15.

To Consider

Should the outside world be involved in such cases? How?

On the Net

The Baltimore Antislavery Society page provides links to information about contemporary slavery not only in African countries such as Sudan, but in many other parts of the world as well:

http://cgibin1.erols.com/bcccsbs/bass/bass.html

Links to information about children's rights can be found at this site:

http://its2.ocs.lsu.edu/guests/wwwlawl/human/children.htm

---

complex theories might otherwise remove. And, above all, they emphasize the *value* of individual human lives. For a sharp contrast to humanistic attitudes and values, see "In the News and on the Net: Slavery."

Maslow's Humanistic Theory

Perhaps the best known of humanistic psychologists is Abraham Maslow (1970), who was primarily concerned with the development of the healthy personality. Fundamental to his position is a belief that we are moved by two systems of needs (Maslow, 1970). The **basic needs** are physiological (food, drink) and psychological (security, love, esteem). The **metaneeds** are higher-level needs. They manifest themselves in our desire to know, in our appreciation of truth and beauty, and in our tendencies toward growth and fulfillment (termed **self-actualization**) (see Figure 2.6). Alternately, these two groups of needs are sometimes termed *growth needs* (metaneeds) and *deficiency needs* (basic needs). The basic needs are called deficiency needs because when they are not satisfied, individuals engage in behaviors designed to remedy this lack of satisfaction. (For example, hunger represents a deficiency that can be satisfied by eating.) The metaneeds are called growth needs because activities that relate to them do not fulfill a lack but lead toward growth.

These needs are assumed to be hierarchically arranged in the sense that the metaneeds will not be attended to unless the basic needs are reasonably well satisfied. In other words, we pay attention to beauty, truth, and the development of our potential when we are no longer hungry and unloved (at least not terribly so). Put more simply, hunger for food is more

FIGURE 2.6

Maslow's hierarchy of needs.

compelling than hunger for knowledge. But keep studying—this is important.

SELF-ACTUALIZATION

Chief among Maslow's metaneeds, and most important for understanding human development, is *self-actualization*. By his own admission, the term is difficult to define (Maslow, 1970). He suggests that it is characterized by the absence of "neurosis, psychopathic personality, psychosis, or strong

Basic Concepts of Maslow's Humanism

Humanistic orientation	■ An orientation that emphasizes the uniqueness and worth of humans as individuals, and that encourages the fullest possible development of human potential.
Phenomenology	■ An approach concerned mainly with how individuals view their own world. Reflects the assumption that each person's world is individual, unique, and not fully knowable by anyone else.
Basic needs	■ Also called *deficiency* needs because, when unsatisfied, they are manifested in a sense of a *lack* of something, and give rise to behaviors designed to remove the deficiency. ■ Include physiological needs (for food, drink, and sex, for example) as well as psychological needs (the need for security, for acceptance and affection, for approval).
Metaneeds	■ Also called *growth* needs because they are expressed not in a lack or deficiency so much as in a desire to grow, to become more than one now is. ■ Include aesthetic and cognitive needs expressed in the need to find such intangibles as truth, beauty, justice, goodness, order, and symmetry. ■ Also include the highest of all human needs, the need for *self-actualization*.
Self-actualization	■ The process or act of becoming, of developing, of enhancing potential, of achieving self-awareness, of growth, of fulfillment. ■ The most central concept in humanistic psychology.

tendencies in these directions" (1970, p. 150). On the more positive side, he claims that self-actualized people "may be loosely described as [making] full use and exploitation of talents, capacities, potentialities, etc." (p. 150). And the reinforcement—the satisfaction associated with true self-actualization—comes from within rather than without. In contrast, satisfaction of lower-level needs, such as those associated with esteem, is associated with external sources of reinforcement (approval and recognition). Using this loose definition, Maslow searched among 3,000 college students and found only one person he considered to be actualized (although there were several dozen "potentials").

Humanism in Review

One way to look at self-actualization is as a process that guides the direction of development rather than as a state that we can attain. The view that children are directed by a need to become (to actualize) and that the process of actual-

ization is essentially positive and self-directed presents a subtle but important contrast to the more mechanistic, more passive, and less inner-directed theories covered earlier in this chapter.

Critics have been quick to point out that humanism does not present a scientific theory in the sense that, for example, behaviorism does. Instead, it presents a general description of the human condition—a description that is viewed by some as too vague and unreliable to contribute much to the development of psychology as a science. Humanists counter by pointing out that science is only one way of knowing, that there is value in the insights provided by more subjective approaches.

One of the most important contributions of the humanistic approach is its recognition of the importance of the self and its emphasis on the uniqueness of each child. Although humanistic theory does not address well the specifics of the developmental process, it might in the end serve to explain facts that are not easily accounted for by other theories. (See Summary Table 2.14.)

■ A FINAL WORD ABOUT THEORIES

We began this chapter by insisting that facts and theories are not worlds apart in terms of "truthfulness"—that theories are intended as explanations of facts. From these explanations, scientists strive for understanding, for prediction, and sometimes for control.

Theories, we should remember, are inventions whose purpose is to simplify, to explain, sometimes to predict. They are never flatly wrong—or entirely correct. And, of course, they do not have to be accepted or rejected in their entirety. When Mahoney (1991) summarized the results of fifteen surveys conducted between 1953 and 1988 to look at the theoretical beliefs of clinical psychologists, he found that through most of this period, the majority described themselves as "eclectic." That is, most preferred to combine features from more than one theoretical position rather than adhere strongly to a single orientation. Interestingly, early in the period, more clinical psychologists considered themselves followers of psychodynamic theory (Freud) than of any other theoretical position (almost half of all practicing psychologists). Even in 1988, while the most common theoretical orientation was still eclectic, the psychodynamic orientation remained a strong second-place contender. Other orientations (cognitive, behavioristic, humanistic) are descriptive of much smaller numbers of clinical psychologists.

The psychodynamic position continues to be very important in clinical psychology, but cognitive orientations have become increasingly common in other areas of psychology, both in current theory and research as well as in educational applications. As so often happens, history will inform us later about the fruitfulness of these approaches. (See Table 2.15 for a summary of approaches to developmental theory discussed in this chapter.)

TABLE 2.15

Approaches to Developmental Theory

APPROACH	REPRESENTATIVE THEORIST	MAJOR ASSUMPTIONS (THEORETICAL BELIEFS)	KEY TERMS
Psychoanalytic	Freud	Individual is motivated by instinctual urges that are primarily sexual and aggressive.	id, ego, superego, psychosexual, fixation, regression
	Erikson	Child progresses through developmental stages by resolving conflicts that arise from a need to adapt to the sociocultural environment.	competence, social environment, developmental tasks, psychosocial
Descriptive	Havighurst	Development consists of a series of culturally determined tasks (competencies) imposed on the individual at different stages of the life cycle.	developmental tasks, social requirements, social adaptation, maturity
Behavioristic	Watson, Skinner	Changes in behavior are a function of reinforcement and punishment.	reinforcement, punishment, stimuli, responses, conditioning
Social–Cognitive	Bandura	Observational learning leads to developmental change; our ability to symbolize and to anticipate the consequences of our behavior is fundamental, as are our estimates of our self-efficacy.	imitation, modeling, eliciting, inhibiting–disinhibiting, self-efficacy
Cognitive	Piaget	Child develops cognitive skills through active interaction with the environment.	stages, assimilation, accommodation, adaptation, schema
Biological	Bowlby, Wilson	Social behaviors have a biological basis understandable in evolutionary terms. The formation of attachment bonds is one example.	attachment bonds, biological fitness, survival value, altruistic genes, sensitive period
Ecological Systems	Vygotsky, Bronfenbrenner	The ecology of development is the study of accommocations between a person and the environment (culture), taking the changing characteristics of each into account.	culture, language, open systems, ecology, microsystem, mesosystem, exosystem, macrosystem
Humanistic	Maslow, Rogers	All individuals are unique but strive toward the fullest development of their potential.	self, positive growth, metaneeds, basic needs, self-actualization

FOCUS QUESTIONS: SUMMARY ANSWERS

1. What purposes do theories serve?

   ▪ Theories are intended to organize and explain important observations. They are best evaluated in terms of usefulness rather than truthfulness.

2. What are the characteristics of a good theory?

   ▪ Theories should reflect "facts," be understandable, and be useful for predicting events as well as for explaining the past.

3. What are the most basic ideas underlying the theories of Freud? Erikson? Piaget? Havighurst? Skinner? Bandura? Sociobiology? Vygotsky? Bronfenbrenner? Maslow?

▪ Freud's theory is based on the assumption that among the most important causes of behavior are deep-seated, unconscious forces; Erikson's psychosocial theory describes development as progression through a series of stages characterized by basic conflicts, the resolution of which results in the appearance of new capabilities and attitudes; Piaget's theory describes cognitive (intellectual) development in terms of *adaptation* resulting from interaction with the environment, describable in terms of four main stages; Havighurst describes development in terms of a series of requirements that are placed on individuals by their society; Skinner's behavioristic (learning-theory) approaches focus on immediate behavior and on environmental forces that affect behavior (punishments and rewards); Bandura's theory of observational learning explains socialization as a function of imitation, and deals as well with the importance of self-efficacy judgments; sociobiologists are concerned with the biological basis of social behavior; Vygotsky's cultural–historical approach emphasizes the importance of culture and especially language; Bronfenbrenner's ecological systems theory looks at interactions and adaptations between the person and changing contexts; and

Maslow's humanism is concerned with human self-actualization and describes two motivational need systems: *deficiency* (basic) needs, which are psychological (esteem, love) and physical (food, drink), and *metaneeds* (growth needs), such as the need to self-actualize.

STUDY TERMS

accommodation, 46

adaptation, 46

anal stage, 33

arousal, 45

assimilation, 46

association, 38

autonomy versus shame and doubt, 35

basic needs, 56

behavior modification, 40

behaviorism, 37

behavioristic theory, 37

classical conditioning, 38

cognition, 45

cognitive, 45

cognitive theory, 40

concrete operations, 47

conditioned response, 39

conditioned stimulus, 39

conditioning, 38

conscience, 32

constructivism, 48

critical period, 49

developmental theories, 37

disinhibitory effect, 42

ecological systems theory, 53

ego, 32

egocentric speech, 52

Electra complex, 33

elicited, 39

eliciting effect, 43

emitted, 40

ethologists, 49

exosystem, 54

external speech, 52

formal operations, 47

id, 32

identification, 33

identity, 35

identity versus identity diffusion, 36

imitation, 42

imprinting, 49

industry versus inferiority, 36

inhibitory effect, 42

initiative versus guilt, 36

inner speech, 52

learned helplessness, 44

libido, 32

macrosystem, 54

mastery-oriented, 44

mechanistic model, 38

mesosystem, 54

metaneeds, 56

microsystem, 54

model, 42

modeling effect, 42

naive theories, 30

negative reinforcement, 40

nominal fallacy, 30

observational learning, 42

Oedipus complex, 33

open systems, 53

operant, 40

operant conditioning, 38

operation, 47

oral stage, 33

phallic, 33

phenomenology, 55

positive reinforcement, 40

preoperational thought, 47

psychoanalytic, 31

psychosexual development, 33

psychosocial, 35

punishment, 40

reciprocal determinism, 53

reinforcement, 40

reinforcer, 40

releaser, 49

respondent, 40

responses, 38

rewards, 38

scheme, 46

self-actualization, 56

self-efficacy, 44

self-referent thought, 44

sensitive period, 50

sensorimotor period, 47

sexual latency, 33

social speech, 52

sociobiology, 50

stimuli, 38

superego, 32

symbolic models, 42

theory, 30

trust versus mistrust, 35

unconditioned response, 39

unconditioned stimulus, 39

zone of proximal growth, 53

FURTHER READINGS

Theorists such as Freud, Erikson, and Piaget were often prolific and sometimes difficult writers. It is generally easier and perhaps more valuable to begin with secondary sources for information about their theories. The following are useful starting points:

Miller, P. H. (1993). *Theories of developmental psychology* (3rd ed.). New York: W. H. Freeman.

Thomas, R. M. (1996). *Comparing theories of child development* (4th ed.). Pacific Grove, CA: Brooks/Cole.

Wadsworth, B. J. (1996). *Piaget's theory of cognitive and affective development* (5th ed.). New York: Longman.

For a clear account of Vygotsky's life and theories, see the following:

Kozulin, A. (1990). *Vygotsky's psychology: A biography of ideas.* New York: Harvester Wheatsheaf.

More detailed information about Bronfenbrenner's ecological systems theory can be found in Bronfenbrenner's own book. The Kindermann and Valsiner book is a collection of relatively high-level chapters that emphasize and clarify how contexts affect development:

Bronfenbrenner, U. (1979). *The ecology of human development.* Cambridge, MA: Harvard University Press.

Kindermann, J., & Valsiner, J. (1995). *Development of person–context relations.* Hillsdale, NJ: Erlbaum.

The first of the next two references is an excellent summary of Bandura's social–cognitive theory. The second is a simple and highly readable account of imitation among both humans and animals:

Bandura, A. (1986). *Social foundations of thought and action: A social cognitive theory.* Englewood Cliffs, NJ: Prentice-Hall.

Wyrwicka, W. (1996). *Imitation in human and animal behavior.* New Brunswick, NJ: Transaction.

Maslow's humanistic psychology is well explained in the following text:

Maslow, A. H. (1970). *Motivation and personality* (2nd ed.). New York: Harper & Row.

The following collection is a contemporary account of the behavioral scientist's view of how antecedents and consequences affect our behavior:

Baer, D. M., & Pinkston, E. M. (1997). *Environment and behavior.* Boulder, CO: Westview.

FOCUS QUESTIONS

1. What is the nature–nurture controversy about?

2. What are the most basic facts of heredity?

3. What are some of the most common genetic defects?

4. What are some common chromosomal defects?

5. What are some common methods of prenatal diagnosis?

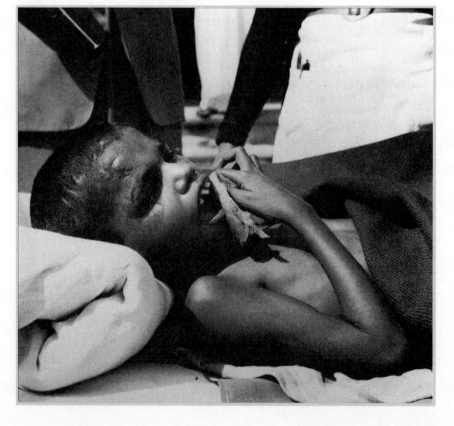

THREE

Gene–Context Interaction

Biology is the only science in which multiplication means the same thing as division.

UNKNOWN

In the legend, Remus and Romulus were orphaned following the imprisonment of their mother, and cast into the Tiber River. When they were later washed to shore under a fig tree, a wolf and a woodpecker found them and raised them. Later, Faustulus, the king's shepherd, found them in the she-wolf's lair and finished raising them. And, in the end, these twins built the city of Rome. ¶ But this is only a legend. In a more recent story, one that begins in 1879, French peasants reportedly glimpse a naked boy running through the forest near Aveyron in France. A year later, they finally manage to capture him, and they immediately put him on display as *L'enfant sauvage d'Aveyron* (the wild boy of Aveyron). Within a few days, he escapes but is eventually recaptured. People are fascinated by this wild creature—naked, speechless, and apparently in every way a wild animal. Itard, a famous physician, takes over the boy's care, convinced he can "civilize" him and teach him to speak. But in spite of Itard's efforts, Victor, as the boy is named, remains more wild than tame. He has little use for clothing, seems insensitive to heat or cold, sleeps as easily on the floor as anywhere, and carries out his toilet functions as the urge moves him. And he never does learn to speak (Lane, 1977). ¶ There have now been at least fifty-four wild children found in different parts of the world, writes Jean-Claude Armen (1974). That these children even survived, he argues, shows the remarkable adaptations of which humans are capable. But that none of them ever succeeded in learning to speak and in becoming fully acculturated also illustrates the extent to which being human requires human experiences in early life. ¶

This Chapter

re these stories of children raised by wild animals (termed **feral children**) convincing evidence regarding the role of heredity and environment in human development? As we see in this chapter, science isn't so certain. For its evidence, it must look elsewhere as well.

This chapter considers an often-asked question: How do genes and experience interact to shape the outcomes of development? How does science begin to solve this puzzle? One argument runs something like this: For human characteristics that are determined mainly by genetic factors, changes in the environment should have little effect. By the same token, vastly different environments should have profound effects on characteristics that depend largely on nurture. Thus, eye color should not change whether a person is reared by natives in the Amazon jungle, by Ihalmiuts in Greenland, by Americans in Boston, or by Canadians in Moose Jaw—or, yes, by wolves and woodpeckers. But the individual's speech will be vastly different in each of these environments.

One way, then, of beginning to sort out and understand the interaction of **heredity** and **environment** is to look at individuals with similar genetic backgrounds—say, **identical twins,** whose genetic similarity is perfect. Investigators can examine the outcomes of the developmental process when each member of the pair is raised in a highly similar environment (twins who are brought up in the same home) or in a highly different environment (twins who are reared apart). Another possibility is to look at **fraternal twins,** whose genetic similarity is about 50 percent—roughly that of any other pair of siblings—but whose environments might be

nearly as similar as those of identical twins reared together. Still another alternative is to look at individuals who are adopted, and to compare them with their adoptive parents, their natural parents, their biological siblings, and their adoptive siblings. And another approach, of course, is to look at genetic material itself, to study its composition and map its organization. Examples of each of these approaches, together with the most important findings of this research, are summarized in this chapter. But first, we look at what is meant by gene–context interaction. And we look, briefly, at feral children.

GENE-CONTEXT INTERACTIONS

The nature–nurture question can be stated very simply: How do genes (nature) and context (nurture) interact to influence human development? (Note that the question is *not* "Which is most important?" but rather "How do they *interact*?") However, answering this question is not so simple.

Feral Children

As we saw, among the early attempts to shed light on nature–nurture interaction are fascinating accounts of children who had allegedly been abandoned in the wilds. Many of these children would, of course, have died. But some of them, legend and folklore inform us, were found by wild animals that took them into their lairs and dens and raised them as their

Studies of twins are very important for unraveling the complexities of gene–environment interaction. These are actually a single set of four-year-old identical twin boys whose mother had dressed them up as girls. The barber changed their hair dramatically, but could do nothing with their smiles.

own (hence the term *feral children,* meaning "wild children"). When recaptured, these children usually don't speak; instead, they run about on all fours and growl or bark at people. Their wild behavior is strong evidence, Singh and Zingg (1942) argued, that the special qualities that make us human are not inherited, but have to be learned.

But the evidence is not at all convincing, claimed Dennis (1951), because there is not a single, fully documented case of a child having been raised by a wild animal.

■ GENIE: A MODERN-DAY WILD CHILD

But there are other accounts of abandoned children that are more reliable. One is the story of a little girl, initially nameless but who later came to be known as Genie. Genie was not abandoned in the wilds, but in a small upstairs bedroom in her own home. Except for brief periods when she was still a toddler, Genie did not leave her room from the age of twenty months until she was almost fourteen—more than twelve years!

Curtiss (1977) describes how Genie's room was completely unfurnished save for a small crib covered with wire mesh, and an infant "potty." Genie was left completely alone in this room, day after day after day—alone and naked, with a sturdy leather harness strapped to her body and fastened to the potty so that she was forced to sit on it for hours. At night, she was sometimes simply left on the potty; other times, she would be stuffed into a sleeping bag specially made to restrain her, much like a straitjacket, and placed inside the crib, imprisoned within the wire mesh. Now and again, someone, usually her father, would come in and feed her—almost always either baby food, soupy cereal, or a soft-boiled egg. Whoever fed her simply stuffed as much food as possible into her mouth; if she spit some of it out, her face would be rubbed in it. If she whimpered or made some other noise, perhaps with her potty or her crib, her father would come in and beat her with a stick. No one was allowed to speak with her during feeding time, or to visit her at other times. Often the father would pretend he was a dog, barking and growling at Genie, and sometimes scratching her with his fingernails. If he just wanted to threaten her, he would stand outside her door and make his most vicious dog noises.

When Genie was thirteen years old, following an especially violent fight with the father, the mother finally took her and left. Shortly after that, Genie was discovered, charges were filed against her parents, and Genie was brought into a hospital. Genie's father committed suicide on the day he was to be brought to trial. And although Genie made some progress, her language and social development remained far below normal. (See Chapter 7 for more details. See also Curtiss, 1977, and Rymer, 1993.)

Two Models of Gene–Context Relationships

Stories such as that of Genie and of other abandoned children are important for psychology because they provide evidence relevant to the heredity–environment (nature–nurture) issue. Whatever characteristics these children share with others who are brought up in more "normal" environments we might assume to be greatly affected by genetic influences, and whatever "human" characteristics they fail to develop we can consider to be more sensitive to environmental forces. Thus, we might begin to understand the relative effects of each in our development.

But the issue is not quite so simple, nor is there a very simple answer. In fact, there have historically been at least two sorts of answers reflecting two different points of view: the *additive* and the *interactive.* The additive point of view assumes that the effects of heredity and environment are, in a sense, additive. That is, heredity accounts for a certain percentage of the variation in a characteristic, and environment accounts for the remainder. This is the model that governed the work of early researchers. For example, Sternberg (1991) points out that in the 1960s, psychology accepted the reasoning that some children were more intelligent than others because they had inherited more "intelligence" from their parents.

By the 1980s, however, the additive model began to give way to the interactive model. Psychologists were now generally agreed that both heredity and environment are important, but not as isolated forces. Rather, it is the interaction between the two that is important (Dalton & Bergenn, 1995).

■ Interaction

Unfortunately, interaction is not a simple concept, and the results of interaction are not always highly predictable. Take something as simple as water and temperature. We know that water and temperature interact to form ice, but can we understand the hardness of ice, its taste, its effect on our skin solely by understanding temperature and water? And is it not true that steam also results from the interaction of water and temperature? The interaction becomes more complex, but it still appears linear and predictable: More heat equals steam; less heat equals ice. Even here, however, interaction is not quite so simple. With changes in air pressure, the interaction of water and temperature changes. Now an even higher or lower temperature is required for the same effect.

As with ice, temperature, and water, interaction among heredity, environment, and human behavior is not a simple additive affair. Relative influences of heredity and environment might change with age, might be different in different contexts, and might vary from one individual to another. Furthermore, quite apart from their interactive role in influencing developmental outcomes, genes and environment can influence each other directly (Lerner, 1991). For example, what we know of evolution makes it clear that gene combinations that underlie adaptive behaviors are more likely to survive in our genetic pools; those that are maladaptive have a poorer chance of surviving. Thus does the environment influence genes. At the same time, it is also clear that individuals select and shape their environments, not only individually but also as cultural groups. Thus do genes influence the environment.

Two great forces, described in terms of at least three pairs of labels, shape human development:

genes	context
nature	nurture
heredity	environment

These forces are not isolated and independent, but do, in fact, affect each other directly and indirectly. In addition, their effects are not *additive*, but *interactive*. What this means is that genes don't account for a certain percentage of a characteristic, and the environment the rest. Rather, the influences of each depend on complex interactions between them, and might vary depending on any of a large number of factors, including the individual's characteristics (such as age or the timing of environmental influences).

The story of Genie provides one example of the complexity of gene–environment interaction specifically in the area of language development. Obviously, the acquisition of language is made possible by our genes. Not only have we been endowed with vocal cords, tongues, mouths, ears, brains, and other structures that make the production and the identification of speech sounds possible, but we also seem to be predisposed to acquire language early in our lives. Genie, who was not exposed to language during this sensitive early period (roughly, the early preschool years), had not learned to speak or to understand others. When she was later exposed to a normal language environment, as well as to direct language instruction, she managed to develop only a small vocabulary and to acquire a limited and uncertain grasp of simple language-production rules. As Rymer (1993) points out, her development of language was far from normal.

It is worth emphasizing again that both the characteristics of the person and those of the context need to be taken into account—as ecological–contextual theory makes clear. We look again at the relationship between person and context later in this chapter; first, however, we take a look at the mechanics of heredity. (See Summary Table 3.1.)

■ THE MECHANICS OF HEREDITY

The mechanics of heredity are complex and sometimes bewildering, its marvels amazing. The mechanics can be simplified somewhat; the marvels are best left for saints and poets.

Conception

Human life begins with the joining of the mother's **ovum (egg cell)** and the father's **sperm cell.** For life to occur, this union is necessary, and because two people of opposite sexes are involved, it ordinarily requires a physical union between a male and a female as well—ordinarily, but not always. **Conception** is also possible with **artificial insemination,** a clinical procedure wherein the father's sperm is introduced directly into the mother (sometimes using anonymous donor sperm so that the identity of the biological father may never be clear).[*]

Another possibility is to insert an ovum from a female donor in a woman whose Fallopian tubes are blocked. A number of groups offer donor egg programs for profit. (One that I just found following an Internet search pays the egg donor $2,500 and charges the recipient around $5,500.) Still another possibility is conception that occurs completely outside the mother's body, either in another woman's body or in vitro (literally, meaning "in glass"). The fertilized egg can then be implanted in the mother to develop as it normally would. (See "Across Cultures: Dolly and Polly, and Polly, and Polly, and….") Surrogate mothering, where one woman bears a child for another, is another possibility—one that can give rise to complicated ethical and legal issues. For example, a California couple in their sixties, using their now-deceased daughter's previously frozen embryos, have found a surrogate mother who is attempting to bear their daughter's child ("Frozen Life: Will Julie Become a Mother…," 1997). Still another possibility is fertility drugs—drugs that attempt to stimulate the production of mature ova.

None of these procedures is a certain solution for all childless couples, and none is a cure for the causes of childlessness. But when successful, they do remove the symptom: childlessness.

■ SEX CELLS

Mature women usually release a single mature ovum about once every twenty-eight days (ordinarily between the tenth and the eighteenth day of their menstrual cycle). Sometimes two or more eggs are produced at once or a single fertilized egg divides, thus making possible multiple births.

All of the woman's ova are present in her ovaries at birth—perhaps as many as a million of them. These are primitive and immature, and more than half of them atrophy before **puberty** (the beginning of sexual maturity). Of those that remain, approximately 400 will mature and be released between puberty and **menopause** (cessation of menstruation). In contrast, a man produces sperm cells at the rate of several billion a month (200 to 300 million every four days or so) and usually continues to produce them from puberty until death.

The ovum is the largest cell in the human body, at approximately 0.15 millimeters in diameter—about half the size of

---

[*]Artificial insemination of the mother is ordinarily a medical procedure. But an Associated Press report describes the case of an inventive woman who used a turkey baster to inseminate herself. She apparently administered herself a number of treatments, *and stood on her head for 30 minutes* after each. "I figured gravity couldn't hurt," said she ("Turkey Baster Used to Help Make Baby," 1993, p. 28). The report also states that the baster, sterilized in the kitchen dishwasher, cost only $2.95.

Dolly and Polly, and Polly, and Polly, and...

olly is a sheep. And so are Polly, and Polly, and Polly, and Polly, and Polly. And that may seem just too enormous a leap across cultures!

But it may not be nearly as far as we might think. You see, Dolly was the first reported successful example of a **clone.** And cloning has some potentially enormous implications for our more human cultures.

Dolly was produced by British scientists using technology that involves using an adult (rather than an *embryonic*) cell. The result: a normal sheep genetically identical to the parent sheep from which the adult cell was taken. This, of course, gives rise to the possibility of producing countless identical sheep—a veritable insomniac's nightmare of countless sheep.

The Polly's are another story—one whose implications may be even more far-reaching. There are five of these clones, but they are clones with a difference. Unlike Dolly, whose genes are those of the parent cell, the Polly's parent cells were modified (*genetically engineered,* so to speak) before they

Each of the five Polly clones, like the one seen here, carries a human protein gene. Scots researchers hope to have her produce medicines.

were implanted. That is, in a process described as **transgenics,** the cells used to clone these sheep had nonsheep genes introduced into them. Three of the Polly's, announced a spokesman for PPL Therapeutics, the company responsible, carry a *human* gene that may be of therapeutic value in the treatment of human disorders ("Sheepish About Human Genes," 1997).

What might this gene be? There are a range of possibilities. Some of the company's sheep already produce various blood-clotting products. Another

possibility is that the altered gene might lead one or more of the Polly's to produce milk containing a protein that might be extracted and given to those who lack it. This might be useful for treating hemophiliacs, certain bone diseases, diabetes, and a variety of other conditions. There is speculation, as well, that the same technique might be employed with other animals, including pigs, whose organs are sometimes used in human transplants. Genetic engineering of cloned pigs could conceivably produce animals with organs better suited for successful transplants (for examples, animals without the protein that is sometimes associated with organ rejection).

To Think About

Is it OK to clone identical individuals? Humans as well as nonhumans? What are some of the negative implications and possibilities? Positive implications? What are the ethics of transgenics, where foreign genes are introduced into a cell prior to implantation?

---

each period (.) on this page. The sperm cell, by contrast, is one of the smallest cells in the body, 0.005 millimeters in diameter. What the sperm cell lacks in size is made up by the length of its tail—fully twelve times longer than the main part of the cell to which it is attached. It is this long tail that enables the sperm to swim toward the ovum.

Carriers of Heredity

The egg cell and the sperm cell, called **gametes,** are the immediate origins of new life. Not only do they give rise to the development of a new human, but they also carry the instructions or the blueprints that determine what that individual will inherit. **Genetics** is the science that studies heredity.

The complex field of genetics is among the fastest growing of all modern disciplines. To try to simplify it accurately in a few paragraphs, or a few pages, is somewhat presumptuous. But we have no choice, so we will strive for clarity and simplicity, if not completeness.

PROTEINS

The basis of all human life—the living, functioning cells of which we are composed—can be reduced to complicated molecules called **proteins.** These, in turn, are made up of different amino acids, of which there are twenty different known kinds (Emery & Mueller, 1992). A specific combination and sequence of amino acids determine the nature and function of each protein. The number of possible combinations is astronomical. Consider that the twenty-six letters that make up the alphabet by means of which you and I are now communicating allow us to generate new combinations of sentences, paragraphs, chapters, even books, virtually indefinitely.

DNA

The basis of life is proteins; the nature and function of proteins are determined by amino acid combinations and sequences. In turn, these combinations and sequences are determined by a special code contained in a substance called deoxyribonucleic acid or **DNA.** This substance consists mainly

FIGURE 3.1

DNA molecules are arranged in sequences of pairs in a spiraling, double-helix structure. Genes, labels for carriers of specific hereditary information, can be thought of as locations or addresses on a segment of the DNA molecule.

of four components, which are arranged in different sequences of pairs in a structure resembling what is termed a **double helix** (see Figure 3.1). In effect, this arrangement of DNA components is the blueprint or genetic code that determines our heredity.

CHROMOSOMES

We have two kinds of cells in our body: **sex cells** (ova or sperm) and body cells (called **somatic cells**). All normal body cells contain identical genetic information. That is, all have the same assortment of DNA molecules—the same genetic code. These DNA molecules are located on rodlike structures called chromosomes. There are twenty-three pairs of these chromosomes in every human body cell. One member of each pair of chromosomes is inherited from our mothers and the other from our fathers. In other words, we inherit twenty-three chromosomes from each of our parents for a total of forty-six chromosomes. The division of body cells involves what is called **mitosis**—a process that results in genetically identical pairs of cells.

Unlike somatic cells, mature sex cells (sperm and ovum) each contain twenty-three chromosomes rather than twenty-three pairs. This is because the gametes (sex cells) result from a special kind of cell division termed **meiosis,** which results in daughter cells that have only half the number of chromosomes of the parent cell (Bascom-Slack, Ross, & Dawson, 1997). And when chromosome pairs in the parent cell divide to form mature sperm (in males) or ova (in females), they do so randomly. That is, individual members of chromosome pairs wind up in any of a mind-boggling number of different possible combinations. And because there are two parents involved, the total number of different individuals that can result from a single human mating is some almost meaningless number larger than 60 trillion.[*]

---

[*]And that does not even take into account that during meiosis segments of chromosomes sometimes "cross over" and exchange places, thereby increasing the number of possible combinations astronomically.

So should we be amazed that we are so much like our parents and siblings? Not really. You see, in these over 60 trillion theoretically possible combinations, there will be a vast amount of redundant information. And much of that redundant information is absolutely fundamental to our humanity. Among other things, it is expressed in the fact that most of us have a single head, two eyes, a brain with a marvelously developed cortex, limbs, digits, and on and on.

But genetics deals less with our sameness than with our variability. It is concerned with the chemistry and the biology that account for differences among individuals of the same species.

SEX CHROMOSOMES

Of the twenty-three chromosomes contained in each sperm and each ovum, one, labeled the **sex chromosome,** determines whether the offspring will be male or female (the other twenty-two are called **autosomes**). As shown in Interactive Figure 3.2, the father produces two types of sperm, one type with a larger sex chromosome labeled X and one type with a smaller chromosome labeled Y. If the sperm that fertilizes the ovum contains an X chromosome, the offspring will be a girl; if the sperm cell contains a Y chromosome, the result will be a boy. Because the mother produces only X chromosomes, it is accurate to say that only the father's sperm can determine the sex of the offspring.

The ratio of males to females at birth is about 105 to 100 (U.S. Bureau of the Census, 1996). But males are more susceptible to various illnesses and diseases, so by the age of five, there are almost as many girls as boys. By age seventy-five, women outnumber men about two to one.

In this figure there is a clue to a fact of which Henry VIII was sadly ignorant as he beheaded a succession of wives for failing to give him a son. Can you figure it out before continuing? Only the male sex cell, the sperm, can contain either an X or a Y sex chromosome; the ovum always contains only the X chromosome. Because an XY pairing determines that the offspring will be male (XX is female), the "failure" of Henry's wives to produce sons was really his fault.

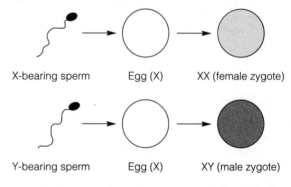

X-bearing sperm   Egg (X)   XX (female zygote)

Y-bearing sperm   Egg (X)   XY (male zygote)

Each sperm cell contains either an X or a Y sex chromosome.

Each normal ovum contains only an X sex chromosome.

An XX pairing results in a female offspring; an XY results in a male.

Genes

The units of heredity carried by the chromosomes are called genes. It still isn't clear just exactly how many genes we have, but most estimates are somewhere between 65,000 and 80,000 (Fisher, 1997). Some chromosomes, especially the sex chromosomes, contain far fewer genes than others (Friedman et al., 1992). These genes, either in pairs or in complex combinations of pairs, determine our potential for inherited characteristics.

■ GENETIC EFFECTS

There are, for example, pairs of genes that correspond to eye color, hair characteristics, and virtually every other physical characteristic of an individual. In addition, other combinations of genes appear to be related to personality characteristics such as intelligence—although the ways in which genes affect personality are not as obvious or as easily measured as the ways in which they affect physical characteristics.

Among many other characteristics known to be largely determined, or at least influenced, by genes are disorders, illnesses, and defects such as some forms of blindness and baldness, hemophilia, alcoholism, and Down syndrome. Some of these are discussed later in this chapter.

■ GENE FUNCTIONING

Genes are arranged in corresponding pairs on chromosomes, one gene being inherited from each parent. From studies of animals and plants (particularly fruit flies and peas), as well as from observations of humans and other animals, scientists have discovered that one of the pair may be dominant over the other. When a **dominant gene** is paired with a corresponding **recessive gene**, the characteristics corresponding to the dominant gene will appear in the individual. For example, we know that the gene for normally pigmented skin is dominant over the gene for albinism (unpigmented skin). Hence, an individual who inherits a gene for normal skin from one parent and one for albinism from the other will nevertheless have pigmented skin. A true albino (completely unpigmented skin) will have inherited a recessive gene for unpigmented skin from each parent. It follows as well that two albino parents will inevitably produce albino children. (See Interactive Figure 3.3 for an illustration of a characteristic related to the presence of a dominant gene.)

If human genetics were limited to the effects of single pairs of genes and their dominance or recessiveness (termed **major gene determination**), genetics would be far simpler. In fact, however, many characteristics are a function of an undetermined number of pairs of genes acting in combination (termed **polygenetic determination**). In addition, genes are seldom completely dominant or recessive under all circumstances. Some genes appear to be dominant over a specific gene but recessive with respect to another. Furthermore, the material of which genes consist (deoxyribonucleic acid, or DNA) occasionally undergoes mutations—changes that may be brought about through X-rays, chemicals such as mustard gas, some drugs, or other causes.

Genotype and Phenotype

Genetic makeup defines **genotype**; manifested characteristics are **phenotype**. That is, phenotype is what can be seen (color

INTERACTIVE FIGURE 3.3

Can you roll your tongue as shown: If you can roll your tongue, would you be prepared to wager that either your mother or your father can also? Tongue-rolling ability is related to the presence of a dominant gene.

Phenotype is defined as the individual's manifested characteristics; genotype is the person's genetic makeup. But genotype can't always be inferred from phenotype. Thus, this infant's brown eyes are part of his phenotype, but the underlying genotype might be two genes for brown eyes or only one because the gene for brown eyes is ordinarily dominant over that for blue eyes.

FIGURE 3.4

Phenotype (manifested characteristics) is influenced by genotype (genetic makeup). But genotype cannot always be inferred from phenotype. A brown-eyed person might have two genes for brown eyes or just one, with a recessive gene for blue eyes.

of hair, for example); in contrast, genotype is hidden and has to be inferred from phenotype or can sometimes be determined through an examination of the matter of which genes are composed.

For characteristics determined by recessive genes, it's possible to make accurate inferences about genotype; that is not the case for those determined by dominant genes. For example, the gene for brown eyes is normally dominant over that for blue eyes. Hence, we can infer that individuals whose phenotype (manifested characteristics) include blue eyes must have two recessive genes for blue eyes (genotype). On the other hand, we can't be certain about the genotype for brown-eyed individuals because they might have two dominant genes for brown eyes or a dominant gene for brown eyes and a recessive gene for blue eyes (see Figure 3.4).

The effects of genotype on phenotype are not quite as simple as the eye-color illustration implies. In fact, most human characteristics, including eye color, are usually the result of combinations of genes (polygenetic determination). The effects of polygenetic determination are not either-or (for example, either blue or brown), but include a whole range of possibilities. Thus it is that individuals are not simply blue- or brown-eyed, but can also have eyes that are green or hazel or blue-green, or a variety of other shades. In addition, some mutations (structural changes) of genes can change a normally recessive gene into a dominant gene (Offner, 1993).

Plomin (1987) summarizes the relationship between genotype and phenotype as follows:

- First, it is clear that genetic differences (genotype) lead to phenotypic differences. Blue-eyed parents are far more likely to produce blue-eyed offspring than are dark-eyed parents.

- Second, characteristics that are influenced by more than one gene tend not to be dichotomous (either-or) but are distributed in a manner that approximates what is referred to as the **normal curve** (a bell-shaped curve where the majority of cases cluster near the average, with fewer and fewer cases deviating farther and farther from the average). For example, height is influenced by genetic makeup. But most people aren't extremely tall or extremely short; instead, most are average, with the fewest numbers at the farthest extremes.

- Third, the environment also makes an important difference to manifested characteristics. Height reflects not only genetic influences but also environmental conditions such as nutrition and health.

Reaction Range and Canalization

The environment makes a great deal of difference for some things (like language learning); for others (like eye color) it makes little apparent difference. Characteristics that are less affected by environmental forces are said to be highly **canalized** (Waddington, 1975). Eye color is a highly canalized characteristic; it typically corresponds to genotype and is unaffected by experience. In contrast, many complex intellectual abilities (the ability to learn to speak several languages, for example) do not appear to be highly canalized but are highly affected by experience.

In evolutionary terms, canalization may be seen as a genetic tendency toward predictable regularity. This predictable regularity ensures that individuals of one species will be much more similar than dissimilar. For characteristics that are not highly canalized, phenotype may be very different from what might have been predicted on the basis of genetic makeup.

THE EPIGENETIC LANDSCAPE

Waddington's (1975) **epigenetic landscape** is an analogy to illustrate the relationship of genetic and environmental forces in development (Figure 3.5). In this illustration, genetic forces are represented by the canals that run down the landscape, the tilt of the figure represents environmental forces, and the ball represents some characteristic of the developing organism. Where the ball ends up represents the final state of that characteristic.

The analogy makes several important points. First, changes in the environment (different tilts) can shift the ball's path and dramatically affect the final outcome; second, for highly canalized traits (deeper channels), far greater environmental forces (changes in tilt) will be needed to influence the final outcome; and third, subtle environmental forces are more likely to affect the course of development early (top of the figure) rather than late (bottom of the figure, where all channels are deeper).

REACTION RANGE

Even for highly canalized characteristics, phenotype (manifested characteristics) seldom results from only genetic influences, but is usually influenced by the environment as well. That is, **epigenesis,** the unfolding of genetically influenced characteristics, is brought about by the interaction of genes and environment. In a sense, it is as though genetic influences (genotypes) make possible a range of different outcomes, with some being more probable than others. This range of possible outcomes is termed **reaction range** (Gottesman, 1974).

FIGURE 3.5

Waddington's epigenetic landscape, a graphic analogy depicting the interaction between environmental and genetic forces. Genetic forces are represented by the valleys and contours of the landscape; they make certain outcomes more probable than others. Environmental forces are represented by changes in the tilt of the landscape. (Based on Waddington, 1975.)

The reaction range for a particular characteristic includes all the possible outcomes for that characteristic given maximum variations in the nature and timing of environmental influences. Thus, your genes at birth might have been such that your most probable adult height would be 6 feet (1.82 meters). But given exceptional nutrition and exercise (or the use of growth and performance-enhancing drugs), you might have ended up being 6 feet 8 inches tall (2.03 meters) and a star basketball player. Or, given inadequate nutrition and early ill health, you might have ended up only 5 feet 6 inches (1.67 meters). Thus does the environment interact with genotype to determine which of the many possible outcomes—that is, which reaction from the range of all possible reactions—will be manifested. One of the important tasks of the psychologist is to determine the nature and timing of experiences that are most likely to have a beneficial influence on phenotype.

Molecular Genetics

Mendelian genetics, named after Gregor Mendel, the nineteenth-century monk who discovered the first secrets of genes, makes inferences about the dominance and recessiveness of genes largely by looking at the characteristics of parents and of offspring. In contrast, **molecular genetics** studies heredity by looking at the actual structure of genes. The techniques of molecular genetics make it possible to examine chromosomes directly, to look at sequences of DNA molecules, to identify their specific chemical components, and to locate chemical segments that correspond to genes. One way of doing this is to use certain enzymes that serve to cut through sequences of DNA (Bodmer & McKie, 1995). When two individuals have identical DNA sequences, the length of the resulting fragments will be identical, but if the sequences are different, the resulting fragments will have different lengths (called **restriction fragment length polymorphisms,** or RFLPs). Thus, RFLPs (pronounced "rifflips") allow geneticists to identify genes on specific chromosomes that are associated with the presence or absence of some observable characteristic. These genes are called marker genes. Marker genes are genes that are common to the general population; they are normally found in all individuals (Emery & Mueller, 1992).

Marker genes have now been discovered for all chromosomes. By 1992, more than 2,500 such genes had been assigned to specific locations on specific chromosomes (McKusick, 1992). Relatively recent discoveries include the gene for Huntington's disease (described later in this chapter), a marker gene for a wide variety of human cancers, and genes associated with Duchenne muscular dystrophy and with some immunodeficiencies (Smith & Notarangelo, 1997).

Offner (1992) cautions that although the emphasis seems to be on identifying genes associated with diseases and defects, genes should not be seen merely as things that cause problems. In fact, our genes are complex sets of instructions

Important Concepts in Heredity

Conception	■ The union of gametes.
Gametes	■ Sex cells: the ovum (egg cell) for females, sperm cells for males. Production of mature sex cells begins at puberty and continues indefinitely for males; it ends at menopause for women.
DNA	■ Deoxyribonucleic acid. Found in the nuclei of all human cells. Assumed to be the basis of organic life. Consists of four chemical bases arranged in an intertwined spiral pattern (double helix) in an enormous number of potentially different combinations.
Chromosomes	■ Microscopic, gene-containing bodies, of which there are 23 pairs in every normal human body cell, one pair inherited from each parent.
Sex chromosomes	■ One of the 23 pairs of chromosomes in cells (the others are called *autosomes*). Determine our sex. Males produce either an X or a Y sex chromosome; females produce only an X. An XY pairing results in a male offspring; an XX pairing results in a female.
Genes	■ Units of heredity.
Cell division	■ The splitting of a cell. For body cells, the process involves *mitosis,* which results in identical daughter cells. For sex cells (ovum and sperm), the process involves *meiosis,* which results in daughter cells with different genetic makeup—which is why no two of us are alike unless we are identical twins.
Major gene determination	■ Where a genetically based characteristic is determined mainly by the presence or absence of a pair of genes, and where characteristics associated with a recessive gene will be manifested only if both corresponding genes are recessive.
Polygenetic determination	■ Where a genetically based characteristic is determined by the interaction of groups of genes.
Genotype	■ The individual's underlying genetic makeup—that is, the individual's particular complement of genes.
Phenotype	■ The individual's manifested characteristics. Sometimes used to infer genotype.
Canalization	■ Describes the extent to which genetically influenced characteristics are resistant to environmental influences. Highly canalized traits are little affected by environmental forces.
Reaction range	■ All the possible outcomes for a particular characteristic given variations in the nature and timing of environmental influences. Reaction range is greatest for least canalized traits.
Mendelian genetics	■ The study of the relative recessiveness and dominance of pairs of genes. The study of heredity through a comparison of the characteristics of parents and offspring.
Molecular genetics	■ The study of heredity based on the structure of genes and chromosomes.
Marker genes	■ Genes whose presence on a chromosome is known to be associated with a specific trait.
Human Genome Project	■ A massive, long-term, international project designed to map the entire human genetic structure.

for putting together normal human beings. However, the importance of studying defective genes lies in the possibility of correcting them or, at the very least, of identifying their presence early—perhaps even before conception.

More than 95 percent of our genes still remain unmapped. A massive, federally funded genetics project is now under way in the United States. Its goal is to provide a complete genetic map of the human being—a map of what is termed the genome, the complete set of genetic instructions contained in our cells (Bodmer & McKie, 1995). (See "In the News and on the Net: The Human Genome Project.")

The implications of success in this endeavor are staggering. Correcting genetic defects might be possible, and so could accurately predicting the outcome of different gene pairings. What happens next? Does medicine play God? Do governments engineer genes to produce the kinds of people they want? Do chromosomal tests become mandatory? Do they become part of who we are, like our Social Security numbers? (See Summary Table 3.2.)

STUDYING GENE–CONTEXT INTERACTION

Genesis means "beginning and unfolding." Our genes are aptly named: They are clearly our beginnings. And, in interaction with our contexts, they are also involved in guiding our development. "Genes do not by themselves produce structural or functional characteristics," says Lerner (1991, p. 27). Instead, they interact with context to produce change. The current emphasis in genetic research is on finding out how context and genes work together. Keep in mind that he Human Genome Project, an enormous project with astonishing implications, is intended to map the entire human genetic structure by the year 2005. The project began in 1990, and is apparently on schedule. Much of what seemed like science fiction a few years ago is now reality. For example:

- Many diagnostic tests are now available to detect both dominant and recessive genes associated with various disorders, and to compute probabilities that offspring will be affected. As well, unborn fetuses can be tested directly. In fact, it is now possible to buy "gene chips" designed to detect gene mutations such as several associated with specific cancers.

- Several biotechnology companies are developing ways of changing genes to correct genetically linked diseases. At least 180 experimental trials are now under way in the US.

- Various clinical trials are also under way in an effort to develop procedures for changing genes in order to prevent the occurrence of diseases and defects.

1. Cookson, C., & Green, D. (1997, Nov. 5). Genetic research gathers steam. *Financial Times*, p. 60.

To Think About

What are some of the ethical and practical implications of these and related advances in genetics?

On the Net

For whatever you want to know about the current state of the Human Genome Project, check the following web address:

http://www.ornl.gov/TechResources/Human_Genome/home.html

genetic and environmental forces do not compete; rather, they work together to increase the individual's adaptation (Lerner, 1993).

Galton's Conclusion

Family members share a wide range of genes and are therefore a good source of information about gene–context interaction. As Plomin (1987) points out, there is 100-percent genetic similarity between pairs of identical twins, approximately 50-percent similarity among siblings who share both parents, and somewhere around 25-percent similarity among stepsiblings who share only one parent.

The high degree of genetic relatedness among members of families is what led Francis Galton, Charles Darwin's cousin, to conclude that intelligence is largely hereditary. He had noticed that most of England's outstanding scientists came from a small number of families. As a result, he argued that parents should be selected for favorable genetic characteristics—a practice termed **eugenics**. Not very good research, surely. Even if Galton's observations were entirely accurate, they didn't prove his point. An environmentalist might argue, for example, that the reason these families produced outstanding scientists was simply that they provided children with environments conducive to the development of genius.

Animal Studies

Gene–environment interactions can sometimes be studied more easily with animals than with humans, not only because certain physiological measurements are sometimes possible with animals but not with humans (brain dissections, for example), but also because animal environments can be controlled far more completely than human environments can. In addition, animal matings can be controlled precisely, and many generations can be produced and studied within a relatively short period of time. Not so with humans. But there are, of course, some serious limitations of animal studies, not the least of which is the difficulty of generalizing findings from animals to humans.

The classic study of genetic influence in rats is that of Tryon (1940), who began by having his rats learn a maze to test their intelligence. Fast learners were then mated with other fast learners, and slow learners were paired with other slow learners. After only eighteen generations, there was no longer any overlap between the groups. The dullest rats among the bright group were now brighter than the smartest of the dull group, and vice versa (see Figure 3.6).

Other animal studies have demonstrated that it is possible to breed different strains of the same species that are predictably different in some identifiable characteristic. For example, in only a few generations mice can be bred for aggression, emotionality, preference for alcohol, and other characteristics (see Cairns, Gariépy, & Hood, 1990). In much the same way, various "personality" characteristics have been developed in different breeds of dogs: fierceness and fighting ability in pit bull terriers, vigilance in German shepherds, obstinacy and contrariness in the Lefrançois hound.

GENE-CONTEXT INTERACTIONS AMONG ANIMALS

But even in rats and dogs and other nonhuman animals, genetics by itself tells only part of the story. For example, consider the song thrush, which dearly loves to eat snails and which does so by grabbing a snail in its beak and smashing the shell against a rock by means of a rapid, sideways motion of its head, back and forth, back and forth (Weisfeld, 1982). This appears to be a genetically influenced behavior

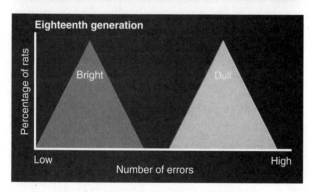

FIGURE 3.6

An approximate representation of Tryon's successful attempt to breed maze-bright and maze-dull rats. After eighteen generations of selective breeding, the dullest rats among the bright group were now brighter than the smartest of the dull group. (Based on Tryon, 1940, p. 113.)

learn during this critical period, it goes through life never knowing how to eat a snail properly, the way other song thrushes do it.[†]

What investigations such as these illustrate most clearly is the complexity of gene–environment interaction, even for behaviors we might assume to be entirely genetically based. In addition, animal studies suggest that behaviors having important adaptive functions become more probable through succeeding generations. Because these behaviors have to do with biological adaptation and the survival and propagation of species, they are typically related to feeding, rest, defense, reproduction, or elimination (Weisfeld, 1982).

GENETICALLY DETERMINED BEHAVIORS IN HUMANS

Are there similar, genetically ordained behaviors among humans? Some researchers think so. These behaviors, they argue, are common to all members of the species—hence common to all human cultures. In addition, they occur in the absence of experiences that might otherwise explain their acquisition. Weisfeld (1982) suggests that these genetically programmed behaviors might include such things as the infant's distress at being separated from the mother or other caregiver (more about this in Chapter 6); the tendency of mothers in all cultures to hold their infants on the left side, whether or not they are right-handed; various facial expressions that have identical meanings everywhere (such as the human smile, which occurs in blind as well as in sighted infants); and human vocalizations, which are initially identical in deaf infants and in hearing infants.

Intervention Studies

Another way of studying gene–environment interactions is through various kinds of interventions—such as enriching or depriving an individual's environment to see what the effects might be.

THE SHERMAN AND KEY STUDY

An early study by Sherman and Key (1932) provides tentative evidence of the effects of a "natural" rather than experimental kind of intervention. The study compared the intelligence test scores of the Mountain children (from isolated families, no newspapers, magazines, or other forms of

because the European blackbird, a close relative of the song thrush that also eats snails, doesn't seem to be able to learn the same smash-the-snail's-shell[*] behavior. But it is also an environmentally influenced behavior because the young song thrush doesn't instinctively know how to smash a snail shell; it learns to do so largely by trial and error during a critical period early in its life. If it's not given an opportunity to

---

[*]Say that four times real fast. Then get back to your studying.

[†]"The cucumber gets crooked from infancy," declared my grandmother, agreeing with many Tunisian grandmothers—but not really clarifying whether it gets crooked for genetic or environmental reasons.

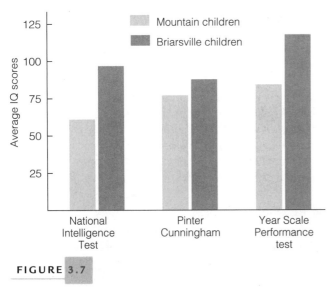

FIGURE 3.7

Comparisons between Mountain children and Briarsville children on some measures of intelligence.

reading material, nor any consistent contact with the outside world) with a control group in a more typical environment (the Briarsville children). The Briarsville children had been exposed to conventional schooling and had access to the offerings of the wider culture through newspapers and so on. Results of the comparison are shown in Figure 3.7. Note that the Briarsville children performed significantly better than the Mountain children on all three measures of intellectual performance.

Sherman and Key argue that these differences reflect the effects of environmental characteristics. But that isn't the only explanation. We don't know, for example, whether the parents of these children were comparable in terms of intelligence; none were tested. Maybe the parents who chose to isolate themselves in the mountains were less intelligent than those who lived closer to the cultural mainstream. It's also possible that they were *more* intelligent.

HEAD START AS INTERVENTION

There is an abundance of more recent and better controlled interventions. One example is Project Head Start, a massive, federally funded U.S. program designed to alleviate, through intervention, some of the possible disadvantages of being born and raised in homes less advantaged economically, socially, and intellectually.

There have been more than 2,000 different Head Start programs (Zigler & Freedman, 1987). Many of these provided services only a few hours a day, and many did not expose children to systematic, well-thought-out experiences. In general, however, the evidence is that higher-quality programs are effective in increasing measured intelligence, and that children exposed to such programs often do better in subjects such as mathematics. In addition, there are usually improvements in more-difficult-to-measure areas such as social functioning (Zigler & Freedman, 1987). Significantly, in a longitudinal study of 128 children, Molfese, DiLalla, and

Bunce (1997) found that the single best predictor of intelligence was the home environment and, specifically, factors that affect the intellectual climate of the home.

Studies of Twins

"If I had any desire to lead a life of indolent ease," Stephen Jay Gould tells us, "I would wish to be an identical twin, separated at birth from my brother and raised in a different social class. We could hire ourselves out to a host of social scientists and practically name our fee. For we would be exceedingly rare representatives of the only really adequate natural experiment for separating genetic from environmental effects in humans" (1981, p. 234). Why is this so? Because identical twins are genetically identical; they result from the splitting of a single zygote, a fertilized ovum, into two genetically identical fertilized eggs (hence **monozygotic** or **identical twins**). The other type of twins results from the fertilization of two different egg cells by two different spermatozoa (hence **dizygotic** or **fraternal twins**). This is possible only when the mother produces more than one egg, resulting in twins who are no more alike genetically than ordinary **siblings**.

Unfortunately for research, the incidence of twins is relatively low—approximately 1 in every 86 births. Furthermore, identical twins are much rarer than fraternal twins—perhaps 1 in 300 births in North America. And that of identical triplets is even rarer: only 1 for every 50,000 births ("The Guinea Pigs," 1997). The precise causes of twin births are not known, although heredity appears to be a factor, because twins are found relatively frequently in some families and not at all in others. Also, older parents are more likely to have twins than are younger parents (Ernst & Angst, 1983).

Twins occur rarely in human births—approximately 1 in every 86 births. Identical twins are rarer—perhaps 1 in 300 or so births among Caucasians and far fewer among the Chinese or Japanese. Twins provide researchers with an excellent opportunity to separate the effects of heredity and environment. Triplets, such as the Koralja trio, who are Jersey City policemen, are even rarer than twins.

INTELLIGENCE

Many studies of twins have looked at correlations for intelligence test scores. Recall from Chapter 1 that a correlation is a measure of relationship usually expressed in numbers ranging from 0 to plus or minus 1. A high positive correlation—say +0.75 to +1.00—means that if one twin has a low or high intelligence test score, the other is also likely to have a correspondingly low or high score. A high negative correlation—say, −0.75 to −1.00—means that a high score for one would be associated with a low score for the other.

In general, the median correlation for intelligence test scores for identical twins is above +0.80, whereas that for fraternal twins is below +0.60 (see Figure 3.8). If members of identical and fraternal twin pairs have had similar environments, these correlations may be interpreted as evidence that measured intelligence is influenced by heredity.

As Figure 3.8 also shows, with decreasing genetic similarity, there is a corresponding decrease in similarity between intelligence scores. Thus, the correlation for cousins is less than that for twins. This, too, is evidence of the influence of heredity.

But these data also support the belief that contexts influence measured intelligence. Because most sets of identical twins have more similar environments than do cousins or siblings, the higher correlation between various intelligence measures for identical twins may be due at least in part to their more nearly identical environments. And the difference between identical twins reared together and those reared apart is additional evidence that environment influences

development. For example, Figure 3.8 reports median correlations of +0.85 and +0.67 for intelligence test scores of identical twins raised together and apart, respectively. Because these twins are genetically identical, environmental forces are clearly important. It is also revealing that as identical twins grow up, their phenotypes (manifested characteristics) become less similar, but, of course, their genotypes remain identical. It seems that the interaction of these identical genotypes with somewhat different contexts leads to progressively more dissimilar developmental outcomes (McCartney, Bernieri, & Harris, 1990).

PERSONALITY

Twin studies also provide evidence that a host of personality characteristics are strongly influenced by genetic factors (Plomin, 1989). In an Australian survey of 3,810 pairs of adult identical and fraternal twins, for example, Martin and Jardine (1986) found high correlations for personality characteristics such as anxiety, depression, conservatism, and introversion/extroversion. Similar results have also been reported in a survey of American adult twins (Pogue-Geile & Rose, 1985).

Perhaps more striking is the finding that some mental disorders have a genetic basis. For example, Gottesman and Shields (1982) found that of twenty-eight pairs of identical twins there was 42-percent concordance for schizophrenia—that is, 42 percent of all schizophrenic members of twin pairs had a schizophrenic twin. The concordance between members of fraternal twin pairs was only 9 percent, from a sample of thirty-four pairs.

FIGURE 3.8

Median correlation coefficients for intelligence test scores from a large number of studies. The high correlation for identical twins shows the strong genetic basis of measured intelligence. The greater correlation for siblings or twins reared together compared with those reared apart supports the view that environmental forces are also important in determining similarity of intelligence test scores. (From T. J. Bouchard and M. McGue [1981]. Familial studies of intelligence: A review, Science, 212, 1055–1059. © 1981 by the AAAS. Used by permission.)

No. of Correlations	34	3	3	8	41	69	2	32	4	2	4	5	6	8	8	16
No. of Pairings	4,672	65	410	982	5,546	26,473	203	8,433	814	200	1,176	345	369	758	1,397	3,817
Median Correlation	.85	.67	.73	.475	.58	.45	.24	.385	.22	.35	.145	.29	.31	.19	.18	.365

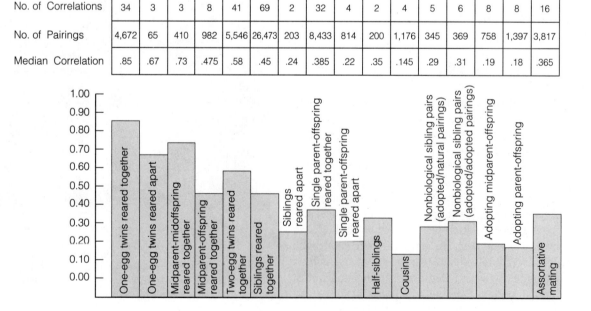

Studies of adopted children and studies of mental disorders among related family members also confirm the finding that some forms of schizophrenia as well as manic-depression have a genetic component (Farmer, 1996). Similarly, there appears to be little doubt that heredity is often involved in the onset of alcoholism. Not only are children of alcoholics about four times more likely to be alcoholics than are members of the general population, but studies of twins have found very high concordance rates for alcoholism (high concordance means that when one twin has a specific characteristic, the probability is high that the other will also have the characteristic). Also, certain racial groups appear to be more prone to alcoholism than others. This is partly explained by the fact that there appear to be detectable, biologically based differences between alcoholic-prone and "normal" individuals. Differences have been found with respect to certain liver enzymes involved in metabolizing alcohol (Emery & Mueller, 1992) and with respect to specific brain receptors that might be associated with responses to alcohol (Blum et al., 1990).

Adopted Children Studies

When it is possible to obtain information about biological as well as adoptive parents, and about natural and adopted children, adopted children studies permit a wide range of comparisons that make it easier to untangle the interaction of genes and context.

In the Texas Adoption Project, which began in 1973, investigators have access to data that include physical as well as cognitive measures of the adopted children's biological mothers (and sometimes fathers as well), in addition to similar measures for the children themselves, their adoptive parents, and other "natural" children in the adoptive home (Horn, 1983; Loehlin, Horn, & Willerman, 1997). This makes it possible to compare relationships between adopted children and their biological mothers with those between the adopted children and their adoptive mothers. Furthermore, these relationships can also be compared with those that exist between the adoptive parents and their natural children. In other words, the design of this study makes it possible to look at correlations in which the members of a pair have common genes but different environments (adopted children and their biological mothers), in which members of a pair share an environment but are genetically unrelated (adopted children and their adoptive parents), and in which there is some commonality with respect to both genes and the environment (adoptive parents and their natural children).

Some of the results of the Texas Adoption Project are summarized in Table 3.3. What is most striking about these findings is that the correlation between adopted children and their biological mothers is higher than that between the adopted children and their adoptive parents—a finding that has been replicated in other studies as well (Turkheimer, 1991). As Loehlin, Horn, and Willerman (1994) point out, the higher the degree of biological relatedness, the higher the correlation for general intelligence scores. Thus, the rela-

TABLE 3.3

IQ Correlations in the Texas Adoption Project

CORRELATION PAIRING	NUMBER OF PAIRS	OBSERVED CORRELATIONS
Share genes only:		
Adopted child × biological mother	297	0.28
Share environment only:		
Adopted child × adopted mother	401	0.15
Adopted child × adoptive father	405	0.12
All unrelated children	266	0.18
Share genes and environment:		
Natural child × adoptive mother	143	0.21
Natural child × adoptive father	144	0.29
Natural child × natural child	40	0.33

Source: From "The Texas Adoption Project," by J. M. Horn, 1983. *Child Development*, pp. 268–275. © 1983 by the Society for Research in Child Development, Inc. Reprinted by permission.

tionship between adopted children and their biological parents is about the same as that between adoptive parents and their own children although the adopted children are not raised by their own parents. Eysenck claims this is strong evidence that genetics is the principal determiner of variation in intelligence (Eysenck & Kamin, 1981). However, it should be noted that these correlations are very low; they do not, by themselves, account for very much variation in intelligence. But, as geneticists would be quick to point out, the degree of genetic relatedness between a child and a natural parent is not nearly as high as that between siblings, and even less than that between identical twins.

An Illustration of Gene–Context Interaction

It seems clear that over the course of generations, environmental contexts exert a selective force on genes; this is one of the basic laws of evolutionary theory (Charlesworth, 1995). We also know that the interaction of genes and environment affects behavior. It is perhaps not so obvious, but no less true, that genes can also influence environment.

Elder, Nguyen, and Caspi's (1985) analysis of the lives of 167 children who lived during the Great Depression (1930s) provides a dramatic example of how genes can affect a child's environment. The Depression was a time of severe economic hardships during which many fathers lost their jobs and their ability to look after their families. As a result, says Elder (1979), some fathers became more punitive and more exploitative; others became more rejecting and indifferent. These changes, notes Elder, were especially difficult for adolescents, whose relationships with parents changed in systematic ways (Elder et al., 1985). Boys' perceptions of the power and attractiveness of their fathers tended to decline, whereas their peers became more appealing. Interestingly, however, adolescent boys did not appear to suffer in terms of confidence, aspirations, and positive self-concept. In contrast, girls tended to lower their aspirations and their self-esteem, and to experience increased moodiness and unhappiness. These negative effects, claims Elder, were not linked so much to economic hardships as to the rejecting behavior of the fathers. And, in general, they were more serious for girls than for boys. But what is most striking is that the least attractive girls suffered most. In Elder, Nguyen, and Caspi's words, "If girls were unattractive, family hardship accentuated fathers' overly demanding, exploitive behavior...[but] only when girls were rated as unattractive" (p. 371). In some cases, economic hardship actually increased the extent to which fathers were warm and supportive of their attractive daughters, sacrificing and going out of their way to provide for them. Thus can a genetically influenced characteristic (physical attractiveness) have a direct effect on the environment.

Related to this, a large number of studies have found that on average, teachers judge physically attractive students to be more socially skillful, more likely to achieve, and even more intelligent (Ritts, Patterson, & Tubbs, 1992).

The lesson to be learned from such studies is clear: If we are to understand the development and the lives of people, it is essential that we take into account the contexts in which they are born and live. In Bronfenbrenner's terms, we need to look at the microsystem (in the Elder study, the adolescent in interaction with father, mother, peers), the mesosystem (family interactions with school or with the adolescent's workplaces), the exosystem (the father's changed relationship with his work setting), and the macrosystem (the dramatic social and economic changes of the Great Depression). An ecological approach to understanding development emphasizes not only the importance of the interactions that define the child's context, but underscores as well the importance of the characteristics of individuals and contexts in interaction. And it provides a framework for beginning to understand how characteristics that have a strong genetic basis (physical appearance or intelligence, for example) can influence interactions in systems that are also influenced by environmental factors (economic conditions, for example).

Human Plasticity

When Snyderman and Rothman (1987) questioned 1,020 American scholars, researchers, and theorists, they found that most believed that intelligence is inherited to a significant degree. But virtually all recognize that human characteristics are influenced by the interaction of genes and changing contexts.

Still, the old nurture–nature controversy—the question of whether certain traits are influenced primarily by heredity or only by the environment, and of how important each is—has not gone away completely. The persistence of this controversy, says Gottlieb (1992), "reflects an inadequate understanding of the relations among heredity, development,

and evolution" (p. 137). It's a controversy sometimes fueled by the belief that we are—or at least should be—equal. And if we are equal, then it cannot be that Jill has an assortment of genes highly likely to lead to charm and intelligence and grace while Mikey starts his life with an assortment of genes that propel him blindly toward low intelligence or schizophrenia.

Or can it? Science suggests that yes, our genes are different, and yes, we have different probabilities of reaching certain outcomes. But science also tells us that genes, by themselves, determine little. They simply underlie potential, making some outcomes more probable than others. Even in the face of highly probable (highly canalized) outcomes, the human being is sufficiently plastic that environmental forces can lead to surprising and wonderful things.

That is the essence of Gottesman's (1974) concept of reaction range, of which we spoke earlier. Reaction range is the range of possibilities implicit in our genes. It includes all the outcomes possible for any given characteristic, taking into account variations in the timing and nature of environmental influences. The concepts of reaction range and of human plasticity are simplified by Stern (1956) in what he calls the **"rubber band hypothesis"** (see Figure 3.9).

In effect, the rubber band hypothesis compares intelligence to a rubber band. Some of us have short bands to begin with (limited inherited potential for intelligence, a short reaction range); others have longer bands. Manifested intelligence is the eventual length of the band after it has been stretched by the environment. Some environments stretch bands a lot; others hardly stretch them at all. Longer bands, of course, stretch more easily than shorter bands.

Do highly demanding environments break bands? Do old bands become frayed and brittle? Do bands stretch more easily when new? Unfortunately, analogies are simply comparisons; they provide no answers for questions like these. (See Summary Table 3.4.)

FIGURE 3.9

The Stern hypothesis, an example of gene–environment interaction. Individuals with different inherited potential for intellectual development can manifest a wide range of measured intelligence as a function of environmental influence.

		Inherited potential	
		Genes for low intelligence	Genes for High intelligence
Environment	Poor	Much below average	Average
	Average	Below average	Quite intelligent
	Excellent	Average or quite intelligent	Genius

Studies of Gene–Context Interaction

INVESTIGATION	OBSERVATION	MAIN CONCLUSION
Anecdotal observation of achievement among British scientists (Galton)	A handful of families have produced most of England's most brilliant scientists.	Intelligence among humans is largely inherited.
Investigations of maze-learning among highly inbred rats (Tryon)	After eight generations, even the dullest of the "bright" rats is "brighter" than the brightest of the dull rats.	Intelligence—or at least maze-brightness—among rats is largely inherited.
Observations of the song thrush's snail-eating behavior (Weisfeld)	The thrush eats snails by smashing their shells against rocks, but must learn to do so through a period of trial and error during a critical period early in its development.	Context and genetic influences interact in complex ways to determine even what seem to be highly "instinctual" behaviors.
Intervention studies such as with Project Head Start	Higher quality programs are effective in increasing measured intelligence, and also contribute positively in less-easy-to-measure areas.	Environmental interventions, especially during critical, earlier periods, can significantly affect developmental outcomes.
A: Comparisons of twins, some reared together, some apart (Plomin, Bouchard, Burt, and many others) **B:** Comparisons of adopted children with biological parents, adoptive parents, and others (Texas Adoption Project)	The higher the degree of biological relatedness, the higher the correlation for measures such as intelligence, some manifestations of mental disorders, and a number of other characteristics. At the same time, shared environments are reflected in higher correlations in many of these same characteristics.	Genes clearly contribute to measured intelligence—as do contexts. In a sense, genes determine potential; the interaction of genes and context determines outcomes. Although we have different probabilities of reaching certain outcomes, we are remarkably plastic within a range of possible outcomes.

GENETIC DEFECTS

But to continue with the analogy, not only are there short and long bands, but there also appear to be some that are defective—and perhaps some that are vastly superior as well. These defects may be evident in one of a variety of genetic diseases or chromosomal disorders.

"Genes are instructions for assembling an organism," says Offner (1993). "It is only when there is a mistake in these instructions that a genetic disease results" (p. 406). In most cases, the resulting disease is linked with recessive rather than dominant genes. The reason for this is simple: Abnormalities linked with a dominant gene are always manifested in all carriers and have much less chance of being passed on to offspring—especially if they lead to early death. In contrast, abnormalities linked to recessive genes are manifested only when the carrier inherits two related recessive genes. Thus, individuals who are carriers of a single recessive gene for some abnormality don't manifest the abnormality and may therefore be completely unaware that they are carriers. Thus, they are more likely to pass the gene on to their offspring—who will, likewise, not manifest the abnormality unless they inherit a second defective gene from the other parent.

Because related individuals (cousins, for example) have so many genes in common, they are also more likely to share defective genes. It is precisely for this reason that the risk of genetic disorders among the children of biologically related parents is so much higher than for children whose parents are not related. In contrast, if a person who is a carrier of a defective recessive gene mates with someone who does not carry the gene, there is only one chance in four that the offspring will inherit the gene and no chance that this offspring will manifest the disorder (because the gene is recessive). Thus, continued matings among individuals who are not biologically related may, over a period of generations, eventually succeed in eradicating or greatly reducing the incidence of the recessive gene in question. By the same token, continued matings among family members might lead to a proliferation of the gene and a corresponding increase in the manifestation of the disorder it underlies (see "At a Glance: Hemophilia Among Royalty" and Figure 3.10).

Huntington's Disease

As we saw, most very serious or fatal genetic disorders are linked with recessive genes (otherwise, all carriers would be affected and would either die before having children or would be aware of the risks involved and refrain from parenthood). However, one exception is **Huntington's disease** (also called Huntington's chorea), which is both fatal and associated with a dominant gene. The reason that the disorder is still present emophilia-A is a sex-linked recessive genetic disorder. Males who carry the recessive gene on their X chromosome are always affected: Their blood-clotting mechanisms don't work properly, and they run the risk of dying from untreated bruises, cuts, or internal bleeding. Females who carry the recessive gene on one X chromosome typically also have the normal *dominant* gene on the other X chromosome. Thus, they don't suffer from the disease, but they can pass the defective gene on to their children. Many of the royal families of nineteenth-century Europe carried the gene. Queen Victoria of England was a carrier, and so were two of her daughters (see Figure 3.10)

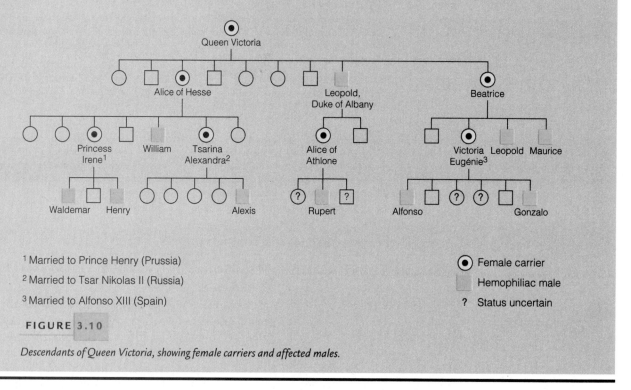

¹ Married to Prince Henry (Prussia)

² Married to Tsar Nikolas II (Russia)

³ Married to Alfonso XIII (Spain)

FIGURE 3.10

Descendants of Queen Victoria, showing female carriers and affected males.

is because it does not ordinarily manifest itself until the age of thirty or forty—after which it leads to rapid neurological deterioration and eventual death.

Until recently, there was no way of determining whether an individual carried the dominant gene for Huntington's disease, so a person whose parents or other relatives had cases of Huntington's could only wait to see whether the disease would eventually strike. Now, however, the gene has been identified, making it possible to determine relatively accurately the probability that an individual will be affected (Bodmer & McKie, 1995). However, because Huntington's disease is fatal and incurable, many individuals who might be carriers of the gene prefer not to be screened. Jacopini and associates (1992) found that fewer than half of those who knew they were at risk intended to take advantage of the screening offered to them. Among the most common reasons for refusing to be tested are lack of treatment or cure, fear of losing health insurance, and inability to "undo" the knowledge (Quaid & Morris, 1993). However, as for other genetically based disorders, there exists the possibility of eventually being able to replace this defective DNA sequence with a normal gene.

Sickle-Cell Anemia

Sickle-cell anemia is a genetic disorder linked to a recessive gene. Approximately 10 percent of all blacks in the United States, and a much lower proportion of whites, carry the recessive gene for sickle-cell anemia (Thompson, Gil, & Abrams, 1992) (Figure 3.11). These 10 percent are **heterozygous** for this gene (having one normal and one abnormal gene); another 0.25 percent of the black population is **homozygous** (carrying two defective genes). Effects of the defective gene are clearly apparent in abnormally shaped red blood cells (sickle-shaped rather than circular), which multiply with lack of oxygen (Figure 3.12). Those who are homozygous for this gene often die in childhood or are severely ill throughout life. Those who are heterozygous are ordinarily healthy except in conditions of low oxygen such as at high altitudes, where they may become quite ill.

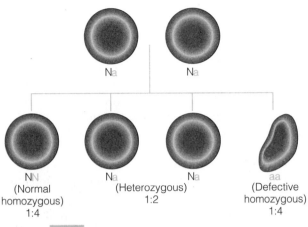

NN

Na   Na

NN
(Normal
homozygous)
1:4

Na   Na
(Heterozygous)
1:2

aa
(Defective
homozygous)
1:4

FIGURE 3.11

An illustration of recessive gene action in the determination of sickle-cell anemia. Parents are heterozygous; that is, they possess one normal (N) and one defective (a) gene, and will therefore not suffer from the disease. A child born to these parents will have one chance in four of not carrying the defective gene, one chance in two of being heterozygous, and one chance in four of possessing two defective genes and therefore suffering from sickle-cell anemia.

PKU

Phenylketonuria (PKU) is a genetic defect associated with the presence of two recessive genes. It occurs throughout the world but is considerably more common among some ethnic groups such as the Gypsies of eastern Slovakia (Kalanin et al., 1994). In individuals suffering from this disease, the liver enzyme responsible for breaking down phenylalanine into usable substances is absent or inactive. Infants who inherit the two recessive genes for PKU appear normal at birth, but with the continued ingestion of phenylalanine (which makes up about 5 percent of the weight of protein), their nervous system deteriorates irreversibly, and they become increasingly mentally retarded (Bodmer & McKie, 1995). Fortunately, however, PKU is easily detected by a routine blood test at birth, and its onset can be prevented by providing children with diets low in phenylalanine from infancy (Curtius, Endres, & Blau, 1994).

PKU is a striking example of a highly canalized tendency that is nevertheless subject to environmental influence. The disorder is clearly genetic, but in the absence of specific environmental influences (the ingestion of phenylalanine), the individual's phenotype will not reflect genotype.

Other Genetic Defects

There are a large number of other genetic defects; in fact, several thousand have now been identified and catalogued.

TAY–SACHS DISEASE

Tay–Sachs disease, associated with a recessive gene, is an enzyme disorder that results in the brain's inability to break down certain fats. Eventually, these build up, preventing neural transmission and leading to the degeneration of brain cells. Affected individuals commonly die before the age of three. Tay–Sachs disease can be detected before birth but cannot yet be prevented or cured (Suzuki, 1994).

MUSCULAR DYSTROPHY (MD)

A degenerative muscular disorder of which there are various forms, muscular dystrophy (MD) is often linked to a recessive gene or is multifactorial. It usually involves an inability to walk, and it may lead to death. The gene for one form of muscular dystrophy, Duchenne muscular dystrophy, has been located. Hence, it is now possible to detect its

FIGURE 3.12

On the left, normal oxygenated red blood cells; on the right, sickle cells.

presence in the unborn child. In addition, parents can be tested to arrive at an estimate of the probability that their offspring will be affected (Kruyer et al., 1994). Considerable research is currently under way in an effort to develop gene-therapy techniques that might either replace the defective gene or prevent its manifestation (Fassati, Murphy, & Dickson, 1997).

■ NEURAL TUBE DEFECTS

Among the most common congenital malformations are neural tube defects, which occur at a rate of 1 for every 500 to 1,000 births (Miller et al., 1990). Neural tube defects may take the form of *spina bifida,* in which the spine remains open at the bottom, or of *anencephaly,* in which portions of the skull and brain are absent. Such defects often lead to severe retardation or death. Although genetically linked, the causes of these defects are multifactorial. They generally develop very early in pregnancy (as early as the first week) and can be detected by means of an **AFP test**—a standard test conducted at about the thirteenth week of pregnancy, which looks at the level of *alphafetoprotein* in the mother's blood. If this substance is present in concentrations higher than usual, further tests such as ultrasound or fetoscopy (described later) are performed to determine whether there is a neural tube defect. In some jurisdictions, AFP screening is routine or even mandatory (as are tests for PKU).

■ DIABETES MELLITUS

Some forms of diabetes, an insulin deficiency disease, are associated with recessive genes, as well as with other factors. Children born to mothers with diabetes mellitus have a two to three times higher risk of birth defects. These can include limb deformities, cardiac problems, neural tube defects, and other problems (Friedman, 1992).

■ NONMEDICAL CONDITIONS

In addition to the several thousand known medical conditions that are clearly genetically linked, there is increasing evidence of a genetic basis for at least some manifestations of emotional and behavioral problems such as alcoholism, depression, anorexia nervosa, infantile autism, and schizophrenia. For some of these conditions, specific marker genes have been located. However, their causes are usually multifactorial; accordingly, they are highly susceptible to environmental influences.

CHROMOSOMAL DISORDERS

Genetic defects are linked to specific recessive or dominant genes, or to a combination of genes; they may also be related to certain environmental conditions. **Chromosomal disorders,** on the other hand, are associated not with specific genes but with errors in chromosomes. Many of these errors result from improper divisions and recombinations during meiosis.

Down Syndrome

The most common chromosomal birth defect, Down syndrome, affects about 1 out of every 680 live births. About twice that many fetuses are affected by the condition, but approximately half result in spontaneous miscarriages during the first third of pregnancy (Dill & McGillivray, 1992). Some children with Down syndrome have characteristic loose folds of skin over the corners of the eyes, producing an Oriental appearance—hence the now uncommon label "mongolism." Also, mental retardation is common among children with Down syndrome, and their language development is often retarded (Kumin, 1994). Not all children are equally affected.

Most cases of Down syndrome are due to failure of the twenty-first pair of chromosomes to separate during meiosis (termed *nondisjunction*). Hence, the resulting gamete (sex cell) has an extra copy of the twenty-first chromosome (thus the alternative medical label **Trisomy 21**). When this gamete is combined with the other gamete during fertilization, the

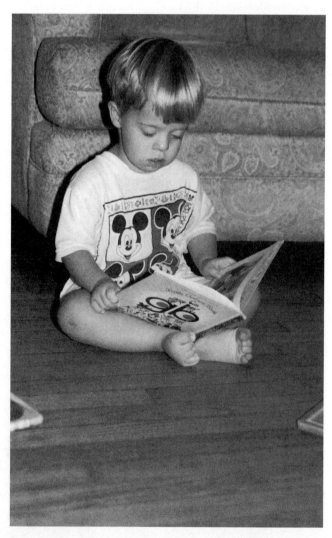

Down syndrome, the most common chromosomal birth defect, is closely related to parental age and is often associated with mental retardation. But not all Down syndrome children are equally affected.

zygote (fertilized egg) has an extra twenty-first chromosome. Nondisjunction of the twenty-first chromosome is closely linked with the age of parents, and most often occurs during meiosis of the ovum rather than of the sperm. As a result, about 95 percent of Down syndrome cases are associated with the mother; the other 5 percent are associated with the father (Antonarakis, 1991). The probability of producing a child with Down syndrome is about 1 in 1,420 for women in their early twenties; it's close to 1 in 30 for women aged 45 (Dill & McGillivray, 1992; see Figure 3.13). Fathers aged 50 to 55 have a 20 to 30 percent greater chance of fathering children with Down syndrome.

Because medical science knows precisely what the genetic cause of Down syndrome is, it is possible to detect its presence in the fetus before birth. Procedures for doing so are discussed later in this chapter.

Abnormalities of the Sex Chromosomes

A number of chromosomal defects are associated with the sex chromosome. Some involve the absence of a chromosome, others involve the presence of an extra chromosome, some involve a fractured or abnormally compressed chromosome, and still others involve a defective gene on an X chromosome. For example, the X chromosome is the site for genes related to defects such as night-blindness, baldness, and hemophilia. Each of these defects is associated with recessive genes, and each is far more common among males than females. Why? Simply because females who inherit the defective gene on one of their two X chromosomes often have the corresponding *normal* gene on the other chromosome. As a result, they are carriers of the defective gene but don't manifest the disorder because the gene is recessive. Males,

FIGURE 3.13

The probability of Down syndrome or some other chromosomal abnormality increases dramatically with age. (Based on Friedman et al., 1992.)

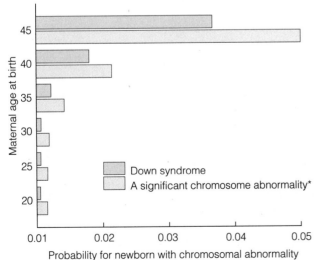

*Excludes unbalanced translocation and XXX

on the other hand, have only one X chromosome; their other sex chromosome is a Y. In many cases, the normal dominant genes that would counter the effect of the recessive gene for one of these disorders are not present on the Y chromosome. Accordingly, males manifest conditions such as hereditary baldness far more often than do females. Yet the gene is passed on from mother to son—not from father to son (because the father always passes on a Y chromosome to his sons, and the mother always passes on the X chromosome).

Of special interest in this connection is **fragile X syndrome,** which is one of the most common causes of *inherited* mental retardation and which has, by many accounts, been greatly underestimated (Patel, 1994; Wiebe & Wiebe, 1994). In fragile X syndrome, the X sex chromosome is abnormally compressed or even broken. Although the condition can also occur in females, it is far more common among males and is one of the reasons that there are more mentally retarded males than females in the general population (Zigler & Hodapp, 1991). Unlike Down syndrome, in which mental retardation is typically apparent very early in life, fragile X individuals often manifest no symptoms of retardation until puberty (Silverstein & Johnston, 1990). Between the years of ten and fifteen, however, there is frequently a marked decline in intellectual functioning, which becomes more severe with advancing age (Maes et al., 1994).

In addition to these chromosomal abnormalities, there are a number of conditions marked by the absence of a sex chromosome or by the presence of an extra chromosome. (See also Summary Table 3.5.) Most common among these are the following:

- **Turner's syndrome** affects 1 in every 2,500 female children (Dill & McGillivray, 1992). These children are born with a missing sex chromosome (designated as 45, X or XO, rather than 46, XX; the "45" indicates the total number of chromosomes). Such children typically have underdeveloped secondary sexual characteristics at puberty but can be helped by injections of the female sex hormone *estrogen* before puberty (Emery & Mueller, 1992).

- **Klinefelter's syndrome** involves the presence of an extra X chromosome in a male child (thus 47, XXY) and is considerably more common than Turner's syndrome (1 out of 1,000 males; Dill & McGillivray, 1992). It is marked by the presence of both male and female secondary sexual characteristics. Boys suffering from this disorder typically have small, undeveloped testicles, high-pitched voices, some breast development, and little or no facial hair after puberty. Therapy with the male sex hormone testosterone is often effective in improving the development of masculine characteristics and in increasing sex drive.

- **Supermale syndrome** is the label sometimes used to describe males with an extra Y chromosome (47, XYY). These males are characteristically tall; sometimes, they are also of lower than average intelligence. Some research evidence has linked this syndrome with criminality, but

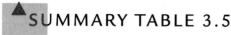
GENETIC DEFECTS	SOME CHARACTERISTICS
Huntington's disease	■ Linked to a *dominant* gene but not manifested until age 30 or more. ■ A serious neurological disorder that is usually fatal.
Sickle-cell anemia	■ Linked to a recessive gene. ■ Far more common among blacks than among Caucasians. ■ Varies in severity and can lead to serious illness with lack of oxygen.
Phenylketonuria (PKU)	■ Linked to recessive genes. ■ Associated with severe retardation developing early in life. ■ Easily detectable at birth. ■ Effects preventable through dietary means.
Tay–Sachs disease	■ Linked with recessive gene. ■ An enzyme disorder usually leading to early death.
Muscular dystrophy	■ Linked with recessive genes. ■ Degenerative muscular disorder. ■ Present in various forms, some of which have marker genes and can therefore be detected, but cannot yet be prevented.
Neural tube defects	■ Genetically linked defects of spinal tube. ■ May be manifested in *spina bifida* or in *anencephaly*.
Diabetes mellitus	■ Some forms linked with recessive gene. ■ An insulin deficiency disease, often controllable.

CHROMOSOMAL DISORDERS	SOME CHARACTERISTICS
Down syndrome	■ Often associated with *nondisjunction* of the 21st chromosome so that offspring has 3 (hence *Trisomy* 21). ■ Most common cause of mental retardation. ■ Closely associated with parental (especially maternal) age.
Fragile X syndrome	■ Linked with an abnormally compressed or broken X chromosome. ■ Far more common among males than females. ■ Highly common cause of mental retardation, often not manifested until adolescence.
Turner's syndrome	■ Female disorder linked with absence of an X chromosome. ■ Sometimes apparent in underdeveloped secondary sexual characteristics. ■ Symptoms sometimes alleviated through injections of estrogen.
Klinefelter's syndrome	■ Male child with an extra X chromosome (XXY). ■ Treatment often involves injections of testosterone.
Supermale syndrome	■ Male child with extra Y chromosome. ■ Often tall. ■ Tentative but poorly established link to criminality.

the conclusion remains tentative (Emery & Mueller, 1992). However, XYY males are often less mature and more impulsive than normal.

tributions are complex and not completely known, it is nevertheless often possible to determine the probability that a child will be affected.

GENETIC RISK

Medical advances and improved nutrition have greatly reduced infections and nutritional deficiencies for which children are hospitalized, note Emery and Mueller (1992). Now, about one in twenty children admitted to hospitals suffer from problems that are at least partly genetic in origin.

For disorders that are linked directly to the presence or absence of known genes, it is sometimes possible to identify affected children before birth. For other disorders, whose origins are only partly genetic or for which the genetic con-

Fetal Diagnosis

Fetal diagnosis is the assessment of the condition of the unborn. There are six principal techniques for fetal diagnosis.

■ AMNIOCENTESIS

In **amniocentesis**, a hollow needle is inserted into the amniotic fluid surrounding the fetus, allowing the physician to obtain 15 to 20 ml of **amniotic fluid**, which contains fetal cells. These can then be analyzed to reveal the absence of chromosomes or the presence of extra chromosomes, as well as the blood type of the fetus and the chemical composition of the amniotic fluid. Many diseases and defects that might affect the unborn child can thus be detected. Because the procedure involves a slight risk of infection and leads to miscarriages in from .5 to 1 percent of cases, it is commonly employed only in those cases where the pregnant woman is older and where there is a probability of fetal abnormality or other complications (Garrett & Carlton, 1994). Amniocentesis is not usually performed until the fifteenth to seventeenth week of pregnancy.

One of the most common uses of amniocentesis has been for the detection of Trisomy 21 (Down syndrome). Because of the moderate risks associated with the procedure, and because incidence of Trisomy 21 increases dramatically with age (see Figure 3.13), the procedure is most commonly used when the mother is thirty-five or more, or when a younger mother is known to be at risk. However, because about 95 percent of pregnant women are under thirty-five, initial screening by age alone misses about 80 percent of Down syndrome fetuses (Kloza, 1990).

Fortunately, there is now another way of screening women who are at higher risk of bearing a child with Down syndrome. Specifically, it has been discovered that the level of alpha fetoprotein (AFP) serum in the pregnant woman's blood is significantly lower than normal. (Recall that AFP levels are routinely assessed to detect the likelihood of neural tube defects, with higher than normal levels indicating a higher probability of problems.) Thus, AFP tests can identify mothers of all ages who are at risk of bearing a child with Down syndrome (Rose et al., 1994).

CHORIONIC VILLUS BIOPSY (CVS)

Chorion biopsy (chorionic villus biopsy or CVS) is a medical procedure for obtaining and examining fetal cells. In CVS, a plastic tube is inserted through the vagina (or a fine needle through the abdomen) to obtain a sample of the **chorion** (Green, 1994). The chorion is part of the placenta (a flat membrane on the inside of the uterus, to which the umbilical cord is attached). It contains the same genetic information as the fetus. The advantage of a chorion biopsy over amniocentesis is that it can be performed as early as seven weeks after conception. Also, because it provides enough fetal cells, chromosomal examination can usually be performed the same day. Amniocentesis, on the other hand, requires a two- to three-week period of tissue culture and does not provide results until well into the second trimester of pregnancy. If the results lead to a decision to terminate the pregnancy, this can be accomplished more simply and more safely in the first trimester. Chorion biopsy procedures are somewhat more experimental than amniocentesis and carry a slightly higher risk of complications, including a higher risk of miscarriage (Green, 1994).

ULTRASOUND

Ultrasound (sometimes called sonogram) provides computer-enhanced, sound-wave generated images of the fetus in "real time." It is among the least harmful and least invasive technique currently available, and it is the method of choice for proving the presence of a living fetus. This technique is the most exact means for estimating fetal age, detecting the position of the fetus, discerning changes in fetal position, detecting multiple pregnancies, and identifying a variety of growth disorders and malformations. In fact, notes Abramsky (1994), it is not only the most common prenatal diagnostic test given to women, but it is also the one that detects the most fetal abnormalities.

Ultrasound images make it possible to see the beginnings of fetal activity, including behaviors such as thumb-sucking; they also allow the physician to examine bone structure, to assess length of bones, to determine relationships among the size and growth of various bodily structures, and even to count fingers and toes. Ultrasound is always used with amniocentesis or CVS to guide the physician, but it is not a substitute for these procedures because it cannot provide actual samples of fetal cells.

FETOSCOPY

Fetoscopy is a surgical procedure that allows the physician to see the fetus. It is used mainly to obtain samples of tissues from the fetus itself, the most important being blood. Fetoscopy can furnish the physician with crucial information about the status of the fetus, especially when there is a possibility of disorders such as hemophilia. However, it carries higher risks than amniocentesis (about a 3 to 5 percent higher probability of miscarriage) (Emery & Mueller, 1992).

RADIOGRAPHY

Some inherited disorders and malformations can be diagnosed through radiography—that is, by means of X-rays of the fetus. However, because of the possibility that X-rays may harm the fetus, sonograms are used instead whenever possible.

PREIMPLANTATION DIAGNOSIS

All fetal diagnostic techniques that we've considered so far can be carried out only after the fetus has begun to develop. However, it is now possible to determine the chromosomal structure of the fetus before the fertilized egg is implanted. One way of doing this is to remove the mature egg and fertilize it with the father's sperm (in vitro fertilization). The zygote is then allowed to multiply to the eight-cell stage, and a single cell is removed and examined for the presence of specific genetic disorders—all within a matter of hours. Removal of a single cell apparently does not affect later development. If no defects are found, the zygote can then be implanted in the uterus (Emery & Mueller, 1992). The great advantage of **preimplantation diagnosis** is that it can identify problems before a therapeutic abortion would otherwise be necessary. However, it is still limited to a handful of advanced, highly specialized medical centers.

Treating Genetic Disorders

Not all genetically based disorders are equally serious. Many can be treated and controlled; some can be cured. For example, the effects of PKU, as we saw, can be prevented through diet.

And in the next chapter, we see how the effects of Rh incompatibility in the fetus, once a usually fatal condition, can be prevented through inoculation of the mother or reversed through blood transfusions. For other conditions, it is sometimes possible to replace deficient enzymes, proteins, vitamins, or other substances (the use of insulin to control diabetes, for example). Similarly, various drugs or even surgery may be used to control and sometimes cure genetic disease (cancer, for example).

Emery and Mueller (1992) suggest that in addition to these medical treatments, there are several other possible though not yet proven treatments. One involves the use of clones (identical copies) of normal genes to replace those that are defective; another is the use of viruses or even of antibiotics to eradicate bacteria or other agents involved in the development of genetically linked diseases (Fisher, 1997).

Genetic Counseling

Although fetal (and preimplantation) diagnosis, along with monitoring changes in the mother, provides powerful tools for detecting potential problems, there are many genetically based problems that medical science cannot determine with absolute certainty. In some cases, however, it's possible to assign a numerical value to the probability of a given outcome. When this occurs, parents and physicians may be faced with difficult decisions involving serious ethical questions. In these situations, genetic counseling offers a valuable service.

■ WHAT IS GENETIC COUNSELING?

Genetic counseling is a branch of medicine and of psychology that attempts to provide counsel to physicians and parents. Such counseling typically strives to assess the probability of a defect occurring, its likely seriousness, the extent to which it can be treated and even reversed, and the best courses of action to follow once a decision has been made about whether to have a child. In many instances, genetic counseling will take place before conception and might take into account the age and health of the mother as well as the presence of genetic abnormalities in ancestors or in siblings. In other cases, genetic counseling will occur after conception (see Table 3.6 and Summary Table 3.7).

TABLE 3.6

Probability of Some Common Genetic Defects

GENETIC DEFECT	INCIDENCE (PER 100 POPULATION)	SEX RATIO (M:F)	NORMAL PARENTS HAVING A SECOND AFFECTED CHILD (%)	AFFECTED PARENT HAVING AN AFFECTED CHILD (%)	AFFECTED PARENT HAVING A SECOND AFFECTED CHILD (%)
Asthma	3.0–4.0	1:1	10	26	—
Cerebral palsy	.2	3:2	1	—*	—
Cleft palate only	.04	2:3	2	7	15
Cleft lip and/or cleft palate	.1	3:2	4	4	10
Club foot	.1	2:1	3	3	10
Congenital heart disease (all types)	.5	1:1	1–4	1–4	10
Diabetes mellitus (juvenile, insulin-dependent)	.2	1:1	6	1–2	—
Dislocation of hip	.7	1:6	6	12	36
Epilepsy ("idiopathic")	.5	1:1	5	5	10
Hydrocephalus	.005	1:1	3	—	—
Manic-depressive psychosis	.4	2:3	10–15	10–15	—
Mental retardation (of unknown cause)	.3–.5	1:1	3–5	10	20
Profound childhood deafness	.1	1:1	10	8	—
Schizophrenia	1.0–2.0	1:1	10	16	—
Spina bifida (neural tube defect)	.3	2:3	5	4	—
Tracheo-esophageal fistula	.03	1:1	1	1	—

Source: Adapted from *Elements of Medical Genetics* (8th ed.) by A. E. H. Emery & R. Mueller. Edinburgh and London: Churchill-Livingstone, 1992. Used by permission.

*No data.

METHOD	PROCEDURE	ADVANTAGES/DISADVANTAGES AND USES
Amniocentesis	Hollow needle inserted through abdomen into amniotic sac to withdraw fluid containing fetal cells.	■ Not usually performed until 15th to 17th week of pregnancy. ■ Useful for detection of chromosomal abnormalities such as Down syndrome.
Chorionic Villus Biopsy (CVS)	Fetal cells obtained from the placenta (lining of the womb) by means of a tube inserted through the vagina.	■ Possible as early as 7 weeks after conception. ■ Provides much the same information as amniocentesis, but much earlier. ■ Higher risk of infection and miscarriage.
Fetoscopy	Surgical procedure involving insertion of instrument that allows physician to "see" fetus and obtain actual samples of fetal tissue.	■ Provides fetal cells for analysis. ■ Useful for detecting disorders such as hemophilia. ■ Higher probability of miscarriage than CVS or amniocentesis.
Radiography	X-ray procedure.	■ Can detect certain malformations. ■ Possible fetal damage from X-ray effects—hence ultrasound typically used instead.
Ultrasound	Sonogram of fetus provides real-time, computer-enhanced image of fetus.	■ Noninvasive, painless, low-risk, without known side-effects. ■ Provides actual image of fetal morphology (shape) and movement. ■ Useful for detecting normal (and abnormal) fetal development and for determining fetal position and age.
Preimplantation Diagnosis	Experimental, highly technical, genetic examination of cells prior to implantation, typically following *in vitro* fertilization.	■ Permits detection of specific genetic disorders prior to pregnancy. ■ May eventually be useful for correcting genetic disorders.

The Future in Genetics

Genetic counseling has traditionally been limited to advising prospective parents about the likelihood of their having a child with a given problem, and providing them with information about their options. And the options have typically consisted of deciding to try to conceive, or not to, or deciding to have a therapeutic abortion, or not to. It may be different in the very near future.

■ REWRITING GENETIC MESSAGES

We now appear to be on the threshold of a new age. Almost daily, there are new discoveries in genetics. We are now able to detect genetic weaknesses, as well as strengths, from the very earliest moments of life. Our mushrooming knowledge of cell biology at the molecular level is opening new doors into the vast and almost uncharted world of genetic engineering. Science is breaking the genetic code. It's learning to read the messages that direct the arrangements of the amino acids that, in turn, define the structure and function of the protein molecules that are the fundamental units of our biological lives. Science has begun to experiment with ways of altering genetic messages, of rewriting the code to enhance the possibilities implicit in our genes or to correct errors. Using recombinant DNA techniques, scientists can use bacteria to reproduce sequences of genetic material. The results include new medications, new refining and manufacturing processes, new products, even new lives.

■ GENETIC SPECULATION

Pergament (1990) suggests that the following developments are possible, perhaps even highly probable, for the twenty-first century:

■ By 2001, it will be possible to separate X- and Y-bearing sperm, to inactivate one or the other, and therefore to select the sex of the child prior to conception.

■ By 2002, science will have discovered how to preserve mature ova that can then be banked and used for reproduction in future generations.*

■ Using technologies of robotics, computers, and genetic engineering, by 2003 the analysis of chromosomes will be simple and accurate.

■ The human genome will have been completely mapped by 2005 so that by 2010 it will be possible to analyze genetic makeup prior to implantation and, using in vitro fertilization, to ensure the genetic health of the zygote.

---

*It happened before 2002. Ova can now be preserved to be fertilized later. And fertilized embryos can also be frozen and, potentially, developed generations from now.

- By 2020, gene scanners will permit detailed analyses of all chromosomes, not only in the egg and sperm, but also in human tissue (kidneys, eyes, bladder, and so on) to detect anomalies and mutations.

- And by 2050, says Pergament, the artificial womb will have been perfected. Now it will be possible to take long-preserved ova and sperm, join them in vitro, and let the artificial womb take over.

ETHICAL ISSUES

There are ethical issues involved here—important ethical issues. Some have to do with the potential dangers of experiments that can, theoretically, produce new forms of life, the consequences of which cannot really be imagined because the nature of that life may be unknown before its creation. Other issues have to do with the morality of altering genetic codes, with the ethics of decisions relating to creating or ending life, with the legality and morality of surrogate mothering and artificial insemination, maybe even with the very definition of life. Responding to these concerns, a Canadian commission (the Royal Commission on Reproductive Technologies) has proposed 293 recommendations to govern genetic research and its applications (Kondro, 1992). The commission advocates jail sentences or fines for researchers trying to clone human embryos, produce human–animal hybrids, or sell human eggs, sperm, embryos, or fetal tissue ("Tough Curbs Urged for Reproductive Medicine," 1993). "This is not a medical policy but a social matter," explained Patricia Baird, chair of the commission. "We must be careful not to commodify human beings, and commercialize human reproduction" ("Baird Sounds Off at Snell," 1994, p. 3).

Perhaps by 2050 these issues will have become more important than the science that gave them birth, and another new discipline will have arisen to deal with them. But we have not yet reached that stage, and we continue to struggle with questions whose answers are not at all clear. Although we know vastly more now than we did even ten years ago, there is still much about our beginnings—and our ends—that we do not understand.

FOCUS QUESTIONS: SUMMARY ANSWERS

1. What is the nature–nurture controversy about?

- It pits those who believe we are what we are because of our genes against those who believe our environments shape us. A more important issue concerns how these forces *interact* to determine the outcomes of development.

2. What are the most basic facts of heredity?

- Conception requires the union of sperm and ovum. The bases of biological life are protein molecules made up of amino acids in complex arrangements determined by a special genetic code contained in sequences of deoxyribonucleic acid (DNA) molecules located on chromosomes. In the chromosomes are the carriers of heredity, the genes. Sex is determined by special chromosomes labeled X and Y (XX equals female; XY equals male; only the father produces a Y).

3. What are some of the most common genetic defects?

- Huntington's disease (a fatal neurological disorder) is caused by a dominant gene. Sickle-cell anemia (the reduced ability of red blood cells to obtain oxygen), PKU (an enzyme disorder that sometimes leads to mental retardation), Tay–Sachs disease (another enzyme disorder leading to brain degeneration and death), and some forms of muscular dystrophy (a degenerative muscular disorder), diabetes (a sugar-processing disorder), and neural tube defects are all examples of genetic disorders associated with recessive genes.

4. What are some common chromosomal defects?

- Chromosomal disorders result from errors in chromosomes and include Down syndrome (Trisomy 21) and disorders associated with errors in sex chromosomes such as Turner's syndrome (linked to an absent sex chromosome); XYY syndrome (super males), affecting men only; Klinefelter's syndrome, affecting men with an extra X chromosome (XXY); and fragile X syndrome (a common cause of mental retardation, especially among males).

5. What are some common methods of prenatal diagnosis?

- Amniocentesis (analysis of amniotic fluid withdrawn through a needle), chorion villus biopsy (analysis of preplacental tissue), fetoscopy (a surgical procedure to obtain fetal blood or skin samples), ultrasound (use of sonar techniques to detect physical characteristics and movement), radiography (X-rays), and preimplantation diagnosis (analysis of zygote cells prior to implantation).

STUDY TERMS

AFP test, 82

amniocentesis, 84

amniotic fluid, 84

artificial insemination, 66

autosomes, 68

canalized, 70

FURTHER READINGS

The following two books present fascinating, and tragic, accounts of the life of Genie, an abandoned child. The first presents details of Genie's life before her eventual discovery at age fourteen; the second is an account of her later treatment and of the professional jealousies and bitterness that followed.

Curtiss, S. (1977). *Genie: A psycholinguistic study of a modern-day wild child.* New York: Academic Press.

Rymer, R. (1993). *Genie: A scientific tragedy.* New York: Harper Perennial.

The first of the following two books is a well-written, somewhat journalistic account of molecular genetics and, specifically, of the Human Genome Project. The second is a far more technical and difficult collection dealing with some of the details of research in molecular genetics applied to medicine:

Bodmer, W., & McKie, R. (1995). *The book of man: The Human Genome Project and the quest to discover our genetic heritage.* New York: Scribner.

Hall, J. C., & Dunlap, J. C. (Eds.). (1997). *Advances in genetics: Incorporating molecular genetic medicine.* San Diego, CA: Academic Press.

Detailed information concerning various approaches to prenatal diagnosis and their uses, advantages, and disadvantages is contained in the following easy-to-read and relatively short book:

Abramsky, L., & Chapple, J. (Eds.). (1994). *Prenatal diagnosis: The human side.* New York: Chapman and Hall.

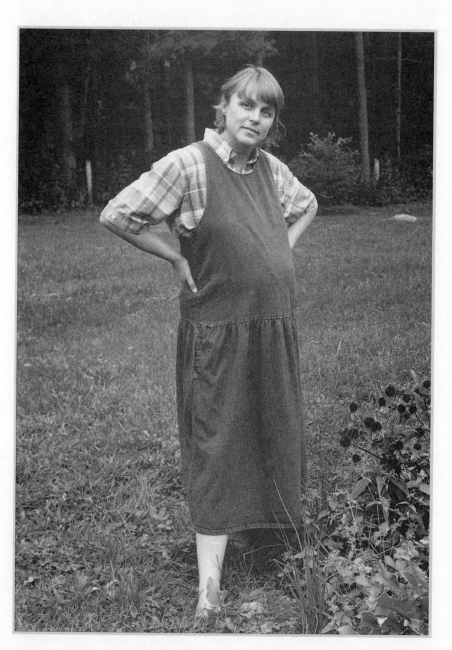

FOUR

Prenatal Development and Birth

"Who was your mother?"

"Never had none!" said the child, with another grin.

"Never had any mother? What do you mean? Where were you born?"

"Never was born!" persisted Topsy.

"Do you know who made you?"

"Nobody, as I knows on," said the child, with a short laugh. "I 'spect I grow'd."

HARRIET BEECHER STOWE
Uncle Tom's Cabin

e know, of course, that Topsy was wrong, that she didn't just "grow'd," that she had to have had a mother. In Topsy's day, there was seldom any doubt about who the mother was—although there might occasionally have been some uncertainty about the father. ¶ Things are no longer so clear-cut. In fact, under some circumstances they are so unclear that even the highest courts in the land are hard-pressed to determine maternity. Ironically, however, sophisticated DNA analyses can sometimes point unerringly to the father. ¶ A case in point is that of one Anna M. Johnson, who agreed to bear a child for Mark and Crispina Calvert in exchange for $10,000 ("Court to Decide Right of Surrogate Mother," 1992). The Calverts later had a disagreement with the surrogate mother, and both parties sought legal custody of the child. The issue is complex: The child was conceived from Mark Calvert's sperm and Crispina Calvert's ovum; Ms. Johnson was then artificially inseminated with the fertilized ovum and bore the child to term. Who is the natural mother? Who is entitled to be the legal mother? ¶ Not the surrogate mother, the California appellate court decided, agreeing with an earlier New Jersey Supreme Court ruling. Because surrogate mothers are not biologically related to the fetus, said the court, they cannot be considered either natural or legal mothers. ¶ Where does that leave the growing numbers of single women who turn to artificial insemination to produce children, not as surrogate mothers but for themselves ("Babies Without Dads," 1992)? And what are the implications of childbearing at age fifty, or even sixty, as is now possible using a previously fertilized, donated ovum? A sixty-year-old European woman recently gave birth to a baby girl ("Mom, 60, Delivers Healthy Girl," 1994). She had lied about her age so that her doctor would implant a zygote into her. The doctor claims he would otherwise have refused. "One has to set an age limit," said he. "I think age 50 is enough" (p. 18). ¶

This Chapter

ometimes **artificial insemination** involves donor sperm but uses the mother's ova, fertilized in the body or outside (in vitro). In such cases, the mother is also a biological parent. But in cases such as Ms. Johnson's and the sixty-year-old mother, both sperm and ovum are donated, and the woman who carries the child serves as a host rather than a biological parent (See "In the News and on the Net: Embryos for Sale.")

Whether **conception** is artificial or natural, however, the fetus usually develops in a highly predictable fashion. The function and structure of each of the body's cells is largely preordained by the genetic material in the twenty-three pairs of chromosomes in the fertilized egg. But even here, as in all of life, development is always subject to a variety of influences.

This chapter traces the normal course of prenatal development from conception through birth, looks at some of the factors that can affect the fetus, and describes childbirth.

▲ **SUMMARY TABLE 4.1**
Detecting Pregnancy

Probable signs	■ Cessation of menses.
	■ Morning sickness.
	■ Changes in breasts.
	■ Increased frequency of urination.
	■ Quickening.
Positive signs	■ Detecting fetal heartbeat.
	■ Palpation of fetus through abdomen.
	■ X-ray or ultrasound detection.
	■ Detection by means of over-the-counter tests for presence of HCG in urine.
	■ Detection by means of blood tests for HCG.

■ DETECTING PREGNANCY

In the absence of chemical tests or a professional medical examination, there are few signs by which women can determine **pregnancy** with certainty before the later stages of **prenatal development.** However, there are a handful of tentative signs, none of which occur very early in pregnancy. Cessation of **menses** (menstruation) is not a certain sign of pregnancy because many other factors can cause it. Morning sickness, although it affects approximately two-thirds of all pregnant women, does not ordinarily begin until about two weeks after the missed period and can easily be mistaken for some other ailment. Frequently during the early stages the breasts enlarge and become slightly painful, and the aureoles darken. Because these symptoms are highly subjective, they are quite unreliable. And movement of the fetus in the womb (termed **quickening**) is not usually noticed by the mother until the fourth or fifth month; by then, most women have realized for some time that they are pregnant.

In addition to these tentative signs of pregnancy, there are more positive symptoms such as the fetal heartbeat, which can be heard with the aid of a **stethoscope.** Similarly, fetal movements can be detected by feeling the abdomen or sometimes simply by observing it. X-rays and ultrasound are two other methods of ascertaining the presence of a fetus.

Several decades ago, the surest medical test of early pregnancy required the aid of a virgin animal such as a rabbit, frog, or mouse.* Fortunately for virgin rabbits and mice, who always had to be killed to complete the test, chemical pregnancy tests are now generally available, even in kit form

for in-home use, and are very widely employed. One study found that an average of five different pregnancy tests were performed for each confirmed pregnancy in a group of women and that more than two-thirds of these were purchased over the counter and performed at home (Voss, 1992). These tests detect changes in the woman's urine through a chemical reaction and are effective as early as two weeks after conception. Specifically, they react to what is termed the **pregnancy hormone (human chorionic gonadotropin,** or HCG) in the woman's urine. Positive indications are highly reliable. However, negative readings are less accurate and should be followed by a second test a week or so later.

An even more accurate test of pregnancy involves examining the woman's blood for a specific subunit of the HCG hormone. Although this test is far more expensive than the home pregnancy test and doesn't yield results as early, it can also be used to estimate the woman's due date (*HealthGuide: Pregnancy,* 1997). (See Summary Table 4.1.)

■ STAGES OF PRENATAL DEVELOPMENT

The **gestation period** (the time between conception and birth) for different species varies considerably: Cows take about as long as people; elephants need 600 days; dogs come to term in approximately 63 days, rabbits in 31, and chickens in 21.

The human gestation period is usually calculated in **lunar months,** each of which has 28 days—hence 10 lunar months or 280 days for pregnancy (counting from the onset of the last menstrual period). However, the actual gestation period is approximately 266 days because fertilization cannot usually occur until 12 to 14 days after the beginning of the menstrual period, which is when **ovulation,** the release of an egg by the ovaries, takes place.

---

*"What for?" harrumphed my grandmother. "Why the jiggers would anyone wanna get a rabbit killed for that unless you're gonna eat it? They'll find out soon enough if they're pregnant."

IN THE NEWS AND ON THE NET

he Columbia–Presbyterian Medical Center in Manhattan has become the first hospital in the United States to openly admit that it designs and sells *made to order* human embryos. Using surplus eggs from women treated at the infertility clinic and sperm from donors representing a wide variety of ethnic, social, and intellectual backgrounds, doctors can produce and freeze embryos. For as little as $2,725 U.S., prospective parents can then purchase and have implanted embryos whose probable characteristics match theirs. Says Dr. Mark Sauer, the director of the infertility clinic at the hospital, "Behind closed doors, the most liberal-minded people are as discrimi-

nating as you can get. So don't accuse us of playing God."

1. Langton, J. (1997, Dec. 1). American doctors selling made-to-order embryos. *The Daily Telegraph* (London), p. 6.

To Think About

There are few legal rules or ethical guidelines for the conduct of fertility clinics. How ethical are embryo supermarkets? Are there ethical issues implicit in giving parents detailed genetic information about their unborn children? To what extent should we be allowed to develop technologies to control conception and birth?

On the Web

An increasing number of clinics buy and sell ova, sperm, and frozen embryos. For example:

http://www.creatfam.com/applicat.htm

The American College of Obstetrics and Gynecology has standardized the terminology used to describe prenatal development by identifying three developmental stages with clear time boundaries. The stage of the **fertilized ovum** or **zygote** (also called the **germinal stage**) begins at fertilization and ends two weeks later, shortly after implantation in the uterus. The **embryo stage** follows and terminates at the end of the eighth week. Finally, the **fetus stage** lasts from the end of the eighth week until the birth of the baby.

Stage of the Fertilized Ovum

Except in cases of in vitro conception, fertilization in the woman usually occurs in the **Fallopian tubes** that link the **ovaries** to the **uterus** (Figure 4.1). It results from the invasion of the tubes by millions of sperm cells, one of which succeeds in penetrating the outer covering of the ovum. Once a single sperm has penetrated the ovum's outer shell, the egg

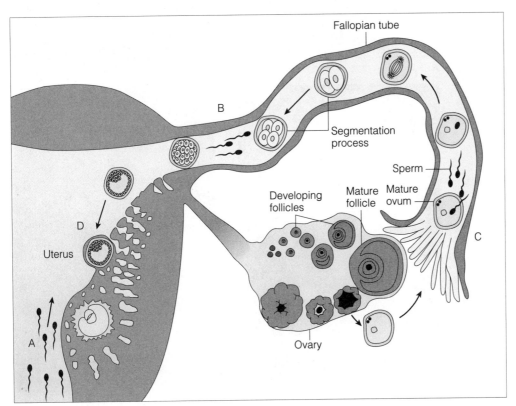

FIGURE 4.1

*Fertilization and implantation. At **A**, millions of sperm cells have entered the vagina and are finding their way into the uterus. At **B**, some of the spermatozoa are moving up the Fallopian tube (there is a similar tube on the other side) toward the ovum. At **C**, fertilization occurs. The fertilized ovum drifts down the tube, dividing and forming new cells as it goes, until it implants itself in the wall of the uterus (**D**) by the seventh or eighth day after fertilization.*

then becomes impenetrable to other sperm. From that moment a human child begins to form, but it will be approximately 266 days before this individual is finally born.

The fertilized ovum (zygote) is then carried toward the uterus by currents in the Fallopian tubes, a process requiring between five and nine days. Cell divisions occur during this time, so the fertilized ovum, which initially consisted of the single cell resulting from the union of sperm and ovum, now contains about 125 cells (Handyside, 1991). Still, it is not much larger at the end of the first week than it was at the time of fertilization, mainly because the cells of which it consists are considerably smaller than they originally were—hardly surprising because the ovum has received no nourishment from any source other than itself.

About one week after fertilization, the ovum is ready to implant itself in the uterine wall. At this stage, many potential pregnancies terminate with implantation failure. For those that continue, the ovum facilitates implantation by secreting certain enzymes and producing tiny, tentaclelike growths (called **villi**) that implant themselves in the lining of the uterus to obtain nutrients from blood vessels. This is the beginning of the **placenta**—the organ that allows nutrients to pass to the fetus and waste materials to be removed while keeping the blood of the mother and the fetus separate. The placenta and the fetus will eventually be connected by the **umbilical cord**, a thick cord about 20 inches (50 cm) long, consisting of two arteries and one large vein. It is attached to the placenta at one end and to what will be the child's

FIGURE 4.2

*Development during the stage of the fertilized ovum (**A**: 4 days after conception); the embryo (**B**: 32 days); and the fetus (**C** and **D**: 8.5 and 15 weeks, respectively).*

A *4 days*

B *32 days*

C *8½ post-ovulatory weeks*

D *15 post-ovulatory weeks*

navel at the other. The umbilical cord contains no nerve cells, so there is no connection between the mother's nervous system and that of the child in utero (in the uterus). Note that the placenta serves as a link between mother and fetus, whereas the umbilical cord links the fetus to the placenta.

The Embryo

The embryo stage, beginning at the end of the second week of pregnancy, follows implantation of the fertilized ovum in the wall of the uterus. The normal course of physiological development in the embryonic and fetal stage is highly predictable and regular (Figure 4.2).

At the beginning of this stage, the embryo is still only a fraction of an inch long and weighs much less than an ounce. Despite the size, not only has there been cell differentiation into future skin cells, nerves, bone, and other body tissue, but also the rudiments of eyes, ears, and nose have begun to appear. In addition, some of the internal organs are beginning to develop so that by the end of the first lunar month, a primitive heart is already beating. By the end of the second lunar month, the embryo is between 1½ and 2 inches (3.8 and 5 cm) long and weighs close to two-thirds of an ounce (19 gm). All the organs are now present, the whole mass has assumed the curled shape characteristic of the fetus, and the embryo is clearly recognizable as human. Arm and limb buds have appeared and begun to grow, resembling short, awkward paddles. External genitalia (sex organs) have also appeared.

The Fetus

By the end of the eighth week of pregnancy, which marks the beginning of the fetal period, the absolute mass of the fetus is still unimpressive. By the end of the third lunar month (ten weeks of pregnancy), it may reach a length of 3 inches (7.5 cm) but will still weigh less than an ounce (25 gm). The head of the fetus is one-third of its entire length; this will have changed to one-fourth by the end of the sixth lunar month and slightly less than that at birth (see Table 4.2 and Figure 4.3).

During the third month of pregnancy, the fetus is sufficiently developed that if it is aborted it will make breathing movements and will give evidence of a primitive **sucking reflex** and of the **Babinski reflex** (the infant's tendency to fan its toes when tickled on the soles of its feet) if stimulated appropriately.

During the fourth lunar month of pregnancy, the fetus grows to a length of 6 inches (15 cm) and weighs approximately 4 ounces (114 g). The bones have begun to form, all

TABLE 4.2

Prenatal Development According to Lunar Months (Weight and Length Approximate)

LUNAR MONTH	WEIGHT	LENGTH	CHARACTERISTICS
1	Negligible	Negligible	Cell differentiation into those that will be bones, nerves, or other cells.
2	2/3 oz. (19 g)	1 1/2–2 in. (3.75–5 cm)	All organs present; leg buds and external genitalia just appearing.
3	7/8 oz. (24.5 g)	3 in. (7.5 cm)	If aborted, will make primitive breathing movements and suck; bones forming, organs differentiated.
4	4 oz. (112 g)	6 in. (15 cm)	
5	11 oz. (308 g)	10 in. (25 cm)	Fetal movement (quickening); lanugo appears.
6	20 oz. (560 g)	12 in. (30 cm)	Heartbeat clearly discernible; eyelids present.
7	2.6 lb. (1.2 kg)	15 in. (37.5 cm)	
8	4 lb. (1.8 kg)	16 in. (40 cm)	All major changes have now occurred; development is largely a matter of increasing weight and length.
9	4.7 lb. (2.1 kg)	17.5 in. (44 cm)	
10	7.5 lb. (3.4 kg)	20 in. (50 cm)	

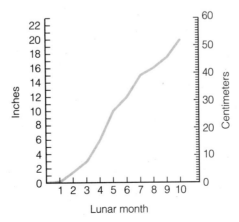

FIGURE 4.3

Approximate weight and length of the fetus at the end of each lunar month of prenatal development.

organs are clearly differentiated, and there may even be evidence of some intrauterine (within the uterus) movement.

By the fifth month, a downy covering (called **lanugo**) begins to grow over most of the fetus's body. This covering is usually shed during the seventh month but is occasionally still present at birth. The fetus weighs approximately 11 ounces (312 g) and may have reached a length of 10 inches (25 cm) by the end of the fifth lunar month.

Toward the end of the sixth month, it is possible to palpate (feel by touch) the baby through the mother's abdomen. The heartbeat, already discernible in the fifth month, is now much clearer. The eyelids have now separated so that the fetus can open and close its eyes. It is approximately a foot (30 cm) long and weighs close to 20 ounces (568 g). If born now in a modern hospital, it might survive with sophisticated care to compensate for the immaturity of its digestive and respiratory systems.

The fetus's growth in size and weight becomes more dramatic in the last few months of the fetal stage. Brain development is also particularly crucial during the last three months of pregnancy, as it will continue to be after birth, especially for the first two years of life. The unborn child's sensitivity to malnutrition is assumed to be related to neurological growth during the late stages of fetal development (Morgane et al., 1993). This sensitivity is sometimes evident in lower developmental scores during infancy and impaired mental functioning among children born to malnourished mothers.

Most of the physical changes that occur after the seventh month are quantitative (Table 4.2). It is now a matter of sheer physical growth: from 15 inches and 2.6 pounds in the seventh month (38 cm; 1,180 g) to 16 inches and 4 pounds in the eighth (41 cm; 1,816 g); from 17.5 inches and 4.7 pounds in the ninth (44 cm; 2,133 g) to 20 inches and 7.5 pounds at the end of the tenth (50 cm; 3,405 g).

Two terms that are sometimes used to describe the general pattern of fetal development are **proximodistal** (meaning, literally, "from near to far") and **cephalocaudal** ("from the head to the tail"). They refer to the fact that among the first aspects of the fetus to develop are the head and internal organs; the last are the limbs and digits. (See Summary Table 4.3.)

DRUGS, CHEMICALS, AND PRENATAL DEVELOPMENT

There are a wide range of influences that can enhance or impede the healthy development of the fetus. Influences that cause malformations and physical defects in the fetus include **teratogens** and **mutagens.** Teratogens affect the embryo or fetus directly and include various maternal illnesses, drugs, chemicals, and minerals. The term derives from *teras,* the Greek word for "monster." Note that the effects of teratogens are not passed on from one generation to another.

In contrast, the effects of mutagens may be transmitted from one generation to another because mutagens cause actual changes in genetic material that can then lead to malformations and defects. Radiation is a well-known mutagen. Thus, deafness caused by a mutated gene (resulting from a mutagen like radiation, for example) may be passed on to offspring; deafness caused by a virus (such as the teratogenic virus *cytomegalovirus*) will not be.

Note that the effects of many teratogens often depend on a variety of factors, both environmental and genetic. That is, the occurrence and the severity of a defect associated with a particular teratogen are often determined by the fetus's genetic background and the timing of the influence, as well as the stresses that might result from the combined presence of other teratogens—not to mention the effects of other external positive influences. Accordingly, the effects of the same teratogen can vary widely from one fetus to another.

Prescription Drugs

Because it is clearly impossible to use human subjects in controlled investigations with chemical substances whose effects may be injurious to the fetus, our information about the effects of drugs on the fetus is often based on studies of animals or on human studies in poorly controlled situations. Generalizing from studies of animals to humans in the case of drugs presents an additional problem, because certain drugs have dramatically different effects on members of different animal species, as well as on children relative to adults (Friedman, 1992). Also, normal adult doses of a drug might well represent huge doses for a fetus weighing only ounces, particularly if the drug crosses the placental barrier easily.

▲ SUMMARY TABLE 4.3
Stages of Gestation
(Prenatal Development)

STAGE	DESCRIPTION
The fertilized ovum	■ Also termed the *germinal stage* or the period of the zygote; begins at fertilization and ends two weeks later, after implantation of the zygote (fertilized egg) in the uterine wall. Still microscopic.
Embryonic stage	■ From end of second to end of eighth week of intrauterine development. During this stage most of the important morphological (pertaining to form) changes occur. Teratogens (influences that cause malformations and defects) are most influential during this period. At the end of this period, the embryo is close to 2 inches (4.5 cm) long and weighs about ⅔ ounce (19 grams).
Period of the fetus	■ From the end of eighth week until birth. Accelerating growth curves toward the end of this period.

FREQUENCY OF DRUG USE

The frequency of drug use by pregnant women and the variety of drugs they consume are uncertain. In a U.S. study of 2,752 mothers of infants without major congenital malformations, 68 percent claimed to have used at least one prescription or nonprescription drug during pregnancy (Rubin, Ferencz, & Loffredo, 1993). In a New Zealand study of 56,037 births between 1982 and 1989, 31 percent of mothers reported using prescription drugs during the first trimester (40 percent used alcohol, and 29 percent smoked cigarettes) (Correy et al., 1992).

SOME TERATOGENIC PRESCRIPTION DRUGS

Among the better-known teratogenic drugs are *thalidomide,* which causes severe physical changes in the embryo; *quinine,* which is associated with congenital deafness; and various *anesthetics* that appear to cross the placental barrier easily and rapidly and cause depression of fetal respiration and decreased responsiveness in the infant. Other apparently teratogenic but less common drugs include *acitetrin,* which is associated with a high risk of miscarriage or fetal malformations, and *tetracycline,* which appears to cause dental staining (Friedman & Polifka, 1996).

It might be reassuring for some to note that a number of widely used sedatives and tranquilizers such as *diazepam* (Valium) and some of the *barbiturates* such as *barbital, phenobarbital,* and *secobarbital* appear to have very small or minimal effect on the developing fetus when used therapeutically. The effects of habitual use and of overdosing is less clear (Friedman & Polifka, 1996).

The prescription drugs mentioned in this section are only a few of the drugs that are known to be harmful to the fetus. There are many others that do not seem to have any immediate negative effects, but whose long-term effects are still unclear. For example, *diethylstilbestrol* (DES) is a drug that was heavily prescribed through the 1940s and 1950s for women who were at risk for spontaneous abortions—and which is still prescribed in some parts of the world (Palmlund et al., 1993). Not until several decades later did medical researchers discover a link between DES use by pregnant women and vaginal cancer among girls subsequently born to these women. Because the effect occurs so long after taking the drug and because it is manifested in only a small percentage of the offspring, it is extremely difficult to detect. For this reason, many medical practitioners discourage the use of any prescription drugs by pregnant women unless absolutely necessary.

OVER-THE-COUNTER MEDICATIONS

Among nonprescription drugs that may also have negative effects on the fetus are aspirin, which may increase the tendency to bleed in both mother and fetus (Stockman, 1990). Although these effects are reportedly unlikely with the mother's occasional use of low doses of aspirin, some evidence suggests that the use of aspirin within one week of delivery may be linked with a higher probability of intracranial hemorrhage in infants, especially those who are premature (Friedman and Polifka, 1996). In addition, a variety of animal studies with rats, monkeys, dogs, cats, and mice have found that aspirin, used in doses comparable to those that might be used when treating rheumatic disease among humans, is associated with a significantly higher probability of fetal malformations as well as subsequent behavioral problems.

Acetaminophen (Anacin 3, Datril, or Tylenol) appears to pose little risk to the unborn fetus in normal therapeutic doses. But in the case of an overdose during pregnancy, the risk of fetal death may be quite high. *Benzocaine* (Orajel or Americaine) poses no known risk to fetal development. The data with respect to a very common antacid and laxative, *magnesium hydroxide* (Milk of Magnesia), are poor in quantity and quality, report Friedman and Polifka (1996), and no animal studies have been reported. It appears that there is no greatly increased risk to the fetus as a result of taking Milk of Magnesia, but there may nevertheless be some minor risk.

There has been some question concerning the effects of megadoses of common vitamins. Evidence suggests that vitamin C (*ascorbic acid*), in usual therapeutic doses, poses little risk to the fetus. Similarly, normal doses of vitamin A (*retinol*) do not appear to have measurable negative effects. However, there is a slight chance that very high doses may increase the risk of anomalies. Vitamin B6 (*pyridoxine*), even in very high doses, is not associated with fetal problems. Finally, evidence suggests that it is unlikely that vitamin D is a teratogen even in very high doses (Friedman & Polifka, 1996).

Although not exactly an over-the-counter drug, the effects of *aspartame,* the increasingly common sugar substitute in diet products (common trade names include Equal and Nutrasweet), may be of interest. It, too, seems unlikely to be a teratogen (Friedman & Polifka, 1996).

IMPORTANCE OF TIMING AND OTHER FACTORS

There are at least four separate factors that determine the potential effect of a drug or chemical on the fetus and that make the task of determining their most likely effects highly complex: the mother's reaction to the drug, drug dosage and frequency of use, interactions with other drugs the mother is taking or might have taken in the past, and the timing of drug use. How these factors interact, and their importance, is often unclear. This is why, for a vast number of substances reviewed in their detailed examination of the effects of drugs on the fetus, Friedman and Polifka (1996) repeatedly include this caution: "A small risk cannot be excluded." In addition, for many drugs, "the quantity and quality of data on which risk estimate is based" are "poor," "very poor," "poor to fair," or just "fair." The data are considered "good" in far fewer than half of all instances.

What does seem clear is that the timing of exposure to possible teratogens is critical. Thus, exposure during the first two weeks after conception may be associated with implantation failure and lead to abortion. In fact, about 30 to 40 percent of all potential pregnancies are lost before they are recognized—that is, in the first two weeks (Simpson, 1991). Exposure during the embryonic stage (weeks two to eight) is generally associated with the most serious structural changes (physical deformities and abnormalities). This is because the embryonic period is marked by the most rapid development of organs. After this stage, the fetus's basic structure has already been formed and is not as vulnerable to external influences (see Figure 4.4).

Chemicals

There are now tens of thousands of chemicals in use in the world, and several thousand new ones are introduced each year. Although the majority of these are "contained" in one way or another—that is, they do not find their way into our air, our water, or our food—and are essentially harmless, others are not so benign. Large numbers of these chemicals are "endocrine-disrupting" and may have subtle, long-term consequences (Colborn, vom Saal, & Soto, 1993). Many tend to accumulate in body fat, and their negative effects can be

transmitted to the fetus either directly or through the mother's milk. Other chemicals have more direct effects, sometimes causing serious fetal malformations or death.

One example of a highly toxic chemical is **methylmercury**, whose effects received worldwide attention following the births of a large number of severely deformed and retarded infants in Minimata Bay, Japan. The deformities were traced to the presence of high levels of mercury in the fish that inhabitants of this community consumed in great quantities; the mercury was, in this case, an industrial waste. The effects of mercury are now known as **Minimata disease.**

Other teratogenic chemicals whose effects are well-known are the **polychlorinated biphenyls** (PCBs) and related chemicals such as *dioxin,* often used in manufacturing herbicides or insecticides. These chemicals appear to be associated with a higher incidence of miscarriage and with physical deformities (Jacobson & Jacobson, 1990). For example, following the leak of *methyl isocyanate* (used to manufacture pesticides) in Bhopal, India, the rate of spontaneous abortions quadrupled (Bajaj et al., 1993).

In addition to the chemicals known to be harmful to the fetus, there are many toxic chemicals whose effects on fetal

FIGURE 4.4

The most serious structural defects in prenatal development are most likely to occur in the first eight weeks, although teratogens can have serious consequences throughout gestation.

development are unknown, although we know how they affect children and adults. Lead is one example. It is present in some fuel emissions, in some paints, in certain metal products, and elsewhere. It accumulates slowly in the body, and when it reaches sufficiently high concentrations, it can lead to serious physical and mental problems in children and adults (Weisskopf, 1987).

On a more reassuring note, although our highly industrialized environments are loaded with synthetic substances and potentially harmful chemicals, we have perhaps overemphasized their danger, says Tierney (1988). Fortunately, only relatively rarely are we exposed to them in sufficient doses or over a long enough period that they affect our health measurably—or become teratogens for the unborn.

Nicotine

The harmful effects of smoking on the smoker, and the effects of "sidestream" smoke on the nonsmoker, have been well documented. Some of smoking's effects on the fetus also seem clear. Among its most consistent effects is a higher

The effects of smoking and alcohol consumption are well-known for adult humans, but among the risks these behaviors pose to human fetuses are low birth weight, miscarriage and fetal death, learning impairment, attention deficits, behavior problems, and impaired language development.

probability of placental problems, in which the placenta becomes detached from the uterine wall, often leading to fetal death or stillbirth, as well as significantly lower birthweight, which, in turn, is associated with a higher probability of subsequent complications. Nicotine use is linked with a higher risk of miscarriage and fetal death, and it is related to a higher incidence of early childhood respiratory infections and diseases (Newman & Buka, 1991).

Caffeine

The effects of caffeine on the human fetus do not appear to be very dramatic. Risk of malformations is rated as "none"; risk of spontaneous abortion is rated as "none to minimal" (Friedman & Polifka, 1996). Note that these risks apply to the ingestion of a "normal" amount of caffeine in drinks such as coffee, tea, or colas. The potential effects of very high doses are unclear. Some studies report cardiac arrhythmias among newborns whose mothers drank very large amounts of caffeinated beverages (Hadeed & Siegel, 1993). And caffeine given to pregnant rats has been associated with birth defects in their offspring—but only in doses far larger than those ordinarily consumed by humans (Jacobson et al., 1985). Following a review of related research, Nehlig and Debry (1994) conclude that caffeine is not a human teratogen, although very high consumption might be toxic for the fetus. In addition, caffeine does not appear to change the composition of the mother's milk and may, in fact, serve to stimulate its production.

Alcohol Consumption and Fetal Alcohol Syndrome (FAS)

Alcohol consumption by pregnant women may be associated with premature birth and with various defects in their offspring. The severity of the defects appears to be directly related to the amount of alcohol ingested by the mother.

The most serious collection of alcohol-related effects in the newborn is labeled **fetal alcohol syndrome (FAS)**; less serious effects are termed *fetal alcohol effects*. The three major features of extreme FAS are facial malformations (low forehead, widely spaced eyes, a short nose and long upper lip, and absence of a marked infranasal depression), retarded physical growth, and central nervous system problems sometimes manifested in mental retardation. Less severe fetal alcohol effects might include learning impairment, attention deficits, behavior problems, and impaired language development (Newman & Buka, 1991). Full FAS occurs in about 6 percent of women who are heavy drinkers, with heavy drinking defined as more than six drinks, glasses of wine, or bottles of beer per day. Less extreme symptoms of FAS would occur in a much higher percentage of children born to mothers who are heavy drinkers. And the effects of a single alcoholic binge at a critical time in pregnancy, note Friedman and Polifka (1996), may cause damage to the fetus.

The current consensus is that even in small amounts, alcohol may be harmful to the fetus, although it may not necessarily lead to fetal alcohol syndrome. For example, one study compared the effects of heavy drinking (four or more drinks a day) with the effects of more moderate drinking (two to four drinks a day) and with those of lighter drinking (fewer than two drinks a day) (Streissguth et al., 1980). Some of the symptoms associated with FAS were found in 19 percent of the children born to mothers in the first group, 11 percent of those in the second, and only 2 percent of those in the third.

The evidence is not all in, and the conclusions are still tentative. However, in summarizing the effects of alcohol on the developing fetus, Brendt and Beckman (1990) conclude that consuming six drinks or more of alcohol per day constitutes a high risk; fewer than two drinks per day is not likely to lead to fetal alcohol syndrome, but may nevertheless be associated with some symptoms such as growth retardation (Euromac Project Group, 1992). And, as Newman and Buka (1991) point out, binge drinking may be especially harmful to the fetus in the early stages of pregnancy. Not surprisingly, an increasing number of medical practitioners recommend that pregnant women refrain from any alcohol use. In Friedman and Polifka's words, "...no safe amount of alcohol drinking during pregnancy has been determined" (1996, p. 15).

Illegal Drugs

As we saw, various prescription and nonprescription drugs used for medicinal purposes can harm the developing fetus; so can legal recreational drugs such as alcohol, nicotine, and caffeine. In addition, many illicit recreational drugs can also affect the fetus adversely.

■ NARCOTICS

Narcotics such as heroin and morphine are not considered to be teratogens. That is, they do not appear to cause malformations or defects in the fetus. However, babies born to narcotics addicts are themselves addicted. These infants suffer a clearly recognizable withdrawal (labeled the **neonatal abstinence syndrome**). Its symptoms may include tremors, restlessness, hyperactive reflexes, high-pitched cries, vomiting, fevers, sweating, rapid respiration, seizures, and sometimes death (Fundaro et al., 1994). Often, these symptoms don't reach a peak until the infant is three or four days old, and may persist for up to six months. Some physicians recommend *methadone* maintenance in low doses for the mother during the later stages of pregnancy and gradual weaning of the infant from methadone after birth. A study involving 223 infants born to drug-addicted mothers, many of whom were on methadone, found a close relationship between the magnitude of the mother's doses and the severity of the infant's abstinence syndrome (Fundaro et al., 1994).

■ MARIJUANA

There is some uncertainty about the effects of marijuana on infants (Food and Nutrition Board, 1990). Some studies suggest that the gestational period is somewhat shorter for heavy marijuana users (Zuckerman & Bresnahan, 1991); other studies report no discernible effects (Fried, 1993). Consequently, Friedman and Polifka (1996) classify marijuana as one of those drugs whose use is unlikely to lead to teratogenic effects on the fetus. However, sensitive tests of cognitive functioning given to children of heavy marijuana users at age six suggest the possibility that there may be some slight, long-term negative effect (Fried, 1996).

■ COCAINE

Marijuana was the drug of the sixties, claim Peters and Theorell (1991), heroin was the drug of the seventies, and cocaine (and "crack"*) became the drug of the eighties and nineties. Cocaine addiction is reportedly about five times more common than heroin addiction in the United States. Some reports claim it has reached epidemic proportions. However, estimates of illegal drug use are seldom very reliable.

Once thought to be relatively harmless, cocaine is now considered not only highly addictive, but also potentially very harmful to the unborn. Like most mood-altering drugs, it crosses the placental barrier easily. And because it is fat-soluble, it remains in the placenta as well as in amniotic fluid where, notes Mullin (1992), the fetus ingests it over and over again. A dose of cocaine lasts about forty-eight hours in the adult; in the fetus it may last four or five days.

We should note at the outset that the information we have concerning the effects of cocaine, as well as that of other illegal drugs, may not be entirely reliable. As Lester and associates (1996) point out, information about the frequency of drug use, its timing, dosages and their purity, and the interaction of various drugs is often unreliable or unavailable. In addition, there may be a systematic bias toward publishing studies whose results support the notion that these drugs do have harmful effects.

In fact, much of the published research indicates that cocaine use is associated with risk of serious pregnancy complications and **congenital** (present at birth) problems. For example, infants born to cocaine and crack users manifest more startle reactions and more tremors than children of nonusers. They are also more likely to manifest disturbances in sleep patterns, feeding difficulties, diarrhea, fever, and increased irritability. On average, they are smaller and may show evidence of growth retardation—for example, delayed age of standing, pulling up to a sitting position, and developing visual and auditory orientation (Mullin, 1992). And not only are they more likely to be stillborn or to abort spontaneously (Rosenak et al., 1990), but they are also more likely to die of **sudden infant death syndrome** (SIDS, described in the next chapter) (Kandall et al., 1993). There is evidence, too, that children of cocaine-addicted mothers are more likely to suffer emotional and physical abuse, and the disadvantages of more disorganized and chaotic child-rearing environments (Hawley et al., 1995).

---

*Crack is easily manufactured from cocaine, is less expensive, and has far more intense and immediate effects than cocaine used more conventionally (see Chapter 12 for more information).

ngel Aldus (not her real name) was born to a cocaine-addicted mother in a county hospital. While in the early stages of labor, her mother was caught in a hospital washroom trying to inject cocaine. In another similar case in Minneapolis, a mother was charged and sentenced to more than two years in jail. "Your crime," said the judge, "is roughly akin to distributing cocaine in the schoolyard" (Logli, 1994, p. 129).

Angel's mother wasn't charged. In fact, her mother left the hospital the moment she felt strong enough, and Angel never saw her again. Angel became one of 22,000 infants abandoned in her hospital crib in 1991—one of 22,000 so-called *boarder babies*. Like Angel, most boarder babies (about 75 percent) have been exposed to drugs prenatally.

Angel was subsequently adopted. But the damage had already been done. At age four, she suffers from a variety of physical problems, including cerebral palsy and bone deformities. As her adoptive mother writes, "My heart breaks for my little girl, who though physically disabled, is intellectually intact as she watches her siblings run and play. She, even at this young age, wonders why she cannot" (quoted in Logli, 1994, p. 127).

To Think About

The economic and social costs of substance abuse by pregnant women are enormous. For example, fetal alcohol syndrome is the leading known cause of mental retardation in North America. Estimates are that each year in the United States, more than 40,000 children are born with defects linked to their mothers' use of alcohol. These defects are permanent.

The conditions described in the preceding paragraph are only a few of the many different negative consequences of maternal cocaine use that have been reported in hundreds of different studies. Some researchers suggest that it might be useful to label these consequences the *fetal cocaine syndrome,* as has been done for alcohol. The most common characteristics of this syndrome include growth retardation, low birthweight, prematurity, irritability, and physical features such as small toenails, a short nose, and **microcephaly** (small head). However, Friedman and Polifka (1996) note that the meaning of this syndrome is still not clear.

There are now close to 1 million children who have been born to crack-addicted mothers, claims Hutchinson (1991). Because crack has been available since 1985, many of these children are now in school. The most seriously affected of them are, in Hutchinson's words, "a new breed, unlike other children with histories of drug exposure. They are in constant motion, disorganized, and very sensitive to stimuli. Crawling, standing, and walking take longer to develop. They are irritable and hard to please. It is hard for them to make friends. They respond less to the environment" (p. 31). (See "Across Cultures: Angel Aldus, Boarder Baby" and Summary Table 4.4.)

MATERNAL CHARACTERISTICS AND PRENATAL DEVELOPMENT

Maternal characteristics such as age and health can have direct implications for the well-being of the fetus. And characteristics such as social class might sometimes have important indirect effects.

Maternal Health

A wide range of diseases and infections are known to affect the fetus. The best known is probably rubella (German measles); others are syphilis, gonorrhea, and poliomyelitis, each of which can cause mental deficiency, blindness, deafness, or miscarriage. Cretinism (subnormal mental development, undeveloped bones, a protruding abdomen, and rough, coarse skin) may be related to a thyroid malfunction in the mother or to an iodine deficiency in her diet. If the deficiency is not too extreme, it can sometimes be alleviated in the child

SUMMARY TABLE 4.4

Drugs and Chemicals That Might Affect Prenatal Development

Note that for any given individual, the occurrence and the severity of an effect may be influenced by (1) the fetus's genetic background; (2) the timing of the influence (often more serious during the embryonic period—weeks two to eight); (3) the interaction of more than one influencing factor; and (4) the mitigating effects of other positive influences.

INFLUENCE	SOME POSSIBLE EFFECTS
Prescription drugs	
thalidomide	severe morphological changes in the embryo; limb reduction.
quinine	congenital deafness.
diazepam (Valium)	little effect in therapeutic doses.
barbiturates	little effect in therapeutic doses.
diethylstilbestrol (DES)	higher risk of cervical cancer.
Over-the-counter drugs	
aspirin	little risk at normal doses; risk of hemorrhaging with high doses.
acetaminophen (Tylenol)	little risk at normal doses; risk of fetal death with overdosing.
benzocaine (Orajel)	no known negative effects.
Milk of Magnesia	no known negative effects.
Vitamins	little apparent risk in normal doses; may pose some risk with massive doses.
Aspartame	unlikely to be a teratogen.
Chemicals	
methylmercury	Minimata disease; mental retardation; blindness; death.
PCBs	higher incidence of miscarriage and deformities; coffee-colored skin pigmentation.
lead	serious physical and mental problems in children and adults.
Nicotine	occasional placental problems; lower birth weight; prematurity; higher risk of fetal death.
Caffeine	little effect in normal doses; excessive consumption may be more toxic.
Alcohol	range of effects ranging from mild to extreme fetal alcohol syndrome; growth retardation; mental retardation.
Illegal Drugs	
narcotics	neonatal abstinence syndrome (withdrawal symptoms).
marijuana	unlikely to be teratogenic, except in massive doses.
cocaine, crack	variety of possible effects, including neurological problems, growth retardation, increased susceptibility to SIDS, increased likelihood of fetal death.

through continuous medication after birth. And AIDS is a more recent, and lethal, threat to the fetus.

■ DIABETES

Diabetes is a maternal condition that can have serious consequences for the fetus. Before the discovery of insulin, fetal death and maternal death were very high. Now, however, mortality rates among diabetic mothers are about the same as those among nonpregnant diabetic women. Management involves careful monitoring of mother and fetus to assess and control sugar levels (simple, self-monitoring procedures are available for in-home use) (Sparks, Jovanovic-Peterson, & Peterson, 1993). With timely diagnosis and proper medical management, fetal deaths are generally below 5 percent (Coustan, 1990). However, there is still a two to four times higher rate of birth defects among these infants. The most common defects include limb, heart, and neural tube defects (Friedman & McGillivray, 1992). Most of these birth defects result from influences that occur early in pregnancy, hence the importance of careful monitoring from the outset.

■ HERPES

Herpes simplex 2 (vaginal and genital herpes) is the most common of all sexually transmitted diseases; it can have serious effects on the fetus, particularly if the mother's infection is active at the time of delivery. The probability of the infant's contracting the virus during birth is extremely high—40 to 60 percent (Eden et al., 1990). Because the newborn does not possess many of the immunities that are common among older children and adults, the herpes virus may attack the infant's internal organs, leading to visual or nervous system problems or death in as many as two-thirds of all cases (Berland, 1991; Eden et al., 1990). As a result, infants born to mothers infected with the herpes virus are often delivered through cesarean section to prevent infection from occurring.

Another form of herpes virus, **cytomegalovirus**, affects the salivary glands and can also be passed on to the fetus during birth. It is one of the main infectious causes of mental retardation, and also an important cause of deafness.

■ ACQUIRED IMMUNITY DEFICIENCY SYNDROME

Acquired immunity deficiency syndrome (AIDS) is another sexually transmitted disease that is of considerable current concern. First reported in the United States in 1981, the disease remains incurable and fatal. In 1994 there were more than 78,000 new cases of AIDS reported in the United States (U.S. Bureau of the Census, 1996). Estimates in 1996 were that, worldwide, more than 20 million people were infected and 4.5 million had developed AIDS. In the United States, almost 1 million people have been infected and more than 300,000 have died (Painter, 1997a). The prognosis is that most of those infected will eventually die from resulting complications. However, the death rate has declined significantly beginning in 1996, largely because of powerful new drugs that have prolonged the lives of those infected (Manning, 1997). In addition, transmission of HIV from mother

AIDS Cases

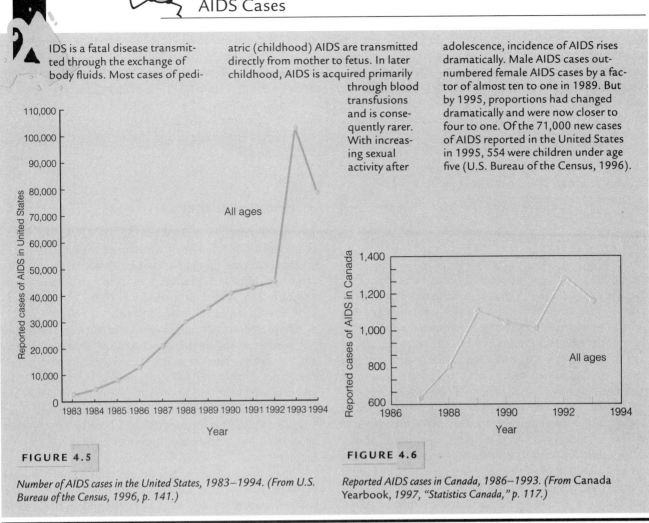

IDS is a fatal disease transmitted through the exchange of body fluids. Most cases of pediatric (childhood) AIDS are transmitted directly from mother to fetus. In later childhood, AIDS is acquired primarily through blood transfusions and is consequently rarer. With increasing sexual activity after adolescence, incidence of AIDS rises dramatically. Male AIDS cases outnumbered female AIDS cases by a factor of almost ten to one in 1989. But by 1995, proportions had changed dramatically and were now closer to four to one. Of the 71,000 new cases of AIDS reported in the United States in 1995, 554 were children under age five (U.S. Bureau of the Census, 1996).

FIGURE 4.5

Number of AIDS cases in the United States, 1983–1994. (From U.S. Bureau of the Census, 1996, p. 141.)

FIGURE 4.6

Reported AIDS cases in Canada, 1986–1993. (From Canada Yearbook, 1997, "Statistics Canada," p. 117.)

---

to newborn infant has also declined because of these same drugs (Painter, 1997b).

AIDS is transmitted through the exchange of body fluids, primarily through blood–blood exchange or through semen–blood exchange. Accordingly, transmission occurs mainly through anal intercourse (because of the thinness of rectal tissues that frequently tear during intercourse), through blood transfusions involving infected blood, and through the communal use of hypodermic syringes. Not surprisingly, AIDS is most common among homosexual males and among intravenous drug users (see Chapter 12 for more information).

Most infants and children with AIDS acquired it directly from their mothers through blood exchange in the uterus or during birth. Until recently, the risk of transmission from infected mother to fetus ranged from 35 percent to 60 percent (Anderson, 1996). With the increasing use of AZT, however, transmission rates have been cut by about two-thirds (Painter, 1997b). Initially, prognosis for an infected newborn was poor, but with the combined use of AZT and antibiotics beginning soon after birth, about one-third of infected

children are surviving eight to ten years or even longer (Hutton, 1996).

Clearly, high-risk women (current or past intravenous drug users or those whose sexual partner[s] include bisexual males and/or men who have been or are intravenous drug users) should be tested for the AIDS antibody before considering pregnancy. (See "At a Glance: AIDS Cases" and Figures 4.5 and 4.6.)

Maternal Emotions and Stress

A once-common folk belief was that the mother's emotional states could be communicated directly to the child. If the pregnant woman worried too much, her child would be born with a frown; if she had a particularly traumatic experience, it would mark the infant, perhaps for life; if she was frightened by a rabbit, the result might be a child with a harelip.

Most of these beliefs about pregnancy are simply tales. Because there is no direct link between the mother's nervous system and that of the fetus, there is little possibility that the mother's emotional state or disorder could be communicated directly to the unborn child. However, because of the close relationship between the mother and the fetus, a number of investigators have pursued the idea that stimuli affecting her will also have some effect on the child, however indirect. One theory is that an anxious mother's chemical balance affects the child physiologically and therefore, indirectly, psychologically. However, given the fact that it is extremely difficult to measure emotional states accurately in both infant and mother, or to control other possible factors that might be associated with stress (such as poverty, medical problems, or inadequate diet), conclusive statements about the influence of maternal emotional state on the unborn are not warranted.

Older Mothers

The mother's age can also be related to the well-being of the fetus. We know, as was pointed out in Chapter 3, that the incidence of Trisomy 21 (Down syndrome) is about forty times higher for women over forty than for women aged twenty or twenty-one. Fragile X syndrome is also more common with increasing maternal age, as are Klinefelter's syndrome and Trisomy 18 (associated with neural tube defects, congenital heart disease, growth retardation, and other problems).

However, given the availability of procedures (such as chorion biopsy or amniocentesis) that make it possible to determine the presence of a number of chromosomal abnormalities and other defects or diseases prenatally, increasing numbers of women, and men, are making the decision to have a family later. The greatest increase in fertility rates in recent years has been among women in their early thirties. About 10 percent of all current births occur to women over the age

of thirty-five, compared with only 6 percent in 1970 (U.S. Bureau of the Census, 1996).

In spite of the association between the mother's age and some chromosomal abnormalities, modern health care makes it possible for many women to deliver healthy, full-term babies at ages that would have entailed much higher risk a few decades ago. In fact, when Spellacy, Miller, and Winegar (1986) compared outcomes for 511 pregnancies of women over 40 with more than 26,000 pregnancies of women between 20 and 30, they found that age posed little risk when factors such as cigarette smoking and maternal weight were taken into account.

Teenage Mothers

Births to teenage girls remain very high relative to the rest of the population—in spite of widespread sex education and sexual abstinence programs (Males, 1993b). In fact, in 1993 more than 12 percent of all births were to girls aged fifteen to nineteen (U.S. Bureau of the Census, 1996). About 30 percent of these were to unmarried teenage parents.

Children born to younger teenage mothers are often at a physical, emotional, and intellectual disadvantage relative to children born to older mothers. There are more miscarriages, premature births, and stillbirths among teenage mothers, and surviving infants are more often the targets of abuse and neglect. In one representative study, for example, Stier and colleagues (1993) compared children born to 219 mothers aged 18 or less with another group of 219 children whose mothers were 19 or more. There were about twice as many instances of physical abuse among children of younger mothers (12.8 percent of all children) and 50 percent more cases of retarded growth. In addition, about four times more of these children experienced changes in primary caregiver

Infants in this high school infant center are among the approximately half-million children born to U.S. teenagers each year. Teenage mothers, half of whom are unmarried, account for 8 percent of all births in the country. When they receive the same medical attention and social support as older women, their children can fare as well.

early in their lives—sometimes because of placement in foster care, sometimes because the mother left home.

As Buchholz and Korn-Bursztyn (1993) point out, however, much of this research fails to take into account the social circumstances of teenage parenthood—the poverty and the lack of social, educational, and medical assistance. It is not the age of the teenage parent that is the important factor as much as the greater financial, social, and emotional stressors she might face. All other things being equal, unless she is very young (below age fifteen), if a teenage mother and her infant receive the same medical attention and social support as an older mother, the health and developmental status of her infant will be normal. Unfortunately, however, all other things are not often equal for teenage mothers. (See Chapter 12 for a more detailed discussion of teenage pregnancy.)

Maternal Nutrition

Nutrition, claim Morgane and colleagues (1993), is the single most important external influence on the fetus and neonate.

EFFECTS OF SERIOUS MALNUTRITION

Nutrition's importance is underlined by the consequences of serious malnutrition such as occurred during the German siege of Leningrad in World War II. During this time, many Russians starved to death in bitterly cold, unheated homes—and birthrates dropped to about 13 percent of what they had previously been (Shanklin & Hoden, 1979). In addition to this dramatic decline in birthrates, there were also great increases in **amenorrhea** (cessation of menstruation, which, incidentally, is not uncommon among anorexic women), low levels of fertility, and an increase in miscarriages.

EFFECTS OF LESS SERIOUS MALNUTRITION

Investigating the effects of malnutrition is difficult because investigators can't always separate these effects from the effects of other factors that often accompany malnutrition (poor sanitation, poor medical care, drug use, and so on). In addition, malnutrition is seldom limited just to the period of prenatal development but usually continues into infancy and even childhood.

Studies with both animals and humans leave no doubt that malnutrition, especially protein deprivation, has negative effects on the developing brain. Thus, Rizzo and his associates (1997) found a significant positive correlation between a variety of measures of children's intellectual performance at the ages of seven and eleven, and measures of the extent to which their mothers had provided these children with nutrients during fetal development. The mothers, 139 of them in this study, were diabetic and had therefore been closely monitored during pregnancy.

The effects of nutrition, note Morgane and associates (1993), depend largely on the type and severity of the deprivation as well as its timing. And although some of the effects of malnutrition are reversible given adequate nourishment and stimulation after birth, long-term intellectual deficits may result from malnutrition that begins before birth and continues for some time afterward.

NUTRITIONAL REQUIREMENTS DURING PREGNANCY

During pregnancy, the mother's energy requirements change so that she now requires somewhere between 10 and 15 percent more calories. Accompanying metabolic changes include an increased synthesis of protein, which is important for the formation of the placenta and enlargement of the uterus; a reduction in carbohydrate consumption, the effect of which is to provide sufficient glucose for the fetus; and increased storage of fat to satisfy the mother's energy requirements (Chez & Chervenak, 1990).

Not only must the pregnant woman increase her protein intake, but there is also an increased need for important minerals (for example, calcium, magnesium, iron, and zinc) and vitamins (mainly B6, D, and E). Recommended dietary allowances for pregnant women range from 25 to 50 percent above those for nonpregnant women (*Recommended dietary allowances*, 1980).

Research indicates that the average intake of these nutrients is often less than what is recommended for American women (Food and Nutrition Board, 1990). Hence, current medical advice emphasizes that what the woman eats is more important than how much. As noted, with respect to brain growth, protein appears to be among the most important ingredients of a good diet.

OPTIMAL WEIGHT GAIN

Current medical advice contradicts the long-held belief that women should be careful to minimize weight gain during pregnancy. Infant mortality is often lower in countries where pregnant women gain significantly more weight than do pregnant women in the United States or Canada. Maternal weight gain leads to higher fetal weight and reduces the risk of illness and infection. Accordingly, doctors who once cautioned women to limit their weight gain to about 10 pounds now suggest that the optimal weight gain for a woman who begins pregnancy at an average weight is somewhere between 25 and 35 pounds (11.5 and 16 kg) (Chez & Chervenak, 1990); it is even higher for women who are initially underweight. For women who are initially overweight, recommended gains are correspondingly lower (15–25 lb.; 7–11.5 kg) (Food and Nutrition Board, 1992). Total recommended weight gain for women carrying twins is 35 to 45 pounds (16–20.5 kg).

Unfortunately, this medical advice is most likely relevant to those least likely to be exposed to it and to those least able to take advantage of it. Malnutrition and starvation are seldom a deliberate choice.

Rh(D) Immunization

There is a particular protein in Rhesus monkeys that is often, but not always, present in human blood. Because this protein was first discovered in the Rhesus monkey, it is called the **Rh factor** (Rh for Rhesus). Individuals who have this factor are *Rh-positive;* those who don't are *Rh-negative.*

A specific component of the Rh blood group, labeled "D," is especially important for the pregnant mother and her fetus. Introduction of Rh(D)-positive blood into an individual who is Rh-negative leads to the formation of antibodies to counteract the D factor—a process termed *immunization* (Bowman, 1990). If these antibodies are then introduced into an individual with Rh(D)-positive blood, they attack that person's blood cells, causing a depletion of oxygen and, in the absence of medical intervention, death.

Unfortunately, this situation can occur in the fetus (termed **fetal erythroblastosis**) when the fetus has Rh(D)-positive blood and the mother is Rh-negative. Because the Rh factor is a dominant genetic trait, this situation will occur only when the father is Rh(D)-positive (and the mother Rh-negative). If blood from the fetus gets into the mother's bloodstream—termed **transplacental hemorrhage**—the mother's blood will begin to produce antibodies. These are usually not produced early enough or in sufficient quantities to affect the first child. Subsequent fetuses may be affected, however.

Transplacental hemorrhage occurs in approximately 50 percent of all pregnant women, either during pregnancy or immediately after birth (Knuppel & Angel, 1990). Hence, the chances of Rh(D) immunization are very high—if, of course, the mother is Rh-negative and the father Rh(D)-positive. At one time, this condition was always fatal. Now, however, it is possible for the physician to monitor antibody levels in the

mother's blood, determining when levels are high enough to endanger the fetus. At this point, there are several alternatives. If the fetus is sufficiently advanced (thirty-two or thirty-three weeks, for example), labor might be induced or a cesarean delivery performed and the infant given a complete blood transfusion immediately (Bowman, 1990). If the fetus is not sufficiently advanced, a blood transfusion may be performed in utero.

PREVENTING Rh(D) IMMUNIZATION

Fortunately, this type of medical intervention is not often necessary due to the development of the drug **Rhogam** (Rh Immune Globulin or RhIG) in 1968. Rhogam is blood that already contains passive antibodies that prevent the formation of additional antibodies.

It has become routine for all physicians to ascertain whether a pregnant woman is Rh-negative and whether she is at risk of immunization. Bowman (1990) suggests that husbands or partners of Rh-negative women should then be screened. If they too are Rh-negative, there is little chance of fetal erythroblastosis. However, because of the possibility of an extramarital conception, mothers who are Rh-negative and their fetuses should be monitored closely throughout pregnancy.

When an expecting mother is at risk of immunization (that is, she is Rh-negative and the father is Rh(D)-positive), Rhogam is sometimes administered during the seventh month of gestation—or within no more than seventy-two hours of delivery, as soon as it has been determined that the fetus is Rh-positive and that the mother is therefore at risk of Rh(D)

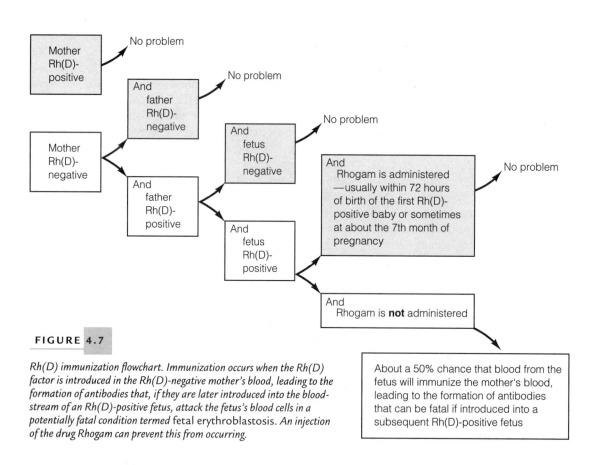

FIGURE 4.7

Rh(D) immunization flowchart. Immunization occurs when the Rh(D) factor is introduced in the Rh(D)-negative mother's blood, leading to the formation of antibodies that, if they are later introduced into the bloodstream of an Rh(D)-positive fetus, attack the fetus's blood cells in a potentially fatal condition termed fetal erythroblastosis. *An injection of the drug Rhogam can prevent this from occurring.*

immunization. Similarly, Rhogam should be administered in the event of the abortion or miscarriage of an Rh(D)-positive fetus if the mother is Rh-negative. The drug needs to be re-administered after the termination of every Rh-positive pregnancy. (See Figure 4.7 for an Rh(D) immunization decision flowchart.) (See also Summary Table 4.5.)

CHILDBIRTH

In the United States, childbirth is something that happens about 4 million times a year although fertility rates (proportion of women having children) have declined (U.S. Bureau of the Census, 1996). In Canada, it happens about one tenth as often (382,870 times in 1995). In China, it is estimated to happen more than 21 million times a year. (See "At a Glance: Births and Deaths in the United States and Canada" and Figures 4.8 and 4.9.)

Surprisingly, what causes the childbirth process to begin remains almost as much of a mystery today as it has always been. Hippocrates, writing more than 400 years before Christ, thought he knew. The child starts the whole process, he informed his readers. When the fetus has grown too big, there simply isn't enough nourishment available, so it becomes agitated—it kicks around and moves its arms, and it ruptures the membranes that hold it in. And then it forces its way out, head first because the head part is heavier than the bottom part (see Liggins, 1988).

Hippocrates was wrong, although there were many who believed his speculation right into the eighteenth century. We now know that fetuses that are dead may go through the process of labor—which would not be possible if they were responsible for initiating it.

There have been many other theories over the years, but, as Liggins (1988) concludes, we still don't have "the final chapter of the 2000-year-old search for the cause of labor" (p. 387). However, even though we don't know its cause, we do understand a lot about the process.

In the world's developed countries, birth is largely a medical procedure, with doctors and other medical personnel working to ensure the safety and comfort of both newborn and mother. They have at their command techniques and procedures to induce labor, to accelerate it, to delay it, even to stop it if necessary. They can administer drugs to lessen the mother's pain, perform blood transfusions on the infant, or deliver through cesarean section.

Elsewhere and in earlier times, birth was a more natural process. It occurred in birthing huts, in fields, in forests, or, perhaps most often, in homes. Birth was sometimes a solitary experience; sometimes there were midwives, healers, or other attendants. In general, it was believed to be far simpler, far shorter, and less painful than birth often is today. Goldsmith (1990) quotes a nineteenth-century traveler who had been trekking with the Guyana women of South America: "When on the march an Indian is taken with labor, she just

SUMMARY TABLE 4.5
Maternal Conditions That Might Affect Prenatal Development

INFLUENCE	SOME POSSIBLE EFFECTS
Maternal health	
Diabetes	■ 2 to 4 times higher rate of fetal defects.
	■ Careful monitoring and control of sugar levels important.
Herpes	■ Highly contagious during birth.
	■ Nervous system problems including mental retardation.
	■ Fetal death.
	■ Cesarean section recommended.
AIDS	■ Mother to infant transmission rate, 10 to 20 percent.
	■ AZT and other drugs have significantly increased survival rate in childhood.
Maternal emotions	■ No direct neurological link between mother and fetus.
	■ Some speculation that maternal chemical changes accompanying intense emotion might affect fetus.
	■ No conclusive statements.
Older mothers	■ Higher risk of some chromosomal problems, including Down syndrome.
	■ Modern health care has reduced age-related risks considerably.
	■ Increasing frequency of childbirth to older mothers.
Teenage mothers	■ About 12 percent of all births.
	■ Social, physical, intellectual disadvantages linked not with the mother's age, but with other conditions such as poverty and associated disadvantages.
Maternal nutrition	■ Serious malnutrition sometimes associated with miscarriages and decline in birthrate.
	■ Less serious malnutrition may lead to negative effects on physical and neurological development.
	■ Increased nutrition requirements for pregnant women.
	■ Optimal weight gain for normal-weight women, 25 to 35 pounds (11.5 to 16 kg).
Rh(D) immunization	■ A possibility only if mother is Rh(D) negative, father Rh(D) positive, and fetus is Rh(D) positive.
	■ If untended, may lead to *fetal erythroblastosis* and fetal death in the absence of a blood transfusion.
	■ Can be prevented through injection of Rhogam within 3 days of birth of first Rh(d) positive child.

Births and Deaths in the United States and Canada

n 1960, when the baby boom was nearing its peak, almost 4.3 million babies were born in the United States. And only 1.7 million people died, leaving a natural population increase of about 2.5 million. Similarly, in Canada an average of 400,000 children were born each year between 1946 and 1966. Now, however, in spite of substantial increases in total population, the number of births have remained fairly constant. This means that the fertility rate (number of births per 1,000 population) has dropped—partly because of more effective contraception and partly because of changed attitudes toward conception and childbearing. Thus, in Canada, the fertility rate has declined from 15.3 per 1,000 in 1975 to 12.9 per 1,000 in 1995. In the United States, it has declined from 18.4 in 1970 to 15.5 in 1993.

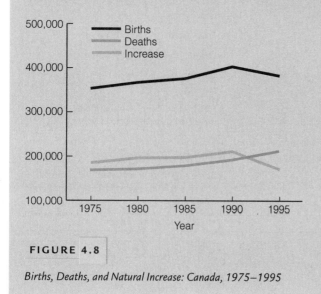

FIGURE 4.8

Births, Deaths, and Natural Increase: Canada, 1975–1995

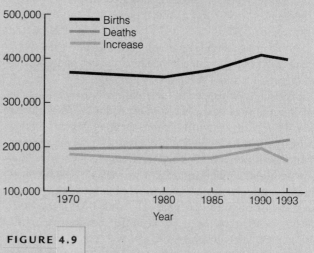

FIGURE 4.9

Births, Deaths, and Natural Increase: United States, 1970–1993

---

steps aside, is delivered, wraps up the baby with the afterbirth and runs in haste after the others" (p. 22).

But we know too that "primitive" birth was (and is) often a tragic experience: Infant mortality was high, and the death of the mother was also not uncommon. A century ago, in most of the world including North America, more than 100 of every 1,000 infants died; that number has now been reduced by almost 90 percent (U.S. Bureau of the Census, 1996; *Canada Yearbook,* 1997). The decline in infant mortality rates is due not only to medical advances, but also to improved sanitation and a consequent reduction in maternal and infant infections. Through the Middle Ages, high risk of death during childbirth (or of subsequent infections) made childbearing a relatively dangerous undertaking for mothers. Even as recently as 1960, of every 100,000 women giving birth in the United States, an average of 37 died (75 percent of these were nonwhites). By 1995, maternal mortality rates had been cut by more than 75 percent (still twice as high for black as for white mothers). During the same period, infant and fetal death rates were more than halved (see "At a Glance: Deaths in Childbirth" and Figures 4.10 and 4.11).

A Clinical View of Labor

Labor is the process whereby the fetus, the placenta, and other membranes are separated from the woman's body and expelled.

The onset of labor is usually gradual and may be described in three stages. That there are exceptions to the normal process has been substantiated by numerous fathers who were caught unawares, taxi drivers who drove too slowly, pilots who did not quite make it, and many others for whom nature would not wait. Although physicians can induce labor, as we saw, the precise natural cause of the beginning of labor remains unknown. Yet labor begins, more often than not, at the prescribed time.

STAGE 1: DILATION

The first stage of labor is the longest, lasting an average of twelve hours but varying greatly in length. Generally, labor is longest and most difficult for the first delivery.

The first stage consists of initially mild contractions spaced quite far apart (like butterflies in my stomach, said one

Each year more than half a million women throughout the world die in childbirth, about 99 percent of them in the developing world. In addition, an estimated 100,000 die of unsafe abortions (Grant, 1993). There are three ways of attacking the problem, says Grant: 1) reduce unwanted pregnancies; 2) prevent complications of pregnancy; and 3) provide medical assistance when there are complications.

FIGURE 4.10

Declining maternal mortality rates from delivery and complications of pregnancy and childbirth, 1960–1990. (Based on U.S. Bureau of the Census, 1996, p. 92.)

FIGURE 4.11

Maternal mortality rates for selected countries per 100,000 live births, 1980–1990. (Based on Bellamy, 1997, pp. 92–93.)

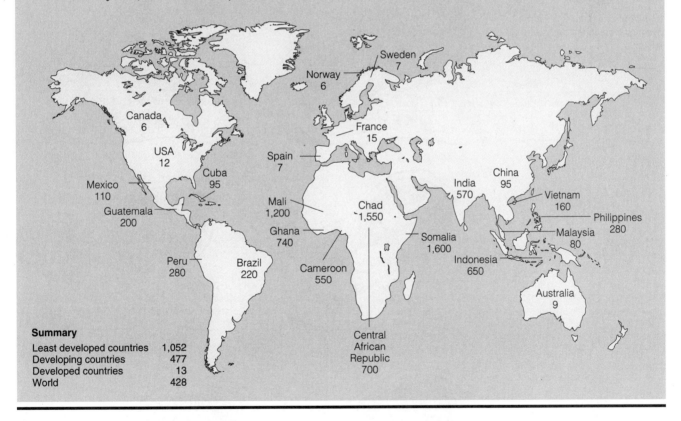

Summary

Least developed countries	1,052
Developing countries	477
Developed countries	13
World	428

woman). Contractions become more painful, more frequent, and longer toward the end of the first stage of birth (like a bear cub in my guts, said another).

In the first stage, the **cervix** (the opening to the uterus) dilates to allow passage of the baby from the uterus, down through the birth canal, and eventually into the world. Contractions are involuntary and exert a downward pressure on the fetus as well as a distending force on the cervix. If the **amniotic sac** (the sac filled with amniotic fluid in which the fetus develops) is still intact, it absorbs much of the pressure in the early stages and transmits some of the force of the contractions to the neck of the cervix. However, if the sac has ruptured or bursts in the early stages of labor, the baby's head will rest directly on the pelvic structure and cervix, serving as a sort of wedge.

■ STAGE 2: DELIVERY

The second stage of birth, delivery, begins when the cervix is sufficiently dilated. It starts with the baby's head emerging (in a normal delivery) at the cervical opening and ends with the birth of the child (Figure 4.12). The second stage usually lasts no more than an hour and often ends in a few minutes. The fetus ordinarily presents itself head first and can usually be born without the intervention of a physician. On occasion, however, complications arise that require some sort of intervention. For example, the head of the fetus may be too large for the opening provided by the mother. In such a case the physician may make a small incision in the vaginal outlet (an **episiotomy**), which is sutured after the baby is born. Complications can also arise from abnormal presentations of the fetus: **breech** (buttocks first), **transverse** (cross-

wise), or a variety of other possible positions. Some of these can be corrected before birth by turning the fetus manually in the uterus **(version)**. Sometimes the fetus is delivered just as it presents itself.*

---

*My grandmother, who was the local midwife in the rural area where I was born (I was born at home—in my parents' bedroom, not on the kitchen table), had a number of strategies to which she would resort when there seemed to be a possibility of complications at birth. These included sending someone to get Mrs. duGrenier, who had a different repertoire of strategies or, more often, praying. Among the Chaga of Tanzania, in East Africa, strategies are somewhat different. When there are complications, everyone assumes it's probably the mother's fault, that she has committed some serious social blunder such as adultery. If that's the case, then it might be sufficient for her to confess her transgression right then and there for the complications to right themselves. Or, as is quite often the case, she has perhaps had a quarrel with her mother- or father-in-law. In that case, she is asked to give up the necklace she's wearing; it is then sent over to the in-laws' house so that they can spit at it, thus removing whatever evil curse is at work (Harkness & Super, 1993). My grandmother would have loved this strategy.

FIGURE 4.12

This cross section shows the normal, headfirst presentation and delivery of a baby.

Toward the end of the delivery stage, the attending physician or nurse severs the neonate's umbilical cord, places silver nitrate or penicillin drops in its eyes to guard against gonococcal infection, and assures that its breathing, muscle tone, coloration, and reflexive activity are normal. Following this, the physician assists in the third and final stage of birth and evaluates the condition of the **neonate**, or newborn, perhaps by means of the *Apgar scale* (discussed later in this chapter).

In the third stage, the **afterbirth**—the placenta and other membranes—is expelled. This process usually takes less than five minutes and seldom more than fifteen. The physician examines the afterbirth carefully to ensure that all of it has been expelled. If it is incomplete, surgical procedures (frequently, dilation and curettage, or D & C—a scraping of the uterus) may be employed to remove remaining portions. At the end of the third stage of labor, the uterus should contract and remain contracted. It is sometimes necessary to massage the abdominal area or administer drugs to stimulate contraction and to guard against the danger of postpartum (afterbirth) hemorrhage.

Cesarean Delivery

In an increasing number of instances, medical intervention bypasses these three stages of birth through a **cesarean delivery**—used in almost one-quarter of all births in the United States (U.S. Bureau of the Census, 1996). (See "At a Glance: U.S. Cesarean Deliveries" and Figures 4.13 and 4.14.) In such cases, birth is accomplished by making an incision in the mother's abdomen and uterus and removing the baby. Cesareans are most often indicated when the mother's labor fails to progress, when previous cesareans have been performed, when the fetus is in a breech presentation, or when the physician detects signs of fetal distress. **Epidural analgesia**, an injection of anesthetic frequently used to relieve childbirth pain, appears to increase the risk of insufficient cervical dilation leading to a cesarean delivery (Thorp et al., 1994).

Cesarean deliveries have clearly saved the lives of many mothers and infants and alleviated much pain and suffering, but the rapid increase in the proportion of cesarean births relative to nonsurgical births is a source of some concern. Although much of this increase clearly results from dramatic improvements in the physician's ability to monitor the fetus prior to birth and during labor, and is associated with higher fetal survival (Iffy et al., 1994), critics suggest that not all cesarean deliveries are necessary. Sperling and colleagues (1994) looked at reasons for cesarean births for all 1989 births in two Danish counties with very different rates of cesarean sections (8.3 percent and 15.2 percent). Their conclusion was that the greater use of cesarean deliveries in the one county could not be accounted for by differences in any of the conditions that ordinarily lead to a decision to perform a cesarean. Deciding factors seemed to be simply differences in obstetric practice as well as differences in maternal expectations and demands.

Lieberman (1987) reports that a number of hospitals have succeeded in dramatically reducing rates of cesarean deliveries without any increase in fetal or maternal problems. This is accomplished largely by reviewing the need for a cesarean delivery in cases where they might simply have been done routinely, as sometimes happens for breech births, twins, or patients who have had previous cesareans.

In North America, childbirth is increasingly occurring in more homelike environments, often with spouse, parents, and others present. And what used to be exclusively medical procedures—like cutting the umbilical cord on this twin—can sometimes be done even by the father.

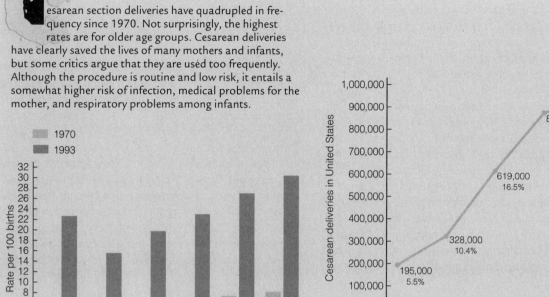

Cesarean section deliveries have quadrupled in frequency since 1970. Not surprisingly, the highest rates are for older age groups. Cesarean deliveries have clearly saved the lives of many mothers and infants, but some critics argue that they are used too frequently. Although the procedure is routine and low risk, it entails a somewhat higher risk of infection, medical problems for the mother, and respiratory problems among infants.

FIGURE 4.13

Changes in rate of cesareans by age, 1970–1993 (per 100 births). (From U.S. Bureau of the Census, 1996, p. 80.)

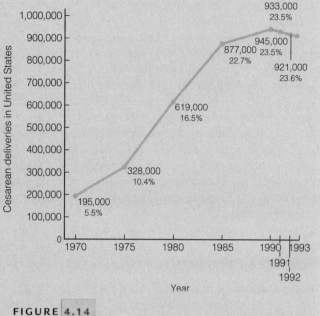

FIGURE 4.14

Cesarean deliveries in the United States, 1970–1993. (Per 100 births.) (Based on U.S. Bureau of the Census, 1994, p. 79, and 1996, p. 80.)

Classifications of Birth

The physical status of the child has traditionally been classified according to the length of time spent in gestation and by weight. A fetus born before the 20th week and weighing less than 500 grams (about 1 pound) is termed a **spontaneous abortion** (or sometimes simply an *abortion* or a *miscarriage*). A fetus delivered between the 20th and 28th week and weighing between 500 and 999 grams (between 1 and 2 pounds) is an **immature birth.** At one time, immature births invariably died; the majority still do, most of them from respiratory failure. But with modern medical procedures, an increasing number survive, some born as much as four months prematurely and weighing under 750 grams (1½ pounds).

The birth of a baby between the 29th and the 36th weeks is called a **premature birth,** provided the child weighs between 1,000 and 2,499 grams (between 2 and 5½ pounds). Complications are more common if the child weighs less than 1,500 grams. A few decades ago, only 20 percent of premature infants in the 1,000 to 1,500-gram range (2 to 5½ pounds) survived. Now between 90 and 95 percent survive.

A **mature birth** occurs between the 37th and the 42nd week and results in an infant weighing over 2,500 grams (5½ pounds). A late delivery is called a **postmature birth.**

Small-for-Gestational Age Infants

All newborns, regardless of whether they are premature, are also classified as **small-for-gestational age (SGA)** when they weigh less than 90 percent of newborns of the same gestational age, as **large-for-gestational age (LGA)** when they weigh above the 90th percentile (that is, in the top 10 percent), or as **average-for-gestational age (AGA)** (Table 4.6).

From a medical point of view, it's important to distinguish between prematurity and being small-for-gestational age (SGA) because the implications of being SGA may be more serious than the implications of being premature but average-for-gestational age (AGA). The premature but average-for-gestational age infant has been developing at a normal rate and, unless very premature, may suffer no negative consequences. However, the small-for-gestational age infant, regardless of gestational age, has been developing less rapidly than

TABLE 4.6

Physical Status of Child at Birth

CLASSIFICATION BY GESTATION	TIME	AVERAGE WEIGHT
Abortion	Before 20th week	Less than 500 g (1 lb.)
Immature birth	20th–28th week	500–999 g (1–2 lb.)
Premature birth	29th–36th week	1,000–2,499 g (2–5½ lb.)
Mature birth	37th–42nd week	Over 2,500 g (5½ lb.)
Postmature birth	After 42 weeks	

CLASSIFICATION BY WEIGHT AND GESTATION	
SGA (small-for-gestational age)	10 percent less than average for infants of same gestational age
AGA (average-for-gestational age)	Within 10 percent of average weight for gestational age
LGA (large-for-gestational age)	10 percent more than average infants of same gestational age

When she was born, Carla Snipe snorted once, recalls her mother, then yelled about as loudly as anyone in the county ever had. Her color was as much red as pink, claims her mother, and she kicked out strongly enough that the nurse was hard-pressed to hang on to the still-slick infant. What would you guess Carla's Apgar score might have been?

SCORE	HEART RATE	RESPIRATORY EFFORT	MUSCLE TONE	COLOR	REFLEX IRRITABILITY
0	Absent	Absent	Flaccid, limp	Blue, pale	No response
1	Slow (less than 100)	Irregular, slow	Weak, inactive	Body pink, extremities blue	Grimace
2	Rapid (over 100)	Good, crying	Strong, active	Entirely pink	Coughing, sneezing, crying

normal. Palo and Erkkola (1993) compared 153 premature SGA infants with another 153 equally premature but AGA infants. The SGA infants were more likely to be delivered through emergency cesarean (82 percent of them) and had a much higher mortality rate (7 percent compared with 4.6 percent).

Neonatal Scales

In almost all North American hospitals it is routine to evaluate the condition of a newborn by means of the **Apgar scale.** The scale, shown in Interactive Table 4.7, is almost self-explanatory. Infants receive scores according to whether each of the appropriate signs is present. Maximum score is 10; average score is usually 7 or better; a score of 4 or less indicates that the neonate must be given special care immediately. The Apgar evaluation is administered at least twice—at one minute after birth and at five minutes after birth (and sometimes at ten minutes after birth). Five- and ten-minute scores are often higher than one-minute scores.

A second important scale for assessing the condition of a newborn infant is the **Brazelton Neonatal Behavioral Assessment Scale (NBAS)** (Brazelton, 1973). Like the Apgar scale, it may be used to detect problems immediately after birth. In addition, it provides useful indicators of central nervous system maturity, as well as of social behavior. The Brazelton scale looks at a total of twenty-six specific behaviors, including reaction to light, cuddling, voices, and a pinprick; it also looks at the strength of various reflexes. The scale is especially useful in identifying infants who might be prone to later psychological problems. Brazelton (1990) suggests that use of the scale has done much to increase our understanding of infant developmental patterns and of infants' states of consciousness. It also provides physicians with information that

Having a baby is as easy as falling off a log.

might be important for them to share with parents. For example, parents of infants who are less responsive to cuddling and to other social stimulation could be alerted to this from the very beginning, and thus these parents could compensate by providing the infant with extra loving contact.

The Mother's Experience: Prepared Childbirth

The preceding discussion of the delivery of a human child is admittedly clinical and maybe a little like the antiseptic hospitals in which most North American babies are born; it doesn't uncover and transmit the magic and the mystery of the process. In an effort to recapture some of this mystery, I spoke with several women whose experience qualified them to make subjective comments more valid than those my imagination might supply.

"What's it like, having a baby?" I asked.

"It's a piece of cake," my first interviewee assured me in her characteristic, clichéd way. "It's as easy as rolling off a log."

"It hurts like #@*#!!" my second interviewee insisted in her usual profane manner. "It's a hell of a big log!"

Combining these impressions, an absolutely clear picture of the situation emerges.

The inexperienced mother sometimes approaches the event with some degree of apprehension; there is often some pain associated with childbirth. However, advocates of **natural childbirth** (also called *prepared childbirth*) claim that through a regimen of prenatal exercises and adequate psychological preparation, many women experience relatively painless childbirths.

Natural childbirth, a phrase coined by a British physician, Grantly Dick-Read (1972), refers to the process of having a child without anesthetics. The Dick-Read process recommends relaxing exercises and psychological preparation for the arrival of the child, all directed toward delivery in which painkillers are unnecessary. Natural childbirth is based on the assumption that alleviating the fear of pain, together with training in relaxation, will result in less pain.

■ LAMAZE AND LEBOYER METHODS

Two popular methods of prepared childbirth are the Lamaze and the Leboyer techniques. The **Lamaze method** teaches expectant mothers a variety of breathing and relaxation exercises. These are practiced repeatedly, often with the assistance of the father or birth partner, until they become so habitual that they will be used almost "naturally" during the actual process of birth. The use of anesthetics during labor is less common among women who are thus prepared, and women's moods tend to be more positive during labor (Leventhal, Leventhal, & Shacham (1989).

The **Leboyer method** is concerned more with the delivery of the infant than with advance preparation of the mother. Leboyer's (1975) technique involves delivering the baby in a softly lit room, immersing the infant almost immediately in a lukewarm bath, and then placing the baby directly on the mother's abdomen. These procedures are designed to ease the infant's transition from the womb to the world—thus the need for soft lights, which do not contrast as harshly with the darkness of the womb as does conventional delivery room lighting, and for a lukewarm bath, which might feel something like amniotic fluid. Leboyer claims that his procedures eliminate much of the shock of birth and result in better-adjusted individuals. Critics suggest that birth in dimly lit surroundings might contribute to the physician's failing to notice important signs of distress or injury and that the dangers of infection are greater under these circumstances than they are when more conventional hospital practices are employed.

■ HOSPITALS OR HOMES: DOCTORS OR MIDWIVES

Not only are many mothers choosing to have their babies by natural means, but many are also deciding where birth will occur. For some, home is that choice; others choose hospital

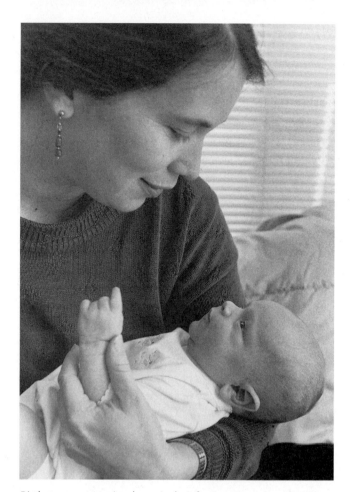

Birth means a staggering change in the infant's environment—from a dark, quiet, cushioned, temperature-controlled world to a hectic world of changing smells, textures, sound, temperatures, and movements. It also means enormous changes in the mother's world.

birthing rooms—a homier and more comfortable alternative than a conventional surgical theater or delivery room—or hospital family suites, where father and other siblings can actually stay. Although most North American births still occur in hospitals, length of hospitalization is considerably shorter than it once was (often only a matter of hours).

Traditionally, in countries such as Britain, the majority of births were attended to by a **midwife** rather than by a physician, a practice less common in North America (Jenkins, 1995). However, with the medicalization of birth, the use of midwives declined even in Europe and their role changed. An increasing number of births were attended to by physicians, and where midwives were used, they were often part of a medical team and were sometimes assigned relatively minor roles (Robinson, 1989).

In many developed nations, midwives have long been engaged in a struggle to have their services recognized and accepted. Partly because of escalating health care costs, there have been recent changes in many countries. Midwifery is increasingly becoming a licensed profession with accredited postsecondary programs (Roberts, 1995).

SEDATIVES IN CHILDBIRTH

For one mother, childbirth may be quite painful; for another mother, it may be a slightly painful but intensely rewarding and satisfying experience. Although the amount of pain can be controlled to some extent with anesthetics, the intensity of the immediate emotional reward will also be dulled by the drugs. In addition, sedatives given to the mother may affect the infant. Children delivered without sedatives are frequently more alert, more responsive to the environment, and better able to cope with immediate environmental demands (Brazelton, Nugent, & Lester, 1987; Shanley, 1994). In short, they may have a slight initial advantage, the long-range implications of which are unclear.

POSTPARTUM DEPRESSION

As many as 10 percent of all women suffer from depression after giving birth (Campbell & Cohn, 1991). It isn't clear whether this **postpartum depression** is due to hormonal changes, to the effects of sedating drugs that might have been used in labor, to disruptions in lifestyle, or to other factors (Dalton, 1980). However, studies indicate that women who receive higher levels of social support (from friends and family, for example) are at lower risk for postpartum depression (Collins et al., 1993). Also, there is evidence that although postpartum depression is not different from other forms of depression, its symptoms tend to be relatively mild (Whiffen & Gotlib, 1993). Hence, the prognosis for postpartum depression is excellent, with most cases improving quickly with time and disappearing completely within a year (Wolman et al., 1993).

The Child's Experience

How do infants react to the process of birth? From their point of view, birth must be an indifferent process: They cannot reason about it, cannot compare it with other more or less pleasant states, can do nothing to alter it, and will not even remember it. But consider the incredibly dramatic difference that birth makes. Up to now, the child has been living in a completely friendly and supportive environment. Receiving nourishment, getting oxygen, eliminating wastes—everything has been accomplished without effort. The uterus has been kept at exactly the right temperature, the danger of bacterial infection has been relatively insignificant, and there have been no psychological threats—we think. But at birth, the infant is suddenly exposed to new physiological and perhaps psychological dangers. Once mucus is cleared from the mouth and throat, the newborn must breathe unassisted for the first time. As soon as the umbilical cord ceases to pulsate, it is unceremoniously clipped an inch or two above the abdomen and tied off with a clamp. And the child is now completely alone—singularly dependent and helpless, to be sure, but no longer a biological parasite on the mother.

DANGERS OF BIRTH

Birth is not without danger for the newborn. In fact, some 61 out of every 1,000 of the world's children die at birth (Bellamy, 1997). A number of others suffer a variety of injuries, including brain damage, often resulting from the tremendous pressure exerted on the head during birth—especially if labor is long and if the amniotic sac has been broken early, in which case the head, in a normal presentation, has been repeatedly pressed against the slowly dilating cervix. In addition, the infant has to pass through an opening so small that deformation of the head often results. (For most infants the head usually assumes a more normal appearance within a few days.)

An additional source of pressure on the child's head may be **forceps,** clamplike instruments sometimes employed during delivery. Although the fetus can withstand considerable pressure on the head, the danger of such pressure is that it may rupture blood vessels and cause hemorrhaging. In severe cases, death may occur; otherwise, brain damage may result because cranial hemorrhage can restrict the supply of oxygen to the brain.

Another possible danger is **anoxia,** a shortage of oxygen to the brain. Anoxia can result if the umbilical cord becomes lodged between the child's body and the birth canal, disrupting the flow of oxygen (referred to as **prolapsed cord**). Anoxia may be related to impaired neurological, psychological, and motor functioning associated with brain damage. (See Summary Table 4.8.)

PREMATURITY

Prematurity is defined by a short gestation period (36 weeks or less) and low birthweight (small-for-gestational age, or SGA—less than 90 percent of average weight for term, usually less than 2,500 grams [5½ pounds]). It is one of the more serious possible complications of birth, affecting approximately 10 percent of all infants born in the United States. Incidence of low birthweight (under 2,500 grams), which often accompanies prematurity, is as high as 50 percent in some countries, such as Bangladesh. In fact, 24 percent of all infants born in the world's least developed countries are classified as low birthweight (Bellamy, 1997).

Causes of Prematurity

We don't know the precise causes of premature delivery (Creasy, 1990). However, a number of factors are related to its occurrence. These include poverty, malnutrition, age, smoking, and a variety of other drugs, all of which are implicated in various infant disadvantages.

Other related factors include illnesses in the mother while she is pregnant. **Gonorrhea** is one such illness that is an important contributor to prematurity in many countries (Donders et al., 1993). In addition, infants from multiple births are more frequently premature than are infants from single births. Finally, a number of infants are preterm in the absence of any of these negative influences and in spite of excellent maternal care, nutrition, and health (see "At a Glance: Birthweight and Prenatal Influences" and Figure 4.15 and Summary Table 4.9).

SUMMARY TABLE 4.8
Concepts in Childbirth

CONCEPT	SIGNIFICANCE
Dilation	first stage of labor, average 12 hours, marked by expansion of the cervix.
Delivery	second stage of labor, usually less than an hour, begins with baby's head emerging, terminates with birth.
Afterbirth	third stage of labor, expulsion of placenta.
Spontaneous abortion	loss of fetus before 20th week.
Immature birth	birth between 20th and 28th week.
Premature birth	birth in 29th to 36th week.
Mature birth	normal birth between 37th and 42nd week.
Postmature birth	birth after the 42nd week.
SGA	small-for-gestational age; weighing at least 10 percent less than average infants of same gestational age.
AGA	between 10th and 90th percentile in weight relative to average infants of same gestational age.
LGA	weighing at least 10 percent more than average infants of same gestational age.
Apgar scale	simple infant rating scale that looks at pulse, respiration, muscle tone, color, and reactivity.
Brazelton scale	more complex infant rating scale that looks at a variety of reflexes and behavioral responses.
Natural childbirth	prepared childbirth, often using a specific technique, designed to minimize the need for medical intervention or anesthetics.
Lamaze method	natural childbirth method marked by relaxation and breathing exercises.
Leboyer method	natural childbirth, emphasizing the delivery of the child in a nontraumatizing environment (soft lights, quiet, warm).
Midwife	someone who assists childbirth; often a trained professional.
Postpartum depression	depression in mother following childbirth; affects as many as 10 percent of all mothers.
Forceps	clamplike instruments sometimes used to assist delivery.
Prolapsed cord	birth condition in which blood flow through umbilical cord is restricted, sometimes leading to fetal damage.
Anoxia	lack of oxygen; sometimes results from a prolapsed cord.

Effects of Prematurity

One of the most obvious possible effects of prematurity is death. Indeed, only a few decades ago the chances of death for a premature infant weighing between 2,000 and 2,500 grams (4½ and 5½ pounds) were approximately six times greater than for an infant weighing 3,000 grams (6 pounds, 10 ounces) or more. Now, however, the majority of premature infants weighing 2,000 grams (4½ pounds) or more survive. In fact, more than 90 percent of infants who weigh as little as 1,000 to 1,500 grams survive (Goldsmith, 1990). Most of these preterm infants spend the first two to three months of their lives in intensive care nurseries, often in incubators (also called isolettes). Chances of survival decrease 10 to 15 percent for each hundred grams below 1,000 (Goldsmith, 1990). However, half or more of those who weigh less than 1,250 grams suffer adverse consequences; one third or more suffer from severe physical or mental handicaps (Beckwith & Rodning, 1991). For research purposes, infants are sometimes classified as low birthweight if they weigh less than

SUMMARY TABLE 4.9
Factors Associated with Higher Risk of Preterm Labor

MAJOR FACTORS

Multiple gestation

DES exposure

Uterine anomaly

Cervix dilated more than 1 cm at 32 weeks

Two previous second-trimester abortions

Previous preterm delivery

Previous labor during preterm, with term delivery

Abdominal surgery during pregnancy

Uterine irritability

MINOR FACTORS

Febrile (fever) illness

Bleeding after 12 weeks

More than 10 cigarettes per day

One previous second-trimester abortion

More than two previous first-trimester abortions

Source: Based on R. H. Holbrook, Jr., R. K. Laros, Jr., & R. K. Creasy (1988), Evaluation of a risk-scoring system for prediction of preterm labor. *American Journal of Perinatology 6,* 62.

Birthweight and Prenatal Influences

Prematurity and low birthweight are among the most serious complications of birth. Low birthweight may contribute to infant death or general developmental retardation, including lower intelligence. Factors implicated in low birthweight include smoking and use of other drugs, malnutrition, maternal age, socioeconomic status, and race. The relationship of age, social class, and race to low birthweight and prematurity is probably due primarily to other associated factors such as poorer nutrition and medical attention. In some of the world's least developed countries, such as Bangladesh, as many as half of all infants are born with low birthweight (under 2,500 grams); in Finland, Ireland, and Norway, only 4 percent of neonates are low birthweight. (In the United States, the percentage is 7; in Canada, it is 6.) On average, 24 percent of infants in the least developed countries, 19 percent of infants in developing countries, and 6 percent of infants in developed countries weigh less than 2,500 grams at birth (Bellamy, 1997).

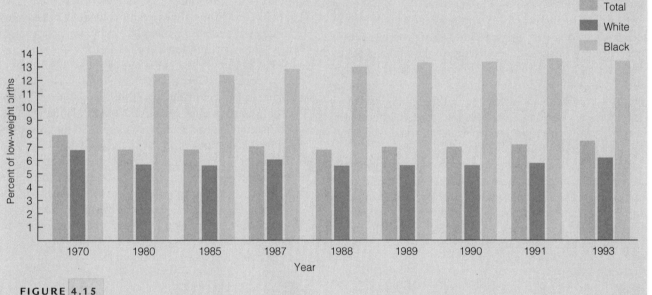

FIGURE 4.15

The relationship of race to low birthweight (less than or equal to 2,500 grams—5 pounds, 8 ounces—for 1970; less than 2,500 grams—5 pounds, 8 ounces—for 1980 through 1993). (From U.S. Bureau of the Census, 1994, p. 79, 1996, p. 85.)

2,500 grams, very low birthweight if less than 1,500 grams, and extremely low birthweight when under 750 grams.

Hack and colleagues (1992, 1993) have been following a group of 249 very low birthweight infants (under 1,500 grams—about 3 pounds) through the first decade of their lives. Comparisons of these children with average birthweight controls reveal lower weight, height, and head circumference at age eight, significantly higher incidence of various illnesses and surgical procedures, and significantly poorer performance on most measures of intellectual func-

tioning, including intelligence, language, reading, mathematics, spelling, and motor abilities. A subgroup of these low birthweight infants who weighed less than 750 grams at birth (about 1½ pounds) were at even greater disadvantage. Almost 25 percent were mentally retarded, about half were in special education classes, 25 percent had vision problems, and 25 percent suffered from measurable hearing loss (Boodman, 1994). These findings have now been confirmed by a number of other studies, including one by Ross, Lipper, and Auld (1991), which found that 48 percent of a group of 88 children who weighed less than 1,500 grams at birth required special educational interventions at age 8—compared with 15 percent of the New York City public elementary school population of which they were part.

Other possible effects of prematurity and/or of prolonged hospitalization following birth include lower intelligence, a higher incidence of cerebral palsy, and general developmental retardation. These effects, of course, are not found among all preterm babies, and are progressively less likely for those infants who are least premature and who weigh the most at birth. Among preterm infants who weigh 2,000 or more grams, subsequent complications are relatively rare.

Prevention of Prematurity

"We still aren't fully aware of all the events that occur to elicit this [birthing] reaction," says Dr. David Olson ("Shortening the Time Between the Bench and the Bedside," 1993, p. 4). If we were, he adds, we might be able to figure out how to prevent premature delivery. At present, all we can do is try to identify women who appear to be at greater risk. This can't be done with certainty because the precise causes of premature delivery are not usually known. However, it's possible to estimate degree of risk given knowledge of the woman's status with respect to the factors most often associated with prematurity—for example, previous preterm delivery, exposure to DES, the presence of more than one fetus, smoking, and uterine anomalies (see Table 4.9). It's also possible to monitor uterine activity and sometimes to detect an increase in activity prior to the onset of preterm labor.

There are a number of different approaches to preventing preterm labor, including bed rest, avoiding sexual intercourse, avoiding the use of antibiotics and other drugs, and suturing the cervix. None of these has been clearly proven to be effective, although there is some evidence that each might sometimes be helpful (Goldsmith, 1990).

Care of Premature Infants

Premature infants born in the twenty-third to twenty-fifth week of pregnancy have a 50-percent survival rate; 85 percent of those born between the twenty-sixth and twenty-eighth week survive ("Shortening the Time Between the Bench and the Bedside," 1993). Nor is prematurity inevitably linked with physical, psychological, or neurological inferiority. With adequate care, many premature infants fare as well as full-term infants.

■ NUTRITION AND MEDICAL CARE

What are the dimensions of that care? First, they include advances in medical knowledge and technology. For example, ventilators make possible the survival of infants whose hearts and lungs are not sufficiently developed to work on

their own; so does intravenous feeding. The contents of intravenous nutrition are especially important because they substitute for nutrients that the infant would ordinarily have received as a fetus. Certain fatty acids appear to be importantly involved in brain growth and neuron development during the last trimester of pregnancy—roughly the period of intrauterine growth that a twenty-seven-week preterm infant would miss ("Preemies' Diet Seen Key to Progress," 1988). Accordingly, the premature infant's nutrition has to include these nutrients at the appropriate time and in the appropriate form. Not surprisingly, hospital care of premature infants is sometimes enormously expensive ("Shortening the Time Between the Bench and the Bedside," 1993).

■ PSYCHOLOGICAL CARE

In addition to important medical advances in the care of premature infants, a tremendous amount of research in the last twenty years has looked at the possibility that at least some of the adverse psychological consequences of prematurity might be due to the lack of stimulation that the preterm infant receives in an intensive care nursery—or, perhaps more accurately, the inappropriateness of the stimulation. Harrison (1985) summarized twenty-four studies that looked at various forms of "supplemental" stimulation for preterm infants. Some investigated the effects of tactile stimulation (stroking, holding); others looked at auditory stimulation (taped recordings of a mother's voice, for example), vestibulary stimulation (oscillating hammock or waterbed), gustatory stimulation (pacifier), or a combination of different kinds of stimulation. In general, the studies support the conclusion that additional stimulation of preterm infants helps their development. Positive effects include greater weight gains, shorter hospital stays, greater responsiveness, and higher developmental scores on various measures. The evidence is clear that the traditional hands-off treatment once given most premature infants is not the best of all possible worlds for them.

A REASSURING NOTE

It is often very disturbing for nonmedical people to consult medical journals and textbooks in search of explanations for their various complaints. Inevitably, they discover that they have all the symptoms for some vicious infection or exotic disease. So if you happen to be pregnant at this moment or are contemplating pregnancy, or are otherwise involved in the process, you might find yourself a little apprehensive. I draw this to your attention only to emphasize that it really isn't that bad (pregnancy, that is). The intrauterine world of the unborn infant is less threatening and less dangerous than our world. Also, it is perhaps reassuring that nature often provides for spontaneous abortions when the embryo or the fetus would have been grossly abnormal. In fact, some

15 percent of recognized pregnancies result in spontaneous abortions, and more than half of these have chromosomal anomalies (Dill & McGillivray, 1992). In most cases when the fetus comes to term, the probability that the child will be normal and healthy far outweighs the likelihood that it will suffer any of the defects or abnormalities described in this chapter.

FOCUS QUESTIONS: SUMMARY ANSWERS

1. What are the common probable and positive signs of pregnancy?

   ■ Early, probable symptoms of pregnancy, such as cessation of menses, changes in the breasts, and morning sickness are uncertain; positive signs include a fetal heartbeat, palpation of the fetus, ultrasounds or X-rays, and chemical tests.

2. What is the normal sequence of prenatal development and birth?

   ■ In stage 1, the *fertilized ovum* moves down the Fallopian tubes and embeds itself in the uterine wall; in stage 2, from week two to week eight, the *embryo* develops so that by the end of the eighth week, all the organs of the infant are present; in stage 3, from week nine until birth, the *fetus* grows mainly in size and weight and neurologically.

3. What factors have the potential of being most harmful to the fetus? When?

   ■ External influences that cause malformations and physical defects are labeled *teratogens. Mutagens* cause changes in genetic material. Teratogens include some prescription drugs (thalidomide or DES—linked with malformations and cancer) and some chemicals (mercury—Minimata disease—and PCBs—linked with spontaneous abortions and physical deformities). Smoking is closely linked with prematurity as well as with low birthweight. Alcohol consumption may lead to *fetal alcohol syndrome* (FAS). Infants born to narcotics addicts are themselves usually addicted at birth. Cocaine is sometimes associated with prematurity, lower birthweight, and developmental problems.

4. What are the principal causes and implications of prematurity?

   ■ Prematurity appears to be linked to social-class variables such as diet and poor medical attention, to the age of the mother, and to smoking. It is associated with a greater possibility of death, physical defects, hyperactivity, and impaired mental functioning.

STUDY TERMS

acquired immunity deficiency syndrome (AIDS), 102

afterbirth, 111

amenorrhea, 105

amniotic sac, 109

anoxia, 115

Apgar scale, 113

artificial insemination, 92

average-for-gestational age (AGA), 112

Babinski reflex, 95

Brazelton Neonatal Behavioral Assessment Scale (NBAS), 113

breech, 110

cephalocaudal, 96

cervix, 109

cesarean delivery, 111

conception, 92

congenital, 100

cytomegalovirus, 102

diabetes, 102

embryo stage, 93

epidural analgesia, 111

episiotomy, 110

Fallopian tubes, 93

fertilized ovum, 93

fetal alcohol syndrome (FAS), 99

fetal erythroblastosis, 106

fetus stage, 93

forceps, 115

germinal stage, 93

gestation period, 92

gonorrhea, 115

herpes, 102

human chorionic gonadotropin, 92

immature birth, 112

labor, 108

Lamaze method, 114

lanugo, 96

large-for-gestational age (LGA), 112

Leboyer method, 114

lunar months, 92

mature birth, 112

menses, 92

methylmercury, 98

microcephaly, 101

midwife, 114

Minimata disease, 98

mutagens, 96

natural childbirth, 114

neonatal abstinence syndrome, 100

neonate, 111

ovaries, 93

ovulation, 92

placenta, 94

polychlorinated biphenyls, 98

postmature birth, 112

postpartum depression, 115

pregnancy, 92

pregnancy hormone, 92

premature birth, 112

prenatal development, 92

prolapsed cord, 115

proximodistal, 96

quickening, 92

FURTHER READINGS

The following is a provocative and straightforward look at childbirth and infant mortality in different parts of the world. It is updated yearly:

Bellamy, C. (1997). *The state of the world's children: 1997.* New York: Oxford University Press.

The following is a detailed, alphabetically organized collection of information on the influence of drugs on the fetus. It deals with both prescription and nonprescription drugs as well as illicit drugs such as marijuana and cocaine:

Friedman, J. M., & Polifka, J. E. (1996). *The effects of drugs on the fetus and nursing infant.* Baltimore, MD: Johns Hopkins University Press.

Bellow's novel is an interesting change of pace from the usual fare of academic references. True, it's fiction, but it's also a chilling account of the potential dangers of lead in our environment:

Bellow, S. (1982). *The dean's December.* New York: Harper & Row.

Shanley's book is a strong argument for making childbirth a natural rather than a medical procedure:

Shanley, L. K. (1994). *Unassisted childbirth.* Westport, CT: Berfin & Garvey.

Those interested in an account of birth in primitive tribes throughout the world might consult the following work:

Goldsmith, J. (1990). *Childbirth wisdom: From the world's oldest societies.* Brookline, MA: East West Health Books.

The following is a detailed discussion of nutrition and weight gain for pregnant women:

Food and Nutrition Board. (1992). *Nutrition during pregnancy.* Washington, DC: National Academy Press.

Those concerned about the implications of HIV and AIDS for childbearing might want to consult the following collection:

Faden, R. R., & Kass, N. E. (Eds.). (1996). *HIV, AIDS and childbearing.* New York: Oxford University Press.

PART TWO

Infancy

"When I use a word," Humpty Dumpty said in a rather scornful tone, "it means just what I choose it to mean—neither more nor less."

LEWIS CARROLL
Alice Through the Looking-Glass

nfans means "without speech." Young infants are *infans:* They have no words upon which to hang meanings. Their meanings, Piaget tells us, are wrapped in sensation and perception. As we see in Chapters 5 and 6, they are meanings of the *here and now.* If the infant sees a bright red ball, the meaning of the ball is a circular redness—a sort of image on the mind's mirror. Or perhaps the ball's meaning is the peculiar, synthetic, rubbery taste of well-chewed balls; or the magic-aliveness of its skin against the palms or the cheeks; or the trajectory of its mysterious bouncing course down the stairs; or all these sensations and actions put together in a shapeless, happy kind of meaningfulness. ¶ That's what *ball* means to the prelinguistic infant. ¶ Later, the infant will discover—or perhaps invent—the actual word *ball.* And with experience and increasing sophistication, *ball* will come to mean much more than the "spherical or nearly spherical object" that my dictionary lists as its first definition. It will also come to mean any number of games played with such objects; the roundish part of something; a poorly thrown, off-base, spherical thing; a dance; a good time; to be especially "with it" as in "on the ball," and on and on. ¶ But when *ball* is a fresh, young word, newly invented by the infant, it means, as Humpty Dumpty insists so scornfully, just what the infant chooses it to mean: a specific round object; the act of throwing anything; a request for Mom or Dad to do something amusing; a means of eliciting approval from some adult; and so on. ¶ *Ball* is seldom just another four-letter word.

FOCUS QUESTIONS

1. What are some of the advantages and disadvantages of breast-feeding?

2. How might the neonate's behavioral repertoire be described?

3. How do infants look?

4. Do infants think? What do they think?

5. What is the basic sequence in language acquisition in early infancy?

OUTLINE

This Chapter

Designing a Newborn

Feeding and Physical Growth of the Infant
    Breast or Bottle
    Infant Growth

Sudden Infant Death Syndrome

Reflexes in the Newborn
    The Orienting Response
    Reflexive Behaviors

Motor Development

Perceptual Development
    Infant Vision
    Visual Preferences
    How Infants Look
    Hearing
    Smell, Taste, and Touch

Cognitive Development
    Infant Memory
    Basic Piagetian Ideas
    The Object Concept
    Sensorimotor Development
    Imitation in Infancy

Language
    Communication
    A Definition of *Language*
    Elements of Language

Language Development in the First Two Years
    Achievements in the Prespeech Stage
    The Sentencelike Word (Holophrase)
    Two-Word Sentences

From Sensation to Representation

Focus Questions: Summary Answers

Study Terms

Further Readings

FIVE

Physical and Cognitive Development: Infancy

Fairy tales are horror stories for children to get them used to reality.

UNKNOWN

pande was born in a traditional "beehive hut" of woven grass and bent saplings. His mother's mattress, upon which he was delivered, was on a mat of straw laid on the hut's hard-polished clay and dung floor. The hut was near the center of the *kraal,* the cluster of huts that housed his parents and all his relatives—which was a good sign because it meant that Mpande's family's social position was important in the *kraal.* ¶ Mpande's mother is a Zulu, a descendent of the ancient clan headed by the man named Zulu, later conquered and united by the great king, Shaka. As a child, Mpande would hear the stories of Shaka's military skill, his zeal for conquest, his leadership. With his age-mates, Mpande would crouch by the fire at night, listening to one of the grandmothers speak of these things. And he would hear the story, too, of how as Shaka's empire and his power grew, he became vain and boastful and so tyrannical that when his mother died, he had 7,000 people killed because their eyes were dry, which meant they did not mourn deeply enough. Only ten years after he became king, two of Shaka's brothers killed him—and few mourned. ¶ Mpande's mother was the second of his father's several wives, all of whom he would eventually learn to call "mother." And all the children of his mothers would be his brothers and sisters as well. As an infant, he would spend the days cradled on his mother's back, listening to her sing, while she scattered the seeds for mealies (maize), sorghum, watermelons, pumpkins, sugar cane, and sweet potatoes. Whenever he was hungry, she would give him her breast. Then he would sleep, reassured by her warmth and her voice, rocked by her movements as she hoed the ground and harvested the corn. ¶ But Mpande's world is a rapidly changing one. Today, only a fraction of the South African Zulus are born and live in *kraals.* Many of the mothers no longer plant crops or make pottery and weave; even fewer of the fathers tend the cattle, which, for centuries, were the center of the Zulu

123

economy. Now many live in cities, where large numbers of the men and boys work in the mines; many of the women work in factories or weave and do beadwork or pottery to sell to tourists. There is little time now for sitting around the fire in the evening and listening to the old ones tell the stories of the people.* ¶

This Chapter

When we contrast our culture with another, we can highlight the extent to which we are products of our contexts. But very few cultures are homogeneous; within each, a tremendous variety of different experiences are possible. As a result, the average child of which we speak in these chapters is a mathematical invention whose meaning rests in the tremendously varied characteristics and accomplishments of all other children. Some of these other children learn to crawl and walk and speak at remarkably young ages; some struggle far longer to learn these things.

We should keep this in mind as we work through this chapter's tables and charts describing the normal and expected achievements of infancy. We should not be too hasty in comparing the progress of our individual infants with that of the wonderful, and mysterious, average infant; nor should we struggle too desperately to correct their deviations before it's too late for them ever to be average.

This chapter looks at the physical, motor, and perceptual development of the average infant, as well as at the characteristics and growth of the infant's mind. The next chapter looks at social relationships and attachments during infancy, and at infant personality. These two chapters cover infancy, a period that lasts from the first few weeks of life to age two.

DESIGNING A NEWBORN

During the first two weeks of life, the newborn is often referred to as a **neonate**. Technically, the neonatal period lasts from birth (immediately after which the infant typically loses weight) until birthweight has been regained.

What kind of creature is the newborn? What does it think, feel, sense? Of what is it capable? These are not easy questions to answer. In fact, it will take us the remainder of this chapter and most of the next to describe the answers that science—and sometimes good sense—have begun to provide. But let us start first with the bare bones of an answer.

Imagine that you have been asked to design an organism that begins life in as primitive a condition as a neonate—that is, with as little physical and motor control as the infant has, and with as unsophisticated an understanding of self and world. Your task is to design this organism in such a way that

---

*Based in part on Bleeker, 1970; Mack, 1980; and Ngubane, 1986.

within two years it can walk, talk, recognize its grandmother, ride a tricycle...yes, even crawl.

So what do you do? You program it for change. Because you're clever, you pay particular attention to change in three areas: biological, intellectual, and social. Biologically, you design a creature that is capable of converting foodstuffs into nutrients, and you program the effects of these nutrients into a sequence of biological growth and maturation that will, among other things, eventually lead to the organism's control of its movements.

Intellectually, you program your little organism to process an enormous amount of information even in the absence of any immediate and tangible reward (such as a cookie or a kiss) for doing so. You provide it with an information-processing system that is automatically geared to focus on the most informative aspects of the environment. Accordingly, your little organism reacts strongly to surprise and novelty; it searches out the unexpected; it develops ways of organizing the information it gathers; it is programmed to invent concepts and ideas.

Socially, you program into the organism a wide range of emotions to serve as motives for action. They drive the organism to seek relationships with other organisms of the same species, to be gregarious, to love, to strive to mean something to others and contribute to the survival of its species.

And one of the crowning achievements in your design of this creature is that you pretune it to attend to speech; you wire it so that it is capable of inventing language and building culture.

Quite a marvelous invention, wouldn't you say? The infant is just such a creature, says Flavell (1985). To summarize: A newborn is a primitive, self-driven little sensing machine designed to mature and grow physically in a predetermined way, programmed as an extraordinarily capable information-processing system, endowed with powerful emotions and gregarious tendencies, and pretuned to speech and to the development of language.

FEEDING AND PHYSICAL GROWTH OF THE INFANT

Still, newborns at birth are almost completely helpless physically. They cannot ensure that their environments are neither too cold nor too warm; they cannot clean themselves; they have no protection against witches, wolves, or one-eyed cats. They can't even find food unless it's put under their very noses.

And then they suck. Sucking is one of those primitive **reflexes** present at birth in virtually all mammals.

Breast or Bottle

The sucking reflex is what ensures the infant's survival. It may seem strange, then, that in Kessen's (1965) words, "the most persistent single note in the history of the child is the reluctance of mothers to suckle their babies" (p. 1).

The breast-versus-bottle battle has raged for many years. In the beginning, the breast side was fought by an army of physicians and philosophers, some of whom argued that breast-feeding was a child's natural right and the mother's duty. Besides, argued Copmenius (quoted in Kessen, 1965), infants pick up many things from their mother's milk, including values: "Who then, unless he be blind, does not see that babies imbibe, along with the alien milk of the foster mother, morals different from those of their parents?" (p. 3). (Does my early delinquency have to do with the morals of cows?)

The other army fighting this apparent battle were mothers who, for one reason or another, were reluctant to breast-feed their infants. Their arguments were generally more personal and more private, and their numbers varied through history, growing through certain decades and lessening again through others.

Is there still a conflict—a breast-versus-bottle controversy? There probably is, although most mothers see the issue as largely a matter of personal choice. The choice is sometimes made on the basis of convenience. It is simply not convenient for many working mothers to breast-feed their infants. Or it is not convenient for women who carry their infants on their backs, or take them to the fields, to also carry bottles with them—or to lead cows or goats around behind them.

At other times, the choice is made on the basis of current fashion. For example, through much of the early part of this century, breast-feeding declined in popularity in North America so that by the early 1970s, fewer than one in four mothers breast-fed their infants. But in the past several decades, breast-feeding has again increased in popularity. One survey reports that 83 percent of women in one Canadian city breast-fed their infants (Kuzyk, 1993). Throughout the rest of the world, the percentage of mothers who breast-feed their infants varies tremendously—from less than one in three in countries such as Liberia, Bangladesh, and Turkey to more than four out of five in countries such as Angola, Haiti, Kenya, and Indonesia (Bellamy, 1997).

What do physicians (and philosophers?) now recommend? Pretty well what they have recommended all along: When possible, mothers should breast-feed their infants. But their reasons have changed over the years; they can now appeal to science. Mother's milk, science tells us, is the best of foods for most newborns. It contains just about the right combination of nutrients, the right proportion of fats and calories, the almost-perfect assortment of minerals and vitamins; it is easier to digest than cow's milk and less likely to lead to allergic reactions. Also, breast-feeding provides infants with a measure of immunity against infections and diseases, and especially against diarrhea, one of the principal causes of infant death in the developing world. Thus, infants who are breast-fed typically have lower mortality rates (Friedman & Polifka, 1996). Furthermore, it helps in population control because **lactation** (the production of milk) delays ovulation (from an average of forty to fifty days after birth

for mothers who don't breast-feed to an average of thirty to forty weeks for those who do; Wang & Fraser, 1994). Accordingly, the World Health Organization strongly recommends advising women in developing countries to return to breast-feeding where this practice has been abandoned. Various programs and approaches have been attempted for this purpose: changing hospital policies, enacting legislation or using other political action, educating mothers and health care workers, even providing material incentives. Success has been mixed (Wilmoth & Elder, 1995). (See "At a Glance: Changes in Breast-Feeding Patterns in the United States" and Figure 5.1.)

In spite of these compelling arguments, it would be misleading not to emphasize that in much of the industrialized world, where sanitation and nutrition are excellent, many bottle-fed infants thrive. For a variety of reasons, breast-feeding may not be possible or desirable for all mothers. In addition, it is worth noting that breast milk is affected by what the mother eats as well as by any drugs she ingests or chemicals to which she is exposed (Byczkowski, Gearhart, & Fisher, 1994). Alcohol, nicotine, barbiturates, stimulants (such as caffeine), sedatives, and prescription drugs can each have an effect on the infant. However, in many cases the amount of the drug that passes from mother to infant through breast milk is very small (Friedman & Polifka, 1996). Accordingly, caffeine use in normal quantities is regarded as being safe while breast-feeding, as is aspirin, unless high doses are used. Drugs such as antidepressants also pass into breast milk, but as Yoshida and Kumar (1996) argue, the benefits of their use for the mother may outweigh any risks to the infant.

Although cocaine is excreted into mother's milk in very low concentrations, there have been reported instances of what is termed *cocaine intoxication* (vomiting, diarrhea, trembling, seizures) among breast-feeding infants. Accordingly, the American Academy of Pediatrics classifies cocaine as one of the drugs to be avoided by nursing mothers (Committee on Drugs, American Academy of Pediatrics, 1994). Clearly, under some circumstances, an infant might fare much better with a cow or a goat.

Infant Growth

More than half a century ago, Scammon (in Malina & Bouchard, 1991) described four different aspects of human growth: genital (the development of sexual characteristics); neural (brain and nervous system); lymphoid (systems, like the lymph glands, tonsils, and appendix, involved in the child's immunities); and general (height and weight, for example). Each of these, as is shown in Figure 5.2, follows a characteristically different pattern of development.

GENITAL GROWTH

Genital growth, which involves the development of sexual characteristics, is negligible in infancy and through most of early and middle childhood. But, as shown in Figure 5.2,

Changes in Breast-Feeding Patterns in the United States

Through much of history, most philosophers, psychologists, religious leaders, physicians, and nurses have been in favor of breast-feeding; some mothers have not. Ultimately, the choice is a personal one.

Breast-feeding may be especially important in developing countries where formulas are often overly diluted or are mixed with contaminated water, leading to malnutrition or to diarrheal dehydration

and sometimes death. There has been a dramatic increase in breast-feeding in the United States in recent years, especially among more highly educated mothers.

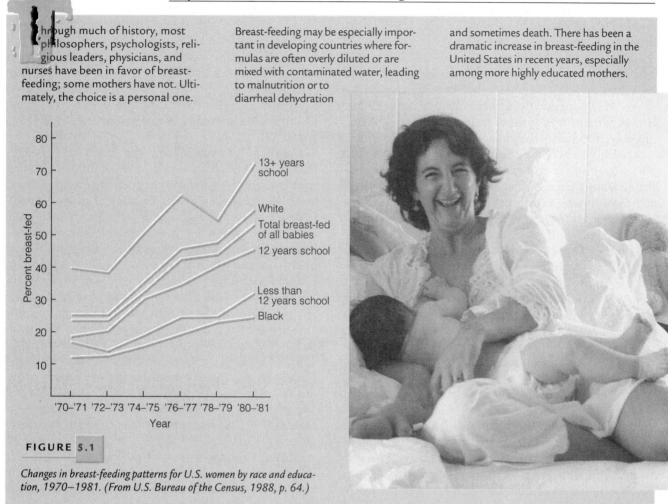

FIGURE 5.1

Changes in breast-feeding patterns for U.S. women by race and education, 1970–1981. (From U.S. Bureau of the Census, 1988, p. 64.)

there is a dramatic spurt between ages twelve and fourteen with the advent of *pubescence*, the series of changes that results in sexual maturity (see Chapter 11).

LYMPHOID GROWTH

The lymphoid system refers to lymph tissues in the body such as in the lymph glands, the tonsils, the thymus (located behind the top of the breastbone), and even in the intestine. The lymphoid system plays an important role in providing immunity and resisting infection. Note that this system develops very rapidly through childhood, peaking in early adolescence. Following adolescence, the tonsils and thymus shrink rapidly so that a normal adult has about half as much lymph tissue as a young adolescent.

NEURAL DEVELOPMENT

The neonate's central nervous system is functionally immature at birth but develops very rapidly early in infancy and is about 95 percent complete by age seven, as shown in Figure 5.2. Its optimal development is highly dependent

upon two factors: adequate nutrition and adequate environmental stimulation. The infant's brain is most vulnerable to the effects of malnutrition prenatally (Crawford et al., 1993); it can also experience serious developmental retardation as a result of postnatal malnutrition. Especially dangerous is protein malnutrition that, claims Udani (1992), affects about 150 million children under age five worldwide. Among other things, severe lack of protein is associated with reduction in brain size, fewer connections among brain neurons, and changes in chemical brain transmitters. Malnutrition is also associated with lower birthweight, and low birthweight babies seem to be more susceptible to nutritional deficiencies (especially deficiencies of several fatty acids that are essential for normal brain development and that are consistently found in breast milk) (Crawford, 1993).

Although severe malnutrition can lead to poor mental development, the often-quoted conclusion that moderate malnutrition leads to lower IQ and retarded mental development is overstated and premature, claims Ricciuti (1991). The human brain appears to be remarkably resistant to per-

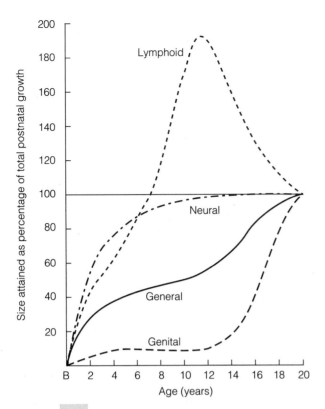

FIGURE 5.2

General growth curves in four areas of human development as described in Growth, Maturation, and Physical Activity (p. 9) by Robert M. Malina and Claude Bouchard, Champaign, IL: Human Kinetics Publishers. Copyright 1991 by Robert M. Malina and Claude Bouchard. Reprinted by permission. And from The Measurement of Man, J. A. Harris et al., University of Minnesota Press, 1930, p. 193. Copyright © 1930 by the University of Minnesota. Reprinted by permission.

manent damage resulting from moderate malnutrition—with the exception, notes DeLong (1993), of brain damage associated with iodine deficiency, which during pregnancy is an important cause of **cretinism** and is also linked with **cerebral palsy** and deafness.

The belief that the effects of malnutrition can be prevented or perhaps reversed through improved nutrition and various supplements is more a statement of social policy than of scientific fact, says Ricciuti (1991). Poor nutrition, Ricciuti explains, is only one facet of a collection of conditions that often accompany poverty—conditions such as poor sanitation, poor medical care, limited intellectual stimulation, and disease.

■ PHYSICAL GROWTH

Physical growth, as shown by the general curve in Scammon's representation (Figure 5.2), occurs in four stages: very rapid growth in infancy and early childhood, slower growth through middle childhood, a very rapid growth spurt in adolescence, and slower growth ceasing in early adulthood.

Although physical growth in infancy is relatively predictable, because of different genetic programs and different nourishment, infants will not be exactly the same at all ages. Average physical development during infancy is shown in

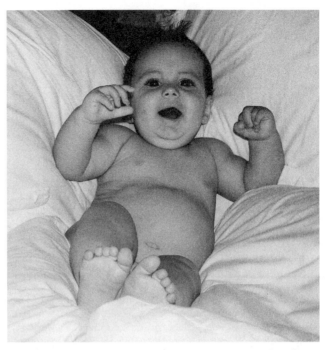

Rates of general physical growth, as well as of neural development, are higher during infancy than during any other subsequent period. Between birth and age 2, this infant will increase his weight by more than 270 percent—and his height by about 72 percent. If rate of change didn't slow down, the average 6-year-old would weigh nearly 400 pounds (182 kilograms) and be about 8.5 feet (2.6 meters) tall.

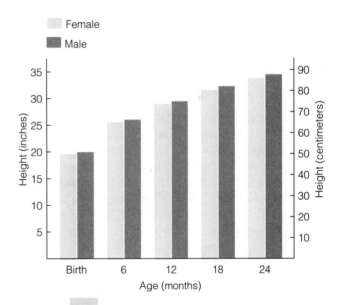

FIGURE 5.3

Height at 50th percentile for U.S. infants, birth to 24 months. (Adapted from Health Department, Milwaukee, Wisconsin; based on data by H. C. Stuart and H. V. Meredith, prepared for use in the Children's Medical Center, Boston. Used by permission of the Milwaukee Health Department.)

Figures 5.3 and 5.4. Note that these are median, or midpoint, values—meaning that 50 percent of all infants of a given age are expected to be taller, and 50 percent will be shorter. Being some distance above or below the norms

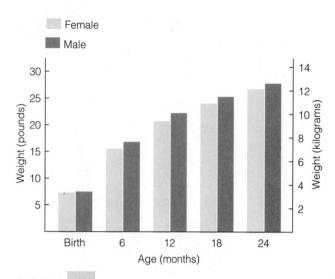

Female
Male

FIGURE 5.4

Weight at 50th percentile for U.S. infants, birth to 24 months. (Adapted from Health Department, Milwaukee, Wisconsin; based on data by H. C. Stuart and H. V. Meredith, prepared for use in the Children's Medical Center, Boston. Used by permission of the Milwaukee Health Department.)

should not, by itself, be cause for alarm. Only when the infant is significantly above or below the average might there be cause for concern. Unfortunately, many of the world's children are significantly below the norm. Bellamy (1997) reports that almost half of all children in the least developed countries are moderately or severely underweight; half suffer from permanently stunted growth. (See Summary Table 5.1.)

SUDDEN INFANT DEATH SYNDROME

In 1993 slightly more than 33,000 infants in the United States died before the age of one, the majority from congenital anomalies, many of which are related to prematurity (U.S. Bureau of the Census, 1996). For the remainder, the single leading cause of death is the mysterious **sudden infant death syndrome** (or SIDS, sometimes popularly referred to as "crib death" or "cot death")—mysterious because a diagnosis of sudden infant death syndrome is not really a diagnosis at all; it is an admission that cause of death is unknown (see "At a Glance: Causes of Infant Deaths in the United States" and Figures 5.5 and 5.6).

DEFINITION

First formally defined in 1969, SIDS is simply "the sudden and unexpected death of an infant who has seemed well, or almost well, and whose death remains unexplained" (Valdes-Dapena, 1991, p. 3). In spite of considerable research, for a long time SIDS could neither be predicted nor prevented. Recently, however, concerted medical efforts have succeeded in reducing SIDS rates from 2.6 per 1,000 in 1980 to 1.8 per 1,000 in 1993—a decline of about 30 percent (U.S. Bureau of the Census, 1996). (See Figure 5.6.)

▲ SUMMARY TABLE 5.1
Feeding and Growth of the Infant

BREAST-FEEDING	
Pros	Optimal combination of nutrients.
	Normally sanitary, uncontaminated (unlike water supply in many countries).
	Imparts immunity against various infections and diseases.
	Greatly reduces incidence of intestinal disorders (especially diarrhea); hence reduces infant mortality.
	Provides opportunity for mother–infant bonding.
Cons	Most prescription and over-the-counter drugs ingested by the mother are excreted in breast milk. In high doses, many are potentially harmful to the infant.
	Street drugs such as cocaine may be harmful to both mother and infant.
	Ultimately a matter of personal choice.

FOUR AREAS OF GROWTH	CHARACTERISTICS
Genital	Development of sex organs
	Negligible in infancy; spurts at puberty.
Lymphoid	Lymph tissues, involved in immunity and disease resistance.
	Rapid development through childhood.
Neural	Nervous system development.
	Immature at birth but rapid development in infancy.
	Highly sensitive to pre- and early post-natal nutrition.
Physical	Changes in height and weight.
	Very rapid in infancy; slower through middle childhood.
	Final spurt at adolescence.

■ SOME COMMON CHARACTERISTICS OF SIDS INFANTS

Although the causes of SIDS are unknown, some SIDS victims share certain characteristics. The most common of these, surprisingly, is age: SIDS occurs during a far narrower age span than almost all other diseases, seldom occurring during the first several weeks of life, peaking between two and four months, falling rapidly to age six months, and then declining more slowly. Fewer than 5 percent of SIDS deaths occur after age one (Hillman, 1991).

Other than age, there are a number of risk factors for SIDS. One is sex, with males accounting for about 60 percent of cases (Hillman, 1991). Other associated factors include heavy wrapping, maternal smoking during pregnancy, and overpproximately 8.4 of every 1,000 infants born in the United States do not survive beyond age one. About two-thirds of these die during the first month, the majority from congenital anomalies (often associated with prematurity). For those who die later, the mysterious and largely unexplained condition sudden infant death syndrome (SIDS) is the single most frequent cause of death. It accounted for almost 4,700 infant deaths in 1993 (U.S. Bureau of the Census, 1996). Reassuringly, however, infant mortality rates in 1993 are only two-thirds what they were in 1980. Much of this decline is due to new information about SIDS and a sharp reduction in frequency of SIDS deaths.

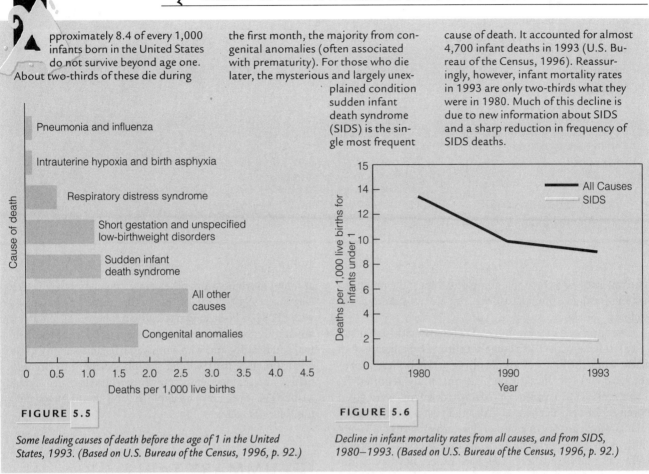

FIGURE 5.5

Some leading causes of death before the age of 1 in the United States, 1993. (Based on U.S. Bureau of the Census, 1996, p. 92.)

FIGURE 5.6

Decline in infant mortality rates from all causes, and from SIDS, 1980–1993. (Based on U.S. Bureau of the Census, 1996, p. 92.)

night home heating (Wigfield, Gilbert, & Fleming, 1994). Finally, and most important for SIDS prevention, a **prone** (stomach down) sleep position is closely associated with SIDS. The evidence seems clear that infants who are put to sleep on their sides or on their backs are at far lower risk for SIDS than infants who sleep prone (Spieker & Brannen, 1996). Research indicates that where there has been a concerted attempt to advise parents to avoid placing their infants prone, there have been dramatic declines in SIDS rates (Wilson, 1997; Anonymous, 1996).

■ SIDS AND NEUROLOGICAL IMMATURITY

Why should this be? One line of speculation is that maturation of the brain may be delayed or abnormal in some SIDS victims (Kopp et al., 1994). Thus, SIDS has sometimes been associated with **apnea**, a temporary paralysis or collapse of the throat muscles that prevents continued breathing and that generally causes the person to wake up. It is also sometimes associated with an abnormality in the diaphragm (Tennyson, Pereyra, & Becker, 1994). One suggestion is that SIDS may result from the infant's inability to learn the voluntary behaviors that eventually replace defensive breathing reflexes. "There is a critical at-risk period for all infants when reflexive defensive responses have faded, but voluntary defensive responses are not yet sufficiently strong," says Hunt (1991, p. 185). Young infants reflexively stick out their tongues when a piece of plastic is put over their mouths. If the object is not dislodged, they typically move their heads from side to side; if that doesn't work, they swing their arms toward their faces. Eventually these behaviors are replaced by more voluntary behaviors. Perhaps the SIDS victim has not learned these voluntary behaviors because of behavioral or neurological problems linked with a slow-to-mature nervous system. And the infant lying prone may experience the added disadvantage of having the mouth and nose covered.

■ PREVENTING SIDS DEATHS

Filiano and Kinney (1994) summarize the findings on SIDS in terms of what they term the triple-risk model. According to this model, SIDS results when all three of the following conditions occur simultaneously: (1) a vulnerable infant, perhaps neurologically immature; (2) a critical developmental period (mainly between 1½ and 4 months); and (3) some ollowing are several web sites with good information about Sudden Infant Death Syndrome (SIDS):

http://www.sids.org/

The American SIDS Institute site (an organization dedicated to the prevention of Sudden Infant Death Syndrome and the promotion of related research, support, and education).

http://www.surry.com/sids.html

General facts about SIDS.

http://www.thebabiesplanet.com/bbsudden.htm

Links to SIDS-related web sites.

http://www.stayhealthy.com/index.html

Wide-ranging health-related information, including SIDS.

The tragedy of SIDS may result from the infant's inability to learn the voluntary behaviors that eventually replace defensive breathing reflexes. This child is being monitored to try to detect patterns that may be associated with SIDS.

external stressor (which might include things like infant infections, temperature fluctuations, or parental smoking (see Fleming, 1994).

One approach to preventing SIDS is to provide parents of at-risk infants with **SIDS home monitors,** which sound an alarm when the infant stops breathing or when there is dangerous change in heart action. In one study reported by Sivan et al. (1997), parents of 261 at-risk infants were given home monitors. Of these at-risk infants, 52 were preterm infants with a history of apnea or heart irregularities, 83 were siblings of SIDS victims, 22 were infants whose mothers were drug-addicted, and 104 had experienced one life-threatening episode. These 261 infants were closely followed until the age of 15. None died, although 5 experienced SIDS-like episodes that required resuscitation.

There are a number of studies, however, in which not all SIDS deaths have been prevented in spite of the use of monitors. In addition, some researchers point out that monitors don't always detect the occurrence of SIDS, nor can all instances be prevented even when they are detected (Noyes et al., 1996).

One of the most effective suggestions for preventing SIDS, as we saw, is placing infants **supine** (on their backs) or, failing that, on their sides. Another, interestingly, is to have them share a room with parents, a procedure that a number of researchers have found to significantly reduce the risk of SIDS (Scragg et al., 1996; Anonymous, 1997).

◼ IN CONCLUSION

As we saw, the probability of SIDS can be reduced through home monitoring, placing infants supine or on their sides, sleeping in the same room with them, and placing emphasis on a drug-free, nutritious pre- and post-natal environment. Nevertheless, SIDS remains unexpected, unexplained, and, by definition, fatal. It occurs throughout the world and appears to have existed many centuries ago, although it would not have been easily recognized or considered important as long

as infant mortality from other causes remained high (Valdes-Dapena, 1991). None of the factors sometimes associated with SIDS has been shown to cause it. Many SIDS victims are apparently thriving infants who seem to be completely normal and healthy, and who simply die, usually silently in their cribs at night. Small wonder that physicians and parents are baffled and that law-enforcement personnel are occasionally suspicious. (See Summary Table 5.2 and "In the News and on the Net: SIDS Sites.")

▲ SUMMARY TABLE 5.2
Sudden Infant Death Syndrome

What it is	◾ the sudden, unexpected, and subsequently unexplained death of an apparently healthy infant, often while apparently sleeping (hence also called *crib death* or *cot death*).
Frequent shared characteristics of SIDS victims: SIDS is most common	◾ between 2 and 4 months of age. ◾ among males. ◾ among infants who sleep prone (on their fronts). ◾ among those who have a sibling who is a SIDS victim. ◾ among those whose mothers are drug-addicted. ◾ among premature infants. ◾ among infants with a history of respiratory or heart problems.
Suggestions for Prevention	◾ Place infants supine or on their sides. ◾ For high-risk infants, use home monitors. ◾ Sleep in the same room as higher risk infants. ◾ Avoid smoking and other drugs, both during pregnancy and after birth.

REFLEXES IN THE NEWBORN

Researching infancy presents some unique problems. Clearly, very young infants cannot be asked to interpret their own responses, nor can they be given instructions about how to behave in experimental situations. How, then, can the investigator determine whether the infant is curious, interested, bored, or confused? How do we know when and if learning has occurred?

The Orienting Response

Part of the answer lies in a group of sometimes almost imperceptible behaviors that have played a significant role in the development of experimental child psychology. These behaviors, collectively labeled the **orienting response**, are evident in our tendency (and that of other animals and birds) to respond to new stimulation by becoming more alert—that is, by attending or orienting to it. It is, as Berg and Berg (1987) put it, a "mechanism that enhances the processing of information in all sensory systems" (p. 268).

In animals such as dogs and cats, the orienting response is clear. On hearing a new sound, for example, a dog will pause, its ears may perk up and turn slightly toward the sound, and its whole attitude says, in effect, "What the *!$! was that?" Although the human infant may not respond so obviously, distinct and measurable changes nevertheless take place. These might include changes in pupil size, heart rate, conductivity of the skin to electricity (**galvanic skin response [GSR]**, also termed *electrodermal response*), and other physiological changes that are observable by using sensitive instruments. These in combination define the human orienting response.

The value of the orienting response to the child psychologist is that it can be used as an indication of attention, because it occurs only in response to novel stimulation to which the individual is then attending. It can also be used as an indication of learning, because it stops when the stimulation is no longer novel. In the same way, a dog might orient visibly when it first hears a cow in the distance, but will cease to do so when the sound has been identified. Such a decrease in the orienting reaction is termed *habituation*. Thus, even though infants cannot tell us whether "mother" sounds the same as "father," whether the color blue looks like red, or whether salt tastes like sugar, we can turn to the orienting response for answers to some of our questions.

Reflexive Behaviors

A **reflex** is, by definition, a simple, unlearned, and largely uncontrollable response to a specific set of circumstances. Most of the behaviors in which the newborn first engages are reflexive—that is, they do not require learning and can easily be elicited by presenting the appropriate stimulus. Some of these reflexes, like the **sucking reflex**, are extremely important to survival. Another **vegetative reflex**, so called because these reflexes are nourishment-related, is the **head-turning reflex**, also called the **rooting reflex**; it can be elicited by stroking the baby's cheek or the corner of the mouth. Vegetative reflexes also include swallowing, hiccuping, sneezing, and vomiting.

A number of common motor reflexes in the newborn have no particular survival value now, but they might have been useful in some less "civilized" time. These include the startle reaction—or **Moro reflex**—which involves throwing out the arms and feet symmetrically and then pulling them back toward the center of the body. There is speculation that the Moro reflex might be important for infants whose mothers live or sleep in trees. If they suddenly fall but react by throwing out arms and legs, they might with luck catch a branch and save themselves. The Moro reflex is sometimes useful in diagnosing brain damage because in normal infants, these reflexes disappear with the development of the brain. As the infant develops control over motor actions, reflexes are inhibited (Mandich et al., 1994). However, the Moro reflex is often present later in life in people with impaired motor function.

Other reflexes that disappear in early infancy are the **Babinski reflex**—the typical fanning of the toes when tickled in the middle of the soles of the feet; the **palmar reflex** (grasping—also called the *Darwinian reflex*), which is sometimes sufficiently pronounced that the neonate can be raised completely off a bed when grasping an adult's finger in each hand; and the swimming and stepping reflexes, which occur when one holds the baby balanced on the stomach, or upright with the feet just touching a surface.

Although reflexes are, by definition, unlearned behaviors, the infant's reflexive behaviors are not completely unmodifiable. Perhaps when the nipple is in the mouth, the infant cannot help sucking, but two things are noteworthy. First, very early the infant begins to exercise a degree of control over some of the circumstances that lead to reflexive behaviors. When the stomach is full, the infant may avert its head or purse its lips tightly, thus avoiding the stimulation that might lead to the sucking response.

Second, beginning very early in life, the infant is capable of modifying some reflexive responses, including sucking—perhaps changing the shape of the mouth or the placement of the tongue to increase the behavior's effectiveness (Widstrom & Thingstrom-Paulsson, 1993). The human organism—programmed to process information, to learn, to change—begins to change very early. (See Summary/Interactive Table 5.3.)

MOTOR DEVELOPMENT

The changes infants go through during the first two years of life, say Hazen and Lockman (1989), are more profound than any that will occur during the remainder of their lives.

Interaction: If you have access to a newborn or young infant, it might be useful for you to provide appropriate stimulation to observe each of these reflexes. With older infants, you might carry out observations of gross and fine motor developments described in Figure 5.7.

REFLEX	STIMULUS	RESPONSE	APPROXIMATE AGE OF APPEARANCE	APPROXIMATE AGE OF DISAPPEARANCE
Sucking	Object in the mouth	Sucks	2–3 months in utero	Becomes voluntary during first year
Head turning (rooting)	Stroking the cheek or the corner of the mouth	Turns head toward side being stroked	Neonate	Becomes voluntary during first year
Swallowing	Food in the mouth	Swallows	Neonate	Becomes voluntary during first year
Sneezing	Irritation in the nasal passages	Sneezes	4–6 months in utero	Present in adult
Moro reflex	Sudden loud noise	Throws arms and legs out symmetrically	Neonate	3–4 months
Babinski reflex	Ticking the middle of the soles	Spreads and raises toes	Neonate	Diminishes by 1 month; disappears by 5–6 months
Toe grasp	Tickling the soles just below the toes	Curls toes around object	4–6 months in utero	Disappears by 9 months
Palmar grasp	Placing object in the infant's hand	Grasps object tightly	4–6 months in utero	Weak by 8 weeks; gone by 4–5 months
Swimming reflex	Infant horizontal, supported by abdomen	Coordinated swimming movements	8–9 months in fetus	Disappears after 6 months
Stepping reflex	Infant vertical, feet lightly touching flat surface	Makes coordinated walking movements	8–9 months in fetus	Disappears after 2–3 months

Within this brief period, initially helpless and completely dependent infants learn to move and to explore, to recognize recurring features of the world, to solve practical problems—and they also learn to represent symbolically and to communicate.

The infant's first movements appear to be largely uncoordinated and purposeless. However, researchers have discovered recurring patterns in these early movements. First, they appear to be cyclical. Beginning prenatally and continuing for about the first four months, the infant's spontaneous movements recur at relatively regular intervals, spaced within minutes (Robertson, 1993a). This appears to be true for both waking and sleeping periods. At first, these **cyclic movements** are typically irregular and rapid, as well as asymmetrical (Grattan et al., 1992). That is, they involve various parts of the body (arms and legs) as well as either side (right or left) at different times. Rapid cyclic movements are typically followed by brief periods of quiescence. Later, the movements become more coordinated and more symmetrical.

Some speculate that these cyclic movements are biologically important in that they provide a sort of built-in way of exercising muscle systems and of beginning to gain control over motor movements. At the same time, periods of quiescence between action provide an opportunity for the infant to interact with the environment. Thus, notes Robertson (1993b), cyclic movements may regulate the infant's interactions. Interestingly, infant movements are typically suppressed during social interaction. In addition, the movement part of the cycle declines abruptly in strength at about two months as the infant begins to pay more attention to ongoing stimulation.

By the age of four months, cyclic motor movements decline and are eventually replaced by more deliberate, controlled movements. There is a close link between the development of control over physical actions and intellectual development. The infant's ability to manipulate and explore is what makes possible the discovery of the properties of physical objects, such as their permanence and their location in space. These discoveries, in turn, are related to the infant's growing ability to reason about objects and to develop concepts (ideas) (Bushnell & Boudreau, 1993). Hence Piaget's (1954) term **sensorimotor** to describe development in the first two years of life.

The order in which children acquire motor skills is highly predictable, although the ages at which these skills appear can vary considerably. Tables of developmental norms, such as that represented by the Denver tests (Figure 5.7), are sometimes useful for assessing a child's progress. However, here as elsewhere, there is no average child.

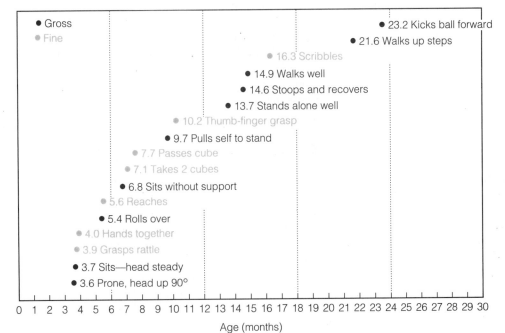

The ages at which children accomplish tasks like these vary considerably. Sitting without support, grasping with finger and thumb, even just raising one's head, all of these are usually precursors to that most wonderful experience, walking!

● Gross
● Fine
                                                      ● 23.2 Kicks ball forward
                                                    ● 21.6 Walks up steps
                              ● 16.3 Scribbles
                    ● 14.9 Walks well
                  ● 14.6 Stoops and recovers
                ● 13.7 Stands alone well
              ● 10.2 Thumb-finger grasp
            ● 9.7 Pulls self to stand
          ● 7.7 Passes cube
          ● 7.1 Takes 2 cubes
        ● 6.8 Sits without support
      ● 5.6 Reaches
      ● 5.4 Rolls over
    ● 4.0 Hands together
    ● 3.9 Grasps rattle
    ● 3.7 Sits—head steady
    ● 3.6 Prone, head up 90°

0 1 2 3 4 5 6 7 8 9 10 11 12 13 14 15 16 17 18 19 20 21 22 23 24 25 26 27 28 29 30

Age (months)

FIGURE 5.7

Age (months) at which 90 percent of norming sample of infants accomplishes described task. (Based on norms from W. K. Frankenburg & J. B. Dodds, 1992, Denver II. (2nd ed.). Training Manual. *Denver, CO: Denver Developmental Materials, Inc. Reprinted by permission of the publisher.)*

oung infants, and especially newborns, are not always very good experimental subjects. When Fantz (1963) wanted to see how newborns react to visual stimulation, one of the most important conditions for selecting subjects was whether they kept their eyes open long enough to be shown the stimuli. And when Meltzoff and Moore (1989) investigated the

newborn's ability to imitate, even though they chose ninety-three well-fed infants who showed no signs of hunger and who remained wide-eyed and alert for at least five minutes before the testing, only forty completed the brief test session. The remainder fell asleep, cried, had spitting or choking fits, or, of all things, had a bowel movement!

FIGURE 5.8

Difficulties in testing infants. Only 40 of 93 infants, ages 13.37–67.33 hours, completed an 8-minute test session. Testing had to be abandoned for the remaining 53 for the reasons shown. (Data from Meltzhoff & Moore, 1989, pp. 954–962.)

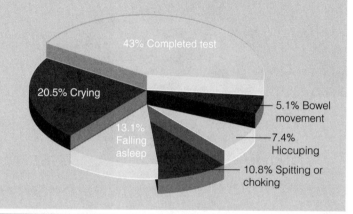

Note that the normal sequence of motor development reflects the two developmental principles mentioned in Chapter 4 with respect to fetal development. First, development is **cephalocaudal** (proceeds from the head toward the feet). For example, infants can control eye movements and raise the head before acquiring control over the extremities. Second, it is **proximodistal** (proceeds in an inward–outward direction). That is, children acquire control over parts of the body closest to the center before they can control the extremities. Thus, they can control gross motor movements before hand or finger movement (see Figure 5.7).

PERCEPTUAL DEVELOPMENT

The experience of human existence depends largely on our ability to make sense of the world and of ourselves. The struggle to discover what things are and what they mean begins in infancy and depends on three closely related processes: sensation, perception, and conceptualization.

Sensation is what happens when physical stimuli are translated into neural impulses that can then be transmitted to the brain and interpreted. Thus, sensation depends on the activity of one or more of our specialized sense organs— eyes, ears, and taste buds, for example.

In its simplest sense, **perception** is the brain's interpretation of sensation. Thus, wavelengths corresponding to the color red affect our retinas in specific ways, causing impulses that are transmitted to the part of our brain that deals with vision, causing us to *perceive* the color red. That we can now think about the color red, compare it to other colors, or make some decision based on it is a function of the third process, **conceptualization.**

In brief, sensation is primarily a physiological process dependent on the senses (the effect of light waves on the retina of the eye), perception is the result of sensation (the recognition that this is a red light), and conceptualization is a more *cognitive,* or intellectual, process (the realization that because this is a red light, I should stop).

Infant Vision

For years, researchers incorrectly assumed that newborns had poorly developed vision with little ability to detect form, patterns, or movements. One of the reasons for this relates to problems in doing research with preverbal infants. Now, however, researchers use increasingly sensitive instruments to detect infant eye movements, visual preferences, and a range of other subtle changes in infant behavior (Friendly, 1993). But there are still difficulties with infant research (see "At a Glance: Infants as Subjects" and Figure 5.8).

FIGURE 5.9

This glass-covered "visual cliff" is used in studies of infants' perception—and fear—of height. Interestingly, infants show little fear of heights until after they have learned to crawl.

VISION AT BIRTH

Is the infant's world fuzzy and blurred, or is it crisp and clear? Is it 20/20 or better—or worse? How can we find out?

Researchers, often using different methods and different criteria, don't always agree. However, a number of important things seem clear. First, infants are far from blind at birth, although some of their visual world may be somewhat fuzzy and blurred. Second, there is a three- to fourfold improvement in the infant's visual acuity between birth and the age of one year (Aslin & Smith, 1988). In fact, by the age of six months, the infant's visual acuity may be close to that of a normal adult. And third, the newborn's visual accommodation is more limited than that of adults. It appears that newborns focus most accurately at a distance of approximately 12 inches (30 cm) (Banks, 1980). Significantly, that is about the distance of the mother's face when she is feeding the infant. This is one of the ways in which the neonate appears to be programmed to perceive important aspects of its environment; there are others.

COLOR AND MOVEMENT

No one has yet determined exactly when color vision is first present in the infant. In Knoblauch, Bieber, and Werner's words, "an efficient screening test for infant colour vision remains an elusive goal" (1996, p. 60). However, indications are that infants are probably not able to discriminate among colors before the age of about two months (Burr, Morrone, & Fiorentini, 1996). By the age of four months, infants can discriminate not only among colors, but even show a preference for certain colors like pure reds and blues (Bornstein & Marks, 1982).

That newborns are sensitive to light intensity is shown by their **pupillary reflexes**, changes in the size of the pupil caused by changes in the brightness of visual stimulation. Also, their eye movements indicate that they are capable of visually following a slowly moving object within a few days of birth and are sensitive to patterns and contours as early as two days after birth. There is evidence as well that infants less than two months of age can perceive high-contrast contours (or edges) but that they cannot yet perceive relationships among different contours or forms (Wattam-Bell, 1996).

DEPTH PERCEPTION

In addition to perceiving color, movement, and form, and demonstrating preferences for these, young infants can also perceive depth. In Gibson and Walk's (1960) "visual cliff" studies, a heavy sheet of glass is positioned over a patterned surface; half of this surface is flush with the glass, and half is some 3 feet lower. An adult standing or sitting on the glass can plainly see a drop or cliff where the patterned material falls away from the glass. So can infants, who, when they are old enough to crawl, typically refuse to cross the deep part, even when their mothers call them from the other side. Thus, perception of depth is present at least from the time that the infant can crawl (Figure 5.9). Interestingly, as Bertenthal and Campos (1990) report, infants who have not yet learned to crawl don't normally show much evidence of fear when lowered onto the deep side—that is, their heart rates don't accelerate significantly. Hence, fear of falling is not entirely innate. These authors argue that through self-locomotion, infants develop the visual–vestibular sense essential to maintaining equilibrium (and related to fear of falling). In addition, locomotion requires them to develop skills of visual attention if they are to avoid colliding with objects; it allows them as well to learn about dangers associated with height, perhaps from parental reactions as they approach stairs or stand on chairs.

Visual Preferences

As we saw, if looking at these colors longer is an indication of preference, very young infants prefer reds and blues. It's possible, but perhaps not likely, that they really don't prefer these colors at all, but are simply puzzled or intrigued by them.

■ FACES OR PATTERNS

In a well-known study of infant visual preference, eighteen infants, ranging in age from ten hours to five days, were shown six circular stimulus patterns of varying complexity, the most complex being a human face and the least being an unpatterned circle (Fantz, 1963). Figure 5.10 shows the percentage of total time spent by subjects looking at each of the circles. That the face was looked at for significantly longer periods of time indicates not only that infants can discriminate among the various figures but also that they prefer faces—or perhaps that they prefer complexity.

It seems, argue de Haan and Nelson (1997), that infants are born with some innate knowledge about faces that allows them to recognize and be attracted to them. De Haan and Nelson suggest that this propensity is probably closely tied to the importance of recognizing primary caregivers if the infant is to form an attachment with them. There is evidence, for example, that by the second day of life infants already prefer their mother's face to that of a stranger (Morton & Johnson, 1991). However, as Leon (1992) points out, studies of infant reactions to their mother's faces have generally provided the infant with the sound of the mother's voice and sometimes with her scent as well. So it isn't clear that infants

actually prefer the sight of the mother rather than her scent or the sound of her voice.

■ ATTRACTIVE AND UGLY FACES

Infants not only recognize faces, but seem to prefer certain kinds of faces over others—and that may be very important. When given a choice of attractive or unattractive dolls, they play with the attractive ones (Langlois, Roggman, & Rieser-Danner, 1990). When confronted by an experimenter wearing either of two professionally constructed, highly realistic masks—one attractive and one unattractive—they withdraw from the attractively masked person far less and show more signs of positive emotions (Langlois et al., 1990). Even at the age of six months, infants seem to prefer faces judged attractive, whether the faces are male or female, young or old, black or white (Langlois et al., 1991).

Why? Perhaps, suggest Langlois and associates (1991), because attractiveness is a sort of facial "averageness." Faces that are unusual may be interesting, but "average" faces are more clearly representative of the ideal human gene pool. Average, and therefore attractive, faces are less likely to carry genes that might be harmful. It is perhaps for this reason that faces created by averaging and digitizing facial features are judged highly attractive (Langlois & Roggman, 1990).

The significance of these observations is threefold. First, as Slater (1996) argues, they point out the importance of the human face for the young infant. Second, it had long been thought that attractiveness is a learned and culturally determined quality, and that young infants would not likely have been exposed to enough models or to enough value judgments to have developed preferences. But this does not appear to be the case. And third, if infants prefer attractive faces, where does that leave ugly parents or grandparents—or brothers and sisters? Or even strangers? Recall the (1985) finding of Elder and colleagues that attractive daughters were better treated by their fathers during the 1930s Depression (see Chapter 3). Are attractive fathers and mothers treated differently by their infants? Their children? If so, what might the implications be for the ecological systems defined by the family?

How Infants Look

Earlier in this chapter you were asked to consider the problem of taking something as primitive as a newborn and designing it so that it would become as sophisticated as a two-year-old—and eventually a twelve-year-old, a forty-two-year-old, a ninety-two-year-old. In designing this little organism, we considered that, among other things, we would have to program it to become an extraordinarily capable information-processing system—a system tuned to notice and respond to the most important features of the environment, and predisposed, as well, to make sense of these features.

Does what we know about the infant's visual system conform to our design requirements? Haith (1980) says yes. The infant, he informs us, does not respond to the visual world in

FIGURE 5.10

Relative duration (percentage of fixation time) of initial gaze of infants in successive and repeated presentations of six circular visual stimuli. The graph depicts infants' preference for the human face and the more complex stimuli. (Based on data in Fantz, 1963, pp. 296–297.)

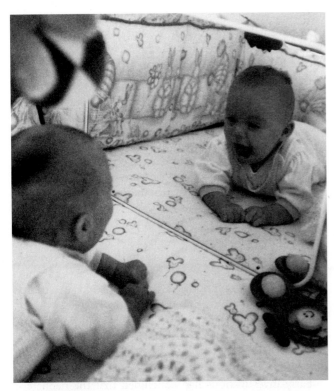

Infants not only recognize faces, but seem to prefer those that are attractive. And what can be more attractive than yours truly in the old mirror, what?

Third, when the newborn looks at a simple stimulus (such as a vertical or a horizontal line), the eyes cross back and forth repeatedly over the edges of the stimulus. The effect is to maintain a high level of firing in the visual cells.

Haith concludes that there appears to be a single important principle that governs the newborn's visual activity: *maximize neural firing.* It's a built-in principle that assures that the newborn's visual activity will lead to the greatest possible amount of information—a vital feature for an organism that has to be an outstanding information-processing system.

RULES THAT GUIDE INFANT LOOKING

This principle—maximize neural firing—is manifested in the rules that govern how babies look (Haith, 1980, p. 96):

- Rule 1. If awake and alert and light not too bright, open eyes.

- Rule 2. If in darkness, maintain a controlled, detailed search.

- Rule 3. If in light with no form, search for edges using broad, jerky sweeps of the field.

- Rule 4. If an edge is found, terminate the broad scan and stay in the general vicinity of that edge. Try to implement eye movements that cross the edge. If such eye movements are not possible in the region of the edge (as is the case for edges too distant from the center of the field), scan for other edges.

This view of the infant's visual perception as rule-governed and information-oriented rather than as stimulus-bound is a dramatic departure from psychology's traditional approach to these matters—a departure that is evident in many other areas of child study as well. This decade's infant—and child—is no longer merely a passive recipient of external influences, but has become active, exploring, information seeking. With regard to perception, Haith (1991) explains, we need to stop looking only at the infant's ability to sense and perceive; instead, we need to ask how perception contributes to the development of the infant's mind.

a simple, reflexive manner, response following stimulus in predictable, mechanical fashion. Instead, infants behave as though preprogrammed to follow specific rules geared to maximizing information. After all, acquiring information is the purpose of looking.

INFANTS LOOK TO SEE

So how do infants look? According to Haith's research, using infrared lights bounced off infants' corneas to reveal movements of their eyes, these are some of the important facts and what they mean:

First, contrary to what we might have expected, infants move their eyes even when there's no light, scanning the darkness in a highly controlled manner, using small movements appropriate for finding shadows, edges, spots. When viewing a uniformly lit but unpatterned field, their eye movements are broader, sweeping movements, suitable for discovering bolder contours. It seems clear that from birth, visual scanning patterns are not simply under the control of external stimuli (after all, scanning occurs in darkness as well as in light) but are internally controlled. It is as though the infant, true to our speculative design, is preprogrammed to obtain information.

Second, newborns actually *look* at stimuli, positioning their eyeballs so that a maximum amount of visual information falls on the fovea—the part of the retina that has the highest concentration of visual cells. It's as though the infant's scanning rules are designed to maximize stimulation—and, consequently, to maximize the gathering of information.

Hearing

Infant dogs, bears, cats—and many other animals—are deaf at birth; the human neonate is not. Instead, the ear is fully grown and potentially functional at about twenty-six weeks of gestation (Smith et al., 1990). In fact, most investigations indicate that neonates are only slightly less sensitive than adults to sound intensity (loudness).

Investigations of infant responsiveness to frequency (high or low pitch) have yielded somewhat inconsistent results partly because of the criteria employed, as well as because subjects of different ages have been used (Aslin, 1987). Studies of older infants usually show that sensitivity to higher frequencies increases with age (Trehub et al., 1991), and the general conclusion that infants (as opposed to newborns) are more sensitive to higher than to lower frequencies is widely accepted. Some researchers suggest that the common tendency of adults to raise the pitch of their voices when speaking to infants or young children is the result of an unconscious recognition of their greater sensitivity to higher frequencies.

■ DISCRIMINATING VOICES

Infants as young as three days can not only discriminate among different voices but also seem to prefer the sound of the mother's voice. In a study where systematic changes in an infant's sucking were reinforced with the sound of a woman reading a book, the infant responded to the sound of its mother but not to that of other women (DeCasper & Fifer, 1980). DeCasper and Fifer argue that this doesn't mean that infants have learned to distinguish their mother's voice from that of other women in the space of a mere three days— or that they've developed a preference for it in the same period of time. They suggest, instead, that these findings are evidence that the fetus can hear sounds while in the uterus, can distinguish among them, and can also learn. In fact, studies with microphones inserted in the uterus indicate that the fetus is commonly exposed to sounds at a level of 70 or more decibels (Smith et al., 1990).* If DeCasper and Fifer's findings and interpretation are correct, they provide evidence of learning **in utero** (Aslin, Pisoni, & Jusczyk, 1983).

Smell, Taste, and Touch

Smell, explains Farbman (1994), is one of the most important senses for driving the behavior of earth's animal species. It should hardly be surprising that newborns are highly sensitive to odors, as well as to tastes and touch. In fact, there is evidence of fetal sensitivity to odors as early as twenty-eight weeks after conception (Bartoshuk & Beauchamp, 1994). Also, animal studies indicate that when certain odors are introduced in the uterine fluid of pregnant animals, the behavior of their offspring is subsequently affected. Bartoshuk and Beauchamp speculate that it's possible that human infants begin to learn about the mother's diet and characteristic odors before they are born.

Within hours of birth, most infants turn their faces when exposed to a strong and unpleasant smell like ammonia. And their facial expressions are distinctly different when they are exposed to the smell of vanilla or of raw fish (Beauchamp, Cowart, & Schmidt, 1991).

In much the same way, they smack their lips when sweet things are placed on their tongues; they pucker their mouths in response to sour tastes. In fact, even premature infants respond differently to sweet than to nonsweet tastes (Bar-

toshuk & Beauchamp, 1994). It seems that the ability to taste and smell is present at birth, and it does not depend on experience. Even at the age of a single day, infants can differentiate among solutions varying in type and concentration of sweetener. And, contrary to what we might have been led to believe about the natural wisdom of the body, infants appear to have an innate liking for sweet things (Beauchamp et al., 1991).

The importance of the newborn's sensitivity to odors and tastes (and that of the fetus) lies in the possibility that certain behaviors and preferences may be learned at a very early age. Recall, for example, the study that indicated that at the age of three days, infants already seem to prefer the voices of their mothers to those of other women. A study by Porter and associates (1991) indicates the same might be true for certain smells associated with the mother. In this study, a group of two-week-old infants were observed in a situation in which they had a choice of turning toward a clean, odor-free pad, or toward a pad worn on their mother's breast. In spite of the fact that these infants were bottle-fed, they typically spent more time turned toward the pad that carried the mother's odor.

■ PAIN SENSITIVITY

Early investigations had concluded that the neonate is remarkably insensitive to much of the stimulation that children and adults would find quite painful. Circumcision doesn't really hurt boy babies, they assured us. But they (whoever they are) were probably at least partly wrong: Boy babies do holler when circumcised! And more recent research indicates that neonates of both sexes are sensitive to pain. McLaughlin and colleagues' (1993) survey of 352 physicians found that the vast majority now agree that newborns feel pain, and most use anesthetics for medical procedures with infants.

■ CAPACITIES OF THE NEONATE

Neonates are remarkably alert and well suited to their environments. They can hear, see, and smell; they can turn in the direction of food, suck, swallow, digest, and eliminate; they can respond physically to a range of stimuli; and they can cry and vomit. Still, they are singularly helpless creatures who would surely die if the environment did not include an adult intimately concerned with their survival. There is much they need to learn, much with which they must become familiar, before they can stand on their own intellectual as well as physical feet. (See Summary Table 5.4.)

■ COGNITIVE DEVELOPMENT

For a long time, Maya Pines (1966) tells us, psychology neglected the infant's mind, as if everyone assumed that babies didn't really have minds, or if they did, they wouldn't be very important at this stage of development. But our views have changed. "Babies are very competent," says Bower (1989). "They are set to use whatever information we give them" (p. ix).

---

*The human hearing threshold is 0 decibels; an ordinary conversation at 3 feet is at about 65 decibels; the noisiest spot at Niagara Falls is at around 75 decibels; with prolonged exposure, hearing damage can result at around 100 decibels. Smith and colleagues (1990) suggest that the fetus is exposed to far higher sound levels than had been anticipated.

▲ SUMMARY TABLE 5.4

Sensation and Perception

in Young Infants

KEY TERMS	DEFINITIONS
Sensation	The effect of stimulation on the sense organs; specifically, the translation of stimulation into neural impulses; a physiological process.
Perception	The brain's interpretation of sensation; the recognition of what is perceived.
Conceptualization	Conscious interpretation of the significance of perception; thinking; a more cognitive process.
Characteristics of infant vision	World somewhat fuzzy at birth.
	Built-in accommodation for about 12 inches.
	Color vision present by about 2 months.
	Ability to perceive depth present by the time infant can crawl.
	Infants look at reds and blues longer than at other colors.
	Recognize and prefer faces within days of birth.
	Prefer mother's face (hence recognize it) within 2 days.
	Prefer attractive to unattractive faces.
Rules of visual perception	Maximize neural firing, maximize information, by
	■ keeping eyes open when awake.
	■ maintaining searching eye movements even in darkness.
	■ searching for edges using broad scans.
	■ when edge is found, changing to shorter eye movements to scan edge.
Hearing	Hearing present even prenatally.
	Sensitivity to higher frequencies may increase with age.
Smell, taste, touch	High sensitivity to odors.
	Preference for mother's smell.
	Preference for sweet tastes.
	Sensitivity to pain present in newborns.

As far back as 1920, Piaget had begun to map the course of the child's intellectual development. Piaget's story of the growth of children's minds tells of their growing awareness of the world in which they live and their discovery or invention of ways of interacting with this world. It is a complex and fascinating story, but it is not the whole story; there are other theories of cognitive development, other explanations of how we come to know. Some of these are termed information-processing approaches. They look at what is involved in memory: deriving information, abstracting, sorting, organiz-

ing, analyzing, and retrieving, for example. We look at memory processes in infancy before we turn to Piaget's theory of cognitive development.

Infant Memory

If neonates are ever to reach the level of competence of the two-year-old, there is a great deal that they must learn and remember: what is edible and what isn't, how to get from here to there, how to ask for things, how to hold a cup, how to get people's interest and attention, and much more.

The neonate's memory is not nearly as efficient and as powerful as yours or mine. Clearly, however, from the very beginning there must be some ability to learn and remember. This primitive ability will eventually develop into the type of memory that is characteristic of the two-year-old, the forty-year-old, the ninety-year-old.

■ STUDIES OF INFANT MEMORY

One common way of investigating memory in very young infants is to use components of the *orienting response* described earlier. For example, researchers might look at the infant's response to the same photograph shown on two different occasions. If the infant remembers something about the photograph, heart rate would not be expected to change in the same way as it might when the infant is presented with a completely new photograph.

A second approach is simply to look at how long it takes for the infant to **habituate** (become accustomed) to a stimulus. Habituation might be revealed in patterns of eye movements (the infant stops looking at the stimulus) or, again, in changes in components of the orienting response, such as respiration or heart rate.

A third measure of infant memory involves the infant's behavior. Sullivan and colleagues (1991) presented one-day-old infants with a novel smell (a citrus odor—in this study, a conditioning stimulus) paired with stroking (a reinforcing stimulus) a total of ten times, each for thirty seconds. Control babies received the stroking or the smell as well, but not the two paired. The next day all infants were given the odor for thirty seconds. Control infants responded indifferently, but those for whom the odor had been paired with stroking turned their heads toward the odor even if they were asleep. But a different odor produced no consistent response—strong evidence of learning (and memory) at the age of one day.

In another study, Swain, Zelazo, and Clifton (1993) had day-old newborns listen to a word, and monitored them as they turned their heads toward the sound. Within a short period of time, these infants habituated (learned) the word and stopped turning. One day later, half of these infants were again exposed to the same word; the other half heard a different word. Again, all infants initially oriented to the word, turning their heads toward it. But those who were exposed to the same word both days habituated significantly more rapidly than those who heard a new word—clear evidence that they remembered something of the word.

PHYSICAL AND COGNITIVE DEVELOPMENT: INFANCY   *139*

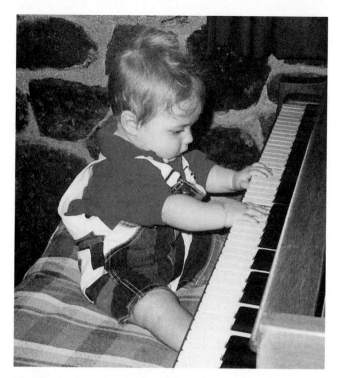

The infant's memory is not as powerful or well organized as yours or mine. It would be too much to expect that this child should remember the sounds that correspond to each key or should be able to organize them into a melody. But that she even recognizes the piano and remembers how to sit and pound its keys is no small feat either.

SUMMARY TABLE 5.5
Development Phases in Infant Memory

PHASE	CHARACTERISTICS
first:	Evidence of memory found in cessation of looking or disappearance of orienting response; with learning, habituation period becomes shorter; memory a fleeting thing, of short duration.
second:	Beginning at around three months; longer term memory evident in intentional actions; recognition of things and people.
third:	By 8 months; infant memories are more abstract, more symbolic; can *pay attention* and *try to remember.*

Still, evidence is that the infant's memory for most things appears to be of relatively short duration. For example, young infants who are conditioned to associate a puff of air with a tone, or a feeding schedule with a bell, may remember from one day to the next—or perhaps for six or ten days. But without any reminders in the interim, all evidence of memory is likely to be gone within a few days (Rovee-Collier, 1987).

■ DEVELOPMENT OF INFANT MEMORY

Perlmutter (1980) describes three sequential phases in the development of infant memory. In the first, the infant's memory seems to be largely a matter of neurons firing when a new stimulus is presented and the firing stopping with habituation. As the infant becomes more familiar with the stimulus (that is, learns and remembers), the period before habituation becomes shorter.

The second phase, which begins at around three months, is related to the infant's growing ability to accomplish intended actions. Infants now actively look and search; they begin to reach, even to grasp; they explore; and they recognize things and people. Recognition is a sure sign of memory.

In the third phase, by the age of eight or so months, infant memories have become much more like our own in that they are more abstract and more symbolic. They remember classes of things like fuzzy objects and big people and pets and building blocks and beets.

Our adult memories, and those of older children, are greatly helped by certain strategies, the most important of which are **organizing, rehearsing,** and **elaborating.** Infants don't systematically use any of these strategies. But two-year-old infants already have some notions about what memory is and understand mental-event terms like *remember, think, know,* and *pretend.* When asked to remember something, they pay attention and they try to remember. These, says Wellman (1988), are strategies in their own right.

There is a great distance between the immature memory of the week-old child who can demonstrate a vague recollection of a familiar smell or sound, and that of the one-year-old who mistakenly yells "Dada" when he sees a stranger's familiar-looking back in the supermarket. There is also a vast distance between this one-year-old's memory and the memory of the twelve-year-old whose intellectual strategies permit mental feats of which the one-year-old cannot yet even dream. (See Chapter 7 for more information about memory.) (See also Summary Table 5.5.)

Basic Piagetian Ideas

Of what can the one-year-old dream? And the infant? Initially, perhaps not a great deal if, as Jean Piaget claims, the infant's world is truly a world of the *here and now.* If it is, in fact, a world that makes sense only when the infant looks at it, hears it, touches it, smells it, or tastes it, there might not be much with which to dream. This Piagetian infant does not have concepts in the sense that we think of them—no store of memories or hopes or dreams, no fund of information with which to think.

But what the neonate has are the sensory systems and the cognitive inclinations that make it into a self-reinforcing, information-processing organism. When Piaget describes the infant, he speaks of an organism that continually seeks out and responds to stimulation and that, by so doing, gradually builds up a repertoire of behaviors and capabilities—and, at the same time, constructs a representation of the world.

ASSIMILATING AND ACCOMMODATING

At first, behaviors are limited mainly to the simple reflexes with which the infant is born, but in time, these behaviors become more elaborate and more coordinated with one another as the infant adapts to the world. And the complementary processes that make **adaptation** possible are those of **assimilation** and **accommodation** (see Chapter 2).

To review briefly, assimilation and accommodation are highly active processes whereby the individual searches out, selects, and responds to information, the end result of which is the actual construction of knowledge. Imagine, for example, a young child walking on a windblown beach, stooping now and again to pick up pebbles and toss them onto the water. In Piaget's view, there is a **schema** involved here—a sort of mental or cognitive representation—that corresponds to the child's knowledge of the suitability of pebbles as objects to be thrown upon the waves, as well as other schemata that have to do with the activities involved in bending, retrieving, and throwing. The pebbles are, in a sense, being assimilated to appropriate schemata; they are understood and used in terms of the child's previous knowledge.

Imagine, now, that the child bends to retrieve another pebble but finds, instead, that she has picked up a stick. The stick is clearly not a pebble and perhaps should not be responded to in the same way. But still, why not? The "throwing things on the big waves" schema is readily available, momentarily preferred. And so the stick too is *assimilated* to the throwing schema, and the child tries to hurl it toward the water. But the new object's heaviness is sudden and surprising, the child's throwing motion inadequate, and the stick falls again upon the sand. Now, when she picks it up again, she doesn't hurl it in quite the same way. Instead, she holds it in two hands tightly grasped with her pudgy fingers, and she pushes hard with her little legs as she throws. In Piaget's terms, she has *accommodated* to the characteristics of this object that make it different from the pebbles she has been throwing.

EQUILIBRATION

To assimilate, then, is to respond in terms of preexisting information; it often involves ignoring some aspects of the situation to make it conform to aspects of the mental system. In contrast, to accommodate is to respond to external characteristics and to make changes in the mental system as a result. One of the governing principles of mental activity, says Piaget, is a tendency toward **equilibration**—that is, a tendency toward maintaining a balance between accommodation and assimilation. At one extreme, if an infant always assimilated and never accommodated, there would be no change in schemata (mental structure) and no change in behavior. Everything would be assimilated to the sucking schema, the grasping schema, the looking schema (that is, everything would be sucked, or grasped, or simply looked at). Such a state of disequilibrium would result in little adaptation and little cognitive growth.

▲ SUMMARY TABLE 5.6
Piaget's Four Factors
That Shape Development

Equilibration	■ The tendency to balance assimilation (responding in terms of previous learning) and accommodation (changing behavior in response to the environment).
Maturation	■ Genetic forces that do not determine behavior but are related to its sequential unfolding.
Active Experience	■ Interaction with real objects and events allow the individual to discover things and to invent (construct) mental representations of the world.
Social Interaction	■ Interaction with people leads to the elaboration of ideas about things, people, and self.

At the other extreme, if everything were accommodated to and not assimilated, schemata—and behavior—would be in a constant state of flux. Now the nipple would be sucked, now it would be chewed, now pinched, now swatted—again, an extreme state of disequilibrium resulting in little adaptation.

FACTORS THAT SHAPE DEVELOPMENT

Equilibration, says Piaget, is one of the four forces that account for the construction of knowledge (Piaget, 1961). That is, it accounts for adaptation and cognitive growth throughout development. Another is **maturation,** a sort of biologically determined unfolding of potential. Maturation—or biology—does not determine cognitive growth but is related to the unfolding of potential. A third factor is *active experience*—the child's interaction with the world. The fourth is *social interaction,* which helps the child develop ideas about things and about people as well as about the self. These four factors—active experience, maturation, equilibration, and social interaction—are the cornerstones of Piaget's basic theory (see Summary Table 5.6).

The Object Concept

The infant's world is a "blooming, buzzing mass of confusion," William James (1892) informed us more than a century ago. In those years, psychologists believed that the neonate's senses didn't function at birth, or functioned very poorly, so that sensations like colors, sounds, smells, and tastes were all indistinct and blurred. As we saw earlier, they were wrong: Children see movements and shapes almost from birth, they can detect and remember odors and faces, and they can hear even before they are born.

Still, James was at least partly right. Why? Because in the infant's *here and now* world, there are no permanent objects.

Our understanding and reasoning about the world demand that things be real, objective, substantive, independent. It would be more than a little confusing if our worlds, like that of this neophyte philosopher, disappeared from our minds with the mere closing of our eyes. Discovering the permanence of objects is one of the great achievements of early infancy.

The nipple exists when the infant sees, touches, or sucks it; when it can't be sensed, it doesn't exist. Imagine what the world would be like, suggest Wellman and Gelman (1992), if we thought objects disappeared and reappeared—that is, if we had no concept of objective objects. This **object concept,** they explain, is absolutely fundamental to our reasoning about the world, which demands that objects be real, out there, substantive, and independent of us. There is no "out there" for infants; they must discover the permanence and objectivity of objects for themselves. This discovery is one of the truly great achievements of infancy.

■ DISCOVERING THAT THINGS ARE REAL

The processes by which infants discover that objects are real and permanent depend on experiencing and exploring the real world. When Stambak and associates (1989) videotaped young infants' responses to different objects such as nesting cups or hollow cubes or rods, they found that even very young infants organize their behaviors in systematic ways, as though actively exploring. Some subjects typically banged different objects with the rod; some explored the insides of the hollow cubes with their fingers or with their hands if the cubes were large enough. It's almost as if these infants had already invented questions and problems and were devising little experiments to find answers.

Not only does the exploration of objects by young infants become increasingly systematic with advancing age, but it also involves more varied activities. Initially, exploration is mainly visual or oral; later, it also becomes manual. By the age of three or four months, most infants use both hands and mouth to explore. And, increasingly, choice of type of exploration depends more and more on the objects being explored: Some things are more easily understood, more meaningful, when held in both hands, licked, drooled on, and gummed emphatically.

■ PIAGET'S CLASSIC OBJECT CONCEPT STUDY

To investigate the infant's understanding of objects, Piaget (1954) showed children an attractive object and then hid it from view. If the object exists only when infants perceive it, reasoned Piaget, they will make no effort to look for it when they can't see it even if they actually saw it being hidden. When children begin to look for an object they can no longer see, this is definite evidence that they can imagine it and therefore know it still exists.

Piaget found that in the earliest stage, children don't respond to the object once it is removed; next, they search for the object, but only in the place where they last saw it; finally, they know that objects continue to exist, and they look for them in a variety of places. This final stage, claimed Piaget, occurs near the middle of the second year of life (about age eighteen months).

■ PIAGET'S UNDERESTIMATION OF INFANTS

Some later investigations of the development of the object concept indicate that the age of acquisition is perhaps younger than Piaget suggests (Wellman & Gelman, 1992). For example, Bower (1989) used infants' orienting response to determine whether they had developed notions of object permanence. In one study, infants are shown a ball and then a screen is moved between the infant and the ball; a few seconds later, the screen is removed. On some trials, the ball has been taken away. When infants do not have object permanence, they should not be surprised if the ball is gone. But they would be surprised to see it gone if they expected it to be there—in other words, if they had acquired notions of object permanence. Bower's main finding is that infants as young as three weeks of age seem to have some notion of object permanence, provided that the object is hidden from view for only a few seconds. When the object is hidden for longer (15 seconds as opposed to 1½ seconds), infants at this age all show surprise when the ball is still present after the screen is removed. Similarly, Baillargeon (1987) found that infants as young as 3½ months seemed to have some primitive notions about the solidity of objects. When one object moved through a space that should have been occupied by another object, they seemed surprised.

It seems, then, that Piaget underestimated the age at which infants begin to develop notions of object permanence. Even one-month-old infants appear to have a short-lived recollection of absent objects. And by the age of three or four months, they have begun to understand that objects are solid and stationary (Baillargeon, 1992). However, it will still be a long time before the three-week-old infant deliberately searches for an object that has not been seen just recently (Bower, 1989).

Sensorimotor Development

Piaget believed that children's understanding of the world throughout most of infancy is determined by the activities they can perform on it and by their perceptions of it—hence

TABLE 5.7

Piaget's Stages of Cognitive Development

STAGE	APPROXIMATE AGE	SOME MAJOR CHARACTERISTICS
Sensorimotor	0–2 years	Motoric intelligence
		World of the here and now
		No language, no thought in early stages
		No notion of objective reality
Preoperational*	2–7 years	Egocentric thought
Preconceptual	2–4 years	Reason dominated by perception
Intuitive	4–7 years	Intuitive rather than logical solutions
		Inability to conserve
Concrete operations†	7–11 or 12 years	Ability to conserve
		Logic of classes and relations
		Understanding of number
		Thinking bound to concrete
		Development of reversibility in thought
Formal operations‡	11 or 12– 14 or 15 years	Complete generality of thought
		Propositional thinking
		Ability to deal with the hypothetical
		Development of strong idealism

*Discussed in Chapter 7.
†Discussed in Chapter 9.
‡Discussed in Chapter 11.

his label for this stage: **sensorimotor period.** Piaget simplifies the infant's cognitive development during this period by dividing it into six substages. Table 5.7 summarizes Piaget's stages of intellectual development from birth through adolescence.

■ EXERCISING REFLEXES (BIRTH TO ONE MONTH)

In Piaget's view, infants learn little that is new during the first month, instead spending much of their waking time exercising the abilities with which they are born (sucking, looking, grasping, and crying). But these activities have an important cognitive function (in addition to the obvious survival function of actions like sucking). By repeatedly performing these activities, the infant eventually develops control over them. By the end of the first month, infants are quite proficient at reaching and grasping, as well as at looking and sucking. However, they still have trouble putting different actions together to obtain a single goal. For example, infants presented with a visually appealing object can look at it but cannot reach toward it. Deliberately reaching and grasping

is a complex activity dependent on the purposeful coordination of looking schemes, reaching schemes, and grasping schemes. This coordination is not usually apparent until the age of three to five months.

■ PRIMARY CIRCULAR REACTIONS (ONE TO FOUR MONTHS)

Early in infancy, children engage in many highly repetitive behaviors (thumb-sucking, for example) called **primary circular reactions.** These are reflexive responses that serve as stimuli for their own repetition. For example, if the infant accidentally puts a hand or a finger into the mouth, this triggers the sucking response, which results in the sensation of the hand in the mouth, which leads to a repetition of the response, which leads to a repetition of the sensation, which leads to a repetition of the response, and so on. This circle of action is called *primary* because it involves the infant's own body.

■ SECONDARY CIRCULAR REACTIONS (FOUR TO EIGHT MONTHS)

During the third substage, a new class of circular reactions appears. These deal with objects in the environment rather than only with the child's body, and are therefore called **secondary circular reactions.** Six-month-old infants engage in various secondary circular reactions, many of them resulting from accidentally doing something interesting or amusing that is then repeated again and again. By kicking, Piaget's young son caused a row of dolls dangling above his bassinet to dance. The boy stopped and watched the dolls. Eventually, he repeated the kicking, perhaps not intending to make the dolls move, but because they had stopped moving and no longer attracted his attention. But again they moved, and again he repeated the action so that, within a very short period of time, he was repeating the behavior over and over—a *secondary circular reaction*. This type of behavior, which Piaget described as *behavior designed to make interesting sights and sounds last,* is especially important because it signals the onset of intention. In Frye's (1991) words, these are behaviors in which infants "knowingly employ means to goals" (p. 15).

■ PURPOSEFUL COORDINATIONS (EIGHT TO TWELVE MONTHS)

The development of intention becomes even more apparent when, in the fourth substage, infants begin to coordinate previously unrelated behaviors to achieve a goal. They can now look at an object, reach for it, grasp it, and bring it to the mouth with the intention of sucking it. It is also during this substage that infants begin to recognize familiar objects and people—which explains why they may now become upset when a parent leaves or when a stranger appears (see Chapter 6).

Also, at about this time, the infant begins to use signs to anticipate events (Mom packing her briefcase is a sign she's leaving—and a signal to holler). Understanding that certain events are signs that some other event is likely to occur is closely related to an understanding of causality. For the young infant, whose logic is not always as perfect as yours or mine, the sign itself is often interpreted as the cause. A child who realizes that Mommy will be leaving when she packs her briefcase may believe that the cause of leaving is the packing of the briefcase—just as the cause of going to bed is taking a bath or putting on pajamas.

■ TERTIARY CIRCULAR REACTIONS (TWELVE TO EIGHTEEN MONTHS)

In the fifth substage, children begin to modify their repetitive behaviors deliberately to see what the effects will be. Rayna, Sinclair, and Stambak (1989) observed a **tertiary circular reaction** in the behavior of a fifteen-month-old girl whose current preoccupation was with breaking objects. Breaking something often seemed to lead to a repetition of the behavior (hence a circular response) but with deliberate variation (hence tertiary—recall that primary and secondary reactions are repetitive with occasional accidental variations). For example, in one session, she picked up a ball of clay, scratched at it until a piece had come off, examined the piece, and then repeated the procedure several times, each time examining the clay on her finger. Next, she noticed a ball of cotton, picked it up, and pulled it into two halves; then she pulled one of the halves into two more pieces, and again, and again. Similarly, in another session, a fifteen-month-old boy who had been tearing apart bits of clay happened across a piece of spaghetti, pressed it to the floor, broke it, picked up the largest piece, broke it again, and repeated the process a number of times. Once finished, he attempted to break a short plastic stick, he tore a sheet of paper into tiny bits, and then he demolished a pipe cleaner. Whoopee!

The most important feature of tertiary circular reactions is that they are repetitive behaviors deliberately undertaken to see what their effects will be—that is, to explore.

■ MENTAL REPRESENTATION (EIGHTEEN MONTHS TO TWO YEARS)

By the end of the sensorimotor period, infants are well on their way to making a transition from an *action-based (motoric)* intelligence to a progressively more *cognitive* intelligence. During this final substage of the sensorimotor period, infants demonstrate that they have begun to learn to represent objects and events mentally. As a result, they can now occasionally combine these representations to arrive at mental solutions for problems, and they are now able to anticipate the consequences of many of their activities before actually executing them. Their behavior is consequently no longer restricted to trial and error, as it was previously. In Piaget's terms, it is as though the child can now begin to *internalize* (represent mentally) actions and their consequences without having to actually carry them out.

As an illustration of mental representation, Piaget describes his twenty-two-month-old daughter's behavior when she was given a partly open matchbox containing a small thimble. Because the opening was too small for her to withdraw the thimble, she had to open the box first. A younger infant would simply grope at the box, attempting clumsily to remove the thimble. But Piaget's daughter appeared instead to be considering the problem, unconsciously opening and closing her mouth repeatedly as if mirroring her thoughts. Finally, she placed her finger directly into the box's partial opening, opened it, and removed the thimble.

The ability to conceptualize the environment is also reflected in infants' mushrooming language development, which, according to Piaget, is greatly facilitated by their imitative behavior.

Imitation in Infancy

In the earliest stages of imitation, infants are able to imitate objects, activities, or people that are immediately present. Stick your tongue out in front of a three-month-old, and a tongue may be stuck right back out at you; open your mouth wide, or your eyes, and the infant might do the same.

■ IMITATION IN VERY YOUNG INFANTS

There is controversy over exactly when the ability to imitate first appears (Wyrwicka, 1996). Some researchers (for example, Meltzoff & Moore, 1989) report that at a mere two weeks of age, infants already are able to imitate simple actions like sticking out the tongue or opening the mouth wide. Reissland (1988) claims to have detected imitation in the first hour after birth. His subjects were twelve awake and alert neonates; models bent over them, widening or pursing their lips as instructed. The results? Infants moved their lips in accordance with lip movements of the models significantly more often than at variance with them. Reissland concludes that the ability to imitate is already present at birth.

Some researchers do not agree that neonates are actually imitating when they stick out their tongue or purse their

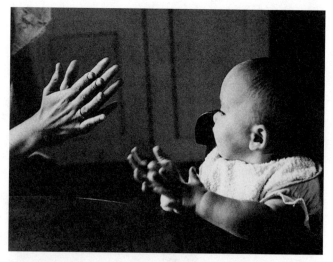

The ability to imitate is a powerful tool for new learning. This little tyke has not only begun to learn how to clap, which can be a socially useful behavior, but she has also learned how to make her mother applaud.

lips in apparent response to a model doing the same thing. Perhaps infants do not truly imitate these facial gestures, but instead simply manifest a generalized, almost reflexive response related mainly to feeding and released by the nearness of the model (Kaitz et al., 1988). It is possible, says Anisfeld (1991), that increased tongue protrusion following modeling occurs because tongue protrusion has been inhibited during modeling.

Meltzoff and Moore (1989) concede that although the evidence supports the conclusion that very young infants have a general ability to match certain adult behaviors, imitative behavior in the newborn is not completely automatic and easily triggered. In addition, many of the imitative behaviors of the very young infant do not continue when the model is no longer present. In other words, the infant is initially capable of imitating only when the model is there or within a very short period of time thereafter. Piaget (1951) suggested that deferred imitation—the ability to imitate something or someone no longer present—is not likely to occur before the age of nine to twelve months.

■ IMITATION IN OLDER INFANTS

Masur (1993) did a longitudinal study of ten boys and ten girls between ten and twenty-one months of age, and found that imitation became increasingly common during this period. The second year of life, claims Masur, is a crucial period for the infant's burgeoning ability to represent mentally and to imitate. And although repetition of familiar repetitive behaviors like tongue protrusion might occur among very young infants, it isn't until the beginning of the second year that infants begin to imitate novel actions. The significance of this transition is that with the capacity to imitate new behaviors, an infant can now use imitation as a powerful tool for new learning—and especially for learning language. In fact, Masur's (1993) research also indicates that there is a dramatic spurt in infants' imitation of novel words in the second half of year two, and that this spurt is reflected in a sudden expansion of vocabulary.

The older infant's imitation is not limited to imitating and learning from adults, but is also evident in peer–peer imitation. Toddlers (older infants) imitating other toddlers is highly evident in child-care facilities. It has also been investigated by Hanna and Meltzoff (1993), who describe a series of experiments in which fourteen- to eighteen-month-old infants readily learned to imitate other "trained" toddlers. In addition, these toddlers demonstrated—in different settings and as much as two days later—that they remembered much of what they had learned through imitation.

■ ACHIEVEMENTS OF IMITATION IN INFANCY

There are at least three different kinds of learning that imitation makes possible for infants, claim Hay, Stimson, and Castle (1991). First, they learn about places by following people around, in much the same way that young kittens and other animals learn about places by following their mothers and siblings. When given the opportunity, infants readily follow their mothers in unfamiliar surroundings; often, too, they will follow strangers or a moving toy. Significantly, once they have followed a leader, they are more likely to go back and explore on their own.

Second, imitation facilitates certain familiar social behaviors, like sharing toys. When experimenters (or parents or siblings) play "give and take" games with infants, infants are subsequently more likely to want to give toys to others.

Third, infants learn new social behaviors by observing them in others. And among the most important of new behaviors that they learn at least partly through imitation are those that have to do with speaking and understanding a language. (See Summary Table 5.8.)

▌LANGUAGE

In the beginning, the infant has no words—only cries. Words are simply more noises.

But for the two-year-old, words are like magic spells that can transform the world. Words can make things appear and disappear; they can change tears into laughter; they have an almost palpable reality, like cats and colors.

And for teenagers and grown-ups, words have still other meanings and other functions. Among other things, words communicate feelings, ask and answer questions, affirm our meaningfulness to others, and theirs to us.

▌Communication

Despite its tremendous power, language is not essential for **communication** (the transmission of messages). Animals that don't have language can nevertheless communicate danger. Whitetail deer wave their tails; pronghorn antelope bristle their rump patches; ground squirrels whistle. Some of these signals communicate danger to other members of the same species.[*]

Communication between humans and other animals also occurs. An animal trainer who instructs his dog to roll over is communicating with the animal (at least when the dog obeys—and perhaps even when the dog does not obey). And the dog who walks to his empty dish, looks at his master, and then begins to growl is not only dangerous but is also communicating very effectively.

---

[*]Some of these signals may also communicate to members of *other* species. For example, the flag-waving of the whitetail deer might not only signal danger to other deer, but might also serve as a signal to predators like wolves (Alcock, 1984). It says, in effect, "Ha, ha, I've seen you, so forget it." And the wolf reads the signal. Because he knows he can't ordinarily catch a healthy deer in a prolonged chase, he lies down and licks his chops and dreams of sneaking up on other deer.

Piaget's Six Substages of Sensorimotor Development with Some Corresponding Achievements in Imitation and Object Permanence

SUBSTAGE AND APPROXIMATE AGE IN MONTHS	PRINCIPAL CHARACTERISTICS	OBJECT CONCEPT AND IMITATION
1. Exercising reflexes (0–1)	Simple, unlearned behaviors (schemes) such as sucking and looking are practiced and become more deliberate.	▪ Preparation for development of object concept. ▪ Some evidence of imitation of facial gestures like opening the mouth.
2. Primary circular reactions (1–4)	Activities that center on the infant's body and that give rise to pleasant sensations are repeated (thumb-sucking, for example).	▪ Fleeting recollection of objects hidden from view for only a few seconds. ▪ "Sporadic imitation," in Piaget's terms.
3. Secondary circular reactions (4–8)	Activities that do not center on the child's body but that lead to interesting sights or sounds are repeated (repeatedly moving a mobile, for example).	▪ Search for objects where they were last seen. ▪ Beginning of systematic imitation (of sounds, for example).
4. Purposeful coordinations (8–12)	Separate schemes become coordinated (such as the ability to look at an object and reach for it); familiar people and objects are recognized; primitive understanding of causality begins, implicit in the use of signs to anticipate events.	▪ Beginning of imitation of new models. ▪ Systematic search for desired objects.
5. Tertiary circular reactions (12–18)	Repetition with variation (repeating a sound with a number of deliberate changes, for example) is experimented with.	▪ Widespread imitation of models, including peers. ▪ Search for objects in a variety of locations.
6. Mental representation (18–24)	Transition between sensorimotor intelligence and a more cognitive intelligence is made; activity is internalized so that its consequences can be anticipated before its actual performance; language becomes increasingly important in cognitive development.	▪ Deferred imitation, the imitation of models and actions that aren't present. ▪ Sophisticated notion of the permanence of objects.

A Definition of *Language*

This communication, however, is a far cry from that made possible by language. The parrot who can say "Polly wants a cracker" is not only boringly conventional but is also probably incapable of saying "A cracker wants Polly, heh, heh" with the intention of conveying a different meaning. The parrot merely mimics. It cannot deliberately rearrange sounds according to established rules to say what it means. It does not know language.

Language *is the use of arbitrary sounds, with accepted referents, that can be arranged in sequences to convey different meanings.* This definition includes what Brown (1973) describes as the three essential characteristics of language: *displacement, meaning,* and *productiveness.*

Language involves displacement because it makes possible the representation of objects and events that are not immediate—that are *displaced*—in both time and space. "The moon was a ghostly galleon," we can say, "tossed upon cloudy seas." Yet neither ghosts nor galleons, nor even moons nor seas, need be where we can touch them or see them. Indeed, what you and I can speak of need not even exist.

One of the primary functions of language is the communication of *meaning.* Although **psycholinguists**—those who study the relationship between language and human func-
tioning—do not always agree on the best definition for meaning, we in our ordinary conversations tend to agree much more than disagree. In fact, it is because you and I have similar meanings for words and sentences that we can communicate as we are now doing.

The third characteristic of language, *productiveness,* means that, given a handful of words, a set of mutually accepted rules about how they can be combined, and agreement about the significance of the various pauses, intonations, and other characteristics of speech, we can produce meanings forever. Language presents so many possibilities for meaningful combinations that almost every day of your life you will say something that no one else has ever said in exactly the same way. Language makes you creative.

Elements of Language

Linguists describe four basic components of language: phonology, semantics, syntax, and pragmatics. Each is essential for effective communication with language.

Phonology refers to the **phonemes,** or sounds, of a language. A phoneme is the simplest unit of language and is nothing more complex than a single sound such as that represented by a consonant or word. There are forty-five phonemes in the English language.

CONCEPT	MEANING
Communication	■ The transmission of a message; does not require language
Language	■ Deliberate use of sounds with accepted referents, arranged in purposeful sequences to convey meaning
Psycholinguistics	■ Scientists who study the relationship between language and human functioning

Elements of Language

Phonology:	Sounds of language; phonemes are the simplest sounds; morphemes, combinations of phonemes, are the simplest meaningful units in a language.
Semantics:	Refers to meaning; significance.
Syntax:	Grammar; the set of rules that govern the accepted, correct use of words to express meaning.
Pragmatics:	Implicit rules governing aspects of communicating with language, including how to conduct conversations, expression, rules of intonation, accents, and so on.

Phonemes can be combined to form **morphemes,** which are the units of meaning **(semantics)** in language. Morphemes may be made up of sounds such as *ing* or *ed*—word endings that affect the meanings of words—or of whole words. Children cannot produce morphemes until they can first pronounce the phonemes. Simply making the sound is not enough; they must be able to make it when they intend to do so, and they must also be able to combine morphemes in meaningful combinations.

Organizing words into meaningful sentence units requires an intuitive knowledge of **syntax,** or grammar, the set of rules governing the combinations of words that will be meaningful and correct for the speakers of that language.

As children practice and master sounds (phonemes), meanings (semantics), and grammatical rules (syntax), they must also learn a large number of unspoken rules and conventions governing conversation. Put another way, they must learn the **pragmatics** of language. An implicit knowledge of pragmatics is what tells children when and how they should speak. It includes uncounted rules and practices governing manners of expression, intonation, accents, and all the other subtle variations that give different meanings to the same morphemes and that might vary appreciably from one context to another. For example, that parents use shorter sentences, speak in higher-pitched voices, and use more concrete names and fewer abstractions when speaking with young children than with other adults is a function of their knowledge of pragmatics.

Phonology, semantics, syntax, and pragmatics are the elements of language. Most of us acquired these elements in an amazingly painless, effective, and efficient way without really being conscious of what we were doing. (See Summary Table 5.9.)

■ LANGUAGE DEVELOPMENT IN THE FIRST TWO YEARS

The transition from the first sounds of the neonate, the cries and the grunts, to the more controlled coos and gurgles, eventually to the babbling, and finally to the word is a fascinating and complex process that is not yet clearly understood.

Early studies of how infants acquire language were often concerned with counting their vocabularies and examining the difference between words they actually used (their **active vocabulary**) and words they didn't use but understood (their **passive vocabulary**). In the early stages of language learning, infants can usually understand many more words than they can use in their own speech. And before using words in speech, many also develop a wide range of communicative gestures (Bates et al., 1989).

Language learning may be divided into two broad stages: the *prespeech stage* and the *speech stage*. In the prespeech stage, which lasts until about age one, meaningful speech sounds are gradually developed. In the speech stage, the child progresses from the first words to an increasingly sophisticated knowledge of grammar, pragmatics, and conversation.

Achievements in the Prespeech Stage

Researchers believe that the ability to use and to understand words grows out of a complex series of interactions between infant and parents. These interactions are referred to collectively as the **language acquisition support system (LASS)** by Bruner (1983). These interactions are reflected in at least four major achievements of the prespeech stage: learning how to take turns, developing a repertoire of gestures, learning to discriminate and produce sounds, and eventually arriving at the first word. In the following four sections, we look at each of these four achievements of the prespeech stage. (See Table 5.10 for a description of the progressive development of infants' language-related abilities, with approximate ages of attainment.)

■ TURN-TAKING

Knowing when and how to take turns is basic to adult conversation. When we have conversations, we wait for the signals that tell us it's our turn, and we give others their signals—well, most of us do; there are some who simply shout a little louder. Most of us have learned the rules that govern turn-taking without really knowing that we have learned them and without, in most cases, being able to verbalize them. Common turn-taking signals include an upward or downward change of pitch at the end of an utterance, the

TABLE 5.10

Age at Which Infants Demonstrate a Given Language Capability

LANGUAGE CAPABILITY	APPROXIMATE AGES	
	50% OF INFANTS	90% OF INFANTS
Responds to bell		at birth.
Laughs	1.9* mos.	3.1 mos.
Squeals	1.7 mos.	4.3 mos.
Says "dada" or "mama," nonspecific	6.5 mos.	9.1 mos.
Imitates speech sounds	5.2 mos.	8.8 mos.
Says 3 words other than "mama," "dada"	13.6 mos.	18.0 mos.
Combines 2 different words	19.8 mos.	2.1 yrs.
Points to six named body parts	19.8 mos.	2.4 yrs.

*For example, 1.9 months equals 1 month and 27 days; 2.4 years equals 2 years and 4 months and 24 days.
Source: From the revised *Denver II* by W. K. Frankenburg and J. B. Dodds (1992). Denver Developmental Materials, Inc., Box 692-19, Denver, CO 80206-0919. Reprinted by permission.

completion of a grammatical clause, a drawl on the last syllable, or the termination of a gesture.

Amazingly, children seem to have a relatively sophisticated awareness of turn-taking signals at very young ages. Elias and Broerse (1996) looked at interactions between forty-eight mothers and their infants when the infants ranged in age from three months to two years. They found a remarkable tendency for mother–infant pairs to interact in alternating fashion. Similarly, Mayer and Tronick (1985) videotaped ten mothers and their infants in face-to-face interaction when the infants were two, three, and five months of age. Analyses of videotapes revealed that not only did infants rarely vocalize when their mothers were speaking, but they seemed to understand the mother's turn-taking signals. They responded not only to head and hand movements, but also to changes in intonation at the ends of utterances, to terminal drawls, and to the completion of grammatical clauses. Accordingly, they cooed and smiled mostly during the mother's pauses. Mothers, for their part, modified the number of turn-taking signals given depending on the child's responsiveness. Thus, even at the age of two months, infants and their mothers are already taking turns.

GESTURES

One of the important achievements of the prespeech stage, says Masur (1993), is the appearance of the intention to communicate, which is first evident in signals and gestures that clearly have meaning for both infant and caregiver. Squirming and gazing intently at the milk bottle are pragmatic (effective) ways of saying to Mama, "If I don't get that *!!$@ing bottle soon, I'm gonna holler!"

Well before they begin to use words, most infants have developed a repertoire of gestures that are clearly meaningful

Language consists of sounds (phonology) that have meaning (semantics) when used according to certain grammatical rules (syntax) as well as practical rules (pragmatics). But communication involves far more than simply language. This toddler already possesses a wealth of nonverbal gestures that makes it far easier to say, "Mom, the cat's digging up your hibiscus again."

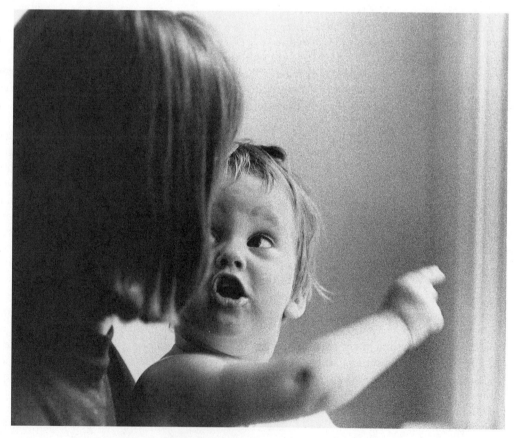

for both infant and caregivers. One of the most common of these gestures, notes Bretherton (1991), is the gaze. Infants use looking not only to indicate what they want, but to direct other people's attention. And they typically alternate the gaze between the desired object and the person whose attention they are trying to direct, as if to try to confirm that the message is being received.

Pointing, another extremely important gesture for most infants, is also used to direct attention, and changes over time, as the infant becomes progressively more aware of situations in which pointing is warranted and is likely to be an effective way of communicating (Franco and Butterworth, 1996). Other common gestures include waving, reaching, grimacing, and so on. Some of these gestures are so common and so important, notes Locke (1992), that their absence may be an early warning of problems in language development. Similarly, problems with turn-taking in early infancy may also be a signal of language delays (Moseley, 1990).

■ SOUND DISCRIMINATION

Communicating through language depends on sounds—the ability of the infant to discriminate among them and the ability to produce them.

Infants appear to be able to discriminate sounds at a very early age. Moffitt (1971) conducted an experiment in which the heart rates of five- and six-month-old infants were monitored while they were exposed to taped recordings of the sounds "bah" and "gah." Changes in heart rate whenever the sound changed indicated that these infants could tell the difference between them. More recent studies, using the same two syllables, indicate that infants require slightly louder sounds than adults to discriminate correctly, especially with noisy backgrounds (Nozza et al., 1990a, 1990b).

With language experience, infants' ability to discriminate reliably among difficult sounds like "sa" and "za" improves. However, if the sounds are not part of their language, they may experience difficulty discriminating among them even as adults—the sounds "la" and "ra" for a native Japanese speaker, for example (Miyawaki et al., 1975).

■ SOUND PRODUCTION

Discriminating among sounds is one aspect of early language learning; producing intended sounds is the other.

Infants as young as three weeks produce three kinds of sounds, reports Legerstee (1991). There are the longer, *melodic sounds* characterized by variable pitch; *vocalic sounds,* which are short, more nasal bursts characterized by relatively uniform pitch; and *emotional sounds* such as laughing, crying, and fussing.

One of the remarkable things about the infants' early sounds is that their emission is context-dependent. In a longitudinal investigation of eight infants, aged three to twenty-five weeks, Legerstee (1991) found that melodic sounds typically occur when mothers are conversing with their infants, that vocalic sounds are more common with unresponsive adults, and that emotional sounds occur far more often in contexts involving other people than in situations where the infant is interacting with an inanimate object such as a doll.

It was long believed that all the sounds of every language in the world are uttered in the babbling of an infant—even in the babbling of deaf infants. This belief leads directly to the conclusion that the ability to produce speech sounds is innate, a conclusion that does not appear to be entirely true. For example, although the first sounds uttered by deaf infants are very similar to those of hearing children, their later vocalizations are typically quite different. These first sounds, say Eilers and Oller (1988), are precursors to the form of babbling in which infants finally utter well-formed syllables with clearly articulated consonants and vowels—a stage that does not occur until some time between seven and ten months. Before then, infants make unarticulated noises: They goo, squeal, growl, whisper, and yell. And although it might be possible to discern many sounds that resemble those found in the world's 5,000 or so languages in these early infant sounds, their utterances remain unsystematic and do not obey the laws of syllables (requiring clarity and a complete vowel of adequate duration).

Infants' first sounds are "soft sounds," notes Bijou (1989), but eventually they gain control over their sound-producing apparatus. Also, they discover that producing sounds is fun, as is evident in the fact that contented infants may spend hours in solitary babbling without any prompting. As a result, by the age of ten months, most hearing children babble clearly, systematically, and repetitively. Children who have hearing problems do not reach this stage until later (Robinshaw, 1996). If the problems are severe enough, most do not progress through the normal stages of language learning (Deal & Haas, 1996). "It cannot be maintained," say Eilers and Oller (1988), "that babbling is independent of hearing" (p. 23).

That babbling is highly dependent on hearing is also clear from a large number of studies that have looked at the babbling of infants exposed to different language environments. Blake and de Boysson-Bardies (1992) analyzed the babblings of three Canadian-English and three Parisian-French infants. Although their babbling was initially highly similar, after the age of one, babbling patterns became predictably distinct. Similarly, a longitudinal study of a French and an American infant revealed progressive differences in babbling relating directly to the infant's language environment (Levitt & Utman, 1992). And comparisons of the babbling of French and Japanese infants show consistent increases in French-only sounds for the French infants corresponding with a rapid decline in French-only sounds for Japanese infants in the second year of life (Halle, de Boysson-Bardies, & Vihman, 1991).

Although certain sounds do appear in the babbling of almost all infants, many other sounds are almost never heard even though they are an important part of some languages. The most common sounds that infants babble are the ones that are easiest given the anatomical structure of their vocal apparatus—consonants such as *b, d, w,* and *m* (described by linguists as *stop, glide,* or *nasal* consonants). Thus, words like *mama, papa,* and *dada* are among the simplest for virtually all infants. In fact, there are some who believe that *mama* and *papa* are common to an astounding number of the world's languages precisely because they are among the first systematic sounds that infants babble. In many of these languages, says Ingram (1991), "'Mama' emerges as a general request for the fulfilment of some need, while 'papa' is a more descriptive term for parents" (p. 711).

■ THE FIRST WORD

It is difficult to determine exactly when infants say their first word. Many infants repeat a sound such as "bah" many times before it becomes associated with an object. The point at which a sound like "bah" ceases to be a babble and become a word (*ball,* for example) may not be entirely clear but has usually occurred by the age of one year.

Not surprisingly, *mama* or *papa* is the first clearly recognizable word spoken by many infants.* The appearance of the first word is rapidly followed by new words that the child practices incessantly. Most of an English-speaking child's first words are nouns: simple names for simple things—the simple things usually being objects or people that are part of the here and now: "dog," "mama," "banket" (blanket), "yefant" (elephant). Verbs, adjectives, adverbs, and prepositions are acquired primarily in the order listed, with the greatest diffi-

---

*"The first word," said my grandmother, "we should pay attention to. Like the Danes say, 'Children and drunkards speak the truth.'" Then she added, "But 'daddy' isn't always the truth."

culty usually being the use of pronouns, especially the pronoun *I* (Boyd, 1976).

But before learning words, infants have begun to show signs that they understand much more than they can say—words that will not be part of their active vocabulary for some time, as well as entire sentences. "Stick out your tongue," she is told by a proud parent, and she sticks out her tongue. "Show Daddy your hand," and she shows it. "Can you wink?" Sure can. Two eyes, though.

To simplify a complex process, the learning of language is described in this text in terms of six sequential stages (based on Wood, 1981). The first of these, just described, is the *prespeech stage,* which lasts until approximately age one. It consists of the crying, the gooing, and the babbling just described; its major achievements are the appearance of the intention to communicate, the learning of gestures for that purpose, learning how to take turns, and eventually learning how to discriminate sounds, to produce them, and to make words from them. The next two stages—those of the *sentencelike word* and the *two-word sentence*—are described in the following sections. The remaining three stages are detailed in Chapter 7 (see Table 5.11).

The Sentencelike Word (Holophrase)

Some time after the sixth month (usually around age one), children utter their first meaningful word. This word's meaning is seldom limited to one event, action, or person but

---

TABLE 5.11

Stages in Children's Development of Grammar

STAGE OF DEVELOPMENT	NATURE OF DEVELOPMENT	SAMPLE UTTERANCES
1. Prespeech (before age 1)	Crying, cooing, babbling.	"Waaah," "dadadada."
2. Sentencelike word (holophrase) (by 12 months)	The word is combined with nonverbal cues (gestures and inflections).	"Mommy." (meaning: "Would you please come here, mother?")
3. Two-word sentences (duos) (by 18 months)	Modifiers are joined to topic words to form declarative, question, negative, and imperative structures.	"Pretty baby." (declarative) "Where Daddy?" (question) "No play." (negative) "More milk!" (imperative)
4. Multiple-word sentences (by 2 to 2½ years)	Both a subject and predicate are included in the sentence types. Grammatical morphemes are used to change meanings (*ing* or *ed,* for example).	"She's a pretty baby." (declarative) "Where Daddy is?" (question) "I no can play." (negative) "I want more milk!" (imperative) "I running." "I runned."
5. More complex grammatical changes and word categories (between 2½ and 4 years)	Elements are added, embedded, and permuted within sentences. Word classes (nouns, verbs, and prepositions) are subdivided. Clauses are put together.	"Read it, my book." (conjunction) "Where is Daddy?" (embedding) "I can't play." (permutation) "I would like some milk." (use of *some* with mass noun) "Take me to the store." (use of preposition of place)
6. Adultlike structures (after 4 years)	Complex structural distinctions made, as with *ask–tell* and *promise.*	"Ask what time it is." "He promised to help her."

Source: Based in part on Barbara S. Wood, *Children and communication: Verbal and nonverbal language development* (2nd ed.), © 1981, p. 142. Reprinted by permission of Prentice-Hall, Inc., Englewood Cliffs, New Jersey.

often means something that an adult would require an entire sentence to communicate—hence the term **holophrase.** Thus, although most holophrases are nouns, they are not used simply for naming. When a child says "milk," she might mean, "There is the milk." She might also mean, "Give me some milk," "I'm thirsty," "I want you to hold me," "Go buy some milk," or "Are you going to do it to the cow again?"

Two-Word Sentences

Not surprisingly, the progression of speech development is from one word to two (roughly by the age of eighteen months)—and later to more than two. There does not appear to be a three-word stage following this two-word stage, but rather a multiword stage where sentences range in length from two to perhaps five or more words.

Masur (1993) notes that there are three widely recognized general language-learning milestones in the first two years of life: The first is the acquisition of communicative gestures in the second half of year one; the second is the appearance of the first words at about age one; and the third is a dramatic vocabulary spurt at about seventeen or eighteen months. The appearance of two-word sentences coincides closely with this sudden acceleration in vocabulary growth (Goldfield & Reznick, 1996).

BABY TALK

When infants are first learning words, the range of syllables available is limited. Many of their words are one- or two-syllable words, which often repeat the same syllable in different combinations ("mommy," "daddy," "baby," "seepy" [sleepy], "horsy," "doggy"). Even when it is incorrect to do so, the child may repeat the syllable in a one-syllable word, as in "car car" or "kiss kiss."

In an attempt to communicate with children on their level, parents sometimes exaggerate the errors committed by their infants. The result is occasionally something like, "Wou my itsy bitsy witta baby come to momsy womsy?" But there is no evidence that parental (or grandparental) models of this type hamper the rapid and correct acquisition of language. In the early stages, the warmth of the interaction may be more important than the nature of the language employed.

TELEGRAPHIC SPEECH

The transition from holophrases to two-word sentences generally occurs at around eighteen months and coincides with a period of increasingly rapid vocabulary growth. Speech at this stage is sometimes described as being telegraphic because it eliminates many parts of speech while still managing to convey meanings. "Dog allgone" is a two-word utterance "telegraphed" from the lengthier adult equivalent, "The dog is not in this location at this time."

Interestingly, mothers often tend to *expand* the infant's telegraphed speech, report Bloom and associates (1996). In addition, much of what they say to their infants takes the form of simply acknowledging the child's verbalizations, repeating them, or clarifying them. Whereas the preponderance of mothers' talk to their infants in this study occurred in response to something the infant had said, most of what infants said was self-generated. That is, most mother–infant "conversations" are initiated by the infant and not by the mother.

EARLY GRAMMAR

Whether precise grammatical functions can be accurately assigned to the infant's two-word utterances is a matter of some debate. The functions of the words *fish* and *eat* in the two-word utterance "fish eat" are, in fact, dependent on the intended meaning. But because the child does not use number agreement (for example, "fish eats" to mean "the fish eats" and "fish eat" to mean "I eat fish") or order ("eat fish" versus "fish eat") to signal meaning, the psycholinguist can never be certain that children at this stage are aware of grammatical functions.

By the age of two, infants have reached the point where they can name all the familiar objects and people in their environment. More than this, they can now combine words into meaningful sentencelike units. They can also use adjectives and adverbs, questions, and simple negatives and affirmatives; and they have begun to learn a variety of subtle and implicit rules governing intonation, inflection, and the conventions that guide conversations.

But there is much more yet to be learned; there remain three stages in our six-stage description of the sequence of language acquisition. The story of that sequence continues in Chapter 7. (See Summary Table 5.12.)

FROM SENSATION TO REPRESENTATION

The term *sensorimotor* describes well the predominant relationship between infant and world, but it does not describe the most important cognitive achievements of the first two years of life—achievements that move the growing person from infancy to childhood. By definition, infants are no longer infants when they are no longer speechless.

Some of the achievements of infancy are apparent in Table 5.13. They include the realization of the independent existence and permanence of objects, a dawning understanding of cause-and-effect relationships, and the learning of language coupled with the effects this has on cognitive development. These achievements, together with children's recognition of their own identities—their selves—represent a dramatic transition from a quasi-animalistic existence to the world of thought and emotions as we know it. But although it is a dramatic transition, at least in its import, it is neither sudden nor startling. Those who follow the lives of individual children closely (and daily) never see the transition from sensorimotor intelligence to preoperational thought. It happens suddenly and irrevocably on the second birthday only in textbooks. Real life is less well organized.

Language Achievement in Infancy

STAGE	TIMING AND CHARACTERISTICS
Prespeech (first year)	
turn-taking	evident in first mother–infant interactions; progressively less co-vocalization with time.
gestures	begin to develop in first weeks; used to communicate prior to language; continue after language achieved; gazing is first highly important gesture.
sound discrimination	language experience contributes significantly to sound discrimination.
sound production	melodic or vocalic sounds, or emotional sounds like crying produced very early; more systematically repetitive sounds of babbling well developed by 7 to 10 months.
first word	first meaningful word by age 12 months—give or take a few months.
Sentencelike Word (by age 1)	
holophrases	by age 1; single words with multiple, enlarged meanings.
Two-word sentences (18 mos.)	
baby talk	often involves repetition of simple syllables; parental imitation does not appear to delay language learning.
telegraphic speech	short sentence constructions used to "telegraph" meanings that could be more accurately expressed in longer sentences.
vocabulary spurt	very rapid increase in vocabulary size toward end of second year.

TABLE **5.13**

Average Ages for Mental Development in Infants

AGE (MONTHS)	MENTAL BEHAVIOR ANTICIPATED
0.2	Regards person momentarily, responding either to speech or to movements.
0.7	Eyes follow moving person.
0.7	Makes definite response to speaking voice.
1.5	Smiles or laughs in response to another person's speaking to and smiling at him or her.
2.0	Visually recognizes mother; expression changes when infant sees mother bending over to talk to him or her.
2.6	Manipulates red ring placed in infant's hand or grasped by infant.
3.8	Carries red ring to mouth during free play.
3.8	Inspects own hands.
4.1	Reaches for cube, even if not actually touching it.
5.1	Laughs or shows pleasure when held and played with.
5.8	Lifts cup with handle.
6.0	Looks for spoon that has fallen.
9.1	Responds to verbal request *not* accompanied by gesture.
12.0	Turns pages of book, even if effort is clumsy.
14.2	Says two words meaningfully (approximations all right if clear).
20.6	Puts two or more words denoting two concepts into one sentence or phrase.

Source: Adapted from *Bayley Scales of Infant Development* by N. Bayley, 1969. Reproduced by permission. Copyright © 1969 by The Psychological Corporation, New York, N.Y. All rights reserved.

FOCUS QUESTIONS: SUMMARY ANSWERS

1. What are some of the advantages and disadvantages of breast-feeding?

   ▪ Human breast milk is infant-specific, easily digested, nourishing, and useful in guarding against the possibility of diarrhea; as well, it provides a degree of immunity to infant illnesses.

2. How might the neonate's behavioral repertoire be described?

   ▪ The behavioral repertoire of the neonate consists largely of reflexes (for example, sucking, Moro, Babinski, palmar [grasping], swimming, stepping, swallowing, and sneezing). Many of these disappear with the development of the brain and the achievement of voluntary control over movements.

3. How do infants look?

   ▪ Infants can detect movement and form shortly after birth, but their accommodation is somewhat inflexible. They are probably unable to see colors before the age of two months or so. The infant's looking seems to be directed by rules that maximize information.

4. Do infants think? What do they think?

   ▪ The neonate's memory is not as efficient, as powerful, or as long term as that of older children or adults, but there is memory for smells and sights within days of birth. By the age of three months, infants actively search and show signs of recognition.

5. What is the basic sequence in language acquisition in early infancy?

■ Four achievements of the prespeech stage of language development (first year) include learning turn-taking (evident in very early mother–child interactions), learning gestures to communicate (especially gazing and pointing), learning sound discrimination (present at very young ages), learning to produce sounds (an important contributor is babbling, which becomes systematic by the age of seven to ten months), and finally producing the first meaningful word.

STUDY TERMS

accommodation, 141
active vocabulary, 147
adaptation, 141
apnea, 129
assimilation, 141
Babinski reflex, 131
cephalocaudal, 134
cerebral palsy, 127
communication, 145
conceptualization, 134
cretinism, 127
cyclic movements, 132
elaborating, 140
equilibration, 141
galvanic skin response (GSR), 131
habituate, 140
head-turning reflex, 131
holophrase, 151
in utero, 138
lactation, 125
language, 146
language acquisition support system (LASS), 147
maturation, 141

Moro reflex, 131
morphemes, 147
neonate, 124
object concept, 142
organizing, 140
orienting response, 131
palmar reflex, 131
passive vocabulary, 147
perception, 134
phonemes, 146
phonology, 146
pragmatics, 147
primary circular reactions, 143
prone, 129
proximodistal, 134
psycholinguists, 146
pupillary reflexes, 135
reflex, 131
reflexes, 124
rehearsing, 140
rooting reflex, 131
schema, 141
secondary circular reactions, 143
semantics, 147

sensation, 134
sensorimotor, 132
sensorimotor period, 143
SIDS home monitors, 130
sucking reflex, 131
sudden infant death syndrome, 128

supine, 130
syntax, 147
tertiary circular reactions, 144
vegetative reflex, 131

FURTHER READINGS

The following two sources are simple, nontechnical descriptions of development in infancy. They offer many practical suggestions that might be useful for parents interested in understanding and promoting the intellectual development of their infants:

Devine, M. (1991). *Baby talk: The art of communicating with infants and toddlers.* New York: Plenum.

White, B. L. (1985). *The first three years of life* (rev. ed.). Englewood Cliffs, NJ: Prentice-Hall.

Nursing mothers who might be concerned about the possible effects of prescription (and other) drugs on their infants might want to consult the following alphabetical compendium of drug effects on both fetus and nursing infant:

Friedman, J. M., & Polifka, J. E. (1996). *The effects of drugs on the fetus and nursing infant.* Baltimore, MD: Johns Hopkins University Press.

The following two books present readable and authoritative accounts of what is known about SIDS:

Guntheroth, W. G. (1995). *Crib death: The sudden infant death syndrome* (3rd ed.). Armonk, NY: Futura.

Sears, W. (1995). *SIDS: A parent's guide to understanding and preventing Sudden Infant Death Syndrome.* Boston: Little, Brown.

This text is a clear and useful account of Piaget's theory:

Wadsworth, B. J. (1996). *Piaget's theory of cognitive and affective development* (5th ed.). New York: Longman.

Bower's book is a stimulating explanation of how experience makes the rational infant even more competent:

Bower, T. G. R. (1989). *The rational infant: Learning in infancy.* New York: W. H. Freeman.

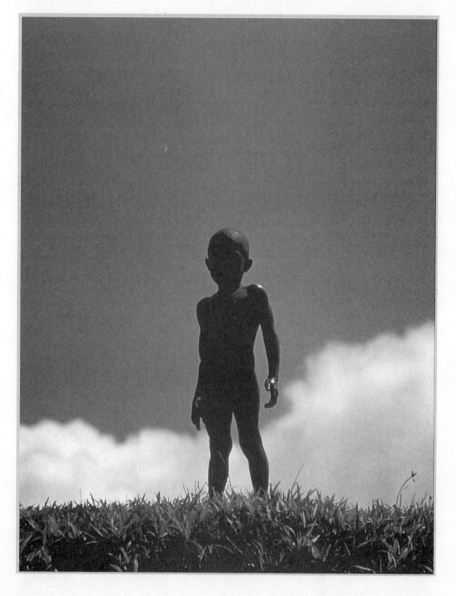

Social Development: Infancy

The face of a child can say it all, especially the mouth part of the face.

JACK HANDY
Deep Thoughts

Barumba was born in the spectacular highlands of New Guinea, an island poised like some prehistoric bird above the continent of Australia. His father had spent the day strutting through the village, showing off his vest of brilliant orange, red, and green parrot feathers, his resplendent collar of green beetle shells, and his skirt of gorgeous plumes plucked from birds of paradise. He knew that if the others in the village looked at him in admiration, it would bode well for his first child. ¶ Barumba's mother, too, had chosen to adorn herself for her first birth. Around both arms, she wore tightly woven, brightly colored armbands of orchid fibers. Around her neck hung the necklace of dog's teeth made for her by her mother, and below it dangled her favorite string of red nuts. And through her nostril she had the long leg bone of a wild guinea fowl. ¶ The contractions were almost continuous now, and the mother knew it would be soon. Anxiously, she watched as the top of the head appeared, long black hair slicked down, now the ears, now the neck—yes! yes! yes! ¶ "He will be a great artist," she yelled out in her excitement, and her husband crashed into the hut, beetle shells clanking, so that he too might see. ¶ Sure enough, the infant's umbilical cord was wrapped around his neck. And, as the Mundugumor have known for centuries, only those infants whose umbilical cords are wound around their necks at birth stand any chance of becoming great artists. Amazingly, they are right. ¶ "Hot dang!" said Barumba's father. ¶

This Chapter

e are a little like the Mundugumor, suggests Pogrebin (1980). We know, of course, that it's ridiculous to think that the position of the umbilical cord is of any consequence. Instead, we look for appendages between the legs of our infants. To a considerable extent, these tell us how to interact with our infants, what sorts of toys they are most likely to enjoy, what their personalities should be. And surprisingly often, our predictions are every bit as accurate as those of the Mundugumor! No?

This chapter looks at the extent to which early influences affect the development of gender roles. It deals, as well, with predominant infant states, infant emotions, infant temperament, and the development of attachments between infants and their caregivers, along with infant reactions to strangers and to separation from those to whom they are attached. It looks, too, at the care of young infants in contemporary societies, at current approaches to parenting, and at the effects these approaches might have on children. Finally, it looks at infants with characteristics different from those of the mythical average child—those with exceptionalities.

INTERACTIONS IN THE FAMILY CONTEXT

Current approaches to understanding the infant experience pay increasing attention to the importance of the infant's interactions with parents, siblings, dogs, and so on. However, discovering the nature of family interactions and their influences is not simple; interpreting them is even more difficult. Traditionally, the analysis has been of two-person, or **dyadic, interactions**—for example, mother–infant, father–infant, infant–sibling. This model, useful though it is, has one major shortcoming: It fails to take into consideration the far more complex nature of the majority of the families into which infants are born, as well as the great variety of indirect effects that parents and families can have on infants (White & Woollett, 1992). Now researchers have begun to recognize that how infants and children affect parents' lives is extremely important (Ambert, 1992).

As an illustration, consider Marlis, an especially difficult infant who cries a lot, refuses her mother's breast unpredictably, and soils her diaper at awkward times almost as if to say, "There, that'll teach ya!" Her mother, in turn, is easily annoyed, impatient, highly emotional, and given to temper tantrums. Brad, on the other hand, is an angel of a baby. He sleeps regularly, seldom cries, loves his mother's breast, and soils his diaper only at regular intervals and always very politely with an apologetic little grimace as if to say, "Phoo and yuk! I sure hate to have to do that!" And Brad's mother is calm, enthusiastic, patient, and absolutely delighted with her infant.

In all likelihood, parent–infant interactions will be very different in these two cases. They will reflect distinct charac-

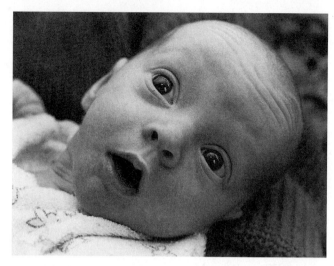

Current developmental models investigate not only how parents influence their infants, but also how infants influence parents. That this child seldom cries or complains, and that she looks so impressed by her mother, will surely have a profound effect on how her mother interacts with her.

teristics of infant and parent. As Ambert (1992) points out, there is a tremendous range of infant and child characteristics, and behaviors, that can have profound effects on parents. To list but a few of the more obvious, child misbehaviors and problems such as truancy, poor academic performance, illnesses, and juvenile delinquency might significantly affect parents' lives. In contrast, more positive child behaviors—for example, in academics or athletics—can also have profound effects on parents. Less obvious but perhaps no less important, there is evidence that the birth of an infant often changes the relationship between husband and wife (sometimes increasing stress and discord, sometimes having the opposite effect); that discordant and conflict-ridden marriages are sometimes related to the development of antisocial behavior in children; that highly supportive marital relationships are related to caregiving skills with young infants; that the birth of an infant can frequently make a good marriage better, although it is less likely to make a bad one good; and that among the key qualities of parenting reflected in cognitive development and adjustment are sensitive mothering (attentiveness, warmth, responsiveness, and stimulation) and involved fathering (doing things with infants, including caregiving and playing) (Ambert, 1992).

But, as Belsky points out, we still know "very little about the direct influence of the child on marital relations and even less about the reverse process of influence" (1981, p. 17). The adoption of a **contextual model** that considers the family in addition to the mother and the father may increase our knowledge considerably.

A wide range of infant characteristics are especially important influences on the infant's developmental context. Among these are the infant states (current general condition), infant temperament (the biological basis of personality), the sex of both parent and infant, and parental personality characteristics.

INFANT STATES

My cousin Arthur cried a good deal of the time when he was an infant.* Crying was one of his predominant **infant states** (state is the general condition of the infant).

Wolff (1966), following a careful study of the behavior of infants, describes six distinct infant states: *regular sleep, irregular sleep, drowsiness, alert inactivity, alert activity,* and *crying* (the last two states are sometimes grouped together and termed *focused activity*). These states are described in Summary/Interactive Figure 6.1. Note that they are essentially descriptions of *central nervous system* activity. Interestingly, there is evidence that these states are present in the fetus, although they are less easily detected at that time. We know, for example, that toward the end of the prenatal period, the fetus spends alternating periods of time sleeping and awake (Groome et al., 1997).

Newborns vary consistently in the amount of time spent in each state, some sleeping more than half the day; others sleeping for only a few hours (Brown, 1964). Similarly, some cry as much as 40 percent of the time and others hardly at

---

*His wife believes that's why he now complains so much as a grown man. "It's his nature," she explains, strangely proud that her husband should have such a nature. "Maybe," says one of my other cousins, rather unkindly, "it's because she doesn't have a nature herself."

all. With increasing age, expected changes include a decline in the amount of time spent sleeping and an increase in alert activity.

Although the average neonate sleeps as much as 75 to 80 percent of the time, for most young infants periods of sleep are relatively short and are interspersed with many brief periods of wakefulness. It isn't clear whether infants dream while they sleep. However, an extremely high proportion of the infant's sleeping time (as much as 50 percent) is characterized by **rapid eye movement (REM) sleep.** And we do know that in children and adults, most dreams occur during REM sleep. The amount of REM sleep declines gradually during **infancy** (from birth to the age of two). By the age of two years, approximately 25 percent of the infant's sleep is of the REM variety—very similar to that of an adult.

Note that the concept of infant state refers simply to the infant's condition of alertness. That is, infant state takes into account whether the infant is sleeping, drowsy, alert, or crying. As we saw, however, infants can differ markedly in the amount of time they characteristically spend in each of these states. Differences in predominant infant states may, in fact, reflect basic, genetically influenced differences in temperament.

INFANT TEMPERAMENT

Differences in the customary ways of reacting and behaving that differentiate adults from one another are generally referred

---

SUMMARY/INTERACTIVE FIGURE 6.1

States reflecting infant's responsiveness to environment: *Predominant states of the infant—that is, the infant's vigilance and wakefulness—vary a great deal from one infant to another. Some sleep more; others cry; some study their environments.*

Interaction: *If you have access to an infant, you might use one or more of the observation techniques described in Chapter 1 (diary description, time sampling, specimen description, or event sampling) to study infant states and perhaps to compare two or more infants. (Based on information in Wolff, 1969.)*

State	Description	Responsiveness	Relative distribution in newborn
Regular (deep) sleep	Largely motionless, eyes closed, regular breathing	No response to mild stimuli	
Irregular sleep	Twitching motions, eyes closed, irregular breathing	Sounds or bright light can elicit grimace or smile	
Drowsiness	Moderately active state precedes or follows sleep; eyes may be closed or open	Responsive to stimuli	
Alert inactivity	Relative inactivity, eyes open, breathing more rapid than regular sleep, examining environment	Highly responsive; maintains examination of world	
Alert activity	High activity, eyes open, rapid breathing	Moderate responsiveness to stimuli	
Crying	High activity, eyes open, low alertness, rapid breathing	Low responsiveness to stimuli	

Relative distribution in newborn: Regular (deep) sleep 33.3%; Irregular sleep 33.3%; Drowsiness 10%; Alert inactivity 10%; Alert activity 8.3%; Crying 5%.

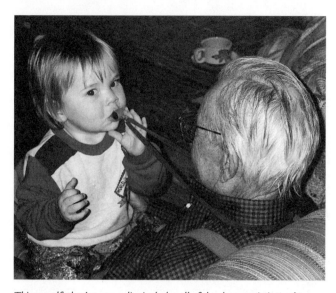

This grandfather's personality includes all of the characteristics and tendencies that have resulted from a lifetime of experiences interacting with some early biological predispositions. Experience has had less time to shape the infant's customary ways of reacting and behaving—which are therefore labeled temperament rather than personality. Experiences such as sitting on Grandpa's knee and blowing a magic whistle might do much to begin to shape this little boy's personality.

to as personality differences. The term **personality** includes all of the abilities, predispositions, habits, and other character istics that make each of us unique (Wiggins & Pincus, 1992).

When psychologists speak of differences among infants, they don't often use the term *personality* because it implies a degree of learning that has not yet had time to occur. Instead, psychologists speak of infant **temperament,** or characteristic emotional responses. Clusters of related temperament characteristics are termed **types.**

One important difference between temperament and personality is that temperament is assumed to have a primarily

genetic basis whereas personality has developed through interaction with the environment. Thus, Buss and Plomin (1985) define *temperament* as "inherited personality traits present in early childhood" (p. 84). That is, a child is born with a certain temperament rather than with a certain personality. Temperament is reflected in the prevailing states we described earlier (crying, for example).

Not surprisingly, individual differences in temperament, to the extent that they can be measured, appear to be present before birth (DiPietro et al., 1996). Furthermore, they are relatively stable throughout infancy (Stifter & Jain, 1996). And, as we see later, they are reflected in later personality traits (Warren et al., 1997).

Part of the reason for a very high current level of interest in infant temperament, suggests Kagan (1992), lies in research with animals that has found marked differences in the characteristics of different animals of the same species and breed—differences that appear to be genetically based, as are temperamental differences. For example, one dog may be highly timid; another from the same litter may be bold and aggressive. Furthermore, recent advances in neuroscience suggest the possibility of identifying actual biological and chemical differences that might account for differences in temperament. However, as Kagan (1992) puts it, "Scientists have not yet discovered that physiology that is reliably and selectively linked to the [temperament]" (p. 994).

Types of Infant Temperament

In the pioneering and best-known investigation of infant temperament, the New York Longitudinal Study (NYLS), Thomas, Chess, and Birch (1968, 1970; Thomas & Chess, 1977, 1981) carefully observed 141 children from 85 highly educated, professional families, and interviewed their parents. They found that there are at least nine different charac-

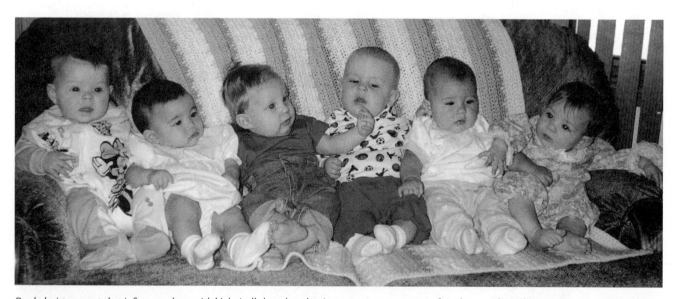

Psychologists suggest that infants are born with biologically based tendencies to react one way more often than another. These tendencies are evident in the infant's temperament. These six urchins are only about half a year old, but already their personalities seem distinctly different.

TABLE 6.1

Nine Temperament Characteristics of Infants

1. Level and extent of motor activity
2. Rhythmicity (regularity of functions such as eating, sleeping, and eliminating)
3. Withdrawal or approach in new situations
4. Adaptability to changes in the environment
5. Sensitivity to stimuli
6. Intensity (energy level) of responses
7. General mood or disposition (cheerful, cranky, friendly, and so on)
8. Distractibility (how easily infant can be distracted from ongoing activities)
9. Attention span and persistence in ongoing activities

Source: From "The Origin of Personality" by A. Thomas, S. Chess, and H. G. Birch, 1970, *Scientific American* 223, pp. 102–109.

teristics that are easily observed in infants (particularly after the infant is two or three months of age) and on which they can be rated as being high, medium, or low (see Table 6.1). Furthermore, certain infants have remarkably similar patterns of characteristics giving rise to three distinct *types* of infant that parents seem to recognize readily. For example, **difficult infants** are characterized by irregularity (lack of rhythmicity) with respect to things such as eating, sleeping, and toilet functions; withdrawal from unfamiliar situations; slow adaptation to change; and intense as well as negative moods. In contrast, **easy infants** are characterized by high rhythmicity (regularity in eating, sleeping, and so on); high interest in novel situations; high adaptability to change; and

a preponderance of positive moods, as well as low or moderate intensity of reaction. And **slow-to-warm-up infants** are characterized by low activity level, high initial withdrawal from the unfamiliar; slow adaptation to change; and a somewhat negative mood, with moderate or low intensity of reaction. Of the original 141 children in the NYLS, 65 percent could be classified as belonging to one of these three temperament types (40 percent easy, 15 percent difficult, 10 percent slow to warm up); the remaining 35 percent displayed varying mixtures of the nine temperament characteristics (see Summary/Interactive Table 6.2).

Assessing Infant Temperament

Infant temperament is evident primarily in the behavior of infants. However, classifications of temperament cannot always be accomplished by observing infants directly, which is a time-consuming and difficult task. More often, researchers rely on parental observation reported in specially designed questionnaires. For example, the Early Infancy Temperament Questionnaire developed by Medoff-Cooper, Carey, and McDevitt (1993) is designed for use with infants younger than four months of age; it is based on Thomas and Chess's (1981) Revised Infant Temperament Questionnaire, which is more suitable for older infants.

There are other ways of classifying infant temperament (see Bates, 1989). For example, Buss and Plomin (1985) classify infants on the basis of *emotionality, activity,* and *sociability* (termed the EAS approach). And Strelau (1989) suggests that temperamental differences might be assessed through physiological measures of the excitability of the nervous systems—that differences in physiological reactions such as brain-wave activity, heart rate, or motor responses may underlie

SUMMARY/INTERACTIVE TABLE 6.2
Infant Temperaments*

Interaction: What sort of infant were you? Ask your mother, your father, a sibling, or someone else who can tell you. Do you see any relationship between who you are now and what you were like as an infant?

TEMPERAMENT TYPE	DESCRIPTION	APPROXIMATE PERCENTAGE
Easy	Regularity in eating and sleeping (high rhythmicity); high approch tendencies in novel situations; high adaptability to change; preponderance of positive moods; low or moderate intensity of responses	40
Difficult	Irregularity in eating and sleeping (low rhythmicity); withdrawal in novel situations; slow adaptation to change; preponderance of negative moods; high intensity of reactions to stimulation	15
Slow to warm up	Low activity level; high initial withdrawal from unfamiliar; slow adaptation to change; somewhat negative mood; moderate or low intensity of reaction to stimulation	10
Varying mixtures	Unclassified	35

*Thomas and Chess (1981) caution that these temperaments do not exhaust all possibilities. In addition, although it is sometimes convenient, as well as apparently logical, to classify infants in these ways, there are wide ranges of behaviors within each category. "Easy" children don't all react the same way to the same situations, nor do all "difficult" children. Note, too, that some 35 percent of all infants appear not to fit any of these categories.
Source: Based on classifications used by Thomas, Chess, and Birch (1968, 1970; Thomas & Chess, 1981) in the New York Longitudinal Study (NYLS).

differences in temperament. For example, Stifter and Fox (1990) showed that measures of heart-rate variability are closely related to infant reactivity in the first year of life.

The Implications of Infant Temperament

Temperament may be defined as the infant's biologically based tendencies to react one way more often than another. Personality is an outgrowth of interaction between innate temperament and environmental influences (Carey, 1989). "An infant's temperament," say Kagan and Snidman (1991), "renders some outcomes very likely, some moderately likely, and some unlikely—although not impossible—depending on experience" (p. 856). As an example, Kagan (1997) found that 20 percent of a large sample (462 infants) of four-month-olds were highly reactive (fearful of the unfamiliar, easily distressed); about 40 percent of this sample were nonreactive (relaxed in the face of the unfamiliar, not easily frightened). At the age of fourteen to twenty-one months, about one-third of the highly reactives continued to be highly fearful in strange situations; in contrast, only 4 percent of the nonreactives were highly fearful. The majority were calm, outgoing, confident. And these patterns, though less clear, were still evident at the age of 4½ years. As Kagan and Snidman (1991) conclude, the temperament *uninhibited to the unfamiliar* (nonreactive), characterized by a tendency to approach in strange situations, is likely to lead to spontaneous, fearless, outgoing youngsters. In contrast, infants who are markedly inhibited in the face of the unfamiliar are likely to continue to be timid at the age of eight years.

Still, given difficulties in classifying infant temperament, and given the fact that there are numerous individual exceptions to our generalizations, predictions of later problem behaviors on the basis of mothers classifying their infants as being of "difficult" temperament are often highly unreliable. For example, Oberklaid and associates (1993) found that maternal classifications predicted only 17.5 percent of children who had behavior problems in preschool—which is hardly more than the percentage of all preschoolers who had problems among this large group of 1,583 children (14 percent). In fact, in this study, sex (male) and socioeconomic status were better predictors than maternal ratings alone.

■ IMPLICATIONS FOR PARENTING

Temperament does not mean, caution Kagan and Snidman (1991), that genetics inevitably determines our personalities—that our contexts are of no importance. In fact, knowing something of an infant's temperament may be very useful in allowing us to alter contexts in beneficial ways. Thomas, Chess, and Korn (1982) suggest, for example, that "easy" children, because of their high adaptability, will respond well to a variety of parenting styles (such as permissive or authoritarian). In contrast, a more difficult infant may require more careful parenting. Because these children adapt more slowly and respond less well to novelty and change, they require consistent and patient parents. Also, given their more intense and more negative moods, they are not likely to react well to highly authoritarian or highly permissive parents. Not surprisingly, researchers report that positive family relationships and contented parents are more often associated with highly rhythmic, "easy" infants than with those who are "difficult" (Wilson, Hall, & White, 1994). And it is probably not just a chance event that a large number of studies report a positive relationship between maternal postpartum depression and infant temperament, with excessive crying being most often identified as a contributing factor (Beck, 1996).

The contribution of temperament to the infant's development, and its relationship to the behavior of parents, presents yet another example of the extent to which parent–child influences are interactive (bidirectional) (Rothbart & Ahadi, 1994). It should come as no surprise that mothers of babies with **colic** (excessive crying behavior, often following eating) tend to rate their infants' moods more negatively. In one investigation of colicky infants, Jacobson and Melvin (1995) report that not only do mothers of colicky infants view their temperaments as more difficult, but they also express considerably more annoyance and intolerance with their infants' temperament.

As an illustration of the interaction of infant temperament with parental behavior, consider the case of Robert, an "easy" child. He adapts readily to change, smiles a lot, is rhythmic in feeding and sleeping routines, responds well to parents and to strangers, and, perhaps most important, appears to be happy. Parents react with pleasure to such a child, note Thomas and Chess (1981). They feel responsible for what Robert is; they think of themselves as wonderful parents. They smile and laugh as they tend to their little Robert, and he smiles right back at them. They gaze at each other, and everything they say and do says, "You're wonderful!"

But Marlis does not smile so much, cries more, eats and sleeps irregularly, is timid in the face of the unfamiliar, and whines and fusses much of the time. Hence, her social progress seems slower than Robert's; the message her parents receive does not say, "You're wonderful, dear parent." Nope. Instead it says, "As a parent, you're just so-so," or worse yet, "As a parent, you ain't worth $%##@!"

Cultural Context and Temperament

Although temperament has a biological basis, it is constantly evolving as a result of child–context interaction. As Kagan (1992) notes, behaviors influenced by temperament are not immutable. In his words, "Membership in a temperamental category implies only a slight, initial bias for certain emotions and actions" (p. 994). Consequently, developmental outcomes are not always easy to predict. The infant who is initially difficult may become an adolescent whose charm, grace, and other good qualities make a mother blush with pride; and the one who is initially easy may, it's true, become a thoroughly reprehensible, no-good #@%^^&. Or worse.

DeVries and Sameroff (1984) point out that what is often important in influencing developmental outcomes is the *goodness-of-fit* between the infant's temperament and immediate context. For example, research indicates that it is often an advantage for an infant to be "easy" in North American contexts and a disadvantage to be "difficult." However, in one study of the Masai in Africa, the opposite appeared to be the case, claims deVries (1989). There, six months after first being classified as "easy" or "difficult," the "difficult" infants seemed to have fared much better. In fact, mortality had been much higher among the "easy" infants. Why? One plausible explanation, according to deVries, is that there had been a serious drought in the region, and many infants had died or suffered from malnutrition and disease. That the "difficult" infants had been least likely to die, speculates deVries, was probably because they yelled and hollered more when they were frustrated and hungry—and succeeded more often in being fed. Thus, a particular environmental characteristic "fit" better with the "difficult" temperament—a temperament that, under most circumstances in our culture, seldom "fits" as well as the "easy" temperament.

In Lerner and colleagues' (1986) terms, the most optimal situation, one where there is high goodness-of-fit between the infant and context, exists when external demands and expectations are compatible with the infant's basic temperament. Conversely, there is a poor fit when the infant's temperament is not in accord with environmental demands. For example, Marlis (who, you may recall, is a difficult infant) reacts loudly and impatiently to frustration. Her father is distressed and annoyed at this behavior because he expects and wants Marlis to be more like Robert. There is a poor fit here, and the result is conflict and strain in the relationship between Marlis and her father.

Difficult temperaments do not always lead to poor fit, nor does the easy temperament always result in high goodness-of-fit. Goodness-of-fit would be higher than expected, for example, if Marlis's father took pride in his daughter's lustiness, her independence, her aggressiveness. And if Robert's parents were concerned at how "easy" he is, afraid that he might not cope well in what they think is a dog-eat-dog world, goodness-of-fit between his temperament and his context might be unexpectedly poor. Here, as elsewhere, we need to consider the characteristics of the person in interaction with characteristics of the context.

INFANT EMOTIONS

"The emotions of one person cannot be directly perceived by another," notes Beckwith (1991, p. 78). This makes it especially difficult to investigate emotions among preverbal infants. Still, we can see infants smile and laugh, and we can hear them cry. And from these behaviors, we can make inferences about what they might be feeling.

Some psychologists, beginning with J. B. Watson (1914), have assumed that the infant is capable of reflexive emotional responses from birth. There are at least three such emotions, claimed Watson: *fear, rage,* and *love.* Because each of these is a reflex, each can be elicited by a specific stimulus. Rage results from being confined or from having movements restricted, fear results from a loud noise or from being dropped suddenly, and love results from being stroked and fondled. Unfortunately, it isn't possible for psychologists to know for certain that the infant's responses to these stimuli are, in fact, what we think of as fear, rage, or love.

Another approach to studying emotions in infants is that of theorists such as Izard and Malatesta (1987), who base their conclusions on examinations of human facial expressions. These, they claim, reveal a number of distinct emotions, including interest (or general excitement), joy, surprise, distress, anger, disgust, contempt, fear, shame, and guilt. They suggest as well that the facial expressions of infants indicate they may be capable of most of these feelings (Termine & Izard, 1988).

It is extremely difficult to separate such closely related emotions as joy and surprise (or distress, anger, and disgust—or shame and guilt). Accordingly, much of the research on infant emotions has looked at behaviors such as crying, smiling, and fear reactions. We look briefly at each of these before considering early infant attachments.

Crying

Infant crying, explains Pinyerd (1994), is one of the infant's main ways of communicating both physiological and psychological distress. However, not all infant cries are cries of pain, hunger, or distress. For example, Sroufe (1996) reports that it is highly common for one-year-old infants to visibly fight back their tears when, in an experimental situation, their caregiver leaves the room for a short while. Strikingly, many of these infants will then burst into tears when the caregiver returns—surely not a sign of distress at all, but more of relief.

Persistent and excessive infant crying, no matter what its cause, can be highly annoying for parents and siblings, and appears to be linked with higher incidence of postpartum depression (Mayberry & Affonso, 1993). Although crying related to hunger or pain can usually be eliminated, persistent crying, the cause of which is neither identifiable nor under the caregiver's control, may be more resistant to treatment (Wolke, Gray, and Meyer, 1994).

KINDS OF INFANT CRIES

Crying that is excessive, persistent, or unusual in quality may be the earliest indication of a physiological problem, notes Pinyerd (1994), hence the importance of mothers and other caregivers being familiar with the infant's normal cries and their meanings.

Wolff (1969) described four common types of infant cries, the most frequent of which is called the *rhythmic cry.* It is the

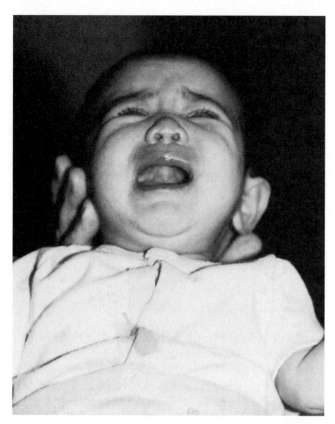

Many infants occasionally engage in rhythmic cries, angry cries, cries of pain, or cries of hunger, each of which most parents can identify and eliminate. But some infants also engage in more persistent cries, the causes of which are not always clear or controllable.

type of cry to which most infants eventually revert after initially engaging in another type of crying. Most experienced parents apparently recognize their infant's rhythmic cries and typically interpret them as meaning that there is nothing seriously wrong.

The *angry cry* is characterized by its protracted loudness and results from more air being forced through the vocal cords. It, too, does not fool an experienced caregiver.

A third distinguishable cry, says Wolff, is that of pain. The infant's *pain cry* is characterized by a long wail followed by a period of breath holding. Other highly useful facial indicators of infant pain include the brow bulge caused by the furrowing of the forehead, and a marked nasolabial furrow, the depression in the upper lip just below the nose (Rushforth & Levene, 1994).

Finally, there is the *hunger cry*. Gustafson and Harris (1990) report that most mothers respond quickly to hunger cries or to cries of pain and that they readily discriminate between the two—although most mothers seem to be more sensitive to the general distress level of the infant than to the cause of the distress. Interestingly, first-time parents tend to respond to infant crying sooner than parents who have more than one child (Donate-Bartfield & Passman, 1985). And mothers are more likely to be attentive than are fathers (Graham, 1993).

The meanings of an infant's cries are apparently not universal. Isabell and McKee (1980) observe that in many primitive cultures where the child is carried about constantly by the mother, mother–infant communication can occur through physical contact. In these cultures, there appears to be little need for the vocal signals of distress that we have come to expect from our infants. For instance, among South American Indian tribes in the northern Andes, infant crying is extremely rare and is invariably interpreted as a sign of illness. Why else would a warm, well-fed, and constantly embraced infant cry?

Smiling and Laughing

Smiling and laughing are central in parent–child interaction. From parents' smiles and strokes, infants learn that they are loved and important; parents, too, look for smiles and other nonverbal gestures in their infants as evidence that they themselves are worthwhile and loved.

Smiling, a universal phenomenon among human cultures, is a fleeting response in the warm, well-fed infant and appears to occur as early as two to twelve hours after delivery (Wolff, 1963). This early smile involves the lower part of the face, not the upper cheeks and eyes, and is described as a reflex smile rather than as a true social smile. Interestingly, children born with no cerebral cortex (**anencephalic**), but with a functioning brain stem so that they survive for a few days after birth, also seem to be able to smile. Luyendijk and Treffers (1992) report that 78 percent of the time, impartial observers watching videotapes of the facial responses of four such children to being touched or having slight pressure applied to them judged the responses as being smiles, grins, or laughter. This suggests that the neural mechanisms associated with early smiling are located in the brain stem, the most "primitive" of brain structures in an evolutionary sense. Thus, these early infant smiles have little to do with comfort, satisfaction, or happiness, but simply reflect bursts of cortical activity (Sroufe, 1996). Typically, such smiles occur when the infant is sleeping. Later, waking smiles will occur in response to physical stimulation such as being jiggled or tickled or having air blown on one's face.

Gewirtz (1965) identified three stages in the development of smiling behavior. The first phase, just described, is *spontaneous* or **reflex smiling**. It occurs in the absence of readily identifiable stimuli and is often, though perhaps incorrectly, attributed to gas pains. **Social smiling**, the second phase, takes place initially in response to auditory and visual stimuli that are social in nature—that is, related to other humans. For example, many four-week-old infants smile readily in response to their caregiver's voice.

Finally, perhaps by the age of 3½ months, the child displays the **selective social smile**, common among children and adults (Gewirtz, 1965). It occurs in response to social stimuli that the infant can identify as familiar. With the appearance of the selective social smile, infants smile less often in response to an unfamiliar voice or face and display more withdrawal behavior and other signs of anxiety in the presence of strangers. (More about stranger anxiety appears in a later section of this chapter.)

Research leaves little doubt that smiles are highly reinforcing for young infants; it is almost as though the infants recognized the smiles' social significance at ages far too young to have learned them. For example, Kaplan, Fox, and Huckeby (1992) report a study in which month-old infants were conditioned to a tone using only a smiling face as a reinforcer. Interestingly, a neutral face was not nearly so effective.

Hodapp and Mueller (1982) note that the development of smiling in infants follows the same general pattern as the development of crying. That is, the early development of these behaviors follows an internal to external progression. Whereas the first instances of smiling and crying are mainly responses to internal states—primarily gastric disturbances—within a short period of time, cognitive elements (such as are needed in recognizing a voice, a face, or an object) are clearly involved.

At about four months, infants begin to laugh in addition to smiling. At first, laughter is most likely to occur in response to physical stimulation such as tickling; later, infants laugh in response to more social and eventually more cognitive situations—seeing other children laughing, for example.

Although the function of laughter in infants has never been very clear, perhaps because it has not been investigated very much, Sroufe (1996) suggests that it probably serves to release tension. Fear, in contrast, signifies a continued building up of tension.

Wariness and Fear

Fear, argued Watson and Rayner (1920), is the infant's unlearned response to loud noises and sudden loss of support. Later, some infants come to fear a wide range of stimuli; others remain relatively unperturbed in the face of environmental changes. Interestingly, whereas many fears appear to have been learned, others don't seem to be. For example, Gullone and King (1997) report that fear of snakes is quite often found among people who have had no experience with snakes.

What do infants fear? Research and the revelations of grandmothers suggest a number of situations and events that might strike fear in an infant's breast. For example, fear of heights appears to be almost universal in infants by the age of thirteen to eighteen months. Fear of strangers is not ordinarily seen before the age of six months and becomes most common by two years. Many other fear-provoking situations typically involve some unexpected change. For example, a jack-in-the-box may be frightening; so might an experimenter or parent wearing a mask. In addition, separation from the mother is frightening for many infants. As Hinde (1983) notes, it seems that as certain objects and people become familiar, infants begin to react with fear to strangers and to unfamiliar objects.

In a detailed longitudinal study of fear, Bronson (1972) found that the most prevalent class of responses for 3- and 4-month-old infants is smiling rather than being uneasy or crying. By the age of 6½ months, however, there is increasing evidence of wariness; by 9 months, there is evidence of learned fears. These findings are in agreement with many others, indicating that infants are not likely to display marked stranger anxiety until after the age of 6 months.

Interestingly, at all ages objects are far less potent than strangers in bringing about reactions of wariness or fear. By the age of nine months, many of Bronson's infants had experienced fear reactions with strangers and seemed to have learned to associate specific features of a person with fear (beards or white smocks, for example). Similarly, wariness of novel objects was very rare before nine months. Situations or objects that make loud noises or move suddenly are most likely to bring about fear reactions in infants (a vacuum cleaner or a jack-in-the-box, for example).

Why are infants sometimes wary and sometimes not? Bronson's research suggests the reason lies in innate temperament interacting with various experiences. The relationship of age to the development of fear may at least partly reflect the fact that certain experiences are unlikely or less frequent at earlier ages—also that the meanings of some experiences depend on the infant's level of understanding. Clearly, a stranger is not a stranger until a familiar person can be recognized as familiar.

But why should some strangers and some novel objects elicit fear? One plausible explanation is Hebb's (1966) suggestion that infants develop certain expectations about their world and that violation of these expectations (*incongruence* is Hebb's term) may lead to fear.

Regulation of Emotions in Infancy

When you or I find ourselves in a frightening situation, when our hearts race and our knees turn to jelly, we do something to control or regulate our emotions. Perhaps we play cognitive games with ourselves: We tell ourselves that we have nothing to be afraid of, that we are such wonderful surgeons or public speakers or students that we will perform marvelously. Or we change the situation so that it isn't frightening anymore, perhaps by avoiding it.

HOW INFANTS CONTROL THEIR EMOTIONS

There is a temptation to think that infants are not capable of this sort of control of emotions: that if they are frightened, all they can do is cry, and if they are delighted, then, like little robots, they must smile. We sometimes think of them as responding almost blindly to the stimulation that the world provides, willy-nilly, for them.

We are wrong; they are not nearly so helpless. Beginning very early in life, infants are capable of what Gianino and Tronick (1988) term **self-directed regulatory behaviors** and **other-directed regulatory behaviors**—behaviors designed to regulate, or control, their emotions.

As an example, Tronick (1989) describes a peek-a-boo game between a mother and her infant. In this little episode, the infant turns away from the mother just before the "peek" and begins to suck on his thumb, staring blankly into space.

TYPE OF EMOTION	SOME DETAILS
Watson's unlearned infant emotions	
fear:	unlearned response to sudden loss of support.
rage:	unlearned response to confinement.
love:	unlearned response to cuddling, stroking.
Types of infant crying	
rhythmic cry:	most common cry; doesn't mean anything is wrong.
angry cry:	cry of frustration.
pain cry:	signals being hurt; intuitively recognized by most mothers.
hunger cry:	meaningful for most caregivers.
Development of smiling	
spontaneous smile:	present within weeks; a result of cortical activity.
social smile:	occurs in response to social stimuli like smiling faces; by age of 4 weeks.
selective social smile:	in response to *recognized* social stimuli such as presence of a caregiver; by 3½ months.
Laughing	by 4 months; first in response to physical stimulation like tickling; later in response to more social and, eventually, more cognitive stimulation.
Fear	evidence of wariness by 6½ months; evidence of learned fears by 9 months; that which is feared is typically unexpected, incongruous; some fears appear more universal, such as fear of heights; some fears seem unlearned, such as fear of snakes.
Strategies for regulating emotions	
self-directed:	ways of controlling emotional reaction that involve infant rather than others (thumb-sucking, for example, or turning away).
other-directed:	means of controlling emotional reaction that involves directing the behavior of others (for example, looking at a parent and gooing to get her to smile).

The mother sits back. Within a few seconds the infant turns to the mother, pulls out the thumb, and contorts his body; his expression is clearly interested. The mother smiles, moves closer, says, "Oh, now you're back!" The infant smiles and crows. Shortly, he goes back to sucking his thumb. But again, after a few seconds, he turns to the mother once more and smiles.

The infant in this instance seems to be attempting to control the mother's behavior. This other-directed regulatory behavior is evident in how he turns back to the mother, how he crows and smiles, how he tries to make her do things that he finds exciting. In effect, by controlling her behavior, he is exercising control over his own emotions. And when things become too exciting, too emotional, he can regulate his emotions by turning away and distracting himself by sucking his thumb and by staring into space, a self-directed regulatory behavior. (See Summary Table 6.3.)

PARENT-INFANT ATTACHMENT

Tronick (1989) argues that the emotion-regulating behaviors of young infants not only control their emotions but are also evidence that the infants' behavior is goal-directed. And one of the important goals of all infants, and adults, is to form and maintain attachments.

Mother-Infant Bonding

Attachment is a relatively general term that includes the host of positive emotions that link parents, children, and other people; *bonding* is a more specific and more biological term. Thus, **mother–infant bond** refers primarily to the very early, biologically based attachment that the mother develops for her infant. Attachment between mother and infant is both biologically and psychologically important. Biologically, the existence of a strong mother–infant bond serves to ensure that mother and infant will stay close to each other—a condition that, for most animals, is extremely important to the infant's survival. Hence, it seems reasonable to suppose that there would be powerful genetically based tendencies to establish such bonds.

Mutual gazing is among the earliest forms of mother–infant interaction and appears to be very important in the formation of emotional bonds. It benefits an infant by keeping the object of its attachment close.

Ethologists (those who study animal behavior in natural settings) inform us that yes, there are powerful preprogrammed tendencies among many nonanimal species. They are evident in the fact that mothers and infants exposed to each other during a **critical period,** generally shortly after birth, typically "bond." In the absence of appropriate experiences during this critical period, bonding fails to occur. As we saw in Chapter 2, theorists such as Bowlby (1958) and Klaus and Kennell (1983) argue that infants kept from their mothers at birth may fail to bond with them. They suggest, as well, that failure to establish a strong mother–infant bond is detrimental to the future adjustment and emotional health of the child, and may be related to such things as child abuse or "growth failure." Growth failure, or **failure to thrive (FTT)** (also called *maternal deprivation syndrome*), is a condition in which an apparently normal infant fails to gain weight, falling to the bottom 3 percent of normal standards. Abramson (1991) reports significantly more expressions of negative emotion among these infants. In addition, the condition is marked by listlessness, loss of appetite, illness, and, in its more extreme manifestations, even death.

■ BONDING MECHANISMS

It is likely that no emotional bond links the infant to its mother immediately at birth. A neonate taken from its mother and given to another will surely never know the difference unless, of course, the facts are disclosed later. But that a bond does form with the primary caregiver(s) is also clear. Wellman and Gelman (1992) point out that the infant has certain biological preadaptations that facilitate the development of this bond. These include perceptual biases such as the infant's built-in visual accommodation for a distance of approximately 8 to 10 inches (about the distance to the caregiver's face during feeding), the young infant's apparent preference for the human face, and a sensitivity and responsiveness to the human voice. They also include some reflexive response tendencies that seem especially designed for social interaction. Like the young of most mammals, for example, the human infant clings and turns and roots and sucks. One of the functions of these vegetative reflexes is surely to ensure that the infant obtains nourishment and survives. But more than this, feeding is among the first important social interactions between caregiver and infant. Almost invariably, feeding leads to the mutual gaze, which is highly significant in the development of attachment and which appears to be universal between mothers and infants in different cultures (Fogel, Toda, & Kawai, 1988).

Schaffer (1984) also suggests that certain biological rhythms are geared to social interaction. Some, like those expressed in the infant states of waking and sleeping, are modifiable and eventually become attuned to the mother's cycles of waking and sleeping. Others, like the rhythms apparent in cyclical motor movements (see Chapter 5), seem to contain many of the elements of a dialogue and may underlie the learning of the turn-taking rules that are a fundamental part of conversations with language.

The Importance of Bonding

The existence of biological preadaptations that facilitate the formation of bonds between caregiver and infant may be evidence that powerful biological forces direct both mother and infant toward mutual attachment. This makes sense because attachment has important survival value—a value that would have been especially apparent at a time when physical survival was threatened by the "hissing serpents and dragons of Eden" (Sagan, 1977). One of the important functions of the infant's distress at being separated from the mother is that it serves to keep her close (Oatley & Jenkins, 1992)—and perhaps to protect the infant from wild beasts.

But now dragons and serpents no longer lurk so blatantly in our forests—or parking lots. But, say Klaus and Kennell (1976), there is nevertheless a critical period very early in our lives during which we must have contact with our mothers so that a bond may form. Bonding failure, they claim, can have serious negative consequences later.

The evidence? Klaus and associates (1972) randomly selected a group of twenty-eight low-income mothers and allowed half of them extended contact with their infants immediately after birth (one hour of the first two hours following birth), as well as five additional hours of contact with their infants on each of the first three days following birth. The remaining fourteen mothers, serving as a control group, saw their infants regularly at feeding time in conformity with hospital routine (Klaus & Kennell, 1976). Interviews and observations one month later indicated that mothers in the extended-contact group were significantly more bonded to their infants, showed more concern for them, and expressed considerably more interest in them. These mothers tended to cuddle their babies more, to engage in more verbal interaction with them, and to spend more time in mutual gazing.

However, it would be premature to conclude that there is a critical period early in the lives of neonates during which contact with the mother (or perhaps some other important caregiver) is of absolutely fundamental importance. As Klaus and Kennell (1983) admit, "The human being is highly adaptable, and there are many fail-safe routes to attachment" (p. 50). Not surprisingly, a raft of subsequent studies has failed to demonstrate convincingly the existence of a critical period for mother–infant bonding (Goldberg, 1983; Schaffer, 1984). This does not mean, of course, that maternal deprivation or rejection is irrelevant. As we saw, these factors can lead to serious conditions like *growth failure.* However, the importance of a crucial few hours immediately after birth has not been clearly established. (See "In the News and on the Net: Host Mothers.")

Studying Attachment

Attachment is a powerful emotional bond, impossible for an infant to describe for us, and not easy to study because many of the experiments that might shed light on the area cannot ulie Garber died about a year ago, at the age of 28. When she knew she was going to die, she decided to have her eggs fertilized and the embryos frozen. And, on her death bed, she apparently asked her mother to find a host mother for her baby, and to be involved in raising the child. Now, following a storm of controversy, Julie Garber's parents have succeeded in getting a court order granting them ownership of their daughter's embryos.

And, for $25,000, they have hired a 23-year-old surrogate mother who, as of this writing, is pregnant with the dead woman's child.

1. Craig, O. (1997, Dec. 2). Surrogate pregnant with dead woman's frozen embryo. *Edmonton Journal*, p. A7.

To Think About

Do you think surrogate parenting is ethical and should be permitted? Under all circumstances?

On the Net

The following web site is that of a national, all-volunteer organization that provides information about, promotes, and supports surrogate parenting:

http://www.opts.com/

---

be performed with humans. For this reason, infant monkeys have sometimes been used instead. (See "At a Glance: Mother-Deprived Monkeys" and Figure 6.2).

Measurements of infant attachment are always indirect. Investigators look at behaviors that are directed toward the object of attachment (crying, smiling, vocalizing, following, clinging, holding, looking at, and so on); they focus on the infant's reaction to strange situations and on physical contact between parents and infant; and they look at the infant's reaction to being separated from a parent.

■ AINSWORTH'S STRANGE SITUATION

How do you determine whether, to whom, and how strongly an infant is attached? One way is Ainsworth and associates' (1978) **Strange Situation procedure,** a procedure often sequenced as follows (each event lasts approximately three minutes):

1. Mother and baby enter a room.

2. Mother puts baby down; stranger enters, speaks with mother, shows baby a toy; mother leaves.

3. If baby cries, stranger attempts to comfort; if baby is passive, stranger attempts to interest it in a toy.

4. Mother returns, pauses in doorway; stranger leaves; mother leaves.

5. Baby is alone.

6. Stranger comes back.

7. Mother returns; stranger leaves.

What the Strange Situation provides is a way of assessing attachment under stress. It permits researchers to determine the infant's anxiety or security in these circumstances. A large number of studies using the Ainsworth procedure with infants reveal attachment behaviors that sort themselves into four broad categories.

Securely attached infants are those who use the mother as a base for exploration—who go out freely and play in the

room but who often reestablish contact, either by looking at the mother, interacting verbally, or returning to her physically. When the mother leaves, these infants are upset and often stop their exploration. During the reunion episodes, they greet the mother warmly and try to reestablish physical contact or some sort of interaction with her. Securely attached infants manifest few, if any, negative reactions toward their mothers during reunion. If upset, they are easily soothed by the mother and return readily to play or exploration.

In contrast, insecurely attached infants are those who display significant negative behavior toward the mother during reunion events. Some of these infants, the **insecure-avoidant** (also termed *anxious-avoidant*), either ignore the mother's reentrance or actively avoid contact with her—sometimes by looking away, sometimes by pushing her away physically. Interestingly, they rarely cry when the mother leaves.

A second group of insecurely attached infants, the **insecure-ambivalent,** are very upset when the mother leaves, their behavior being evidence of strong attachment. However, the mother's reappearance does not soothe their distress. Strangely, these infants sometimes display anger when the mother returns. The anger is sometimes very subtle; for example, they might push the mother away even when they appear to want to be held (hence the ambivalence).

A final group, originally termed unclassified by Ainsworth and associates (1978), is now often termed **disorganized/disoriented.** These infants typically display any of a range of disorganized or disoriented behaviors, such as crying for a parent at the door and then moving quickly away when they hear the parent approaching, approaching the parent with the head turned away, or standing motionless with no clear reaction during the Strange Situation (see Summary/Interactive Table 6.4).

Stages of Attachment

The why of infant attachment is clear: After all, the infant's very survival demands a solicitous caregiver. What better

Mother-Deprived Monkeys

nfant monkeys who are raised in isolation later experience serious developmental problems, often manifested in an inability to achieve sexual relations (Harlow, 1958; 1959). Female monkeys raised under such conditions, who then have infants of their own, will often reject them. But when the mothers of infant monkeys are replaced by a substitute, infants typically form a strong attachment to the substitute. Research that has compared infant monkeys' attachment to cloth-covered and wire mother-substitutes indicates that quality of physical contact is especially important for infant monkeys.

FIGURE 6.2

Amount of time spent by infant monkeys on cloth and wire surrogate mothers. The results show a strong preference for the cloth mother regardless of whether the infant was fed on the wire model or on the cloth model. (From Harry F. Harlow, Love in infant monkeys, Scientific American, 1959, 200, 68–74. Copyright 1959 by Scientific American, Inc. All rights reserved. Used by permission.)

▲ SUMMARY/INTERACTIVE TABLE 6.4

Types of Infant Attachment

Interaction: In first grade, George Leroy used to get such severe stomachaches that he often had to be taken home to his mother. "He's always been like that," claimed his mother. "Why, when he was little, he used to raise a stink every time I had to leave him. And one time, when I come back from bowling or something, he up and heaved his potty at me, he was still so mad, and the dang thing was about ... as heavy as a brick." According to Ainsworth's classification, what sort of attachment did George display toward his mother?

ATTACHMENT CLASSIFICATION	COMMON BEHAVIOR WHEN MOTHER LEAVES OR RETURNS
Securely Attached	▪ Uses mother as a base from which to explore; upset when she leaves but quickly soothed when she returns; greets her positively on return.
Insecure-Avoidant	▪ Rarely cries when mother leaves; ignores or actively avoids her when she returns, sometimes pushing her away or pointedly not looking at her.
Insecure-Ambivalent	▪ Very upset when mother leaves; often angry when she returns, sometimes pushing her away.
Disorganized/Disoriented	▪ Contradictory, disorganized reactions to separation and reunion; may cry for mother but run away when she returns, or approach her while looking away.

Source: Based in part on *Patterns of Attachment* by Ainsworth et al., 1978, Hillsdale, NJ: Erlbaum.

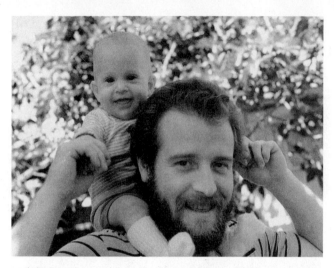

In the preattachment phase, infants seem predisposed for human interaction; in the attachment-in-the-making phase, they cry, look at, and smile to draw and hold attention; in the clear-cut-attachment phase, they can finally crawl over to the attachment object, climb on—and sometimes cling for dear life.

way to ensure that the caregiver will be there when needed than to program into the human gene pool powerful parent–infant attachment tendencies? However, nature does not program the attachment itself; it develops later. Nor do genes limit attachment to the biological mother or father.

Bowlby describes four phases in the infant's development of attachment. Through each phase, the infant's behavior seems to be guided by a single overriding principle: keep the attachment object close. And in most cases, that attachment object is the mother.

PREATTACHMENT

The *preattachment* phase spans the first few weeks of life and is marked by the preadaptations that seem to predispose the infant for human interaction: things like their preference for the human voice and face, their movements in synchrony with adult speech, and their built-in visual accommodation for about the distance of the mother's face (Wellman & Gelman, 1992).

ATTACHMENT IN THE MAKING

During the second phase, *attachment in the making,* there is marked emphasis on behaviors that promote contact with important adults—for example, crying and smiling as well as sucking, rooting, clinging, looking at, and following with the eyes. The second phase culminates in clearly identifiable attachment during the second half of the first year of life. At this time, the infant manifests the "selective social smile"—the smile that occurs in recognition of familiar faces. At the same time, smiling in response to unfamiliar faces becomes less common.

CLEAR-CUT ATTACHMENT

Clear-cut attachment becomes evident with the infant's development of **locomotor abilities.** Now infants are able

to attract the mother or father's attention not only by smiling, crying, reaching, and so on; they can also crawl over and grab a leg; they can climb up and wrap themselves around a neck; they can cling to the strings that hang from the rear of old aprons. In brief, they can indicate very clearly what (and whom) the objects of their attachment are.

GOAL-CORRECTED ATTACHMENT

Some time in the second year, Bowlby (1969) informs us, the infant enters a phase of *goal-corrected attachment.* The infant has now developed notions of self and has begun to understand something of the point of view of others. Gradually, infants learn to make inferences about the effects of their behaviors, as well as about their parents' behavior; and they learn to affect the behavior of parents in ways more subtle than crying, smiling, yelling, or toddling over and grabbing hold. (See Summary Table 6.5.)

The Implications of Attachment Patterns

As we saw earlier, some infants are *securely attached* to their caregivers; others are more *insecure* or even *disorganized.* Among other things, securely attached infants are those who have achieved a good balance between the security of attachment and the ability to explore. Insecurely attached infants are more anxious, often about both their attachment and their exploration.

Patterns of attachment appear to reflect relatively stable qualities. For example, Main and Cassidy (1988) found infant attachments at the age of one year to be highly predictable of attachment behaviors at the age of six. However, stability is not the case when major changes occur in the infant's context such as somebody leaving or dying (Waters, Hay, & Richters, 1986). Similarly, infants who are maltreated often display marked instability of attachment, and are also more likely to be insecurely attached (Schneider-Rosen et al., 1985). Reassuringly, however, the more sensitive the new caregiver is, the more likely the infant is to form secure attachments (Howes & Segal, 1993).

There is increasing evidence that securely attached infants—who, as we noted, are in the majority in North American cultures—fare better in the long run (in these cultures). These infants are often more competent, better problem solvers, more independent, more curious, and perhaps more resilient. In one study, children who experienced high levels of support from their mothers—which is closely related to secure attachment—fared significantly better in kindergarten (Pianta & Ball, 1993). In contrast, insecurely attached infants are somewhat more likely to be overly dependent and to experience problems in school. Thus, in a study reported by Shaw and associates (1996), infants who had been classified as disorganized at the age of twelve months were significantly more likely to have problems involving disruptive behavior at age five. Those who had been classified as disorganized and whose mothers perceived them as of "difficult"

The Beginning

At the very beginning there is the egg. And although its form and functions seem vastly removed from those which mark us as adult humans, this tiny fertilized egg contains the secrets of our destiny.

PART TWO

Infancy

In some ways, we humans begin with very little. Indeed, we can neither walk, nor fly nor swim. So singularly helpless are we that we would surely die without caregivers singlemindedly devoted to our survival.

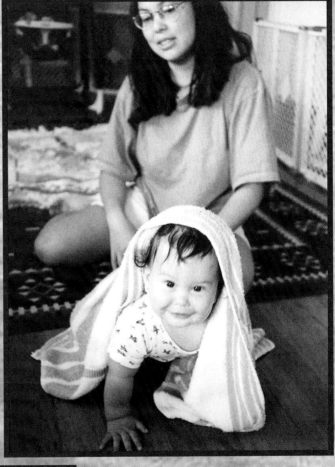

At first we are strangers to the world, strangers to ourselves, familiar only with a tiny handful of sights and sounds and smells—mostly those related to the mother or other important caregivers.

M uch of growing up involves becoming progressively more familiar with what is out there, with what things and people and animals mean, what we can do with them, what they can do to us and with us.

In time, we gain control of our movements, and we begin to learn how to accomplish some of the things we intend. But there is much that we cannot yet do, much that remains strange and unfamiliar.

Early Childhood

The processes of growing up, of learning, and becoming are intimately linked with play. Play, in its many forms, is the very essence of childhood, its magic and joy.

Play is also childhood's teacher. For in the sensorimotor play of the child, there are physical skills to be learned and practiced; and through imaginative play, the mind opens and blossoms.

In the social games of early childhood, children learn many of the rules and roles that will serve them later when life is more serious, less playful. As it might be, for example, in school.

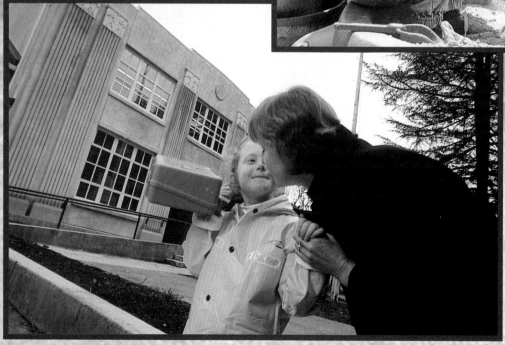

PHASE	APPROXIMATE AGE	IMPORTANT BEHAVIORS
Preattachment	First month	Crying, smiling, rooting, clinging, sucking, looking at; movements synchronized with adult speech; discrimination of mother's voice.
Attachment in the making	Into second half of first year	Singling out objects of primary attachment; selective social smile—directed more toward attachment objects/persons than toward the unfamiliar.
Clear-cut attachment	Second half of first year	Continued use of behaviors designed to draw attention—smiling, crying, squirming; use of newly developed locomotor skills to approach attachment object/person.
Goal-corrected attachment	Second year	Begins to adopt mother's point of view and to make inferences about mother's behavior; manipulation of mother's behavior in more subtle ways following gradual recognition of cause-and-effect relationships.

Source: Based on Bowlby (1969).

(as opposed to "easy") temperament were also more likely to be excessively aggressive.

Clearly, attachments are a function of interactions. Furthermore, the nature of these interactions, and their outcomes, will be influenced by the characteristics of both infant and caregiver (or other significant people in the child's context). Hence the importance of the family—and of the culture in which the family is embedded, because it, too, influences child-rearing practices and attitudes toward children. Our North American macrosystem is relatively child-centered: It emphasizes the rights of children, and it encourages parents to provide physically and psychologically safe environments. Not surprisingly, then, more than two-thirds of infants appear to be securely attached (perhaps it should be surprising that as many as one-third are not!).

Elsewhere in the world, cultures reflect different values, and sometimes child-rearing practices and attitudes toward children are quite different. In some of these cultures, insecurely attached infants are far more common than in North America (for example, Germany, Japan, and Israel; see Sagi, Ijzendoorn, & Koren-Karie, 1991).

Whether parents should attempt to change their infants' predominant patterns of attachment—and indeed, whether they would be very effective in doing so—are important issues. Unfortunately, they are also very complex issues. What does seem clear is that all infants must be provided with an opportunity to develop attachments that will provide them with the security they need to engage in the exploration of a bewildering, exciting, and sometimes frightening world. Those opportunities are not always related solely to the presence of the mother. Grandparents, siblings, uncles, and aunts can also be important. So can fathers.

Fathers and Infant Attachment

Our traditional views of the family and of mother–father roles have typically focused on the importance of the mother in the early social development of the infant—and on the father's relative unimportance. Most of our developmental theorists (Freud, for example) argue that the father becomes important after the age of two or three. Furthermore, many of these theorists have viewed the infant as largely incompetent—as passive and reflexive, as being moved by primitive physiological needs but seldom by a need to discover and to know. Little wonder that the father has not been seen as playing an important role.

Some of these traditional values are still the norm in many of the world's cultures. For example, Ho (1987) reports that in China, looking after the young is still largely a female function; the father's role is more that of a disciplinarian. There, traditional values stress filial devotion and respect—that is, children, and especially sons, are taught to respect and obey their fathers (and grandfathers). Recently, however, there appears to have been a dramatic decline in some of these filial values. At the same time, fathers have begun to involve themselves more in child rearing.

In North America, too, important changes are rapidly altering our conception of the father's role. These include an increasing number of "father-assisted" childbirths, in which the father has an opportunity to interact with the infant as early as does the mother. In addition, changing work patterns and changing male–female responsibilities in the home have done a great deal to change the role of the father with his infant (McBride & Darragh, 1995). As Lamb (1987) notes, mothers continue to be extremely important to the infant, but they are not unique. Fathers and other caregivers are also tremendously important. In fact, considerable research indicates that newborns and young infants may form attachments almost as strong with fathers as with mothers (Geiger, 1996). In addition, infants tend to form very similar attachments (secure or insecure, for example) with both parents (Fox, Kimmerly, & Schafer, 1991).

Nevertheless, it is still true that the most common family roles are those where the mother changes the diapers, feeds the infants, clothes them—in short, does the nurturing. Many studies find, for example, that fathers' interactions with their infants are still mostly in the form of playing rather than caregiving (Geiger, 1996). One study reports that 50 percent of a sample of Australian fathers and 43 percent of a sample of U.S. fathers had never changed a single infant diaper (Russel, 1983). These stereotyped gender roles appear to be most common among those of lower social status, the less well educated, and, not surprisingly, those who are male (Hoffman & Kloska, 1995).

■ FATHERS AS PARENTS

In summarizing the research on father–infant attachment, Collins and Gunnar (1990) conclude that fathers are as competent and as important as mothers in a caregiving role. But there are some systematic differences between mother–infant and father–infant interactions. Fathers spend more time in play interactions with their infants; mothers spend more time in nurturant roles (feeding, bathing, changing). As a result, some infants—especially males—display more **affiliative behaviors** toward fathers than toward mothers (Lamb, 1980). Affiliative behaviors are defined as behaviors that demonstrate a social relationship that stops short of being attachment. Evidence of affiliation includes smiling, looking at, laughing, and giving; evidence of attachment might include seeking to be close, clinging, wanting to be picked up, putting the head in the lap, snuggling, and so on. It appears that infants (especially males) begin to affiliate with their fathers at a very young age when they are given the opportunity to do so (Phares, 1992). And in an unfamiliar situation, the departure of both the father and the mother is followed by signs of distress, whereas the departure of a stranger leads to an increase in play behavior (Bridges, Connell, & Belsky, 1988).

What research has established is that the father is far from irrelevant in the early development of the infant. However, the mother typically has considerably more contact with young infants than does the father.

■ FEAR OF STRANGERS AND SEPARATION FROM PARENTS

One way of investigating parent–child attachment, as we saw, is Ainsworth's Strange Situation; it looks at the effects of very short-term separations and attempts to measure what is called **separation protest**. A second type of study looks at the consequences of longer-term separation, such as might result from divorce or the death of a parent. A third group of studies explores parent–child attachment by looking at the reactions of infants to strangers.

■ Fear of Strangers

Fear of strangers occurs in many infants, but not usually before the age of six to nine months. It appears that once

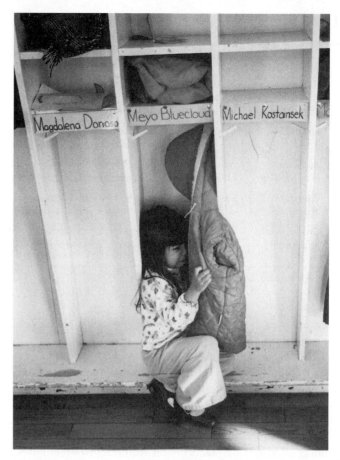

Even when you know your mother is coming back to get you at the end of the short preschool day, you can be afraid and lonely. This little girl may find some comfort in her own coat, and in her own cubicle, but she is still anxious and distressed.

infants have become familiar with their environment—that is, once they have developed certain expectations of events that are most likely to occur—they may be uneasy and afraid when these events do not occur. A common early reaction to the unexpected, Shreeve (1991) explains, is freezing (not doing anything) and mutism (not saying anything). These responses are, in fact, common fear responses in young infants and children.

The belief that fear arises from the occurrence of the unexpected is sometimes labeled the **incongruity hypothesis** (Hebb, 1966). Infants who are in contact with the largest number of people (strangers and siblings) are less likely to manifest fear, react with the least amount of fear, and stop being afraid of strangers at an earlier age (Gullone & King, 1997), providing support for this hypothesis. Infants exposed to many strangers at early ages will necessarily confront the "unexpected" less often than those whose early exposure to strangers is limited.

■ PREVENTING STRANGER ANXIETY

Not all infants react the same way to the departure of a parent or the arrival of a stranger. As we saw, infants exposed to many strangers and siblings are less likely to be fearful of strangers. In one study, Jacobson and Wille (1984) studied the reactions of ninety-three children, aged fifteen to eighteen months, to brief periods of separation from their mothers. They found that previous separation experience was closely related to the amount of distress the children manifested, but the relationship was curvilinear. That is, distress did not increase in linear fashion with increasing separation experiences, but declined with moderate exposure to separation. Specifically, children who had experienced moderate amounts of maternal separation were best able to cope with the absence of their mothers; it was as though they had learned that the separation would only be temporary. Those who had experienced either very little or a great deal of separation were the most distressed—perhaps because they had had too little opportunity to learn about separation or because they had learned that separation would be frequent or prolonged.

One way of minimizing infant distress at being left with strangers, then, might be to ensure that the infant has frequent, short-term exposure to strangers (and siblings). In addition, the strangers' behavior may be critically important. For example, a study by Gunnar and colleagues (1992) looked at the effects of exposing infants to strangers for periods of thirty minutes (recall that the Ainsworth Strange Situation typically exposes infants to strangers for only about three minutes). They measured infant fear through the infant's behavior, as in the Ainsworth procedure, and also by looking at elevations of cortisol in the infant's saliva—a common measure of stress. They found that when caregivers were instructed to be warm and responsive and to interact with the infant, indications of anxiety were significantly lower than when caregivers were more distant (although not insensitive to the infant's distress). Not surprisingly, there is also evidence that mothers who are themselves attentive and interactive (rather than dismissing or preoccupied) are less likely to have highly fearful infants (Crowell & Feldman, 1991).

Trying to prepare young preschoolers in advance for an upcoming separation from the mother doesn't always work as intended. Adams and Passman (1983) had one group of mothers of 2- to 2½-year-old children discuss their upcoming departure for three days preceding the event; a second group did not prepare their children in advance. And, at the time of departure, some of these mothers in both groups provided a brief explanation of their departure and then either left immediately or lingered for one minute; others left as they normally would.

Amazingly, children who had not been prepared in advance showed less distress after the mother's departure than children whose mothers had discussed their departure during the previous three days. And those whose mothers did not linger after explaining they were leaving also showed less distress than those whose mothers lingered for sixty seconds. One possible explanation, argue Adams and Passman, is that the lengthy preparation actually teaches children to become alarmed. In the same way, lingering just prior to departure may teach the child that displaying anxiety might serve to delay the departure (Adams & Passman, 1981).

SECURITY BLANKETS

A variety of inanimate objects such as blankets, teddy bears, and even thumbs, often called **transitional objects,** may also serve to reduce the fears of infants and young children. These objects are termed *transitional* because they become the focus of children's affection and attention while they are in transition between a state of high dependence on the parent and the development of a more independent self (Winnicott, 1971). According to this view, the development of self requires separation from the parent and *individuation*—the recognition of one's own individuality. The process of separating and becoming independent gives rise to anxiety; the blanket or the teddy bear serves to comfort the child.

No less than half of all middle-class American children show strong attachments to inanimate objects, report Passman and Halonen (1979), the two most common of which are, not surprisingly, the blanket and the pacifier. A large number also suck their thumbs, most often to fall asleep (Lee, 1992; Ozturk & Ozturk, 1990) but also as a refuge against fear and stress (Lookabaugh & Fu, 1992).

In one study, Passman and Weisberg (1975) compared the effectiveness of mothers and blankets in reducing a child's anxiety in a strange situation. They found that as long as they had their blankets close by, children who were attached to their blankets played and explored as much and displayed no more anxiety than those who were not attached to blankets but whose mothers were present. In situations of higher stress (high arousal), however, the mother is more effective than a blanket in reducing anxiety (Passman & Adams, 1982). Lookabaugh and Fu (1992) also report that children who are attached to inanimate transitional objects, including their thumb, cope more effectively in stressful situations than children with no such attachment.

In North American cultures, attachment to blankets, teddy bears, pacifiers, and other inanimate objects seems to be normal in the sense that a majority of children manifest these attachments. But, some parents worry, is the child who is attached to these inanimate, nonsocial objects perhaps more insecure, less well adjusted, than the child whose attachments are more social?

Not likely, says Passman (1987). In a study of 108 preschoolers, he found little relationship between attachment to blankets and general fearfulness. "Blanket-attached children," he concludes, "are thus neither more insecure nor more secure than are others" (p. 829).

So if you are anxious and cannot bring your mother with you, do bring your blanket...or whatever.

Longer-Term Separation from Parents

Studies of the long-term effects of parent–infant separation sometimes look at children who have been adopted and therefore separated from their primary caregivers. Obviously, infants adopted soon after birth, before they have formed strong attachments with caregivers, are not likely to respond in the same way as older children. In fact, in one study of

TABLE 6.6

Immediate Impact of Long-Term Mother–Child Separation on Infants 3 to 16 Months

IMPACT	PERCENTAGE
No disturbances	15
Mild disturbances	36
Moderate disturbances	23
Severe disturbances	20
Extreme disturbances	6

Source: Based on data provided by Yarrow and Goodwin (1973).

TABLE 6.7

Severity of Reaction to Maternal Separation According to Age

AGE	SLIGHT OR NO REACTION	MODERATELY SEVERE TO VERY SEVERE REACTION
Less than 3 months	100%	0
3–4 months	60	40
4–5 months	28	72
6 months	9	91
9 months	0	100

Source: Based on data provided by Yarrow and Goodwin (1973).

seventy adopted children, none showed even slight negative reactions before the age of three months; in contrast, all who were nine months or more manifested moderate or very severe negative reactions (Yarrow & Goodwin, 1973). In this study, only nine children were adopted before the age of three months, however; the remainder were placed at ages ranging from three to sixteen months. Only 15 percent of all the children were completely free of all disturbances; the remainder showed disturbances of varying severity (see Tables 6.6 and 6.7). These disturbances were most obvious in the infant's sleeping schedule and were also evident in feeding behaviors, social reactions (withdrawal, for example), and emotional behavior (crying). Disruptions in social reactions included decreased social responsiveness, increased stranger anxiety, and specific disturbances in interactions with the new mother evident in feeding difficulties, colic, digestive upsets, and, most strikingly, physical rejection of the new mother or excessive clinging to her. In addition, developmental scores were lower in 56 percent of the cases following adoption.

We know that the permanent loss of a parent, as happens through death or sometimes through divorce, can have an adverse effect on many significant aspects of the infant's development. What about regular but temporary loss of parental contact, as happens in many forms of child care?

INFANT CARE

In 1975, fewer than one-third of all U.S. women aged eighteen to forty-four were in the work force within one year of having a child; now more than half are. As a result, more than one out of every two North American preschool children is now in child care (U.S. Bureau of the Census, 1996; see "At a Glance: Working Mothers in the United States" and Figures 6.3 and 6.4). And, with increasing numbers of mothers going back to work within weeks of childbirth, the fastest growing type of child-care facility is infant care. Given what we know about the importance of caregiver–infant interaction and attachment, questions relating to the effects of child

care on the social, emotional, and intellectual development of infants become critically important. (See Chapter 8 for a discussion of the effects of child care on older children.)

Gamble and Zigler (1986) summarize a large body of research that has looked at the effects of child care on the infant's attachment to parents and on different aspects of social behavior. An important concern of this research has been to determine whether child care either can prevent the formation of parent–infant attachments or can serve to redirect that attachment toward a different caregiver. Reassuringly, all available evidence suggests not. Apparently, the infant's primary attachment to parents can be established in a wide variety of circumstances and is highly resistant to disruption. Konner (1982) reports that it occurs in societies as disparate as the !Kung, where infants are in immediate contact with their mothers twenty-four hours a day, and in the Israeli kibbutzim, where infants have contact with their mothers only for a short period each afternoon and on weekends.

Clarke-Stewart, Gruber, and Fitzgerald (1994), following a detailed investigation of the effects of child care, conclude that good quality child care does not detract from parent–child relationships, nor does it decrease the influence of the family. In fact, it seems clear that good quality day care has measurably positive effects on measures of both cognitive and social development. In Clarke-Stewart, Gruber, and Fitzgerald's study, day-care children were consistently more advanced than children who stayed at home with their mothers: "This advance showed up on all our measures of development: cognitive development, social competence with unfamiliar adults, independence from the mother in an unfamiliar situation, general obedience and competence at dinnertime, compliance with requests made by a researcher, social interaction with a peer friend, and social competence with an unfamiliar peer" (1994, p. 233).

The point that needs to be underlined is that *quality child care* has measurably beneficial effects on children. Where child care does have apparently detrimental effects on infants, these effects are often associated with poorer-quality child care (Bowman, 1993). Unfortunately, however, there is little control of the standards of infant care centers and homes.

Working Mothers in the United States

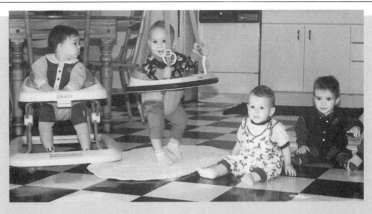

etween 1960 and 1997, the percentage of married women in the work force doubled (from 30.5 percent to 61.1 percent). The number of married women in the work force who had given birth within the previous year and who lived with their husbands increased by about 50 percent between 1975 and 1997. By 1997, more than half of women with children under 1 *and husbands at home* worked. As a result, more infants than ever before are in some type of child care.

FIGURE 6.3

Increase in percentage of mothers who live with husbands and work outside the home. Note by comparison that growth in employment is far more modest for wives without minor children at home. (From U.S. Bureau of the Census, 1994, p. 402 and 1996, p. 400.)

FIGURE 6.4

Changes in percentages of women who enter the work force within one year of giving birth. (From U.S. Bureau of the Census, 1996, p. 82.)

And the better child-care options are often too expensive for parents whose children may be most in need of them. With respect to center infant care, desirable characteristics include a low caregiver-to-child ratio; appropriate equipment and toys; adequate indoor and outdoor spaces; an organized, goal-directed schedule of age-appropriate activities; and qualified caregivers. (See Chapter 8 for a more detailed discussion of the characteristics of high-quality child care.)

As Lerner and Abrams (1994) put it, "Research has not been able to clearly link maternal employment to any detriments in infant or toddler cognitive and intellectual development" (p. 178). The focus must now change, says Silverstein (1991). Instead of continuing to search for the negative consequences of mothers' working and of alternate child care, research should focus on documenting "the negative consequences of not providing high-quality, affordable day care" (p. 1025).

Research on the effects of alternate forms of infant care has found no consistent negative effects of quality care. Nor does being looked after by someone else while parents work appear to disrupt parent–infant bonds like this mother and child.

PARENTING INFANTS

Parenting is a difficult and extremely important task with far-reaching consequences. Sadly, it's not a task for which all parents are highly suited—either by training or by temperament. When O'Brien (1996) studied an ostensibly average sample of 413 parents of children aged 9 months to 3 years, she found high general agreement that raising children is a difficult and sometimes frustrating undertaking. Most irritating for parents were infant behaviors such as whining, demanding attention, interrupting ongoing activities, and refusing to do as asked. Nor did parenting become easier with experience. In fact, parents who had more than one child typically reported more difficulties and more frustration than did those with a single child.

In the same way as quality of infant care can have measurable effects on children, so too can quality of parenting. Following a review of research that has looked at the effects of parents on infants, Belsky, Lerner, and Spanier (1984) describe six important dimensions of parenting: *attentiveness, physical contact, verbal stimulation, material stimulation, responsive care,* and *restrictiveness*. The first five of these have positive effects on the infant's social, emotional, and intellectual well-being; the last is more negative. That is, parents who are attentive to their children (for example, look at them more); who touch them, play with them, cradle and rock them; who speak to them and who provide them with objects to look at, to touch, to taste, to smell; and who are responsive to their cries and to their other signals of distress, amusement, interest, or amazement are more likely to have intellectually advanced and emotionally well-adjusted infants. Those who are restrictive in that they verbally and physically limit the infant's freedom to explore may, to some extent, influence their intellectual development negatively.

In summary, parents most likely to promote optimal cognitive development during infancy are those who serve as, or give the child access to, the greatest sources of stimulation (speaking, holding, touching, responding to, providing toys, and so on); those who are restrictive—that is, those who limit the amount of stimulation to which the infant is exposed—are likely to have the opposite effect. (See Chapter 8 for further discussion of parenting styles.)

Cultural Similarities

In general, children rate their mothers and fathers differently with respect to important dimensions of parenting such as warmth and control. In China, says Ho (1987), mothers look after children; fathers discipline them. Perhaps it isn't surprising that Berndt and associates (1993) found that Chinese children (as well as children from Taiwan and Hong Kong) see their mothers as warmer and less controlling than fathers.

▲ SUMMARY TABLE 6.8
Important Conclusions in Care and Parenting of Infants

- More than half of all mothers with chldren under 1 work outside the home.

- Nonparental infant care does not disrupt affectional bonds between parents and infants.

- High-quality care has measurably beneficial effects on the cognitive and social development of children.

- High-quality care is characterized by low caregiver-to-infant ratio, an organized schedule of age-appropriate activities, adequate indoor and outdoor space, adequate toys and equipment, and qualified caregivers.

- The influence of parents is not lessened by the impact of out-of-home infant care.

- Parenting is a difficult task for which not all parents are equally suited.

- The six most important dimentions of good parenting are attentiveness, physical contact, verbal stimulation, material stimulation, responsive care, and lack of excessive restrictiveness.

Interestingly, children in Western societies express very similar views of their parents (Collins & Russell, 1991). No matter how involved fathers are in child rearing, mothers are typically seen as more affectionate, warmer, and less strict. This is not surprising given that mothers are the ones who feed, wash, and clothe children—in other words, who nurture them (Hodapp & Mueller, 1982). In contrast, fathers play with them—or discipline them. Thus, even in these earliest parent–infant interactions, gender has begun to make a difference. (See Summary Table 6.8.)

EARLY GENDER TYPING

Sex differences in attitudes and behaviors are evident in **gender roles** (or **sex roles**). A gender role is the particular combination of attitudes, behaviors, and personality characteristics that a culture considers appropriate for the individual's anatomical sex—in other words, that is considered masculine or feminine. **Gender typing** describes the processes by which boys and girls learn masculine and feminine roles.

To some extent, masculinity and femininity are clearly the products of genetically ordained physiological and hormonal differences between males and females. That is, contrary to what was once the dominant theory, psychologists no longer believe that infants are born sexually neutral and that they develop notions of sexual identity as a function of their upbringing. The contemporary view is that although sexual iden-

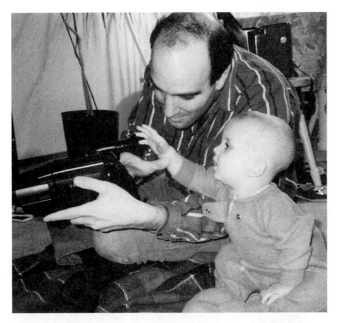

Male and female characteristics stem from biology as well as from the countless gender-related messages that result from the behaviors and expectations of parents and siblings. Thus, this young lad may already have begun to learn not only that video cameras are smooth black things but also that men are generally more interested in electronics than are women. But will he ever learn to set the clock on his VCR?

tity results from the interaction of genetic predispositions and environmental influences, there is an innate predisposition toward a male or female gender identity (Diamond, 1996).

Note that cultures often determine which behaviors will be considered masculine or feminine. In some cultures, for example, the aggressiveness and dominance that we think of as masculine characterize women, and the more nurturant traits that we associate with women are more common for men (see Chapter 12 for more details). Clearly, cultures and families have a great deal to do with the eventual gender roles of their children.

When Does Gender Typing Begin?

The assigning of gender roles begins at the very beginning— or even before, when parents wonder, "Hey, should we take a chance and paint the room blue? But, shoot, it might be a girl! Maybe we'd better stay with something neutral, like desert tan, and we can add the blue or the pink later."*

When an infant is born, the attending physician or midwife doesn't say, "Holy jeepers, lady, it's a baby!" No. The key word is not *baby;* it's *boy* or *girl* (unless, of course, prenatal diagnosis has already spoiled the surprise). The simple anatomical fact of being boy or girl tells mother and father and

---

*My aunt Eugenie, who had ten kids, never had this problem: "I only had one room," she explains, "and it would have been a darn sight too expensive to paint it each time." All ten grew up with no apparent gender confusion.

all the significant others what to think and how to react. The knowledge that it's a "boy" or "girl" even colors the parents' perceptions. When Rubin, Provenzano, and Luria (1974) asked thirty parents to describe their day-old infants as they would to a relative or a close friend, without any hesitation they spoke of their alert, strong, well-coordinated, firm, and hardy sons. In contrast, they described their daughters as weaker, finer-featured, softer, less attentive, more delicate. Yet these parents, especially the fathers (who were most guilty of exaggerating the sex-appropriate characteristics of their sons), had scarcely had any opportunity to interact with and get to know their infants. And hospital records indicated clearly that these male and female infants were indistinguishable in terms of weight, muscle tone, activity, responsiveness, and so on.

But many parents waste little time making their new infants sexually distinct: They color the boy-infants blue, the girl-infants pink. Because of the connotations associated with these colors, they emphasize long-established sexual stereotypes. And in much the same way, the names parents give their infants reinforce their sometimes unconscious beliefs about male–female differences. Kasof (1993), for example, shows how male names (like John or Michael) are seen as more attractive, more intellectually competent, stronger. In contrast, many female names (like Edith) carry connotations of being less attractive, more old-fashioned, and less able.

◼ EXCEPTIONAL INFANTS

The Lifespan is mainly about the physical, intellectual, and social development of the average person. However, it is worth repeating that this average person is simply a useful mathematical invention, that none of us is "average" in all ways. Instead, we are *individuals,* each different from every other. But there are so many of us—approaching 6 billion now— that to keep things clear and simple, psychology has to speak of the mythical average.

Still, we need to keep in mind that our average is a fiction and that the individual—Tara, Trevor, Tammy, Tommy—is our reality and our main concern. We also need to keep in mind that some of these individuals depart so dramatically from our average—are so *exceptional*—that they are worthy of study in their own right.

Exceptionality is a two-sided concept: There are, on the one hand, those who are exceptionally gifted; on the other, there are those who lack normal abilities and competence. Furthermore, exceptionality is found in each of the three major areas of human development: social, physical, and intellectual (see Figure 6.5).

In this section, we deal briefly with some of the most common manifestations of physical and social–emotional exceptionality in infancy. In Chapter 9, we look at physical and at intellectual exceptionality in childhood; in Chapter 10, we discuss social–emotional exceptionality.

	Normality	
	Physical	
Visual impairment Hearing impairment Motor skill disorders Other physical loss, injury, or disease		Superior athletic ability Superior sensory ability
	Social-Emotional	

Autism
Schizophrenia
Hyperactivity
Conduct disorders
  (aggressiveness,
  delinquency, withdrawal,
  severe shyness)
		Invulnerability
		Leadership

	Intellectual	

Mild, moderate, severe,
  and profound retardation
Learning disabilities
		Giftedness
		Superior intellectual,
		  creative, and
		  motivational qualities

FIGURE 6.5

The physical, social–emotional, and intellectual dimensions of exceptionality.

Motor Skill Disorders

Not all children learn to walk, tie their shoes, or dance as expected; some experience developmental delays and other problems in acquiring motor skills.

■ CEREBRAL PALSY

Cerebral palsy, also labeled **significant developmental motor disability,** is a collection of symptoms (a syndrome) that includes motor problems and may also include psychological problems, convulsions, or behavior disorders. It is most often defined as a *nonprogressive* motor function disorder (Davis, 1997). It was originally known as **Little's disease** after the surgeon who first described it, but is, in fact, not a disease. It varies in severity from being so mild that it is virtually undetectable to being sufficiently serious that it is manifested in paralysis.

Cerebral palsy is most often a **congenital disorder;** that is, it is present at birth in more than two-thirds of all cases. It is often associated with brain damage, although the damage is often mild and nonspecific. Hence, lack of oxygen at birth (termed **perinatal asphyxia** or *anoxia*) is estimated to cause as many as 20 percent of all cases of cerebral palsy (Patel & Edwards, 1997). Not surprisingly, it is far more common among highly premature infants. Spinillo and associates (1997) report that 12.3 percent of the survivors among a group of infants born between the 24th and the 33rd week of gestation had this disorder. In another study, 18 percent of infants born before the 33rd week of gestation were later found to have cerebral palsy (Allen & Alexander, 1997). Cerebral palsy can also result from maternal infection and disease, as well as from postnatal brain injury sometimes

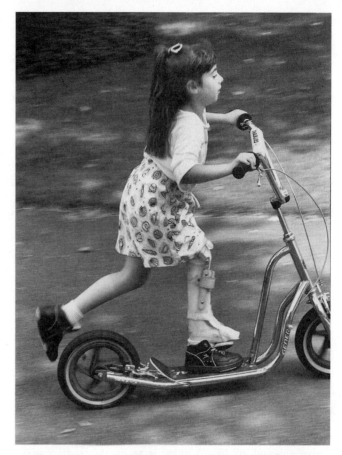

Many of the physical and motor problems of infancy and childhood are so mild as to be almost undetectable; others may be evident in paralysis. Some, like that of this little girl whose leg is about three inches shorter than the other, may require special devices or sometimes surgery. A positive self-image and acceptance by others are especially important for children with physical problems.

resulting from diseases such as meningitis or encephalitis. Still, in somewhere between 17 and 60 percent of all cases, the cause is unknown (Davis, 1997).

One of the most common symptoms of cerebral palsy is *spasticity* (inability to move voluntarily) in one or more limbs, or *dyskinesia* (abnormal movements) (see Table 6.9). Limb disorders in cerebral palsy may also be accompanied by disorders of facial movements (termed *orofacial praxis*), sometimes evidenced in the inability to control facial expressions (Dewey, 1993). The motor impairments of cerebral palsy are sometimes sufficiently severe that it is difficult to assess the child's intellectual ability. As a result, it was often assumed that intellectual deficits were common among those suffering from cerebral palsy. However, more recent evidence suggests that fewer than half of cerebral palsy victims are mentally retarded (Erickson, 1987).

Physical therapy is sometimes effective in improving motor control and coordination of children with cerebral palsy (Pape et al., 1994). Also, electrical stimulation of certain muscle groups is sometimes effective (Hazelwood et al., 1994). In some cases, brain surgery is effective in decreasing spasticity (Kaufman et al., 1994).

TABLE 6.9

Categories of Cerebral Palsy (Classified by Body Functioning)[*]

Cerebral palsy is a nonprogressive motor disorder that is most often congenital (present at birth). It varies tremendously in extent and severity of symptoms. Although it is often associated with prematurity (between 10 and 20 percent of infants born before the 33rd week of gestation) and with perinatal asphyxia, its precise cause remains unknown in as many as half of all cases.

Ataxia	Manifested in balance problems and an uncertain walk. Affects approximately one out of four of those with cerebral palsy.
Spastic	Characterized by loss of control over voluntary muscles. Movements tend to be jerky and uncontrolled. Some symptoms in two out of five cerebral palsy victims.
Athetosis	Marked by trembling, drooling, facial gestures and other involuntary and purposeless muscle activity (fluttering of the hands, for instance—in contrast with the rigid, jerky movements of spasticity). Often affects speech as well. Frequently found in combination with spasticity. Affects one out of five cerebral palsy individuals.
Tremor	Involves shaky movements, most often of the hands, sometimes visible only when the individual is voluntarily attempting to do something. Involves less extensive movement than athetosis or spasticity.
Rigidity	Caused by strong opposing tension of flexor and extensor muscles, resulting in fixed and rigid bodily postures (sometimes referred to as lead-pipe cerebral palsy).
Mixed	Involves a combination of characteristics descriptive of one or more of the common classifications. Most cerebral palsy victims fall within this category, although the majority are described in terms of their most predominant combination of characteristics.

[*]Note: It should be stressed that the effects of cerebral palsy are sometimes so mild as to be undetectable. At other times, they are serious enough to cause death in infancy.

OTHER MOTOR SKILL DISORDERS AND PHYSICAL PROBLEMS

There are motor skill disorders that are not associated with brain damage or cerebral palsy. These are often evident in delayed development among children, many of whom also have other developmental disorders such as mental retardation, autism, or even attention deficit disorders (Deuel, 1992). These disorders may be apparent in difficulties in learning motor tasks such as walking, running, skipping, and tying shoes; they may also be apparent in difficulties in carrying out motor activities. A common label for these problems is **developmental coordination disorder.**

According to the *Diagnostic and Statistical Manual of Mental Disorders (DSM-IV)* of the American Psychiatric Association, a developmental coordination disorder exists when

(1) the person's performance of activities requiring motor coordination (such as crawling, walking, sitting, handwriting, sports) is markedly below what would be expected for the person's age; (2) the disturbance interferes with academic achievement or activities of daily living; and (3) the disturbance is not due to a known physical disorder (such as cerebral palsy) (American Psychiatric Association, 1994).

There are many other physical problems of infancy and childhood that sometimes require special services—diseases and conditions such as muscular dystrophy, cancer, asthma, diabetes, and the absence of one or more limbs, as well as paralysis, to name but a few. Some are congenital, some result from infections and diseases after birth, and others result from accidents of various kinds. Many cases are associated with serious emotional and social problems that are often related to difficulties the child experiences in being accepted by others and in developing a positive self-concept. Hence, a great deal of what special education programs, parents, and therapists can do for physically exceptional children relates to their emotional and social well-being.

Epilepsy

Epilepsy is a seizure disorder whose origins are sometimes genetic and sometimes unknown (Berkovic & Scheffer, 1997). Seizures involve abnormal electrical activity in the brain. The more serious forms of epilepsy (sometimes termed **grand mal** as opposed to **petit mal**) can often be controlled with drugs. Petit mal seizures, which last between one and thirty seconds, are seen in a momentary "absentness" of the child and are often accompanied by rhythmic, fluttering movements of both eyelids. These seizures may occur very often and are sometimes interpreted by parents or teachers as a sign that the student is deliberately not paying attention. Medication can successfully prevent the occurrence of petit mal seizures in the majority of cases. Also, in many cases medication can be discontinued with no further recurrence of seizures. Echenne and associates (1994) report that one form of infant epilepsy, termed *benign infantile epilepsy*, is associated with a dominant gene and can easily be controlled with antiepileptic drugs. The treatment typically lasts no more than sixteen months and is effective in preventing further seizures. More serious forms of epilepsy, where seizures are frequent and interfere significantly with normal functioning, are sometimes treated by means of brain surgery. A **hemispherectomy,** in which the two halves of the brain are surgically separated, is sometimes highly effective in relieving patients of seizures (Vining et al., 1997).

Autism

Tim was an apparently normal, healthy child, the second child born to a couple in their early twenties. He was an "easy" infant who cried very little and who, in fact, appeared most contented when left alone. The mother later recalled that he didn't smile as a young infant and that he didn't appear to recognize her. Still, he progressed apparently normally through his first year, learned to walk at the young age of nine months, displaying advanced motor development, seldom tripping or falling as most toddlers do.

But at the age of two, he had still not learned to speak. An examination showed his hearing to be normal. His parents hoped he would be a "late bloomer." But even at the age of three, Tim still did not respond to his parents' speech. In addition, he had developed few social skills, and he engaged in unusual and repetitive behaviors—like spinning the wheels of his toy car or sitting and rocking his body endlessly.

Tim's condition is rare. It is what is labeled **autism**, a disorder described by the American Psychiatric Association (1994) as a **pervasive developmental disorder**. The causes of autism are unclear although some cases appear to be linked with a chromosome abnormality (Vostanis et al., 1994); others may be associated with defects or damage in the part of the brain called the cerebellum (Ciesielski & Knight, 1994).

Autistic disorder is apparent mainly in the infant's failure to develop normal communication skills. In those infants who initially learn language and then develop autism later, there is almost invariably significant language loss (Kurita, 1996). Its other features include a lack of normal responsiveness to other people, bizarre responses to aspects of the environment, a pattern of developmental delays, and, very often, any of a number of repetitive, stereotypic behaviors (Morrison & Rosales-Ruiz, 1997). Also, some autistic children are self-destructive; others engage in destruction of things (Celiberti et al., 1997). Comparisons of videotapes of the first birthdays of eleven autistic infants with those of eleven normal children revealed a number of behavioral signs that seem to differentiate the two groups: These had to do with pointing, showing others different objects, looking at other people, and turning in response to hearing one's name (Osterling & Dawson, 1994).

Among the major symptoms of autism, the APA (1994) lists the following: (1) severe and consistent impairment in social relationships (for example, inappropriate emotional responses, lack of awareness of feelings of others, abnormal social play, inability to make friends); (2) significant impairment in verbal and nonverbal communication (for example, absence of babbling, lack of facial expressiveness, absence of imaginative activity as in "make-believe" games, abnormal speech production, inability to initiate or maintain a conversation); and (3) markedly restricted range of interests and behaviors (for example, stereotyped movements like spinning or head banging, persistent preoccupation with parts of objects like repeatedly smelling or feeling something, serious distress over trivial changes in environment, unreasonable insistence on routines, and preoccupation with one activity).

Although the autistic disorder usually manifests itself before the age of three, it sometimes develops later (Mesibov & Van Bourgondien, 1992). The most common treatment is to use tranquilizers and antipsychotic drugs. Although there is little evidence that these medicines are very effective in alleviating the condition, they are useful in making patients more manageable (McCormick, 1997). Psychotherapy (psychoanalysis, for example) has not proven very effective, although some forms of behavior therapy (based on conditioning theories described in Chapter 2) beginning early in the child's life and sustained over a long period of time are sometimes helpful (Hagopian, Fisher, & Legacy, 1994). In general, the long-term prognosis for autistic children is not good, with only a very small percentage ever recovering sufficiently that they can be classed as "completely normal." (See Summary Table 6.10.)

▲ SUMMARY TABLE 6.10
Some Manifestations of Exceptionality in Infants

Exceptionality is a two-sided concept; it includes both ends of extreme deviations from average functioning and abilities. Here we look only at one end.

EXCEPTIONALITY	SOME CHARACTERISTICS
Cerebral palsy (significant developmental motor disability)	
definition:	a congenital, nonprogressive motor disorder.
causes:	unknown in many cases; perinatal asphyxia in about 20 percent of all cases; often associated with prematurity.
manifestations:	symptoms range from nearly imperceptible to almost total paralysis; sometimes evident in spasticity (inability to move voluntarily) and dyskinesis (abnormal movements).
Developmental coordination disorder	
definition:	difficulties in learning or carrying out motor activities, not associated with brain damage or cerebral palsy.
symptoms:	delayed or below average performance of common motor activities; resulting impairment of normal activities.
Epilepsy	
definition:	a seizure disorder of varying severity.
types:	*grand mal*—major seizures; *petit mal*—milder form of epilepsy.
causes:	sometimes genetic; often unknown.
treatment:	drugs can often be used to control seizures; in severe cases, brain surgery may be employed.
Autism (pervasive developmental disorder)	
etiology:	unclear; sometimes linked with a chromosomal abnormality.
symptoms:	impairment in social relations; impairment in communication; restricted range of interests, sometimes marked by repetitive and/or self-injurious behaviors.
treatment:	one or more of drug therapy, behavior therapy, or psychotherapy; prognosis for long-term normalcy not good.

THE WHOLE INFANT

There is something frustrating about fragmenting the developing infant into such psychologically convenient categories as description of capabilities, physical development, motor development, social–emotional development, and intellectual development. We lose the individual in the interminable and sometimes confused array of beliefs, findings, tentative conclusions, convincing arguments, and suggestions. The theoretical infant is a hypothetical average. And although many infants are very close to the hypothetical average child when they are one month old, fewer are still average at the age of two months, even fewer at the age of six months, and almost none by the age of one year. By the time the child becomes as old as you or I, the average individual will no longer exist but will appear only in the oversimplified theories of the social scientist or in the files of the market researcher who wants to know what the "average" person is wearing this spring.

Each person is an integrated whole whose intellect, emotions, and physical being all interact; each part is inextricably linked with and dependent upon every other part of the living organism. However, if we attempt to describe a person in that way, the sheer complexity of the task might over-whelm us. And so we continue to speak of the isolated forces that affect human development as though they exist apart from the integrated, whole person. But it bears repeating that our divisions, although necessary, are artificial and sometimes misleading.

FOCUS QUESTIONS: SUMMARY ANSWERS

1. How might infants influence their caregivers?

   ■ Influence in infant–parent interactions is bidirectional and strongly affected by the characteristics of both parent and infant as well as by the larger context.

2. Are infants born with certain personalities?

   ■ Individual personality differences among infants define temperament, which is assumed to have a strong genetic basis. Three broad infant temperaments are difficult, easy, and "slow to warm up." In North America, "easy" may be an advantage.

3. How important is early contact between parent and infant?

   ■ Forming an attachment with a caregiver is one of the most important tasks of early infancy. There appear to be powerful genetic tendencies toward the formation of caregiver–infant bonds (evident in infants' preference for the human voice and face, as well as in response tendencies such as rooting and sucking reflexes). (Bonding refers to the biologically based processes by which parents and infants form attachment links.)

4. Is it better for mothers to stay home with their infants?

   ■ High-quality infant care does not appear to disrupt parent–infant bonds or to prevent their formation, has no consistent negative effects, and is associated with superior cognitive and social development.

5. Is the nonaverage abnormal? What is exceptionality?

   ■ Exceptionality has both positive and negative dimensions, and may be evident in cerebral palsy, epilepsy, a variety of diseases, congenital physical problems, and physical problems resulting from accidents. Emotional exceptionality may be apparent in childhood-onset pervasive developmental disorders (like autism), which are rare but very serious early forms of emotional disorders.

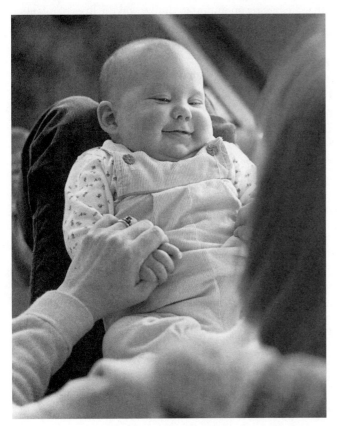

Infants are individuals, not averages. Their intellect, emotions, and physical being all interact. Their complexity defies description, and that complexity only increases as they grow into children, adolescents, then finally adults.

FURTHER READINGS

The following two books underline the role of family systems in influencing developmental outcomes:

Ambert, A. M. (1992). *The effect of children on parents.* New York: Haworth.

White, D., & Woollett, A. (1992). *Families: A context for development.* New York: Falmer.

A good summary of research and applications in temperament research is contained in this text:

Carey, W. B., & McDevitt, S. C. (Eds.). (1989). *Clinical and educational applications of temperament research.* Berwyn, PA: Swets North America.

Although fathers continue to be far less involved in the nurturant aspects of child rearing than mothers, evidence suggests that the qualities that define good caregivers are not gender-specific. The first of the following two references presents a strong argument for "generative" fathering, in which fathers become more actively involved in all aspects of parenting; the second describes a study that looked at gender differences in the nature and quality of parenting:

Hawkins, A. J., & Dollahite, D. C. (Eds.). (1997). *Generative fathering: Beyond deficit perspectives.* Current issues in the family series, Vol. 3. Thousand Oaks, CA: Sage.

Geiger, B. (1996). *Fathers as primary caregivers.* Westport, CT: Greenwood.

There is not enough child care in North America, nor is there enough quality child care, say Clarke-Stewart, Gruber, and Fitzgerald in the first of the following three books. The other two detail changes in contemporary North American society that are having an important impact on the lives of infants:

Clarke-Stewart, K. A., Gruber, C. P., & Fitzgerald, L. M. (1994). *Children at home and in day care.* Hillsdale, NJ: Erlbaum.

Hernandez, D. J., & Myers, D. E. (1993). *America's children: Resources from family, government, and the economy.* New York: Russell Sage.

Hayes, C. D., Palmer, J. L., & Zaslow, M. J. (Eds.). (1990). *Who cares for America's children? Child care policy for the 1990's.* Washington, DC: National Academy Press.

Pogrebin's book is a provocative analysis of the role that parents play in gender typing their infants:

Pogrebin, L. C. (1980). *Growing up free: Raising your child in the 80's.* New York: McGraw-Hill.

Sroufe's book is a thorough and relatively high-level look at the development of emotions in children:

Sroufe, L. A. (1996). *Emotional development: The organization of emotional life in the early years.* New York: Cambridge University Press.

PART THREE

Early Childhood

When you think that the eyes of your childhood dried at the sight of a piece of gingerbread and that a plum-cake was a compensation for the agony of parting with your mamma and sisters; O my friend and brother, you need not be too confident of your own fine feelings.

WILLIAM MAKEPEACE THACKERAY
Vanity Fair

ith the proliferation of day care, perhaps preschoolers no longer sense so profound an agony at parting from Mama. Perhaps, too, with the reduction in the size of the family, there are no sisters to bring to the eyes tears of sadness—or of joy. ¶ Still, it's true that preschoolers often don't need more than a piece of gingerbread or a plum-cake to dry their tears. At the same time, they don't need a very serious personal crisis to make them cry. ¶ As we see in the next two chapters, their understanding of the world is different from ours. So, too, are their emotional responses. It is as though the line between joy and sorrow has not yet been firmly drawn; it is easily crossed. Tears and laughter come more easily. I can move Jennie from gladness to tears if I take her stuffed toy from her. But now, if I give her a cookie (or a plum-cake), she smiles. ¶ We, too, can still cry when someone takes our stuffed toys. But what will dry our grown-up tears? Where are our gingerbreads and our plum-cakes?

SEVEN

Physical and Cognitive Development: Early Childhood

Tis the eye of childhood,
That fears a painted devil.

WILLIAM SHAKESPEARE
Macbeth, II, ii

'm seven years old. I'm dressed like a pirate because it's Halloween, and I'm ringing Mr. Delisle's doorbell, hoping Mrs. Delisle will answer because she always puts more stuff in our bags. My four-year-old sister, Paulette, is standing next to me, dressed in some yukky girl-costume like a fairy. My mother made me bring her. "Trick or treat," she's chanting, saying it like "treat" has two syllables. ¶ Shwack! The door wrenches open, and there stands Mr. Delisle. For some twisted reason, he's wearing one of those disgustingly monstrous masks. "Death to all at the hand of the painted devil!" he yells, scaring the living begory out of us, and Paulette has a small accident right there and runs home crying. ¶ "Her, she was scared," I tell my mom. "Me, I just drank too much soft drink."

n retrospect, I might have been wrong. It's likely that for both Paulette and me, experience had not yet drawn its thick black line between reality and fantasy. It's a line that we adults are so careful to keep firmly in view. Preschoolers scarcely know that it exists. For the first seven or eight years of life, Pearce (1977) informs us, the child often does not bother to check thinking against reality. Thinking is wishful, fantastic. It somehow assumes that reality can be changed or controlled by thoughts, that thoughts enter the real world and make of it what we wish—or, sometimes, what we fear. When Vikan and Clausen (1993) questioned four- to six-year-olds, they found that children firmly believe that people can be influenced, even controlled, by wishful thoughts and magical behavior just as readily as by rewards or persuasion. Thus it is that a magic spell can produce a witch or a princess, a silver thread or a pot of gold; and a kiss can cure a booboo, and a mother can make a dragon smile. Thus it is, too, that a painted devil can strike terror in a child's heart.

In this chapter, we examine the early development of thinking in preschool children, tracing their astounding achievements as they begin to glimpse the logic that governs the real world—perhaps, in the process, losing some of the ability to see things through the eyes of childhood as a more adultlike vision takes over. We look, too, at preschool education and at the development of language. But first, we turn to physical growth and motor development in children ages two to six.

PHYSICAL GROWTH IN THE PRESCHOOLER

At birth, the fetus has been growing at a rate of about 24 centimeters and 10 kilograms (9.4 inches and 22 pounds) per year (Tanner, Whitehouse, & Takaishi, 1966). During infancy, however, there is a rapid reduction in rate of growth—a **growth deceleration.** As a result, between ages 2 and 6, the child gains 6 to 8 centimeters and about 2 kilograms (2 to 3 inches and 4.4 pounds) per year. As we see in Chapter 11, at adolescence there is a dramatic, but relatively brief, acceleration of growth, but by about age 16 for girls and 18 for boys, growth rates are almost zero. (See Figure 7.1 for a representation of velocity curves—or speed of growth—for weight for boys and girls.)

In spite of the deceleration in growth rates in infancy through the preschool period, there are nevertheless phenomenal changes that take place during this period, as a comparison of the 6-year-old with the 2-year-old shows (see Figures 7.2 and 7.3). Not only do preschoolers gain an average of an additional 30 centimeters and 9 kilograms (about 1 foot and 20 pounds), but there are also some marked differences in rates of change for various parts of the body. These differences are reflected in the very different, and far more adult, appearance of the 6-year-old compared with the 2-year-old. For example, the thick layers of fat that give 1-year-old

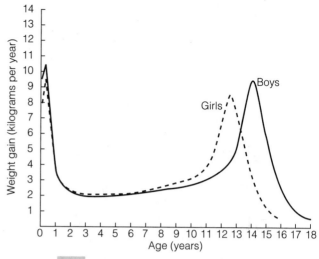

FIGURE 7.1

Body weight velocity curves (speed of growth) for boys and girls, from birth to age 18. The shape of the curves is much the same for height. (From Tanner, Whitehouse, Takaishi, Archives of Diseases in Childhood, *1966, vol. 41, pp. 454–471. Reprinted by permission.)*

infants their babyish appearance begin to disappear slowly during the second year of life and continue to recede gradually. Because these tissues grow much more slowly than other tissues, by the time children have reached age 6, their layers of fat are less than half as thick as they were at age 1.

Not only does the relative amount of fatty tissue change during the preschool years, but its distribution also changes as a result of the more rapid growth of bone and muscle. The squat appearance of infants is explained by the fact that their waists are usually as large as their hips or chests. Six-year-old children, in contrast, have begun to develop waists that are smaller than their shoulders and hips. This becomes even more evident in early adolescence.

The relatively larger infant waists are due not only to layers of fat but also to the size of the internal organs, many of which grow at a much more rapid rate than other parts of the body. Given space limitations between the child's pelvis and diaphragm, the abdomen often protrudes. This condition changes as children grow in height during the preschool years.

Other aspects of body proportions that account for the different appearance of the six-year-old include changes in the ratio of head to body size (shown in Figure 7.4). The head of a two-month-old fetus is approximately half the length of the entire body; at birth, it is closer to one-fourth the size of the rest of the body; and by the age of six, it is close to one-eighth the size, which is a short step removed from the head-to-body relationship typical of the normal adult with a normal-sized head: one-tenth. Thus, from the age of two to six, the head changes from approximately one-fifth to one-eighth of total body size—a significant enough change to be noticeable. Because of this, and because of changes in the distribution of fat and in the space that the child now has for internal organs, the six-year-old looks

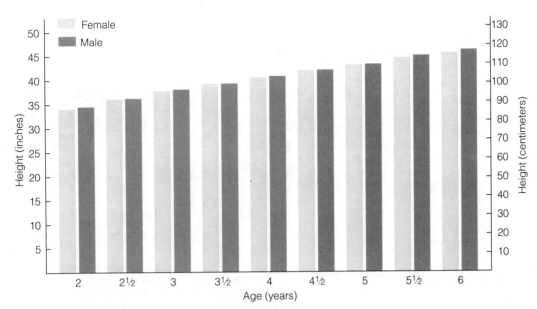

FIGURE 7.2

Height at 50th percentile
for U.S. children ages 2 to 6.
(Adapted from the Health
Department, Milwaukee,
Wisconsin; based on data
by H. C. Stuart and H. V.
Meredith, prepared for use
in Children's Medical Center, Boston. Used by per-
mission of the Milwaukee
Health Department.)

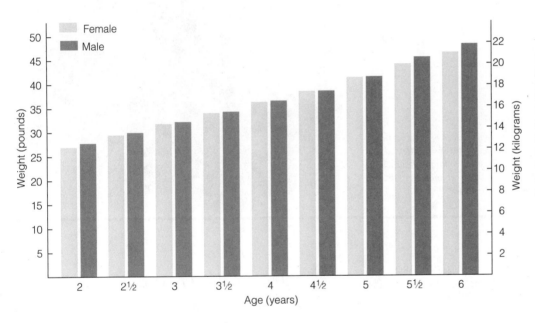

FIGURE 7.3

Weight at 50th percentile
for U.S. children ages 2 to 6.
(Adapted from the Health
Department, Milwaukee,
Wisconsin; based on data
by H. C. Stuart and H. V.
Meredith, prepared for use in
Children's Medical Center,
Boston. Used by permission
of the Milwaukee Health
Department.)

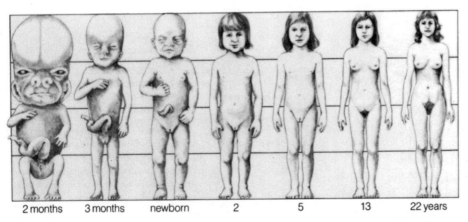

FIGURE 7.4

Changes in form and proportion of the
human body during fetal and postnatal
life. (From Jensen et al., Biology, 1979,
p. 233. Used with permission of the
Wadsworth Publishing Company.)

Preschoolers' Health Problems

ost preschoolers occasionally suffer from illness or injury serious enough to require medical attention or to keep them home. In fact, only twenty or thirty of every one hundred preschoolers will *not* have an upper-respiratory infection at least once (a cold, for example), and almost one-third will suffer some physical injury. Between ages five and seventeen, the rates for colds and other infections, and for digestive system problems decline; those for injuries increase. On average, rate of injury is about 30 percent higher for males than females (U.S. Bureau of the Census, 1996; see Figure 7.5).

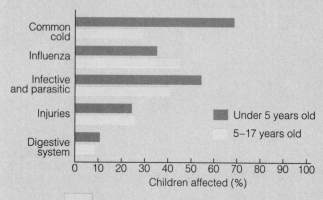

FIGURE 7.5

Preschoolers' and older children's susceptibility to injury and illness. The graph shows the percentage of children who will be affected at least once by the indicated condition, and the condition is sufficiently serious to require medical attention or staying at home. (Adapted from U.S. Bureau of the Census, 1996, p. 143.)

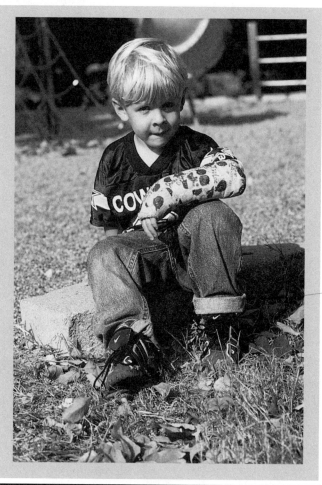

remarkably like an adult; the two-year-old looks more like a typical baby. (See "At a Glance: Preschoolers' Health Problems" and Figure 7.5.) (See Summary Table 7.1.)

MOTOR DEVELOPMENT

Learning to walk is the infant's most significant motor achievement, with extremely important social and cognitive implications. Infants who can walk (or at least crawl) can approach those to whom they are attached, and they can also leave them to explore places that they would otherwise see only from somebody's arms—or looking over the edge of some wheeled baby-thing. Self-locomotion facilitates the process of becoming familiar with the world.

Infants not only learn to walk, but also practice and eventually learn to coordinate a wide range of other motor activities. By age two, they are remarkably adept at picking up objects, stacking blocks, unlacing shoes, and a host of other actions.

▲ **SUMMARY TABLE 7.1**

Some Principles of Preschool Physical Growth

PRINCIPLE	COMMENTS
The period is marked by growth deceleration.	For example, weight gains drop from about 10 to 2 kilograms per year between ages 2 and 6.
Male/female growth rates are approximately equal.	Because males are slightly taller and heavier at birth, they remain so throughout childhood.
There are marked differences in rates of change for different parts of the body.	The most dramatic involves head-to-body ratio, which, at birth, is about 1:4 but becomes about 1:8 by age 6. Also, fatty tissues decline proportionally, while relative bone and muscle mass increases.

In early childhood, children continue to progress in motor development, their locomotion becoming more certain as they lose the characteristic wide-footed stance of the toddler (from 18 months to 2½ years). As their equilibrium stabilizes and their feet move closer together, their arms and hands also move closer to their bodies. They no longer need as wide a stance to maintain their balance—nor do they always need to keep their arms out as if they were perpetually walking a rail. Still, they fall far more often than you or I.

But it doesn't hurt so much.

Developmental Timetables

Most parents are keenly interested in the developmental progress of their infants and children. They feel proud of their offspring's accomplishments and are sometimes distressed and worried when their children do not develop as rapidly as they expect—or as rapidly as someone else's children.

Here, as in all areas of human development, there are no absolute norms, no definite, preestablished levels of performance that must be reached by certain ages. Our definitions of what is normal are vague and inexact. Still, psychology and medicine provide us with indications of what we might expect—that is, with **developmental timetables**—and these timetables may be used as benchmarks against which to evaluate our children, if we must.

Many different scales of infant and child development might be used for these purposes. As we saw, there are neo-

natal scales with which to assess the physiological and neurological condition of the newborn (for example, the *Brazelton Neonatal Behavioral Assessment Scale* or the *Apgar*). There are also scales to assess motor and mental development in infancy (for example, the *Bayley Scales of Infant Development*). And there are developmental scales that span infancy and childhood (for example, the *Denver II* or the *Gesell Developmental Schedules*). Each of these instruments typically provides simple tasks that can be presented to the infant or child, or describes observations that can be made. Each also provides specific tables of norms describing what sorts of infant or child behaviors can be expected at different ages.

The Denver Developmental Screening Test, for example, was initially designed primarily to permit identification of infants and children suffering from developmental delays (Frankenburg et al., 1981). It has subsequently been revised and restandardized with various ethnic groups, and it is now known as the **Denver II** (Frankenburg & Dodds, 1992). It provides age norms corresponding to the levels at which 25, 50, 75, and 90 percent of children are expected to demonstrate a given capability. Four different areas are examined by the test: language, personal–social, fine motor, and gross motor. (See Table 7.2 for examples of fine motor and gross motor tasks pertinent to early childhood.) A child is considered to be developmentally delayed when incapable of

TABLE 7.2

Age at Which Norming Sample of Children Accomplish Described Task*

MOTOR TASK	APPROXIMATE AGES	
	50 PERCENT	90 PERCENT
Gross		
Kicks ball forward	18.3 mos.*	23.2 mos.
Throws ball overhand	20.3 mos.	2.9 yrs.
Balance on 1 foot 1 second	2.5 yrs.	3.4 yrs.
Broad jump	2.7 yrs.	3.2 yrs.
Balance on 1 foot 5 seconds	4.3 yrs.	5.4 yrs.
Walks heel to toe	4.6 yrs.	5.7 yrs.
Fine		
Scribbles	13.2 mos.	16.3 mos.
Tower of 4 cubes	19.2 mos.	23.8 mos.
Imitates vertical line	2.4 yrs.	3.2 yrs.
Tower of 8 cubes	2.2 yrs.	3.5 yrs.
Picks longer line	3.3 yrs.	5.3 yrs.
Draws person, 3 parts	3.7 yrs.	4.6 yrs.
Draws person, 6 parts	4.6 yrs.	5.6 yrs.

Norms of developmental timetables tell us that most two-year-olds cannot yet stack eight jars, nor can they stand on one foot for a whole second. But the first of these tasks can be accomplished with a little parental help. And, as for the second, it isn't really necessary to stand on one leg in order to dance the Great Jar Tower Dance.

*For example, 18.3 months equals 18 months and 9 days; 2.5 years equals 2 years and 6 months.
Source: From the revised *Denver II* by W. K. Frankenburg and J. B. Dodds, 1992. Denver, CO: Denver Developmental Materials, Inc. Reprinted by permission of the publisher.

performing a task of which 90 percent of children of the same age are capable. Isolated developmental delays are not considered serious. But when a child is delayed on two or more tasks and in more than one area, further assessment may be required.

Developmental delays are not always evidence of genetically based problems or permanent neurological damage. Sheard (1994) reports, for example, that iron-deficient infants often perform less well on tests of intellectual and motor development. Reassuringly, however, treatment of these children with iron supplements often leads to marked improvement.

Motor Development and the Growth of Intellect

There appears to be a very close relationship between timetables for motor development and other aspects of development. In infancy, for example, learning to crawl, and eventually to walk, seems important for developing notions of depth (Bushnell & Boudreau, 1993). Similarly, the development of a variety of other motor skills in the preschool period seems to be closely related to the child's growing intelligence. In fact, motor skills that demonstrate increasing control and coordination of fine-muscle movements are often used as items on measures of intelligence. Among these are the skills required for tracing geometric figures or for copying them freehand. Gesell (1925), whose work maps out in detail the sequential progression of children's motor development, reports that before age two the child is usually incapable of copying a circle or a horizontal line although the two- to three-year-old can do so quite easily. By the age of four, children can also copy a cross but are unable to copy a diamond (see Figure 7.6).

The ability to draw the human figure also seems to reflect the preschooler's increasing conceptual sophistication. Thus, the preschooler's first attempts are typically crude lines with a head but no body or distinct limbs. In time, progressively more details and increasingly exact proportions are added. As far back as 1926, Goodenough (1926) used these observations to devise a simple intelligence test for children, the Goodenough Draw-a-Man test. Later, more politically correct revisions titled it the **Goodenough–Harris Drawing Test** (Harris, 1963) or the Draw-a-Person test (Naglieri, 1988) (see Figure 7.7). More recent evidence suggests there is a close relationship between the preschooler's drawings of human figures and cognitive development assessed in terms of Piaget's stages (discussed later in this chapter) (Chappell & Steitz, 1993).

Motor and Social Development

Most aspects of development are related to one another. Thus, motor development is related not only to the child's intellectual development but also to social development. For example, a child's play, particularly with **peers,** is often influenced by motor skills because various aptitudes are called for in different games. A child who is still incapable of jumping with both feet is not likely to be invited by older children to join in a game of jump rope; a child who cannot grasp marbles skillfully may be left out of the traditional springtime marble games.* Conversely, the child who is precocious in physical and motor development is likely to be the first one asked to participate in games—indeed, may be the one to

---

*Not always, said my grandmother. Sometimes kids just want somebody there who's gonna lose their marbles for sure.

FIGURE 7.6

Usual order of difficulty, with very approximate ages, for copying simple geometric designs reasonably well. Because of the close relationships between motor and intellectual development in early childhood, many intelligence tests for young children include items such as these.

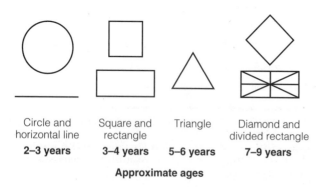

Circle and horizontal line	Square and rectangle	Triangle	Diamond and divided rectangle
2–3 years	**3–4 years**	**5–6 years**	**7–9 years**

Approximate ages

A   B

initiate them. Clearly, then, physical development and motor development have an important influence on the child's social development; game playing is one important means of socialization (more about this in Chapter 8). (See Table 7.3 for a summary of some physical and motor achievements of early childhood.)

THE PRESCHOOLER'S MIND

Infants, notes Rovee-Collier (1996), are not simply incompetent adults who get better and better as they age and grow and develop. Rather, they are highly competent organisms within their own particular niches, displaying remarkable adaptations in their responses to the immediate demands of their environments. What we should ask, she insists, is not so much "what do children do?" but "why do they do it?"

Still, the infant's responses are often startlingly different from those that you or I would make in the same situation. And that difference may serve to inform us about "why" children do what they do. For example, Fabricius and Wellman (1993) had children aged four to six judge the distances covered by different routes to the same location. Sometimes the routes were direct, at other times they were indirect, and still other times, some object placed along the route served to segment it. Many of these children insisted that the indirect and the segmented routes were shorter. Why? Perhaps, as Piaget thought, because these children focused only on one aspect of the route, or perhaps because they have difficulty representing the routes mentally.

But we don't expect our preschool children, much less our infants, to have adultlike memories or to be completely logical. We are seldom surprised when a 4-year-old is misled by appearances; we express little dismay when our 2½-year-old calls a duck a chicken. These instances of perception-dominated and illogical thinking simply amuse us; that is what we expect of young children.

But we would be surprised if our 7-year-olds continued to think segmented routes were shorter than other identical routes or if they continued to insist on calling all reasonably shaggy-looking pigs "doggy." We expect some intellectual (or cognitive) differences between preschoolers and older children. Among cognitive skills that differentiate older children from preschoolers are those having to do with memory.

TABLE 7.3

Physical Characteristics of the Child Age 2 to 5

AT 2 YEARS BEGINS TO	AT 3 YEARS BEGINS TO	AT 4 YEARS BEGINS TO	AT 5 YEARS BEGINS TO
Walk	Jump and hop on one foot	Run, jump, and climb with close adult supervision	Gain good body control
Run	Climb stairs by alternating feet on each stair	Dress self using buttons, zippers, laces, and so on	Throw and catch a ball, climb, jump, skip with good coordination
Actively explore environment	Dress and undress self somewhat	Use more sophisticated eating utensils such as knives to cut meat or spread butter	Coordinate movements to music
Sit in a chair without support	Walk a reasonably straight path on floor	Walk balance beam with ease	Put on snowpants, boots, and tie shoes
Climb stairs with help (two feet on each stair)	Walk on balance beam	Walk down stairs alone	Skip
Build block towers	Ride a tricycle	Bounce and catch ball	Jump rope, walk in a straight line
Feed self with fork and spoon	Stand on one foot for a short time	Push/pull wagon	Ride a two-wheel bike
Stand on balance beam	Catch large balls	Cut, following lines	Roller skate
Throw ball	Hop	Copy figure X	Fold paper
Catch	Gallop	Print first name	Reproduce alphabet and numbers
Jump	Kick ball		
Push and pull	Hit ball		Trace
Hang on bar	Paste		
Slide	String beads		
	Cut paper with scissors		
	Copy figures 0 and +		

Source: From G. W. Maxim (1993). *The very young* (4th ed.). Columbus, OH: Merrill, p. 80. © 1993 by Macmillan College Publishing Company. Reprinted by permission of Prentice Hall Inc.

Infantile Amnesia

Most of us are victims of a curious phenomenon called **infantile amnesia**: We remember virtually nothing about our infancies. So powerful is infantile amnesia that Newcombe and Fox (1994) found that nine- and ten-year-old children were unable to recognize photographs of most of their preschool classmates. In contrast, adults easily remember over 90 percent of photographs of elementary school classmates even decades later.

No one knows for sure why we experience infant amnesia. It isn't simply because our infancies are so far behind us, because a fifty-year-old remembers things that happened thirty years earlier but a ten-year-old remembers little of what happened only six years before. One theory is that parts of the infant's brain associated with memory are insufficiently mature to permit long-term remembering; another is that the infant's memory strategies are too primitive to allow the organization and associations required; still another is that there can be no memory of personal events before the infant develops a strong sense of self with which to associate them (Howe & Courage, 1993).

Our memories of early childhood are usually better than those of our infancies, but they too are full of shadows. What we retain are often global sorts of impressions, vague feelings, jumbles of emotions and events. In fact, time robs even our adult memories of crispness and clarity.

The Preschooler's Memory

Still, from the very beginning, the infant clearly has some ability to learn and to remember. But, as we saw in Chapter 5, the neonate's memory is very brief. The effects of simple conditioning procedures sometimes last only hours, or perhaps a day. Yet the infant is not long confused about whether this is his mother's voice or her face. Recognition of things like voices and faces is a certain sign of memory. But there are some important differences between the memories of infants and those of adults. Chief among them is that the infant does not deliberately and systematically organize, group, rehearse, or elaborate material to remember it—and these four activities are the most important memory strategies of adults and older children.

■ INCIDENTAL MNEMONICS

A number of researchers argue that the younger preschooler rarely uses systematic **memory strategies** for remembering. For example, they do not systematically rehearse (Gathercole, Adams, & Hitch, 1994), nor are they consciously aware of the possibility of using strategies (Hashimoto, 1991). Most of what the preschooler remembers is the result of what Wellman (1990) calls **incidental mnemonics**. Incidental mnemonics are not deliberate; hence, they are not really strategies. They are what happens when someone pays attention, for whatever reason, and later remembers, or when someone

is exposed to the same thing often enough that it becomes familiar and known. Remembering, in these cases, is not the result of a deliberate and systematic attempt to elaborate or to rehearse but is, in a sense, involuntary.

■ PRESCHOOLERS' MEMORY STRATEGIES

Although younger preschoolers do not appear to use or to be aware of deliberate and systematic strategies for remembering, they nevertheless do use primitive sorts of strategies. For example, Wellman (1988) asked three-year-olds to bury a toy in a sandbox before leaving the room with the experimenter. Some of the children were asked to remember where they had buried the toy; others were asked if there was anything they would like to do before leaving, but were given no instructions about remembering. Strikingly, half the children who had been instructed to remember the toy's location marked it by placing a mound over the object, by marking the sand, or sometimes by placing another toy on top of it; only 20 percent of the no-instruction group did likewise (see Figure 7.8).

Marking the toy's location is an intelligent and effective strategy. As we noted, however, many of the preschooler's memory strategies are not so effective. Heisel and Ritter (1981) asked three- and five-year-olds to hide an object in one of 196 separate containers arranged in a 14-foot-square matrix, and instructed some of them to remember where they had hidden the object. Significantly, many of the children in both age groups used memory strategies when they had been instructed to remember. The strategies used by the five-year-olds were often very effective—namely, hiding the object in one of the corner locations, because these could be remembered and relocated very easily. But what is perhaps most striking is that the three-year-olds' strategies, while every bit as consistent as those of the older children, were often very ineffective. Almost half these three-year-olds tried to hide the object in the same location on every trial, thus demonstrating that they were using a systematic strategy, but the location was typically somewhere near the center of the array. As a result, when they were later asked to find the object, these children fared almost as poorly as those who had not used strategies.

■ FIGURE 7.8

Three-year-olds were asked to hide a toy in a sandbox. Half of those who were asked to try to remember where the toy was hidden (the instructions group) marked its location; only 20 percent of the no-instructions group did likewise. Preschoolers may be capable of using simple memory strategies, but often do not do so spontaneously.

Percentage of children who marked the hidden toy's location in the sandbox mother in the little town of Martensville, Saskatchewan, noticed a diaper rash on her 30-month-old child. This led to suspicions of child abuse, at the center of which was a baby sitting service. Subsequently charged were Ron Sterling, Linda Sterling, their 25 year old son, Travis, 5 other males, and one minor female—with a total of 190 counts of physical and sexual abuse against two dozen children. Children were later to testify that they had been driven to a "devil's church" and made to drink urine and eat feces. One child swore he'd had an axe handle driven into his penis. Others said they had been victimized with penis-shaped vibrators. And after photographs of a building thought to be the "devil's church" were circulated, some children remembered being locked up in the wire cages that were evident in the photographs. Public hysteria ran high.

But there were no scars on any of the children, no physical evidence of abuse, and the wire cages were too small to have held any of the children. Interviews of the children were repeated numerous times, and were allegedly carried out by people who had little experience in such matters. After a sensational 3-month trial, the Sterling parents were acquitted, although the son was found guilty of some charges. But these convictions, too, were later overturned.

1. Eisler, D. (1997). A cautionary tale. *Maclean's*, Feb. 10.

To Do

As a major paper, research the proposition that young children make unreliable witnesses in criminal trials.

On the Net

For links to web sites dedicated to exposing what some people consider to be modern-day witch hunts primarily involving child sex abuse or satanic rituals, see the following:

http://www.vix.com/men/falsereport/index.html

The overuse of an inappropriate memory strategy is one of the most common mistakes made by young children trying to remember, says Wellman (1988). An important developmental change in memory strategies is a gradual reduction in the use of faulty strategies and an increase in more effective strategies.

Two things are noteworthy about the young preschooler's primitive memory strategies, says Wellman (1990): First, they seldom involve deliberate reorganization or elaboration, or even rehearsal; second, many of the preschooler's mnemonic strategies are faulty in the sense that they are misused and often do not lead to an improvement in memory. Still, older preschoolers sometimes do use deliberate, although not always highly effective, strategies to help them remember. The use of more effective strategies increases dramatically in elementary school.

DEVELOPMENT OF EARLY MEMORY STRATEGIES

The preschooler's increasing ability to remember results in part from increasing familiarity with things and events. For example, Saarnio (1993) showed that the more familiar preschoolers were with certain scenes, the better they were able to remember objects in the scenes. Still, preschoolers are easily distracted and may, on occasion, confuse their inventions and fantasies with reality. See, for example, "In the News and on the Net: A Witchhunt."

The development of memory skills may also depend on social interaction. (Recall from Chapter 2 that Vygotsky [1977] argues that the child's learning process is guided by interaction with adults or more advanced peers.) When Harris and Hamidullah (1993) asked mothers to teach their four-year-olds to remember different things (like the names of four cartoon characters or the location of animals in a zoo), the mothers spontaneously used strategies. The most common strategy used was rehearsal (repeating and having children repeat). In addition, many mothers combined these verbal rehearsal strategies with nonverbal strategies such as pointing out cues (like spots on the cartoon dog whose name was "Spotty the Dog").

Ornstein, Baker-Ward, and Naus (1988) describe five stages in the early development of memory strategies:

- Stage 1. In the beginning, the infant doesn't deliberately use strategies to remember.

- Stage 2. The preschooler may occasionally use primitive strategies, but these don't always result in memory improvement.

- Stage 3. In the early elementary school years, children use somewhat more effective strategies, but are often distracted by irrelevant information.

- Stage 4. Later, strategies become increasingly effective and are applied in a variety of settings.

- Stage 5. Finally, as a result of repeated practice with memory strategies, their use becomes habitual and automatic.

In summary, preschoolers are clearly able to remember. But in most cases, memory results not from the deliberate use of memory strategies, but from incidental mnemonics—for

Stages in the Development of Memory Strategies

There is little memory of the events of infancy, a phenomenon labeled *infantile amnesia*. And few preschoolers deliberately use systematic memory strategies. Instead, they use *incidental mnemonics*, sort of accidental strategies that result from paying attention or simply being exposed to something often enough. Five stages describe the development of the common, adult memory strategies of *rehearsing*, *organizing*, and *elaborating*.

1. In the beginning, no deliberate use of strategies

2. Occasional use of primitive, but often ineffective, strategies

3. More systematic use of strategies in early elementary school years, but child is often distracted by irrelevant information

4. Increasingly effective strategies applied in different settings

5. Use of strategies has become habitual and automatic

TABLE 7.5

Piaget's Stages of Cognitive Development

STAGE	APPROXIMATE AGE	SOME MAJOR CHARACTERISTICS*
Sensorimotor*	0–2 years	Intelligence in action.
		World of the here and now.
		No language, no thought, no notion of objective reality at beginning of stage.
Preoperational†	2–7 years	Egocentric thought.
Preconceptual	2–4 years	Reason dominated by perception.
Intuitive	4–7 years	Animistic thinking.
		Intuitive rather than logical solutions.
		Inability to conserve.
Concrete operations‡	7–11 or 12 years	Ability to conserve.
		Logic of classes and relations.
		Understanding of numbers.
		Thinking bound to concrete.
		Development of reversibility in thought.
Formal operations§	11 or 12 to 14 or 15 years	Complete generality of thought.
		Propositional thinking.
		Ability to deal with the hypothetical.
		Development of strong idealism.

*Discussed in Chapter 5.
†Discussed in this chapter.
‡Discussed in Chapter 9.
§Discussed in Chapter 11.

example, paying attention to something or being exposed to it more than once. In contrast, the elementary schoolchild often deliberately uses memory strategies.

One of the important differences between the older memorizer and the preschooler is that older children have acquired some understanding of the processes involved in learning and remembering. They have developed intuitive notions of themselves as information processors, capable of applying strategies and of monitoring and changing them as required. In the current jargon, they have developed some of the skills involved in **metamemory** (defined as the knowledge that children have about the processes involved in remembering). (More about the memories of older children appears in Chapter 9.) (See Summary Table 7.4.)

PIAGET'S VIEW OF PRESCHOOLER

The infant's intelligence, as we saw in Chapter 5, is a sensorimotor intelligence: It involves immediate sensation and perception. The intelligence of the preschooler is more conceptual, more symbolic. It is, in Piaget's term, **preoperational.**

An **operation** is a thought characterized by some specific logical properties—a logical thought. When DeVon believes he has more gum when he rolls it into a fat ball and less when he spreads it out like a thin pancake on his sister's pillow, he is demonstrating preoperational (or prelogical) thinking. His thinking is not yet characterized by **reversibility.** That is, he doesn't yet understand either the possibility or the implications of undoing an action mentally.

Piaget divides the preoperational period (ages two to about seven years) into two subperiods: The first, lasting from two to four, is termed **preconceptual;** the second, from four to seven, is called **intuitive** (Table 7.5).

Preconceptual Thinking

Toward the end of the second year, and especially with the advent of language, infants begin to symbolize. Now they can represent their actions mentally and anticipate consequences before the action actually occurs. Also, they have begun to develop some understanding of causes—of actions as means to ends.

PRECONCEPTS

As children begin to symbolize, they develop the ability to internalize objects and events in the environment and to relate them by their common properties. Thus, they develop **concepts.** But these concepts are not as complete and logical as an adult's; they are **preconcepts.** Preconcepts enable the child to make simple classifications necessary for identifying things. Thus, children recognize a man because they have a building concept that tells them that a man is whatever walks on two legs, has hair, wears pants, and speaks in a gruff voice. By noting their characteristics, children can identify dogs, birds, elephants, and houses. However, what they frequently cannot do is distinguish among different individuals belonging to the same species. Piaget (1951) illustrates this with his son, Laurent, who pointed out a snail to his father as they were walking. Several minutes later they came upon another snail, and the child exclaimed that here again was the snail. The child's failure to recognize that similar objects can belong to the same class and still be different objects—that is, they can retain an identity of their own—is an example of a preconcept. A related example is the preschooler who steadfastly continues to believe in Santa Claus even after seeing ten different Santas on the same day. For the child, they are all identical.

There are three other striking features of the child's reasoning processes during the preconceptual period, evident in transductive reasoning, syncretic reasoning, and animism.

■ TRANSDUCTIVE REASONING

There are two main types of logical reasoning: *deduction* and *induction*. To deduce is to go from the general to the particular. For example, from my knowledge that mammals give birth to live young, I might deduce that a specific mammal such as a three-toed sloth gives birth to tiny live sloths. In contrast, to induce is to go from specific examples to a broader generalization. After observing a number of barn swallows build nests of a mixture of mud and a cementlike type of saliva, I might generalize that all barn swallows build similar nests.

Transductive reasoning goes not from general to particular or particular to general, but makes inferences from one particular to another—that is, from one instance to another, often based on superficial similarities. It is very much like inductive reasoning except that it is based on a single case rather than many. If I find that one red-headed person has a particularly charming personality, I might transduce that all red-headed persons will also be charming. Transductive reasoning can occasionally—and somewhat accidentally—lead to a correct inference; it can also lead to totally incorrect conclusions. Consider the following example:

A flies; B flies; therefore, B is A.

Clearly, if A is a bird and B is also a bird, then A is a B and vice versa. If A is a plane and B is a bird, the same reasoning process leads to an incorrect conclusion. Thus it is that a young preschooler can unashamedly insist that cats are dogs and chickens are turkeys.

■ SYNCRETIC REASONING

The preschooler's classification behavior reveals **syncretic reasoning**, in which different objects are grouped according to the child's limited and frequently changing rules. For example, a two-year-old child who is placed in front of a table bearing a number of objects of different kinds and colors and who is asked to group objects that go together might reason something like this: The blue truck goes with the red truck because they both are trucks, and this thing goes with them because it's blue and that truck is blue. Here's a ball and here's a marble and they go together, and here's a crayon that's yellow like the ball so it goes with them too.

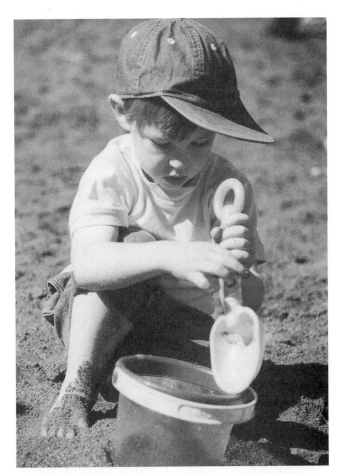

The preschooler's logic, says Piaget, is less than perfect: It tends to be intuitive and egocentric, and it relies on perception more than on reason. Still, it represents enormous advances over the infant's primitive understanding. Although this preschooler still suspects little about the logic that governs things like conservation of substances like sand, he has developed highly useful and completely adequate notions of quantity of sand and of ways of getting it from beach to pail—and perhaps eventually onto the floor of his mother's bedroom.

The important point is that preschoolers' classification rules change constantly; they see little reason to use the same rule consistently. We adults, whose thinking is not so magical, do not have the same luxury.

■ ANIMISM

There are other ways in which the thinking of the preconceptual child is more magical than ours. Piaget (1960) recounts a conversation he had as he walked with a young child. "Does the sun move?" Piaget asked (p. 215). "Yes," the child answered, going on to explain to Piaget that the sun followed him wherever he went, that it turned when he turned, and that it must surely be alive because otherwise it couldn't follow the way it does.

This, the belief that inanimate objects are alive, describes what Piaget labeled **animistic thinking**. Animistic thinking is what leads two- or three-year-olds to argue that the moon and the wind are alive. And if pressed to substantiate their beliefs, to explain how they know these things are alive, sometimes they argue that it is because they move that one knows they're alive.

"But cars move too," the clever psychologist interrupts. "Are they alive?" But animism has its limits, and most children at this stage don't think cars are alive. In fact, suggests Bullock (1985), whereas animistic thinking is sometimes characteristic of very young preschoolers, it is far less common among four- and five-year-olds. Furthermore, animism seems to apply far more readily to such things as the sun, moon, wind, and clouds—about which even we adults don't always know a great deal—than it does to rocks and trees and cars and dead cats.

Intuitive Thinking

The period of intuitive thinking begins at about age four and ends at approximately seven. It is termed *intuitive* because although children solve many problems correctly, they do not always do so using logic. During this period their thinking is said to be intuitive, egocentric, perception-dominated, and characterized by classification errors.

■ AN EXAMPLE OF INTUITIVE THINKING

In one of Piaget's problems, three balls are shown to a child and then inserted into a hollow cardboard tube so that the child can no longer see them. The balls are blue, red, and yellow. At first, when the tube is held vertically, the child knows clearly which ball is on top. Then the tube is turned a half rotation (180 degrees), and the child is asked which ball is now at the top. Alternatively, it may be turned a full rotation, one-and-one-half turns, two turns, and so on. Piaget found that as long as preschoolers could continue to imagine the position of the balls inside the tube, they could answer correctly. But they couldn't discover a rule that would have allowed them to solve the problem through reason (a rule about the relationship between odd and even numbers of turns or half-turns and the location of the balls, for example). They solved the problem through intuitive mental images rather than logical reasoning.

■ CLASSIFICATION PROBLEMS OF THE PRESCHOOLER

To demonstrate the preschooler's problems with classification, a Piaget-type problem presents the child with a collection of objects made up of two subclasses—for example, a handful of wooden beads of which fifteen are brown and five are blue. The child readily admits that all are wooden beads, and the experimenter then divides the beads into the subclasses, brown and blue, and asks whether there are more brown beads or more wooden beads. The trick is obvious, you say? Not to the child at this stage of development. "There's more brown beads," the child replies, as though breaking down a class into its subparts destroys the parent class.

■ PRESCHOOLER EGOCENTRICITY

In one Piaget study, a girl doll and a boy doll are placed side by side on a piece of string in plain view of a child. Now the experimenter, holding one end of the string in each hand, steps behind a screen so that the dolls are hidden from the child's view. The child is asked to predict which of the dolls will appear first if the experimenter moves the string toward the right. Let's assume that the boy doll appears first. The experimenter then hides the dolls again and repeats the same question: "Which of the dolls will come out first if they are moved to the same side?" The procedure is repeated several times regardless of whether the child answers correctly. A normally intelligent child will answer correctly for every early trial. What happens in later trials is striking: The child eventually makes the opposite and clearly incorrect prediction! If asked why, one of the more common answers is that it just isn't fair that the same doll comes out first every time; now it's the other doll's turn. Children inject their own values, their own sense of justice, into the experimental situation, demonstrating their egocentric thought processes. The term **egocentric** is not derogatory but simply points out an excessive reliance on the thinker's individual point of view coupled with a corresponding inability to be objective.

Egocentric thought is also demonstrated by the preschooler's inability to imagine what a mountain looks like when seen from another point of view—for example, the top or bottom or another side. It's apparent too in what Piaget terms *egocentric speech,* the characteristic self-talk of the budding young linguist who repeats words and sounds to himself—much as a young prelingual infant might babble—but using real words.

■ RELIANCE ON PERCEPTION

The preschooler's perception also dominates thinking, as is easily shown in Piaget's **conservation** problems (see Chapter 9). In a typical conservation of mass problem, for example, a child is shown two identical balls of modeling clay and acknowledges that there is the same amount of clay in each. One of the balls is then flattened into a thin pancake, broken into small pieces, rolled into a long snake, or otherwise deformed. The child now believes that the ball of clay that has been altered contains either more or less clay because it looks that way. The preoperational child relies on the appearance of the object rather than on any of the logical rules that will later govern thinking (for example, nothing has been added to or taken away from the clay, so it must still contain an identical amount). Figure 7.9 illustrates simple tasks that can be used to demonstrate some of the important prelogical characteristics of the preschooler's thought processes.

Replications of Piaget's Work

Literally hundreds of studies have been conducted to investigate Piaget's view of the child's progression through stages of cognitive development. With a few exceptions, most have found that the sequence described by Piaget is valid, not only in European and North American countries, but in many other parts of the world as well. However, some evidence shows that Piaget's estimates of the ages of attainment are, in

FIGURE 7.9

Preconceptual period: 2–4 years

Preconceptual

Similar objects are assumed to be identical.

Transductive

a dog
(is furry, likes balls)

(is furry, likes balls, must also be a dog)

Reasoning from particular to particular.

Syncretic

"Put those that go together on the table."

Groupings according to idiosyncratic and changing criteria.

Animistic

"It seems to move when I do. It must be following me."

Some inanimate objects are responded to as though they were alive.

Intuitive period: 4–7 years

Intuitive

Tube is rotated; child must predict order of balls, but cannot do so unless the rotations are so few that they can be "imagined."

Perception-dominated

1 2
A

1 2
B

Child admits two balls of clay are "the same" in **A**. In **B**, where one has been flattened, child thinks amount has been changed.

Egocentric

Boy and girl dolls are behind screen. They are always brought out on the same side so that boy always appears first. Child eventually predicts the other doll should be first: "It's her turn."

Prone to errors of classification

Child realizes some flowers are daisies, fewer are tulips, but answers "Daisies" to the question: "Are there more flowers or more daisies?"

effect, underestimates for some North American and European children on specific tasks. One type of study that illustrates this point concerns Piaget's "mountain" problems.

In the original study, children observed three mountains of unequal height set on top of a table. They were allowed to walk around the display, becoming familiar with all sides of the mountains. Later they sat on one side of the table, a doll was placed on the other side, and they were asked to select photographs representing the doll's point of view. Piaget found that children in the preoperational period usually indicated that the doll would see the same things they themselves saw, a finding that he interpreted as evidence of egocentricity.

When Piaget's mountain task is made simpler, the child sometimes responds quite differently. Liben (1975) asked preschoolers to describe what a white card would look like from their point of view and from the experimenter's point of view if, for example, the experimenter, but not the children, wore green-tinted glasses. A correct, nonegocentric response in this case would be that the card would look green to the experimenter. Liben found that almost half the three-year-olds answered correctly, and most of the older children had no difficulty with the questions. Similarly, when Hughes (reported in Donaldson, 1978) presented preschoolers with a situation in which they had to determine whether a "policeman" could

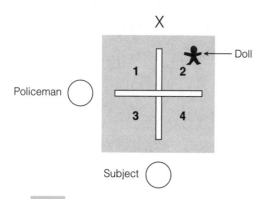

X

Doll

Policeman

1 2

3 4

Subject

FIGURE 7.10

Arrangement for the Hughes experiment. Subjects had to determine whether a doll hidden in 1, 2, 3, or 4 could be seen by the policeman. In a later part of the experiment, a second policeman was placed at X. The child now had to decide where the doll would have to be hidden so as not to be seen by either policeman. Preschoolers had little trouble answering correctly.

see a boy doll from a vantage point quite different from the child's, subjects had little difficulty determining what the policeman's point of view would actually be (Figure 7.10).

■ WAS PIAGET WRONG?

Do these studies mean that Piaget's conclusions about the preoperational child's egocentricity are invalid? The answer is no. Donaldson (1978) points out that all these studies present the child with problems that are really very different from the problem of the mountains. The child who can accurately predict whether a policeman can see into an area when the policeman is on the opposite side of the table from the child should not be expected to be able to describe what the physical array would look like to the policeman. Among other things, doing so would require that the child be able to reverse left and right (in other words, that the child realize the policeman's left is the child's right)—a task that is sometimes difficult even for adults, as those of us who have occasionally been surprised by our movements in mirrors can testify.

What these and related studies most clearly point out is that egocentricity and other characteristics of children's thinking are far more complex than had been suspected. As Lourenco and Machado (1996) point out in their defense of Piaget against his critics, there have been widespread misinterpretations of Piaget's theory. Many have assumed, for example, that the most important aspects of the theory have to do with discovering the ages at which children achieve certain understandings and capabilities. In fact, the central aspects of the theory have more to do with the processes by which children interact with the world, how they develop ideas, and how conflict among ideas leads to cognitive change and to the construction of progressively more logical representations of reality (Siegler & Ellis, 1996).

Some of Piaget's critics have been concerned that Piaget's emphasis, especially when dealing with the preschooler, has been on what children cannot do, on their mistakes and their incomplete and sometimes laughable logic. More recent em-

phases have done better justice to what preoperational children can do rather than what they cannot do.

Cognitive Achievements of the Preschooler

As Flavell (1985) notes, in light of what we know of preschoolers' cognitive achievement, it is inappropriate and misleading to think of them as preoperational or preconceptual. For example, there have been monumental advances in the child's ability to represent the world symbolically, highly evident in the use of language. Thus, when Smith (1979) asked four-year-olds questions of the type "A basenji is a kind of dog but not a poodle. Is a basenji an animal?" many answered correctly. Similarly, many had no difficulty with questions of the form "An abalone is a kind of food but not a plant. Is an abalone a vegetable?" These are class-inclusion questions; they require knowledge of class membership (animals include dogs; nonplants are not included among vegetables). They depend on the child's ability to reason by relating concepts. In addition, children's ability to classify and their understanding of number are quite phenomenal.

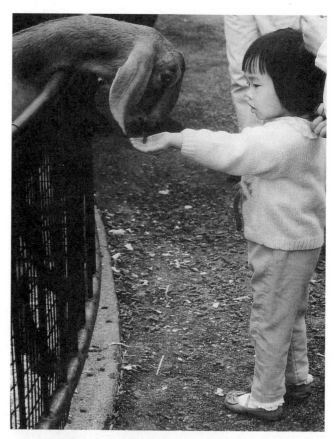

Among the cognitive achievements of the preschooler are remarkable advances in language and in understanding numbers, as well as a budding new ability to classify and to relate concepts. These achievements, notes Piaget, are highly dependent on the child's experiences with real objects—such as goats.

NUMBER CONCEPTS

English-speaking children's first number word, interestingly, is most often *two*. It typically appears shortly after the first birthday, at which time it might mean a whole collection of things, or it might mean exactly two of something (Sophian, 1996). For the next little while, children may practice number names, and might repeat them in memorized sequence as in "One, two, three, go." And by the time they become older preschoolers, there are few of them who cannot count objects and who do not understand that six jellybeans is more than four. Indeed, most will tell you without prompting that six is exactly two more than four or that if you had six jellybeans to begin with and your little brother ate four of them, you would have only two left. Children invent their own solutions for problems of this kind, claims Aubrey (1993). As a result, they come to school with a wide range of competencies, not all of which are taken into account by the school curriculum.

Gelman (1982; Gelman & Gallistel, 1978) identifies the rather remarkable sorts of knowledge that underlie the preschooler's understanding of number. First there are *number abstraction skills* that give the child an understanding of numerosity—of how many things there are in a collection of, say, snails in one's pockets. Second, there are *numerical reasoning principles* that allow the child to reason about or predict the outcome of certain simple numerical operations, such as adding to or taking from. Finally, there are the principles that allow children to count. We adults take these principles completely for granted although they are remarkably complex and wonderfully logical. And, amazingly, preschoolers discover and use them without anyone needing to actually teach them.

To some extent, psychology's preoccupation with what preschool children cannot do has often obscured their achievements. Number abstraction and numerical reasoning skills are important and complex cognitive abilities that illustrate dramatically some of these achievements. Also, their language development is nothing short of phenomenal. In short, preschoolers are a tremendous cognitive distance from sensorimotor children.

Can their capabilities be influenced through preschool education? Should they be? (See Summary Table 7.6.)

PRESCHOOL EDUCATION

Such questions are not without controversy. On one side are those like Elkind (1987), who fears that we push our children so relentlessly toward competence that the hurried child misses much of childhood, or Sigel (1987), who deplores the hothouse atmosphere of many early childhood programs. There are a number of misconceptions about preschool education, say Canning and Lyon (1991). One is the assumption that children need to be given experiences not provided in most homes; another is the belief that structured experiences (such

SUMMARY TABLE 7.6
Some Characteristics of Preoperational Thought

An operation is a thought subject to certain rules of logic—hence a *logical* thought. A *preoperation* is a thought that stops somewhat short of being completely logical. In spite of their remarkable achievements in language learning and number competence, preschoolers are described by Piaget as *preoperational*. Instead of being completely logical, their thinking may work like this:

PRECONCEPTUAL PERIOD (2–4 YEARS)

Preconceptual	Similar objects (like the toy at home and the one at the neighbor's) are considered identical.
Transductive	Reasoning from particular to particular; conclusions on the basis of a single example.
Syncretic	Changing criteria when grouping objects.
Animistic	Believing inanimate objects are alive, have a will, intend to do things.

INTUITIVE PERIOD (4–7 YEARS)

Intuitive	Reasoning based on mental images, on feeling rather than on logic.
Perception-dominated	Where appearances contradict logic, go with appearances.
Egocentric	Inject personal point of view into equation; inability to adopt another's point of view.
Prone to classification errors	Confusion among classes and their subclasses, as though dividing a class into its components destroys the parent class.

as learning to play the violin as a toddler or being taught a second language) will inevitably have a beneficial effect on the child's development in general. This "myth of early experience," write Canning and Lyon, has led us to forget that "the adult's role in preschool environments should be to provide appropriate play opportunities and be available to children" (p. 2).

On the other side of the debate are those who reason that preschool children can benefit tremendously from formal academic instruction. Even infants can be—and should be—taught basic reading skills, says Doman (1984). Accordingly, there has been a strong trend toward providing progressively more structured educational programs at the preschool level. This trend, says Rescorla (1991), stems from psychology's emphasis on the importance of early experience, a perception of decline in achievement of North American students relative to other groups (for example, the Japanese), and parents' desire for their children to be the best. It stems, as well, from the observation that in developing countries such as India, children who are exposed to preschool education typically manifest significant intellectual advantages over those who aren't (Pandey, 1991).

In many parts of the world, preschools are rare and elitist. But in North America, they are nearly universal—in spite of ongoing debate about whether their main purpose should be academic preparation or social development.

There is no simple and clear resolution to this debate—which may be one reason why there are so many different forms of preschool education programs. Some are distinct—that is, they are describable in terms of specific principles and procedures. However, the majority are highly eclectic. They include kindergartens, nursery schools, preschools, play schools, intervention programs, compensatory education programs, even day-care centers (day care is discussed in Chapter 8). They are found in schools and homes, in church basements and community centers, in parks and shopping malls, in universities and technical schools, even in office buildings. Their offerings are a varied mixture dictated in part by the ages of their charges, the resources available, the wishes of parents, the restrictions and mandates of local laws and regulations, and the inclinations and capabilities of instructors and caregivers.

Preschools and Primary Schools in the Nonindustrialized World

As in many other poor cities in the world, when cars stop at busy intersections in Manila and Quezon City in the Philippines, children rush out to sell things or to beg for money. "They are called 'street children,'" writes Tsuchiyama (1992). "They have dropped out of school. ...They sleep on the roadside" (p. 56).

In fact, almost 20 percent of children in the Philippines aged six to eleven are not enrolled in school, one-third of all children don't graduate from fourth grade, and kindergartens and other forms of preschool education are extremely rare (Tsuchiyama, 1992). That, too, is the case in Africa as well as in most other developing countries, where fewer than 50 percent of all children attend primary schools, and many drop out before they finish (Bellamy, 1997). In fact, taken as a whole, in the world's least developed countries only 56 percent of males enroll in primary school—and only 45 percent of females! And only slightly more than half of these actually reach fifth grade. Fewer than one-quarter of the males who

enroll in primary school also enroll in secondary school, but only about one in ten of the females do so.

But the picture in the developed world is vastly different. Ninety-seven percent of both males and females in the world's industrialized countries attend elementary school, and an amazing 99 percent of these reach fifth grade. Ninety-nine percent of the *females* go on to enroll in secondary school—and 97 percent of the males. (See Figure 7.11.)

In most of the world's poorer countries, only a tiny percentage—those from rich families—have access to preschool education. But in North America and much of Europe, our children have free (even compulsory) access not only to elementary and high school education, but also to a tremendous assortment of preschools. The following sections present very brief summaries of some forms of preschool education.

Nursery Schools

For many years, **nursery schools** were among the most prevalent form of preschool education. They typically take

FIGURE 7.11

Primary school enrollment in the world's countries. (Based on data from Bellamy, 1997, p. 98.)

Preschool Enrollment

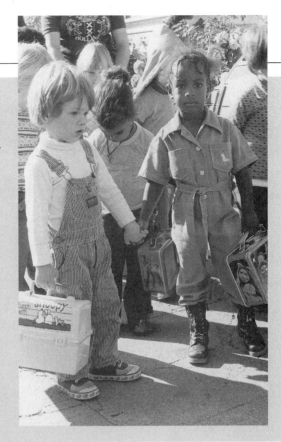

n 1994, 53 percent of all new mothers went back to work within one year of giving birth (U.S. Bureau of the Census, 1996). The number-one reason for going back to work is financial need; career development and personal enjoyment are also important reasons (Volling & Belsky, 1993). Of the more than 12 million U.S. children ages 3 to 5 in day care in 1994, over 7½ million were in nursery schools and kindergartens. Only 11 percent of the 5-year-olds were not enrolled in pre-primary schools.

FIGURE 7.12

Pre-primary school enrollment, 1994, for U.S. children ages 3 to 5. (Adapted from U.S. Bureau of the Census, 1996, p. 162.)

in very young preschoolers and emphasize social and emotional development. In contrast, **kindergartens** usually take in children in their last year prior to the beginning of primary school; their emphasis is often as much or more on academic preparation for first grade as it is on social and emotional activities. Whereas well-run kindergarten programs typically include activities such as counting and letter recognition, the principal activities of nursery schools consist of games, dancing, singing, listening to stories, and so on—many of the functions that are also performed by good day-care facilities. In fact, as Caldwell (1991) points out, so close are the functions of day-care facilities and of nursery schools (and other preschools) that many of today's day-care facilities are equivalent to what were once called "nursery schools" (see Chapter 8 for a discussion of day care). Caldwell coins a new term for the function of these day cares: *educare*. (See "At a Glance: Preschool Enrollment" and Figure 7.12.)

Kindergartens

Not long ago, kindergartens were usually considered an optional preschool program. Now, a majority of North American children attend kindergartens, most of which are housed in regular schools, funded in the same manner as schools, and staffed by teachers whose certification requirements are the same as those who teach at more advanced levels. In many ways, kindergartens are part of regular school. Many no longer simply prepare the child for the first-grade tasks of learning to read and write and count; they actually engage in the heady business of teaching these things (if the children don't already know them). One of the big differences between kindergartens and regular schools, in most (but no longer all) jurisdictions, is that kindergartners can go home at lunchtime and stay there the rest of the afternoon, or they can stay home all morning and go to school only in the afternoon.

But perhaps we are hurrying our children too much, Elkind (1981a) warns. Perhaps we should let them slow down and be children—let them play and dream and do magical things that don't require knowing how to read and write and count real numbers in perfect sequence. Marcon (1993), for example, reports a study in which children who attended kindergartens in which the emphasis was mainly on social–emotional development fared as well in the long run as did children who attended more academic kindergartens. (In fact, these children were less likely to be retained a grade in elementary school!)

Not only are we hurrying our children, says Elkind (1987), but many parents are also miseducating them. These are "Gold Medal" parents whose burning ambition is to produce a star basketball or hockey player, a world-class gymnast, a violin prodigy. Or they are "College Degree" parents whose babies are destined for Harvard or MIT. For these parents, children have become symbols of parental ambitions and proof of parental success.

iroki had seemed exceptionally intelligent and creative to some American observers in Komatsudani, a preschool on the east side of Tokyo. When they mentioned this to Fukui-sensei, the teacher, she seemed puzzled. "Hiroki's intelligence is about average," she said, "about the same as most other children." But, the observers protested, he seems gifted. He finishes his work so fast, and then he entertains the children with his wonderful songs. No, protested the teacher, speed isn't the same thing as intelligence. "And his entertaining the other children," she added, "is a reflection not so much of intelligence as it is of his great need for attention" (Tobin, Wu, & Davidson, 1989, p. 24).

The teacher's response to individual talents and weaknesses might be one of the important differences between Japanese and North American preschools—a difference evident as well in the nature of the classroom activity. Whereas North American schools tend to emphasize individual activity with some group activities (such as reading), Japanese schools are characterized by far more of what the Early Childhood Education Association of Japan labels "all-together classroom activity." Thus, in Komatsudani, some of the activities on a typical day included an early-morning exercise song, during which children formed a circle and went through a series of

group exercises; the end-of-exercise, go-to-your-room song, during which the teacher led the students in a running file to the classroom, each child removing shoes at the doorway; the morning song sung in unison by the children and played on an organ by Fukui-sensei, the teacher; chanted roll-call attendance, followed by a group counting song; a workbook project; group lunch; a group rest period, heads on your tables; a major origami (paper-folding) group project; and a teacher-read story using *kami shihai* (a "paper show" in which the story is told in pictures on one side of cards held up by the teacher, who simultaneously reads the story written on the backs of the cards) (Tobin et al., 1989).

Another difference between Japanese and North American preschools—a direct result of the greater emphasis on group activities in the Japanese preschool—is their much larger size. Government guidelines suggest that classes should not be larger than forty students. In one study, average size of preschools was around thirty-four students (Hinago, 1979).

And a final difference may be that Japanese parents are more demanding than many North American parents. Even at the preschool level, they have begun to measure the accomplishments of their children. One study reports that 71 percent of all children aged three to five can already boast of

some accomplishment (swimming, ballet, gymnastics, calligraphy, violin, and so on), and 100 percent of the five-year-olds have achieved some accomplishment (Horiuchi, 1979).

To Think About

Ohba (1979) suggests that Japanese society is characterized by an intense "my homeism," a powerful sort of family cohesiveness that finds expression in parents' strong wish that children excel, and in unrelenting pressures put on children to do so. Elkind (1981a) says the same is true of much of North American society, where parents often push their children relentlessly, hurrying them through their childhoods. What do you think?

We have to strike a balance, Elkind (1981a) urges, between the spoiled child, who remains a child too long, and the **hurried child**, who does not remain a child long enough, and whose life might be plagued by "a fear of failure—of not achieving fast enough or high enough" (p. xii). (See "Across Cultures: Hiroki's Preschool.")

Compensatory Programs

Compensatory preschool programs are designed to make up for initial deficits in children. The best-known and most massive compensatory education program ever undertaken in the United States was **Project Head Start**, which began in 1964 and which was conceived as part of the American war on poverty. The program allocated huge sums to the creation of eight-week summer programs for children from disadvantaged backgrounds. Almost three decades later, the Head Start

budget had grown to nearly $3 billion, and almost 800,000 preschoolers are enrolled in the program ("Bush Calls for Unprecedented Increase," 1992).

Because of the variety of approaches used in these projects, it has been difficult to assess their effectiveness. Many early studies indicated that children enrolled in Head Start programs continued to be inferior to more advantaged children who had not been exposed to such programs, and critics were quick to conclude that huge amounts of money had been squandered in poorly planned, poorly executed, and basically ineffective programs. However, subsequent research has sometimes found quite dramatic improvements resulting from Head Start programs. Previous researchers, say Lee, Brooks-Gunn, and Schnur (1988), often failed to look at initial differences between groups exposed to Head Start and comparison groups. When they found that disadvantaged groups were still disadvantaged after the programs, they concluded that the programs had not worked. A study of

969 subjects conducted by Lee and associates found that although Head Start programs did not eliminate the difference between Head Start children and comparison groups, they did reduce it.

Following a review of various studies of Head Start programs, Haskins (1989) concludes that such programs have an immediate, positive impact on children. In addition, many programs also appear to have long-term benefits. Barnett (1993) reports, for example, that twenty-five years after a compensatory preschool program, the economic benefits to the participants (and the community) were far in excess of the costs of the program. Many of these long-term benefits are evident in "life success measures" such as reductions in teenage pregnancy, delinquency, unemployment, and reliance on welfare assistance (Barnett, 1992).

■ GOOD COMPENSATORY PROGRAMS

One of the reasons that studies of Head Start programs have not always reported positive results, claims Zigler (1994), is that the types of programs used and their implementation have sometimes left a lot to be desired. It is now generally recognized that the better programs have measurably beneficial effects on children. The important question, say Zigler and Styfco (1996), is this: What are the characteristics of good compensatory programs?

Various authorities suggest a number of important considerations. McCartney and Howley (1992) argue that one of the essential requirements for an effective intervention program is that the family as a child-rearing unit be taken into account, and that an attempt be made to provide conditions that will ameliorate a negative home environment. Accordingly, health, nutrition, housing, and employment need to be raised to an adequate level for intervention programs to be effective. And parents need to be involved directly in the program (White, Taylor, & Moss, 1992).

What are the best forms of preschool intervention? It depends, of course, on what the goals are. If we measure success in terms of preparation for academic tasks, the most effective forms of intervention are typically highly specific, "model" approaches. These are usually based on identifiable theories and characterized by well-formulated approaches and carefully developed materials (Dowell, 1997). Of hundreds of different possible examples, one of the better known is the **Montessori method,** which dates back to the turn of the century (Montessori, 1912). It was initially developed for use with mentally retarded children, but has proven highly effective and popular as a general program. Unlike most preschool programs, it is designed for use in elementary and high school as well.

One of the distinctive features of the Montessori approach is the use of specially developed materials for teaching sense discriminations. Montessori believed that all learning stems from sense perception and can therefore be improved by training the senses. Among the best known of her materials are large letters of the alphabet covered with sandpaper, which are used to teach the child to read. The prescribed teaching method requires not only that children look at the letters, but also that they trace the shapes with their fingertips, saying the sound of the letter and getting a tactile sensation of it at the same time. (See Figure 7.13 for examples of some Montessori materials.)

Evaluations of Montessori programs have generally been quite positive, in spite of the criticism that such programs, given their highly structured nature, might stifle the child's creativity. For example, a study of the long-term effects of preschool programs found that the highest achievers in grades six, seven, and eight were males who had been exposed to a preschool Montessori program (Miller & Bizzell, 1983).

Maria Montessori began to develop her program mainly to improve the functioning of mentally retarded children in

FIGURE 7.13

Some traditional Montessori materials.

Solid geometrical insets

Lacing frame   Buttoning frame

Plane geometrical insets

Sound boxes

Dark color to light color

Color boxes

Plane geometric forms
(in three series)

▲ SUMMARY TABLE 7.7
Dimensions of Preschool Education

Preschool education is far from universal, being rare or nonexistent in many of the world's least developed countries. Often, only those whose parents are wealthy have access to it. But in the United States, about half of all children ages three to five are enrolled in one of the following forms of preschool education (almost 90 percent eventually attend kindergarten):

Nursery schools	■ Take children at very young ages.
	■ Emphasis on social development and play.
	■ Highly positive short- and long-term effects of good nursery schools.
Kindergartens	■ Take children in final year prior to first grade (hence mostly 5-year-olds).
	■ Often use a structured, relatively academic program.
	■ Compulsory in many jurisdictions.
Compensatory programs	■ Programs designed to compensate for disadvantages sometimes associated with poverty.
Head Start programs:	Best known of U.S. compensatory programs.
	Take many different forms; high-quality programs can be very effective.
Montessori approach:	One possibility for compensatory programs.
	Emphasis on prescribed drills and routines designed to train the senses and lead to skills in reading, writing, and arithmetic.
	Also used beyond the preschool level.

Italy. Not surprisingly, one of its main emphases is on the development of language skills. (See Summary Table 7.7.)

■ LANGUAGE LEARNING IN THE PRESCHOOLER

Language, defined as "the use of arbitrary sounds with established and accepted referents, either real or abstract, that can be arranged in sequence to convey different meanings," is still, as far as we know, uniquely human.

Some Nonhuman Primate Studies

When psychologist Hayes and his wife tried to teach a chimpanzee to speak, they failed (Hayes & Hayes, 1951). It seems that the chimpanzee's vocal apparatus simply does not lend itself to speaking a language.

More recently, Savage-Rumbaugh and associates (1993) raised a child and an ape with the same caregiver, exposing both to the same language environment. When the child was

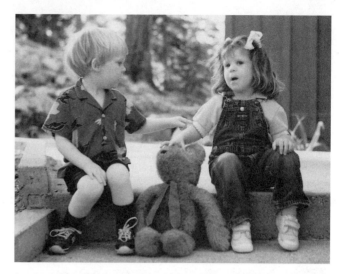

Language (though not communication) is, as far as we know, a uniquely human phenomenon, the purposes and functions of which are staggeringly important. Even when raised with humans and their children, nonhuman primates—and teddy bears—do not acquire the ability to speak.

two and the ape was eight, both were asked to respond to 660 novel sentences. And both did about equally well, indicating that although the ape had not learned to speak English, it had learned to comprehend it. In fact, it seems that apes, chimpanzees, and bonobos (and perhaps other primates as well) share some language and communication abilities with us, claim Langs, Badalamenti, and Savage-Rumbaugh (1996)—at least when it comes to comprehension.

Comprehension, most linguists agree, precedes the ability to speak. One of the major differences between apes and humans, in an evolutionary sense, Rumbaugh and Savage-Rumbaugh (1996) speculate, may be that when humans raised themselves up on their hind legs to become bipedal, there followed adjustments in their vocal tract and in the soft palate. These adjustments made the production of speech sounds possible. Thus, the capacity to comprehend speech might have existed some millions of years before the capacity to produce it; apes are still at that first stage.

Since the Hayes's attempt to teach a chimpanzee to speak, a succession of researchers have undertaken to teach chimpanzees American Sign Language. Its big advantage is that it does not require chimpanzees (or gorillas) to make sounds, but simply to make gestures. A number of these individuals report what seemed like remarkable success (for example, Fouts, 1987). However, critics insist that none of the chimpanzees in question have actually learned a language. Detailed examinations of videotapes of "sign-speaking" chimpanzees seemed to indicate that what they had learned was simply to imitate—to associate a symbol or gesture with food, or to use some movement or gesture to make some demand associated with reinforcement (Terrace, 1985). But the debate is by no means over, and researchers continue to report the development of "communicative" or "conversational" competence among various nonhuman primates (for example, Greenfield & Savage-Rumbaugh, 1993; Miles, 1997).

Language Development in Infants

The human brain, notes Gibson (1996), equips infants remarkably well to learn language—as we saw in the Chapter 5 discussion of the first three stages of language development (see Table 5.11 in Chapter 5). Thus, in the first short year of life (the prespeech stage), there is a dramatic transition from crying, gurgling, cooing, and babbling to the utterance of meaningful speech sounds. At around the age of one, the sentencelike word appears, accompanied by a repertoire of gestures, cries, and inflections that serves to communicate meaning. And by the age of eighteen months, the infant readily uses two-word sentences (duos). Increasing language sophistication now makes it possible for the infant to combine words with different modifiers to ask questions, make declarations, express denial, or issue commands. And through the last six months of the infant's second year, there is an astonishing vocabulary spurt. As Smith (1995) notes, the two-year-old is so good at learning words that if you show her a new object like, say, a tractor, and you tell her, "Hey, this is a tractor," from that day on, she will likely be able to recognize and correctly name every tractor she encounters for the rest of her life!

The story continues here with a discussion of the remaining three stages.

Multiple-Word Sentences

At around age 2½, children move from two-word combinations to multiple-word sentences. "Allgone" becomes "Banana is gone" and eventually "The banana is gone" or "My banana is gone."

Although the child's speech continues to be somewhat telegraphic, children now make increasing use of **morphemes** to express meaning (Brown, 1973). Recall that these are the smallest units of meaning in language. They include all words, as well as grammatical endings such as *ed* and *ing,* suffixes, prefixes, articles, and so on. The use of grammatical morphemes is what allows the child to transform the verbs *go* to *going, jump* to *jumped, eat* to *eated,* and *do* to *dood.* Morphemes in the English language tend to be acquired in about the same order both by children who develop normally and by those who experience delays in language development (Paul & Alforde, 1993).

As children learn to combine words in longer expressions and to use a greater variety of morphemes to change meanings, they often become highly creative in their use of language. Examples of their inventiveness are found in the words they create as they reinvent the grammatical rules of their language and discover the meanings of its many morphemes. "Daddy unpickmeup," insisted my youngest linguist, squirming to be put down. "You already feeded me." Similarly, his three-something-year-old sister, having learned that "pitch black" was very black, insisted that other things can be "pitch clean," "pitch empty," or "pitch big."

More Complex Changes

The power of the child's language takes a bound with the development of the ability to make meaningful transformations using *conjunction, embedding,* and *permutation* (Wood, 1981)—a development that occurs between the ages of 2 1/2 and 3 or 4. Simple conjunction is illustrated by the combining of two sentences. "Where?" and "We go" now become "Where we go?" Embedding is inserting. For example, the word *no* may be embedded in the sentence "I eat" to form a sentence with the opposite meaning: "I no eat." Permutation involves changing word order to change meaning. At first, children use intonation instead of permutation. For example, the sentence "I can go" may be a simple declaration when the *I* or the *can* is emphasized but becomes a question when *go* is emphasized. A simple permutation from "I can go" to "Can I go?" achieves the same meaning with much less ambiguity.

As children begin to show an understanding of various adult-accepted rules for transforming sentences, they also behave as though they had an implicit understanding of the grammatical function of various words and phrases. They now use nouns as nouns and not as verbs, adjectives are no longer treated as verbs, and nouns are further categorized as plural or singular. Evidence of children's understanding of this type of categorization is evident in their appropriate use of verbs and of such determiners as *that, the, those,* and *these.* For example, the child will now say "That box is empty"; an earlier error might have taken the form of "This boxes is empty."

Adultlike Structures

The further refinement and elaboration of speech requires mastery of countless subtle and intricate grammatical rules that we all use unconsciously. Some of these rules govern the arrangement of words in meaningful expressions; they specify what is (and is not) grammatically acceptable and meaningful. They tell us that "the fat mosquito" is a correctly structured phrase, but "Fat the mosquito" is not (although "Fat, the mosquito" might be). Other rules permit us to transform phrases or to combine them to create a variety of meaningful statements. Thus, there are rules that allow us to transform a passive sentence into an active one ("The dog was bitten by the man" to "The man bit the dog") or a negative to a positive ("I did not go" to "I went"). Much of this learning occurs in the first elementary grades. (See Summary Table 7.8.)

EXPLANATIONS OF LANGUAGE DEVELOPMENT

Each of us uses language as if we had a relatively complete understanding of a tremendous range of grammatical rules.

Spoken language *production* appears to be uniquely human; comprehension may not be because some evidence suggests that other primates might also be capable of some degree of language *comprehension*. Language learning in infancy progresses through learning turn-taking, the use of gestures, sound production and discrimination; the appearance of the first word (the *holophrase* if its meaning is large enough); and eventually highly telegraphic two-word sentences. Toward the last six months of infancy, there is often a remarkable vocabulary spurt. In the preschool period, language learning continues as follows:

STAGE	TIMING AND CHARACTERISTICS
Multiple-Word Sentences	By 2 to 2½ years.
	Sentences include both subject and predicate.
	Grammatical *morphemes* such as *ing* or *ed* are used to change meaning.
	Use of language is often highly inventive.
More Complex Changes	Between 2½ and 4 years.
	Use combinations, permutations, and embedding to alter meanings.
	Rapidly developing implicit knowledge of grammatical and structural rules of language.
Adultlike Structures	After 4 years.
	Continued mastery of complex rules for transforming sentences and for accurately conveying meanings.
	Use of language becomes potentially highly generative.

Yet, unless we are taught these rules formally, we can't explain them. In fact, linguists have not yet been able to work out a complete set of consistent and valid rules even for a single language.

The remarkable thing is that, in an amazingly short time, young children acquire a working knowledge of a very complex system of rules. How?

There are two principal classes of explanations for the development of language. One emphasizes the role of experience (learning); the other emphasizes the importance of biology (hereditary predispositions). Current evidence suggests that biology and experience are both important but that each, by itself, does not present an entirely adequate explanation.

The Role of Biology

Some, like Chomsky, believe that language is innate, that our brains have evolved in such a way as to make language development not only possible but almost inevitable. Rymer (1993) quotes Chomsky in an interview: "If you were to put prelinguistic children on an island, the chances are good that their language facility would soon produce a language. Maybe not in the first generation. And that when they did so, it would resemble the languages we know. You can't do the experiment because you can't subject a child to that experience" (p. 38). (However, Genie's experience is that experiment—a natural experiment—as we see below.)

Others, like Piaget, argue that language arises mainly from interactions with the environment and results from the infant's being able to abstract and represent sensorimotor schemata. Piattelli-Palmarini (1994), following an extensive analysis of a debate that took place between Piaget and Chomsky in 1975, gives the nod to Chomsky. The evidence, Piattelli-Palmarini argues, strongly suggests that the human brain is "language specific"—that it is prewired for language. Furthermore, Chomsky's theory of language development (and that of Lenneberg, 1969) is critical-period based. It argues that the critical period for learning language is before age five and that, almost invariably, language learning is pretty well complete by puberty.

THE EVIDENCE FOR BIOLOGY

There are several observations that support the hypothesis of a strong biological influence on language learning. For example, there is the fact that the earliest speech sounds of infants from very different backgrounds—even those of children whose parents are deaf—are highly similar. There is also the ease and astounding rapidity with which children learn language, in a sense reinventing the grammar of the language as they learn, and making only a fraction of the mistakes they might be expected to make if they were learning primarily through reinforcement, imitation, and trial and error. Finally, there is the observation that many of the mistakes children do make are not imitative but appear to result from the over-application of rules that are themselves correct.

These observations have given rise to a number of biological theories to explain language learning, the best known of which is Chomsky's (1957, 1965) theory of a **language acquisition device (LAD).** Simply put, it attempts to account for the infant's apparent predisposition for acquiring language by assuming that we are born with some special language-learning capacity. Children behave as though they were prewired for grammar, says Chomsky. How else are we to explain the fact that they make so few errors while learning syntax?

In effect, LAD is more a metaphor than an explanation. As a metaphor, it says that infants behave as if they already have at their command a range of cognitive skills, of language-related predispositions. And from this observation, we might infer that there must be some innate neurological prewiring at birth. But as Rice (1989) observes, this is not a completely satisfactory explanation of how these things work. Metaphors are not machines; they are simply comparisons.

GENIE'S STORY

Genie's story, described briefly in Chapter 3, provides another line of evidence for the Chomsky biological and critical period hypothesis. Recall that Genie was abandoned from the age of twenty months until almost fourteen years. When she surfaced, she made few sounds other than a peculiar laugh. For example, when angry, she wouldn't yell or scream; instead, she would scratch or gouge her face, urinate, smear mucus on herself, or blow her nose loudly into her clothes—or all of these. Rymer (1993) speculates that because she had been prevented from making noise by her father, she had learned to turn her emotions inward. When she really needed to make a noise, she would use other things to do so like dragging a chair, banging objects, or scratching her nails on a balloon.

At first, Genie's vocabulary seemed to be increasing relatively rapidly. She would often drag people around pointing at things and asking that they be named. But, at least for the first year, her expressions remained limited to short, largely incoherent verbalizations. A year and a half after being "found," Genie would only rarely put two words together, and almost never three. And, unlike normal children, who, after they reach the two-word-sentence stage, typically experience an explosion of rapid language learning, Genie continued to plod along. Even four years later, the kinds of sentences she would build when pushed to do so included confused combinations like "Where is may I have a penny?" or "I where is graham cracker on top shelf?" She continued to have no understanding of personal pronouns, totally confusing *I, me,* and *you,* never quite able to figure out who she was and who was somebody else. Nor did she ever learn to respond to "hello" with "hello," or even to understand the meaning of "thank you."

Scans of activity in Genie's brain subsequently showed that her left hemisphere remained virtually unresponsive to language (it's normally centrally involved in language functions). This is additional evidence that early experience may be essential for organizing the brain in the first place—during a critical period.

At the time of Rymer's writing, Genie had apparently regressed to a largely nonverbal existence and lived in a home for retarded adults. In the last photos Rymer saw of her, Genie was twenty-nine, a large, bumbling person with an expression of "cowlike incomprehension" on her face, an inmate of an asylum, totally withdrawn from the world.

In support of Chomsky's theory, Curtiss (1977) writes, "Language grows like an organ. When it comes to physical growth, no one asks why—why do arms grow? Learning a language is like learning to walk, a biological imperative timed to a certain point in development. It's not an emotional process" (p. 205).

The Role of Experience

In spite of the role of biology in language learning, little doubt exists that there is an overwhelming amount of learning involved in making the transition from the first meaningful sound to the fluent conversations of the six-year-old. Yet most children accomplish this learning apparently effortlessly and in much the same sequence across different cultures. Strangely, however, adults who are initially without language (because of isolation, for example) do not fare as well—as Genie's story illustrates. Similarly, adult learners who try to acquire a second language usually experience more difficulty doing so than do young children, and even if they are successful, their pronunciation will typically be characterized by a variety of errors that would not be found among those who learned the language at a younger age. There appears to be a sensitive period early in life when learning one or more languages will be easiest.

■ PARENTS AS TEACHERS

That children acquire the speech patterns, idioms, accents, and other language characteristics of those around them makes it clear that learning is centrally involved in language acquisition. Parents and other caregivers play an important role as language models: They provide the child with models of correct language as well as of the subtle rules governing conversations and the communication of messages. In addition, parents also serve as important dispensers of reinforcement for the child's verbalizations.

In Chapter 5 we spoke of the bidirectionality of parent–child influence, noting that what a caregiver does influences the infant and, no less true, what the infant does influences the caregiver. We see evidence of bidirectionality of influence in the development of language as well. The infant's level of language comprehension and use appears to have subtle but marked effects on the behavior of parents. Bruner (1978) refers to a fine-tuning theory of mother–infant interaction— "mother" because she is more often the principal caregiver than is the father. Virtually all mothers, he notes, alter their speech patterns according to the understanding of their children. It is as though the mother becomes a teacher, not because she consciously intends to be but because she "fine-tunes" her responses and behaviors to the immediate demands of her child. Furthermore, there is a consistency and regularity in the mother's altered speech patterns. One mother typically employed four sequential types of statements when "reading" to her young son. First she would say "Look": an attention-getting utterance. Next she would pose a standard question—"What is that?"—pause, and provide a label: "It's an X." Finally, following the child's response, she would say, "That's right." Additional evidence of fine-tuning occurred whenever the child responded earlier in the sequence. If, for example, he said "Truck" as the page turned, the mother would go immediately to her final response: "That's right."

■ CHILD-DIRECTED LANGUAGE (MOTHERESE)

In later stages of language development, the role of the mother as sensitive, fine-tuned teacher becomes even more apparent. The language mothers employ when talking to their children—sometimes called **motherese** (or *child-directed language*)—is quite different from what they would normally use when speaking with adults. Motherese is a good example of pragmatics in language; the mother adjusts her speech to the requirements of the situation. Thus, mothers tend to use simpler, shorter, and more repetitive utterances. In other words, they reduce (by simplifying and repeating). On other

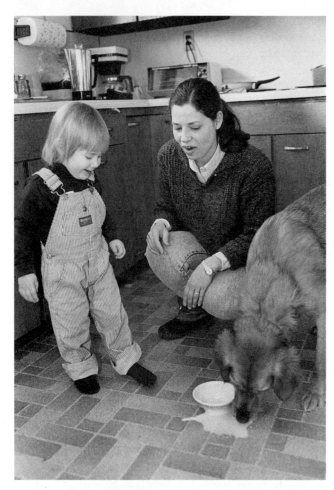

centered on the present and only seldom on the past or future, almost as though they knew, with Piaget, that the young infant's world is a world of the here and now.

Some children are fast language learners; others are much slower. For example, one study found a difference of 30 months between the fastest and the slowest learners among a sample of 128 3½-year-olds (Wells, 1985). One of the differences between the fastest and the slowest learners may be the extent and quality of the motherese to which they are exposed. Hampson and Nelson (1993) videotaped a sample of forty-five toddlers and analyzed their speech and that of their mothers. They found that the mothers of the most linguistically advanced children used a higher percentage of object names in their speech—and fewer commands. Also, Pelaez-Nogueras and Gewirtz (1993) report that motherese that imitates infant's vocalizations appears to reinforce them.

In summary, there is growing evidence that the mother (or father) plays a crucial role in the development of language and that this role goes well beyond providing a suitable model of the family's language. Unconsciously, parents modify their speech and become teachers—perhaps far better teachers than they could possibly be trained to be. (See Summary Table 7.9.)

When interacting with their infants, parents unconsciously tend to use shorter, grammatically simpler, higher-pitched, present-tense expressions. They also ask more questions and name more objects and actions. This child-directed speech, also called motherese, contributes to language learning.

▲ SUMMARY TABLE 7.9
Influences in Language Learning

SOURCE OF INFLUENCE	THEORISTS AND SOME SUPPORTING EVIDENCE
Biology	■ Chomsky (LAD) and Lenneberg.
	■ Earliest sounds made by all infants (even those who are deaf) are highly similar.
	■ The ease and rapidity with which children learn complex grammars.
	■ The difficulties people experience when trying to learn a language later in life.
	■ The observation that many errors children make are not learned but appear to result instead from the fact the grammars they have invented don't yet admit exceptions.
	■ The case of Genie; little language exposure for first 14 years of her life; relatively little language recovery later.
Experience	■ Bruner and Piaget.
	■ Children not exposed to language don't naturally invent it (Genie's case).
	■ The enormous difficulties deaf children experience in learning language.
	■ The specifics of language reflect the child's language environment.
	■ Motherese (child-directed language) appears important for the child's language learning.

occasions, mothers expand the child's expressions. A child might say, "Daddy gone," to which the mother might reply, "Yes, Daddy is gone." Moerk (1991) points out that most expansions are corrections and that corrections of this kind are especially important in early language learning.

Studies of motherese in different languages have typically found that the most important features of mother-to-infant speech appear to be universal. For example, Grieser and Kuhl (1988) found this to be true even in a language such as Mandarin Chinese, which is very different from English in that it is tonal (inflection and intonation are far more meaningful). Mothers' speech in Mandarin Chinese also tends to be grammatically and semantically simpler, and pitched at a higher frequency.

There are other, perhaps more subtle, ways in which the speech of the mother (or other caregivers, as well as siblings) is influenced by the presence of infants. Thus, typical caregiver speech is simpler, higher pitched, characterized by exaggerated intonation, made up of shorter sentences, and consists of a higher than normal percentage of questions. In addition, the speech of caregivers vis-à-vis their infants is almost always

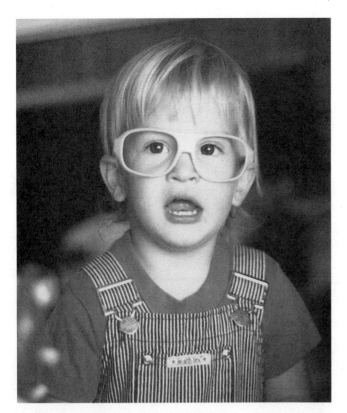

The preschooler's memory is not as impressive as yours or mine; they don't yet recognize the power of strategies like organizing or elaborating or rehearsing. But, remarkably, if you ask this bespectacled young scholar either "¿Como te llamas?" or "What's your name?" he will answer without hesitation, and correctly. And if he is exposed to two language environments throughout the preschool years, by the time he is six he will have learned a second language far more competently than would most adults over the same period of time.

CHANGING LANGUAGE CONTEXTS

In 1900 almost 90 percent of the United States population was white; most of the remainder was black. Hispanics were few enough in number that they weren't included as a category in census tables (U.S. Bureau of the Census, 1996).

By 1982, almost 75 percent of schoolchildren in the United States were still non-Hispanic white. But now, about 10 percent were Hispanic; the remainder included a varied mixture of ethnic groups. Ten years later, in California, the "minority" had become the "majority," with 52 percent of students belonging to "minority" categories (Garcia, 1993). Projections are that by 2020, 70 percent of beginning first-grade students will belong to nonwhite groups, and the percentage of white, non-Hispanic school-age Americans will have dropped to about 50 percent while the Hispanic group will have increased to around 25 percent. In fact, in 1995, 27 percent of the total population of California was Hispanic (U.S. Bureau of the Census, 1996). (See "At a Glance: Changing Demographics" and Figure 7.14.) The educational implications of these changes are considerable. In 1982, most schoolchildren spoke English—the dominant, standard, ma-

jority language. Now more than 15 percent speak a different language at home, and in over half of all cases, that language is Spanish (U.S. Bureau of the Census, 1996).

Effects of Bilingualism

There are two views with respect to the psychological effects of being **bilingual** (proficient in two languages). One maintains that there is a limited amount of cognitive space available for language and that learning two or more languages places such a strain on cognitive capacity that the individual suffers. According to this view, the second language competes with the first, and, in the end, the individual is not as proficient in either language as the **monolingual** individual. This competitive view is based in part on early studies of bilingualism, which often concluded that bilingual children were handicapped. Not only did they perform less well on measures of ability (such as intelligence tests), but they also tended to do less well in either language.

The second view maintains that there is no competition among languages and no clear limitation of cognitive resources necessary for language learning. This view is based on research indicating that "all other things being equal, higher degrees of bilingualism are associated with higher levels of cognitive attainment" (Hakuta & Garcia, 1989, p. 375).

Subtractive bilingualism is the term coined by Lambert (1975) to describe the negative influence of a second language. **Additive bilingualism** describes situations in which learning a second language has a positive influence on the first. And **transitional bilingualism** describes a common situation in which the dominant language replaces the minority language within a few generations.

TRANSITIONAL BILINGUALISM

For most children whose early environment includes two languages, learning a second language does not appear to be much more complicated than learning to ride a bicycle. In the end, however, for most individuals there is a dominant or preferred language. Few individuals become what Diaz (1983) calls **balanced bilinguals**—people who are equally fluent and comfortable in both languages. That, suggests Moffatt (1991), may be because most children learn languages sequentially rather than simultaneously, and rarely are the two languages equally valued in the society. This may be especially true in North American societies where the dominant language is highly reinforced but second languages often are not. As Pease-Alvarez and Hakuta (1992) put it, "Don't worry about English; they are all learning it; instead, if you are going to worry, worry about the lost potential in the attrition of the second language" (p. 5). In fact, note Hakuta and D'Andrea (1992), in many instances the bilingualism that has characterized parts of North America has been purely "transitional": Within three or four generations, the native language is completely replaced by the dominant English language.

Changing Demographics

As recently as 1980 in the United States, the dominant language was standard English and about three-quarters of all schoolchildren were white. But in some states like California, more than half of current schoolchildren have a language other than English as their first language. That percentage is expected to reach 70 within two decades—at which time it is expected that fewer than half of all schoolchildren in major urban schools throughout the United States will speak English as a first language. This will have important implications for education.

Part of the reason for these changing demographics is smaller family size among white groups (in 1992, 3.18 for white married couples, 3.62 for African Americans, and 4.02 for Hispanics). In addition, net immigration rates continue to be much higher for nonwhite races. Projections are that by the year 2050, the percentage of the U.S. population

that is white will have decreased by about one-third; the Hispanic portion will have more than doubled (U.S. Bureau of the Census, 1996).

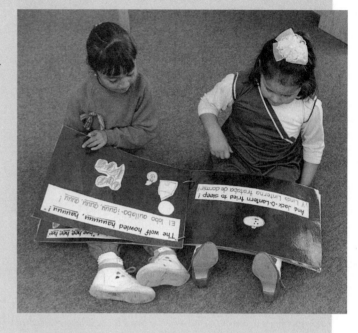

FIGURE 7.14

U.S. population by origin status, 1995, with projections to 2050 (Data from U.S. Bureau of the Census, 1996, p. 19).

▪ SUBTRACTIVE BILINGUALISM

Research indicates that for some minority group children, whose first language is the minority language, learning a second language may be a subtractive experience *in the sense that they become progressively less functional and fluent in their first language as their language skills improve in the second* (Pease-Alvarez & Hakuta, 1992). This does not happen because learning the second language actually interferes with learning or remembering the first, but for one, or often all, of the following reasons:

- The majority language (the second language in this case) is usually the dominant language in the media and in the community; hence, the minority language receives little support and reinforcement outside the home and tends to be used in less-valued social roles and milieus.

- Parents, and sometimes children, often actively discourage use of the minority language in the home.

- The minority language employed in the home is sometimes not a very good model. It is often characterized by idiom and colloquialism, by vocabulary impoverishment, by improper grammar, and by idiosyncratic pronunciation.

- If the minority language is not part of the children's schooling, they are unlikely to read or write in it. Thus, they may develop a relatively high level of oral proficiency in the minority language while developing little competency in reading or writing it.

For all of these reasons, competence in the minority language suffers, and the bilingual experience becomes subtractive.

▪ ADDITIVE BILINGUALISM

In contrast, learning a second language for children whose first language is the majority language appears to be largely an additive experience. For example, such is the case for many

English-speaking children enrolled in French immersion programs in Canada and in Spanish immersion programs in the United States. The evidence seems clear that these programs can be very successful in developing linguistic skills, as well as in contributing to general academic achievement (Garcia, 1993). Although most students who go through immersion schooling don't develop as high a level of proficiency as native speakers, their language deficiencies don't seem to interfere with their use of the second language. In addition, these students typically achieve at least as well as comparable students in conventional English programs in academic subjects and on measures of social and cognitive development.

Bilingualism in Schools and Society

There has been a staggering amount of research on the effects of bilingual programs, says Cziko (1992). But the conclusions are neither clear nor simple. One of the problems, as Lam (1992) notes, is that some programs are exceptionally good, and others are not; some teachers are more effective than others; some students learn more easily.

The current view is that a second language does not interfere with the first; in fact, level of proficiency and rate of learning of the second language are closely related to proficiency in the first. Furthermore, the higher the level of proficiency in the second language, the more likely that there will be measurable cognitive benefits (Ricciardelli, 1992).

Still, bilingualism and bilingual programs remain a controversial and emotionally charged issue. Interestingly, they are also a relatively recent issue, because although North American societies have been multilingual and multicultural from the very beginning, education has more often been unilingual. This has often posed problems for students and teachers—problems that, Brisk (1991) notes, were traditionally viewed as problems with students rather than with the educational system. As a result, in most cases schools accepted no responsibility for any problems that a minority-language child might experience. Teachers simply assumed that the problem would rectify itself with exposure to traditional schooling. If it didn't ... well, too bad, students would simply have to fail.

A more recent emphasis in education has been for schools to accept responsibility for problems related to minority languages. A common educational response has been to establish bilingual or English as a second language (ESL) programs. The main purpose of these programs, says Brisk, has been to prepare students to fit into the traditional, English-only school curriculum.

Brisk (1991) argues that as our societies become increasingly multilingual and multicultural, schools must become more responsive to the needs of students. What schools should be focused toward, say Collett and Serrano (1992), is becoming truly inclusive—that is, truly multicultural. Schools should not simply admit students from different backgrounds and then try to make them all the same by preparing them to fit into a traditional English-only curriculum. Serafini (1991) argues that recognizing and encouraging diversity in schools, and valuing competence in more languages than simply English, may do much to reduce racism.

■ THE OTHER SIDE

It would be astounding were we all to agree. We don't. In the United States, powerful, well-funded, and highly vocal groups of **English Only** and **U.S. English** advocates argue that English should be designated the official language—as it now has been in several dozen states, most recently Virginia and Georgia (U.S. English Press Releases and Newsletters, 1997). Many English Only (or English First, or U.S. English) members are strongly opposed to publicly funded bilingual education. In contrast, groups such as **English Plus** advocate expanding bilingual programs both for adults and for children.

The debate is sometimes tense and often highly emotional. Different jurisdictions respond to it in different ways. Ignoring it is not an option; it doesn't go away.

■ LANGUAGE, THINKING, AND COMMUNICATING

Clearly, language is centrally involved in successful adjustment to virtually all aspects of society. Not only does language allow children to direct the behavior of others according to their wishes (as when they ask for something), but it also provides a means for acquiring information that would otherwise be inaccessible (as when they ask questions, listen to stories, or watch television). Nelson (1996) suggests that the child who cannot speak or cannot understand the language that surrounds him is a lot like some illiterate adults who sometimes go to great lengths to hide their weakness, to convince people that, yes, they do know what the sign over there

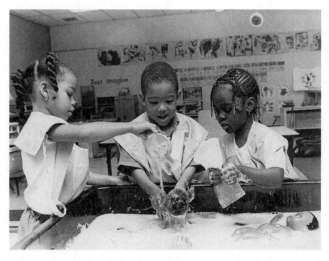

Language is central to children's social interaction. Although there is much that can be communicated with gestures and grunts, the complexities of bathing dolls are far more clearly conveyed in words and sentences. So are the dolls' names.

says, and no, they simply forgot to fill out the form again. There are children, says Nelson, who become very wise at pretending to understand a verbal message when they have no idea what it means.

Speech and Language Problems

We assume that by the time children reach school age, their language skills will be sufficient for them to understand and follow instructions, express interests and wants, tell stories, ask questions, carry on conversations—in short, communicate. Sadly, that is not always the case.

There are a number of different language and speech problems, each of which can vary tremendously in seriousness. At one extreme are children who, because of severe mental retardation, neurological damage or disease, mental disorders such as autism, or deafness, are essentially nonverbal. Their communication might consist of a few gestures or signs.

There are others whose speech is largely incomprehensible, sometimes because conceptual development is so poor that thought sequences seem illogical and speech becomes largely nonsensical, and sometimes because of speech production problems like those reflected in poor articulation, voice control problems, and stuttering.

And there are those whose language development is less advanced than normal, perhaps because of mild mental retardation or because of a learning disability reflected in language deficits. The predominant view is that these children don't learn different language forms or acquire language differently; their skills simply develop more slowly. Some of these children are of normal or above-normal intelligence and have no deficits other than their problems with language. However, because of our schools' predominantly verbal teaching and testing methods, many of these children are viewed as intellectually handicapped, and their language problems may be interpreted as the result of inferior ability rather than as the cause of poor achievement.

Speech problems and delayed language development are most common among children who have some other handicap—that is, retarded children and others suffering from motor, neurological, or mental disorders. They are relatively uncommon among the majority of children.

It is not clear what causes language problems in the absence of other handicaps. Although an impoverished and unstimulating home context may sometimes be implicated, in some cases children of apparently normal intelligence from advantaged backgrounds experience significant developmental delays or language impairments (Rice, 1989).

Early diagnosis of speech and language problems is especially important, notes Ruben (1993), because of the critical period in early childhood during which most language learning occurs. It is also important because of the significant correlations that have been found between retarded language development and subsequent behavior and emotional problems, including a greater probability of criminality (Stattin & Klackenberg-Larsson, 1993). Part of the explanation for this relationship, explain Benasich, Curtiss, and Tallal (1993), may lie in the drop in intelligence that often accompanies significant language impairment in early childhood. These children may subsequently experience far more difficulty coping both in school and in society.

Thinking and Language

One of the reasons that children with language problems are often at a disadvantage may have to do with the relationship between thinking and language. And although the nature of that relationship isn't entirely clear—hey, psychologists are never short of theories.

One extreme position, the **Whorfian hypothesis**, maintains that language is essential for thinking (Whorf, 1956). This position is based on the assumption that all thinking is verbal and that thought is therefore limited to what is made possible by language. There are two forms of the Whorfian hypothesis. The strongest form argues that thought depends on language and that thought will not occur in the absence of language. The weaker version maintains that language influences thinking.

To accept the more extreme position would be to deny that those who are prelinguistically deaf and who have not learned an alternate communication system can think. We would also have to believe that the prelinguistic infant cannot think and that, among those who have begun to develop language, thought is restricted to subjects and ideas for which the thinker has appropriate language. And we would have to believe that cows cannot think.

We don't believe all these things. So we accept, agreeing with psychologists such as Piaget and Vygotsky, that thought often precedes language. Piaget (1923), for example, points out that the development of certain logical concepts often precedes the learning of words and phrases corresponding to those concepts. Words such as *bigger, smaller,* and *farther* do not appear to be understood until the concepts they represent are themselves understood. Both Vygotsky and Piaget argue that language and thought first develop independently. Thus, there is considerable evidence of what we consider to be thought among preverbal children and nonhuman animals. But after the age of two, language and thought become more closely related. After that age, thought becomes increasingly verbal, and language acquires the capacity to control behavior.

In brief, both research and good sense inform us that our sophisticated thought processes are inextricably bound with language—as are our belief systems, our values, and our world views (Hunt & Agnoli, 1991). So convinced are we of this that attempts to bring about difficult social changes often begin with attempts to change language. Antiracist and antisexist movements are a case in point. In the first edition of this text, it was acceptable to use masculine pronouns as though all children, all psychologists, and, indeed, all significant people were male. Speaking of one of Blaise Pascal's *Pensées,* for example, I wrote this: "One of the paradoxes of human existence is that despite man's great intelligence it is impossible for him to know where he came from or where he is going" (Lefrançois, 1973, p. 351).

That this type of chauvinistic sexism is no longer acceptable in our language may eventually be reflected in its eradication from our thoughts and those of our children.

Communicating and Conversing

Language is more than a collection of sounds whose combinations refer to objects and actions and whose expression conveys our meanings. And it is more than a means for thinking and expressing our thoughts. Language is the means by which we draw information from past generations, record our own small contributions, and pass them on to generations that will come later. It is the great binding force of all cultures.

But infants and preschoolers, newly learning language, are not concerned with its great cultural contributions. Their first interest is in communicating—and the first communications are simple assertions ("that dog," "see Daddy," "my ball") or requests ("milk!" "more candy"). The second concern is with conversation.

A conversation is an exchange typically involving two or more people (although some people do talk to themselves—and answer). It is generally verbal, although it can consist of a combination of gestures and verbalization, or it can consist entirely of gestures as in the case of ASL (American Sign Language). Genuine conversational exchanges begin around age two. Initially, they are highly telegraphic, as is the child's speech; there aren't many variations possible when your sentences are limited to a single word. A short excerpt from an intelligent conversation with one of my offspring illustrates this:

Him: Fish.

Me: Fish?

Him: Fish!

Me: Fish? Fish swim.

Him: Fish! Fish! (The conversation becomes more complex.)

Me: There are fish in the lake. (An original thought, meant to stimulate creativity.)

Him: Fish. (Nodding vigorously and pointing, this time, in the general direction of the lake—I think.)

From this primitive, repetitive conversation, children progress to more complex expressions and begin to learn the importance of subtle cues of intonation, accentuation of words, rhythm of sentences, tone, and accompanying gestures. They learn, as well, about the implicit agreements that govern our conversations—the well-accepted rules that determine who shall speak and when, whether interruptions are permissible and how they should occur, what information must be in-

cluded in our conversations if we are to be understood, and what we can assume is already known.

Thus, more or less, does the infant progress from a sound to a word, from one word to two, from an expression to a conversation, from a conversation to a book....(See Summary Table 7.10 on page 212.)

FOCUS QUESTIONS: SUMMARY ANSWERS

1. How are motor development and intellectual development related?

   ◼ Motor skills are important for exploration of the environment and the development of intellectual skills, and are often used as an index of normal or expected cognitive development.

2. What are the most important intellectual achievements of preschoolers?

   ◼ Preschoolers can classify and solve simple class-inclusion problems, have a remarkable understanding of number that reflects both number abstraction skills (understanding of numerosity, based on universal counting principles) and numerical reasoning (understanding of some of the effects of transformations), and have made enormous strides in language learning.

3. Is exposure to preschool education good, bad, or irrelevant?

   ◼ In general, good preschool programs have measurably positive effects on cognitive and social development. However, some fear that emphasis on formal instruction at the preschool level hurries children unnecessarily and robs them of their childhood.

4. How do children learn language?

   ◼ Imitation and reinforcement are not completely adequate explanations for the observation that the earliest speech sounds of all infants are very similar, that infants make few directly imitative mistakes as they learn language, and that there appears to be a critical period for language learning early in life. Chomsky advances the metaphor of a language acquisition device (LAD), which suggests that children learn language as if they were neurologically predisposed to do so. The mother (and other caregivers) play an important role as language teachers.

Important Concepts and Issues in Bilingualism and the Contributions of Language to Thinking and Communicating

CONCEPT AND ISSUES	EXPLANATION/COMMENTS
Changing demographics	■ Rapid increase in proportion of children who speak a language other than English at home.
	■ Projected huge increase in proportion of Spanish-speaking Americans in coming decades.
Transitional bilingualism	■ Tendency for minority languages among bilingual individuals to be largely replaced by the dominant language (English in North America) within 3 or 4 generations.
Subtractive bilingualism	Where learning a second language subtracts from proficiency in the first—not because of competition for cognitive space or actual interference among languages, but for one or more of the following reasons:
	■ Dominance and reinforcement of majority language in the media.
	■ The home discouraging use of minority language.
	■ Use of poor, relatively illiterate, unschooled models of the minority language.
Additive bilingualism	■ Where learning a second language improves performance in the first (and contributes to general academic achievement); most common when there is high proficiency in the first language.
The bilingualism controversy	Controversial and emotional issues relating to:
	■ Provision of bilingual school programs at public expense.
	■ Use of more than one language in an official capacity.
	■ Issues fueled by lobby groups such as *U.S. English* and *English Only* on the one hand, and *English Plus* on the other.
Language and speech problems	■ Hamper communication.
	■ Often associated with deafness, mental retardation, neurological damage, or mental disorders such as autism.
	■ Take various forms (comprehension problems, speech production problems, developmental delays).
	■ Sometimes associated with later behavioral and emotional problems.
Contribution of language to thinking	■ Extreme Whorfian Hypothesis (not widely accepted): There is no thinking without language; language is essential for thought.
	■ Moderate Whorfian Hypothesis (more generally accepted): Language influences thinking.
Language and Conversation	■ Communicative exchange between two or more individuals does not depend on language, but is highly facilitated by it.
	■ Communication among generations is also highly dependent on language.

STUDY TERMS

additive bilingualism, 207

animistic thinking, 193

balanced bilinguals, 207

bilingual, 207

compensatory preschool programs, 200

concepts, 192

conservation, 194

Denver II, 187

developmental timetables, 187

egocentric, 194

English Only, 209

English Plus, 209

ESL, 209

Goodenough–Harris Drawing Test, 188

growth deceleration, 184

hurried child, 200

incidental mnemonics, 190

infantile amnesia, 190

intuitive, 192

kindergartens, 198

language, 202

language acquisition device (LAD), 204

memory strategies, 190

metamemory, 192

monolingual, 207

Montessori method, 201

morphemes, 203

motherese, 205

nursery schools, 198

operation, 192

peers, 188

preconcepts, 192

preconceptual, 192

preoperational, 192

Project Head Start, 200

reversibility, 192

subtractive bilingualism, 207

syncretic reasoning, 193

transductive reasoning, 193

transitional bilingualism, 207

U.S. English, 209

Whorfian hypothesis, 210

FURTHER READINGS

A simple, layperson's description of physical growth, play, parenting, and preschools is found in the following text:

Lee, C. (1990). *The growth and development of children* (4th ed.). New York: Longman.

Wellman's book is a fascinating look at how preschoolers view the world and especially at what they know about thinking and about states of mind:

Wellman, H. M. (1990). *The child's theory of mind.* Cambridge, MA: MIT Press.

Wadsworth's book is a clear summary of important aspects of Piaget's system:

Wadsworth, B. J. (1996). *Piaget's theory of cognitive and affective development* (5th ed.). New York: Longman.

The following collection presents a useful look at preschool programs and early intervention:

Zigler, E. F., Kagan, S. L., & Hall, N. W. (Eds.). (1996). *Children, families, and government: Preparing for the twenty-first century.* New York: Cambridge University Press.

Language development is described in more detail in the first of the following two books; the second looks at the complex relationship between language and thinking:

Berko-Gleason, J. (Ed.). (1993). *The development of language* (3rd ed.). Columbus, OH: Merrill.

Nelson, K. (1996). *Language in cognitive development: Emergence of the mediated mind.* New York: Cambridge University Press.

Cummins and Swain provide an account of bilingual education programs and their effects:

Cummins, J., & Swain, M. (1986). *Bilingualism in education: Aspects of theory, research and practice.* London: Taylor & Fry.

EIGHT

Social Development: Early Childhood

To love playthings well as a child, to lead an adventurous and honourable youth, and to settle when the time arrives, into a green and smiling age, is to be a good artist in life.

ROBERT LOUIS STEVENSON
Virginibus Puerisque

ata Sakharam Narvankar is a girl of the "sweeper class" who lives in Gujerat, India. Her life, says Rice (1972), is an unending, unchanging cycle of poverty and work. She lives in a hutment, an abject cluster of tenement housing—little huts made of woven palms and thatched roofs through which the sun and the rain pass freely. In Lata's world, children begin to work as soon as they can toddle. The older ones, the four- and five-year-olds, look after the babies. Also, they cook and clean and shop for small handfuls of food when they can. If they live where people have money, their daily work is to beg. Lata, who is twelve, works as a "sweeper" in an apartment during the day—washing, cleaning, sweeping, swabbing. At night, she returns to her poverty. Without hesitation, she gives all her earnings, 21 rupees a month, to her mother. When asked what she would do if she had a lot of money, she doesn't know what to say; the possibility is so remote that she has never dreamed about it. "There are very few childhood games," writes Rice (1972), "no toys, no schooling, no entertainment...." (p. 19). ¶ Olivia Miller is the same age as Lata Sakharam Narvankar. She lives in Moose Jaw, Saskatchewan, in a comfortable middle-class house. She is expected to go to school 198 days a year; her mother also asks her to help with simple household chores on an occasional basis. And she is expected to keep her room reasonably tidy. Her room is about the size of Lata's entire hutment and has far more valuable things in it than belong to all of Lata's family. In fact, there is vastly more forgotten money in Olivia's piggy bank than an entire year of Lata's wages. ¶ And, yes, Olivia is expected to play and amuse herself, alone and with others, during most of her very abundant free time. Even much of school involves play. ¶

This Chapter

They are very different worlds, those of Olivia Miller and Lata Sakharam Narvankar. We should not too quickly assume that our developmental generalizations might apply equally to both. Nor should we dupe ourselves into thinking that having learned a few trivial details about the lives of two individuals, we actually know something important about their cultures. Quick sketches such as these are very misleading; they omit too many details and, especially in cases such as Lata's with which we tend to be less familiar, they lead us too easily to inappropriate generalizations.*

Play is only one of the many topics of this chapter. It looks as well at preschoolers' social development and at their expression and control of emotions. It also explores the development and the implications of gender roles, which, even in the preschool period, are enormously significant. Finally, the chapter examines the role of the family in the early socialization of the child, focusing on current issues such as separation and divorce, single-parent families, remarriage, and alternate forms of child care, paying attention to the general effects of day care and to the characteristics of high-quality care.

----

*As an antidote to the tendency to think of all Indian children as downtrodden, oppressed, and doomed to joyless and playless childhoods, you might consult the following book on children's play in different cultures, especially the chapter that deals with play in the East Indian context: Roopnarine, J. L., Johnson, J. E., & Hooper, F. H. (Eds.). (1994). *Children's play in diverse cultures*. Albany, NY: State University of New York Press.

One of the important developmental tasks of the preschool period, claims Erik Erikson, is to develop a sense of initiative, of personal competence, and of autonomy. Raking the grass "all by myself, don't help me" is no trivial thing for this girl's development.

PROCESSES OF SOCIALIZATION

Preschoolers do not have the same sense of self, the same understanding of emotions (or the same control over them), or the same understanding of what is appropriate behavior and what isn't as do older children (or adults). Socialization (or social learning) is fundamental in the development of these important things. Simply defined, **socialization** is the process by which children learn behaviors appropriate for people of their gender and age. It is also through socialization that they learn and acquire the traditions, the beliefs, the values, and the customs of their groups.

What is learned through socialization is determined largely by the cultural context. Thus, in some societies, children might learn to be aggressive and fearless; in others, they might be socialized to be timid and fearful—a fact that makes our average child even more of a myth. But the processes by which socialization occurs are highly similar in different cultural groups.

Erikson's Psychosocial Stages

One well-known theory of social development is that advanced by Erik Erikson. It describes sequential stages of social development, each of which is characterized by conflicting tendencies or desires, and each of which requires the attainment of some new competence. Because of the theory's strong emphasis on social development, it is often labeled a theory of **psychosocial** development. The first three of Erikson's stages span the years from birth to around the end of the preschool period.

The first Erikson stage, **trust versus mistrust,** lasts through most of infancy. The principal task for the infant in this stage is to develop sufficient trust in the world to be able to go out and begin exploring it actively. Throughout this period, the most important influence in the infant's life is clearly the principal caregiver(s)—most often the mother.

The second stage, **autonomy versus shame and doubt,** spans the first year or so of the preschool period. At this time, children begin to discover that they are responsible for their own actions—a discovery that is closely linked with the development of intentionality. The child's developing autonomy depends on opportunities to explore and to be independent, says Erikson (1959). Hence the need for a balance in parental control. Overprotection can lead to doubt and uncertainty. Yet there is clearly a need to continue to protect; the young preschooler cannot be permitted unsupervised and unlimited freedom to explore.

The third stage, **initiative versus guilt,** spans the remaining preschool years. The new sense of competence required of the child involves a sense of initiative—a sense of personal agency. But there still lingers a desire to retain the comfort and security that come from allowing other people—especially parents—to maintain control and responsibility.

In summary, according to Erikson, much of "growing up" during the preschool period involves developing a sense of an *autonomous* self—a self that is capable of forming intentions and of behaving in ways that are effective. Development is greatly facilitated by the infant's physical exploration of the environment, as well as by mushrooming language skills that make it possible to explore in other ways—as, for example, when the four-year-old bombards caregivers with questions. The development of social competence through the preschool period also requires achieving progressive independence from parents. The overprotective parent who does not easily permit independence may make the child's progression through Erikson's stages more difficult. (See Chapter 2 for more details; see also Table 8.1.)

Socialization Through Imitation

Erikson (1968) believed that **imitation** is one of the important means by which preschool children become socialized, especially in the first two or three years of life. Later, **identification** (a process whereby children do not merely imitate models but adopt their values and beliefs—in a sense, growing to be like them) becomes more important.

One important theory of social learning based on imitation, discussed in Chapter 2, is that proposed by Albert Bandura. To summarize briefly: Bandura's theory explains the effects of imitation partly in terms of rewards and punishments, but gives a tremendously important role to the informative function of models and to the observer's understanding and interpretation of that information. It is what the observer imagines and expects that is important in learning through imitation.

Bandura describes three separate effects of imitation. There is the **modeling effect**, evident in learning new behavior; the

Children learn a tremendous range of behaviors through imitation— behaviors like licking the spoon to test the broth. Less obvious, but perhaps far more important, imitation is also central in transmitting values and beliefs.

inhibitory effect and the **disinhibitory effect**, in which the rewards or punishment a model receives serve to bring about (disinhibit) some previously suppressed behavior or, alternately, to inhibit current behavior; and the **eliciting effect**, in which the model's behavior serves to evoke a related behavior in the observer.

Imitation-based theories of social learning are useful for explaining how children in nontechnological societies learn how to do things like set snares and traps or wield brooms and corn-grinding stones. But most of us no longer need to learn how to operate a corn-grinding stone or lay out a trap. So what do we learn from social imitation in more complex societies?

Cooperation and Competition

Among other things, perhaps we learn important social tendencies like **cooperation** and **competition**. In fact, there is considerable research to support the belief that children are socialized to be cooperative or competitive by the predominant way of life—the mores, the traditions, of their immediate social environment. As a result, children from different social groups can be remarkably different in terms of cooperation and competition.

■ STUDYING COOPERATION

Studies of cooperation and competition have often used the four-person cooperation board developed by Madsen (Madsen & Lancy, 1981). This is simply an 18-inch paper square covered with a piece of paper set up as shown in Interactive Figure 8.1 (Madsen, 1971). Note that when a child holds each of the strings at the four corners, the pen can be made to trace a line through any or all targets, as long as participants cooperate; if, on the other hand, they choose

TABLE 8.1

Erikson's Psychosocial Stages of Preschool Development

STAGE	APPROXIMATE AGE	PRINCIPAL DEVELOPMENTAL TASK
Autonomy vs. shame and doubt	18 months to 2 or 3 years	Developing a sense of control and mastery over actions; learning that one is autonomous, that intentions can be realized; overcoming the urge to return to the comfort of trusting parents, and especially the mother, to do all important things.
Initiative vs. guilt	2 or 3 to 6 years	Developing a sense of self, largely through identifying with parents; developing a greater sense of responsibility for own actions; achieving progressive independence from parents.

Cooperation board: Examine the layout. Imagine that you are the child sitting in position 1; three other children occupy positions 2, 3, and 4. Each of you has grasped the string that runs from the cone at the center. You know that if you pull hard enough, the cone will slide toward you and the pen will draw a line right to your corner. The four of you are asked to draw a line through each of the target circles in order, from 1 to 4. What do you need to do to suc-ceed? Suppose, now, that the target circles are moved so that each is placed directly under the string at the four corners of the board. To win this game, you have to pull the pen so that it traces a line through your circle. But there doesn't have to be just one winner; all four can win. Suppose, further, that you know you are the strongest one of the four and that if you pull hard enough, no one else can win. *How do you think you would have acted as a child? (Adapted from Madsen & Lancy, 1981, p. 397.)*

to compete, then the strongest child will succeed only in pulling the pen to one corner. In a variation of this proce-dure, target circles might be drawn under the strings at each of the four corners so that a child might win (and prevent others from winning) by competing.

■ COMPETITION AND COOPERATION IN DIFFERENT CULTURES

Madsen and Lancy (1981) used the cooperation board to look at competition and cooperation among two groups of Papua New Guinea children: the Imbonggu, a highly intact tribal group whose traditional way of life is based on cooper-ation, and the Kila-Kila, a more heterogeneous group heavily influenced by rapid modernization and living in an urban-ized setting characterized by violence and crime.

First, children, in groups of four, were simply instructed to draw a line through the numbered circles, in order, and were rewarded as a group for being successful (each child was given a coin). The objective was simply to determine whether children were able to cooperate when so instructed and when rewarded for doing so.

After three one-minute trials under this "group reward" condition, subjects were then asked to write their names next to one of the circles (either to their right or left) and were told they would receive a coin each time the line passed through their circle. Now, in order to be successful, subjects had to cooperate.

The results of the study are striking. There were no differ-ences between the Imbonggu and Kila-Kila on the first three trials. Each of the groups improved on every trial, and by the third trial, each succeeded in crossing an average of slightly more than twelve circles. But the results on the fourth, fifth, and sixth trials, where subjects were being rewarded in-dividually rather than as a group, are intriguing. Whereas the Imbonggu continued to improve on each of the trials—a clear sign that they continued to cooperate—the perfor-mance of the Kila-Kila foursomes deteriorated dramatically. In fact, two-thirds of the Kila-Kila groups did not cross a sin-

gle circle on the fourth trial; in contrast, the Imbonggu group that cooperated the least still managed to cross six circles (Figure 8.2).

These marked differences in competitive and cooperative tendencies, claim Madsen and Lancy (1981), are due to dif-ferences in immediate cultural contexts. Thus, there are soci-eties whose world view is predominantly peaceful and that socialize their children to be nurturant and helpful to oth-ers rather than fiercely competitive. These societies, explains Bonta (1997), tend to devalue achievement because it often results in competition. At the same time, they are more likely to exemplify and to reward cooperative behavior. Hence, it comes as little surprise that research reveals that rural people, for whom cooperation has often been linked with comfort, if not survival, tend to be more cooperative than city dwellers. Thus, rural Mexican children have been found to be more

FIGURE **8.2**

Differences in cooperation and competition between Imbonggu and Kila-Kila children. (Adapted from Madsen & Lancy, 1981, p. 399.)

cooperative and less competitive than urban Mexican children—as have kibbutz Israeli children compared with urban Israeli children, Blackfoot Indians compared with urban Caucasians in Canada, urban and rural Colombians, urban and rural Maoris in New Zealand, and various other groups (Madsen & Lancy, 1981).

COMPETITION AND COOPERATION IN NORTH AMERICA

North American societies are often contrasted with cooperative societies of the kind described by Bonta (1997). We socialize our children to compete, explain Johnson and Johnson (1994). We have structured our most powerful socializing agency, our schools, in such a way that competition is usually the best way to succeed. Thus, students are engaged in a fierce struggle to see who is best, and only one, or a few, can be best. This ensures that students work primarily on their own, *competitively* rather than *cooperatively*. Not surprisingly, many are highly competitive, but many are not. And, in general, females are often found to be more cooperative than males (for example, Segal, Connelly, & Topoloski, 1996).

We tend to think of competition and cooperation as opposites. In fact, explains Charlesworth (1996), they might be more closely related than we think. That is, most individuals are not one or the other in all circumstances; our behavior changes depending on our immediate goals, the people with whom we're interacting, our mood, and a host of other factors. Thus, schools can be structured so that some activities are intensely competitive and others cooperative. And the same children may do very well (or very badly) in either case.

One of the characteristics of highly heterogeneous societies such as ours is that the models they present are highly varied. In advanced societies, many of these are **symbolic models,** which need not be real, immediately present people. These may include characters in literature or movies, verbal and written instructions, religious beliefs, or folk heroes (such as musicians or athletes). One of the most powerful transmitters of these symbolic models may well be television (about which we say more in Chapter 10). (See Summary Table 8.2.)

■ SOCIALIZING EMOTIONS

Socialization, or social learning, Parke (1994) explains, is fundamental in the development of emotions among preschoolers. Young children, he notes, do not have as fine a control as we do over the emotions they feel—or over their expression. They control their emotions more through behavior than through cognition; thus can they make a frightening pack of wild things disappear just by closing their eyes. And they are more easily moved to tears and to laughter than we are. Put another way, their emotions are not completely socialized.

The socialization of emotions involves at least three things: learning to interpret emotions, achieving some control over

CONCEPTS	EXPLANATIONS/COMMENTS
Psychosocial development	Erikson's label for development through a series of social crises, the resolution of which leads to important social competencies. The theory describes two preschool stages: ■ *Autonomy vs. shame and doubt* (developing control over personal actions; learning that one is autonomous). ■ *Initiative vs. guilt* (developing a sense of self; assuming greater responsibility for one's actions; becoming more independent from parents).
Imitation	Very important socializing process. According to Bandura, manifested in three distinct effects: ■ Modeling (learning of new behaviors). ■ Inhibition-disinhibition (suppression or reappearance of deviant behaviors). ■ Eliciting (behaviors not identical to those of model but related to them).
Cooperation and competition	■ Cooperation: act of working jointly toward a shared goal. ■ Competition: contending with someone else for an individual goal. ■ Competitive/cooperative tendencies strongly influenced by models that cultures provide.

them, and learning when, where, and how displaying them is appropriate and expected.

■ Interpreting Emotions

Initially, the infant does not know how to interpret the feelings of others. Facial expressions of joy or sadness, for example, are meaningless for the one-month-old infant. But sometime between the ages of three and six months, there appears a growing recognition not only that others are capable of emotional reactions, but that these can be inferred from expressions and from behavior. By the age of nine months to one year, infants in ambiguous situations actively search other people's faces as though looking for a clue that might guide their own behavior. This is referred to as **social referencing.** Denham (1993) observed twenty-eight mother–toddler pairs and found a very high correspondence between the infant's emotional responses and the mother's emotional displays. Similarly, many kindergarten students respond with obvious facial distress (sad expressions) when they hear an infant cry—clear evidence that they have learned to interpret the infant's emotional expressions (Eisenberg et al., 1993).

When they see others crying, they are likely to feel sad—perhaps even to cry. And if others laugh and are happy, they, too, are more likely to be joyful.

In spite of their growing ability to interpret their emotions and those of others, preschoolers' verbal descriptions of emotions remain relatively imprecise. When Brown, Covell, and Abramovitch (1991) asked preschoolers how they would feel following a story event associated with happiness, sadness, or anger, they typically responded in terms of an intense emotion. And when, later in the story, an event occurred that would lead to a lessening of the emotion, preschoolers often thought they would feel a different emotion. If they had been sad earlier, now they would be happy. Strikingly, it seldom occurred to them that they might be more or less sad or happy. In contrast, older children in the same study often thought they would feel a different degree of the same emotion.

If specifically asked to describe what they think someone else is feeling, preschoolers might infer that someone feels "good" or "bad" because he or she is crying or laughing. They don't yet look for underlying causes upon which to base inferences. Yet when Boyatzis, Chazan, and Ting (1993) read brief stories describing a boy's emotion to 3½-year-old children, most had little difficulty selecting the photograph that accurately reflected the emotion in question. Interestingly, girls in this study (which also included 5-year-olds) were better than boys at identifying emotions.

Not surprisingly, early in the preschool period, children cannot readily tell the difference between emotions that are real and those that are a pretense. Thus, if someone falls but jumps up and "laughs it off" in embarrassment, the two-year-old is likely to conclude that the person is happy. In contrast, three- to five-year-olds often have little difficulty distinguishing between real emotions and "sham" emotions (Banerjee, 1997). Furthermore, their understanding of emotions is sufficiently sophisticated that they can easily predict the most likely parental reactions to their own emotions (Denham, 1997).

Regulating Emotions

As we saw in Chapter 6, even very young infants are capable of simple behaviors whose effect is to control the emotions they feel. For example, a frightened infant might close his eyes, suck his thumb, or snuggle his face in his mother's lap—an example of what Gianino and Tronick (1988) call self-directed regulatory behaviors. Alternatively, an infant might push away an object that is frightening her—an example of other-directed regulatory behaviors.

Preschoolers, with their ever-expanding mobility and rapidly developing cognitive and social skills, become increasingly adept at avoiding situations that lead to negative emotions and at seeking out and maintaining those associated with good feelings. But, a little like infants, their control of emotions is situational and behavioral rather than cognitive. When they hear the ice cream truck's bell, they run to get Mother—or money—and when the frightening part of

the story comes, they close their eyes and cover their ears. In the Brown, Covell, and Abramovitch (1991) investigation in which children were questioned following emotion-related events in stories, the younger children saw emotions as being situation-specific. Hence, to change a feeling, change the situation. A child who is sad over losing a favorite toy will nevertheless be happy when she goes to bed. Why? "Because I won't have to look for it."

In contrast, the older child's control of emotions is more cognitive. One way of not feeling sad about a lost toy, the older child insists, is not to think about it—or to think a happy thought. Most of us are more like older than younger children. And our emotions have clearer links with our cognitions (Mathews & MacLeod, 1994).

Eisenberg and associates (1997) note that learning how to regulate (control) emotions, especially negative emotions like fear, has a significant bearing on the quality of the child's social interactions and adjustment. They suggest, too, that parental encouragement of the expression of negative emotions may be an important contributor to how well children cope with negative emotions.

Emotional Expression

Infants are easily moved to tears or to laughter. It doesn't shame them to cry in front of strangers, nor does it ever embarrass them to laugh; they don't yet know what it is to feel foolish. But preschoolers are a little more restrained; they have begun to learn what researchers call **emotional display rules.**

One aspect of display rules has to do with learning when and how it's appropriate to display certain emotions; another deals with understanding the emotional expressions (emotional displays) of others. Part of display rule learning involves discovering that expressed emotion doesn't always correspond with underlying emotion. Even young children are able to smile when they lie or pretend it doesn't hurt when it would be embarrassing to cry.

It is not clear how preschoolers learn simple display rules such as the rule stating that if you are disappointed with a gift, you should not cry in front of the giver—not that preschoolers are always successful in doing so. Even we adults are not always able to hide our feelings. If someone gives us a rose when we fully expected a whole garden, we might find it very difficult to smile, even though our socialization is far more advanced than that of children.

Among the many activities and experiences of childhood that contribute to the socialization of the child, perhaps none is more important than play. (See Summary Table 8.3.)

CHILD'S PLAY

Defined most simply, **play** is activity that has no long-range goal, although it might have some immediate objectives (to

▲ SUMMARY TABLE 8.3
Processes in Socializing Emotions

PROCESSES	EXPLANATIONS/COMMENTS
Interpreting emotions	■ Emotional expressions are not highly meaningful for young infants. ■ By age one, infants try to clarify ambiguous emotional situations by looking at other people's reactions *(social referencing)*. ■ Preschoolers interpret others' emotional responses relatively well and can show empathy. ■ Verbal descriptions of emotions remain inexact.
Regulating emotions	■ Young preschoolers' regulation of emotional reactions is situational and behavioral rather than cognitive. ■ Older preschoolers realize emotions can be controlled to some extent through thoughts.
Expressing emotions	■ Infants easily moved to laughter or tears. ■ Preschoolers learn *emotional display rules*—when and how to display emotions. ■ They also learn that the emotion displayed does not always accurately reflect underlying emotion.

hop from here to there, to make a sand hill, to fly a kite, to pour a cup of pretend tea). Play is what children, and grown-ups, do for the fun of it. But that play has no ultimate purpose does not mean it is unimportant and useless. In fact, it is extremely important for all aspects of the child's development: social, physical, and intellectual.

Why Play?

Among animals, ethologists tell us, play has two important functions: First, it is useful in developing and exercising physical skills that might be important in hunting or escaping from predators; second, it serves to establish social position and to teach acceptable behaviors, such as in the mock-fighting, rough-and-tumble play of lion cubs or chimpanzees.

In some ways, many of the functions of play among children are not very different from those among animals. Some forms of physical play are useful in developing and exercising physical skills, and might also contribute to social adaptation. In addition, play involving physical exploration is closely linked to attention and learning (Ruff & Saltarelli, 1993).

More imaginative play may have quite different functions. Imagining involves important cognitive abilities related to symbolizing, imitating, anticipating, and problem solving. Children's growing awareness of self and of others, and their gradual realization that we are all thinking beings, have their roots in play, claims McCune (1993). Not surprisingly, research

reports positive correlations between play and level of cognitive development (Tamis-LeMonda & Bornstein, 1993). It also reports a close relationship between play and measures of social competence, such as are evident in friendships (Park, Lay, & Ramsay, 1993). It is no surprise that play can successfully be used as a form of therapy for children experiencing learning problems, depression, socially inappropriate behavior, and a variety of other social and emotional problems (Landreth, 1993).

Types of Play

One of the simplest ways of classifying play is to make a distinction between two types of play activities: **practice play** (or **sensorimotor play**) and **pretend play** (or **imaginative play**). Each of these can be solitary (played alone) or social (played with others).

Practice Play

Practice play is mainly physical activity and is evident among the young of many animals (for example, a kitten chasing a ball). It involves manipulating objects or performing activities simply for the sensations that result, and it is a very common form of infant and preschool play. It may consist of motor activities such as creeping, crawling, walking, running, skipping, hopping, manipulating objects and parts of one's own anatomy, and so on. It is evident in the countless solitary games of young preschoolers.

Pretend Play

Many of the preschooler's solitary games are not simply practice play, but also *pretend* play. Even infants as young as age one can pretend, although their pretending usually takes the form of simulating common activities—for example, pretending to eat or pretending to sleep. By age two, however, a wide range of make-believe games becomes possible as children learn to transform objects, people, and activities into whatever they wish. In pretend play, boys are often superheroes such as Superman (or super antiheroes such as dragons or monsters); girls are often mothers or nurses (Paley, 1984). Many of these pretend games are suggested by the immediate environment, notes Jaffke (1996). Thus, a picture, a crooked stick, a broken teacup, a squished worm … each can inspire a new game. (See Summary Table 8.4.)

■ REALITY AND FANTASY

Preschoolers are sometimes uncertain about the difference between reality and fantasy. Three-year-old Mollie wants to play a pretend game with the other nursery school children, but she knows some pretend bad thing is going to happen. The child is scared because "What if the bad thing doesn't know it's pretend?" (Paley, 1986, p. 45).

SUMMARY TABLE 8.4
Types of Play*

TYPE	EXAMPLE
Practice (sensorimotor) Play	
Solitary:	Bouncing a ball, up, down, up, down . . . .
Social:	Playing baseball.
Pretend (imaginative) Play	
Solitary:	Giving a doll pretend tea.
Social:	Dramatizing monsters in a group.

*Note that these simple categories of play are not mutually exclusive. A single "game" or play session might involve elements of practice and pretend games, and might be solitary in some respects and social in others. Also, there are different types of social play (see Table 8.5).

"Go to sleep, Mollie," Libbie orders. "There might be something dangerous. You won't like it."

"I know it," Mollie says. "But I got a bunk bed at home and I sleep there."

"Bunk beds are too scary," Amelia says.

"Why are they?" Mollie looks worried.

"It's a monster, Mollie. Hide!" (p. 45).

But Mollie protests that there are no monsters in her house today. Still, she is unwilling to take any chances:

"I'm going to be a statue," Mollie whispers. "So he won't see me" (p. 45).

Now Frederick comes roaring in on all fours. "I'm a lion. I'm roaring," he says.

"Is he scaring you, Mollie?"

"No."

"Is anyone scaring you?"

"The bunk bed," she answers solemnly (p. 45).

Mollie, like many other three-year-olds, can create her own ghosts and monsters, and she has developed her own ways of dealing with them. If they threaten too frighteningly, she can become a statue so they won't see her, or she can hide by the teacher—or she can, ultimately, resort to her knowledge that the monsters are pretend monsters.

But when others create monsters, Mollie can never be quite certain that they are truly *pretend* pretend. Perhaps, just perhaps, one of them might be *real* pretend.

We, of course, do not suffer from the same limitations as does Mollie (nor do most of us enjoy quite as boundless an imagination). We have somehow learned to tell the difference between fantasy and reality; we can dismiss our monsters if they frighten us. Can't we?

■ DAYDREAMING AND IMAGINARY PLAYMATES

One type of imaginative play that becomes increasingly prevalent as the preschooler ages is **daydreaming**. Unlike other types of imaginative play in which the child actively engages in fantasy, daydreaming is imagining without the activity. Daydreaming is a normal and healthy activity, engaged in by adults as well as children.* Not surprisingly, however, teachers tend to perceive students with attention problems as being more prone to daydreaming than are more attentive children (Stanford & Hynd, 1994).

Daydreaming, which is a solitary form of imaginative play, sometimes gives rise to the **imaginary playmate**—constant companion and friend to approximately half of all preschool children. These imaginary friends, complete with names and personalities, are spoken to, played with, teased, and loved by their creators. In one study, Taylor, Cartwright, and Carlson (1993) interviewed a dozen four-year-olds who had imaginary playmates, asking them to describe their imaginary friends—which they did quite readily. The remarkable thing is that when these children were interviewed again seven months later, their descriptions had hardly changed; they were every bit as stable as descriptions of real friends.

There is little information about the role that imaginary companions might play in the preschooler's development. However, some evidence suggests that the creation of an imaginary playmate is often associated with more advanced language and social development, and may predict later creativity (Singer & Singer, 1990).

■ CONTRIBUTIONS TO A THEORY OF MIND

Pretend play, says Leslie (1988), contributes to one of the cognitive capacities that sets us apart from other species: Specifically, it eventually enables us to think about ourselves and about others as thinkers—as organisms capable of having different states of mind. When Mother puts a banana in her ear and says "Hello," four-year-old Nancy recognizes at once that the banana is a pretend telephone. But there is no confusion here between reality and fantasy; she still knows very clearly that this is a banana. What is also clear to Nancy, however, is that Mother can have different states of mind—and that she can too. Nancy has begun to develop a **theory of mind,** says Leslie. And one important aspect of this theory is the recognition of others and of self as thinkers capable of deliberately selecting and manipulating ideas—even pretend ideas. Here, in the preschool period, is the dawning of what psychologists label **metacognition**—knowing about knowing.

Social Play

Recall that both practice and pretend play can be solitary or social. Although both are important to the healthy and happy development of the child, **social play** has tremendous implications for the child's social development.

Social play is any type of play that involves interaction among two or more children. Thus, both practice and pretend play are social when they involve more than one child. Skipping rope alone in the darkness of one's basement is a solitary sensorimotor activity; skipping rope out on the play-

---

*I don't do so much of it anymore. I keep hearing my grandmother: "Quit daydreaming, Guy! Hoe the dang potatoes!"

There are many forms of social play, including situations where a player simply watches others play (onlooker play), games where children play side-by-side but not together (parallel play), sessions where players interact with each other but still play independently, and cooperative play where children share goals and allocate roles—as in this scene, where the lass in front drives the train as her passengers climb aboard.

ground with others turning the rope, "pepper, pepper, salt and…," is a cooperative or social activity. Similarly, creating elaborate and fantastic daydreams in the solitude of one's bedroom is private imaginative play, but playing "let's pretend"—"you be the veterinamen [sic] and I'll be the dog"—is social imaginative play. One of the defining characteristics of social play, notes Sawyer (1997), is that it is essentially rule-governed. That is, almost all instances of true social play involve at least implicit understanding or agreement about some aspects of the play—in other words, some primitive rules.

Parten (1932) describes the play behavior of preschoolers as being solitary or as reflecting one of five different kinds of social play distinguishable in terms of the type and amount of peer interaction involved. Although these develop sequentially, they also overlap.

SOLITARY PLAY

In solitary play, the child plays alone with toys or engages in some solitary motor activity, paying little attention to other children. Much of the child's play before the age of two appears to be solitary.

PRIMITIVE SOCIAL PLAY

Although infant play is mainly solitary, there are some forms of **primitive social play** that sometimes occur even before the age of six months. Many of these, like "peek-a-boo" games, and play that includes tickling, tossing, and related activities, typically occur with parents or older children. Some, like the "chase" games of toddlers or the "touch me and I'll touch you" game, are examples of nonsolitary play among infants (Brenner & Mueller, 1982).

ONLOOKER PLAY

As the label implies, **onlooker play** consists of a child watching others play, but not participating actively. Onlooker play occurs throughout childhood. Often, the onlooker may talk with the players, perhaps even giving them advice or asking questions.

PARALLEL PLAY

In **parallel play**, children play side by side, often with similar toys, but do not interact, do not share the activities involved in the game, and do not use any mutually accepted rules. Parallel play is nevertheless social play of a primitive sort because it involves two or more children who apparently prefer to play together even if they do not interact. Some research indicates that the presence of toys often detracts from social interaction and leads to parallel or perhaps solitary play, particularly among very young children (Vandell, Wilson, & Buchanan, 1980). Not surprisingly, in the absence of toys, children are more likely to interact with one another.

ASSOCIATIVE PLAY

With advancing age, children become more interested in interacting with peers and are more likely to include toys in what is termed **associative play**. This type of play involves interaction among children, even though they continue to play separately. In associative play, children sometimes share toys, but each child plays independently without mutually accepted goals or rules. Goncu (1993) reports that this type of shared play becomes increasingly common between ages 3 and 4½.

COOPERATIVE PLAY

Children who play cooperatively help one another in activities that require shared goals and perhaps even a division of roles. Although most research on the preschooler's play behavior indicates that associative and **cooperative play** are not common before the age of four or five, there is sometimes evidence of cooperation in the play of much younger children.

It is largely through cooperative social play that preschoolers form friendships. Not surprisingly, the best-liked children appear to be those who are most cooperative (as well as least aggressive and least difficult) (Denham & Holt, 1993). Patterns of interactions in preschool friendships appear to be quite stable (Park et al., 1993).

An important example of cooperative social play is found in the drama that children sometimes enact in their pretend play:

"You be the baby."

"I be the baby."

"I be the mother."

"You be the mother. I be the baby."

"If you're bad…if you wee-wee your diaper, well, you know…" (making an abrupt spanking gesture, but smiling broadly all the while).

Garvey (1977) found that the most common roles in dramatic play were mother–infant, mother–child, and mother–father. She also found that children often reveal their fears and worries, their hopes and aspirations, in their dramatic play. Social play of this kind is more than just fun; it provides an important opportunity for acquiring and practicing behaviors involved in social interaction, for developing cooperative behaviors, for learning how to resolve conflict, for making friends, and for fostering imagination and creativity.

Cultural Differences in Play

Play appears to be universal among all cultures, but its frequency and the forms it takes are strongly influenced by the preschooler's context (Hughes, 1990). For example, in societies where children have to assume work responsibilities at very early ages, there is less childhood play—an observation that is also often true of children who are economically and socially disadvantaged (Schwartzman, 1987). (See also Interactive Figure 8.3 for information about where British children play.)

INTERACTIVE **FIGURE 8.3**

British children's favorite play places: Can you recall the five favorite play places (activities) of your childhood? Robin Moore (1986) asked 48 boys and 48 girls ages 9–12 to make maps or drawings of their favorite play places and then interviewed each child. He also accompanied 24 of them to their favorite play places and interviewed their parents. How do their favorite play places and activities compare with yours? (From Moore, 1986.)

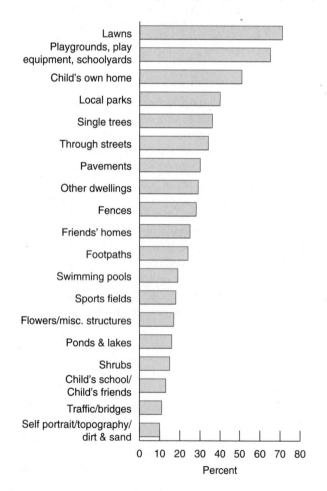

Children learn many of their first play behaviors in interaction with principal caregivers, note O'Reilly and Bornstein (1993). One would therefore expect that among the poor, many mothers would be preoccupied or busy and would devote less time to interacting with infants. Bowman (1993) reports that this expectation has been corroborated in the finding that the play of poor children is sometimes less complex and involves less advanced usage of language.

Not only are there cultural and social group differences in play, but there are also gender differences. Not surprisingly, when college students are asked to select toys for a child who has been described as masculine, feminine, or gender-neutral, toys selected tend to be strongly stereotyped to reflect the child's gender (Fisher-Thompson, Sausa, & Wright, 1995). (See Summary Table 8.5.)

DEVELOPING GENDER ROLES IN EARLY CHILDHOOD

Gender is one of those visually conspicuous characteristics on which we base our judgments of people and our reactions to them, says Fiske (1993) (others are age, race, and physical appearance). In most cultures, including ours, there are usually marked differences between the ways in which males and females are expected to think, act, and feel. The range of behaviors considered appropriate for males and females—that is, considered masculine or feminine—together with the attitudes and personality characteristics associated with each define **gender roles**. The learning of sex-appropriate behavior is **gender typing**. Gender typing, as we saw in Chapter 6, begins from the very earliest moment when the mere fact

▲ SUMMARY TABLE 8.5

Classifications and Examples of Children's Social Play

CLASSIFICATION	POSSIBLE ACTIVITY
Solitary play	Child plays alone with blocks.
Primitive social play	"Peek-a-boo."
Onlooker play	Child watches others play "tag" but does not join in.
Parallel play	Two children play with trucks in sandbox but do not interact. They play beside each other, but not together.
Associative play	Two children play with dolls, talk with each other about their dolls, lend each other diapers and dishes, but play independently, sharing neither purpose nor rules.
Cooperative play	"Let's pretend. You be a monster, and I'll be the guy with the magic sword and. . . ."

Children begin to learn gender-typed behavior at very young ages.

that the child is male or female determines much of what a parent's reactions to the infant will be.

Gender Schemas

"One of the first social dimensions that children notice is sex," claim Serbin, Powlishta, and Gulko (1993, p. 1). Very early in life, they begin to develop what researchers label **gender schemas** (also sometimes termed *gender scripts*). Gender schemas are the child's knowledge about characteristics associated with being male and female (Levy, 1993). Much of this knowledge consists of **stereotypes** such as those associated with common occupations or with predominant personality characteristics. All normally socialized children develop these stereotypes, these notions of what males and females are like. But sometimes there are important differences in the beliefs and attitudes of different children about appropriate gender roles. These differences, as Crouter, Mchale, and Bartko (1993) have shown, are often related to the gender roles that parents display in the home. Thus, children of working mothers, and especially those whose mothers occupy nontraditional roles, tend to be more **androgynous** in their gender role stereotypes—that is, they display a greater balance, a greater acceptance of both masculine and feminine characteristics, interests, and activities as appropriate for either gender. Children use their gender schemas as guides for interpreting and understanding the behavior of others, as well as for directing their own behavior.

Cognitive Gender Attainment Theory

By the age of two or three years, children can not only correctly label people "man" or "woman" (or "boy" or "girl"), but they can also predict the sorts of activities or occupations that would be most likely for specific individuals, knowing nothing about them other than their gender. But even though children begin to discriminate between male and female very early in life—that is, they begin to develop *gender schemas* early—it isn't until later in the preschool period that they finally understand that gender is a permanent category that can't easily be changed (Serbin et al., 1993). At the same time, children begin to assume the role they associate with their sex. And their understanding of this role, claim Levine, Resnick, and Higgins (1993), determines and constrains much of their behavior. Because boys are not supposed to cry, Miguel tries hard not to. And because girls aren't supposed to like computers, Sarah ignores the thing on her brother's desk.

■ THREE EARLIER THEORIES

One long-held theory concerning the development of gender roles was based on Freud's (1963) suggestion that boys learn to behave as "boys" and girls as "girls" at least partly through *identifying* with their parents and with other males and females. In his terms, the values, the behaviors, the beliefs, and the attitudes of each sex become the child's as they are *introjected*. **Introjection**, in this context, is something like borrowing. It involves the unconscious process of taking someone else's inferred attitudes, beliefs, desires, and so on, and making them part of one's own belief system.

A second important explanation of gender typing is **social learning theory**. As we saw in Chapter 2, this theory holds that parents, siblings and other children, and powerful symbolic models such as television and story characters suggest sex-appropriate behaviors for children. And as these behaviors occur, they, in turn, are reinforced by the models and by society. Thus do boys learn to be masculine and girls learn to be feminine.

A more cognitive explanation suggests that gender typing results from the preschooler's growing understanding of the *meaning* of gender. Kohlberg (1966) describes two broad stages—two levels of understanding—that reflect the child's increasing awareness of gender:

■ Stage 1. **Basic gender understanding** describes the initial stage where the infant recognizes that there are two different genders and that he is a boy or she is a girl. Although many eighteen-month-old infants can identify themselves as being a boy or a girl, many at this age still cannot readily determine whether other children are boys or girls.

■ Stage 2. **Gender constancy** refers to the realization that gender is permanent and unchangeable. It reflects the child's eventual understanding that superficial changes (in ways of behaving or dressing, for example) are irrelevant to basic gender. Gender constancy is generally achieved by most children by the end of the preschool period.

Kohlberg argues that once children become aware of their gender identity and its meaning, they actively participate in organizing their behaviors as well as their environments to conform to sex-appropriate patterns. Thus, having decided that she is a female, a girl selects feminine toys and behaviors. And having decided that he is a male, the boy leaves the doll corner except when he raids it with his phasers and missiles or haunts it as a pretend monster. Not surprisingly, the most widely used indicators of gender typing at the preschool level are based on selection of toys and activities. In the elementary school years, more abstract measures of self-perception are possible (Boldizar, 1991).

Cognitive Gender Schema Theory

A more recent theory of gender typing, **gender schema theory**, has been proposed by Bem (1981, 1989). Essentially, it represents a combination of some of the elements of each of both social learning theory and Kohlberg's cognitive theory. That is, it recognizes that both the child's growing understanding of the nature and meaning of gender and the models, reinforcements, and punishments that the immediate environment provides interact to shape the nature of the child's gender roles (Martin & Halverson, 1987).

According to gender schema theory, the child begins with no understanding of the nature of gender—that is, without what Kohlberg labels *basic gender identity,* the recognition that one is male and female. With the development of notions of gender identity, the child begins to acquire notions of what it means to be a boy or a girl. These notions come largely from the information implicit in the models that the child's culture provides and from the ways in which parents and others tend to reinforce sex-appropriate behaviors—and perhaps to punish, in subtle ways, those that are less appropriate.

As we noted earlier, children's gender schemas—that is, their notions of what males and females are and *should be*—are already quite well established in the late preschool period. These schemas color children's perception of the world and serve to organize their understanding of the behavior of others, as well as to guide their own behavior. In rare cases, however, some children experience significant difficulty developing a strong and clear notion of personal gender identity and being comfortable with that identity. This problem, technically labeled **gender identity disorder**, is sometimes evident in situations where boys feel themselves to be girls or wish desperately that they were (Soutter, 1996). It is also sometimes apparent in cases where girls wish themselves male (Fridell et al., 1996). In Fridell and associates' investigation of twelve girls with gender identity disorder, they found that these girls were rated as significantly less attractive than other normal girls. It's not clear whether this might have been a contributing factor in the disorder.

In some cases, gender identity disorder is pervasive and leads affected individuals to undergo sex-change procedures. In certain cases, the disorder can apparently be corrected. Soutter (1996) reports the case of three boys, all of whom suffered from gender identity disorder and two of whom had gone so far as to give themselves girls' names. Following longitudinal therapy involving acceptance by teachers and protection from ridicule and teasing, all three had developed clear masculine gender identities in adolescence.

Gender Differences and Stereotypes

There are obvious biological differences between the sexes; that there are also psychological differences is less obvious and certainly far more controversial. Nevertheless, as is shown in Chapter 12, there are some small (and declining) differences between males and females in some areas—perhaps most notably in aggressiveness, where males have the doubtful distinction of being considerably more aggressive.

That our common stereotypes (fixed beliefs) of masculinity and femininity are still clearly different is apparent even at very young ages. For example, Henshaw, Kelly, and Gratton (1992) asked fifteen boys and fifteen girls aged eight to nine to give an experimenter advice about whether a boy (John) and a girl (Sally) would like masculine toys (cricket bat, train set, skateboard), feminine toys (doll, skipping-rope, baby carriage), or neutral toys as a present. Only 7 percent of the children thought John would like girls' toys; in contrast, almost half thought Sally would like boys' toys.

In the same study, children were also asked whether John and Sally would like activities such as karate, football, and climbing trees (masculine activities), activities such as dancing, gymnastics, and skipping (feminine activities), or more neutral activities. They were also asked similar questions relating to traditionally male occupations (farmer, bus driver, judge) and to those that have traditionally been female (cook, secretary, librarian). Finally, they were asked whether a stylized drawing of a cat with either a pink bow, a blue bow, or a yellow bow would be a boy or a girl cat. Results, summarized in Figure 8.4, indicate that the children clearly differentiated between masculine and feminine interests and activities. Perhaps more striking, they also reveal that boys' roles are more constrained than those of girls. That is, it is considered less likely and less appropriate that a boy be interested in a girls' toy or activity than that a girl show interest in boys' things. As Henshaw and associates (1992) put it, boy sissies are more strongly sanctioned than girl tomboys: "Girls in trousers are acceptable in a way that boys in dresses will probably never be" (p. 230). Or, in the words of one of the children who participated: "Skipping's for girls—I wouldn't skip and my friends wouldn't skip" (p. 234).

In much the same way, pink is for girls and blue is for boys, even for cats. Not a single child thought the pink cat would be a boy cat—or vice versa. Ten percent thought the yellow cat might be male; 27 percent thought it might be female.

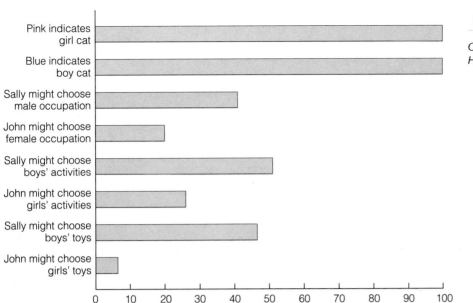

FIGURE 8.4

Children's gender stereotypes. (Based on Henshaw, Kelly, & Gratton, 1992.)

GENDER DIFFERENCES IN PLAY

When they are only three, Paley (1984) informs us, boys will gladly pretend to be babies, mothers, fathers, or monsters. Most are as comfortable wearing the discarded apron and the nursery school teacher's high-heeled shoes as the fire fighter's hat or the ranch hand's boots. They play in the "doll corner" as easily as do the girls. (See Interactive Figure 8.3 for information about where children play.)

But when preschoolers reach age five, the atmosphere in the doll corner changes dramatically. Now when there are pretend games, the boys are monsters and superheroes; in the pretend games of the girls, there are princesses and sisters. But these are not the only changes that come with age. In Paley's (1984) words,

> In the class described in this book, for example [a kindergarten class], you hop to get your milk if you are a boy and skip to the paper shelf if you are a girl. Boys clap out the rhythm of certain songs; girls sing louder. Boys draw furniture inside four-story haunted houses; girls put flowers in the doorways of cottages. Boys get tired of drawing pictures and begin to poke and shove; girls continue to draw. (p. xi)

GENETIC INFLUENCES

Do these early differences in male/female interests and behaviors primarily reflect the influence of social context? Or are they partly biologically based?

The evidence is not entirely clear or complete, but there are strong indications that at least some male/female differences are biological. The evidence is clearest with respect to the greater aggressiveness of males than females. Males are more aggressive than females at an early age, this finding is consistent in most cultures and also for nonhuman primates, and the injection of male hormones into pregnant mothers affects the subsequent aggressiveness of female children who are in utero at the time (Jacklin, 1989; Maccoby & Jacklin, 1980).

SOCIOCULTURAL MODELS AND EXPECTATIONS

However, we should not conclude that the greater aggressiveness of males in our culture is inevitable given probable genetic differences in overt aggression. The influence of cultural factors cannot be discounted. For example, many occupations requiring physical aggression and strength have traditionally been restricted to males, whereas those requiring nonaggressive, passive, nurturant behavior have been considered more appropriate for females. Hence, the models society provides for children are clear.* Children see them everywhere: on television, in books, in schools, on the playground. The message is clearly that there are certain behaviors, attitudes, and interests that are appropriate—and others inappropriate—for one's sex (Henshaw et al., 1992). The same message is clear, as well, in the sorts of behaviors society reinforces in children. For example, male popularity depends primarily on athletic ability and toughness; female popularity depends on attractiveness, social skills, and academic achievement (Adler, Kless, & Adler, 1992).

Finally, gender role messages are evident in the way parents treat their children—how they dress them, what toys they buy for them, what they expect of them, how they react to their displays of aggression or nurturance (Witt, 1997). In fact,

---

*My grandmother liked to point out that most soldiers, police officers, wardens, and politicians who control the machinery of collective violence are men—as are most murderers, rapists, muggers, and scoundrels. But there are exceptions.

SUMMARY TABLE 8.6

Important Theories and Concepts in the Development of Gender Roles

CONCEPT/THEORY	EXPLANATIONS/COMMENTS
Gender schema	■ Personal knowledge about the characteristics, behaviors, interests, and so on that define masculine and feminine.
Freudian gender attainment theory	■ The belief that gender schemas develop as a function of identifying with parents.
Social learning gender attainment theory	■ The belief that gender schemas result from the influence of models and the reinforcements that cultures provide regarding sex-appropriate behaviors.
Cognitive gender attainment theory	■ The belief that gender schemas arise from the cognitive understanding of the meaning of gender identity, the development of gender constancy (the notion that gender is permanent, unchangeable), and the subsequent organization of interests and activities to conform with the appropriate gender roles.
Gender schema theory	■ Recognizes that elements of both cognitive explanations (the child's growing understanding of the meaning of gender) and social learning explanations (the influence of models and reinforcements) shape gender roles.
Gender identity disorder	■ Profound discomfort with one's anatomical sex.
Gender stereotypes	■ Fixed beliefs about behaviors and interests that are masculine or feminine.
Gender differences in play	■ Reflect basic cultural stereotypes; recognized by preschoolers at very young ages.
Influences on gender roles	■ Some evidence of genetic influences, especially in greater overt aggressiveness of males; considerable evidence of strong cultural and familial influences.

the family is probably the greatest single socializing influence in the life of the preschooler. (See Summary Table 8.6.)

THE FAMILY

Our vision of the "typical" North American family is still often that of a **nuclear family**—mother, father, and one or two children—with father as breadwinner, although mother, too, might work (as opposed to an **extended family,** which includes many other relatives as well). But in Canada in 1995, 15 percent of all families with children were lone-parent families (*Canada Yearbook,* 1997). In the United States in 1995, 22 percent of **family households** were single-parent families. In the United States, 53 percent of the black family

households were single parent, as were 32 percent of the Hispanics and 18 percent of the whites (U.S. Bureau of the Census, 1996). Hence, the traditional "white, two parents, and children" definition of the North American family is no longer correct. "There is no single correct definition of what a family is," Fine (1993, p. 235) writes. It might be white, African American, Hispanic, or some other mix; it might be one- or two-parent; it might be an intact family or a blended family ("stepfamily"); it might be a gay or a lesbian family. The average size of the U.S. family in 1995 was 3.2; in Canada, it was 3.0. This represents a drop of about half a child per family household since 1960. (See "At a Glance: Changes in the Family" and Figure 8.5.)

Not only is the family difficult to define, but it is also very private and highly dynamic. That it is highly private means that researchers seldom have access to the most intimate aspects of its functioning. And that it is dynamic—that is, changing not only with the addition or loss of members but also as relationships among its members change—means that the relationships and influences within the family do not expose themselves clearly and simply to the scrutiny of the social scientist. Hence, it is difficult to research the family. There is much about which we can only speculate.

Parenting Preschoolers

The family serves three principal functions in North American societies, claims Westman (1991): (1) It has a sustenance function (to provide food, shelter, clothing); (2) it has developmental functions (through caregiving and parenting); and (3) it has advocacy functions (through ensuring the child's access to education, health care, a safe environment, and so on).

In Chapter 6 we reviewed findings that the most important features of caregiving for the infant are attentiveness, physical contact, verbal stimulation, material stimulation, responsive care, and absence of restrictiveness. As infants age and as their verbal, motor, and intellectual abilities blossom, important dimensions of parenting begin to change. But parenting is no less important for older children than it is for preschoolers.

PARENTING STYLES

Baumrind (1967) looked at the kinds of parenting associated with three distinct groups of children: one of buoyant, friendly, self-controlled, and self-reliant children; another of discontented and withdrawn children; and a third of children who lacked self-reliance and self-control. Baumrind found some consistent and striking differences among the parenting styles of the mothers and fathers of these children. Parents of children in the friendly, self-controlled, self-reliant group were significantly more controlling, demanding, and loving than parents of either of the other groups. Parents of the discontented and withdrawn children also exercised much control but were detached rather than warm and loving. And

Changes in the Family

The average size of the family has declined in recent decades and is now at about 3.2 persons in the U.S. in 1995 and 3.0 in Canada—a drop of more than one-half child since 1960. As population has increased, the number of married couples has also increased. But whereas in the United States families with both spouses present increased by about 33 percent between 1960 and 1995, the number of male-headed families increased by a whopping 125 percent in the same period. Yet there are still about six times more female-headed households—some 9.8 million in the United States in 1995 (compared with 1.7 million male-headed households). In Canada, about 15 percent of all families are nontraditional, one-parent families. In both countries, this represents an increase of close to 150 percent in the last three decades (U.S. Bureau of the Census, 1996; *Canadian Sourcebook*, 1997).

FIGURE 8.5

Changes in U.S. average family size and increases in single-parent families, 1960–1995 (From data in U.S. Bureau of the Census, 1996, p. 58.)

parents of the children low in self-esteem were warm but highly permissive.

On the basis of studies such as these, Baumrind identifies three different styles of parenting, each of which is characterized by different types of parental control (Baumrind, 1989): permissive, authoritarian, and authoritative.

Permissive parenting is a nonpunitive, nondirective, and nondemanding form of parental control. Permissive parents allow children to make their own decisions and to govern their own activities. They don't try to control through the exercise of the power that comes from authority, physical strength, status, or the ability to grant or withhold rewards, but they might, on occasion, try to appeal to the child's reason.

Authoritarian parenting is grounded on firm and usually clearly identified standards of conduct. These are often based on religious or political beliefs. The authoritarian parent values obedience above all, and exercises whatever power is necessary to make the child conform. Children in authoritarian homes are given no responsibility for personal decisions, nor are they involved in rational discussion of the family's standards.

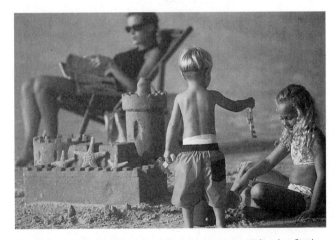

Parenting styles range from extreme permissiveness to rigid and unflinching control. Child-care experts typically reject these highly-permissive or highly-authoritarian extremes, instead recommending authoritative parenting—parenting that is based on reason and that permits independence, but that also values obedience and high standards of personal conduct.

Authoritative parenting falls somewhere between permissive and authoritarian control. It uses firm control but allows for rational discussion of standards and expectations; it values obedience but tries to promote independence. Authoritative parents, in contrast with authoritarian parents, are those whose standards derive more from reason than from religious or political beliefs (Table 8.7).

Interestingly, the parenting styles of mothers and fathers within families tend to be more alike than different. Bentley and Fox (1991) compared the responses of fifty-two pairs of mothers and fathers of one- to four-year-olds to the Fox Parenting Inventory (Fox, 1990). The scale measures three areas of parenting: expectations ("My child should use the toilet without help"), discipline ("I yell at my child for whining"), and nurturance ("I read to my child at bedtime"). Although mothers received higher nurturance scores than fathers, mothers and fathers did not differ on expectations or discipline.

■ NOVICE AND EXPERT PARENTS

Some parents are probably better at parenting than others. In Cooke's (1991) terms, some are *novices* and some *experts*. How are the two different? Among other things, experts are better at sensing the child's needs and goals, especially in problem-solving situations; they have better general knowledge of child development and child rearing; they have consciously thought about their roles and their goals; and they foster activity that provides their children with opportunities to be self-directive. These characteristics of expert parents are most evident in competent children—that is, in children whose measured achievement compares favorably with that of other children.

Effects of Parenting

Do parents really matter?[*] And if so, which of these parenting styles is best? The Freudian model says yes, parents matter a great deal because children are extremely sensitive to the emotional experiences of their early lives and especially to their relationships with their parents. And the behavioristic model says yes, too, because children are highly responsive to the rewards and punishments of their environments.

■ CONFLICTING FINDINGS

But the research has not always been entirely clear. For example, **retrospective studies** (looking backward in time, often using interviews or questionnaires) with delinquent and otherwise disturbed adolescents and adults have generally found that their childhoods were marked by a variety of traumas sometimes associated with alcoholic or abusive parents, poverty, authoritarianism, rejection, and a variety of

---

[*] "Why do you ask questions like that?" snorted my grandmother, "when you already know the answer." "What's the answer?" I challenged, and she retorted with half a dozen of her proverbs: "Does a cat eat mice? Does a one-legged duck swim in circles? Is the pope catholic? Does a bear...."

TABLE 8.7

Parenting Styles

STYLE	CHARACTERISTICS	EXAMPLES
Permissive	Laissez-faire; nonpunitive; child responsible for own actions and decisions; autonomy more important than obedience; nondemanding	"Okay. I mean sure. Whatever you want. You decide."
Authoritarian	Dogmatic; very controlling; obedience highly valued; self-control and autonomy limited; little recourse to reasoning	"You're going to darn well study for 40 minutes right now. Then you say your prayers and go right to bed. Or else!"
Authoritative	Based on reason; permits independence but values obedience; imposes regulations, but allows discussion	"Don't you think you should study for a while before you go to bed? We'd like you to get good grades. But you know we can't let you stay up that late. It isn't good for you."

other factors. In one such study, women whose partners were alcohol-dependent reported significantly more problem behaviors among their children (Tubman, 1993). But when researchers try to predict which of a group of children will be maladjusted and which will be happy and well adjusted, they are unsuccessful about two-thirds of the time (Skolnick, 1978). Indeed, some very successful, well-adjusted individuals have home environments that should place them at high risk. It seems that predicting the effects of child-rearing practices is far more difficult than explaining these effects after the fact.

More recent research has often found significant relationships among certain dimensions of parenting and child personality and behavior. For example, Benasich and Brooks-Gunn (1996) found a high correspondence among measures of mothers' knowledge of child development and child rearing and measures of home environment as well as measures of child IQ at thirty-six months. Mothers with the highest knowledge scores in this study also tended to have children who manifested the fewest behavior problems. Similarly, Weiss and Schwarz (1996) found that children whose parents were excessively authoritarian were more likely to have problems relating to adjustment, academic achievement, and substance abuse as college students.

■ BAUMRIND'S ADVICE

Following extensive investigations of the relationships between behavior and characteristics of parents and the personalities of their children, Baumrind (1977, 1993) concludes that there is no one best way of rearing children. Like McClelland (1973), she argues that there are no specific child-rearing practices that should be advocated rather than others (breast-feeding, toilet training, and coloring with oils, for example), but there are some general characteristics of parents, reflected in their behaviors and attitudes toward their children, that clearly have highly positive effects—and negative ones, too. She found, for example, that parents who were firm and directive were more likely to have children who would be responsible (as opposed to socially disruptive and intolerant of others) and active (as opposed to passive)—a finding also confirmed in other studies (for example, Kochanska, Clark, & Goldman, 1997). But what she advocates is not *authoritarian* but *authoritative* parenting—parenting that is firm but reasonable, demanding but warm, nurturing, and loving. Better-than-adequate parenting by parents who are confident of their parenting skills, she insists, can optimize the development of both children who are normal and those who are at risk (Baumrind, 1993).

There is evidence that Baumrind's advice is sound. Bronstein and colleagues (1993) report a number of studies that have found a link between authoritative parenting and positive child outcomes—and between lax parenting and poorer child adjustment. Similarly, Kuczynski and Kochanska (1995) report a study of preschoolers in which they found a clear relationship between authoritative child rearing and the child's personal and social competence. Kochanska (1997), too, reports positive outcomes for children of mothers characterized by high empathy and cooperative but authoritative parenting styles.

■ CHILD-CARE ADVICE

Parents do make a difference. As McCartney and Jordan (1990) note, the conclusions of parenting research have not always been clear because researchers have tended to use simple models that were not adequate for the complexity of the interactions involved. If the conclusions are to be valid and useful, they argue, researchers must adopt models that not only emphasize the complexity of parenting but that also recognize the possibility that parenting styles that are excellent for certain children in given circumstances may be quite disastrous for other children—or under different circumstances.

There are nevertheless some recognizably good—and bad—ways of parenting. "At the most simple level," says Christopherson (1988), "if the children are basically happy, the parents are probably not doing too much that is wrong" (p. 133). At a more detailed level, he offers seven guidelines for child-rearing practices (pp. 133–136):

■ Behavior and relationships with others depend on the extent to which the child's basic needs are met.

■ Parents need to recognize each child as a unique individual.

■ The faith, honesty, confidence, and affection between the parent and child affects the quality of the parent–child relationship.

■ Parents should separate the worth of a child from the behavior.

■ The child should be allowed as much freedom as possible to make mistakes and discoveries, but to do so with safety, respect for the rights of others, and for the social convention.

■ Parents should arrange the environment to encourage prosocial behavior.

■ Parents should be ready to lend support directly or indirectly through physical or verbal guidance.

Learning How to Parent

In many close-knit, nonindustrialized societies, the old ones show the young ones how to parent. There is evidence that, at least to some extent, the same thing happens in our more complex, industrialized societies. Ijzendoorn (1993) surveyed a large number of parenting studies and found a significant amount of what is termed intergenerational transmission of parenting styles. It seems that we have a tendency to parent as did our own parents.

■ SOURCES OF CHILD-CARE ADVICE

But not all parents simply rely on their own intuition, common sense, and intelligence, or on the transmitted wisdom of their parents and grandparents. Many others turn to one or more of three major groups of commercial child-care advisors: (1) the medical profession, whose doctors and nurses readily provide advice relating to psychological as well as physical health; (2) books; and (3) parenting courses.

■ PARENTING COURSES

There are a handful of well-known and widely established parent education courses, most of which require relatively lengthy training and practice sessions. Some of these have proven especially valuable for children with learning and behavior problems (Thompson, Grow, & Ruma, 1993).

Parenting courses are almost invariably based on a recognition of the rights of children and take into consideration their needs and desires. They treat children as important human beings and discourage punitive approaches to parental control (such as shouting, threatening, physical punishment, and anger-based behaviors), instead encouraging reasoning. The ultimate aim of most of these courses is to foster a warm, loving, and nurturant relationship between parent and child. And the principal method by which each of the various techniques operates involves communication.

In short, most parent education programs encourage parents to be authoritative (firm, democratic, reasonable, respectful) rather than authoritarian (harsh, controlling, demanding, dogmatic, powerful) or permissive (laissez-faire, noncontrolling, weak); in addition, they teach specific techniques to help parents become authoritative. The major weaknesses of these programs include the fact that the solutions they provide are often too simple for the complexity of the problems with which parents must occasionally deal, they typically do not take into account important differences

CONCEPT	EXPLANATIONS/COMMENTS
Nuclear family	■ Parent(s) and immediate children.
	■ No longer as common as proportion of lone-parent families increases.
Functions of parenting	■ To provide basics (food, shelter. . . .).
	■ Developmental functions (through caregiving, parenting).
	■ Advocacy functions (access to education, health . . .).
Parenting styles	
Permissive:	Nonpunitive, uninvolved, nondemanding.
Authoritarian:	Dogmatic, demanding, controlling.
Authoritative:	Reason-based, permits independence, values obedience.
Effects of parenting styles	■ Authoritative parenting associated with positive outcomes.
	■ Mother's knowledge of child care and of children associated with positive outcomes.
	■ Punitive, controlling, harsh, demanding parenting may be associated with negative outcomes.
Sources of parenting information	■ Parents, grandparents, intuition, and the medical profession.
	■ Child-care books.
	■ Parenting courses, most of which advocate *authoritative parenting* based on *reason* and reflecting *respect and love* for the child.

among children of different ages and of different sexes, and they sometimes mislead parents into thinking that all answers are to be found in a single method (Brooks, 1981). (See Summary Table 8.8.)

FAMILY COMPOSITION

The family, says Hoffman (1991), is a dynamic (changing) and interactive social unit. Parenting styles define one feature of this unit; so do other factors such as birth order, family size, and spacing of siblings.

Birth Order

About a century ago, Galton (1896) noticed that there was a preponderance of firstborn children among great British sci-

entists. Since then, research has attributed many advantages to being the firstborn (or an only child). Among them are more rapid and more articulate language development, higher scores on measures of intellectual performance, higher scores on measures of achievement motivation, better academic performance, better peer relations, fewer symptoms of stress, more curiosity, a higher probability of going to college, and a higher probability of being a president and, of course, a king or queen (see, for example, Gaynor & Runco, 1992; Pilkington, White, & Matheny, 1997).

There are a number of plausible explanations for the observed effects of **birth order.** Certainly, these effects are not due simply to being a firstborn, a middle, or a lastborn child; in White and associates' words, they result instead from "the pattern of behaviors and attitudes that emerge from family experiences" (1997, p. 89). What being firstborn means, says Marjoribanks (1997), is that the child is initially exposed to a family environment with "undiluted" resources. Siblings who come later are born into a family where the attentions of the parents are less focused on the one (and first) child, and their interactions with each child are different in subtle but apparently highly important ways.

Family Size

In general, although things may be "cheaper by the dozen," the larger the family, the more limited the advantages to the children. In fact, many investigators report lower intelligence test scores among members of larger families (for example, Zajonc, 1976; Zajonc & Mullally, 1997). These same researchers also report distinct birth order effects. Thus, the most advantaged individuals, *taken as a group,* are firstborn children in very small families (or, of course, *only* children, who, by definition, are firstborn in the smallest of possible families). And the least advantaged are those born later, those born in very large families, and, as we see in a moment, those born in families where there is little spacing among siblings.

Zajonc's explanation of these findings takes the form of what he labels the **Confluence Model.** According to this model, homes are characterized by a measurable quality termed **intellectual climate.** Intellectual climate is measured as follows: Each person in the family is assigned a value relating to age. Parents, for example, are given 30 points each, a newborn, 0, and other children, values ranging from 0 to 30 according to their ages. The intellectual climate of the home is computed very simply by summing these values and dividing by the number of individuals in the family (thus giving the average intellectual climate of the home). Thus a newborn child born into a two-parent family is born into a family with an intellectual climate of $(30 + 30 + 0)/3 = 20$. But had the child been a twin, the intellectual climate would have been five points lower ($[30 + 30 + 0 + 0]/4 = 15$).

Put another way, a measure of intellectual climate reflects the many different home-based environmental factors that might contribute in important ways to the development of a child's intellect—things like the nature and frequency of conversation with intelligent adults and older siblings, opportunity to interact with appropriate play and learning materials, and guidance and assistance from more competent adults and older siblings. It follows from this model that the best home environment is that which has the greatest number of adult models who interact with the child, and the least conducive to intellectual development is that where the resources of the family are shared among a large number of siblings, causing what Marjoribanks refers to as *resource dilution*. Thus, Zajonc's *confluence model* takes into account not only birth order and family size, but also **family spacing**—that is, length of intervals between siblings.

Age Intervals

Family size and birth order, taken together, are important predictors of academic success, achievement, and even creativity; the prediction becomes even more powerful if a third variable is introduced into the equation: that of *family spacing* or *age intervals*. Simply put, children whose siblings are significantly younger or older seem to be at an advantage. Close spacing among siblings has repeatedly been found to be associated with intellectual disadvantages and, occasionally, peer-adjustment and parent–child relation problems as well (Pilkington, White, & Matheny, 1997).

The influence of age intervals, like that of birth order and family size, is probably best explained in terms of the sorts of family relationships and interactions that are most likely to result. A child whose siblings are much older or much younger, Gaynor and Runco (1992) explain, is more likely than other children to be perceived by parents as special. Furthermore, on average, there may well be less dilution of

resources in families where children are widely spaced. And, by definition, the measured intellectual climate in a home with closely spaced children becomes progressively lower with each new child. With multiple births, of course, the spacing is zero, and the index of intellectual climate is accordingly lower. (See "In the News and on the Net: *Sept d'un Coup*.")

SOME CAUTIONS

Before we go running off bragging that we're firstborns or only children—or complaining that we're not—we should note that the contributions of birth order, family spacing, and family size to intelligence and academic achievement are not overwhelmingly high. Furthermore, there are many other critically important factors that a simple model like the *confluence model* doesn't take into account, not the least of which is the influence of genes. In addition, it's difficult to separate the effect of family size from the effects of social class, religion, or rural versus urban environment. Larger families are far more common among the poor, the culturally deprived, and certain ethnic minorities. When these factors are taken into account, socioeconomic status often emerges as a more important predictor of intelligence and academic achievement than does family size or birth order.

We should always bear in mind that the conclusions of our social sciences are usually based on the average performance of large groups of individuals. Within these groups, there are those whose behavior does not come close to matching the predictions that social science might make based on its conclusions. Thus, there are saints and geniuses whose siblings numbered in the tens and twenties, all closely spaced, and there are poltroons and oafs who were born first into tiny little families. (See Summary Table 8.9.)

Zajonc's Confluence Model argues that powerful, home-based influences on intellectual development, such as the nature and frequency of conversation and guidance involving intelligent adults and older siblings, create a measurable intellectual climate in the home. The measure of intellectual climate is the average of the values assigned to each family member. Because these values increase with age, firstborn and only children have an advantage over those born later or born into large families, for whom family resources are more diluted. Hence, the model takes into account birth order, family size, and family spacing.

Birth order	▪ On average, firstborns and only children have an advantage on measures of intelligence, achievement, adjustment, probability of leadership, and so on.
Family size	▪ There is an inverse relationship between size of family and measures of intellect.
Family spacing	▪ Other things being equal, the more closely spaced the family, the greater the disadvantage to its children.
Cautions	▪ Birth order, family size, and family spacing do not, in and of themselves, account for any variations in measures of intellect or adjustment; they do so indirectly by influencing interactions in the family.
	▪ Family composition predictions of intelligence and adjustment don't take into consideration other important factors such as genetics, social class, and poverty.
	▪ There are countless exceptions to generalizations based on family composition variables.

■LONE-PARENT FAMILIES

Close to half of all American children are spending (or will spend) an average of six years in a family with only one parent. The large majority of these one-parent families, most of which are headed by mothers rather than fathers (see Figure 8.5), result from separation or divorce; a smaller proportion result from the death of a parent or from bearing children out of wedlock. Amato and Keith (1991) cite projections that parents of 38 percent of white children and 75 percent of black children in the United States will divorce before the children are sixteen.

Does Separation or Divorce Have Negative Effects?

There is considerable controversy over the most likely effects on children of parental separation and divorce. One large body of research seems to show clearly that the effects are primarily negative and that they are also highly general. Other recent studies present far less negative outcomes.

For example, Rodgers (1996) did a **meta-analysis** of a large number of studies that had looked at the effects of divorce. (A meta-analysis combines the results of separate but related studies in an attempt to arrive at a single, valid conclusion.) He concludes that the negative effects of divorce have often been *understated* and that they present as great a risk for children's mental health and happiness as other important early life factors. On the other hand, Burns, Dunlop, and Taylor (1997), following a critique of Rodgers's conclusions, suggest that the effects of divorce on child outcomes are very weak—that, in fact, the child's gender, father–child and mother–child relations, and father's occupation are, by themselves, better predictors of important child characteristics such as anxiety, depression, and self-concept. But that the effects of divorce might be relatively weak compared with those of other variables in the child's life does not make them unimportant (Rodgers, 1997). In fact, other meta-analyses of the impact of divorce, such as one reported by Amato and Keith (1991), find significant negative effects on school achievement, behavior, adjustment, self-concept, and relations with both the remaining and the departed parent. In Bronstein and associates' (1993) words, "Children from divorced families are more likely to experience behavioral, social, emotional, or academic problems" (p. 268).

Possible Negative Effects of Divorce

The Amato and Keith (1991) meta-analysis concludes that the negative effects of divorce are related to the ages of the children. In almost all investigations, the most serious effects are on children in the middle age groups—mainly elementary and high school—with college students least affected. Frieman (1993) also reports that parental breakup often results in dramatic changes in classroom behavior. And, strikingly, parental divorce can even lead to a reduction in children's eventual lifespan. In fact, Friedman and associates (1995) found a reduction of an average of eight years in the longevity of both men and women whose parents had divorced when they were children. Subjects were 1,261 participants in the **Terman study.**

What might the negative effects of divorce be on children of different ages? Wallerstein and Kelly (1976, 1980) conducted a longitudinal investigation of age-specific effects of divorce among a group of sixty families. For the youngest group (two- to three-year-olds), negative effects were sometimes evident in regression manifested in loss of toilet habits, bewilderment, and clinging behavior directed toward strangers. Three- and four-year-old preschoolers showed loss of confidence and self-esteem, and were quick to blame themselves for the departure of the father. The next age group (five- and six-year-olds) seemed less affected developmentally, although some of the daughters tended to deny the situation and to continue expecting their fathers' return. The

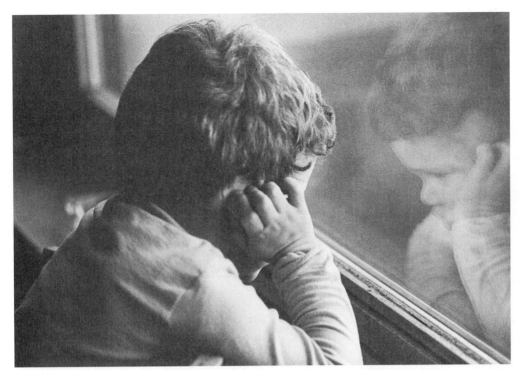

The negative effects of loss of a parent (through death or divorce) appear to be most severe for children aged three to nine—although studies indicate that the effects of divorce may have become less negative in recent decades. Still, even when there are no apparent behavioral or developmental problems, there is often lingering sadness.

seven- and eight-year-olds were understandably frightened by the divorce and intensely saddened, many of them missing their fathers constantly. Many of these children also live in fear of making their mothers angry, perhaps imagining that she too might leave them. Nine- and ten-year-olds initially react with apparent acceptance, many of them trying to understand why the divorce has occurred. But their outward calm covers feelings of anger, sometimes intense hostility toward one or the other parent (or both), and shame (Wallerstein & Kelly, 1976). About half suffered from varying degrees of depression, low self-esteem, poorer school performance, and poorer relationships with peers. The adolescent group (ages twelve to fourteen) reveals a much deeper understanding of their parents' divorce (Springer & Wallerstein, 1983). Many adolescents were keen observers and analyzers of interactions between their parents, and were able to evaluate the situation objectively. Unlike younger children, they were much less likely to harbor feelings of guilt about the divorce or hostility toward one or both parents. However, some of these children, who initially seemed to cope well, later manifested varying degrees of anger, resentment, and maladjustment—an example of what Wallerstein (1989) labeled the "sleeper" effect.

Some researchers have suggested that boys are more adversely affected by divorce than are girls, although the Amato and Keith (1991) meta-analysis indicates that sex differences are not very pronounced. Other than for the fact that boys sometimes exhibit more unhappiness or emotional distress following a divorce than do girls, there is no consistent pattern of greater negative effects for boys than girls. In short, there is no greater incidence of behavior problems, of difficulty in school, of lowered self-esteem, or of problems with parent–child relationships.

Why Divorce or Separation Might Have Negative Effects

Why should divorce or separation of parents have an effect on the mortality of their children? Perhaps for a variety of reasons, suggest Tucker and associates (1997), following a further investigation of the Terman subjects ("Termites," they called them). Among these reasons were the following: Men whose parents divorced were themselves more likely to divorce as adults, which is itself sometimes associated with shorter life expectancy; men of divorced parents obtained less education; women whose parents divorced were more likely to smoke, and were also more likely to divorce their own husbands later.

There are several other reasons why divorce might affect children negatively, explains Amato (1993). These include the absence of one of the parents, problems associated with adjusting to the remaining parent, conflict between parents, economic hardship, and generally stressful life changes. They include, as well, the child's relationship with the departing parent both before and after the divorce or separation.

■ FATHER (OR MOTHER) ABSENCE

Much of the research in this area has focused on, and has attributed negative consequences to, the father's absence. We might expect that father absence could affect children either because the roles traditionally filled by the father would no longer be filled (or might be filled less adequately by the mother, who must also continue to carry out her own roles) or because the absence of the father has an effect on the mother, who then interacts with her children differently. Interestingly, bad father–child relations are sometimes a better

Characteristics of North American Families

Dramatic increases in divorce rates now mean that in the United States, more than one child in four lives with only one parent, and almost nine times out of ten, that parent is the mother (Figure 8.6). In Canada, 13 percent of all families are lone-parent families. Unfortunately, the median income for mother-only families is about half that for father-only families (and less than one-third that for two-parent families) (Figures 8.6, 8.7, 8.8, and 8.9).

United States, 1991

FIGURE 8.6

Living arrangements of U.S. children. (From data in U.S. Bureau of the Census, 1996, p. 58.)

Canada, 1994

FIGURE 8.7

Living arrangements of Canadian children. (From data in 1997 Canadian Sourcebook, pp. 5–8.)

FIGURE 8.9

Median family income of mother-only, father-only, and two-parent U.S. families with children under 18, 1992. The median is the midpoint; half the families in each category earn more than the median and half earn less. (From data in U.S. Bureau of the Census, 1996, p. 468.)

FIGURE 8.8

Average income, Canadian families, 1994. (From data in 1997 Canada Yearbook, p. 179.)

---

predictor than divorce of negative consequences such as anxiety, depression, and poor self-esteem (Burns et al., 1997). In this connection, psychologists have coined the label **parental alienation syndrome (PAS)** to describe a cluster of symptoms often associated with alienation from one or the other parent. PAS appears to be one possible, highly distinctive outcome of divorce, especially where the family has been characterized by a high degree of stress and conflict (Rand, 1997). It is sometimes evident in the child choosing, or being forced into, an alliance with one parent against the other. In severe cases, notes Rand, the love bond between child and alienated parent can be completely ruptured. Possible adverse effects on the child are serious.

■ ECONOMIC IMPACT

The economic circumstances of the one-parent home are, on average, considerably less advantageous than those of the

two-parent family. In both Canada and the United States, the average income in mother-headed homes is only about 60 percent that of father-headed homes (and 30 percent that of married-couple families). More telling, almost half of single-mother families are below the poverty level, compared with only 7 percent of married couples with children (U.S. Bureau of the Census, 1996; *Canadian Sourcebook*, 1997). The change from relative affluence to poverty can be especially difficult for children whose peers are more advantaged. Economic hardship also increases the risk of trouble with the law and is associated with a higher probability of not finishing school. (See "At a Glance: Characteristics of North American Families" and Figures 8.6, 8.7, 8.8, and 8.9.)

■ FAMILY CONFLICT

A third explanation for the negative effects of divorce relates to stresses associated with conflict between parents, both before and during the process of separation. Smith, Berthelsen, and O'Connor (1997) report that 42 percent of the fifty-four preschoolers in their study of children living in homes characterized by spousal violence exhibited behavioral problems serious enough to require intervention. In fact, one of the most striking findings revealed in the research summarized by Amato and Keith (1991) is that children living in high-conflict but intact families fared *less well* than children whose parents had divorced: They manifested more adjustment difficulties, lower self-esteem, and more behavior problems. Conversely, in a study of 225 divorced fathers, Arditti and Michaelena (1994) found that those who had the most positive relationships with their wives both before and after the marital breakup also experienced better postdivorce relationships with their children.

■ PARENTAL DISENGAGEMENT

Peterson, Leigh, and Day (1984) present what they refer to as a "middle range theory of the potential impact of divorce." It is a theory that deals with two principal variables. The independent variable is the degree of **parental disengagement.** (An independent variable, recall, is a variable that, in an experiment, is manipulated by the experimenter; it is the variable that is expected to have an effect on outcomes.) The dependent variable is the child's social competence. (A dependent variable, remember, is that which is presumably affected by the independent variable.) So the degree of parental disengagement—which ranges from varying levels of marital discord through temporary separation, long-term separation, divorce, and death—may affect the child's social competence, which is manifested in the child's ability "to engage in social relationships and possess adaptive psychological qualities" (Peterson et al., 1984, p. 4).

In examining the relationship of these two variables— parental disengagement and the child's social competence— Peterson, Leigh, and Day (1984) take into account much of the wealth of research in this area and reduce it to a handful of conclusions:

■ The higher the degree of disengagement, the greater the impact on the child. In other words, divorce would generally be more stressful than temporary separation. By the same token, a situation in which one of the parents breaks all ties with the child would be more stressful than one in which both parents continue to maintain close ties with the child.

■ The severity of the immediate crisis brought about by the divorce is closely related to the negative impact of divorce. Children who have been abused or neglected by a parent are less likely to view the divorce as a very serious calamity, and are likely to experience a lower degree of stress.

■ The more accurate the child's perception of the parents' relationship prior to marital breakup, the less negative the consequences. Those who incorrectly view their parents' relationship as "happy" immediately before separation or divorce suffer the highest stress.

■ The more positive and amicable the parents' relationship following marriage breakup, the less negative the effect on the child.

■ The closer the relationship between the leaving parent and the child prior to marital breakup, the more serious the effect on the child.

■ Age is related to the severity of consequences in a curvilinear fashion, with the most serious consequences occurring for children between the ages of three and nine, and the least severe occurring before and after those ages.

The Lessening Impact of Divorce

Note that the Terman studies, which reveal a rather frightening relationship between divorce and longevity, began about seven decades ago. For a variety of reasons, divorce appears to have been a far more negative event in the days of our parents and grandparents than it is today. In fact, in the Rodgers meta-analysis of divorce effects, the oldest studies consistently reported greater negative effects (Rodgers, 1996). More recent studies, as we have noted, often report substantially weaker effects. In Burns, Dunlop, and Taylor's words, "Our data suggest that not all children of divorced families suffer adverse consequences" (1997, p. 136). Their point is that the emphasis should be on identifying children who are most likely to experience negative effects, and to take steps to prevent or lessen these effects.

Why should results of current research on the effects of divorce show a weakening of negative effects relative to those conducted some decades ago? There are a variety of possible reasons. One is that some of the earlier research may have been flawed. Demo (1993) argues that much of the research failed to take into consideration the predivorce status of the children involved. For example, the Wallerstein and Kelly longitudinal study describes troubled children of various ages following their parents' divorce, but because there is no information concerning what these children were like before the divorce, it does not follow logically that their present condition was caused by the divorce. In fact, these children might have been negatively affected by parental conflict before the parents separated.

A second reason for the less negative conclusions of more recent research, suggests Kurdek (1993), is that these conclusions have often reflected an unacknowledged bias toward the traditional family structure and a pervasive negative attitude toward divorce.

Third, the fact that more recent investigations are finding less negative effects on children may be because divorces in the 1950s and 1960s were less common, less culturally acceptable, and more difficult to arrange. Consequently, both children and parents had to cope with more disapproval and were provided with less support. Mothers found it more difficult to arrange for satisfactory child care and to obtain the kind of employment that would provide them with both the time and the money for their child-caring commitments.

In Conclusion

There are several dangers implicit in interpreting studies such as these. One is that we might inadvertently stress either the negative or the positive aspects of divorce. Although divorce is often a trying time for children, living in conflict (and sometimes with physical and mental abuse) can also be very trying. At a certain point, family conflict in the intact home may have negative effects on children far greater than the potentially negative effects of divorce. Before that point is reached, divorce often is the best solution, both for parents and for their children. It bears repeating that some loving single parents can effectively overcome whatever trauma might be associated with the loss of one parent, and that there are countless two-parent families in which parenting is inadequate and love is seldom if ever shown.

Much of the current emphasis in this area is no longer on establishing whether or not divorce and separation have negative effects, and how pervasive and serious these might be. Rather, an increasing number of researchers are trying to uncover the characteristics of postdivorce parenting and of child and family support that are most likely to prevent or lessen negative consequences of marital dissolution (Katz & Gottman, 1997). For example, Baris and Garrity (1997) suggest that parents who plan their divorce so as to lessen conflict and stress, and so as to provide for continued co-parenting, are less likely to have children who are negatively affected.

Most children (and parents) adapt to life in a single-parent home within two or three years of the initial disruption. Richards and Schmeige (1993) interviewed seventy-one single parents. They found that money was the number-one problem for mothers; difficulties with the ex-spouse were a greater problem for men. Both men and women reported that parenting became easier over time. However, at about the time that adjustment to life in the one-parent family seems almost complete, remarriage often occurs. And that, too, can require major readjustments. (See Summary Table 8.10.)

CHILDREN IN STEPFAMILIES

About 60 percent of all first marriages now end in divorce, and the majority of those who divorce remarry. Thus, about half of all American children spend at least some time in a one-parent family. And about one-quarter of all children will live with at least one stepparent before adulthood (Mason & Mauldon, 1996).

A stepfamily is the family grouping that results from the remarriage of a widowed or divorced parent and in which, consequently, only one of the two married adults in the family is the child's biological parent. More than one in every six American families with children under eighteen is a stepfamily (U.S. Bureau of the Census, 1996), and projections are that this proportion may reach 50 percent by the year 2000.

▲ SUMMARY TABLE 8.10
Possible Consequences of Divorce on Children

Some possible negative effects	■ Lower self-esteem and achievement, unhappiness, depression.
	■ Behavior and adjustment problems.
	■ Shortened lifespan (due to factors such as higher incidence of smoking, depression, subsequent divorce, lower educational attainment, poorer employment).
	■ Effects related to age in curvilinear fashion: worst for children aged 3 to 9, least severe before and after this range.
Possible reasons for negative effects	■ Father absence, which might affect child directly, or indirectly because of its effect on the mother.
	■ Resulting poverty and loss of educational and other opportunities.
	■ Effects of family conflict and stress (which may well be more severe than the potential effects of divorce).
Lessening impact of divorce	■ Some flaws in earlier studies may have exaggerated negative consequences of divorce.
	■ Negative consequences may historically have been worse because of biases in favor of the traditional family and lack of social and economic support for one-parent families.
	■ Consequences of separation or divorce are not invariably negative or long term.

Interestingly, stepfamilies are no more enduring than first marriages, with about 60 percent ending in divorce (Pill, 1990). In addition, remarriages in which there are stepchildren are more likely to dissolve than if there are no children, especially if the children are older—above nine (Visher & Visher, 1996).

Possible Problems in Stepfamilies

Does this mean that parenting is more difficult in stepfamilies? Perhaps. Clearly, the number and complexity of relationships that can exist within a stepfamily are much greater. For example, the marriage of a man and woman who have both been married previously and who both have children can create a staggering number of new relationships involving the biological relatives of each of the stepparents, not to mention previous spouses and their parents, siblings, uncles, aunts, and cousins. In addition, there has been considerable legal ambiguity surrounding the rights and obligations of stepparents and stepchildren, especially in cases where the stepfamily breaks up (Mason & Mauldon, 1996).

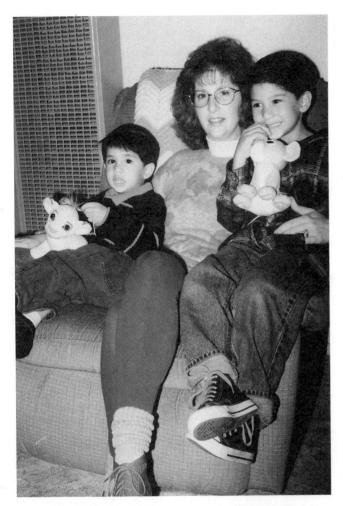

Although children sometimes experience problems adjusting to life in a stepfamily, the effects of stepfamilies on children are often highly positive. This stepmother hardly looks like the wicked stepmother of fairy tales.

The remarriage of the parent in a one-parent family sometimes brings new problems for a child who not only has had to cope with the initial disruption of the family through death or divorce but must now cope with another reorganization of the family. And whereas remarriage is almost invariably seen as a highly positive gain for the parent because it reestablishes an important relationship, it is often seen as a loss by the child because it implies a change in the relationship between the child and the natural parent. Many children experience feelings of abandonment following the remarriage of a parent (Kaiser, 1996).

In addition to the loss, real or imagined, of some of the biological parent's attention and perhaps affection, the stepchild must now also deal with establishing new relationships with the stepparent, with stepsiblings if there are any, and perhaps with a new set of grandparents and other relatives. Furthermore, the stepchild's role in the family often changes. This can be particularly difficult for adolescent children. Their newly developed adult roles, sometimes accelerated by the absence of the parent (for example, the boy has become "man of the house" following his biological father's departure), can be severely disrupted by the appearance of a new

stepparent. Similarly, the creation of a new stepfamily can disrupt established patterns of control and discipline and sometimes lead to serious problems ("You're not my dad! I don't have to listen to you!").

Other possible problems sometimes associated with the stepfamily include sexual fantasies and inclinations between stepsiblings as well as between children and their stepparents (and resulting feelings of guilt and confusion), stepsibling rivalry and competition, ambivalence about the stepchild's role in the family, confusion over whether and how the departed parent should continue to fit into the child's life, and the need for the child to abandon the fantasy or wish that the natural parents might one day be reunited.

The Positive Side

Fortunately, the effects of stepfamilies on children are often highly positive. Pasley, Dollahite, and Ihinger-Tallman (1993) report that well-functioning stepfamilies are no different from well-functioning intact families, although it's true that there is a sometimes difficult period of early adjustment. Interestingly, stepparents who have previously been parents tend to adjust more easily to the stepparenting role. Also, those who ease more slowly into the new stepparenting roles fare better than those who try to assume the role too quickly—especially with respect to control and discipline.

The fairy-tale stereotype of the stepfather or stepmother as the wicked wielder of terrible powers is, in fact, a fairy tale. Clearly, many stepparents are kind and considerate people who want to love and be loved by their stepchildren. When the initial adjustments have been made, the stepchild might, in a great many cases, be as fortunate as many in intact nuclear families.

NONPARENTAL CAREGIVERS

In the old days, most North American children spent their preschool years in intimate contact with their mothers. Today, an increasing number of children are cared for during the day by others. In fact, child care by someone other than a parent is now the norm for more than 50 percent of all U.S. preschool children—a percentage that is climbing (Clarke-Stewart, Gruber, & Fitzgerald, 1994). About 75 percent of mothers of preschoolers now work, and it is becoming increasingly common for many mothers to go back to work within weeks of childbirth. In 1993, 53 percent of U.S. women went back to work within one year of giving birth (U.S. Bureau of the Census, 1996). As a result, infant child care is the fastest growing type of supplemental care in the United States.

Nonparental child care takes a variety of forms, ranging from situations in which families can afford to hire a private, in-the-child's-home caregiver to substitute for the mother during her absence, to institutionalized centers for large numbers of children with many caregivers. Most common, however, are private homes that look after perhaps a half-dozen youngsters—referred to as family child care. About half of all children are cared for by grandparents or other relatives (Hofferth, 1992). Although family child care is the most common form of early child care, most of the research in this area has focused on institutional centers.

In addition to arranged care for children, there are self-supervised or **latchkey children,** so called because their parents sometimes hang keys around their necks so they can let themselves into their homes after school. Some studies report that self-supervision is sometimes associated with more behavior problems (Vandell & Ramanan, 1991). However, many find no measurable difference between self-supervised children and those who are looked after by their parents.

General Effects of Child Care

Given the proliferation of nonparental child care, it's important to ask whether it's as good for infants and preschoolers as parental care and what the characteristics of good child care are. There is no lack of research. The early emphasis in much of this research was to determine whether infants and preschoolers cared for by someone other than their mother might suffer harmful consequences relating to difficulties in forming affectional bonds with their mother. In spite of this largely negative orientation, a review of several dozen early studies found few significant differences in social, intellectual, and motor development between child-care and home-care children (Bronfenbrenner, Belsky, & Steinberg, 1977). More recent research has generally corroborated these findings. As Bowman (1993) puts it, "In general, nonfamily care and education have not been found to jeopardize the development of young children" (p. 109). In fact, the opposite may well be true. It seems clear, argue Clarke-Stewart, Gruber, and Fitzgerald (1994), that high-quality child care has positive effects on children's social and intellectual development.

Characteristics of High-Quality Child Care

As a result, child-care research now often focuses on the characteristics of programs that seem to have the most positive effects on children, as well as on the characteristics of children for whom nonparental care is most likely to be a positive or a negative experience. Not surprisingly, this research reveals that children who are most in need are most likely to benefit from high-quality child care. For example, Caughy, DiPietro, and Strobino (1994) looked at the effects of nonparent child care among 867 five- and six-year-old children. Children from the more impoverished homes in the sample typically fared better on later tests of reading and arithmetic, especially if they had been placed in child care before the age of one, and also when the child care occurred in a center rather than in a private home. Children from more optimal

home environments did not show the same advantages of child care. Interestingly, when Holloway and associates (1995) interviewed mothers to discover what it was they would ideally want from preschool child care, one of their most common desires was that child care prepare their children for school.

How can parents determine what is likely to be good or bad child care? Clarke-Stewart, Gruber, and Fitzgerald (1994) suggest that these are some of the characteristics of high-quality child care:

- Qualified caregivers—that is, caregivers who have the training and the inclination to provide children with the sorts of experiences that are conducive to intellectual and social growth.

- A well-designed program that provides educational and social experiences not readily available in the home.

- Low caregiver–child ratio so that there is a high degree of interaction between each child and caregivers.

- An environment that is not highly discipline oriented. In the Clarke-Stewart, Gruber, and Fitzgerald (1994) study, children who received less discipline (in the sense of fewer demands, less control, less punishment, more choices, and more responsibility for responses) were more advanced cognitively, more obedient, and more likely to get along with peers.

- Ample opportunity for interaction with peers.

- A stimulating physical setting.

- A high degree of agreement between parents and caregivers' goals and beliefs about children and child care.

Poorer quality child-care programs are easily recognized, note Endsley and Bradbard (1981), by the characteristics they have in common. These might include unsanitary and unhealthy physical surroundings, obvious physical hazards, excessive overcrowding, high adult–child ratios (exceeding 1 to 20 or, in the case of infants, 1 to 10), lack of activities and materials that are interesting and challenging to young children, untrained staff who are at best thoughtless and insensitive and at worst reject and abuse young children, and disregard for parents' feelings about child rearing (p. 32). Interestingly, parents who are most satisfied with their child-care arrangements are those for whom there is the greatest amount of agreement with respect to child rearing (Britner & Phillips, 1995).

Licensing requirements for establishing child-care facilities vary tremendously throughout North America and are usually nonexistent for smaller, family-based centers (Hernandez & Myers, 1993). As a result, although there are many high-quality facilities available, there are others whose environments are of far lower quality. To evaluate these facilities, Endsley and Bradbard (1981) suggest that parents should obtain personal references and, perhaps most important, visit the centers, observe them in operation, and talk with the people in charge. Sadly, however, most of us are likely to spend

Characteristics of High- and Low-Quality Child Care

Higher quality	• Qualified caregivers.
	• Well-designed program.
	• Low caregiver–child ratio.
	• Noncontrolling, choice-filled environment.
	• High child–child interaction.
	• Stimulating physical setting.
	• Caregiver–parent agreement regarding child rearing.
Lower quality	• Unsanitary, unhealthy, hazardous physical surroundings.
	• Overcrowding.
	• Adult–child ratios exceeding 1 to 20 (or, in the case of infants, 1 to 10).
	• Lack of stimulating program.
	• Untrained, uninvolved staff.
	• Disregard for parents' feelings about child rearing.

more time looking, comparing, and obtaining references when buying a car than we are when finding someone to care for our children. (See Summary Table 8.11.)

FOCUS QUESTIONS: SUMMARY ANSWERS

1. What do preschoolers understand of what others feel?

   ▪ Initially, they understand relatively little, but eventually they learn how to interpret the feelings of others (sometimes using social referencing). Also, they learn to control their emotions (through increasingly behavioral means), and they learn rules of emotional display (when and how to express emotions).

2. What is the importance of play in early childhood?

   ▪ Practice play may be useful for developing and exercising important physical skills, as well as for establishing social position and teaching acceptable forms of behavior. Pretend play is closely related to cognitive development and the development of the child's theory of mind.

3. To what extent are masculinity and femininity determined by early experiences?

   ▪ Gender roles (behaviors that are masculine or feminine) result from an interaction of genetic and contextual forces. Sex differences in childhood are evident in the tendency of boys to play more physically, in the toys they select and are given, and in the roles they assume in their pretend games. A cognitive explanation for gender typing describes two stages: *basic gender identity* (recognizing maleness or femaleness) and *gender constancy* (realizing that gender is stable, permanent, and unchangeable). *Gender schema theory* expresses the belief that gender typing involves cognitive elements (recognition of gender and gender constancy) and social influences, both of which shape gender roles.

4. How important is parenting? Family size? Position in the family?

   ▪ Firstborn and only children often have some achievement and intellectual advantages over their siblings—as do children whose siblings are much younger or older than they are. Children from larger families sometimes do less well than children from smaller families on measures of intellectual performance. These observations are due mainly to the social and economic characteristics of large and small families, and to the influence of birth order, birth interval, and family size on the relationships most likely to develop between children and their parents.

5. What are the effects of divorce on children?

   ▪ Some of the possible negative effects of divorce and separation on children include lower self-esteem and achievement, profound unhappiness, and, on occasion, a shorter lifespan. Immediate effects are most serious for three- to nine-year-olds. These effects may be due to absence of a parent, family conflict, economic hardship, and stressful life changes, and are more serious with greater parental disengagement. An increasing number of more recent studies find few long-term negative effects of divorce, perhaps because it is now more common and more socially accepted.

STUDY TERMS

androgynous, 225

associative play, 223

authoritarian parenting, 229

authoritative parenting, 230

autonomy versus shame and doubt, 216

FURTHER READINGS

Paley's books offer a fascinating, often delightful, description of life in the preschool. The first of these short books follows three-year-old Mollie through a year of nursery school, revealing her excitement and her fears in the little dramas that are an intrinsic part of Paley's classes. The second follows the lives of a kindergarten class, providing fascinating insights into how children struggle to arrive at their own understanding of what it means to be a boy or a girl:

Paley, V. G. (1986). *Mollie is three: Growing up in school.* Chicago: University of Chicago Press.

Paley, V. G. (1984). *Boys and girls: Superheroes in the doll corner.* Chicago: University of Chicago Press.

The following book presents a brief but detailed analysis of the games children play and of the role of play in development:

Hughes, F. P. (1990). *Children, play, and development.* Boston: Allyn & Bacon.

The Hernandez and Myers book presents a detailed analysis of recent changes in North America that are having an important impact on child care:

Hernandez, D. J., & Myers, D. E. (1993). *America's children: Resources from family, government, and the economy.* New York: Russell Sage.

An informative look at the importance of how children are cared for, and a description of some of the characteristics of quality child care, is provided by the following text:

Clarke-Stewart, K. A., Gruber, C. P., & Fitzgerald, L. M. (1994). *Children at home and in day care.* Hillsdale, NJ: Erlbaum.

PART FOUR

Middle Childhood

"Suppose there are two mobs?" suggested Mr. Snodgrass.

"Shout with the largest," replied Mr. Pickwick.

CHARLES DICKENS
Pickwick Papers

s we see in Chapters 9 and 10, there are more than just two mobs in middle childhood. All compete for the child's attention. "This way," the mobs clamor. "Everybody is going this way. You should go where everybody is going." ¶ "Study!" schools say. "It's important for your future!" ¶ "Play!" friends and peers urge. "It's a ton of fun!" ¶ "Watch!" television demands. "Never mind playing and studying. Watch and then run out and buy what I sell you!" ¶ "Read!" the newsstands coax. "Look at the pretty pictures. Become a comic-book collector!" ¶ "Caution!" parents advise. "Find some balance, my child. Study, play, watch, read. Be cautious. And do the dishes!" ¶ Is the child just some piece of clay to be shaped by the strongest or the most-determined hands? Or is there a *self* that emerges through childhood and into adulthood—a self that evolves from the budding consciousness of the infant, that learns intention and willfulness and the making of choices, that develops notions of worth and feelings of effectiveness, or sometimes of powerlessness? ¶ Perhaps, Mr. Snodgrass, even if there are two very large and very loud mobs—or even a dozen of them— you should not simply shout with the largest. ¶ If you have a self, you might first want to listen to what each has to say.

1. What is the most common nutritional problem of childhood?

2. What is Piaget's view of important intellectual changes in middle childhood?

3. What model of human memory is basic to current information-processing approaches?

4. What are the dimensions of intellectual exceptionality?

NINE

Physical and Cognitive Development: Middle Childhood

Some folks are wise, and some are otherwise.

TOBIAS SMOLLETT
Roderick Random

hen Barbara Follett was only four, she became fascinated by her mother's old portable typewriter. And when she had barely turned five, she typed a long letter to her friend, Mr. Oberg. One paragraph reads: ❡ *The goldfinches come every afternoon and eat their supper on the clump of bachelor's-buttons right on the left-hand side of the path that leads from the back door to our road. There are ten goldfinches, five males and five females. Before they eat their suppers, they sit on the clothesline and swing in the breeze. I wish you could be here to see them.* (McCurdy, 1966, p. 4) ❡ At the age of six, she was writing poetry and long prose stories filled with the beauty of nature and with childish love and enthusiasm: ❡ *The butterflies are coming fast now. Sometimes I sit down in a chair and suddenly I see a white Butterfly fly in circles about the potato patch; and I jump from my seat and run after it and see it alight and I tiptoe up to it, and I am just about to open my fingers to take it by the wing when away it would fly.* (McCurdy, 1966, p. 22) ❡ At the age of nine, she had finished a book, later published under the title *The House Without Windows*. It is an enchanting story of a little girl who runs away into a world of animals and meadows, later into the sea, and finally into a world of eternal snows where she is utterly alone until a flurry of butterflies carries her off into invisibility. The story ends: ❡ *She was a fairy—a wood nymph. She would be invisible forever to all mortals, save those few who have minds to believe, eyes to see. To these she is ever present, the spirit of Nature—a sprite of the meadow, a naiad of lakes, a nymph of the woods.* (McCurdy, 1966, p. 67) ❡ When Barbara Follett was thirteen, she published a second book consisting of a series of letters she had written while sailing. And on Thursday, December 7, 1939, when she was only twenty-four, she walked out of her apartment in Brookline and was never seen again. To this day, her disappearance remains a mystery. ❡

This Chapter

Barbara Follett never attended school. As professor Howard Mumford Jones, when reviewing her first book, wrote, "there seems to be no sane reason why she should ever go to one" (quoted in McCurdy, 1966, p. vii).

Barbara Follett's story is not the story of the average child in middle childhood; it's the story of a unique individual. But it, too, provides glimpses into the minds of children. The purpose of this chapter is to clarify those glimpses. It traces the continued growth of the child's mind through **middle childhood** (approximately ages six to twelve), looking at how children know and remember, how they solve problems, how they develop notions of themselves as effective processors of information. It deals with the growth of normal intelligence, as well as with exceptionality. But it first looks at physical development.

PHYSICAL GROWTH AND MOTOR DEVELOPMENT

The physical development of many of the world's children is far from optimal—sometimes because of inadequate diet and sometimes simply because of lack of exercise. In the world's most undeveloped countries, 41 percent of children under age five are significantly underweight (more than two **standard deviations**[*] below the normal weight for their age). About 10 percent of these children suffer from **wasting** (defined as more than two standard deviations below normal weight for average children of that height), and an alarming 50 percent suffer from moderate to severe **stunting** (defined as more than two standard deviations below average height relative to normal children of the same age). Not surprisingly, the mortality rate for these countries is 170 per 1,000 children under age 5 (Bellamy, 1997). (See Figure 9.1.)

In contrast, the under-five mortality rate for the world's most developed countries is only about 9 children per 1,000, and the percentage of children who are underweight is negligible. In fact, estimates are that as many as 20 percent of all North American children may be obese. These observations underline the importance of knowledge about the normal course of physical development and about the contributions of nutrition and exercise to physical and mental well-being.

Changes in Height and Weight

Although girls tend to be slightly shorter and slightly lighter than boys from birth to the end of the preschool period, the growth rates for each are almost identical. This pattern changes in middle childhood. As Figures 9.2 and 9.3 show, although

---

[*]A standard deviation is a measure of variation from the average. A weight that is two standard deviations below average would be in the bottom 2.3 percent of the population.

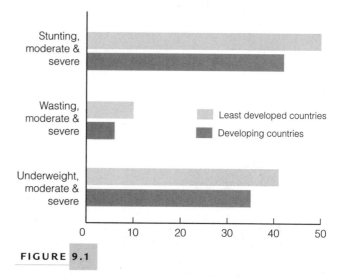

FIGURE 9.1

Manifestations of malnutrition in nonindustrialized countries. (Based on data from Bellamy, 1997, p. 98.)

the average girl is three-fourths of an inch (2 cm) shorter at the age of six, she has caught up with and surpassed the average boy by the age of eleven and is still slightly taller at the age of twelve. With respect to weight, girls are close to 2 pounds (1 kg) lighter at the age of six and do not catch up with boys until the age of eleven. Between the ages of eleven and twelve, however, girls undergo a sudden spurt of weight gain that puts them 3 pounds ahead of boys in a single year. Chapter 11 points out that not until the age of 14½ do boys overtake girls in weight, and at 13½ they exceed girls in height.

FAT AND FAT-FREE MASS

A common way of describing the mass of the human body is in terms of components referred to as **fat-free mass** and **fat mass**. Fat-free mass, also termed *lean body mass* and consist-

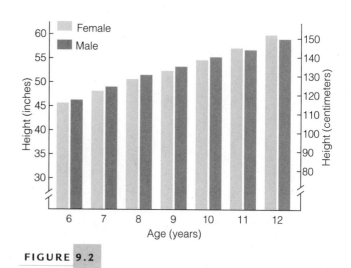

FIGURE 9.2

Height at 50th percentile for U.S. children. (From the Health Department, Milwaukee, Wisconsin; based on data by H.C. Stuart and H. V. Meredith, prepared for use in Children's Medical Center, Boston. Used by permission of the Milwaukee Health Department.)

ing mainly of bones, organs, and muscle tissue, is the most stable part of body mass. Fat mass, consisting mainly of white adipose tissue (fat cells), is more susceptible to the influences of diet and exercise. In the average adult male, about 85 percent of body weight is accounted for by fat-free mass and only 15 percent is fat mass. In contrast, almost 30 percent of the weight of average adult females is fat mass (Malina & Bouchard, 1991).

In infancy, fat mass is relatively high in both males and females (about 25 percent of total body weight). The pattern for boys is a gradual reduction of percentage of fat mass through middle childhood, with a very slight increase during the growth spurt at adolescence. Following this growth spurt, there is continued slow decline until the adult ratio of about 15 percent fat mass is reached at around age twenty. For girls, the reduction in proportion of fat mass is even more gradual until early adolescence, when there is again a very gradual increase until the adult ratio of close to 30 percent is reached at about age twenty (Malina & Bouchard, 1991). In general, then, girls tend to retain a higher percentage of body fat than boys, whereas muscle development is more rapid in boys (Smoll & Schutz, 1990). (Figure 11.3 in Chapter 11 shows growth curves for fat mass in males and females.)

■ THE GROWTH SPURT

Toward the end of middle childhood there occurs a sudden growth spurt in both height and weight. It is generally taken to signal the beginning of sexual maturation (and of adolescence). On average, this spurt begins almost two years earlier for girls than for boys. Average age of maximum rate of growth in height (termed **peak height velocity**) is 11.4 for girls and 13.4 for boys (Malina, Bouchard, & Beunen, 1988). For some, however, the growth spurt can occur years later or earlier than average. As a result, there are sometimes dramatic height differences among children of the same ages during middle childhood. This can be a source of embarrassment

and worry for some children. At a time when peer approval has become among the most important things in life, it may be seen as a great misfortune to be either precocious or retarded in physical development. Nature sometimes compensates for initial discrepancies so that the early-maturing child stops growing while others catch up—or so that the late-maturing child suddenly blossoms and rapidly overtakes the others. And sometimes it doesn't. (See Chapter 11 for a discussion of the psychological effects of early and late maturation.)

Nutrition and Health

If they are well nourished, between the ages of six and twelve, children grow 2 to 3 inches (4.4–6.6 cm) and gain about 5 to 7 pounds (approximately 2–2.75 kg) each year. Normal gains in height are a better indicator of the long-term adequacy of the child's nutrition than are weight gains; gains in weight often reflect the shorter-term effects of nutrition. Hence the significance of the observation that 42 percent of children in developing countries and 50 percent of those in the least developed countries are stunted (Bellamy, 1997) (see Figure 9.1).

Nutrients are found in various classes of food and drink, among the most important of which is water. It makes up slightly more than 60 percent of the body weight of children (and of adults). Also critical are carbohydrates, fats, proteins, and various minerals and vitamins. In fact, during middle childhood, the recommended daily allowances of substances like calcium and most vitamins and minerals are almost as high for children as for adults (Food and Nutrition Board, 1989).

Unfortunately, as we saw in Chapter 1, many of the world's children are not well nourished, and many millions die of starvation each year. Although starvation is uncommon in North America, malnutrition is not. Malnutrition takes one of two forms: overnutrition, often leading to obesity, and undernutrition, often reflected in the intake of foods low in protein and essential vitamins and minerals.

■ OBESITY

The most common nutritional problem among children in North America is **obesity,** which may affect more than 20 percent of all children (Looney & Plowman, 1990). Obesity is defined medically as weighing more than 20 percent more than average for one's height, age, and sex. It is a serious condition that is difficult to rectify. Its relationship to cardiovascular and other health problems is well-known; its implications for the child's social and emotional well-being are perhaps less obvious but no less real. Not only does the severely obese child often find it difficult to participate in games and activities that are an important part of the lives of many children, but such a child may be subjected to the ridicule and ostracism often reflected in derogatory nicknames. It's hardly surprising that when Braet, Mervielde, and Vandereycken (1997) compared 139 obese nine- to twelve-year-olds with 150 normal children, they found that the obese

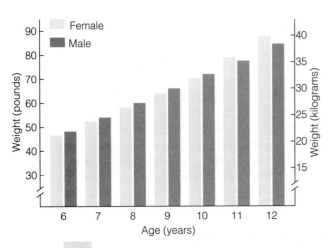

FIGURE 9.3

Weight at 50th percentile for U.S. children. (From the Health Department, Milwaukee, Wisconsin; based on data by H.C. Stuart and H. V. Meredith, prepared for use in Children's Medical Center, Boston. Used by permission of the Milwaukee Health Department.)

group reported far more negative self-perceptions. Moreover, they scored lower on tests of general self-worth, and their parents reported far more behavioral and emotional problems for them than did parents of normal children.

Obesity in children is linked to several factors. Overeating of both fat and energy (calories) is clearly the most important: Children simply take in more than they expend in growth and activity. This, of course, does not mean that the obese child eats excessively all the time. In fact, many obese children might eat only slightly more than they require each day, but the cumulative long-term effect is obesity.

Also important is the child's genetic background: Some children are clearly more susceptible to obesity than others. Those whose parents are themselves obese are more likely to also become obese than are children of slim parents (Malina & Bouchard, 1991). Similarly, when one member of an identical twin pair is obese, the other is also more likely to be. Interestingly, however, studies of identical twins indicate that those who are genetically predisposed to being thin are much less likely to show the consequences of overeating. It's as if their bodies are programmed to burn more calories (Bouchard et al., 1990).

Another possible factor in childhood obesity, often overlooked partly because it may be confounded with heredity, is the influence of parents who themselves have eating and nutrition problems. For example, Franzen and Gerlinghoff (1997) report a number of **case studies** where mothers with eating disorders also have children with similar eating disorders. In these cases, the influence of the mother may be partly a function of modeling and a function of the nutritional opportunities provided for the children.

A fourth important factor in childhood obesity is inactivity. Children who lead sedentary lives, who spend much of their day watching television, are more likely to gain excess weight. Watching television is especially important in contributing to weight gain, not only because it is physically passive but also because it encourages high-calorie snack and drink consumption. In fact, one treatment for obesity involves efforts to make children more knowledgeable about the media, and especially about the nature and purposes of advertising. Unfortunately, media advertising is not only highly pervasive but extremely effective with children. Thus, when Levine, Smolak, and Schermer (1996) undertook a ten-week *media resistance* program with 386 fourth- and fifth-grade students, they were not highly successful in bringing about more critical evaluation of mass media.

A fifth factor in obesity is the use of food as a reward—or a punishment. Children who are given "treats" for good behavior may learn to reward themselves with junk food—or to console themselves in the same way.

Although obesity is difficult to reverse, it can be prevented in most children even when genetic background predisposes the child to gaining excess weight. Two factors need to be controlled: exercise and diet. Children need to be encouraged to develop good eating habits. Care must be taken to ensure that they consume adequate amounts of proteins, vitamins, minerals, and fibers—and also that they resist the ever-

Notwithstanding widespread beliefs to the contrary, today's school children are not *less fit than was the case several decades ago—especially if they live in environments that allow them to participate in active games and sports such as this school soccer match.*

present temptation of junk food. In other words, this presupposes that children (and their parents) have a high level of knowledge about nutrition and about the relationships among exercise, nutrition, and health. As Mobley (1996) points out, this is not highly likely to be the case for very young children. When she tested three- to six-year-olds' health knowledge, she found that preschoolers tended to learn safety items first (for example, how and when to cross a street) and nutrition and health promotion items much later. Contrary to popular wisdom, the body does not automatically hunger for specific minerals, vitamins, or other nutrients it might lack. Nor does it drive us to exercise when television beckons. Even animals do not select the most nutritious meal when there are other more appealing alternatives (Galef, 1991).

A number of programs have been designed for improving children's knowledge of nutrition and exercise habits. For example, Hopper and associates (1996) report on a school-based exercise and diet program involving ninety-seven children in grades two and four, with parental participation. The object of the program was to decrease fat and cholesterol intake while at the same time increasing the use of systematic exercise. The authors report a high degree of success, with children in experimental groups not only displaying greater knowledge of nutrition but also consuming more fruit, grain, and cereal than control group children. The most positive results were for those children whose parents were most involved in the program. (See "In the News and on the Net: Michelin Man on Diet.")

■ DISEASES AND INFECTIONS

Although the development of vaccines has drastically reduced the incidence of diseases and infections among children, the majority of children nevertheless suffer occasionally from various problems. Most common are respiratory infections such as colds, although these are about half as common he French tire company *Compagnie Generale des ETS Michelin* recently announced that *l'Homme Michelin* will soon appear with a new body. Ostensibly to celebrate the 100th anniversary of the company, but perhaps as much in response to this age's preoccupation with physical appearance, the Michelin man is about to lose at least some of his bulging waistline.

Almost twice as many U.S. children are now obese than was the case 20 years ago—an estimated 14 percent of U.S. children above age 6. Two factors that most accurately predict a child's chances of being obese are whether or not the parents are obese, and whether the child is obese as an *older* child (rather than obese as a preschooler). Genetic tendencies toward obesity become a serious problem primarily when accompanied by overeating, poor nutrition, and lack of exercise.

1. Thinner Michelin Man. (1997, Dec. 4). *Edmonton Sun*, p. 2.

2. Childhood Obesity. KRON-TV, September 24, 1997.

To Consider

Obesity remains the number-one nutritional problem among North American children. Do you suppose things such as the Michelin Man's slimmer profile might have an effect on this problem? Why or why not?

On the Net

A web site that provides links to a wide variety of sites dealing specifically with obesity as well as with nutrition, dieting, and weight reducing programs is the following:

http://www.loop.com/~bkrentzman/ links/obesity.links.html

after age five as before. About 69 percent of children under five suffer from a cold at least once a year, but only 29 percent of those ages five to seventeen do so (U.S. Bureau of the Census, 1996). Less common are communicable diseases such as chicken pox, mumps, mononucleosis, and measles. Very uncommon are vaccine-preventable diseases such as tetanus, poliomyelitis, pertussis (whooping cough), and smallpox. Rabies, too, is uncommon.

Motor Performance

Children's strength and muscular control develop significantly during the years from six to twelve. Early in this period, their control of large muscles is considerably better than their control over smaller muscles (an explanation for the inelegant writing of first- and second-grade children). By the end of middle childhood, control over the small muscles is much improved.

■ SEX DIFFERENCES IN MOTOR PERFORMANCE

Changes in locomotor skills, agility, coordination, and physical strength vary not only by age but also show consistent differences between the sexes. These differences may be important in explaining some of the child's interests. For example, throughout middle childhood, the boy's physical strength (measured in terms of grip strength) is superior to the girl's even though the average girl is taller and heavier than the boy. Similarly, boys consistently outjump girls after

the age of seven, presumably because boys have greater leg power and arm–leg coordination for jumping than do girls. Malina and Bouchard (1991) also cite evidence that boys do better than girls in tests of kicking, throwing, catching, running, and broad jumping. But girls surpass boys in a number of motor skills during middle childhood, particularly when the skills require muscular flexibility, balance, or rhythmic movements, such as those in hopscotch and rope skipping and some forms of gymnastics, as well as in the ability to balance on one foot (Morris et al., 1982).

Not surprisingly, these differences are consistent with the gender typing of these activities. That is, rope skipping and hopscotch have traditionally been more feminine than masculine; throwing balls, catching, running, and jumping are considered more masculine. In addition, the differences between boys and girls, while consistent, are seldom very great. There is typically a great deal of overlap, so in activities in which boys are better than girls, some girls are better than some boys; conversely, where girls are, on the average, better than boys, some boys are nevertheless better than some girls (Lockhart, 1980). However, it's important to note that although sex differences in motor skills are usually very small during middle childhood, after adolescence the disparity increases dramatically (Smoll & Schutz, 1990), generally in favor of the males.

Through middle childhood, sex differences are found not only in the execution of motor skills relating to sports or to track-and-field events, but also with respect to play behavior. For example, Boulton (1996) reports that eight- to eleven-year-old boys engage in far more rough-and-tumble play

Children's motor coordination, agility, and strength increase dramatically through middle childhood. The skills required for this girl's participation in a strikingly complex rope skipping game are tremendously important to her self-concept and happiness.

than do girls. They chase each other, fight and wrestle, tug, push, pull, hit, and restrain in ways that many girls would find quite unacceptable.

EXPLANATIONS OF SEX DIFFERENCES

Boulton (1996) speculates that sex differences in aggressive behaviors and rough-and-tumble play may be partly genetically based, and may be related to the male's traditional need to establish social dominance over rivals. Certainly, young boys are far more likely than young girls to display their anger in physical aggressiveness (Murphy & Eisenburg, 1996). However, the extent to which sex-related differences in motor skills, both in childhood and later in adolescence, result from innate biological differences between the sexes and the extent to which cultural norms, expectations, and experience are involved is not clear. We do know that at least for some activities, proportion of adipose (fatty) tissue is closely related to performance for both boys and girls. In a comparison of the motor performance of more than 2,000 children ages nine to seventeen, Smoll and Schutz (1990) found that fatness alone accounted for as much as 50 percent of the variance between males and females. Given the much greater percentage of fat mass retained by females from early childhood on, some of the observed male–female differences in motor performance are probably related to this biological difference. However, with advancing age, sex differences in motor performance are increasingly influenced by environmental factors.

It bears repeating that sex differences in motor skills are often trivial. And although some of these differences are a function of innate biological differences, social expectations and environmental opportunities also influence the activities in which youngsters become interested and proficient.

Physical Fitness

There is a widespread belief that schoolchildren are not as fit today as was the case several decades ago. The belief is based in part on the observation that as many as 20 percent of school-age children are obese. It also stems from the fact that many children spend much of their time watching television, playing and working with computers, or engaged in other relatively nonactive endeavors. And evidence does suggest that teenagers are not as active now as they were even ten years ago (Center for Disease Control, 1992).

Does this mean that today's children are relatively unfit? No, claim Pangrazi and Corbin: "Recent research suggests that they are more fit than previously reported" (1993, p. 14). Part of the confusion stems from the fact that definitions of physical fitness have changed from a concern with performance on various tests of speed, skill, strength, and flexibility to a concern with more health-related criteria like stamina and body fat percentage. Children are only slightly fatter now than they were twenty years ago, claim Looney and Plowman (1990); more than 80 percent meet high standards of physical fitness (Corbin & Pangrazi, 1992).

Some Physical and Sensory Problems

Not all children are born with normal physical skills or sensory abilities, nor do all have the same potential to develop. Those who differ markedly from the average are termed *exceptional.*

Exceptionality is evident in all areas of human development: physical and motor, intellectual, and social–emotional. In each area, it may be positive (evident in extraordinary talents and skills), or it may be negative (apparent in deficits and disorders). Later in this chapter, we look at both the positive and negative dimensions of intellectual exceptionality in middle childhood. Here we look briefly at physical and sensory problems.

VISUAL IMPAIRMENT

Those who can see at 20 feet what a "normal" person can see at 20 feet are said to have 20/20 (or normal) vision; those who can see at 20 feet what normal people see at 200 feet are said to have 20/200 vision and are classified as legally blind if their corrected vision in their better eye is no better than 20/200. Accordingly, many individuals who are classified as legally blind do, in fact, see; this is one reason why the term **visually impaired** is highly preferable to *blind*. Approximately half of all legally blind children can read large type or print with the help of magnification. For the **special needs** teacher, it is especially important to determine whether a child will be able to learn to read visually or will have to learn to read by touch. For those who can read visually, the "special" qualities of education might not need to go beyond providing magnifying equipment or large type, unless there are other problems involved.

Special classrooms and special teachers for visually impaired children are much less common than they once were; many of these children are now being educated in regular classrooms, a practice termed **mainstreaming** (about which more is said later in this chapter). But those who must learn to read braille require special equipment and teachers. Note, however, that there is an unusually high prevalence of visual disorders among those with severe mental handicaps (as many as 25 percent are *severely* visually handicapped (Kwok et al., 1996). These children also have a much higher than normal incidence of hearing impairment.

■ HEARING IMPAIRMENT

Deafness is the inability to hear sounds clearly enough for the ordinary purposes of life. The **hard of hearing** are described as those who suffer from some hearing loss but who can function with a hearing aid and sometimes without.

A useful way of describing deafness is to distinguish between prelinguistic and postlinguistic deafness—in other words, between loss of hearing that occurs prior to learning a language and that which occurs later. Unfortunately, in nine out of ten deaf children, loss of hearing was congenital (present at birth) or occurred within the first two years, often resulting from infections such as **otitis media.**

Otitis media is the second most common reason why parents bring their children to doctors (the first involves upper respiratory infections). It's a middle ear disease that may be accompanied by mild to severe loss of hearing and can sometimes last for months. Because it is highly common in infancy, when the child is acquiring language, otitis media can be associated with retarded language growth and related cognitive problems. The milder forms of otitis media, lasting only a few weeks, are often treated effectively with antibiotics. More severe, recurring (chronic) cases lead to build-up of fluid in the middle ear, which causes deafness. In these cases, treatment often involves surgically inserting tubes in the ear to allow the fluid to drain (Feagans & Proctor, 1994).

In terms of cognitive development, deafness generally presents a far more serious handicap than does visual impairment, largely because of the severe difficulties it presents for learning to understand and to speak—hence the historical, but no longer popular, expression "deaf and dumb" or "deafmute." There is little evidence that the visually impaired are intellectually handicapped as a result of their blindness, but the same is not true of those who are hearing impaired. The academic achievement of children who are deaf often lags behind, a problem that can be attributed largely to language deficiencies. This observation, of course, applies to the prelinguistically deaf and not to those whose loss of hearing occurred after they had already learned a language.

In addition to the academic problems associated with deafness, there are often emotional and social problems. These problems probably result from lack of social interaction, in turn resulting from impaired ability to communicate through language.

The education of the deaf generally requires specially trained teachers and often occurs in institutions. Understandably, the principal emphasis is on the acquisition of language—usually a combination of American Sign Language (ASL), finger spelling, and speech reading (lipreading).

The education of children with only a partial hearing loss may also require special instruction, particularly if the loss is manifested in speech disorders. Although many children with partial hearing are capable of following conversations if the conversations are at close range or sufficiently loud, they often experience difficulty in distinguishing among consonants for which there are no visual clues (for example, *p–b, t–d,* and *f–v*). Their own speech may consequently be affected. Special education for these children can often be implemented without removing them from regular classrooms, simply by providing special instructional sessions for them. Itinerant teachers (who travel from class to class) are often used for this purpose.

■ OTHER PROBLEMS

A number of other physical problems in middle childhood sometimes require special education or services. These include diseases and conditions such as muscular dystrophy, cancer, asthma, diabetes, and the absence of one or more limbs, as well as paralysis. Some are congenital, some are caused by infections, and others result from accidents of various kinds. In many cases, serious emotional and social problems are associated with them. As Zigler and Hodapp (1991) note, the handicapped child is often a source of stress in the family—especially in those that are economically disadvantaged or headed by a single parent. As a result, some (though far from all) handicapped children may experience difficulty in being accepted by others and in developing a positive self-concept. Hence, a great deal of what special education programs, parents, and therapists can do for physically exceptional children relates to their emotional and social well-being.

The Physically Gifted

The main emphasis in exceptionality has long been on those individuals whose exceptionalities have placed them at a disadvantage. But there are exceptional individuals at the other end of the spectrum as well. Although increasing attention is being paid to cognitive giftedness, particularly as it is manifested in intellectual and creative endeavors, much less attention has been focused on systematically identifying those who possess exceptional physical skills and on providing special education programs so that these children might develop their "full human potential." Indeed, there is an increasingly noticeable lack of research on the emotional, social, and intellectual characteristics of the physically gifted and on how their development might be enhanced. But we do provide scholarships for those who are inclined toward competitive athletics. (See Summary Table 9.1.)

▲ SUMMARY TABLE 9.1

Important Concepts in Physical and Motor Development, Middle Childhood (Ages 6–12)

CONCEPT	EXPLANATIONS/COMMENTS
Abnormal physical growth	Among under-5-year-olds in the less developed countries of the world: ■ 41% are underweight. ■ 10% suffer from wasting. ■ 50% suffer from stunting.
Normal physical growth	■ Boys are taller and heavier than girls from birth until around 11. ■ Girls have a higher proportion of fat- to fat-free mass. ■ Peak height velocity (growth spurt) occurs earlier for girls (around 11.4) than for boys (around 13.4).
Obesity	■ Characteristic of as many as 20 percent of children in North America. ■ Sometimes serious implications for physical health as well as self-concept, peer relations, and happiness. ■ Linked to overeating, genetics, parental influence, inactivity, and using food as a reward. ■ Can be prevented or lessened through programs on nutrition and exercise.
Diseases	■ About 70 percent of all under-5 children have at least one cold or upper respiratory infection per year. ■ Between ages 5 and 17, rate drops to about 30 percent per year.
Sex differences in motor performance	■ In middle childhood, boys *on average* are stronger than girls, jump higher, throw farther. . . . ■ Girls surpass boys in skills requiring flexibility, balance, and rhythmic movements. ■ These differences relate to heredity as well as cultural interests and expectations.
Physical/sensory problems	■ Children with visual impairment (less than 20/200 vision in better corrected eye defines legal blindness) are often taught in regular classrooms (mainstreamed). ■ Severe hearing impairment poses more serious problems for cognitive development.
Physical giftedness	■ Relatively little attention is paid to identifying the physically gifted and developing their full potential.

■ COGNITIVE DEVELOPMENT: PIAGET'S VIEW

Physical and motor development are two important aspects of development through middle childhood; closely related is intellectual development, one description of which is provided by Jean Piaget in his account of **concrete operations**. Recall that the Piaget child approaches this period by way of the *sensorimotor period* (birth to two years) and two preoperational subperiods: *preconceptual thought* (two to four years) and *intuitive thinking* (four to seven years) (see Table 9.2).

According to Piaget, the child's thinking toward the end of the intuitive stage is egocentric, perception-dominated, and

TABLE 9.2

Piaget's Stages of Cognitive Development

STAGE	APPROXIMATE AGE	SOME MAJOR CHARACTERISTICS*
Sensorimotor*	0–2 years	Intelligence in action. World of the here and now. No language, no thought, no notion of objective reality at beginning of stage.
Preoperational†	2–7 years	Egocentric thought.
Preconceptual	2–4 years	Reason dominated by perception.
Intuitive	4–7 years	Animistic thinking. Intuitive rather than logical solutions. Inability to conserve.
Concrete operations‡	7–11 or 12 years	Ability to conserve. Logic of classes and relations. Understanding of numbers. Thinking bound to concrete. Development of reversibility in thought.
Formal operations§	11 or 12 to 14 or 15 years	Complete generality of thought. Propositional thinking. Ability to deal with the hypothetical. Development of strong idealism.

*Discussed in Chapter 5.
†Discussed in Chapter 7.
‡Discussed in this chapter.
§Discussed in Chapter 11.

intuitive. As a result, it is marked by contradictions and by errors of logic. With the beginning of the period of concrete thought, many of these deficiencies disappear and are replaced by more logical thinking. Recall, however, that although Piaget's descriptions serve to highlight some of the important features of preschooler thinking, they do not always do justice to the child's cognitive achievements. In addition, not only are there tremendous individual variations in performance on the various Piagetian tasks by different children of the same ages, but very minor changes in the tasks used can sometimes lead to very different responses.

The Conservations

Conservation refers to the realization that quantities do not change unless something has been added or taken away. In Chapter 7, for example, we described a situation in which a child is shown two equal balls of modeling clay and asked whether there is still as much clay in each after one has been flattened. The preoperational child's belief that amount has changed because the deformed ball looks different is an example of failure to conserve. The eventual realization that the transformed object does not have more or less substance than it previously had marks not only the acquisition of concepts of conservation but also the transition between preoperational thought and concrete operations.

■ CONSTRUCTING KNOWLEDGE

The significance of the acquisition of conservation is not so much that children are no longer deceived by the problem but rather that they have now developed certain basic logical rules, evident in much of their thinking. That is, in the course of what Kuhn (1984) calls *meaning-making* (or what Piaget called *constructing knowledge*), the child has discovered that a certain logic governs things and relationships—that the game of knowing has rules. These rules make it possible for

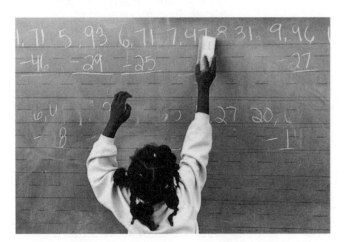

The schoolchild, says Piaget, discovers a new logic to guide thinking and to erase the contradictions and the confusion of earlier developmental stages. But there are important new discoveries yet to come, and tremendous individual variations in the ease and confidence with which different children master them.

children to overcome many of the errors that characterized their thinking during the preoperational period. In a sense, they free the child from reliance on perception and intuition; like some of us, children can now rely on logic. Put another way, they can rely on **operations** (thought processes governed by rules of logic) rather than on **preoperations.**

Just because children now attempt to use logic in constructing knowledge does not mean that they will always respond correctly (Smith, 1993). In fact, one of the most dramatic and clearest illustrations of an incomplete logic used in the construction of knowledge occurs during the late preoperational period and leads to an incorrect answer. When a young child—say, three or four years of age—is asked to draw what the water would look like in a tilted jar, the most common response is, in Thomas and Lohaus's (1993) words, "a scribbling or the like" (p. 9). At this early stage, children lack any clear notion of lines, water levels, and so on. But in response to the same problem, a five- to seven-year-old brings a clever but inappropriate logic to bear on the matter—a logic that, according to Piaget, reflects the child's understanding that the water level in a container is ordinarily parallel to the bottom of the container. The child's drawing is therefore something like that shown on the left side in Figure 9.4—rather than the correct response, which is shown on the right. As Kuhn (1984) points out, the child has never actually seen anything like the drawing on the left. Therefore, it doesn't reflect actual experience with the world as much as the child's attempts to make sense—to construct meaning—out of experience.

Interestingly, later investigations show that almost half of adolescents and adults also fail this water levels task (see Thomas & Lohaus, 1993). They suggest this may be because not all errors on the task are due simply to the absence or misapplication of an appropriate rule (appropriate logic). Some result from what they term field effects—a tendency to be misled by the appearance of the problem. Thus, among many adolescents and adults who fail the problem, the more the jar is tilted, the greater the tendency to make an error.

■ RULES OF LOGIC

Part of constructing knowledge involves a gradual recognition of the logic that governs things. Three rules of logic

FIGURE 9.4

*Young children typically draw fluid level in a tilted jar as shown in **A** rather than **B**—not because they have ever seen anything like **A** in the real world, but because the logic they use in their attempts to make meaning out of their experiences is not always appropriate.*

A   **B**

that are discovered (or invented) during concrete operations are important for the acquisition of conservation: identity, reversibility, and compensation. Each can be illustrated by the conservation-of-quantity problem in which children must decide whether amount has changed in a deformed ball of clay. Children who answer correctly (who have acquired conservation) may be reasoning in one of three ways: Nothing has been added to or taken away from the flattened object, and it must therefore be identical to what it was (**identity**); the pancakelike shape can be reformed into the original ball, in which case the pancake and the ball must contain the same amount (**reversibility**); or the flattened object appears to have more material because it is larger, but its thinness makes up for its diameter (**compensation**).

Once the child has learned about identity, compensation, and reversibility, do the rules apply to all thinking? The answer is no. There are about as many different kinds of conservation as there are characteristics of objects that can vary

in quantity. In addition to conservation of amount (or mass, involving liquids or solids, or discontinuous material like beads, beans, or baubles), there is conservation of number, length, area, volume, and so on. If the rules of logic that make these conservations possible were completely general, they would all be acquired at the same time. When children realize that amount of clay does not change when a ball is flattened, they should also realize that an amount of water does not change when it is poured from a tall, thin vase into a shallow, wide bowl. But, as Figure 9.5 shows, approximate ages at which the various conservations are acquired span several years.

Additional evidence that the child's rules of logic at the concrete operations stage are not completely general are found in what are called *extinction* studies. In these studies, children who have already acquired a specific conservation are given evidence that their reasoning is incorrect. The argument is that if a conserver truly believes that conserva-

FIGURE 9.5

Some simple tests for conservation with approximate ages of attainment.

1. Conservation of substance (6–7 years)

A

The experimenter presents two identical modeling clay balls. The subject admits that they have equal amounts of clay.

B

One of the balls is deformed. The subject is asked whether they still contain equal amounts.

2. Conservation of length (6–7 years)

A

Two sticks are aligned in front of the subject. The subject admits their equality.

B

One of the sticks is moved to the right. The subject is asked whether they are still the same length.

3. Conservation of number (6–7 years)

A

Two rows of counters are placed in one-to-one correspondence. The subject admits their equality.

B

One of the rows is elongated (or contracted). The subject is asked whether each row still has the same number.

4. Conservation of liquids (6–7 years)

A

Two beakers are filled to the same level with water. The subject sees that they are equal

B

The liquid of one container is poured into a tall tube (or a flat dish). The subject is asked whether each still contains the same amount.

5. Conservation of area (9–10 years)

A

The subject and the experimenter each have identical sheets of cardboard. Wooden blocks are placed on these in identical positions. The subject agrees that each cardboard has the same amount of space remaining.

B

The experimenter scatters the blocks on one of the cardboards. The subject is asked whether each cardboard still has the same amount of space remaining.

tion is a logical and necessary consequence, there should be strong resistance to extinction of that logic. To simplify, consider a typical extinction experiment in conservation of weight. First, subjects are presented with two identical clay balls. Conservers agree that both weigh an equal amount and continue to maintain that this is the case, even after one or both of the balls have been deformed or broken into little pieces. At this point, however, the experimenter asks that participants verify their conservation response by means of a balance scale. But it's a trick! The scale is "rigged" so that one of the balls now weighs more than the other.

In more than twenty-five separate extinction experiments, subjects believed evidence that contradicted their original conservation response (Miller, 1981). Young conservers (and sometimes older ones) do not always behave as if they believe these rules of logic to be necessarily true in all relevant cases. However, further questioning of subjects reveals that they don't doubt the certainty of the logical rule but are simply not always clear about when to apply the rule. Miller's (1981) research indicates that even young children realize that social rules, for example, are arbitrary and uncertain but that Piagetian rules of logic are more universal. However, the rigged balance scale presents a real-life problem rather than a problem in logic. Specifically, in this situation, children are not deciding whether the logical rule is correct (they know it is) but whether the scale is correct.

In a similar series of experiments, Winer and McGlone (1993) asked children and college students misleading conservation questions such as "When do you weigh more, when you are walking or running?" Or, after presenting two equal rows of checkers in a conservation of number problem and then spreading one out, they asked, "Who has more, you or I?" Strikingly, some college students show lack of conservation in these circumstances—and even more grade three and six students do likewise. Why? Perhaps, though not likely, because we are acquiescent, suggest Winer and McGlone. Or maybe because subjects are responding to what they think the experimenter means rather than says ("She probably means 'Who looks like they have more?' rather than 'Who actually has more?'"). Or, most likely, this simply illustrates that both children and adults are capable of thinking at various levels of sophistication; even after we have learned a dozen elegant rules of logic, we don't always behave as though we had.

Acceleration of Conservation

Some researchers and educators have been keenly interested in the question of whether the intellectual abilities described by Piaget can be taught. The assumption is that teaching Piagetian concepts might provide a way of speeding up the developmental process, increasing children's cognitive capabilities, and maybe even making them more intelligent. Thus, many researchers have looked at the possibility of accelerating the development of concepts of conservation—concepts that are simply defined, easy to measure, and highly significant in general cognitive development. But the results have

generally been mixed, with many researchers failing to bring about significant change, while others have reported some success, especially with children with delayed development (see, for example, Campbell & Ramey, 1990; Perry, Pasnak, & Holt, 1992). The evidence does not support the conclusion that development can be altered easily and significantly through short-term training programs. Conservation can be accelerated, but training programs need to be detailed and systematic, especially if the children are still some distance from acquiring conservation naturally (Furth, 1980). Whether such efforts, when successful, contribute significantly to intellectual development—or to happiness and self-esteem—remains unclear.

Classes, Seriation, and Number

During concrete operations, children not only acquire various conservations, but also acquire or improve three other abilities.

CLASSES

For example, they achieve the capacity to understand **class** inclusion and to reason about the composition and decomposition of classes. Ten-year-old Anna scoffs at the ridiculous simplicity of a question that asks whether there are more roses or more flowers in a bouquet of fifteen roses and five tulips. She now understands that roses make up a subclass of the larger class, flowers. Similarly, she has little difficulty multiplying two classes in the problem "If there are black balls and white balls, and some are large while others are small, how many different kinds of balls are there?" (The answer is illustrated in Interactive Figure 9.6.) Tom, her five-year-old brother, on the other hand, does not easily understand this problem. Nor can he answer the flowers problem correctly. But he too, as we saw in Chapter 7, demonstrates some ability to deal with class inclusion problems when he answers the following problem correctly: "A Siamese is a cat but not an alley cat. Is a Siamese an animal?"

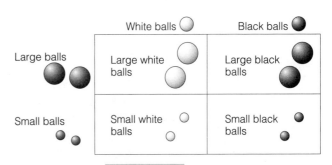

INTERACTIVE FIGURE 9.6

Suppose X comes in exactly two shapes, each of which can be either black or white. How many different X's are there? Right. There are four. The concrete operations child may have some difficulty with this simple classification problem because it's too abstract. X is not concrete enough. The problem is simpler if we ask, instead, "How many kinds of balls do we have if we have big and small black ones, and big and small white ones?" Such a problem can be used to test a child's ability to classify objects.

A second achievement of the period of concrete operations is an understanding of **seriation** (ordering in sequence). One of Piaget's seriation tasks involves presenting the child with a series of objects—for example, a group of dolls, each a different length so that the objects can be arranged from longest to shortest. The bottom row of Figure 9.7 illustrates the arrangement desired, quickly produced by the child in concrete operations. A typical preoperational response to this problem is to place several of the dolls in order while ignoring the fact that others may fit in between those that have already been positioned. If the next doll the child selects is too short to be placed where the child intended it to be (at the upper end), it is placed without hesitation at the other end, even though it might be taller or shorter than the doll that is already positioned there. The child does not understand that if *A* is greater than *B,* and *B* is greater than *C,* then *A* must also be greater than *C.* Understanding this concept eliminates the necessity of making all the comparisons that would otherwise be necessary.

■ NUMBER

Understanding seriation also makes a more complete understanding of number possible because the **ordinal properties** of numbers (their ordered sequence—first, second, third, and so on) depend on a knowledge of seriation. Similarly, the **cardinal properties** of numbers (their quantitative properties—the fact that they represent collections of different magnitude) depend on a knowledge of classification. As we saw in Chapter 7, many preschool children already have an impressive knowledge of number, a fact Piaget largely overlooked as he searched for the limitations of preoperational versus operational thought.

A Summary of Concrete Operations

An operation is a thought that is characterized by rules of logic. Because children acquire conservation early in this period, and because these concepts are manifestations of operational thinking, the period is called operational. It is concrete because children's thinking deals with real objects or those they can easily imagine. Children in the concrete operations stage are bound to the real world; they don't yet have the freedom made possible by the more advanced logic of the formal operations stage: freedom to contemplate the hypothetical, to compare the ideal with the actual, to be profoundly unhappy and concerned about the discrepancy between this world and that which they imagine possible. (See Summary Table 9.3.)

■ THE CHILD'S MEMORY

In Piaget's view of the child's cognitive development, the emphasis is on the discovery (construction) of logic. Memory, claims Piaget, reflects how much knowledge the child has about logical rules (Reyna, 1996). A somewhat different emphasis in cognitive development looks not at the construction or discovery of reality so much as at the *processes* by which children learn and remember. This emphasis defines what is sometimes labeled the **information-processing approach.**

The Information-Processing Approach

It begins, as all views of the developing person must, with the observation that a newborn infant is very different from

FIGURE **9.7**

A test of a child's understanding of seriation. The elements of the series are presented in random order, and the child is asked to rearrange them in sequence of height. The top row was arranged by a 3½-year-old, the bottom by an 8-year-old.

Some Characteristics of Concrete Operational Thinking

An operation is a thought subject to certain rules of logic—hence a *logical* thought. The development of operations is the major achievement of the concrete operations period (roughly ages seven to eleven or twelve). But the logic that defines these operations tends to be applied to real, *concrete* objects and events rather than to more abstract situations—hence the label *concrete operations*.

NEW DEVELOPMENTS	EXPLANATIONS/OBSERVATIONS
Ability to conserve	Defined as the realization that certain quantities don't change unless something is added or taken away.
	Depends on and illustrates three rules of logic:
	■ **Identity:** nothing has been added or taken away; hence, quantity is unchanged.
	■ **Reversibility:** whatever has been done can be undone to prove that quantity has not changed.
	■ **Compensation:** misleading perceptual features are compensated for by other equally misleading but opposite perceptual features.
	Concepts of conservation cannot easily be taught prior to the time they would be acquired naturally.
Reasoning about classes	■ Abstract understanding that breaking a class into subclasses does not destroy the parent class.
Number knowledge	■ Ability to reason about classes is reflected in clearer understanding of ordinal (first, second, third . . .) and cardinal (one, two, three . . .) properties of number.

an older child—or an adult. Among other things, infants do not know that day follows night, which itself follows day; that butterflies whisper to each other when they perch on buttercups in the sunshine; or that tigers have tails. In fact, they are strangers to their very own hands and feet, strangers to the world. These things are not familiar to them. And, as Rheingold (1985) points out, the process of development is a process of becoming familiar with the world.

The difference between the newborn, who is almost totally unfamiliar with everything around, and the older child, who has learned about tigers, tautologies, and tarantulas, can be described in a number of ways. We can say, with Piaget, that the developing child, through the processes of assimilation and accommodation, has constructed a sort of reality that conforms, more or less, to certain logical rules, which, in turn, characterize and make possible a sequence of orderly stages.

Or we can say that the developing child begins with no **knowledge base,** few strategies for dealing with cognitive material, and no awareness of the self as a knower or as a

processor of information. This approach permits us to view development as the business of acquiring a knowledge base, developing **cognitive strategies,** and gradually developing an awareness of self as a knower. This is an information-processing approach to cognitive development.

Accordingly, the information-processing approach looks at three things: the knowledge base and its creation, the processes and strategies by which information becomes part of the knowledge base or is retrieved from it, and the emergence of the child's awareness of self as a player of what Flavell (1985) calls *the game of cognition*. The first two of these relate to human memory because the individual's knowledge base is made up of what is in memory, and the strategies that enable the child to develop and use a knowledge base are those that permit adding things to or retrieving things from memory. The third component, the recognition of the self as a knower capable of using and evaluating strategies, involves what is termed **metacognition.** Literally, *metacognition* refers to knowing about knowing.

The Structure of Memory

The information-processing model views the child as a consumer and processor of information—as a little organism that sheds its ignorance as it builds up a store of memories. The most common description of this model is based on the work of Atkinson and Shiffrin (1971), which describes three types of information storage: sensory memory, short-term memory (also called *working memory*), and long-term memory. Each of these is distinguished primarily by the amount and nature of processing that it involves. The term *processing* refers to mental activities such as sorting, analyzing, rehearsing, and summarizing (see Figure 9.8).

■ SENSORY MEMORY

Sensory memory refers mainly to sensation—the momentary impressions associated with sensory stimulation. It requires virtually no cognitive processing. You cannot, at every moment, be aware of all the sights, sounds, tastes, smells, and feelings that are immediately possible—that require only that you pay attention. Hence, most of the sensory stimulation that surrounds us is not processed at all but has only a fleeting (less than one second) and unconscious effect on memory.

■ SHORT-TERM MEMORY

Your ability to recall the beginning of a sentence as you read it illustrates **short-term memory** (or working memory). If you can't remember the beginning of the sentence, it is usually because you aren't paying attention. In a sense, then, short-term memory is equivalent to **attention span.** Attention span has two main limitations: First, its capacity in adults appears to be limited to about seven items (plus or minus two; Miller, 1956); second, it seems to hold material only for seconds rather than minutes.

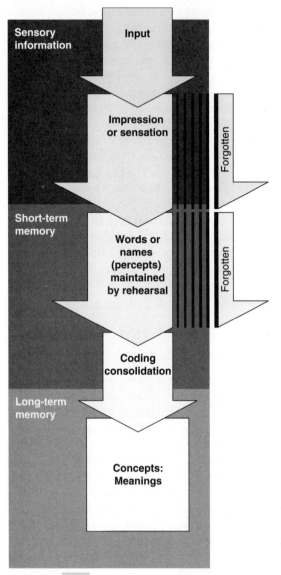

Sensory information — Input

Impression or sensation — Forgotten

Short-term memory — Words or names (percepts) maintained by rehearsal — Forgotten

Coding consolidation

Long-term memory — Concepts: Meanings

FIGURE 9.8

The three components of memory. Sensory information first enters sensory memory. From there it may go into short-term memory, where it is available as a name or word, for example, as long as it is rehearsed. Some of the material in short-term memory may then be coded for long-term storage, where it might take the form of meanings and concepts. These three components of memory do not refer to three different locations in the brain or other parts of the nervous system, but to how we remember—or, more precisely, how we study memory. (From Guy R. Lefrançois, Theories of Human Learning: Kro's Report *[3rd ed.]. [Pacific Grove, CA, 1995]. Copyright © 1995, 1982, 1972 by Brooks/Cole Publishing, a Division of International Thomson Publishing Inc. Reprinted by permission of the publisher.)*

But these storage limitations are not as serious as they might seem. Although we seem to be able to attend to only about seven items at once, a process called **chunking** (grouping items into related units) can be used to increase memory capacity significantly. Miller (1956) illustrates chunking by reference to a change purse that can hold only seven coins. If you put seven pennies into this purse, its capacity is seven cents. However, if you fill it with seven groupings (chunks) of coins, such as nickels, dimes, or quarters, its capacity increases dramatically.

A common measure of short-term memory is to have subjects try to repeat a sequence of unrelated numbers they have just heard—a task that is used on a number of intelligence tests. Average adolescents and adults are able to repeat correctly six or seven (or sometimes even nine) digits. In contrast, six-year-olds will typically succeed in repeating only two or so.

The child's limited working memory may be very important in explaining some aspects of cognitive development. Siegler (1989), for example, suggests that children are often unable to solve certain problems simply because they cannot keep in mind all relevant information simultaneously. And Case (Case et al., 1988) claims that the most important constraint on the child's ability to understand and solve problems is simply a limitation on short-term storage space.

Sensory memory, as we saw, does not involve cognitive processing but is a fleeting impression, almost like an echo. In contrast, short-term memory is highly dependent upon rehearsal or repetition. When I look up and dial a new telephone number, by the time I have finished dialing, I will usually no longer remember the number.

LONG-TERM MEMORY

But if I think I might need the number again tomorrow, there are several things I can do. One is to write it down so that I will not have to remember it. That would impose little cognitive strain. I would not have to use any of the strategies required to move material from short-term to long-term storage. Still, it would require the use of **long-term memory;** tomorrow I would have to remember not only that I made a note of the number but also where the note is. And I would have to remember a tremendous range of other information as well, including how to translate telephone numbers into the orderly and sequential act of dialing, how to speak and listen with a telephone, and so on. Put another way, even as habitual a behavior as using a telephone requires a tremendous knowledge base. And our knowledge base is, in effect, our long-term memory. It includes everything we know—about ourselves, about the world, about knowing.

Long-term memory has three important characteristics. First, it is highly stable. What you can remember today of what you learned in high school, you are relatively likely to remember tomorrow or next week, or next year.

Second, long-term memory appears to be generative rather than simply reproductive. That is, we remember main ideas, termed **gist memory,** and tend to generate (make up) details on the basis of our knowledge of **scripts**—that is, our knowledge of what goes with what, of what ordinarily follows what. Research on children's memories indicates that they, too, tend to fill in gaps according to their personal scripts. In one study, Johnson, Bransford, and Solomon (1973) presented subjects with the following short passage:

John was trying to fix the birdhouse. He was pounding the nail when his father came out to watch him and to help him do the work.

Memories that we can put into words, like how to divide numbers or our telephone numbers, define explicit (or declarative) memory. But many of the things we know are implicit (or nondeclarative). How to do the perfect double-twisting somersault is one of those implicit memories; so, too, is how to do the primitive, double-legged, twisted frog-dive.

When subjects were later shown these sentences along with others, one of which was

John was using the hammer to fix the birdhouse when his father came out to watch and to help him do the work.

they overwhelmingly agreed that they had seen the last sentence rather than the two that they had actually seen. Note that the hammer was not even mentioned in the original text. It seems that participants recalled the central ideas of the two sentences and "generated" the hammer because hammers are what we use to pound nails. Their birdhouse-building scripts, like yours and mine, use hammers.

The third characteristic of long-term memory is that understanding facilitates remembering—as would be expected

given that we tend to "generate" on the basis of our understanding. Paris and Lindauer (1976) asked children to remember the simple sentence "The workman dug a hole in the ground," adding "with a shovel" for half their subjects. One of the recall procedures was to present subjects with cue words (in this case, *shovel*). Significantly, the word *shovel* served equally well as a cue for children who had not seen the word in the original sentence. Clearly, the cue word would have been totally meaningless for children who did not initially understand that holes can be dug with shovels. (Some of the characteristics of these three components of memory are summarized in Table 9.4.)

Four Types of Long-Term Memory

When the centipede was asked how it managed to walk with its many legs, it was stunned to realize it had never really thought about the problem. It just simply knew how. But, the story goes, it now began to think about it, trying to understand the process, to figure out which leg moved where, when, which next, and on and on until, finally, the poor thing wound up totally confused and helpless, its legs wrapped in dozens of little knots.

■ DECLARATIVE VERSUS NONDECLARATIVE MEMORY

There is much that we, too, know not consciously or in words, but perhaps in our muscles or maybe in some unconscious part of our nervous systems—things like how to ride a bicycle, or our unthinking reactions to things that frighten or excite us. Memories of this kind are labeled **nondeclarative memory** or **implicit memory** (simply because they can't be put into words).

In contrast, memories relating to our addresses, people's names, the meanings of words, and so on *can* be put into words. Such memories make up **declarative memory**, also called **explicit memory**. The main distinction between declarative and nondeclarative memory, explain Squire, Knowlton, and Musen (1993), is that declarative memory is *conscious*

Source: From G. R. Lefrançois (1997). *Psychology for teaching* (9th ed.). Belmont, CA: Wadsworth, p. 165.

TABLE 9.4

Three Levels of Memory

	SENSORY	SHORT-TERM	LONG-TERM
Alternate Labels	Echoic or iconic	Primary or working	Secondary
Duration	Less than 1 second	Less than 20 seconds	Indefinite
Stability	Fleeting	Easily disrupted	Not easily disrupted
Capacity	Limited	Limited (7±2 items)	Unlimited
General Characteristics	Momentary, unconscious impression	Working memory; immediate consciousness; active, maintained by rehearsal	Knowledge base; associationistic; passive; the result of encoding

memory for facts and events; nondeclarative memory is *unconscious* memory.

SEMANTIC VERSUS EPISODIC MEMORY

There appear to be at least two distinct types of declarative long-term memory, explains Tulving (1991). On the one hand, there is stable, abstract, general knowledge about the world—the sort of knowledge you need to understand language, for example. This type of declarative knowledge makes up **semantic memory.** In addition to this general, abstract body of long-term memories, each of us has a large store of personal memories—memories of things that have happened to us personally, of little episodes in our lives. These memories make up **episodic memory.** Episodic memory is autobiographical knowledge. (See Figure 9.9 for a summary of the different types of and labels for long-term memory.)

Main Processes in Long-Term Memory

Three basic processes are involved in remembering: rehearsing, elaborating, and organizing.

REHEARSING

Rehearsing involves repetition and is important in maintaining information in short-term memory as well as in transferring material from short- to long-term storage. The simplest rehearsal strategy is to name the material (five, five, five, one, two, one, two) over and over again until it seems unlikely that it will escape. Most children younger than five do not rehearse in order to remember and cannot easily be taught to

do so (Wellman, 1990). In fact, the majority do not spontaneously rehearse until the age of seven or eight.

ELABORATING

To elaborate is to extend material or add something to it to make it more memorable. For example, **elaborating** might consist of forming associations between new material and existing knowledge, or of forming mental images that go beyond (elaborate on) the actual material. Elaboration that relates to the meaning of what is being learned seems most effective. Bradshaw and Anderson (1982) had children try to recall sentences such as "The fat man read the sign." Those who elaborated this sentence to something like "The fat man read the sign warning of thin ice" significantly improved their ability to remember that the man in question was fat. Younger children do not spontaneously elaborate to improve their recall. By age twelve, however, most have learned that certain strategies are better than others and have begun to use them deliberately.

ORGANIZING

Organizing refers to grouping and relating material. Chunking material into related groups is one example of organization. Assume, for example, that you have been asked to memorize the following list as rapidly as you can: pencil, horse, pen, house, barn, cat, apartment building, bear, typewriter. Some of you will immediately notice that the list can easily be organized into three groups of related items (animals, dwellings, writing instruments) and will use this organization to help remember the items. Interestingly, young children will not spontaneously organize material the way

FIGURE **9.9**

Different types and labels for long-term memory. Researchers describe different long-term memory systems that are distinguishable in terms of the kind of material stored in each. (From Guy R. Lefrançois, Theories of Learning: Kro's Report *[3rd ed.]. [Pacific Grove, CA: Brooks/Cole, 1995], p. 263.)*

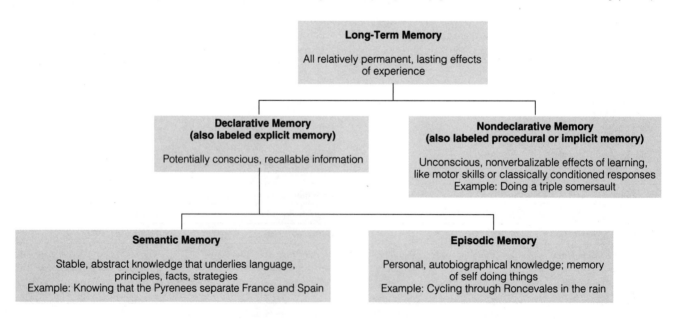

you would. Their use of strategies is more limited than yours; they know less about knowing.

Developmental Changes in Memory

An information-processing model of memory is particularly useful for looking at the development of memory because it leads to several predictions about infant and child memory that can be tested directly. For example, we would expect that for the types of memory that involve little cognitive processing, young children might not perform very differently from older children or adults, but that where processing strategies are necessary, there would be more differences between them.

SENSORY AND SHORT-TERM MEMORY

In general, research supports this prediction: Recall that does not depend on strategies does not appear to change very much as the child develops. For example, recognition memory, a task that does not ordinarily involve complex strategies, is highly accurate from early childhood on (Nelson, 1993). Similarly, comparisons between adults and children with respect to sensory and short-term memories—neither of which requires any strategy more elaborate than simple repetition—have found few significant differences. Apparently, short-term and sensory memory change little from childhood to adulthood because they do not require the use of elaborate or cognitively demanding strategies.

LONGER-TERM MEMORY

Recall that is highly dependent on the use of strategies should improve as the infant's recognition and understanding of strategies improves. This prediction is also supported by the evidence. As we saw earlier, very young children don't rehearse and organize as systematically as do older children. Paris and Lindauer (1982) note that research has found significant developmental changes in memory under at least four sets of circumstances: when the memory task requires intentional memorization, when the material is unfamiliar, when specific organizational strategies are required, and when the task requires a change in the learner's strategies.

Not surprisingly, research indicates that children become progressively better at remembering as they get older. Between the ages of five and ten, for example, they make progressively fewer errors in tasks that require them to identify facial photographs that they have seen for anywhere from 5 to 20 seconds (Davies, 1993). Nevertheless, they consistently make more errors on these sorts of tasks than do adults, who find facial recognition very easy.

It isn't clear that children become better memorizers as they age solely because they develop better memory strategies. There is at least one other reason, argues Reyna (1996): It's simply that they *know* more. We have understood for some time, for example, that experts in specific fields are far better at remembering things that relate to those fields. Thus, chess masters can recall chess positions with an accuracy that non-

chess experts find amazing. In much the same way, as children learn more about certain domains, their memories in those domains increase dramatically. In fact, when younger children know significantly more than older children in a specific area, they can outperform them on memory tests for newly presented material relating to that area.

CHILDREN AS WITNESSES

But how do younger children fare as witnesses in courts of law, where children are increasingly being called upon to testify in various cases, many of which have to do with abuse? How accurate and reliable is their testimony? How well do they actually remember? Unfortunately, there are no simple rules by which courts can determine whether a child's testimony is reliable. Like adult witnesses, who sometimes remember things that have never happened, children, too, often misremember or can be led to remember things that never happened (Hayes & Delamothe, 1997).

Davies (1993) reviewed a large number of studies that have looked at children's memories. Among other things, these studies lead to some important observations. First, the younger the child, the less the amount of information provided. Interestingly, however, the proportion of errors (of actual misinformation) stays relatively constant from childhood to adulthood. But adult recollections typically include far more detail.

Second, children are remarkably poor at judging people's ages, although they are more willing to estimate age than other physical characteristics, like weight or height. Before age ten, children seem not to be very aware of the sorts of cues that adults use for estimating age. Thus, adults can easily arrange in order photographs of a single individual taken at different ages, a task that young children typically fail.

Third, after age six, children often perform about as well as adult witnesses in tasks that require them to identify a "criminal" from an array of photographs. A common study exposes "witnesses" to a staged event and later asks them to select a "perpetrator" from a series of photos, or from an actual lineup of possible perpetrators. In seven different studies reviewed by Davies, very young children (three-year-olds) did more poorly than older children and adults. In general, however, older children and adults were about equally accurate, although accuracy ranged from very low in some studies (17 percent) to almost perfect in others.

Fourth, although young children are about as likely as adults to correctly identify a perpetrator, they are significantly more likely to *incorrectly* identify a suspect when the perpetrator is not present either in a photograph or in a lineup (Dekle et al., 1996).

Fifth, delays between the enactment of a crime and the testing of children's recollections do not seem to significantly reduce the accuracy of a child's memory.

It's important to note that the results of studies of children as witnesses are not entirely consistent. Although they indicate that children's memories improve with age, they also show that the elementary schoolchild's reliability as a witness is not significantly poorer than that of an older child, or even of an adult. In Davies's (1993) words, "Thus, to use the results of studies that have simply found significant developmental effects as a reason for excluding children from giving testimony would be quite wrong" (p. 152). However, appearing in court can be a highly stressful experience for child witnesses, particularly when they are victims. Some jurisdictions go to considerable effort to prepare child witnesses and have enacted laws to protect them from the sorts of cross-examination procedures that might be employed with adult witnesses (Sas, Wolfe, & Gowdey, 1996). In some jurisdictions—for example, Scotland—child witnesses are sometimes allowed to testify in surroundings more friendly than a courtroom, perhaps with parents or other supportive individuals present, while their testimony is transmitted to the courtroom via video (Flin, Kearney, & Murray, 1996).

Metacognition and Metamemory

In general, younger children are less capable of organizing material to facilitate their recall; in addition, they seem to be less aware of the importance of doing so (Short, Schatschneider, & Friebert, 1993). In other words, they seem to know less about knowing—to understand less about understanding. They are not reflective about themselves as knowers and seem not to have recognized the special skills that allow them to know and remember: They still lack the skills of **metacognition**—the skills that would allow them to monitor their progress, to estimate the effects of their efforts to learn, and to predict their likelihood of success in remembering. The skills of metacognition are what tell us that there are ways to organize material so that it will be easier to learn and remember, that there are rehearsal and review strategies that are more effective for one kind of learning than another, and that some kinds of learning require the deliberate application of cognitive strategies. Because memory is inseparably linked with cognition, metacognition includes what is sometimes termed **metamemory**—knowing about remembering.

Metacognitive skills seem to be largely absent in younger children. This does not mean that they use no memory or learning strategies; it simply means that they are not aware of them—that they do not consciously apply them. When Moynahan (1973) asked young children whether it would be easier to learn a categorized list of words or a random list, children below the third grade selected either list; children in the third grade were more likely to select the categorized list. Paradoxically, even when children are capable of engaging in useful memory strategies, they often do not. Hence, it may be important to teach children when and how to use the strategies, as well as the strategies themselves (Mayo, 1993).

Mulcahy (1991) points out that teachers are often not very systematic about teaching memory skills and other cognitive strategies. As a result, children are usually left to decide on their own whether a strategy should be used, what strategy, when, and how. Not surprisingly, then, they often know about a strategy but do not spontaneously use it.

Teaching Cognitive Strategies

Teachers have traditionally not taught cognitive strategies systematically in schools. Instead, they simply assume that students will learn them incidentally. However, a number of programs have been designed to teach children cognitive strategies (see Royer, Cisero, & Carlo, 1993). For example, Mulcahy (1991) uses a Socratic dialogue question-and-answer teaching method to lead students to a recognition of their own cognitive strategies. Similarly, Collins, Brown, and Newman (1989) suggest a *cognitive apprenticeship* approach where **mentors** (parents, teachers, peers, siblings) serve as both models and teachers. The object is to provide learners with cognitive strategies so that they are equipped to explore, organize, discover, and learn on their own. Research makes it plain, claim Perkins, Jay, and Tishman (1993), that instruction in the skills that define metacognition can significantly improve learning and memory.

The Game of Cognition

Metacognition and metamemory deal with our knowledge about how we know—our awareness of ourselves as players of what Flavell calls the game of cognition. The object of the game of cognition is to pay attention, to learn, to remember, to retrieve from memory, and to do a variety of things such as sorting, analyzing, synthesizing, evaluating, and creating.

There is more than one way to play the game of cognition. Some people play it very badly. They learn slowly, remember inaccurately, and seem lost and clumsy when faced with tasks requiring evaluation, synthesis, or creation. Others play the game very well. Their responses are quick and accurate, their syntheses elegant, their creations startling.

Children do not play the game of cognition as well as adults. Why? Research reviewed in this section suggests at least four reasons: Children do not have (or do not use) strategies that are as effective, they lack basic knowledge about the world, their metamemory skills (their awareness of the need to monitor, to evaluate, to use strategies) are absent or less well developed, and their short-term memory capacity is more limited. These four factors, says Peverly (1991), account for the development of memory. They are the tools of intelligence. (See Summary Table 9.5.)

INTELLIGENCE

"Intelligence is what the tests test," Boring (1923, p. 35) informed us. This simple definition of what is not a simple concept is useful and not entirely tongue-in-cheek. Weight is not a simple concept either. Yet to say that weight is what a scale measures is useful and accurate. A butcher need not know the scientific definition of weight to use the scales. Perhaps a psychologist or a teacher need not know what intelligence is to make use of the results of intelligence tests.

▲ SUMMARY TABLE 9.5

Important Concepts
in Memory Development

CONCEPT	EXPLANATIONS/COMMENTS
Information-processing approach	An approach to understanding intellectual processes that looks at how individuals acquire, process, and remember information. It is concerned with three things: ■ **Knowledge base:** storehouse of information (knowledge). ■ **Cognitive strategies:** processes used for learning and remembering. ■ **Metacognition:** individual's awareness of self as a processor of information, and awareness of processes used in acquiring and remembering information.
Sensory memory	■ Fleeting (less than one second). ■ Momentary sensory impression.
Short-term memory	■ Also called *working memory*. ■ Less than 20 seconds' duration. ■ Easily disrupted. ■ Defines attention span (7±2 items). ■ Active; maintained by rehearsal.
Long-term memory	■ Indefinite duration. ■ Not easily disrupted. ■ Unlimited. ■ Defines *knowledge base:* all relatively permanent, lasting effects of experience. ■ Results from active memory processes such as rehearsing, organizing, elaborating.
Memory strategies	■ **Rehearsing:** repeating over and over and. . . . ■ **Organizing:** grouping related items; comparing and contrasting. ■ **Elaborating:** linking with related ideas; expanding.
Types of long-term memory	■ **Declarative:** also termed *explicit:* potentially conscious, recallable information. ■ **Nondeclarative:** also termed *implicit;* unconscious, nonverbalizable, like motor skills. ■ **Semantic:** type of declarative memory; stable, abstract knowledge of things, facts, principles. . . . ■ **Episodic:** type of declarative memory; personal, autobiographical; memory of self doing things.
Developmental changes in memory	■ Sensory and short-term memory, which don't depend on strategies, don't change much with age although short-term memory capacity increases. ■ Long-term memory improves with development of memory strategies, expansion of knowledge base, expansion of short-term memory capacity, and development of awareness of self as knower and of strategies as useful tools (metamemory).

Then again, perhaps we do need to know, because there is a fundamental difference between measuring weight and measuring intelligence. We agree about weight; we know what it is. We define it precisely, and our scales measure accurately: They measure exactly what they are supposed to measure and nothing else (they are **valid**). And they measure consistently, yielding the same measurement for the same weights over and over again (they are **reliable**).

Approaches to Defining *Intelligence*

But we don't know exactly what intelligence is. Some theorists argue that it is a quality of human functioning that depends on some basic, general capacity or trait in the person—that if you have a lot of this general something (referred to as *g*), your behavior will be intelligent. In contrast to this **general factor theory**, some theorists believe that intelligence is split into several separate abilities like memory or reasoning or mathematical computation skills. This approach is labeled **special abilities theory**.

■ FLUID AND CRYSTALLIZED ABILITIES

One view that is especially useful for our purposes combines these two approaches: It is that advanced by Cattell (1971). On the one hand, he explains, there are certain abilities that seem to underlie much of our intelligent behavior—a sort of a general factor. He labels these abilities **fluid abilities** (or fluid intelligence). Fluid abilities are reflected in the individual's ability to solve abstract problems and in measures of general reasoning, memory, attention span, and analysis of figures. Because these abilities are not learned, they are relatively unaffected by context.

In contrast to these basic fluid abilities is a grouping of intellectual abilities that are mainly verbal and that are highly influenced by culture, experience, and education. These **crystallized abilities** (crystallized intelligence) are reflected in measures of vocabulary, general information, and arithmetic skills.

Several developmental predictions can be based on the notion of fluid and crystallized intelligence. First, because fluid intelligence is independent of experience, it should remain constant throughout most of development, perhaps increasing slightly as the nervous system matures through childhood and adolescence, and maybe decreasing somewhat in old age as the nervous system ages. Second, because crystallized intelligence is highly dependent on experience, it should increase with increasing experience, perhaps right through old age. These predictions have received some support (Kaufman et al., 1996). (See Chapters 15 and 17.)

■ A CONTEXTUAL APPROACH

A second view that is useful in a study of the human lifespan is that of Sternberg (1984), who sees intelligence as a quality of human functioning best defined in terms of the context in which it occurs. In this **contextual theory of**

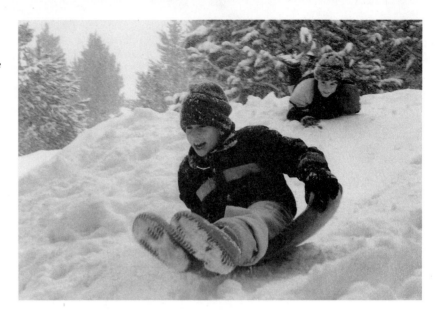

Although psychologists present a staggering array of different definitions for intelligence, most agree that it is a quality that contributes to adaptation in a real-life, practical sense. Thus, to use a lid to slide down the hill when the old sled has busted itself against a tree may be a very intelligent thing to do. Avoiding the tree in the future might be even more intelligent.

intelligence, intelligence is what makes adaptation possible, and adaptation occurs in specific contexts. Thus, certain behaviors may be highly intelligent in one context but quite unintelligent in others. In Sternberg's (1984) words, intelligence is the "purposive selection and shaping of and adaptation to real-world environments relevant to one's life" (p. 312).

How do we find out what intelligence is in a particular context? One way, according to Sternberg, is to ask people. In North American cultures, for example, people might tell you that the most intelligent individuals are those who have high practical problem-solving ability, high verbal ability, and a high level of social competence. Elsewhere, the definition might be somewhat different.

Another way of looking at intelligence, Sternberg (1985) suggests, is to look at its three major components: *metacomponents*, *performance components*, and *knowledge-acquisition components*.

The **metacomponents** are the cognitive strategies of which we spoke earlier. This component of intelligence includes what we have been discussing as metacognition or metamemory. Thus, it includes skills involved in planning, monitoring, and evaluating cognitive performance.

Performance components relate to actually doing—in contrast to the metacomponents, which are involved in selecting problems and procedures, responding to feedback, changing procedures, and so on. Put another way, the metacomponents of intellectual functioning define its executive functions—its decision-making functions. *Performance* refers simply to the execution of decisions made at the metacomponent level. Thus, performance components include actual activities such as reasoning, rehearsing, encoding, analyzing, and remembering.

The **knowledge-acquisition component** refers to what is actually achieved in the process of learning. It includes processes used in acquiring information, such as separating the important from the unimportant, organizing, and comparing new with old information (see Figure 9.10).

> Intelligence is adaptation to real-world environments and involves selecting and shaping the environment using the three components of intelligent activity.

● **Metacomponents**

Executive skills involved in planning, monitoring, and evaluating cognitive activity

● **Performance components**

Processes actually used in carrying out tasks, such as encoding, inductive reasoning, and remembering

● **Knowledge-acquisition components**

Processes used in acquiring new information, such as separating important from unimportant information (selective encoding), relating items of information (selective combination), and comparing new information with old (selective comparison)

FIGURE 9.10

Sternberg's contextual view of intelligence and the three components of intelligence.

Multiple Intelligences

Cattell's description of fluid and crystallized intelligence, and Sternberg's description of the components of intelligence have one very important thing in common: Both emphasize that intelligence is an activity—an information-processing activity. This contrasts sharply with the older view that intelligence is a quantity or a mysterious quality that some people have a great deal of, and others not so much. The view that intelligence is an activity (or a collection of activities) opens up the possibility that it can be improved through training and practice.

It's also important to recognize not only that intelligence is an activity, but that it can be manifested in different areas. In fact, suggests Gardner (1983) in his **theory of multiple intelligences,** we don't have one but rather *seven* different kinds of intelligence, each relatively independent from the other: logical–mathematical, linguistic, musical, spatial, bodily–kinesthetic, interpersonal, and intrapersonal (see Table 9.6).

Most of our experience in measuring intelligence, notes Gardner (1993), has been in the area of mathematical, linguistic, and logical tasks. This view of multiple intelligences requires the development of new tasks to tap previously ignored areas. It suggests as well that educational experiences have sometimes been too narrow—that they may have overlooked the development of one or more of our *intelligences.*

Measuring Intelligence

The principal use of intelligence tests is for prediction. An intelligence test score is, in effect, a prediction that an individual will do well (or not do well) on tasks that require intelligence, like passing a grade or succeeding in college.

Among the most widely used intelligence tests are the Stanford-Binet and the Wechsler. These are **individual intelligence tests;** they can be administered to only one child at a time and only by a trained tester. Hence, they are quite expensive, but they yield a richer picture of intellectual functioning than do **group intelligence tests**—tests that can be administered to a large group at one time and that are commonly of a paper-and-pencil variety.

The Stanford-Binet yields scores in four areas: verbal reasoning, quantitative reasoning, abstract/visual reasoning, and short-term memory. It also provides a composite score that is described as a measure of "adaptive ability" and that can be interpreted as an **Intelligence Quotient (IQ).** The IQ derives its meaning from the fact that we know that the average IQ of large, unselected populations is around 100 and that it is distributed as shown in Interactive Figure 9.11. Note that approximately two thirds of all individuals have measured IQs that range between 85 and 115. Fewer than 2.5 percent score above 130 or below 70.

The Wechsler Intelligence Scale for Children (3d ed., 1991), also called the WISC-III, yields a composite IQ score comparable to that obtained with the Stanford-Binet. The tests differ in several important ways, however. Most notably, the WISC-III also yields separate standardized scores for various subjects, as well as a verbal IQ and a performance IQ (in addition to the composite IQ). Deficiencies in language background are sometimes apparent in discrepancies between verbal and performance scores.

Wechsler tests are also available for adults (WAIS-R: Wechsler Adult Intelligence Scale Revised, ages 16 to 75) and for preschool children (WPPSI: Wechsler Preschool and

TABLE 9.6

Howard Gardner's Seven Intelligences

INTELLIGENCE	POSSIBLE OCCUPATIONS	CORE COMPONENTS
Logical–Mathematical	Scientist Mathematician	Sensitivity to and capacity to discern logical or numerical patterns; ability to handle long chains of reasoning.
Linguistic	Poet Journalist	Sensitivity to the sounds, rhythms, and meanings of words; sensitivity to the different functions of language.
Musical	Composer Violinist	Abilities to produce and appreciate rhythm, pitch, and timbre; appreciation of the forms of musical expressiveness.
Spatial	Navigator Sculptor	Capacities to perceive the visual–spatial world accurately and to manipulate the mental representations that result.
Bodily–Kinesthetic	Dancer Athlete	Abilities to control one's body movements and to handle objects skillfully.
Interpersonal	Therapist Salesperson	Capacities to discern and respond appropriately to the moods, temperaments, motivations, and desires of other people.
Intrapersonal	Person with detailed accurate self-knowledge	Access to one's own feelings and the ability to discriminate among them and draw upon them to guide behavior; knowledge of one's own strengths, weaknesses, desires, and intelligences.

Source: From H. Gardner and T. Hatch (1989). Multiple intelligences go to school: Educational implications of the theory of multiple intelligences. *Educational Researcher,* Vol. 18, No. 8, pp. 4–10.

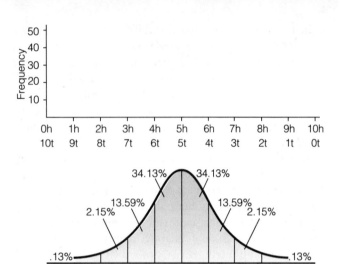

INTERACTIVE FIGURE 9.11

On a sheet of paper, draw two axes as shown at top.

Now shake 10 coins in a cup, roll them out, count the heads and tails, and record them. Do this at least 50 times, although 500 would be better. When you are finished, plot your results. The resulting graph should be a close approximation of the figure above, which is a normal curve *depicting the theoretical distribution of IQ scores. Note that average events (an average IQ of 100, an equal number of heads and tails) are most frequent, and more unusual events (10 heads or 10 tails, IQs above 130 or below 70) are least frequent. Only 2.28 percent of the population scores above IQ 130 or below 70. Two-thirds of the entire population scores between IQ 85 and 115.*

TABLE 9.7

The Wechsler Intelligence Scale for Children Revised (WISC-III)

VERBAL SCALE	PERFORMANCE SCALE
1. *General information.* Questions relating to information most children have the opportunity to acquire. (M)	1. *Picture completion.* Child indicates what is missing in pictures. (M)
2. *General comprehension.* Questions designed to assess child's understanding of why certain things are done as they are. (M)	2. *Picture arrangement.* Series pictures must be arranged to tell a story. (M)
3. *Arithmetic.* Oral arithmetic problems. (M)	3. *Block design.* Child is required to copy exactly a design with colored blocks. (M)
4. *Similarities.* Child indicates how certain things are alike. (M)	4. *Object assembly.* Puzzles to be assembled by subjects. (M)
5. *Vocabulary.* Child gives meanings of words of increasing difficulty. (M)	5. *Coding.* Child pairs symbols with digits following a key. (M)
6. *Digit span.* Child repeats orally presented sequence of numbers in order and reversed. (S)	6. *Mazes.* Child traces way out of mazes with pencil. (S)
	7. *Symbol Search.* Child performs symbol location task that measures mental and visual processing speed search skills. (S)

Note: (M) = mandatory; (S) = supplementary.

Primary Scale of Intelligence, ages 4 to 6½). The various subtests of the WISC-III are described in Table 9.7.

Developmental Changes in IQ

A normal six-year-old child can correctly repeat two or three digits if they are presented clearly and distinctly at a rate of approximately one per second, but would not be expected to repeat four digits in reverse order. An average three-year-old can quickly identify legs, arms, hands, nose, and mouth on a doll, but might hesitate if asked to point to the infranasal depression. Clearly, there is a marked improvement in children's problem solving, remembering, language, reasoning, and so on. Does this mean that intelligence improves?

The answer, of course, depends on how intelligence is defined. If it's defined simply in terms of being able to do those things we consider to be examples of intelligent behavior (such as remembering, reasoning accurately, and expressing oneself clearly), then the answer is yes—children become more intelligent with age. But if intelligence is defined psychometrically (that is, in terms of how we measure it), the answer is no because measured IQ is not an absolute indicator of what or how much a child can do. Instead, it is a measure of what a child can do compared with other children of similar ages and experience. And because children improve at similar rates and in similar ways, then the average child's

measured intelligence does not change from year to year. By definition, it stays right around 100.

But, as we have said more than once, there is no average child; the average is merely a mathematical invention. What about the individual?

The individual, research informs us, may display a great variety of intellectual developmental patterns. As a result, measured differences between two individuals do not necessarily remain constant. For some children, measured IQ may increase over a period of years, or it may decrease, or it might go up and down like a bouncing ball. For the majority, however, measured IQ is relatively stable; it fluctuates within a range that would be expected given the imprecision of the tests. This indicates, claim Gustafsson and Undheim (1992), that the factors that underlie intelligence are relatively stable.

Misconceptions and Facts About IQ

The IQ is not always clearly understood, nor is it always used intelligently. A number of misconceptions are still common.

■ MISCONCEPTION 1

IQ is a mysterious something possessed in lesser or greater quantities by everyone. In fact, the IQ is simply a mathematical expression based largely on an individual's ability to perform selected tasks in prescribed circumstances. It does not reveal mystical, hidden qualities that would otherwise be known only by clever psychologists who have dedicated their lives to the pursuit of the hidden truth.

■ MISCONCEPTION 2

IQ is a constant. I have *x* amount, you have *y*, and that's that. Not so, claim Salomon, Perkins, and Globerson (1991). There is evidence that interaction with new technologies like computers and television may be increasing measured intelligence. And there is also striking evidence that schooling increases intelligence (Husén & Tuijnman, 1991). But even if intelligence did not change, measures of IQ are not constant; they can vary tremendously from one testing time to another. This might not mean, of course, that whatever underlies intelligent behavior is unstable and highly variable. It might mean, instead, that we simply cannot measure it very well.

■ MISCONCEPTION 3

IQ tests measure all the important things. Not really. As Weinberg (1989) notes, IQ tests tell us nothing about social intelligence or about adaptation, motivation, or emotion. Nor do they reveal anything about athletic ability, creativity, self-concept, or a host of important personality variables.

■ MISCONCEPTION 4

IQ tests are fair. Many intelligence tests are culturally biased; they penalize children whose backgrounds are different from the dominant white, middle-class majority. They are culturally biased because they are constructed with the middle-class child in mind and because they are usually standardized on samples of middle-class children. Not surprisingly, children from minority groups often do less well on these tests than their like-aged, middle-class white counterparts. However, the most recent revisions of the Wechsler and the Stanford-Binet have taken this weakness into account and have used more representative norming samples. Accordingly, they are now much more culture fair to minorities.

■ FACT

IQ is related to academic and job success. In an important article, McClelland (1973) argued that intelligence tests bear very little relationship to success in life or in careers. This article had a profound influence on psychologists as well as on popular thinking, and led quickly to widespread skepticism about intelligence testing. In fact, formal intelligence testing has been abandoned in many school jurisdictions, often at the insistence of parents. But McClelland's conclusions are wrong, claim Barrett and Depinet (1991), following a detailed review of relevant research: "The evidence from these varied scientific studies leads again and again to the same conclusion: Intelligence and aptitude tests are positively related to job performance" (p. 1016).

Still, the controversy over the use and usefulness of intelligence tests will not be quickly resolved. These tests have weaknesses and limitations, yet they can be very useful. Unfortunately, although they are widely used, they are not always well understood—hence the need to urge that information derived from such tests be used in a restrained

and intelligent way. This means that no important decisions should be based on a single test without considering information from other important sources. And perhaps nowhere is this admonition more true than when we are dealing with exceptional children. (See Summary Table 9.8.)

■ INTELLECTUAL EXCEPTIONALITY

Exceptionality refers to mental, physical, or social–emotional functioning that is significantly better or poorer than average.

Thus, there are those who are exceptionally gifted, who possess extraordinary talents, and there are those to whom nature and nurture have been less kind. Here we speak of both dimensions of intellectual exceptionality: mental retardation on the one hand, and intellectual giftedness or very high creativity on the other.

Mental Retardation

Mental retardation is a complex, multifaceted exceptionality that can vary tremendously in severity.

■ DEFINITION

The most obvious feature of **mental retardation** is a general depression in the ability to learn; a second important feature involves problems in adapting. These features are reflected in the widely accepted definition presented by the American Association on Mental Deficiency (AAMD) (AAMD Ad Hoc Committee on Terminology and Classification, 1992, p. 5):

> Mental retardation refers to substantial limitations in present intellectual functioning. It is characterized by significantly subaverage intellectual functioning existing concurrently with related limitations in two or more of the following applicable adaptive skill areas: communication, self-care, home living, social skills, community use, self-direction, health and safety, functional academics, leisure, and work. Mental retardation manifests before age 18.

The meaning of this definition may be clarified by looking at each of the key terms involved. First, *significantly subaverage intellectual functioning* is defined in terms of test scores on one or more of the well-known individual intelligence tests—for example, the Stanford-Binet or the Wechsler. An IQ of 70 is the accepted (and admittedly inexact) cutoff between normality and mental retardation.

Second, *limitations in … adaptive skill areas* are significant maturational deficits that are most often manifested in inability to learn or in inability to reach the levels of independence, social responsibility, and social effectiveness that would normally be expected of others of similar age and experience. Failure to learn to dress oneself during the preschool period might be one indication of an impairment in adaptive behavior; failure to toilet train would be another (Reschly, 1990).

Finally, the definition specifies that the deficits must be manifested during the developmental period—a period that extends from conception to age eighteen.

■ IDENTIFICATION

In practice, mental retardation is most often identified and defined by performance on intelligence tests, with some occasional, though limited, attention to adaptive behavior, a characteristic that is difficult to measure or define. This excessive reliance on measured intelligence is sometimes unfortunate for at least two reasons: First, measures at the lower levels of mental retardation are extremely unreliable because almost nobody in the norming samples ever scores below 50 (Reschly, 1992); second, intelligence may be reflected more accurately— and more usefully—in the individual's level of adaptation than in more abstract measures of IQ, especially for those from different cultural or language backgrounds.

The AAMR provides a detailed discussion of what is meant by "adaptive behavior" and how it might be assessed. For example, adaptation during infancy and early childhood is evident in the child's development of sensory motor skills, the ability to communicate, the appearance of self-help skills, and progressive socialization. During later childhood, children would also be expected to learn and apply basic academic skills, develop age-appropriate reasoning and judgment, and develop social skills evident in participation in group activities. During adolescence, in addition to the continued age-appropriate development in all these areas, the individual would also be expected to assume more adult roles reflected in work and social responsibilities. Various standardized inventories are available for assessing level of adaptive behaviors (see Reschly, 1990).

■ PREVALENCE

Estimates of the prevalence of mental retardation vary. The normal distribution of intelligence in the general population suggests that 2.68 percent of the population should score below IQ 70 (Reschly, 1992). But if level of adaptation is taken into account, the figure is closer to 1 percent (Patton & Polloway, 1990).

As we noted in Chapter 6, the existence of multiple developmental problems is not uncommon (Hooper, 1992). Thus, many children who are mentally retarded also manifest other developmental disorders. For example, Coulter (1993b) reports that many mentally retarded children also have cerebral palsy. And of these, about half also suffer from epileptic seizures.

■ CHARACTERISTICS OF MENTAL RETARDATION

The causes of mental retardation are so varied that it is almost always classified in terms of severity rather than cause. The American Association on Mental Retardation distinguishes among four categories of retardation: mild, moderate, severe, and profound. The American Psychiatric Association makes exactly the same distinctions but allows for more overlap between categories. The categories are defined in terms of scores on intelligence tests (Figure 9.12). Overlapping categories that are of more practical use for special-needs educators distinguish among educable, trainable, and custodial retardation.

The largest proportion of intellectually handicapped children (approximately 75 percent) is characterized by **mild retardation.** Most of these children are not identified as being retarded until they have been in school for some time.

FIGURE 9.12

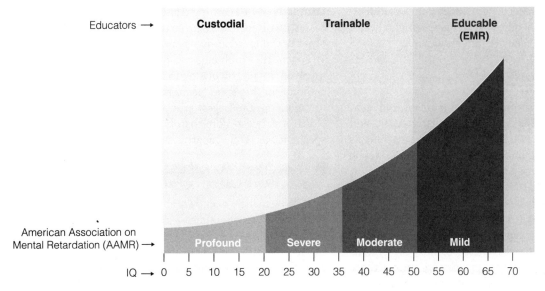

Educators → **Custodial**   **Trainable**   **Educable (EMR)**

American Association on Mental Retardation (AAMR) → Profound   Severe   Moderate   Mild

IQ → 0 5 10 15 20 25 30 35 40 45 50 55 60 65 70

Two common classification schemes for mental retardation. Note that these classifications are based entirely on measured IQ. In practice, adaptive skills would also be taken into account. The AAMR classifications shown here are based on the Stanford-Binet or Cattell tests. The Wechsler Scales have a different distribution and therefore different cutoff points: 55–69 (mild), 40–54 (moderate), 25–39 (severe), below 25 (profound).

They ordinarily develop social and language skills and experience relatively normal motor development. The majority are capable of acceptable academic achievement in elementary school. This is the group described as **educable mentally retarded (EMR).**

Children classified as having **moderate retardation** compose another 20 percent of the retarded group. These children can learn to talk during the preschool period; most will also learn to walk, although their verbal and motor skills may be inferior to those of normal children. Many moderately retarded children are mainstreamed—that is, educated in regular schools though often with special teachers and equipment.

Severe mental retardation is usually associated with poor motor development, few communication skills (although these sometimes develop slightly later in life), and a high degree of dependence throughout life. Children marked by **profound mental retardation** may not learn toilet or dressing habits; in addition, many do not learn to walk.

Learning Disabilities

There are a significant number of children in schools who, in the absence of perceptible emotional or physical disturbances and without being mentally retarded, experience serious learning difficulties in one or more areas. Such children have sometimes been described as suffering from *hyperactivity, learning dysfunction, cerebral dysfunction, minimal brain damage, perceptual handicaps, dyslexia, perceptual disability,* or simply as being slow learners. Each of these terms is relatively nonspecific, often confusing, and sometimes meaningless. In 1963, Samuel Kirk proposed a new term that would, in effect, include all the conditions previously described by these and other labels: **learning disability.** It does not carry the stigma attached to such terms as brain damage or cerebral dysfunction, nor does it complicate our understanding with excessive categorization (Hammill, 1993).

■ DEFINITION

The term *learning disability* is now widely used to describe a variety of conditions. Unfortunately, these conditions are not always easily defined or identified. U.S. Public Law 94–142, which provides funding programs for special education, includes a definition of learning disabilities that serves as a guideline for the allocation of funds. However, the definition is open to several interpretations and has led to considerable controversy. As a result, various jurisdictions have modified existing definitions and have established their own criteria for learning disabilities. None of these definitions and criteria says what a learning disability actually is; each simply stipulates behaviors and conditions considered symptomatic of the condition. In addition, because of the very general nature of most definitions, many researchers have proposed more precise definitions for what appear to be relatively specific disabilities (for example, Cole, 1993; Stanovich, 1993).

In spite of the considerable disagreement concerning what learning disabilities are and are not—and how many there really are (Kavale, 1993)—most definitions emphasize four characteristics of a learning disability:

■ There is a marked disparity between expected and actual behavior, which is often apparent in an uneven pattern of academic achievement.

■ There is an uneven pattern of achievement. Although learning-disabled children do reasonably well in many subjects, there are specific subjects and areas in which they are unable to do certain things that other children do quite easily.

■ Children with a learning disability typically experience problems in one of the basic psychological processes involved in language or in arithmetic. Hence, the condition is often evident in disorders of listening, thinking, talking, reading, writing, spelling, or arithmetic.

■ Finally, the problems associated with learning disabilities are not the result of other problems relating to hearing, vision, or general mental retardation.

■ IDENTIFICATION OF LEARNING DISABILITIES

Initial indications of learning disabilities are typically tentative and probabilistic. The most obvious characteristic, and the one most likely to be noticed by parents and teachers, is general academic retardation. Note, however, that academic retardation does not define a learning disability, although it often occurs as a result of the child's problems with reading, writing, and other aspects of the language arts.

Other general symptoms are sometimes associated with learning disabilities. These can include inattentiveness, mood shifts, hyperactivity, and impulsiveness (see Table 9.9). Short-term memory problems are not uncommon among those with learning disabilities (Swanson, 1993). Some research indicates, as well, that children with learning disabilities are more likely to abuse drugs than those not so classified, perhaps because of their poorer school performance and subsequent adjustment problems (Karacostas & Fisher, 1993). By the same token, adolescents with learning disabilities may be at slightly higher risk of suicide (Huntington & Bender, 1993).

A variety of tests are used in identifying the learning disabled. These are designed to provide information concerning three aspects of the student's characteristics and functioning. They measure general intelligence, examine basic psychological processes involved in learning and remembering, and look at the possibility that other factors—such as visual problems, hearing deficits, physical or health handicaps, low intelligence, or environmental disadvantages—might be involved. The first and third of these (measuring intelligence and eliminating other defects) are relatively straightforward, but the second (assessing basic psychological processes) is not. One of the problems is that there isn't widespread agreement on what these processes are. Certain tests, such as the

TABLE 9.9

Some Symptoms That May Be Associated with Learning Disabilities

- Inattentiveness (short attention span)
- Impulsiveness
- Hyperactivity
- Frequent shifts in emotional mood
- Impaired visual memory (difficulty in recalling shapes or words)
- Motor problems (difficulty in running, hitting a ball, cutting, writing)
- Disorders of speech and hearing
- Specific academic difficulties (reading, writing, spelling, arithmetic)

Source: Based in part on *Minimal Brain Dysfunction in Children: Terminology and Identification* (by S. D. Clements, 1966) (NINDB Monograph No. 3). Washington, DC: U.S. Department of Health & Human Services; and Edmonton (Alberta) Public School Board (1978) *Learning Disability. No. 7.*

Detroit Tests of Learning Aptitude, attempt to look at processes involved in activities such as reading and are sometimes useful for identifying specific weaknesses.

Given the problems of definition and identification involved, it's not surprising that faulty categorization is very common in this area. Now children with learning disabilities make up the largest group of special needs students in North America—more than two-thirds of all students with special needs (U.S. Department of Education, 1991).

■ PRINCIPAL MANIFESTATIONS OF LEARNING DISABILITIES

Relatively little is known about the origins and causes of specific learning disabilities—although brain damage or some other neurological impairment is suspected in many cases (Mercer, 1990). Various diseases and infections, malnutrition, and other environmental or genetic factors might also be involved.

Learning disabilities are most often classified according to the specific area of disability and are labeled according to whether they involve oral or written speech, comprehension or production of speech, or particular problems in spelling or arithmetic. By far the most frequently diagnosed learning disabilities are those that have to do with language—especially with reading.

A common learning disability manifested in reading problems is **developmental reading disorder**—also called *dyslexia* or *specific reading disability* (Stanovich, 1992). The main feature of developmental reading disorder, according to the American Psychiatric Association, is impairment in recognizing words and understanding what is read. These difficulties are not related to mental retardation, physical problems such as deafness, or inadequate schooling (American Psychiatric Association, 1994). Developmental reading disorder is usually first manifested in problems associated with learning to read and may later be evident in spelling difficulties. Individuals with developmental reading disorder are typically of average measured intelligence but, in spite of ample opportunity to learn to read, are usually several years behind in reading skills. Remedial teaching can sometimes be highly effective in overcoming some of the effects of developmental reading disorder.

The American Psychiatric Association also recognizes what is labeled **developmental arithmetic disorder** (American Psychiatric Association, 1994). Its essential feature is significant impairment in developing arithmetic skills in the absence of other problems such as mental retardation. Developmental arithmetic disorder may be evident in computational problems (difficulties in adding, subtracting, multiplying, or dividing) or in problems in processing visual or auditory information. Accordingly, reading problems are sometimes associated with arithmetic disabilities (Semrud-Clikeman & Hynd, 1992).

In addition to reading and arithmetic disorders, learning disabilities also include what are referred to as **process disorders**—that is, they are sometimes labeled in terms of a deficit in a basic psychological process. Thus, there are deficits relating to perception (some students are confused by words that sound or look alike), memory (sometimes evident in problems associated with remembering and generalizing what has been learned), and attention span (a condition labeled "attention deficit disorder" that is sometimes associated with restlessness, hyperactivity, low frustration tolerance, and distractibility). In practice, however, it is often difficult to separate a basic process disorder from a disorder that is manifested in a specific subject area.

Learning disabilities, as they are presently defined, are usually treated in the regular classroom. Alternately, learning disability specialists, many of whom specialize in reading or writing skills, may work with these children in the regular classroom. In a declining number of cases, they are given no special treatment.

Intellectual Giftedness

Intellectual giftedness may be apparent in two related aspects of cognitive functioning: high intelligence and high creativity. But in the same way that mental retardation is defined not only in terms of performance on an intelligence test but also in terms of adaptive behavior, intellectual giftedness, too, cannot easily be identified solely on the basis of scores on measures of intelligence or creativity. In recent years, there has been a strong move away from basing definitions of giftedness solely on intelligence scores, and also taking into account motivational and personality factors (Morelock, 1996).

U.S. Public Law 91–230 defines giftedness as follows:

Gifted and talented children are those identified by professionally qualified persons, who by virtue of outstanding abilities, are capable of high performance. These are children who require differentiated educational programs and/or services beyond those normally provided by the regular school programs in order to realize their contribution to society.

The law goes on to state that capacity for high performance may involve demonstrated achievement, or the potential for high achievement, in one or more of the following areas: general intellectual ability, specific academic aptitude, creative thinking, leadership ability, visual and performing arts, and psychomotor ability.

A common estimate is that somewhere between 3 and 5 percent of the school population might be considered gifted (Hallahan & Kauffman, 1991). However, special education programs are provided for nowhere near this number. This is especially true of the gifted who are culturally disadvantaged (Patton, Prillaman, & Tassel-Baska, 1990).

Among these highly gifted are the creative.

Identifying the Gifted and Creativity

One of the major problems in the area of giftedness, says Porath (1996), has to do with the definition and identifica-

tion of the qualities in question. In practice, these qualities have most often been defined in terms of scores on tests: Intellectual giftedness is defined as a very high measured IQ, and high **creativity** is defined as an extraordinarily high score on a test designed to measure creativity. And the school administrator who must make a decision about who will be labeled "gifted" (and who, at least by implication, will be labeled "not gifted") also looks at test scores and perhaps asks teachers for their nominations. There are serious problems with this approach, notes Grossman (1995). First, there is considerable ambiguity about the meaning of high IQ or high creativity scores; second, what is represented by these tests is often quite different from the definitions that government agencies or school jurisdictions have adopted; and third, identifying a group of students as gifted and talented also means, by implication, identifying an even larger group who do not qualify. There are serious ethical and equity issues here.

■ SOME MEASURES OF CREATIVITY

Intelligence, as we saw, is typically measured with one or more of a variety of intelligence tests. Creativity, too, can be assessed with tests, but there is considerable disagreement about their validity, their reliability, and their meaningfulness. As a result, researchers often use a combination of measures, including personality inventories, biographical and activity inventories, and behavioral measures (Heinzen, 1991). Personality inventories focus on what are considered to be the characteristics of creative people (for example, openness, flexibility). Biographical and activity inventories are based on the assumption that past creative activity is the best predictor of future creativity. They look at the extent to which individuals have already been creative. And behavioral measures try to predict future creativity by looking at specific

Giftedness may be apparent in high intelligence and high creativity, as well as in personality characteristics. But perhaps most important for those who eventually become eminent is not only that they be highly gifted but also that their family contexts encourage and provide opportunity for the development of their special talents.

behaviors such as performance in school. With all of these approaches, there is, in Heinzen's (1991) words, tremendous "diversity and lack of coherence" (p. 8).

In studies of creativity, the most frequently used measures are open-ended tests that require subjects to produce a variety of different responses. These are sometimes called **tests of divergent thinking.** Individuals think divergently when they produce a number of different solutions for a single problem. In contrast, measures of intelligence typically present items that require **convergent thinking**—the production of a single correct response.

Most production measures of creativity are based on Guilford's (1950) assumption that the most important factors involved in creative ability are **fluency, flexibility,** and **originality.** Accordingly, the open-ended tasks require the production of a variety of different responses that can then be scored in terms of these factors. For example, one item asks subjects to think of as many uses as they can for a brick. Counting the total number of responses gives a measure of fluency. Flexibility is revealed in the number of shifts from one class of uses to another (for example, shifting from responses where bricks are used for building purposes to ones where they are used for holding objects down). Originality is revealed in the number of unusual or rare responses. Interactive Table 9.10 gives one example of a creativity item and how it might be scored.

Interestingly, when children are given tests of divergent (creative) thinking and told to be creative, their scores typically increase (Runco, 1986a). This finding has sometimes been used as a basis for arguing that children who normally score high on creativity tests simply perceive the test differently. However, it is significant that children who improve most on measures of originality when they are asked to be creative are those who score highest on measures of giftedness in the first place.

Runco (1986b) makes the important point that while measures of creativity reflect creative potential, they do not reflect creative performance. The greatest achievers—those who eventually attain eminence in the world—are characterized by more than just high scores on measures of intelligence and creativity.

■ SOME CHARACTERISTICS OF CREATIVE AND GIFTED CHILDREN

A number of studies have looked at the characteristics of creative and gifted children. None of them presents a simple description of what these children are like—probably because each is unique, very different from the others. Hoge and Renzulli (1993), for example, looked at the self-concepts (the self-esteem) of gifted students in an effort to discover whether the gifted have higher evaluations of themselves. It might be reasonable to expect that they would have, argue Hoge and Renzulli, given that their accomplishments should be superior to those of more ordinary individuals. Also, if they are labeled "gifted," that too might have a positive effect on their self-concepts. But there is the possibility, they also caution,

Sample Answers and Scoring Procedure for One Item from a Creativity Test

Without looking at the answer section of Table 9.10, write down as many uses as you can think of for a nylon stocking. Some people run out of ideas very quickly; others continue to generate them for a long time. Some people's ideas are very common; others are highly unusual. Open-ended questions such as these can be used to measure creativity. See the sample answers and a scoring procedure for the nylon stocking item.

ITEM: How many uses can you think of for a nylon stocking?

ANSWERS:

*	Wear on feet.
#*	Wear over face.
*	Wear on hands when it's cold.
$*	Make rugs.
*	Make clothes.
#$*	Make upholstery.
$*	Hang flowerpots.
*	Hang mobiles.
#$*	Make Christmas decorations.
$*	Use as a sling.
$*	Tie up robbers.
#$*	Cover broken windowpanes.
#$*	Use as ballast in a dirigible.
$*	Make a fishing net.

SCORING:

*	Fluency:	14	(total number of different responses)
$	Flexibility:	9	(number of shifts from one class to another)
#	Originality:	5	(number of unusual responses—responses that occurred less than 5 percent of the time in the entire sample)

that the high expectations that are sometimes placed on the gifted might lead them to greater feelings of frustration and dissatisfaction, and might be evident in lower rather than higher self-concepts.

Hoge and Renzulli looked at fifteen studies that compared the self-concepts of gifted and nongifted children. Their conclusions? "In general, gifted children displayed slightly higher self-concept scores than more average children" (p. 458). Not surprisingly, this finding was most evident in measures of what is termed academic self-concept—the children's evaluations of their academic abilities. However, a review of seven studies that had looked at the possibility that labeling a child "gifted" might increase self-esteem found no relationship between labels and self-concept.

In general, research on the personality characteristics of gifted children indicates that they are different from the nongifted in a number of dimensions. For example, they are generally more highly motivated to learn and to achieve (Porath, 1996); they have been found to be more playful or, as Runco (1996) puts it, more "childlike in their behavior and thinking" (p. 3); and indications are that they are more open to emotion in their fantasy and in their play (Russ, 1996).

It is worth noting, as well, that very often more of those identified as gifted in secondary school are male rather than female. This fact, argues Randall (1997), is largely a reflection of social pressures, expectations, and role models that present tremendous challenges for gifted girls. As one thirteen-year-old girl put it, "It's almost a sin to be too smart in junior high" (Randall, 1997, p. 46). It's little surprise that among the "hidden gifted," defined as underachieving gifted children, the proportion of females to males decreases with advancing grade level (Lupart & Pyryt, 1996).

Other research indicates that the gifted are, in fact, probably better players of what is sometimes called the game of cognition. Both Swanson (1992) and Cheng (1993) found that the gifted children manifest higher metacognitive skills. That is, they are more aware of their cognitive processes and better at selecting and applying cognitive strategies and at evaluating their effectiveness.

An older study by Wallach and Kogan (1965) looked at the personality characteristics of highly creative children and compared them with those of children identified as being highly intelligent. Among other things, the highly intelligent but less creative students in this sample tended to be addicted to school and were well liked by teachers. In contrast, highly creative but less intelligent students were most frustrated with school and suffered most from feelings of inadequacy. The most favored group, not surprisingly, were those who were high on both intelligence and creativity. These students were most in control of their behaviors and were capable of both adultlike and childlike behaviors. (See Figure 9.13.)

■ THE ROOTS OF EMINENCE

For practical purposes, there is seldom a need to separate high intelligence and high creativity. Not only is there a close relationship between the two, but programs for gifted and talented children are seldom tailored for one or the other. And studies of eminent individuals—that is, of those who have achieved fame and recognition on the basis of outstanding performance in any area—typically find that these individuals are both highly intelligent and specially gifted in a creative sense (Runco, 1996).

But eminent individuals are something other than just highly intelligent and specially gifted. Countless individuals score extremely high on all our measures of giftedness and intelligence but never approach eminence. A follow-up of the Terman (1925) studies of genius, for example, found that very few of the original sample ever attained eminence (Oden, 1968). Nevertheless, a relatively high proportion of the men—but a significantly lower proportion of equally gifted women—achieved at high levels academically and in their careers. For women in the Terman Study, suggests Holahan (1996), the

	Measured intelligence	
	High	Low
Divergent thinking (creativity) High	High contol over their own behavior, capable of adultlike and childlike behavior	High internal conflict; fustration with school; feelings of inadequacy, can perform well in stress-free environment
Low	Addicted to school, strive desperately for academic success; well liked by teachers	Somewhat bewildered by environment; defense mechanisms include intensive social or athletic activity, occasional maladjustment

FIGURE 9.13

Characteristics of children identified as high and low on measures of intelligence and creativity. (Based on studies reported by Wallach & Kogan, 1965.)

single most important factor militating against their achieving at a high level was the perceived incompatibility between a working career and a home-making career. These women, mostly born around 1911, would have been young women in the 1930s through the 1950s, at which time dual-career families were far rarer than they are today. Thus, their contexts had an important influence on the course of their lives.[*]

What is special about those few gifted individuals who achieve eminence? Perhaps a number of personality characteristics—qualities such as high motivation and persistence—and, perhaps most important, the right family and cultural context. Family background seems to have been an important factor in the lives of a majority of those who have achieved eminence.

Albert and Runco (1986) warn that perhaps we have taken too simple and too cognitive a view of giftedness and that, as a result, we have been guilty of neglecting important personality and family variables. They suggest that seven important factors are involved in the development of eminence. If children are to become eminent, it is best that they

■ be both intelligent and creative

■ develop the values, motivation, and abilities that allow them to undertake important or highly unusual work

■ have a family context that encourages the development of these values and drives

■ find a "fit" between talents and career demands, such that the demands of the career are sufficiently challenging to lead to eminence

---

[*]"I'm not sure I believe that. Some people, no matter what kind of experiences you give them, they'll always be stupid," said my grandmother, quoting yet another proverb—this time, a Rumanian one: "He who washes the head of an ass wastes both water and soap."

- have a family that provides the right combination of experiences (that is, musical, athletic, academic, and so on)

- have a family history consistent with appropriate experiences and values (that is, grandparents, who were influenced by their parents, also influenced their children, who now influence the children of whom we speak)

- be subjected to family direction consistent with the development of the gifted child's talents (rather than unrealistic, overly demanding, or uncaring)

Notice how important the family is in Runco's suggestions. In much the same way, Christian and Morgan (1993) offer numerous suggestions for parents of gifted children, advising them on how to cope with the interests, the energy level, the challenges of the gifted. Karges-Bone (1993), too, argues that the most important source of influence in the life of the gifted child is the family.

Trends and Controversies in Special Needs Education

There are a number of trends and controversies in implementing special services for exceptional children. Some of these are summarized briefly here.

■ MAINSTREAMING

First, there has been a gradual shifting of responsibility for children with special needs from special organizations and institutions to the public school systems. In part, this trend reflects a growing recognition that children who are disadvantaged should have an opportunity to lead lives as nearly normal as possible. Deinstitutionalization and non-segregation are the natural consequences of this trend, and perhaps nowhere is this more obvious than in the **mainstreaming** movement.

To mainstream is to place in regular classrooms children who might once have been placed in "special" classrooms or even in institutions. The mainstreaming movement followed the passage of U.S. Public Law 94–142 in 1975. This law requires, among other things, that school jurisdictions provide special services for exceptional children in "the least restrictive environment" possible. Subsequently, various court decisions interpreted "the least restrictive environment" to mean the regular classroom. The effectiveness of special classrooms for mildly retarded children had been called into question, and a consensus seemed to be growing that mildly retarded children would do better in regular classrooms.

Mainstreaming remains controversial for several reasons (Chester, 1992). First, the inclusion of special needs students in the regular classroom is expensive and difficult for school administrators, particularly because the law stipulates a need for extensive, unbiased testing. Second, caring for special needs students sometimes presents a difficult burden for classroom teachers who are not always trained for

this responsibility. Third, there is evidence that some exceptional children might fare better in segregated classrooms—or, alternatively, that the regular classroom might fare better without these students. For example, Simon (1992) argues that behaviorally disruptive children with serious aggressive tendencies might function better in segregated classrooms with specially trained teachers.

The bulk of the research indicates, however, that inclusive education can meet the needs of exceptional children and that the self-concepts of mainstreamed students are typically better than those of segregated students. As Sobsey (1993) puts it, "The majority of the research to date shows both educational and social advantages for integrated settings over segregated alternatives" (p. 1). However, he advises that in many cases, the needs of the exceptional child can best be served through adaptive education—that is, by providing intensive, individualized, "special" programs for these children within the regular classroom.

■ LABELING

A second controversy concerns the use of labels. Critics of the use of labels argue that they are unfair because (1) a disproportionate number of minority group children are labeled (and perhaps mislabeled, owing to the biased nature of many of our tests), (2) the imposition of a label changes the child's environment by affecting the child's self-concept, and (3) labels contribute to a growing tendency to view exceptional children as being quantitatively rather than qualitatively different from normal children.

In spite of these objections, labeling has definitely not been abandoned, although there has been a concerted attempt to use more euphemistic (less stigmatizing) labels, to use them more judiciously, and to avoid making labels serve as explanations. It has never been very useful to label Johnny "dyslexic" and then to say that he can't read because he's dyslexic. Here, as elsewhere, labels name and classify; they do not explain. (See Summary Table 9.11.)

■ THE MAGICAL CHILD

"The parents of the magical child lead him into the world by example," Pearce (1977) tells us. "At seven, he is open to suggestion, able to construct the abstractions needed for moving into the world...he is fascinated with the world and becomes analytic. He wants to take the world apart and see what makes it tick" (p. 213).

In Piaget's terms, the child of whom we have spoken in this chapter is ready to construct a knowledge system that will lead to a mounting understanding of the world.

Or, in the language of information-processing theory, the child seeks to develop a knowledge base, to discover processes and strategies for dealing with knowledge, and to develop a sense of self as perceiver, knower, and rememberer.

SUMMARY TABLE 9.11

Important Concepts in Intellectual Exceptionality

CONCEPT	EXPLANATIONS/COMMENTS
Mental retardation	Significantly subaverage intellectual functioning associated with impairments in adaptive behavior during the developmental period. May be: ■ **mild**—the largest group, capable of elementary school achievement (educable). ■ **moderate**—measured IQ in high 30s to low 50s; generally learn to talk and walk in preschool period, with noticeable impairment. ■ **severe** or **profound**—limited motor and verbal learning.
Learning disability	■ Marked disparity between expected and actual performance. ■ Uneven pattern of achievement. ■ Disability often evident in basic psychological process *(process disorder),* in problems with written language *(developmental reading disorder),* or in problems with basic computational skills *(developmental arithmetic disorder).*
Giftedness	■ The gifted and talented are those whose abilities permit them outstanding performance. ■ High creativity may be identified in terms of personality characteristics, motivation, and high ability to innovate. ■ Tests of creativity (of *divergent thinking*) are typically open-ended tests that require the production of multiple responses that may be scored in terms of fluency (number of responses), flexibility (number of different classes of responses), and originality (unusualness of responses). ■ For social and cultural reasons, girls are often underrepresented in programs for the highly gifted. ■ The roots of eminence include high ability, a nurturant family and cultural context, and an appropriate combination of motivational and personality characteristics.
Education for special needs	■ *Mainstreaming* involves placing children with special needs in ordinary classroom. It is mandated in many jurisdictions, but remains controversial. ■ The use of labels is often discouraged because they are often biased against minority groups, and they can have a negative effect on the labeled child's environment (for example, in terms of changes in parental and teacher expectations).

As we noted, infants are not expected to know that day follows night, that butterflies whisper to each other when they perch on buttercups in the sunshine, and that there is a smooth, cold logic that can be invented to explain the mysteries of numbers and classes and series, although perhaps not the whispers of butterflies. Those are among the discoveries of later childhood.

But happily, the grand mysteries of cognition are not all solved through middle childhood. There is yet a concreteness to the child's logic, a limit to the reaches of imagination. We continue the story in Chapter 11.

FOCUS QUESTIONS: SUMMARY ANSWERS

1. What is the most common nutritional problem of childhood?

   ■ Obesity (linked to overeating, underexercising, and genetic background) is the most common childhood nutritional problem in North America.

2. What is Piaget's view of important intellectual changes in middle childhood?

   ■ First, children develop concepts of conservation (the realization that certain transformations do not change the quantitative features of objects) that reflect the development of important rules of logic that now influence thinking. Also, they acquire abilities relating to classification, seriation, and number.

3. What model of human memory is basic to current information-processing approaches?

   ■ Information-processing approaches to cognition look at knowledge base, strategies for dealing with cognitive material, and awareness of the self as a knower or as a processor of information. Memory may be described in terms of three components: sensory memory (the momentary effect of sense impressions), short-term memory (similar to attention span—seconds long, highly limited), and long-term memory (indefinite duration—requires cognitive processing). Long-term memory may be declarative (explicit, verbalizable) or nondeclarative (implicit, nonverbalizable). Declarative memory may be semantic (stable, abstract knowledge base) or episodic (memory for personal events).

4. What are the dimensions of intellectual exceptionality?

   ■ One dimension includes mental retardation (characterized by a general depression in the ability to learn,
   defined in low measured intelligence and poor childhood adaptation) and learning disabilities (include
   a wide range of specific learning problems not associated with mental retardation, often manifested in
   language-related problems [developmental reading
   disorder], in computational problems [developmental
   arithmetic disorder], or in problems with basic psychological processes [process disorder]). The other
   dimension includes intellectual giftedness, which is
   manifested in exceptional intelligence, exceptional
   creativity, and high motivation.

STUDY TERMS

attention span, 257

cardinal properties, 256

case studies, 248

chunking, 258

class, 255

cognitive strategies, 257

compensation, 254

concrete operations, 252

conservation, 253

contextual theory of
   intelligence, 263

convergent thinking, 272

creativity, 271

crystallized abilities, 263

deafness, 251

declarative memory, 259

developmental arithmetic
   disorder, 270

developmental reading
   disorder, 270

educable mentally retarded
   (EMR), 269

elaborating, 260

episodic memory, 260

explicit memory, 259

fat mass, 246

fat-free mass, 246

flexibility, 272

fluency, 272

fluid abilities, 263

general factor theory, 263

gist memory, 258

group intelligence tests, 265

hard of hearing, 251

identity, 254

implicit memory, 259

individual intelligence
   tests, 265

information-processing
   approach, 256

Intelligence Quotient (IQ),
   265

knowledge-acquisition
   component, 264

knowledge base, 257

learning disability, 269

long-term memory, 258

mainstreaming, 251, 274

mental retardation, 268

mentors, 262

metacognition, 257, 262

metacomponents, 264

metamemory, 262

middle childhood, 246

mild retardation, 268

moderate retardation, 269

nondeclarative memory, 259

obesity, 247

operations, 253

ordinal properties, 256

organizing, 260

originality, 272

otitis media, 251

peak height velocity, 247

performance components,
   264

preoperations, 253

process disorders, 270

profound mental
   retardation, 269

rehearsing, 260

reliable, 263

reversibility, 254

scripts, 258

semantic memory, 260

sensory memory, 257

seriation, 256

severe mental retardation,
   269

short-term memory, 257

special abilities theory, 263

special needs, 251

standard deviations, 246

stunting, 246

tests of divergent thinking,
   272

theory of multiple
   intelligences, 265

valid, 263

visually impaired, 251

wasting, 246

FURTHER READINGS

The following book is a highly readable and excellent analysis of Piaget's view of cognitive development:

   Wadsworth, B. J. (1996). *Piaget's theory of cognitive and
   affective development* (5th ed.). New York: Longman.

This collection is a detailed look at research that explores
children's memories:

   Nelson, C. A. (Ed.). (1993). *Memory and affect in development: The Minnesota Symposia on Child Psychology* (Vol.
   26). Hillsdale, NJ: Erlbaum.

The following text is a clear and useful account of developmental disorders in infancy and childhood:

   Hooper, S. R., Hynd, G. W., & Mattison, R. E. (Eds.).
   (1992). *Developmental disorders: Diagnostic criteria and
   clinical assessment.* Hillsdale, NJ: Erlbaum.

A current collection of articles dealing with the development
of creativity and its relationship to personality and emotion is
found in this book:

   Shaw, M. P., & Runco, M. A. (Eds.). (1994). *Creativity
   and affect.* Norwood, NJ: Ablex.

TEN

Social Development: Middle Childhood

A manner rude and wild
Is common at your age.

HILLAIRE BELLOC
Bad Child's Book of Beasts

isho City, Japan: When he was only ten, his classmates began to taunt and bully Koyoteru Okouchi, a student at Tobu Junior High School in Nisho City, central Japan. The bullying worsened rapidly, and soon the bullies began demanding that he give them money. When they thought he might refuse, they dunked him in the nearby river. After three years of bullying, they had extorted more than $10,000 from him, much of which he had stolen from his parents and grandparents after selling his books and his computer software. "If only I'd had the courage to say no," Koyoteru wrote just before he hanged himself. He was only thirteen. And even in his final note, he doesn't name his tormentors, speaking of them only as "the usual four" ("Bullies Drive Teen to Suicide," 1994). ¶ *New York, U.S.:* David Harris, age twelve, is dead. Lewis Santiago Pagan is accused of killing him. Lewis is a shy, awkward giant of a boy, already six feet tall and weighing more than 200 pounds at age thirteen. David was a puny 4 feet 5 inches; he weighed only 80 pounds. But, in spite of his size, David had joined a group of bullies who ridiculed and taunted Lewis, pulling his legs out from under him and making him fall. In the end, Lewis pulled out a large "Rambo-type" knife and stabbed David three times in the chest, killing him. "It seems that Lewis had finally had enough," said Detective Kim Royster ("'Gentle Giant' Stabs Boy for Taunts," 1994). ¶ As a result of incidents such as these, a number of school jurisdictions have begun to look at bullying as a serious problem that needs to be prevented rather than simply dealt with in response to a crisis. In Norway, for example, following the suicides of three different victims of bullying in one year, a national antibullying campaign has been established (Tattum & Herbert, 1993). ¶

279

This Chapter

e know that not all children are bullies—or victims. Nor are all of them rude and wild through middle childhood. Some, of either sex, must also be polite and gentle and well behaved. Given a thousand eight-year-olds, will they be found to be more rude than polite? More wild than restrained?[*]

This chapter presents the beginning of an answer. It looks at how children are socialized through the middle years, how they become caring and concerned individuals, and how they develop notions of who they are and of their self-worth. It examines the role of parents, peers, and friends in shaping the developmental process. It looks, too, at how important school and television are in the child's context.

Much of the wildness—and the rudeness—of middle childhood is playful. Sadly, some is not. There are dysfunctional families where children are neglected and abused, sometimes in shocking ways. This chapter closes with a look at child maltreatment, followed by a discussion of social–emotional exceptionality.

SOCIAL COGNITION

Cognition refers to knowing, *metacognition* is knowing about knowing, and **social cognition** refers to an awareness of others as selves that, like our own selves, are also capable of feelings, motives, intentions, and so on. The purpose of social cognition, says Fiske (1993), is for people to make sense of others.

The Origins of Social Cognition

Social cognitions have their roots in the infant's realization that there are things out there that are persons and others that are nonpersons (Wellman & Gelman, 1992). At about the same time, infants begin to develop a sense of self and to form bonds, usually to their caretakers. Thus begins the process of socialization.

But the infant's social cognitions unfold slowly and reflect many of the limitations that characterize nonsocial cognitions. Recall how young infants and even preschoolers have difficulty adopting another person's point of view, as is illustrated by Piaget's mountains problem (in which children view a three-dimensional "mountain" display from one angle and are asked to describe what it would look like from a different angle). In much the same way, infants and preschoolers cannot easily make inferences about what other people

are thinking or feeling. Still, recent research suggests that preschoolers may be far better social thinkers than had been thought.

Theories of Mind

"Current research," write Wellman and Gelman (1992), "reveals sophisticated reasoning about the mental states of self and others in 3- to 5-year-olds" (p. 351). It seems that preschoolers have already begun to develop a theory of mind. This implicit theory of mind is based on an understanding that others have mental states—that is, that they have thoughts, emotions, wishes, beliefs. It is essential that children have a **theory of mind** if they are to understand others and interact intelligently with them.

If four-year-old Elizabeth does not have a theory of mind—that is, does not understand that her mother has her own thoughts and beliefs—then it would not occur to her to lie when her mother asks, "Did you poke that hole in your bedsheet, Elizabeth?" Intentional deception, claim Ruffman and colleagues (1993), requires that children understand not only that people can believe different things, but also that it is possible to make people believe things that are false. Three-year-olds have considerable difficulty deceiving others or understanding deception. But the four-year-old has no such problem—strong evidence, claim Ruffman and associates (1993), of the beginning of a theory of mind.

The roots of a theory of mind are found in the behavior of even younger children. "Children as young as 2 years old are, in some respects, quite competent social reasoners, and so they must have some kind of 'theory of mind,'" writes Perner (1991). They show awareness of others' mental states in their conversations, their play, their fighting. Two-year-olds who tease a sibling or steal a favorite toy or call each other names act as if they know the likely effects of their behaviors.

Young children also show evidence of a theory of mind in their understanding of fairy stories. Many of these stories, argues Hinchcliffe (1996), use language that refers to intentions, feelings states, and understandings of characters that would be largely meaningless to a child unable to attribute psychological states to others.

Play, and especially imaginative (fantasy) play, may have much to do with the development of the child's theory of mind. Taylor and Carlson (1997) looked at the development of theories of mind in three- and four-year-old children by presenting them with tasks that required different kinds of understanding, each dependent on the ability to attribute states of mind to others—for example, distinguishing between appearance and reality, as when people laugh when they have hurt themselves; believing things that are false; and being able to adopt the mental point of view of another. They also looked at differences among these children in terms of fantasy play and identified those who created imaginary characters such as imaginary playmates, and they looked at the relationship between measures of play and measures of

---

[*]"The answer," said my grandmother, using an uncharacteristically profane Spanish proverb to explain herself, "is they're not really that wild. A lot of them pee in the bottle just to hear the thunder." I didn't have time to find out what she meant.

theory of mind. Not surprisingly, these two sets of measures were closely related; the most fantasy-prone children were also those with the most clearly developed theories of mind.

ROLE TAKING AND EMPATHY

Early investigations of the development of empathy (the ability to recognize and share the feelings of others) often asked children to recognize the emotion that would accurately reflect the reaction of a person in a story. In one study, for example, Selman (1980) told children the following story:

> Holly is an 8-year-old girl who likes to climb trees. She is the best tree climber in the neighborhood. One day while climbing down from a tall tree, she falls off the bottom branch but does not hurt herself. Her father sees her fall. He is upset and asks her to promise not to climb trees anymore. Holly promises.
>
> Later that day, Holly and her friends meet Shawn. Shawn's kitten is caught up in a tree and can't get down. Something has to be done right away, or the kitten may fall. Holly is the only one who climbs trees well enough to reach the kitten and get it down, but she remembers her promise to her father. (p. 36)

Children were then asked whether Holly knows how Shawn feels about the kitten, what Holly thinks her father will do if she climbs the tree, how Holly's father will feel if he knows she has climbed the tree, and what the child being questioned would do in the same situation.

Selman summarizes the development of the child's ability to understand and verbalize another person's point of view in five stages, numbered 0 to 4. These are shown in Summary Table 10.1. In general, they describe the preschooler as largely unaware of others' states of mind and as developing a gradually more sophisticated and abstract understanding of the thinking of others through middle childhood.

One possible conclusion from studies such as Selman's is that infants and preschoolers are largely ignorant of the states of minds of others until the age of six or seven—that, as Moore and Frye (1991) put it, they have not yet learned to see the world through others' eyes. However, as we saw, preschoolers' ability to deceive and their apparent anticipation of the consequences of their behavior indicate that they do have some understanding of others' mental states. But preschoolers' understanding remains limited. They cannot easily imagine themselves in someone else's mental state or verbally explain or predict another person's behavior. As an illustration, Durkin and Howarth (1997) showed children aged five to nine one of several pairs of short videos. One group of children saw a video in which a man and child carry a picnic basket to a car. The man puts the basket down while he goes to the other side to open the vehicle. Three young men walk by, and one of them sneaks over and steals the basket. But just at that moment, the man turns back to the basket in time to catch the thief.

A second group saw an identical video except that in this version, the man does not return to the basket in time to see

SUMMARY TABLE 10.1
Selman's Developmental Progression in Social Cognition

PERSPECTIVE-TAKING STAGE	DESCRIPTION	TYPICAL RESPONSES TO CAT STORY (SEE TEXT)
0. Egocentric (to 6 years)	There is no perspective but mine. People feel the way I would in that situation.	"Her daddy will be happy 'cause he likes the kitten."
1. Social-Informational (6–8)	Okay, so others have a point of view too, but they would feel the way I do if they had the same information.	"He'd let her climb if he understood how she felt."
2. Self-Reflective (8–10)	Actually, we can have different points of view. There's hers, and there's mine. I can see mine; she can see hers.	"He'll be mad 'cause he doesn't want her to climb trees."
3. Mutual (10–12)	Well, maybe I can see hers and she can see mine. We can even talk about our different points of view.	"Holly and her father can talk to each other. They will understand each other. They can work it out."
4. Social and conventional (12–15+)	Actually, within the context of discombobulism, and taking into consideration the teachings of MUMU and the charter of personal delimitations, her point of view is totally philanthropic. On the other hand. . . .	"It depends on whether her father thinks the cat's life or Shawn's feelings are more important than obedience. Besides. . . ."

Note: These reflect children's ability to *verbalize* their perspectives and their understanding of other perspectives. However, their actual behavior reflects more advanced understanding of other people's thoughts, beliefs, and feelings during the preschool period.

the thief take it. Later, both groups of children are questioned about what they saw, who the thief was (a simple question, even for the five-year-olds), and whether the man in the video would know who the thief was. The question, it turns out, is extremely difficult for five-year-olds when the video witness has different information than the child. Most kindergartners are likely to confuse what they themselves saw and know with what they think the man in the video would know. In contrast, the older children manifested growing ability to differentiate between their own view and that of the video character. Still, however, when older children made errors, they were almost invariably errors in which they attributed their own perspective to the video character. The implication, note Durkin and Howarth, is that kindergarten children are unlikely to be able to understand a good deal of the social information that is implicit in television programs, including information about motives, intentions, guilt, and so on.

Clearly, the preschooler's theory of mind is less sophisticated than that of the older child. But just as clearly, important developments have occurred in the preschooler's growing capacity to understand belief, intention, and other aspects of mind.

SELF-ESTEEM

The child's theory of mind, says Astington (1991), "is the understanding children have of their own and others' minds....This understanding enables children to predict and explain actions by ascribing mental states...to themselves and to other people" (p. 158). Thus, theory of mind implies an awareness of self and of others as distinct selves. Put another way, it implies a **self-concept**. Self-concept is one aspect of what we refer to in Chapter 2 as *self-referent thought*—thought that has to do with the **self** (thought that is *self-reflective*).

Self-concept is a general term that refers to the description we would arrive at if asked to describe our roles and our personality characteristics (Kahne, 1996). One aspect of self-concept is evaluative; it refers primarily to how we evaluate ourselves, what we think of ourselves. This aspect of self-concept is better labeled **self-esteem** (also called **self-worth**). People have high self-esteem (positive self-concepts) when they think well of themselves, and low self-esteem (or negative self-concepts) when they don't think much of themselves.

Some aspects of the self-concept are not evaluative. They have to do with abstract, cognitive notions of what the self is rather than with whether the self is good or bad, worthwhile or worthless, lovable or detestable, moral or immoral.

Two Approaches to Self-Esteem

How do we develop notions of self-esteem? How do we decide whether or not our selves are worthwhile? Historically, there have been two major approaches to answering these questions.

JAMES'S APPROACH

William **James's approach to self-worth** (1892) says this: My self-worth is a direct function of the difference between what I would like to be and what I think I am. The closer my actual self (as I perceive my self) is to my ideal self (the way I would like to be), the more I will like myself, and, hence, the higher my self-esteem.

COOLEY'S APPROACH

Cooley's approach to self-worth (1902) argues as follows: My self-worth is a direct function of what I think others think of me; my worth is reflected in their behavior toward me (hence, his expression *looking-glass self*). If people avoid me, that is evidence that I am not very worthy; if they seek me out, the evidence is more positive. Those who are most im-

One of the most important aspects of our self-concepts is evaluative—whether we like or don't like ourselves. For those whose notions of self-esteem (or self-worth) are highly positive, smiling and laughing are easy.

portant in serving as mirrors in whose behavior I can view my self are people who are most important to me. Hence, for the preschooler, parents and siblings are most important; for the elementary schoolchild, peers and teachers also become important—and perhaps coaches, mentors, tutors, religious leaders, and so on (see Table 10.2).

Investigations and Implications of Self-Esteem

There are a number of scales for measuring self-esteem (for example, the Rosenberg Self-Esteem Scale and the Harter

TABLE 10.2

Two Theories of the Basis of Self-Esteem

THEORY	EXAMPLE OF REASONING PROCESS
James: discrepancy between actual and ideal self (what I would like to be versus what I think I am)	"I'm a blonde, which is what I would want to be if I had a choice. My skin is clear, and I like my eyes—nice blue. Physically, I know I'm well, pretty attractive. But I've just been pulling off C's in school, which is the pits. I want at least B's."
Cooley: looking-glass self (what I think important others think of me)	"Willie asked me out. Billy asked me out. Sam looks at me as if he wants to ask me out, and he could go out with anybody in the school. I must be pretty attractive."

TABLE 10.3

Areas in Which Children Evaluate Their Self-Worth

AREA	DESCRIPTION
1. Scholastic competence	How competent, smart, the child feels with regard to schoolwork.
2. Athletic competence	How competent the child feels at sports and games requiring physical skill and athletic ability.
3. Social acceptance	How popular or socially accepted the child feels with peers.
4. Behavioral conduct	How adequate the child feels with regard to behaving in the way one is supposed to behave.
5. Physical appearance	How good-looking the child feels, how much the child likes such characteristics as height, weight, face, hair.

Note: Children's estimates of self-worth are based on (1) what significant other people think of the child's capabilities and worth (Cooley's looking-glass theory) and (2) the extent to which the child lives up to personal ideals and aspirations (James's discrepancy between aspirations and competence theory). Both kinds of evaluations occur in the five areas described here.
Source: From "The Determinants and Mediational Role of Global Self-Worth in Children," by S. Harter (1987).

Self-Perception Profile for Children—see Hagborg, 1993, for a look at the validity of these measures). These scales typically ask children questions about how well they think they perform in various areas considered important for developing notions of self-worth. For example, the Harter scale asks questions relating to five areas: athletic, scholastic, social, physical, and moral.

In some of Harter's (1987, 1988) studies, children were asked how important they think it is to do well in these areas. Thus, investigators could look at the difference between actual performance (competence) and the child's wishes, and arrive at a measure relating to James's approach.

Children were also asked to what extent they felt their importance is recognized by others, how well others treat them, whether they think they are liked, admired, and respected. This line of questioning provides information relating to the regard in which others hold the child (Cooley's approach).

Finally, children were asked questions relating to a more global concept of self-esteem—questions relating to how well they like themselves as people.

Use of questions such as these provides answers for a number of important questions: Are discrepancy-between-actual-and-ideal-self-based estimates of self-esteem (James's theory) or "looking-glass" estimates (Cooley's theory) actually related to general concepts of self-esteem? Are discrepancies between competence and the ideal more important in one area than another (for example, are athletics more important than scholastics)? Are there developmental changes in areas of importance? Is the source of approval and social regard important?

■ SOME IMPORTANT FINDINGS

Harter (1987) provides answers for a number of these questions based on her investigations of children in grades three through eight (approximately eight to thirteen years of age). Prior to the age of eight, children do not seem to have a single, clearly defined, and measurable notion of self-worth; accordingly, younger children are not included in Harter's samples.

First, although children have a general estimate of personal worth, they also make individual estimates of self-worth in at least five separate areas: scholastic competence, athletic competence, social acceptance, physical appearance, and behavioral conduct (Table 10.3). In other words, some children may see themselves as athletically competent (good and worthwhile), but these same children may have decided that they were not "good" in a moral sense—or that they are not as worthwhile scholastically. There is evidence that self-concept is relatively stable, although self-esteem might increase or decrease depending primarily on the child's experiences (Block & Robins, 1993).

Second, Harter's studies indicate that the child's judgments of self-worth reflect both major sources described by James and Cooley. That is, the difference between competencies (in each of the five important areas) and the child's aspirations and desires is reflected in estimates of self-worth. At the same time, how others regard the child also has an important influence on self-esteem.

Third, not all five areas are equally important to every child. High or low competence in important areas will have a more powerful influence than competence or incompetence in less important areas. If athletics are more important than being good (behavioral conduct), not being a good athlete will be more damaging to self-esteem than behaving immorally. In Harter's studies, physical appearance is the most important area in determining self-worth, both for the younger (grades three to six) and the older (grades six to eight) children. Children who see themselves as attractive are most likely to like themselves. For both these age groups, behavioral conduct (goodness of behavior in a moral sense) was least important (see Table 10.4).

TABLE 10.4

Correlations Between Children's Self-Worth and Perceived Inadequacies in Specific Areas

	ELEMENTARY SCHOOL: GRADES 3–6	MIDDLE SCHOOL: GRADES 6–8
Physical appearance	.66	.57
Social acceptance	.36	.45
Scholastic competence	.35	.36
Athletic competence	.33	.24
Behavioral conduct	.30	.26

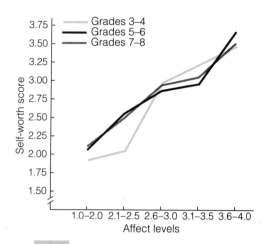

FIGURE 10.1

The relationship between mood and self-concept. In Harter's study, children who were sad (low affect level) had the lowest opinions of themselves. (From S. Harter, "The Determinants and Mediational Role of Global Self-Worth in Children," in Contemporary Topics in Developmental Psychology, *p. 234, N. Eisenberg (Ed.). © 1987 John Wiley & Sons, Inc. Used by permission of the publisher.)*

Fourth, as we noted, some sources of social regard and support are more important than others. For example, it might not matter very much that some nameless fan yells disparaging remarks while ten-year-old Willie stands at the plate waiting for a pitch, but it might matter a great deal if his coach later makes the same remarks. In Harter's (1987) studies, the most important sources of support in determining self-worth, for both the younger and the older children, are parents and classmates, rather than friends or teachers. It is noteworthy that parents retain their importance through these years, because this contradicts a popular belief that as peers become more important, parents must become less important. It is also significant that classmates are typically more important than are friends. This may well be because classmates' opinions can be seen as more objective; the evaluation of friends, on the other hand, could be more biased.

Fifth, estimates of self-worth are closely linked with affect (emotion or mood), which, in turn, has much to do with motivation. As Harter (1988) comments, elementary schoolchildren who like themselves (who have high self-esteem) are the happiest; in contrast, those who do not think very highly of themselves are more likely to feel sad or even depressed. Also, children who are happy are most likely to feel motivated to do things; those who are sad are least likely to want to do things. Figure 10.1 depicts the relationship between mood and self-worth scores for three groups of children from grades three through eight. Note that for all three groups, very low affect scores (sadness bordering on depression) are associated with very low self-worth scores; conversely, high affect is associated with high measures of self-worth.

SOME IMPLICATIONS

Some of the practical implications of self-worth seem clear. To the extent that positive self-esteem is closely related to happiness and to high motivation—and, by the same token, to social adjustment and general well-being—parents, teachers, and others who share responsibility for rearing youngsters must be concerned with far more than their cognitive development or their physical well-being. They must do what they can to ensure that the evaluation that every child places on the self is a positive judgment. In fact, enhance-

ment of children's self-esteem is one of the key recommendations of most parenting programs and may be especially important for children at risk for developmental problems (Cutright, 1992; Silvestri, Dantonio, & Eason, 1994). And developing high self-esteem has often been adopted as one of the principal goals of schools (Kahne, 1996).

Unfortunately, the causes of feelings of self-worth are not simple. They include factors over which we have limited control like scholastic competence or physical appearance. But they also include things over which we have more control—like our personal estimates of our children and our communication of love and support.

We are not alone in determining children's self-worth. Friends, classmates, teachers, and parents are all important. (See Summary Table 10.5.)

FRIENDS, PEERS, AND PARENTS

"Friendships of children," writes Berndt (1989), "appear to exist in a kind of never-never-land, a world of fun and adventure that adults rarely if ever enter and cannot fully understand" (p. 332). But science, in her careful and analytic way, asks questions whose answers might increase understanding—questions like "How do children view friendship?"

Children's Views of Friendship

For the three- to five-year-old, claims Selman (1980, 1981), a friend is merely a playmate and friendship is nothing more complex than "playing together." At this stage, children have

CONCEPT	EXPLANATIONS/COMMENTS
Self-concept	■ General concept referring to our views of our roles and characteristics.
Self-esteem	■ Also termed *self-worth*. The evaluative aspect of our self-concepts—whether or not we think well of ourselves.
James's approach to self-esteem	■ Self-esteem is high to the extent that there is little discrepancy between what we would like to be (ideal self) and what we think we are.
Cooley's approach to self-esteem	■ Self-esteem reflects what we think others think of us.
Findings relating to children's self-esteem	■ Estimates of self-worth are made in at least five areas: scholastic competence, athletic competence, social acceptance, physical appearance, and behavior. ■ Both the James and the Cooley approaches are reflected in children's self-esteem. ■ Physical appearance is the most important area for most children; popularity is second; behavioral conduct is less important. ■ Parents and classmates are important sources of social approval. ■ Children with high self-esteem tend to be happier and more highly motivated.

The very young view friends as those with whom one plays; older children understand that friendships grow over time and involve sharing, trust, respect, and mutual interests. Among these children who gather in Central Park to play soccer, there are likely to be a number of "best" friends.

no concept of friendship as an enduring kind of relationship. A friend is simply someone who happens to be present and who plays with the child. And if they are asked how friendships are formed, they are likely to say, "By playing together." If asked to describe a friend, they will speak of activities but not of traits or characteristics ("He plays with me" or "He doesn't hit me").

Even in the preschool period, however, patterns of interactions among pairs of friends appear to be relatively stable over time. Park, Lay, and Ramsay (1993) studied twenty-four pairs of preschool friends (average age forty-six months) and found high correlations between observations made one year apart. Pair interactions tended to be highly consistent in terms of characteristics like how happily the children played together, what strategies were used for resolving conflicts, and how well children shared.

By the age of eleven or twelve, children understand that friendships develop over time and that they involve a reciprocal sharing of thoughts and feelings and a high degree of mutual trust. When asked to describe friends, they are likely to speak of qualities ("She understands people; she's so sincere") and of mutual interests ("We like a lot of the same things"). Whereas younger children assume that the best friends are those who live close by and who want to play,

older children realize that the best friends are those who share interests, who are mutually supportive, who like each other. A five-year-old assumes that to become friends it is necessary only to play together; a twelve-year-old believes that to become friends it is necessary to get to know one another. Accordingly, it is hardly surprising that highly aggressive children seek out the friendship of other highly aggressive children—even though these friendships tend to be characterized by "frequent, lengthy, and intense conflicts" (Snyder, Horsch, & Childs, 1997, p. 145). By the same token, the least aggressive children among the seventy-two boys and girls in the Snyder, Horsch, and Childs study were most likely to form friendships with others like themselves. And the pattern continues from preschool right through adolescence when, in the authors' words, "aggressive adolescents seek out peers with similar antisocial characteristics who provide further modeling, opportunity, and reinforcement for antisocial behavior" (p. 145).

Dimensions of Childhood Friendships

"Not having friends," writes Bullock (1994), "contributes to loneliness, low self-esteem and inability to develop social skills" (p. 95). Peer relations, she argues, are necessary for healthy development.

■ BEST FRIENDS

Strictly speaking, only one of our friends can be our best friend; none of the others can be more than second best. However, in common usage, *best friend* refers to a close type of friendship in which several people can be best friends all at the same time.

Most six- to twelve-year-old youngsters have more than one best friend, although that is not always apparent in the research. Berndt (1988) points out that if children are asked to name their best *friend*, they will obligingly name only one person. But if they are asked to name their best *friends,* they gladly name a number of people. And if the question is changed only slightly, and they are asked instead to indicate whether each child in their class is a best friend, a friend, or not a friend, some children will name most of the class as best friends.

■ SEX DIFFERENCES

Most children have a number of close friends who are most often of the same race and grade, who share common interests, and who are almost invariably of the same age and sex. In a study of friendship patterns among four- to nineteen-year-olds of both sexes attending an ungraded school where children of all ages interacted with others of different ages, Gray and Feldman (1997) found very few instances of age-mixing (where age-mixing was defined as involving children separated by at least twenty-four months). And where age mixing did occur, it almost invariably involved athletic activities and games rather than conversation. Similarly, gender mixing was rare except for the youngest children (below age seven) and the older ones.

Both boys and girls usually have two or three close friends rather than just one best friend. And for both sexes, friendships tend to be highly mutual: If one child indicates that a second is a best friend, the second child will very likely also have chosen the first as a best friend. As Hartup (1983) notes, reciprocity is a prominent characteristic of all childhood friendships.

One of the main differences between girls' and boys' friendships is that girls' relationships tend to involve more kindness, empathy, and self-revelation (Clark & Bittle, 1992). That is, girls' friendships are often more intimate. In addition, the pattern in elementary school, notes Erwin (1993), is for boys to have more friends than girls and to play in larger groups. Furthermore, as we noted in Chapter 8, they play more aggressively and more competitively at all ages.

■ IMPORTANCE OF FRIENDS

There is little doubt that having friends is extremely important to all normal children. Sadly, however, Bullock (1994) reports that between 6 and 11 percent of elementary school-age children have no friends. More than half the children referred for emotional or behavioral problems have no friends or have difficulty in peer interactions.

Rubin (1980) suggests that, among other things, friendships contribute significantly to the development of social skills (such as being sensitive to other people's points of view, learning the rules of conversation, learning sex- and age-appropriate behaviors). In addition, interactions with friends are involved in developing notions of self and self-worth. Friendships may also be important in developing feelings of belonging to a group, and may therefore play a crucial role in the development of notions of cultural identity. Not surprisingly, children who have no friends are at much higher risk of dropping out of school (Bullock, 1994).

It is also clear that friends have powerful influences on each other. Berndt (1988) summarizes research that has found that a child's academic performance can be positively or negatively influenced by choice of friends. Similarly, friends may serve to encourage or discourage deviant behaviors (such as delinquency or drug use).

Close friends are one source of influence on the developing child; peers are another.

Peer Groups

A **peer group** is a group of equals. Most individuals in our society have a peer group, excluding hermits, whose peers, by definition, are also isolated and therefore of little consequence to their development.

The peer group is one of the major transmitters of cultural expectations and values, particularly during middle childhood. As we saw, during these years the peer group typically consists of like-sexed children who are also of similar ages. During the elementary grades, younger children are typically less well accepted; so, too, are those who are excessively shy (Lemerise, 1997).

Parents and Peers

In infancy and early childhood, parents have traditionally been the center of the child's life—although with increasing numbers of children in day-care facilities, the importance of peer groups during the preschool period has increased significantly in recent decades. By the beginning of middle childhood, peers have assumed tremendous significance. And as children's interests and allegiance shift gradually toward peers, there are important changes in the ways in which they interact with and conform to their parents.

In early childhood, parental authority is largely unquestioned. This does not mean that all children always obey their parents. Sometimes temptation or impulse are just too overwhelming. And sometimes, too, parents overstep the unwritten but clearly understood boundaries of authority. As Braine and colleagues (1991) note, parental authority does not extend to immoral acts, nor can it be permitted to infringe on important areas of personal jurisdiction, such as choice of friends.

In later childhood and adolescence, parental authority is subjected to more constraints, and the child's area of control increases. Berndt (1979) asked 251 children in grades 3, 6, 9, and 11–12 to respond to hypothetical situations in which parents or peers urged them to do something antisocial, something prosocial, or something neutral. As expected, Berndt found that conformity to parents decreased steadily with age, and so did conformity to peers, except with regard to antisocial influences, which increased until about grade 9 (age 14), before beginning to decline again (see Figure 10.2).

Here, as in other areas of human development, relationships and interactions are complex and influence one another. Accordingly, it is misleading and overly simplified to consider parent–child relations on the one hand, and child–peer relations on the other, and to compare and contrast

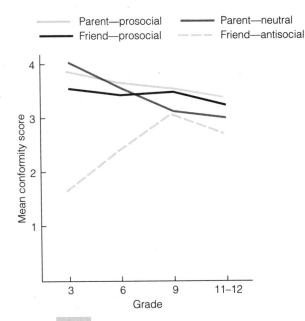

FIGURE 10.2

Changes in average conformity scores as a function of age and source of pressure. (From T. J. Berndt, "Developmental Changes in Conformity to Peers and Parents," Developmental Psychology 15, pp. 608–616. © 1979 by the American Psychological Association. Reprinted by permission of APA and the author.)

them as though they were isolated and unrelated. There is evidence, for example, that the kind of relationship a child has with parents is very closely related to later relationships with peers. Fuligni and Eccles (1993) found that children who felt their parents did not relax their power and provide them with more opportunities for decision making as they neared adolescence were more likely to be extremely peer oriented.

There is considerable evidence that supportive parenting leads to good peer relationships. Thus, securely attached infants (see Chapter 6) are more likely to later have good relationships with peers. Similarly, authoritative–democratic

That these young lads are happy buddies may have a lot to do with their relationships with their parents. Supportive parenting, research suggests, leads to good peer relations.

(as opposed to authoritarian–restrictive) parenting is associated with the most positive peer relationships (Dekovic & Janssens, 1992).

Peer Acceptance

Peer acceptance or rejection (**sociometric status**) is typically assessed using one of two methods: *peer ratings* or *peer nominations*. In a peer-rating study, each member of a group (for example, a classroom) might be asked to rate all other members of the group in terms of how well they like them, whether they would like to play with them, how smart they are, how popular, and so on. A study using peer nominations might ask participants to name the three individuals they like best, the three they like least, the three smartest kids, and so on. Data gathered in this way can then be analyzed to provide an index of sociometric acceptance or rejection, and can sometimes be depicted pictorially in a **sociogram** (Figure 10.3). Information of this kind is sometimes useful in research that looks at the qualities associated with popularity or social isolation.

Sociometric Status

We are not all equally loved and sought after by our friends. Indeed, not all of us have friends. Some of us are social isolates. **Social isolates** are those who do not often interact

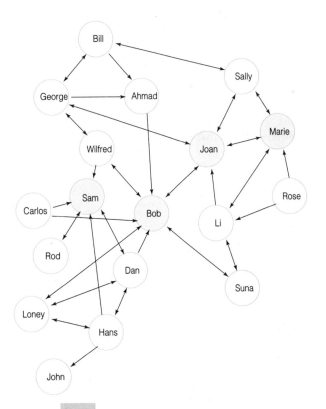

FIGURE 10.3

A sociogram of friendships in a fourth-grade classroom.

with peers, or those who are seldom selected as "best friend" by anyone. These two definitions are different, says Gottman (1977). Some children are liked and accepted but do not interact much with their peers; on the other hand, some children are very low on everybody's list of "my best friends" or "who I would most like to be with" or "who I would most like to be like," but they nevertheless interact frequently with peers.

FIVE LEVELS OF SOCIAL STATUS

In an attempt to investigate these definitions and clarify the nature of social isolation, Gottman studied 113 children in depth. His observations suggest five distinct categories of children (see Table 10.6). *Sociometric stars* are those who are consistently "especially liked." *Teacher negatives* are usually in conflict with teachers and might be either high or low on measures of peer acceptance. *Mixers* are those who interact often with peers; they too might be high or low on measures of acceptance. The *tuned out* are those who are usually not involved with what is going on—who are tuned "out" rather than "in." The tuned out, rather than being strongly rejected, are simply ignored. And, finally, *sociometric rejectees* are those who are disliked not only by their peers but are actively rejected by everyone. These are the children who are the butts of all the cruel jokes and taunts.

QUALITIES RELATED TO PEER ACCEPTANCE

In general, children who are friendly and sociable, and who evaluate others positively, are more easily accepted than those who are hostile, unsociable, withdrawn, or indifferent (Rabiner, Keane, & Mackinnon-Lewis, 1993). Similarly, children who are intelligent and creative are more accepted than those who are slow learners or retarded. Size, strength, athletic prowess, and daring are particularly important characteristics for membership in boys' peer groups; maturity and social skills are more important for girls, especially as they approach adolescence. Attractiveness is important for both (Hartup, 1983).

The observation that friendly, socially competent children have more friends (have higher status, as the sociologists put

TABLE 10.6

Five Categories of Social Status

CATEGORY	CHARACTERISTICS
Sociometric stars	Especially well liked by most.
Mixers	High peer interaction. Some well liked, others not.
Teacher negatives	Typically in conflict with teachers. Some are liked, others not.
Tuned out	Not involved—are ignored rather than rejected.
Sociometric rejectees	Not liked very much. Rejected rather than simply ignored.

Source: Based on Gottman (1977).

it) raises an interesting and important question: Are the characteristics of high-status (accepted) and low-status (rejected) children the cause or the result of their status? Does a friendly child have many friends because she is friendly, or is she friendly because she has many friends? Similarly, does social rejection lead to socially incompetent behavior, or is the socially incompetent behavior present to begin with, and lead to social rejection?

A review of a large number of studies strongly suggests that popular children are popular because they are more competent socially and that unpopular children lack social skills (Newcomb, Bukowski, & Pattee, 1993). In other words, how a child interacts with others is a primary cause of social status. The most socially competent children quickly sense what is happening in an unfamiliar social situation and are able to modify their behaviors accordingly. Thus, they are less likely to engage in behaviors that are inappropriate or unexpected than are socially incompetent children. In addition, Bryant (1992) found that the most socially preferred children are those most likely to use calm approaches to resolve conflicts. In contrast, children most likely to be rejected by peers are those who react to conflict either with anger and retaliation or with avoidance.

QUALITIES RELATED TO PEER REJECTION

Among characteristics often associated with peer rejection are those that make the child different or that are perceived as undesirable. Thus, in a study of tolerance and rejection, Crystal, Watanabe, and Chin (1997) found that children who were different from their peers were most likely to be rejected. In this study, the nontypical children were either highly aggressive, withdrawn, learning disabled, unathletic, or poor. Similarly, in a study of 362 eight- to eleven-year-olds, Pope, Bierman, and Mumma (1991) found that aggressive, hyperactive, and immature boys were likely to be rejected. Parkhurst and Asher (1992) also found that rejected students tend to be the most aggressive or, interestingly, the most submissive. In fact, one of the strongest predictors of peer rejection, claim Rys and Bear (1997), is physical aggression, especially among boys (among girls, physical aggression is relatively rare). Related to this, Juvonen (1991) reports that those who engage in behaviors others consider deviant (rule breaking, for example) are more likely to be rejected.

Consequences of Peer Acceptance and Rejection

Research indicates that the quality of children's relationships with their peers is very important for their happiness and adjustment (La Greca & Stone, 1993). Rejected children, Crick and Ladd (1993) report, are more lonely, more socially anxious, and more likely to avoid social situations. They are also more likely to drop out of school (Garnier, Stein, & Jacobs, 1997).

Ollendick, Weist, and Borden (1992) ranked the sociometric status of 296 fourth graders and, five years later, evaluated the academic performance and social adjustment of 267 of these children. Those classified as "rejected" fared significantly more poorly on both sets of measures. Similarly, Vitaro, Tremblay, and Gagnon (1992) found that preschoolers classed as "rejected" two years in a row were significantly more likely to manifest later behavior problems such as fighting, withdrawal, or hyperactivity than were children identified as "rejected" only one of two years.

Note that although peer rejection may be associated with poorer adjustment, that is certainly not always the case. In a study of 881 children in grades three through five, Parker and Asher (1993) found that many children who are not very popular nevertheless have very close and very satisfying friendships. There are wide individual differences in the sociability of different children. Not all are outgoing, talkative, expansive; many appear withdrawn and shy. We should not make the mistake of assuming that children who appear shy are also lonely and friendless. Nor should we assume that they are likely to be rejected by their peers or socially tuned out. Some of these children are extraordinarily socially competent. Many have a large number of close friendships. Some might, in fact, be among Gottman's sociometric stars. (See Summary Table 10.7.)

THE INFLUENCE OF THE SCHOOL

Outside of the family, say Asp and Garbarino (1988), the school is the most pervasive socializing influence in the life of the child. Schools are centrally involved in teaching children much that is necessary for their effective interaction in our increasingly complex world. In fact, note Stevenson and colleagues (1991), the influence of the school is so pervasive in our societies that much of what developmental psychologists view as "normal" development is, in fact, a reflection of what children learn in schools.

How Schools Affect Measured Intelligence

Schools do more than socialize children and teach them important information and skills; there is evidence that they also increase measured intelligence. For example, there has been a massive increase in IQ scores in the Netherlands since the 1950s. This increase, argue Husén and Tuijnman (1991), is due to changes in context, the most important of which may be formal schooling. Similarly, Flynn (1987) found that in fourteen industrialized countries there has been an increase of about 15 IQ points in one generation.

There is additional evidence that formal schooling is closely tied to measured intelligence. For example, Ceci (1991) reviewed studies that show a relationship between level of schooling (grade attained) and IQ, between missing school and declines in IQ, between delayed school entrance and lower IQ, and between increasing school attendance in an area and general increases in measured IQ. And Stevenson and associates (1991) found significant differences in cognitive development between Peruvian children who attended school and those who didn't. Perhaps more striking, they found remarkable similarities in the cognitive functioning of first graders from such diverse cultural backgrounds as Peru, Taiwan, Japan, and the United States—almost as though the experiences of first grade had already begun to wipe out

▲ SUMMARY TABLE 10.7

Childhood Friendships, Sociometric Status, and Well-Being

	CONCLUSIONS/EXPLANATIONS/COMMENTS
Dimensions of childhood friendships and peer acceptance	■ Initially (preschool period), friends are simply "someone to play with"; later, they become someone with whom there is much in common and much to share. ■ Most children have more than one "best" friend. ■ There is little age- or gender-mixing among childhood friendships. ■ Friendships are important for the development of social skills as well as for self-esteem and happiness. ■ Peer groups are one of society's major transmitters of culture. ■ Friends tend to select each other on the basis of similarities in age, gender, interests, and personality. ■ Aggressive boys often seek out others who are also aggressive; they serve as models and as sources of reinforcement for each other. ■ Socially competent, friendly children are most likely to be accepted by peers. ■ Overly aggressive, socially incompetent, and "atypical" children are more likely to be rejected.
Levels of sociometric status	■ *Social isolates* interact little with peers, but are not necessarily rejected. ■ *Sociometric stars* are especially well liked by most. ■ *Mixers* interact a great deal; some are liked, others not. ■ *Teacher negatives* are in conflict with teachers; some are liked, others not. ■ *Tuned out* are not involved; they are ignored rather than rejected. ■ *Sociometric rejectees* are not liked; they are rejected rather than simply ignored.

Schools are central in teaching children both the academic and the social skills required for successful adaptation to an increasingly complex world. Here a teacher helps a class to locate the Mt. Everest home page on the worldwide web.

what would otherwise have been highly noticeable differences. The evidence, claim Husén and Tuijnman (1991), supports the conclusion "that not only does child IQ have an effect on schooling outcomes, but also that schooling per se has a substantial effect on IQ test scores" (p. 22).

The Effects of Teacher Expectations

One illustration of how schools can affect children is found in the classic Rosenthal and Jacobson (1968a, 1968b) study of how teacher expectations can become self-fulfilling prophecies. The study involved administering students an intelligence test in the spring of the school year, telling teachers this was a test designed to identify academic "bloomers" (students expected to blossom next year), and later "accidentally" allowing teachers to see a list of likely bloomers. In fact, these bloomers were a randomly chosen group of about 20 percent of the school's population. No other treatment was undertaken.

■ THE SELF-FULFILLING PROPHECY

Amazingly, many teachers observed exactly what they expected. The experimental group not only scored higher on measures of achievement than a comparable control group, but also scored higher on a general measure of intelligence.

Hundreds of replication studies have been undertaken since the original studies. Not all of them provide very clear evidence of the existence or importance of teacher expectation effects (see Meyer, 1985). However, there is some evidence that many teachers develop predictable patterns of expectations and that these affect student behaviors and outcomes (Ozar, 1994; Wang, Haertel, & Walberg, 1993). These are often more positive for children from more advantaged socioeconomic backgrounds, as well as for students who are more attractive, more articulate, who sit close to the

teacher and speak clearly, and who are given the most positive labels—"learning disabled" rather than "retarded." Not surprisingly, even children have stereotypes about others who are labeled, and react accordingly. Miller, Clarke, and Malcarno (1991) observed nine- to fourteen-year-old children interacting with others described as being either "special education" students or regular students. The labels alone had a significant impact on how these children interacted.

Unfortunately, a quick overview of the results of studies such as these makes them seem far more dramatic and important than they actually are. In addition, there is a tendency to assume that negative expectations are more potent and more pervasive than are positive expectations. That is not the case.

Mastery-Oriented Versus Helpless Children

Teacher expectations, it seems, might affect the performance of some students. Can the student's own expectations also have an effect? Attribution theory suggests yes.

An **attribution** is an assignment of cause or blame for the outcomes of our behaviors. If I think my stupidity is due to my having hit my head on a low branch when I was ten, then I attribute my stupidity to that event. Attribution theories look for regularities in how we attribute causes to the things that happen to us (Weiner, 1980, 1994).

We saw in Chapter 2 that children are different in how they typically assign responsibility for their successes or failures. Some accept personal responsibility for the consequences of their behavior. They are said to have an **internal orientation** or internal **locus of control** (or to be **mastery-oriented** or persistent; Dweck, 1986). Others are more likely to attribute successes and failures to circumstances or events over which they have no control, and are described as having an **external orientation** or locus of control (in Dweck's terms, they are characterized by **learned helplessness** rather than by persistence). Thus, mastery-oriented children are most likely to attribute their successes to ability or effort (factors that are personal, or factors over which they at least have personal control); in contrast, helpless children are more likely to attribute their successes or failures to luck or the difficulty of the task (factors over which they have no personal control) (see Interactive Table 10.8).

■ HOW MASTERY-ORIENTED AND HELPLESS CHILDREN DIFFER

Differences between mastery-oriented and helpless children are often highly apparent. First, mastery-oriented children tend to be more achievement-oriented. They undertake tasks that are more challenging and strive harder to do well in them (Erdley & Dweck, 1994).

Second, mastery-oriented and helpless children react very differently to successes and failures. When Diener and Dweck (1980) arranged a problem situation so that all chil-

In Chapter 3, you were asked to figure out what Henry VIII didn't know that might have influenced his habit of beheading various wives who failed to give him sons. Did you succeed or fail? Why? Are you one of those who characteristically accept personal responsibility for successes and failures? Or are you more likely to invoke luck, the difficulty (or easiness) of the task, or other factors over which you have no control? How do you explain your high (or low) grades to yourself? Your reasons reveal important things about your personality and achievement motivation.

EXTERNAL	INTERNAL
Difficulty (task easy or too difficult).	Ability (intelligence, skill, or the lack thereof).
Luck (bad or good).	Effort (hard work, industriousness, self-discipline, or laziness, distractions, lack of time).

SUMMARY TABLE 10.9
The Influence of the School:
Five Summary Points

1. Formal school is closely tied to measured intelligence.

2. What teachers expect of students may influence their performance (a self-fulfilling prophecy).

3. Teacher expectations, both positive and negative, sometimes reflect biases and stereotypes based on labels, gender, and other identifiable student characteristics.

4. Students who tend to assume responsibility for the outcomes of their behaviors (internal locus of control, or mastery orientation) appear to have an advantage in terms of motivation and achievement.

5. Students who attribute the outcomes of their behaviors to factors beyond their control (external locus of control, described as learned helplessness) are at a disadvantage in terms of motivation and achievement.

dren would experience an unbroken sequence of eight successes, helpless children still predicted they would not do very well if they had to repeat the eight tasks. These children found it difficult to interpret success as indicating that they are capable. Even after succeeding, they continue to underestimate future successes and overestimate future failures. In contrast, mastery-oriented children were confident they would continue to perform as well. And even when they were given a series of failure experiences, they continued to see themselves as capable and to predict future success experiences. They have higher expectations of themselves.

There appear to be some clear advantages to being mastery-oriented, especially in school. For this reason, a number of programs have been developed to change attributions. These are based on the assumption that the tendency to attribute outcomes to internal or external factors is at least partly learned, and can therefore be changed (Ames, 1992).

Schools clearly have a profound influence not only on the learning of "things," but also on social learning. (See Summary Table 10.9.) Another source of profound influence on both of these classes of learning is television.

THE POWER OF TELEVISION

We don't know for certain what to think of television. Surely we must like it; very few of our homes don't have at least one set. Yet we've invented all sorts of pejorative labels for it: *the idiot box, the vidiot, the one-eyed monster, the rug-rat babysitter, the plug-in drug, the boob tube*. It's almost as though we fear it—or at least fear what it might do to our children. And for some time now, our prophets of doom and gloom have been spreading the alarm. Television, they croak as they lurch about

our villages, will have highly negative effects on children. Some of these prophets claim that television is producing a generation of passive people—inactive, lethargic, apathetic. Others argue that the violence characteristic of much of television is creating a generation of violent people. Still others fear that television has a corrupting influence through its transmission of undesirable values, including the message that immorality is often rewarded. There is also the possibility, warn the alarmists, that, given the amount of the child's time it consumes, television may have a harmful effect on family relationships, on the social development of children, and on badminton, bicycling, bird-watching, and bingo. Although the research evidence is incomplete, we have enough answers to partially respond to these criticisms and to present a more balanced impression of the actual influence of television on the lives of children.

Children's Viewing Patterns

In 1950, there were about 100,000 television sets in North American homes; one year later, there were more than 1 million. Now it is no easy thing to find any home without at least one set (Gunter & McAleer, 1990). A conservative estimate is that preschoolers spend more than a third of their waking time watching television. Even nine-month-olds watch about ninety minutes of television a day (Cohen, 1993/1994). Many young children spend more time watching television than they spend in conversation with adults or siblings. In fact, by age eighteen, many children will have spent about 50 percent more time watching television than going to school and doing schoolwork combined. Only sleeping will have taken more time than watching television (Huston et al., 1990).

Young Children's Comprehension of Television

What children see and understand from television might be quite different from what you or I might see. Not only do they lack the experiences that we have, but their conceptual bases are more fragmented, less complete. Researchers now recognize that how children process television information must be closely related to whatever effects television might have (Geiger & Newhagen, 1993).

Hayes and Casey (1992) report that preschoolers understand very little of the emotions and motives of characters—hardly surprising given their social cognitions. Accordingly, the preschooler responds to the most striking features of what is actually happening—the sights, the sounds, the action. What they don't understand, notes Evra (1990), they simply ignore. But even at the age of five or six, children use fairly sophisticated cognitive skills to understand television's messages. And those with the most advanced verbal skills have a much higher level of comprehension (Jacobvitz, Wood, & Albin, 1991). With advancing age, children become progressively more sensitive to motives and more attentive to implications of actions for the characters involved. And research indicates that their memory for what they see on television may be far better than for what they read. Walma van der Molen and van der Voort (1997) presented 152 fourth and sixth graders with brief sequences of children's news items, either televised or in written form. When these children were subsequently tested for their recollections of what they had read or seen, the television-presented material proved significantly more memorable than the printed material.

But what is it that children see on television—and remember? In spite of the fact that there are increasing numbers of channels dedicated to commercial-free, nonviolent children's programming, much of what children see is rapid action, constant change, high noise level, slapstick violence (Hough & Erwin, 1997). And much of the violence is unrealistic, excessive, and carried out by characters clearly identified with some of our culture's negative stereotypes. For example, following a detailed analysis of the content of television programming, Diefenbach (1997) reports that one recurring stereotype links mental disorders with violence. The mentally ill, he notes, account for ten times more violence than other television characters (and close to twenty times more violence than people in the real world!). One very important question concerns the effects of television violence on children.

Overt and Social Aggression

Violence is an extreme form of what is termed **overt aggression.** Violence implies overt physical action and the possibility of real harm or injury to people or objects. Overt aggression is not always violent. It includes a range of forceful human actions intended to dominate, to frighten, perhaps even to hurt physically.

Our psychological research, if not our powers of observation, makes it clear that overt aggressiveness is predominantly a male characteristic. This has led many to mistakenly assume that *aggressiveness* is a male, but not a female, trait. In fact, although *overt* aggressiveness is primarily a male propensity, there are less obvious but, at least in some ways, no less harmful forms of aggression that are engaged in more by girls than by boys. These forms of aggression are labeled **social aggression** (or sometimes **relational aggression**). They are so labeled because the primary goal of social aggression is to harm people by disrupting their social relations. Overt aggression seeks to do harm through physical damage, note Crick, Casas, and Mosher (1997); in contrast, social aggression seeks to do harm by damaging peer relationships. Thus, the methods of overt aggression are kicking, punching, pushing, and gouging eyes; the methods of relational aggression are ridicule, social exclusion, rumor mongering, malicious teasing, contempt, and disdain.

Social aggression, report Galen and Underwood (1997), is recognized by children, and especially by girls, as highly hurtful—in fact, as often more hurtful than overt aggression. Evidence suggests that children who are victims of social aggression often suffer from adjustment problems and unhappiness (Crick, 1966). At the same time, in the same way as overtly aggressive children are most likely to be rejected by peers, so too, children who engage in high levels of social aggression are also more likely to suffer peer rejection (Grotpeter & Crick, 1996).

Unfortunately, those concerned with the effects of television violence on children's aggressiveness have not usually distinguished between overt and social aggression. The research predominantly looks at the effects of extreme overt aggression (violence, in other words) on manifested aggressive behavior. There is much that we don't yet know about the extent of relational aggression in television programs, or about the effects that television's portrayal of social aggression might have on child viewers.

■ LABORATORY RESEARCH ON TELEVISION VIOLENCE

But we do know that television programming for children (and for adults) is marked by a very large number of violent images. Many of these, note Potts and Henderson (1991), have to do with injury-related events. Not only are these far more common on television than in real life, but their negative consequences are often trivialized, and they often happen in "humorous" circumstances.

In an early series of studies, Bandura and his associates (Bandura, 1969; Bandura, Ross, & Ross, 1963) exposed children to violent models that were either live actors, films of real people, or films of cartoon characters. Following exposure to a violent model (typically, the model was aggressive toward an inflated rubber clown), children were given objects similar to those toward which the model had been aggressive and were observed at play through a one-way mirror. In most studies of this kind, a majority of the children who have been exposed to models of violence behave aggressively;

Several decades ago, visiting with friends typically meant playing games, talking, inventing fantasies; now it often means jointly watching television. Because it's so difficult to find comparison groups of children who have not been exposed to television, research remains somewhat uncertain about the effects of television viewing.

in contrast, those who have not been exposed to violent models most often respond nonaggressively.

Although these studies have been widely interpreted as evidence that violence on television leads to violence in real life, there are at least three reasons why this kind of generalization may be unrealistic. First, the aggression displayed in an ordinary television program is directed against people rather than against inanimate objects, and children learn early in life, through socialization, that aggression against people is normally punished. Second, the experimental situation generally exposes the child to objects identical to those aggressed upon by the model, and usually immediately afterward. But a child who watches a violent scene on television is rarely presented immediately with an object (or person) similar to the one on whom the televised violence was inflicted. Third, striking a rubber clown with a mallet, kicking it, or punching it after seeing a model do so may not be a manifestation of aggression at all. The child has simply learned that these are appropriate and expected behaviors with this inanimate object.

■ NATURALISTIC RESEARCH ON TELEVISION VIOLENCE

Studies of television viewing under more natural circumstances may provide clearer information about its impact. Unfortunately, it's difficult to find children who have not been exposed to television and who can therefore serve as control groups for these studies; hence, there are few of them.

One study reported by Williams and Handford (1986) looked at sports participation of children without television compared with children who had access to only one channel and others who could access four channels. Not surprisingly, they found that the greater the access to television, the less likely the children were to participate actively in sports.

A study conducted by Joy, Kimball, and Zabrack (1977) involved children in a town where television was just being introduced. Two years later, comparisons of these children with comparable children in another town that still had no

American children watch many hours of television a week, most of it characterized by violent themes and acts. The weight of the evidence indicates that televised violence does increase viewer aggression, but how serious and long-term these effects are is unclear.

television found a measurable increase in aggressive behavior among the television children. Similar results were also reported in Sweden, where researchers found high positive correlations between television viewing and aggressiveness (Rosengren & Windahl, 1989). Note, however, that these studies do not prove that viewing violent television programs causes aggression. It may be that children who initially preferred violent programs would have been more aggressive and more prone to delinquency than other children even if they had not been exposed to these programs.

■ CROSS-CULTURAL COMPARISONS

A series of studies looked at the effects of television violence on aggressiveness in children from five countries: the United States, Finland, Israel, Poland, and Australia (Huesmann & Eron, 1986). Not only are these cultures very different, but television accessibility and the nature of television programming vary tremendously. For example, in the Israeli kibbutz, children watched TV for only one or two hours a week and were almost never exposed to television violence. In contrast, American children watched twenty or more hours of television, most of it characterized by violent themes and violent acts.

The main conclusion advanced by Huesmann and Eron is essentially the same as the conclusion reached by the Surgeon General's Report on Television and Social Behavior more than a decade earlier: Television violence does have an adverse effect on some children. Second, the relationship between television viewing and aggression appears to be interdependent. That is, the most aggressive children tend to select the more violent television programs and to view more of them; at the same time, those who watch more violent programs tend to be more aggressive.

In conclusion, most research summaries that have looked at the relationship between aggression and television viewing reach similar conclusions. As Rosenkoetter, Huston, and Wright (1990) put it, "Most professional reviews...have concluded that the weight of evidence indicates that television violence does increase viewer aggression" (p. 125). But, as Evra (1990) emphasizes, the most recent studies indicate that the long-term impact of television violence may, in fact, be negligible.

OTHER POSSIBLE NEGATIVE EFFECTS OF TELEVISION

Another possible negative effect of violence on television is the instillation of fear in some children—an effect that, for some, may be more serious than increased aggressiveness. In fact, a survey conducted by Ridley-Johnson, Surdy, and O'Laughlin (1991) found that parents are as concerned about fear-related influences of television as about aggression-related effects.

There is a possibility, too, that television may have changed the nature of children's play. Cohen (1993/1994) notes not only that children who watch more television may participate less in sports, but also that the influence of parents and peers seems to have declined with the television generation. Television is now a primary source of information and influence, he argues. It not only reinforces models of social behavior, but creates them as well. So important is it that children and, indeed, families often arrange their schedules (and their furniture) around television.

Positive Effects of Television

However, the potential effects of television are not all negative. Evidence shows, for example, that the language development of preschoolers can be significantly improved with educational television (Koutsouvanou, 1993). Similarly, children who watch the news show *Channel One* in the classroom do learn more news than those who don't (Greenberg & Brand, 1993). At the same time, they are also motivated to want to buy the products they see advertised, even when they don't understand the meaning of the commercials (Mac-Neal, 1992).

There is evidence, too, that in the same way that television might be instrumental in undermining values such as non-violence, family stability, cooperation, altruism, and gender equality, so too might it serve to bring about and strengthen these values. Baran, Chase, and Courtright (1979) found that cooperation could be increased in young children after exposure to an episode of *The Waltons* that dealt with coop-

eration in problem solving. Similarly, research with episodes from *Mister Rogers' Neighborhood* and with a number of other deliberately prosocial programs found clear evidence of improvement in prosocial behaviors such as friendliness, generosity, cooperation, creativity, empathy, racial tolerance, and others (Rosenkoetter et al., 1990). Unfortunately, however, as Cohen (1993/1994) points out, only rarely does commercial television teach these messages.

Rock Videos, VCRs, and Video Games

What messages does the new television-related technology provide, and what is their potential influence on children?

ROCK VIDEOS

Close to the cutting edge of television technology, and sometimes very close as well to the edge of what society's evolving tastes and morals find acceptable, are rock videos. They are very simple: Take a popular, avant-garde, rock-type song; create images to accompany the lyrics; and combine the two in a frenetic, jarring, surprising, evocative, and sometimes bizarre way. The result? A dazzling, seductive, intriguing, audiovisual experience that has transformed the music industry—and that has alarmed some parents and educators as well. Why? Because, as one commentator put it, "Some of them are sending messages that are questionable, to say the least: anti-work, anti-marriage, anti-family, pro-violence, pro-casual sex, pro-woman-as-victim" (*Television and your children,* 1985, p. 52).

Rock videos, says Luke (1988), have much the same faults that are found in commercial television: They are racist, sexist, violent, and highly commercialized. Although research on their effects is still rare, it is likely that they will be at least as influential as more ordinary television programs. Indeed, they might even be more influential given their technological slickness, the addictive quality of their lyrics and their rhythms, and their popularity with the teen and preteen generation. At the same time, their popularity might also be used to advantage in some circumstances, perhaps as a motivational tool in the classroom. For example, Berg and Turner (1993) report a project in which sixth-grade students created their own music videos based on great works of art as well as on their own art.

VCRs

About 70 percent of American homes now have VCRs (Clifford, Gunter, & McAleer, 1995). Their rapid proliferation brings an additional worry for those concerned about the potentially harmful effects of television. Rosengren and Windahl (1989) point out that parents and society either do not have, or often don't exercise, significant control over children's selections of the video recordings that they rent for home viewing. In most areas, it is possible for children to rent videos that depict aggression and standards of morality that would not be considered acceptable on broadcast television. Similarly, the increasing availability of quasi-private channels through home satellite systems means that increasing numbers of children may be exposed to extreme forms of violence and pornography at very young ages (Nelson, 1992). There is clearly a need for more research to ascertain the probable effects of this exposure and to identify the parameters that might interact to make some children more vulnerable than others.

VIDEO GAMES

Video games have been a source of concern for some parents as well, particularly in light of their quasi-addictive qualities and their overwhelmingly violent themes. However, Griffiths's (1991) review of relevant studies indicates that frequent players are no more maladjusted, conduct disordered, or likely to use drugs than infrequent players or nonplayers. Although some studies report greater incidence of aggressiveness among frequent players, at least half do not.

The Two Sides of the Television Controversy

"Television," writes Neuman (1991), "is a wonderful nemesis for those inclined to fret over the education of the young. It has been accused of robbing youngsters of childhood, reducing attention spans, and impairing children's ability to think clearly" (p. 158). She goes on to describe how television has been blamed for poor achievement, aggression, illiteracy, and so on. But, following a review of the research, she concludes, "The charges against the medium have been unwarranted" (p. 158).

That is one side of the controversy. The other side is summarized by Cohen (1993/1994): "Research data support past warnings of the potential negative effects associated with frequent television watching, especially among younger viewers" (p. 103).

An increasing number of researchers are now arguing that schools should teach children the basic skills of television literacy—skills relating to distinguishing between reality and fantasy, making wise choices among available programming, and limiting viewing and engaging in other important social and intellectual activities such as conversation, reading, and playing (Cohen, 1993/1994). The long-range goal, some authors argue, should be to eliminate advertising for children. This, they believe, would have a significant impact on programming. And ultimately, it might serve to reduce violence in the contemporary family. (See Summary Table 10.10.)

CHILD MALTREATMENT

There are a frightening number of crimes against persons in the United States each year—crimes like rape, robbery, and assault. In 1994 almost one out of every three households was touched at least once by crime. An astounding 47 percent of the offenders were friends, relatives, or at least acquain-

SUMMARY TABLE 10.10
Television and Aggression: Eight Summary Points

1. For many children, only sleeping takes up more time than watching television.

2. What children understand from television depends on their age and prior knowledge.

3. Aggression is defined by actions tended to dominate, to control, to frighten, to humiliate.

4. The most masculine form of aggression is *overt*, involving actual physical action (kicking, punching, slapping, shooting), the most extreme forms of which define *violence*.

5. The most feminine form of aggression is *social* or *relational*, involving acts that seek to harm persons by disrupting their social relations (ridicule, social exclusion, malicious gossip, contempt, and disdain).

6. The weight of evidence indicates that televised violence does increase viewer aggression, but how long-term these effects are is unclear. Other possible negative effects relate to the instillation of fearfulness in children and the disruption of normal social development by reducing play behavior.

7. Possible positive effects include enhanced language development, expansion of knowledge base, and the inculcation of prosocial values, given appropriate television programming.

8. The long-term effects of rock videos, VCRs, and video games are unknown, but the intensity of their attractiveness to children is clear.

tances of the victims; that percentage rises to an astonishing 67 percent in cases of rape or sexual assault. In addition, there are now over 1.2 million substantiated instances of child abuse and neglect each year in the United States, and about twice that number reported (U.S. Bureau of the Census, 1996).

Children are surrounded by violence—in the home, on television, in school. Boulton (1993) surveyed more than 100 elementary school boys and girls. More than half reported they had engaged in at least one physical fight during the preceding year, mainly in retaliation for teasing or because of disagreements over the way games were being played. Boys engaged in more fights than girls.

Some argue that much of the violence in our society begins with violence in the home and that much of the violence in the home begins with cultural values that, at least implicitly, have maintained it is acceptable for parents to use physical force to control and to punish their children (de Jonge, 1995).

Prevalence of Child Maltreatment

Reported cases of **child maltreatment** increased dramatically through the 1980s—from 3.5 per 1,000 population in 1980 to more than 10 per 1,000 in the 1990s (U.S. Bureau

AT A GLANCE

Child Maltreatment

Reported instances of child abuse and neglect have risen dramatically in recent decades—from 10.1 cases per 1,000 children in 1976 to more than 30 cases per 1,000 in 1986

(the numbers in Figure 10.5 are per 1,000 *population*, and are therefore lower). A total of more than 2.9 million children were victims of reported maltreatment in 1994. Of these children, 46.3 percent were male; 52.7 percent

were female (the sex was unknown in 1 percent of reported cases). It is unclear to what extent rising rates represent an actual increase in maltreatment and to what extent they reflect increased awareness and reporting by teachers, physicians, relatives, and family acquaintances.

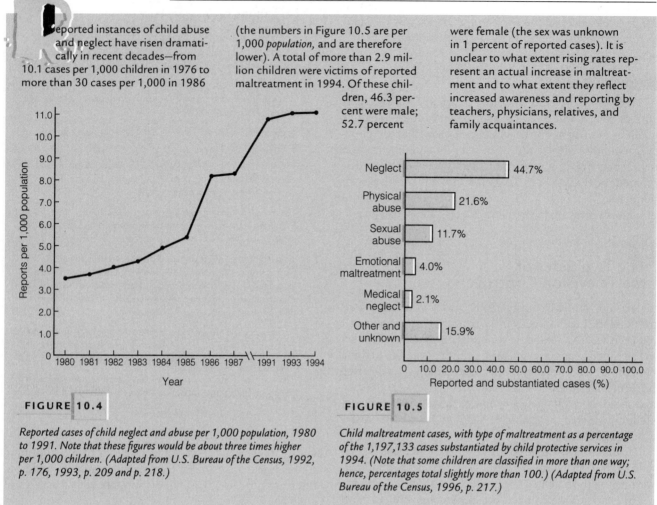

FIGURE 10.4

Reported cases of child neglect and abuse per 1,000 population, 1980 to 1991. Note that these figures would be about three times higher per 1,000 children. (Adapted from U.S. Bureau of the Census, 1992, p. 176, 1993, p. 209 and p. 218.)

FIGURE 10.5

Child maltreatment cases, with type of maltreatment as a percentage of the 1,197,133 cases substantiated by child protective services in 1994. (Note that some children are classified in more than one way; hence, percentages total slightly more than 100.) (Adapted from U.S. Bureau of the Census, 1996, p. 217.)

---

of the Census, 1996).* In 1991 nearly 2.7 million children were subjects of reported child abuse and neglect cases. Of these, nearly 1 million cases were substantiated. In 1994 the number of substantiated cases of child maltreatment had risen to 1.2 million (see "At a Glance: Child Maltreatment" and Figures 10.4 and 10.5). However, it isn't clear whether this means that child maltreatment is actually increasing or whether reporting and detection are more thorough. Still, given the difficulty of obtaining information from parents and even from doctors in cases of child abuse, this figure may represent a very conservative estimate. Murray, Henjum, and Freeze (1992) surveyed a sample of 110 college students and found that a shocking 22 percent of the women had been sexually abused as children (6 percent of the men); about three-fourths had experienced physical punishment (spanking, slapping, hitting). And in Wellman's (1993) sample of 824 college students, 6 percent of the males and 13 percent

of the females reported being sexually abused as children or adolescents.

In a survey of child abuse in the United States, Straus and Gelles (1986) found that 43 percent of a sample of 1,428 parents had used some form of physical violence on a child at least once during the past year (see Table 10.11). An astounding 2.9 percent admitted to having used a knife or a gun on one of their children at least once in their lifetimes—small wonder that one out of every five murders in the United States is committed among immediate family members in their own home.

Nature of Child Maltreatment

Not all child maltreatment involves physical abuse. For example, Uchiyama's (1994) analysis of 250 cases of child maltreatment in Japan identified eight classes of maltreatment: inappropriate care, excessive punishment, sexual abuse, injuries requiring medical attention, child abandonment, in-

---

*Note that these figures are per 1,000 *population*. Instances of abuse and neglect are about three times greater per 1,000 *children*.

TABLE 10.11

Violence Against Children in the United States, 1985

TYPE OF VIOLENCE	RATE PER 1,000 CHILDREN AGED 3 THROUGH 17[*]
Minor violent acts	
Threw something	27
Pushed, grabbed, shoved	307
Slapped or spanked	549
Severe violent acts	
Kicked, bit, hit with fist	13
Hit, tried to hit with something	97
Beat up	6
Threatened with gun or knife	2
Used gun or knife	2
Violence indexes (cases)	
Overall violence	620
Severe violence	107
Very severe violence	19

[*]For two-caretaker households with at least one child three to seventeen years of age at home.
Source: Adapted from "Societal Change and Change in Family Violence from 1975 to 1985 as Revealed by Two National Surveys" by M. A. Straus and R. Gelles, 1986, *Journal of Marriage and the Family, 48,* 465–479. Copyright 1986 by the National Council on Family Relations, 3989 Central Ave., N.E., Suite 550, Minneapolis, MN 55421. Reprinted by permission.

fanticide, killing of a child, and abandoning the corpse of a child. Some of these are clearly more extreme than others.

Current research makes distinctions among five classes of child maltreatment: physical abuse, neglect, emotional maltreatment, medical neglect, or sexual abuse. A sixth, very serious, form of child maltreatment, *shaken baby syndrome,* is actually a specific kind of physical abuse.

PHYSICAL ABUSE

Physical injury to the child is the main criterion of **physical abuse.** However, the distinction between what is abuse and what is permissible punishment (or attempted control) by a parent is not at all clear and may vary dramatically from one situation to another.[*] In some cultures, for example, parenting may involve levels of violence that would be viewed as abusive in other contexts. Segal (1995) reports a survey of 319 middle-class professionals in India, of whom more than 90 percent reported that during the past year they had used violence as a means of conflict resolution with their children.

---

[*]My grandmother and most of her cohorts, who belonged to a different culture and a different period, firmly believed in the necessity of punishment. "The mare's kick won't hurt the colt," she'd say—which is an old Spanish proverb. Or, borrowing from the English, she'd assert, "The rod breaks no bones."

A frightening 41 percent of these revealed that their use of violence might have been more "abusive" than "acceptable."

In many North American societies, some forms of violence are widely accepted as a parenting tool. This is reflected in the observation that many institutions charged with the care of children resort to physical punishment and sometimes other forms of abuse as a means of control (Jones, 1995). It is evident, as well, in the rather large number of religion-related instances of abuse that are reported each year. Bottoms and associates (1995) obtained detailed information on 1,652 cases of abuse perpetrated by ministers and priests that were later reported to mental health professionals. Some have to do with attempting to rid a child of supposed demons, and others simply reflect the ministerings of religious authority.

As a result of the occasional confusion between what is acceptable and unacceptable, many physicians are uncertain about what to report (Warner & Hansen, 1994). Similarly, a survey of 264 elementary schoolteachers and 47 principals revealed that school personnel have widely differing notions of what abuse is (Tite, 1993). In addition, most prefer to deal with suspected abuse informally rather than file formal complaints with the authorities. (See "In the News and on the Net: Children in Cages.")

SHAKEN BABY SYNDROME

A specific, particularly horrifying, kind of physical abuse called **shaken baby syndrome** is seen with alarming frequency by physicians and other professionals. Essentially, shaken baby syndrome is infant abuse by whiplash-shaking of the infant (Chiocca, 1995). This results in the brain being battered against the inside of the skull. Effects can include severe brain injury and neurological damage often leading to death. Symptoms of fatal shaken baby syndrome include loss of consciousness, comatose states, convulsions, and respiratory distress. Death often occurs relatively soon after the traumatic infant shaking episode (Nashelsky & Dix, 1995).

Cases of shaken baby syndrome that are not fatal are nevertheless often accompanied by serious retinal damage caused by hemorrhaging (bleeding) of the retina. Blindness or partial loss of vision is relatively common (Matthews & Das, 1996). The nature of these retinal hemorrhages is sufficiently different from hemorrhages resulting from other causes that they are often used as evidence that the infant has been criminally shaken (Betz et al., 1996).

Head injury from shaken baby syndrome is, in fact, the most common cause of death among physically abused infants. Hence the importance of understanding the motives and the circumstances that might trigger a perpetrator's actions. Hence, too, the importance of determining who is most likely to be a perpetrator.

Not surprisingly, difficult, colicky, crying infants are more likely to be abused than are happy, easy infants (Wong, Wong, & Yech, 1995). As well, slightly more of the victims are male than female (Starling, Holden, & Jenny, 1995). Perhaps more surprising, fathers appear to be about twice as likely as mothers to be guilty of shaking their infant. Starling,

Children in Cages

7-year-old girl was found in a dog cage in a cold, dark, basement after her 11-year-old brother walked into a nearby police station in Brillion, Wisconsin. In spite of below-freezing temperatures, the boy was barefooted and wore no coat. The girl had apparently been in the dog cage, a tiny, two foot square cage, for most of the past two weeks, with nothing but a single blanket—evidently as punishment. She and her 4 other siblings (aged 16 months to 11 years) have been placed in foster care. Their 28-year-old parents face charges of felony child abuse.

Meanwhile, in Auburn, Washington, a 14-month-old boy, who was discovered when police were evacuating a burning building, is believed to have been left alone in his crib for 5 days with little food or water—although his mother, LaDawn Jump, reportedly brought him peanut butter and jelly sandwiches or cheese on occasion. The boy's thumb was covered with raw sores. Doctors believe this was probably because most of the time, the toddler had nothing else to eat. The mother apparently had a new boyfriend and was afraid the toddler's presence might chase him away. She had previously been arrested for suspected child abandonment, and now faces new charges.

1. U.S. parents kept girl, 7, in dog cage, say police. (1997, Nov. 20). *Edmonton Sun*, p. 43.

2. Tot gnawed on his thumb during five days alone: cops. (1997, Nov. 20). *Edmonton Sun*, p. 43.

To Debate, Research, or Write Up

Examine the proposition that in the same way as people are not permitted to drive cars until they have demonstrated some minimum level of car-handling competence and knowledge of traffic rules, so too should prospective parents be required to demonstrate their ability and willingness to care for children.

On the Net

The National Child Protection Clearing House is dedicated to providing a forum

for ideas related to the prevention of child maltreatment. The web site:

http://www.aifs.org.au/external/nch/pubs.html

Holden, and Jenny (1995) identified confessed or convicted abusers in 151 cases of infants suffering from shaken baby syndrome. Male perpetrators were more than twice as common as female perpetrators. Fathers were guilty in 37 percent of cases, boyfriends in 20.5 percent, and mothers in only 12.6 percent. Perhaps most surprising, female babysitters accounted for 17.3 percent of these 151 cases.

PHYSICAL NEGLECT

Physical neglect involves acts of omission rather than commission and is usually evident in parents' failure to ensure that children have adequate nourishment, shelter, clothing, and the other important things of contemporary life. Physical neglect is somewhat more difficult to detect than physical abuse, but nevertheless makes up almost half of reported abuse cases (U.S. Bureau of the Census, 1996).

MEDICAL NEGLECT

More than 25,000 cases of **medical neglect** were substantiated in the United States in 1994 (U.S. Bureau of the Census, 1996). A large number of these involve parents lacking in the knowledge or financial resources required to provide their children with adequate medical treatment. Others are cases where medical help has been withheld for religious reasons (Bottoms et al., 1995).

EMOTIONAL ABUSE

Emotional abuse, sometimes referred to as *psychological abuse,* consists of parental behaviors that cause emotional and psychological harm to the child but that are not instances of physical abuse or neglect—for example, continually shaming or ridiculing children (especially in public), isolating them, confining them in small spaces, severely verbally abusing them, depriving them of emotional contact and comfort, blaming, yelling, and other behaviors that might be classified as involving mental cruelty (Burnett, 1993). The effects of emotional abuse, unlike those of physical abuse or neglect, are often invisible. Consequently, instances of emotional abuse are seldom reported—and substantiated even less often (only 4 percent of all substantiated cases in 1994). However, the long-term effects of emotional abuse and neglect are sometimes more serious than those of physical abuse. They may come to light years later and may involve serious adjustment and emotional problems (Rowan, Foy, & Rodriguez, 1994).

SEXUAL ABUSE

Sexual abuse is a form of child maltreatment in which sexual behaviors are forced upon a child. Victims of sexual abuse are primarily female and are often very young—in fact, they are sometimes still infants. Incest is often but not always involved in the sexual abuse of children.

Estimates of the prevalence of sexual abuse vary considerably. There are several reasons for this. One is the problem of definition. Sexual abuse may be defined as an unwanted sexual act involving physical contact; it may also be defined as any of a number of actions that do not involve physical contact (for example, a proposition or suggestion, verbal enticements, exhibitionism). Estimates vary depending on the researcher's definition. Lamb and Coakley (1993) point out that a variety of types of cross-gender sexual play among children may be considered sexual abuse, depending on the researcher's definition. In their survey of 128 female undergraduate students, 44 percent might be considered by some to have experienced sexual abuse. Using less global definitions, however, estimates are much lower—for example, 13 percent in the Wellman (1993) survey.

A second problem in arriving at accurate estimates has to do with the extreme social taboos that surround all forms of incest, especially father–daughter incest (Schmidt, 1995). Estimates of these acts have typically been based on cases reported to courts or other legal jurisdictions or that come to light in the course of mental health treatment, and are probably gross underestimates.

A third problem is that many of the victims are too young to understand what is happening or to be reliable witnesses. Hence, researchers sometimes rely on relatively vague methods, such as reenactment with dolls or children's drawings, to detect possible victims of sexual abuse (Sadowski & Loesch, 1993).

Because of these problems, estimates of sexual abuse are largely meaningless. For example, Finkelhor and colleagues' (1986) survey of ten studies found prevalence rates of sexual abuse ranging from a low of 6 percent of the sample to 62 percent. We do know, however, that about 12 percent of all substantiated cases of child maltreatment in the United States in 1994 involved sexual abuse—a total of 139,980 cases (U.S. Bureau of the Census, 1996).

The Finkelhor and colleagues (1986) review indicates that there are some broad characteristics that might serve to identify situations where the risk of sexual abuse is higher than normal. To begin with, girls are at considerably higher risk than are boys, although boys too are at some risk. Those who live alone with their fathers, or who live with stepfathers, are at higher risk, as are those whose mothers are employed outside the home or who are ill, disabled, battered, or alcoholics. A review by Powell (1991) found that marital dissatisfaction, a poor mother–daughter relationship, social isolation of the family, a history of child abuse in the family, and violence in the home all increased the likelihood that a daughter would be sexually abused. Note, however, that these are extremely broad categories that include so many individual exceptions that their predictive value is severely limited.

The Consequences of Maltreatment

The most serious possible physical consequences of child abuse—child death—is substantially underdiagnosed, claims Kotch (1993), following an analysis of 92 cases of fatally injured children in New Zealand and another 393 cases of children who were intentionally injured. Other possible physical consequences include blindness, deafness, disfiguration, and additional atrocities.

Apart from these physical consequences, there are serious emotional and psychological consequences, not all of which are highly apparent. These can result perhaps as readily from physical abuse and neglect as from emotional or sexual abuse.

■ SOME EFFECTS OF MALTREATMENT

Abused children are often frightened, confused, and unhappy; their behaviors may range from complete social withdrawal or regression to behaviors characteristic of younger children to uncontrolled aggression, truancy, and delinquency. Leiter and Johnsen (1997) also report that the school achievement of sexually abused and neglected children, on average, is significantly poorer than that of those who are not maltreated. Not surprisingly, their social relationships also suffer, as Salzinger, Feldman, and Hammer (1993) found in a comparison of eighty-seven physically abused children with eighty-seven nonabused children. The abused children had fewer friends and lower sociometric status, and were rated as more aggressive by their peers and more disturbed by their teachers.

■ POSSIBLE EFFECTS OF SEXUAL ABUSE

Among adolescents who have been victims of sexual abuse, there is a higher than normal incidence of running away, attempted suicides, emotional disorder, and adolescent pregnancies—particularly if the father was the abuser. One investigation of forty-one rural mothers who had been pregnant as teenagers found that an astounding 54 percent had been sexually abused before the age of eighteen (Butler & Burton, 1990).

Kendall-Tackett, Williams, and Finkelhor (1993) reviewed forty-five studies that have looked at the consequences of sexual abuse on children aged eighteen or younger. About one-third of the victims of abuse appeared to have no symptoms;

Emotional abuse of children (shaming and ridiculing them, for example) can have effects that are even more serious—though less immediately apparent—than those of physical abuse.

a full two-thirds did. The most commonly studied childhood symptom of sexual abuse—and perhaps one of the most common effects of sexual abuse—is *sexualized behavior.* Sexualized behavior includes sexual play with dolls, inserting objects in vaginas and anuses, excessive masturbation, seductive behavior, asking for sexual stimulation from others, and more advanced sexual knowledge than expected. Other effects of sexual abuse include anxiety, depression, fears, poor self-esteem, and behavior problems.

Rowan, Foy, and Rodriguez (1994) provide evidence that the long-term effects of sexual abuse can be serious and persistent. Among a group of forty-seven adults sexually abused as children who later sought therapeutic help, 69 percent manifested symptoms of **posttraumatic stress disorder.** This condition may be apparent in symptoms such as fatigue, depression, loss of appetite, and obsessive thoughts.

■ THE ABUSIVE FAMILY CONTEXT

Child abuse may be viewed as a symptom of a dysfunctional family. When Madonna, Van Scoyk, and Jones (1991) compared thirty families in which there had been reported incest with comparable but nonincest families, they found clear patterns of dysfunction in the incest families. Not only were these families typically characterized by very rigid belief systems, but one parent was generally highly dominant. In addition, these families were characterized by parental neglect and emotional unavailability of parents, and by lack of autonomy among children. There is evidence, as well, that in families where children are abused, spouse abuse is also common (McKay, 1994).

Membership in an abusive family system would be expected to have negative effects not only on the victims of abuse, but on other family members as well. Accordingly, it is perhaps not surprising that when Jean-Gilles and Crittenden (1990) compared reported abuse victims to their siblings, they found remarkable similarities between the two. Siblings were also frequently subjected to abuse (often not reported) and manifested similar behavior problems. The common view that one child in a family serves as a scapegoat and that the others are spared is largely inaccurate and misleading, claim Jean-Gilles and Crittenden. Thus, our attempts to understand, prevent, and treat child abuse and neglect need to take into consideration the entire family as a dynamic, functioning system.

■ CHARACTERISTICS OF ABUSIVE PARENTS

Child maltreatment sometimes appears to be a lower-class phenomenon because parents of abused children tend to be from lower socioeconomic levels and have lower educational achievements. They are also more likely to be unemployed and on social assistance (Trickett et al., 1991). However, higher-class parents may simply be better at hiding child maltreatment. When the poor and uneducated need help, they go to the police; when the well-to-do need help, they hire professional counselors.

Many abusive parents have themselves suffered abuse as children, but only a small number of child abusers may be classified as "psychotic" or as suffering from some other personality disorder (Dubowitz, Black, & Harrington, 1993). However, many abusive parents share one or more of the following traits: limited knowledge of child rearing; low tolerance for common infant behaviors, such as crying; and misinterpretations of children's motivations for crying (Emery, 1989). An investigation of twenty-eight abusive families found that parents in these families were less satisfied with their children, found child rearing difficult and unsatisfying, lived with more anger and conflict, and were less likely to reason with their children than simply to forbid certain behaviors (Trickett & Susman, 1988). In addition, there is evidence that drug abuse can be a major contributing factor in child abuse and neglect (Blau et al., 1994).

■ WHO IS MALTREATED?

In 1994 almost 14 percent of all abused children were under age one; one-quarter were between two and five, and 35 percent were ten or older. Fifty-three percent of the total were female (U.S. Bureau of the Census, 1996).

Among the factors that contribute to the likelihood of an infant's being abused are prematurity, the presence of deformities, being a twin, being born to a mother who has often been pregnant, and being born to a very busy or depressed mother. In addition, there is some evidence that infants of difficult temperament (who adjust to change less easily, who cry more, whose routines are less predictable) are more often victims of abuse. Thus, children who are abused are sometimes characterized by extreme irritability, feeding problems, excessive crying, and other behaviors that are annoying to parents (Ammerman, 1990). Not surprisingly, toddlers and preschool children who are abused also often manifest a variety of behavior problems, the most common of which include excessive crying and aggressiveness. However, these may often be the consequences, rather than the causes, of abuse. Not surprisingly, attempts to identify children who are most at risk for abuse on the basis of their temperaments and early behaviors have not been very successful (Berthier et al., 1993).

In the United States, there is an overrepresentation of nonwhite children among those abused. This higher incidence appears to be related to a variety of socioeconomic factors, including poverty, lower educational levels of parents, larger families, and a higher likelihood of having a father substitute in the home.

■ WHAT CAN BE DONE?

Although it is unlikely that child abuse can be completely eliminated—particularly because physical force is a widely accepted child-rearing technique in contemporary societies and also because of the privacy of the family—a number of things can still be done. Gaudin (1993) suggests several approaches that might reduce the frequency and seriousness of child abuse. These include direct interventions to remedy neglect and abuse, family-focused interventions to prevent recurrence, efforts to strengthen and preserve functional families, group approaches involving both victims and perpetrators, and legal intervention where necessary.

Some prevention strategies have tried to discover ways of predicting which parents or children are most likely to be involved in child abuse so that something can be done before the problem occurs. Unfortunately, although abused children have a number of characteristics in common, many of these characteristics are also found among nonabused children (Berthier et al., 1993). Similarly, although we know that certain racial, economic, and social factors are involved in child abuse, we cannot reliably predict who is most likely to be abused (or abusive). Prevention based on prediction remains difficult, costly, and susceptible to the error of false identification (Jordan, 1993).

Other preventive strategies that might be highly effective in the long term include Jordan's (1993) suggestion that parents and communities be more closely involved in both prevention and remediation. Specific programs, such as the "Talking About Touching" program for use with young children, can increase children's knowledge about abuse and also can suggest ways of avoiding it (Madak & Berg, 1992). There is a need, too, argues Moriarty (1990), for screening procedures and preemployment testing to ensure that potential child molesters and abusers are not employed in situations in which children are easy victims. Unfortunately, this is very difficult because there is no clear personality profile that easily identifies potential child maltreaters—other than perhaps criminal conviction or psychiatric diagnosis in the case of pedophiles.

Neither the problem nor its solution is simple. (See Summary Table 10.12.)

■ SOCIAL–EMOTIONAL EXCEPTIONALITY

Among the possible consequences of child maltreatment are a variety of adjustment problems and **emotional disorders** (or *behavior disorders:* the terms are used interchangeably in this section). These problems tend to be both varied and highly individualistic; they are not easily classified or even defined. Many of the problems result from the interactions of a variety of other factors.

The expression *emotional disorder* is used to include a wide range of nonphysical exceptionalities ranging from relatively minor behavior problems to serious mental disorders such as autism or schizophrenia. Terms that are frequently used synonymously to refer to children with problems in this area are *behavior disordered, emotionally disturbed,* and *socially maladjusted.* Each of these terms describes children who are troubled and who may also cause trouble for parents, teachers, peers, and others (Kovacs, 1989).

Note that the labels describing social and emotional problems are only descriptions, not explanations. Children who are diagnosed as having "attention deficit hyperactivity disorder" are so labeled because they display a common set of

▲ **SUMMARY TABLE 10.12**
Definitions and Findings in
the Study of Child Maltreatment

CONCEPT	EXPLANATIONS/COMMENTS
Violence	■ Extreme form of overt aggression, highly common as revealed in crime rates, analysis of television content, and incidence of child maltreatment.
Child maltreatment	■ Can take the form of neglect, physical abuse, sexual abuse, emotional maltreatment, or medical maltreatment.
Physical abuse	■ Evident in physical injury, as in "shaken baby syndrome."
Shaken baby syndrome	■ Possible effects of violently shaking an infant; whiplash type of neurological injury, often fatal or leading to blindness and other serious problems.
Physical neglect	■ Child maltreatment involving omission rather than commission (for example, failure to provide adequate nutrition or shelter).
Medical neglect	■ Failure to provide child with necessary medical attention.
Emotional abuse	■ Child maltreatment involving various forms of "mental cruelty" such as ridiculing, shaming, humiliating, ignoring, isolating.
Sexual abuse	■ Child maltreatment where victim is forced to participate in sexual behaviors (ranging from talking, looking, touching, fondling, to other sexual acts).
Possible consequences of child maltreatment	■ Physical consequences can include blindness, deafness, disfigurement, loss of limbs, paralysis, death. ■ Emotional consequences can include depression, aggression, sexual maladjustment, school failure, profound unhappiness.
Who abuses, who is abused, what can be done	■ Abuse is often a symptom of a dysfunctional family. ■ Abusive parents may themselves have been abused as children and manifest low tolerance for "annoying" child behaviors. ■ Slightly more girls than boys are abused; more irritable infants are somewhat more susceptible. ■ Abusers are more often male than female. ■ Two types of possible intervention include apprehension and punishment of abusers, and social as well as therapeutic programs.

behavioral and emotional symptoms, but the label serves in no way to explain these behaviors and symptoms.

Problems associated with defining and identifying social–emotional maladjustment are far more difficult than those relating to physical exceptionality. Whereas reasonably competent individuals can usually arrive at an agreed-on diagnosis of visual or hearing impairments, the same does not hold for the common social–emotional problems such as *autism, childhood depression,* and *attention deficit disorders.*

Prevalence, Classifications, and Contributing Factors

Estimates of the prevalence of emotional disorders vary considerably depending on the criteria used for identification and on whether estimates include mild as well as severe instances of disturbance. Tuma (1989) reports data indicating that about 15 to 19 percent of U.S. children and adolescents suffer from problems requiring some form of mental health services.

CLASSIFICATIONS

Classifying emotional disturbances in childhood presents a number of special difficulties. First, because many childhood disorders are characteristically different from adult behaviors, models of adult affective disorders are not always appropriate. For example, a number of behaviors that might be symptoms of underlying disorders in adults are relatively common in younger children: Uncontrollable laughter and temper tantrums are common and expected in childhood, but among adults, these behaviors might seem bizarre and might be a symptom of some underlying disorder (Kazdin, 1989).

Second, for some behaviors, developmental changes have to be taken into account. One example is that of apparent problems that become less frequent and less serious with increasing maturity. Lying, for example, is quite common among six-year-old boys, but becomes far less frequent by adolescence. A second example is that of behavioral and emotional problems that are manifested in different symptoms as the child ages. Kazdin (1989) illustrates this by reference to the youngster who initially threatens and shoves other children who are in his way, but whose aggressive behavior will later take other forms more appropriate for his age—for example, fighting or using weapons.

Finally, there are disorders that are primarily childhood problems; others are more common in adulthood. For example, **hyperactivity** (discussed in the next section) appears to be primarily a childhood disorder, although there is now evidence that many children do not "outgrow" it (Henker & Whalen, 1989). In contrast, serious affective (emotional) disorders such as depression and mania were long thought to be adult rather than childhood disorders. We now know, however, that although children rarely suffer the manic disorders, they do suffer depression (Kovacs, 1989).

CONTRIBUTING FACTORS

The factors that contribute to the development of behavior disorders vary a great deal as well. These are often classified in one of two ways: **genetic–congenital** and **social– psychological.** Possible genetic and congenital causes include

chromosome abnormalities, maternal malnutrition, maternal infections, and birth injury. Social–psychological contributing factors include neglect, maltreatment, malnutrition, head injuries, and diseases and illnesses, as well as conditions within the family, such as stress associated with conflict. In addition, poverty, parental abuse, parental rejection, physical handicaps, age, sex, and racial and religious discrimination have been implicated (Kazdin, 1989). Also, there is evidence that cognitive problems such as mental retardation or learning disabilities are sometimes related to behavior problems (Cole, Usher, & Cargo, 1993).

Attention Deficit Hyperactivity Disorder

In contrast to well-adjusted, resilient children, as many as 3 percent of elementary schoolchildren suffer from varying degrees of **hyperactivity** (American Psychiatric Association, 1987). Of these, a significant number also suffer from attention problems and are classified as having **attention deficit hyperactivity disorder (ADHD).** Attention problems can also exist without hyperactivity (**attention deficit disorder [ADD]**). Many ADHD children experience considerable difficulty adjusting to school and home and are considered to have relatively serious problems (Zentall, 1993).

In general, ADHD is marked by excessive general activity for the child's age (often taking the form of incessant and haphazard climbing, crawling, or running); difficulty in sustaining attention and apparent forgetfulness; and impulsivity (tendency to react quickly, difficulty taking turns, low frustration tolerance). The criteria described by the APA also stipulate that the duration of the child's hyperactivity be at least six months.

CAUSES AND DIAGNOSIS

The causes of ADHD are unclear although the fact that between 80 and 90 percent more males than females are so diagnosed suggests that it is at least partly genetic. There is evidence that it is largely a maturational problem involving the central nervous system. Not only is the activity level of hyperactive children often similar to that typical of children four or five years younger, but many of these children— though not all—seem to outgrow their symptoms after adolescence (Henker & Whalen, 1989).

Other explanations for ADHD have sometimes implicated neurological impairment or brain damage and dietary or vitamin-linked causes. However, the evidence for either of these causes is weak (Erickson, 1992). There is some suggestion, too, that between 5 and 10 percent of hyperactive children react badly to certain food dyes and that these children might therefore be helped through dietary means (Ross, 1980).

Diagnoses of ADHD, or simply of hyperactivity, are sometimes—perhaps even often—made inappropriately by parents and teachers who are confronted by children who are restless and who find it difficult to do the quiet things that adults

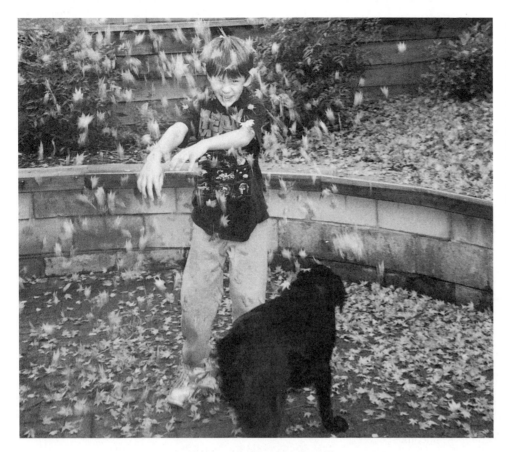

Attention deficit hyperactivity disorder (ADHD) is sometimes inappropriately diagnosed by parents and teachers in response to children's normal restlessness or to learning problems related to other causes. Although the boy shown here has been diagnosed as having ADHD, the disorder is not readily apparent on the playground or in the park—where high levels of physical activity are normally expected. It is more evident in school, where sustaining attention often requires curtailing physical activity.

sometimes demand. Strictly speaking, attention deficit hyperactivity disorder as defined by the American Psychiatric Association (1994) needs to begin before the age of seven to differentiate it from disorders that might arise as reactions to stressful events or illness. In addition, children must manifest a combination of symptoms for a period of at least six months. These symptoms might include any, or most, of the following:

- often fidgets with hands or feet or squirms

- is easily distracted by outside stimuli

- has difficulty remaining seated

- often blurts out answers to questions before they have been completed

- finds it difficult to wait to take turn in group situations

- often shifts from one uncompleted activity to another

- often seems not to be listening

- often interrupts or intrudes

- often talks excessively

- has difficulty working quietly

- has difficulty maintaining attention

Clearly, not all children suffering from this disorder will display the same combination and seriousness of symptoms. However, given the fact that the condition appears easy to diagnose (it is defined largely in terms of observable behav-

iors) and that it can therefore easily be overdiagnosed, extreme caution should be exercised before applying the label to any child.

■ TREATMENT

The most common treatment for a child diagnosed as having an attention deficit disorder with hyperactivity involves the use of stimulant drugs such as dextroamphetamine (Dexadrine) and methylphenidate **(Ritalin).** This might seem strange given that stimulants ordinarily increase activity and the ADHD child already suffers from excessive activity. However, these drugs appear to sedate rather than stimulate ADHD children (Swanson et al., 1991). Their use, some argue, is effective in preventing continued achievement declines in school (Weber, Frankenberg, & Heilman, 1992), as well as in increasing the manageability of the children. Some evidence suggests that these drugs are about twice as effective as behavior modification (primarily the use of rewards) in controlling problem behavior in many ADHD children, as well as in improving academic achievement (Pelham et al., 1993). Nevertheless, drug therapy with ADHD children remains a controversial treatment. These drugs can also have some negative side effects such as weight loss, growth retardation, and mood changes (Henker & Whalen, 1989).

As McClure and Teyber (1996) point out, ADHD children are often greatly in need of teacher and family support. These children have considerable difficulty completing tasks and may have relatively few success experiences to help them overcome the growing suspicion that they might be "dumb" or in other ways inferior. Such children are highly vulnerable, argue McClure and Teyber, and require firm but affectionate discipline.

Other Behavior Disorders

There are a number of other, sometimes serious, behavior disorders of childhood and adolescence, not all of which can easily be classified. Many of these are problems of socialization seen in aggressive, hostile, and essentially antisocial behavior—as in, for example, extreme noncompliance (labeled **oppositional defiant disorder** by the APA). Extreme aggressiveness is relatively common among ADHD children (Stormont-Spurgin & Zentall, 1996). Alternatively, conduct disorders might be evident in withdrawal, social isolation, or extreme shyness. Not surprisingly, aggressive and hostile behaviors (delinquency, vandalism, and so on) are likely to be dealt with—or at least punished. Social isolation and extreme shyness are much more likely to be ignored.

Other social disorders may be manifested in lying, stealing, inability to form close relationships with others, temper tantrums, disobedience and insolence, extremely negative self-concepts, and related behaviors and attitudes.

Anorexia nervosa is another disorder that might be classified as a conduct or behavior disorder. It involves drastic changes in eating habits, leading to serious—sometimes fatal—weight loss. Because it affects adolescents far more often than any other age group, it is discussed in Chapter 11.

Treatment of children exhibiting conduct and personality disorders depends largely on the severity of the disturbance. In cases of moderate or mild disturbance, teachers and parents can often cope adequately; with the occasional help of professional personnel, they can sometimes do much more than cope. More severe disturbances may require therapeutic and sometimes judicial intervention.

Stress in Childhood

Many of the emotional and behavioral problems of childhood, and perhaps a number of the physical problems as well, are related to something we call **stress**—a difficult concept that everybody understands at least intuitively.

STRESS DEFINED

In the physical sciences, stress is a force that is exerted on a body, sometimes causing deformation or breakage. In psychology, stress is a nonphysical force that is exerted on an individual, sometimes causing negative change. Skinner and Wellborn (1994) suggest that there are two approaches to defining stress. One is concerned with stimuli, the other with responses. Stimuli are said to be stressful when they make excessive demands on the individual; responses are stressful when they are accompanied by the physiological changes of high arousal such as increased heart rate, perspiration, and trembling.

THE EFFECTS OF STRESS

Lazarus (1993) classifies stress in terms of the severity of its effects. Thus, there is *harm,* which implies actual damage; *threat,* which implies the possibility of damage; and *challenge,* which implies demands that can be met.

This classification recognizes that stress is clearly not always negative. Challenge, and even threat, may lead to what are essentially adaptive physiological responses. In such cases, stress prepares the individual for action. The sudden shot of adrenaline and the acceleration of heart rate when we are threatened or challenged increase the effectiveness of our running, our fighting, or our speechmaking.

But under other circumstances, we may have an overload of stress and suffer harm. The implications of this overload vary from one individual to another, but are clearly not limited to adults. As we saw in Chapter 6, infants and preschoolers can suffer profound distress at the loss of a parent or sometimes even as a result of temporary separation from a parent. The effects may be apparent in sleeping or eating disturbances, as well as in a general listlessness that may border on depression (Honig, 1993).

Among children, the effects of stress might include physical complaints (such as stomach pains, sometimes caused by ulcers, or asthma) or emotional problems (such as persistent fears, high anxiety, or even depression) (Johnson, 1986).

CHILD STRESSORS

Many of the things that children fear, notes Kupetz (1993), are a source of considerable stress for them. She warns that parents often trivialize these fears because they judge them by adult standards ("Don't be silly, Guy, there's nothing in the closet. Hey, you guys, did you hear what Guy's scared of now?"). Parents need to realize that children's fears are real, and they need to help children reduce the stressors in their lives.

Fears are just one source of childhood stress; Elkind (1981a) describes several others, many of which are more common to this generation of children than they were to earlier ones. They relate to *stimulus* or *demand overloads.* There is, for example, *responsibility overload,* in which young children whose parents work are made responsible for tasks like looking after younger siblings, buying groceries, preparing meals, cleaning the house, and so on. There is *change overload,* in which children from mobile families are shunted rapidly from one community to another, transferred from school to school, and left with a sequence of caregivers. *Emotional overload* may result when children are exposed to emotion-laden situations that impact directly on their lives, but over which they have little control (parents quarreling, for example). Finally, there is *information overload,* resulting largely from the tremendous amount of information to which television exposes the child. Add to all these potential sources of stress the sometimes exorbitant achievement demands that are placed on the child by school, parents, and society. "Hurry," they all say to Elkind's (1981a) *hurried child.* "Hurry! Grow up! There isn't much time!"

Clearly, not all children are exposed to the same stressful situations, nor will all react in the same way. Some children remain unperturbed in the face of events that might prove disastrous for others. Nevertheless, psychology provides a number of ways of assessing stress in the lives of children or at least of determining potential for stress. Many of these are based on the assumption that all major changes in a person's life are potentially stressful and that, although most individuals can cope with a limited number of changes, there eventually comes a breaking point. Accordingly, these stress scales simply ask individuals to identify all major changes they have recently experienced. Some changes are clearly more important than others (the death of a parent compared with changing schools, for example). Values are assigned accordingly. Table 10.13 is one example of this approach for children.

Social–Emotional Giftedness

Here, as elsewhere, exceptionality has two dimensions: the disadvantaged, among whom are the autistic, the depressed, the hyperactive, and those exhibiting personality and conduct disorders; and the advantaged, to whom we have paid little special attention.

Among the advantaged are the highly resilient, sometimes labeled **invulnerables** or "superkids." Invulnerables are children who, because of their biological history and environment, are at greater psychiatric risk than others but who adapt unharmed. Werner (1993) describes a number of risk factors: birth problems, poverty, and family environments marked by alcoholism, mental illness, or conflict. Each of these has been linked with subsequent emotional and behavior problems in children. Significantly, however, many children whose backgrounds include one or even all of these characteristics nevertheless grow up to be well-adjusted, socially competent adults. In Werner's (1993) study of at-risk children, for example, about one-third of the at-risk children grew up to be apparently strong, well-adjusted individuals. (That 129 children, fully two-thirds of the original sample, developed serious learning or behavior problems in elementary school, manifested delinquent behavior in adolescence, or experienced mental health problems at some point in development is also highly significant.)

Werner's research on high-risk infants who turned out well suggests that resilient infants share a number of common characteristics. For example, as infants, most seem to be characterized by easy temperaments. They are outgoing, adjust quickly to change, cry little, establish eating and sleeping routines, and are alert and responsive. As elementary school students, they concentrate well and are active and sociable. And perhaps most important, their environments typically include some clear source of support that helps them withstand stress. Support often takes the form of substitute parents (perhaps grandparents or older siblings), as well as close friends.

The importance of understanding why some children survive and even thrive in high-risk situations and why others

TABLE 10.13

*Stressful Events in Children's Lives**

LIFE-CHANGE EVENT	POINTS
Parent dies.	100
Parents divorce.	73
Parents separate.	65
Parent travels as part of job.	63
Close family member dies.	63
Personal illness or injury.	53
Parent remarries.	50
Parent fired from job.	47
Parents reconcile.	45
Mother goes to work.	45
Change in health of a family member.	44
Mother becomes pregnant.	40
School difficulties.	39
Birth of a sibling.	39
School readjustment (new teacher or class).	39
Change in family's financial condition.	38
Injury or illness of a close friend.	37
Starts a new (or changes) an extracurricular activity (music lessons, Brownies, and so forth).	36
Change in number of fights with siblings.	35
Threatened by violence at school.	31
Theft of personal possessions.	30
Changes responsibilities at home.	29
Older brother or sister leaves home.	29
Trouble with grandparents.	29
Outstanding personal achievement	28
Moves to another city.	26
Moves to another part of town.	26
Receives or loses a pet.	25
Changes personal habits.	24
Trouble with teacher.	24
Change in hours with baby-sitter or at day-care center.	20
Moves to a new house.	20
Changes to a new school.	20
Changes play habits.	19
Vacations with family.	19
Changes friends.	18
Attends summer camp.	17
Changes sleeping habits.	16
Change in number of family get-togethers.	15
Changes eating habits.	15
Changes amount of TV viewing.	13
Birthday party.	12
Punished for not "telling the truth."	11

*If scores for a one-year period total 150, stress exposure is average; if between 150 and 300, there is a higher probability of stress-related symptoms; above 300, serious consequences are even more probable.
Source: From *The Hurried Child* (pp. 162–163) by David Elkind. 1981. Reading, MA: Addison-Wesley Publishing Co., Inc. Adapted with permission of the publisher.

▲ SUMMARY TABLE 10.14

Definitions and Findings in Childhood Social–Emotional Exceptionality

CONCEPT	EXPLANATIONS/COMMENTS
Emotional Disorder	■ Used interchangeably with *behavior disorder* to include a wide range of nonphysical exceptionalities ranging from relatively minor behavior problems to serious mental disorders such as autism or schizophrenia.
Genetic–Congenital	■ Disorders whose causes are inherited or at least present at birth (such as chromosomal and genetic problems as well as the effects of maternal malnutrition or birth injury).
Social–Psychological	■ Causes that are not genetic–congenital but contextual (such as neglect, maltreatment, malnutrition, head injuries, diseases and illnesses, as well as conditions within the family, like stress).
Hyperactivity	■ Strong compulsion to engage in physical activity; restlessness; often accompanied by attention deficits.
Attention Deficit Disorder (ADD)	■ Disorder marked by consistent problems in paying attention.
Attention Deficit Hyperactivity Disorder (ADHD)	■ Serious attention deficit disorder with accompanying hyperactivity; often treated with stimulant drugs (Ritalin); often overdiagnosed.
Oppositional Defiant Behavior	■ Emotional disorder marked by extreme noncompliance; other emotional disorders include extreme shyness, aggression, and a variety of other manifestations of serious maladjustment.
Stress	■ In a psychological sense, a force that exerts pressure on an individual causing an effect ranging from *challenge*, to *threat*, to *harm*. Childhood stressors include fears as well as *demand overloads* (excessive responsibilities, emotional burdens, information overload, and parental as well as school pressures).
Invulnerables	■ Describes children exposed to risks that would surely claim large numbers of other children in similar circumstances, but who thrive and emerge unscathed—perhaps even stronger.

do not is related directly to the possibility of "inoculating" children against risk or of ameliorating risk for those who are most vulnerable, suggests Anthony (1975). Perhaps exposure to a certain amount of adversity may be crucial for the development of resistance to disturbance. At the same time, exposure to too many stresses may have just the opposite effect. It may be that there is a particular combination of personality characteristics or genetic predispositions that, in interaction with a stressful environment, produces a highly adjusted, healthy person. The critical problem is to identify this combination of characteristics and environment in an effort to maximize the development of human potential. The emphasis is dramatically different from that which focuses on identifying and treating disorders.

Exceptional social and emotional competence may be seen not only in those who survive high risk but also in exceptional individuals whose early lives and biological history present no unusual psychological threats. Among these socially gifted children may well be found the leaders of tomorrow. Perhaps we should provide "special" education not only for those with handicaps but for the socially gifted as well. (See Summary Table 10.14.)

■ FOCUS QUESTIONS: SUMMARY ANSWERS

1. What do children know of the states of minds of others?

   ■ Social cognition refers to an awareness of ourselves and of others as being capable of feelings, motives, intentions, and so on; it implies a *theory of mind*. Selman's five stages of role taking reflect the child's ability to verbalize other perspectives: egocentric (to age 6: one point of view), social–informational (6–8: my view is correct, others less informed), self-reflective (8–10: people are aware only of their views), mutual (10–12: people recognize and talk about each other's views), and social and conventional (12–15+: abstract recognition of different views).

2. What is self-esteem, and why might it be important?

   ■ Self-esteem refers to personal evaluations of the self (James's view: discrepancy between the actual and aspirations; Cooley's view: a reflection of how we think others evaluate us). After age eight, children can make global assessments of self-worth and can make separate evaluations in five areas: scholastic, athletic, physical appearance, social acceptance, and morality. High self-worth is associated with happiness; low self-worth is associated with sadness and depression. In turn, these moods are linked with motivation.

3. What role do friendships play in a child's development? How important are friends and peers?

   ■ For preschoolers, friendship is playing together; in middle childhood, friendships involve enduring, reciprocal relationships. Friends and peers are critical for positive self-concepts and for learning sex-appropriate values and attitudes.

4. Does television have a primarily negative, positive, or neutral effect on children?

   ■ There is evidence of a relationship between television viewing and aggression. Overt aggression (physical actions) is more masculine; relational aggression (intended to disrupt social relations) is more feminine. Television might enhance language development and knowledge base, and prosocial television themes can have positive effects.

5. How prevalent and how serious is child maltreatment?

   ■ Violence touches many North American homes each year, some of it in the form of child maltreatment, which may be physical abuse (punching, kicking, beating, *shaken baby syndrome*), physical neglect (failure to provide food, clothing, shelter), medical neglect (failure to provide health care), emotional abuse (habitual ridicule, scolding, ostracism), or sexual abuse (sexual behaviors forced upon the child). Any of these forms of abuse can have serious and long-lasting physical and psychological consequences.

STUDY TERMS

anorexia nervosa, 304

attention deficit disorder (ADD), 302

attention deficit hyperactivity disorder (ADHD), 302

attribution, 290

child maltreatment, 295

Cooley's approach to self-worth, 282

emotional abuse, 298

emotional disorders, 301

external orientation, 290

genetic–congenital, 302

hyperactivity, 302

internal orientation, 290

invulnerables, 305

James's approach to self-worth, 282

learned helplessness, 290

locus of control, 290

mastery-oriented, 290

medical neglect, 298

oppositional defiant disorder, 304

overt aggression, 292

peer group, 286

physical abuse, 297

physical neglect, 298

posttraumatic stress disorder, 300

relational aggression, 292

Ritalin, 303

self, 282

self-concept, 282

self-esteem, 282

self-worth, 282

sexual abuse, 298

shaken baby syndrome, 297

social aggression, 292

social cognition, 280

social isolates, 287

social–psychological, 302

sociogram, 287

sociometric status, 287

stress, 304

theory of mind, 280

violence, 292

FURTHER READINGS

The Frye and Moore book presents an intriguing account of children's development of intuitive theories of mind; the collection edited by Gauvain and Cole contains a wide-ranging collection of fascinating articles on various aspects of development from birth through adolescence:

Frye, D., & Moore, C. (Eds.). (1991). *Children's theories of mind: Mental states and social understanding.* Hillsdale, NJ: Erlbaum.

Gauvain, M., & Cole, M. (Eds.). (1993). *Readings on the development of children.* New York: W. H. Freeman.

This book is a detailed analysis of the dimensions and importance of childhood friendships:

Erwin, P. (1993). *Friendship and peer relationships in children.* New York: John Wiley.

For a discussion of the relationship between physical punishment and aggression in children, see the following:

McCord, J. (Ed.). *Coercion and punishment in long-term perspectives.* New York: Cambridge University Press.

The much-studied impact of television on the lives of children is reviewed in:

Clifford, B. R., Gunter, B., & McAleer, J. (1995). *Television and children: Program evaluation, comprehension, and impact.* Hillsdale, NJ: Erlbaum.

The following collection presents articles that look in depth at child abuse and neglect, at the characteristics of victims and perpetrators, and at programs designed to prevent the occurrence of child abuse or to treat its effects:

Fontes, L. A. (Ed.). (1995). *Sexual abuse in nine North American cultures: Treatment and prevention.* Thousand Oaks, CA: Sage.

A clear, comprehensive look at childhood behavior disorders is presented in:

Kazdin, A. E. (1995). *Conduct disorders in childhood and adolescence* (2nd ed.). Thousand Oaks, CA: Sage.

Adolescence

Youth is the time to go flashing from one end of the world to the other both in mind and body; to try the manners of different nations; to hear the chimes at midnight; to see sunrise in town and country; to be converted at a revival; to circumnavigate the metaphysics, write halting verses, run a mile to see a fire, and wait all day long in the theatre to applaud "Hernani."

ROBERT LOUIS STEVENSON
Virginibus Puerisque

There is little of revivals and fires, or of theaters and sunrises, in the two chapters that summarize the adolescent experience—although there is something of scarification, circumcision, and the taboos of primitive rites of passage. There is also a good deal about one of the most important developmental tasks of this period: the selection and formation of an identity. It is in adolescence that we struggle to decide who we are, and that we begin to flesh out the dream of who we will be. ¶ In these chapters, there is much, too, about newly expanding powers of mind and body— powers that make it possible to go flashing from one end of the world to the other, trying different manners, hearing chimes, and being converted at revivals—powers that make it possible to write halting verses. Mostly about love.

1. Is adolescence a universal phenomenon, or is it largely cultural?

2. What are the universal biological features of adolescence?

3. What are the most common eating disorders of adolescence?

4. What is adolescent egocentrism?

5. Is being good or bad a fundamental part of our personalities?

Physical and Cognitive Development: Adolescence

They always take a new name, and are supposed by the initiation process to become new beings in the magic wood.

MARY KINGSLEY
West Africa

*Based partly on O'Hagan, H. (1979). "Tay John." In D. Gutteridge (Ed.), *Rites of passage.* Toronto: McClelland & Stewart.

hen Kumkleseem approached manhood, everyone waited to see what would happen. A boy sees things with the eyes of a child, things that men can no longer see. But the child must die, say the old ones, so that the man can be born and walk in the world that other men have made. "The boy says 'I.' The man says 'We!' and this word that the man speaks is the word of his greatest magic" (O'Hagan, 1979, p. 38). ¶ Toward the end of his childhood, Kumkleseem did all the things that boys must do if they are to be men. Whenever the camp moved, he waited until it was far out of sight before running after it. In this way, his legs would become hard and his breath long, and he would never be left behind. And every day, he walked into the ice-cold river and the people beat him with willow sticks when he came out so that he might learn to endure all hardship without complaint. And when the nights grew cold, he lay outside all night, naked and with no robe, sometimes holding his hands in the flowing water through the night. But even when he had become the fastest runner and the best hunter, he was still not a man, for he had not yet gone alone to a place of his own choosing and fasted and prayed for the vision that would reveal to him the shape and texture of his life as a man. ¶ And so one night Kumkleseem left and walked far out into the awesome valley where men of his tribe do not walk for fear their voices will be taken and they will be left only with the voices of coyotes. For twelve days he was gone and when he returned, lean and hard from his fasting, he sat by the fire and would not eat until he had spoken. ¶ "You have come far," said Tis-Kwinit. ¶ "I have gone far," Kumkleseem answered, telling them of the voices he had heard, the things he had seen after he had walked four days and then sat four days, looking and listening while the mountains pressed in on him at night so that he could not move his elbows. "On the ninth day I turned back the way I had come. Now I am here," he finished. ¶ "What you say is good," said Tzalas. And Kumkleseem was a man.*

311

This Chapter

Becoming a man, or a woman, is not quite so clear in most of our western industrialized societies. We no longer know where to go for our visions. Besides, if we had a vision to relate, would anyone listen to us around the campfire?

This chapter looks at some of the implications of these changes. It looks, as well, at some of the important changes adolescents go through—things like the momentous physical changes that mark the transition from childhood to adolescence. These changes have tremendous implications for social development (covered in the next chapter). It also discusses some of the implications of early and late maturation, and some of the physical concerns of adolescence that may be manifested in eating disorders. Later sections in the chapter deal with the growth of logic and with egocentrism in adolescence. The chapter concludes with a discussion of moral development and behavior. But first it looks at the transition to adulthood and at some of the chicken-blood-and-whiskey-type rites that sometimes accompany this transition.

BETWEEN CHILD AND ADULT

Adolescence is the transition between childhood and adulthood—the period during which the child has achieved sexual maturity but has not yet taken on the roles and responsibilities, or the rights, that accompany full adult status.

In contemporary industrialized countries, adolescence is relatively easily defined, say Schlegel and Barry (1991): It spans the period of the teen years. But in preindustrial societies, it is not always clear that the period even exists.

Primitive Rites de Passage

In some preindustrial societies, passage from childhood to adulthood is clearly marked by ritual and ceremony collectively termed **rites de passage.** Interestingly, even in totally unrelated societies, these rites often have several common features. Most rites of passage involve four steps: First is separation, a period during which the child is separated from the group. A common **taboo** (forbidden behavior) during this period is that of brother–sister or mother–son contact.

Second, prior to becoming an adult, children are trained in behaviors expected of adults. Sometimes this involves teaching through telling. Or it might involve showing the child by example.

The third step is the **initiation** itself—the actual rituals that mark passage from childhood to adulthood. These ceremonies are often accompanied by feasting because they are a time of celebration, but they are also usually a time of pain

and suffering. Thus, many initiation ceremonies include fasting, **scarification** (the inflicting of wounds with resulting scars), and circumcision.

The final step of the passage rite is **induction** (absorption into the tribe). Inductees now know, without any doubt, that they are full-fledged, adult members of their social group.

Rites of passage can serve a number of useful functions. They impart a sense of adult responsibility to children, and they lessen the ambiguity that might otherwise exist between childhood and adulthood. In addition, many primitive rites reinforce certain important taboos such as those having to do with incest. Bloch and Niederhoffer (1958) suggest this may be the main reason for separating boys and girls, as well as parents and their opposite-sexed children, prior to initiation.

Another important function of a passage rite is that it creates a strong psychological bond between the initiate and the tribe, as well as among initiates. At the same time, it helps to sever bonds between the child and the immediate family. It is as if initiates are being told that they now belong to the tribe and not the family, that they can look to it for support and strength, but that they must also defend and protect it.

Today's Rites de Passage

These nonindustrialized societies do not have a long period of adolescence as we know it. There is only childhood, the passage, and adulthood. They are sometimes referred to as **discontinuous societies** because they provide a clear break between important developmental stages.

We, on the other hand, live in **continuous societies.** There are no clear boundaries between developmental stages—no formal rites of passage. Our young ones are exempted from the separation, the training, the initiation, and the induction—even the scarification. Instead, they are put through a period labeled "adolescence"—a period of life that G. Stanley Hall (1916) described as the most troubled, the most stressful, and the most difficult of all stages of development. According to Hall's theory, all adolescents go through a period of **sturm und drang** (storm and stress). He believed that because this period of upheaval and turmoil is biologically based, it is largely inevitable, and it must also be common to all cultures. We now know that this view is fundamentally incorrect and misleading, and that this developmental period is not tumultuous for the majority of adolescents.

In contemporary Western culture, there have not been formal rites of passage (except, perhaps, the Bar Mitzvah or the Bat Mitzvah, in which the Jewish boy or girl becomes an adult at the age of thirteen through religious ceremony, and the "coming-out" party in certain social groups). Our "rites" of passage have historically been indefinite and confusing. They have included a wide range of events that can span many years: getting a driver's license, being old enough to vote or to drink, losing virginity, beginning work, growing (or trying to grow) a mustache, starting to date, and graduating from high school.

In many nonindustrialized societies, the passage from childhood to adulthood is unmistakably marked by rites and ceremonies. Our contemporary societies are somewhat less clear about the passage. Thus, even after graduation from high school, which is often considered to be one of the clearest signs of passage from childhood, there are many who will not adopt the roles and responsibilities of adulthood for a long time.

There are writers who claim that secondary schools now serve as rites de passage similar to the traditional rites of many nonindustrialized societies. They have all the same characteristics, Fasick (1988) argues. They exemplify *separation* (children are segregated into schools) and *training* (the adolescent is formally socialized for the responsibilities of adult life), and the high school graduation is an *initiation* and *induction* ceremony. Fasick suggests that this ceremony is almost universal for much of the middle and working class; for many adolescents, it clearly marks passage from the world of childhood to a world of adult responsibilities.

There are a relatively large number of writers who now suggest that formal rites of passage might not only be very useful for psychological and social reasons, but that adolescents may also have a strong need (or at least a strong desire) to take part in such rituals (Christie & Dinham, 1991; Gill, 1992). Butler (1993) argues, for example, that because they lack institutionally approved rites of passage, many adolescent college students use alcohol as a rite of passage. He suggests that colleges and universities should look at implementing approved rites of passage. Similarly, Redding and

Dowling (1992) point out that many adolescent girls and their families are developing rites of passage that mark progress through college (dances, parties, graduation dinners, presents).

In the United States, there are now an increasing number of African American rites of passage programs, many of them linked to specific schools and communities. Warfield-Coppock (1992) describes twenty such programs. These are typically organized and supervised programs that include training in life skills and social skills, as well as social events. Some also include opportunities for volunteer community service (Trotter, 1991). Their goal is often to foster greater cultural awareness, to enhance the development of self-esteem, and to ease the transition from childhood to adulthood.

BIOLOGICAL AND PHYSICAL CHANGES

As a psychological phenomenon, adolescence may not be common to all cultures, but the biological changes of this period are universal (Montemayor & Flannery, 1990).

Biologically, adolescence is the period from the onset of puberty to adulthood. **Puberty** signifies sexual maturity; **pubescence** refers to the changes that result in sexual maturity. These changes occur in late childhood or early adolescence. Although adulthood is not easily defined, age twenty is a convenient, although arbitrary, beginning point. The beginning of adolescence is even more variable and occurs at different ages for the sexes, but age twelve is often used as an approximation.

Physical Changes

Only during infancy do humans experience a more rapid period of postnatal growth than they do at adolescence.

HEIGHT AND WEIGHT

After infancy, everything slows down to a gain of maybe 2 or so kilograms per year (as opposed to about 10 at birth). But the **growth spurt** that signals impending sexual maturation once more sees weight velocity abruptly climb back up to almost 10 kilograms per year. Then there is a very rapid decline again so that, about 5 years after the onset of the growth spurt (by age 16 for girls and about 18 for boys), weight and height velocity approximate zero. (See Figure 7.1 in Chapter 7 for a depiction of male and female weight velocity curves between birth and age 18.)

The rapid changes in height and weight characteristic of pubescence begin before the age of 12 and are shown in Chapter 9 (Figures 9.1 and 9.2). Figures 11.1 and 11.2 show average height and weight changes for boys and girls from 12 to 18. On average, by the age of 11½ girls surpass boys

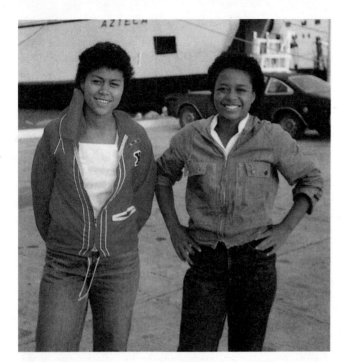

Adolescence, as a biological phenomenon defined in terms of a period of rapid sexual maturation, is universal (although it occurs at different ages among different groups). But as a psychological phenomenon, sometimes marked by a prolonged period of readjustment, it appears to be highly culture-specific.

BODY COMPOSITION

As we saw in Chapter 9, the body composition of boys and girls is different throughout childhood, with boys having relatively more **fat-free mass** and less **fat mass**; the two, taken together, determine body weight. During the adolescent growth spurt, boys' proportion of fat decreases even more because fat-free mass grows at a faster rate than does fat mass. This is not the case for girls, however, so average sex differences in proportion of body weight due to fat mass are magnified (see Figure 11.3).

STRENGTH AND MOTOR PERFORMANCE

Changes in muscular strength, aerobic performance, and motor capacity also reflect the physical growth spurt, especially in boys. Malina and Bouchard (1991) report a high, positive correlation between the maturity level of adolescent boys and their performance in running, jumping, and throwing, as well as in measures of strength. Thus, boys who mature earlier tend to be stronger and faster, and to perform better in sports. In contrast, girls' motor performance does not appear to be closely related to maturity status, so younger, less mature girls frequently outperform more mature girls. One explanation for this is that with increasing maturity, the girl develops a higher proportion of fat relative to fat-free mass. As a result, sex differences in many areas of motor performance increase in favor of males (Beunen & Malina, 1988). This is especially evident in competitive athletics, where male records almost invariably surpass female records.

Pubescence: Sexual Changes

Pubescence refers to all the changes that lead to sexual maturity. These changes, which are universal, are precipitated by a dramatic increase in **hormones** produced by **endocrine**

in height and maintain a slight advantage until 13½. Girls outweigh boys at approximately 11, but by 14½, boys catch up to and surpass girls.

An additional physical change, of particular significance to boys, is a rapid increase in the length of limbs. As a result, many boys acquire the gangling appearance often associated with early adolescence, exaggerated by the fact that their rate of purchasing clothes is often considerably behind the rate at which they outgrow them.

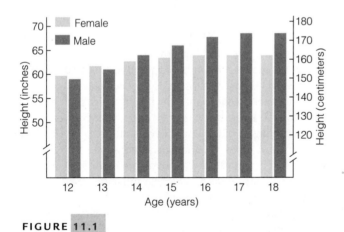

FIGURE 11.1

Height at 50th percentile for U.S. children. (From the Health Department, Milwaukee, Wisconsin; based on data by H. C. Stuart and H. V. Meredith, prepared for use in Children's Medical Center, Boston. Used by permission of the Milwaukee Health Department.)

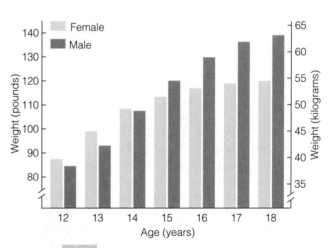

FIGURE 11.2

Weight at 50th percentile for U.S. children. (From the Health Department, Milwaukee, Wisconsin; based on data by H. C. Stuart and H. V. Meredith, prepared for use in Children's Medical Center, Boston. Used by permission of the Milwaukee Health Department.)

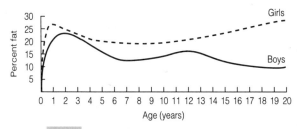

FIGURE 11.3

Growth curve for fat mass in boys and girls. Distinct average sex differences in ratio of fat-free to fat mass may account for many of the observed sex differences in motor performance. (Adapted from Malina & Bouchard, 1991.)

The physical growth spurt manifests itself with changes in muscular strength, aerobic performance, and motor capacity. Sex differences in many areas of motor performance increase, as is evident in competitive athletics, where male records usually surpass female records. This girl has obviously not noticed that she is in the minority where athletic prowess is concerned.

glands such as the **gonads** (*testes* in boys and *ovaries* in girls) (Dubas & Petersen, 1993). Most signs of pubescence are well-known. Among the first in both boys and girls is the appearance of pigmented pubic hair, which is straight initially but becomes characteristically kinky during the later stages of pubescence. At about the same time as pubic hair begins to appear, the boy's testes begin to enlarge, as do the girl's breasts. The girl then experiences rapid physical growth, her first menstrual period (**menarche**, a relatively late event in pubescence), the growth of **axillary hair** (armpit hair), the continued enlargement of her breasts, and a slight lowering of her voice. The boy's voice changes much more dramatically than the girl's, and he, too, grows rapidly, particularly in height and length of limbs. Boys also acquire the capacity to ejaculate semen, grow axillary hair, and eventually develop a beard.

The changes of pubescence that relate directly to the production of offspring involve **primary sexual characteristics.** These include changes in the **ovaries** (organs that produce ova in the girl) and the **testes** (organs that produce sperm in the boy) so that these organs are now capable of producing mature ova and sperm.

Changes that accompany the maturation of the sex organs but that are not directly related to reproduction are said to involve **secondary sexual characteristics.** The appearance of facial hair in the boy and the development of breasts in the girl, voice changes, and the growth of axillary and pubic hair are all secondary sexual characteristics.

The ages at which primary and secondary sexual characteristics develop vary a great deal, but the sequence of their appearance is more predictable—although not entirely fixed. Tables 11.1 and 11.2 summarize that sequence.

TABLE 11.1

Normal Sequence of Sexual Maturation for North American Girls

SEQUENCE	PHYSIOLOGICAL EVENT
1	Beginning of adolescent growth spurt.
2	Appearance of unpigmented pubic down.
3	Breast elevation ("bud" stage).
4	Appearance of pigmented, kinky pubic hair.
5	Increase in size of vagina, clitoris, and uterus.
6	Decline in rate of physical growth.
7	Menarche.
8	Development of axillary (armpit) hair; continued enlargement of breasts; slight lowering of the voice.
9	Increase in production of oil, increased perspiration; possible acne.

Note: The first of these changes may occur as young as age 7¼; the last may not be completed before age 16. Average age of menarche is 12.

TABLE 11.2

Normal Sequence of Sexual Maturation for North American Boys

SEQUENCE	PHYSIOLOGICAL EVENT
1	Appearance of unpigmented pubic down; growth of testes and scrotum (sac containing testes).
2	Beginning of adolescent growth spurt.
3	Enlargement of penis.
4	Appearance of pigmented, kinky pubic hair.
5	Lowering of voice; appearance of "down" on upper lip.
6	First ejaculations occur.
7	Decline in rate of physical growth.
8	Development of axillary (armpit) hair; growth of facial hair.
9	Increase in production of oil; increased perspiration; possible acne.
10	Growth of chest hair.

Note: The first of these changes may occur as young as age 9½; the last may not be completed before age 18. Average age of first ejaculation is 12 to 14.

Puberty: Sexual Maturity

Puberty is sexual maturity—the ability to make babies. However, it is very difficult to determine exactly when a person becomes fertile. Although research has often used the girl's first menstrual period (**menarche**) as an indicator, a girl is frequently infertile for about a year after her first menstruation, so the menarche is not an accurate index of puberty; nevertheless, it is a useful indication of impending sexual maturity (Malina, 1990).

It is almost impossible to arrive at a clear index of sexual maturity for boys, although first ejaculation (**spermarche**) is sometimes taken as a sign comparable to menarche. However, the probability that a boy can become a father immediately after first ejaculation is slight—although not zero—as the concentration of sperm in the semen remains very low for the first year or so.

▪ AGE OF PUBERTY

The average age for puberty in North America is about 12 for girls and 14 for boys, immediately following the period of most rapid growth (the growth spurt). Consequently, the age of puberty may be established by determining the period during which the person grew rapidly. The period of rapid growth may begin as young as 8.7 for girls compared with 10.3 for boys (Malina, 1990). However, there is a wide age range. Some girls may not reach sexual maturity until age 16 and some boys not until age 18 (Dubas & Petersen, 1993). And in other parts of the world, sexual maturity may occur much earlier or much later. For example, in New Guinea, menarche occurs at ages ranging from an average of 15.5 to 18.4. Similarly, among a large sample of Nigerian boys, spermarche occurred at an average age of 14.3 (Adegoke, 1993).

The Implications of Early and Late Maturation

Like the average child, the average adolescent whose growth is depicted in Figures 11.1 and 11.2 is an abstraction, an invention designed to simplify a very complex subject. Hence, although the average adolescent matures at about twelve or fourteen depending on sex, some mature considerably earlier and some considerably later. The timing of this event may be very important to the child.

▪ EFFECTS FOR BOYS

The research indicates quite consistently that early maturation may be a definite advantage for boys. Early-maturing boys are typically better adjusted, more popular, more confident, more aggressive, and more successful in heterosexual relationships. In addition, they appear to have more positive self-concepts (about which more is said in the next chapter). In contrast, adolescent boys who mature later than average are, as a group, more restless, more attention-seeking, less

confident, and have less positive self-concepts (Crockett & Petersen, 1987).

▪ EFFECTS FOR GIRLS

Findings are less consistent for girls. However, most studies indicate that on measures of adjustment, early-maturing girls are initially at a disadvantage—in contrast to early-maturing boys. Dubas and Petersen (1993) summarize the main findings: Early-maturing girls are more likely to have poorer self-concepts, to feel depressed, to date earlier but also to engage in more disapproved behavior, such as getting drunk and skipping school, and to be concerned about their body weight. On average, early-maturing girls weigh more than girls who mature later and are more likely to develop long-lasting eating problems (Brooks-Gunn, 1988). Stattin and Magnusson (1990) also report higher incidence of sexually precocious behavior and violations of social norms among early-maturing girls.

However, there is evidence that the initial disadvantages of early maturation for girls may disappear later. For example, although Simmons and Blyth (1987) found more conduct problems and lower academic success among early-maturing girls, these disadvantages had later disappeared. It appears, claim these authors, that the effects of early and late maturation in girls depends on their ages. Early maturation is a disadvantage in the very early grades (fifth or sixth), when most girls have not yet begun to mature and when the early-maturing girl is likely to find herself excluded from peer group activities. At a later age, however, when most of her age-grade mates have also begun to mature, the early-maturing girl may suddenly find herself in a more advantageous position. Her greater maturity is now something to be admired.

▪ A CONTEXTUAL EXPLANATION

As Petersen (1988) notes, pubertal change is most stressful when it puts the adolescent out of step with peers, especially if the change is not interpreted as desirable. And the consequences of maturational timing are most clearly understood in terms of their effects on relationships and interactions that are important to the adolescent. Thus, early maturation may enhance peer relations for boys largely because early-maturing boys often excel in activities and abilities that are highly prized in the adolescent peer culture. Not only are they larger and stronger and therefore more likely to be better athletes, but they are also more socially mature and hence more likely to lead in heterosexual activities. Furthermore, evidence suggests that relations with parents are better for early-maturing boys (and for late-maturing girls) (Savin-Williams & Small, 1986).

Early-maturing girls, on the other hand, are more likely to be out of step with their peers. Given the fact that girls are on the average two years in advance of boys in physical maturation, the early-maturing girl may well be four or more years in advance of like-aged boys—which might not contribute positively to her social life. Nor is her sexual precocity as likely to be admired by her immature age-peers as is the sexual precocity of early-maturing boys.

Rapid physical changes during adolescence, sometimes apparent in changing body shape, skin eruptions, obesity, and physical awkwardness, may be a source of concern for some adolescents. However, some changes can often be a source of pride and of increasing feelings of self-worth.

From an ecological perspective, what we know of the implications of maturational timetables presents an excellent example of child characteristics interacting with one another (specifically, degree of sexual maturity interacting with age) to determine important elements of the child's ecology (namely, the nature of interaction with parents and peers). But we should note that the child's ecology is unique to that child. Thus, although there may be some general advantages or disadvantages associated with the timing of pubescence, there are many individual exceptions to our generalizations. Not all early-maturing boys and girls are characterized by the same advantages or disadvantages of early maturation, nor are all those who mature later affected in the same way.

Some Concerns of Adolescents

In Harter's (1990) studies of the self, physical appearance is one of the most important factors in determining self-worth. Hence, it is not surprising to find that in a major survey, almost half of all teenagers list their appearance as one of their major concerns (Bibby & Posterski, 1992). In this connection, one of the items most frequently mentioned as the greatest worry for both adolescent boys and girls is the presence of blackheads or pimples ("zits"). Acne is a pervasive problem for many teenagers, a large number of whom consult physicians in search of relief. Treatments sometimes involve dietary change (to diets lower in fat content), the use of special soaps and lotions, abrasive cleaners, drugs, and even abrasion of the skin to stimulate new skin growth (Martin, 1991/1992).

But physical appearance is *not* teenagers' most persistent or universal worry. A massive, thirteen-nation survey of adolescent concerns reveals that the most-often mentioned cause of adolescent worry concerns schooling issues—most specif-

ically, fear of academic failure (Gibson-Cline, 1996). Second as a source of concern is family issues; third is personal identity and self-concept problems. Not only is this pattern of adolescent concerns common to adolescents in all thirteen countries, but it is common to both the advantaged and the nonadvantaged in these countries. Interestingly and significantly, however, patterns of concerns are different for a third group from these nations: those in the *poverty* group. Not surprisingly, for the poorest children, family matters—specifically, those having to do with money and extreme poverty—are more pressing concerns than academic failure (Ondis et al., 1996). (See Figures 11.4, 11.5, 11.6, and 11.7.)

In a survey of 3,600 Canadian adolescents from 150 different schools, the adolescents' greatest worry concerned life beyond graduation—"What am I going to do after high school?"—a problem that affected approximately two-thirds of all respondents. Other important concerns had to do with money, achievement in school, boredom, loneliness, and the

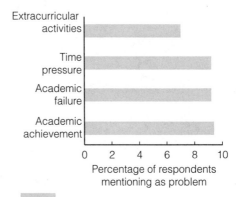

Percentage of respondents mentioning as problem

FIGURE 11.4

Four sources of concern most often mentioned by middle-class U.S. male adolescents. (Based on Gibson-Cline, 1996, p. 217.)

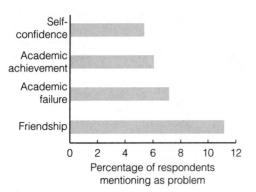

FIGURE 11.5

Four sources of concern most often mentioned by middle-class U.S. adolescent girls. (Based on Gibson-Cline, 1996, p. 217.)

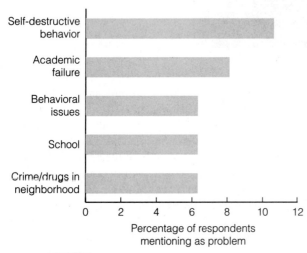

FIGURE 11.6

Five sources of concern most often mentioned by poorer U.S. adolescent boys. (Based on Gibson-Cline, 1996, p. 217.)

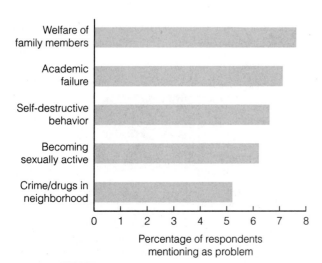

FIGURE 11.7

Five sources of concern most often mentioned by poorer U.S. adolescent girls. (Based on Gibson-Cline, 1996, p. 217.)

TABLE 11.3

Personal Concerns of Adolescents

CONCERN	PERCENTAGE INDICATING "A GREAT DEAL" OR "QUITE A BIT" OF CONCERN
What am I going to do when I finish school?	68
Finances (40% of respondents worked part-time)	54
School concerns	50
Time (not enough time to do the things they want)	48
Appearance	44
What is the purpose of life?	44
Boredom	43
Height or weight	43
Loneliness	35
Feelings of inferiority (poor self-image)	29
Sex	28
Parents' marriage	20

Source: Adapted from R. W. Bibby and D. C. Posterski, *The emerging generation: An inside look at Canada's teenagers,* Table 4.1, p. 60. Toronto: Irwin, 1985. Reprinted with permission of Stoddart Publishing Co., Ltd.

parents' marriage (see Table 11.3). Almost half indicated that their physical appearance was a matter of considerable concern, and about the same number were worried about their height or weight (Bibby & Posterski, 1985). Unfortunately, these concerns are sometimes evident in some serious eating disorders. (See Summary Table 11.4.)

NUTRITION AND EATING DISORDERS

Most adolescents, especially if they are very active physically, expend a very large number of calories each day. However, some take in more than they need; others take in fewer.

Nutritional Requirements

Estimates are that normal, active adolescents require approximately 50 percent more calories during adolescence, and especially during the growth spurt, than they did earlier—or that they will through the rest of their lives. At the same time, they require proportionally more vitamins and minerals. Especially important for bone growth is calcium, of which many adolescents don't get enough. Many are also iron deficient. Iron is particularly important for girls because of blood loss during menstruation, and for boys because of increased muscle mass. Moreover, teenagers who are pregnant have an even greater need for calories, minerals, and vitamins. Un-

SUMMARY TABLE 11.4

Concepts and Occurrences in the Adolescent Transition

CONCEPT/EVENT	EXPLANATIONS/COMMENTS
Rites de passage	• Collective term for ceremonies that accompany major life transitions in certain cultures. The most dramatic often have to do with admission to adulthood. Often include elements of taboos, preparation, initiation, and final induction.
Discontinuous versus continuous societies	• Societies that clearly demarcate passage from one stage to another (for example, through rites de passage) are termed discontinuous; ours is continuous. Nevertheless, some school graduation ceremonies embody elements of passage rites, as do other events, such as obtaining a driver's license, graduating, and getting married.
Puberty versus pubescence	• Puberty is sexual maturity; pubescence includes all of the changes that lead to sexual maturity.
Physical changes of adolescence	• Heralded by the growth spurt; about 2 years earlier for girls than boys; include changes in relative fat-free versus fat mass, with boys having less fat mass after puberty.
Sexual changes of pubescence	• Primary sexual changes (directly linked with ability to reproduce) include changes in testes and ovaries, evident in production of sperm and ova. • Secondary sexual changes include changes in body hair, voice changes, and breast changes.
Early maturation	• Seems an advantage for boys; initially a disadvantage for girls, but disadvantages disappear later. • Effect of early and late maturation best understood in terms of culturally reinforced roles and the extent to which it puts adolescent out of step with peers.
Adolescent concerns	• School concerns seem predominant through much of the world except for the poorest adolescents, for whom family matters, money, crime, and related issues may be greater concerns. Physical concerns are also important for many teenagers.

fortunately, many are malnourished, sometimes because of lack of information, but more often because of cultural models that stress the importance of thinness (Story, 1997).

Parents are frequently alarmed not only at how much their teenagers eat, but also at what they eat, fearing either that the refrigerator will always be empty or that the fast foods their offspring gorge on will be detrimental to their health.

Nutritionists, whose concern is less with empty refrigerators than with empty calories, are quick to point out that there are certain classes of "fast" foods that are nutritious. For example, milk shakes and other ice-cream products are rich in calcium; potatoes contain vitamin C; there is protein in cheese and in meats. But there is a need, too, for fruits and vegetables, and for balance. And there is a need, as well, to make sure that adolescents have adequate nutritional information—although that will not necessarily change their behavior. For example, Chapman and associates (1997) evaluated the effectiveness of a nutrition education program presented to a group of thirty-six girls from high school football teams. Following the program, these girls did, in fact, have a significantly higher level of knowledge about nutrition. But there was no improvement in their food choices. (The authors caution, however, that this might have been due to the short duration of the study.)

Do adolescents not eat well because they don't know any better? Or do most of them know as much as they need to about nutrition? Perhaps they do, suggest Baranowski and associates (1997). When given access to fruits and vegetables during school lunches, for example, they often select them. However, they are much less likely to eat fruits and vegetables at home or when they eat out. And given the social functions served by fast-food establishments, adolescents are likely to eat out as often as parents or pocketbooks permit. Hence, it isn't so much lack of nutritional information as availability of food, the wonderful taste of gravy-smothered fries, and the eating habits of peers and models that may determine the adolescent's eating habits.

Clearly, not all adolescents have bad eating habits. But for many that do, two different sorts of problems, other than those of malnutrition, may result: problems of obesity resulting largely from overconsumption and underexercise, and problems more closely related to "dieting" in its various forms, including "yoyo" dieting and binge eating followed by fasting.

Body Mass Index

How do you decide whether you are overweight, underweight, or just about right? Nutritionists and physicians today often use **body mass index (BMI)**, rather than weight alone, when discussing obesity or excessive thinness. Your body mass index is simply a number that reflects the relationship between your height and your weight. In the metric system, it's calculated simply by dividing your weight in kilograms by the square of your height in meters. To get exactly the same index using pounds and inches, multiply your weight in pounds by 703, and then divide by the square of your height in inches.

What does BMI mean? It doesn't define fitness, nor does it provide a good indication of muscle to fat. But it does provide a crude measure of the extent to which an individual is underweight or overweight. According to the National Academy of Sciences' diet and health report, a BMI of 21 to 26 is optimal (Sizer & Whitney, 1997). A BMI of 27.8 for men and 27.3 for women is the cutoff point for obesity. A BMI of 32 or more is generally considered to be more severely overweight; above 45 brings extremely high risks. At the other extreme, a BMI below 20.7 for men and 19.1 for women is

Body Mass Index (BMI)

Calculate your BMI by multiplying your weight in pounds by 703 and dividing the result by the square of your height in inches. Or, using the metric system, divide your weight in kilograms by the square of your height in meters. The resulting number will probably be in the twenties. If it's much higher or much lower, its meaning is roughly as follows:

MEN	WOMEN	MEANING
Below 20.7	Below 19.1	Underweight
20.7 to 27.8	19.1 to 27.3	Normal range
27.8 to 31.1	27.3 to 32.2	Moderately overweight
31.1 to 45.4	32.3 to 44.8	Severely overweight
>45.4	>44.8	Morbid obesity

Source: Based in part on Sizer, F. S., & Whitney, E. N. (1997). *Nutrition: Concepts and controversies* (7th ed.). Belmont, CA: West/Wadsworth.

considered underweight, and also carries risks. (See Interactive Table 11.5.)

Obesity

Obesity, the most common nutritional problem among both children and adolescents, affects up to a quarter of all North American teenagers (Whitney & Hamilton, 1984). Although obesity in infancy is not a good indicator of obesity in later life, obesity in childhood and adolescence is (Malina & Bouchard, 1991).

The increased medical risks for cardiovascular disease that obesity poses are serious and well-known; its psychological risks are less apparent. However, there is little doubt that obesity can contribute to peer rejection, to negative peer interactions, to low self-esteem, and to unhappiness (Baum & Forehand, 1984). It is also associated with poorer performance in school, although it isn't clear whether this is because obese adolescents are subject to discrimination, because they are expected to do less well, because they avoid participation, because teachers involve them less, because they lack self-esteem or independence, or for other reasons (Morrill et al., 1991).

About 25 percent of the variation in fat distribution among individuals is genetic, explain Malina and Bouchard (1991); another important influence has to do with lifestyle. Among children, obesity is often associated with a combination of high-fat foods and low physical activity (Muecke, Simons-Morton, & Huang, 1992). Contrary to what might be expected, psychology has not found that any particular combination of personality characteristics, family structure, or child-rearing pattern is highly predictive of obesity (Burgard, 1993; Crawford & Shapiro, 1991). Put most simply, other than for rare glandular and metabolic problems, and in spite of genetic contributions, obesity in adolescents—and others—is caused by taking in more calories than are

expended. Weight reduction can therefore be achieved by consuming fewer calories and by expending more.

Unfortunately, the problem is not so simple. Its alleviation requires nutritional information that not all adolescents have or are interested in acquiring, and it requires changing habits that are not only self-rewarding but encouraged by the media, and that are consequently extraordinarily persistent. And the problem is compounded by the fact that the weight levels that Western societies consider ideal, both aesthetically and for health reasons, may not be "reasonable weight levels" for those who are severely obese (Brownell & Wadden, 1992). Because these "ideal" weights seem unattainable, they discourage rather than encourage weight loss. As a result, obesity continues to be a very significant North American problem, and its alleviation, a major industry.

Strangely, despite the prevalence of obesity, contemporary Western societies place tremendous emphasis on physical attractiveness, which, especially among girls, is clearly defined as thinness.

Anorexia Nervosa

Translated literally, **anorexia nervosa** means "loss of appetite as a result of nerves." It describes a complex and only partly understood condition that may be increasing in frequency.

Anorexia is defined medically as involving a loss of at least 15 to 25 percent of "ideal" body weight, this loss not being due to any detectable illness. The American Psychiatric Association (1994) definition includes as criteria intense fear of gaining weight, disturbance in body image, and significant weight loss.

Anorexia nervosa almost always begins with a deliberate desire to be thin and consequent dieting, and ends in a condition in which the patient seems unwilling or unable to eat normally. Many affected females cease menstruating relatively early following initial dieting, and many become excessively active and continue to engage in strenuous exercise programs even after their physical conditions have deteriorated significantly (Warah, 1993). In the absence of medical intervention, anorexia nervosa can be fatal.

PREVALENCE

Estimates of the prevalence of anorexia vary considerably depending on the criteria used (Martin, 1993). Although surveys often find that only about 1 percent of the population is severely anorexic, when estimates of anorexia are based just on eating attitudes and habits, estimates are much higher. For example, in a study of 191 athletes, Stoutjesdyk and Jevne (1993) found that 10.6 percent of the females and 4.6 percent of the males scored in the "anorexic" range on a test of eating attitudes. Following a detailed review of thirty-three years of literature on eating disturbances, Shisslak, Crago, and Estes (1995) report that at least twice as many people have **partial syndrome eating disorders** as have fully defined disorders. Many of these are binge eaters with periods of normal eating interspersed among binges, or they are n investigation by Penner, Thompson, and Coovert (1991) indicates that very thin, anorexic women consistently overestimate their body size, whereas average-size, nonanorexic women do not. Anorexia, severely restricting eating is just one of the eating disorders that relates to our current cultural emphasis on being thin. Bulimia—alternating food binges with severe dieting and self-induced vomiting and diarrhea—is perhaps three or four times more common than anorexia (Figure 11.8).

FIGURE 11.8

*Prevalence rates for eating disorders among adolescents. The low-socioeconomic sample (**A**) consisted of 328 females and 384 males; the high-socioeconomic sample (**B**) consisted of 314 females and 235 males. Note that clinical bulimics meet all DSM-III criteria for bulimia, Bulimia-1 individuals meet all criteria except one, and Bulimia-2 individuals meet all criteria except two. (Data from Lachenmeyer & Muni-Brander, 1988.)*

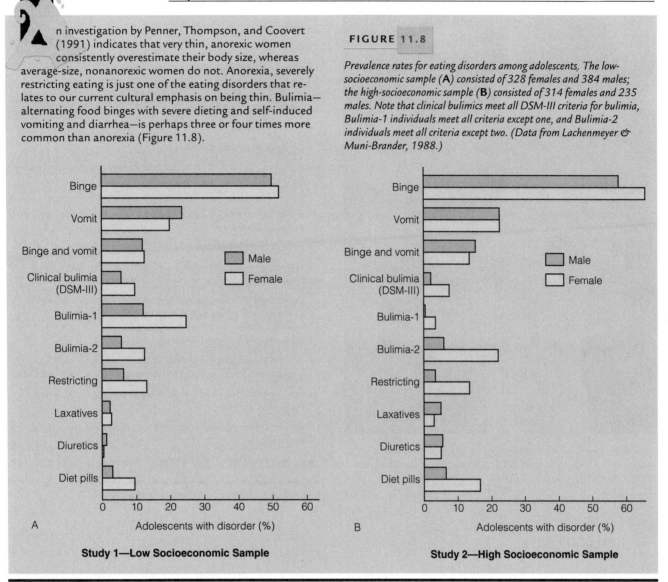

A — Study 1—Low Socioeconomic Sample

B — Study 2—High Socioeconomic Sample

individuals who subject themselves to severe fasts in between normal eating periods (see "At a Glance: Eating Disorders Among Adolescents" and Figure 11.8).

CAUSES

The causes of anorexia nervosa are neither simple nor well understood, probably because there are a variety of possible contributing factors. Endocrine imbalances are sometimes, although infrequently, involved. In general, however, the condition is thought to be primarily psychological. It has often been associated with factors such as excessive concerns about body shape, low self-esteem, disorderly eating habits, and chronic dieting (Shisslak, Crago, & Estes, 1995). Similarly, Keel, Fulkerson, and Leon (1997), following a longitudinal study designed to uncover some of the precursors of

eating disorders, report that they are closely linked with distorted body image and disordered eating habits. Anorexia has also sometimes been linked with depression, as well as with feelings of personal ineffectiveness (Lyon et al., 1997). In addition, its onset among adolescent girls often coincides with the beginning of dating—perhaps because the girl's appearance becomes more important to her at this time (Smolak, Levine, & Gralen, 1993). Some speculate that anorexic individuals are typically those who do not feel that they are in control of their lives but who discover that they can control their body weight; in the end, control becomes an obsession. Others suggest that lack of positive self-image coupled with the emphasis that society places on thinness (particularly among females) may be manifested in anorexia in those cases where the person attempts to obtain approval by dieting.

Distortion of body image is a common symptom of anorexia nervosa. Many very thin anorexic women, looking into perfectly good mirrors, consistently overestimate their body size.

TABLE 11.6

Possible Medical Consequences of Bulimia Nervosa

- Dehydration.

- Constipation.

- Abnormal heartbeat, atrial flutter, fibrillation.

- Increased susceptibility to cold.

- Menstrual irregularities.

- Abdominal distention.

- Excessive weight fluctuations.

- Dehydration and fluid shifts, sometimes resulting in headaches and fainting. Problem more serious if diuretics are used or if bulimia follows prolonged fasting.

- Electrolyte imbalance, aggravated by laxative or diuretic use as well as by repeated vomiting.

- Hypoglycemic symptoms.

- Malnutrition-related problems (might include cardiovascular, kidney, gastrointestinal, or blood problems as well as insomnia).

- Dental/oral problems sometimes associated with loss of enamel as a result of frequent exposure to stomach acidity during vomiting episodes. Other possible gum, salivary duct, and tongue problems associated with emesis (vomiting).

- Specific gastrointestinal difficulties, sometimes associated with ipecac abuse. Prolonged use can lead to cardiac problems and death.

- Laxative-related problems, which vary depending on the nature of the laxative abused.

- Insomnia resulting from malnutrition, nocturnal binges, or underlying depression.

- Various neurological and endocrine problems.

Source: Based on Goode (1985) and Brown (1991).

Bulimia Nervosa

Whereas anorexia nervosa is characterized by not eating (in spite of the fact that some anorexics occasionally do go on eating binges), **bulimia nervosa** (or simply bulimia) involves recurrent episodes of binge eating. It is, in fact, a more common eating disorder than anorexia, with a higher than expected proportion of males (Lachenmeyer & Muni-Brander, 1988).

The American Psychiatric Association (1994) describes bulimia nervosa in terms of recurrent episodes of binge eating (rapid consumption of large amounts of food in a short time). Other criteria for a diagnosis of bulimia nervosa include a feeling of lack of control over eating behavior; regular episodes of self-induced vomiting, use of laxatives or diuretics, strict dieting or fasting, or vigorous exercise; a minimum average of two binge-eating episodes per week; and persistent overconcern with body shape and weight.

Typically, foods consumed during a binge are high in calories and are eaten inconspicuously. Abdominal pain is a common result, as are frequent weight fluctuations. Other possible medical consequences of bulimia nervosa are listed in Table 11.6. Unlike anorexia, bulimia does not usually present an immediate threat to life—although its eventual medical consequences can be quite serious.

CAUSES

One important contributing factor in the increasing incidence of bulimia nervosa is the tremendous emphasis that society places on thinness. Not surprisingly, among characteristics that most clearly differentiate bulimic girls from those who are nonbulimic are a greater desire to be thin, a higher degree of dissatisfaction with their bodies, and chronic dieting. In addition, bulimic females are more likely to see themselves as being overweight and tend to be significantly more depressed (Ledoux, Choquet, & Manfredi, 1993). Miller, McCluskey-Fawcett, and Irving (1993) report that adolescents who were sexually abused are at higher risk of being bulimic. So, too, are those whose parents have the highest frequency of addictive problems (alcoholism, drug use, overeating, and gambling), as well as those who are most inclined toward perfectionism (Brouwers & Wiggum, 1993).

Some Treatments

Anorexia nervosa and bulimia are frightening and baffling conditions for parents. Anorexia is especially frightening because it can be fatal, and it is baffling and frustrating because it may seem to parents that the anorexic adolescent deliberately and totally unreasonably refuses to eat. And neither pleas nor threats are likely to work. What is?

Because anorexia and bulimia are not, in most instances, primarily biological or organic disorders, their treatment is often complex and difficult. There are no drugs or simple surgical procedures that can easily cure these conditions. In some extreme instances, patients respond favorably to antidepressant drugs; at other times, it is necessary to force-feed them to save their lives. Generally, however, successful treatments have typically involved one of several forms of psychotherapy. Among these, what is termed **cognitive-behavior therapy**—the use of reinforcement and/or punishment combined with more rational approaches—has sometimes been dramatically effective (Wilson & Fairburn, 1993). For example, Wilfley and associates (1993) significantly reduced binge eating among fifty-six bulimic women using group cognitive-behavioral therapy. Similarly, Agras and colleagues (1994) reduced binge eating in bulimic women using individual cognitive-behavioral therapy, accompanied by antidepressant medication.

There are some who argue that one of the main causes of anorexia and bulimia is dieting and that to treat these disorders effectively, it is necessary to treat dieting. And perhaps to treat dieting, it is necessary to change the social and cultural conditions that have placed such a tremendous value on thinness. (See Summary Table 11.7.)

ADOLESCENT INTELLECTUAL DEVELOPMENT

Jean Piaget's view of intellectual development begins with a description of infants *assimilating* aspects of the environment, *accommodating* to others, *equilibrating* (balancing) the two processes, and constructing progressively more advanced views of reality. In time, the infant succeeds in separating self from world, in representing aspects of the world symbolically, and in dealing with knowledge in increasingly logical ways. And by the end of *concrete operations,* the child understands the logical necessity of conservation, can solve a variety of problems, and can classify, seriate, and deal with number at a surprisingly sophisticated level.

In the following sections, we continue our examination of intellectual development, looking first at Piaget's contributions and then at information-processing approaches.

▲ SUMMARY TABLE 11.7
Nutritional Needs and Eating Disorders of Adolescents

CONCEPT	EXPLANATION/COMMENTS
Nutritional needs	■ Approximately 50 percent increase in need for calories in adolescence. ■ Greatly increased need for vitamins and minerals such as calcium and iron. ■ Nutritional awareness is not always reflected in food choices.
Body mass index	■ A crude measurement of obesity or excessive thinness, computed by dividing weight in kilograms by square of height in meters.
Obesity	■ Defined as weighing more than 20 percent of normal for age, height, and sex. A BMI in the high 20s or greater. ■ Most common nutritional problem in North America. ■ Some genetic contribution.
Anorexia nervosa	■ Excessive thinness related to loss of appetite/refusal to eat, linked to obsessive desire to be thin, distorted body image, fear of gaining weight. ■ Sometimes fatal.
Bulimia	■ Characterized by recurrent episodes of binge eating, persistent overconcern with body weight and image, dieting, fasting, use of laxatives and emetics, dramatic weight fluctuations. ■ Relatively common. ■ Bulimia and anorexia are sometimes treated with cognitive-behavior therapy.

Piaget's View: Formal Operations

Some of the important distinctions between concrete and **formal operations** are illustrated in children's responses to the following Inhelder and Piaget (1958) problem: Participants are presented with five test tubes that contain different unidentified chemicals; a combination of these chemicals will result in a yellow liquid. This phenomenon is demonstrated for participants so they know that one special tube, which is kept apart, is the catalyst for the desired reaction. What they are asked to do is discover which combination of the other four tubes is the correct one. They are allowed to experiment as necessary to solve the problem.

Typical ten-year-olds begin by combining two of the chemicals, then two more, then again two. If, by chance, they arrive at a correct solution, they exclaim, "There, those two! That's the solution." But if they are asked whether they can find any

With the advent of adolescence, claims Piaget, there develops the potential for a more advanced form of logic—a logic that is more complex and more abstract than that of the younger child.

other solutions, their strategy changes little. They continue to combine pairs of liquids, or even three or four at once. Their behavior is unsystematic, and if they are unlucky or not persistent enough, they may be incapable of discovering even one correct combination.

Intelligent fifteen-year-olds behave quite differently. As illustrated in Figure 11.9, they can solve the problem by systematically combining the tubes by twos, threes, and finally all four, yielding all possible combinations. In the end, there will be no doubt in their minds that they have found all correct combinations.

■ FORMAL VERSUS CONCRETE THINKING

In this experiment, there are clues to some of the important differences between the child's thinking during the stage of concrete operations and thinking characterized by formal operations.

First, ten-year-olds begin their solution by attempting actual combinations; their hypotheses are real behaviors. In contrast, the bright fifteen-year-old begins by imagining all the possibilities and then tries them. There is a fundamental difference in the orientations. The first reflects the concrete nature of the child's thought; the second reflects the adolescent's ability to deal with the hypothetical.

Second, the experiment illustrates the logical capacity of the adolescent's thinking. Because ten-year-olds consider every combination as a separate and unrelated hypothesis and because they arrive at these combinations in a haphazard way, they are likely to overlook possibilities in the process. In contrast, adolescents first consider the range of all possible combinations. The concrete logic that was sufficient to deal with

classes and seriation is replaced by what Piaget terms the **logic of propositions.** This form of logic is a much more powerful tool for dealing with the hypothetical—with statements that need not relate to reality but are simply characterized by the possibility that they can be true or untrue (in fact, this is the definition of a **proposition:** a verbal statement that can be true or false).

■ IMPLICATIONS OF FORMAL THINKING

The adolescent's newly acquired capability to deal with the hypothetical might not be very obvious, or perhaps even very important, if it were manifested only in problems of chemistry and physics. But formal operations extend well beyond the realms of science. They are apparent in new preoccupations with understanding the self as an abstraction (Harter, 1990), in an egocentric reliance on logic (Lapsley, 1990), and in an intense new idealism. Children can now contemplate states of affairs that do not exist, they can compare the ideal to the actual, they can become profoundly distressed at the failure of preceding generations to prevent the confusion that they observe around them, and they can be puzzled by some of the profound questions that have always tormented philosophers. It is precisely the adolescent's ability to deal with the hypothetical that made it possible for 44 percent of the subjects in Bibby and Posterski's (1985) study to claim that they were very concerned about the purpose and meaning of life. Such questions do not often suggest themselves to the ten-year-old.

With the idealism of formal operations, there also comes a belief in the omnipotence of thought. The *egocentrism* of adolescence (which we discuss later in this chapter) can be seen

FIGURE 11.9

All possible combinations of the four test tubes to which the fifth can be added. The experiment required the subject to discover the combination(s) that will yield a yellow liquid when potassium iodide is added. The correct solutions have a light gray background.

Diluted sulfuric acid   **Water**   **Oxygenated water**   **Thiosulphate**   **Potassium iodide**

in the belief that reason and logic provide all the answers and in an apparent inability to adopt the point of view that admits that we do not have all the answers, and that even if we did, social, political, and other human realities sometimes oppose their implementation. It is this unshakable belief in the power of thought that may underlie the adolescent's absolutely insistent political, social, and religious arguments with parents and others.

An Information-Processing View

Piaget's stage-bound description of intellectual development, although it provides many important insights into cognitive functioning, is not always an accurate description of the child's capabilities. Ironically, whereas Piaget seems to have underestimated the cognitive achievements of infants and preschoolers, he may have overestimated those of the adolescent. There is evidence, for example, that the abstract and logical thinking of formal operations, which is not ordinarily present at the beginning of formal operations (at age eleven or twelve), is often not even present among adults.

A complementary approach to understanding intellectual development is the **information-processing approach.** As we saw in Chapter 9, information-processing theories are concerned with three important aspects of cognition: the acquisition of a knowledge base, the development of cognitive (information-processing) strategies, and the development of metacognitive skills.

To review briefly, the **knowledge base** consists of all the concepts, ideas, information, and so on that we have in memory. Infants begin life with very little knowledge base. The knowledge base derives from the individual's experiences; schools do a great deal to expand and organize the knowledge base.

Cognitive strategies are the procedures involved in learning and remembering. They include strategies such as organizing and rehearsing.

And the skills of **metacognition** relate to information that the knower has about the processes of knowing and remembering, and to awareness of the self as an information processor.

The information-processing approach to cognitive development looks at the individual's knowledge base, development of strategies for processing information, and self-awareness as a processor of information. The skills reflected in this girl's playing of the flute are based on years of experience and practice that have enriched her knowledge base, gradually transforming her from novice into expert.

As metacognitive skills increase, so too does the child's ability to analyze performance, to predict the likelihood of success, to change strategies, to evaluate, and to monitor.

An information-processing view of development describes how each of these three aspects of information processing (knowledge base, processing skills, and metacognitive skills) changes with age and experience.

CHANGES IN KNOWLEDGE BASE

Knowledge base grows with increasing experience and exposure to schooling. Anderson (1980) describes how children progress from being novices in all areas to being experts in at least some areas—especially in certain games, in aspects of social interaction, in certain levels and classes of school subjects, and perhaps in hobby-related or cultural pursuits. One of the important differences between experts and novices has to do with knowledge base. But the difference is not simply that experts know more (have more content in their knowledge bases), but also that they have formed more asso-

ciations among the things they know. Their knowledge is richer in the sense that it suggests more relationships. The artist who is an expert in color does not understand the color blue in the same way I, a novice, might. My pitiful understanding permits me to relate blue to robin eggs, morning skies, and northern lakes; the expert might relate it to these as well, but might also break it down into a dozen hues whose subtlety and associations have no meaning for me. More than this, the expert might well understand blue as a wavelength, might understand its relationships to other waves of different lengths, and might have a sense of its crispness or fragility that quite escapes me.

CHANGES IN PROCESSING

If development is a process of shedding some of the novice's ignorance and acquiring increasing expertise, then it follows that expertise involves more than changes in knowledge base—that it must also involve changes in information-processing capacity. Among other things, information-processing capacity depends on the availability of appropriate strategies—and it depends on attention span.

That attention span increases with age is clear. Intelligence tests such as the Stanford-Binet require that subjects try to recall sequences of digits presented at one-second intervals. Whereas a preschool child might correctly recall a string of two or three digits, an adolescent might easily recall six or seven.

Changes in the availability of appropriate strategies are not as easily investigated, partly because it is not always simple to identify a strategy and determine whether it is present. However, Piaget's investigations of concrete and formal operations suggest that the strategies available to older adolescents are substantially different, and considerably more powerful, than those available to the younger child. For example, Demetriou, Efklides, and Papadaki (1993) show how the strategies that adolescents use become progressively more systematic and specialized, enabling them to do things like form hypotheses, design experiments, and even build models and theories. In addition, adolescents have more ready-made solutions for problems. Thus, there are many Piagetian tasks that present real problems for a younger child but that can be solved almost from memory by an older child. A six-year-old might need to "figure out" whether there is still the same amount of material in a deformed object; the adolescent need not "figure."

METACOGNITIVE CHANGE

One additional important area of developmental change in information processing involves the child's understanding of the self as a processor of information and an increasing understanding of the processes of cognition. As we saw in Chapter 9, metacognitive skills seem to be largely absent in young children but are clearly present in older children and adolescents. These changes make the adolescent more of an expert knower and information processor. But they do not eliminate the adolescent's egocentrism. (See Summary Table 11.8.)

SUMMARY TABLE 11.8
Two Approaches to Describing Adolescent Intellectual Development

APPROACH	EXPLANATIONS/COMMENTS
Piaget's Formal Operations	■ Ages 11–12 on. ■ Ability to deal with abstractions, with the hypothetical (logic of propositions). ■ Apparent in new preoccupations with understanding self as an abstraction, in an egocentric reliance on logic, and in a new sense of abstract idealism.
Information Processing	Describes changes in three areas: ■ Knowledge base (increases in specific knowledge; more relations and associations among items of information). ■ Processing capacities (increases in memory and attention capacities; more sophisticated cognitive strategies). ■ Metacognition (increasing awareness of self as information processor; increasing ability to monitor, evaluate, and control cognitive activities).

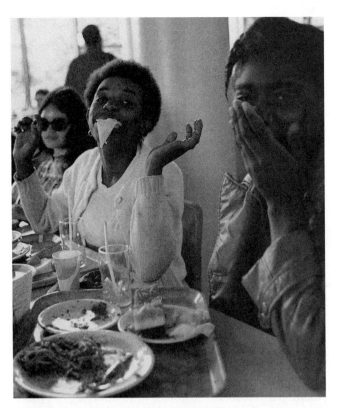

The concept of the adolescent's imaginary audience is a recognition of the adolescent's self-consciousness and egocentrism—a recognition of the fact that many adolescents act as though they think others are always watching and judging them. Whether this girl thinks her imaginary audience is shocked and disgusted, mildly amused, or very impressed at how much pizza she can put in her mouth at one time might have important implications for her behavior.

ADOLESCENT EGOCENTRISM

In Piagetian theory, **egocentrism** is not a derogatory term as it might be in ordinary usage. It refers less to a selfishness than to a cognitive and emotional self-centeredness and is apparent in children's inability to be completely objective in their understanding of the world and in their interactions with others. During sensorimotor development, for example, infants are egocentric in that they cannot easily differentiate between self and the physical world: Objects exist only when they are being looked at, tasted, felt, or smelled—a rather extreme egocentrism. And in the preschool period there is evidence of egocentrism in the children's centeredness on the perceptual features of objects when they respond incorrectly to conservation problems.

The egocentrism of the adolescent is not as extreme or naive as that of the infant. It is characterized by an inability to differentiate between objects and events that are of concern to others and those of concern to the adolescent. As Jahnke and Blanchard-Fields (1993) note, it's a sort of confusion between the adolescent's thoughts and the thoughts of others. **Adolescent egocentrism** is sometimes apparent in behaviors that seem to be motivated by the adolescent's belief that everybody is watching and is terribly concerned—that there is, in other words, an *imaginary audience* that is always pass-

ing judgment. It is also apparent in the adolescent's private conviction that he or she is special—a conviction that defines the *personal fable*. These two concepts—the imaginary audience and the personal fable—are the two main dimensions of adolescent egocentrism (Vartanian & Powlishta, 1996).

The Imaginary Audience

The adolescent's **imaginary audience** is a hypothetical collection of all who might be concerned with the adolescent's self and behavior. It is the *they* in expressions such as "They say…" or "They predict.…" Social psychologists inform us that each of us behaves as though "they" are watching and care. But the imaginary audiences of most adults are less important than those of adolescents. According to Elkind (1967), it is because of this imaginary audience to which the adolescent is continually reacting that young adolescents are often very self-conscious. It is also because of this same audience that many become so concerned with their hair, their clothing, and other aspects of their physical appearance. It is as though adolescents believe that others are as deeply concerned about them as they themselves are and that these others constantly judge them.

MEASURING THE IMAGINARY AUDIENCE

How does research investigate beliefs such as these? How can psychology locate an imaginary audience?

The answer is with one of several instruments such as Elkind and Bowen's (1979) **Imaginary Audience Scale (IAS)** or Enright, Shukla, and Lapsley's (1980) Adolescent Egocentrism–Sociocentrism Scale. The IAS is based on the assumption that individuals who act as though an imaginary audience is watching them will be self-conscious. Accordingly, the scale is really a measure of self-consciousness. Items for the IAS were selected from a pool of suggestions given by students who were asked to describe situations they might find embarrassing. The final scale consists of twelve items, the first four of which are reproduced in Interactive Table 11.9.

A number of investigations using the IAS or the Enright scale have found considerable variability in the ages at which children become egocentric (Jahnke & Blanchard-Fields, 1993). However, the evidence seems clear that egocentrism is an important phenomenon of adolescence. And although it typically declines following early adolescence, when Peterson and Roscoe (1991) gave the IAS to female college freshmen, they found that their scores were even higher than those of young adolescents. Peterson and Roscoe reason that being placed in a new social environment results in a greater self-protectiveness and consequently a greater self-consciousness.

The Personal Fable

Adolescent egocentrism is reflected not only in the imaginary audience but also in the elaboration of fantasies, called **personal fables.** Not surprisingly, the adolescent is the hero in these fables. The fantasies have a number of identifying themes, the most common of which are "I am special." "Eagles and gods do not do untidy things upon me." "I will not get pregnant." "I will not become addicted to these drugs I take only for recreation." "Mom, you just don't understand what real love is." "Neither do you, Dad!"

One of the characteristics of the personal fable is a sense of invulnerability. Unfortunately, it is often sadly inappropriate, as is evident in the fact that adolescents—especially males—have the highest accident rate of all age groups except those over sixty-five (U.S. Bureau of the Census, 1996).

Elements of the personal fable run through the lives of most of us. We all believe that we are somewhat special. But these beliefs appear to be greatly exaggerated in adolescents and may partially account for their casual attitude with regard to taking risks.

IMPLICATIONS OF THE IMAGINARY AUDIENCE AND THE PERSONAL FABLE

Understanding adolescent self-consciousness might not only do a great deal to clarify the adolescent experience for us, but might also have a number of practical implications. For example, Elkind (1981b) suggests it might contribute in important ways to our understanding of vandalism, teenage pregnancy, drug abuse, and other related behaviors. And, in-

INTERACTIVE TABLE 11.9

The Imaginary Audience Scale (IAS)

Instructions: Please read the following stories carefully and assume that the events actually happened to you. Place a check next to the answer that best describes what you would do or feel in the real situation.

1. You have looked forward to the most exciting dress-up party of the year. You arrive after an hour's drive from home. Just as the party is beginning, you notice a grease spot on your trousers or skirt. (There is no way to borrow clothes from anyone.) Would you stay or go home?

_____ Go home.

_____ Stay, even though I'd feel uncomfortable.

_____ Stay, because the grease spot wouldn't bother me.

2. Let's say some adult visitor came to your school, and you were asked to tell them a little bit about yourself.

_____ I would like that.

_____ I would not like that.

_____ I wouldn't care.

3. It is Friday afternoon, and you have just had your hair cut in preparation for the wedding of a relative next weekend. The barber or hairdresser did a terrible job, and your hair looks awful. To make it worse, that night is the most important basketball game of the season and you really want to see it, but there is no way you can keep your head covered without people asking questions. Would you stay home or go to the game anyway?

_____ Go to the game and not worry about my hair.

_____ Go to the game and sit where people won't notice me very much.

_____ Stay home.

4. If you went to a party where you did not know most of the kids, would you wonder what they were thinking about you?

_____ I wouldn't think about it.

_____ I would wonder about that a lot.

_____ I would wonder about that a little.

Source: From D. Elkind and R. Bowen, Imaginary audience behavior in children and adolescents, *Developmental Psychology*, 1979, 15(1), 38–44, p. 40. Copyright 1979 by the American Psychological Association. Reprinted by permission of the author.

terestingly, measures of self-consciousness have been found to be among the best predictors of whether sexually active, unmarried adolescent girls use contraception (Green, Johnson, & Kaplan, 1992; Johnson & Green, 1993). Similarly, Greene and associates (1996) found that measures of adolescent egocentrism (specifically, measures of the imaginary audience and personal fable) could be highly useful for predicting a wide variety of risk-taking behaviors, including sexual behaviors associated with risk of HIV infection. And Montgomery, Haemmerlie, and Zoellner (1996) report that among a college sample of eighty students, high scores on an Imaginary Audience Scale were significantly related to risk taking, specifically as it relates to excessive drinking of alcohol.

One of the important motives that might underlie decisions relating to risk-taking behavior may relate directly to

Adolescent Risks and Violent Death

e have reason to worry about our young people," write Lavery and colleagues (1993). "Adolescents are at high risk for accidental injury, violence, and the initiation of lifestyles and habits which present long-term health risks" (p. 277). Their risk-taking behavior is manifested in drug abuse, dangerous hobbies, and automobile and other accidents, and is especially evident in the incidence of violent death among white adolescent males. Violent death among blacks is more common than among whites but does not reveal the same pattern of higher incidence in adolescence. This might be because death among blacks involves a higher proportion of homicides, which continue at a high rate after adolescence, and perhaps because of more limited access to automobiles. For both blacks and whites, violent death is considerably lower for females than for males (Table 11.10).

TABLE 11.10

1993 U.S. Death Rates (per 100,000) by Age for Accidents

	WHITE		BLACK	
AGE	*Male*	*Female*	*Male*	*Female*
15–24	99.1	28.2	242.2	39.9
25–34	92.0	24.8	197.3	46.2
35–44	82.9	24.9	169.9	40.1
45–54	70.5	24.3	137.2	28.7
55–64	71.7	26.7	112.1	31.9
65 and older	157.1	78.6	164.3	70.8

Source: U.S. Bureau of the Census, 1996, p. 101.

what the adolescent expects the reaction of the imaginary audience to be. Teachers, parents, counselors, and friends are all members of that audience. Mine is made up mainly of popes and presidents.

High-Risk Adolescent Behavior

Adolescents—especially males—engage in a variety of reckless behaviors, many of which have potentially devastating consequences (see "At a Glance: Adolescent Risks and Violent Death" and Table 11.10).

MANIFESTATIONS OF ADOLESCENT RECKLESSNESS

Where I live, automobile insurance rates for a sixteen-year-old, accident-free male driver are about four times higher than they are for *moi*. Why? Not because I am technically a better driver, but simply because more sixteen-year-olds drive at high speed when sober, and even more of them drive at high speed when drunk. Over one-third of all drunk drivers involved in fatal accidents are aged sixteen to twenty-four. Yet this age group represents fewer than one-fifth of all licensed drivers. More than three-fourths of the 35,000 fifteen- to twenty-four-year-olds who died in 1993 died as a result of accidents, suicide, or homicide (U.S. Bureau of the Census, 1996).

About 50 percent more sexually active teenage girls than sexually active twenty-five- to forty-four-year-olds do not use contraception. And over 1 million unmarried teenagers become pregnant in the United States each year (U.S. Bureau of the Census, 1996).

Adolescents have the highest rate of illegal drug use of any age group (Arnett, 1992). In 1990, 40 percent of all serious crimes in the United States were committed by those under eighteen (U.S. Bureau of the Census, 1996).

WHY ADOLESCENTS TAKE RISKS

Adolescents' reckless behaviors, explains Arnett (1992), involve doing things that they recognize as dangerous, but they deliberately underestimate the danger and ignore precautions that could be taken. When Beyth-Marom and colleagues

(1993) asked adult and adolescent subjects to describe the possible consequences of high-risk behaviors like drinking and driving, their responses were remarkably similar. Adolescents *know* the risks involved in their behaviors; they can anticipate their possible outcomes as clearly as can adults. But they consistently underestimate risks associated with activities in which they themselves engage. Benthin, Slovic, and Severson (1993) had adolescents rate perceived risks and benefits of thirty high-risk activities like smoking, drug use, drinking, and sex. Not only did participants perceive lower risks for their own high-risk behaviors, but they also perceived greater benefits. And, strikingly, they consistently overestimated the extent to which their peers engaged in the same activities.

Adolescents' tendency to underestimate the probability of bad outcomes for themselves is one factor that explains risk taking, claims Arnett (1992). It is, in fact, a reflection of their personal fable of invulnerability—their frequently expressed belief that "It won't happen to me." A second is the personality trait labeled **sensation seeking**, which may be related to levels of sex hormones. Sensation seeking implies a desire to take risks for the sensations involved. Driving motorcycles, waterskiing, and using drugs have all been shown to be related to high scores on the sensation-seeking scale. Third, a wealth of research suggests that peer influences contribute to the likelihood of reckless behavior (Arnett, 1992). Finally, some high-risk-takers are adolescents who score high on measures of social maladjustment (Lavery et al., 1993).

The Cautious Adolescent

Although adolescence is a period of greater apparent recklessness than any other period of life, it would be misleading not to emphasize that the majority of adolescents are not reckless. In 1995, more than 7.7 million American sixteen- to nineteen-year-olds worked—and more than 11 million were in school. And school, for a lot of them, is serious, nonreckless work. In fact, more than 4 million of the 11 million in school were also employed. In Canada, almost half of all fifteen- to nineteen-year-olds were employed (*Canada Yearbook,* 1997). It is also worth noting that in a 1994 U.S. survey, 92.7 percent of all twelve- to seventeen-year-olds did not use marijuana, 99.6 percent had never used cocaine, and more than half had never used alcohol (U.S. Bureau of the Census, 1996).

Clearly, the adolescent is not totally unrestrained, reckless, and immoral. (See Summary Table 11.11.)

MORAL DEVELOPMENT

Morality involves interactions between people in which questions of trust, ethics, values, and rights are involved. Most of us believe implicitly that some people are good and others less good—that goodness or evil is an intrinsic part of what we are, of ourselves. When we judge people to be morally

▲
SUMMARY TABLE 11.11
Adolescent Egocentrism

CONCEPT	EXPLANATIONS/COMMENTS
Adolescent egocentrism	■ Cognitive and emotional self-centeredness reflected in the imaginary audience and the personal fable.
Imaginary audience	■ Describes the adolescent's belief that others are watching and care; reflected in self-consciousness, and measured by means of scales that tap self-consciousness.
Personal fable	■ The belief that we are unique, special, correct, lucky, and invulnerable—more or less.
Implications of high egocentrism as reflected in the imaginary audience and personal fable	■ Measured egocentrism found to be related to the probability of various high-risk behaviors associated with drug use, pregnancy, and unsafe sex, among others. ■ Adolescent recklessness evident in high incidence of accidental and violent deaths, especially among males. ■ Not all adolescents are highly egocentric—or highly reckless.

"good" or "bad," says Kohlberg (1964), we might be referring to any one of three things: their ability to resist temptation, the amount of guilt that accompanies failure to resist temptation, or the individual's evaluation of the morality of a given act based on some personal standard of good and evil. These dimensions of morality are not necessarily very closely related. A person may repeatedly violate some accepted code of conduct—behave immorally, in other words—yet feel a great deal of guilt. A second may engage in exactly the same behavior and feel no guilt. Yet both may judge the act equally evil. Who is most moral?

Morality as a Cognitive Phenomenon

Carroll and Rest (1982) suggest that there are four steps involved in behaving morally: First, moral behavior requires recognizing a moral problem and being sensitive to the fact that someone's welfare is involved. Second, it is necessary to make a judgment about what is right and wrong—about what ought to be done in a given situation. Third, the individual needs to make a plan of action that takes into account relevant ideals and values. Finally, the plan must be put into action.

It is entirely possible, Narváez and Rest (1995) argue, to fail to act morally because of a deficiency in only one of these components. Research on **bystander apathy,** stimulated by the now-famous murder of Kitty Genovese, is a case in point (Latané & Darley, 1970). Kitty was a New Yorker who, returning home from work at 3 o'clock one morning, was set upon by a maniac and murdered. The murder took an entire half hour to complete and was watched by at least thirty-

Behaving morally requires four things: recognizing a problem, evaluating it in terms of personal values, deciding what ought to be done, and acting. One of the characteristics of adolescence, says Piaget, is a newfound idealism linked with the adolescent's ability to imagine a better world—and a willingness to get one's hands dirty trying to improve it.

eight of Kitty's neighbors in a fashionable residential district, most of them from their windows. No one tried to help her; no one yelled at the murderer; no one even called the police. Table 11.12 shows how the behavior of the bystanders might be interpreted in light of Carroll and Rest's analysis of what is required for moral behavior.

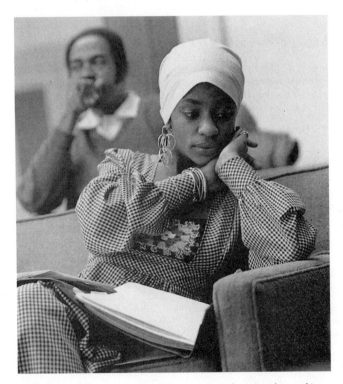

Some view morality as a cognitive phenomenon in that it involves making judgments about right and wrong as well as about actions that ought to be taken. Guidance for moral judgment and action is sometimes found in religions or in the behavior of others. Some, like this woman, look for moral advice in the written word.

Piaget's Two-Stage Approach

Carroll and Rest's view of morality, which closely follows the work of Kohlberg (1969, 1980) and Piaget (1932), is clearly based on the individual's cognition (understanding) of a situation. Not surprisingly, research indicates that moral reasoning and behavior are closely linked with metacognition (for example, Swanson & Hill, 1993).

Piaget's description of moral development is also cognitive. He investigated children's morality by telling them stories and asking them to judge how good or bad the characters were—essentially a cognitive activity. In one story, for

TABLE 11.12

Carroll and Rest's Four Components of Moral Behavior Illustrated by Reference to the Kitty Genovese Murder

MORAL BEHAVIOR REQUIRES:	POSSIBLE REASONS FOR NOT INTERVENING IN THE MURDER:
Moral sensitivity (recognition of a moral problem)	Failure to recognize seriousness of situation ("It's only a lover's quarrel.")
Moral judgment (deciding what ought to be done)	Inability to devise a plan of behavior compatible with ideals and values ("How can I save her life without endangering mine?")
Moral motivation (conscience; ideals; that which guides moral action)	Individual's values run counter to helping someone in this situation ("If he wants to kill her, hey, it's up to him.")
Moral action (implementing moral or immoral behavior)	Unable to implement the plan they might have devised ("I should restrain the attacker physically, but I'm not strong enough.")

example, a child accidentally breaks fifteen cups and another deliberately breaks a single cup. Is one worse than the other?

Younger children, notes Piaget, often judge guilt by the apparent consequences of the act: The child who has broken the largest number of cups or who has stolen the greatest quantity of goods or the largest amount of money is more evil—and should be punished more—than the one who deliberately broke only one cup, stole just a few things, or took just a little money.

Based on children's responses to these stories, Piaget identified two broad stages in the evolution of morality. In the first stage, lasting until about age eight or ten, children respond in terms of the immediate consequences of behavior, manifesting a morality that is governed by the principles of pain and pleasure. Thus, good behaviors are those that have pleasant consequences; bad actions have unpleasant consequences. Accordingly, the child responds primarily to outside authority, because authority is the main source of reinforcement and punishment. Piaget labels this first stage of moral development **heteronomy.** The morality of this stage is a morality of *obedience,* notes DeVries (1997). It reflects what Piaget thought to be a predominantly authoritarian relationship that typically exists between young children and their parents.

In the second stage, beginning at around age eleven or so, morality comes to be governed more and more by the individual's own principles and ideals. As a result, moral judgments become less obedience-bound, more autonomous—

hence Piaget's label of **autonomy** for the second stage. Autonomous morality, suggests Piaget, reflects a change from the authoritarian, obedience-oriented parent–child relationship of earlier years to a more cooperative and more mutually respectful relationship (DeVries, 1997).

Kohlberg's Morality of Justice and Reason

Kohlberg (1969, 1980), whose work has had an enormous influence in this area, studied moral development by posing moral dilemmas to groups of children, as well as to adolescents and adults. These dilemmas took the form of stories, one of which is paraphrased and illustrated in Interactive Table 11.13.

Children's responses suggest three levels in the development of moral judgments, each consisting of two stages of moral orientation (shown in Table 11.13). The three levels are sequential, although succeeding levels never entirely replace preceding ones, making it almost impossible to assign ages to them.

■ PRECONVENTIONAL

At the **preconventional level,** the child believes that evil behavior is that which is likely to be punished and that good behavior is based on obedience or the avoidance of the evil of

INTERACTIVE TABLE 11.13

Kohlberg's Levels of Morality

Kohlberg identified levels of moral judgment in children by describing to them situations involving a moral dilemma. One example is the story of Heinz, which can be paraphrased as follows:

Heinz's wife was dying of cancer. One special drug might save her, a drug recently discovered by a local druggist. The druggist could make the drug for about $200 but was selling it for ten times that amount. So Heinz went to everyone he knew to try to borrow the $2,000 he needed, but he could only scrape together $1,000. "My wife's dying," he told the druggist, asking him to sell the drug cheaper or let him pay later. But the druggist refused. Desperate, Heinz broke into the drugstore to steal the drug for his wife. Should Heinz have done that? Why? (Kohlberg, 1969, p. 379)

Interaction: As a crude assessment of your moral development, write out your responses to these questions, and then compare them with the illustrative responses given below.

Level I Preconventional	Stage 1: Punishment and obedience orientation	"If he steals the drug, he might go to jail." (Punishment.)
	Stage 2: Naive instrumental hedonism	"He can steal the drug and save his wife, and he'll be with her when he gets out of jail." (Act motivated by its hedonistic consequences for actor.)
Level II Conventional	Stage 3: "Good-boy, nice-girl" morality	"People will understand if you steal the drug to save your wife, but they'll think you're cruel and a coward if you don't." (Reactions of others and the effects of the act on social relationships become important.)
	Stage 4: Law-and-order orientation	"It is the husband's duty to save his wife even if he feels guilty afterwards for stealing the drug." (Institutions, law, duty, honor, and guilt motivate behavior.)
Level III Postconventional	Stage 5: Morality of social contract	"The husband has a right to the drug even if he can't pay now. If the druggist won't charge it, the government should look after it." (Democratic laws guarantee individual rights; contracts are mutually beneficial.)
	Stage 6: Universal ethical*	"Although it is legally wrong to steal, the husband would be morally wrong not to steal to save his wife. A life is more precious than financial gain." (Conscience is individual. Laws are socially useful but not sacrosanct.)

*None of Kohlberg's subjects ever reached Stage 6. However, it is still described as a "potential" stage. Kohlberg suggests that moral martyrs like Jesus or Martin Luther King exemplify this level.

Source: Based on Kohlberg (1969, 1980).

disobedience (Stage 1). Similarly, the child's judgments tend to be **hedonistic:** Good is that which is pleasant, and evil is that which has undesirable consequences (Stage 2).

■ CONVENTIONAL

The second level, a morality of **conventional** role conformity, reflects the increasing importance of peer and social relations. Thus, moral behavior is behavior that receives wide approval from significant people—parents, teachers, peers, and society at large (Stage 3). Similarly, conforming to law becomes important for maintaining adults' approval (Stage 4).

■ POSTCONVENTIONAL

At the highest level, the **postconventional level,** the individual begins to view morality in terms of individual rights and as ideals and principles that have value as rules or laws, apart from their influence on approval (Stage 5). Stage 5 moral judgments are rare even among adults, and Stage 6 judgments, based on fundamental ethical principles, are even rarer. Colby and Kohlberg (1984) suggest that there is some doubt as to whether Stage 6 should even be included as a stage in moral development.

■ A SEVENTH STAGE?

But Kohlberg (Colby & Kohlberg, 1984) also spoke of the possibility of a seventh stage—a mystical, contemplative, religious stage—a metaphorical stage in which, through the "logic of contemplation and mystical logic…we all know that the deepest feeling is love and the ultimate reality is life" (Hague, 1991, p. 283).

Recent Research on Morality

There is little doubt that Kohlberg's contribution to the understanding of morality is enormous. At the same time, a large number of researchers have found reason to criticize his approach and his conclusions. Among other things, these researchers point out that Kohlberg's view of morality is overly narrow, that the dilemmas he used to study morality might not have been especially meaningful for most of his subjects, and that by restricting his samples to males, he overlooked a dramatically different form of female moral reasoning. We look at each of these criticisms briefly.

■ A LESS RESTRICTED VIEW

Kohlberg's emphasis is clearly on morality as a question of justice and of rational decision making, note Walker and associates (1995). It assumes that the most moral individuals are those who make the most ethical *abstract* judgments, the ones who weigh the far-reaching consequences of their judgments and actions using individually determined principles of morality. But, argue Walker and associates, when you ask people to describe *real* moral dilemmas they have faced and you get them to discuss what they did and why, you quickly discover that there are at least three fundamentally important aspects of actual, day-to-day moral behavior that Kohlberg's dilemmas do not take into account.

First, adult moral decisions typically reflect real, practical considerations—that is, they take into account the actual implications of a moral action. They weigh responses to questions such as "Will I lose my job? Will he be arrested? What's in it for me?"

Second, individuals' responses in situations requiring moral decisions and actions reflect their cultural background. Kohlberg had argued that the development of his moral stages is universal. In fact, Walker and associates point out, the dominant values of a culture often determine how a person will respond to a moral dilemma—and will determine, as well, what that culture defines as moral. In China, for example, **filial piety** is seen as one of the highest virtues. The notion of filial piety says, in effect, that not only in their childhood, but also throughout their lives, people should display the highest devotion to their parents, that the welfare of parents always comes first, and that parents should always be obeyed, and at all ages (Wu, 1981). Not surprisingly, when Walker and associates included Chinese participants in their study of morality, they found that the judgments of even the adult respondents often reflected Kohlberg's lowest, obedience-oriented levels of morality.

Third, Kohlberg's approach fails to consider the importance of religion or faith or spirituality in morality. In real life, actions are often judged moral or immoral based on the extent to which they promote or violate explicit rules of faith—or, very often, explicit rules of law.

■ MORE MEANINGFUL DILEMMAS

Kohlberg's view of morality is thought to be too restricted in that it does not take into account the influence of religion or culture, or the practical implications of behavior. Critics also argue that it presents moral dilemmas that are not very meaningful for most respondents and that, for this reason, responses might not be very meaningful. When you ask people to describe real moral dilemmas they have recently faced, or to describe the most important or the biggest dilemma they *ever* faced, the vast majority of moral problems described have to do with relationships—not with abstract notions of right and wrong, or with seemingly remote issues such as whether or not to steal a drug for a dying person.

Some researchers suggest, further, that Kohlberg's moral dilemmas are perhaps too verbal and too abstract for children. They ask that the child understand and keep in mind very complex situations involving a number of actors, they require the manipulation of a variety of elements and circumstances, and often they don't provide enough information (but if they did, they would be even more complex). As a result, it appears that the Kohlberg dilemmas underestimate children's moral reasoning. When questions are made simpler, or when children and adolescents are observed in naturalistic settings, researchers sometimes find evidence of very sophisticated moral reasoning at very young ages. For example, children as young as six or seven are likely to consider the actor's intentions in judging the severity of an act, report Darley and Shultz (1990). Also, young children often take into account other factors, such as whether an authority permits the act to occur (Tisak, 1993). Thus, children will judge an act more harshly if it intentionally causes harm, or if the consequences could have been foreseen, than if the action's harm is unintentional and could not have been expected. Similarly, preschoolers, like older children, readily differentiate between lies and the truth, and judge lies as being less moral than the truth (Bussey, 1992). Says Buzzelli (1992), even preschoolers are not really "premoral": "As early as the second year of life, children begin to use standards in evaluating their own behavior and the behavior of others" (p. 48).

■ ALSO LOOKING AT WOMEN

Reasoning that Kohlberg's abstract dilemmas were not very meaningful for most people, and even less meaningful for women, Gilligan (1982) examined morality by interviewing twenty-nine pregnant women while they were actually facing the very real moral dilemma of needing to make a decision about having an abortion. Her findings reveal that these women's moral judgments were less the *justice*-oriented judgments that adult males typically make in response to the Kohlberg stories, but they were judgments based on compassion and caring.

Women, notes Gilligan, appear to progress through three stages in their moral development. In the first stage, the woman is moved primarily by selfish concerns ("This is what I want . . . what I need . . . what I should do . . . what would be best for me"). In the second stage, the woman progresses through a period of increasing recognition of responsibility to others. And the final stage reflects a morality of "nonviolence." At this stage, the woman's decision is based on her desire to do the greatest good both for self and for others.

Male–Female Differences in Morality

If Gilligan's description of female moral development is accurate, it reflects a number of important differences between male and female morality. In contrast with Kohlberg's description of male moral progression from what are initially hedonistic (pain–pleasure) concerns toward a conventional, rule-regulated morality, Gilligan describes female morality as progressing from initial selfishness toward a recognition of social responsibility. Boys are perhaps more concerned with law and order than with caring and compassion. Women's is a morality of caring rather than of abstract justice (Stander & Jensen, 1993).

Nunner-Winkler (1984) elaborates Gilligan's position by reference to Kant's (1797/1977) distinction between negative and positive moral duties: Negative duties are illustrated in rules such as "Do not kill" and "Do not steal." These rules are absolute and clear; you follow them, or you do not. In contrast, positive duties are open-ended. They are reflected in rules such as "Be kind" and "Be compassionate." There are no boundaries or limits on positive duties. They don't specify how kind, to whom, how often, when.

Negative duties, says Nunner-Winkler, reflect the justice orientation of males; females feel more obliged than males to fulfill positive duties, which relate more closely to caring and compassion.

Do women and men see the world differently and make different moral judgments? Some research says yes. Stimpson and colleagues (1991) asked college students to rate eighteen adjectives having to do with "interpersonal sensitivity" and "caring." Females consistently rated these adjectives higher in terms of goodness than did males. Similarly, Eisenberg and associates (1991) found that girls' prosocial reasoning was higher than boys in late childhood and adolescence.

But other research finds less clear evidence of sex differences in morality. Muss (1988) reviewed a number of studies and concluded that the distinctions between male and female morality are not very clear. He reasons that if Gilligan's descriptions are correct, it follows that females should, on average, be more altruistic, more empathetic, and more concerned with human relations; in contrast, males should be less altruistic. But research on altruism, cooperation, and other forms of prosocial behavior has not found these differences. Note, however, that these findings do not invalidate Gilligan's basic conclusions. It may well be that males and females are equally altruistic, but their altruism might stem from fundamentally different orientations, reflecting very different moralities. Females may, as Gilligan suggests, be altruistic because of their concern for humanity; males may be just as altruistic because of their adherence to principles and ideals that stress the injustice of being unkind.

One of the important contributions of Gilligan's approach is that it underlines the need to be aware of the possibility that many of our theories and conclusions in human development are not equally applicable to males and females. In Gilligan's (1982) words, the sexes speak in a different voice. Neither voice is louder or better; they are simply different.

Implications of Research on Moral Development

Some of the most important implications of research on morality relate to the observation that individuals who operate at the lowest levels (hedonistic) are more likely to be delinquent than those who operate at higher levels. As Gibbs (1987) notes, the delinquent's behavior generally reflects immature moral reasoning and egocentricity. Individuals who operate at higher levels of morality are more likely to be honest and to behave in a generally moral way. Similarly, altruism in children is highly related to level of moral development (Eisenberg, Miller, & Shell, 1991). Even the political choices of adolescents appear to be related to moral development (Thoma, 1993).

Can moral reasoning and behavior be improved?

■ SCHOOL INFLUENCES

There is considerable evidence that moral judgments and behaviors can be influenced by specific programs in schools (Damon & Colby, 1987). Specific techniques used in these programs include simply discussing moral dilemmas, evaluating the ethical implications of human behavior, role-playing situations involving specific moral dilemmas, modeling procedures, and direct teaching. For example, Stoll and Beller (1993) report that by using a combination of approaches they succeeded in bringing about significant behavior change in a group of student athletes over a three-year period (evident in a decline in fighting, increased caring for others, better classroom behavior, and even an improvement in grades).

A comprehensive program designed to increase prosocial behavior among elementary schoolchildren is described by Battistich and colleagues (1991). This program included activities in the school as well as in the home. Activities were geared toward developing prosocial values and interpersonal understanding, and made extensive use of cooperative learning and discussion of rationales for rules and reasons underlying moral behaviors. The authors report that after five years, the children in the program engage in more spontaneous prosocial behavior in the classroom, have improved perspective-taking skills, and are better at resolving conflicts. However, they caution that differences between program children and other comparable children are slight and often inconsistent. In addition, it isn't always easy to measure the effects of programs such as this.

■ FAMILY INFLUENCES

In addition to what schools and educators might attempt to do, the values and behaviors of parents are highly instrumental in determining the values of their children (Kochanska, Murray, & Coy, 1997). There are ways, argue Colby and Damon (1995), in which people's values and goals can be translated into extraordinary moral commitment. In a world where immorality is highly visible, if not highly rampant, there is much that needs to be done. One approach is through parenting.

Research reveals a clear relationship between parenting styles and children's morality. Specifically, the internalization of moral rules is fostered by two things: (1) the frequent use of discipline that points out the harmful consequences of the child's behavior for others and (2) frequent expression of parental affection (Hoffman, 1979). Most forms of parental discipline, Hoffman argues, contain elements of "power assertion" and "love-withdrawal." That is, discipline usually involves at least the suggestion of the possibility of loss of parental love as well as something like deprivation of privileges, threats, or physical punishment. The main purpose of this "power assertion," according to Hoffman, is to get the child to stop misbehaving and pay attention. From the point of view of the child's developing morality, however, what is most important is that there now be an accompanying verbal component. The purpose of this verbal component is to influence the child cognitively and emotionally—perhaps by bringing about feelings of guilt or of empathy, and by enabling the child to foresee consequences. The verbal component might simply admonish ("Don't do that"); ideally, however, it should go beyond the admonishment to describe

▲ **SUMMARY TABLE 11.14**
Ideas and Findings in Moral Development

CONCEPT/THEORY	DESCRIPTION/EXPLANATIONS
Morality	■ An aspect of human interactions or judgments that implies recognition of right and wrong, virtue, principles, ethics. . . .
Carroll and Rest's four steps involved in moral behavior	■ Moral sensitivity (recognizing a moral issue). ■ Moral judgment (deciding what *ought* to be done). ■ Moral motivation (making a plan according to values). ■ Moral action (implementing the plan).
Piaget's two stages	■ Heteronomy (obedience-based morality reflecting authoritarian parent–child relationship). ■ Autonomy (self-determined principles, reflecting mutually respectful parent–child relationship).
Kohlberg's stages of moral development	■ Level 1—Preconventional (Stage 1: obedience oriented; Stage 2: pain–pleasure driven). ■ Level 2—Conventional (Stage 3: good-boy, nice-girl morality; Stage 4: law-and-order orientation). ■ Level 3—Postconventional (Stage 5: morality of social contracts; Stage 6: universal ethical principles).
Contrasts between newer research and Kohlberg's views	■ Less-restricted models include consideration of practical implications of moral judgments, influence of culture, and influences of religions, faith, and laws. ■ Use of more meaningful, real-life dilemmas. ■ Recognition of gender differences.
Some male–female differences	■ Some evidence suggests that male morality is more a morality of law and order, of justice, of right and wrong. ■ In contrast, female morality may be more a morality of caring and compassion. ■ Both might be equally moral, and equally altruistic, but for different reasons and perhaps in different ways.
Implications of research on morality	■ Our future may depend on the extent to which we can direct school, cultural, and family influences toward the development of morality.

the consequences ("Don't do that because..." or "If you do that, the cat might...").

The future of this world depends on the morality of our children. (See Summary Table 11.14. See also "In the News and on the Net: Gang Murder.")

eena Virk, described by her class-mates as "plump and insecure," dreamed of being a nurse, a writer, an artist. Too, she dreamed of having friends, of fitting in; but, sadly, she had no friends. Still, on a Friday night, Reena, age 14, found herself in the company of those with whom she had sought friendship, at a party by the river. The entire story has not yet been told, but apparently someone stubbed a cigarette on Reena's forehead, pro-voking her into a fight with not one, but an entire group of girls. She was brutally beaten and left somewhere along the Gorge, a river that runs through Victoria on Vancouver Island. Later, the story goes, at least one boy and one girl returned to finish the sav-age beating, breaking Reena's back,

her legs, and her neck, and then throw-ing her into the Gorge. Later that week, police became aware of rumors in city high schools about a girl having been killed. Subsequently Reena's body was discovered and, to date, 7 girls and 1 boy have been charged—all between 14 and 16 years old.

1. Jimenez, M. (1997, Nov. 25). "Worst nightmare" for slain girl's parents. *Edmonton Journal*, p. A3.

To Do

Bullying and gang violence, the popu-lar media inform us, are becoming in-creasingly common. Is there evidence that this is true? Why might it be true? Or, if it isn't true, why might it *seem* to be true?

On the Net

For practical information on crime prevention, see the U.S. Department of Justice's Justice for Kids and Youth web site:

http://www.usdoj.gov/kidspage/

FOCUS QUESTIONS: SUMMARY ANSWERS

1. Is adolescence a universal phenomenon, or is it largely cultural?

  ■ The biological aspects of adolescence are universal; the psychological implications may not be—as is evident in the absence of a prolonged period of tran-sition from childhood to adulthood in many nonin-dustrialized (discontinuous) societies, where specific rites of passage are clear signals of maturity (the rites often include separation, training, and initiation—sometimes with scarification and circumcision) and induction into the tribe. Continuous societies have no formal rites of passage.

2. What are the universal biological features of adolescence?

  ■ There is a spurt in rate of height and weight increase during adolescence that occurs about two years ear-lier for girls than for boys. Boys retain relatively less fat mass than girls. The changes of pubescence (in primary sexual characteristics, directly related to reproduction, and in secondary sexual characteristics,

not directly related to reproduction) lead to puberty (sexual maturity).

3. What are the most common eating disorders of adolescence?

  ■ Because of rapid muscular and skeletal growth, ado-lescents require large amounts of protein and miner-als such as calcium. Most also expend a relatively large number of calories, but obesity is still the most common nutritional problem of adolescents in North America. Anorexia involves significant weight loss, refusal to maintain weight, and distorted body image. Bulimia is defined in terms of recurrent episodes of binge eating (often followed by "purges") that are accompanied by the realization that the behavior is not normal and by feelings of guilt or self-deprecation.

4. What is adolescent egocentrism?

  ■ Adolescent egocentrism describes a self-centeredness that leads adolescents to believe that others are highly interested in their thoughts and behaviors (a self-consciousness). It is evident in the *imaginary audience* (an imagined collection of people assumed to be con-cerned with the adolescent) and the *personal fable* (feelings of invulnerability and uniqueness). Adoles-cents' greater propensity for taking high risks may be linked to their sense of invulnerability and uniqueness.

5. Is being good or bad a fundamental part of our personalities?

  ■ Carroll and Rest describe four components of moral behavior: (1) recognizing a moral problem (moral sensitivity), (2) deciding what ought to be done (moral judgment), (3) devising a plan of action according to values (moral motivation), and (4) implementing the plan (moral action). Failure to act morally may be the result of a deficiency in any one of these four components. Gilligan's work suggests that men and women differ in their moral development—that men become progressively more concerned with law and order whereas women respond more to social relationships and to the social consequences of behavior.

STUDY TERMS

adolescence, 312
adolescent egocentrism, 327
anorexia nervosa, 320
autonomy, 332
axillary hair, 315
body mass index (BMI), 319
bulimia nervosa, 322
bystander apathy, 330
cognitive strategies, 325
cognitive-behavior therapy, 323
continuous societies, 312
conventional, 333
discontinuous societies, 312
egocentrism, 327
endocrine glands, 314
fat mass, 314
fat-free mass, 314
filial piety, 333
formal operations, 323
gonads, 315
growth spurt, 313
hedonistic, 333
heteronomy, 332
hormones, 314
imaginary audience, 327
Imaginary Audience Scale (IAS), 328
induction, 312

information-processing approach, 325
initiation, 312
knowledge base, 325
logic of propositions, 324
menarche, 315, 316
metacognition, 325
morality, 330
obesity, 320
ovaries, 315
partial syndrome eating disorders, 320
personal fables, 328
postconventional level, 333
preconventional level, 332
primary sexual characteristics, 315
proposition, 324
puberty, 313
pubescence, 313
rites de passage, 312
scarification, 312
secondary sexual characteristics, 315
sensation seeking, 330
spermarche, 316
sturm und drang, 312
taboo, 312
testes, 315

FURTHER READINGS

An excellent account of contemporary adolescence, viewed against the backdrop of historical changes in adolescence, is provided by:

Kett, J. F. (1977). *Rites of passage: Adolescence in America, 1790 to the present.* New York: Basic Books.

The following collection presents a fascinating look at the adolescent experience in thirteen nations through a coordinated research program that permits comparisons among them:

Gibson-Cline, J. (Ed.). (1996). *Adolescence: From crisis to coping: A thirteen nation study.* Boston: Butterworth/Heinemann.

Burton's book describes eating disorders, provides case examples of them, and describes an approach toward treating them:

Burton, E. (1993). *Eating disorders: Personal construct therapy and change.* New York: John Wiley.

Sugar's book provides a detailed look at the biological and psychological changes experienced by adolescent girls, and examines a wide range of other topics such as the role of the family, delinquency among adolescent girls, and adolescent motherhood:

Sugar, M. (Ed.). (1993). *Female adolescent development.* New York: Brunner/Mazel.

The first of the following two books is a useful introduction to the complicated area of research in morality. The second is a somewhat more difficult collection of research articles that deal with the development of morality in everyday life.

Kurtines, W. M., & Gewirtz, J. L. (Eds.). (1995). *Moral development: An introduction.* Boston: Allyn & Bacon.

Killen, M., & Hart, D. (Eds.). (1995). *Morality in everyday life: Developmental perspectives.* New York: Cambridge University Press.

FOCUS QUESTIONS

1. Is adolescence typically a time of strife and conflict?

2. How important are parents and peers throughout adolescence?

3. Are there real and important psychological differences between the sexes?

4. What are the principal sexual beliefs and behaviors of adolescents?

5. How common and serious are adolescent delinquency, drug abuse, and suicide?

TWELVE

Social Development: Adolescence

It's all that the young can do for the old, to shock them and keep them up to date.

GEORGE BERNARD SHAW
Fanny's First Play

chool One: On a recent morning at a central-city high school in New York City, a fifteen-year-old boy walked up to two of his schoolmates, pulled out a 38-caliber pistol, and shot one in the head and the other in the chest; both died. A friend of one of the dead boys, very upset, called another friend to tell him what had happened. As he spoke to him on the phone, he heard a clicking sound. "What's that noise?" he asked. "I'm playing Russian roulette," said the other. And then bang! He lost the game and became the third violent student death in that school that morning (Knox, Laske, & Tromanhauser, 1992). ¶ Perhaps as many as 20 percent of all high school students in the United States carry weapons to school, and even more claim to carry guns. Many of those who carry weapons are members of gangs that consist mainly of racial minority groups. Many attend schools in deteriorating city centers and live in an atmosphere of crime and poverty. They see school not as a neutral place for learning but as just another piece of turf over which to fight. ¶ *School Two:* "Does anyone carry weapons in your school?" I ask a handful of teenagers, all students at a large suburban high school. Ray, whose parents are both doctors, is an outstanding student (90+ average) in a special advanced academic program. He plays the cello, enjoys badminton, hockey, and football, and swims and wrestles. His ambition is to go into medicine, specializing in general practice. "I don't know anyone who would have a weapon in this school," he says. "That, like, would suck, man." ¶

This Chapter

chools—and families—can vary tremendously in the sorts of experiences they provide and the values they encourage. These are extremely powerful influences on the adolescent's social development.

This chapter looks at adolescent social development, not only in the North American context, but also in other more universal contexts. It deals with the evolution of the self, with emerging gender roles, with sexual beliefs and behaviors, and with some manifestations of adolescent turmoil and rebellion.

Keep in mind that change is fundamental through the entire lifespan. Our attitudes and our values are not fixed immutably, bound always to reflect the social, religious, political, educational, and family contexts from which we emerged at adolescence.

Things that seem "cool" today might well "like suck" tomorrow.

Contexts might be seen as exercising an equalizing influence. The pressure of a single ecology tends to produce individuals with similar values and attitudes. Clearly, however, we don't all turn out the same. Not a single one of us is average in every respect. Our selves and our identities are solely our own. Still, they, too, reflect our contexts.

SELF AND IDENTITY

The **self** is crucially important to a study of adolescence—as it is to all of psychology. In fact, Banaji and Prentice (1994) report that in the six years immediately preceding 1993, more than 5,000 articles have been published on the self.

Self is a difficult and complex concept, not easily defined—which is probably why it has been redefined by so many hundreds of psychologists over the years. Few, however, have made the concept much clearer than did the alleged "father" of psychology, William James, more than a century ago.* "A man's self," wrote James in the highly masculine jargon of those times, "is the sum total of all that he can call his" (1890, p. 291). In this definition, *self* is a *conscious* awareness of one's characteristics. As we saw in Chapter 10, notions of self also include important evaluative aspects. Thus, we have notions of our selves as being good or bad. In other words, we have feelings of **self-esteem** (or *self-worth*).

The term **identity** is often used as though it were synonymous with *self*. In fact, however, the terms have somewhat different meanings in psychology. The term *identity* is most closely related to the writings of Erikson, who sees the concept as signifying a sort of wholeness, a sense of being, that has its roots in childhood and reaches its greatest importance

in adolescence. In Erikson's words, "The young person, in order to experience wholeness, must feel a progressive continuity between that which he has come to be during the long years of childhood and that which he promises to become in the anticipated future..." (1968, p. 87).

Put more simply, in Erikson's writings on adolescence, identity means individuals' own notions about who they are and who they are becoming—their *self-definition*. And this sense of identity relates specifically to different areas of life. As will be illustrated shortly, the adolescent's achievement of identity may be at different levels of development with respect to social relations, politics and ideology, and schooling and career development. One of the important tasks of adolescence is to develop a strong sense of identity in all, or most, of these areas.

Self-Esteem in Adolescence

At the same time, it appears to be extremely important for adolescents to develop and maintain high, positive evaluations of themselves—that is, positive notions of self-esteem.

Self-esteem, as we saw in Chapter 10, is a reflection of how well one likes oneself in general. In childhood, notions of self-esteem reflect the individual's evaluations of different aspects of the self, such as *athletic, scholastic, social, physical,* and *behavioral* (Harter, 1983). For those who think being a good athlete is most important for being liked, evaluations of their worth as athletes contribute significantly in determining general feelings of self-worth.

In adolescence, the evaluation of self becomes more cognitive, say Byrne and Shavelson (1987). It is based on a more objective (rather than emotional) understanding of who and what the self is—rather than mainly on how well adolescents like themselves or how competent they think they are in important areas.

CHANGING NOTIONS OF SELF

Between late childhood and late adolescence, explain Hart and Yates (1996), important changes take place in the child's views of the self—changes that reflect what is important and, by implication, what isn't. When asked about the self, the preadolescent child tends to emphasize the importance of personal qualities and personal effort and how these relate to success and status in different areas ("I'm tall, which is why I'm good at basketball"; "I'm smart, which is why I have a lot of friends"). The organizing principle for notions of self revolves around personal characteristics and personal effort.

In contrast, the young adolescent tends to organize notions of self around *social acceptance* and *social relations*. When asked about the self, responses might include statements such as "I'd like to be thinner, because girls would like me more"; "I'm glad I'm athletic because I've made a lot of friends in sports."

In later adolescence, note Hart and Yates (1996), personal values, principles, and beliefs become important organizing influences for the adolescent's developing notions of self

---

*"And who's the bejiggered mother, then?" asked my grandmother. I didn't know.

("I'm glad I live on a farm because I don't want a career outside my home; I just want to have a really large family"; "It's a good thing I'm intelligent because I want to be a teacher and help underprivileged children work toward better lives").

But no matter how the child or the adolescent organizes notions of self, what the person thinks of himself or herself—in other words, notions of self-esteem—remains critically important.

THE IMPORTANCE OF SELF-ESTEEM

Low self-esteem, explain Zimmerman, Copeland, and Shope (1997) following a review of related research, has been found to be linked with depression, substance use, delinquency, suicide, and poorer performance in school.

Research suggests that the self-esteem of adolescents can be described in terms of one or sometimes a combination of four distinct trajectories. On the one hand are youth whose self-esteem is consistently high; on the other are those who lack significantly in self-esteem. A third group includes those whose self-esteem is slowly rising. And a fourth is made up of those whose self-esteem is rapidly declining (Hirsch & Dubois, 1991).

In a four-year longitudinal study involving more than 1,100 students in grades six through ten, Zimmerman and associates (1997) investigated some of the characteristics of individuals in each of these four groups and looked, as well, at the implications of high or low, and rising or declining, self-esteem. Reassuringly, the largest group comprised those whose self-esteem was consistently high throughout the

four-year period, and the smallest group was those with low self-esteem. About 20 percent of the group had moderately high and rising self-esteem; another 20 percent had steadily decreasing notions of self-worth (see Figure 12.1).

Zimmerman and associates looked at the relationship between membership in each of these self-esteem categories and a variety of factors, such as susceptibility to peer pressure, academic achievement, tolerance for deviance, and alcohol use and misuse. Their most important findings were, not surprisingly, that those with consistently high self-esteem, as well as those with moderately high but rising self-esteem, were, in their words, "developmentally healthier" at tenth grade than were those in the other two groups. These youths

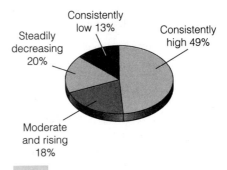

FIGURE 12.1

Percentage of respondents in each of the four self-esteem categories in Zimmerman and associates' study. (Based on data in Zimmerman et al., 1997.)

were significantly more resistant to peer pressure, had higher average grades, and reported less tolerance for deviant behavior or alcohol misuse. In contrast, those with the lowest self-esteem, or with rapidly declining self-esteem, fared significantly less well.

It is worth noting that although self-esteem is relatively stable for many adolescents, for others it may change in important ways over time. Those for whom self-esteem is increasing are at considerably less risk for negative developmental outcomes than are those for whom self-esteem is rapidly declining.

Facets of the Self

It may be a little misleading and oversimplified to speak of self-esteem as though it were a simple trait about which psychologists can easily make reliable judgments such as "It's consistently high"; "It's moderate but rising"; or "It's declining rapidly." In fact, because *self* is a multifaceted concept, there are notions of self in many different areas. And, in some cases, the individual may have quite different estimates of the worth of each of these different facets of self.

The term **self-image** is used extensively in adolescent research to mean something very similar to self-esteem or self-worth. Thus, the Offer Self-Image Questionnaire, a widely used instrument for assessing self-image, has teenagers report on their attitudes toward and feelings about themselves in a number of different areas (Offer, Ostrov, & Howard, 1981). Like Harter (1983), Offer assumes that the adolescent has a multiplicity of selves that can be considered and evaluated separately:

- *Psychological self.* Reflects adolescents' emotions, their conceptions of their bodies, and their ability to control impulses.

- *Social self.* Consists of adolescents' perceptions of their relationships with others, as well as their morals and their goals.

- *Sexual self.* Reflects attitudes and feelings about sexual experiences and behavior.

- *Familial self.* Consists of adolescents' feelings and attitudes toward parents and other members of their family.

- *Coping self.* Reflects psychological adjustment and how effectively the adolescent functions in the outside world.

The Offer questionnaire investigates these five facets of self by presenting adolescents with a series of statements (for example, "Being together with other people gives me a good feeling") and having them select one of six alternatives relating to how well the statement describes them (ranging from *describes me very well* to *does not describe me at all*). (See Table 12.1.) Each descriptor in the questionnaire is worded both positively and negatively.

TABLE 12.1

Facets of Self in the Offer Self-Image Questionnaire

IMPORTANT ASPECTS OF SELF	RELEVANT SELF-EVALUATIVE QUESTIONS
Psychological self	Do I like my body? Am I in control of myself? What are my wishes? My feelings? My fantasies?
Social self	Am I friendly? Outgoing? Do people like me? What kind of morals do I have? What are my aspirations? Am I a loner?
Sexual self	How do I feel about sex? What do I think of pornography? Am I sexually attracted to others? Sexually attractive to them? Comfortable with my sexuality?
Familial self	How do I feel about my parents? Home? Siblings? Other relatives? Do I prefer to stay home? Do people at home like me? Need me? Want me?
Coping self	How effective am I? How well do I cope with what others demand? What school demands? What I demand? Am I well adjusted? Reasonably happy? How decisive am I?

The Offer questionnaire was developed more than twenty years ago (scoring procedures have changed since then) and has now been given to tens of thousands of adolescents. Results provide important data concerning the adolescent experience.

In a massive study, appropriate translations of the Offer Self-Image Questionnaire were administered to 5,938 adolescents in ten different countries (Australia, Bangladesh, Hungary, Israel, Italy, Japan, Taiwan, Turkey, the former West Germany, and the United States) (Offer et al., 1988). One of the objectives was to compare adolescents' self-images in each of these countries and arrive at a better understanding of what is universal about adolescence in today's world and what might be specific to given cultural contexts. Adolescents included in the study were both male and female, classified into two age groups: younger (ages thirteen to fifteen) and older (ages sixteen to nineteen).

THE UNIVERSAL ADOLESCENT

What is similar about adolescence in these ten countries? A surprising number of things. The "universal adolescent," to use Offer and associates' phrase, resembles most other adolescents in some ways with respect to each of the major facets of self-image:

- *Psychological.* The universal adolescent is usually happy and optimistic, and enjoys being alive.

- *Social.* The universal adolescent enjoys the company of others, is caring and compassionate, and places great value on school, education, and preparation for adult work.

- *Sexual.* The universal adolescent is confident about the sexual self, and willing to talk and think about sex.

- *Familial.* The universal adolescent expresses strongly positive feelings toward parents, a high degree of satisfaction with home life, and good feelings about relationships at home.

- *Coping.* The universal adolescent expresses confidence in his or her ability to deal with life, and feels talented and able to make decisions.

THE CONTEXT-BOUND ADOLESCENT

But there are differences, too, across these cultures. For example, adolescents from Bangladesh were consistently lower on impulse control. Forty-two percent of the Bengali (Bangladesh) adolescents reported being constantly afraid; many admitted feeling inferior to other people, as well as feeling sadder, lonelier, and more vulnerable. Why? Context seems the most plausible explanation. This was the poorest of the countries sampled. Lack of economic opportunities and adequate medical care, coupled with widespread disease and starvation, might well lead to feelings of vulnerability and fear.

Other cross-national differences included the very high value placed on vocational and educational goals by American adolescents and the very low value placed on them by Hungarian and Israeli teenagers—probably because vocational choice is a complex and important developmental task for American adolescents. For most Israeli and Hungarian adolescents, choices are more limited or are largely predetermined by society.

Not surprisingly, there were marked differences in the sexual attitudes of adolescents from some countries. In particular, Turkish and Taiwanese adolescents reported extremely conservative sexual attitudes and behaviors—clear evidence of the extent to which such attitudes are influenced by cultures (see Table 12.2). Similarly, Israeli adolescents reported the most positive family relationships, again not very surprising given Israel's emphasis on family and community.

STORM AND STRESS?

In spite of the very real differences that exist among adolescents of different cultures and different backgrounds, recall that among the most consistent findings of the Offer and associates (1988) study was that most adolescents are usually happy and optimistic. Furthermore, most are happy with their families and their homes, they are caring and compassionate, and they are confident in their abilities to cope with life. And, as we just saw, far more of them have positive than negative self-esteem.

So is this period, as G. Stanley Hall (1916) believed, a period of **sturm und drang** (storm and stress)? Hall had argued that this would be the case for most adolescents in all cultures because the mood swings, the irritability, and the conflict of this period are related directly to a dramatic increase in sex hormones. Most psychologists no longer believe this to be true. When Buchanan, Eccles, and Becker (1992) examined the research, they found that the most important determiners of adolescent moods and behavior are not the hormones that rage through their bloodstreams, but rather nonbiological, contextual factors. Not surprisingly, if the Offer and associates (1988) cross-national study were to be summarized in a single paragraph, it might read something like this: Contrary to what has been a popular view of adolescence since G. Stanley Hall's pronouncements about the storm and stress of this period, adolescence throughout the world is predominantly a positive, nonturbulent, energetic, growth-filled period.

At the same time, approximately 15 percent of North American adolescents describe themselves as anxious, depressed, confused, and emotionally empty (Offer, Ostrov, &

TABLE 12.2

*Sexual Self: Sample Items Showing Consistent Cross-National Differences Across Age and Gender**

| | PERCENT ENDORSEMENT | | | | | | | | |
ITEM	Australia	Bangladesh	Hungary	Israel	Italy	Taiwan	Turkey	United States	West Germany
Dirty jokes are fun at times.	82	33	39	78	69	43	19	78	69
I think that girls/boys find me attractive.	53	63	58	68	55	41	59	73	63
Sexually I am way behind.	20	26	11	10	7	33	19	24	11
Thinking or talking about sex scares me.	7	50	13	6	7	27	22	10	6
Sexual experiences give me pleasure.	67	44	65	72	67	22	49	74	67
Having a girl-/boyfriend is important to me.	69	77	68	75	76	52	74	73	82

*Items presented (1) were on a scale on which at least one country was consistently high (or low) in all four age-by-gender cells and (2) were consistently high (or low) for that country for that scale. Consistently high (or low) was defined in terms of being in the upper (or lower) third of nine countries in all four age-by-gender cells. Percentages shown are the average percent endorsement for that item for the country across four age-by-gender cells.
Source: From *The Teenage World: Adolescents' Self-Image in Ten Countries* by D. O. Offer, E. Ostrov, K. Howard, and R. Atkinson, 1988. New York: Plenum. Reprinted by permission of the author and publisher.

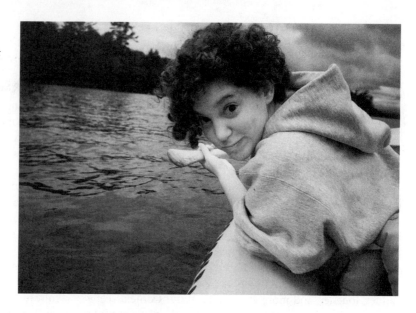

Contrary to some earlier beliefs, the identity crises of adolescence are not invariably marked by "storm and stress." Many adolescents explore life's alternatives and reach adult commitments with little apparent turmoil and conflict.

Howard, 1984). This percentage is, in fact, significantly higher than for preadolescents.

■ STRESS AND LIFE CHANGE

A number of researchers have suggested that one of the main reasons for higher **stress** during this period is that adolescents experience more significant changes in their lives than do younger children (Mullis et al., 1993). To investigate this belief, Larson and Ham (1993) gave questionnaires to 483 fifth to ninth graders and their parents to obtain a measure of important events in their lives. They also obtained a measure of students' emotions by having them rate their moods at various times. There were two especially important findings: (1) Young adolescents experienced significantly more life-change events than preadolescents, many of them family based (not getting along as well with parents, someone going to the hospital, someone in the family being in trouble with the law). In addition, they experienced more school-based changes (disciplinary action, changing schools, being suspended), as well as relationship-based changes (breaking up with a girl- or boyfriend), and other events like being sick or being cut from a sports team. And (2) young adolescents reported significantly more negative affect (emotion) than preadolescents. As Larson and Ham (1993) conclude, "Higher rates of daily distress experienced in adolescence may be partly attributed to the greater number of negative life events encountered" (p. 130). This pattern of negative affect in response to negative life experiences, they add, "is not the universal storm and stress described by early theorists....But it is experienced by a substantial minority and it does suggest that for some, early adolescence is a pivotal point in the development of positive versus negative adjustment to daily life" (p. 138).

Identity Development in Adolescence

When there are storms in adolescence—and stresses too, of course—these are sometimes related to turbulence that occa-

sionally surrounds the development of identity—the sense of wholeness and purpose of which we spoke earlier.

The notion that one of the most important aspects of all development is the development of a sense of personal identity is central to Erik Erikson's theory (discussed in Chapter 2). Recall that the fifth of Erikson's eight developmental stages is termed **identity versus role diffusion.** By the term *identity*, Erikson (1968) means a sort of wholeness that derives from the past but that also includes future goals and plans. The primary developmental crisis facing the adolescent, says Erikson, is the conflict among accepting, choosing, or discovering an identity and the diffusion of the adolescent's energies resulting from conflict and doubt concerning choice of identities. As Nightingale and Wolverton (1993) note, adolescents don't often have carefully prepared, socially approved, and highly appreciated roles in contemporary industrialized societies. As a result, they are left to struggle alone with the problems of establishing these roles—in other words, with the problems of developing an identity.

Resolution of adolescents' identity crises can take a variety of forms, the most common of which is the selection of an identity that conforms to societal norms and to individuals' expectations of themselves. Erikson points out that one of the major social functions of prolonged adolescence is simply to serve as a breathing space (an **adolescent moratorium,** in his terms) during which adolescents can experiment with different roles in their quest for identity. He is not particularly alarmed that some of these roles constitute what he terms **negative identities** (delinquency and other forms of rebellion, for example), because in most cases they are temporary, eventually giving way to more acceptable and happier identities.

Erikson's description of this developmental stage has been clarified by Marcia's investigations of the development of identity in adolescence (Kroger, 1993; Marcia, 1966, 1993). Building on Erikson's work, Marcia identifies four distinct types of identity status on the basis of whether the adolescent has undergone (or is currently undergoing) a crisis and on whether a commitment has been made to a specific identity. Recall that identity refers to individuals' notions about who they are and are becoming.

IDENTITY DIFFUSION

Adolescents in a state of **identity diffusion** are characterized by a total lack of commitment, as well as no experience with an identity crisis. These are individuals whose political, social, and religious beliefs are ambiguous or nonexistent, and who have no vocational aspirations. Individuals who have not developed a mature sense of identity by late adolescence are sometimes recognizable as full-time fun seekers (what Marcia calls "playboys") or as disturbed individuals characterized by high anxiety, low self-esteem, and lack of self-confidence (Marcia, 1980).

FORECLOSURE

Foreclosure is a strong commitment to an identity without having experienced a crisis. Foreclosure is clearly illustrated in instances where political, religious, and vocational decisions have been made for the adolescent and are accepted without question. This is often the case, for example, in close-knit religious or political communities where the roles and the beliefs of each individual are determined by others. It is also the case when adolescents simply allow parents or, sometimes, peers to make important identity-related decisions for them. These adolescents do not go through an identity crisis. Their most striking characteristics appear to be high adherence to authoritarian values (obedience and respect of authority) (Marcia, 1980).*

MORATORIUM INDIVIDUALS

According to Erikson, one of the important functions of adolescence is to serve as a time during which it is not essential to be fully committed to one lifestyle, one vocation, one set of beliefs—a moratorium during which the adolescent can explore the tremendous variety of alternatives that might be available. Moratorium adolescents have vague, changing commitments; in this sense, they are in crisis. But it is a useful crisis for most adolescents, because in the absence of a moratorium during which to explore, there is a danger of premature commitment (as in the case of foreclosure) or of continuing lack of commitment (as in identity diffusion).

IDENTITY ACHIEVED

Adolescents who have experienced a crisis (a moratorium) and made a choice (a commitment) are described as **identity achieved.** Marcia (1980) reports that adolescents who have achieved an identity are more independent, respond better to stress, have more realistic goals, and have higher self-esteem than adolescents in any of the other three categories. How-

---

*Some, like Côté and Levine (1988), point out that the negative aspects of adopting a "ready-made" identity have been unfairly emphasized. On the positive side, some of the "foreclosed" choices that adolescents adopt are admirable. My grandmother agreed. "Look at Cecile," she said as proof. Cecile is a nun.

TABLE 12.3

*Marcia's Descriptions of Identity Status in Terms of Crisis and Commitment**

STATUS	CHARACTERISTICS
Identity diffusion	No crisis; no commitment (ambiguous belief systems; no vocational commitment).
Foreclosure	No crisis; strong commitment (commitment predetermined by political, social, or religious affiliation).
Moratorium	Crisis; no commitment (period of exploration of alternatives).
Identity achieved	Crisis finished; commitment made.

*A crisis is defined as a period of active and conscious decision making during which various alternatives are examined and evaluated. Commitment is acceptance of a combination of political, social, religious, and vocational alternatives. Level of crisis and commitment may be different in each of these areas.

ever, he also emphasizes that identities are never static and absolutely permanent. Even when the adolescent appears to have achieved an identity, further changes often occur. For example, some college students move in and out of identity crises before finally achieving a final commitment. And, as we will see in Chapter 13, the Peter Pans among us may never resolve our identity crises. (See Table 12.3.)

CAREER PREPARATION AND IDENTITY FORMATION

We treat adolescents, especially older adolescents, differently than we do younger children, note Hart and Yates (1996). We give them more responsibility, and we expect more responsible behavior of them. Why? In a nutshell, because they have developed more adult identities.

It's important to note that Marcia's description of identity formation assumes that identity develops independently in different areas such as those relating to careers, schooling, and social relations. Not all adolescents will have achieved the same level of adultlike responsibility in each of these areas at the same time. For example, an adolescent who is married and has a child has achieved an apparently high level of identity (and concomitant responsibility) with respect to social relations. But that same adolescent might be at a stage of *identity diffusion* or *moratorium* with respect to schooling and career development—that is, she might still be considering various alternatives, experimenting with different identities, trying to develop a sense of purpose and continuity.

Not surprisingly, there are often marked gender differences in the importance of identity formation in different areas. Following a study involving more than 3,000 Dutch youth (ages twelve to twenty-five), Meeus, Dekovic, and Iedema (1997) report that identity having to do with the development of mature social relations is typically more important for girls than for boys. In contrast, identity relating to school and to careers is more important for boys than for girls.

Among the choices that are most important for identity formation, notes Blustein (1997), are precisely those that have to do with occupation or career. Their importance during adolescence, relative to the importance of achieving identity in social relations, or in politics and ideology, has much to do with the fact that in contemporary industrialized societies, the development of a career is typically expected to occur prior to the assumption of adult social roles or the development of political ideologies. This becomes increasingly true as the average age of marrying and of having a first child increases into the twenties or later (U.S. Bureau of the Census, 1996). Preparation for a career, on the other hand, is something that most adolescents begin to think about well before leaving school. It is, as Kracke (1997) notes, a singularly important choice in identity formation.

Current identity problems in the area of career preparation and development have often been related to high unemployment rates. Youth, and especially those who leave school early, make up a disproportionate percentage of the unemployed, note Meeus, Dekovic, and Ledema (1997). For some, unemployment is a source of considerable distress that can be manifested in a variety of adjustment problems, including serious unhappiness, depression, and loss of self-esteem. But these authors also found that the reaction of different individuals to unemployment varies considerably. For many, the experience doesn't entail obvious negative consequences. (More about career development appears in the next chapter.) (See Summary Table 12.4.)

PARENTS, PEERS, AND SOLITUDE

The development of self and identity does not occur in a vacuum, but rather in a specific social context—a social ecology describable in terms of a wealth of interactions and influences. And at every age throughout childhood and adolescence, peers and parents are a fundamental part of this context.

Relationships Between Adolescents and Their Parents

Developmental psychologists generally agree that one of the things that happens throughout childhood and especially at

SUMMARY TABLE 12.4

Ideas in the Development of Self and Identity in Adolescence

IDEAS	DESCRIPTION/EXPLANATIONS/RELATIONSHIPS
Self	■ Associated with William James.
	■ Defined as the sum total of an individual's characteristics as perceived by the individual; what I think I am.
Identity	■ Associated with Erik Erikson.
	■ A sense of wholeness, of purpose; a clear notion of what and who one is and will be; implies continuity and goals, and relates to different areas of our lives such as social relations, political and religious beliefs, and schooling and careers.
Self-Esteem	■ Personal evaluation of the worth of the self (self-worth).
	■ Changes, developmentally: organized around personal characteristics in late childhood; social relations in early adolescence; ideals and principles in later adolescence.
	■ Research suggests that more adolescents have high than low self-esteem.
	■ High self-esteem seems important for healthy development.
Some Facets of Self	■ Based on Offer's research.
	■ Important facets of self include the psychological, social, sexual, familial, and coping.
The Universal Adolescent	■ Usually happy and optimistic, gregarious and caring, sexually confident, positive in relation to family, and confident regarding the ability to deal with life's problems.
	■ Notions of self are affected by the adolescent's context (for example, culture).
	■ Hall's view of adolescence as a period of storm and stress describes a minority of adolescents—but a sizeable and important minority.
Identity Development	■ According to Marcia, describable in terms of four kinds of identity status distinguishable in terms of crisis and commitment. Status may be different in different areas (social, career, political . . .): identity diffusion (no crisis, no commitment), foreclosure (no crisis, strong commitment), moratorium (crisis, no commitment), and identity achieved (crisis passed, commitment made).
	■ Achieving identity with respect to social relations may be more important for girls than for boys; career and school-related identity status may be more important for boys.
	■ Achieving identity sometimes poses serious problems, especially in terms of high youth unemployment.

Dependence on parents decreases during the teen years, and allegiance to peers increases. The lad with the pointed hair is not imitating his father's coiffure.

adolescence is an emotional distancing of child from parents (Grotevant, 1994). Thus, at the risk of oversimplifying, we can describe the socialization of the adolescent in terms of three stages based on changing roles of parents and peers (see Table 12.5). The first, a *preadolescent stage,* is marked by the child's high social, emotional, and physical dependence on parents, and is characterized by low conflict. The second, spanning early adolescence, involves increasing independence—that is, increasing emotional distancing—and sometimes increasing conflict as well. And the third, beginning in later adolescence, is marked by declining conflict and the achievement of relative independence.

In spite of the near universality of the adolescent's emotional distancing from parents, it would be misleading to assume that adolescents and parents eventually end up far apart emotionally. The expression *emotional distancing* as a description of changing adolescent–parent relationships is accurate and useful only as an indication of adolescent emotional dependence on parents relative to that characteristic of the preadolescent. In fact, adolescents and parents typically

remain very closely attached emotionally. This attachment, Grotevant (1994) explains, serves as a buffer for adolescents, protecting them from some of the stresses and anxieties of growing up and adjusting to a complex world. In addition, continued strong attachment to parents has repeatedly been shown to be closely related to the development of positive self-image. In a study of 167 adolescents, O'Koon (1997) found not only that strong attachments to parents continued right into late adolescence (and presumably beyond) but also that those adolescents who were most attached to their parents were, on average, those with the highest self-esteem.

■ PARENTING ADOLESCENTS

The transition from childhood to adulthood is not only a question of emotional distancing, but also one of earning or being assigned adult responsibilities, notes Brannen (1996). However, contemporary industrialized societies often give young people conflicting messages concerning both their rights and their responsibilities. As we have seen, in these *continuous* societies there typically isn't a single accepted age at which a child becomes adult—not a single act or event that would ensure this status. Thus, adolescents may be allowed to vote at one age, to purchase alcohol or tobacco at another, to get married at yet a different age, perhaps to go to war at yet another. These contradictions don't simplify the task of parenting adolescents.

Much of parenting involves protecting children from their own immaturity. For young children, whose immaturity is clearly reflected in their dependence, this role poses little conflict. But for adolescents, whose immaturity is less (and who, in most cases, don't recognize their immaturity), parenting is a far more difficult function. Yet, as Glasgow and associates (1997) point out following an investigation of the effect of parenting styles on adolescents, it's clear that the

TABLE 12.5

Three Stages of Socialization

STAGES	TIME FRAME	CONFLICT
High dependence on parents	Early childhood	Low
Decreasing dependence on parents and increasing independence	Late childhood Early adolescence	Increasing Increasing
High independence	Late adolescence Early adulthood	Decreasing Decreasing

importance of parenting doesn't decline as children become adolescents. Glasgow and associates corroborate Baumrind's (1989) often replicated finding that *authoritative* parenting presents clear advantages over other parenting styles. In the Glasgow and associates' study, the most negative results were those associated with parents who were not only highly permissive, but essentially neglectful in the sense that they were mainly uninvolved.

Parenting adolescents, says Alvy (1987), involves more than simply protecting them from their immaturity. It also includes providing basic resources and care, guiding and supporting development (providing opportunities for intellectual, social, emotional, and spiritual growth, fostering self-esteem), and advocacy (supporting and helping adolescents in relation to institutions or groups such as schools and employers).

There are several reasons, suggest Small and Eastman (1991), that rearing adolescents in contemporary society might be more difficult and might lead to more conflict than in the past. First, the period of adolescence has increased significantly in all industrialized countries. Hurrelmann (1990) notes that most adolescents attend schools and postsecondary institutions through their teen years and beyond, and many remain economically dependent on the family for all or much of that time. This has led to greater uncertainty about the responsibilities of parents. Parents have also become confused about how best to prepare adolescents for entry into an increasingly complicated and rapidly changing world with competing sources of information and values. There are also more dangers about which to worry—high-risk and potentially harmful activities, substances, and influences, such as drugs and radical cults. Finally, increases in family breakup and increased mobility of family members have led to an erosion of the family, so parents of adolescents have fewer sources of advice or support.

Partly because of the responsibilities and difficulties of parenting adolescents, and partly because of the changing roles and relationships of parents and adolescents, this period frequently involves conflict.

■ PARENT–ADOLESCENT CONFLICT AND EARLY HOME LEAVERS

Several decades ago, the predominant view was that conflict was the main characteristic of parent–adolescent relationships. As Kaplan (1984) put it, "The irrevocable giving-up of the love relationships of childhood entails an extended and painful emotional struggle" (p. 141). However, the more current view is that although parent–adolescent conflict is not uncommon, parents continue to have a significant influence on the thinking and behavior of their adolescents. Interestingly, the greatest conflict occurs in early adolescence (during puberty) and often declines in later adolescence. The reason for this, suggest Paikoff and Brooks-Gunn (1991), is that conflict typically arises because the changing needs and interests of the adolescent require a readjustment in the family system. Once this adjustment has been made, conflict declines. And when it doesn't, then perhaps the adolescent becomes an **early home leaver.**

There are, of course, a vast number of reasons why an adolescent might be an early home leaver or a **late home leaver.** Clearly, parent–adolescent conflict is not the principal reason why children leave home. In fact, there is evidence that in many cases, where parent–adolescent relationships are warmest and most positive, adolescents find it easier to leave home and even to move farther away geographically (Sherrod, 1996). And in some cases, when relations have been conflicted and strained, adolescents remain close, almost as though they had not quite finished their growing up. Still, one of the better predictors of children leaving home early, reports Tang (1997), is the structure of the family. Specifically, after an analysis of nearly 10,000 cases of early (before age eighteen), on-time (between ages eighteen and twenty-four), and late (after age twenty-five) home leavers, Tang found that those most likely to leave home early were from nonbiological or nonintact families. This may be partly because of greater caregiver–adolescent conflict in these families; it could also be because attachments might not be as close.

It would be misleading to suggest that parents and their adolescents are typically in conflict. In fact, as Smetana (1995) points out, there are important areas of parent–child interaction that are seldom the basis of conflict. For example, parents and their adolescents typically agree with respect to most larger moral issues, almost as if children had adopted their parents' moral beliefs and made them their own. Where there is conflict, notes Smetana, it typically has to do with interpersonal relations—most often with sibling relationships or with peer relationships. It is hardly surprising that Bibby and Posterski (1992), following their survey of nearly 4,000 adolescents, ascribe "turbulence on the home front" to conflict over peer relationships. In this survey, freedom and friendship ranked first and second in terms of importance; family life was a distant ninth (see Interactive Figure 12.2).

Peer Groups

"Adolescents have an urgent need to belong," says Drummond (1991, p. 283). Not only do the peer group and friends satisfy emotional needs, but they are also an important source of information and opportunity for socialization. The adolescent peer group is, in many ways, like a separate culture that eases transition from childhood to adulthood.

Adolescent peer groups vary in size, interests, social backgrounds, and structure. They might consist of two or three like-sexed persons (buddies, pals, best friends), larger groups of like-sexed individuals, or couples. Yet another type of peer group comprises persons of both sexes who "hang out" together. In addition, there are gangs, close-knit groups of individuals distinguished by their conflict with authority (more about gangs later). Most adolescents belong to several groups at the same time. Indeed, friends (who are typically part of the peer groups) are the adolescent's most common source of enjoyment (Bibby & Posterski, 1992).

A number of distinctly different peer groups appear to be common to most contemporary high schools. For example, Brown and colleagues (1993) studied 3,781 students in six

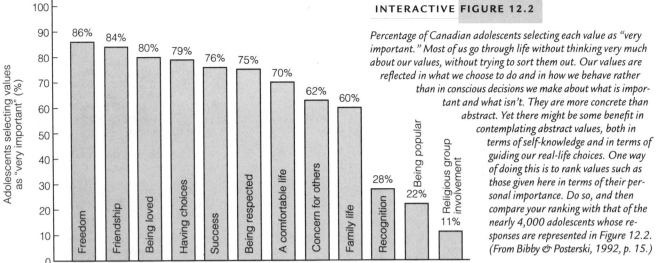

Percentage of Canadian adolescents selecting each value as "very important." Most of us go through life without thinking very much about our values, without trying to sort them out. Our values are reflected in what we choose to do and in how we behave rather than in conscious decisions we make about what is important and what isn't. They are more concrete than abstract. Yet there might be some benefit in contemplating abstract values, both in terms of self-knowledge and in terms of guiding our real-life choices. One way of doing this is to rank values such as those given here in terms of their personal importance. Do so, and then compare your ranking with that of the nearly 4,000 adolescents whose responses are represented in Figure 12.2. (From Bibby & Posterski, 1992, p. 15.)

different U.S. high schools in an effort to identify their peer group affiliations. They were also interested in determining the extent to which parents are a source of influence in the lives of contemporary adolescents. On the basis of their research, they identified six distinct peer groups (or "crowds") in these schools.

All schools, Brown and colleagues (1993) note, have an "elite" peer group composed of two distinct crowds. On the one hand are the "jocks," consisting of students committed to athletics and not overly focused on academics, but who are nevertheless interested in pleasing teachers and in getting acceptable grades. Their interest in drugs is generally limited to alcohol. Also among the elite group are the "populars," who are more strongly committed to academics than the jocks, but who are also "moderately" interested in drug use and in delinquent behavior.

At the opposite end of the scale in terms of social status is a group labeled "outcasts" and made up of "loners" and "nerds"—children who are socially awkward and inept, and whose social status is very low. Other fringe groups include some smaller groups described by Brown and associates (1993) as more "alienated." They include "druggies," "greasers," and others who are heavily involved in drug use or delinquency, and who are often rebellious in school and society. Their values and behavior stand in sharp contrast to those of the "brains" or "eggheads," who are strongly focused on academic achievement, who value close relationships with parents and authority, and who carefully avoid drugs and delinquency. Their social standing is "marginal."

Finally, the largest peer group is composed of "normals." Brown and colleagues (1993) note that these children tend to avoid deviant activities but are not clearly or strongly enough

Having friends and being loved were two of the three most important things in the lives of the nearly 4,000 adolescents studied by Bibby and Posterski; freedom was the other. Not surprisingly, acceptance by peers and the development of close relationships are among adolescents' greatest sources of joy and self-esteem.

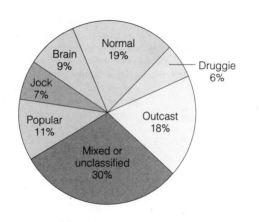

Classification	Description
Popular	Socially competent; academically oriented; moderately involved in drugs and delinquency
Jock	Focused on athletics; drug involvement limited to alcohol; interested in acceptable grades and good relations with parents and teachers
Brain	Strong focus on academic achievement; close relationships with teachers; pointed avoidance of drugs and delinquency
Normal	Largest group; the "average"; avoid deviant activities; no overriding focus on drugs or achievement
Druggie	Strong focus on drugs, delinquency; inattentive to school and authority
Outcast	"Loners" and "nerds"; low social competence, low self-image; low involvement in deviant behavior; average or above-average academic achievement

FIGURE 12.3

"Crowds" in the typical U.S. high school. These six groups accounted for 70 percent of the 3,781 students who were rated in a study of six high schools. (Based on Brown et al., 1993.)

focused on any other activity to be identified as belonging to another distinct group (see Figure 12.3).

Perhaps the most revealing finding of the Brown investigation is that parents play a critical role in determining their children's most likely peer affiliations. Not only are parents instrumental in shaping their children's social skills and values, but they also exercise considerable influence over peer choice through their selection of neighborhoods in which to live as well as through their selection of schools, school programs, and leisure activities (such as sports). Brown and colleagues (1993) report that some specific parenting practices—such as monitoring the adolescent's activities, encouraging achievement (academic or athletic), and being involved in joint decision making with the adolescent—are closely reflected in adolescent behaviors and values, especially with regard to things like academic achievement and drug use.

The influence of parents on adolescents may also be evident in the observation that "brains" tended to be overrepresented among children living in intact families, and that children from stepfamilies or one-parent families were underrepresented among "brains" but overrepresented among "druggies." As Brown and associates (1993) put it, "Parenting practices and family background characteristics cannot determine a teenager's crowd affiliation, but their influence should not be discounted."

Solitude

In spite of their strong, almost insistent, need for the companionship of friends and peers, adolescents spend about one-quarter of their *waking* hours alone, reports Larson (1997). In fact, on average, they spend *more*, rather than *less*, time alone as they move from childhood into adolescence. And most of the time, they do so voluntarily rather than because they

have no friends, or because other circumstances force them to be alone.

Is **solitude** good or bad for the adolescent? The question is probably too simple for a complex issue, but Larson found a positive relationship between time spent alone and measures of contentment and psychological well-being—providing that the adolescent didn't spend an inordinate amount of time in solitude. In his study of 483 children from fifth through ninth grade, Larson found that the best adjusted youngsters were those who spent an intermediate amount of time alone.

Common sense has sometimes suggested that adolescent girls spend significantly more time than boys in conversation, and correspondingly less time in solitude. As is often her habit, common sense is again only half right. Following a survey of more than 2,000 seventh- and ninth-grade boys

Adolescents spend a lot of their waking hours alone, not because they lack friends, but because there is much for them to think about. While making the transition from childhood into adolescence, moderate amounts of time spent alone seems to be directly related to positive adjustment.

and girls, Smith (1997) reports that girls do, indeed, spend more time in conversation than do boys. But they also spend more time alone. That is one gender difference common sense might not have been gifted enough to see; are there others? (See Summary Table 12.6.)

GENDER DIFFERENCES AND STEREOTYPES

Perhaps if we're to be informed clearly in this area, we will have to look to science rather than to common sense.

Science tells us, first, what common sense already knew: Probably the most salient of all human characteristics are those that indicate membership in one of two categories: male or female. As biological categories, male and female are relatively easily identified and defined. But at another level, they are psychological and sociological categories. And here, science struggles a little more.

These psychological and sociological categories, science tells us, are evident in the sometimes dramatic (and sometimes very subtle) differences in the behaviors that are expected of males and females—hence that are considered masculine or feminine. These differences in behavior, together with the attitudes and personality characteristics associated with them, are what define **gender roles** (sex roles). **Gender** refers specifically to the psychological characteristics typically associated with biological sex. Thus, there are two sexes, male and female, and two corresponding genders, masculine and feminine. Bem (1974) also argues that there are individuals who share relatively equally the characteristics of both genders, and labels these individuals **androgynous**. The learning of sex-appropriate behavior (of gender roles) is referred to as **gender typing**. Explanations of gender typing are presented in Chapter 8.

Common Gender-Role Stereotypes

Very early in life, children begin to learn about the behaviors that their culture finds acceptable and desirable for their sex. For example, in North America, boys might learn to play with toy trucks and guns, to be interested in wrestling and play fighting, and to engage in boisterous, loud sports. Girls might learn to play with dolls and houses, to be interested in arts and books, and to like to cook and sew. These, and many other activities and interests, are parts of the **sexual stereotypes** that characterize our societies.

Sexual stereotypes are preconceived, typically unquestioned beliefs about male–female differences. In some cases, they are superficial and trivial; in others, they are more fundamental. Some might reflect basic, undeniable anatomical differences; others are influenced more by context. They are clearly evident in the workplace, for example, where stereotypes held by both men and women often determine not only which jobs will be available for either sex, but also which jobs will be gladly accepted by one or the other (Ridgeway,

▲ SUMMARY TABLE 12.6

Concepts Relating to Peers, Parents, and Solitude in Adolescence

CONCEPTS	EXPLANATIONS/ELABORATION
Changing relationships with parents	■ Increasing independence through adolescence, sometimes accompanied by increasing conflict. ■ Emotional distancing is normal and does not imply loss of affection. ■ Adolescent–parent attachment is closely related to positive self-image.
Parenting adolescents	■ Society presents conflicting criteria of maturity and adult responsibility for adolescents. ■ The importance of parenting does not decline in the transition from childhood to adolescence. ■ Authoritative parenting is related to positive developmental outcomes; neglectful parenting is sometimes related to more negative outcomes.
Parent–adolescent conflict	■ Not generally descriptive of most parent–adolescent relationships. ■ Conflict seldom involves questions of morality; it most often concerns social relationships (siblings and friends). ■ Other things being equal, children from nonintact and nonbiological families are more likely to leave home early.
Peers	■ Satisfy important emotional needs; also a source of information and support. ■ Types of high school peer groups include normal (largest group; nondeviant); popular (socially competent and academically oriented); jock (athletic focus); brain (academic focus); druggie (drug focus; delinquency group); and outcast ("loners" or "nerds"; low self-image).
Solitude	■ A common adolescent state by choice (¼ of waking hours). ■ Moderate, rather than excessive, solitude related to positive adjustment. ■ Girls spend more time in conversation than boys; they also spend more time in solitude.

1997). In general, North American sexual stereotypes associate the male figure with active, work-oriented, and positively evaluated activities and the female figure with more passive, home-oriented, and less positively evaluated roles (Long, 1991). Not surprisingly, Morrison and associates (1997) found that male adolescents were more likely than females to hold these stereotypes. However, in some respects, sexual stereotypes are biased *against* men, note Fiebert and Meyer (1997) following a survey of sexual stereotypes of college students. For example, women are seen as more caring, more nurturant, and less aggressive than men.

Gender roles define patterns of behavior commonly associated with being male or female. Our gender-role stereotypes see males as aggressive, boisterous, and physical—and females as more passive, gentler, more home oriented. Increasingly, however, our gender-based stereotypes need revising. For example, we do not, in our stereotyped images, see young teenagers like this 12-year-old-girl and 14-year-old boy, holding hands and sliding in the mud just for the pure joy of it.

■ GENDER-ROLE PREFERENCE: THE CHANGE-SEX QUESTION

Boys and girls still have little difficulty in identifying personality characteristics that are stereotypically masculine or feminine. Not only do they agree as to what boys and girls should be like, but they also agree that masculine characteristics are more desirable. "If you woke up tomorrow and discovered that you were a girl, how would your life be different?" Tavris and Baumgartner (1983) asked a group of American boys. "Terrible," "A catastrophe," "I would immediately commit suicide" were some typical answers. But when girls were posed the same question—that is, what would happen if they discovered they had become a boy?—they responded quite differently: "Great," "Now I can do what I want," "Now I can be happy." Patterns of responses were clear: Girls often responded positively to the "change-sex" question; boys did so extremely rarely. This difference was evident in children as young as age eight and as old as age seventeen. Sexual stereotypes appear to be learned very young and to be very pervasive.

Five years later, Intons-Peterson (1988) asked the same question of eleven-, fourteen-, and eighteen-year-old Swedish and American adolescents to see if there had been any measurable changes in the intervening years. Her expectation was that gender stereotypes would not be as marked in Sweden as in the United States and that male and female reactions to the change-sex question would not reflect as decided a preference for the male sex (because of the Swedish government's explicit, family-based social program aimed at equalizing the sexes).

As expected, the male gender in the United States was still associated with the "hard-driving, macho image of lore" (Intons-Peterson, 1988); females were seen as less aggressive, gentler. And although these differences were also apparent in the Swedish samples, they were not as extreme. Swedish samples were more likely to view women as capable and effective and men as being emotional and tender.

Responses to the change-sex question were essentially identical to what they had been in 1983. Although a majority of females were content with their gender, most responded in terms of the positive aspects of becoming male. They wrote that they would now enjoy athletics more, that they would travel and stay out later at night, that they would study less but think more about a career. They also felt that they would be more aggressive and less emotional, that they would be less concerned about their appearance, and that they would need to become interested in fighting and in "showing off."

Most males still responded very negatively to the thought of becoming female. They saw themselves becoming burdened by menstruation and concerned with contraception and pregnancy. They expected to be more passive, weaker, and restricted more to indoor activities. They thought, too, that they would become more interested in permanent sexual relationships and be more emotional.

Interestingly, these gender differences are more apparent for the eighteen-year-olds than for the younger group, especially in Sweden. This might be evidence that attempts to eradicate sex stereotypes and to achieve greater gender equality are beginning to have an effect.

■ Gender Differences

Gender stereotypes reflect widely held beliefs about gender. Some of these beliefs may well be accurate, and others not.

■ BIOLOGICAL DIFFERENCES

There are obvious biological and physical differences related to anatomical sex. We know that males are taller and heavier than females (except for a brief period in late childhood) and that females mature approximately two years earlier than males. Other biological differences include the fact that, beginning from puberty, male blood pressure is higher than that of females; female heart rate is between two and six beats higher than that of males; fat-free mass in males is relatively higher than in females, as is metabolic rate; and among males, physical energy is greater, recuperative time is less, and muscle fatigue is slower to occur.

In many ways, however, males are the weaker sex—even from the very beginning. About 50 percent more sperm bear the male (Y) than the female (X) sex chromosome, but there aren't 150 male infants born for every 100 females because the male sperm is more fragile. And so it continues throughout life. At birth, there are about 105 males for every 100 females, but males are more vulnerable to most infections and diseases, so that by adolescence, numbers of males and females surviving are approximately equal; by age 65, there are almost 150 females living for every 100 males (U.S. Bureau of the Census, 1996).

Not only are males more fragile and less long-lived, but they are also more prone to learning, speech, and behavior disorders, greatly overrepresented among the retarded and the mentally disordered, and more prone to bed-wetting, night terrors, and hyperactivity (Shepherd-Look, 1982).

PSYCHOLOGICAL DIFFERENCES

Biological differences between the sexes are generally clear and agreed upon; psychological differences are far less obvious and far more controversial.

In an early review and summary of much of the important research in this area, Maccoby and Jacklin (1974) had concluded that there are clear differences between the sexes in four areas: verbal ability (favoring females), visual/spatial ability (favoring males), mathematical ability (favoring males), and aggressiveness (lower among females).

But at least some of these gender differences no longer seem as clear in this decade as they did in 1974—evidence perhaps that because they resulted mainly from socialization processes, they reflected a cultural context that has changed dramatically in the last several decades.

VERBAL ABILITY

For example, the once-apparent greater verbal ability of females relative to males no longer appears very general, is usually very small, and is not apparent at early ages. In fact, in a large-scale survey of cognitive abilities among young adolescents, Rosen (1995) found no significant differences between boys and girls on measures of verbal ability. Similarly, Robinson and associates (1996) found no gender differences in verbal measures for high-ability preschoolers.

VISUAL/SPATIAL ABILITY

Males often do better than females in tests of visual/spatial ability, beginning even in the preschool period (Livesey & Intili, 1996). And these differences appear to be general across a variety of cultures. For example, Amponsah and Krekling (1997) found significant, and highly similar, gender differences on measures of spatial/visual ability among adults in Ghana and Norway. Tests of spatial ability require that the subject visualize three-dimensional objects and be able to rotate or otherwise manipulate them mentally. For example, a three-dimensional block design test is often used with young children. As Chipman (1988) notes, there isn't a great deal of information about the importance of spatial ability, although some researchers argue that this gender difference may be related to differences in mathematics achievement.

MATHEMATICS AND SCIENCE

There is some evidence that males perform better than females in mathematical skills beginning in early elementary school (Robinson et al., 1996). The same appears to be true for sciences such as chemistry and physics, with gender differences in these subjects *increasing* after adolescence (Burkam, Lee, & Smerdon, 1997). Differences are most evident at the highest levels of mathematics achievement, where males consistently outnumber females. Hedges and Friedman (1993) report that there are about twice as many males as females in the top 5 percent in tests of mathematical ability—and about six times more in the top 1 percent. Interestingly, gender differences in mathematics and science are much smaller in the earlier years. Hence, the fact that females do not continue to do as well may be explained by culturally determined interest and motivational factors (Kaiser-Messmer, 1993).

Significantly, in the same way that gender differences in verbal performance have declined and, in many instances, completely disappeared, so too have differences in mathematics performance. Hyde, Fennema, and Lamon (1990) did a meta-analysis of 100 studies in this area involving more than 3 million subjects. Their conclusion? Girls actually show a slight superiority in mathematical computation in elementary and junior high school, but differences in favor of males emerge in high school, and are most evident in problem solving.

AGGRESSION

As we saw in Chapter 10, males are generally more aggressive than females (Windle & Windle, 1995). Recall, however, that this conclusion applies primarily to **overt aggression**—that is, to physical and verbal aggression. There is now evidence that females may be equally aggressive with respect to **social aggression** (relational aggression) rather than overt aggression (Galen and Underwood, 1997). Overt aggression seeks to do physical harm; its methods include kicking, punching, pushing, and breaking or ripping off extremities. Social aggression seeks to do harm by disrupting peer relations; its methods include ridicule, exclusion, vicious gossip, contempt, and disdain.

Gender differences in aggression are assumed to have a biological as well as a cultural basis. For example, they have been shown to be related to the male sex hormone, **testosterone.** But because aggression is strongly influenced by culture, gender differences in aggression are sometimes very different in different sociocultural contexts (Mead, 1935).

In conclusion, studies of gender differences in academic achievement reveal some small and declining differences largely explainable in terms of culturally based interests and opportunities. They do not provide data that would be sufficient for making inferences about specific individuals. Linn and Hyde (1989) point out that gender differences in height

CONCEPTS	EXPLANATIONS/ELABORATION
Gender roles	■ Defined by the behaviors typical of males and females; reflect behaviors considered probable and appropriate for one's sex; define what a culture considers masculine and feminine.
Gender stereotypes	■ Fixed, unexamined beliefs about persons based on their membership in a gender category. ■ Common North American gender stereotypes ascribe active, powerful, positively valued roles to males and more nurturant, more passive roles to females.
Gender-role preference	■ Research using the *change-sex question* indicates that males are sensitive to the negative aspects of being female; girls respond more to the positive aspects of being male. These gender differences in role preference may be decreasing.
Gender differences	■ Typically small and may be decreasing. ■ Often evident for *overt aggression*, which is a highly masculine trait; *relational aggression* is a more female characteristic. ■ There are culturally mediated differences in science and math achievement favoring boys, especially after late childhood.

Changes in hormone levels affect sexual arousal directly. There appears to be a long-term trend for initiation of sexual activity at progressively earlier ages, but regular sexual activity may not commence for a year or more after loss of virginity.

and strength are far more significant and far more stable. Interestingly, so are gender differences in career accessibility and in earning power—as well as in social attitudes toward careers and roles most appropriate for males and females (Morinaga, Frieze, & Ferligoj, 1993). Not only are psychological gender differences very small, but they may not be very important. Perhaps it would be far more useful to try to understand how interests and abilities develop and interact. (See Summary Table 12.7.)

ADOLESCENT SEXUALITY AND TEEN PREGNANCY

Sex is an area of profound preoccupation for many adolescents[*]—an area that consumes a great deal of their time and energy.

In psychology, sex is many things. To begin with, of course, it is simply a category—male or female—that is usually easily defined by some obvious biological differences. Sex is also a psychoanalytic term that, in Freud's writings, becomes the

___

*"Humph! Grown-ups too!" said my grandmother when she first read this. "Take your Uncle Renald, for example...." But that's another story.

source of energy that motivates all of us from birth to death. But sex is more than a psychoanalytic term or a biological dichotomy. It can mean (as it does in this section) nothing more, or less, complicated than the physical union between male and female, or variations thereof, or the wish thereto, or the fantasy thereof.

Sexual Beliefs and Behavior

There have been some major changes in sexual attitudes and behavior in recent decades. These are reflected in three areas, says Zani (1991): standards, attitudes toward sexual behavior, and age of sexual initiation.

THE DOUBLE STANDARD

The old **sexual double standard** has largely crumbled in many industrialized societies. This standard said, basically, "Boys will be boys, but girls, well, they should behave." In the 1950s, when Kinsey and his associates (1948, 1953) first began to research sexual activity, the standard was in full force. At that time, most males reported experiencing orgasm before marriage, but only 30 percent of females reported doing so. By the mid-1960s, incidence of premarital intercourse among females had risen to about 40 percent—still some distance shy of males' reported 60 percent (Packard, 1968). By the 1980s, however, percentages were about equal at around 75 or 80 (Darling, Kallen, & Van Dusen, 1984), and by the 1990s, females' percentages had increased even more to around 80 to 85 percent (Chase-Lansdale & Brooks-Gunn, 1994) (see Figure 12.4).

ATTITUDES TOWARD SEXUALITY

Recent decades have seen dramatic changes in attitudes toward sexuality. These are reflected not only in the demise of the double standard, but also in an increased openness about sexuality and in a wider acceptance of premarital sex. This does not mean that sex has become totally casual and matter-of-fact among today's adolescents. In fact, the vast majority of teenagers do not think it is appropriate to have intercourse when dating casually, but more than half believe it proper when in love and dating only one person (Roche & Ramsbey, 1993) (Figure 12.5). For the majority of adolescents, the critical factor is whether the partners have a caring and com-

mitted relationship. The new standard holds that sexual activity is permitted for both sexes providing there is affection between partners (Table 12.8). However, male attitudes toward premarital sex among casual acquaintances continue to be more liberal than those of females.

AGE OF INITIATION

Average age of sexual initiation has declined in recent decades. A study of more than 600 Italian adolescents found that about one-third of the girls and one-quarter of the boys had had sexual intercourse before age fifteen (Zani, 1991). Smith (1997) reports similar findings for the United States, as do Cooksey, Rindfuss, and Guilkey (1996). These authors note that there appears to be a long-term trend for initiation of sexual activity at progressively earlier ages, especially for white U.S. teenagers, relative to blacks. Brooks-Gunn and Furstenberg (1989) point out that it is not uncommon for teenagers to have sex at fourteen or fifteen and then not to repeat the activity for another year or more.

Among the most obvious antecedents of sexual activity are the biological changes of pubescence. Changes in hormone levels affect sexual arousal directly; in addition, changes

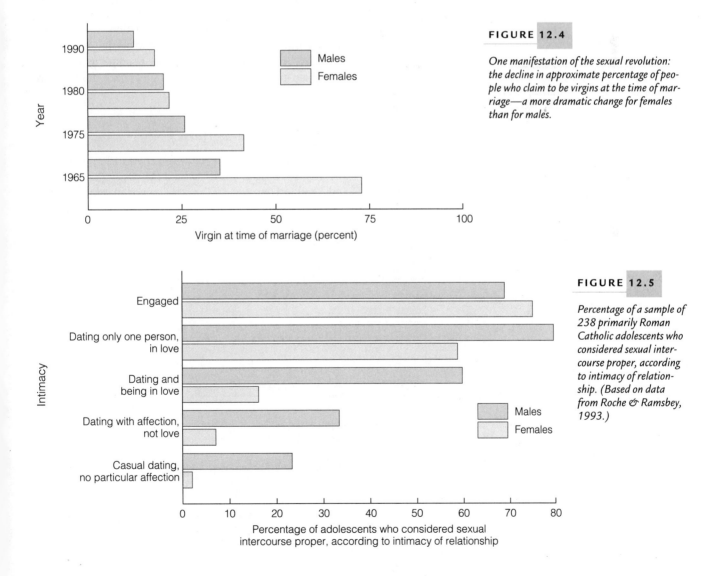

FIGURE 12.4

One manifestation of the sexual revolution: the decline in approximate percentage of people who claim to be virgins at the time of marriage—a more dramatic change for females than for males.

FIGURE 12.5

Percentage of a sample of 238 primarily Roman Catholic adolescents who considered sexual intercourse proper, according to intimacy of relationship. (Based on data from Roche & Ramsbey, 1993.)

TABLE 12.8

What Adolescents Consider Appropriate Dating Behavior

IF TWO PEOPLE ON A DATE LIKE EACH OTHER, DO YOU THINK IT IS ALL RIGHT FOR THEM TO:	MALE	FEMALE	TOTAL
Hold hands?			
Yes, first date.	92	91	92
Yes, after a few dates.	7	9	8
No.	1	0	0
Kiss?			
Yes, first date.	84	80	82
Yes, after a few dates.	16	19	18
No.	0	1	0
Neck?			
Yes, first date.	59	42	50
Yes, after a few dates.	38	52	45
No.	3	6	5
Pet?			
Yes, first date.	42	16	28
Yes, after a few dates.	50	63	56
No.	8	20	15
Have sexual relations?			
Yes, first date.	19	3	11
Yes, after a few dates.	51	33	42
No.	29	59	44
If they love each other.	1	5	3

Note: Based on a survey of 3,600 high school students, aged fifteen to nineteen. Source: Based on Bibby and Posterski, *The emerging generation: An inside look at Canada's teenagers*, Table 5.1, p. 76, Toronto: Irwin, 1985. Reprinted by permission of Stoddart Publishing Co., Ltd.

in secondary sexual characteristics, such as breast enlargement in the girl or lowering of the boy's voice, may serve as important sexually linked stimuli. Other important factors

linked to age of first sexual intercourse include a number of specific events and behaviors, including parental divorce, drug use, and age of dating (Dorius, Heaton, & Steffan, 1993). Peers also influence whether or not an adolescent is likely to engage in sexual intercourse. Significantly, adolescents typically overestimate the amount of sexual activity engaged in by their peers, and underestimate the age of first intercourse (Roche & Ramsbey, 1993; Zani, 1991). (See Figure 12.6.)

■ MASTURBATION

The most common form of sexual outlet for adolescent males and females is **masturbation.** Although contemporary attitudes toward masturbation are that it is normal, pleasurable, and harmless, some adolescents continue to feel guilty and ashamed about masturbating. Males masturbate more frequently than females and often have more liberal attitudes toward the acceptability of masturbation; college experience tends to have a liberating effect on women's attitudes toward masturbation (Davidson & Darling, 1988).

For males, first ejaculation (**spermarche**), sometimes through a nocturnal emission or through masturbation or intercourse, is usually the first sign of pubescence. But unlike the girl's menarche, it is often a secretive affair. In Adegoke's (1993) sample of Nigerian boys, only half told someone—usually a friend—about their first ejaculation. Sixty percent of these boys were not prepared for the event. Zani (1991) notes that because of males' reluctance to admit ignorance or innocence in sexual matters, most do not seek information.

Adolescent Pregnancy

Estimates suggest that there are as many as 12 million sexually active teenagers in the United States—7 million males and 5 million females. Of the 5 million or so sexually active

FIGURE 12.6

Teenagers' reported sexual behavior and their beliefs about what others do when dating and in love. (Based on data from Roche & Ramsbey, 1993.)

Births to Unmarried Teenagers

In the United States, an increasing number of infants are being born to unmarried women. In 1970, about one in ten births was to an unmarried mother (10.7 percent); by 1994, the proportion had risen to almost one in four (23 percent). In 1993, nearly one-third of all births to unmarried women were to adolescents aged fifteen to nine-teen—some 357,000 infants. This figure represents about one-third of all teenage pregnancies The others are births to married teenagers or are pregnancies terminated by abortion or other fetal loss (see Figures 12.7 and 12.8).

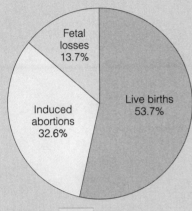

FIGURE 12.7

Pregnancy outcomes for U.S. teenagers (aged 15–19), 1991. (Based on U.S. Bureau of the Census, 1996, p. 84.)

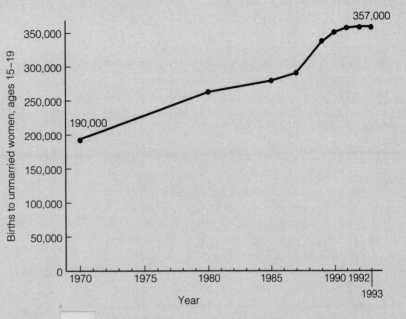

FIGURE 12.8

Births to unmarried mothers aged 15 to 19, 1970–1993. (Based on U.S. Bureau of the Census, 1996, p. 79).

females, approximately 1 million become pregnant each year (see "At a Glance: Births to Unmarried Teenagers" and Figures 12.7 and 12.8). The teenage birthrate in the United States accounts for 11.2 percent of all births; it also accounts for 20 percent of all abortions (U.S. Bureau of the Census, 1996; see Figure 12.9). Who gets pregnant? Why? What are the outcomes and implications of teenage pregnancy?

WHO GETS PREGNANT?

It's important to note that although teenage pregnancies, by definition, involve teen mothers, it is misleading and in-accurate to treat the situation as though it were solely a teen problem. In fact, notes Males (1993a), in 69 percent of all teenage births where the mother is a teenager, the father is an adult. Even in cases where mothers are younger than fifteen, more than half of the fathers are adults.

Teenage pregnancies are not restricted to any particular social, economic, religious, or ethnic group. However, in the United States, pregnancies are more common among black than white teenagers. In 1993, 22.7 percent of all births to black mothers were to teenagers; 11 percent of white births were to teenagers. For mothers of Hispanic origin, 16.8 per-

cent of births were to teenage mothers (U.S. Bureau of the Census, 1996).

Teenage pregnancies are also more common in economically depressed areas (Wilcox et al., 1996). Some have speculated that teenage pregnancy often leads to dropping out of school, to poverty, and to eventual dependence on social assistance. Not so, argues Gordon (1996) following a survey of pregnant or at-risk girls in an inner-city high school. The pattern is more often that the girls are poor to begin with. Many also have low academic skills. These two factors, argues Gordon, appear to result in pregnancy more often than pregnancy results in poverty. In fact, in Gordon's sample, most of the pregnant girls *wanted* to be pregnant.

Compared with married mothers of the same age, socio-economic status, and religious background, unmarried teenage mothers often have lower educational and occupational status, more often come from broken homes, are more likely to have been sexually abused, and are more likely to engage in other high-risk behaviors such as drinking and abusing drugs (Langer & Tubman, 1997; C. Smith, 1996). Many are likely to have had initial intercourse at lower than average ages (C. Smith, 1997).

The vast majority of teenage pregnancies are unplanned. Among reasons for the increasing rates of teenage pregnancy, note Black and DeBlassie (1985), are changes in social attitudes toward sexual activity and toward pregnancy. Pregnancy no longer brings shame and humiliation; accordingly, there is less pressure, both on boys and girls, to prevent conception.

Second, there are many psychological factors that might motivate sexual intercourse, leading to pregnancy: loneliness and alienation, often part of life in socially and economically depressed surroundings; the girl's wish to "get back" at overprotective parents; the boy's wish to establish the "macho" image that some male societies still reinforce. Not surprisingly, girls from poorer families are more likely to become pregnant (Males, 1993b), as are those from rigid, authoritarian families (Romig & Bakken, 1990).

Third, there is the adolescent's egocentrism—the personal fable that stresses the special invulnerability of the teenager and that is premised on the belief that "It won't happen to me." This, coupled with the adolescent's sensation-seeking tendencies, may account for some teenage pregnancies (Arnett, 1992). Johnson and Green (1993) found that the more mature (cognitively, as well as in terms of age and grade) and the less egocentric the female teenager, the more likely she was to use contraception.

Fourth, and perhaps most important, the majority of pregnancies occur accidentally and as a consequence of ignorance or misinformation concerning sex and contraception. More than half of all teenagers do not use contraception at the time of first intercourse, and perhaps a third continue to use none later (Arnett, 1992). Significantly, approximately half of all pregnancies occur within six months of first intercourse. Many teenagers do not know where to get birth control information, and of those who have adequate information, many are only intermittently sexually active. For them, the cost of the safest birth control methods makes their use prohibitive. In addition, use of an IUD (intrauterine device), oral contraceptives, or of a diaphragm requires the cooperation of a physician. As a result, of those who do employ contraception, many are forced to use the least reliable methods: withdrawal, rhythm (attempting to time intercourse to coincide with the woman's cyclical periods of infertility), and condoms. Brooks-Gunn and Furstenberg (1989) argue that we need to know much more about teenage sexual activity and attitudes toward condoms in order to encourage their use (see Figures 12.9 and 12.10).

■ IMPLICATIONS

Pregnancy for an unmarried teenager is often a serious problem. As Chase-Lansdale and Brooks-Gunn (1994) put it, "Normative developmental sequences and life transitions are irrevocably altered or delayed, and risks to healthy development in multiple domains occur" (p. 208). Many teenage pregnancies result in a dramatic disruption of the mother's educational and career plans. There are also much higher health risks with teenage pregnancy and delivery, both for

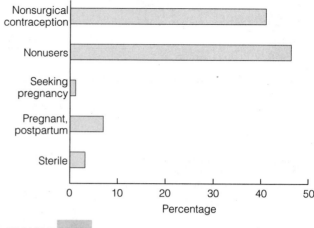

FIGURE 12.9

Reproductive status of U.S. women, ages 15 to 24, 1990. (Based on U.S. Bureau of the Census, 1996, p. 84.)

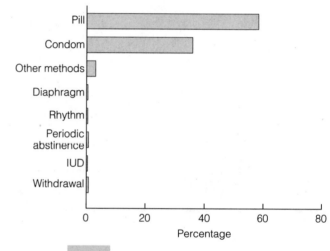

FIGURE 12.10

Choice of contraceptive method by the 41.2 percent of U.S. women, ages 15 to 24, who used nonsurgical contraception in 1990. (Based on U.S. Bureau of the Census, 1996, p. 84.)

mother and for infant. Moreover, the economic and social conditions under which the majority of teenage mothers are forced to live, and the emotional stresses associated with these conditions, as well as with child rearing, can be a heavy burden. Not surprisingly, divorce rates for teenage marriages are much higher than for marriages that occur later.

In addition to disadvantages of teenage pregnancy for the mother, there are also disadvantages for the offspring. Donnelly and Voydanoff (1991) summarize these as follows: "Children [of unmarried adolescent mothers] are more likely than those of older mothers to experience a number of difficulties as they grow and develop. These difficulties include poverty and its associated problems, physical problems, lower educational attainments, problem behaviors, maltreatment and the increased likelihood of becoming adolescent parents" (p. 404).

Teenage parents, note Passino and colleagues (1993), tend to be less socially competent than their nonpregnant peers. They also manifest higher levels of stress and are less sensitive to the needs of their infants. One study that compared child-rearing knowledge and attitudes of adolescent mothers with those of older mothers found that the teenage mothers were not only significantly lower on measures of parenting knowledge, but also scored higher on indicators of authoritarian parenting (Camp, 1995). Although the economic disadvantages of teenage childbearing often disappear over time, as Furstenberg, Brooks-Gunn, and Chase-Lansdale (1989) put it, "The children of teenage mothers however, are distinctly worse off throughout childhood than the offspring of older childbearers" (p. 313).

The implications of teenage parenthood are clearly more direct and more applicable for mothers and children than for fathers, a great many of whom are not involved in any pregnancy-related decisions or in child rearing—and the majority of whom are not teenagers (Males, 1993b). However, school dropout rates are higher for teenage fathers even when they do not marry the mother (Marsiglio, 1986).

However, these observations and conclusions do not apply to all teenage parents. Many are sensitive, caring, and competent parents. Sadly, the probability that this will be the case, given their relative immaturity and lack of experience and information, is not overwhelmingly high.

■ WHAT TO DO?

Not all teenage mothers are economically disadvantaged, have inadequate job skills, and raise children who experience developmental problems. Still, as Roosa (1991) puts it, "The vast majority of adolescent mothers and their children would benefit by postponing early pregnancies."

Given the staggering economic, psychological, and social costs of adolescent parenthood, the United States Public Health Service has, since 1981, funded a variety of pregnancy prevention programs. The majority of these are offered in junior high schools through sex and family-life education programs. Their objectives are to decrease adolescent pregnancy by changing sexual attitudes and sexual behavior. For legal, and sometimes moral, reasons, many are abstinence programs that do not permit discussion of contraception or abortion (Jorgensen, 1991).* Others offer free access to contraception, provide information about sexuality and contraception, and attempt to influence sexual attitudes and to expand adolescents' life options (Chase-Lansdale & Brooks-Gunn, 1994).

Selman and Glendinning (1996) classify pregnancy prevention policies into two main groups: programs that attempt to affect teenage pregnancy directly (such as sex education in schools, the provision of contraception, and access to free legal abortions) and those that approach the problem more indirectly (the provision of educational and employment opportunities for adolescent girls, making access to welfare

and housing more difficult for teenage mothers). The more direct methods work, at least to some extent, they argue, but the indirect methods don't. In particular, they argue that welfare does *not* serve as an incentive for teenage girls to become pregnant—a point also made by Wilcox and associates (1996).

Sex education, pregnancy prevention programs, and the provision of contraception in schools remain controversial. When McKay (1996) surveyed parents to uncover their attitudes toward sex education courses, he found that more than 90 percent of respondents either agreed very strongly or disagreed very strongly with the idea of providing sex education for students. There are parents who fear that sex education and easy access to contraception may serve to increase adolescent sexual behavior and to foster values that run counter to those of the family and the community. Because of this, and because of the danger of sexually transmitted diseases, many parents advocate sexual abstinence programs (see Hess, 1990). However, adolescents are not always highly motivated to participate in such courses, especially when what the programs teach contradicts their values and their behaviors. As Gordon (1996) notes, if these programs are to succeed with adolescents, they must recognize that the problem is not adolescent sexual activity but rather teenage pregnancy.

Many pregnancy prevention programs have not been based on systematic research or knowledge about the antecedents of pregnancy, and most have not involved the adolescent's family and peer systems. Not surprisingly, many have not proven highly effective (Males, 1993b). However, indications are that with more sensitive and careful program development and evaluation, and with further refinement of preventive strategies, program results can be positive (Haynes, 1993; M. A. B. Smith, 1994). Such programs need to take into account the realities of contemporary life—realities that, for example, not only condone but encourage sexual intercourse and that include adult men having sex with teenage girls. Given these realities, abstinence programs may be too simplistic (and too unrealistic), argue Brick and Roffman (1993). When Christopher and Roosa (1990) investigated the effects of an adolescent pregnancy prevention program that focused on self-esteem and resisting peer pressure, and that taught that sex should occur only after marriage, program dropout rates were very high. Nor was there any evidence that the program was effective in reducing sexual activity.

■ HOMOSEXUALITY

Homosexual experiences during adolescence do not appear to be very common. Evidence suggests that approximately one out of every ten adolescent boys, and perhaps half that number of girls, have isolated sexual experiences with someone of the same sex, usually during early adolescence (Dreyer, 1982). Estimates of the number of these who subsequently adopt a homosexual or bisexual lifestyle are extremely unreliable, but are probably considerably less than the 8 or 9 percent who have had adolescent homosexual experiences. In Michael and colleagues' (1994) comprehensive survey of the sexual behaviors of 3,432 randomly selected adults, only 2.8 percent of men and 1.4 percent of women claimed to be

---

*"Abortion's pretty controversial, leave it alone," my grandmother warned, borrowing an old Salvadoran proverb: "Never kick a dead donkey from the rear end."

homosexual or bisexual. That homosexual groups have become more visible and more outspoken in recent decades may account for the popular perception that their numbers have increased.

Causes of homosexuality are not known, although there are a variety of theories: genetic, social learning, hormonal. And it is extremely difficult, in most cases impossible, to alter sexual preference.

Sexually Transmitted Diseases

There are more than two dozen known **sexually transmitted diseases (STDs)**—also known as **venereal diseases**. Among the most common are chlamydia, gonorrhea, and herpes. Less common are syphilis and AIDS, although both of these are increasing. Reported yearly cases of syphilis in the United States almost doubled between 1980 and 1991 (134,000 cases reported in 1991 compared with 69,000 in 1980). However, numbers appear to be decreasing once more (82,000 cases in 1994; U.S. Bureau of the Census, 1996). Significantly, STD rates are more than twice as high among teenage girls than would be predicted on the basis of rates among teenage boys. The reason for this, suggests Males (1993b), is the high rate of intercourse between adult males and teenage females.

CHLAMYDIA

Chlamydia may be the most common of the STDs, although the dramatic increase in infection rates may be largely a function of better screening procedures (Division of STD Prevention, 1995). This disease was rarely seen until very recent years and still goes largely undetected. Estimates are that as many as one of every ten sexually active women has chlamydia—twice as many as have gonorrhea. It is now one of the leading causes of infertility among women (Roberts, 1996). In the majority of women, chlamydia presents no symptoms in its early stages (approximately 80 percent); this is also the case for about 20 percent of infected men. In later stages, abdominal pain may cause the victim to seek medical help, but by then the woman is often infertile. Chlamydia can be treated easily and effectively with antibiotics.

GONORRHEA

Gonorrhea has declined dramatically since 1980, when there were more than 1 million cases reported in the United States, but it is still a highly common STD, with about 418,000 reported cases in the United States in 1994 (U.S. Bureau of the Census, 1996). Symptoms in the male usually include a discharge from the penis and pain during urination. Symptoms in the female are more subtle and often go unnoticed. The disease can normally be treated simply and effectively with penicillin and related drugs. Like some other sexually transmitted diseases, it can sometimes be prevented through the use of a condom or simply by washing the genitals thoroughly after intercourse.

GENITAL HERPES

Genital herpes is caused by a virus and remains incurable, although the virus can remain inactive for long periods of time. An estimated 500,000 new cases are reported each year. The disease is believed to be contagious only when lesions are present (like tiny cold sores, commonly found on the penis and scrotum in males, and on the vulva, vagina, and cervix in females). Newer drugs can provide effective control of symptoms.

AIDS

Acquired immune deficiency syndrome (AIDS) is a sexually transmitted disease caused by the **human immunodeficiency virus (HIV)**—an organism that appears to mutate rapidly, thereby increasing the difficulty of treating it (Alcamo, 1993). At present, it is incurable and fatal. It is transmitted through the exchange of body fluids, principally blood and semen. Largely for that reason, AIDS has been found primarily among four high-risk groups: intravenous drug users who often share needles, homosexual males who engage in anal intercourse, hemophiliacs who have been exposed to the virus through blood transfusions, and certain groups of Haitians who engage in rituals involving blood exchange. As of 1992, 244,939 cases had been reported in the United States; of these people, 166,467 had died (U.S. Bureau of the Census, 1994; see Figure 12.11).

FIGURE 12.11

Number of AIDS cases reported in the United States in 1995. Total number of cases was 71,547. Of these, 81 percent were male, 41 percent were blacks, and 16 percent were Hispanics. Highest number of cases were reported in California (15.6 percent) and New York (17.3 percent); lowest were in Arkansas (0.4 percent) and Oklahoma (0.4 percent). (Based on U.S. Bureau of the Census, 1996, p. 142.)

Middle Childhood

The half-dozen years of middle childhood are enthusiastic and joyous years, marked by some of our most stunning physical and intellectual triumphs. Sometimes they bring small failures too.

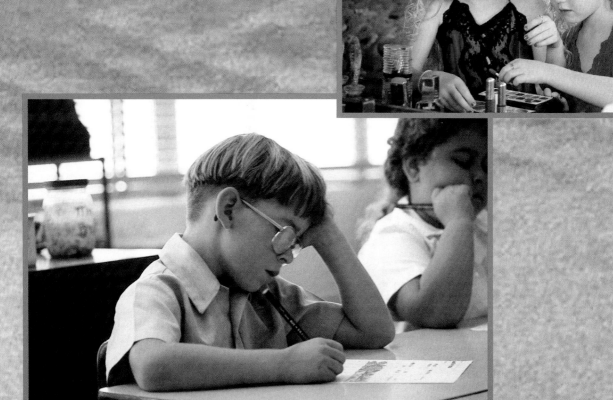

In Shakespeare's "As You Like It," middle childhood is the age of the "whining schoolboy, with his satchel and shining morning face, creeping like a snail unwillingly to school." Not so. For many, school—and the friends therein—is close to the very center of life. Parents, too, have their importance.

Adolescence

Finally we teeter uncertainly between childhood and adulthood, often unready or unwilling to leave all our childish things behind.

nd then, bang, pubescence strikes. And the hormones that go raging through our veins wrest our attention from our childish toys and games and turn it squarely to matters we had not much thought of before.

In adolescence, some of us struggle mightily with our identities, uncertain of who we are—perhaps even more uncertain of who we want to be or can be or should be.

Early Adulthood

Early adulthood brings a whole new set of important developmental tasks. Unlike Peter Pan, we can't all stay young and be just a boy or a girl the rest of our lives.

ome of us have to go out and weed the garden and make computers and stuff. Much as we might prefer to remain children, early adulthood insists that we make decisions relating to career and economic independence.

Early adulthood also urges that we make important lifestyle decisions: to cohabit, to stay single, to get married, to join a commune? Our most common adult lifestyle in North America has always been heterosexual marriage—although marriages no longer last as long as they once did.

his week hundreds of high school students attending Jamestown High in Jamestown, New York, discovered that they might be infected with the HIV virus. These are girls who had sex with Nushawn Williams. There were 28 of them, Nushawn admitted (and dozens more elsewhere). But what's different about Jamestown is that it's just a small town (34,000 residents). So when new HIV cases began to show up, one after another, the county medical commissioner became suspicious—and traced the cases back to Nushawn Williams. He may be what the medical profession refers to as a *super transmitter* who carries a particularly virulent mutation of the virus. Chances of infection are enormously higher with such individuals. At present, at least 9 of the 28 girls who had sex with Williams are known to be infected; the youngest was only 13 when she knew Williams. These nine girls are thought to have exposed at least another 70 sex partners to the virus. The final count remains unknown.

1. Lauter, D. (1997, Oct. 28). Man infects 9 with AIDS virus in semirural NY. *Los Angeles Times*, p. 1.

2. Mandel, M. (1997, Nov. 2). Terror comes to town. *Edmonton Sun*, p. News 10.

To Think About

A special court order was obtained to release Nushawn William's identity and to circulate his photograph among potential victims. Under what circumstances, if any, do you think authorities should be permitted to take such action? How about in the case of convicted sex offenders who have served their sentences?

On the Net

For a frequently updated web site dealing with all aspects of HIV and AIDS including incidence and treatment, and including, as well, links to a wide variety of other AIDS- and HIV-related sites, see the AIDS Virtual Library:

http://planetq.com/aidsvl/

Another useful web source is:

http://www.critpath.org/

Because there may be as much as a ten-year lag between exposure to the virus and development of symptoms, reported cases reflect what was happening ten years ago. The World Health Organization predicts that worldwide, 4 million women will have died of AIDS by the year 2000 ("AIDS Will Kill 4M Women by 2000: WHO," 1993). Homosexual and drug-related transmission are still most common. However, heterosexual transmission is the norm throughout most of the world and is expected to become more common in North America as well ("Sleeping with the Enemy," 1991). In fact, relative incidence of AIDS among women in the United States has increased dramatically. Between 1981 and 1986, only 7 percent of reported cases were female, but in 1995, 19 percent of all new cases were female (U.S. Bureau of the Census, 1996).

Adolescents appear to be relatively well informed about AIDS and how it is transmitted (Lamport & Andre, 1993), and as many as one-third claim they have changed their sexual behavior because of fear of AIDS. That means, however, that two-thirds have not.

There is some indication that sexual activity—especially unprotected sexual activity—among homosexual males has declined in the wake of widespread accounts of increases in the incidence of AIDS and other STDs (Stall, Coates, & Hoff, 1988). (See "In the News and on the Net: HIV Supercarrier" above.)

OTHER STDS

Among other STDs is **acute pelvic inflammatory disease (PID)**, a complication that can result from diseases such as gonorrhea or chlamydia. It is a major health problem, affecting more than 1 million U.S. women a year (Quan, 1994). The resulting inflammation of the cervix and Fallopian tubes can lead to infertility or tubal pregnancies, especially following repeated infections. In one study of 1,309 women who had been diagnosed as having acute pelvic inflammatory disease, 12.1 percent were found to be infertile. Of the others who did become pregnant, 7.8 percent had tubal pregnancies (Westrom, 1994).

Genital warts are also sexually transmitted. They are caused by a virus and affect about 1 million people in the United States each year. They are not usually dangerous, and can be removed. Sexual transmission is also the leading cause of hepatitis B, which accounts for about 5,000 deaths in the United States each year ("Sleeping with the Enemy," 1991). (See Summary Table 12.9.)

ADOLESCENT TURMOIL

A large majority of adolescents pass exuberantly through the teen years, enjoying their increased powers of mind and

ISSUES	EXPLANATIONS/RESEARCH FINDINGS
Double standard	■ Sexist attitudes that historically condoned sexual activity for men but not for women.
Changes in adolescent sexual beliefs and behavior	■ Demise of double standard. ■ Earlier age of sexual initiation. ■ Debunking of taboos surrounding masturbation.
Teen pregnancy	■ An increasingly common occurrence (12 percent of all births in the U.S. in 1994; ⅓ of all births to unmarried women). ■ More common among the poor, the uneducated, the sexually abused.
Possible reasons and motives for teen pregnancy	■ Unplanned, indirect result of changing attitudes toward sexual activity, coupled with strong biological urges of adolescence. ■ Psychological factors such as loneliness and alienation. ■ The personal fable; it won't happen to me. ■ Ignorance and misinformation regarding pregnancy and conception control.
Implications of teen parenthood	■ Possibility of negative consequences linked to interruption of schooling and career paths. ■ Possibility of negative consequences of associated poverty. ■ Stress associated with new responsibilities for which the mother isn't well prepared. ■ Negative implications for offspring.
Social policies for preventing pregnancy	■ Direct interventions include sexual education, providing contraception, and free legal abortion. ■ Indirect interventions include providing educational and employment opportunities for teenage girls, and reducing easy access to welfare assistance.
Homosexuality	■ A relatively uncommon sexual orientation, the actual incidence of which cannot easily be determined. ■ No clear agreement on causes; highly resistant to attempted orientation reversals.
STDs	■ Chlamydia (often asymptomatic; highly common; important cause of infertility). ■ Gonorrhea (common; easily treated with penicillin). ■ Herpes (cold-sore type lesions; common; incurable but controllable). ■ AIDS (caused by HIV virus; generally fatal; highest risk groups are IV drug users and homosexuals). ■ PIDs (pelvic inflammatory diseases; important cause of infertility).

body, successfully overcoming or avoiding the turmoil that besets their less fortunate peers. But for others, perhaps some 15 percent who describe themselves as anxious or confused or depressed, adolescence can be a turbulent and troubled time (Offer, Ostrov, & Howard, 1984). Clearly, then, the turmoil topics—delinquency, gangs, drugs, suicide—relate only to the minority. But they are an important minority.

Delinquency

Delinquency is a legal rather than a scientific category. A delinquent is a juvenile who has been apprehended and convicted for transgression of established legal rather than moral laws. Adults in similar situations are criminals rather than delinquents.

When delinquency is defined in this manner, surveys of its prevalence can be based directly on police and legal records. These records indicate a tremendous increase in the delinquency rate in recent decades. There are almost as many crimes committed by adolescents and younger children as by people over twenty-five (U.S. Bureau of the Census, 1996). However, many of the offenses for which juveniles are apprehended and brought to court are status offenses such as truancy, running away, sexual promiscuity, underage drinking, or driving without a license. But 31 percent of all *serious* crimes committed in the United States in 1994 were committed by those under eighteen (see "At a Glance: Gangs, Violence, and Delinquency" and Table 12.10).

A number of factors appear to be related to delinquency, but because most of the studies that have investigated delinquency simply indicate correlations, it is impossible to identify delinquency's specific causes. Age, for example, is related to delinquency, but we have no evidence that it causes delinquency. Other related but not necessarily causal factors include social class, intelligence, peers, parents, personality, and sex.

■ SOCIAL CLASS

Research on the relationship between social class and delinquency is ambiguous and inconclusive. Although the lower classes, as well as some racial subgroups, are greatly overrepresented among delinquent groups, it is by no means clear that there are, in fact, many more delinquents among these groups. Because of the nature of law enforcement systems, their often unconscious prejudices, and their consequently greater likelihood of recognizing and apprehending delinquents among minority and lower-class groups, it is hardly surprising that more of these adolescents are classified as delinquents. At the same time, to the extent that delinquency is a form of rebellion sometimes motivated by the desire for material possession, it is reasonable to expect that more of the poorer adolescents would be delinquent. Furthermore, lower-class parents tend to look to the police for help with their children; middle-class parents go to therapists.

■ INTELLIGENCE

There is a large body of evidence linking delinquency with lower than average measured intelligence (Binder, 1988).

Gangs, Violence, and Delinquency

andom and unprovoked violence, sometimes perpetrated by gangs and sometimes by individuals, is as frightening as it is unpredictable. Violence that is not random, but that is based on allegiance to ideology and on hatred of identifiable groups (as is the case for some racist groups), is no less terrifying. Although the number of delinquency cases dealt with by U.S. courts has not changed very much in recent years (in the United States, 1.05 million cases in 1975 and 1.49 million in 1991), incidence of violent juvenile offenses in the United States increased from 57,000 cases in 1982 to 120,000 cases in 1993. With respect to violent offenses, males outnumber females by approximately 7 to 1. As a result, more than 80 percent of all juveniles held in custody in 1993 were male.

TABLE 12.10

Number and Types of Delinquency Cases Disposed of by U.S. Juvenile Courts in 1993

All delinquency offenses	1,490,000		Property offenses (*continued*)	
			Motor vehicle theft	61,000
Violent offenses	122,000		Arson	8,000
Criminal homicide	3,000			
Forcible rape	6,000		Delinquency offenses	795,000
Robbery	36,000		Simple assault	166,000
Aggravated assault	78,000		Vandalism	117,000
			Drug law violations	89,000
Property offenses	573,000		Obstruction of justice	96,000
Burglary	150,000		Other*	327,000
Larceny	354,000			

*Includes stolen property offenses, trespassing, weapons offenses, other sex offenses, liquor law violations, disorderly conduct, and miscellaneous offenses.
Source: Adapted from U.S. Bureau of the Census, 1996, p. 217.

However, this should not be taken as direct evidence that lower intelligence causes delinquency. Quay (1987) notes that much of this difference in measured intelligence may be accounted for in terms of lower verbal ability. This puts children at a disadvantage in social interaction as well as in school. Consequently, they are more likely to get into trouble with teachers, school administrators, parents, and perhaps friends as well.

PEERS

Peer groups, particularly in the form of gangs, can also contribute to delinquent behavior. Like other peer groups, the delinquent gang reinforces its dominant values and also serves as a model for translating these values into actual behaviors. Lindstrom (1996) describes this as a "spreading effect." His investigations indicate that not all youths are equally affected by their peers, but that some are, in effect, more susceptible than others. Correctional institutes for juveniles, which are comprised primarily of delinquent peer groups, may be one example of the influence of peers on delinquent behavior. Not surprisingly, more than half of all admissions to most correctional institutions are, in fact, readmissions.

A study reported by Claes and Simard (1992) indicates that delinquent adolescents are more likely to make friends outside of school than are nondelinquents. Not surprisingly, they are also more likely to commit antisocial acts with their friends.

PARENTS

The father is perhaps the most influential parent with respect to juvenile delinquency. Fathers of delinquent boys are

often more severe, more punitive, more prone to alcoholism, more rejecting, and more likely to have engaged in delinquent behavior themselves (Peiser & Heaven, 1996). At the same time, many parents of delinquent adolescents are likely not to have monitored or disciplined their children closely while they were growing up (Klein et al., 1997). Not surprisingly, children of adolescent mothers are also more likely to engage in delinquent behaviors (Chase-Lansdale & Brooks-Gunn, 1994).*

There is evidence, too, that father absence may be related to delinquency (Amato & Keith, 1991). Some speculate that father absence may contribute to delinquency in sons, perhaps by failure to provide adequate male models, perhaps as a function of protest against female domination, or perhaps simply because of inadequate supervision. Girls, too, appear to be more prone to delinquency in father-absent homes or where the mother is viewed as cold and rejecting (Kroupa, 1988).

PERSONALITY

Many studies have looked at the possibility that delinquency is at least partly a function of the individual's personality characteristics. Results are generally inconclusive although there is some evidence that high impulsivity (low impulse control), high need for stimulation (danger-seeking orientation), and low self-esteem are related to delinquency (St. C. Levy, 1997). With respect to low self-esteem, we noted earlier that delinquents typically think less well of themselves than do nondelinquent adolescents.

---

*"It's not always the parents," said my grandmother. "Many a good cow has an evil calf!"

Gangs are social groups that organize themselves spontaneously and whose defining characteristic is found in conflict with other groups or with established society. Gangs tend to encourange delinquent values and behaviors.

■ SEX

The incidence of delinquency is about four times higher among boys than girls. This may be partly explained by the male's greater aggressiveness. Traditionally, delinquency among males has involved more aggressive transgressions, whereas girls were apprehended more often for sexually promiscuous behavior, shoplifting, and related activities. Evidence indicates that this pattern is now changing, as more girls become involved in aggressive delinquent acts, including breaking and entering, car theft, and even assault. Drug-related offenses also account for an increasing number of detentions. Interestingly, in a study of female delinquency, Caspi and colleagues (1993) found highest risk for delinquency among girls who matured earliest. Early-maturing girls were far more likely to know—and be friends with—delinquent boys than was the case for girls who matured later.

In summary, a complex set of psychological and social forces impinges on the potential delinquent, although no single factor can reliably predict delinquent behavior. Social class, age, sex, home background, intelligence, personality, relationship with the father, and peer influences are all implicated, but these don't give a complete picture. Clearly, many adolescents from the most deprived of backgrounds are not delinquents, and many from apparently superior environments are.

Adolescent Gangs

Sociologists define a **gang** as a group that forms spontaneously, that interacts on a face-to-face basis, and that becomes aware of its group membership through conflict with some other group or, perhaps more often, with some representatives of established society. A gang may consist of different numbers of individuals from a wide variety of backgrounds and locales, although it typically includes a fairly homogeneous group of people who at least live close to one another and who often attend the same school. But most important, a group does not become a gang until it comes into conflict with something external. It is hardly surprising, then, that the word *gang* has always been closely associated with juvenile delinquency, truancy, rebelliousness, and other disturbing behaviors.

Lasley (1992) reports that gangs are primarily composed of adolescents. As gang members age, they typically drop out and are replaced by younger members. Hence, many gang members are school-aged; as a result, gangs pose a real danger in some schools. Burke (1991) describes how wearing highly prized clothing (like certain sports jackets) can place an individual in danger, and how some high school girls participate in gang activities, often by hiding gang members' drugs and weapons in their school lockers.

Of special current concern are gangs whose members often engage in violent behaviors simply because of an apparent taste for violence and mayhem. Some British soccer riots and the occasional school-holiday violence seen in some North American resort areas are examples of this kind of violence. Also of concern is gang violence premised on fundamental beliefs and principles that are focused against specific groups or institutions. Here in Edmonton, for example, two members of a group identifying themselves as neo-Nazi skinheads beat up and blinded a sixty-year-old man who had, more than a decade earlier, expressed anti-Nazi views ("The 'Scene' and the Skinheads," 1990). Their admitted philosophy is clearly racist; their dream is of an all-white society; their music is counterculture, frenetic, and anarchistic; their dress, hairstyles, and makeup are intended to shock and outrage; and violence is their modus operandi.

Violence among delinquent gangs is often an expression of a new identity that gang members adopt. Adolescents who join small, highly cohesive, counterculture groups are provided with a set of beliefs and principles that are sometimes very well articulated. Their allegiance to the gang is not only a rejection of family, school, and larger cultural values, but is also an embracing of the values and of the individuals in their new community.

But not all adolescents who are dissatisfied, disillusioned, or in need of the community of groups join gangs in protest. A significant number of the severely dissatisfied drop out of society. Lest another stereotype be fostered, we must point out that the methods of dropping out described here are undertaken by both the adventurous and the timid, the weak and the strong, the deluded and the rational—and frequently they are not attempts to drop out but rather attempts to intensify the experience of living.

Drugs

Drug use is an almost inescapable fact of contemporary life. Drugs are with us constantly in the guise of coffee, tea, headache tablets, cocktails, and thousands of other forms. People have known about drugs for centuries, although they have not always known the chemical components of the substances they ate, drank, chewed, applied to wounds, inhaled, put in ears, or otherwise used on their persons.

The most commonly abused drugs in North America are classified in Table 12.11. The U.S. Bureau of the Census (1996) reports declines between 1974 and 1994 in the use of hallucinogens, tranquilizers, marijuana, and even cigarettes. However, there are some indications that alcohol use and abuse have increased during this time. The United States has the highest rates of illegal drug use among industrialized nations (Newcomb & Bentler, 1989). (See "At a Glance: Changing Patterns of Drug Use" and Figure 12.12.)

■ SOME DEFINITIONS

The American Psychiatric Association distinguishes among a number of drug-use terms. **Drug abuse** refers primarily to the recreational use of drugs and is not considered a disorder unless it impairs social or occupational functioning. **Drug dependence** is a disorder ordinarily resulting from the repeated use of a drug and is manifested in a strong desire to continue taking the drug—either for the pleasant sensations that might result or to escape feelings of withdrawal.

The APA distinguishes between **physiological dependence,** commonly called *addiction,* where the desire to continue taking the drug is at least partly organically based (for example, not taking it will lead to unpleasant physiological reactions), and **psychological dependence,** sometimes called *habituation,* where the desire to continue taking the drug has to do mainly with its psychological rather than its physiological effects. **Drug tolerance** refers to changes that occur in the user so that with the passage of time, more and more of the drug is required to produce the desired effect.

Widiger and Smith (1994) make the important point that there are no infallible rules for identifying clearly when drug use is a problem for a given individual. The APA's *Diagnostic*

TABLE 12.11

Classification of the Most Frequently Abused Drugs

CLASS	EXAMPLES
Narcotics	Opium Morphine Heroin Codeine Methadone
Sedatives (downers)	Barbiturates (Phenobarbital, Seconal, Nembutal) Tranquilizers (Valium, Librium, Vivol) Alcohol
Stimulants (uppers)	Cocaine Crack Amphetamines (Benzedrine, Dexedrine, Methedrine)
Hallucinogens (psychoactive, psychotropic, psychedelic, psychomimetic)	LSD PCP Mescaline Psilocybin Marijuana
Inhalants	Glue Paint thinner Aerosol sprays Solvents
Unclassified (or sometimes classified as stimulant)	Nicotine
"Designer" Drugs	Any of a combination of chemicals and drugs, often manufactured by amateur chemists

and Statistical Manual (DSM-IV) recognizes that drug use and abuse exist on a continuum marked by increasing lack of control (*dyscontrol* is the term employed). To some extent, whether or not drug use is abuse depends on the drug, the organism, and the context. Thus, use of certain drugs that are toxic or that are likely to have serious adverse consequences is probably abuse, use of drugs by young children or adolescents may be abuse because of the possibility that drug use will interfere with important aspects of development and adjustment, and use of drugs in inappropriate contexts (at work or in school) is also more likely to be abuse.

■ WHO USES DRUGS?

Researchers have sometimes assumed that there is a drug-use continuum that reflects psychological health and adjustment: At the most positive extreme is the drug abstainer, at the most negative extreme is the frequent drug user or the addict, and in between are infrequent users who occasionally experiment with drugs. However, a longitudinal study conducted by Shedler and Block (1990) contradicts this view. The study looked at psychological characteristics of children from preschool through age eighteen. At age eighteen, children were identified as drug abstainers, drug experimenters, and drug users. As expected, drug users were found to be the least well adjusted, the most impulsive, and n the 1960s, social prophets loudly trumpeted their fears that drugs were taking over the lives of adolescents, that coming decades would witness drug-related social upheavals and political catastrophes that could scarcely be imagined. But recent decades have seen a decline in the use of drugs in most categories.

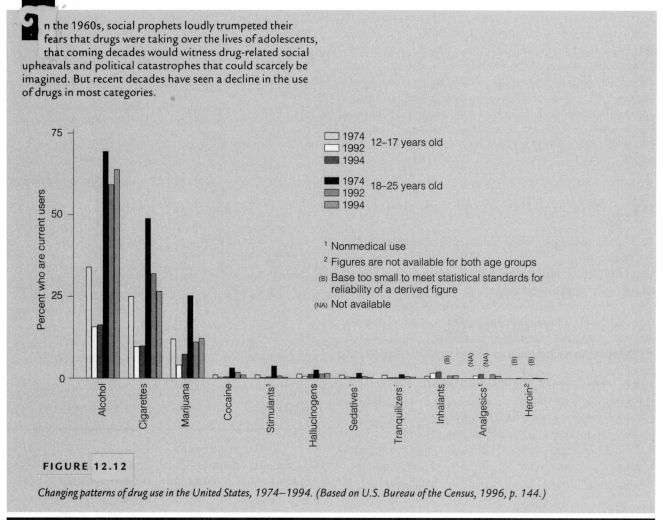

FIGURE 12.12

Changing patterns of drug use in the United States, 1974–1994. (Based on U.S. Bureau of the Census, 1996, p. 144.)

the most likely to suffer from emotional problems. But the abstainers were not the best adjusted of the three groups; the drug experimenters were. In Shedler and Block's (1990) words, "The picture of the abstainer that emerges is of a relatively tense, overcontrolled, emotionally constricted individual who is somewhat socially isolated and lacking in interpersonal skills" (p. 618).

In the Shedler and Block study, children who later became frequent drug users were often identifiable by a complex set of common characteristics even as young as age seven. Often, these children did not get along as well with their peers, were less advanced in moral judgments, were more impulsive, displayed less self-reliance, had lower self-esteem, and were more prone to emotional distress. At age eleven, these children continued to be more emotional, less attentive, and less cooperative, and reacted poorly to stressful situations. In short, frequent drug users often appear to have been relatively maladjusted as children (Luthar & Cushing,

1997). Low self-esteem is perhaps the single personality variable that is most often implicated in drug abuse.

There also appear to be gender differences in drug user characteristics. Male drug users are often more aggressive or more shy as children; females are more likely to show symptoms of emotional disorders like depression, to have attempted suicide, to have been abused as children, and to have a family history of drug abuse (Toray et al., 1991). For both males and females, father alcoholism is also a strong predictor of drug abuse, as is punitive or affectionless parenting (Clausen, 1996).

REASONS FOR DRUG USE

Experimentation with drugs is primarily an adolescent phenomenon. And when teenagers are asked about their decisions to use or not to use drugs, they seldom refer to morality, social convention, or even parents or the law. Even nonusers claim that the decision is a matter of personal choice dictated by prudence and not by morality. And perhaps the most important factor in making that personal decision is the individual's perception of dangers associated with a drug. Frequent drug users are most likely to discount a drug's harmfulness (Nucci, Guerra, & Lee, 1991).

The reasons for drug use are many and complex, and are not to be found solely in the personality characteristics of the frequent drug user. As we saw, environmental factors such as father alcoholism or maltreatment as a child may also be implicated. The fact that children of alcoholics may be as much as four times more likely to become alcoholics than children of nonalcoholics also suggests the possibility of a genetic contribution (Marlatt et al., 1988). However, the meaning of this relationship is not entirely clear. It might mean that there are genetically determined physiological (chemical, hormonal, or metabolic) characteristics that make one person more susceptible than another to alcoholism. It might also mean that the social and economic implications of being raised in the home of an alcoholic parent are conducive to alcoholism.

One of the most important influences in the adolescent's decision to use drugs relates to the influence of peers. Dinges and Oetting (1993) surveyed more than 100,000 junior high and high school students. Among other things, they found that adolescents who used a specific drug almost invariably had friends who also used the same drug. In their words, "Drug-using friends are a necessary condition in the evolution of drug use" (p. 263). Swaim and colleagues (1993) report similar results with samples of American Indian adolescents.

Reasons for first using (and not necessarily eventually abusing) drugs often have to do with a simple urge to experiment (Pearl, Bryan, & Herzog, 1990). However, those who subscribe to the **gateway drug-use theory** believe that early use of drugs like alcohol and nicotine serves, in a sense, as a gateway to the use of other drugs (Pentz, 1994). Rarely does the adolescent begin with drugs like cocaine or heroin. However, this doesn't mean that most adolescents who use these gateway drugs will become drug abusers. In fact, the vast majority will not. Newcomb and Bentler (1989) argue that there is little evidence to support the belief that experimentation with drugs presents a significant danger to later health and psychological well-being.

Use of drugs is most likely to become misuse, Segal (1997) suggests, among individuals with poor self-esteem who also experience the strong pressures of a peer drug culture and who are not reared in a growth-fostering environment (parental neglect, abuse, alcoholism; poverty; inadequate schooling; and so on). The type of drugs experimented with is also very important. Some drugs have a higher potential for physiological and psychological dependence than others (heroin and freebase cocaine, or crack, for example). In addition, genetics may well be involved in the nature and intensity of the individual's reaction.

The fact that there are genetic, social, and personality variables that appear to be related to the likelihood of drug use and abuse should be interpreted with caution. The evidence does not warrant the conclusion that these inevitably cause drug abuse. Nor, as experience clearly shows, does the apparent absence of these factors guarantee that a given adolescent is safe. As Polson and Newton (1984) point out, one of the most common refrains heard when parents are first confronted with the fact of their child's drug use is "Not my kid, couldn't happen to my kid."

Sadly, perhaps, it could.

Implications of Teenage Drug Use

It is clearly unrealistic to expect that adolescents will not experiment with drugs. As Newcomb and Bentler (1989) note, the vast majority will have puffed on a cigarette or sipped somebody's alcoholic drink well before adolescence. In adolescence, not to drink occasionally—and perhaps not to smoke cigarettes or try marijuana—would, in many instances, not be socially normal. Society's focus, these authors claim, should be on delaying drug experimentation for as long as possible to allow for the development of social and intellectual adaptive skills. The emphasis should perhaps be less on preventing use than on preventing abuse.

The short-term implications of drug abuse among adolescents are sometimes painfully obvious. For example, alcohol is implicated in a staggering number of fatal, teenage automobile accidents. Less dramatic, but no less real, drug abuse may be reflected in poorer school achievement, dropping out of school, failure to adjust to the career and social demands required for transition to young adulthood, deviance, and criminality. Watts and Wright (1990) report very high correlations between use of alcohol, tobacco, marijuana, and other illegal drugs and delinquency. In their study of black, white, and Mexican American adolescents, frequent drug use was the best predictor of both minor and violent delinquency. Similarly, Dawkins (1997) found that substance use (especially the use of alcohol and marijuana) was closely associated with violent, as well as nonviolent, crime among adolescents. Not surprisingly, in a study of 312 young offenders, history of previous offenses was an even better predictor of subsequent crime than was drug use.

The long-term implications of teenage drug abuse have been examined by Newcomb and Bentler (1988), who looked at seven different aspects of the lives of young adults (including family formation, stability, criminality, mental health, and social integration). They found that teenagers who had used large amounts of drugs were more likely to have left school early and to have consolidated family and career plans earlier. Those who had used a variety of drugs had often adopted adult roles less successfully; their attempted careers and marriages were more likely to have failed.

The long-term medical consequences of drugs such as nicotine and alcohol have also been extensively researched and are well-known. In the following sections we look at these and at some other commonly used drugs.

MARIJUANA

Marijuana, whose active ingredient is **tetrahydrocannabinol (THC)**, is derived from hemp, a tall annual plant appearing in male and female forms. It is variously known as hashish, bhang, grass, ganja, charas, marijuana, muta, grefa, muggles, pot, reefer, gauge, stick, Acapulco Gold, Panama Red, Panama Gold, Thai stick, jive, Indian, Jamaican, tea, and dope. It is ordinarily smoked although it can also be eaten or drunk. Its main psychological effect is a pleasant emotional state. If taken in sufficient doses and in sufficiently pure forms, it may evoke the same types of hallucinogenic reactions sometimes associated with stronger drugs like LSD.

Whether marijuana is physically addictive remains controversial. Gold (1989) suggests that it may be addictive following prolonged use; others believe that it has not been shown to be addictive or especially harmful (Royal College of Psychiatrists, 1987). In one study in which 382 habitual marijuana users participated in a program designed to help them stop, many experienced considerable difficulty and distress (Stephens, Roffman, & Simpson, 1993).

The physiological effects of marijuana use depend largely on the dosages and the frequency of use. Minor cardiovascular changes (increased heart rate, for example) are common even with very low doses. The respiratory system may be adversely affected with prolonged use and heavier doses (marijuana produces more tars than tobacco, and these contain a higher concentration of certain cancer-causing agents) (Cox et al., 1983).

The fear that marijuana is the first step toward heroin addiction has generally been discounted. There is no evidence that marijuana users develop tolerance to marijuana as users do to some other drugs like heroin. Hence, the marijuana user does not need to go to more powerful drugs to continue to achieve the same "high." Nor is there any evidence that using marijuana leads to a psychological craving for heroin.

■ LSD

D-lysergic acid diethylamide tartrate, or **LSD-25**, is the most powerful hallucinogen known. Because it is a synthetic chemical, it can be made by anyone who has the materials, the equipment, and the knowledge. The most common street name for LSD-25 is acid; others are barrels, California sunshine, blotters, cubes, domes, flats, wedges, purple haze, jellybeans, bluecaps, frogs, microdots, and windowpanes. Its use appears to have declined recently (U.S. Bureau of the Census, 1996).

LSD-25 (ordinarily referred to simply as LSD) is usually taken orally, commonly in the form of a white, odorless, and tasteless powder. Its effects vary widely from one person to another, as well as from one occasion to another for the same person. The predominant characteristic of an LSD experience (called an "acid trip") is the augmented intensity of sensory perceptions. On occasion, an acid trip is accompanied by hallucinations, some of which may be mild whereas others may be sufficiently frightening to lead to serious mental disturbance in the subject even after the immediate effects of the drug have worn off.

■ ALCOHOL

Alcohol, the most commonly used and abused drug in contemporary society, is a central nervous system depressant. In relatively moderate doses, its primary effect is to suppress inhibition, which is why many individuals who have consumed alcohol behave as though they had taken a stimulant. In less moderate doses, the individual progresses from being "high" or "tipsy" to intoxication. Literally, to be intoxicated is to be poisoned. Behavioral symptoms of varying degrees of intoxication may include impaired muscular control, delayed reflexive reactions, loss of coordination and balance, impaired vision, uncertain speech, faintness, nausea, amnesia (blackouts), and, in extreme cases, paralysis of heart and lung muscles sometimes leading to death (Reid & Carpenter, 1990).

Alcohol is physiologically addictive, although prolonged or excessive consumption is generally required before symptoms of physical addiction are present. Signs of psychologi-

The most commonly used drug among North American teenagers is alcohol. It is a physiologically addictive drug that, with prolonged excessive use, can have serious health consequences. One of its main effects is to suppress inhibition. Thus, it has made this young man far more willing to sing for what he assumes is an adoring public. Unfortunately, it has not made him a better singer.

TABLE 12.12

Students Reporting Drinking with Friends

AGE	NEVER (%)	SOMETIMES (%)	USUALLY (%)	ALWAYS (%)	AT LEAST SOMETIMES (TOTAL %)	TOTAL NUMBER OF STUDENTS
12	72	24	2	2	28	163
13	62	29	6	3	38	142
14	34	37	23	6	66	242
15	20	42	28	10	80	208
16	13	35	35	17	87	249
17	12	41	33	14	18	219

Source: Brown and Finn (1982, p. 15).

cal dependency (a strong desire to continue taking the drug) may appear considerably sooner. One of the major physiological effects of alcohol is its contribution to **cirrhosis** of the liver—one of the ten leading causes of death in the United States. In addition, it is implicated in more than half of all motor vehicle deaths, a large number of which involve adolescents (Beatty, 1991).

Alcohol consumption among adolescents is widespread. Most surveys report that extremely few teenagers have not tried alcohol at least once (Newcomb & Bentler, 1989). Close to 20 percent of adolescents aged fourteen to seventeen are considered problem drinkers (see Table 12.12).

Why do adolescents drink? There are clearly many reasons, including social pressure, experimentation, insecurity, and other personal problems, as well as simply for the sensation of being "tipsy," "high," or "drunk." Why do adolescents want to get drunk? To feel good, have fun, celebrate, let off steam, cheer up, forget worries, feel less shy, and impress friends, they claim (Brown & Finn, 1982). But when they are asked what their actual behaviors and feelings are when they are drunk, although a large number do "feel good" and "laugh a lot," a significant number fall asleep, feel unhappy, cry, damage property, and get into fights—and approximately one-third at all age levels occasionally get sick.

When is alcohol consumption by adolescents deviant or a problem? Is it a problem only when the adolescent gets into trouble? Does it become a problem when alcohol consumption becomes habitual or excessive or when it interferes with normal social or physical functioning? Or is it always a problem because the behavior is generally illegal? There are no easy answers.

■ COCAINE

Cocaine is ordinarily a white powder derived from coca leaves. Also known as coke, big "C," snow, gold dust, star dust, flake, Bernice, or Corine, it is most commonly inhaled vigorously through the nostrils, although it can also be injected.

In moderate doses, the primary effect of cocaine, like that of other stimulants, is one of euphoria and high energy. In higher doses, it can lead to hallucinations and sometimes convulsions. For some decades it was widely believed that cocaine is nonaddictive and largely harmless. It is now considered to be extremely dangerous (Cheung, Erickson, & Landau, 1991). Indications are that it may be as addictive as heroin (Ringwalt & Palmer, 1989).

Cocaine is sometimes purified to produce **crack** (*freebase cocaine*), which has a more profound effect on the user. Some users mix it with heroin and inject it intravenously (called a speedball). Crack appears to be particularly attractive to adolescents for several reasons. First, it is far cheaper than cocaine. Second, its effects are almost instantaneous and intensely euphoric. And third, so much glamour and misinformation have surrounded the so-called recreational use of cocaine that many adolescents think there is nothing to fear.

Crack is easily and quickly manufactured by cooking down ordinary powdered cocaine with bicarbonate of soda (or mixing it with a petroleum product such as ammonia). Small pieces of the resulting off-white, rocklike, moldy-smelling solid are then chopped up and smoked, usually in a waterpipe. The euphoric effect or "rush" occurs within five to ten seconds and is far more intense than that associated with inhaling ordinary cocaine—the reason being that the concentrations of cocaine that reach the brain are many times higher than is the case with inhalation. Consequently, there is a far higher risk of overdosing with crack, of experiencing convulsions, or even of dying. Many users of crack experience an overwhelming compulsion to use it again as soon as possible, even after using it only once. The use of crack is also associated with psychological changes, the most common of which involve strong feelings of paranoia. Many users also become violent (Washton, 1989), and some commit suicide.

■ OTHER DRUGS

Other drugs used by some adolescents include various hallucinogens such as STP and MDA (methyl amphetamines), PCP (phencyclidene), inhalants, various barbiturates and other milder tranquilizers, and a range of new molecular variations of these and other chemicals (such as "ecstasy"), sometimes collectively labeled "designer drugs." Of these, alcohol is still the drug of choice, both among adolescents and adults (see Table 12.13 for some symptoms of drug use and abuse).

Suicide

Suicide, the deliberate taking of one's life, is final—an end that is sought when individuals can see only two choices: life as it is now or death. Evidently, they prefer to die.

Suicide is not a pleasant topic—it so violently contradicts our implicit belief in the goodness of life. Consequently, a powerful social stigma is associated with the act, and the event is often covered over both by the information media and by the attending physician. As a result, we know only of suicides of people whom we have known (and sometimes not even then), of particularly prominent persons (not always

TABLE 12.13

Symptoms of Drug Use and/or Abuse

DRUG	SIGNS AND EARLY SYMPTOMS	LONG-TERM SYMPTOMS
Narcotics	Medicinal breath. Traces of white powder around nostrils (heroin is sometimes inhaled). Red or raw nostrils. Needle marks or scars on arms. Long sleeves (or other clothes) at inappropriate times. Physical evidence may include cough syrup bottles, syringes, cotton swabs, and spoon or cap for heating heroin.	Loss of appetite. Constipation.
Sedatives	Symptoms of alcohol consumption with or without odor. Poor coordination and speech. Drowsiness. Loss of interest in activity.	Withdrawal symptoms when discontinued. Possible convulsions.
Stimulants	Excessive activity. Irascibility. Argumentativeness. Nervousness. Pupil dilation. Dry mouth and nose with bad breath. Chapped, dry lips. Scratching or rubbing of nose. Long periods without sleep. Loss of appetite. Mood shifts. Changes in friends. "Hangover" symptoms.	Loss of appetite. Possible hallucinations and psychotic reactions.
Hallucinogens, marijuana	Odor on breath and clothing. Animated behavior or its opposite.	None definite.
LSD, PCP, MDA, STP	Bizarre behavior. Panic. Disorientation.	Possible contribution to psychoses. Recurrence of experiences after immediate effects of drug.
Inhalants	Odor of glue, solvent, or related substance. Redness and watering of eyes. Appearance of alcoholic intoxication. Physical evidence of plastic bags, rags, glue, or solvent containers.	Disorientation. Brain damage.

those either), or of people who commit the act so flagrantly that it compels attention.

There are relatively few scientific investigations of suicide, its causes, and the personalities of those who deliberately choose their time and method of departure. Do children commit suicide? How often? How about adolescents, disillusioned idealists that they are, caught up in the stress and turmoil of the transition to adulthood? Here are some facts.

■ RATE

The suicide rate in the United States is 12.1 per 100,000. Relatively few children under the age of fifteen commit suicide (1.7 per 100,000 in the United States). Suicide rates increase slowly from adolescence and then more rapidly after age sixty-five (U.S. Bureau of the Census, 1996). The most dramatic recent increase in suicide rates is among those aged fifteen to nineteen, where suicide rates nearly doubled between 1970 and 1990 (U.S. Bureau of the Census, 1996). Interestingly, suicide rates are consistently higher in New World countries (Canada, the United States, Australia, and New Zealand) than they are in Old World countries (England, Wales, Scotland, Northern Ireland, and Ireland) (Cantor et al., 1996). And, for some unexplained reason, the most advanced countries—that is, those with the highest life expectancies and the lowest infant mortality rates—have had the highest recent increases in youth suicide rates (Lester, 1995). (See "At a Glance: Adolescent Suicide" and Figure 12.13.)

■ SEX DIFFERENCES

At all age levels, far more females than males attempt suicide, but about four times more of the males are successful. More than 25,000 males committed suicide in the United States in 1994, compared with slightly more than 6,000 females. Some have argued that this is because males who attempt suicide are more serious about wanting to die than are the girls. It may also be because the more violent and instantaneous methods employed by males (for example, guns in 66 percent of all cases) do not provide much opportunity for help. In contrast, the slower and more passive methods most often employed by females (such as poisoning, which is used 35 percent of the time) often allow time for rescue.

■ PSYCHOLOGICAL EXPLANATIONS

There are many psychological explanations for suicide. For example, there are biological theories (suicide is due to bad genes, psychiatric disorders, biochemical changes of adolescence, and the like); psychoanalytic theories (suicidal adolescents are those whose unconscious death wish is exaggerated by deficient ego development during this critical period); psychological stress theory (suicide results from a perceived inability to cope with stress associated with rapid and demanding life changes); sociological theories (social norms sometimes sanction suicide by providing the adolescent with the opportunity to die for the group—alternately, groups sometimes exclude the adolescent, thus causing depression and leading to suicide); social learning theories (suicidal behavior is suggested by the behaviors and atti-

Adolescent Suicide

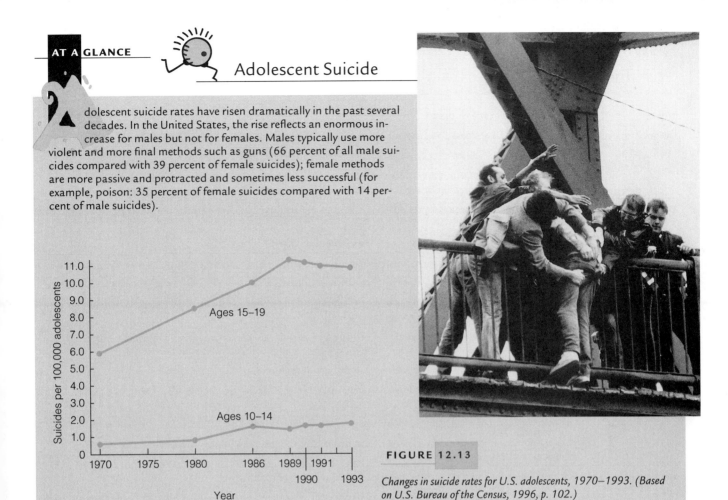

dolescent suicide rates have risen dramatically in the past several decades. In the United States, the rise reflects an enormous increase for males but not for females. Males typically use more violent and more final methods such as guns (66 percent of all male suicides compared with 39 percent of female suicides); female methods are more passive and protracted and sometimes less successful (for example, poison: 35 percent of female suicides compared with 14 percent of male suicides).

FIGURE 12.13

Changes in suicide rates for U.S. adolescents, 1970–1993. (Based on U.S. Bureau of the Census, 1996, p. 102.)

tudes of friends, family, or other important people); and ecological theory (individual, environmental, and social factors contribute to suicidal tendencies).

Henry and associates (1993) suggest that of these, the most useful may be the ecological approach. Not only does it take into account most of the explanations included in other theories, but it provides a way to understand how suicide might result from the combined effects of a variety of factors. Thus, reasons for adolescent suicide can include a range of family-based problems (Bronfenbrenner's microsystem), such as death in the family, parental abuse or alcohol use, suicide by other family members, and inability to satisfy parental expectations. They can also include wider social problems (meso-, exo-, or macrosystems). For example, Henry and colleagues (1993) report that suicide rates are about ten times higher among Native American youth, perhaps partly because of economic, social, and even cultural factors associated with hopelessness. In the same way, certain characteristics of contemporary societies—such as high mobility, family instability, lack of intergenerational cohesiveness, poor economic conditions, high unemployment, and expensive and sometimes inaccessible postsecondary education—might all contribute to a greater likelihood of suicide (Wetzler et al., 1996; Stack, 1993).

INDIVIDUAL EXPLANATIONS

Although adolescent suicide might result from the combined effects of these various factors, it is often precipitated by a single event such as the death of a parent or friend, fear of pregnancy, rejection by a close friend, or arrest (Gutierrez, King, & Ghaziuddin, 1996). Meneese, Yutrzenka, and Vitale (1992) found that the best predictors of adolescent suicide for males are depression and lack of family cohesiveness; for females, the best predictors are depression and level of anxiety (as a personality characteristic). In a study by Clerici, Carta, and Cazzullo (1994), drug addiction, and especially inability to obtain sufficient heroin, was related to suicide. Depression and conflict-filled family relationships have also been found to be strong predictors of suicide; so too has failure in school or a recent serious loss. And, for females, a history of sexual abuse and assault is also predictive of suicidal tendencies (Bagley, Bolitho, & Bertrand, 1997). Shreve and Kunkel (1991) suggest that the shame that accompanies these conditions may be the determining motive.

Adolescent suicide, like most adult suicides, rarely occurs without advance warning. The most common warning is one or more unsuccessful attempts at suicide. Other warning signs include statements such as "I wish I were dead,"

TOPICS	EXPLANATIONS/RESEARCH FINDINGS
Delinquency	■ A legal category defined by the apprehension and conviction of a juvenile for transgression of some law.
	■ Thirty-one percent of all serious U.S. crimes are committed by adolescents aged 18 or less.
	■ Factors sometimes predictive of delinquency include any or a combination of (or sometimes none of) lower social class, lower IQ, school failure, punitive or neglectful parenting, father absence, high impulsivity, and being male rather than female.
Gang	■ A spontaneously formed group of individuals in face-to-face interaction who come into conflict with other groups or with some manifestation of authority (or both).
	■ Of current concern are gangs that engage in random or directed violence.
Drugs	■ Adolescent rates of drug use appear to have declined in recent years.
	■ Drug abuse refers to the recreational use of drugs where such use impairs social or occupational functioning.
	■ Drug dependence refers to a physical need to continue taking a drug (physiological dependence, or addiction) or a strong urge to do so (psychological dependence, or habituation).
	■ Adolescents who experiment with drugs are not necessarily more maladjusted than those who don't; reasons for drug use are complex and include an urge to experiment, peer pressure, and some genetic and personality factors.
	■ Drug abuse is sometimes linked with poorer self-esteem, as well as abusive, neglectful, or punitive parenting.
	■ Short-term consequences of abuse of drugs like alcohol include high accident rates, poorer school performance, and delinquency.
	■ Long-term implications of drug abuse include negative social as well as medical consequences.
	■ The drug most commonly abused by adolescents is alcohol. Other abused drugs include various narcotics, sedatives, stimulants, inhalants, and hallucinogens.
Suicide	■ Suicide rates for male adolescents have increased dramatically in recent decades.
	■ More girls than boys attempt suicide; approximately one-quarter as many are successful (two-thirds of male attempts involve firearms).
	■ Precipitating or contributing factors in suicide may include some significant loss or failure, death of a close friend, depression, and poor family relations.
	■ Approximately 99,988 of every 100,000 adolescents do not commit suicide in any given year.

"Nobody would miss me if I weren't here," and "I wish I'd never been born."

Suicide is still the solution of an isolated few. Most of us choose to wait for death and hope that it will be a long time in coming. And for most adolescents, life is only occasionally turbulent and stressful; generally, it abounds with joy and excitement. (See Summary Table 12.14.)

ANOTHER NOTE

Suicide would not have been a very pleasant note upon which to end this chapter. Nor would it have been very realistic. Indeed, closing the chapter with the "turmoil topics," as we

have, is misleading. As Astroth (1993) points out, adolescents today have lower rates of suicide, drug abuse, unwed pregnancies, and drunk driving than do young and middle-aged adults.

It bears repeating that the adolescents whose lives are described among these last pages are not our "average" adolescents. "As a group," note Hart and Yates (1996), "adolescents are in many ways considerably more healthy than is usually acknowledged" (p. 208). Thus, our average adolescents are more joyful than sad, more exuberant than depressed, more confident than self-deprecating. They like order more than chaos, purpose more than dissipation—and junk food more than drugs.

And they laugh and smile a lot more than they cry.

That's a better note upon which to end.

FOCUS QUESTIONS: SUMMARY ANSWERS

1. Is adolescence typically a time of strife and conflict?

   ■ Adolescence is not generally a period of storm and stress. Rather, the universal adolescent is mainly happy and optimistic; caring, concerned, and sociable; confident and open about sexual matters; and strongly positive toward the family.

2. How important are parents and peers throughout adolescence?

   ■ Social development progresses from a stage of relative dependence on the parents to a stage of relative independence. The role of parents in adolescence is to provide resources, protect adolescents, guide their development, and serve as advocates for them. Increasing allegiance to peers does not necessarily entail a high degree of parent–adolescent conflict. The adolescent's acceptance by peers is profoundly important for social and psychological well-being. High-status (well-liked) children tend to be happier, more cheerful, more active, and more successful. Nevertheless, moderate amounts of solitude are important for positive adjustment.

3. Are there real and important psychological differences between the sexes?

   ■ Gender refers to characteristics associated with biological sex (masculine or feminine). Stereotypes view the male gender as dominant, active, and more positively valued, and the female gender as more passive and nurturant. Some gender differences are biological, evident in the greater fragility of the males (higher mortality). Gender differences in mathematics and spatial ability (favoring males) and in verbal ability (favoring females) are small and best explained in terms of culturally determined interests and opportunities rather than in terms of genetically ordained differences.

4. What are the principal sexual beliefs and behaviors of adolescents?

   ■ The sexual revolution among adolescents is evident in the disappearance of the double standard, an increase in sexual activity (greater among females than males), and a lowering of the age of first intercourse. Almost half of young adolescents consider

sexual relations permissible if partners have been together a number of times and have developed a caring relationship. Approximately 20 percent of sexually active teenage girls become pregnant each year, and almost half give birth. The most common sexually transmitted diseases are gonorrhea, herpes, and chlamydia; syphilis and AIDS are rarer.

5. How common and serious are adolescent delinquency, drug abuse, and suicide?

   ■ Delinquency is a legal category defined by apprehension and conviction of a juvenile for a legal transgression; it is associated with social class, sex, self-esteem, intelligence, home, and peer influences (such as gang membership). Incidence of drug use among adolescents appears to have leveled off in recent years. Alcohol is still the drug of choice, nicotine is second, and marijuana is a close third. Predictors of the likelihood of drug abuse among teenagers include drug use among peers or parents; delinquency; stressful life changes; parental neglect, abuse, or abandonment; and low self-esteem. Suicide is uncommon, although its frequency among adolescents has more than doubled in recent decades. More girls than boys attempt suicide, but fewer are successful.

STUDY TERMS

acquired immune deficiency syndrome (AIDS), 360

acute pelvic inflammatory disease (PID), 361

adolescent moratorium, 344

androgynous, 351

chlamydia, 360

cirrhosis, 369

cocaine, 369

common sense, 350

crack, 369

delinquency, 362

D-lysergic acid diethylamide tartrate, 368

drug abuse, 365

drug dependence, 365

drug tolerance, 365

early home leaver, 348

foreclosure, 345

gang, 364

gateway drug-use theory, 367

gender, 351

gender roles, 351

gender typing, 351

genital herpes, 360

gonorrhea, 360

human immunodeficiency virus (HIV), 360

identity, 340

identity achieved, 345

identity diffusion, 345

identity versus role diffusion, 344

late home leaver, 348

LSD-25, 368

masturbation, 356

negative identities, 344

overt aggression, 353

FURTHER READINGS

Frydenberg presents a detailed analysis of the dozens of different ways in which adolescents have learned to cope with the stresses in their lives:

Frydenberg, E. (1997). *Adolescent coping: Theoretical and research perspectives.* New York: Routledge.

The following two books present a detailed look at identity in adolescence. The first is an insightful collection that looks at the development of identity; the second contains fascinating interviews with some of the principal researchers and theorists in this area:

Adams, G. R., Gullotta, T. P., & Montemayor, R. (Eds.). (1992). *Adolescent identity formation* (Vol. 4). Newbury Park, CA: Sage.

Kroger, J. (1993). Ego identity: An overview. In J. Kroger (Ed.), *Discussions on ego identity.* Hillsdale, NJ: Erlbaum.

The sociology of the family in different cultures from the growing child and the adolescent's point of view is the subject of the following collection of articles:

Brannen, J., & O'Brien, M. (Eds.). (1996). *Children in families: Research and policy.* Washington, DC: Falmer.

This volume is a collection of articles that looks at the incidence, methods, and reasons relating to adolescent suicide:

Whitaker, L. C., & Slimak, R. E. (Eds.). (1990). *College student suicide.* New York: Haworth.

PART SIX

Early Adulthood

Sing on! sing on! I would be drunk with life,
Drunk with the trampled vintage of my
youth.

OSCAR WILDE
The Burden of Itys

It's not always an easy thing to grow up, to leave one's childish toys and become an adult. There are important psychosocial tasks to be accomplished first, the psychologists tell us in their peculiar jargon. As we see in the next two chapters, there are competencies to be acquired, crises to be conquered, old attitudes and old ways of thinking to be discarded. There are mature commitments to be made to careers, to friends and spouses and family, perhaps even to dogs and horses and other beasts. There is intimacy to be explored and earned and given. ¶ These are the trappings of adulthood, not of adolescence and childhood. The things of childhood and adolescence must be left behind, trampled in the dust of childish years where wild oats were once sown. ¶ If we do grow up, will our trampling of the vintage of our youth leave us with a wine so sweet it will make us want to sing with joy through our young adulthood? ¶ Or will it leave us with only a vinegar to pucker our lips and furrow our brows and snatch the song from our hearts?

FOCUS QUESTIONS

1. Is early adulthood a period of physical growth, decline, or stability?

2. What is normal (and average) sexual behavior and responsiveness for young adults?

3. How do people select careers? Why is work important?

4. Is the thinking of the young adult different from that of children and adolescents?

THIRTEEN

Physical and Cognitive Development: Early Adulthood

Peter: "Would you send me to school?"

Mrs. Darling (obligingly): "Yes."

Peter: "And then to an office?"

Mrs. Darling: "Very soon."

Peter (passionately): "I don't want to go to school and learn solemn things. No one is going to catch me lady, and make me a man. I want always to be a little boy and to have fun."

JAMES BARRIE
Peter Pan

rmand Delisle, like Peter Pan, decided one day he would rather not grow up. "I'm never gonna grow up," he informed his mother in his sweet little voice, crinkling his nose in that so-cute way of his. "I'm always gonna be your little boy." ¶ "Yeah, right," she said. "Now go out and feed the chickens." But she should have taken him more seriously because Armand, unlike the rest of us who merely flirted with the enchantment of not growing up, developed an unshakable devotion to the idea. He meant what he said. As a result, he didn't have to take school very seriously. So he played more sports than anyone else, and he also missed more school, mostly for hunting or fishing. Mr. Delisle tried quite often to straighten him out, but it didn't help. And Mrs. Delisle...well, she kept him feeding the chickens whenever he happened to be around at the right time. ¶ The rest of us eventually left, went on to other things, mastering the developmental tasks of early adulthood right and left—getting jobs, cars, marriages, careers, children, mortgages.... ¶ Armand is fifty-something now. He still lives at home with his parents. He sometimes says he's looking after the farm, but the hired man really does that. Mostly he fishes and hunts and looks for people who want to play golf or go to Europe. ¶

377

This Chapter

iley (1983) speculates that increasing numbers of young people, like Armand Delisle, are unwilling to grow up. These individuals suffer from **Peter Pan syndrome.** They are unwilling or unable to accept the ordinary responsibilities that come with increasing maturity. Accordingly, they are reluctant to make career decisions, to become economically independent, or, even more, to become emotionally independent and to accept responsibility for others.[*] They are also anxious and lonely because they don't relate well to others who have matured more normally.

But most of us cannot stay little boys and girls and just have fun. We have to go off and learn solemn things. And we have to feed the chickens.

This chapter describes some of what is involved in "growing up"—that is, in making the transition from childhood to adulthood. It deals with the first major stage of adulthood, imaginatively termed **early adulthood** (20 to 40–45); **middle adulthood** (40–45 to 65–70) and **later adulthood** (65–70 onward) follow in *The Lifespan*. This chapter looks at physical development, health, sexual behavior and reproduction, work and careers, and cognitive change in early adulthood. Keep in mind, however, that many of the important activities and events of adulthood can occur at any age.

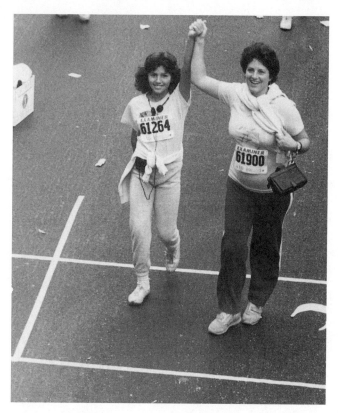

Early adulthood stretches across a wide reach of years—from the end of adolescence to the beginning of middle age at about 45. Thus, this mother and daughter are both young adults, although each is at a different end of that span.

THE TASKS OF EARLY ADULTHOOD

As we saw in Chapter 11, adolescence is generally considered to begin with pubescence (changes leading to sexual maturity) and to end with adulthood. Unfortunately, for those of us who would like things to be simple, both of these events can occur at very different times for individuals of the same sex and do occur about two years apart for individuals of different sexes. Thus, adolescence, as a transition period, has rather fuzzy boundaries.

Some writers describe another developmental period in late adolescence and early adulthood that is often labeled **youth.** Coleman (1974) defines *youth* as the period from age fourteen to age twenty-four—because nobody can be called an adult prior to the age of fourteen and nobody can still be classed a child after the age of twenty-four. That, of course, is not to say that all fourteen-year-olds are childish and all twenty-four-year-olds are mature—witness our Peter Pans. Our definitions are only definitions; they do not alter the exceptions that reality provides.

Early adulthood includes the years between the end of adolescence (or, sometimes, the end of youth) and about age forty or forty-five—which signals the beginning of middle adulthood. However, the period is better understood in terms of the physical, intellectual, and social changes that occur

rather than simply in terms of having attained a given age. One approach to understanding these changes is to look at some of the important developmental tasks of this period.

Developmental tasks are sequential milestones that reflect the acquisition of some major new competence or the occurrence of a social event with important psychological consequences. Some developmental tasks arise from physical maturation; others are more closely tied to social demands and expectations. For example, maturation-related developmental tasks of infancy include learning to walk and talk; two developmental tasks of childhood that are more culturally based are learning how to get along with peers and developing basic skills in reading, writing, and arithmetic. These are achievements with immediate and obviously important consequences for children.

Most of the developmental tasks of adolescence and early adulthood have consequences that are not as immediate, that are more future oriented (Nurmi, 1991). Thus, many of the tasks that are set for adolescents by teachers, parents, and social contexts have to do with expectations and goals for the future. As we saw in the last chapter, even the adoption of an *identity* in adolescence is future oriented insofar as it involves commitment to career, lifestyle, and values.

The developmental tasks of early adulthood, too, are transitional and future oriented: Most of them are important in terms of their future implications for career and family. And as adolescents age into young adulthood, Nurmi (1991)

---
[*]Apropos of which my grandmother muttered, "Why buy the cow when you can have the milk for free?"

informs us, they become even more future oriented. Havighurst and Coleman each describe two somewhat different sets of developmental tasks characteristic of early adulthood.

Havighurst's Tasks of Early Adulthood

Robert Havighurst's (1972) tasks for adolescence and young adulthood are shown in Summary/Interactive Table 13.1. (Later stages are shown in Tables 15.1 and 18.2.) These have to do primarily with establishing a family, a career, and a place in the community—all future-oriented activities. They include things such as courting and selecting a mate, learning to live happily with a partner, starting a family and assuming a parental role, and rearing children (topics that we cover in the next chapter). They include, as well, beginning a career or an occupation (a topic covered in the final sections of this chapter).

There are two important things to keep in mind when looking at developmental tasks. First, they are highly culture specific. They reflect competencies and achievements that are important and relevant primarily in North American societies, as well as in many industrialized societies elsewhere. However, many of these developmental tasks would be totally irrelevant in other societies.

Second, although developmental tasks describe what is common and expected in a given context, failure to achieve a developmental task, or achieving it earlier or later than expected, is not evidence of abnormality. Clearly, not all young adults want a mate. Similarly, some cannot, some will not, and some should not have children. Nor do all need to select and develop a career.

Coleman's Transitional Tasks

According to Coleman (1974), a successful transition between childhood and adulthood requires meeting two classes of developmental objectives. The first concerns the individual's own capacities and abilities, and is referred to as *self-centered;* the second has to do with how the individual relates to others and is termed *other-centered* (see Table 13.1).

Self-centered objectives have to do with the development of skills required for achieving economic independence. They include skills relating to specific occupations or careers, which might be acquired through postsecondary schooling or through the cultivation of some special talent such as that of a musician or singer. They also include skills relating to the management of one's own affairs—for example, handling financial matters and resisting the lure of easy credit. Less obvious, but perhaps no less important, are tasks such as finding and looking after a living space, arranging for utilities, cooking, making decisions about leisure time, and on, and on. And a third self-centered objective has to do with acquiring the skills that are required to be an intelligent consumer, not so much of goods as of the "cultural riches of civilization" (Coleman, 1974, p. 4).

▲ SUMMARY/INTERACTIVE TABLE 13.1

Developmental Tasks of Early Adulthood

Developmental tasks are important social and psychological milestones in human development. Note that they are highly context specific. In contexts where accomplishing a task is seen as highly important (or essential), failure to do so may be linked with considerable distress and unhappiness. However, societies such as ours tolerate and encourage such a wide range of lifestyles and values that failure to accomplish one or more tasks is sometimes totally inconsequential. How many of the tasks of adolescence—and young adulthood—have you now accomplished? How many of the transitional skills have you mastered? Which of those that remain are important to you?

HAVIGHURST'S DEVELOPMENTAL TASKS

PERIOD	TASKS
Adolescence	1. Developing conceptual and problem-solving skills.
	2. Achieving more mature relationships with male and female peers.
	3. Developing an ethical system to guide behavior.
	4. Striving toward socially responsible behavior.
	5. Accepting the changing physique and using the body effectively.
	6. Preparing for an economically viable career.
	7. Achieving emotional independence from parents.
	8. Preparing for marriage and family life.
Young adulthood	1. Courting and selecting a mate.
	2. Learning to live happily with partner.
	3. Starting a family and assuming parent role.
	4. Rearing children.
	5. Assuming home management responsibilities.
	6. Beginning career or occupation.
	7. Assuming appropriate civic responsibilities.
	8. Establishing a social network.

COLEMAN'S TRANSITIONAL SKILLS

SELF-CENTERED SKILLS	USEFUL FOR
Work and occupational skills	Attaining economic independence.
Self-management skills	Making reasonable decisions in the face of wide choices.
Consumer skills	Learning how to use and enjoy culture as well as goods.
Concentrated involvement skills	Succeeding in undertakings; making significant contributions in many areas.

OTHER-CENTERED SKILLS	USEFUL FOR
Social interaction skills	Effective commerce in a variety of situations with different people.
Skills relating to management of others	Assuming responsibility for those who are dependent.
Cooperative skills	Engaging in joint endeavors.

A final self-centered skill required for effective participation in adult society is the ability to engage in concentrated activity. That is, a completely successful transition to adulthood requires individuals to dedicate themselves to certain endeavors, unlike Peter Pan. In many cases, these endeavors will be job-related; in other cases, they might relate to community activities, specific hobbies, religious beliefs, or political interests. Coleman suggests that the greatest of human achievements in all areas are usually the result of concentrated activity.

Among other-centered objectives, Coleman lists three types of experiences that contribute significantly to the adoption of mature social roles. These include the opportunity to interact with a variety of individuals from many different social classes, races, age groups, religions, and occupations; experience in situations where the individual is responsible for others; and experience in activities where the outcomes depend on the cooperation of a number of individuals.

Acquiring these skills should facilitate the transition to adulthood and result in better-adjusted and happier adults.

The Transition to Adulthood

When does childhood finally become adulthood? There is no simple, widely accepted answer. In general, however, the beginning of adulthood coincides roughly with attaining economic and emotional independence from the family. Accord-

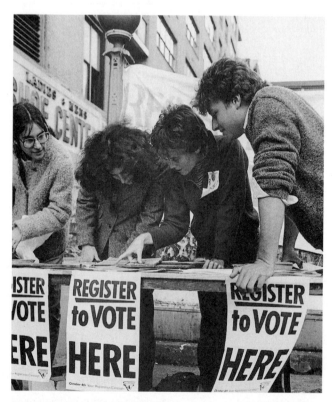

Our continuous societies don't tell us very clearly when adolescence ends and adulthood begins. But, taken together, events such as graduation, getting a driver's license, obtaining permanent employment, getting married—even voting—are important signs of having grown up.

ingly, the most common manifestations of independence are finding some means of financial support (obtaining a job, for example) and establishing a new home, sometimes alone but very often with a friend or a mate. As we saw in Chapter 12, some children leave home early; others stay much longer than normal. Sherrod (1996) notes that where parent–adolescent relations are warmest and most positive, adolescents often find it easier to leave home. And sometimes where relationships have been strained, adolescents find it difficult to leave or to move far away, almost as though they still had some unfinished growing-up business to take care of. We saw, too, that those from nonintact homes (those living in stepfamilies or in single-parent families) are also more likely to leave home early (Tang, 1997).

One of the consequences of today's complex, technological societies has been a prolongation of the transition to adulthood. Simply achieving puberty no longer provides the child with the skills required for optimal participation in adult life. In the days of our grandparents, being able to make babies might have been sufficient qualification for admission to the rank of adulthood. Today, however, a great many of us are required to spend an increasing amount of time learning the skills—the "solemn things"—that we are likely to need later. And during this time, whether we are in college, in the military, unemployed, or elsewhere, we are likely to be neither child nor adult but somewhere in between.

However, we should note again that this swiftly brushed picture of the transition to early adulthood paints only one of several possible scenes. Growing up today does not always entail a prolongation of adolescence—a period of what some term *youth*. There are many who still enter the work force during adolescence. And among these, many become adult in all significant ways far before others of identical age. Similarly, even in the time of our great-grandparents and before, during a period when we imagine life to have consisted largely of idyllic meanderings through pastoral scenes, many people prolonged their adolescence for long periods, unable or perhaps simply unwilling to become adult. Then, as today, there were some people who knew very clearly that we do not all have to become adults (in terms of work roles, responsibilities, and attitudes toward self, others, and life in general). There are those who can dream and play—like children—through the entire lifespan. Let others feed the chickens.

PHYSICAL DEVELOPMENT, NUTRITION, AND HEALTH

One of the reasons that developmental psychology has traditionally been concerned with children and not with adults is simply that children change a great deal—sometimes very rapidly and dramatically; changes among adults are usually less dramatic and less uniform. Hence, the temptation is to think of adulthood as a plateau—a resting state following development and preceding decline. It is worth emphasizing again that contemporary models of lifespan development recognize that change occurs throughout the entire lifespan.

Early adulthood sees the peak of our lives in terms of physical strength, stamina, and endurance, as well as intellectual capacity. This camp counselor can not only run faster than his charges, throw a ball farther, and chop more wood, but inside the binder on his lap he has hidden inventions that will amaze and astound them.

In the area of physical development, adulthood clearly is not a plateau. Although change might not be as predictable or as dramatic as it was in earlier years, there are still some small mountains to climb and a few slopes to descend.

Physical Performance

In the first years of early adulthood, climbing small mountains is no problem, but how steep might the slope look from the threshold of middle age? In the words of the philosopher, "It depends."

Early adulthood is potentially the peak of our physical development in terms of speed, strength, coordination, and endurance, as well as in terms of general health. If we remain fit and active during our twenties and early thirties, we can lift more, run faster, throw farther, work longer, climb higher, and crawl lower than at any other time in our lives. Indeed, our periods of **peak physical performance** are likely to be somewhere between our mid-twenties and our mid-thirties. It is not surprising that Lehman's (1953) studies of the ages at which people were most likely to achieve in a variety of fields found that the twenties and sometimes the early thirties were periods of highest achievement for sports requiring strength, stamina, and coordination (see Table 13.2).

The evidence is clear, Ward (1994) adds, that exercise need not be vigorous or difficult to maintain fitness and flexibility, but that moderate exercise, provided it occurs for three or four thirty-minute periods a week, can be just as effective. However, the evidence also suggests that many young adults

TABLE 13.2

Age Ranges: Peak Athletic Achievement

	AGE RANGE (YEARS)
Professional football players	22–26
Professional prizefighters	25–26
Professional hockey players	26
Professional tennis players	25–29
Leading chess contestants	29–33
Professional golfers	31–36
World billiards records	31–36

Source: From *Age and Achievement* by H. C. Lehman, 1953, Princeton, NJ: Princeton University Press. Copyright 1953, © 1981 by the American Philosophical Society. Reprinted by permission of the publisher.

do not exercise and, as a result, manifest low levels of physical fitness. Pierce and colleagues (1992), who evaluated the fitness levels of 258 male and female college students, report finding relatively low levels of cardiovascular fitness, an indication of a lack of physical activity. Interestingly, however, strength measures for these students remained high.

In a similar study, Glenmark and colleagues (1994) evaluated fifty-five men and twenty-six women at the age of sixteen and again at the age of twenty-seven, looking at both exercise levels and various measures of strength. They, too, found relatively high levels of strength in early adulthood, regardless of physical activity level. Strangely, it seems that there is relatively little correlation between physical exercise and muscle strength, especially for men.

The normal developmental pattern with respect to physical strength sees a very gradual decline following the peak years. This decline is often not particularly noticeable until the forties and is most apparent with respect to back and leg strength.

In addition to a gradual loss of strength following the peak in early adulthood, there is a more noticeable loss of stamina, usually related to poorer aerobic functioning (heart–lung efficiency). Few forty-year-olds can still compete with younger individuals in athletic events and sports requiring strength and endurance (marathons or hockey, for example). For this reason, in the same way that competitions in childhood are made more fair by assigning competitors to age-determined classes, so adult competitions are sometimes separated into age classes. But whereas the older age groups typically outperform the younger groups in childhood, the opposite is true in adulthood. Masters' class (over-forty) marathons are won with slower times than the open classes.

It is important to note that here, as elsewhere, many of the changes and declines of age are neither dramatic nor inevitable. Thus, declines in physical endurance and strength before the age of fifty are scarcely noticeable, so early adulthood is best described as a period of stability rather than one of decline. And with proper exercise and training, many individuals are able to continue performing physically at high levels well into old age—witness Rontoyannis's (1992) seventy-nine-year-old long-distance runner.

Flexibility

Improvements in motor performance after adolescence are highly dependent on practice. Perhaps nowhere is this more evident than in measures of range of joint motion (**flexibility**). In fact, without training, flexibility begins to decline at about the age of twelve. Decline is gradual and often goes unnoticed but, in the absence of training, continues through early adulthood. But with continued exercise, says Ward (1994), the rate of decline for most measures of fitness, including flexibility, slows significantly. In fact, sixty-year-old master athletes can often outperform thirty-year-olds who are customarily inactive. Rontoyannis (1992) reports the case of a seventy-nine-year-old elite long-distance runner whose performance and physiology remained very close to those of other runners who were half a century younger.

Although exercise slows the rate of decline in flexibility, it does not completely prevent it. Flexibility often diminishes even for athletes and others who work physically, simply because few sports and occupations require a full range of motion in all joints. For example, the seventy-nine-year-old runner studied by Rontoyannis (1992) had lost considerable joint flexibility relative to younger runners although he could perform as well as many of them. Loss of flexibility is not nearly as apparent in the case of gymnasts and dancers, whose training is directed toward maintaining flexibility, and who typically retain a high range of motion in all joints through early adulthood. Flexibility can be maintained through training, and perhaps increased through appropriate exercises, even when these are begun very late in life.

Declining flexibility results largely from the fact that certain motions are not generally required in ordinary life. As a result, the individual is often unaware that range of joint movement is gradually decreasing. When it becomes most apparent—for example, in the shorter steps and reduced pelvic rotations of older walkers—it is often dismissed as one of the inevitable consequences of aging. But it may not be completely inevitable given continued high-flexing activity throughout life.

The Senses

There are no dramatic age-related changes in the functioning of our senses through early adulthood: All our senses continue to function about as well at the end of early adulthood as they did at the beginning.

However, there are a number of more subtle changes. Their effects are generally felt so gradually that they are seldom noticed as they are occurring. Morioka and associates (1990) looked at vision and hearing among more than a thousand normal individuals aged five to twenty-four. Both visual accommodation and hearing declined systematically, but very slowly, with age. It seems that the lens in the eye is subject to the effects of aging almost from birth, becoming progressively less flexible and changing its shape so that most individuals become increasingly farsighted as they age.

Hearing, like vision, changes only slightly in early adulthood but, on average, begins to decline in the thirties; decline accelerates after middle age (Belsky, 1990). Losses that do occur are typically more common for men than for women. Hearing losses in early adulthood are most often the consequence of environmental factors, such as prolonged exposure to noisy environments, rather than the effects of age.

Changes in touch sensitivity, as well as in taste and smell, are not apparent in early adulthood.

Health

In the same way that early adulthood is characterized by the peak of physical strength and endurance, as well as of sensory capacity, so is it characterized by the peak of physical health. In particular, many of the infections of childhood become far less common in early adulthood and remain so throughout life. With increasing age, however, there is increased susceptibility to chronic (recurring) medical complaints, such as back and spine problems and heart ailments. Whereas the leading causes of death among young adults are accidents, heart disease and cancer are the leading causes of death among men after age forty-five and among women after age thirty-five (U.S. Bureau of the Census, 1996). In this connection, there have been some dramatic changes in the most common causes of death during the last several decades. In 1940 the leading cause of death was pneumonia and influenza, followed closely by tuberculosis. Fifty years later, influenza and pneumonia accounted for fewer than one-twentieth as many deaths as heart disease and cancer, which now lead the list. And in 1994, tuberculosis accounted for only about 1.2 of every 200,000 deaths in the United States (U.S. Bureau of the Census, 1996).

The majority of adults (over 80 percent) consider themselves to be in "good-to-excellent" health in early adulthood (Bayer, Whissell-Buechy, & Honzik, 1981). Toward the end of this period, however, there is a gradual increase in the number who suffer from a variety of complaints, and a corresponding increase in the number who become more concerned with exercise and health (Hooker & Kaus, 1994). Among women, the most common complaints relate to the reproductive system. These may involve attempts to become pregnant, pregnancy itself, problems relating to menstruation, ovarian cysts and tumors, and infections. Among men, the most common complaints relate to the digestive system; men have three times the incidence of stomach ulcers that women do.

Another sex difference with respect to adult health is that women generally report more illnesses than do men. Ironically, their life expectancies continue to be significantly higher. Some theorize that women are more sensitive to their bodies and are perhaps less likely to dismiss symptoms as inconsequential. Accordingly, they are more likely to seek medical help and thus to report more illnesses. Also, they are more likely to receive assistance when it will be most effective.

Nutrition and Diet

Our strength and stamina, the impressiveness of our peak performances, how long and healthily we live, and perhaps even our level of happiness may have a lot to do with how nutritious our diets are.

■ THE FOOD GUIDE PYRAMID

One of the most important guides for healthy eating used by modern nutritionists is known as the **Food Guide Pyramid.** This guide was first distributed by the United States Department of Agriculture in 1992. As shown in Figure 13.1, it includes five essential food groupings. Recommended daily intakes are represented by the area of the pyramid taken up by each food group. Note that there is a range of recommended servings for each group. The lower limit is intended for people who consume about 1,600 calories a day; the upper limit is for those whose intake is closer to 2,800 calories. What is meant by one serving is described for each food group in Figure 13.1. At the very tip of the pyramid is a sixth

FIGURE 13.1

Food Guide Pyramid, U.S. Department of Agriculture. The sizes of food-group areas of the pyramid represent recommended daily servings for adults. The lower limit is for an average daily consumption of 1,600 calories a day; the upper limit is for 2,800 calories. What counts as a single serving is roughly as follows:

Bread, cereal, rice, and pasta group:	1 slice of bread; ½ cup of cooked cereal; 1 cup of rice or pasta
Vegetable group	1 cup raw leafy vegetables; ½ cup cooked vegetables; ¾ cup vegetable juice
Fruit group	1 medium piece fresh fruit; ½ cup chopped, cooked, or canned fruit; ¾ cup fruit juice
Milk, yogurt, cheese group	1 cup milk or yogurt; 1½ ounces natural cheese; 2 ounces processed cheese
Meat, poultry, fish, beans, eggs, and nut group	2–3 ounces cooked lean meat, fish, or poultry; ½ cup cooked beans; 1 egg; 2 tablespoons peanut butter
Fats, oils, and sweets group	Use sparingly!

KEY
Fat (naturally occurring and added)
Sugar (added)

Fats, Oils, & Sweets
USE SPARINGLY

Milk, Yogurt, & Cheese Group
2–3 SERVINGS

Meat, Poultry, Fish, Dry Beans, Eggs, & Nut Group
2–3 SERVINGS

Vegetable Group
3–5 SERVINGS

Fruit Group
2–4 SERVINGS

Bread, Cereal, Rice, & Pasta Group
6–11 SERVINGS

food grouping that includes fats, oils, and sweets. Recommended daily intake of this group is expressed simply: *use sparingly.*

How well do adults eat? Not very well, apparently. Lehmann (1996) reviews a raft of studies that indicate that the elderly, in particular, are seriously undernourished. And there is evidence that this might also be the case for the young. Millen and associates (1996) compared the dietary patterns of 3,659 adult men and women (ages twenty to seventy) to Food Guide Pyramid guidelines. On the whole, neither men nor women ate very well at all. Men were characterized by low intakes of whole grains, fruits, vegetables, and complex carbohydrates; on the other hand, they had very high intakes of beer and liquor, as well as of high-fat animal foods. Women also had high intakes of alcohol and of various sources of hidden fats. As well, their diets were generally deficient in fruit, vegetable, starch, and dairy intake. And, note the authors, many compounded their poor nutrition habits with chronic dieting.

On a more optimistic note, per capita consumption of red meat in the United States has declined by about 10 percent since 1970; during the same period, consumption of poultry products has almost doubled. Egg consumption has also declined (about 25 percent). Less optimistically, consumption of fats and oils has increased by more than 30 percent, and consumption of milk has been cut by one-third (U.S. Bureau of the Census, 1996).

We know that good nutrition is essential for physical well-being. It's also clear that good nutrition is fundamentally involved in our emotional well-being. Its relationship to mental functioning isn't quite so clear. However, when Wachs and associates (1996) looked at the relationship between diet and measured IQ among adult Egyptians, they found a small but significant relationship between nutrition and intelligence. Specifically, for both men and women, it seems that intake of animal protein was positively related to intellectual performance.

■ OBESITY

In the Millen and associates (1996) investigation of adult nutritional habits, chronic dieting was one of the most common nutritional problems of women. And, in some cases, dieting and loss of weight are highly recommended; unfortunately, in many other cases, dieting is the result of this age's sometimes alarming preoccupation with thinness.

As we saw in Chapter 11, **obesity** is sometimes defined as the condition of being 20 percent or more above normal (average) weight for one's age and sex. **Body mass index (BMI),** which is essentially a ratio of weight to height, is commonly used as a crude index of relative weight. (See Table 11.5 for an explanation of the meaning of BMI and how to compute it.) Although BMI provides a useful guide, it doesn't take into consideration other important variables, such as cardiovascular fitness and fat-mass to lean-mass ratios.

At present, 27.5 percent of all persons in the United States are considered obese (more than 20 percent above ideal weight), with more males than females in that category (29.6 and 25.6 percent, respectively) (U.S. Bureau of the Census,

1996). The most serious medical consequence of obesity is a substantially higher risk of cardiovascular disease and early death. The psychological consequences are less clear. But given current cultural standards of physical attractiveness, and given the importance of being physically attractive, many individuals sense enormous pressure to be thin. Hence the preoccupation with dieting, even among those who, by BMI standards, are normal or essentially underweight. The irony, too, is that dieting is only occasionally successful in bringing about long-term weight loss; in many cases, weight reduction is inconsequential or temporary (G. T. Wilson, 1994).

Unless it is combined with exercise.

Exercise and Lifestyle

Participate! Play tennis! Play racquetball! Play squash! Dance! Join a spa! Take an exercise class! Skate! Ski! Swim! Run! Jog! Well, at least walk.

Literally millions of adults, many of whom have engaged in virtually no unnecessary physical activity since high school or college—and perhaps not even then—embark on exercise programs in early or middle adulthood. In fact, slightly more than 40 percent of all persons above eighteen claim to exercise or play sports regularly (U.S. Bureau of the Census, 1996). And many undertake these programs with the same dedication and determination that they bring to their careers—and perhaps to other aspects of their lives. Why? Simply, to be happy and healthy. That is, after all, what most of us want. Exercise, we are told, will make us healthier, may enable us to live longer, and should make us trimmer, more fit, and perhaps even more attractive, given our contemporary cultural standards of physical attractiveness.

How valid are these claims? Research leaves little doubt that exercise contributes significantly to good health. Numerous studies of cardiovascular fitness have repeatedly found higher levels of fitness and lower incidence of coronary heart disease among those who exercise regularly than among those whose lives are more sedentary (Ward, 1994). In addition, exercise is important in reducing the percentage of body fat and in increasing muscle and bone density (Sambrook, Kelly, & Eisman, 1993).

Active lifestyles are characteristic of an increasing number of young adults. Such lifestyles not only contribute to increased health and happiness, but are also an important way of meeting people.

oday, my radio spoke of obesity. The image that we once had of the *gordito* (fat person) as a jovial, happy-go-lucky person is no longer valid, said the announcer. In addition to the health risks of obesity, newer research shows that:

- obese women are, on average, 20 percent less likely to succeed in finding a mate

- obese men are 11 percent less likely to be successful in that undertaking

- the average income of obese persons in the United States is significantly lower than is average for others of their age and sex

1. *Ronda de Actualidades, Radio Nacional de España (Sin Fronteras*, Nov. 2, 1997).

To Do

Using library or computer resources, see if you can verify these observations. List other discoveries about obesity that result from your search.

On the Net

See

http://zorba.uafadm.alaska.edu/coop-ext/efnep/pyramid.html

for information and suggestions regarding applications of the Food Guide Pyramid. See

http://odphp.osophs.dhhs.gov/pubs/1997.htm#Nutrition

for information regarding free copies of the Food Guide Pyramid.

But does exercise make us happier? Does it affect us psychologically? Blumenthal and associates (1982) say yes. They investigated the effects of exercise on a group of sixteen subjects, aged twenty-five to sixty-one, who had registered for a ten-week adult fitness program. At the beginning of the program, all subjects were administered a battery of three psychological tests to assess mood, anxiety, and some general aspects of everyday functioning, such as sleep patterns and social habits. A control group, consisting of healthy but sedentary individuals of similar age, was also administered these same tests.

The exercise program for the sixteen experimental subjects consisted of a ten-minute routine of stretching exercises, followed by forty-five minutes of walking or running, three times a week over a period of ten weeks. All exercise periods were under medical supervision. Control-group members continued as before, without any regular exercise program.

At the end of the ten-week period, individuals in both the experimental and the control groups were again administered the three psychological instruments. The results are clear and striking. Whereas the groups had initially been similar on each of these instruments, the experimental group now felt less tension, fatigue, depression, and confusion, and experienced significant reductions in immediate and general anxiety. And, as expected, physiological measures indicated significant improvements in the experimental groups.

Additional evidence of the psychological benefits of exercise is provided by Puretz, Haas, and Meltzer (1996), who presented questionnaires to 497 women who exercised regularly. Responses indicated that about one-quarter of these women had initially been motivated by a desire to lose weight; about an equal number had started exercising for health reasons. Now all continued to exercise (more than half had been doing so for over five years) not only because of their desire for continued weight control and feelings of good health, but as much for the pleasure and tension reduction that also resulted. (See "In the News and on the Net: Fat Chance.")

Drug Use and High-Risk Behaviors

Whereas exercise generally has a positive effect on health and well-being, recreational use of drugs typically does not. Of the drugs used by young adults, alcohol and nicotine are by far the most common. In fact, they are the two that show only slight decline after age twenty-five; marijuana, cocaine, stimulants, and all others show a marked decline (U.S. Bureau of the Census, 1996). The health consequences of nicotine use and heavy alcohol consumption are well-known.

There is some evidence that the health-related behaviors of young adults are often quite similar to those of adolescents—that is, their exercise habits, their attention to nutrition, and their participation in high-risk behaviors may not be very different. For example, a survey of 1,408 randomly selected Texas college students revealed the following (Wiley et al., 1996):

- Eighty-nine percent had recently consumed alcohol.

- One-third considered themselves regular smokers.

- Eighty-one percent had had sexual intercourse.

- One-quarter of the sexually active men had had more than ten sex partners.

- Fewer than half of all sexually active subjects, male and female, had used a condom during their last intercourse.

During middle adulthood, however, there appears to be a sharp reduction in a variety of high-risk behaviors. U.S. Census data indicate, for example, that use of virtually all drugs, including alcohol and cigarettes, declines after the age of twenty-five. Still, one-quarter of all U.S. residents above age eighteen are current smokers, 60 percent don't exercise regularly or play sports, 27 percent are overweight, and 45 percent don't eat breakfast (U.S. Bureau of the Census, 1996).

Stress

The effects of **stress** on the health of the young adult are not as clear as those of drugs such as alcohol and nicotine. This is largely because stress is far more difficult to define and measure than is alcohol or nicotine use. In addition, its effects are more subtle and may involve a greater number of systems. Interestingly, one of the effects of stress seems to be an increased probability of abusing alcohol and drugs (Labouvie, 1990).

As we saw in Chapter 10, *stress* may be defined in terms of stimuli that make excessive demands on the individual, or in terms of responses that are accompanied by the physiological changes of high arousal. We saw, too, that in some ways a stress response is an adaptive response. The physiological changes of arousal—the sudden spurt of adrenaline, for example—are useful in mobilizing the individual's systems for responding. However, prolonged exposure to stress can eventually lead to a "stress overload" and to a consequent breakdown of the adaptive response.

Excessive stress in childhood is sometimes evident in sleeping or eating disturbances, depression, and a variety of physical complaints. The consequences of stress for adults are perhaps not very different from those for children. Thus, stress is linked to several physical complaints that sometimes appear in early adulthood, including gastrointestinal problems such as ulcers, heart problems, and high blood pressure (Longstreth & Wolde-Tsadik, 1993).

In general, high stress is often associated with **anxiety**, and high anxiety is one of the most common of all psychiatric symptoms. There is evidence that stress in adulthood can interact with other stressors to which the individual might have been exposed in childhood, increasing the probability of psychiatric disorder and of drug and alcohol abuse. For example, Landerman, George, and Blazer (1991), who studied a sample of 3,801 adults, found that those who had recently been exposed to stress and who had, as children, been exposed to stress associated with parental mental illness or divorce were now more likely to suffer from depression and were more vulnerable to alcohol abuse.

■ SOURCES OF STRESS

Sources of stress in everyday life might include a variety of frustrations, demands, and conflicts having to do with social relationships, spouse and children, career, and so on. They might also include significant events or changes. Several theorists suggest that all change is stressful—even pleasant changes such as going on vacation. In Chapter 10, there is a scale of potential changes in the lives of children ranked in terms of their probable stressful impact. Interactive Table 13.3 presents a similar scale for adults, the **social readjustment rating scale.** In an early study involving 400 subjects, Rahe (1972) reported that those who claimed scores of 150 or lower on this scale in the preceding year were likely to remain healthy; those whose scores were above 300 were much more likely to develop physical as well as mental problems. Similarly, Monroe and associates (1996) found that under some circumstances, undesirable life events increased the likelihood of a recurrence of severe depression among individuals who had already suffered an episode of depression.

■ INDIVIDUAL RESPONSES TO STRESS

Not all adults respond to stressful events in the same way. Psychology and medicine have sometimes found it useful to distinguish between two types of individuals, identifiable largely in terms of the level of stress that seems to permeate their lives. These types, well popularized in literature, are labeled "Type A" and "Type B" (Friedman & Rosenman, 1974).

Type A individuals are hard-driving, aggressive, ambitious, impatient, and competitive (D. F. Smith, 1994). These are individuals who drive themselves mercilessly, who sense most keenly the unrelenting pressures of time and the urgency of their lives. In contrast, **Type B individuals** are slow, relaxed, easygoing. They speak more softly, tend to impose few deadlines on themselves, and do not, in general, respond to life with the same sense of urgency that drives Type A's.

Type A and B individuals are often identified by means of the Jenkins Activity Survey, which asks questions such as "Do people sometimes tell you that you eat too fast?" or "Do the people with whom you work see you as being aggressive and achievement oriented?" (Jenkins, Zyzanski, & Rosenman, 1971). Researchers have found that about 40 percent of the population is Type A; the remainder is Type B. Clearly, however, the types are less a dichotomy than a continuum: Some Type A individuals would manifest extremes of Type A behavior, and others would be only slightly different from Type B individuals.

The medical profession has found this typology particularly useful because of an apparent relationship between Type A behavior and coronary problems (Deary et al., 1994). Some studies indicate that Type A individuals are approximately twice as likely as Type B individuals to suffer fatal heart attacks. Small wonder that being a Type A individual has sometimes been accorded the same weight as a contributor to coronary problems as high blood pressure, high cholesterol level, smoking, and obesity. However, subsequent research has not always found as high a relationship between Type A behavior and coronary problems as did earlier research. But what this research has been finding is that certain components of the Type A personality are more important than others in contributing to health problems. In particular, Type A individuals who are hostile and angry seem to be more prone to coronary problems than Type A's who are simply highly achievement oriented, aggressive, and fast paced (Deary et al., 1994).

Social Readjustment Rating Scale

Major, and even minor, changes can be sources of stress. Some theorists suggest that all change is stressful and that its effects are cumulative. You can obtain a rough estimate of the stress in your own life by using the scale reproduced here. Simply total the life-change unit values associated with each of the life events you have experienced during the past twelve months. Scores of 150 or less are associated with continued health and happiness; scores above 300 are sometimes associated with later problems. However, these generalizations are based on averages and do not reflect countless individual exceptions. Some people are remarkably resistant to stress; others buckle more easily.

RANK	LIFE EVENT	MEAN VALUE (LIFE-CHANGE UNITS)	RANK	LIFE EVENT	MEAN VALUE (LIFE-CHANGE UNITS)
1	Death of spouse.	100	23	Son or daughter leaving home.	29
2	Divorce.	73	24	Trouble with in-laws.	29
3	Marital separation.	65	25	Outstanding personal achievement.	28
4	Jail term.	63	26	Spouse begins or stops work.	26
5	Death of close family member.	63	27	Begin or end school.	26
6	Personal injury or illness.	53	28	Change in living conditions.	25
7	Marriage.	50	29	Revision of personal habits.	24
8	Fired at work.	47	30	Trouble with boss.	23
9	Marital reconciliation.	45	31	Change in work hours or conditions.	20
10	Retirement.	45	32	Change in residence.	20
11	Change in health of family member.	44	33	Change in schools.	20
12	Pregnancy.	40	34	Change in recreation.	19
13	Sex difficulties.	39	35	Change in church activities.	19
14	Gain of new family member.	39	36	Change in social activities.	18
15	Business readjustment.	39	37	Mortgage or loan less than $10,000.	17
16	Change in financial state.	38	38	Change in sleeping habits.	16
17	Death of close friend.	37	39	Change in number of family get-togethers.	15
18	Change to different line of work.	36	40	Change in eating habits.	15
19	Change in number of arguments with spouse.	35	41	Vacation.	13
20	Mortgage over $10,000.	31	42	Christmas.	12
21	Foreclosure of mortgage or loan.	30	43	Minor violations of the law.	11
22	Change in responsibilities at work.	29			

Source: From "The Social Readjustment Rating Scale" by T. H. Holmes and R. H. Rahe, 1967, *Journal of Psychosomatic Research, 11,* pp. 213–218. Reprinted by permission of Pergamon Press, Ltd.

D. F. Smith (1994) suggests that, at least to some extent, Type A personalities may be physiologically based. Nevertheless, it is worth noting that through training in relaxation, and with proper motivation, Type A individuals can become more like Type B's (Ovcharchyn, Johnson, & Petzel, 1981). At the very least, such individuals might learn to relax sufficiently so that they can effectively rid themselves of the damaging effects of stress, although they continue to be hard-driving Type A's in the workplace. (See Summary Table 13.4.)

SEX AND REPRODUCTION

The most dramatic changes in the reproductive system throughout the entire lifespan are those that occur in adolescence. It is then, as we saw in Chapter 11, that profound hormonal changes trigger the well-known series of develop-

ments that defines pubescence and that leads eventually to puberty (sexual maturity). Within approximately a year of the girl's first menstrual period and the boy's first ejaculation of semen (although sometimes sooner), each is capable of becoming a parent.

Normal Sexual Responses

For most, a sexual response is a personal, private, and poetic thing. But science has little patience with poetry and privacy; it insists on being clinical even about the most profound of life's mysteries.

The normal sexual response in both males and females, science informs us, is best described as a four-stage event: excitement, plateau, orgasm, and resolution (Masters & Johnson, 1966). **Excitement** is a preparatory phase leading to sexual arousal. Major changes that mark the excitement phase in females include vaginal lubrication and expansion and

▲ SUMMARY TABLE 13.4
Physical Development, Nutrition, and Health

TOPICS	EXPLANATIONS/RESEARCH FINDINGS
Physical performance	■ Peak physical performance occurs mid 20s to mid 30s. ■ Exercise is important to maintain fitness and flexibility. ■ Following the peak, there is a gradual loss of stamina (poorer aerobic functioning) and a less noticeable decline in strength.
Flexibility	■ In the absence of training or exercise, flexibility (range of joint motion) declines beginning at age 12.
Senses	■ No dramatic age-related changes in sensory functioning through early adulthood.
Health	■ A reduction in acute infections and diseases of childhood. ■ Increase in more chronic conditions. ■ Majority of early adults in good health.
Nutrition and diet	■ Food Guide Pyramid is a graphic representation of recommended daily intake of 5 food groups. ■ Some evidence suggests that the elderly are undernourished; many of those younger make bad nutritional selections. ■ Obesity is a serious nutritional problem, highly resistant to long-term change as a result of dieting (unless combined with exercise). ■ Chronic dieting and excessive preoccupation with weight is another serious nutrition-related problem.
Exercise and lifestyle	■ Physical and health benefits. ■ Benefits in terms of psychological well-being and happiness.
Drug use and high-risk behaviors	■ Many young adults engage in high-risk behaviors not very different from those of some adolescents (drug misuse; unprotected sex; high alcohol consumption). ■ Drug use and high-risk behaviors decline after 25.
Stress	■ Excessive stress may have negative physical and psychological consequences. ■ Sources of stress include a variety of demands and frustrations, as well as major life changes. ■ Type A individuals have lives that seem more permeated by stress (hard driving, ambitious, aggressive). ■ Type B individuals seem less stressed (relaxed, easy-going, nonaggressive).

distension of the vagina; in males, excitement is characterized by erection of the penis.

The **plateau** is a period of continuing sexual arousal following initial excitement but preceding orgasm. Among women, the plateau entails continued swelling of the vagina, some changes in the labia ("lips" surrounding vaginal opening), breast enlargement and sometimes nipple erection, increased heart rate and blood pressure, and occasionally a flushing of chest, neck, and face. Among men, the plateau is marked by a maintenance of the erection, enlargement of the testes, occasional nipple erection, and a sharp increase in pulse rate, blood pressure, and respiration rate.

The orgasmic phase in women entails between five and fifteen contractions of the outer third of the vagina, some uterine contractions, some muscle spasms, and a marked increase in respiration. **Orgasm** in men may involve explosive contractions of the urethra as sperm is emitted (**seminal emission** or ejaculation), muscle spasms, rapid increase in respiration rate, and maximum heart and blood pressure levels. However, in many cases, especially among older men, orgasm does not necessarily involve seminal emission (Gibson, 1992). The two events are confused, says Gibson, because they ordinarily occur together for younger men.

In both males and females, **resolution** involves a rapid return to a preexcitement state.

There are two important differences between male and female response patterns. First, immediately following the male orgasm, there is a period, termed refractory, during which the male is incapable of a second orgasm. This period may be as short as a few minutes or as long as several hours. (See Figure 13.2.)

Second, whereas the usual male pattern of sexual response is a single excitement–plateau–orgasm–resolution cycle, there are three common patterns of female sexual response. The first (A in Figure 13.3) involves excitement, the plateau, an ensuing orgasm, and the possibility of one or more subsequent orgasms (without recycling through the excitement phase), followed by the resolution after the final orgasm. The second (B) is marked by a longer plateau and a slower resolution, but no orgasm. And the third (C) is a faster response cycle that goes relatively directly from excitement to orgasm and returns equally rapidly to a normal state.

In both men and women, the entire sexual response cycle is typically accompanied by physical sensations that vary from mildly to intensely pleasurable. In light of this, and given its biological significance, it is little wonder that sexuality is among the most important of human motivations and behaviors.

Adult Sexual Behavior

Following a series of ninety-minute interviews with 3,432 randomly selected adults aged eighteen to fifty-nine, Michael and associates (1994) report on some of the sexual practices of American men and women. Among their findings:

Male sexual response. (Based on Masters & Johnson, 1966.)

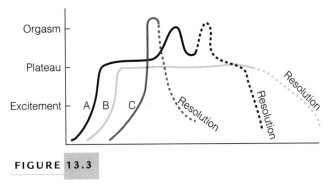

Three female sexual response cycles. (Based on Masters & Johnson, 1966.)

- Only 3 percent of all respondents claimed to have had five or more sex partners during the preceding year. The vast majority, more than 80 percent, reported having only one partner, or none.

- The majority of married people (75 percent of the men and 85 percent of the women) claim that they are faithful to their spouses.

- On average, American males report they have had six sex partners during their lifetimes; women report they have had two.

- Forty-one percent of married couples have sex at least twice a week.

- Married people and couples who live together have sex more often than single people.

- Seventy-five percent of married women and 95 percent of married men report always or almost always having an orgasm during sex.

The results of this survey, the authors point out, indicate that most people are not having sex as often as had been thought, and that they are doing so primarily with their spouses or partners with whom they live.

There are two kinds of problems that can interfere with sexual responsiveness and reproduction: sexual dysfunctions and infertility.

Sexual Dysfunctions

Sexual disturbances of various kinds are often temporary and appear to be relatively common. But because of the secrecy that surrounds these issues, most people who suffer from these dysfunctions think that they are rare and experience needless anxiety. In one longitudinal survey that consisted of four interviews of a sample of young adults over a ten-year period (between ages twenty and thirty), one out of two of the females and one out of three of the males reported sexual disturbances (Ernst, Foldenyi & Angst, 1993).

The most common **sexual dysfunction** among men who consult sex therapists is **erectile dysfunction** (impotence)—the inability to achieve or to maintain an erection. This condition is more common with increasing age. In as many as 50 percent of all cases, it may have physical or medical origins; in others, its roots are more psychological. Among its possible causes are certain drugs (Fleischhacker et al., 1994), as well as anxiety and depression (Holzapfel, 1993).

Premature ejaculation—the inability to control ejaculation—is a relatively common sexual dysfunction among men in early adulthood, but becomes less common with increasing age (Gibson, 1992).

Retarded ejaculation—essentially the opposite of premature ejaculation—is characterized by an inability to achieve orgasm during sexual intercourse. In many cases, retarded ejaculation is situational—that is, it is manifested in some situations but not others. Evidence suggests that stress and anxiety are often involved.

Female sexual dysfunctions include inability to derive pleasure from sexual intercourse; **vaginismus,** or involuntary contractions of the vagina that make intercourse painful or impossible; and inability to achieve orgasm. Inability to achieve orgasm is not viewed as a problem unless the woman expects that she should experience one. As we saw, a female sexual response cycle without an orgasm is common and pleasurable for many women.

Hypoactive sexual desire is yet another sexual dysfunction that appears to be highly common but that is not easily defined or treated (Trudel, Ravart, & Matte, 1993). Put simply, hypoactive sexual desire is manifested by a lower than normal interest in sexual activity. It affects both males and females, but appears to be more prevalent among females. Katz, Frazer, and Wilson (1993) report that there has been a significant increase in lack of sexual desire among young adults in recent years. Their data suggest that much of it is related to higher general sexual anxiety associated with fear of AIDS.

All of these sexual dysfunctions can be treated, sometimes by means of psychological–sexual therapy, sometimes medically. Of them, only severe vaginismus, retarded ejaculation, and impotence are likely to result in infertility—the inability to produce children.

Infertility

With puberty, most men and women not only acquire the capacity to respond sexually but also develop strong urges to do so. There appear to be few major changes in these urges or in the capacity to respond through early adulthood—although frequency of sexual intercourse declines rapidly within the first few years of marriage (see Chapter 14). Some evidence indicates that men might, on the average, be slightly less easily aroused toward the end of early adulthood, and achieve orgasm more slowly. At the same time, through early adulthood, women apparently become more capable of achieving orgasm during intercourse (Gibson, 1992).

Biologically, women and men are capable of producing healthy infants throughout early adulthood. As we saw in Chapter 3, however, the probability of genetic and birth complications increases with advancing age of both parents, but especially the mother.

Infertility (the inability to conceive a child), however, is a relatively common problem among both men and women. Among women, it is most often due to blocked Fallopian tubes, the blockage usually resulting from infections such as chlamydia and acute pelvic inflammatory disease (Quan, 1994). In addition, fertility in women drops slowly from the age of twenty. One reason is that ovulation, which may initially occur regularly, sometimes becomes less predictable as menstrual cycles become less regular. Nor does ovulation always occur with every cycle. Thus, on the average, even when they are fertile, older women do not become pregnant as easily as younger women.

Infertility in women is also sometimes associated with alterations in the menstrual cycle, or complete cessation of menstruation (amenorrhea) as a result of strenuous exercise. This is essentially an adaptive response to metabolic stress in the body, notes Bonen (1994). This type of infertility is temporary, however, and usually reverses with a change in exercise patterns.

Fertility among men also decreases very gradually through early adulthood, largely because of a decrement in the production of sperm. However, this decrement is very slight before middle age—most men in very late adulthood still produce sperm. However, the number of viable sperm produced by elderly men is ordinarily too small to make conception very likely. In a small number of cases (about 1 percent), infertility among men is related to tumors on the testes, to brain tumors, or to other uncommon medical problems (Jarow, 1994).

It's important to note that decreasing fertility among men and women in early adulthood is not a primary aging process—that is, it is not an inevitable consequence of age. In fact, the principal causes of changes in fertility rate during this period are infections and diseases. And although these become more probable with advancing age, they are not a result of aging.

As is discussed in Chapter 14, many women are now having children somewhat later than in the past. Although the

▲ SUMMARY TABLE 13.5
Sex and Reproduction in Early Adulthood

TOPICS	EXPLANATIONS/RESEARCH FINDINGS
Four phases of normal sexual response	■ Excitement (preparatory phase; erection/lubrication). ■ Plateau (continued sexual arousal). ■ Orgasm (climax; highly individual, especially in women where multiple orgasms or different kinds of orgasmic response are possible; generally involves explosive contractions with ejaculation in men). ■ Resolution (rapid return to preexcitement phase).
Adult sexual behavior	■ Appears not to be highly promiscuous. ■ Sexual activity may not be as frequent as once believed.
Sexual dysfunctions	■ Defined as inability to perform normally sexually. ■ Among males, most common dysfunctions are erectile dysfunction (impotence), premature ejaculation (inability to withhold ejaculation), and retarded ejaculation (inability to achieve ejaculation). ■ Among women, most common dysfunctions are vaginismus (painful contractions of the vagina), inability to derive pleasure from intercourse, and hypoactive sexual desire (low sex drive).
Infertility	■ Inability to conceive. ■ Most common cause among women is blocked fallopian tubes, often due to chlamydia or pelvic inflammatory disease. ■ Among men, possible causes include too low sperm count, problems with the testes, or other medical problems.

overall birthrate has scarcely risen in North America in recent decades, the number of first births to women over the age of thirty has increased by more than 35 percent (U.S. Bureau of the Census, 1996). One reason for this is that recent decades have seen some profound changes in female work and career patterns. (See Summary Table 13.5.)

■ WORK AND CAREER PREPARATION

One of the most important developmental tasks for making a successful transition from youth to adulthood is finding some sort of "adult" employment. But finding employment is far more than simply a mundane developmental task; it is fundamentally important to who and what we are. And the ease with which we make the transition from nonwork to work, either at the beginning of our adult years or at the end (or, perhaps, even in the middle), is fundamentally important to our well-being.

Employment: Some Definitions

Although terms such as *career, vocation, job,* and *occupation* are often used interchangeably, their precise meanings are somewhat different. The narrowest of these terms is **job**, which refers to the specific tasks or duties that the worker performs. Thus, one of the jobs undertaken by a caretaker might be to empty wastebaskets. In much the same way, there are jobs associated with being a lawyer or a dentist—specific tasks that are part of the individual's work responsibilities.

Occupation is a more general term than *job;* it refers to a broad employment classification such as accounting, clerking, selling, or being a mechanic. Occupations are categories of work that cover a variety of related jobs.

The term **career** is far broader than either *occupation* or *job.* It does not refer to any specific occupation or employment but to an entire range of related occupations. Thus, a career will often span an entire lifetime of work and may include a host of related occupations (each with its own jobs). A career in food services, for example, might include such occupations as busboy, waiter, bartender, food manager, convention manager, and chain food-services supervisor. It is possible, of course, to have more than one career in a single lifetime.

In its strictest sense, the term **vocation** refers to a "calling" and has traditionally been restricted to the clergy and to certain white-collar professions. Thus, one can have a vocation for the ministry, a vocation for medicine, or a vocation for the law; it is less appropriate to refer to a laborer's or a secretary's vocation.

In this text, as in many other contexts, **work** is often used as a general term to include all manner of occupations, careers, professions, jobs, and vocations.

Why Work?

Work serves a variety of economic, social, and psychological purposes. Its economic functions include what we usually mean when we speak of "making a living"—that is, they have to do with the satisfaction of physical needs. In industrialized societies such as ours, however, the economic benefits of work often go considerably beyond putting a chicken (or a zucchini, for those who prefer) in our pots. Many people can put a dozen or more chickens in their pots. That's one sign of "success."

The social purposes of work are reflected in opportunities for social interaction and the development of friendships. More than this, work provides people with status and responsibility, and gives them reasons for feeling important and wanted.

The psychological purposes of work, closely related to its social purposes, have a lot to do with the development of confidence and self-esteem. It is through working and earning that people achieve a sense of self-worth and satisfaction. More than this, it is from our work that many of us derive important aspects of our identities. It is no accident that many of us answer the question "What do you do for a living?" with "I am a(n) (fill in the blank)." In a sense, we are what we do.

Changes in Work Opportunities

In recent decades, there have been some startling changes in the nature of the work that people do in Western societies. We went very rapidly from societies that were primarily agricultural to societies that were increasingly industrial. Now we have entered a third phase—that of the technological society. The technological society mechanizes production and services; it thrives on the collection, storage, analysis, and dissemination of information; and it creates a vast array of new jobs while at the same time eliminating a great many others. In addition, it requires a far more educated work force than was the case a scant few decades ago (Hansen, 1993).

Coupled with the rapid industrialization of society, there are some continuing demographic trends. The population of the entire industrialized Western world is rapidly aging. This means that there will be proportionally fewer children and young adults in coming decades, and proportionally more middle-aged and older adults. These changes are reflected very clearly in the fact that the most rapidly growing occupational categories are related to health care.

■ JOB TRENDS

Today's high-tech society presents an incredible array of jobs, an increasing number of which have replaced unskilled, low-education occupations. Furthermore, the nature of these jobs is in a constant state of flux, as are the markets that provide employment. For example, since 1976, there has been an increase of more than 50 percent in technical and related occupations, as well as in managerial and administrative jobs—and similar increases in professional specialties and in marketing. During the same period, service occupations increased by only 28 percent, and manufacturing and labor jobs by only 3 percent; meanwhile, forestry, farming, and fishing occupations declined by 8 percent (Silvestri & Lukasiewicz, 1989).

Forecasts of future occupations have been controversial and unreliable, notes Bailey (1991). On the one hand are those who argue that rapid technological advances leading to increasing automation will greatly reduce the demand for unskilled, low-level employment, and that most of the jobs created in the future will require education and training beyond the high school level (Johnston & Packer, 1987). On the other hand are those who note that modern technology is increasingly successful in reducing the need for trained and educated workers, and that the ultimate effect of this is that less rather than more education will be required of many

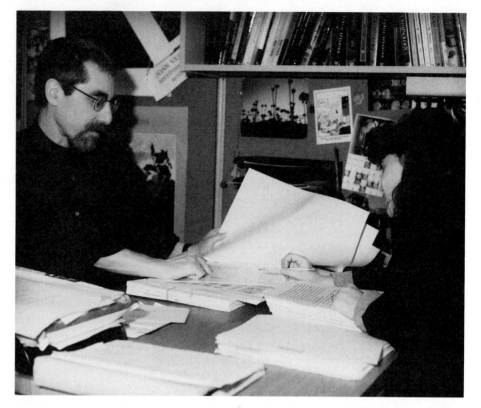

Rapidly developing technological societies present increasingly frequent changes in work opportunities. There is little guarantee that the book-building in which these two are engaged will not have been replaced by some new, computer-driven job—maybe next week.

workers in the future—witness the "dumbing down" of cashier jobs as one example, where electronic bar-code readers automatically enter prices, or the use of icons of tiny hamburgers, fries, or sodas on multikeyed, computerized registers so that fast-food employees need not even know how to read or recognize numbers (let alone add or subtract).

Our best guess, says Bailey (1991), is that there will be a gradual increase in the need for highly educated workers, although lower-skill occupations such as sales, janitorial and cleaning work, and food or beverage service occupations are projected to have a very large absolute growth (see "At a Glance: Projected Job Trends, 1994–2005" and Figure 13.4). And the need for upgrading within occupations will become greater as workers are forced to keep up with rapidly changing technology.

■ OTHER JOB CHANGES

Other important changes in employment include the fact that more than half of all adult women are now in the work force (U.S. Bureau of the Census, 1996; *Canada Yearbook,* 1997), an increase in part-time work, significantly higher educational levels among workers, and a reduction in the number of people available for lower-paying jobs. In addition, there is a vastly increased job turnover rate and much higher job mobility, not only among different occupations within a single career but also among different careers. How is the young adult (or adolescent) to choose from among so many careers? Or the older adult, for that matter? Do we naturally drift toward a career? Do our personal talents and interests urge us gently down the right paths? Or should we be guided? And if we are to be guided, how should it be done?

Theories of Career Choice

There are two general groups of theories that have influenced much of the thinking in career guidance. One is based on the notion that individuals and jobs should be matched with respect to the individual's interests and talents and the job's requirements. This approach is sometimes referred to as **job–person matching**. The other emphasizes the development of career-related abilities rather than simple job-interest matching and is illustrated by Super's **life-span, life-space approach** and by Ginzberg's **developmental career model**. A third family-based model combines aspects of these two basic models, but pays more attention to the individual's context.

■ JOB–PERSON MATCHING: STRONG AND HOLLAND

Guidance counselors who adopt the job–person matching model attempt to identify talents that are essential for specific occupations, administer batteries of tests to discover talents, and then try to match the two. The matching generally takes into account the individual's interests as well as talents. Interests are very often measured using the highly respected **Strong Interest Inventory**. Strong's inventory, now more than seventy years old, was designed primarily to measure vocational interest and was developed largely by looking at the characteristics that people in different occupations had in common. The original inventory contained only ten different scales, but more have been added over the years. One way of validating these scales has been to administer them to adolescents or young adults and then look at whether the occu-

Projected Job Trends, 1994–2005

There are hundreds of jobs today that didn't exist a mere one or two decades ago. Yet the fastest-growing job markets are those that have existed for centuries. Seven of the ten jobs projected to grow fastest by the year 2005, for example, are health-care related—a direct result of our aging population coupled with advances in medical knowledge and technology.

The most rapidly declining job markets result from the use of computers and automation technology in the work-place. Retail salespersons is currently the single largest job category (almost 4 million workers in 1994) and is projected to be the largest in 2005; second is general managers and top executives, with janitors close behind (U.S. Bureau of the Census, 1996).

FIGURE 13.4

Fastest-growing and fastest-declining jobs: moderate estimates, 1994–2005. (Based on U.S. Bureau of the Census, 1996, p. 409.)

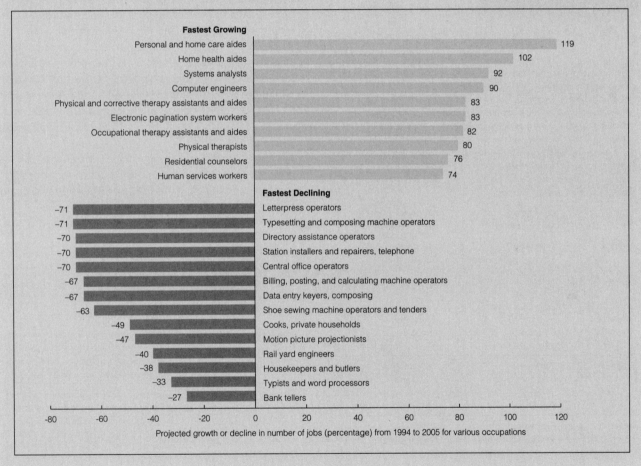

pations they select match the interests indicated by their test performance. A recent review of the history of this instrument concludes that it has become a highly valid predictor of vocational choice (Donnay, 1997).

A well-known example of the job–person matching approach is that of Holland (1992, 1994), whose **Holland**

Vocational Preference Inventory owes much to the Strong. It identifies six specific combinations of traits and interests, labeled "coping styles": realistic, intellectual, social, conventional, enterprising, and artistic. Evidence indicates that these styles are highly stable in given individuals, even over a long period of time—hence their usefulness in career guidance

(Helwig & Myrin, 1997). The six styles, and recommended occupations, are summarized in Interactive Table 13.6.

Trait–interest matching approaches to career guidance have proved highly useful and continue to be widely used both in schools and in placement and employment offices (Stoltz-Loike, 1996). Computer-assisted career guidance (CACG) systems are widely used to match individuals with careers, to suggest alternatives, or to permit exploration of various careers. There are a large number of such systems available (Sampson & Reardon, 1990; Sampson, Reardon, & Lenz, 1991).

■ DEVELOPMENTAL CAREER MODELS: GINZBERG AND SUPER

Developmental career models are concerned less with matching jobs and persons than with understanding and facilitating the chronological development of career decisions.

INTERACTIVE TABLE 13.6

A Job–Person Matching Model Based on Holland's Coping Styles

You who have recently made (or may soon make) a career decision might find it interesting to examine the goodness-of-fit between your characteristics and interests and the decision you have made (may make). If you have a realistic notion of your characteristics and interests (shown in column 2), you can assess your type (column 1) and see whether what you plan to do is anything like the corresponding list in column 3. If the match seems strained, don't be alarmed; perhaps you don't know yourself very well. Besides, global matching models of this kind are not sufficiently sensitive to slot everybody into the very best of all possible careers, and, for many, there may be a very wide range of nearly best of all possible careers.

TYPE	CHARACTERISTICS AND INTERESTS	RECOMMENDED JOB SETTINGS
Realistic	Concrete Mechanically oriented Motor activity	Gas station Construction Labor Skilled trade Farm
Intellectual	Abstract Creative Introverted	Research Academics
Artistic	Subjective Creative Intuitive Emotional	Performing arts Visual arts
Social	Extroverted Socially concerned High verbal ability High affiliative needs	Social work Teaching Counseling
Enterprising	Domineering Adventurous Impulsive Extroverted	Leadership roles Planning roles Real estate development
Conventional	Unimaginative High self-control Want social approval Systematic	Accounting Banking Business/clerical

These models typically view career choices as beginning in childhood and as involving a gradual, decision-making process. Among the best known of developmental guidance models are those advanced by Ginzberg (1972) and Super (1990, 1994).

Ginzberg's model describes three sequential preadult stages in career development: the fantasy period, the tentative period, and the realistic period (see Table 13.7).

The fantasy period lasts until approximately age ten or twelve and is often characterized by highly unrealistic notions of career choice. This is the stage during which children want to be astronauts, baseball players, physicians, or presidents.

During the tentative period (ages eleven to sixteen), adolescents gradually become aware of the requirements of different careers, as well as of their own personal interests and capabilities. Slowly and tentatively, they begin to think about matches between their interests and abilities and the various career opportunities that might be open to them. They also become increasingly aware of the values and rewards attached to different occupations, and they evaluate these as well.

The realistic period begins about age seventeen and involves the beginnings of career decisions. However, final decisions might be some distance in the future, particularly in view of the extent to which postsecondary education extends adolescence and often postpones the need to enter the work world. Even after a career choice has been made, it will remain tentative for some time.

Ginzberg speaks of three substages within the realistic period. The first, exploration, consists of actively investigating, and even trying out, some of the various options. Explo-

TABLE 13.7

Ginzberg's Developmental Guidance Model

STAGE	APPROXIMATE AGES	MAJOR CAREER EVENTS
Fantasy	To 10 or 12	Unrealistic notions of career possibilities; child wants to be a president, an astronaut, a ballerina, an actress, a famous explorer, a cowboy.
Tentative	10–12 to about 16	Growing awareness of requirements of different careers; increasing realization of personal interests and capabilities; keener awareness of the status and rewards associated with different careers.
Realistic	Late adolescence through early adulthood and even later	Involves beginnings of career decisions through active exploration of alternatives; commitment to a clear career choice (crystallization); undertaking series of activities necessary for implementing choice (specification). For many individuals, the process of career evaluation continues through life, and different career choices may be made in mid-ladder.

ration often occurs when first entering the job market or in the early years of college or other postsecondary education. The individual then moves from exploration to crystallization, which entails a relatively firm commitment to a career. The final stage, specification, involves doing the things required to implement the career decision.

According to Ginzberg's developmental model, career evaluation occurs first in early adulthood and often continues through much of the remainder of the lifespan. Increasingly, when people's evaluations of their careers reveal less satisfaction and happiness than had been anticipated, alternate career decisions are made; this can occur at almost any time throughout the lifespan. As is discussed later, middle-of-the-lifespan career choices are made not only by women returning to the work force after raising children or entering it for the first time, but also by men who might already have devoted many of their working years to climbing the ladders of a career whose summits they no longer wish to reach—or whose slopes they find too steep or too unrewarding.

Super's *life-span, life-space* theory of career development extends over the entire lifespan and takes into account the possibility of "recycling"—that is, of starting over again at various stages of career development (Freeman, 1993). It describes five lifespan stages in the development of a career (described in Table 13.8). These are much like Ginzberg's descriptions for the early stages, but extend into early and middle adulthood.

Super describes four different things that need to be taken into account by those interested in understanding and in guiding careers: First, *individual differences,* as might be reflected in a test such as the Strong Interest Inventory, are very important. Second, the career counselor must be concerned with the individual *development*—that is, with the person's

level of preparation and maturity, as might be reflected in schooling, for example. Third is the influence of *context,* which includes things such as the individual's culture and parental occupations.

Finally, the career counselor needs to look at the individual's other roles (Savickas, 1997). Among other things, Super recognized the interaction of the career—or, very often, *careers*—with the individual's characteristics as well as with the many other roles that each of us plays in life. Life is a little like a rainbow with its many arcs, explains Super, coining the expression **life–career rainbow.** The reach of the rainbow's arc represents the lifespan nature of our many roles. Each band in the arc represents a single role like, for example, that of student, citizen, worker, homemaker, leisurite, spouse, parent, pensioner. For each of these roles, there are choices to be made and reevaluated and often changed. And if we are lucky, the roles that define our lives also color them with the vibrant, poetic hues of the rainbow.

One of the advantages of Super's approach, notes Herr (1997), is that it doesn't make a number of assumptions often made by other career guidance models. For example, it doesn't assume that the young adult will leave home to establish a commitment to work—and to intimacy as well. Clearly, with the industrialization of our societies and the prolongation of youth, it has become increasingly common to delay leaving home—or to return after initially leaving. As a result, career plans and intimate relationships are sometimes highly developed before the young adult leaves. And even after the young adult leaves, the family continues to be an important source of influence on careers.

Many career development models also assume that adolescents and young adults have a relatively unlimited number of options from which to select a career. This may be true

TABLE 13.8

Super's Life-Span, Life-Space Career Development Model

STAGE	AGE RANGE	SUBSTAGES	MAJOR POSSIBLE OCCURRENCES
Birth/Growth	0–14	Fantasy. Interest. Capacity. Tentative.	Initially unrealistic notions of career choice; eventual recognition of own interests and capacities; more realistic tentative choices.
Exploration	14–25	Trial transition. Implementing. Specifying. Crystallizing.	Beginnings of career decisions; exploration of alternatives; preparation for career; eventual commitment.
Establishment	25–45	Stabilization. Advancement or frustration.	Continued development and stabilization of career; resolution of occasional crises.
Maintenance	45–60	Innovation, stagnation, or updating.	Possible career changes ("recycling"); possible skills/knowledge improvement; possible stagnation.
Decline	60–death	Deceleration. Disengagement.	Retirement; career change; post-retirement career; life management.

for some, but it does not take into consideration the various constraints, such as economic opportunity, employment availability, gender, race, and intelligence, that sometimes restrict career choice. As Phillips (1997) explains, Super's approach has shifted the focus in career guidance from the nature of what is being chosen to the characteristics of the chooser, as well as to the other roles that the chooser plays.

Super also rejects the assumptions that career exploration begins late in adolescence, that career choice and development progress in a linear and irreversible fashion, and that the process is complete with the adoption of a career (Super, Savickas, & Super, 1996). It's now clear that career exploration may start in early childhood, may involve a variety of abandoned choices that require starting over again, and in many cases is a lifelong process. Hence the need for a career exploration model that takes into account the influence of interactive contextual factors such as the family, the social environment, and the individual's characteristics.

Work Selection

It would be naive and misleading to suggest that most of us make our career choices following well-reasoned decisions based on what we know of our interests and abilities—that each of us undertakes a careful examination of available careers and a thoughtful analysis of their requirements as well as of their potential contributions to our eventual growth and satisfaction. In general, most adolescents and young adults simply don't know enough about themselves or about potential careers to engage in this sort of analysis. There is a huge gap, argues Lent (1996), between social policies that espouse the value of career preparation and what actually goes on in practice. This gap is evident in a survey of current practices in American secondary schools which found that there is shockingly little career preparation going on in high schools (Bloch, 1996). And this is especially true for those students who go directly to work upon leaving school. Where there is career preparation, it is typically designed to benefit those who are going on to universities or to other postsecondary educational institutions.

The fact is that many of us select our careers (or are selected for them) in very different ways. Among the most important factors in determining our career interests, report Naylor and associates (1997) following a survey of Australian youth, are the occupations and educational levels of our parents, as well as our sex and the continued gender typing of many occupations.

Fortune, too, may play a role. It might provide a variety of chance happenings that mold great chunks of our lives. A father dies and leaves his child a business, a farm, or a family to look after; a teenage girl becomes pregnant; a dedicated young doctor marries into great wealth. Events such as these can profoundly influence the course of an individual's career, as can the simple availability of jobs. For those who attempt to enter the labor market directly from high school, or even

before completing high school, the first job obtained is likely to be the one that is first available. And in many cases, the individual's eventual career may be related to this first accidental job.

Employability, too, is an important factor in determining our careers. Bynner (1997) argues that employment opportunities for any given individual are as much, or more, a function of that person's employability than of that year's employment market. And among the factors that make some people highly employable and others much less so are a number of basic skills. Bynner's analysis suggests, for example, that general skills such as those involved in reading, in mathematics, and in organizing, and general personal characteristics such as self-esteem, which is often reflected in being at ease or uneasy in an interview, are critically important. Less important are specific work-related skills such as keyboarding or construction skills.

Socioeconomic background also influences choice of careers, with people from higher levels being most likely to obtain postsecondary education or training, and consequently being most likely to select professional, white-collar, and high-technology occupations. People from lower levels are more likely to be found in blue-collar occupations. (See "Across Cultures: Shashi Kanta, Dreamer.")

■ CAREER SELF-EFFICACY EXPECTATIONS

Also very important in determining choice of career are the individual's expectations of performing competently and successfully—a notion that in today's jargon is labeled **career self-efficacy expectations.** Stoltz-Loike (1996) reviews a large number of studies which indicate that, other things being equal, individuals are most likely to select careers in which they have high expectations of being competent and successful—hence high perceptions of **self-efficacy.** Recall that self-efficacy refers to our personal estimates and predictions of our effectiveness in dealing with the world. Self-efficacy expectations appear to be tied to a number of factors, not the least important of which is previous achievement (Kelly, 1993). Gender, too, has much to do with career choice and with self-efficacy expectations. Despite rapidly changing social conditions, stereotypes of appropriate male–female career divisions are still prevalent and may limit the number of choices girls think they have and affect their estimates of the likelihood of succeeding in these careers. Not surprisingly, women in nontraditional careers tend to have high notions of self-efficacy (Read, 1994). Similarly, career women in the Israeli kibbutz, compared to more traditional noncareer women, see themselves as more independent and emotionally stable, and also manifest higher levels of self-esteem (Lobel, Agami-Rozenblat, & Bempechat, 1993). In this connection, it's interesting to note that males often have lower self-efficacy expectations when considering cross-gender careers than do females in the same situation (Gillespie & Hillman, 1993). In other words, females are more likely to expect to be competent in male-typed careers than males are in female-typed careers.

ACROSS CULTURES — Shashi Kanta, Dreamer

want to become a doctor. Indian medicine is sweeter, western medicine is bitter," says Shashi Kanta, a fifteen-year-old girl whose father is principal of a school in Anangpur, where they live. Her father interrupts the interview and says in English, which Shashi doesn't understand, "It is impossible for a village teacher to educate his children as doctors. It's too expensive" (Rice, 1972, p. 121).

"We are Banyas," Shashi continues, explaining how, because they are members of a business caste, they do not mix with some of the lower castes like the sweepers (a caste whose principal occupation is to look after other people's houses). Because the caste system is officially frowned upon by the government, the castes are often mixed in the schools, although there are still some schools where the lower castes are not allowed to come inside. Instead, they sit on the veranda and listen to the lessons through the windows. "I believe in a democratic way of life," says Shashi, "but I couldn't marry someone from another class." She explains how her father will find her a husband. In her village, girls marry at the age of ten or twelve, but because she will go to university to become a doctor, her father will wait until she is

twenty-three or twenty-four before finding her a husband.

"It is a dream, this wanting to be a doctor," says her father in English so that Shashi does not know what he says. "All my children are dreamers. We must face the facts. It is a tragedy. It is too expensive" (Rice, 1972, p. 124).

To Think About

Among the important developmental tasks of early adulthood are those relating to selecting and preparing for both a career and a lifestyle. And in more than 90 percent of all cases in North America, the lifestyle involves marriage—at least once. Consider how different your decisions, and options, in early adulthood might be in a culture such as Shashi's.

Job Satisfaction

Not many decades ago, the primary motivations for work were money, perhaps security, and often duty. And the emphasis was on being a successful, productive worker. But, as Kuder (1977) notes, it is no longer sufficient just to have a job; we also want to be happy in our work and to feel that our contributions are worthwhile. In Terkel's (1972) words, work is "a search for daily meaning as well as daily bread, for recognition as well as cash, for astonishment rather than torpor; in short, for a sort of life rather than a Monday through Friday sort of dying. Perhaps immortality, too, is part of the quest" (p. xiii).

■ HOW HAPPY ARE WORKERS, AND WHY?

How satisfied and happy are most of us with what we do? Here, as in the more general areas of satisfaction with their lives, few adults are willing to describe themselves as very dissatisfied or very unhappy (see Chapter 16). In a wide-scale study of workers, Dawis (1992) found that at least three-

quarters of all workers at any age level describe themselves as being satisfied with their jobs and happy. Interestingly, however, if given an opportunity, about half of them would change their occupations.

There is evidence, too, that the longer people stay in a job, or *expect* to stay in it, the more prone they are to like it (Coward et al., 1995). Why do we become progressively more happy with our jobs? In addition to the fact that work gives meaning to a great many lives and that we want to be satisfied, perhaps finding it difficult to admit even to ourselves that we might not be, there are at least three reasons why people might become happier with their work as they age. The first and most obvious is that those who are truly unhappy with their careers will often change them early in their lives. The second is that it is possible to grow to love (or at least accept) a career that at first seems unpleasant. And third, as we age, many of us might modify our original dream, dropping our aspirations, lowering our estimates of what our contributions and rewards should be; perhaps we become satisfied with less as it becomes clearer that we are unlikely to be given more.

Work that reflects personal interests, that is challenging, and that provides adequate income is most likely to lead to job satisfaction. It may also be very important that employment provide workers with leisure—with time in which to study or travel, to build and grow, or perhaps just to fish and dream.

Stoltz-Loike (1996) summarizes research which indicates that a number of different factors appear to be closely related to the satisfaction that workers experience with their occupations. Highly important is the extent to which the job reflects personal interests. Also crucial is the extent to which it requires full use of the worker's capabilities and provides an opportunity to develop ideas. Workers who feel **empowered** are more satisfied, more loyal, and perform at higher levels, reports Wallace (1995). Income also contributes to job satisfaction, as does the supportiveness of the work environment.

FAST TRACKERS AND DEAD ENDERS

Not all people are bound to succeed, as success is commonly defined in the economically driven corporate world. Not all will climb the high ladders of corporate achievement to accumulate great power and status, to become, as Kanter (1981) puts it, **fast trackers.** Many more will simply be **dead enders**—those who never reach the summits toward which the "fast trackers" climb so rapidly. Dead enders, Kanter tells us, include those who initially enter occupations that have low ceilings, those who are in high-ceiling employment but who fail somewhere along the line, and those who simply take the wrong paths. Low-ceiling jobs are those that do not ordinarily lead to advancement; they include many labor and clerical jobs. High-ceiling occupations include opportunities for advancement. Dead enders in low-ceiling employment are relatively satisfied; those in high-ceiling employment but who fail to climb upward are among the least satisfied. And those who simply climb the wrong ladders in the beginning find themselves at an intermediate level of satisfaction. There are, of course, other definitions of success. And *dead ender,* because of its negative connotations, is not a good label for all those who enter low-ceiling occupations. There are sources of job satisfaction that have absolutely nothing to do with climbing corporate ladders. (See Summary Table 13.9.)

COGNITIVE CHANGE IN ADULTHOOD

Our predominant models of human development have historically assumed that most of the major developmental changes occur early in the lifespan, that after infancy, childhood, and adolescence, we are characterized more by stability than by change. However, the current lifespan view of human development has largely rejected this model in favor of the belief that there are some important positive changes that occur throughout the lifespan. This model insists that much of development is not complete at adolescence and that the human being remains highly changeable throughout much of life. It maintains that the principal characteristic of adult human development is change rather than stability.

The evidence that might clarify this issue, notes Alwin (1994), is not entirely clear. However, much of it points to the likelihood that characteristics such as intelligence are far more stable than changing. This, of course, does not mean that change is not possible and does not occur; what it means, in effect, is that the rate of change slows very dramatically in adulthood.

Still, some aspects of intellectual functioning seem to change in systematic and predictable ways. Different theorists describe this change with different approaches.

Schaie's Stage Theory of Adult Development

Schaie (1977–1978) suggests that the ways in which adults use their intellects are, in some ways, fundamentally different from those characteristic of children and adolescents.

SUMMARY TABLE 13.9
Work and Career Preparation

TOPICS	EXPLANATIONS/RESEARCH FINDINGS
Some definitions:	■ **Job:** narrow term; specific tasks worker does (writing memos). ■ **Occupation:** more general employment classification (accountant). ■ **Career:** broader term; a range of related occupations (an academic career). ■ **Vocation:** refers to a "calling" (certain religious or professional vocations). ■ **Work:** inclusive term (jobs, occupations, careers, vocations).
Changing work opportunities	■ Fastest growing job opportunities are mainly health-care and computer related. ■ Fastest declining jobs are those where technology reduces need for workers. ■ Notable job trends include increasing female employment in many job sectors, more part-time employment, and a wide variety of new job classifications.
Holland's job–person matching	■ Career guidance model based on matching individuals' interests to jobs (using tests like Strong Interest Inventory or Holland Vocational Preference Inventory). ■ Holland test describes six "coping styles"; realistic, intellectual, artistic, social, enterprising, and conventional.
Ginzberg's developmental career mode	Focus on facilitating the chronological development of career decisions through three phases: ■ fantasy (to 10–12; often unrealistic). ■ tentative (10–12 to 16; growing awareness of jobs and of personal interests and abilities). ■ Realistic (late adolescence through early adulthood; active exploration, choice, implementation, and evaluation).
Super's life-span, life-space theory	■ Career development is a lifelong process; theory allows for ongoing change. ■ Five major career development stages: growth to age 14 or so; exploration through youth; establishment through early adulthood; maintenance until close to retirement; decline. ■ Considers four important influences on career development; interests; development and preparation; culture and context; and the individual's different roles (represented graphically in *life career rainbow*).
Work selection	■ There is relatively little systematic career preparation in high schools. ■ Career choice is often a function of parental occupation and education, social class, gender, employability, good or bad luck, and expectations of success (self-efficacy).
Job satisfaction	■ Job satisfaction is related to length of time employed, how much responsibility workers have, the extent to which occupations make full use of talents and capabilities, and social support in the workplace. ■ *Fast trackers* are not always more satisfied than so-called *dead enders*.

Although he concedes that Piaget's stage of formal operations is, in effect, the highest level of logical thinking that is likely to be attained, he argues that the commitments and social realities of adult life exert powerful influences on how adults think. Accordingly, he proposes a four-stage theory to describe adult cognitive development.

The first stage, labeled the **acquisition stage**, spans childhood and adolescence. As the label implies, it is marked by the continued *acquisition* of information and of ways of solving problems and thinking logically. During this stage, notes Schaie, the emphasis is seldom on the practical or social implications of what is learned.

Early adulthood brings an **achieving stage**, during which the individual becomes increasingly concerned with learning things that will be useful—in careers, in hobbies, in marriage, in child rearing. In contrast to the *acquisition stage,* learning is now directed toward real, long-term goals.

Middle adulthood brings new social responsibilities and new social realities that are now reflected in what Schaie labels the **responsibility stage.** Long-term goals are now reevaluated in the light of the individual's current situation. Perhaps family responsibilities require a restructuring of priorities. Perhaps, too, social responsibilities, reflected in community leadership roles or in political and religious involvement, bring about new *executive* roles (Schaie speaks here of an **executive stage** that is also part of the cognitive development of middle adulthood).

Finally, late adulthood brings a **reintegration stage**, during which the individual may turn cognitive activities toward a reevaluation and reexamination of life and personal goals. As we see in Chapter 18, it is during this period that many choose to do what is termed a **life review.** A life review, which can occur at any stage in the lifespan, involves analyzing one's life in terms of earlier goals and accomplishments, reexamining important relationships, searching always for meaning and meaningfulness.

Note that the focus in all four of Schaie's developmental stages is always on what is most important and makes the greatest amount of sense for the individual. Thus, acquiring information and developing cognitive strategies are important for the child and the adolescent struggling through school, and struggling as well to acquire the skills required for effective commerce in the adult world; achieving is important for the young adult trying to make a success of career and lifestyle choices; being responsible comes to the fore as children age and the demands of political, social, and religious involvement become more insistent; and reintegrating makes sense for those whom age and life's circumstances have moved beyond the responsibilities of an earlier time.

Dialectical Thinking: Riegel and Basseches

Riegel (1970, 1972, 1976) and Basseches (1986) suggest that thinking becomes more *dialectical* with age. *Webster's Third New International Dictionary* defines *dialectics* as "the process of self-development or unfolding (as of an action, event, idea, ideology, movement, or institution) through the stages of thesis, antithesis, and synthesis...." It further defines *dialectical* as being "marked by a dynamic internal tension, conflict, and interconnectedness of its parts or elements." Dialectical thinking, notes the *Oxford English Dictionary*, relates to a series of contradictions and their solutions—to conflict and change.

Dialectical thinking, says Riegel, is evident in the adult's increasing recognition of conflict, of contradiction and uncertainty. Riegel argues that our conventional views of development as a series of stages or plateaus characterized by a state of balance or equilibrium are incorrect and misleading. According to Riegel, lifespan human development is best viewed as sequences of conflicts, crises, or contradictions and their continued resolution. The concept of dialectics is implicit in the view that conflicts or crises arise from contradictory actions and reactions—the classical situation of a thesis leading to an antithesis and finally being resolved in a synthesis.

More specifically, dialectical thinking is evident in the individual's recognition, acceptance, and resolution of conflicts. For example, a young adult's sexual maturity might lead toward behaviors that are culturally problematic. From this lack of synchrony between desires and opportunities, conflict arises, and conflict is the root of dialectical processes. Resolution of conflicts may lead to new developments, new behaviors, new ways of thinking. And when the reorganization is sufficiently dramatic, says Riegel, we might be tempted to recognize a stage or a plateau. But a dialectical view does not emphasize the plateau or the equilibrium—as does Piaget's theory, for example. Instead, it views development as a continuous process because the organism and society are never static. Change is constant, and complete synchrony is rare and fleeting.

Both Riegel (1973a) and Basseches (1986) propose a fifth Piagetian stage—a *dialectical stage*. In this fifth stage, there are no clear plateaus—no levels of cognitive accomplishment clearly evident in the ability to solve a new class of problems. Instead, there is a renewed realization that development occurs on different levels, that it is replete with contradictions, that not all problems and conflicts can be permanently

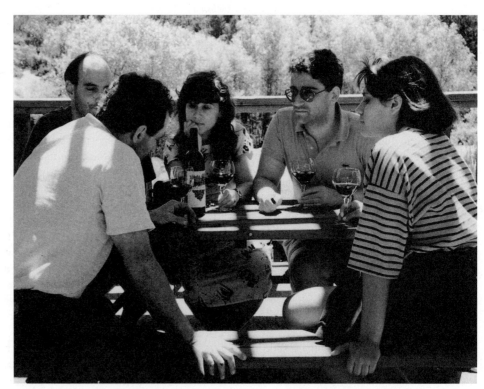

Adolescents and young adults strive to be logical thinkers, says Piaget, searching for correct, reason-driven solutions to the world's problems. But with age, thinking becomes more pragmatic, more attuned to contradictions, more relativistic, more tolerant of ambiguity. These differences are often apparent in the discussions and arguments of older and younger adults—even at friendly family picnics.

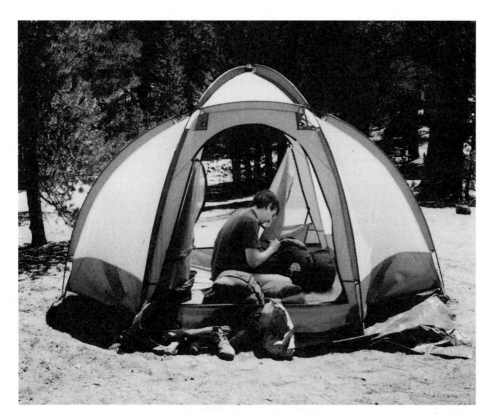

The thought processes of mature adults sometimes reflect a type of wisdom not available to adolescents and others who rely primarily on cold logic to drive their conclusions and decisions. It recognizes that little is completely black or white—although simple, logical truths can sometimes be found in instructions.

resolved, that it is appropriate to change one's beliefs and to accept contradiction and uncertainty. "The developmental and aging processes…are founded upon the ability to tolerate contradictions and insufficiencies in action and thought," Riegel informs us (1973b, p. 482).

In summary, dialectical thinking is a uniquely adult mode of thinking that involves recognition of ambiguities and contradictions, and increasing tolerance of these. In the same way that concrete operations make it possible for the schoolchild to reason about real classes and objects, so dialectical operations make it possible for the adult to reason about social and political systems, interpersonal relationships, and so on. Unlike formal reasoning, which is highly constrained in the sense that it is limited by rules of logic, dialectical thinking is more intuitive, more subject to value judgments. Formal reasoning, claims Basseches (1986), is rarely used in the real world, although it might occasionally be used in science or in a formal testing situation—or perhaps to confirm the results of intuition. Dialectical thought, on the other hand, can be applied to problems relating to intimate personal interactions, artistic activities, business transactions, the sciences, and so on.

Labouvie-Vief's Pragmatic Wisdom

Much adult reasoning, Labouvie-Vief (1980) argues, occurs in very different contexts than does child and adolescent reasoning. Reasoning that involves the manipulation of classes or the consideration of all possible alternatives might be entirely appropriate for many of the problems that children

face, especially in schools. But these ways of thinking are not very suitable or useful for many of the situations that the adult faces. Because of the realities of adult responsibilities, because of the practical demands of certain contexts, and because of ethical constraints, the reasoning that evolves in adulthood is different from the reasoning of the preadult. It is, in Labouvie-Vief's (1980) words, a form of reasoning that is "marked by specialization, concrete pragmatics, and pressures towards social system stability" (p. 141). As a result, in adult thought, there is often a trade-off between the most scientific or most logically correct of possible alternatives and a desire for social stability—or for the most ethical alternative. It is as though age and experience grant adults a kind of wisdom—a dialectical wisdom—that allows them to factor more variables into their problem-solving activities than formal operations allow (Labouvie-Vief & Lawrence, 1985).

Schaie, Riegel, Basseches, Labouvie-Vief, and others who are concerned with the cognitive processes of adults present a compelling argument that the logic of systems such as Piaget's does not adequately describe the thinking of adults (Stevens-Long, 1990). They argue that with adulthood there may come an increasing recognition of ambiguity and contradiction, greater tolerance for these, and the learning of new, dialectical ways of thinking. These are ways of thinking that allow the ongoing resolution of problems but that bring into play a variety of important considerations other than simple logic—for example, ethics, feasibility, and social implications.

Although it is still too early to evaluate the impact and the usefulness of these ideas, their emphasis on aspects of development that have largely been ignored may lead to important insights about changes in thinking through the lifespan.

SUMMARY TABLE 13.10
Three Approaches to Adult Cognitive Development

SCHAIE'S STAGES	DIALECTICAL THINKING	PRAGMATIC THINKING
■ *Acquisition* (to adolescence; Piaget's formal operations; acquisition of information without regard for its long-term implications). ■ *Achieving* (early adulthood; concerned with achieving long-term goals). ■ *Responsibility* (middle adulthood; concerned with immediate responsibilities of career and family; *executive stage* reflects concern with wider social, political, religious responsibilities). ■ *Reintegration* (reevaluation of goals and of life after retirement from work and other responsibilities.	■ Associated with Riegel and Basseches: a fifth Piagetian stage. ■ Dialectical thinking stems from contradiction and is designed to reach a resolution (thesis + antithesis = synthesis). ■ Dialectical thinking allows the application of thought to ambiguous situations, to intimate personal interactions, to business, to politics, to all of life.	■ Associated with Labouvie-Vief. ■ Pragmatic thinking is thinking that is sensitive to ethical constraints and practical and social considerations. ■ Scientific considerations grant the judgments of the young a cold, sharp exactness; pragmatic considerations grant wisdom to the judgments of the old.

These notions might also do much to resolve what has been an ongoing controversy about the nature of age-related changes in intellectual ability. (See Summary Table 13.10.)

A CONTEXTUAL REMINDER

This chapter is clearly rooted in the Western industrialized world as, of course, is most of this book. That is probably as it should be because I am of that world, and most of you are as well. But it is worth repeating once more that much of what we have to say about human development reflects the contexts in which we live and work. Thus, what we believe about the vigor and health of young adulthood, the excellent functioning of the senses, the benefits of exercise, and the relative absence of disease may well be true and important in our Western industrialized world, but not the least bit true in Sierra Leone, where the average life expectancy is forty, or Afghanistan, where it's forty-five (Bellamy, 1997). There, the normal course of physical development is quite different.

Similarly, we can make grand pronouncements about how work must not only put chickens in our pots but also fill our souls with a sense of value and purpose. But these assertions would mean nothing if we were speaking of the aboriginals of the Amazon basin. These people have no careers comparable to ours; they have no corporate ladders to climb—or from which to fall. What they have is a compelling need to go out into the jungle every day of their lives and gather enough food to survive yet another season.

Do you suppose that their thoughts are dialectic? Do you think that they struggle to balance pragmatics and morals in the resolution of issues of profound social and economic importance?

Or is their thinking different, their intelligence more of their context?

FOCUS QUESTIONS: SUMMARY ANSWERS

1. Is early adulthood a period of physical growth, decline, or stability?

   ▪ Adulthood is not a plateau. Peak physical performance occurs from the mid-twenties to the mid-thirties. In the absence of training, flexibility declines gradually from about age twelve but can be maintained and even improved into adulthood with training. There are no dramatic age-related changes in the functioning of the senses through early adulthood. In early adulthood, there is a decreased susceptibility to common infections, but a somewhat greater incidence of chronic complaints. Accidents are the principal cause of death prior to age forty-five, and heart disease and cancer after age forty-five.

2. What is normal (and average) sexual behavior and responsiveness for young adults?

   ▪ The human sexual response cycles through excitement (preparation), plateau (mounting arousal), orgasm, and resolution. Sexual dysfunctions in the male include premature ejaculation, retarded ejaculation, and erectile dysfunction; in the female, hypoactive sex drive, inability to attain orgasm or pleasure from sexual intercourse, and vaginismus. Infertility increases gradually through early adulthood. The most common causes are blocked Fallopian tubes in the female (often due to acute pelvic inflammatory disease) and low sperm count in men.

3. How do people select careers? Why is work important?

■ Work serves economic, social, and psychological functions. Jobs are specific tasks or duties; occupation is a broad employment classification (such as being a mechanic); career refers to a range of related occupations; vocation refers to a "calling" (like to the ministry). A job–person matching approach to career choice (Holland) tries to match individual interests and talents with work requirements; developmental guidance models (Ginzberg) describe sequential stages of exploration and preparation for a career (fantasy, tentative, realistic); life-span, life-space theory (Super) describes lifelong developmental stages in career development, taking the individual's various roles and the influence of context into account. In practice, career selection is highly influenced by family and other contextual influences, career self-efficacy expectations (anticipations of being competent and successful), and other factors such as race, sex, and economics. Fortune also plays a role.

4. Is the thinking of the young adult different from that of children and adolescents?

■ Schaie describes four stages in adult intellectual development: *acquisition* (formal operations), *achievement* (directed to long-range goals in early adulthood), *responsibility* (constrained by career, family, and social responsibility in middle adulthood), and *reintegration* (reevaluation at retirement). Riegel and Basseches suggest that with adulthood there may come an increasing recognition and tolerance of ambiguity, conflict, and contradiction, and the learning of new (dialectical) ways of thinking that allow the ongoing resolution of problems. Labouvie-Vief describes adult thinking as potentially more pragmatic—that is, more attuned to the constraints of social realities, of ethics, of feasibility.

STUDY TERMS

achieving stage, 399
acquisition stage, 399
anxiety, 386
body mass index (BMI), 384
career, 391
career self-efficacy expectations, 396
dead enders, 398
developmental career model, 392
developmental tasks, 378
dialectical thinking, 400
early adulthood, 378
empowered, 398

erectile dysfunction, 389
excitement, 387
executive stage, 399
fast trackers, 398
flexibility, 382
Food Guide Pyramid, 383
Holland Vocational Preference Inventory, 393
hypoactive sexual desire, 389
infertility, 390
job, 391
job–person matching, 392
later adulthood, 378
life–career rainbow, 395
life review, 399
life-span, life-space approach, 392
middle adulthood, 378
obesity, 384
occupation, 391
orgasm, 388

peak physical performance, 381
Peter Pan syndrome, 378
plateau, 388
premature ejaculation, 389
reintegration stage, 399
resolution, 388
responsibility stage, 399
retarded ejaculation, 389
self-efficacy, 396
seminal emission, 388
sexual dysfunction, 389
social readjustment rating scale, 386
stress, 386
Strong Interest Inventory, 392
Type A individuals, 386
Type B individuals, 386
vaginismus, 389
vocation, 391
work, 391
youth, 378

FURTHER READINGS

In the following chapter, Alwin explores in detail the stability of intellectual and personality characteristics throughout the lifespan, and concludes that there is perhaps more stability than change in these areas:

Alwin, D. F. (1994). Aging, personality, and social change: The stability of individual differences over the adult life span. In D. L. Featherman, R. M. Lerner, & M. Perlmutter (Eds.), *Lifespan development and behavior* (Vol. 12). Hillsdale, NJ: Erlbaum.

The first of the following two books presents a detailed and comprehensive look at career education and vocational guidance, which should be of particular value for those who are concerned with career education at different stages in the lifespan. The second is a collection of articles that attempts to integrate different theories of career development:

Drummond, R. J., & Ryan, C. W. (1995). *Career counseling: A developmental approach*. Englewood Cliffs, NJ: Prentice-Hall.

Savickas, M. L., & Lent, R. W. (Eds.). (1994). *Convergence in career development theories*. Palo Alto, CA: CPP Books.

The following collection, edited by Baltes, presents a varied and insightful look at cognitive development and functioning in adulthood:

Baltes, P. B., & Staudinger, U. M. (1996). *Interactive minds: Lifespan perspectives on the social foundation of cognition.* New York: Cambridge University Press.

Those interested in the surprising sexual habits of Americans might want to consult this book:

Michael, R. T., Gagnon, J. H., Laumann, E. O., & Kolata, G. (1994). *Sex in America: A definitive survey.* New York: Little, Brown.

Because of the computer, says Papert, today's children have new, self-directed methods of accessing knowledge. The impact on the thinking of tomorrow's adult may be considerable:

Papert, S. (1993). *The children's machine: Rethinking school in the age of the computer.* New York: Basic Books.

FOCUS QUESTIONS

1. What are the main challenges of early adulthood?

2. What are some of the dimensions of personal intimacy?

3. What kinds of changes have there been in the family? What is the family life cycle?

4. How common is family violence? Acquaintance rape?

Social Development: Early Adulthood

Lord, what fools these mortals be!

WILLIAM SHAKESPEARE
A Midsummer Night's Dream

s was the custom in the seventeenth century, when the parents of Maria Gonçales of São Paulo arranged for her marriage after carefully selecting the family into which she would marry, they also settled on a dowry price. Dowries in São Paulo, as in most countries of the world where such practices were followed, were given to both the husband and the daughter, or sometimes just to the husband or his family. Dowry marriages were typically arranged by parents, and the purpose of the dowry was to help the young couple start out. In Brazil, daughters' dowries were often much larger than the inheritance that a son would receive, sometimes being a very large fraction of the father's entire estate. In addition, sons were often expected to contribute to the dowry, as might, too, uncles and other relatives. So when Maria Gonçales married, her dowry included not only her eventual and complete share of her father's estate (termed her *legítima*), but also one chest, one tablecloth and six napkins, six silver spoons, six plates, two towels, eight scythes, eight hoes, eight wedges, ten head of cattle, one horse and saddle, and at least sixteen Indians. Her brother received far fewer household items—only three pigs and just five Indians (Nazzari, 1991). ¶ When Shudhra of Shahjahapur married—some 300 years later, on an entirely different continent, and in a very different culture—the customs were strikingly similar. Not only was her marriage arranged, but the dowry price was settled on beforehand. It included not only that her mother, her only surviving parent, pay for all the expensive rituals and rites, but that she also spend many thousands of rupees on jewelry, clothes, furniture, utensils, and household articles, and then perhaps 25 percent as many rupees again on gifts of cash and objects for the groom's parents and other relatives. But Shudhra's husband was not happy with the dowry. It was not everything that he had been promised. And so, seven days after the marriage, he arranged to have Shudhra killed. "He wanted a scooter," explained Shudhra's distraught mother. "I had promised one and I wanted to give it also. But my means were limited. Besides the expenditure at the marriage of my daughter had gone much beyond my expectations" (Kumari, 1989, p. 70).

This Chapter

ove, McAdams (1984) informs us, and *power* are the two basic themes that seem to be common in all our lives. These themes surface repeatedly in the fantasies and dreams in which we are the larger-than-life heroes. The love theme is revealed in our concern with personal relationships and in our need to be liked and wanted. The power theme manifests itself in our wish that others recognize our strength and leadership. And one or both are also evident in marriage and dowry systems. Sadly, they are often evident in violence and murder as well.

This chapter looks at both love and violence. It begins with an exploration of the complex and sometimes perplexing topic of love and then examines the sorts of relationships and lifestyles we have invented to satisfy our needs. It discusses marriage and sex as well as nonmarital lifestyles. It looks at the characteristics of the changing family. Finally, it concludes with an examination of violence in the family, and of sexual violence.

ERIKSON'S THEORY: PSYCHOSOCIAL DEVELOPMENT

Recall from Chapter 2 that Erikson's theory of **psychosocial development** describes a series of eight stages through which individuals progress as they develop (Erikson, 1959, 1987) (see Figure 14.1). Each of these stages involves the resolution of an important conflict that arises out of the individual's social interaction—hence the label "psychosocial theory." Progression from one stage to the next requires the resolution of this conflict, an achievement that evolves through the development of a new competence. But the conflicts specific to each stage are never completely resolved during that stage; they continue, in one form or another, throughout life. As we develop and grow, our social environments change, and as a result, so do our most important conflicts.

With the advent of adulthood, the adult is faced with a series of new social demands that require additional adjustments. These, too, may be viewed in terms of competing tendencies—crises that will be resolved through the development of new competencies. Erikson describes three developmental stages that span adulthood and old age: (1) intimacy and solidarity versus isolation, (2) generativity versus self-absorption, and (3) integrity versus despair (the last two of these are discussed in Chapters 16 and 18, respectively).

FIGURE 14.1

Overview of Erikson's psychosocial theory.

Intimacy Versus Isolation

Erikson believed that the search for identity does not always end with puberty but may continue through adolescence and beyond. This was the case, for example, among 623 university professors surveyed by Côté and Levine (1992).

RELATIONSHIPS WITH THE OPPOSITE SEX

One of the principal ways in which adolescents and young adults achieve a sense of personal identity and self-worth is through feelings of intimacy with others. According to Erikson (1980), for the majority of young adults, although not for all, the intimacy they seek will come through a relationship with someone of the opposite sex. But here, as in other stages of the lifespan, there is a conflict—in this case, a conflict between the need to make a commitment and an unwillingness to do so. The individual has an urge to remain independent, to retain a hard-won sense of personal identity; in addition, there is a fear of commitment. Both of these mitigate against intimacy. As a consequence, says Erikson, many young adults enter into sexually intimate relationships that involve little emotional commitment. Erikson and Hall (1983) describe these relationships as primarily "genital" (phallic or vaginal) and claim that they may lead to feelings of extreme isolation.

Even after young adults have gone beyond the family to find intimacy—and perhaps passion and commitment too—parents continue to have considerable influence on their emotional lives. They remain an important source of support and help in times of need; and a reason for joy and laughter.

The culmination of this developmental period, and the resolution of the conflict between a need for intimacy and a drive for independence, is to be found in a balance that permits the commitment and the mutuality of love but that also allows the individual to retain an independent identity.

■ RELATIONSHIPS WITH PARENTS

The young adult's search for intimacy and independence requires a redefinition and realignment of relationships with parents. As we saw, this process begins in early adolescence and is sometimes marked by conflict—although conflict is not the main characteristic of most parent–adolescent relationships.

Miller and Lane (1991) note that the adolescent's happiness is more closely related to the quality of the parental relationship than the peer relationship. Adolescents who describe their relationships with parents as supportive and emotionally warm have a higher sense of well-being than those who see themselves in conflict. Might this also be the case for young adults?

Miller and Lane presented questionnaires to seventy-two college undergraduates in an attempt to discover the nature and importance of their relationships with their parents. One of their clearest findings is that these students, both male and female, felt closer to their mothers and spent more time with them than with their fathers. Both parents appeared to have considerable emotional influence on their young adult children. "Adolescents achieve autonomy by asserting themselves in a context of close and supportive relations with parents," claim Miller and Lane, "rather than by distancing themselves from them" (1991, p. 180). In early adulthood, close parental relationships continue to be important, but the development of a close relationship with someone else is also very important.

According to Erikson, the crowning achievement of early adulthood is most often found in marriage and child rearing. This view has been criticized and is often rejected. There are many individuals who lead happy, well-adjusted lives but who do not express their need for intimacy in a lifelong marital commitment. And although Erikson describes a social pattern that is still relatively common, it is perhaps no longer as common in the late twentieth century as it was in the middle of the century.

Research on Erikson's Model

Although a theory such as Erikson's cannot easily be tested, several studies have attempted to confirm some of its most important beliefs. Many of these have used the **Erikson Psychosocial Stage Inventory** or a modification of this test. Evidence indicates that it presents a reliable and useful measure of the extent to which a given individual has succeeded in progression through Erikson's stages (Leidy & Darling-Fischer, 1995).

One of the best-known studies of Erikson's model with adults is the longitudinal study initiated by Glueck and Glueck (1950) in their investigation of juvenile delinquency. For their study, they had selected a control group of 392 nondelinquent, noncollege, inner-city residents. Later, Vaillant and Milofsky (1980), followed by Snarey (1993), used these same subjects (about which there was a tremendous amount of information), interviewing them at ages fourteen, twenty-five, thirty-one, and forty-seven for a study based on Erikson's theory.

One of the objectives of these studies was to determine which of Erikson's developmental stages most accurately described individual subjects. For example, assignment to Stage 4 (industry versus inferiority) would reflect the extent to which the subject "did things beside and with others" and would be determined by summing scores assigned for doing home chores, adjusting to school academically, and participating in extracurricular jobs and related tasks. Assignment to Stage 5 required that the subject have achieved some sense of identity, most often evident in the fact that he or she would now be self-supporting and relatively independent of the family. Stage 6 (intimacy), as defined by Erikson, requires that the subject be involved in a long-lasting and interdependent relationship. For the men in this study, cohorts of the early- to mid-1920s, this relationship typically involved marriage.

Vaillant and Milofsky introduce an additional stage between Erikson's sixth and seventh (appropriately numbered Stage 6a), termed career consolidation versus self-absorption. Erikson had originally believed that career consolidation occurred during the fifth stage (identity formation), an observation that might have been more accurate in an early sociocultural context in which career decisions were often made earlier than they are now. Assignment to the seventh stage, **generativity,** was based on evidence of the individual's having assumed responsibility for others. The most common indication of

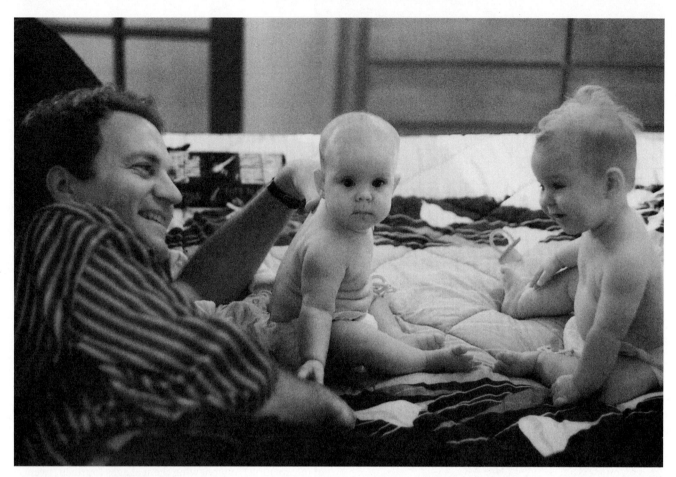

One of the new developmental competencies that Erikson describes as being characteristic of early adulthood is that of becoming generative—an achievement that might be evident in work roles, in community responsibilities, and in producing and caring for children. Does this mean that the person who has two jobs—or twin girls—is twice as developmentally competent?

generativity in this study involved caring for adolescents, as well as various wider community involvements.

Once the results of the questionnaires and interviews had been sorted, Vaillant and Milofsky looked at three hypotheses, each of which was supported by their observations. First, they predicted that because Erikson's model is open-ended, people should reach the various stages at different ages. In their data, for example, although between 30 and 40 percent of the middle-aged men (around age forty-seven) could be described as generative, almost 20 percent were still struggling with the identity issues of adolescence.

Second, if the model is to be useful and generalizable, it should be relatively independent of social class and education. In fact, social-class membership and educational level were not related to the subject's developmental level. Although there were very marked contrasts between the two major groups involved in this study (on the one hand, a sample raised in an inner-city, high-crime, low-status area; on the other, a college sample), approximately equal proportions of each of these groups were assigned to each stage at any given age.

Third, because the model is developmental, progression through each of the stages should be sequential. That is, an individual should not reach Stage 6 or 7 before having achieved Stage 4 or 5. As expected, progression through the stages appeared to be remarkably sequential. Achieving identity and being self-supporting seemed to be a requirement for developing a committed and intimate relationship. By the same token, intimacy seemed to precede career consolidation, which, in turn, preceded generativity.

Snarey (1993) also reports strong support for Erikson's theory, especially in his conclusion that parents, and particularly fathers, play a critical role in their children's development. Similarly, Brookins (1996) found that young people's measures of self-esteem were highly correlated with their scores on the Erikson Psychosocial Stage Inventory. In his study, those who had achieved identity status by late adolescence had significantly more positive self-concepts than those who were still struggling to do so.

It's important to note that because Erikson's theory is an open-ended model, aging does not in any way guarantee the achievement of psychosexual maturity. The term *stage,* which Erikson uses to describe sequential developmental achievements, is metaphorical rather than literal. These are less stages than organized and somewhat predictable changes in commitments and relationships. Accordingly, terms such as *developmental level* or *developmental task* would probably be more appropriate.

▲ SUMMARY TABLE 14.1

Psychosocial Developments
of Early Adulthood: Erikson

STAGE	CRITERIA/SPECULATION/RESEARCH FINDINGS
Identity Vs. Identity Diffusion	■ Achieved identity status important for transition from adolescence to adulthood.
	■ Research indicates that older adolescents/ young adults who have achieved identity have higher self-esteem (feel better about themselves).
Intimacy Vs. Isolation	■ According to Erikson, achieving intimacy is the most important task of early adulthood.
	■ Often reflected in relationships with someone of the opposite sex.
	■ Requires a redefinition of relationships with parents, who continue to be fundamentally important.
	■ Research on Erikson's model indicates that people reach various stages at different ages, social class is unrelated to progression through stages, and progression through stages is sequential.

The single most important developmental task of early adulthood, Erikson tells us, is to achieve intimacy. By intimacy, he means something very close to what others call love. (See Summary Table 14.1.)

▮ LOVE, MATE SELECTION, AND LIFESTYLE CHOICE

Freud (1935) put it very simply: There are two things that are essential to being a healthy adult: **love** and work; Erikson (1987) agreed.

Love was the province of the poet long before science claimed it. And even now, poets may know more about love than does science. Of the wonder and joy and all-consuming nature of love, the poets have had little doubt; about its practical value, they remain less certain. "True love," writes the poet Szymborska (1995), "Is it normal, is it serious, is it practical/What does the world get from two people who exist in a world of their own?" But we have little time for the poetry of love; here we can deal only with its science.

Romantic/erotic love, the marital therapist Grunebaum (1997) informs us, using the label *romantic/erotic* to distinguish this kind of love from that which might exist between a mother and a child, or between brothers or friends, is an all-consuming thing. How do we recognize romantic/erotic love? By its three main characteristics, says Grunebaum:

■ Feelings of longing for the other, including a desire to be emotionally and sexually intimate with him or her.

■ A notion that the other is special, ideal, essential for one's happiness.

■ A preoccupation with and overvaluation of the other.

But definitions such as these, meaningful though they might be, are not quite enough for science, with its penchant for measurement and investigation. So science provides us with ways of measuring love, if not of completely understanding it. Rubin's (1970) Loving and Liking Scales are one attempt to provide a way of measuring interpersonal attraction (see Table 14.2). The scales are based on the assumption that those who like each other sense that they have things in common, evaluate each other positively, and appreciate each other's company. But loving, as we saw, implies deeper feelings, feelings of deep caring, strong attachment, and intimacy. Love brings with it a degree of emotional interdependence, a quality of exclusiveness and absorption. If you simply like someone, that person does not dominate your thoughts and your dreams, nor are you concerned that someone else might also like the same person. Love, on the other hand, often brings with it a measure of fierce possessiveness and the possibility of jealousy and pain—perhaps the possibility of ecstasy as well.

▮ A Model of Love

Interpersonal attraction is no simple thing, Sternberg (1986) informs us. There are at least eight varieties of it including nonlove, romantic love, liking, fatuous love, infatuation, companionship, empty love, and consummate love (see Interactive Table 14.3). What differentiates these states from one another is the combination of **intimacy, passion,** and **commitment** involved in each. Accordingly, Sternberg has given us a **triangular theory of love.** But the triangle in this theory is not the classical male–male–female or female–female–male love triangle. It is the intimacy–passion–commitment triangle (see Figure 14.2).

TABLE 14.2

Several Items from Rubin's Loving and Liking Scales *

LOVING-SCALE ITEMS

1. I feel that I can confide in [　] about virtually everything.
2. If I could never be with [　], I would feel miserable.
3. One of my primary concerns is [　]'s welfare.

LIKING-SCALE ITEMS

1. I think that [　] is unusually well adjusted.
2. I would highly recommend [　] for a responsible job.
3. [　] is the sort of person whom I myself would like to be.

*Each scale is ranked 1 to 9 to indicate degree of agreement.
Source: From "Measurement of Romantic Love" by Z. Rubin, 1970, *Journal of Personality and Social Psychology, 16,* pp. 265–273. Copyright 1970 by the American Psychological Association. Reprinted by permission of the author.

Sternberg's Model of Love

Do you have a main relationship? Is it love? How can you tell for sure? One way, says Rubin, is to use scales with items such as those in Table 14.2, which attempt to separate loving from merely liking. Another way is to analyze the dimensions of your relationship. The Sternberg model describes eight possible relationships, each of which is defined in terms of the balance among passion (physical attraction), intimacy (affection, mutual disclosure), and commitment (conscious decision to love, to share, to be together). Does your main relationship fit one of these categories?

RELATIONSHIP	BALANCE OF COMPONENTS	POSSIBLE ATTITUDE
Nonlove	No passion, no intimacy, no commitment.	"Who? I didn't notice him."
Infatuation	Passion; no intimacy or commitment.	"I just want to be with him—physically, you know."
Liking	Intimacy; no passion or commitment.	"She's nice to talk to."
Romantic love	Passion and intimacy; no commitment	"He's for me; he's the one! At least for the time being."
Companionate love	Intimacy and commitment; no passion.	"She's like a sister! We're in it for the long haul."
Fatuous love	Commitment and passion; no intimacy.	"I need him . . . can't leave. But I need to talk to you."
Empty love	Commitment; no passion or intimacy.	"We'll stick it out. But just because of the kids."
Consummate love	Intimacy, passion, and commitment.	"I want him. I like him. I'm his. Forever."

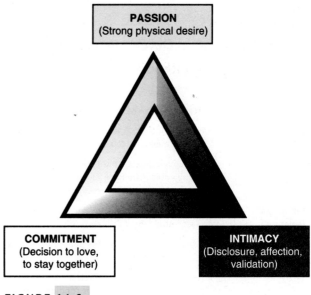

FIGURE 14.2

Sternberg's triangle of love. Different combinations of these three components determine the nature of the love relationship.

In this model, intimacy refers to emotions that bring people closer together—emotions such as respect, affection, and support. Feelings of intimacy are what lead two people to want to share things, perhaps to disclose personal, private things.

Passion is a strong, sometimes almost overwhelming, desire to be with another person. Passion is often, although not always, sexual. Sternberg suggests that passion is a feeling that builds rapidly but then gradually subsides.

Commitment implies a decision-making process and may involve either a short-term or a long-term decision. On a short-term basis, commitment requires making the decision that one is in love. From a long-term point of view, commitment involves deciding to cultivate and maintain the loving relationship. In practice, this often implies a decision to share living arrangements and sometimes the raising of a family, either in marriage or otherwise.

Sternberg's (1986) theory of love holds that it is the particular combination of these three components—intimacy, passion, and commitment—that determines the nature of the relationship. As Interactive Table 14.3 shows, for example, empty love involves commitment but is devoid of passion or of intimacy ("By $%#$, we'll stay together until the children are gone. Then adios!") **Consummate love,** on the other hand, has all three components. And, interestingly, so does high creativity, says Pyryt (1993). Eminent creative achievers, he claims, are those whose relationship with their work shows evidence of the same sort of intimacy, passion, and commitment that are characteristic of consummate love.

There is a pattern to the development of many relationships, Sternberg suggests. Thus, two individuals might begin with nonlove—no passion, commitment, or intimacy. In time, as intimacy grows, nonlove might give way to infatuation, which has passion but no commitment or intimacy—or perhaps to romantic love, which now adds intimacy but is still short of commitment. Eventually, consummate love might evolve as commitment is brought into the relationship. And perhaps the end result will be marriage or some other long-term commitment, reflecting the resolution of the crisis that Erikson describes for early adulthood.

But even consummate love is not a static, unchanging thing. Sternberg (1986) points out that passion is usually very high early in a consummate relationship. But with the passage of time, it diminishes; at the same time, however, commitment and intimacy might increase. Sternberg suggests that intimacy and commitment are generally viewed as being more important for a lasting love relationship than is passion. However, the breakdown of a marriage, notes Grunebaum (1997), most often stems from emotional problems linked directly to romantic/erotic love (that is, to romantic love and sexual attraction)—evidence of their importance in a lasting relationship.

In trying to explain how this thing called love begins, psychology points its finger at physical attraction, similarity, and propinquity (physical proximity). And in trying to describe its dimensions, it looks at the balance among intimacy, passion, and commitment. But always, it speaks only in generalities. Thus, concerning the love that makes these twins laugh, it says much less than might a poet.

The Rules of Attraction

How does this thing called love begin? And when it has happened, how does one know that it is true love and not puppy love? A romance and not a crush? An *amour* and not an infatuation?

It begins, social psychologists tell us, with **interpersonal attraction,** and interpersonal attraction seems to be strongly influenced by three things: physical attraction, similarity, and proximity. The first of these, physical attractiveness, is important in determining whether people want to see each other again after they have met.

Similarity and physical proximity (often referred to as **propinquity** in social psychology) are related variables. People who are in close proximity are typically those who attend the same schools, churches, or colleges, or who go to the same country clubs, bars, or bingo parlors. By the same token, people who go to the same schools, churches, and other places are likely to be similar in a lot of important ways. Accordingly, there is a high tendency for individuals to select mates from very similar backgrounds and who are, therefore, very similar in social class, race, age, education, and religious background. Research conducted by Burleson, Kunkel, and Szolwinski (1997) provides evidence, as well, that people are most attracted to others whose complexity of

cognitive functioning is at a level similar to theirs—or, perhaps, at a somewhat higher level but not at a lower level. For example, highly abstract, flexible, open thinkers are most attracted to others who are cognitively similar and less attracted to more rigid, compartmentalized thinkers.

Selecting a Mate

Physical attraction, propinquity, and similarity. Put the three together and *voilà,* a potential mate!

Perhaps. But often, it isn't quite so simple. You see, there are dozens, perhaps hundreds, of potential candidates who might all, at one time or another, be sufficiently attractive, sufficiently near, and sufficiently similar to become a potential mate for any given person—well, perhaps not any given person but many given persons.

When South (1991) surveyed 2,000 adults, he found that mate selection is highly influenced by the perceived characteristics of the potential mate. Men placed high value on physical attractiveness and on youthfulness of women; in contrast, women placed higher value on the potential mates' employment stability and earnings. But mate selection followed by marriage is not the only choice, although it is the most common. By the age of sixty-five, more than 95 percent of all adults have been married at least once (U.S. Bureau of the Census, 1996). This figure is very similar to what it was in 1970. The most striking change between 1970 and 1995 is a sharp increase in the age at which people first marry.

Cohabitation, homosexuality, singlehood (with or without children), and a variety of communal living arrangements are among the other lifestyles that young adults might select. We look briefly at each of these before turning to the most common adult lifestyle: marriage.

Cohabitation

Cohabitation, living together without being married, was a rare and scandalous occurrence a mere handful of decades ago. For today's cohorts, it is neither rare nor scandalous.

■ INCIDENCE

In 1970, there were 523,000 unmarried couples living together in the United States—196,000 of whom had children under age 15. This represented only 1.2 percent of all couples—about 1 family out of 100. By 1995, 1 family out of every 16 was unmarried (6 percent of all couples), more than 3.6 million unmarried couples. And more than 1.3 million of them had children under 15 (U.S. Bureau of the Census, 1996). The proportion of unmarried couples is about the same in Canada, where in 1991, about 726,000 couples were classified as **common-law marriages**—an increase of 7.4 percent in a single decade (*Canada Yearbook,* 1997; Statistics Canada, 1995).

Throughout much of Europe, the number of unmarried cohabiting couples has increased even more rapidly than it has in North America. In Sweden, more than one out of every eight couples is not married, and close to 40 percent of all infants are born to unmarried couples.

■ REASONS

Couples live together without marrying for several reasons. Among college students, for example, it has become increasingly common to share accommodations for financial reasons. Sexual relations might or might not be part of the arrangement. Among couples whose relations are intimate, cohabitation is sometimes preferred over marriage because the legal obligations are different, partners want intimacy and passion without long-term commitment, or marriage is simply being delayed. In many cases, cohabitation serves as a sort of "trial marriage" during which couples explore their compatibility and assess the rewards that each is likely to obtain from a permanent relationship. Few cohabiting couples view their arrangement as long-term and permanent. Most plan eventually either to marry the person with whom they currently live or to marry someone else. In fact, however, perhaps as many as two-thirds of all cohabiting couples do not marry each other. Some evidence indicates that white, cohabiting American women are somewhat more likely to marry their partners if they become pregnant; among black women, pregnancy does not increase the likelihood of marriage (W. D. Manning, 1993).

Basic lifestyle choices that young adults make (or allow circumstances to make for them) include singlehood, homosexuality, cohabitation, marriage, or one of a variety of communal living arrangements. Of these, marriage is by far the most common, although numbers of unmarried couples, approximately one third of whom have children, have increased dramatically in the last two decades.

■ WHO COHABITS?

Cohabitation, note Schoen and Weinick (1993), is a distinctly different lifestyle than marriage. Among other things, cohabitors are somewhat less likely to select partners who are highly similar in terms of age, religion, or race—all important variables in mate selection for marriage. At the same time, they are more likely to select those with a similar educational background.

Very generally, those who cohabit have a tendency to be somewhat younger than those who marry. They are also, on average, less religious (in terms of church attendance, for example) and somewhat more unconventional, particularly in terms of family-related values (Demaris & MacDonald, 1993). In the United States, more blacks than whites and more individuals from large population centers than from smaller or more rural areas cohabit (Raley, 1996). Education and employment levels tend to be lower among men who cohabit than among married men. Interestingly, the opposite is true for women. Cohabitant women tend to be better educated and are more often employed than married women.

Other important differences between cohabiting and married couples include the observation that there is usually less commitment in cohabitation. That is, unmarried couples typically do not have the same personal commitment to continuing the relationship over the long term or to maintaining it through difficulty; also, unmarried couples usually do not have the same impediments to terminating the relationship (Hall, 1996). Often, there are few possessions that need to be divided or disposed of, no continuing financial obligations, and no ongoing responsibilities caused by children. But that, of course, is not always the case.

■ COHABITATION AND LATER MARRIAGE

As noted, the majority of those who cohabit view their relationship as temporary. Most intend to eventually marry, although not necessarily to marry the person with whom they are living.

The research is impressively unanimous in indicating that cohabitation is not especially good preparation for later marriage. For example, Thomson and Colella (1992) found that couples who had cohabited before marriage reported poorer quality marriages, viewed marriage less favorably, and were more likely to divorce. Similarly, Stets (1993) found that prior cohabitation with someone other than the current spouse had an especially negative effect on the current marriage.

One possible reason that cohabitation might be associated with less marital satisfaction or stability later is that those who cohabit tend to be more unconventional and to have less traditional views of the family. However, Demaris and MacDonald (1993) found that these factors were largely unrelated to later marital instability.

Another possibility is that some of those who cohabit are more inclined to want to explore relationships, less reluctant to do so, and more willing to make and to change commitments.

■ COMMON-LAW RELATIONSHIPS

In some jurisdictions, cohabitation has legal status and can, therefore, entail the same sorts of legal responsibilities that are more explicit in conventional marriage. When cohabitation defines a legally recognized union of partners, it is termed a **common-law marriage.** Common-law marriages apparently originated on the frontier, where ministers, priests, rabbis, and ships' captains were scarce, and where couples were often forced to exchange "marriage" vows, sometimes in the presence of witnesses but often in private as well. Subsequently, these common-law marriages were upheld as being valid in the courts. The result is that, to this day, if it can be established that a couple intend to live together with the same commitments as a married couple, theirs may be a legal, common-law marriage.

A word of caution is appropriate at this point. There is a danger, when summarizing research of this nature, to mistakenly assume that what is generally true must also be true in individual cases. That, of course, is clearly not the case. For example, to say that unmarried couples are, on the average, younger than married couples is not to deny the fact that there are fifty-, sixty-, and even ninety-year-old couples living together but unmarried. Similarly, to say that unmarried couples typically do not share the same kind and degree of commitment as do married couples is not to deny the fact that there are many couples who are firmly committed to their relationship but who have decided not to marry. It would be highly misleading to suggest that the characteristics of those who cohabit and the possible consequences of cohabitation are as simple as they might appear in this handful of paragraphs. Here, as in so many other areas where social scientists ferret, there are too many exceptions to count.

Homosexuality

Several lifestyles are available to those whose sexual preferences are directed toward members of their own sex (homo-

sexual) rather than toward members of the opposite sex (heterosexual). Here, as elsewhere, however, things are seldom simply an either/or proposition; there are degrees of attraction to one or both sexes.

Estimates of the number of people who are considered to be homosexual vary a great deal and tend to be highly unreliable. In a wide-scale survey in the United States, 2.8 percent of the male respondents and 1.4 percent of the female respondents claimed to be gay or bisexual; about 8 percent of the men and 4 percent of the women had had at least one homosexual experience (Michael et al., 1994).

Homosexuality is still viewed with fear (**homophobia**) and prejudice by many. For example, Berkman and Zinberg (1997) found very high levels of homophobia even among social workers. And those who were not clearly homophobic were nevertheless strongly biased in favor of heterosexuals. Even on university campuses, for example, there are numerous instances of violations of homosexual students' rights to free assembly, access to university services, and so on (Liddell & Douvanis, 1994). For example, D'Augelli (1993) looked at incidents of reported harassment and violence toward lesbians and gay men on a university campus. Fully three-quarters of respondents had been verbally harassed, and one-quarter had been threatened with violence and had been afraid for their safety. The most common episodes of harassment involved verbal insults, which had been experienced by 77 percent of respondents; 14 percent had had personal property damaged; 8 percent had had objects thrown at them; some were spat at, punched, hit, or beaten.

Although it has been deleted from the American Psychiatric Association's manual of mental disorders, many still view homosexuality as deviant and unnatural. In fact, it is only in the last half of this century, note Bullough and Bullough (1997), that homosexuality has begun to be viewed with more tolerance and understanding. In spite of this, there are continuing efforts to reorient the sexuality of homosexuals. Haldeman (1994), following an extensive review of the sexual reorientation literature, reports that there is little evidence that any of these treatments are effective.

Indications are that perhaps fewer than half of homosexual men live as couples, whereas approximately three-quarters of lesbians live in pairs (Harry, 1983). Research on the nature of homosexual couples reveals that, contrary to a popular stereotype, it is uncommon for one partner to adopt the "feminine" role and the other the "masculine" (Bell & Weinberg, 1978).

In addition to obvious differences in sexual orientation, there are several notable differences between homosexual and heterosexual couples. First, most of the literature indicates that couple relationships among homosexuals, especially among gay males, tend to involve younger individuals and not to last as long. Sarantokos (1996) reports relatively high levels of conflict among eighty-two cohabiting homosexual couples. Most of these couples (forty-two lesbian and forty gay) also manifested low levels of commitment and stability. Harry (1983) cautions, however, that many studies might underrepresent older and longer-lasting relationships by drawing most of their samples from gay bars and gay associations, both of which tend to be frequented by younger people.

A second difference concerns sexual exclusivity. Whereas contemporary standards within marriage stress the importance of sexual fidelity, this appears to have been less the case among gay men and women (Peplau, 1981). However, fear of AIDS seems to have reduced promiscuity among gay males, a fact that has resulted in a decline in the number of other sexually transmitted diseases in the gay population (Lamanna & Riedmann, 1988).

Approximately 25 percent of gay men and 33 percent of gay women have been or are married. Of these, many have children. Gay fathers who leave their wives very seldom gain custody of their children. However, some do, and a number establish gay stepfamilies with a male partner. Crosbie-Burnett and Helmbrecht (1993) studied forty-eight such families. They report that happiness in such families was closely tied to the extent to which the gay stepfather was included in family activities and child-rearing decisions. Relationships of gay fathers with their children often remain close and caring even after the children have been told of their father's sexual orientation. The same appears to be true of lesbian mothers, far more of whom retain custody of their children after they have divorced and established a homosexual couple relationship. In addition, in an increasing number of jurisdictions, it has become possible for lesbian couples to adopt children. Following a study of children of both gay and lesbian parents, Patterson (1997) reports no apparent problems among these children. On average, these children showed normal levels of adjustment and self-esteem.

Homosexual relationships may differ from heterosexual relationships in important ways, but the need to love and be loved is common to all people regardless of sexual orientation—and regardless, too, of whether individuals choose to cohabit, to marry, or to remain alone and single.

Singlehood

Single adults include not only those who have never married but also those who are divorced, separated, or widowed. There is strong evidence that each of these categories is growing. The age of marriage has increased dramatically in the last several decades, thereby prolonging the period of singlehood before marriage. In 1960, only 30 percent of women ages twenty to twenty-four had not yet married, but by 1980, that figure had risen to 50 percent; by 1995, it had reached 66.8 percent (U.S. Bureau of the Census, 1994). As we saw previously, the number of unmarried couples living together in the United States increased sixfold between 1970 and 1995. During that period, the number of one-parent families also increased dramatically. Almost one out of every three children (31 percent) under the age of eighteen is now in a one-parent home—more than twice as many as in 1970 (U.S. Bureau of the Census, 1996). In Canada, the proportion of one-parent families is considerably smaller at 13 percent (*Canada Yearbook*, 1997).

■ NEVER-MARRIEDS

Close to 5 percent of the population never marries (95 percent do at least once) (U.S. Bureau of the Census, 1996). The never-marrieds make up the largest group of singles, accounting for almost 20 percent (see "At a Glance: The Never-Marrieds" and Figure 14.3).

Among the never-marrieds are those who have deliberately chosen never to marry, those who have temporarily postponed marriage for one reason or another, and those who have been unsuccessful in finding a mate. Accordingly, several social factors have contributed to the increasing number of never-marrieds, as well as to the rising age of first marriage. Among them are the greater number of women going to college and beginning careers before marriage; expanding career opportunities for women; more women than men at the "most marriageable age"; the increasing divorce rate, which, for some, has reduced the appeal of marriage; the widespread acceptability of cohabitation; and the increasing availability of birth control methods.

One of the important implications of these social changes is that many of the never-marrieds who have deliberately postponed marriage, often for an education or a career, and who see their singlehood as temporary, may end up in a state of involuntary, rather than voluntary, singlehood. This may be especially true of women whose increasing age and increasing educational, social, or professional status may serve to dramatically reduce the number of men who are likely to be suitable mates.

We should hasten to point out that unlike a character in a novel by Jane Austen, who exclaims, "Lord, how ashamed I should be of not being married before three and twenty!" today's generation typically sees no shame in singlehood. Indeed, among men it is not uncommon to take pride in being "le gai bachelor," and perhaps these attitudes are becoming increasingly common among women as well. However, research reported by Lewis and Moon (1997) indicates that many single women are highly ambivalent about being single. Although they are often aware of the advantages and disadvantages of their lifestyle, and although many express a relatively high degree of contentment, for some there remains a feeling of loss, perhaps almost of grief. In addition, notes Linn (1995), many women experience strong social and psychological pressures to have a child. And this, too, can sometimes be a source of conflict and sorrow.

■ THE SEPARATED AND DIVORCED

As we have seen, there are many among the never-married who are voluntarily single, either temporarily or permanently. The singlehood characteristic of the separated and divorced, although it may well result from a deliberate decision to end a marriage, was initially unplanned and may not be quite so voluntary.

Chances of a marriage ending in separation or divorce have increased dramatically in recent decades. More than one in three marriages now end in divorce; indications are that this proportion may soon reach 50 percent (O'Leary &

inglehood includes adults who have never married, as well as the widowed, separated, and divorced. Numbers of the separated and divorced have increased dramatically in recent decades, as have numbers of older wid-

ows. But in 1995, by the age of sixty-five, just as many people had been married at least once as had been the case in 1970. The big change is that age of first marriage had risen dramatically. For example, in 1970, by

the age of twenty-nine, about 80 percent of all males and 90 percent of all females had been married. By 1995, these figures had been reduced to about 49 percent for males and 65 percent for females.

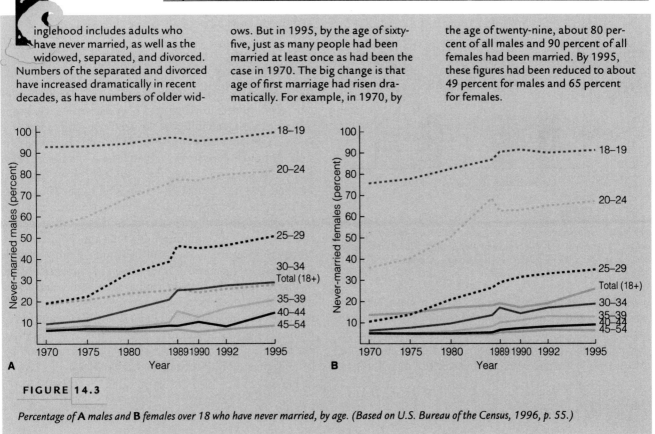

FIGURE 14.3

*Percentage of **A** males and **B** females over 18 who have never married, by age. (Based on U.S. Bureau of the Census, 1996, p. 55.)*

Smith, 1991). However, the majority of those who divorce will remarry. More men remarry than women, and they tend to remarry sooner after divorce (five out of six men and three out of four women typically remarry within three years). Obviously, divorce does not disillusion those who have already been married. And happiness ratings are about the same for people in a second marriage as for comparable people in their first. However, people who have divorced and remarried often report more happiness in their second than in their first marriage (Benson-von der Ohe, 1984).

Because more divorced men than women remarry, because they do so sooner, and because men die sooner than women, there are more separated, divorced, widowed, and never-married women than men in all age groups, but especially at the upper age levels.

Cold statistics do not reveal the potential emotional impact of divorce. In Chapter 8, we looked at this impact on children, more than one of every four (31 percent) of whom are currently living with only one parent—75 percent of them with the mother, 12.5 percent with the father, and the remaining 12.5 percent living with neither parent (U.S. Bureau of the Census, 1996). We noted, among other things, that there are large individual variations in the extent to which children

are chagrined or disturbed by their parents' divorce; these differences are sometimes related to the child's age and sex.

There are large variations in adult reactions to divorce as well. For women, the effects of divorce often include substantial, and sometimes very serious, reductions in income. In 1994 the median income of a female-headed home in the United States was $18,236, that of a male-headed single-parent home was about 52 percent higher at $27,751, and median income in the two-parent home was $44,959 (U.S. Bureau of the Census, 1996). In Canada in 1994, income in a male-headed lone-parent family was 45 percent more than in a comparable female-headed family ($29,141 compared with $15,901). Median income for a two-parent family was $56,362 (*Canada Yearbook,* 1997). (See Figure 14.4.)

In addition to having to cope with reduced income, divorced women must adjust to different living arrangements, establish new social relationships, and sometimes assume a new work role in addition to the old homemaker role (Fine & Fine, 1992). Remarriage also brings a need for new adjustments, and typically also leads to a reduction in support from the ex-husband (Hill, 1992).

The lives of men are often changed less by divorce than those of women, particularly if they continue in the same

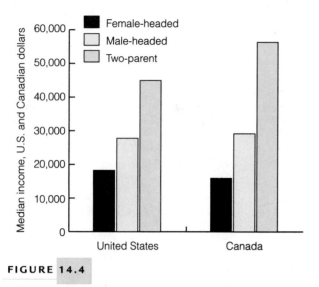

FIGURE 14.4

The cost of single parenting. Note that figures are in U.S. and Canadian dollars, respectively, and cannot be compared directly. (Based on U.S. Bureau of the Census, 1996, p. 469; and Canada Yearbook 1997, *p. 179.)*

work roles. But men, too, need to adjust to new living arrangements and a continued need for intimacy. It is worth noting that studies of happiness typically find that married men are happier than those who are not married, and among the least happy are those who are divorced (Campbell, 1981).

Clearly, however, divorce is not inevitably difficult and traumatic for everyone. And, as we noted in Chapter 8, there are conflict-ridden and unhappy marital relationships in which the partners involved, and the children, may be far better off in different situations.

Communes

Communes are yet another possible lifestyle. But unlike most other choices, this one does not necessarily exclude any other lifestyle. Communes are, by definition, communities— joint, cooperative attempts to carve a happy or useful lifestyle. Although they present a lifestyle that is different from, and hence an alternative to, the lifestyles we have looked at thus far, they are compatible with any of them. Thus, there are communes for conventionally married couples, as well as for people involved in group marriages; there are homosexual and heterosexual communes, religious and political communes, utopian communes, and all manner of other possible communal arrangements. Some communes are established so that members can do their own, presumably unconventional, "thing"; others function primarily to pool individual resources as a means of coping more effectively with society. And still others result from fundamental religious beliefs that can more easily be encouraged and practiced in relative isolation from society. (See Summary Table 14.4.)

SUMMARY TABLE 14.4
Love, Mate Selection, and Lifestyle Choices

CONCEPT	DEFINITIONS/RESEARCH FINDINGS/FACTS
Love	▪ As much the province of the poet as the scientist.
	▪ Science uses scales such as the Liking, Loving scales to measure it.
	▪ Romantic/erotic love characterized by strong feelings of longing, a desire to be intimate, a preoccupation with and overvaluation of the loved one, and a belief that the other is necessary for one's happiness.
	▪ Sternberg's triarchic theory of love describes 8 kinds of love based on the balance among passion (physical desire), intimacy (closeness, affection), and commitment (decision to share).
	▪ Love begins with interpersonal attraction, which requires physical attraction, similarity, and propinquity (geographical closeness); hence, mates are more often alike than different in most important ways.
Lifestyle Choices	▪ Most common is **marriage** (discussed in the next section).
	▪ **Cohabitation** (incidence has increased dramatically in recent decades; occurs for many reasons; may involve long-term commitment but, on average, doesn't; is more common among better educated women, college students, and blacks compared with whites).
	▪ **Common-law relationships** (cohabitation involving the type of commitment that entails varying degrees of legal status in different jurisdictions).
	▪ **Homosexuality** (varying estimates of prevalance; still subject to the effects of homophobia and heterosexist bias, with occasional discrimination and harassment; some evidence of less sexual exclusivity among homosexual couples; no evidence of less than normal adjustment or self-esteem among children [adopted or biological] of gay or lesbian couples).
	▪ **Singlehood** (includes the never-married, widowed, separated, and divorced; sometimes voluntary, sometimes not; can be a source of distress and conflict, especially when involuntary; single parenthood sometimes entails significant economic hardship).
	▪ **Communes** (a community; a group joined by common beliefs and purpose; may take just about as many forms as there are different beliefs and purposes).

MARRIAGE AND HAPPINESS

Although we have a choice of many lifestyles, marriage is the choice of the vast majority. However, it is perhaps notable that we choose it somewhat later than did our parents—and they later than theirs. The median age of first marriage for men is 25.9, and for women it is 24.0 (U.S. Bureau of the Census, 1996) (see Figure 14.5).

In most Western industrialized societies, there is only one officially approved form of marriage: that where each partner is entitled to only one other partner—**monogamy.** Having more than one wife or husband is illegal in North America and is termed **bigamy** by the courts. **Polygamy** is a more general expression for the same state of affairs. It includes **polygyny,** where the man is permitted to have more than one wife, and **polyandry,** where a wife is permitted more than one husband. Murdock (1957) looked at 554 of the world's societies and found that only 24 percent sanctioned only monogamy. The vast majority (75 percent) permit polygyny; only 1 percent permit polyandry (see Table 14.5). Note, however, that even in those societies that permit one or more forms of polygamy, these are typically the exception rather than the rule. Often only the old and the wealthy can afford more than one wife (or husband). Often, too, only the very highly placed in the social hierarchy are permitted polygamy. Even today, however, in certain African countries such as Transkei, polygyny is not uncommon (Cherian, 1990).

Although contemporary Western societies do not permit polygamy, they do permit what Mead (1970) calls *serial monogamy:* We are free to marry, divorce, and remarry an unlimited number of times. (See "At a Glance: Changes in Marriage" and Figure 14.6.) In addition, various group-sex arrangements, mate swapping, open marriages, and other forms of sexual and emotional permissiveness, while not a dominant part of the current social mainstream, are nevertheless not altogether uncommon.

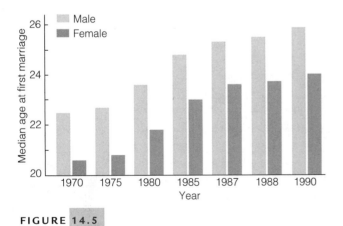

FIGURE 14.5

Median age of first marriage for men and women in the United States. (Based on U.S. Bureau of the Census, 1996, p. 105.)

TABLE 14.5

Common Forms of Marriage Among 554 of the World's Societies

TYPE OF MARRIAGE	NUMBER OF SOCIETIES	PERCENTAGE
Monogamy	135	24
Polygamy	419	76
Polyandry	4	1
Polygyny	415	75

Source: Based on data reported in "World Ethnographic Sample" by G. P. Murdock, 1957, *American Anthropologist, 59,* pp. 676–688. Reprinted by permission of the American Anthropological Association.

Premarital Sex

Indications are clear that monogamy is not what it used to be. This is particularly true for the many women whose roles were determined largely by the well-known double standard that was rampant until recently and that still rears its head on occasion in various male bastions: "Boys will be boys, you know." It went without saying that "girls will not be girls; if they must be anything, they will be angels." As we saw in Chapter 12, approximately as many women as men are now nonvirgins when they marry (see Figure 12.3, Chapter 12).

Contrary to some popular predictions, however, the sexual revolution did not translate itself into widespread, indiscriminate, totally recreational sex, although there is clearly more of this type of sexual activity now than there was when my grandfather sowed his particular species of oats. True, the sexual revolution of these past decades does manifest itself in greater sexual permissiveness. But it is a permissiveness that, with some notable exceptions, insists on affection. And even when dating and in love, 40 percent of the males and more than 80 percent of the females in Roche and Ramsbey's study of 268 college students did not engage in sexual intercourse (see Figure 12.5, Chapter 12). In addition, incidence of premarital sex among this sample had dropped significantly for girls in the preceding five years, although this was not the case for boys. Among girls, high self-esteem and positive attitudes toward school and family are closely related to the decision not to engage in premarital sex (Plotnick, 1992).

Extramarital Sex

Among the several alternatives to the traditional marital relationship are a number that propose sexual nonexclusivity—that condone extramarital sexual relations (see Table 14.6). Although extramarital sex (**adultery,** if a spade is to be called a shovel) is apparently not entirely uncommon, most societies discourage its practice, often on the grounds that it threatens the family unit. However, there is ample evidence of a powerful double standard here, as there is with respect to

Changes in Marriage

arriage is as popular an institution as ever, but recent years have seen significant changes. Both men and women are now marrying about three years later than they were two decades ago. In addition, fewer marriages are the first marriage for either partner (more are remarriages). Interestingly, for marriages that end in divorce (approximately half), the median duration has not changed in almost two decades—it is still about seven years. (Does this prove the existence of the seven-year itch?)

FIGURE 14.6

A *Median duration of first marriage, and* **B** *changes in composition of first and subsequent marriages, 1970–1990. (Based on U.S. Bureau of the Census, 1996, pp. 104, 105.)*

premarital sex. In Japan and in many European countries, it is quite acceptable for a man to have a mistress, providing he is reasonably discreet about the affair and continues to meet his family obligations. The same behavior is far less easily tolerated among married women and, indeed, is often grounds for punishment or divorce; such is seldom the case when the man is the adulterer.

A recent survey of more than 3,000 men and women in the United States reveals that extramarital sex is not overwhelmingly common. In this survey, 85 percent of the mar-

TABLE 14.6

Alternative Nonexclusive Marital Lifestyles

TYPE	CHARACTERISTICS
Open marriage	Major concern is with the independence and growth of individual partners and the development of mutually accepted rules governing the relationship.
Extramarital sex	Mostly nonconsensual, secretive, clandestine "sexual affairs" that tend to be of short duration.
Nonsexual extramarital relationships	More open, nonsexual opposite-sex relationships involving dinners and movies, for example; apparently widely approved by college populations.
Sexually open marriage	An open arrangement designed to permit sexual adventuring by either or both partners with other individuals in independent relationships that do not threaten the marriage.
Swinging	Concerned with recreational sex rather than with relationships and often involves groups and mate swapping.
Group marriage	An uncommon alternative usually involving four adults (two spouse pairs).

Source: Based on "'Open' Marriage and Multilateral Relationships: The Emergence of Nonexclusive Models of the Marital Relationship" by D. L. Weis, 1983. In *Contemporary Families and Alternative Lifestyles: Handbook on Research and Theory* (pp. 194–215), E. D. Macklin and R. H. Rubin (Eds.), 1983, Beverly Hills, CA: Sage. Used by permission of the publisher.

AT A GLANCE

Marriage and Divorce

Divorce rates in the United States more than doubled between 1960 and 1975, and have remained relatively constant since then, at about 4.8 per 1,000 population. At present, about half of all marriages end in divorce. The majority of those

who divorce remarry, about half of them within five years. Although marriage rates have declined slightly in very recent years, marriage is still about twice as common as divorce. In Canada, marriage rates are only slightly more than half as high as in the United

States (5.5 per 1,000 in 1995 compared with 9.1 in the United States). However, divorce rates are also proportionally lower, meaning that there are correspondingly fewer second marriages (U.S. Bureau of the Census, 1996; *Canada Sourcebook*, 1997).

A

B

FIGURE 14.7

A *Marriage rate and* **B** *divorce rate per 1,000 population. (U.S. Bureau of the Census, 1996, p. 104.)*

---

ried women and 75 percent of the married men reported that they were faithful to their spouses (Michael et al., 1994).

Types of Marriage Relationships

We know that about half of all new marriages now end in divorce (see "At a Glance: Marriage and Divorce" and Figure 14.7). We know, too, that some spouses, even if they remain married all their lives, will not always be sexually faithful. But we also know that married people describe their lives in more satisfactory terms and see themselves as being happier than those who remain single (or who are separated, divorced, or widowed).

To describe a marriage as being either "good" or "bad" is usually oversimplistic. There can be much that is good and much that is bad in any marriage. But it might be helpful to know what a "good" marriage can be like. Lavee and Olson (1993) provide us with some answers. They studied 8,385 marriages, analyzing them in terms of nine major dimensions, such as personality issues, communication, conflict resolution, financial management, sexual relationships, and relationships with children, family, and friends. Subsequently, they identified seven different types of relationships, each of which reflects different values and emphases with respect to the nine dimensions studied.

At one extreme is the *vitalized couple,* in which each of the spouses expresses a high degree of satisfaction with all aspects of the marriage. At the other is the *devitalized couple,* in which both are dissatisfied with all aspects of the marriage. *Financially focused couples* are bound by material and financial goals in relationships marked by dissatisfaction with all aspects of the marriage except the financial. The *conflicted couple* shows dissatisfaction with the couple-related issues (communication, personality, conflict resolution) but higher satisfaction with external issues like leisure-time activities. In contrast, the *harmonious marriage* is characterized by high accord with respect to couple-related issues but less agreement regarding external activities. *Traditional couples* experience considerable stress with interspousal relationships but share high satisfaction with respect to family and religious values. And *balanced couples* are generally satisfied with most aspects of their marriage in spite of some problems in different areas.[*]

In the Lavee and Olson (1993) study, 40 percent of the more than 8,000 couples could be described as devitalized

---

[*]"Frank and me," said my grandmother, "We had a pretty good marriage. He never said too much."

"En boca cerrada no entran moscas," I hit her with a Spanish proverb, sort of a retaliation for all the sayings she's thrown at me over the years. "Flies don't go into a closed mouth," I translated for her.

"Don't kick a dead donkey in the rear end," she threw back at me, not for the first time—which I still can't figure out.

(high dissatisfaction with all aspects of the marriage) and only 9 percent as vitalized (high satisfaction with all aspects of the relationship). Membership in other categories was relatively evenly distributed (see Figure 14.8).

These seven types of marriages describe the nature of the relationships that are possible between husband and wife, but they do not describe whether a marriage is good or bad. In fact, note Lavee and Olson, happy (and unhappy) families can differ a great deal. Some happy couples might be happy with all aspects of their marriage (in this study, only about 9 percent were, however), and some might be quite dissatisfied with certain aspects of their relationship but still describe themselves as generally happy. Thus, even among the most happy of marriages (the vitalized), almost one-quarter of the women and 16 percent of the men admitted to having considered divorce. It is perhaps equally significant, however, that among the least happy couples (those in devitalized relationships), 25 percent of the women and 37 percent of the men claimed that they had *not* considered divorce. Hence, each of these different types of relationships can be characteristic of an enduring marriage.

■ MARITAL DISCORD

But each can also be marked by considerable marital discord, which can be an extremely serious problem, say O'Leary and Smith (1991). Not only do difficulties with relationships cause great distress and unhappiness among married couples, as well as among their children, but they are the most important factor in many suicides. Relationship problems are also involved in a large number of family homicides.

The reasons for marital discord are complex and varied. O'Leary and Smith (1991) review a number of studies suggesting that marriage partners tend to select each other for similarity of personality traits, values, goals, and other important characteristics. Apparently, a basic wisdom guides this selection process, because degree of similarity is predictive of marital adjustment and satisfaction; by the same token, dissimilarity may be associated with marital discord.

Also related to marital discord are certain personality variables associated with depression and emotional instability—characteristics such as impulsivity, fearfulness, poor social adjustment, and what is termed **dysphoria,** which means a general unhappiness (Beach & O'Leary, 1993). In addition, those who initially hold nontraditional views about marriage and family life are more likely to be less satisfied with their marriages (Lye & Biblarz, 1993).

Research indicates that marital dissatisfaction tends to increase over the early years of marriage as partners are required to make difficult adjustments, and perhaps to reassess their expectations of everlasting, idealized romantic love (Belsky &

FIGURE 14.8

Lavee and Olson's seven types of marriage. (Based on Lavee & Olson, 1993.)

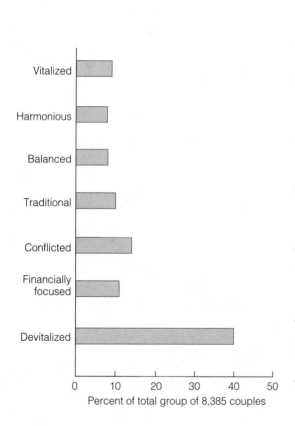

Type of marriage	Main characteristics	Percent in category	Percent dissatisfied with marriage	
			Male	Female
Vitalized	High satisfaction with all aspects of the marriage	9	1.2	2.7
Harmonious	High accord regarding couples-related issues; less accord regarding external issues	8	5.9	9.7
Balanced	Generally high satisfaction but with varied problem areas	8	4.1	10.8
Traditional	High stress with interspousal relations; high satisfaction with family and religious values	10	12.4	23.9
Conflicted	Dissatisfaction with couples' issues like communication; satisfaction with external issues like leisure time	14	24.2	38.4
Financially focused	Bound by material and financial goals; low satisfaction with other aspects of relationship	11	31.3	45.8
Devitalized	High dissatisfaction with all aspects of marriage	40	39.7	57.6

Rovine, 1990). Not surprisingly, about one-third of all divorces occur within the first four years of marriage (U.S. Bureau of the Census, 1996).

Marital discord is often characterized by misunderstanding among partners, poor communication, misinterpretation of actions and intentions, and limited engagement in shared activities (Kayser, 1996). A large number of marriage enhancement programs have arisen to remedy these conditions and restore harmony to discordant marriages. Many of these, note O'Leary and Smith (1991), have not been systematically investigated and may have no beneficial effects. However, others have been shown to be effective for some couples.

■ MARITAL SATISFACTION

The simple longevity of a marriage may be a poor indicator of marital satisfaction. Indeed, a great many abjectly miserable marriages endure, and a number of perfectly contented marriages may end too abruptly.

We ask a great deal of our marriages. Our forebears asked mostly that marriage bring them a workable, child-rearing arrangement with a clear division of duties and responsibilities. Now we expect marriage to make us happy; we think happiness is our right. And if it does not come sooner, we seldom wait for it to come later. We simply try again.

But are the married happier? More satisfied? The evidence suggests yes. When compared with unmarried individuals, married people at all ages report higher levels of satisfaction and happiness. Coombs (1991) reviewed 130 studies of the relationship between marriage and well-being, concluding that "Married men and women are generally happier and less stressed than the unmarried" (p. 97).

Happiness in marriage does not appear to be a static, unchanging thing. Although some studies find little relationship between length of marriage and measures of marital happiness, most studies indicate that there is a curvilinear relationship between the two. Couples tend to report highest levels of satisfaction in the early, prechildbearing years of marriage, least satisfaction through the childbearing years, and a return to higher levels of satisfaction in later years (see Figure 14.9). The lowest point with respect to marital happiness, report Vaillant and Vaillant (1993) following a forty-year study of 169 college men and their wives, is approximately twenty years into the marriage. Researchers have hypothesized that the presence of children puts considerable strain on a couple. And twenty years into the marriage coincides with the teen-rearing years. The requirements associated with raising children, and especially teenagers, make tremendous demands on the time and energy of parents. In addition, this is often the time when career demands on the father are greatest. As a result, time for interaction between spouses and for leisure activities becomes scarce.

In spite of the fact that marital happiness often declines in midmarriage, absolute levels of happiness, as we saw earlier, tend to be higher for the married than for the single, although perhaps not markedly so. And happiness, of course, is relative and highly individualistic. It does not allow itself to be easily measured.

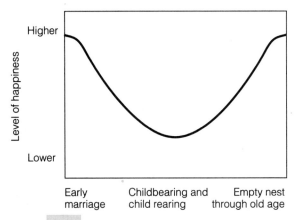

FIGURE 14.9

Graphic representation of U-shaped curvilinear relationship between level of marital happiness and stage in family life cycle. Note that the lower levels of reported happiness through the child-rearing years do not indicate unhappiness. Note, too, that happiness is highly individualistic and highly varied. Clearly, not all marriages follow this idealized pattern.

■ WHO AMONG THE MARRIED ARE HAPPIEST?

Skolnick (1981) provides some insights into who among the married might be happier and why, following intensive interviews with 232 members of the Oakland Guidance Study and the Berkeley Guidance Study. In this study, several social factors appeared to be closely related to marital satisfaction. For women, the most important of these was age at first marriage. In general, the older the woman, the more likely she is to be happily married later on. That teenage marriages break up twice as frequently as older marriages is additional corroboration of this finding. For men, the social variable most highly related to marital satisfaction is occupation, with socioeconomic status, a closely related variable, being almost equally important. In general, executives and professionals tend to be more happily married than other men. And for both men and women, amount of education is positively related to marital satisfaction, as is socioeconomic status and absence of children. Contrary to what might be expected, couples who are voluntarily childless report higher levels of happiness than couples with children (Somers, 1993).

Skolnick also looked at the contribution of personality variables to marital happiness. Like most other researchers, she found that opposites do not attract and complement each other or live happy lives because the strengths of one make up for the weaknesses of the other. Quite the contrary, similar people are attracted to each other. Indeed, the more similar members of a pair were, the more likely they were to report high marital satisfaction. This was particularly true of cognitive variables such as intelligence and impulsiveness or reflectiveness. It is also true of social characteristics. Couples in which both members share some major social characteristic (for example, both are highly aggressive or highly sociable) tend to live in greater harmony than those in which each is the opposite of the other. In fact, following a study of 59 dating and 107 newlywed couples, Botwin, Buss, and Shackelford (1997) conclude that how alike members of a couple are is one of the best predictors of marital and sexual satisfaction.

Finally, Skolnick (1981) reports that those marriages that were rated most satisfactory were typically those in which spouses liked, admired, and respected each other. In contrast, spouses who had discordant personalities, who were critical of each other, and who saw their relationship as utilitarian (rather than as personally close) were more likely to have unhappy marriages. Related to this, Rankin-Esquer and associates (1997) found that the happiest couples tend to be those couples where each member grants the other a high degree of autonomy, encouraging a sense of independence and individuality, while at the same time retaining a sense of closeness, of relatedness.

Sex, too, appears to be related to marital happiness, with both men and women selecting it as one of their favorite activities—and many singling out unsatisfactory sexual relations as the reason for unhappy marriages. Trudel, Landry, and Larose (1997) examined the relationship between low sexual desire and marital adjustment among forty couples, in twenty of which at least one of the partners had expressed lack of sexual interest. Among these couples, frequency of sexual activity was no more than twice per month. The other twenty couples had no desire-related problems and engaged in sex at least twice per week. As expected, couples with sexual desire problems were significantly less happy with their marriages. But whether their poor marital adjustment resulted from a lack of sexual desire, or whether the lack of desire caused the poor adjustment, isn't clear.

On average, frequency of sexual intercourse is highest for the first few years after marriage and then declines rapidly for the next few years. Subsequent average declines are more gradual (see Figure 14.10). Initial declines probably have more to do with the woman becoming pregnant and with the resulting pressures, time constraints, and lack of privacy associated with child rearing than with declining sexual interest. Most evidence suggests, in fact, that males do not experience a noticeable reduction in sexual interest until well into middle age, and 40 percent of married couples claim they have sex at least twice a week (Michael et al., 1994). Women, too, report little reduction in sexual interest or, indeed, in sexual responsiveness through the bulk of their adult years. Solnick and Corby (1983) report that some women are still capable of orgasm well into their seventies and eighties. (See Summary Table 14.7.)

THE CHANGING FAMILY

A marriage is simply the legal union of two individuals. However, its social function goes considerably beyond these two individuals; it makes possible the family, of which, historically, there have been two types. The one most common in

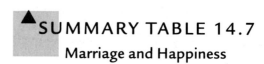

SUMMARY TABLE 14.7
Marriage and Happiness

CONCEPT	COMMENTS/RESEARCH FINDINGS
Kinds of marriage	■ Monogamy (one spouse) most common form in the industrialized world; other primarily recreational options include open marriages, group marriages, and extramarital sex. ■ Premarital sex is highly common; extramarital sex is much less so.
Seven types of marriage from most to least common	■ Devitalized (high dissatisfaction with all aspects of marriage). ■ Conflicted (dissatisfaction with couples' issues; more satisfaction with external issues). ■ Financially focused (bound by material goals; low couple satisfaction). ■ Traditional (high intercouple stress; satisfaction with family and religious values). ■ Vitalized (high satisfaction with all aspects of marriage). ■ Balanced (high satisfaction; some problem areas). ■ Harmonious (high couples' issues satisfaction; less satisfaction with external issues).
Marital discord and satisfaction	■ The married are generally happier than those not married. ■ The happiest are those who are most similar in personality, values, goals. . . . ■ Where members like and respect each other, granting each other autonomy while maintaining high relatedness, marital satisfaction is higher. ■ Sexual desire and activity are important components of most happy marriages; lack of desire is a common source of discord.

FIGURE 14.10

Average frequency of intercourse per month according to years of marriage. (Based on L. A. Westoff and C. F. Westoff, From Now to Zero, *1971. Reprinted by permission of Little, Brown & Co., Inc.)*

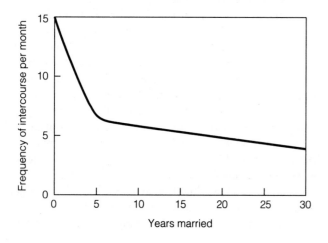

Western societies consists of parents and their immediate children, and is termed the **nuclear family.** That which is most prevalent throughout the world includes grandparents and assorted other relatives in addition to children and their parents, and is termed the **extended family.**

Some widely held notions about what "proper" or "ideal" families are like are based directly on a no longer entirely realistic belief that North American families are nearly all nuclear, mother–father–children families—or, ideally, should be. This image, note White and Woollett (1992), is widely portrayed on television. But it is a misleading image because of some dramatic and well-known changes in the family (see Figure 14.11). Among other things, the North American nuclear family is much shorter-lived (about half of all first marriages end in divorce, and in an average of about seven years), far more couples cohabit without marrying, there has been a sharp increase in one-parent families, and increasing numbers of children are being raised in stepfamilies.

In spite of these changes, the nuclear family is still the most prevalent child-rearing unit in North America. Whereas in 1970, 85 percent of American children lived with both parents, in 1995, the percentage was still 69 (76 percent of whites, 63 percent of Hispanics, and 33 percent of blacks; U.S. Bureau of the Census, 1994). Hence, the following discussion of the family is based primarily on a description of systematic changes in the intact nuclear family with the coming and leaving of children, and with the aging of parents. However, bear in mind that this is a description of only one of North America's many families.

FIGURE 14.11

Decline in percentage of children living at home with both parents, 1970–1995. (Data from U.S. Bureau of the Census, 1996, p. 65.)

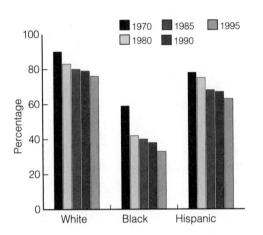

The Life-Cycle Approach: Duvall

A family may be thought of as having a life cycle—a beginning, a growing and changing, and eventually an ending. The **family life cycle** concept provides a useful basis for describing the family and its functions. One example of this approach, described here, is provided by Duvall (1977). He identifies eight sequential stages in the evolution of the family. These stages often overlap and can also be very different for different families. In the main, however, they describe a relatively common progression identifiable in terms of a series of important developmental tasks, most of which relate to child rearing (see Interactive Figure 14.12). But keep in mind that the family cycle described here applies primarily to

INTERACTIVE FIGURE 14.12

Duvall's eight stages of the family life cycle: At which stage of the cycle is your parents' family? Your family, if you are married? What are the tasks and responsibilities of those stages? (From Duvall, 1977, p. 148. Based on data from the U.S. Bureau of the Census and from the National Center for Health Statistics, Washington, DC.)

1. Married couples without children
2. Childbearing families (oldest child birth–30 months)
3. Families with preschool children (oldest child 30 months–6 years)
4. Families with schoolchildren (oldest child 6–13 years)
5. Families with teenagers (oldest child 13–20 years)
6. Families launching young adults (first child gone to last child leaving home)
7. Middle-aged parents (empty nest to retirement)
8. Aging family members (retirement to death of both spouses)

ince 1970, the average age at first marriage has increased by about three years. In addition, as increasing numbers of women have entered the workplace, some have delayed having children; others have decided not to have any. As a result, overall birthrate in the United States has dropped by about 20 percent in the last two decades (from 87.9 per 1,000 women between ages 15 and 44 in 1970 to 67.6 in 1993). As is shown in Figure 14.13, the peak childbearing years in 1970 were between 20 and 24; in 1991, they were between 25 and 29. In Canada, birth rates have also dropped by about 20 percent since 1975 (Figure 14.14).

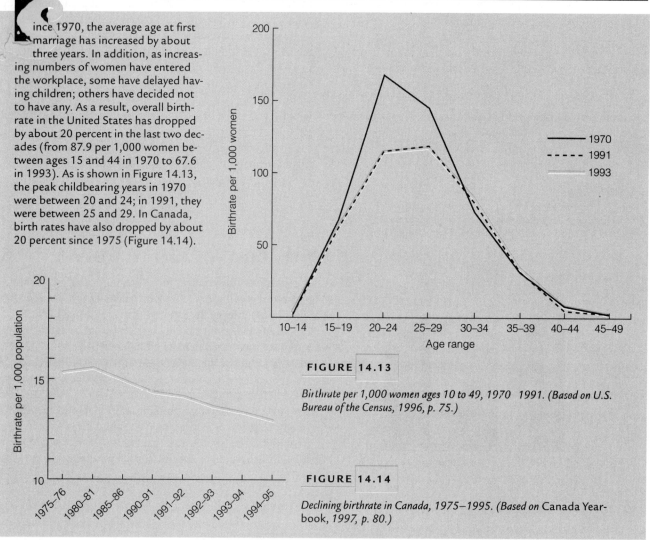

FIGURE 14.13

Birthrate per 1,000 women ages 10 to 49, 1970–1991. (Based on U.S. Bureau of the Census, 1996, p. 75.)

FIGURE 14.14

Declining birthrate in Canada, 1975–1995. (Based on Canada Yearbook, 1997, p. 80.)

"traditional" first-marriage, child-rearing families. In addition, this approach neglects the many important influences on the family other than children—such as careers, as well as relationships with parents, friends, siblings, and spouse. Also, it concentrates on the influence of the first, and thus oldest, child, and ignores the impact of other children. Finally, it applies primarily to North American cultures and very little to cultures such as the Chinese, where the role of children is very different—not only because of different emphases and rituals, but also because of the responsibility that children bear for their elderly parents (Hamilton, 1996). However, other approaches that include more factors become too complex to be very practical.

The first five of Duvall's eight stages span the period of early adulthood and are described briefly here. The sixth and seventh last through middle adulthood and are discussed in Chapter 16; the eighth stage is covered in Chapter 18.

■ STAGE 1: TO HAVE CHILDREN?

Most families begin as a childless couple, a period that, in Duvall's model, lasts for approximately two years. In fact, however, when Duvall developed his model, the largest number of births occurred to women between ages twenty and twenty-four, but in 1991, women had more children between the ages of twenty-five and twenty-nine than at any other period—and women aged thirty to thirty-four had almost as many (see "At a Glance: Changing Birthrates and Age of Childbearing" and Figures 14.13 and 14.14). Hence, the first stage (sometimes called the honeymoon stage) might now last much longer.

The first stage often brings with it three important sets of developmental tasks: those having to do with selecting and developing a career (or finding and keeping a job), those relating to sexual fulfillment and the development of a harmonious marriage, and those relating to whether and when to have children, a decision that is often more complicated in families in which both partners have careers.* As Wilk (1986) points out, in the dual-career family, the decision to start a family (or not to do so) will be affected by at least four groups of considerations. The first two of these, lifestyle and career issues, are most relevant to women who work. The other two, marriage and psychological issues, affect all potential parents.

Lifestyle issues involve questions relating to how the presence of children might change the partners' activities, the impact of potential reduction of income coupled with the costs associated with child rearing, and decisions that have been made or are being made by important reference groups such as friends and co-workers.

Career issues relate to whether the wife is satisfied with her career and her future career prospects, and whether the development of her career can survive one or more interruptions. The transition to a parenting role is sometimes more difficult for dual-career families, and especially for mothers in these families (Romanin & Over, 1993).

Marriage issues have to do with how happy each of the partners is with their marriage, how stable they think it is, and how they think it will respond to the introduction of children. As we noted earlier, the family is a dynamic system. It changes as its composition changes, and it changes, as well, in response to changes in its larger context. It is, in the jargon of this age, an ecological system, composed of complex and ever-changing relationships that give it a life of its own. The strength and viability of this system, its likely effects on children, and the likely effects of children on it are all important factors—not only for dual-career families but also for others.

Psychological factors that are important in making a childbearing decision affect all potential mothers—and all potential fathers as well. They have to do with individual values and preferences and are related to a host of other variables, the most important of which might be the potential parents' relationships with their own parents when they were children. There are some who do not want children for personal reasons. (Wilk's [1986] decision-making model is summarized in Figure 14.15.) (See also "In the News and on the Net: Abortion Wars.")

There are those for whom the question is difficult; sometimes it is simply put off as a result. There are some, too, who do not ask or answer the question but who simply let nature or luck answer it for them. And there are others for whom the answer is so clear that they scarcely need to ask themselves the question.

Stages 2–5: Child Rearing

The next twenty years of Duvall's family life cycle are the childbearing and child-rearing years. However, keep in mind

---

*My grandmother was of another era. "Humphf," she snorted when she read this. "Like the Japanese say, 'Children are treasures more precious than a thousand granaries!'"

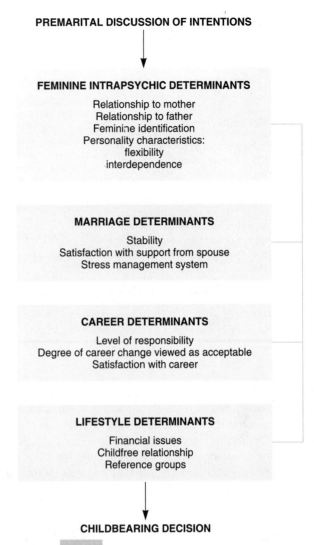

FIGURE 14.15

A dual-career childbearing decision model. (From C. A. Wilk, Career Women and Childbearing. *© 1986 Van Nostrand Reinhold. Used by permission.)*

that this stage now often occurs much later than was recently the case. And for those who do not have children, it simply doesn't happen.

STAGE 2: INFANCY

The infancy stage of the life cycle begins with the birth of the first child and lasts approximately two and a half years. Much of the literature that deals with this period, note Seltzer and Ryff (1994), deals with the effects of parents and parenting on infants rather than on parents. A lifespan view of the family life cycle changes that focus. It recognizes, for example, that this is a period of very rapid changes and adjustments in the family, bringing a variety of demands for both mother and father. Among other things, the mother is called upon to develop and clarify her roles as mother, wife, and person; she needs to learn how to care for and cope with infants and young preschoolers; she needs to maintain a satisfying relationship with her husband; and she must, through innipeg gynecologist and obstetrician Jack Fainman is reported to be in stable condition after being shot in the right shoulder yesterday. His attacker fired through the window of Dr. Fainman's home. Dr. Fainman is associated with the performing of abortions. He is the third gynecologist who has been shot in Canada in recent years—all in November near Canadian Remembrance Day. One police theory is that these shootings are related and are an expression of extreme anti-abortion sentiments.

1. Roberts, D. (1997, Nov. 13). Abortion link pursued in shooting. *Toronto Globe and Mail*, p. A1.

To Consider

Few issues are as controversial and as emotional as the abortion issue. You might consider expressing your thoughts on the issue (or clarifying them) and attempting to determine their bases. Are your opinions grounded in religion? In emotion? In science? In law? Were they initially borrowed, or did you develop them yourself?

On the Net

Links to pro-choice web sites may be found at:

http://www.caral.org/abortion.html

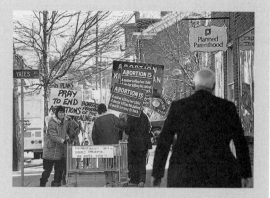

For links to anti-choice sites, go to:

http://www.caral.org/7.anti.html#anti

---

all this, nevertheless maintain some sense of personal autonomy. The father, too, is required to make numerous adjustments, including reconciling conflicting conceptions of his role as father, accepting new responsibilities for parenting, conforming to changes in schedules, coping with the reduced time and attention that the wife can now devote to him, and maintaining a satisfying marital relationship and a

Current lifespan models of the family life cycle recognize that among the most profound and predictable changes in the development of the family are those relating to having and raising children. Not only will his family exert tremendous influence on this infant, but the infant's presence and personality will also shape the nature of his family—even affecting how mother and father relate to each other.

sense of autonomy and self-worth. Not surprisingly, evidence reported by Seltzer and Ryff (1994) suggests that parents whose infants were characterized by "easy" rather than "difficult" temperaments adjust more easily to parenthood and see it as a more positive experience.

■ STAGE 3: PRESCHOOL

As the first child reaches the preschool age, the family enters the third stage of Duvall's family life cycle. It begins when the first child is two, ends with school age (six), and brings with it a continuation of most of the developmental tasks that were first introduced in the preceding stage. Few of these tasks are ever completely resolved during any one phase of the cycle. Indeed, important tasks such as maintaining a sense of autonomy and worth while striving for the development of a mutually satisfying and happy marriage continue from the beginning to the very end of the family life cycle. In addition, the presence of preschoolers in the family brings additional demands for income, space, equipment, time, and attention, as well as a new set of child-rearing responsibilities and problems. And to complicate matters, only those families with a single child can be described as being in only one developmental phase at one time. For many families, there is considerable overlap among stages as additional children are born.

■ STAGE 4: PRETEEN SCHOOL YEARS

The fourth stage, much longer than any of the first three, spans the preteen school years of the oldest child (six to thirteen). It brings three important developmental tasks, none of which is exclusive to this developmental phase, but all of which are fundamentally important to the happy and effective functioning of the family: providing for children's special as well as ordinary needs, enjoying life with children, and encouraging children's growth. Although these tasks are difficult and demanding, most parents raise their children without a great deal of deliberation or guidance, relying primarily on intuition, folk wisdom, and their recollection of the child-rearing techniques of their parents. Interestingly, a study of 454 couples indicates that parents who had more socialization experiences related to child rearing (for example, babysitting, teaching, being a camp counselor, looking after siblings, or taking parenting courses) were happier parents who more easily made the transition to parenthood (Gage & Hendrickson Christensen, 1991).

STAGE 5: TEEN YEARS

The fifth phase in the family life cycle spans the teen years of the oldest child (thirteen to twenty) and brings with it the occasional parenting problems of adolescence. These present many family developmental tasks, including working out possible financial problems, reallocating the sharing of responsibilities, bridging the communication gap between generations, and, all the while, continuing to maintain the marriage relationship. Seltzer and Ryff (1994) cite evidence that parents who have strong commitments to their occupations are less likely to experience conflict and stress related to the increasing independence of their adolescents.

An Evaluation of the Life-Cycle Approach

It is important to keep in mind that life-cycle approaches such as Duvall's describe common patterns in traditional families. However, increasing numbers of families are no longer traditional. As a result, many of the important events that serve as transitions from one stage to another in the evolution of the family now occur much later than they once did, or don't occur at all. Not only are young adults getting married at later ages, but many are also delaying the start of a family. And increasing numbers of adult children continue to live with their parents. In fact, Aquilino (1990) reports that about 45 percent of parents ages forty-five to fifty-four who have adult children have an adult child living at home.

Approaches such as this also tend to oversimplify very complex and highly dynamic relationships. They are based on assumptions that might not always be correct—for example, that families with more than one child go through the same sorts of changes as families with only one child. Nor can they take into account the impact of family crises such as death and divorce, and they say little about the vast number of families that do not fit the once-traditional mold of working father and homemaking mother. Divorce, one-parent families, career mothers, and a variety of other family situations that have become increasingly common in recent decades present different sets of problems and tasks. In spite of this, however, we should not forget that no matter the nature of their families, children still progress in similar ways through their infancies and childhoods, into their adolescence, and finally into the world. And it is children who, after all, define the very existence and nature of the family. (See Summary Table 14.8.)

▲ SUMMARY TABLE 14.8
The Changing Family

Major recent changes in the family	■ Once-traditional family (mother, working father, child) no longer nearly as common (20 percent reduction in number of under-18s living with parents).
	■ Increase in average age of first marriage.
	■ Increase in age of having first child.
	■ Declining birthrate and family size.
First 5 of Duvall's 8 stages of the family life cycle	1. Married couples (to have or not to have children).
	2. Child rearing: infancy (birth of oldest child to 30 mos.; major adjustment in marital roles).
	3. Child rearing: preschool (challenge of juggling demands of marital relationship, child rearing, and continued autonomy).
	4. Preteen years (challenge of providing for children's emotional and physical needs while still maintaining a healthy marital relationship and satisfying personal needs for growth).
	5. Teen years (time of high career demands and sometimes difficult parenting responsibilities).
A caution	■ The Duval description of major events in the family life cycle is largely inapplicable to lone-parent families, to many minority-culture families, to gay and lesbian families, and to many others.

SEXUAL AND FAMILY VIOLENCE

Prophets and others who specialize in gloom and related states have been warning us for some time that violence is rapidly becoming a way of life in contemporary societies. And perhaps they are correct. Certainly, rates for many violent crimes have increased in recent years (Figure 14.16). In particular, sexual violence seems to have increased dramatically in recent decades (Figure 14.17).

Although it might be tempting to assume that violence typically involves strangers and that surrounding ourselves with friends and family will therefore protect us, that, sadly, does not appear to be the case. Indeed, more than 25 percent of all assaults and homicides that are reported to police involve members of the same family, and 47 percent of all crime victims know the perpetrator. More than two-thirds of all rapes, crimes that most of us attribute to disturbed strangers in dark parking lots, are committed by acquaintances or relatives—or "dates." One-third of all female murder victims are killed by boyfriends or husbands (U.S. Bureau of the Census, 1996). As Gelles (1978) puts it, "We have discovered that violence between family members, rather than being a

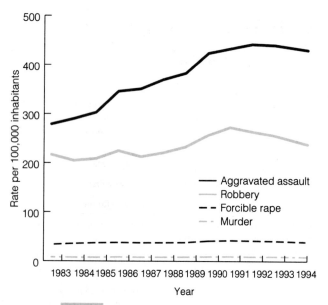

FIGURE 14.16

Increases in rates of selected crimes in the United States, 1983–1994. (Based on U.S. Bureau of the Census, 1996, p. 201.)

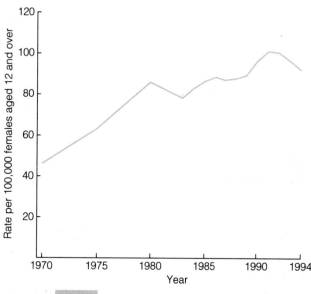

FIGURE 14.17

Rate of forcible rape, 1970–1994. Rate per 100,000 females aged 12 and over. (Based on U.S. Bureau of the Census, 1996, p. 205.)

minor pattern of behavior, or a behavior that is rare and dysfunctional, is a patterned and normal aspect of interaction between family members" (p. 169). In a national survey, Resnick, Kilpatrick, and Dansky (1993) found that more than a third of American women had been exposed to some violent, traumatic event (such as sexual assault or homicide) involving themselves or some close friend at some time in their lives.

Violence in the family takes a variety of forms. It is clearly evident in the observation that the majority of parents admit to using physical force to punish children, and is even more dramatically apparent in instances of child abuse (discussed in Chapter 10). In 1994 there were more than 1 million substantiated cases of child abuse in the United States; about three times that number were reported to authorities (U.S. Bureau of the Census, 1996).

Family violence is present, as well, in countless episodes of aggression among siblings. Indeed, violence among siblings seems to be highly prevalent among young children, although it diminishes rapidly with increasing age. In a sample of 2,143 families, Straus (1980b) found that 74 percent of all three- to four-year-old children who had siblings occasionally resorted to some form of physical aggression in their interactions. Thirty-six percent of those ages fifteen to seventeen behaved in similar fashion.

Interspousal Violence

Interspousal violence, explain Alpert, Cohen, and Sege (1997), includes fatal and nonfatal violence where one or both partners use physical force or some other means (such as a gun) with the intention of hurting or injuring the other. Violence in the family is also evident in child maltreatment as well as in the verbal aggression that Stets (1990) found almost invariably accompanying physical violence. And surprisingly, the latter is almost as common as the former. In Straus and Gelles's (1986) investigation of American families, 3.8 percent of all husbands admitted to activities that the authors define as wife beating. These activities include kicking, biting, hitting with the fist or some other object, threatening with a knife or a gun, or actually using a knife or a gun. And an amazing 4.6 percent of all wives admitted to similar activities with respect to their husbands. However, Straus cautions that wife beating tends to be hidden and secretive more often than is husband beating, and that wives are, in fact, far more often victims than are husbands (Straus & Kurz, 1997).

The picture presented by surveys such as these is probably only a partial sketch, given the privacy of the family. Its affairs are not easily accessible to social science or to law enforcement agencies. In addition, our prevailing attitudes concerning the right of parents to punish their children physically, the normality of siblings fighting, and, yes, even the right of a husband to beat his wife tend to obscure the prevalence and seriousness of violence in the family.

Why do some husbands beat their wives? There is no simple answer. Some, probably a minority, might be classified as suffering from a psychological disorder. In one study involving 100 battered wives, 25 percent of the husbands had received psychiatric help in the past. And, according to the wives, many more were in need of such help (Gayford, 1978). Many of these husbands came to their marriages with a history of violence. Many had been physically abused and beaten as children. And compared with the general population, more of them were chronically unemployed and poorly educated.

Other factors that contribute to violence in the family include the high incidence of violence in society, cultural attitudes that accept violence as a legitimate reaction in certain situations, and our predominantly sexist attitudes toward the roles of husband and wife in contemporary marriage.

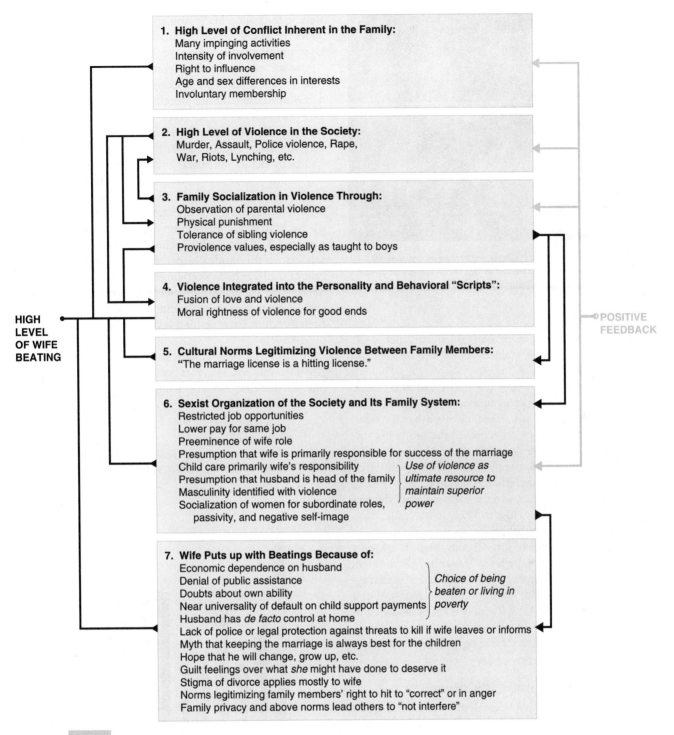

HIGH LEVEL OF WIFE BEATING

1. **High Level of Conflict Inherent in the Family:**
   Many impinging activities
   Intensity of involvement
   Right to influence
   Age and sex differences in interests
   Involuntary membership

2. **High Level of Violence in the Society:**
   Murder, Assault, Police violence, Rape,
   War, Riots, Lynching, etc.

3. **Family Socialization in Violence Through:**
   Observation of parental violence
   Physical punishment
   Tolerance of sibling violence
   Proviolence values, especially as taught to boys

4. **Violence Integrated into the Personality and Behavioral "Scripts":**
   Fusion of love and violence
   Moral rightness of violence for good ends

5. **Cultural Norms Legitimizing Violence Between Family Members:**
   "The marriage license is a hitting license."

6. **Sexist Organization of the Society and Its Family System:**
   Restricted job opportunities
   Lower pay for same job
   Preeminence of wife role
   Presumption that wife is primarily responsible for success of the marriage
   Child care primarily wife's responsibility   ⎱ Use of violence as
   Presumption that husband is head of the family   ⎱ ultimate resource to
   Masculinity identified with violence   ⎰ maintain superior
   Socialization of women for subordinate roles,   ⎰ power
       passivity, and negative self-image

7. **Wife Puts up with Beatings Because of:**
   Economic dependence on husband
   Denial of public assistance
   Doubts about own ability   ⎱ Choice of being
   Near universality of default on child support payments   ⎱ beaten or living in
   Husband has *de facto* control at home   ⎰ poverty
   Lack of police or legal protection against threats to kill if wife leaves or informs
   Myth that keeping the marriage is always best for the children
   Hope that he will change, grow up, etc.
   Guilt feelings over what *she* might have done to deserve it
   Stigma of divorce applies mostly to wife
   Norms legitimizing family members' right to hit to "correct" or in anger
   Family privacy and above norms lead others to "not interfere"

→ POSITIVE FEEDBACK

FIGURE 14.18

Some of the factors accounting for the high incidence of wife beating (solid lines) and positive feedback loops maintaining the system (colored lines). (From Straus, 1980a. Used by permission of the University of Minnesota Press.)

These and other contributing factors are summarized in Figure 14.18.

Sexual Assault and Acquaintance Rape

One form of violence that is not restricted to the family, but that is pertinent there as well, is **sexual assault.** Sexual as-sault can range from sexual innuendo and unwanted suggestions to forcible **rape.** The expression **sexual harassment** is sometimes used to denote the milder forms of sexual assault, short of rape. Sexual assault is an increasingly common problem with a range of sometimes extremely negative consequences. In 1994, 92.1 out of every 100,000 American women over the age of 12 were subjected to attempted or actual forcible rape—a total of more than 102,000 incidents. This

Prevalence of sexual assault is as difficult to ascertain on campus as it is elsewhere. Research indicates that unwanted sexual contact on campus most often occurs with an acquaintance and often involves the use of alcohol.

represents an increase of more than 98 percent since 1970, when the rate per 100,000 women was 46.3 (U.S. Bureau of the Census, 1996).

Rape is ordinarily defined as forcible sexual intercourse. Some jurisdictions—a declining number—stipulate, further, that rape is possible only with someone other than a spouse. In this legal definition is a reflection of the sad belief that women are somehow the property of their husbands, that husbands have the right to use physical force on their wives. Hence the reluctance of law enforcement agencies to charge husbands with assault when wives are victims. English common law maintains that a man is still king in his castle, however humble that castle might be.

In a declining number of jurisdictions, then, it is legally impossible for a man to rape his wife—although he might well be guilty of sexual violence variously labeled "sexual aggression," "sexual coercion," or "sexual victimization." But it is not legally impossible for a friend, a date, or an acquaintance to rape his partner. In fact, such behaviors are shockingly common and are often termed courtship violence, date rape, or **acquaintance rape**.

■ ACQUAINTANCE RAPE ON CAMPUS

Ward and associates (1991) speak of four different kinds of rape that occur on college and university campuses (and elsewhere, too, of course): (1) the *stranger incident,* in which the perpetrator attacks an unknown victim; (2) the *party incident,* in which victim and perpetrator know each other from a single social function during or after which the assault occurs; (3) the *acquaintance incident,* in which the man and woman know each other casually; and (4) the *date incident,* in which the man and woman have an ongoing relationship.

Prevalence of sexual assault on college campuses is difficult to ascertain, as it is elsewhere. There are problems of definition, as well as problems having to do with underreporting. Koss (1988) found that only 58 percent of rape victims reported the incident to anyone at all; a mere 5 percent

went to the police. Many women are uncertain or ambiguous about the seriousness of the incident, and many think that little or nothing can be done.

In a survey of 531 college women, Finley and Corty (1993) found that one out of every six women had experienced some sort of sexual assault the preceding year. Vicary, Klingaman, and Harkness (1995) surveyed 112 adolescent girls from a rural Appalachian school system and found that 8 percent had experienced actual rape or incest, and about one-quarter had been victims of sexual abuse at the hands of dates or boyfriends. Other reports indicate that more than 80 percent of secondary schoolgirls and 60 percent of boys are victims of unwanted sexual attention or action at some time in their school career. For example, Lee and associates (1996) surveyed 1,203 secondary school students from 79 public schools. In this study, 92 percent of the girls and 83 percent of the boys had experienced the mildest form of sexual harassment (sexual comments, jokes, gestures, or looks), and 17 percent of the girls and 13 percent of the boys had been forced to do something sexual beyond kissing (see Figure 14.19).

In a survey of 861 college students, Ward and associates (1991) found that 34 percent of the women had experienced unwanted sexual contact (kissing, fondling, or touching in a

FIGURE 14.19

Percentage of students having ever experienced 14 forms of sexual harassment. (Data from Lee et al., 1996, p. 411.)

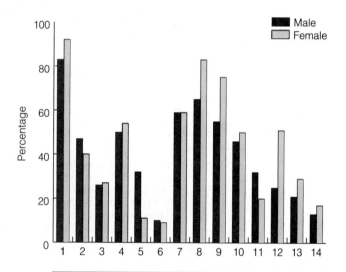

Key to types of sexual harassment:
1. Made sexual comments, jokes, gestures, or looks
2. Showed you sexual pictures, photographs, messages, etc.
3. Wrote sexual messages about you on bathroom walls, etc.
4. Spread sexual rumors about you
5. Said you were gay or lesbian
6. Spied on you as you dressed or showered at school
7. Flashed or mooned you
8. Touched, grabbed, or pinched you in a sexual way
9. Intentionally brushed up against you in a sexual way
10. Pulled at your clothing in a sexual way
11. Pulled your clothing off or down
12. Blocked your way or cornered you in a sexual way
13. Forced you to kiss him/her
14. Forced you to do something sexual, other than kissing

sexual way), 20 percent had been subjected to attempted sexual intercourse, and 10 percent had experienced unwanted completed sexual intercourse. The majority of these episodes occurred with an acquaintance at a party; about three-quarters involved alcohol use by the male, and one-half involved alcohol use by the female; and in almost half the cases of unwanted intercourse, no one was told later. And what is perhaps most striking in this study is that the men's recollections of sexual incidents were dramatically different from the women's. Only 9 percent of the men recalled having sexual contact with an unwilling woman, and another 9 percent claimed they had attempted intercourse with an unwilling partner (women reported 34 and 20 percent, respectively); a mere 3 percent of men admitted they had actually completed intercourse (women reported 10 percent).

■ RAPE MYTHS

Other research indicates that many students don't view date rape as a particularly serious problem. In one survey of 172 college men and women, only about half thought date rape was a problem, and very few believed it was a major problem (Walton, 1994). Even among college students, males are highly likely to subscribe to a number of what are referred to as **rape myths**—unfounded, culturally based beliefs about rape (Kopper, 1996; Workman & Orr, 1996). Some common rape myths are as follows: that many, or maybe most, women actually want to be raped; that women who dress, walk, or look a certain way are unconsciously—or perhaps consciously—signaling their willingness to engage in sexual activity; that if a woman drinks and then experiences unwanted sexual activity, she is largely to blame; that women who deliberately arouse men are responsible for what follows; that men, once aroused, cannot easily control themselves; that men have absolutely no control over being aroused or not; and that women are victims in the true sense only when attacked by some deranged, sex-crazed stranger but not when attacked by a boyfriend or someone else with whom they've been interacting.

It bears repeating that these are myths. Yet Workman and Orr (1996) found that a significant number of college students, especially males, believed that in the event of an unwanted sexual episode, women wearing short skirts would be more to blame than those wearing longer skirts. Similarly, a large number of the 742 undergraduates in a study conducted by Stormo, Lang, and Stritzke (1997) thought that if the victim had been drinking, she would be more to blame, and the perpetrator less. In fact, argue Los and Chamard (1997), the media are largely responsible for propagating these myths and for shifting the emphasis from woman as victim to woman as partner-in-crime. Part of this shift in emphasis, they argue, stems from a shift from coverage of sexual assaults perpetrated by strangers to coverage of acquaintance rape, which the media view as more benign, or at the very least, more ambiguous.

In brief, *rape myth mentality* tends to assign responsibility for date rape to the victim, believing that the woman probably wanted to have sex and that she should have foreseen the man's actions. In this sense, sexual assault is a form of vio-

▲ SUMMARY TABLE 14.9
Sexual and Family Violence

ISSUE	RESEARCH/COMMENTS
Violence in the family	■ Rising incidence of some crimes like sexual assault. ■ Victims and perpetrators of ¼ of assaults and homicides are from the same family. ■ Almost half of all crime victims know the perpetrator. ■ High incidence of violence in the family evident in physical discipline of children, high rates of child maltreatment, and high rates of interspousal violence. ■ Some perpetrators of violence are maladjusted; others apparently simply reflect long-standing cultural practices and myths surrounding male rights and dominance. ■ Males are also quite often victims of interspousal abuse.
Sexual assault and acquaintance rape	■ Sexual assault: episodes ranging from sexual innuendo to rape. ■ Rape: forcible sexual intercourse (older laws specified *with someone other than a spouse*). ■ Acquaintance rape is relatively common in schools (and, of course, elsewhere). ■ Assignment of blame, especially by males, often reflects one of several *rape myths* that misrepresent male and female sexuality and the meanings of sexually linked behaviors.

lence that reflects an attitude of male dominance and female passivity; it reflects, as well, an implicit assumption of the male's rights to sexual satisfaction under certain circumstances. That these attitudes are slowly changing is evident in what is termed **rape shield law**, which prohibits the victim's sexual history or apparently promiscuous behaviors being used against her (Julian, 1993).

Many campuses organize and support workshops designed to increase student awareness of sexual violence, as well as to reduce male callousness toward date rape and to debunk the myths that still surround sexual aggression. These often result in significant attitude changes among males, reports Lonsway (1996). Interestingly, male students who live in coeducational residences and fraternities typically have less traditional views of gender and are less accepting of rape myths (Schaeffer & Nelson, 1993). (See Summary Table 14.9.)

■ THE CONTINUING EVOLUTION OF SELF

Family violence and sexual assault would not have been a happy topic with which to end this chapter. It is shocking

SOCIAL DEVELOPMENT: EARLY ADULTHOOD

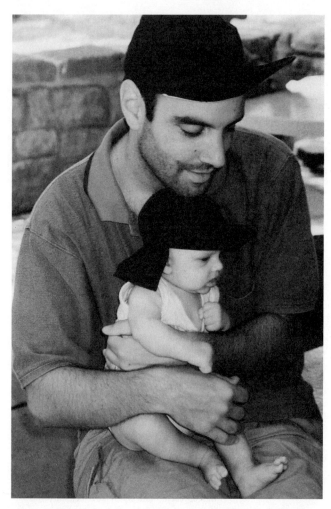

Kegan describes five great stages in the continuing evolution of self. The infant shown here is still at the age of the impulsive self, driven by basic needs and urges, unfettered by more adultlike notions of reality. His father's self is an interindividual self, defined mainly in relationships with others—including relationships with the infant. But even in the adult, there remain elements of each of the earlier selves: impulsive, imperial, interpersonal, and institutional.

occupations throughout life remain fixed at the level of gratification of impulses.

The second self, the *imperial self,* struggles to take over the power and the control that were previously held by parents. The imperial self strives toward the development of personal competence and the achievement of personal control. Much energy is directed toward gaining power and becoming self-sufficient. Developmentally, this self corresponds to Piaget's preoperational and early school period and to Erikson's initiative versus guilt. The imperial self derives from relationships with school, family, and peers.

As the self continues to evolve, the imperial self gradually transforms into the *interpersonal self*—a self that recognizes the mutuality of relationships and searches for reciprocity. Whereas the imperial self is oriented toward power and control, the interpersonal self orients itself around inner feelings and interpersonal relationships. Self-definition—being meaningful—is no longer expressed simply in competence and control but is now found in the feelings that others have toward the self. Males, argue Geller, Johnson, and Madsen (1997), construe their selves in a different way than females do. Their self-definition is thought to be more independent and perhaps less interpersonal. In contrast, women are thought to develop a more *interdependent* view of themselves—hence to emphasize relationships more.

The self of the transition through adolescence to young adulthood is the *institutional self.* It is a self that is embedded in culture, work, and love. In Erikson's view, it is a self that creates its meaning through the selection and cultivation of a personal identity.

The self of early adulthood is a more *interindividual self*—a self oriented toward adult relationships. It is the interindividual self that searches for the special combination of passion, intimacy, and commitment that makes up consummate love.

The interindividual self of the young adult, like Kegan's other selves, is all that has come before it. At every stage, we retain elements of the selves that we have been. Thus, the interindividual self continues to develop the abilities and the competencies that admission to the public world of adulthood demands; at the same time, it retains an orientation toward independence and reciprocal interpersonal relationships. (See Summary Table 14.10.)

Through all of young adulthood, as through all of life, the self struggles to remain meaningful—to mean something. And, to this end, explains Jopling (1996), we sometimes lie to ourselves—not deliberately as a practiced liar might, but unconsciously. We lie to ourselves by creating certain illusions about our selves. These illusions are reflected in the somewhat exaggerated opinions we develop of our personal characteristics and the overly optimistic scenarios we weave of our most likely futures. They are, in a sense, the remnants of our *personal fables,* and they follow us through life. These self-deceptions are important to our happiness and to our mental health, claims Jopling. They allow us to feel special and personally powerful and well loved.

Power and love, said Freud, are the themes of our lives.

and distressing to consider that more than 3 million men and women and more than 2 million children in the United States are victims of severe violence each year. The topic smacks too much of power and too little of love.

Love and power are the two themes that run through our dreams. They are the themes that unify the stories of our lives, that give purpose and direction to our actions. It is through expressions of love and power that we achieve meaning—that we become meaningful. Being meaningful is the essence of Kegan's (1982) view of the evolution of the self.

Kegan describes five stages in the evolution of the self—five major transformations in the relationships that link individuals and their contexts. The first, the age of the *impulsive self,* describes a self that is embedded in impulses and perceptions. This is the self of Piaget's sensorimotor and preoperational child. But the correspondence to these periods is only conceptual, not chronological. There are many adults whose selves do not evolve beyond this level and whose pre-

LABELS FOR MAJOR TRANSFORMATIONS IN THE SELF	MAIN CHARACTERISTICS	LIFE PERIOD
Impulsive self	Concern with gratification of impulses.	Infancy, but aspects of all selves may remain dominant throughout life.
Imperial self	Concern with personal competence and control.	Early and middle childhood.
Interpersonal self	Concern with relationships of reciprocity.	Adolescence.
Institutional self	Concern with culture, with work.	Youth.
Interindividual self	Concern with adult relationships, with intimacy and love.	Adulthood.

The overriding goal is to achieve meaning, to become meaningful. And the expression of that goal is found in the two themes that run through our lives: love and power.

FOCUS QUESTIONS: SUMMARY ANSWERS

1. What are the main challenges of early adulthood?

   ▪ According to Erikson's psychosocial theory of stages characterized by basic conflicts and their resolution, the young adult struggles with *intimacy versus isolation* as relationships with parents and peers change. During this period, the young adult strives to achieve intimacy, often through a reciprocated love relationship with someone of the opposite sex.

2. What are some of the dimensions of personal intimacy?

   ▪ Liking implies positive evaluation; romantic/erotic love implies absorption, attachment, and intimacy (a capacity for pain as well as ecstasy). Sternberg's model describes eight varieties of love (or nonlove), identifiable on the basis of combinations of passion (strong physical desire), intimacy (affection, disclosure), and commitment (a decision to be in love, to stay together).

Important antecedents of interpersonal attraction (which underlies love) include physical attractiveness, similarity, and propinquity (physical proximity). One basic lifestyle choice is to marry or not to marry. Nonmarried lifestyles include singlehood, cohabitation, homosexual relationships, or one of a variety of communes.

3. What kinds of changes have there been in the family? What is the family life cycle?

   ▪ Recent changes in the family include an increase in age of first marriage, increase in age of childbearing, and a declining birthrate as well as a large increase in nontraditional families. Duvall's family life cycle includes eight task-defined stages: the initial childless years (important tasks center on whether or not to have children, and other career and self-related developmental tasks), the first child, the phase of the preschool child, a school-aged phase (seven years), a teenager phase (seven years), a "launching" phase (eight years), the empty nest to retirement period (fifteen years), and a retirement-until-death phase.

4. How common is family violence? Acquaintance rape?

   ▪ Incidence of many types of violent crimes continues to increase, with almost half of all violent acts perpetrated by acquaintances or relatives of the victim. Family violence is evident in interspousal violence, child abuse, and sexual assault, including acquaintance rape. Sexual assault is a general term for a variety of unwanted sexual attention or acts ranging from actions sometimes described as *harassment* to forcible sexual intercourse (rape). Assignment of blame, especially by males, often reflects *rape myths,* prevailing misconceptions about the role of victims in sex crimes and about the nature of male and female sexuality.

STUDY TERMS

FURTHER READINGS

The following short book presents a thoughtful look at interactions in the family, including discussions of topics such as child abuse, stress in the family, and how couples adjust to parenthood:

White, D., & Woollett, A. (1992). *Families: A context for development.* New York: Falmer.

Berner's book is a highly readable account of some of the second-generation effects of divorce: What sort of parents are those whose own parents were divorced?

Berner, R. T. (1992). *Parents whose parents were divorced.* New York: Haworth.

A current, highly informative, balanced view of violence in the family is Gelles's book:

Gelles, R. J. (1997). *Intimate violence in families* (3rd ed.). Thousand Oaks, CA: Sage.

The following volume is a highly respected collection of chapters dealing with different aspects of lifespan development. Of particular relevance to Chapter 14 is the following contribution, which reviews research dealing specifically with parenting:

Seltzer, M. M., & Ryff, C. D. (1994). Parenting across the lifespan: The normative and nonnormative cases. In D. L. Featherman, R. M. Lerner, & M. Perlmutter (Eds.), *Lifespan development and behavior* (Vol. 12). Hillsdale, NJ: Erlbaum.

PART SEVEN

Middle Adulthood

Women sit or move to and fro, some old, some young.

The young are beautiful—but the old are more beautiful than the young.

WALT WHITMAN
"Beautiful Women"

re the old really more beautiful than the young? Almost everything that we see and hear in this century's youth-worshiping context would have us think not. "Think young!" "Feel young!" "Be young!" we are told. When your face begins to fall, you must lift it. Cream and rejuvenate your wrinkles. Restretch your sagging skin. Color your graying hair. Starve yourself if that's what is needed to maintain your hips and your belly. Dance and drink and sing all night even if you would rather dream by the fire. ¶ We struggle so desperately to delay or hide the signals of aging. We do not mature gracefully. ¶ Yet, as we see in Chapters 15 and 16, the middle-aged have more of almost everything we work so hard to achieve—hence more of everything we value. On average, it is the middle-aged who have the most money, the greatest number of possessions, the most power, perhaps even the most love. ¶ In many ways, middle adulthood is the very peak of life's mountain. ¶ But how steep is the downhill side?

Physical and Cognitive Development: Middle Adulthood

To youth I have but three words of counsel—work, work, work.

OTTO VON BISMARCK

lexander Mironov's father wanted to be a cosmonaut. Many of his friends wanted to be diplomats or engineers or soldiers. Some thought they would like to be bankers or teachers, or even professors. These were all highly patriotic jobs: Mother Russia would be pleased. ¶ But, since the collapse of the former Soviet Union, Russia is no longer the mother she once was. And so Alexander Mironov does not dream of being a cosmonaut, as did his father. Nor does he dream of being an engineer or a soldier. Nor do his friends have those dreams. ¶ "I would like to be a killer," says Alexander flatly. ¶ "But, surely, you are joking, heh, heh," says his grandmother. "It is now too crowded a field," she adds, making her own small joke. "Last year you said you wanted to be a banker, to make lots of money." ¶ "That was last year," says Alexander. And, yes, he thinks, the field *is* crowded. He has just read that in the past four years there have been 116 attempted killings of bankers in Russia, 79 of which succeeded (Philps, 1997). There are more than 500 documented contract killings a year in his country (Lally, 1997). It is reported that the killers are very highly paid. Vladimir Kovalenko's uncle is known to be a killer, a member of the famous Russian Mafia. He has a car, membership in the Red Turtle Club, his own apartment, skinny women with blond hair. He is now in Slovakia, where there is much work; there have been 111 killings there in the past nine months (Reuters, 1997). ¶ And so, at least half seriously, Alexander Mironov dreams of being a killer. ¶

This Chapter

Alexander Mironov is not alone among Russian youth. In a recent survey of 1,000 Moscow high school students, 2 percent chose killer as the most prestigious of occupations; scientist and college professor were mentioned by only 1 percent of respondents. The majority now want to be accountants or lawyers or entrepreneurs because those occupations are associated with good income (Lally, 1997). And more of them want to be gangsters and racketeers than cosmonauts or professors or even soldiers.

Work is one of the topics of this chapter; it is extremely important for a great many adults through the middle years—though few admit dreams of becoming killers. In addition, the chapter deals with the physical changes of this period—changes in appearance, in the senses, in organ functioning, and in general health as well as major changes in the reproductive system, particularly in women. It looks, as well, at cognitive changes and at the controversy over whether some aspects of intellectual functioning suffer from the ravages of age. In its final sections, it looks at the changing workplace and at the role of careers in the lives of men and women. Finally, it turns to leisure.

MIDDLE ADULTHOOD

To keep things clear and simple, **middle adulthood** is defined as the two-decade span from the age of forty or forty-five to around sixty or sixty-five. Unfortunately, however, age does not tell us very much about the social and emotional lives of most adults—nor even all that much about their physical lives. Here, as elsewhere in the lifespan, there are those we think of as being old before their time, and there are those we consider young for their age. In general, however, the very old think of the middle-aged as young, and the very young think of the forty-year-old as very old.

And those who are middle-aged? How do they see themselves and their lives?

The answer depends, of course, on the individual. For those whose identities are closely bound to their physical selves, the advent of the middle years can be a source of consternation and perhaps even grief. As is discussed in this chapter, there are, in the middle years, some subtle but largely inevitable and irreversible changes in the body—changes that, given our contemporary definitions of physical attractiveness, are often viewed as negative. But for those whose identities—whose personal meaningfulness—stem more from relationships, from knowledge and intelligence, from cultural competence and success, and from the power that results, the middle years can be a source of profound happiness.

For most adults, the middle years are very busy years. From a career point of view, these are often the most productive and the most successful years of adulthood. Middle-aged workers, on average, already earn and possess more than younger workers, continue to earn and accumulate more, have more competence, and wield more power.

From a social point of view, middle adulthood often involves more close interpersonal relationships than any other period in the lifespan—relationships with aging parents, with children and grandchildren, with siblings and co-workers, and with half a lifetime's worth of friends and acquaintances.

But it is also in the middle years that something happens to our perceptions of time—something initially quite subtle, but nevertheless significant. Our psychological perceptions of time are tied to our ages; they are also very personal. For the very young, days last forever. As Wordsworth put it in "To a Butterfly," "Sweet childish days, that were as long as twenty days are now." But as we get older, the opposite happens, and twenty days now seem no longer than one used to be. And when we reach a point close to the middle of life, Neugarten (1968) tells us, our perception of time changes in yet another way: We stop thinking in terms of how long we have lived; now we begin to think in terms of how much time we have left.

And if there is much we still want to do, perhaps we must now run a little faster. But, alas, we tire more easily. Besides, the days have shrunk.

Do they lengthen again in old age? We look at this question in Chapter 18.

Some Tasks of Middle Adulthood

Havighurst (1972) describes **developmental tasks** as culturally determined responsibilities that represent competencies or achievements important for happiness and adjustment. There are a different series of such tasks at every stage of the lifespan, he informs us (see Chapters 2 and 13). Those that are important for middle adulthood are summarized in Table 15.1. They include problems of adjusting to physiological changes, as well as to work and leisure; these are the subjects of this chapter. In addition, Havighurst's developmental tasks for the middle years deal with relationships with children, parents, spouse, and the community; these are the focus of Chapter 16.

PHYSICAL CHANGES OF MIDDLE ADULTHOOD

Aging is a linear, time-bound, biological process. Some of its consequences, like loss of hair or hair pigmentation, are clearly visible; others, like reduction in the efficiency of various organs, are not so obvious.

Appearance

Although the normal changes in appearance that occur in the middle years typically bear little relationship either to

TABLE 15.1

Middle Adulthood and Havighurst's Developmental Tasks

Middle adulthood spans roughly ages forty or forty-five to sixty or sixty-five. It brings new challenges and requires new adjustments. And it brings a change perception of time: from time lived to time left. Havighurst's developmental tasks describe some of the challenges in middle adulthood:

- Assisting children in the transition from home to world.

- Developing adult leisure activities.

- Relating to spouse as a person.

- Reaching adult social and civic responsibility.

- Maintaining satisfactory career performance.

- Adjusting to physiological changes of middle age.

- Adjusting to aging parents.

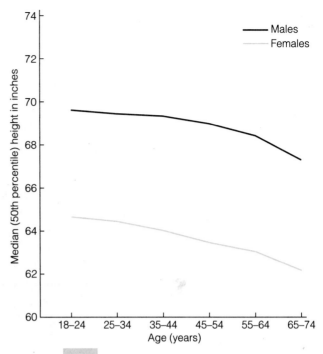

FIGURE 15.1

Decrements in adult median height for men and women. (Based on U.S. Bureau of the Census, 1996, p. 149.)

health or physical functioning, for those whose meaning is closely bound to their physical selves, they can be tremendously important.

Our cultural standards of beauty and attractiveness, closely tied to physical appearance, dictate that peak attractiveness will generally occur during early adulthood. This is particularly true for females and is evident in the physical appearance of the models employed by the advertising industry. It is also evident in the enormous salaries that many of these models command before age twenty-five; witness as well the period of peak income for movie actresses and models, which has traditionally been near the beginning of early adulthood, or between ages twenty-three and twenty-seven—although there are indications that this has changed somewhat in recent years. Men, whose attractiveness (or ugliness) seems, for cultural reasons, not to be so close to the skin, have typically fared somewhat better as older models and actors.

Physical changes that account for our progressively changing appearance are highly varied and initially very subtle. The most obvious are changes in height and weight. After the late teens or early twenties, height does not generally increase. However, after the age of 45 (sometimes earlier and sometimes later), there are frequently decrements in height. On the average, lifetime decrements are greater for women, at about 4.9 centimeters (almost 2 inches), than for men, at 2.0 centimeters (about ¾ inch). Thus, as Figure 15.1 shows, the median height of American men aged 18 to 24 is about 177 centimeters (just under 5 feet 10 inches), and that of men aged 45 to 54 is closer to 175 centimeters (about 5 feet 9 inches). Median height for women aged 18 to 24 is under 164 centimeters (slightly less than 5 feet 4.5 inches), but at age 45 to 54, median height has dropped to around 161.5 centimeters (5 feet 3.6 inches).

Although changes in height are usually so gradual that they are not often detected, changes in weight are often far less subtle. Recall that by age twenty, about 30 percent of

the body weight of females, and 15 percent of the weight of males, is fat mass (Malina & Bouchard, 1991). Figure 15.2 presents the results of a study that looked at relative distributions of fat among 520 adults (215 males, 305 females) between the ages of eighteen and eighty-five. Note that by the middle years, percentage of fat has increased to about 40 for females and close to 30 for males. Fatty accumulations also tend to be distributed differently in men and women. Typically, excess fat first finds its way around the middles of men; it is more likely to be deposited on the hips of women.

FIGURE 15.2

Relative amounts of body fat by age and sex. (From Novak, 1972, p. 440. Reprinted by permission of the Gerontological Society of America.)

Physical and sensory changes throughout adulthood are gradual and almost imperceptible. But slowly our hair recedes and fades, our skin loses elasticity and gains wrinkles, our joints become less flexible, and our stamina and endurance decline. And eventually there comes a day when we require glasses—perhaps even more than one pair. For those whose sense of self-worth is closely tied to their physical selves, these changes can be difficult.

With the increase of fat mass relative to fat-free mass in both men and women, there is a loss of about 40 percent of muscle and about 30 percent of muscle strength between ages twenty and seventy (Rogers & Evans, 1993). However, weight and aerobic training through middle and older age can change this "normal" pattern of muscle atrophy dramatically. Loss of muscle and of strength, note Rogers and Evans, need not be considered an inevitable consequence of aging.

Other physical changes that contribute to the adult's changing appearance include loss of skin elasticity, thinning of hair, loss of flexibility in joints, gradual recession of gums (hence the expression "long in the tooth"), and the appearance of longer, stiffer hair in the eyebrows, ears, and nose (Lemme, 1995). In addition, even among adults who remain trim, there is a gradual thickening of the torso but an eventual thinning of the legs and arms. It is partly for this reason that a skinny old person does not look like a skinny young person.

Although most of the physical changes of the middle years are very gradual and seldom dramatic while they are occurring, we resist them with incredible passion and vigor, especially early in the middle years. We have made a cult of being and looking youthful. Each year we spend billions on lotions, creams, potions, herbs, toupees, dyes, tonics, salves, pigments, tinctures, and unguents designed to make us at least look young—not to mention countless billions more spent on chemical, surgical, or natural cosmetic aids and on various exercise, weight-reducing, and rebuilding and repair programs for aging bodies.

There are, of course, extremely wide individual variations not only in the speed with which we age physically but also in the ways we age. Some of us will lose all our hair; the hair of others will turn snowy white. And some, like my paternal great-grandfather, will retain a thick head of raven-black hair right into their tenth decade of life. I should be so lucky!

The Senses

Like most of our physical systems, our senses are subject to the influences of time. Vision, for example, is best at around age twenty and typically remains relatively constant until age forty. Because of gradual thickening of the lens, loss of lens elasticity, and increased lens density, most individuals become more farsighted beginning in middle age. There is also a gradual loss of light-sensitive cells in the eye beginning around midlife, which might account for some loss of visual acuity (Curcio et al., 1994). In one longitudinal study of aging, it was found that by the age of fifty, 88 percent of the women and all of the men had at least one pair of eyeglasses (Bayer, Whissell-Buechy, & Honzik, 1981). **Glaucoma** (increased pressure in the eye that can cause blindness if not treated) and **cataracts** (clouding of the lens caused by fibers) are also associated with aging. Both become more common after age fifty. About 12.3 men out of every 1,000 between the ages of 45 and 64 have diagnosed cataracts. Between ages 65 and 74, the percentage increases sixfold, to 79 per 1,000. Cataract rates are almost twice as high for women (21.9 between 45 and 64; 140 between 65 and 74) (U.S. Bureau of the Census, 1996).

Hearing losses are also very gradual during the early years of adulthood but are typically more severe for men than for women. **Presbycusis** is the term used for hearing losses associated with age that are apparent in an inability to hear high-pitched sounds. The U.S. Bureau of the Census (1996) reports that hearing complaints before age forty-five are relatively low (43 per 1,000 for men); between forty-five and sixty-four, however, they increase to 191.9 out of 1,000—almost one out of every five men. Rates for middle-aged women are drastically lower, at 87.5 per 1,000.

Changes in the ability to taste appear to be very slight until later adulthood, although by the age of fifty, some individuals are less sensitive to spices, salts, and sugars—a fact that most are not likely to have noticed. Loss of taste sensitivity is common during adulthood—a condition that might be linked to heavy drinking and smoking as well as to the excessive use of salt. In later adulthood, loss of taste sensitivity often leads individuals to flavor their foods with quantities of salt and pepper that children would find almost unpalatable.

Health and Organ Function

Although health generally continues to be good through the middle years, there is a gradual decline in the efficiency of most major organ systems. For example, beginning in early adulthood, the volume of blood that the heart pumps declines very slowly. At the same time, there is frequently a gradual accumulation of plaque on the insides of blood vessels (**atherosclerosis**) and a progressive thickening and hardening of artery walls (**arteriosclerosis**). This increases blood pressure and also increases the probability of a stroke (caused by a blockage of blood flow to part of the brain) and heart attack (the result of a blockage of blood flow to the heart muscle). (See "At a Glance: Health in the Middle Years" and Figures 15.3 and 15.4.)

Other organs that become less efficient through the middle years include lungs, stomach, and liver. The lungs, for example, take in progressively less air with each breath as the person ages. This is mainly because the amount of air that remains in the lungs after expelling a breath increases. Part of the reduced lung efficiency of older people is due to loss of lung tissue elasticity, as well as to increasing rib cage stiffness (Johnson, Badr, & Dempsey, 1994). As a result of declines in lung efficiency, middle-aged adults suffer from more pulmonary chronic complaints such as emphysema and tuberculosis.

Various diseases to which individuals become more susceptible with age include cancer, arthritis, hypertension (high blood pressure), and **osteoporosis,** a thinning and weakening of the bones. Women are much more prone to this latter condition than are men. And although it does not commonly become serious until later adulthood, it often begins in midlife or earlier. A diet rich in calcium (low-fat milk products, vegetables such as broccoli and turnips, and seafood products such as sardines and salmon), as well as in protein and vitamin D, can help prevent osteoporosis or reduce its seriousness (Allen, 1993). So can exercise, which contributes to bone growth and strength. In one study of 111 women, regular exercise contributed significantly to reducing the development of osteoporosis (Brodigan, 1992).

In addition to exercise, **hormone replacement therapy (HRT)** is sometimes recommended after menopause (discussed shortly) or after a woman's ovaries have been surgically removed. However, estrogen therapy is somewhat controversial, given its link with a higher incidence of cancer. As a result, an increasing number of women, notes Wilbush (1994), resist the advice of their physicians with respect to

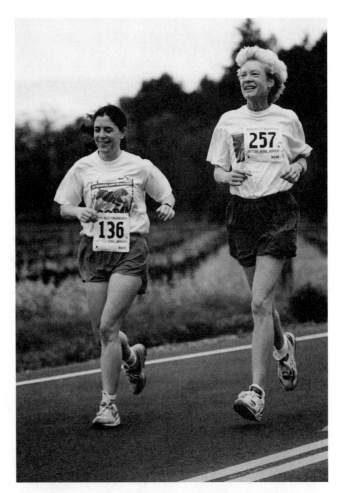

Physical exercise can do much to keep joints flexible, bodies trim, cardiovascular functioning optimal, and bone loss in check. Perhaps as important, physical fitness is closely related to feelings of positive self-worth and happiness. Being able to keep up with your younger friend doesn't hurt either.

hormone therapy. However, the evidence suggests that although risk of cancer does increase with long-term estrogen replacement, there also results a dramatic reduction in fatal heart disease—as well as a reduction in hip and other bone fractures. On the basis of a number of longitudinal studies, Gorsky and colleagues (1994) have calculated that if 10,000 women aged fifty were to be placed on estrogen replacement therapy, by age seventy-five, 574 deaths would have been prevented and an additional 3,951 years would have been added to their lives.

Nutrition and Exercise

Not all middle-aged persons experience the same declines in organ functioning, nor are all equally susceptible to various diseases and infections. Genes continue to be extremely important influences on health at all stages in the lifespan. We know that susceptibility to many forms of heart disease, as well as to different kinds of cancer—the two leading causes of death in the middle years—is partly inherited. At the same

Health in the Middle Years

During the midlife years, there is a gradual decline in strength and stamina, as well as in the functioning of the senses. But for most adults, health continues to be relatively good through the middle years. In fact, there is a marked decline in susceptibility to many acute conditions, such as infections and colds. However, there is an increase in chronic conditions, such as arthritis and heart disease (Figures 15.3 and 15.4).

FIGURE 15.3

Decline in rate of acute conditions with advancing age. (Based on U.S. Bureau of the Census, 1996, p. 143.)

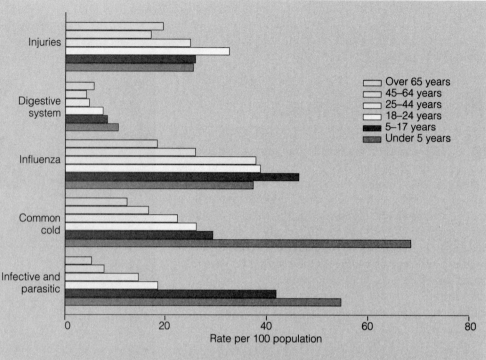

FIGURE 15.4

Increase in rate of chronic conditions with advancing age. (Based on U.S. Bureau of the Census, 1996, p. 143.)

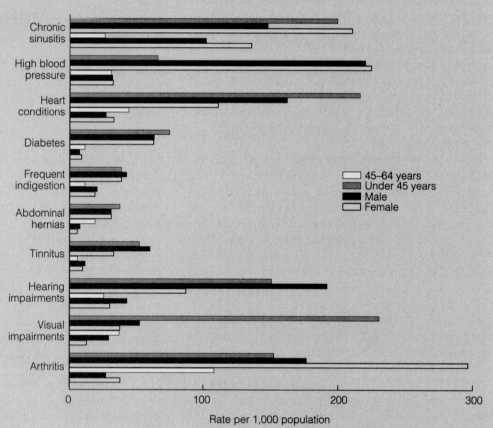

time, however, exercise and diet can each play a significant role in preventing disease and in delaying the effects of age.

Obesity, for example, is clearly implicated in heart disease. And 27.5 percent of all people over eighteen in the United States are overweight (U.S. Bureau of the Census, 1996). Given that, on average, weight declines in later life, this probably means that well over 30 percent of young and middle-age adults are overweight.

There is evidence, too, that certain cholesterols contribute to atherosclerosis, that alcohol is a prime cause of cirrhosis of the liver, and that excessive salt intake is related to heart disease. And as we saw in Chapter 13, when Millen and associates (1996) assessed the eating patterns of 3,659 adult men and women (ages twenty to seventy) in light of recommendations of the **Food Guide Pyramid**, they found widespread evidence of poor nutritional behaviors among adults. For example, both men and women had excessive intakes of alcohol and fats but too-low intakes of fruits and vegetables, as well as of dairy products. In spite of this, however, per capita consumption of fruits and vegetables has increased since 1970. But, then, so too has consumption of fats and oils (U.S. Bureau of the Census, 1996).

Millen and associates (1996) note, as well, that many adults compound the negative effects of their poor nutrition habits with chronic dieting, as well as with smoking. More than 25 percent of all adults over eighteen consider themselves current smokers (U.S. Bureau of the Census, 1996). Interestingly, there is striking relationship between income and smoking, as well as between frequency of exercise and income. The lowest income groups smoke significantly more and exercise much less. As a result, it's hardly surprising that about 25 percent more of the lowest income group (below $10,000 per year) are obese, compared with the higher income group (above $50,000 per year). Similarly, as shown in Figure 15.5, there is a close relationship between educational level and health-related behaviors such as exercise, smoking, and avoiding obesity.

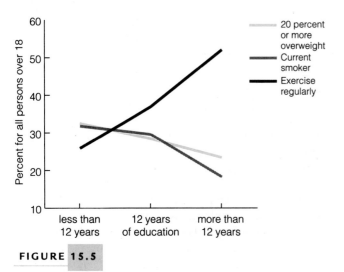

FIGURE 15.5

Relationship between educational level and health-related behaviors. (Based on U.S. Bureau of the Census, 1996, p. 146.)

Not only does cigarette smoking contribute to emphysema, to lung cancer, and to other forms of cancer, but it also contributes negatively to bone density. Hopper and Seeman (1994) studied twenty-one pairs of identical twins, one of whom had smoked at least five years more than the other. Their conclusion: Women who smoke a pack of cigarettes a day through their adulthood will, on average, have 5 to 19 percent less bone density at menopause.

Exercise, for its part, can do a great deal to keep the middle-aged strong and healthy. Research has repeatedly found that those who exercise regularly are more fit and less prone to coronary heart disease (Ward, 1994). This is largely because exercise increases cardiac output, improves circulation and decreases fatty accumulation in blood vessel walls, helps keep arteries and veins flexible, prevents obesity, and increases muscle and bone density (Sambrook, Kelly, & Eisman, 1993). And, as we saw in Chapter 13, exercise can also contribute significantly to a general sense of well-being. (See "In the News and on the Net: Walk Tall.")

The Climacteric and Menopause

One area of physical change that is important for understanding the adult years involves changes in the sex glands and is commonly referred to as the change of life or, more properly, the **climacteric.** The term originates from two Greek words meaning "critical time" and "rung" (as of a ladder). Use of the expression is perhaps unfortunate; it implies too strongly that the rung is critical—that it might break or not be reached, or cause pain and suffering.

■ A PHYSIOLOGICAL EVENT

Among women, the climacteric involves **menopause,** the cessation of menstruation. Clinically defined, *menopause* is "the cessation of menses for a period of at least 12 months as a consequence of the irreversible ovarian failure" (Bellantoni & Blackman, 1996, p. 415). Among men, the climacteric is more subtle, which has led to some debate concerning whether it is fruitful or even appropriate to speak of a male climacteric or change of life.

The secretion of the sex hormones by the ovaries (primarily estrogen) and the testes (primarily testosterone) is among the most important changes of pubescence (see Chapter 11). These hormones are closely involved in the development of secondary sexual characteristics (breasts, facial hair, voice changes, and so on), as well as in sexual interest and behavior. Their production continues, relatively unabated, from puberty through early adulthood. But by the late thirties or early forties among women, and perhaps by the early fifties for men, the production of sex hormones begins to decrease. Among men, this decrease is often very gradual and not easily noticed.

Among women, changes in production of sex hormones are considerably less gradual and far more noticeable and are linked with the woman's declining store of ova. Women are born with about 800,000 immature ova. By puberty, half of alking is a pretty ordinary, pretty natural thing to do. Most of us learn the skill in our infancies and continue to use it through the rest of our lives, never paying much attention to it. In some ways, it's a lot like breathing; we just do it. So when, about 12 years ago, a new magazine appeared on the newsstands with the title *Walking,* comedian George Carlin took a few shots at it: "What are they going to come up with next," he quipped, "A magazine called *Breathing?*" Ironically, a decade later, walking has become the most popular fitness related activity in North America. Experts suggest that if we walk 30 or so minutes at a time, three or four times a week, we will feel better, look better, and perhaps live longer! But now, we should also think a little about how we walk. Walk tall, we're told, because our pos-

tures aren't all they should be. Also, take more rapid steps rather than longer ones, spring off the toes, land on the heels, and roll forward, arms bent and swinging. And, for maximum benefit, find some hills to walk up.

1. Krucoff, C. (1997, Oct. 27). More folks improving step by step. *Los Angeles Times,* p. S3.

To Think About

Examine your own lifestyle in terms of nutrition and exercise. Does your diet approximate recommended guidelines? Your exercise?

On the Net

For a site, updated daily, that provides links to various sources of nutrition- and exercise-related information, see

http://www.fitnesslink.com/

For information and suggestions regarding applications of the Food Guide Pyramid, see

http://zorba.uafadm.alaska.edu/coop-ext/efnep/pyramid.html

---

these have died; and by the early forties, few—if any—are left. Only about 300 or so will ordinarily mature and be potentially fertilizable in the woman's lifetime.

Among the first signs of menopause in women are changes in menstrual pattern: irregularity, skipping of menstrual periods, or noticeably reduced discharge during menstruation. Eventually, menstruation stops entirely. In North America, this can happen at any time between forty and sixty; on average, it occurs at age fifty.

POSSIBLE PHYSIOLOGICAL CONSEQUENCES

Irreversible ovarian failure, the clinical definition of menopause, implies that the ovaries cease producing sex hormones, the most important of which is **estrogen.** More than 90 percent of a woman's hormone is produced by the ovaries; only a small amount is produced by other glands such as the **adrenal glands** (Schiff, 1996).

With the cessation of ovarian function come a number of physiological consequences. One, clearly, is that the woman is no longer able to conceive a child. But, as we saw in Chapter 4, this doesn't mean that she cannot have a fertilized embryo implanted and carry it to term.

Other physiological changes include a corresponding decline in bone mass, a gain in fat-mass relative to the rest of the body, and some negative changes in immune system functioning (Bellantoni & Blackman, 1996). These changes are evident in a somewhat higher risk of osteoporosis, heart disease, and urinary tract problems. However, the extent to which the probability of these outcomes increases varies consider-

ably for different women and may well be insignificant for most (Schiff, 1996).

One of the better-known possible physiological consequences of menopause involves changes in blood vessel functioning that become apparent in what are termed **hot flashes.** During these episodes, skin temperature may fluctuate by as much as 7 degrees Celsius, the skin may erupt in perspiration, and the woman may sense considerable physical discomfort. In severe cases, hot flashes may occur as many as three times an hour. In such cases, sleep disturbances are not uncommon. On average, women who suffer from hot flashes will do so for about a year; however, some may experience them for five or more years (Bellantoni & Blackman, 1996).

NONPHYSIOLOGICAL SYMPTOMS

Strictly speaking, menopause is a biological event with discernible causes and clear biological effects—specifically, cessation of ovulation and menstruation, and consequent permanent infertility. Nevertheless, because the changes of menopause affect most of the body's organs, notes Hargarten (1994), they can also lead to any of a variety of psychological symptoms. For example, the hot flashes of menopause are sometimes accompanied by dizziness, headaches, mood fluctuations, tremors, and weakness. In as many as one-third of all women, these symptoms are serious enough to cause the women to consult a physician, and are medically labeled the **climacteric syndrome** (Porcile et al., 1994). One of the occasional symptoms of this climacteric syndrome is depression, which increases during the climacteric (Coleman, 1993). However, as Schiff (1996) argues, there is little evidence to suggest that menopause is a direct cause of depression. It's far more likely that the depressions that sometimes occur during this period are associated with any of a variety of other factors such as changes in life satisfaction, stress, lowered self-esteem, anxiety about the future, and health concerns.

Interestingly, in many countries of the world, incidence of climacteric syndrome is much lower than in the West. Datan, Rodeheaver, and Hughes (1987) report, for example, that among five different Israeli subcultures, where loss of fertility is a welcome event, the psychological consequence of menopause is typically positive. Similarly, Haines, Chung, and Leung (1994) found significantly fewer acute menopausal symptoms among a sample of Chinese women in Hong Kong.

Beyene (1989), who studied menopause among Mayan and Greek peasant women, also found evidence that many of its symptoms are context-specific. For example, the most common menopausal symptom among the Greek women was hot flashes. Cold sweats, insomnia, and irritability were also relatively common; depression was rare, but did occur occasionally. In contrast, none of the Mayan women experienced any of these symptoms. About one-third of them experienced headaches and dizziness (more than 40 percent of the Greek women reported these symptoms), and about one-fifth experienced hemorrhaging (12 percent of the Greek women reported hemorrhaging).

These differences, claims Beyene, cannot be accounted for solely in terms of role changes or cultural expectations, given marked similarities among the peasant women in their attitudes toward menopause and in the social implications of the event. In other areas, such as diet and childbearing patterns, however, the women were very different. Mayan women typically had protein-deficient diets, consisting primarily of corn and very rarely of meat or eggs; Greek women ate meat and cheese, and a variety of legumes. Also, more than half of the Mayan women had five or more children (one in five had eight or more); more than 60 percent of the Greek women had two children or fewer. More cross-cultural studies are needed to clarify the role of these and other variables, says Beyene.

■ TREATMENT

Where problems accompanying menopause are sufficiently serious, they are sometimes treated with estrogen replacement therapy (ERT). In effect, this therapy serves to replace some of the estrogen that is no longer being produced after menopause. As we saw, ERT is also sometimes used in an attempt to reduce the risk and seriousness of osteoporosis. For example, Porcile and colleagues (1994) used an oral contraceptive containing low levels of estrogen with thirty women at menopause. They found a clear reduction of the symptoms of climacteric syndrome. In addition, exercise is one of the important treatments for climacteric syndrome. Hargarten (1994) reports that exercise can reduce most of its symptoms.

Symptoms similar to those that occasionally accompany menopause have sometimes been reported by men, although there is little evidence that they might be tied to hormonal changes that are common to most men. In fact, hormonal changes among men are seldom sufficient to lead to infertility, although they often do lead to a reduction in the number of viable sperm that are produced. It may be significant that when Solstad and Garde (1992) investigated men's beliefs about a male climacteric, the proportion of men who believed in the reality of the phenomenon decreased with advancing age. However, this might reflect the fact that a relatively large number experienced no symptoms. And that 18 percent of the fifty-one-year-old men in the sample thought they had experienced (or were experiencing) the climacteric may also be revealing. Solstad and Garde (1992) conclude that the male climacteric is simply a general label for a variety of nonspecific, unexplained physical complaints.

Sexuality

Janus and Janus (1993) report that more than 80 percent of men and almost 70 percent of women aged thirty-nine to fifty claim to have sex at least weekly. These figures are almost identical to those for younger adults. And the numbers among thirty-nine- to fifty-year-olds who claim to have sex daily (15 percent of men and 10 percent of women) are also almost identical to those for younger age groups. Apparently, sexual interest and behavior among men and women change little with the advent of the middle years. However, there are often some slight changes in sexual functioning. For example, although women continue to be interested in sex and continue to be capable of orgasm, there is often some reduction in vaginal lubrication with arousal following menopause (Bellantoni & Blackman, 1996). Among men, changes in sexual functioning are gradual and vary a great deal from one individual to another. It may now take longer, and more direct penile stimulation, for the man to achieve an erection, both before and after intercourse, and the erection might not always be as firm as it was some decades ago. In addition, ejaculation will typically be less forceful and will not necessarily occur with every orgasm (Gibson, 1992).

Unfortunately, these highly common changes are seldom discussed openly and are often interpreted as evidence of rapidly declining sexual prowess—an event that can lead to considerable anxiety concerning sexual performance and that is often implicated in the man's resulting impotence. In fact, the process of aging does not entail the loss of ability to perform sexually. (See Summary Table 15.2.)

■ AGE-RELATED COGNITIVE CHANGES IN MIDDLE ADULTHOOD

Many of the physical changes of aging are obvious. We can see the wrinkles and the sags, the graying and the thickening, the bending and the slowing. However, cognitive changes

▲ SUMMARY TABLE 15.2
Physical Changes in Middle Adulthood (Ages 40–45 to 60–65)

TOPICS	EXPLANATIONS/RESEARCH FINDINGS
Changes in appearance and sensory functioning	■ Gradual loss of height, muscle mass, and strength: more apparent in women. ■ Loss of skin elasticity; redistribution of fat; increase in fat relative to nonfat. ■ Increased vision and hearing problems (more cataracts; increased presbycusis). ■ Lower heart–lung efficiency. ■ Increasing atherosclerosis (plaquing of blood vessels) and arteriosclerosis (hardening of vessels); increasing osteoporosis (weakening, thinning of bones).
Nutrition and exercise	■ Exercise can do much to maintain flexibility, muscle mass and tone, cardiovascular functioning, and a sense of well-being. ■ More than 25 percent of North Americans are overweight. ■ Nutritional habits of many are poor (excessive oils, fats, sweets, and alcohol; insufficient fruits and vegetables). ■ More than half of all adults don't exercise regularly; 25 percent are current smokers.
The climacteric and menopause	■ Climacteric signals change of functioning of sex organs; menopause is cessation of menses as a function of irreversible ovarian failure. ■ Physiological consequences of menopause include inability to conceive a child, immune system changes, and higher susceptibility to heart disease, urinary tract problems, and osteoporosis and hot flashes (with symptoms severe enough to require attention in as many as ⅓ of women). ■ Menopause is occasionally accompanied by emotional side effects, sometimes including mood swings and depression. ■ Evidence suggests that menopause may be less a direct cause of these effects than other changes associated with the meaning of these changes and resulting changes in life satisfaction and self-esteem. ■ ERT (estrogen replacement therapy) is often effective in relieving symptoms of menopause and appears to reduce risk of osteoporosis and heart disease; it remains somewhat controversial because of a possible link to higher probability of certain cancers.
Sexuality	■ There is little change in sexual desire or capacity in middle age. ■ Sexual functioning may change somewhat with reduced vaginal lubrication following menopause and a longer period for sexual arousal for the man.

are not so obvious. Do they even occur? We have had little difficulty in answering this question with respect to childhood and adolescence, when, at every succeeding age, we could detect increases in comprehension and reasoning, and in the ability to analyze, synthesize, and solve problems. The task is not so simple with respect to adults and has led to considerable controversy. Does cognitive ability—like strength, vision, and the elasticity of our skin—reach a peak in early or middle adulthood, enter a period of stability, and then begin a downhill slide—slow and imperceptible at first but gradually more rapid until, in the words of Shakespeare, we reach again our "second childishness"? Or does it continue to grow so that, when we are finally old, we might also be truly wise?

Does Measured Intelligence Change with Age?

At first glance, it might not seem very difficult to answer these questions. After all, if cognitive ability is reflected in the **In-telligence Quotient (IQ)**, all we should need to do is administer appropriate tests to the appropriate people, and voilà, an answer: Intelligence increases fantastically with age, intelligence decreases with age, intelligence doesn't change, or intelligence changes this way to begin with, then that way, and then that way.

What do the experts tell us? Some of them suggest that a certain amount of intellectual decline with age is inevitable; others argue strongly that the belief that intellectual decline with age is highly significant and largely inevitable is at least partly a myth.

The Evidence

It turns out that the questions are not so simple, and the evidence is not so clear. And much of the controversy stems from the fact that the complexity of the question and the inadequacy of the evidence have not always been recognized.

While some measures of intellectual functioning sometimes begin to decline very slowly toward the end of middle age, measures that reflect the accumulated effects of experience (what Cattell labels crystallized abilities) often continue to increase through middle adulthood.

CROSS-SECTIONAL STUDIES

The first studies that looked at age-related changes in intelligence were typically **cross-sectional**; they compared the performance of groups of individuals of different ages. Almost invariably, when the intelligence test scores of older subjects were compared with those of adolescents or young adults, the adults did less well (Schaie, 1996). On general intelligence tests such as the Stanford-Binet and the WAIS (Wechsler Adult Intelligence Scale), the highest scores are almost always obtained by adolescents (or young adults), with progressively lower scores for older age groups. The same is also true of measures of specific mental abilities such as knowledge of verbal meaning, inductive reasoning, and number concepts (see Figure 15.6).

But the meanings of these findings are not quite so clear-cut. For one thing, patterns of decline are not consistent across all abilities. Some abilities (for example, verbal ones) decline less than others (inductive reasoning, for example) (Fillit, 1997). And, more important, cross-sectional studies cannot take into account the influence of **cohort** variables. Recall that a cohort is a group of individuals born within the

same time period. In effect, what a cross-sectional study does is compare different cohorts. When it compares seventy-year-olds to twenty-year-olds in 1995, it is comparing a group of individuals born in 1925 with one born in 1975. Clearly, these cohorts have been exposed to dramatically different environmental influences. Among other things, individuals born in 1925 have spent considerably less time in school, were not exposed to television and computers in their childhood, are often totally unfamiliar with the types of items in most intelligence tests, may never have been exposed to electronically scored answer sheets with their fine print and their demand for careful eye–hand coordination, and might be quite intimidated by the entire testing procedure. Thus, the older cohort's lower scores in cross-sectional studies (such as are illustrated in Figure 15.6) might not result from a natural decline in intelligence with age but might simply reflect the historical disadvantages experienced by that cohort.

LONGITUDINAL STUDIES

Longitudinal studies do not share this weakness. Recall that a longitudinal study compares the performance of the same individuals at different times. For example, a study that presents intelligence tests to a group of twenty-year-olds in 1955 and presents the same test to the same individuals in 1975 and again in 1995 is longitudinal. It provides far better data for reaching conclusions about changes that are age-related rather than specific to cohort variables (Schaie, 1994). However, the findings might be valid for only one cohort.

■ SEQUENTIAL STUDIES

As we saw in Chapter 1,* **sequential designs** combine elements of longitudinal and cross-sectional studies and avoid some of the disadvantages of each. One good example is Schaie's (1983b, 1994, 1996) investigation of intelligence, a thirty-five-year longitudinal study (the Seattle Longitudinal Study) with intelligence testing of all subjects at seven-year intervals and the addition of new samples at each of the testing times. Subjects ranged in age from twenty-five to eighty-eight. Thus, the study permitted comparison of different cohorts (cross-sectional) as well as the investigation of each of four cohorts over the thirty-five-year period. The results of the cross-sectional part of the study were as expected: There appears to be an age-related decline in performance on the different subtests of the Primary Mental Abilities Test, two of which are shown in Figure 15.6. However, when different cohorts are compared with each other, it becomes apparent that the earlier-born cohorts are at a general disadvantage—strong evidence that at least part of the decline in intellectual functioning is due to cohort-related influences (such as schooling) rather than to age. And this possibility is further supported by the results of the longitudinal part of the investigation. Vastly simplified, these results show much less decline within cohorts over the thirty-five-year period. In fact, for some abilities such as verbal meanings, performance continues to increase slightly after age twenty-five; at age eighty-eight, individuals still perform as well as at age twenty-five (see Figure 15.7). But for other abilities, such as spatial orientation, there is, in fact, some decline (see Figure 15.8).

---

*"Who remembers Chapter 1 when they get to Chapter 15?" my grandmother used to say. "Sometimes you got to repeat things." So I do. Briefly.

A Conclusion

Most researchers now agree that the current evidence supports two conclusions:

1. There is a decline in some measures of intellectual capacity or performance with age.

2. Some measures of intellectual capacity are stable or continue to increase through early and middle adulthood and sometimes even into old age.

It is instructive and revealing to look at the nature of the abilities that remain stable or continue to increase, and those that decline. In general, it seems that those capacities that depend on underlying physiological mechanisms—on a smoothly functioning nervous system, for example—are most likely to decline with age. These capacities define what Cattell calls **fluid intelligence.** Fluid abilities don't improve with experience but seem to depend more on some underlying, basic capacity. They are reflected in general reasoning, memory, attention span, and analysis of figures.

Capacities that depend more on experience are most likely to remain stable or even to increase. After all, why shouldn't general information, vocabulary, and the other legacies of experience not continue to increase over the years? These capacities define **crystallized intelligence;** they are reflected in measures of vocabulary, general information, and arithmetic skills.

Our reasoning suggests that fluid abilities, which depend on a smoothly functioning nervous system, should decline with age; by the same token, crystallized abilities, which depend on experience, should remain stable or perhaps increase. That this is generally the case is, in fact, supported by

FIGURE 15.7

Comparison of cross-sectional and longitudinal age differences for verbal meaning. (Adapted from Schaie, 1986. Used by permission of Brookhaven National Laboratory.)

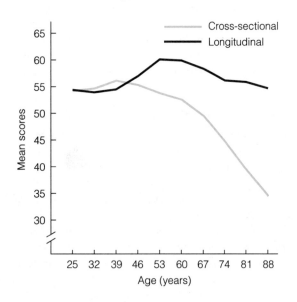

FIGURE 15.8

Comparison of cross-sectional and longitudinal age differences for spatial orientation. (Adapted from Schaie, 1986. Used by permission of Brookhaven National Laboratory.)

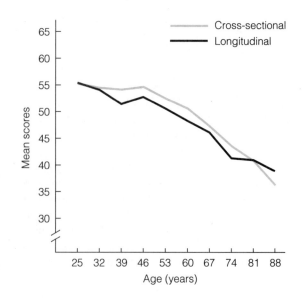

the evidence. For example, Kaufman and associates (1996) looked at performance on tasks representing crystallized and fluid intelligence among almost 1,200 individuals aged fifteen to ninety-four. In general, crystallized abilities (those most dependent on experience) were relatively well maintained; in contrast, performance on tasks representing fluid abilities (those more dependent on functioning of the nervous system) showed declines with increasing age. Figure 15.9 illustrates these patterns. As Schaie (1996) concludes, "[scores on] Verbal Reasoning, Space, and Reasoning attain a peak plateau in midlife from the 40s to the early 60s, whereas Number and Word fluency peak earlier and show very modest decline beginning in the 50's" (p. 351).

■ FACTORS AFFECTING DECLINE AND STABILITY

Alwin (1994) points out that although it is generally true that some capacities decline with age while others might increase slightly, intellectual performance through the middle years (and sometimes well into old age) is marked more by stability than by anything else. Furthermore, notes Schaie

FIGURE 15.9

Smoothed curves summarizing several studies on aging and fluid intelligence and several studies on aging and crystallized intelligence. (From Horn & Donaldson in Brim & Kagan, 1980, pp. 469–471.)

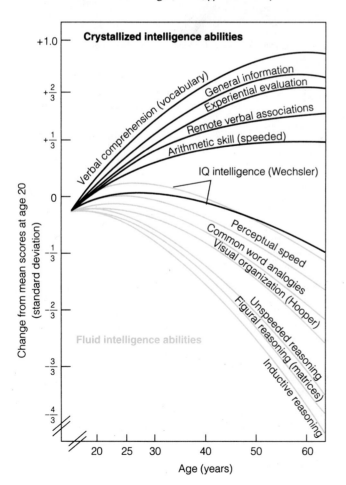

(1996), the evidence is clear that the average age of peak functioning with respect to different cognitive abilities has shifted upward during the past several decades and is continuing to do so. What this means, he argues, is that profoundly important social and environmental influences that are peculiar to each cohort have much to do with intellectual performance.

It's also clear that patterns of intellectual changes can be very different for different individuals. As an example, for some individuals in the Berkeley Growth Studies, there were significant increases in measured IQ between ages seventeen and eighteen, and again between ages thirty-six and forty-eight (Honzik, 1984). As might be expected, these increases are related primarily to better performance on crystallized (culture-influenced) measures. Not surprisingly, the people most likely to continue to perform well or even to improve their performance as they age are those whose spouses were significantly more intelligent than they themselves were to begin with (in terms of measured IQ). There appears to be little doubt that continued intellectual stimulation and opportunity to stretch the capacities that define intelligence are closely related to maintaining or improving peak performance. It is worth noting, as well, that those who experienced the greatest intellectual declines in the Berkeley studies were often heavy drinkers or those who had suffered some illness. Similarly, Tranel, Benton, and Olson (1997), in a longitudinal study of cognitive changes between age sixty-five and, in some cases, eighty-nine, found that those who experienced the greatest declines in cognitive functioning were also those who suffered from chronic diseases and were in poor health. In their words, "significant health problems...are associated with deterioration in neuropsychological functioning" (p. 94). In the absence of health problems, however, their view is that "mental decline across a broad spectrum of cognitive abilities should not be viewed as an inevitable correlate of the aging process, even in persons in the 9th decade of life" (p. 94).

Most researchers do not deny that decline is frequently observed with advancing age. However, the majority maintain that it is not always inevitable and irreversible. As Bromley (1990) notes, the reasons for decline may often be physical factors such as reduced oxygen supply to the brain—which may in turn be due to reversible conditions such as illnesses, stress, or even lack of exercise. We need to distinguish, argues Willis (1997), between **normal cognitive decline** and **pathological cognitive decline.** Normal cognitive decline would be evident in decrements caused by normal, age-related changes in neurological and physiological systems associated with intelligent functioning. Pathological decline refers to decrements associated with various conditions such as illness, trauma, or disease that are often, but not inevitably, a consequence of aging.

The most sensible conclusion at this point is an optimistic one. Decline in important areas such as verbal ability, reasoning, and numerical skills is usually inconsequential until well into the sixties. Given appropriate environmental stimulation, not only will many cognitive abilities not decrease with age, but some may actually continue to increase well into old age (Schaie, 1993). Wisdom, which we discuss in Chapter 17 (along with other aspects of cognitive change), may be a case in point.

Thinking in Middle Adulthood

As we saw in Chapter 13, current views of adult thinking have changed remarkably in recent decades. We know that adults continue to learn through much of the lifespan, both formally and incidentally (Rossing, 1991). It is inevitable that this learning should be reflected in their thinking.

Researchers such as Labouvie-Vief and Riegel argue that the problems that adults face, and the circumstances of their lives, exercise a profound influence on their cognitive processes. The formal logic of a Piagetian system might be suitable in an academic setting, or perhaps even for the adolescent who has not yet learned that there are reasons why logic is not always the only—or even the best—approach. Real-life problems often require experience and intuition as much as logic, and their solutions need to reflect practical realities (pragmatics).

Basseches (1984) and Riegel (1976) suggest that a uniquely adult form of reasoning evolves through early adulthood and into the middle years. It is a form of thinking that is dialectical. Not only are adult dialectical thinkers more sensitive to contradictions—and more tolerant of them—but they have also learned a series of procedures (dialectical schemata) for dealing with contradictions. Thus, they have an ability to reason about political and social systems, as well as about interpersonal relationships, that is not commonly found in younger individuals. And perhaps that is why, for many adults, the middle years are the most creative of the entire lifespan.

Creativity in the Middle Years

Perhaps the most convincing evidence of the middle-aged person's continuing intellectual competence is found in creative performance.[*] Among the first studies in this area were Lehman's (1953) estimates of the age ranges during which peak creativity, leadership, and achievement occurred. He found that the peak in most areas (the sciences, mathematics, music) occurred in the thirties, except for the writing of novels and other books (excluding poetry), which peaked in the forties. Achievement in athletics peaks much earlier, generally during the twenties.

Later analyses revealed that Lehman's studies had used some questionable procedures (including failing to take sub-

---

[*]"Which clearly doesn't end in middle age," snorted my grandmother. "Look at Monet and Michelangelo and Picasso. They all painted when they were in their eighties and nineties. And Grandma Moses was 100 when she did her last painting, and Freud wrote a book when he was 83. And look at Mr. Delisle, why don't you, and that poem he wrote me last spring."

"But it's not evidence you need," she shot back when I made some little comment. "It's respect."

ject mortality into account) and that his estimates of ages of peak performance were therefore biased toward the younger age groups. The problem was that many creative people in his samples didn't live long enough to show that it's possible to be creative in old age. When Dennis (1966) replicated the Lehman study, including in his sample only men who lived at least until the age of seventy-nine, he found that the age of peak achievement in most areas is substantially higher than Lehman had estimated (see Table 15.3). In fact, peak production seldom occurs before the forties, and sometimes even the fifties and sixties. And in many areas, it continues well into the seventies.

When peak production declines during the middle years, this does not always mean that the capacity for creative production has also declined. Diamond (1986) points out that many highly successful adults find their creative output reduced precisely because of their success. In many fields, those who are the highest producers are also those who are most likely to be promoted. Administrative responsibilities might then severely reduce the individual's output. Furthermore, assessing creative potential solely on the basis of measurable production is misleading. As Sasser-Coen (1993) argues, creativity in the second half of life is often evident in qualitative improvements rather than in quantity of production.

In many areas, creative production is based not only on the special predispositions and talents that make up the creative personality (see Chapter 9) but also on a large store of

TABLE 15.3

Creative Output by Decade for Men Living to Age 79 or More

AREA	NUMBER OF MEN	NUMBER OF WORKS	DECADE					
			20s	30s	40s	50s	60s	70s
Scholarship								
History	46	615	3	19	19	22	24	20
Philosophy	42	225	3	17	20	18	22	20
Scholarship	43	326	6	17	21	21	16	19
Sciences								
Biology	32	3,456	5	22	24	19	17	13
Botany	49	1,889	4	15	22	22	22	15
Chemistry	24	2,420	11	21	24	19	12	13
Geology	40	2,672	3	13	22	28	19	14
Invention	44	646	2	10	17	18	32	21
Mathematics	36	3,104	8	20	20	18	19	15
Arts								
Architecture	44	1,148	7	24	29	25	10	4
Chamber music	35	109	15	21	17	20	18	9
Drama	25	803	10	27	29	21	9	3
Librettos	38	164	8	21	30	22	15	4
Novels	32	494	5	19	18	28	23	7
Operas	176	476	8	30	31	16	10	5
Poetry	46	402	11	21	26	16	16	10

Source: From "Creative Productivity Between the Ages of 20 and 80" by W. Dennis, 1966, *Journal of Gerontology* 21, pp. 1–18. Reprinted by permission of the publisher.

Age-Related Cognitive Changes in Middle Adulthood

CONCLUSIONS	EVIDENCE/EXPLANATIONS
There are age-related declines in measured intelligence.	■ Almost all pertinent cross-sectional studies find that younger adults outperform older adults.
The superior performance of younger relative to older adults is not necessarily evidence of an inevitable age-related decline in measured intelligence, but is evidence that more recently born cohorts have had social experiences conducive to better intellectual functioning.	■ Differences between older and younger adults on longitudinal studies are often considerably smaller than is the case in cross-sectional studies; at identical ages, more recent cohorts outperform cohorts born earlier.
Intellectual abilities that are highly dependent on experience and culture are less likely to decline with age.	■ Considerable research indicates that *crystallized* abilities such as verbal comprehension and general information decline little or not at all until well into old age.
Intellectual abilities that are highly dependent on neurological, sensory, and physiological functioning are most susceptible to age-related declines.	■ Many studies indicate that *fluid* abilities such as inductive reasoning and perceptual speed begin to decline in middle adulthood, and manifest the greatest losses in old age.
Pathological cognitive decline, which can occur early in the lifespan and be quite severe, is often confused with normal cognitive decline, which is far more moderate.	■ In longitudinal studies, the clearest cognitive decrements are almost invariably manifested by those who suffer from serious ill health.
There are significant individual differences in patterns of cognitive stability and decline.	■ Many individuals show little or no cognitive decline; some show stability or even dramatic recovery following a period of loss.
Creativity is not invariably doomed to decline with advancing age.	■ In many fields, creative output continues unabated into the upper decades of life.

relevant information and experience. Dennis's finding that creative output in most areas seldom peaks before the middle years should come as no surprise. In fact, there are some who believe that creativity in later life is unique in that it is based not only on talent but also on wisdom (Hildebrand, 1990). (See Summary Table 15.4.)

■ WORK IN MIDDLE ADULTHOOD

Not only are the middle years the most creatively productive, but they are also the most productive in the area of careers

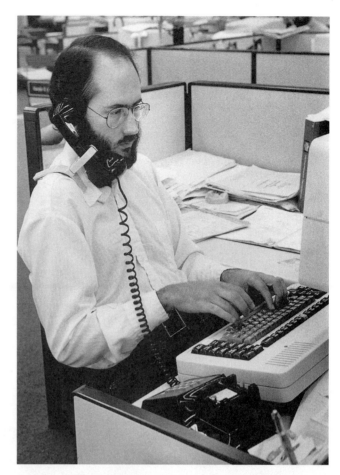

Among male–female differences in the work place are differences in income, in job status, in administrative positions, and in the nature of the jobs that are most typically male or female. But profound social changes are rapidly reducing and eliminating these differences. This man answering the phone and booking appointments for his boss while she conducts an important board meeting is a situation that would have been relatively unlikely a handful of decades ago.

and jobs. Middle-aged adults hold more administrative and high-level positions than younger workers, and they earn more. In general, they are more competent.

In Chapter 13, we discussed the nature and rewards of work, changes in attitudes toward work as well as in employment opportunities, and processes involved in selecting and preparing for careers. As we saw, there have been major changes in employment opportunities in recent decades. No one has been more affected by these changes than women.

Women in the Workplace

Between 1900 and 1970, the percentage of adult women working for a salary in North America more than doubled (from 20 to 45 percent; Sheppard, 1976). By 1993, about 58 percent of women between 18 and 44 were employed (U.S. Bureau of the Census, 1994) (see "At a Glance: Women in the Work Force" and Figures 15.10, 15.11, and 15.12).

Women in the Work Force, Canada and the United States

t the turn of the nineteenth century, fewer than 20 percent of American women were in the work force. By midcentury, the percentage had almost doubled, and by 1995, it had nearly tripled. During this time, the percentage of men in the work force hardly changed. However, between 1960 and 1995 the percentage of married men in the work force declined from 89.2 to 77.5. During the same period of time, the percentage of married women working increased from 31.9 to 61.0 (Figures 15.10 and 15.11). In Canada, female participation in the work force increased from 45.6 percent in 1976 to 57.4 in 1995 (Figure 15.12). During the same period, men's participation in the labor force declined from 77.8 to 72.5 (Figure 15.13).

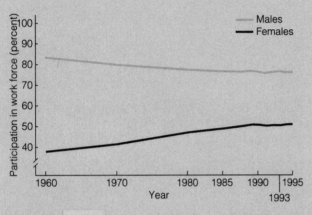

FIGURE 15.10

Increase in percentage of women in U.S. work force, 1960–1995. (From U.S. Bureau of the Census, 1996, p. 399.)

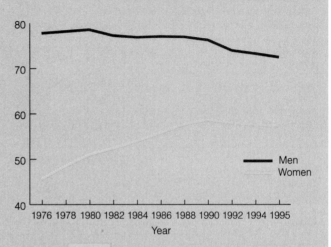

FIGURE 15.12

Increase in percentage of women in Canadian work force, 1975–1995. (From Statistics Canada, 1996, p. 207.)

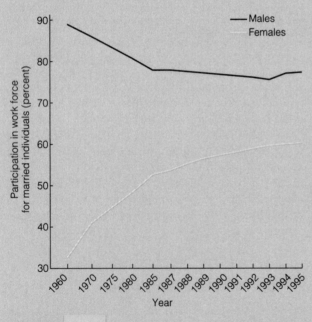

FIGURE 15.11

Changes in U.S. work force participation for married men and women, 1960–1995. (From U.S. Bureau of the Census, 1996, p. 399.)

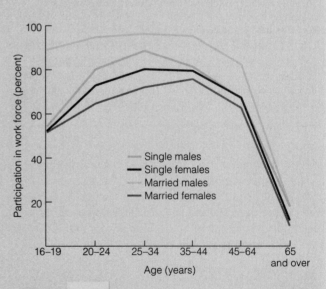

FIGURE 15.13

Work force participation rates by age, sex, and marital status in the United States, 1995. (From U.S. Bureau of the Census, 1996, p. 399.)

Inequity in the Workplace

espite dramatic changes in the workplace, certain forms of employment are still primarily male, and others female. In the United States in 1995, for example, more than 12 million precision production jobs (mechanics, construction trades, repairs) were held by males, and only about 1 million by females. In contrast, nearly 15 million clerical, support, and receptionist positions were held by females, and only about 3 million by males. In the United States, the average income of female workers in 1994 was only 66 percent that of males. The ratio of female–male earnings for all full-time workers in Canada in 1994 was even lower at 62 percent. Gains since 1967 have been small (see Figure 15.14), and a woman with four years of college can still expect to earn less than a man with no more than a secondary school education (see Figure 15.15).

In spite of these continuing inequities in the workplace, there have been some dramatic changes in recent decades—changes not only in the number of women working, but also changes in the nature of the work they do. Rogers (1993) reports that there has been a literal explosion of job classifications for women, and that many of the more sexist job titles have now disappeared.

FIGURE 15.14

Changes in ratio of female-to-male earnings in Canada, 1977–1994. (Based on Statistics Canada, 1996, p. 215.)

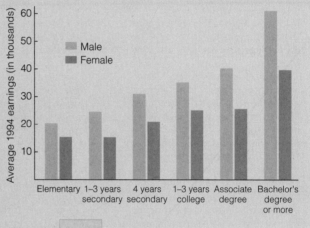

FIGURE 15.15

U.S. male and female earnings by educational attainment in 1994. (Based on U.S. Bureau of the Census, 1996, p. 471.)

Figure 15.13 shows the relative distribution of the U.S. work force in 1995 by age, sex, and marital status. Not surprisingly, the period of peak employment for females—especially for married females—occurs somewhat later than that for men (ages 35 to 44 rather than 25 to 34). It coincides with children being older or leaving home.

Male–Female Differences at Work

Fewer women than men work for a salary—52.6 percent of all women over sixteen in 1995, compared with over 79.1 percent of all men (U.S. Bureau of the Census, 1996). As mentioned previously, typical female occupations are not yet on a par with male occupations in terms of status, prestige, or income. For example, 97 percent of receptionists, 99 percent of secretaries, 92 percent of teachers' aides, and 87 percent of telephone operators are women. In contrast, women make up only 4 percent of airplane pilots and navigators, 4 percent of mechanics, 2 percent of the construction trades, and 12 percent of administrative supervisors (U.S. Bureau of the Census, 1996).

Average income for females in the United States is about 66 percent that of males. In Canada, it's about 62 percent. Women with four years of college earn about as much as men who have only completed high school (U.S. Bureau of the Census, 1996; Statistics Canada, 1996). Those with high school diplomas earn less than men who have never gone to high school (see "At a Glance: Inequity in the Workplace" and Figures 15.14 and 15.15).

Social Changes

In my grandmother's era, women who continued their education or who took one of various job-training courses often hen Takashi Wagatsuma was ready to get married, he followed the traditional Japanese customs for the pure *miai* marriage. This required a formal introduction, an approved meeting or *miai,* and the posing of the question by both his parents and hers. The *miai* marriage is recognizable by four themes, says Blood (1967): observing traditional formalities, relying on the initiative of others, absence of premarital interaction, and lack of love. As Takashi later put it, "Ours was a pure *miai* marriage and a very rational one. I must confess that in the marriage decision there was, to a certain extent, a calculating, self-interested aspect. I thought that after the calculation, affection for her would naturally arise in me" (Blood, 1967, p. 20).

When Hiroshi Koyama of Kyoto wanted to get married, he followed none of the traditional procedures. For him, there were no go-betweens, no arranged meeting or *miai,* no formal exchange of presents (the *yuino*). He met his future bride "through the mere chance of working together." "My case may safely be called a pure love match," claimed Hiroshi. "During the whole process of arranging for marriage no interference broke in from the parents or friends" (Blood, 1967, p. 21).

Omiai, arranged marriages, are still very common in Japan, accounting for more than one-third of all marriages. And when Blood (1967) compared such marriages with love marriages, he found that both husbands and wives tended to be more satisfied with arranged marriages, especially with respect to what Blood refers to as the structural aspects of marriage—things like the respect that husband and wife have for each other and how well each performs expected duties. Only with respect to the more dynamic aspects of marriage, such as sexual satisfaction and companionship, was there a very slight difference in favor of love marriages.

To Think About

A Japanese man, speaking about differences between traditional Japanese marriages and American marriages, comments that there are many things in marriage more important than sexual or emotional passion—things like the household and the honor of the

family, duty and respect, work, and, yes, deep companionship. He finds it sad that Americans have so little in their lives that they need so much from their marriage—and must, therefore, almost always be disappointed: "Americans are highly unrealistic about marriage: They expect too much from that single relationship" (Hamabata, 1990, p. 124). What do you think?

---

claimed that they were doing so in order "to have something to fall back on later." These women typically assumed that they would get married and raise children while the husband earned their bread. Having to "fall back" was something that would happen only in the wake of some great misfortune like illness or death of the husband or, heaven forbid, separation or divorce.

Not so any longer. Changing social conditions are reflected not only in the increasing numbers of women who have entered the work force but also in the fact that the expected family pattern, where the man works outside the home and the woman inside, describes fewer than 20 percent of all contemporary American families. Approximately 70 percent of two-parent families also have two wage earners (U.S. Bureau of the Census, 1996). Increasing numbers of families have deliberately chosen not to have children. Furthermore, single-parent families headed by a woman are now as common as the more traditional two-parent family, where the man is the sole wage earner. Clearly, there have

been some profound changes in the American family. (See "Across Cultures: Takashi Wagatsuma and Hiroshi Koyama Get Married.")

Dual Careers

Families with two wage earners now appear to be the norm rather than the exception. However, a two-earner family is not necessarily a **dual-career family**. A career, as we saw, is defined by a relatively systematic progression through a series of related occupations. Unlike a simple job, a career demands commitment and loyalty; typically, it requires a greater investment of time and energy.

A dual-career family is one in which both the husband and the wife have separate careers and the career of neither is sacrificed for the other—or for the family. Among college populations, the notion of a dual-career family has apparently become increasingly popular. In one survey, more than

Early Adulthood (continued)

For many, early adulthood sees the establishment of the mother-father-children nuclear family. For others, there are other options.

Middle Adulthood

Middle adulthood is, in many ways, the peak of our life's mountain— or perhaps it's more like a high plateau. During these years, we have more of everything that our societies prize: money, wealth, prestige, power— perhaps even love.

uch about the middle adult years seems stable and predictable. Still, there are now increasing signs of change in our physical powers, signs that age will not be denied.

*D*uring middle adulthood, social and family relationships
often change, sometimes in dramatic and distressing ways;
often in very happy ways.

Middle adulthood embraces an enormous span of years. At the very beginning of this span we might be new parents, perhaps embarking on new careers, new relationships. At the end, we might be grandparents, newly retired.

Late Adulthood

In one of the last of his seven ages of man (and woman too), Shakespeare speaks of a justice, "in fair round belly, full of wise saws." We are no longer so certain that the old are wise. But we agree that a round belly is not so fair.
And even in late adulthood, we continue to struggle against the effects of aging.

or many, there is still much to be
done in late adulthood—and
perhaps far less time in which
to do it. In the first ages of our lives,
when we rest, we dream of things
we have not yet done. In the last of
our ages, the dreams that color our
resting reach more often toward
the past than the future.

The End

All the world's a stage, said Shakespeare, and we are all merely players. Each of us, should we live so long, play seven acts— seven ages. The last scene of all, he writes, that ends this strange eventful history . . . mere oblivion, sans teeth, sans eyes, sans taste, sans everything.

80 percent of both male and female college students indicated that they were interested in having a dual-career family (Nadelson & Nadelson, 1980).

Surveys of dual-career couples reveal that they often share several common characteristics. Typically, the husband and the wife have very similar values, possess relatively high-level job skills, are self-reliant and independent, and have high incomes. It is also quite common for these couples either not to have children or to have small families, which are typically started only after the wife has already established her career (Hertz, 1986).

Dual-career families sometimes entail unique sets of problems. One of the most common affects the wife rather than the husband and results from the fact that many wives not only are members of a dual-career partnership but are also involved in a **double career** (also referred to as a *double-track career*). The difference between a dual career and a double career is simple: Dual careers exist where two people develop separate and individual careers; a double career exists when a single person assumes the responsibilities of two careers at the same time.

Double Careers

Double careers are common among wives who are responsible for their careers outside the home and who must also assume responsibility for a tremendous range of home-related tasks: cooking, cleaning, supervising, child rearing, and so on. Many, note DeMeis and Perkins (1996), are almost required to be "supermoms." What is perhaps surprising is that most college students and, indeed, most young couples believe strongly that if both husband and wife are to have individual careers, each should share domestic responsibilities equally. Ironically, however, this is not often the case in practice. In a survey of 287 fully employed, married women, Pina and Bengtson (1993) found marked inequity in division of household chores. Similarly, Demo and Acock (1993) found that among all family groupings in a sample of 2,528 families (stepfamilies, single-parent families, and two-parent families), women did between two and three times more housework than their spouses or cohabiting mates. In light of this, it's hardly surprising that Ward (1993) found that working outside the home does not seem to contribute to the woman's marital happiness.

One of the possible results of the tremendous burden of responsibilities that the double-tracked woman carries is high stress—which can affect fathers as well as mothers (Deater-Deckard & Scarr, 1996). In severe cases, the result might be **burnout**—a term used to describe a situation in which the individual no longer feels able to cope. Ways of preventing burnout, or of relieving its effects, might include abandoning or postponing one spouse's career, enlisting the husband's help with domestic duties (difficult in practice), making children increasingly responsible for their own care, or hiring domestic help or "nannies."

Many of the problems of double-career women relate not only to inequities in allocation of domestic duties, but have to do as well with child care. Often, there are problems associated with availability of care, its cost, and its quality (Neugebauer, 1994). In addition, as Joshi and Davies (1992) have documented, women who work and have children not only bear the cost of looking after and raising these children, but also suffer considerable lifetime losses of earning relative to women who have never interrupted their working careers to have children.

Career Changes

Career changes in midlife, notes Levinson (1981), are not uncommon. These often result from the reevaluation of dreams that sometimes occurs in the forties, and from the individual's changing views of life and of the self. Increasingly, however, career changes occur not only at midlife but throughout the individual's working career. Drummond and Ryan (1995) note that employment longevity is rapidly declining and that more employers are now hiring workers on a job or contract rather than a career basis. The average tenure (in years) for all workers in all occupations is under seven. In 1994 about 22 percent of males and 19 percent of females over twenty were unemployed because of plant closings, job abolishment, or "slack" work (U.S. Bureau of the Census, 1996).

▋ VOLUNTARY CAREER CHANGES

Clearly, not all career changes are voluntary. But for those that are, there are many reasons people might choose to change careers. Midlife changes and reevaluations (discussed in the next chapter) are one reason. Often, men abandon careers that have demanded too much time and energy, and that have not allowed enough time for family and other personal concerns. These might be abandoned in favor of more gentle, less aggressive pursuits, suggests Levinson (1978, 1990). In contrast, at midlife many women become more career-oriented, more aggressive, more interested in exploring their strengths and talents, and in testing their limits in different settings (Sheehy, 1981). Their career changes might be motivated accordingly.

Technological changes present another reason for voluntarily making career changes. Sometimes these lead to restlessness about the permanence and value of present careers. Alternatively, these changes can open up exciting new fields and, rather than chasing people from careers, might attract them instead.

Another relatively common reason for voluntary midlife career changes is the emptying of the family nest. When the little ones have flitted away, the parents are freed. They now have less reason to fear the risks that might come with career changes. In addition, mothers who have interrupted their schooling or their careers to raise children can now resume the interrupted activity. If the mother begins to earn a second family income, the resulting reduction in the

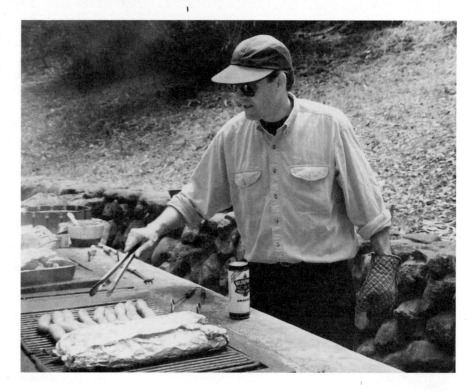

Voluntary changes of career do not have the same psychological implications as involuntary changes. It's the best time of my life, says this former accountant who has sold his practice to set up a business that caters family and company picnics.

financial risk involved will sometimes lead to the father's changing careers.

Not surprisingly, studies that have looked at the characteristics of people who voluntarily decide to change careers have often found these people to be more self-reliant, somewhat more willing to take risks, and generally characterized by feelings of control and power—what is now termed **career self-efficacy** (Mathieu, Sowa, & Niles, 1993). However, this is not to say that all people who change careers are more in control, more self-reliant, and more characterized by feelings of self-efficacy. Some who make career changes are marked more by fluctuating and unstable interests, a high fear of failure, and emotional problems than by high feelings of competence.

■ INVOLUNTARY CAREER CHANGES

From a psychological point of view, people who deliberately choose to change careers may be in a much better position than those whose career changes are involuntary. As my cousin Luke could easily testify, should he be willing, there are five reasons for making an involuntary career change, and he experienced them all.

To begin with, he was fired. A career change resulting from being fired is perhaps the most difficult to cope with and often gives rise to a reaction not unlike the grief that might follow the loss of a loved one (Jones, 1979).

A second reason for involuntary career change is the loss of a career because of changes in the workplace. If all the oil fields dry up, many oil-related careers are involuntarily disrupted. This, Luke insisted, happened to him!

Third, some careers are of short duration by their very nature. These "early-leaver" careers include most professional sports and certain high-risk and highly demanding occupations. Luke had a brief but incredibly successful career as a chicken sexer until age, some three months later, lessened his tactile sensitivity and forced him into an early retirement.

Fourth, involuntary career changes are sometimes necessitated by illness or injury. In Luke's case, an assortment of temporary injuries forced yet another involuntary switch in careers.

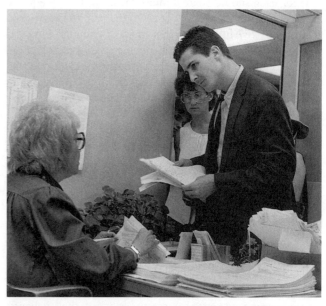

Involuntary career changes—like getting fired, for example—can be highly devastating not only because of their economic implications, but also because of their blow to the individual's feelings of worth and competence.

And fifth, of course, is mandatory retirement. In some cases, retirement, whether mandatory or not, is quite voluntary; in many, however, it isn't. "I didn't want to quit, no way," Luke is reported to have said. "But what the heck. Elizabeth's got a good job anyway. D'you wanna go fishing?"

Increased leisure may be one of the benefits of an involuntary career change.

LEISURE

Is work the most important thing in our lives? Do we, as we struggle to grasp the slippery rungs of corporate, academic, social, and financial success, sometimes become addicted to this thing called work? Do those who no longer stop to smell the roses even remember that roses are out there?

There are roses out there. We need only the **leisure** to notice. Leisure, Aristotle claimed, is the purpose of everything else we do. *Leisure* may be defined as discretionary time—time during which we have no obligation to do anything specific, time that we spend as we choose.

Lu and Argyle (1994) investigated the relationships between leisure activities and general happiness among a group of 114 subjects. Sixty-eight percent of this group reported that they were committed to some kind of leisure activity. Interestingly, those with higher self-esteem tended to devote their leisure to voluntary work, those marked by high levels of cooperativeness were more likely to join clubs, and those who were somewhat more neurotic were most likely to select private hobbies.

Perhaps the most important finding of the Lu and Argyle study is that commitment to leisure activities is closely related to happiness. Yet our culture remains somewhat ambivalent about leisure; it is not entirely certain how to treat it. The work ethic that drove our forebears, and that still drives sizable numbers of us, sees virtue and grace in work but sees little value in leisure. Accordingly, we continue to be socialized to work but not to play. We are taught a thousand subtle tricks for navigating through the courses of our work lives, but we are seldom given any advice about how to play. Indeed, we are seldom even told that we should play, or why.

But we should. Leisure can not only make us happier, but it also helps relieve the effects of stress—effects that can sometimes be very damaging. And what we do with leisure, like what we do with work, can have a tremendous impact on our self-esteem. In fact, leisure activities can sometimes provide us with identity in much the same way as work might. For example, Luke, for a brief period, did not simply cut the tops off tall trees; he was, you better believe it, a lumberjack! But even while he was being a lumberjack, there were times when he would swell with rushes of well-being when someone would say about him, "That Luke there, he's quite a poker player."

Although our cultures have traditionally emphasized work far more than leisure—and, in fact, often continue to define

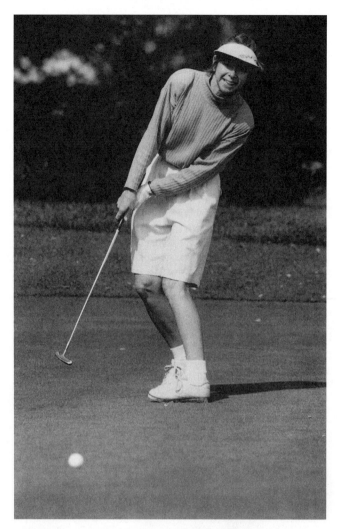

Although our cultures have traditionally emphasized work over leisure, increasing industrialization and technological advance may result in increasing leisure—and in a belated recognition of its importance. A hole in one—well, even in four or five—can do a great deal for self-esteem and happiness.

leisure as time off work—there are signs of ongoing change. Current emphases in an increasing number of career guidance and counseling programs are no longer on setting goals and making whatever sacrifices are necessary to obtain them in the distant future—after which come the gold watch and the phases of retirement. Instead, people are urged to find occupations that are pleasant and satisfying for them. More than this, these occupations must not only involve rewarding activities but also provide people with the income and, far more importantly, with the leisure required for a truly high-quality life.

If we learn to make the most of our leisure activities, then there is a very good chance that work will not be the only important thing in our lives when, and if, we reach for our gold watches and our pension checks. Not only will we have smelled so many more roses, now dead, but we may have learned where the new ones grow. (See Summary Table 15.5.)

SUMMARY TABLE 15.5
Some Observations About Work and Leisure in Middle Adulthood

- The middle years are the most productive, the most powerful, and the most remunerative of the work years.

- About three times more women work now than was the case at the turn of the century.

- Much female employment is still in lower-paying, lower-status jobs; women earn about two-thirds as much as men on average.

- Dual-career families, where the careers of both wife and husband are developed equally with equitable sharing of household and child-rearing responsibilities, are rare; females in two-career families are often in a *double-career* situation, where they have full responsibility for their career and major responsibility for home- and child-related tasks.

- Voluntary career changes might be undertaken because of changing interests, changes in the marketplace, or changes in family or life circumstances.

- Involuntary career changes, which sometimes have negative consequences, can result from being fired, changes in the workplace, the nature of the career, or mandatory retirement.

- Our societies have traditionally emphasized the work ethic and have prepared us poorly for leisure, which can have important implications for our emotional well-being.

FOCUS QUESTIONS: SUMMARY ANSWERS

1. What are the principal physical and sensory changes of middle age?

   - Physical changes of middle age include cessation of growth in height (a slight decrement in later years), the accumulation of fatty tissue, loss of skin elasticity, thinning of hair, stiffening of joints, loss of muscle tone, and reduction in muscle tissue. Sensory changes include a gradual reduction in visual acuity, greater farsightedness, and a gradual loss of hearing ability, particularly for higher tones. Major organ systems slowly become less efficient after early adulthood. Signs of arteriosclerosis (hardening of artery walls) are common, and people become more susceptible to heart disease, cancer, arthritis, cirrhosis, hyperten-

sion, and osteoporosis, but less susceptible to acute infections.

2. What is the climacteric? How is it related to the midlife crisis?

   - By the late thirties or early forties for women, and perhaps by the fifties for men, the sex glands' production of hormones decreases, leading to the climacteric or "change of life" (not dramatic among men, cessation of menstruation, or menopause, among women). Menopause is sometimes accompanied by physical symptoms ("hot flashes," trembling, dizziness, and headaches) that are occasionally treated with hormone replacements. Sexual interest and functioning are ordinarily maintained after the climacteric (some reduction in vaginal lubrication for women, slower sexual arousal for men).

3. Does measured intelligence change with age? Does it decline in middle or old age?

   - Cross-sectional studies find cohort-related evidence of intellectual decline with age. Longitudinal studies show that abilities dependent on experience (verbal and numerical abilities, for example) tend not to decline as early or as much. In contrast, abilities less dependent on experience (*fluid,* like reasoning or attention span) do not fare as well. *Normal cognitive decline* describes predictable, age-related changes in mental functioning; *pathological cognitive decline,* which is more dramatic and less common, describes decline due to conditions like serious ill health.

4. What sorts of gender-related changes have occurred in the workplace and in child care in recent decades?

   - The percentage of adult women who work has tripled in this century. More than half of two-parent families have two wage earners. Some involve *dual careers* (husband and wife have independent, equal careers); many involve *double careers* (inequitable division of home-making and child-rearing responsibilities so that one partner, usually the wife, juggles two careers). Women's occupations still tend to be lower than men's in status and income, and still reflect many old stereotypes.

STUDY TERMS

adrenal glands, 446	cataracts, 442
arteriosclerosis, 443	climacteric, 445
atherosclerosis, 443	climacteric syndrome, 446
burnout, 457	cohort, 449
career self-efficacy, 458	cross-sectional, 449

FURTHER READINGS

The following is a short, highly readable book that covers many of the topics of this chapter:

Genovese, R. G. (1997). *Americans at midlife: Caught between generations.* Westport, CT: Bergin & Garvey.

Schiff's book is a remarkably thorough and informative book dealing with all aspects of the psychological and physiologi-cal changes of menopause. At the same time, it is very easy to read:

Schiff, I. (1996). *Menopause.* New York: Random House.

The following three books look at cognitive change in the middle years and beyond. Schaie's is a clear summary of his well-known, thirty-five-year study of aging; the Rogers and Fisk book is a somewhat more academic collection of pertinent research articles; and the Fillit and Butler book is a brief look at the significance of cognitive decline in later life and at the effectiveness of various interventions:

Schaie, K. W. (1996). *Intellectual development in adulthood.* New York: Cambridge University Press.

Rogers, W. A., Fisk, A. D., & Walker, N. (1997). *Aging and skilled performance: Advances in theory and applications.* Mahwah, NJ: Erlbaum.

Fillit, H. M., & Butler, R. N. (Eds.). (1997). *Cognitive decline: Strategies for prevention.* London, England: Greenwich Medical Media.

The following book looks at career counseling at each of the major stages of the lifespan, including young and middle adulthood as well as later stages:

Drummond, R. J., & Ryan, C. W. (1995). *Career counseling: A developmental approach.* Englewood Cliffs, NJ: Prentice-Hall.

Social Development: Middle Adulthood

Children are treasures more precious than
a thousand granaries.
Old Japanese Proverb

n the street of Wang's Broken Tea Cup, Weng Fu, the beggar, stood and shouted thunderously, "Who'll buy? Who'll
buy? What young man wishes to buy a father?" Young men
gathered around, making sport of Weng Fu. A richly dressed
youth held out some money and Weng Fu reached for it.
But it was only a jest; the youth closed his hand on the
money before the beggar could grasp it, and ran off laughing. Weng Fu lurched after him, reaching for the money.
Someone stuck out a foot and tripped the old beggar, who
fell into the mud. ¶ Ah Tzu, an orphan, tugged at the beggar's rags to help him rise. "Will you buy me for a father?"
asked the beggar. "Certainly," answered the boy, "where is
your house?" So Weng Fu took the boy to a house with a
roof of straw so thin it would stop no rain, and with holes
in the walls. "Give me all your money," said the beggar, "that
I might eat, and while I am gone, braid me some sandals."
And the beggar left, returning later with a silver tray laden
with wonderful food. "You haven't finished the sandals,"
said he. "Work while I eat." And the beggar ate at great
length, making loud noises of appreciation while Ah Tzu finished the sandals. "Now," said Weng Fu, "there is a bean
cake in the cupboard which you may eat." Ah Tzu got from
the cupboard a single dried-up bean cake. "But I am still
hungry," said the beggar. "Give me half the cake." And he
took three-fourths of the dried-up cake, leaving only a small
corner that had been chewed by mice. ¶ For three days, Ah
Tzu stayed in the beggar's house, protecting it, serving his
new father, guarding his jewels, and beating away thieves.
Then the house caught fire, and the two had to flee. But at
the door, Weng Fu turned and said to Ah Tzu, "There is a
brick on the floor in the far corner of the house; get it for
me." Ah Tzu did so, risking his life for a worthless brick. "Ah,"
said his new father, "I have lost my ribbon. Go now to the
emperor and ask him for one of his discarded queue rib-
bons for Weng Fu, the beggar." Ah Tzu did so, even though

he knew he would receive nothing from the emperor but a rope for his own neck. Trembling like a leaf, he knelt in front of the emperor and made his request. "No, my son, I shan't give you a ribbon for old Weng Fu. He no longer exists," said the emperor—who was Weng Fu. Having no children, he had gone out as a beggar to find someone pious enough, obedient enough, to be his beloved son and heir.[*]

This Chapter

This is one of hundreds of stories told to Chinese children, stressing the value of filial piety. Among important cultural values reflected in stories of filial devotion, says Wu (1981), are the beliefs that (1) from the earliest age, children should show great devotion to their parents; (2) parents' welfare comes before that of children; and (3) children should be obedient and try to make their parents' lives pleasant and comfortable no matter what.

Clearly, our Western societies place less emphasis on filial devotion than do many Eastern societies. Still, throughout the lifespan, connections between children and parents are among the most important of all social relationships—as is made clear in this chapter, which looks at relationships between middle-aged parents and both their children and their aging parents.

The chapter looks, as well, at the seasons of our lives, at how these follow each other, nose to tail, in a straight line. In childhood, when all our seasons stretch unbroken before us, we know that they—and we—will last forever. Even as adolescents, our own special egocentrism, our fable of invulnerability, convinces us that our own personal winters will never come.

But somewhere in the middle years, Neugarten (1990) tells us, there is a change in our perception of personal time. Age is no longer simply a question of how long we have lived, but more a question of how much—or how little—there is yet to come. And our youthful myth of immortality and invulnerability crumbles. "Death takes on a new reality," says Neugarten. "It becomes personalized, i.e., it could happen to oneself" (1990, p. 31).

Perhaps middle age is only the autumn of our lives, but our springs and summers are gone. Still, as we see in Chapters 17 and 18, our winters might yet be our very best seasons.

This chapter begins with a look at some of the theories that try to clarify the seasons of our adult lives, especially the stages and transitions of the middle adult years (forty or forty-five to about sixty or sixty-five). It deals in turn with theories described by Erikson, Peck, Levinson, Sheehy, and Gould; then it asks an important question: Is there a period in our middle years when, overwhelmed by existential anguish, we struggle more desperately with the meaningfulness of our lives? Is there, in the popular jargon, a **midlife crisis?**

The chapter looks at these questions and examines as well the importance of relationships with spouse, with children,

---

[*]Based on Chrisman (1968).

At midlife, some of us go through a crisis linked with a reluctance to age. This man's new car may be one manifestation of this crisis.

with aging parents, and with friends. Then it examines personality changes in middle adulthood; finally, it presents a recipe for happiness and satisfaction.

THEORIES AND DESCRIPTIONS OF MIDDLE ADULTHOOD

Our intuitive notions about the life cycle, says Nanpon (1991), agree remarkably well with those of the experts—except that younger people tend to view the later stages of life as occurring at earlier ages. He asked 100 beginning psychology students to trace a "life" line across a sheet of paper, mark it off into major life stages with specific age boundaries, label each of these stages, and describe the key characteristics of each. Students were free to describe as many or as few stages as they wished.

Most students described the expected preadult stages: infancy, the preschool period, preadolescence, and adolescence. Many described adulthood as beginning at eighteen, and a large number thought age twenty-five represented a significant transition to life as a couple (or its equivalent). The next important transition was age forty, which students saw as the beginning of a transition between adulthood and old age. For a remarkable number (25 of the 100), age fifty was seen as the end of professional life and the beginning of old age. Another forty-eight thought old age began later, at about age sixty.

Our intuitive notions of stages of the life cycle, says Nanpon, are typically tied to important sociocultural events—for example, access to school, voting or drinking age, average ages of marriage and retirement. Erikson's theory, too, is tied to social and cultural demands.

Generativity Versus Self-Absorption: Erikson

Erikson's theory of **psychosocial development** describes crises and conflicts at every developmental stage. These arise mainly from social demands placed on the individual. Prog-

or most of her life, Farzana Begum lived with her parents in the small city of Hydarabad in Southern India. The Begums were poor—so poor that they despaired ever being able to afford the dowry that prospective grooms demand, and have a right to expect under the centuries-old Muslim traditions that govern such things in Farzana's world. The high cost of looking after daughters and of marrying them, and the much higher prestige associated with parenting sons, is one of the reasons why, even today, female infants are sometimes killed at birth. It was hardly surprising, then, that when representatives of a wealthy Arab from the Middle East came to Farzana's parents and offered them $30 for their daughter, they took it—in spite of the fact that, strictly speaking, such transactions are illegal. Having been sold, and bound, in any case, to obey her parents, Farzana went to marry her new Arab husband. A year later, after

she had borne him a son, he cast her aside. Now Farzana is back in her village, humiliated and outcast, her life destroyed by the shame that taints women collectively labeled as "Arab affected."

1. Filkins, D. (1997, Oct. 27). India's marriage pipeline to the Mideast. *Los Angeles Times*, p. 1.

To Do

Although most officials deny the existence of this pipeline of women from India to the Mideast, the evidence is that countless young girls are sold to wealthy purchasers every year. Some end up in marriages that work; many find themselves in the role of servant, slave, or sex object (or all three). Develop a major paper on the topic.

On the Net

Information about the status and health of women in many of the world's

developing countries can be found in the Demographic and Health Surveys page, funded primarily by USAID:

http://www.info.usaid.gov/

---

ress at each stage requires acquiring a competence or an attitude that resolves the conflict underlying the crisis. In early adulthood, for example, the individual confronts the profoundly important task of achieving intimacy and, at the same time, overcoming an urge to remain independent, to retain the autonomy and the personal identity that have been achieved in earlier developmental stages. These urges make it difficult to achieve the commitment that is required for genuine, mutual intimacy. Hence the conflict, and hence, too, the stage's name: **intimacy versus isolation.** (For a different look at the need for intimacy—or perhaps the need for domination—see "In the News and on the Net: Women for Sale.")

In the middle adult years, individuals are faced with a new developmental task and a new crisis: **generativity versus self-absorption.** With increasing maturity, the adult needs to establish the sorts of caring and work relationships that will benefit the world and the community—that is, to be generative or productive rather than absorbed in self. Generativity can be evident in different areas. One is work. As we note in Chapter 13, for many, work is far more than a means of earning a living or of "killing time." It can be a way of being someone, a means of self-discovery and self-expression, an essential aspect of feeling worthwhile, as well as a means of contributing to family and society in significant ways.

Another way of expressing generativity is through the establishment of a family—by producing children and acting as a parent. Note, again, Erikson's continuing emphasis on the individual's relationship to the sociocultural environment.

As in all of Erikson's stages, there is a crisis, a conflict here. Generativity requires a concern for others. People are gener-

ative when they rear and guide their children or the children of others, when they contribute to the community through political, social, or economic involvement, and when they contribute through their work. But even the most selfless and the most generative of individuals are occasionally tempted to look inward at themselves. There is an urge to become preoccupied with things that affect the self—things such as health, the accumulation of money, the enjoyment of life. Resolution of the crisis does not require abandoning all thoughts of self, but rather achieving a balance between self-interests and the interests of others.

Peck's Extension of Erikson's Theory

Although Erikson's description is valid and useful, argues Peck (1968), the fact that he covers the entire last forty or fifty years of life in only two stages provides too little detail to account for some of the critical issues during those years. Peck suggests that there are several additional crises related primarily to the physical and mental changes of adulthood, as well as to some of the more common social changes. These crises describe an additional seven stages, the first four of which are applicable primarily to middle age; the last three relate to old age (see Figure 16.1).

■ VALUING WISDOM VERSUS VALUING PHYSICAL POWERS

Middle age is marked by a gradual decline in stamina, elasticity, muscle tone, and other components of strength,

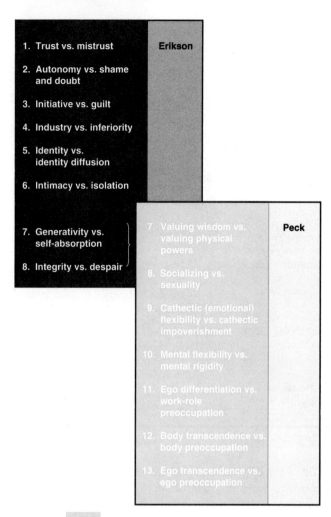

FIGURE 16.1

Erikson's theory revised. Peck defines seven additional adult developmental tasks during the last two stages of Erikson's scheme.

endurance, and athletic prowess. These physical changes make it progressively more difficult for laborers to toil without pain, for professional athletes to continue participating in their sports, or for fathers to beat their sons at racquet sports or Indian leg wrestling. As these changes occur, it becomes more important for individuals to place greater emphasis on nonphysical activities. The athlete must develop other competencies; the laborer must work differently or change employment; and the father might consider less physically demanding sports, such as billiards or darts, or more cerebral competitions, such as chess or poker—hence the label for this particular psychosocial conflict.

■ SOCIALIZING VERSUS SEXUALITY

Hormonal changes through middle age often result in changes in sexual interest, behavior, or capability. And some of the important interpersonal relationships that characterize early adulthood, and that might initially have had a strong sexual component, change accordingly. Friendship, trust, emotional and moral support, companionship, and other dimen-

sions of social relationships may become more important as sexuality becomes less so.

■ EMOTIONAL FLEXIBILITY VERSUS EMOTIONAL IMPOVERISHMENT

Social, as well as physical, changes in the middle years also require adaptation and change. The third of Peck's stages illustrates this: Through middle age (sometimes much earlier and sometimes much later), many of our emotional ties are strained or ruptured for any of a variety of reasons—people die, children leave home, couples separate and get divorced, careers end, and dogs run away. Adjusting to these emotional changes often requires considerable emotional flexibility.

■ MENTAL FLEXIBILITY VERSUS MENTAL RIGIDITY

In the same way that changes in our emotional lives require us to be able to form new relationships and sometimes to forget old ones, so a variety of social and cultural changes require us to accept new ideas and sometimes to reject old ones. Hence the need for mental flexibility. We cannot always rely on old beliefs and opinions or on old attitudes. (The last three of Peck's stages correspond to Erikson's final stage; all are discussed in Chapter 18.)

Theories such as those of Erikson and Peck do not lend themselves easily to specific age-related predictions for any given individual. Nor can they easily be validated experimentally. However, in a sample of adults aged twenty-two to seventy-two, McAdams, St. Aubin, and Logan (1993) found evidence of higher generativity among the middle-aged group than among younger adults. They defined generativity in terms of the individual's concerns, behaviors, and commitments that are aimed at providing for the next generation. They also found that the most generative individuals tended also to be the happiest.

One of the principal contributions of these approaches lies in the insights they provide for understanding the concerns and preoccupations of adults. That, too, is the principal usefulness of the two descriptions we consider next: Levinson's seasons and Sheehy's passages.

Seasons of a Man's Life: Levinson

In a widely read book, Levinson (1978) attempts to organize the lives of forty men around universal themes and changes. The book is based on five to ten separate, in-depth interviews with each man. Following these interviews, Levinson advanced a description of adult development, an account of the seasons of a man's life. Like Erikson's and Peck's accounts, this description deals primarily with psychological change and social change, and their relationship to each other.

Levinson (1981) suggests that the human lifespan divides itself roughly into five major eras or ages: preadulthood (birth to twenty-two), early adulthood (seventeen to forty-five), middle adulthood (forty to sixty-five), late adulthood (sixty to eighty-five), and late late adulthood (eighty to death). Within these eras, he identifies a sequence of stages that appear to be common to each of the forty subjects. These are described here and summarized in Figure 16.2.

■ EARLY ADULTHOOD

Each of Levinson's stages involves a major developmental task. For example, the transition into early adulthood requires separating from the family and establishing a separate iden-

FIGURE 16.2

Levinson's description of major developmental periods through early and middle adulthood. (From D. J. Levinson, The Seasons of a Man's Life. Copyright © 1978 by Daniel J. Levinson. Reprinted by permission of Alfred A. Knopf, Inc.)

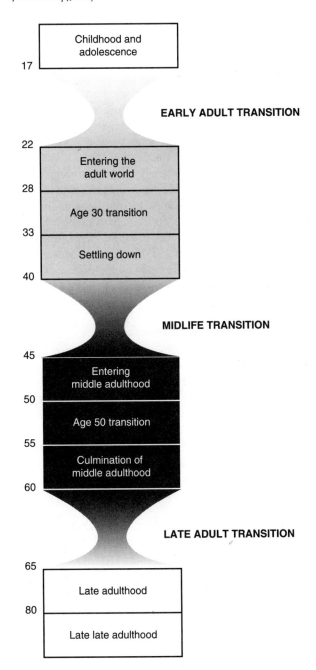

tity; entering the adult world involves exploring career roles as well as establishing stable adult roles.

Of major significance toward the end of this period—at around age thirty—is the adoption of what Levinson refers to as a "dream." **Levinson's dream** is an idealized fantasy that includes the goals and aspirations of the dreamer. In one sense, the dream is a tentative blueprint for the dreamer's life. In Levinson's (1978) words,

> These are neither night dreams nor casual daydreams. A "dream" of this kind is more formed than a pure fantasy, yet less articulated than a fully thought-out plan....In its primordial form, the Dream is a vague sense of self-in-adult-world. It has the quality of a vision, an imagined possibility that generates excitement and vitality. (p. 91)

The majority of men's dreams have to do with occupations. Some men also include marriage and family goals in their dreams, or sometimes personal growth or spiritual goals (Gooden & Toye, 1984). Women's dreams are more likely to involve marriage and family goals (Roberts & Newton, 1990).

Individuals often reexamine career and lifestyle choices during early adulthood, especially during the age-thirty transition, and reevaluate them in terms of the dream. Divorce and career changes sometimes result.

The next period, settling down (late thirties), is marked by major efforts to lay the groundwork for accomplishing the dream in all-important areas: career-related, social, economic, political, family-related, and so on.

■ THE MIDLIFE TRANSITION

Probably the most highly popularized of all adult developmental stages is the midlife transition—often referred to as the **midlife crisis**. The main developmental task of this period is to come to grips with successes and failures relative to the dream. Otherwise, suggests Tamir (1982), the dream may continue to exercise the same power that it held when the dreamer had more time, energy, and perhaps opportunity to achieve it.

Drebing and Gooden (1991) looked at the importance of the dream in the lives of sixty-eight men ages thirty-six to fifty-five. They found that 78 percent of these men had formed a dream in early adulthood. Of the men who had developed a dream (primarily occupational in nature), 38 percent claimed to have been largely successful in fulfilling it whereas 10 percent had failed. Others were in the process of trying to alter their dreams, either by changing them or by adding to them.

The most important findings from this study have to do with the importance of the dream's outcome to the individual's sense of well-being. The most depressed, anxious, and purposeless individuals in this sample (that is, those who most clearly were experiencing a crisis) were those who had never developed a dream. And those who had failed in their dreams were also significantly more depressed and anxious, and had lower scores on a measure of purpose in life than those who had been successful in their dreams. Interestingly, those who were still pursuing dreams, often modified from earlier aspirations, were characterized by higher levels of emotional well-being.

The urgency of the need to reexamine the dream in midlife is aggravated by the fundamental change that now occurs in the individual's perception of time. As Neugarten (1968) described it, people change from a perspective of "time from birth" (age, in other words) to one preoccupied with "time until death." We now realize, as Corlett and Millner (1993) put it, that we are closer to old age than we ever thought we'd be. Any of a variety of what Levinson calls "marker events" can contribute dramatically to this change in time perspective: death of parents, children leaving home, death of friends and age peers, sickness, and so on. Following these and other less dramatic events (such as being beaten at tennis or golf by one's son), individuals become progressively more conscious of their own mortality and of the idea that there may not be enough time to achieve the dream. For many, it now becomes fundamentally important to modify the dream—to change commitments and lifestyles and to emphasize those aspects of life that might have been neglected. For some men, the result is a resolution to spend more time with family and friends—and perhaps less with work and career. For others, it might involve a complete abdication of earlier responsibilities and commitments—and new commitments to what are sometimes dramatically different lifestyles.

ENTERING MIDDLE ADULTHOOD

Individuals enter middle adulthood at about age forty-five. Some bring with them renewed commitment to family and career; others, following the crises of the preceding period, enter middle adulthood with new lifestyles. All, according to Levinson (1978), experience fundamental change following the midlife transition, even if they continue in the same external roles. Detailed examination of the lives of his subjects leads him to observe that there are typically changes in relationships with work, family, and others—sometimes for better and sometimes for worse. Thus, there is tremendous variation in the extent to which men find their lives satisfactory during this period.

AGE-FIFTY TRANSITION

Levinson (1978) provides only a quick sketch of developmental phases after the age of forty-five. He suggests that at about age fifty, another period of transition involves tasks very similar to those of the midlife transition: namely, to reexamine accomplishments and relationships in relation to the dream espoused in early adulthood. For those who have accomplished this task inadequately in their early forties, there may be a crisis similar to that of the midlife; for others, the period may be relatively free of turmoil.

CULMINATION OF MIDDLE ADULTHOOD

Following this period of transition, there is a relatively stable "settled" period during which the individual's career will begin to wind down. In a final period of transition, bridging middle and late adulthood, the key tasks will involve reconciling the dream with reality, accepting again the notion of one's own mortality, and preparing for what are sometimes drastic changes brought about by retirement and all that it entails.

Seasons of a Woman's Life: Levinson

Critics of Levinson's work suggested that the seasons of a woman's life don't necessarily follow the same cycles as those of a man. In response, Levinson (1996) undertook detailed interviews with a group of forty-five women in much the same way as he originally had with the forty men. And, in general, he found that women go through similar stages as do men, but with a number of important differences.

GENDER-BASED DREAMS

For example, the dreams of Levinson's men tended to focus primarily on their work and careers. But the women's dreams embraced family as well as careers. In general, the women tended to be less career-oriented than the men, less driven to climb corporate ladders or accumulate the visible, material trappings of success. Levinson terms this phenomenon **gender-splitting**. He claims that gender-splitting is a powerful and probably universal phenomenon, evident in the fact that most women placed more weight on the family than on the career aspect of the dream.

The dreams of women, notes Levinson, are more complex than those of men. Not only do they reflect career as well as family aspirations, but they are also subject to rapidly changing social conditions that affect women more than men—changes in work opportunities, in the stability of the family, in gender stereotypes, and so on. As a result, women's dreams are more subject to revision and change than are those of men. And fewer women are completely happy with the outcomes of their dreams.

CAREER TRANSITION

A second important developmental difference between adult men and women, notes Levinson, is that women tend to complete their preparation for a career, and to begin their careers, later than men. Whereas most men are well into the beginnings of their careers by the age-thirty transition, many women are just starting their preparation at that point. In addition, for many men, a special relationship with a respected **mentor** is an important part of preparation for and development of a career. However, relatively few women in Levinson's sample had mentors—perhaps because there are fewer available.

In summary, Levinson's account of the adult lifespan describes major tasks during developmental phases that last between five and seven years. The tasks typically involve making important choices about family, lifestyle, and career. In an overly simplified sense, for men, the primary preoccupation during early adulthood revolves around work: climbing the ladder, being recognized, achieving success, being somebody in the community. For many women, the dream includes establishing a home and starting a family as well as a career.

Between ages forty and forty-five, the individual confronts his or her dreams and evaluates life in relation to earlier goals and ambitions. This confrontation often translates itself into a crisis ("Where am I going? What do I want out of life? What is really important?"). Subsequently, the dream may change, and different things may become more important.

Sheehy's (1976) journalistic account of the lives of 115 men and women also describes a developmental progression very much like that described by Levinson—but with a number of important differences.

Sheehy's Passages

Sheehy (1976, 1981), a journalist, suggests that the word *crisis* is often interpreted too seriously. It hints of impending catastrophe, of calamity just around the corner. For this reason, *crisis* is not entirely appropriate to describe most of the events that characterize the adult lifespan—hence her substitution of the term **passages**. Sheehy's passages are very similar to Levinson's stages, but the labels have been changed (see Interactive Table 16.1).

It is in her description of entry into middle adulthood, the **deadline decade,** that Sheehy departs most significantly from Levinson. This phase, corresponding to Levinson's midlife transition, is accorded a longer age span by Sheehy (ages 35–45, compared with 38–43), in recognition of the possibility that midlife crises can occur much later or much earlier than Levinson had thought.

■ MALE–FEMALE DIFFERENCES AT MIDLIFE

A second important observation made by Sheehy is that although the general developmental pattern for men and women is highly similar, the midlife passage often occurs considerably earlier for women—frequently at about age thirty-five (compared to forty or forty-five for men). Even more important, resolution of this crisis sometimes takes a dramatically different form for men than for women.

Highly simplified, Levinson's view is that men spend much of their early twenties deciding on a "life structure," commit themselves to career and life-plan decisions during their thirties, and then subject their lives to profound reexamination at about age forty. The result is a midlife crisis of varying severity, the resolution of which is often seen in the man's subsequently greater concern with family and self than with aggressive, achievement-related goals.

In contrast to this general male pattern, says Sheehy, not only do women begin their reexamination of goals and priorities considerably earlier, but their resolutions often take a different twist. Whereas many men become more passive, more oriented toward feeling—perhaps more "feminine"—many women become more active, more aggressive—perhaps a little more "masculine" (Hyde, Krajnik, & Skuldt-Niederberger, 1991). As Gutmann (1990) puts it, resolution of the midlife crisis often sees a "return of the repressed." Specifically, the man's repressed femininity and the woman's repressed masculinity begin to assert themselves in a gradual movement

Sheehy's Adult Transitions

Each transition of the lifespan entails far more tasks than can be described here. Where do you fit in Sheehy's sequence? What do you see as the most important psychological tasks that you now face? Look, as well, at Gould's transformations, described in Table 16.2. To what extent do you still hold the false assumptions of earlier ages? Or did you ever?

PASSAGE LABEL	PRINCIPAL TASKS AND CHARACTERISTICS
Pulling Up Roots (18–22)	Separating individuality from that of parents; leaving security of parental home.
The Trying Twenties (23–27)	Trying on life's alternatives; developing capacity for intimacy; career and lifestyle choices.
Catch 30 (28–33)	Emphasis on stability and on "making it"; rooting and extending; first sense of stagnation.
Deadline Decade (35–45)	Midlife crisis; realization of mortality; reexamination of youthful illusions and dreams; turmoil.
The Comeback Decade (46–55)	Danger zone; need to balance work and play, time lived with time left, and changes in placement within generations.
The Freestyle Fifties (50s)	Phenomenon of second life; movement from stagnation to peak excitement; for men, more interest and enjoyment in environment and social relationships; for women, more aggressive, managerial commitments.
The Selective Sixties (60s)	Ability to separate the truly important from the trivial; development of distinctive personality; possibility of high excitement about life.
The Thoughtful Seventies (70s)	Healthiest and happiest individuals are independent, highly involved, and plan ahead. Highly developed ability to think abstractly.
The Proud-to-Be Eighties (80s)	Detached contemplation; need to find balance between demanding and giving help and comfort; pride in survival and in continued competence.

Source: Based on Sheehy (1976, 1981).

toward the greater **androgyny** (combination of masculine and feminine characteristics) that is often part of old age. However, evidence suggests that for most people, these changes are very subtle and often unnoticeable (Hucyk, 1996).

As Sheehy notes, one of the ways in which couples can sometimes resolve their midlife dilemmas and find new excitement and meaning in the next decades is to "renegotiate" traditional roles. Perhaps the wife can contribute salary and vacations to the family—and the husband can provide nurturance, laundered clothing, and pot roasts.

The *freestyle fifties* are characterized by individuals who have accepted who they are. Transition through the *selective sixties* frequently involves a new recognition of what is most important in life—friends, family, loving, caring, sharing. These attitudes carry on into the *thoughtful seventies,* when individuals are in an excellent position to contemplate important philosophical, religious, social, and political abstractions—and on into the *proud-to-be eighties,* when some individuals find new vigor and pride in existence. In Sheehy's (1981) words, "The approach of the final passage transforms the grains in the hour-glass to the dust of gold and cinnamon—precious enough to be spent well and to be savored in the smallest ways" (p. 53).

Gould's Transformations

Gould's transformations provide yet another description of adult development. Gould (1972, 1978) studied a large sample of more than 500 men and women between the ages of sixteen and sixty. However, the most unusual aspect of his sample was that members were outpatients at a psychiatric clinic (at the University of California, Los Angeles) involved in group therapy. Subjects in this sample were divided into different groups according to age and were interviewed by psychiatrists, who attempted to uncover feelings and statements that would be most characteristic of each age group. In this way, Gould hoped to arrive at a sequential description of important changes in the adult lifespan. Following these initial interviews, questionnaires were sent to a sample of 524 individuals who were not psychiatric patients. These questionnaires were based primarily on patients' statements that appeared to be characteristic of specific age groups. This aspect of the study was intended simply to corroborate initial findings and to establish that the patient population was not fundamentally different from a nonpatient population.

Gould's description of adult development is summarized in Table 16.2. At first glance, it appears to be very similar to that advanced by Levinson and Sheehy. Thus, early preoccupations center on separating from the family and establishing an adult identity (work, family, social responsibility); crises occur about age thirty and again at forty, the latter being tied to a recognition of mortality and a sense of urgency with respect to goals.

Closer examination reveals that Gould's transformations present a different emphasis from that of Levinson's seasons or Sheehy's passages. Gould, a psychiatrist, is concerned less with the individual's relationship to work, career, dreams, and family, and more with the person's self-consciousness—that is, with the individual's understanding of the self and with the gradual transformations that change a child's consciousness into an adult's consciousness. Thus, development is described through developmental tasks that involve getting rid of the false, "childish" assumptions of early years and replacing them with more adult assumptions. For example, between ages sixteen and twenty-two, the principal false (or immature) assumption that dominates the individual's life concerns the rightness of parents: "I'll always want to be with my parents and believe in them—and they can always rescue me if I need help." Accordingly, the major developmental task of this early period is that of leaving home—but not simply in a physical sense. To really "leave" home is to discard these false assumptions concerning the rightness and potency of parents and to accept that parents can be wrong. We do this intellectually, says Gould (1990), long before we are successful in doing it emotionally.

In a similar fashion, progress through the lifespan requires shedding a variety of other false assumptions and adopting ones that are more realistic (see Table 16.2). The result, according to Gould, is greater self-understanding and greater self-acceptance.

TABLE 16.2

Gould's Transformations

AGE	MAJOR FALSE ASSUMPTIONS	MAJOR TASKS
16–22	"My parents will always be my parents. I'll always believe in them."	Move away from home; abandon idea that parents are always right.
22–28	"If I want to succeed, I need to do things the way my parents do." "If I make mistakes and need rescuing, they'll rescue me."	Become independent; explore adult roles; abandon idea that things will always turn out right if done in the manner of parents.
28–34	"Life is pretty straightforward, especially if you're on the right track. There aren't too many contradictions."	Explore aspects of inner self; become more sensitive to emotions; begin to realize inner contradictions.
34–45	"I have all the time I need. I am doing the right thing."	Recognize and accept idea of one's own mortality; develop strong sense of personal responsibility; reassess values and priorities.

Is There a Midlife Crisis?

Popular literature, rather than psychological research, may be largely responsible for the currency of the expression **midlife crisis** or *midlife identity crisis*, notes Gullette (1997). Unfortunately, books such as Levinson's and Sheehy's are not based on the kind of investigation that science demands. But they are nevertheless intriguing and suggestive, and sometimes they can lead to important insights. Still, what does science say about the midlife crisis?

First, as is her custom, science begins by defining more clearly what is meant by the expression *midlife crisis*. A **life crisis**, psychology informs us, involves some identifiable, discrete change or life event that brings with it some degree of distress, challenge, or hazard (Lieberman, 1996). Hence, a *midlife crisis* is such an event or change occurring during the midlife period. But to describe the midlife as involving a specific *midlife crisis*, argues Shek (1996), it must be shown that such a crisis is a *normative* event during the midlife—in other words, that it is a common occurrence in most lives.

The research isn't entirely clear. Shek (1996) administered a Midlife Crisis Scale to more than 1,500 Hong Kong adults to determine the extent to which they were aware of changes, concerns, or major dissatisfactions that might qualify as crises. Although there were crises in many of these lives, there was little evidence of a common crisis such as might define the *midlife crisis.*

Costa and McCrae (1980) looked at distress among men ages thirty to seventy, assuming that distress is an emotion that would accompany a serious midlife crisis. In this study, however, distress did not peak in the middle years; in fact, it was higher for younger than for older adults. Similarly, Long and Porter (1984) report that for many women, the changes that occur at midlife (children leaving home, perhaps resuming a career) are often liberating. Although these changes require major readjustments, the eagerness with which many women embrace them hardly connotes a crisis. And the Waskel and Phelps (1995) survey of midlife crises among 370 females aged 30 to 60 found that many women did not recognize a midlife crisis in their own lives. Others had or were experiencing what they thought was a midlife crisis, but precipitating factors varied considerably. Sometimes they were identified as a personal change, such as a change in personality; at other times, crises were related to changes in work, or to other external events.

These studies do not establish that the concept of a midlife crisis is invalid but suggest, instead, that the notion of a *universal* crisis at this stage is probably inappropriate. The best answer to the question "Is there a midlife crisis?" is simply that yes, there sometimes is, but it isn't universal. Medicine, for example, recognizes its existence as a collection of midlife symptoms of distress. These are often tied to individuals' concerns about dying (Ellman, 1996; Waskel, 1995).

Most researchers agree that the middle years involve major transitions that require change if the individual is to cope and remain reasonably happy. During this period, the increasing frailness of aging parents, or their death, underlines for the middle-aged their own potential frailty and their own inevitable mortality. Sometimes the realization leads to a difficult adjustment—and sometimes to a crisis. However, there are important transitions throughout the lifespan, and major adjustments to be made at all levels. Furthermore, crises are tied less to age than they are to events. Hence, crises that occur in midlife for some might occur much earlier or much later for others.

In summary, it is misleading to refer to the midlife as a period of universal crisis. However, it is not misleading to suggest that at some point in middle adulthood, many individuals will reevaluate their lives, and some will suffer frustration and regret at the outcome. For some, the situation may evolve into a crisis; for others, it may be interpreted as simply another opportunity for growth. (See Summary Table 16.3.)

FAMILY RELATIONSHIPS

Of all the stages in the span of our lives, the middle years have the potential for the greatest number of different family relationships. A middle-aged couple can have relatively young

SUMMARY TABLE 16.3
Theories and Descriptions of Midlife Development

CONCEPTS/ THEORIES/ISSUES	EXPLANATIONS/ COMMENTS/EVIDENCE
Generativity versus self-absorption: Erikson	▪ Successful resolution of main psychosocial task of middle adulthood is evident in *generative* undertakings that might be work- or family-related.
Peck's elaboration of Erikson	▪ Four middle-age psychosocial tasks reflected in competencies that value wisdom over the physical, socializing rather than sexuality, emotional flexibility over rigidity, and mental flexibility rather than rigidity.
Levinson's Seasons of a Man's Life	▪ Important event at transition into midlife is formulation of the *dream*, a semiarticulated fantasy that includes the work- and family-related goals and aspirations of the dreamer.
	▪ Important event in midlife is evaluation of life vis-à-vis the dream, sometimes evident in a midlife crisis.
Levinson's Seasons of a Woman's Life	▪ Differ from male seasons in that the *dream* places more weight on family, less on career; *career transition* tends to occur later; mentors play a more minor role.
Sheehy's Passages	▪ Midlife passage (and crisis) occurs earlier for women (35 rather than 40 or 45).
	▪ At midlife, there is often a slight reversal of masculine/feminine roles.
Gould's Transformations	▪ Growing up into adulthood involves rejecting a series of false beliefs and assumptions relating to parents.
Is there a midlife crisis?	▪ Crises are events that entail distress, challenge, danger. There are crises in midlife, often associated with changing time perspective (time left to live rather than time since birth) and fear of mortality. But there is little evidence that the midlife crisis is common enough to be *normative.*

children or children who are themselves on the threshold of the middle years. They can have grandchildren who are infants and some who are old enough to have given them great-grandchildren. They can have parents who are still in the upper reaches of middle adulthood or parents who are very old. Add to this all the possibilities of aunts and uncles, cousins and nephews and nieces, brothers and sisters, in-laws, step-relatives, and so on, and the web of possible relationships can become enormously tangled.

Or it can be brilliantly simple. Clearly, there are many individuals who have no children and few, if any, family connections. Their midlife experiences might be vastly different from those described here.

Relationships with Children

For those whose lives include families and children, two stages of Duvall's eight-stage description of the family life cycle are directly pertinent: the **launching phase** and the **empty nest phase** (see Figure 14.10 in Chapter 14). Keep in mind, however, that because Duvall's approach describes the most common child-rearing patterns in traditional families, it does not take into consideration the possibility that the major events and tasks that define the stages might occur much later, or sometimes earlier, in many families. Nor is it suitable for cultural contexts different from ours. In addition, there is a tendency to oversimplify when discussing complex relationships within simple stages. At the same time, however, the simplification is sometimes an advantage, providing a way to organize and understand facts.

LAUNCHING

The launching phase, the sixth in Duvall's cycle of the family, begins with the first child's leaving home and ends when the youngest child departs, an average of about eight years. Hence, during the launching phase, there are often adolescents still in the home, and the problems and challenges of parenting adolescents continue. One of these challenges has to do with resolving conflict with teenagers while continuing to maintain a rewarding and smoothly functioning marital relationship. Following a longitudinal study of parenting, Vuchinich, Vuchinich, and Wood (1993) report that parental agreement is important for solving a family's problems. Interestingly, however, when agreement is so strong that it is seen as a coalition, it may have the opposite effect. This, they suggest, is because strong parental coalitions may frustrate the adolescent's need to develop autonomy.

Other challenges and problems brought about by the launching phase include the need to rearrange physical facilities and resources, additional expenses relating to the launching (college or wedding expenses, for example), and reassigning responsibilities among grown and growing children. Clearly, the launching phase will be longer, more expensive, and perhaps more difficult in those families in which there are many children and in which the space between the oldest and youngest child is greatest. In addition, given that the U.S. National Survey of Families and Households reports that the level of support given children (both economic and social) often declines very little until the thirties, some of the responsibilities of the launching phase may last many years (Cooney & Uhlenberg, 1992).

THE EMPTY NEST

The empty nest phase, the seventh in the family life cycle, begins with the launching of the last child and lasts perhaps fifteen or more years. The average age of the mother at the beginning of this stage is about fifty-two (fifty-four for the average father). Although the family continues to function as an important social unit and to encourage the development of autonomy among its sons and daughters, its primary de-

Contrary to what we might expect, for married couples the period of the "empty nest"—that is, the period immediately following what Duvall terms the "launching phase"—is among the happiest of the stages of the family life cycle.

velopmental tasks shift away from children and refocus on the husband and wife. Among these tasks are those that relate to maintaining a sense of well-being, developing and enjoying career responsibilities, dealing with aging parents, and establishing and maintaining a useful or enjoyable position in the community.

Although folklore has often associated the departure of children with unhappiness and even depression among parents, especially among mothers, remarkably consistent research findings contradict this belief (Gerson, 1995). As an example, Rollins and Feldman (1981) looked at marital satisfaction through Duvall's stages among 850 couples. Like other researchers, they found that the majority (around 80 percent) of husbands and wives thought that their marriages were "going well" either all or most of the time. But they also found that happiness and satisfaction tend to be highest in the first stage of the cycle (prior to the advent of children) and begin to decline with the first child, reaching a low at about the time that the oldest child is entering adolescence. By the time of the empty nest stage, happiness and satisfaction again begin to increase, and continue to do so until the retirement years (see Figure 16.3). Not surprisingly, many parents look forward to their children's leaving and establishing their own independent lives as adults. And many are distressed when, because of economic and employment conditions, their adult children either do not empty the nest as expected or return after having left (Halpern, 1994). There are, also, the special problems faced by aging parents of children with disabilities. If they have continued to assume primary responsibility for the care of these children, aging sometimes brings fears related to who will care for their children when they no longer can (Mengel, Marcus, & Dunkle, 1996). For many, this can be a source of considerable distress.

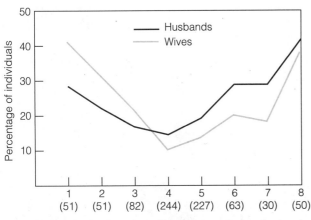

FIGURE 16.3

Percentage of individuals at each stage of the family life cycle (from stage 1, "beginning families," to stage 8, "retirement") reporting their marriage was going well "all the time." (Figures in parentheses indicate the number of husbands and wives in each stage. There was a total of 1,589 cases.) (From Rollins & Feldman, 1981, p. 308. Used by permission of Columbia University Press.)

An earlier study of 1,746 couples conducted by Nock (1979) had concluded that the most happily married couples are those without children, whether they are couples who have not yet had children, couples who will never have children, or couples whose children have already left home. In addition, childless couples are least likely to contemplate divorce. Connidis and McMullin (1993) showed that the relationships are somewhat more complex than this. Specifically, it isn't simply the fact of having or not having children that is important, but rather how close parents and children are. Not surprisingly, those who are closest are happiest. Similarly, those who are childless by choice are happier than those who are involuntarily childless.

In summary, in the majority of cases, both mothers and fathers evaluate the nest-emptying experience positively more often than negatively (Gerson, 1995). Typically, relationships with children who have left home remain close and positive, and parents continue to support their children and to advise them on all kinds of subjects, ranging from careers to child rearing. In fact, when children and their parents interact and advise one another, most of the advice flows from parent to child no matter whether the children are twenty or fifty (Cohler & Grunebaum, 1981).

Relationships with Aging Parents

For most of us, the realization that our parents are not the strongest and the wisest people in the whole world is a reluctant discovery. In childhood, we have little doubt about what Father and Mother are, and what they can do. Even through adolescence, when logic and experience should teach us better, we remain convinced that in at least some ways, our par-

Increasing life expectancy means that more middle-aged parents and their children are likely to know parents and grandparents for very long periods of time—which can be a source of tremendous joy and comfort. It can also present some middle-aged parents with the challenge of caring both for children and for aging parents at the same time.

ents are still the biggest and the best. And so it continues through early adulthood.

But finally there comes a day, usually some time in the middle years, when we look at our parents and make the shocking discovery that our childhood convictions were an illusion. It is a sobering and sometimes distressing realization. Midlife brings with it not only the problems of adjusting to the changes that age brings our parents, but also a dramatic role-reversal in which the child must now look after the parent. This role-reversal is sometimes a source of considerable stress, argue Sherrell and Newton (1996). But caring for parents is, for increasing numbers of middle-aged adults in industrialized countries, a normal developmental task. And so, too, is the eventual challenge of adjusting to the death of one or both of them.

In North America, aging adults do not commonly move in with their children unless financial need or health problems compel them to do so—although they often move closer to them. It is the parent generation, not the children, that most insists on independence, say Sherrell and Newton (1996).

However, as parents become more frail, there is a greater need for children to provide assistance and support—sometimes financial, often emotional and physical. Not surprisingly, the closer the relationship between parent and child has been in the past, the more likely the now-adult child is to care for aging parents. Also, daughters are more likely than sons to provide this care although, as Lee, Dwyer, and Coward (1993) discovered, this is so primarily because far more aging mothers than fathers are in need of care (fathers don't live so long). Same-gender care, they point out, is the rule rather than the exception. Thus, when it is fathers who need to be cared for, sons are more likely to assume the responsibility.

Adjusting to the death of a parent is a sometimes difficult developmental task that is often accompanied by intense grief and sometimes depression (Moss, Moss, & Rubinstein, 1993). If the care has been prolonged, and especially if the aged parent has been seriously ill or physically or mentally incompetent, grief often lessens rapidly following death (Collins et al., 1994). Parental death, interestingly, is one possible cause of marital strife in the middle years (Guttman, 1991).

Although divorce has become enormously more common in recent decades, marriage continues to be as popular as it ever was. About 95 percent of all Americans marry at least once. Some do it over and over again.

Relationship with Spouse

The middle years, notes Maltas (1992), are the prime of life, a time of joy and plenty, but there is often "trouble in paradise." The "trouble" of which Maltas speaks is marital strife, a relatively common midlife occurrence.

■ MARITAL DISRUPTION

Marital disruption affects all stages of the lifespan. As Pearson (1996) points out, middle age often brings major new challenges even to relationships that have already survived forty or more years: retirement, chronic illness, death of friends or relatives, loss of children. In Chapter 6, we looked at its implications for infants and young children; in Chapter 8, we examined how children of different ages react to the separation of their parents; and in Chapter 14, we looked at the effects of divorce on husbands and wives. We noted that currently about 50 percent of all marriages end in divorce and that the vast majority of those who divorce will also remarry, most within three years. (See "At a Glance: Marriage and Divorce" and Figures 16.4 and 16.5.)

Research suggests that divorce in middle age can be difficult for both the husband and the wife. In general, the longer the couple has been married, the more difficult the adjustment. Lingering unhappiness, bitterness, and even depression are not uncommon (Maltas, 1992).

Divorce is often more difficult for middle-aged women than for men, for several reasons. The fact that men often receive more emotional and psychological support outside the home, particularly in a one-wage-earner family, may make it easier for men to make the transition out of a marital relationship. In addition, women are more likely than men to suffer economic hardship following divorce. And perhaps most important, the chances of finding someone suitable for an intimate relationship or for remarriage are lower for middle-aged women than for men. When Schneider and associates (1996) followed 249 widows and 101 widowers for two years following the deaths of their spouses, they found that a full 61 percent of the men were remarried or at least involved in a new romance. In contrast, 81 percent of the women had neither a new marriage nor a new romance. Not surprisingly, the women most likely to remarry were the youngest in the group. But for men, the best predictors of remarriage were education and income level rather than age.

Several factors combine to reduce the chances of a widow finding a suitable partner. For one thing, by middle age, more men than women have died, so the total pool of men has been reduced; for another, our contemporary standards of physical attractiveness penalize women more than men (Bogolub, 1991). Not surprisingly, middle-aged men tend to remarry younger women.

Remarriage

Among the adjustments and changes that are sometimes required following remarriage in middle age are those having to do with the marital relationship itself. Often, difficult interpersonal adjustments are required of two individuals who have had half a lifetime to establish their own habits and expectations. And, explain Moss and Moss (1996), if one of the partners has recently lost a spouse, the survivor's continuing tie with the deceased can have a significant effect on the new marriage. In addition, there may be the need to establish relationships with an entirely new set of in-laws, as well as perhaps stepchildren.

We should note, however, that these adjustments and changes are not necessarily problems, although they can be challenges. And divorce in middle age is not always traumatic. In addition, remarriage and the creation of stepfamilies have

Marriage and Divorce

aking into account population in-creases, wedding bells ring about as often now as they did in the days of our grandparents. In any given year, around 9 marriages take place for every 1,000 people. But when our grandparents or great-grandparents agreed to marry and remain married "until death do us part," they were far less likely to break the agreement. In 1910, there was less than 1 divorce per 1,000 population; 85 years later, that number had increased by a factor of about 5. Median age of divorce for men is now about 35.6; for women, it's 33.2 (U.S. Bureau of the Census, 1996). Because half of all divorces occur after these ages, a relatively large number occur in the middle years (Figures 16.4 and 16.5).

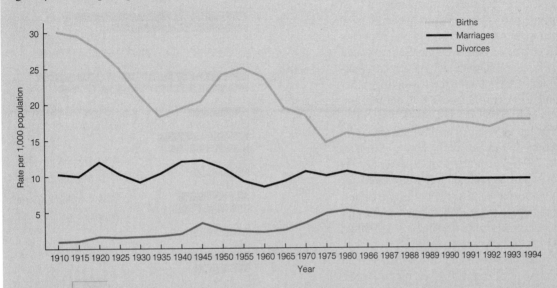

FIGURE 16.4

Changes in marriage, divorce, and birthrates per 1,000 population, 1910–1994. (From U.S. Bureau of the Census, 1996, p. 104.)

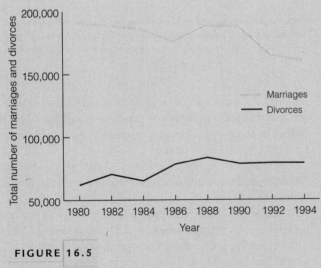

FIGURE 16.5

Marriages and divorces in Canada, 1980–1994. (From Statistics Canada, 1996, pp. 172, 173.)

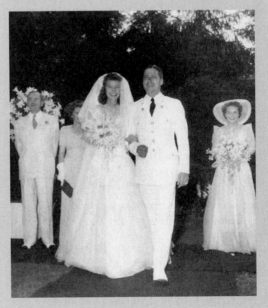

some definite benefits. For example, whereas divorce often brings economic hardship, remarriage generally eliminates that hardship. Furstenberg (1987) reports that remarried women are about as well off as women in their first marriage. They are about as likely to work and no more likely to consider their economic situation a problem. At the same time, on the average, remarried women are far better off economically than those who have not remarried.

In addition to the possible economic benefits of remarriage, there are clearly some emotional benefits. Not surprisingly, remarried men and women consider themselves to be happier than do those who are divorced.

Stepparenting

Remarriage where one or both of the partners have children from a previous marriage can sometimes lead to complicated patterns of relationships among members of the resulting stepfamily—and which can become even more complicated with the pregnancy of the wife (Dimmock, 1992). Such families, notes Dietz-Omar (1991), often remain evolving rather than established families for a prolonged period of time, and are sometimes marked by less cohesion and satisfaction among their members. Both stepparents and stepchildren often have difficulty accepting the other as part of the family (Sanders, Nicholson, & Floyd, 1997). Furstenberg and Spanier (1984) found that when members of stepfamilies were asked for their subjective impressions of family life, both parents and children who were members of stepfamilies had somewhat more negative evaluations than those who belonged to intact nuclear families. Stepfamilies are seen as less relaxed and less close, and as more tense, complex, and disorganized, than traditional families (Fursternberg, 1987; see Figure 16.6).

In spite of these findings, on the whole, both children and parents have positive evaluations of life in a stepfamily. And when the stepfamily consists of their biological mother and a stepfather (rather than their biological father and a stepmother), stepchildren rate their stepfamilies about as positively as do children with both biological mother and father.

The stepfamilies that result from remarriages in middle age, if they include children at all, are more likely to include older rather than younger children. And even when older children have been living with one of the partners prior to the remarriage, it is not uncommon for them to move out at the time of remarriage. Still, remarriage typically requires adjustment, especially during the first year or two of the new marriage. These first years are a time of negotiation and bargaining; they are a time for establishing roles and defining norms (Pasley et al., 1996).

But ultimately, as we have seen, the majority of those who have remarried will rate their lives as "very happy." (See Summary Table 16.4.)

PERSONALITY IN MIDDLE AGE: PLASTER OR PLASTIC?

We are persons; our **personality** characteristics are what make us what we are. As personalities, we can be described in terms of several characteristics, or **traits**. Some people are bold and assertive; others are retiring and submissive. Some

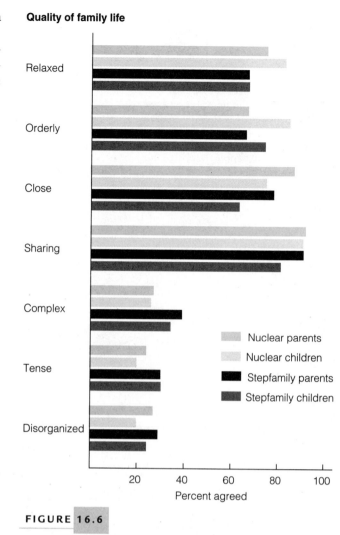

Quality of family life

Nuclear parents
Nuclear children
Stepfamily parents
Stepfamily children

Percent agreed

FIGURE 16.6

Percentage of parents and children who agreed that their family life conformed with the listed descriptions in the preceding few months. (From Furstenberg, 1987, p. 50. Reprinted by permission of the Guilford Press.)

are anxious; others are secure. Some are depressive; others are optimistic; conservative or experimenting; emotional or stable; trusting or suspicious; relaxed or tense; practical or imaginative; and on and on.

One way to simplify the study of human personality is to group related traits together into what are sometimes called **types.** This is what Costa and McCrae (1978, 1994) did, resulting in what they label the **NEO typology:** *N* for **neuroticism,** *E* for **extraversion,** and *O* for **openness.** These three types include most of the personality variables that would be of interest to those doing research on personality changes throughout the lifespan. Neuroticism includes such traits as anxiety and depression. And a common belief has been that many older people become more depressed with age. Extraversion includes traits such as those sometimes labeled "sensation seeking" (adventurousness) and "activity." Again, we have often assumed that both adventurousness and activity decline with age. And openness refers primarily to the individual's receptivity to new experiences and might

- Of all life's ages, the middle years have the potential for the greatest number of different relationships.

- In Duvall's family life cycle, the *launching phase* begins when the first child leaves home and ends when the last one leaves; it is often marked by the special problems of parenting adolescents.

- The *empty nest phase* begins when the last child has left; on average, marital satisfaction and happiness begin to rise again with the emptying of the nest.

- Relationships with aging parents often involve *role-reversal*, with children now caring for their parents almost as a normal developmental task; the role is often a difficult one for middle-aged children, as is adjusting to the death of parents.

- Marital disruption is not uncommon in middle age, and appears to be more difficult for women than for men, the majority of whom remarry relatively quickly.

- Remarriage often brings adjustment problems, sometimes associated with ambiguities surrounding the roles of stepparents and stepchildren; on average, the remarried are happier than the divorced or widowed.

also be reflected in measures of dogmatism, rigidity, and authoritarianism.

An important question in the study of the development of personality concerns the extent to which people change with age. As Roberts (1997) puts the question, are we dealing with "plaster or plasticity"? If we are plaster, then is the cheerful, outgoing twenty-year-old likely to be a cheerful, outgoing sixty-year-old? If we are more plastic, then there might be major developmental changes in personality traits that occur with age. If so, are these changes consistent and predictable?

Cross-Sectional Research: We Are Plastic

In a widely reported study of aging, Neugarten (1964) studied groups totaling more than 1,000 subjects aged forty to ninety, trying to identify general patterns of personality change. As we saw earlier, Neugarten observed a tendency for men and women to alter their dominant approaches to life in middle adulthood: Males became less aggressive, more passive, more concerned with emotions and with internal states—in short, they became somewhat more "feminine." In contrast, women often became more aggressive, more active, and more concerned with achieving personal goals (Helson & Wink, 1992).

A similar study, also conducted by Neugarten (1968), looked at the self-concepts of 100 middle-aged men and women. All these individuals were highly articulate, well-

educated, successful business and professional leaders. Interviews revealed that most felt that middle age is "the prime of life." As one of the subjects put it, "There is a difference between wanting to feel young and wanting to be young" (Neugarten & Datan, 1981, p. 281). Although subjects would have liked to retain the appearance and vigor of youth, most would have been reluctant to give up the competence, confidence, power, and other rewards that had come with maturity.

Middle age, Neugarten informs us, is characterized by a tremendous increase in self-awareness and introspection and by greatly heightened self-understanding. Accordingly, the prevalent theme of these middle years is the reassessment of self. And, as we saw, the result of this reassessment often takes the form of greater femininity for males and greater masculinity for females. Gutmann (1990) suggests that one of the reasons for this change lies in the fact that the roles that men and women play with respect to child rearing during their early adulthood require that women be unaggressive and nurturant if they are to be good mothers and that men be aggressive and active if they are to be successful breadwinners. Following midlife, when men and women are finally freed from parenting roles, they are able to concentrate on those aspects of their personalities that had previously been repressed.

Two important points must be noted here. First, these patterns of personality change are far from universal, and they are not usually very dramatic. In other words, most men do not become highly (or even noticeably) feminine after age fifty-five, and most women do not become dramatically more aggressive. In fact, in an important longitudinal study of personality changes (discussed in more detail shortly), Costa, McCrae, and Arenberg (1983) point out that although there were declines in masculinity scores for their male subjects, these were so slight that at current rates of decline it would take 136 years for an "average" 75-year-old man to reach the average masculine score of the women in the sample!

Second, to the extent that this slight change in gender roles after the midlife is due to the different roles played by men and women, it follows that changing conceptions of gender roles with respect to parenting, economic support of families, and decision making may do a great deal to lessen personality differences that now exist between younger males and females. In the end, it may be far less likely that males will become less aggressive or females more active and aggressive. In other words, the changes in male and female personality characteristics in middle adulthood described by Neugarten might well be cohort-specific rather than age-related. This, of course, makes them no less real or important, but might significantly alter our explanations and our understanding.

Longitudinal Research: We Are Plaster

Although a number of cross-sectional studies, such as those described above, report some small but relatively consistent changes in personality with age, these studies do not warrant the conclusion that change is a function of age. It bears repeating that cross-sectional studies cannot separate the effects of age from those of the cohort.

Using data from the Baltimore Longitudinal Study, Costa, McCrae, and Arenberg (1983; Costa and McCrae, 1994) performed a series of studies employing sophisticated sequential designs (see Chapter 1). These designs allow researchers to separate age effects from those related only to the specific cohorts being examined, as well as from the effects of time of testing.

A variety of personality tests were employed in the Baltimore study, with testing occurring every one or two years after 1958, and including samples spanning all age decades between twenty and eighty.

The results of these studies can be summarized very simply: For almost all the personality scales used, there is no consistent change related to age. In fact, not only is there no consistent change, but there is firm evidence of considerable stability through the entire age range for all important traits that make up the NEO model (neuroticism, extraversion, and openness to experience), plus two new traits—conscientiousness and agreeableness. Two exceptions are scores on the general activity and masculinity scales of the Guilford–Zimmerman Temperament Survey. As we noted earlier, masculinity scores tend to decline for males and increase for females. Similarly, measures of general activity level also tend to decline with age. However, changes on both these scales tend to be very small.

McCrae and Costa (1994), following their extensive sequential investigation of personality change, conclude that there is overwhelming evidence for stability of personality traits. As Alwin (1994) puts it, "The general conclusion in the literature is that personality traits increase in relative stability in young adulthood and grow to high levels of stability in adulthood" (p. 159).

Plaster or Plastic? A Conclusion

So are we plaster, as McCrae's research indicates? Or are we more plastic, in the manner described by Neugarten? The answer, says Chiriboga (1996), is both. The consensus, he explains, is that personality predisposes us to a relatively high degree of stability in important characteristics throughout the lifespan. Thus, there is what he terms *continuity*. This does not mean, of course, that there is no possibility of significant personality change in the course of the lifespan. In fact, for some traits, in some situations, there is remarkable *discontinuity*. And sometimes this discontinuity is predictable—for example, Neugarten's finding that some women become somewhat more masculine at midlife and some men become more feminine. Similarly, Wink (1996) reports a tendency for highly autonomous women to increase in impulse control and on a factor labeled *personal agency*. And Jones and Meredith (1996) found that some characteristics such as self-confidence, outgoingness, and dependability were more

▲ **SUMMARY TABLE 16.5**
Stability and Change in Personality in Middle Age

- Personality traits are any distinct, consistent quality in which one person can be different from another; types are clusters of related traits.

- The NEO typology clusters traits into three main groupings: *neuroticism* (anxiety, depression, excessive emotionality), *extraversion* (sensation seeking, sociability, adventurousness), and *openness* (receptivity to the new; flexibility).

- A basic question in lifespan personality research is this: To what extent is personality continuous (unchanging; plaster) or discontinuous (changing; plastic)?

- Some research (e.g., Neugarten's) indicates predictable discontinuity, with males becoming somewhat more feminine and women more masculine at midlife.

- Other research (e.g., McCrae and Costa's) indicates high stability.

- The best current conclusion seems to be that our mythical average adult is both plaster and plastic—that there is remarkable consistency in personality across the lifespan but that socializing experiences continue to exercise their influence, bringing about systematic changes in some individuals.

susceptible to change over the lifespan than was assertiveness or warmth.

Here, as elsewhere, our conclusions apply to a mythical average person rather than to the individual. And we do know that there are sometimes remarkable and dramatic changes in people's personalities. Miserable, cranky individuals sometimes become very agreeable; some very agreeable people sometimes become quite unbearable. These changes might be brought about by some major event in a person's life such as a near-death experience, the loss of a loved one, or the winning of a lottery; or they might simply be the result of sheer personal effort. Or they might result from systematic, orderly experiences.

In summary, as Roberts (1997) notes, there is clearly a consistency to personality so that there is a high correlation between what the adult is at middle age and what that same person was earlier in life. At the same time, the socializing experiences of life, including those of family, friends, and work, continue to have an influence throughout life, so that change is possible throughout the lifespan. Is happiness also possible throughout life? (See Summary Table 16.5.)

HAPPINESS AND SATISFACTION

"Taking all things together, how would you say things are these days—would you say you are very happy, pretty happy,

Most adults see themselves as relatively satisfied and happy—although some are less so than others. Among the happiest are those who are healthy, who have adequate income, and who have positive self-concepts. And, other things being equal (are they ever?), the married are happier than the single, widowed, or divorced.

or not too happy?" (Campbell, 1981, p. 27). When this question was first asked in a psychological survey in 1957, more than one person in three described themselves as being "very happy"; one in ten were "not too happy." The remaining 54 percent thought they were "pretty happy." But by 1972, only one in four people selected "very happy," a finding that seems strange in view of the tremendous growth in prosperity between 1957 and 1972, and the accompanying rise in the standard of living. Is happiness inversely related to owning two cars and having quail and other exotic meats in many pots? Does it increase or decrease with age? Who is most likely to be happy?

These are fundamentally important questions to each of us, for it is happiness, in any of its many disguises, for which we all strive.*

likely to be satisfied tomorrow, next month, and perhaps even next year. In this context, to be satisfied is to confess either to the fulfillment of one's goals and aspirations or to a resignation to the way things are.

Happiness, on the other hand, is more subject to the fluctuations of mood. It is a personal, highly subjective feeling, easily sensed and interpreted by each of us but not always easily communicated to others. Nor can it readily be tied to satisfaction. Campbell, Converse, and Rodgers (1976) found that although "completely satisfied" individuals most often saw themselves as being "very happy," many were only "pretty happy." And a large number of individuals were dissatisfied with the major domains of life, such as job, health, housing, and marriage, but nevertheless felt "pretty happy" or even "very happy."

Are the Satisfied Happy?

Contrary to what we might have expected, **satisfaction** and **happiness** are different. Nor do they always go hand in hand. Satisfaction is a relatively stable dimension. If I am satisfied with my job, my spouse, or my life in general today, I am still

Who Is Happiest?

Who are the happiest people? The rich or the poor? The married or the single? The young or the old? Some tentative answers are available, following extensive interview studies reported by Campbell and associates (1976). These studies involved randomly selected samples that were representative of the entire population of the United States. The samples ranged in size from 2,164 to 3,692 individuals and totaled more than 12,000 subjects. Interviews were conducted on five

---

*"I struggle for happiness, too," said my grandmother. "But I'll have mine after my lifespan instead of right now, like you. Heck, you can't even wait 'til after supper."

separate samples and provided information about satisfaction with various important dimensions of life, self-estimates of happiness, and detailed information about sex, age, marital status, and so on.

A word of caution is appropriate at the outset. The results of studies such as these have to be interpreted tentatively, primarily because of the highly subjective nature of some of the questions involved. Not only might there be systematic differences in the ways in which different groups interpret the questions, but there might also be systematic biases in the ways in which people choose to respond.

■ HEALTH

Not surprisingly, health is among the most important of all variables in predicting whether people will describe themselves as being happy. Those who suffer serious or chronic health problems are most likely to be unhappy or even depressed. Health concerns are also among the important causes of suicide.

■ AGE

Age-related changes in satisfaction and happiness are somewhat difficult to separate from those associated with major personal events, particularly because many of these events (marriage, childbearing and child rearing, career advancement, and retirement) are closely tied to chronological age. Thus, it is difficult to determine whether our popular notions of youth as a time of carefree abandonment and happiness and of old age as a period of contentment and serenity are accurate portrayals of age-related changes.

Campbell's (1981) research, as well as other studies reviewed by him, indicates that there has been a systematic change in professed happiness of young people since the early 1970s. Fewer of them report a high level of happiness. The same is not true of older people. As Campbell (1981, p. 176) put it, "In 1978…the young people were less positive than any of the older generations except the very old." Campbell suggests that social, political, and other cohort-specific environmental variables might well account for these observations.

Among the most surprising findings, at least on the surface, is the observation that adolescents and young adults are also typically less satisfied than older people (Morganti et al., 1988) (see Figure 16.7). But, as Campbell (1981) explains, this finding is perhaps not so surprising when one considers the possibility that younger adults may be dissatisfied not because their lives are objectively less satisfying than those of older adults but because they have not yet resigned themselves to not fulfilling all their dreams and aspirations. In contrast, adults past middle age might well have resigned themselves to the objective realities of their lives, feeling less able to make significant changes in them.

■ PERSONALITY

Are some people, by the nature of their personalities, happier than others? Common sense would seem to say yes: We

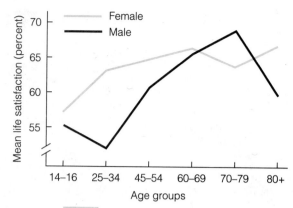

FIGURE 16.7

Differences in life satisfaction by age and group. (From Morganti et al., 1988, p. 50. Reprinted by permission of Baywood Publishing Company and John Morganti.)

often describe people as being basically happy or basically unhappy. And, at least to some extent, research agrees. Lu and Shih (1997), for example, gave a battery of tests and questionnaires to a random sample of 191 people aged 18 to 65. Their results indicate that *extraverts* (characterized by adventurousness, high activity level, sensation seeking, and high sociability) were typically the happiest. In contrast, those who scored high on *neuroticism* scales (high anxiety, depression, excessive emotionality) were among the least happy.

Botwin, Buss, and Shackelford (1997) also report research that shows a relationship between personality and happiness—but, in this case, an indirect relationship. What they found in a study of marital happiness was not so much that specific personality types were associated with higher happiness, but that high congruence between spouses contributed significantly to happiness. Both men and women, explain the authors, typically have pretty clear ideas about the personality characteristics of the sorts of people they would like to marry—in most cases, personality characteristics similar to their own. And most people tend to select mates who conform with these ideals. Ultimately, the more alike the spouses are, the higher the degree of happiness.

■ RELIGIOSITY

Lewis and associates (1997) looked at the relationship between measures of religiosity (primarily attitudes toward Christianity) and happiness among more than 200 undergraduate university students. They found no evidence that the more religious people were happier.

■ MARRIAGE AND CHILDREN

Other intriguing findings from the Campbell studies are that single women are happier than single men, married people are typically happier than the unmarried (single, widowed, or divorced), divorced women are less happy than divorced men, childless couples are as happy as couples with children, and couples whose children have left home continue to report high levels of satisfaction and happiness. As we saw, the empty nest does not always lead to unhappiness.

The finding that the married are more happy than those not married has been widely corroborated. Lauer, Lauer, and Kerr (1995), for example, summarize research which indicates not only that the married are happier and more satisfied, but also that marriage is conducive to physical and mental health. Thus, death rates are measurably lower for those who are married, and referral rates for emotional problems are lower.

As we saw earlier, happiness and marriage appear to be related in a curvilinear fashion, with the least happy years being the child-rearing years and the happiest being the first years of marriage and the years following the emptying of the nest. In Lauer, Lauer, and Kerr's (1995) investigation, more than 90 percent of 140 retired couples described themselves as being happy, very happy, or extremely happy.

■ OTHER CONTRIBUTORS TO HAPPINESS

In a study of 162 women, Kopp and Ruzicka (1993) discovered that the more roles a woman is called upon to assume, the happier she is likely to be. In this study, women who occupied two or more of the roles of partner, mother, and out-of-home employment were happier than women who had only one role. This finding might seem counterintuitive but is supported by other research that indicates that work involvement is positively related to happiness.

Another intriguing but totally unexplained finding is that television watching in general is associated with lower levels of happiness, but watching television soaps is positively correlated with happiness (Lu & Argyle, 1993)!

A Recipe

If psychology were to be so bold as to attempt to provide us with a recipe for happiness, it would first look at what have been found to be the most consistent correlates of reported happiness. From the Berkeley Guidance Study, we learn that there are several conditions in early adulthood (specifically, age thirty) that serve as good predictors of happiness at age seventy (Mussen, Honzik, & Eichorn, 1982). For women, these include satisfaction with their marriages (compatibility with their husbands) and satisfaction with their husbands' jobs. For men, the most important early predictors of later happiness are health, stamina, energy level, their wives' emotional stability, job satisfaction, and marital compatibility.

From the Campbell research, psychology would conclude that health and marriage are important for happiness. Research reported by Markides and Martin (1979) agrees: Health, income, and activity level are three common correlates of happiness. The Sears (Sears & Barbee, 1977) longitudinal study would add that for men, working into the sixties and maintaining an intact marriage are important for

A Tentative Recipe for Happiness in Adulthood

Satisfaction is a relatively stable feeling associated with the extent to which our goals and aspirations are fulfilled; happiness is more subject to fluctuations linked to current events in our lives. What sorts of things are most closely associated with happiness in your life? Does your list correspond with that which psychology provides in this tentative recipe for happiness?

MOST IMPORTANT INGREDIENT	OTHER IMPORTANT INGREDIENTS
Health	Work involvement
	Marriage
	Emotionally stable spouse
	Adequate income
	Stamina
	Energy level
	Friendship
	An extraverted personality
	Positive self-concept
	High personal autonomy
	Television soaps

Source: Gleaned from scattered pieces of psychological research.

happiness; for women, working and being married are also important. The Morganti and associates (1988) study found that satisfaction increases with age (until very old age) and that it is highly correlated with health, self-concept, and personal autonomy (control). (See Interactive Table 16.6.)

Psychology's recipe for happiness might include all the foregoing and might add, as well, that we should try to die at least as early as our spouses. But psychology would not dare be so bold or so flippant. (See Summary Table 16.7.)

▲ SUMMARY TABLE 16.7
Psychology's Conclusions Regarding Happiness and Satisfaction

- Satisfaction implies fulfillment of goals or resignation to the way things are.

- Happiness is more subject to fluctuations of mood and is reflected in transient feelings of well-being, of joy, of euphoria....

- Younger people are often less *satisfied* but not necessarily less happy.

- Other things being equal, the happiest are the healthy, the married (especially before and after the child-rearing period), the sociable and extraverted, those highly involved with their work, and those with high stamina and energy level.

FOCUS QUESTIONS: SUMMARY ANSWERS

1. What are the major transitions and periods of stability of middle adulthood?

   ▪ Erikson describes the conflict of the middle years as one of generativity (being productive in work, community, family) versus self-absorption (temptation to become self-absorbed). Levinson describes several important developmental tasks (such as leaving home and making lifestyle decisions) in the adult seasons of our lives. Between these phases are important transition periods, the most highly popularized of which is the midlife transition, which entails a serious reexamination of the individual's life, particularly in relation to the "dream." Sheehy's lifespan passages give the midlife crisis a wider age range (thirty to fifty), place it earlier for women than for men, and recognize that resolution of the midlife crisis often results in a "turning inward" among men and the opposite among women. Gould describes several transformations whereby a childish consciousness, characterized by false and immature assumptions (particularly concerning parents), is gradually replaced by a more adult consciousness. Research suggests that midlife crises are tied more to events than to age and that the majority of individuals do not have a full-blown crisis during middle age. But some do.

2. Do relationships with friends, family, and spouse become less important with age?

   ▪ No. Middle age in Duvall's family life cycle includes the launching phase (from first to last child leaving home) and the empty nest phase (from last child leaving to retirement). Relationships with departed children tend to remain close, and the empty nest does not ordinarily lead to serious unhappiness. Relationships of middle-aged individuals with their aging parents often involve role-reversal (child tending for parent) and often require adjusting to the parents' dying. Divorce in middle age is less common than at earlier ages and is often harder for women. Remarriage is more common for men than for women after a middle-age divorce (diminishing pool of men). Remarriages in the middle years bring substantial emotional, and sometimes economic, benefits, but may require major readjustments, especially if children are involved.

3. Is personality pretty well established by adolescence? Or does it continue to change in adulthood?

   ▪ Some research suggests that males and females become less gender typed and more androgynous through middle age. The magnitude of these changes is very small. Longitudinal investigations of personality change using sequential designs support the hypothesis that there is far more stability than change with age. The best conclusion is that there is considerable stability in personality but that specific traits can vary as a result of situational influences.

4. Who is most likely to be happy?

   ▪ Satisfaction relates to the extent to which various objective aspects of our lives correspond with our goals and aspirations. Happiness is an emotional state, susceptible to fluctuations of mood. Married individuals report more happiness than those who are alone (single, widowed, or divorced); childless couples report as much happiness as those with children; couples whose children have left home (the empty nest) do not, as a result, report lower levels of happiness; extraverted personality characteristics are more closely associated with happiness; and perceived health is closely related to happiness. But psychology does not yet have a complete recipe for happiness.

STUDY TERMS

androgyny, 469

deadline decade, 469

empty nest phase, 472

extraversion, 476

freestyle fifties, 469

gender-splitting, 468

generativity versus self-absorption, 465

happiness, 479

intimacy versus isolation, 465

launching phase, 472

Levinson's dream, 467

life crisis, 470

mentor, 468

midlife crisis, 464, 467, 470

NEO typology, 476

neuroticism, 476

openness, 476

passages, 469

personality, 476

proud-to-be-eighties, 469

psychosocial development, 464

satisfaction, 479

selective sixties, 469

thoughtful seventies, 469

traits, 476

types, 476

FURTHER READINGS

Probably the best sources of additional information with respect to descriptions of the lifespan are original books written by Levinson, Sheehy, and Gould. Jacobs's much shorter account is based on the lives of women and provides some interesting insights into female adult development:

Gould, R. L. (1978). *Transformations: Growth and change in adult life.* New York: Simon & Schuster.

Jacobs, R. H. (1979). *Life after youth.* Boston: Beacon.

Levinson, D. J. (1978). *The seasons of a man's life.* New York: Knopf.

Levinson, D. J. (1996). *The seasons of a woman's life.* New York: Knopf.

Sheehy, G. (1976). *Passages: Predictable crises of adult life.* New York: Dutton.

Sheehy, G. (1981). *Pathfinders.* New York: Morrow.

The first of the following three books, a collection of Neugarten's papers, provides an insightful and important look into the research and theorizing of one of the most important lifespan personality researchers in recent decades, the second is a high readable account of how culture determines the meaning of aging, and the third presents a variety of descriptions of middle adulthood:

Neugarten, D. A. (Ed.). (1996).*The meanings of age: Selected papers of Bernice L. Neugarten.* Chicago: University of Chicago Press.

Gullette, M. M. (1997). *Declining to decline: Cultural combat and the politics of the midlife.* Charlottesville: University Press of Virginia.

Lachman, M. E., & James, J. B. (Eds.). (1997). *Multiple paths of midlife development.* Chicago: University of Chicago Press.

The classic studies of satisfaction and happiness in the United States, conducted by Campbell and his associates beginning in 1957, are summarized in the following book:

Campbell, A. (1981). *The sense of well-being in America: Recent patterns and trends.* New York: McGraw-Hill.

PART EIGHT

Late Adulthood

The years like great black oxen tread the world,
And God, the herdsman goads them on behind,
And I am broken by their passing feet.

WILLIAM BUTLER YEATS
"The Countess Cathleen"

In our youths, we scarcely know there are great black oxen that tread the world. We believe we are alone, gifted and special, with our paths stretching out forever before us. In those carefree years, we know with the certainty of youth that there will always be roses along the way and that we will always know to smell them. ¶ But even then, if we allow ourselves to think of it, we realize that the great black oxen march relentlessly and that they will catch up to us one day. Even as children, if we look to the horizon, we can see their shadows. It is inescapable. ¶ They are not malevolent, God's great beasts. It is not that they have singled us out, you and I, that they have decided it is us upon whose bones they will tread. But they cannot slow down, the oxen of our years, and we can go no faster. ¶ In Part Eight, the breaths of God's great black oxen are hot upon the backs of our subjects. But the bones that are broken in these chapters are accidental. And it would be a mistake to think that the beasts that age brings rumbling behind us always bring pain and fear. There is much of late adulthood that is hopeful and wonderfully happy. ¶ When, as old men and old women, our years have finally caught up with us and the beasts are no longer simply shadows, perhaps they will have become our friends. Maybe then we will see that they do not care to chew on our roses. ¶ In the end, they will break our bones, God's great black oxen. But that won't be until Part Nine.

FOCUS QUESTIONS

1. What is ageism? How does it affect the elderly?

2. How are lifespan and life expectancy different? Can either be changed?

3. What are some of the most common physical changes in late adulthood?

4. What are some of the most common intellectual changes in late adulthood?

Physical and Cognitive Development: Late Adulthood

"You are old, Father William," the young man said, "And your hair has become very white; and yet you incessantly stand on your head—Do you think, at your age, it is right?"

LEWIS CARROLL
Alice in Wonderland

elp me, Guy," she says. "Prop me up in the corner so's I don't fall down." I wrap my hands around her gray-socked ankles and ease her feet back, planting one against either wall. My grandpa's coveralls, which she has put on not because she needs a work-out suit but more to preserve her modesty, slip down past her bony knees, exposing her blue-veined shanks. ¶ "Hey," I say, "I'll get the hammer and nail your feet smack to the wall so's you don't fall down!" Gawd, what a sense of humor! But my grandmother doesn't laugh; this is serious. Her Digest lies open on the table, and I can see the title of the article she has just read: "Shrink Your Varicose Veins!" it promises, "And Increase Your Intelligence," the subtitle adds, as a less consequential side benefit of standing on your head ten minutes a day. ¶ "OK," says she, "beat it. I'll find my own way down." I look at her for a minute, her inverted face framed by the thick green cushion under her head, her features all upside-down slack, her wrinkles drooping unexpectedly toward her forehead. I can't tell whether she's smiling or grimacing in pain, or whether it's just gravity pulling her lips in the wrong direction. ¶ "Beat it," she croaks again. "OK," I say, and I go out thinking I'm going to go across the road to where I can watch the barn swallows building their mud-and-spit nest against the beam on the church porch—and I run smack into Father Paradis halfway to the gate. ¶ "Your grandmother home?" he asks. ¶ "Sure, go on in," I say, gawd forgive me, which he does. And then I hear what I imagine is my grandmother finding a very quick way down (good thing I didn't actually nail her feet), and Father Paradis, all embarrassed, excusing himself, saying "I'll come back later," and he passes me even before I reach the gate. ¶ "Is there something wrong with your grandmother?" he asks. "She's standing on her head." ¶

e don't expect our old people to stand on their heads.

Nor do we expect our youth to sit in rocking chairs, reminiscing about the good old days. We expect that people will act their ages. And we have certain widely held beliefs about what is appropriate behavior for different ages.

Unfortunately, the expectations our society has for old people are sometimes inaccurate and prejudicial. Negative expectations of this kind that are based solely on age define **ageism**. Ageism is one of the topics of this chapter.

The chapter looks as well at important changes in the demographics of old age, brought about by dramatic increases in life expectancy (although not in lifespan). It discusses various explanations for why we age and examines some of the important physical changes that are part of the aging process. Finally, it looks at intellectual changes in old age and at the growth of wisdom.

LATE ADULTHOOD: CHANGING DEMOGRAPHICS AND CHANGING ATTITUDES

When does old age actually begin? Most of us think of age sixty-five as the boundary between middle and old age, perhaps because sixty-five has been a common retirement age. In addition, Social Security and pension programs for the aged, as well as the various concessions that some public and private entities grant the "elderly," are typically for those aged sixty-five and above.* In fact, however, variability among individuals is at least as great at age sixty-five as it is at any other time in the lifespan. It's important to keep in mind that there are sixty-five-year-olds whose interests, activities, and vitality are comparable to those of an average fifty-year-old. And, of course, there are some who are "old before their time."

Carving Up Old Age

Although it's convenient and simple to group all those above age sixty-five in a single category, we should also bear in mind that there is a tremendous spread of years between a sixty-five-year-old and an eighty-five- or ninety-year-old. As a result, says Fisher (1993), a single stage of adulthood is totally

---

*"That's not true anymore," complained my grandmother. "Used to be you had to be sixty-five to get stuff like that. But now they got stuff for people who're only fifty-five, or sometimes just fifty, like deals in stores and traveling and condominiums." She cocked her head and pointed her cane dangerously toward me, adding in her cynical, sly way: "But it's not that you guys are getting old younger. It's that the marketing people who run the world know where the numbers and the money are. So there!"

inadequate if we are to understand the changes and the complexity of this phase of life. And, given that so many people are living so much longer, dividing up old age and recognizing the possibilities make increasing sense. Fisher interviewed seventy-four people aged sixty or more and identified five distinct possible phases of older adulthood. These are described in the next chapter, which deals with the social and emotional changes of this period.

Neugarten (1990), too, suggests that it might be fruitful to divide old age into periods. She describes three major categories: The **young-old**, roughly between ages fifty-five and seventy-five, are those who are still highly active physically, mentally, and socially (although they may be retired from their main careers). The **old-old** are those for whom physical activity is more limited and who may be less concerned with finding productive ways to spend their time. For many of the old-old, family and social relationships are highly important. And the **oldest-old** are those above eighty-five, who currently make up about 1 percent of the population in North America. And even this group, says Neugarten, is very heterogenous, including highly competent individuals as well as others for whom the effects of decline have become more apparent and more rapid.

These unimaginative and somewhat clumsy labels reflect our lack of more common terms with which to discuss the elderly and are another indication of how we have historically had little interest in aging. Unfortunately, being called "old-old" or even "young-old" may not be looked on with great favor by those who are now often labeled "seniors" or "senior citizens." "Oldest-old" would be even less palatable.

Changing Demographics

Numbers of older people have increased dramatically, both in absolute terms and as a proportion of the overall population. For example, while the population of the United States increased almost two and a half times during the first six decades of this century, the number of people over the age of sixty-five increased by a factor of more than five. This tremendous increase is due in part to a high birthrate early in the century, as well as to immigration policies that increased the number of young people in North America. Initially, therefore, there were relatively few old people. Dramatic increases resulted not only because the children of the high-birthrate group had grown up but also because medical advances, as well as changes in nutrition, have contributed to our increased life expectancies. The net result is that currently, about one in eight people in Canada and the United States is sixty-five or more (see "At a Glance: The Demographics of Aging" and Figures 17.1, 17.2, and 17.3). And the percentage continues to increase. Projections are that by the year 2000, almost 14 percent of the population will be over sixty-five; that percentage is expected to increase to 20 percent by the year 2030 (U.S. Bureau of the Census, 1996). At present, the fastest growing age group in the United States is above age eighty.

The demography of old age has changed dramatically in the last 30 years. Between 1960 and 1995, the percentage of people age 65 and older in the United States and in Canada increased by about 50 percent (Figures 17.1 and 17.2). The greatest percentage increase occurred at the upper levels: The percentage of those age 85 and older more than tripled. Because of increased longevity, percentages of those widowed declined during that period, but the percentage of those divorced more than doubled (Figure 17.3).

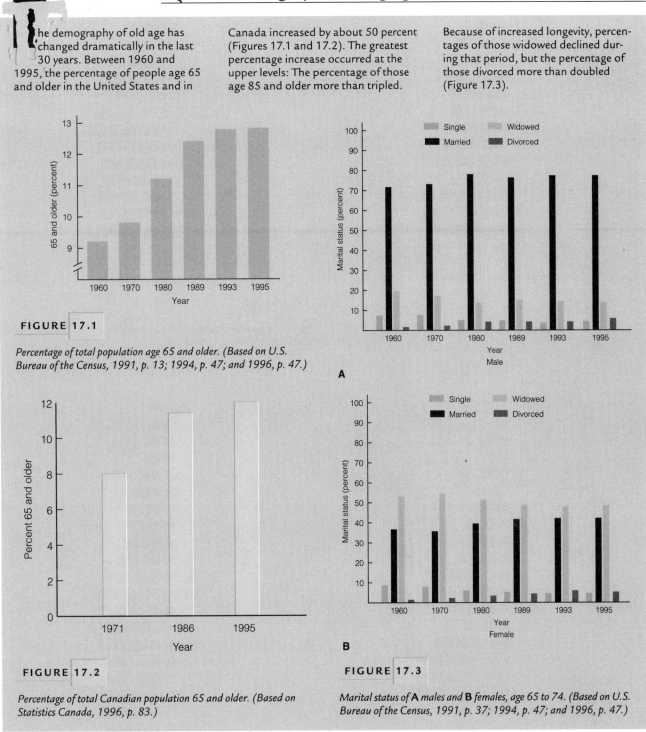

FIGURE 17.1

Percentage of total population age 65 and older. (Based on U.S. Bureau of the Census, 1991, p. 13; 1994, p. 47; and 1996, p. 47.)

FIGURE 17.2

Percentage of total Canadian population 65 and older. (Based on Statistics Canada, 1996, p. 83.)

FIGURE 17.3

*Marital status of **A** males and **B** females, age 65 to 74. (Based on U.S. Bureau of the Census, 1991, p. 37; 1994, p. 47; and 1996, p. 47.)*

One of the reasons for predicting a continued increase in the proportion of older people is the effect of the population bulge created by the postwar baby boom (evident in Figures 17.4 and 17.6). As this bulge moves into old age, the numbers of old people relative to younger people will increase dramatically (Figures 17.5 and 17.7). The net effect is increased even more by declining birthrates. As a result, the age-population pyramids shown in Figures 17.5 and 17.7 are not pyramids at all—as they would be if birthrates remained relatively constant and if deaths occurred primarily from "natural" causes (rather than as a result of wars or other events that kill primarily within selected age groups).

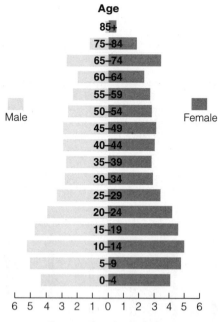

FIGURE 17.4

Age–sex population pyramid for the United States: 1970. (Based on U.S. Bureau of the Census, 1996, p. 16.)

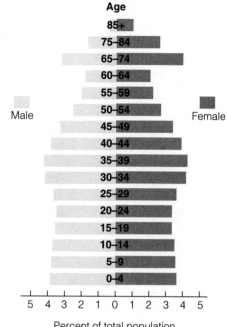

FIGURE 17.5

Age–sex population pyramid for the United States: 1995. (Based on U.S. Bureau of the Census, 1996, p. 16.)

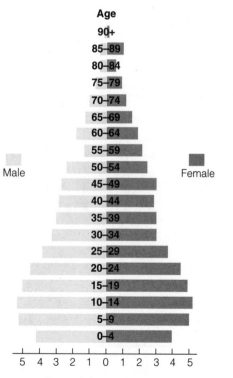

FIGURE 17.6

Age–sex population pyramid for Canada: 1971. (Based on Statistics Canada, 1996, p. 82.)

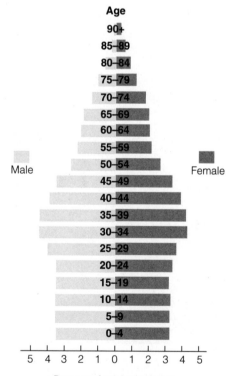

FIGURE 17.7

Age–sex population pyramid for Canada: 1995. (Based on Statistics Canada, 1996, p. 82.)

Attitudes Toward the Elderly

"How old are you?" Few questions are more important to any of us when we first meet someone. Of course, it isn't always proper to ask; there are many for whom age is very private.

But if we do ask and find out how old someone is, what have we actually discovered? A great deal, most of us think, because we all have definite opinions about what people of different ages *should* be like. For example, we know that children should be immature and impulsive; that adolescents should be moody and sometimes rebellious; that young adults should be adventurous, bold, and energetic; that middle-aged adults should be responsible, controlled, and strong; that older adults should be cautious, rigid, and narrow-minded; and that the very old should not be totally competent in all areas. Armed with these tidbits of folk knowledge, we glibly judge people to be "old" or "young" for their age. And, in fact, our judgments are probably often accurate and useful. At other times, however, our age-based expectations are inaccurate and highly prejudiced. *Ageism* is the term used to describe *negative* attitudes toward a group that are based solely on age.

Ageism

Ageism is most common with respect to old age. It is evident, say Powell, Branco, and Williamson (1996), in age discrimination in the workplace, in housing, and in education. It is apparent, as well, in the negative, constraining images that often lead the young to describe the elderly in terms such as "used up," "ready to die," "narrow-minded," "prejudiced," "worn-out," and "incompetent." When Ng, Giles, and Moody (1991) asked people what kind of information they would ask of a driver involved in an automobile accident so that they might assign responsibility, they found that responses were highly dependent on the age of the driver—but not the sex. Younger drivers would be asked about their driving conduct. (Had they been drinking? Had they been in previous accidents? How fast were they going?) But older drivers would be asked about their competence. (How was their vision? Their health? Were they licensed to drive? Were they mentally capable? Were they physically capable?) Implicit in these questions are negative age-related stereotypes of the old.

Negative attitudes such as these are sometimes manifested in age discrimination in which older and younger people are treated differently simply on the basis of age. For example, medical treatment of the elderly often reflects ageism. Not only do the medical professions assign a lower priority to research dealing with diseases associated with aging, but expensive medical screening such as that undertaken for cancer is more likely to be provided for the young than the old, even though there is far more cancer in those above age sixty-five (Derby, 1991). Similarly, the care of the aged is often inferior to that provided for a younger person in the same circum-

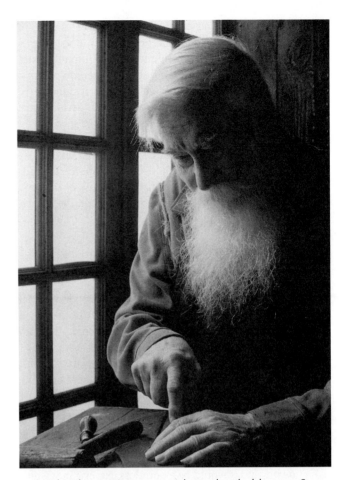

Ageism describes negative stereotypes that are based solely on age. Stereotypes which suggest that old age brings a dramatic decline in ability fail to take into account the value of experience or to recognize the possibility that wisdom comes with age.

stances, often because medical personnel don't understand the changes of aging very well (Bader, 1994).

Another example of ageism may be found in immigration policies, which have traditionally favored the young and which, earlier in U.S. history, allowed parents to bring their children from foreign countries but often did not permit them to bring their parents. Similarly, ageism is illustrated in age-based mandatory retirement. And it is evident in the negative media portrayals of the old as doddering, feeble-minded, wrinkled, and laughable men and women, standing weakly and foolishly on the last of their worn legs.

Child-Directed Speech

Ageism is evident as well in the speech that is often used when communicating with the elderly, speech that is highly reminiscent of that of mothers to their infants. Thus, speech directed to the old is often higher-pitched, sentences are shorter, ideas are presented in their simplest forms and are often repeated, delivery is slower and more careful, and there is more use of body language such as widening of the eyes and exaggerated gestures and expressions. This type of speech, say Bunce and Harrison (1991), reflects a view of the elderly as helpless and incompetent. In addition, it communicates lowered expectations and fosters negative stereotypes that might lead to lower self-esteem on the part of the elderly, withdrawal from social interaction, and poorer performance (Giles et al., 1992). Unfortunately, child-directed speech, and other manifestations of ageism, are not uncommon among health care workers in charge of the elderly (Grant, 1996). Many among the elderly find child-directed speech degrading. However, there is evidence that with some of the very old, clear and very simple communication might be associated with better performance (Bunce & Harrison, 1991).

Other Negative Attitudes

Ageism describes negative attitudes that are prejudicial because they are based on age alone. Attitudes that are based on fact, even though they might be negative, do not illustrate ageism. Thus, the sometimes gloomy pictures that we have of social, physical, and psychological changes in very old age might, to some extent, be fact—negative and uncomfortable fact, to be sure, but fact nevertheless. And social policies that appear to favor the young might often be based not on a stereotyped and prejudiced ageism but on the sometimes painful recognition that the elderly present much greater risks of decline in all areas. Indeed, they are at much greater risk of death, and it would be a pointless exercise in wishful thinking to behave as if this were not the case.

One of the reasons why ageism might appear to be more prevalent now is that it is only recently that the old have become numerous. In addition, attitudes toward the old sometimes reflect environmental, economic, political, and social conditions. For example, in harsh and demanding environments, where survival is at a premium, the old quickly become a burden. And, in the same way that children who were an economic burden were sometimes killed during the Middle Ages, there are societies in which the elderly were also killed or customarily committed suicide (Mowat, 1952; Simmons, 1960).

Lest this paint too cynical a picture, let me hasten to point out that many people are not guilty of ageism or of unfairly negative attitudes toward the elderly. Nor, as is made clear in this chapter, does everything suddenly become gloomy with the advent of old age. The rapidly growing proportion of old people in contemporary society is having a profound effect on public opinion as well as on social policy. The middle-aged and the elderly are increasingly breaking traditional age barriers. Many go back to school, begin new careers, marry for the first time, or devote themselves to dramatically new lifestyles at ages that would have been considered far too advanced only a few decades ago. People such as Segovia, Picasso, Grandma Moses, or Freud, all of whom played music, painted, or wrote into their eighties, nineties, or even, in Grandma Moses's case, at age 100, do much to relieve us

▲ **SUMMARY TABLE 17.1**
**Changing Demographics
and Attitudes: Late Adulthood**

- Late adulthood (65+) spans a tremendous age range and includes great heterogeneity; hence Neugarten's division of the period into the young-old (65 to 75 or so), the old-old (75 to 85), and the oldest-old (above 85).

- In recent decades, there has been a 50% increase in the percentage of the North American population above 65, partly because of an aging population bulge and partly because of increased life expectancy; at the oldest ages, women outnumber men substantially.

- Ageism describes age-based negative stereotypes; ageism directed toward the elderly is often evident in the workplace, in education, in health care, in child-directed speech, and in media portrayals.

- Some factual attitudes toward the elderly are nevertheless painful and negative; they recognize declines that often accompany aging, and the elderly's greater risk for a variety of negative outcomes.

of lingering age-related negative stereotypes. (See Summary Table 17.1.)

■ LIFESPAN AND LIFE EXPECTANCY

In North America, life expectancy has increased by almost one-quarter of a century in little more than three-quarters of a century. At the turn of the century, the average individual did not live fifty years; now we can reasonably expect to live to about age seventy-seven—less if we are male, more if we are female. Table 17.2 presents life-expectancy data for seventeen countries. Note the tremendous variation for different countries. In addition, in most of these countries, there is a wide discrepancy between male and female longevity. In Canada and the United States, for example, women live an average of between seven and eight years longer than men, a fact that is partly explained in terms of the greater susceptibility of men to stress-related disease (heart disease, for example) and to their traditionally less restrained lifestyles (more automobile accidents, for example) (see "At a Glance: Male and Female Longevities" and Figure 17.8). But part of the explanation must also lie elsewhere, because male infants and children are also more likely to die than are female infants and children. Although approximately 105 males are born for every 100 females, the numbers of each still alive are equal by early adulthood. And by age 65, fewer than 70 males are still alive for every 100 females. Above age 85, there are more than 250 females for every 100 males (Figure 17.9). Social and cultural sex biases may have favored males; nature has been less kind.

Male and Female Longevities

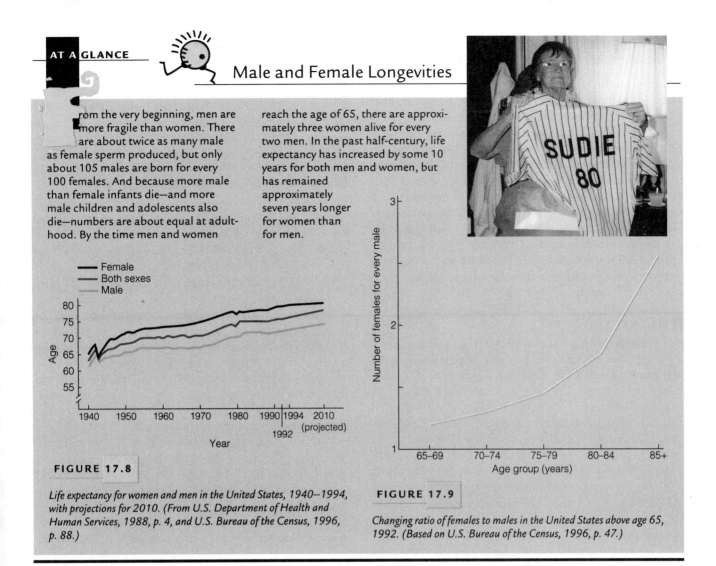

From the very beginning, men are more fragile than women. There are about twice as many male as female sperm produced, but only about 105 males are born for every 100 females. And because more male than female infants die—and more male children and adolescents also die—numbers are about equal at adulthood. By the time men and women reach the age of 65, there are approximately three women alive for every two men. In the past half-century, life expectancy has increased by some 10 years for both men and women, but has remained approximately seven years longer for women than for men.

FIGURE 17.8

Life expectancy for women and men in the United States, 1940–1994, with projections for 2010. (From U.S. Department of Health and Human Services, 1988, p. 4, and U.S. Bureau of the Census, 1996, p. 88.)

FIGURE 17.9

Changing ratio of females to males in the United States above age 65, 1992. (Based on U.S. Bureau of the Census, 1996, p. 47.)

TABLE 17.2

Life Expectancies at Birth in Selected Countries

COUNTRY	LIFE EXPECTANCY AT BIRTH (YEARS)	COUNTRY	LIFE EXPECTANCY AT BIRTH (YEARS)
Sierra Leone	39	Germany	76
Uganda	52	France	77
Bangladesh	55	Australia	77
Indonesia	62	Canada	77
Nicaragua	66	Sweden	78
Russian Federation	68	Spain	78
China	68	Japan	79
United Kingdom	76	Hong Kong	79
United States	76		

Source: From Bellamy, C. (1997). *The state of the world's children: 1997.* New York: Oxford University Press, pp. 88–89.

Theories of Biological Aging

Although improved nutrition and medical care have given us twenty-five more years than our late-nineteenth-century predecessors, our **lifespans** (the maximum length of life in the absence of disease or accident) still remain virtually identical to what they have always been. If we live until age 65, our **life expectancy** (the average anticipated years of life) is another 15.4 years for males and 19.0 for females (U.S. Bureau of the Census, 1996)—only a few years more than it was almost a century ago. In other words, although it is now far more likely that we will reach old age (approximately two-thirds of us can expect to reach age seventy), the very oldest among us will, in the end, live no longer than the very oldest who lived a long time ago. If disease, accident, or boredom doesn't claim us, old age surely will.

▪ GENETIC THEORY

Although we do not yet know exactly why we age, there are several theories of biological aging. A **genetic theory of aging** holds, for example, that cells are programmed to die—that, in other words, the limits to life are biological and are inherent in the cells of which we are composed or in the protein matter that binds the cells (collagen) (Koli & Keski-Oja, 1992). When tissue cultures are raised in the laboratory, these cultures initially regenerate and multiply at a high rate. But eventually, they begin to atrophy and finally die. What is perhaps most striking about this observation is that whereas cultures based on human embryonic lung tissue regenerate perhaps fifteen times before dying (more if the donor is younger, less if older), cultures from animals with shorter lives regenerate correspondingly fewer times. In fact, there is an almost perfect relationship between the normal lifespan of organisms and the number of times that cultures derived from their tissue will regenerate (Brouwer, 1990). Only certain defective, usually cancerous, cells regenerate indefinitely (Harmon & Allan, 1997).

▪ CELL MALFUNCTION THEORIES

There are several other theories of aging that also relate directly to body cells. **Cell error theory** suggests that, with the passage of time, certain changes occur in DNA material so that the cell eventually ceases to function. These changes are seen as errors rather than as genetically preprogrammed occurrences. DNA damage, notes Simic (1992), can be detected through urinalysis and can be tempered through reduction of calorie intake.

The **toxin theory of cell malfunction** maintains that there is a gradual buildup of foreign material in the cell. Although much of this material is poisonous, initially it is present in insufficient quantities and does not affect cell function. With the passage of time, however, it continues to accumulate until the cell dies. One of the consequences is a reduced ability to combat infections and disease (Koli & Keski-Oja, 1992).

The **free-radical theory** argues that portions of cells sometimes become detached during normal metabolic processes.

Many of these "free radicals" are highly unstable chemical compounds that may interact with various enzymes and proteins in the body and significantly affect the cell's ability to function normally (Harman, 1993).

A last cell-related theory is **cross-linking theory**, which describes a process whereby bonds ("cross-links") form between molecules or parts thereof, changing the properties of the component cells and altering their functioning.

▪ ORGAN AND SYSTEM THEORIES

In addition to these genetic and cell-based theories of biological aging, other theories speculate that various body systems undergo age-related changes that eventually lead to their breakdown or malfunction. Such theories sometimes argue that aging results from reductions in the efficiency of body systems that control temperature, blood-sugar level, and so on (Davies, 1990). Perhaps best known among these theories is the **theory of immune system malfunction.** This is the system designed to guard against foreign invaders. It protects us from cancer, for example, as well as from a variety of infections. With advancing age, however, not only does the immune system weaken so that it can less effectively protect us from infection and disease, but it also sometimes makes errors and interprets some of our own cells as invaders. This process, known as **autoimmunity,** leads to the production of antibodies that may attack the body itself. Autoimmunity is thought to be involved in some diseases of aging, such as rheumatoid arthritis (Luqmani, Gordon, & Bacon, 1994).

Aging, says Harman (1993), is essentially the accumulation of changes that accompany age. Some of these changes are due to the environment and to disease; others are related to inborn processes of aging. Furthermore, the causes underlying the changes of age interact with one another, hence the importance of a variety of explanations (see Table 17.3).

TABLE 17.3

Theoretical Explanations for Why We Will Die in Any Case

THEORY	EXPLANATION
Genetic	Cells are preprogrammed to die.
Error	Cellular changes lead to cells becoming nonfunctional as a result of errors that occur in DNA material over time.
Toxin	The gradual buildup of foreign material in the cells eventually becomes toxic, and the cells die.
Free-radical	Portions of cells become detached, interact with various chemicals and enzymes, and eventually impede the cells' ability to function normally.
Cross-linking	Bonds form among cells, changing their properties and altering their functioning.
Immune system breakdown	Immune system weakens with age and provides less protection against viral and bacterial invasion or, in a process known as autoimmunity, loses the ability to recognize foreign invaders and begins to attack the system it previously protected.

Longevity in North America

Harman (1993) suggests that by optimizing the environment and controlling and treating disease, it might be possible to add as much as five years to life expectancy. As far as science knows, however, our lifespans are the upper biological limits of our lives. And our life *expectancies* will seldom reach the limit of our *spans*. Some of us will die sooner, others later. Why these differences in **longevity?**

Several factors contribute to longevity. As we see in Table 17.2, culture, or at least some of the complex of variables associated with it, is one such factor, and as Figure 17.8 shows, sex is another. Women live longer than men, whites longer than blacks, and Americans longer than Ugandans, *on average*. Some of the reasons for this are clearly environmental and relate to nutrition, medical care, health habits, and various vices and virtues having to do with lifestyle—exercising, drinking, smoking, and so on. Other reasons for longevity are genetic and relate to inherited susceptibility to various diseases, as well as to other genetically linked strengths and weaknesses.

A variety of other factors have also been found to be linked to longevity. These include physical condition (overweight individuals have shorter life expectancies; those who exercise are more likely to live longer), nature of occupation (people whose jobs require little physical activity die earlier

on the average), locale (rural people live longer than those in urban environments), wars (life expectancies of those actively engaged in such contests are understandably less), and religious calling (nuns live longer than monks; other things being equal, both live longer than you and I). In addition, the unmarried tend not to live as long as those who are married, and professional athletes have life expectancies that are several years longer than those of nonathletes (Tucker et al., 1996; Sarna et al., 1993). There is a tendency, as well, for those described as Type B personalities (relaxed, easygoing) as opposed to Type A (aggressive, hard-driving, hurried) to live longer (Shimonaka, Nakazato, & Homma, 1996). Similarly, some evidence suggests that those with a better sense of humor, as well as those who are more curious and exploring, live longer (Ridley & Harrison, 1996; Swan & Carmelli, 1996). These and other factors are summarized in Interactive Table 17.4.

So should we all become athletic monks and nuns, and move to the country and tell each other jokes? Perhaps not,

Life expectancy at birth for North American males is now around 72; for females, it's about 79. Certain lifestyle factors (like smoking and drinking, or exercising and avoiding wars) can affect longevity. But factors over which we have little control are perhaps most influential in determining how long we live. Thus, the long lives of these 94-year-old identical twin dentists may well reflect the effects of genetics and of early nutrition and care.

INTERACTIVE TABLE 17.4

A Recipe for Longevity

How long can you expect to live? On average, about 77 or 78 years in Canada and the United States—more if you are female, less if male. But some of us will live longer; others will die sooner. Sex is only one of the factors that influences longevity. You cannot control your sex, and you have only limited control over the possibility of accidental death. But perhaps you can control some of the other factors associated with longevity, listed here. You may live longer if:

- You are female.
- Your ancestors lived long lives.
- You are a large tortoise and not a housefly.
- You remain physically active well into old age.
- You are highly educated.
- Your employment is of high status.
- You continue to be employed well into old age.
- You are a monk or a nun.
- You are married or cohabit full time.
- You have a good sense of humor.
- You exercise moderately on a regular basis.
- You drink moderately and don't smoke.
- You avoid wars, accidents, and homicidal maniacs.
- Your job requires physical activity.
- You are not overweight.
- You sleep less than nine hours per night.
- You are curious as an old person.
- There is no incidence of cardiovascular diseases, cancer, chronic bronchitis, or thyroid disorders among your close relatives.
- You live in the country rather than in the city.
- You undergo regular medical examinations.

because the most important factors in determining a long life are those over which we have no control—namely, genetic factors, the environments of our grandmothers and of our mothers before and during pregnancy, and our own experiences in early childhood. Sadly, we can far more easily shorten our lives than lengthen them. That is, the good that we might do by *not* smoking or drinking is not likely to equal, in terms of years, the bad that we might do were we to smoke and drink. And perhaps living a long time is not very important. We have to be concerned with the quality of our lives as well as with their length.

Longevity Elsewhere

In most parts of the world, only two or three people out of every 100,000 live to be 100, one in 1 million reaches 105, and only one in 40 million lives to be 110 (Hayflick, 1975). Occasionally, however, the popular press tantalizes us with visions of healthy old people, sometimes 120 or more years of age, living in some faraway place. There are at least four such groups of people, including the Vilcabambans in Ecuador, the Hunzukuts in the Karakoram Range of Kashmir, and the Abkhasians in parts of the Caucasus of the Georgian Republic. Scientists have visited each of these parts of the world, interviewed the inhabitants, and attempted to determine what they might have in common (Leaf, 1973). They found, for example, that some long-lived individuals smoked and drank rum and never bathed; others climbed up and down mountains and bathed in ice-cold streams. Some ate chicken but no pork or other fatty meats; others ate mutton and goat; still others were largely vegetarian. Most were illiterate, medical care was primitive or nonexistent, and infant mortality was high.

Unfortunately, none of this information is very valuable because scientists were unable to verify the ages of the older people in these societies. None had valid birth records, and many of the older people seemed to systematically exaggerate their ages by as many as 40 years (Hayflick, 1975).

Models of Aging

Although there is no proof that people in these cultures live longer than North Americans or western Europeans, their aging nevertheless appears to be very different. Old Abkhasians, for example, are vigorous and strong, and never completely retire. In addition, they continue to walk up and down the mountain slopes, to swim in icy streams, and sometimes to father children at remarkable ages (Benet, 1976).

Why do the Abkhasians age so well? There are two plausible reasons, says Benet. One is genetic: Those who have survived in the harshness of the mountain country may have served to select for a better genetic pool. The other is social-environmental: Among other things, the Abkhasian culture stresses the importance of physical work but sees no virtue in

overexertion; the common diet consists primarily of fruit, vegetables, and meat; and the culture expresses different attitudes toward aging in that individuals do not retire or lose status with age. Infusino and associates (1996) describe a very similar situation with respect to forty **centenarians** living in a remote region of Italy (the Calabrian region). Most of these very old people continued to perform physical tasks and activities associated with daily life, and also manifested very good mental performance and very low levels of depression. In general, they continued to feel important and valued in their culture.

In contrast, in the Western world, little is asked of the individual for the first twenty or so years of life, a contribution is expected during the middle thirty or thirty-five years, and after age sixty or sixty-five, little more is expected. This *discontinuity* between productive and nonproductive life, is, in effect, a clear social signal that differentiates between being useful and being useless, between being culturally valued and not being valued, between being wanted and not being wanted.

It is highly revealing that in societies such as ours, like Jack Benny, we are more likely to claim we are thirty-nine than seventy-nine when we find ourselves somewhere in between. It is also revealing that "looking one's age" is considered negative (as in "He's sure been looking his age lately"). Many people only reluctantly allow themselves to look their age, resorting to facelifts, skin tonics, hair transplants, and the hundreds of other means that our culture defines as cosmetic improvement.

Still, many people genuinely look forward to aging. Perhaps, as the proportion of the aged continues to increase, many more will do so. (See Summary Table 17.5.)

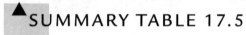

SUMMARY TABLE 17.5
Lifespan, Life Expectancy, and Longevity

- Life expectancy is the expected or predicted length of an average life for a person of a given age and sex within a specific culture; longevity is the actual length of a person's life; lifespan is the maximum length of life in the absence of accident or disease.

- Theories to explain aging include genetic theory (cells are programmed to die); cell error theory (cellular changes lead to death); toxin theory (accumulation of toxins in cells causes cell death); free-radical theory (portions of cells detach and impede functioning); cross-linking theory (bonds form among cells, changing their functioning); and immune system breakdown theory (age-related malfunctions of the immune system).

- Factors related to longevity include sex, genetics, physical activity, nutrition, and medical care.

- In some cultures, the aged continue to be a valued and useful part of society; in others, that is less the case.

PHYSICAL CHANGES IN OLD AGE

The lifespan view of human development recognizes that change occurs at all stages. But it also recognizes that many, though by no means all, of the physical, social, and cognitive changes of the final stage involve decline. The technical term for this period of decline is **senescence**. Senescence can begin at very different ages for different individuals, and the losses it entails are not always dramatic or rapid. In addition, manifestations of aging are not identical for all individuals. Some results of aging are nearly universal and are sometimes referred to as **primary aging**. Loss or atrophy of brain cells is one primary change of senescence, as is gradual loss of cells from all organ systems (Booth, Weeden, & Tseng, 1994). Various forms of degeneration are also part of senescence. One example is the loss of calcium in bones, leading to **osteoporosis**. Another is **arteriosclerosis**—a gradual hardening of the arteries—which begins very early in life and becomes progressively more serious, although its severity varies greatly among different individuals.

Physical Appearance

Most of the physical changes characteristic of old age begin well back in middle age and progress slowly through the remainder of the lifespan. For example, as we saw in Chapter 13, both strength and endurance peak in early adulthood (through the twenties and sometimes early thirties), and begin to decline very slowly from that point. In the same way, height usually reaches its maximum in early adulthood and begins to decline very slowly after age forty-five, partly because of tendons that shrink and harden, feet that become flatter, a spinal column that shortens, and muscles that have begun to atrophy. The combined result of these changes can often be seen in the characteristically stooped posture of the very old.

Among the many changes that contribute to the appearance of age, perhaps none are more apparent than those that occur in the skin, on the face, and on the head. Our skins are truly marvelous things. Indeed, it is difficult to imagine a better wrapping for our bodies—totally flexible, self-regenerating and self-repairing, sensitive to heat and cold as well as to pain, highly elastic, porous yet impervious to wind and rain, and totally washable. But with age, these wrappings become thinner and far less elastic, and are often flecked with little splotches of brown pigment (popularly called "liver spots") as well as with warts, bristly hairs, and the blackish bruises of tiny leaks in blood vessels. As fatty cells die, old skin is no longer sufficiently elastic to cover the loss; it sags and droops under our arms and chins, and it creases and wrinkles. And the wrinkles of the very old are quite different from those of the middle-aged. No longer do they follow the contours of muscles that have repeatedly stretched the skin in the same

Signs of aging are clear in changes in our skin as it becomes less elastic, thinner, dotted with brown splotches, wrinkled, and creased—changes that can be accelerated by a lifetime of exposure to the elements.

way—the laugh lines on the cheek, the "crow's feet" at the corners of the eyes, and the frown lines on the forehead. The wrinkles of the very old are an almost random arrangement of tiny little creases running in all directions between larger crevices. But these are the wrinkles of the very old; there is a long space of time between the appearance of our first wrinkles and the wizening of very old age.

Other physical changes that have begun in middle age (or earlier) also continue. Hair becomes thinner or loses pigment; wear on remaining teeth (if any still remain) becomes more apparent, and gums continue to recede. Thus, the caricature of the "old codger" might be either "toothless" or "long in the tooth."

The timing and the exact manifestations of these changes are sometimes very different in different individuals. Nutrition and physical activity can affect their appearance, as can genetic background.

Fitness and Exercise

When older adults were asked to throw tennis balls as hard and as well as they could, investigators found that they threw with about the same motions and velocities as nine- or ten-year-old

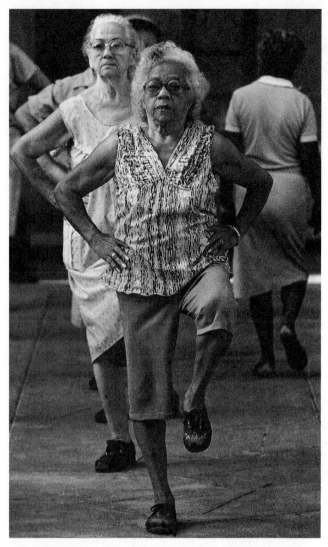

Exercise and training can do a great deal to maintain and even improve muscular strength and endurance, flexibility, and stamina well into late adulthood. In a program designed to keep Cuba's aging population fit and healthy, elderly Havana residents participate in morning exercises.

children (Williams, Haywood, & Vansant, 1991). Clearly, with age, there is ordinarily a steady decline in flexibility, strength, stamina, and various aspects of physical performance. This decline is related not only to the gradual deterioration of muscles but also to the shortening and stiffening of tendons and ligaments, to the weakening of bones, to loss of aerobic capacity, and to loss of motor neurons (Booth et al., 1994). The important point, however, is that much of this decline does not result from primary aging processes. Hence, much of it is avoidable, and some is reversible.

In the absence of sustained training, for example, flexibility declines gradually from about age twelve. But when Voorrips and colleagues (1993) tested fifty elderly women, they found that those who were more physically active had significantly greater flexibility, as well as better scores on most measures of physical performance.

Evidence of the benefits of fitness and exercise is perhaps most dramatic in the case of older athletes. Many elderly

master athletes, notes Ward (1994), perform better on some measures than do sedentary men who are thirty years younger—and perform enormously better than the elderly who are also sedentary. For example, many older adults cannot perform a single sit-up or a modified push-up, yet competitors at a Seniors' Games event, which included such activities as track and field, tennis, swimming, golf, softball, and horseshoes, performed at levels far beyond expectation, often exceeding performance levels of groups ten to thirty years younger (O'Brien & Conger, 1991). In fact, seventy-year-old male athletes demonstrated higher grip strength than 60 percent of seventeen- to nineteen-year-olds. And seventy-year-old women were as flexible as teenagers. As the authors conclude, "Seniors who are physically active in late life are advantaged in terms of strength, muscular endurance, and joint flexibility into their years beyond age seventy" (p. 78). It is also worth noting that these athletes were remarkably positive about life: They had plans and goals for the future, and they felt useful, important, and wanted.

In addition to the benefits that exercise has for physical fitness, it also has clear and significant positive effects on health. Among other things, it strengthens bones and muscles, reducing the risk of falling and breaking bones (Pendergast, Fisher, & Calkins, 1993); it improves cardiopulmonary functioning (Willoughby, Roozen, & Barnes, 1997); it improves circulation and abates the risk of arteriosclerosis (Seals et al., 1994); and it may even improve functioning of the immune system (Nieman & Henson, 1994) as well as mental functioning (Etnier & Landers, 1997; Tomporowski, 1997). There is recent evidence, too, that simple relaxation exercises can have a measurable effect on creative functioning among the elderly (Krampen, 1997).

The World Health Organization's recently released guidelines for physical activity among older persons summarize the benefits of exercise as follows (Chodzko-Zajko, 1997):

1. Physiological benefits:
   - regulating blood glucose levels
   - improving sleep
   - increased cardiovascular endurance
   - strengthening of muscles and bones
   - improved flexibility and balance
   - improved speed of movement

2. Psychological benefits:
   - relaxation
   - reduction of stress and anxiety
   - enhanced mood and general sense of well-being
   - cognitive improvements
   - improved mental health

3. Social benefits:
   - formation of new friendships
   - widened social and cultural networks

4. Benefits for society:
   - reduced health and social care costs
   - enhanced productivity of older adults

World Health Organization guidelines suggest that exercise for the elderly should be simple, relaxing, and enjoyable—all extremely important considerations in view of the fact that many of the elderly are highly reluctant to participate in exercise programs. When Whaley and Ebbeck (1997) asked why, the most often cited reason was "I get enough exercise elsewhere." Other frequently cited excuses included lack of time, inconvenience, and distaste for the types of activities involved. What the WHO guidelines recommend are daily programs including activities such as stretching, aerobic exercise, strength training, walking, dancing, swimming, cycling, or even bed or chair exercises. The physical and emotional well-being of the elderly may owe a great deal to such programs—as well as to nutrition.

Nutrition and Health

Nutrition is as important among the elderly as it is throughout life. But, notes Lemme (1995), the elderly often make greater efforts to maintain healthy lifestyles than do those who are younger. This may be partly because those who have retired have more time for such endeavors; it might also be because of a heightened awareness of mortality, and a greater determination to stall the effects of aging.

In addition to the normal, but reduced, requirements that the elderly have for each of the basic food groups, there is also a greater need for mineral and vitamin supplements. For example, both vitamin D and calcium are important in arresting bone loss and preventing osteoporosis—as is exercise. At the same time, fat intake should be limited whereas fiber intake often needs to be increased. Especially important is **hydration**—that is, intake of sufficient water and other fluids (Bloom, 1996).

■ HEALTH CARE

Because of demographic changes in the industrialized world, most evident in the rapidly increasing proportion of the very old, there is tremendous interest in the consequences of aging, and especially in the burden these elderly might place on medical systems (Mosley, 1994). In 1994 in the United States, for example, 1.4 million people over age 65 were home health care patients (U.S. Bureau of the Census, 1996). More than one million of them had expenses paid by Medicare; 120,000 were on Medicaid. Services provided included skilled nursing, social services, counseling, medication, nutritional guidance, and physical therapy.

We noted earlier that susceptibility to diseases changes from childhood through middle adulthood. Whereas the young are more susceptible to acute infections (colds, for example), those who are older suffer more from chronic complaints (back problems, heart disease). This pattern continues into old age. In addition, whereas the old are perhaps less susceptible to acute infections, they experience greater difficulty in coping with them. Upper respiratory infections are not often fatal among children, but they sometimes are among the very old.

The most common chronic conditions in people above the age of sixty-five include arthritis, hypertension, hearing impairment, heart conditions, visual impairments, and arteriosclerosis. Other diseases to which the elderly are susceptible include **Parkinson's disease**, which is linked to a deficiency in the neurotransmitter dopamine and which is often characterized by coarse tremors, generalized weakness, slow movement, sleep disturbances, and sometimes depression; cancer; kidney and urinary problems; and acute brain syndrome, which may be characterized by confusion, speech disturbances, hysteria, paranoia, or other symptoms of mental disturbance, but which, to the extent that it is acute (as opposed to *chronic,* or recurring), will generally respond to treatment. **Acute brain syndrome** often results from drug overdoses, toxic drug combinations, or excessive ingestion of alcohol. The elderly are particularly susceptible to acute brain syndrome, not only because of age-related changes in the brain and nervous system but also because many elderly people take an alarming number and variety of prescription drugs. In addition, there is evidence that a number of the elderly are addicted to illegal drugs. Their preferred drugs, notes Rosenberg (1995), are heroin and marijuana, as well as alcohol. And, because of some of the neurological and physiological changes of age, the elderly are often far more susceptible to the ill-effects of these drugs and are likely to experience more medical complications.

We saw, too, that the elderly are more susceptible to osteoporosis. Hence, the bones of the old are more brittle than those of the young. This, combined with an approximately fourfold increase in the likelihood of falling, means that their bones are far more likely to break (Pendergast et al., 1993). And, unfortunately, they mend more slowly and with more difficulty. Finally, Alzheimer's disease, discussed next, is an important disease of old age.

There is a danger, when listing the possible ailments of the aged, that we will confound aging with disease. Some diseases become more common with age, but they are not caused by age, and are therefore not an inevitable consequence of aging. Our focus, claims Butler (1989), should be on the extraordinary potential of the elderly.

■ ALZHEIMER'S DISEASE

Alzheimer's disease is a brain disorder first identified by Dr. Alois Alzheimer in 1906. It occurs more in older than younger individuals, but may occur in people as young as forty or as old as eighty or more. Estimates are that it might affect as many as 2 percent of individuals over the age of sixty-five and 5 percent of those over seventy-five. Physiologically, it involves a tangling and plaquing of nerve fibers visible under microscopic examination of the brain, as well as a gradual shrinking of the brain (Wisniewski, Silverman, & Wegiel, 1994). Until recently, Alzheimer's could be conclusively diagnosed only following a neurological examination after death. Now, however, it has been discovered that those with Alzheimer's are extraordinarily sensitive to eyedrops commonly used by ophthalmologists to dilate the pupil. Whereas the pupils of normal patients typically dilate about

4 percent, those with Alzheimer's dilate at least 13 percent (Gorman, 1994).

Among the earliest symptoms of Alzheimer's is progressive loss of memory. Individuals suffering from the disorder gradually forget all sorts of information, including how to do things they have done all their lives. In fact, one test for screening Alzheimer's patients is a simple **Clock Drawing Test,** which requires participants to draw or identify the features of a traditional clock face (Brodaty & Moore, 1997). They can become confused and disorganized, easily lost—even in their own homes—and bewildered. Perhaps even more frightening, in the early stages of the disease (which can run over an eight- to twenty-year course), they are often fully aware of what is happening to them. This awareness, note Seltzer and associates (1997), can greatly increase the caregiver's burden, especially when the caregiver is a family member. Eventually, Alzheimer's patients may not recognize people they have always known, and in advanced cases, they may lose all sense of their personal identity. Affected individuals eventually revert to a speechless childishness; it is necessary to feed them, dress them, sit them on the toilet, and lead them around by the hand.

It appears that Alzheimer's may have a variety of causes, some of which may interact with one another. For example, some cases of Alzheimer's appear to be genetic and have been associated with a specific DNA mutation (Lee et al., 1997). This genetically linked form of Alzheimer's has an earlier onset (before age sixty-five) and, typically, a much more rapid progression. Other possibilities include viruses (perhaps contracted in childhood but inactive or ineffectual until old age), metals (higher concentrations of zinc and aluminum have been found in the brains of some Alzheimer's victims [Goudsmit, Neijmeijer-Leloux, & Swaab, 1992]), defects in brain neurotransmitter substances, and malfunctions of the immune system.

Alzheimer's remains a progressive and irreversible condition. There are several potential treatments, including diet control of aluminum, attempts to reduce aluminum concentrations in victims, and the delivery of neurotransmitter substances to patients' brains by means of tiny pumps and plastic tubes that are surgically implanted. In addition, the emerging research on the genetic basis of some manifestations of Alzheimer's suggests the possibility of identifying those who are at risk, perhaps even before birth (Post, 1994)—a possibility that entails difficult ethical questions, particularly because the disease is seldom manifested until old age.

Lest this brief examination of the health consequences of aging paint too grim a picture, let me hasten to point out that although some 86 percent of the elderly suffer from one or more major conditions, the majority do not consider their health to be a very serious problem. Remarkably few are bedridden, dependent, or hospitalized.

Sensory Changes

As we saw in Chapter 15, beginning in early adulthood, there are very gradual changes in most of the sensory systems.

■ VISION

Virtually all individuals require at least one pair of prescription eyeglasses by the end of middle age, with men generally requiring them at younger ages than women. The most common problem is farsightedness **(presbyopia),** which is related to decreasing elasticity and thickening of the lens, and its consequent inability to focus clearly on nearby objects. The lens also becomes less transparent with age. Peripheral vision, depth perception, color vision, and adaptation to the dark also become poorer, and sensitivity to glare increases (Perlmutter, 1994). In addition, the vast majority of people over seventy have at least the beginning of cataracts. Most cataract problems can be corrected with surgery, although over half of the blind are found among the elderly. About eleven percent of those over seventy-five have visual impairments (U.S. Bureau of the Census, 1996). Blindness often results from glaucoma—increased pressure in the eyeball.

In spite of these potential problems, the vast majority of old people function very well with glasses.

■ HEARING

One of the major sensory changes associated with aging is **presbycusis,** the loss of hearing due to aging. This loss is often associated with changes in the inner ear, including the loss of hair cells, which are involved in translating vibrations into nerve impulses, and also the loss of nerve cells along auditory pathways. Often, too, hearing losses are caused or accelerated by prolonged exposure to loud noise. Symptoms of presbycusis often begin in midlife and become more serious after the age of sixty. They are more common for men than for women. About 30 percent of males and 18 percent of females above age sixty-five have hearing impairments. Above age seventy-five,

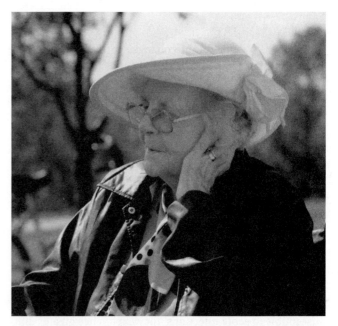

One of the main sensory changes associated with old age is hearing loss, a problem that is more severe and more common for men than for women. The consequences of hearing loss, especially when it leads to social withdrawal, can be quite serious. Fortunately, advances in hearing-aid technology can sometimes compensate for hearing loss.

algarian Tom Spear has just renewed his driving license after passing the required medical and eye examinations. He is now 101; his license is good for another two years. "I was very privileged to be able to comply with all of the requirements," said Mr. Spear. "But I've had a safe driving record for life. I treasure it very dearly—and will continue to do so."

1. Calgarian, 101, on the road again. (1997, Oct. 4). *Edmonton Journal*, p. A11.

To Do

Consult library, news, or Internet sources to find examples of remarkable achievements at advanced ages.

On the Net

The American Physical Therapy Association Section on Geriatrics web page provides interesting information about seniors, including information on the outstanding accomplishments of some of them:

http://geriatricspt.org/geriatricspt. html

percentages of those with hearing impairments increase to 45 percent for men and 30 percent for women.

Among the elderly, hearing losses are most evident in decreased sensitivity to higher tones and in difficulty in discriminating among different sounds (Macrae, 1991). It is partly for this reason that older people sometimes find it very difficult to follow conversations when there is background noise (other conversations, radio or television, or children playing, for example). The desire that many older people have for quiet environments may well be related not to an aversion to noise so much as to a desire to follow normal conversation without strain.

The psychological consequences of a hearing loss can be quite serious. Elderly people whose impairment is severe enough to seriously limit the ability to understand speech may be prevented from enjoying such pastimes as playing cards, watching television, and attending movies and concerts. Even more serious, hearing-impaired elders may deliberately avoid social interaction and also suffer loss of self-esteem. The result may be loneliness and depression.

The physical changes that lead to hearing loss among the elderly can sometimes be corrected simply by removing earwax, or occasionally through surgery. But in other cases, they are irreversible and irremediable. However, the hearing system is only one of the components involved in communication. Fortunately, something can often be done about other components: The acoustic signal, for example, can be amplified and sometimes clarified by means of a hearing device, and the environment can be altered to eliminate background noise. Something as simple as placing furniture so that speakers must face each other can be highly helpful. And the speaker can take pains to speak loudly (without shouting), to face the listener with mouth and lips in full view and uncovered, and to enunciate clearly and distinctly.

■ OTHER SENSES

Many older people frequently find that food does not taste as good as it once did. Some use far more salt, pepper, and other spices than they did when younger, because both smell and taste become less acute in old age. In fact, in one study, subjects over sixty-five were about ten times less sensitive to odors

than subjects between eighteen and twenty-six (Murphy et al., 1991). This diminishment is due to a combination of loss of nerve cells, changes in parts of the brain related to smell and taste, and the cumulative effects of lifestyle factors such as drinking alcohol, smoking, and perhaps eating spicy foods.

Reaction Time and Attention Span

Late adulthood comprises a substantial portion of the lifespan; it can last more than thirty years. As a result, it is highly misleading to make general statements about capacities and declines of this period as if they were common to the entire period. It is extremely important to keep in mind that the sensory losses and the physical changes that we have described thus far may be undetectable at the very beginning of late adulthood, and often occur so gradually that they are not easily noticed until very late in life—if at all.

Changes in reaction time and attention span are no different. Although it has long been established that reaction time slows significantly in late adulthood, it is not true that all elderly people are markedly slower than younger people. On the average, however, people over sixty-five do not react as rapidly, either physically or mentally (Botwinick, 1984). That is, they do not reach conclusions or make decisions as rapidly, nor do they respond as quickly. And evidence suggests, as well, that for some of the elderly, there is a reduction in attention span, especially when what is being attended to needs to be thought about (Perlmutter, 1994).

As we see later in this chapter, slower reaction time and attention problems are one explanation for the poorer performance of the very old on timed cognitive measures. It is also part of the explanation for their worsening performance in sports that require rapid reactions (tennis, for example). And it explains in part why older people have proportionally more traffic accidents. But there are, of course, other explanations for the poorer performance of some of the elderly. These include changes in both physical functioning and sensory abilities. And, clearly, not all of the elderly are equally affected by the declines of old age. See, for example, "In the News and on the Net: On the Road at 101."

Society is uncertain about the sexuality of the very old, preferring to think of them as affectionate, perhaps, but essentially sexless. Yet research shows that the majority, providing they have partners, continue to be sexually active. These newlyweds are 84 and 76.

Sexuality

One of the myths that we have long entertained with respect to the old is that they are essentially sexless—affectionate and emotional, perhaps, but generally devoid of either the desire or the ability for sexual expression. It bears repeating that this view is a myth. In one study of more than 4,000 men and women above age fifty, the vast majority reported that they were sexually active. Even after the age of seventy, two of every three women and four of every five men continued to be sexually active (Brecher, 1984; Figure 17.10). And the majority of women who are sexually inactive simply lack sexual partners, most often because their partners have died (Gibson, 1992).

There are, nevertheless, some differences in sexual responsiveness between the young and the old. In the female, after

the **climacteric** there is a gradual shrinking and loss of elasticity in the uterus, a thinning of the walls of the vagina, and a loss of fatty tissue and elasticity surrounding the vagina. In addition, lubrication may occur more slowly and be less plentiful. As a result, some women may experience pain and irritation during intercourse. However, these changes are much less noticeable in some women than in others. Furthermore, in most women, the clitoris remains sensitive to stimulation, so the vast majority of women who were capable of orgasm when younger will not lose this capability.

Among men, there is a higher incidence of erectile impotence with advancing age. This condition may be related less to age than to other factors, such as heart or circulatory disease, diabetes, and certain types of surgery or medication (Gibson, 1992). In addition, older men often require more time and stimulation to achieve an erection, tend to be less active sexually than younger men, and may experience less intense orgasms (Kennedy, Haque, & Zarankow, 1997).

Although sexual activity, defined in terms of intercourse or orgasm, clearly declines with advancing age, there is little evidence that sexual interest does likewise (Schlesinger, 1996). When the definition of sexual activity is broadened to include a variety of activities such as caressing and holding, it becomes clear that sexuality can continue to be important throughout the upper reaches of the lifespan. However, we should note that sexual behavior is a highly private matter for many, and perhaps even more so for the cohorts that have thus far reached old age. In addition, among these cohorts, extramarital sexual activity has not been widely accepted. Because the majority of very old women are not married but the majority of very old men are, opportunities for sexuality in old age may be limited for many women and less so for men. Succeeding cohorts may tell a different story. In fact, increasing numbers of the elderly are now living as heterosexual cohabiting couples (Hatch, 1995). And

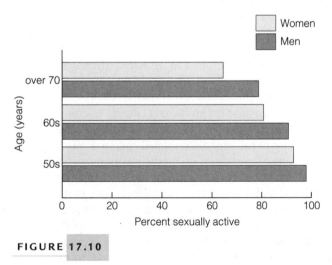

FIGURE 17.10

Change in sexual activity with age. (Based on Brecher, 1984, p. 313.)

the main impediment to cohabitation for many elderly women is simply the increased unavailability of men. (See Summary Table 17.6.)

SUMMARY TABLE 17.6
Physical Changes in Old Age:
Issues and Findings

CONCEPT/ISSUE	EXPLANATIONS/COMMENTS/EVIDENCE
Senescence	■ Technical term for period of decline at end of lifespan; *primary aging* refers to changes that are nearly universal, such as loss of calcium in bones, or atrophy of brain cells.
Changes in physical appearance	■ Shrinking and hardening of tendons, flattening of feet, shortening of spinal column, loss of skin elasticity, loss of hair and hair pigmentation, loss of fatty cells and skin elasticity, receding of gums, wearing of false teeth....
Fitness	■ Gradually declines with loss of flexibility and strength; reaction time is slowed; fitness can be improved and maintained through nutrition and exercise.
Exercise	Four classes of benefits: ■ Physiological (improved blood sugar regulation, sleep patterns, cardiovascular fitness, muscle strength, bone strength, flexibility, and reaction speed). ■ Psychological (greater sense of well-being, relaxation, better mental health). ■ Social (more friends, improved social networks). ■ Society (reduced health-care costs, increased productivity).
Nutrition	■ Reduced need for calories; high need for minerals and vitamins, such as vitamin D and calcium to reduce bone loss; low need for fats; high need for hydration.
Health and health care	■ Suffer less from acute complaints, but have longer recovery time. ■ Suffer more from chronic complaints. ■ Serious diseases of aging include Alzheimer's and Parkinson's. ■ High health-care costs for the elderly.
Sensory losses	■ Both vision and hearing suffer losses with age (presbyopia—farsightedness—and presbycusis—auditory system degeneration, most evident in loss of higher frequency sounds).
Reaction time	■ Slows with advanced age, as does attention span, although changes are often not very dramatic.
Sexuality	■ Given the availability of sexual partners, and in the absence of serious illness or disease, most of the elderly continue to be sexually interested and active.

COGNITIVE CHANGES AMONG THE ELDERLY

Although the physical changes of late adulthood are extremely important, perhaps equally important for daily functioning is the individual's ability to maintain an adequate level of functioning in the cognitive resources involved in remembering, thinking, and problem solving.

Memory

We are, in effect, what we remember. To lose one's **memory** is also to lose one's identity. But loss of one's identity through memory loss is relatively rare, although it is sometimes the eventual outcome of Alzheimer's disease. Less extreme losses of memory, however, may not be uncommon with age. Indeed, one of our stereotypes of old age is the belief that old people have considerable difficulty learning new things and remembering recent events. Another related belief is that old people can remember things that happened long ago better than things that happened recently. We examine the validity of some of these beliefs in the following sections.

DIVISIONS OF MEMORY

Remembering, as we saw in Chapter 9, may be described in terms of **short-term memory**, which is much like attention span, or **long-term memory**, which includes all our knowledge base. In addition, long-term memory consists of **declarative memory** (conscious or explicit memory), which includes **semantic memory** (stable, abstract knowledge) and **episodic memory** (autobiographical memory). Long-term memory may also be **nondeclarative memory** (nonverbalizable or implicit) (see Chapter 9 and Figure 17.11 for more clarification).

SHORT-TERM MEMORY

One of the most common measures of short-term memory, also common in many intelligence tests, is the *digit-span test*: Numbers are read out at one-second intervals, and the testee tries to remember as many as possible. A five-year-old child might recall three or four numbers; a young adult will remember about seven; a middle-aged adult will also remember seven or so. Between sixty and eighty, however, there is an average loss of one or two digits. This, Poon (1985) suggests, is not a very significant decrement and may not be especially important for cognitive functioning.

NONDECLARATIVE MEMORY

Implicit, nonverbalizable knowledge like how to ride a bicycle or how to read and write is largely unaffected by age. Even motor skills that have not been practiced for years are not ordinarily forgotten, even if the coordination, balance, and strength to execute them are not always available (Perlmutter, 1994).

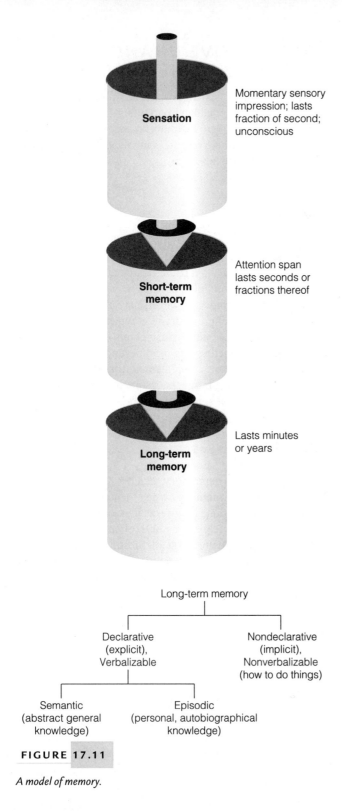

FIGURE 17.11

A model of memory.

Labels within the figure:

Sensation — Momentary sensory impression; lasts fraction of second; unconscious

Short-term memory — Attention span lasts seconds or fractions thereof

Long-term memory — Lasts minutes or years

Long-term memory
- Declarative (explicit), Verbalizable
  - Semantic (abstract general knowledge)
  - Episodic (personal, autobiographical knowledge)
- Nondeclarative (implicit), Nonverbalizable (how to do things)

■ EPISODIC AND SEMANTIC MEMORY

Semantic memory (abstract, verbalizable, general knowledge) is highly dependent on experience. Consequently, it, too, shows few age-related declines until well into old age. In fact, notes Perlmutter (1994), it can sometimes give the older person an advantage, or at least a way of compensating for slower reaction time or slower decision making.

Episodic memory (personal, autobiographical knowledge of individual experiences) is not nearly as resistant to the effects of aging. This is true for younger adults (try to remember the presents you received last Christmas, for example) and even more so for the elderly.

Some measures of long-term memory are more sensitive than others; that is, they are more likely to provide evidence of memory. For example, **recognition recall**, in which the task is simply one of recognizing, is easier than **free recall**, in which the task is one of generating a correct recollection from memory. Measures of recognition often show little decline with age, but such is not the case for free recall. In one study, Bahrick, Bahrick, and Wittlinger (1975) found virtually no changes in the ability of individuals to recognize the names and photographs of those with whom they went to high school, whether they were tested 1.3 months or almost 50 years after leaving school. During the entire span, recognition hovered around 90 percent. But when the task is changed so that individuals are asked to *recall* rather than *recognize* those with whom they went to school, the rate drops dramatically (see Interactive Figure 17.12).

■ SOME CONCLUSIONS

There is general agreement, say Craik and Jacoby (1996), that memory abilities decline with age. But it seems that some sorts of abilities decline far more than others. As we saw, free recall tasks are more difficult than recognition tasks and tend to show more effects of aging. Similarly, responses that re-

INTERACTIVE FIGURE 17.12

Free recall and name recognition as a function of age. How many of the names of your 12th-grade classmates can you recall and write down at this moment? Of your 8th-grade classmates? How many of those you have forgotten do you suppose you would recognize if you were shown a list of names that included them? The graph depicts the results of a study in which subjects who had left school between 1.3 months and 50 years earlier were asked either to recall the names of their former classmates or to recognize them from lists. (From Bahrick, Bahrick, & Wittlinger, 1975, pp. 62, 66. Reprinted by permission of the American Psychological Association and H. P. Bahrick.)

quire habitual behaviors—termed **automatic responding**—seem less affected by age than responses that are more conscious. Driving a car to work using the same route every day eventually involves largely automatic responses at every choice point (such as interchanges or intersections), but stopping along the way to mail a letter requires a disruption of the automatic response and demands conscious, voluntary effort. As we know, even the young can be absentminded and fail to turn into their postal stations. The old, it seems, are even more so (Craik & Jacoby, 1996).

Memory for verbal material and for sequences, too, appears to suffer with age. Smith and associates (1997) administered memory tests to 349 elderly people. They found that performance on a variety of memory tests, such as memory for story sequences, deteriorates with age.

The most important conclusions warranted by the evidence are the following:

1. Short-term memory is not dramatically affected by the passage of time, although attention span (short-term memory span), which is normally somewhere around seven (plus or minus two) items, declines at an average of perhaps one item per decade after age sixty.

2. Episodic memory losses are evident from early adulthood on, but become more apparent in old age; nondeclarative and semantic memory are more resistant to aging.

3. There are important changes in the brain that probably underlie memory loss in old age. By age ninety, the brain weighs about 10 percent less, largely because of loss of neurons (Spence, 1989). This reduction in brain mass is related to declining speed of responding in the elderly.

Note that observed memory declines are seldom very noticeable before age seventy. But by that age, says Fillit (1997), there is generally "significant, but manageable, decline in cognitive abilities" (p. 1). The greatest differences between older and younger subjects generally relates to *timed recall of unfamiliar material* and may underestimate the elderly person's memory because of a tendency to respond more slowly. Not surprisingly, age differences in long-term memory are not nearly as apparent when the materials are highly meaningful and relevant to people's lives (Ratner, Padgett, & Bushey, 1988).

The general pattern of declining memory in old age is not universal; there are many older people who maintain remarkable cognitive skills throughout life. It is continuing potential we should emphasize, says Perlmutter (1988), not deficits.

Intelligence

Maintaining a high level of cognitive resources is essential, note Poon and colleagues (1992), for successful, independent adaptation to old age. Among our important cognitive resources are memory and intelligence. Although there is a general age-related decline in memory, some important aspects of memory, as we saw, are less affected. Is this also the case with other aspects of intelligence?

■ DECLINE OR STABILITY

Research reviewed in Chapter 15 leads to several observations and conclusions:

- Cross-sectional comparisons of intellectual performance have typically found far more striking evidence of intellectual decline than longitudinal studies, which suggests that cohort (or generational) influences may be involved (Schaie, 1997). To the extent that this is correct, it is likely that the next generations will show even less decline in measured intelligence.

- Longitudinal studies of changes in intelligence find less general decline in performance before age sixty-seven. For some specific abilities, there is little measurable decline prior to the ninth decade of life (Schaie, 1994).

- Intellectual abilities that are most likely to decline in old age are those that Cattell termed **fluid abilities.** Declines are most apparent in timed tasks such as code substitution, reaction time, and inspection time in analysis of figures (Nettelbeck & Rabbitt, 1992). Functioning well on these tasks is highly dependent on intact physiological systems but relatively independent of experience. Hence, their decline may be associated with physiological changes such as loss of neurons in the brain and reduced delivery of oxygen to the brain (Cheung & Hachinski, 1997).

- Abilities that are least likely to decline and that may, in fact, continue to improve well into old age are the **crystallized abilities.** These are highly dependent on culture and experience and are evident in verbal skills and general information. Thus, older people sometimes do less well on the performance scales of the Wechsler tests; these require motor coordination, speed, dexterity, and spatial–visual abilities. In contrast, older people may continue to do as well on the verbal scales of the Wechsler tests (vocabulary, information, comprehension) (Mortensen & Kleven, 1993). These scales deal with familiar, rather than unfamiliar, items and do not reward speed (or punish slowness) as do the performance scales.

- Among the oldest-old (above age 85), most measures of intellectual performance, including those of crystallized abilities, show decline (Korten et al., 1997). Nor does high ability serve as insurance against decline. In a study comparing cognitive decline in a group of eminent academics and a group of elderly blue-collar workers, Christensen and associates (1997) found that decline was pretty well universal, especially on tests of nonverbal intelligence, and that there were essentially no differences between the two groups. Poon and colleagues (1992) gave a series of tests to a sample of 165 people aged between 60 and 100. All of these subjects, including the centenarians—the 100-year-olds—lived in private homes and were independent or semi-independent.

Fluid intelligence (picture arrangement; block design)
Crystallized intelligence (vocabulary; arithmetic)
Primary memory (learning word pairs)
Secondary memory (recall of word pairs)
Tertiary memory (recall of familiar information)
Problem solving (practical problems)

FIGURE 17.13

Measures of cognitive competence with 60-, 80-, and 100-year-olds. (Based on Poon et al., 1992, pp. 31–46.)

As Figure 17.13 shows, there is decline in all areas between ages 60 and 100—except in a measure of problem solving. This measure dealt with practical questions highly relevant to day-to-day adaptation: what to do in the case of electrical failure, child-care questions, how to deal with prank telephone calls, banking questions, and so on. It is highly significant that the elderly in this sample not only maintained their practical, problem-solving abilities, but actually improved them.

In summary, there is some decline in intellectual performance with advancing age on the average. It must be stressed, however, that decline is not usually significant until near age seventy or beyond and that it is not universal in two senses: First, it does not affect all aspects of intellectual functioning equally; second, it does not affect all individuals equally. We need to keep in mind, too, that cognitive decline is often a sign of *pathological decline* (due to illness or disease) rather than *normal decline* (due to age: hence common to everybody) (Willis, 1997). In fact, in a ten-year longitudinal study, Tranel, Benton, and Olson (1997) found little evidence of cognitive decline among individuals aged seventy-five to eighty-nine except where there were significant health problems.

IQ Fluctuations and Terminal Drop

When summarizing research of this kind, there is always the danger of mistakenly assuming that what is generally true should apply to all "normal" people. Not so. There are, in fact, thirty-year-olds who experience measurable and sometimes very rapid and highly significant declines in intellectual functioning. In the same way, there are sixty-, seventy-, and eighty-year-old people who also experience declines in intellectual functioning. Is age the cause, always and inevitably, in the case of the older people? The simple answer is no. There is evidence, for example, that intellectual decline can occur throughout the lifespan as a result of illness (Cheung & Hachinski, 1997). Because the elderly are more at risk of chronic illness than the young, observed differences in intellectual performance might conceivably be related to illness, or perhaps to drugs taken to counteract illness, rather than to age itself.

One curious observation based on studies of intellectual change in old age concerns the phenomenon labeled **terminal drop**, first labeled by Kleemeier (1962) after he noticed that among subjects who died during the course of his longitudinal study, there were many whose measured intelligence started to drop sharply not long before death. Subsequently, other researchers noticed much the same thing: Many people experience a sudden drop in intellectual performance one or two years prior to dying (Berg, 1996). This finding has sometimes been explained in terms of a general decline in functioning that might be associated with poorer health preceding death. Thus, sudden declines in IQ scores might be an early indication of a physical change and impending illness.

Not all cognitive declines are *terminal* in the sense that they herald death (Bromley, 1990). Some may simply reflect the older person's deliberate *disengagement* from life. As Lapierre, Bouffard, and Bastin (1992/1993) discovered, the aspirations of the very old tend to be directed toward issues having to do with self-preservation; aspirations related to the outside world and to self-development are more characteristic of those not quite so old. One manifestation of this disengagement or turning inward might be a drastic reduction in motivation to do well on measures of intelligence.

As we have seen, not all elderly persons suffer the same degree of cognitive decline as they age. Fillit (1997) suggests that those who are most likely to maintain a high level of cognitive functioning well into old age are those characterized by the following:

- avoidance of cardiovascular and other chronic diseases
- a favorable environment (high socioeconomic status)
- involvement in a stimulating environment
- a flexible personality in middle age
- marriage to a spouse with high cognitive status

- maintenance of high levels of perceptual processing speed

- high satisfaction with life accomplishments

- maintenance of vision and hearing (p. 2)

Problem Solving and Intuition

Strikingly, however, as Poon and associates (1992) found, even the very old often continue to do remarkably well on measures of practical problem-solving ability. Yet they often don't do nearly as well on more abstract problems. Why?

One possibility is that they approach problems at a more concrete, less abstract level. In the game 20 Questions, for example, adolescents and middle-aged adults typically ask general, abstract questions that allow them to eliminate large numbers of alternatives at once ("Is it alive?" "Is it vegetable?"); in contrast, the very young and the very old are more likely to ask very specific questions to test concrete hypotheses immediately ("Is it my baseball cap?" "Is it my gold star?"). In Bromley's (1990) words, "Old subjects tend to pay attention to irrelevant information, to miss or forget the point of the exercise, to let personal experience substitute for logical reasoning" (p. 198).

■ MYTHICAL THINKING: MYTHOS

These findings do not necessarily mean that older persons are less capable of abstract and rational thought than adolescents. They might mean, instead, that older adults simply approach problems differently, and with very different motivation. As we saw in Chapter 15, the thinking of older adults may be more pragmatic and more attuned to social and economic realities. As a result, abstract questions might not seem very meaningful or important to them. Hence, when older adults are faced with abstract formal reasoning tasks, they tend to personalize them (Datan et al., 1987). Instead of applying the deductive system that would lead directly to the correct solution, they rely on more personal and intuitive ways of thinking. Labouvie-Vief (1986) labels this approach **mythos** (for mythical, as opposed to *logos* for logic). Mythos is a form of thinking that is subjective, personal, and intuitive. But it is not, she insists, inferior to a formal, logical approach; it is simply different. The two types of thinking coexist, and in some adults, they reach a balance. In others, perhaps, there is an imbalance—an overreliance on intuition and pragmatics, and an underreliance on logic. It is as if the pendulum has now swung fully from the other extreme that once characterized adolescence, in which the thinker believed in the omnipotence of logic.

■ COMPETENCE OF THE ELDERLY

Applying the cold rules of logic in solving a game of 20 Questions or a problem in algebra reflects one kind of competence, but it's the sort of competence that may not be too relevant to the life of the very old. The competence they require is that which allows them to use phones, to understand how and when to take medication, to look after personal finances, to shop, to keep house, and to understand a television guide. And, report Willis and Schaie (1994), a remarkable percentage of the elderly are fully competent in these important areas.

Life, perhaps a little like school, is full of problems that require solutions and that demand decisions. But the problems presented to us in school are well defined and conform nicely to the methods of solution that we have been carefully taught. They have reassuringly simple answers, unique solutions that fit and that earn check marks and gold stars and smiles and hugs and pretty rainbows.

Many of life's problems are not so simple. Nobody presents them to us clearly defined; nobody teaches us the precise and appropriate methods for solving them; they have no simple, unique solutions; they tend to be long-term problems requiring long-term decisions, rather than short-term problems with immediately available solutions. Life's problems are open-ended and context-bound. Problems of human relationships, of history, of politics, of economics, cannot neatly be factored and solved. And there isn't always someone there to give us our gold stars and our hugs or to stamp neat check marks onto our life's work.

In many ways, adulthood requires a different kind of thinking—not a schoolchild's thinking, which accepts teacher-determined problems and applies prelearned strategies in an attempt to reach the correct solution, but thinking that is concerned more with identifying problems, with deciding which ones are in need of solution, and with determining which solutions are pragmatic and ethical. Although older persons might not play the game of 20 Questions at as abstract and complex a level as the young adult, their solutions to real-life problems might be just as effective.

Learning in Adulthood

The reality of eventual decline in the performance of physical and intellectual tasks cannot be denied. However, in most cases, these declines do not significantly affect the older person's ability to adjust to changes or to cope with the demands of everyday life throughout most of late adulthood. For most individuals, learning can, and does, continue throughout the lifespan. In fact, it is possible to significantly improve the memories of older people through systematic training programs. However, as Kruse, Lindenberger, and Baltes (1993) found in a study of memory training, even with very intensive training, elderly subjects are often unable to reach the levels that younger subjects reached after only a few training sessions.

Increasingly, older people are going back to school after retirement. As a result, adult education programs are proliferating. Many of these specialize in high-interest courses, responding to the fact that many older people take classes primarily out of personal interest. For many, retirement means

For many, new learning enriches the years of later adulthood. Many adult education programs specialize in high-interest courses; others are designed to be more practical and sometimes lead to second careers. This intense lady may well throw such a fine mess of pots that they will beg her to sell them at the Saturday market.

that they can finally do what they have wanted to do for a long time.

There are also others who undertake programs for more practical reasons, who see potential economic benefit from learning. For example, it is increasingly common for a retired person to take courses in order to launch a cottage industry—market gardening, hydroponics, ceramics, freelance accounting, writing, and on and on. Second careers often

begin in middle adulthood, but there are some that begin in late adulthood as well.

Learning programs that are geared to the very old need to consider some of the possible differences between the old and the young. For example, the learning environment needs to be comfortable, well lighted, and free from distracting background noises. The stimuli used should consider the probability that some learners will have hearing or vision losses. Accordingly, speech should be clear, distinct, and unhurried; printed materials should be nonglossy (to reduce glare), and typefaces should be bold and high-contrast; and steps should be taken to ensure that the material presented is interesting, personally relevant, and not overly demanding. It is a social failing that our culture, unlike that of the Chinese (Ho, 1983), does not encourage reverence for the elderly. The old can contribute a great deal to society—witness Picasso, Segovia, and George Burns. Even if they do not paint, play, act, write, or grow orchids, the elderly are perhaps much wiser. (See Summary Table 17.7.)

WISDOM

Wisdom is a particular quality of human behavior and understanding that has long been associated with old age. This quality appears to combine the types of intuition, emotion, and knowledge that are not easily available to those whose experiences span only a few years. Thus it is that we believe the ancients—the old ones—to be wise.

Perlmutter (1994) defines *wisdom* as a combination of intellectual, emotional, and behavioral characteristics that are apparent in "exceptional knowledge and understanding of life matters, unusual judgment and communication skills,

SUMMARY TABLE 17.7
Cognitive Changes Among the Elderly: Issues and Findings

CONCEPT/ISSUE	EXPLANATIONS/COMMENTS
Memory	■ There are age-related memory declines in late adulthood.
	■ Recognition fares better than recall (at all ages, but especially among the elderly).
	■ Automatic responses are less disrupted by age than conscious, voluntary actions.
	■ The elderly perform less well on timed tasks, better on tasks that are more practically meaningful.
	■ Memory losses are often a sign of *pathological decline* (due to illness or disease) rather than *normal decline* (due to age: hence common to everybody).
Intelligence and competence	■ There is general cognitive decline with age, especially among the oldest-old.
	■ Fluid abilities (dependent on a smoothly functioning nervous system—i.e., as gauged by digit span or memory tests) fare less well than crystallized abilities (dependent on culture and experience—i.e., as gauged by verbal tasks).
	■ Prior to death, there is often a significant drop in measured intelligence, termed *terminal drop*.
	■ Cognitive decline before very old age is often *pathological* rather than *normal*.
	■ The thinking of the old may be more pragmatic, more intuitive, more mythical than logical (*mythos* rather than *logos*).

Wisdom is a special combination of patience, intelligence, kindness, and practical decision-making capacity more often associated with the old than with the young. It rests not so much on logic as on an ability to draw from life's lessons and to balance alternatives in the face of uncertainty. It is not a quality possessed by all the old, nor is it guaranteed by great intelligence. Thus, Einstein was considered brilliant but was not often described as wise—although he might well have been. The puppet thinks so.

and extraordinary social sensitivity and interpersonal skill" (p. 123).

Wisdom is not a highly obvious and easily measured human characteristic, which might account for its relative absence in psychological literature. Peck (1968), in his elaboration of Erikson's theory, is one of the few developmental theorists to mention wisdom specifically as an age-related characteristic. According to Peck, as physical strength and endurance decline, one of the important developmental tasks that faces the adult is that of valuing wisdom rather than physical powers. But what, precisely, is wisdom? How does it develop? And does it truly belong only to the old?

Some Philosophical Conceptions

Psychology suggests a few tentative answers for these questions, but in the main, biblical history and ancient philosophy deal most thoroughly with wisdom. Clayton and Birren (1980) present a review of some of the important literature. Among other things, they note that although wisdom is universally acknowledged as a quality most commonly found in

older persons, Eastern and Western beliefs concerning how it is most likely to be acquired differ somewhat.

In the West, there have been three paths to wisdom—all of which need to be followed if the individual is to be truly wise. The first is that of formal education, which has historically emphasized the ability to make intelligent judgments and thoroughly reasoned decisions. The second path involved listening to and learning from parents or other important and influential mentors. The third path to wisdom is that of faith—in some ways a far easier path than the first two: Some individuals are simply chosen to be wise. These people are given wisdom in the same way that others are given long noses or curly hair.

Eastern conceptions concerning paths to wisdom are somewhat different. In the main, these are tied to religion, but unlike the Western belief that having faith might be sufficient to be granted wisdom, most Asian religions require great sacrifice and dedication on the part of those who would be wise. These religions often prescribe specific behaviors and regimens, such as meditation or fasting, that must be followed by those who are disciples of wisdom. Most have in common the belief that wisdom (often referred to as *enlightenment*) requires long periods in the presence of a master teacher.

Both Western and Eastern conceptions of wisdom view it as a type of knowledge that leads to a greater understanding of reality (of life, its meaning and purpose, and so on). And if the descriptions of its development provided by East and West are accurate, it is unlikely that the young will be very wise. (See "Across Cultures: Shyam Narayam Tidori, Guru.")

Psychological Conceptions

Historical views of wisdom, notes Assmann (1994), range from a conception of wisdom as a problem-solving capacity applied to practical problems, to ill-defined notions of cosmic consciousness or religious salvation. Our implicit views of wisdom, perhaps closer to current psychological views, say four things about wisdom. Specifically, those who are wise

- know more than other people
- know things at a greater depth than others
- know things that other people can't understand
- know what is good for them and for others

Wisdom and Age

Clayton and Birren (1980) looked at how wisdom is seen by individuals of different ages and at whether it is typically associated with the elderly. They presented twenty-one-year-olds, forty-nine-year-olds, and seventy-year-olds with fifteen terms that might be considered to be related to wisdom (for example, *intuitive, pragmatic, understanding, gentle,* and *sense of humor*). These were presented in 105 pairs, and

Shyam Narayam Tidori, Guru

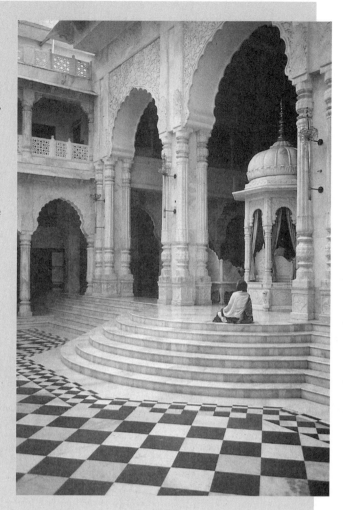

"When I met Shyam Narayam Tidori," writes Edward Rice (1972), "I felt for the first time in my life that I was in the presence of an ancient man. He is a guru, a spiritual guide" (p. 35).

"We are gurus," Shyam informs Rice, "that is priests and teachers, my father and his father and my brothers and I, as far back as anyone can remember." Why? Because they are Brahmins, the caste of priests, gurus by heredity. "We are the face of Brahman, the Absolute, the One Reality which is the Ground and Principle of all beings," says Shyam. He explains that his special devotion is to the Lord God Shiva, the benevolent God, an idol in the temple to which he goes morning and night. In the morning, he offers the Lord God Shiva leaves from the bel tree and pours water on the idol; in the evening, he places lighted lamps around its feet. It is part of *kharma*, part of the balance of good and evil. Life is an almost endless series of cycles of which there are more than 8 million. When a man dies, his soul simply goes into another womb. Which womb—fish, animal, bird—depends on whether his *kharma* is good or bad. And when the soul has accumulated enough good deeds, it then goes to heaven, a place that it will never want to leave. But without a guru, no man can ever hope to attain salvation, or *mukti*.

So spoke Shyam Narayam Tidori, guru. He was only seventeen.

To Think About

Even at age seventeen, Shyam Narayam Tidori already had disciples, young men he had initiated into the secrets of Hinduism, men into whose ear he had whispered the secret mantra, the sacred verse that they would never, in their entire lives, reveal to anyone else. In the Western world, we tend to think of wisdom as something achieved only by those who are intellectually gifted, who have studied much, who have lived a long time, and who convince others by their words and behaviors that they possess some rare qualities of judgment and decision making. Can a seventeen-year-old, like Shyam Narayam Tidori, be truly wise?

---

subjects were asked to judge how similar each pair was. (For example, are *wise* and *aged* highly similar? Are *experienced* and *knowledgeable* alike?) In general, this study revealed that most subjects tend to associate wisdom with age—although older subjects were not very likely to see themselves as being wise.[*]

Why might the old be wiser than the young? Perhaps, suggests Basseches (1984), because the old do not always apply the straightforward rules of logical, deductive thought to the solution of real-life problems. Instead, their thinking is *dialectic*. Their wisdom stems from the ability to recognize contradictions and to deal with them, from their understanding that knowledge is relative rather than absolute, that reality abounds with contradictions, and that the most effective kind of thinking is contextual—that is, it arises from the practical, real-life circumstances that surround contradictions.

Interestingly, these characteristics of dialectical thinking are very similar to Dittmann-Kohli and Baltes's (1986) description of what is involved in the ability to make wise decisions. Specifically, they suggest that wise decision making requires (1) some level of skill or expertise relevant to the problem at hand, (2) emphasis on the practical aspects of solutions, (3) a related emphasis on the problem's context, (4) a recognition of uncertainty, and (5) relativism in judgment and behavior. In other words, wisdom is a sort of marriage between knowledge and a pragmatic or practical intelligence. Dittmann-Kohli and Baltes suggest that as a result of the wisdom that older people acquire, they are better able to resolve complex interpersonal problems.

It is perhaps significant that, historically, positions of greatest responsibility requiring fundamentally important decisions are seldom entrusted to the young. With some notable exceptions, presidents, popes, emperors, and kings and queens have generally been older rather than younger. Lehman (1953) found that even in industry and commerce, the

---

[*]Said my grandmother, borrowing an old Lebanese proverb, "Better a mountain goat than a city philosopher!"

CONCEPT/ISSUE	EXPLANATIONS/COMMENTS
Western conceptions	There are three paths to wisdom: ■ formal education. ■ learning from parents and other influential mentors. ■ having faith.
Eastern conceptions	The path to wisdom is tied to religion and requires great and long sacrifice and dedication, and guidance by a master teacher.
What psychology says	Those who are wise: ■ know more than others. ■ know at greater depth than others. ■ know things others cannot understand. ■ know what is good for themselves and others. We think of the old as more wise than the young, partly because they've had more experience, partly because they think *dialectically,* trying to balance contradictions and practicalities and intuitions. Leadership is often reserved for the elderly.

peak age for leadership was above sixty-five. Perhaps even more significant, Dennis (1966) reports that maximum creative output in the fields of history and philosophy occurs in the sixties, seventies, and beyond. And there are countless examples of outstanding achievement in art, music, literature, and psychology by individuals well into old age. (See Summary Table 17.8.)

■THE IMPLICATIONS OF DECLINE

Although it might be somewhat distressing to contemplate the increasing probability of decline with age, most of us will in the end cope successfully and even happily with aging—should we be lucky enough to live that long. We are, after all, human, and part of being human is being resilient, remembering the good things and always having hope. There is little evidence that age robs us of any of these qualities.

There are other reasons, too, why the aged might cope successfully with whatever declines and losses they experience. To begin with, changes often occur so slowly that it is often possible to adapt to them without making any major adjustments. In addition, other people of the same age also experience similar changes, and that, presumably, makes life easier. Even more dramatic and perhaps more personal changes that might initially appear to be totally devastating

(knowledge of a serious health problem or death of a spouse, for example) can usually be adapted to. It is important to keep in mind that physical and cognitive decline is only one feature of the lives of the very old. Increasing wisdom and peaceful reflectiveness may be others. As the studies of life satisfaction that we review in the next chapter clearly show, happiness and joy can continue to come from many sources.

■FOCUS QUESTIONS: SUMMARY ANSWERS

1. What is ageism? How does it affect the elderly?

   ■ The elderly are often the object of *ageism* (negative prejudices that are based solely on age), evident in media portrayals, in expected behaviors, in health care, in discrimination, and in child-directed speech.

2. How are lifespan and life expectancy different? Can either be changed?

   ■ Life expectancies (but not lifespans) have increased nearly 50 percent since 1900. In the industrialized world, women can expect to live about eight years longer than men. Aging may be due to a combination of genetic factors (lifespan limits are programmed in cells), cell malfunctions (cell errors, toxins, free radicals, or cross-linked cells hamper normal cell functioning), or immune system defects. Longevity is related to sex, physical activity, nutrition, race, mobility, education, occupation, employment, locale, heredity, and other factors such as cultural expectations, attitudes toward aging, and lifestyle.

3. What are some of the most common physical changes in late adulthood?

   ■ *Senescence* describes biological decline as a function of age. Among nearly universal characteristics of aging are arteriosclerosis and increased susceptibility to cancer, arthritis, and acute brain syndrome. Visible physical changes of age include loss of skin elasticity and consequent wrinkling, loss of hair or hair pigmentation, loss of teeth or recession of gums, and loss of strength, stamina, and flexibility. The elderly are less susceptible to acute infections but more prone to chronic conditions (arthritis, hearing losses, heart disease, visual impairment, and arteriosclerosis) as well as to diseases like Alzheimer's (brain deterioration characterized by memory loss, disorientation, and eventual death) and Parkinson's (neurological disease marked by tremors and fatigue). The elderly become more farsighted *(presbyopia)*, may suffer hearing loss *(presbycusis)* and reduced taste and smell sensitivity, and may not react as quickly mentally or physically. Old age brings some decline in sexual interest and activity, but in most cases, sexual activity can continue well into old age.

4. What are some of the most common intellectual changes in late adulthood?

   ■ There are memory declines with age. Short-term memory is not dramatically altered by the passage of time, although its capacity may slowly diminish. Procedural memory (how to do things) and semantic (abstract knowledge) memory are quite resilient; episodic (autobiographical) memory, conscious actions (as opposed to automatic), nonmeaningful material, and timed tasks all suffer more. Decline is often *pathological* (due to illness or disease) rather than *normal* (a nearly universal result of aging). Longitudinal studies find general cognitive decline among the elderly, especially after seventy. Much of the decline is in fluid abilities (attention span, speeded abstract tasks); crystallized abilities (dependent on experience) fare much better. Just prior to dying, measured IQ sometimes drops *(terminal drop)*, perhaps because of health problems or *disengagement*. Older adults often do not do as well as younger individuals on tasks requiring abstract reasoning. Labouvie-Vief describes the thinking of older adults as more intuitive and more personal *(mythos)* rather than formal and logical *(logos)*.

STUDY TERMS

acute brain syndrome, 499

ageism, 488

Alzheimer's disease, 499

arteriosclerosis, 497

autoimmunity, 494

automatic responding, 505

cell error theory, 494

centenarians, 496

climacteric, 502

Clock Drawing Test, 500

cross-linking theory, 494

crystallized abilities, 505

declarative memory, 503

episodic memory, 503

fluid abilities, 505

free-radical theory, 494

free recall, 504

genetic theory of aging, 494

hydration, 499

life expectancy, 494

lifespans, 494

FURTHER READINGS

The following collection contains a number of articles that detail the physiological and biological changes of aging:

Schneider, E. L., & Rowe, J. W. (Eds.). (1996). *Handbook of the biology of aging.* New York: Academic Press.

The first of the following two books might be of interest to those concerned with the problems facing elderly women and adjustments sometimes required of them; the second book is a highly readable, sociological look at the status and roles of the elderly in contemporary North American societies:

Rosenthal, E. R. (Ed.). (1990). *Women, aging, and ageism.* New York: Harrington Park Press.

Powell, L. A., Branco, K. J., & Williamson, J. B. (1996). *The senior rights movement: Framing the policy debate in America.* New York: Twayne.

The following is a straightforward description of the physiological changes in sexual interest and functioning that occur among the elderly, and a candid look at their sexual lives. It is especially valuable for those who counsel the elderly:

Gibson, H. B. (1992). *The emotional and sexual lives of older people: A manual for professionals.* New York: Chapman and Hall.

Fillit and Butler's collection is a very succinct and readable but highly informative collection of articles dealing with cognitive decline:

Fillit, H. M., & Butler, R. N. (Eds.). (1997). *Cognitive decline: Strategies for prevention.* London, England: Greenwich Medical Media.

EIGHTEEN

Social Development: Late Adulthood

Old age is no such uncomfortable thing if one gives oneself up to it with a good grace, and don't drag it about "To midnight dances and the public show."

HORACE WALPOLE
Letter

here's two kinds of old folks," says my grandmother, as she hoists another sack of potatoes up onto her shoulder. "There's those who don't much like to sit still as long as they got the strength, God willing, and they'll keep doing their share and more." She trudges through the garden toward the house, her feet sinking into the sandy brown dirt, leaving indistinct prints between the rows. When she reaches the back of the house, she dumps the potatoes emphatically down the chute. ¶ "So what if they want to go dancing once in a while?" she asks, almost angry. It's me she's asking, but it's not me she wants an answer from, because I'm not the one who said anything. It's my mother who said, sort of as a joke I thought, "You're pretty old to go to dances, don't you think?" ¶ "The other kind," my grandmother continues just a little scornfully, shaking the dust out of the empty potato sack, "is like Old Man Boutin, who'd just as soon eat and sleep, and rock on the porch a little if the weather's warm and there's no mosquitos." She slings the empty sack over her shoulder and heads back out across the garden, toward where my mother's digging the big, red-skinned Norlands out of the ground. ¶ "Me," says my grandmother in a voice so there's no doubt everybody hears her, "my only rocking's gonna be on the freakin' dance floor." ¶

This Chapter

or many, old age is a time of withdrawal and rocking chairs; for others, "midnight dances and the public show" are more appealing, and digging potatoes is sort of fun just because you can, by gosh, still do it.

Is one preferable to the other? Does one imply more successful aging? These are two of the questions this chapter addresses. It also looks at the *life review,* the process of examining and evaluating the course of one's life and of coming to terms with the future. It examines, as well, the impact of retirement from work, the continued development of important relationships with others, and alternative living arrangements for the elderly. It concludes with a discussion of satisfaction and happiness.

DESCRIPTIONS OF DEVELOPMENT IN LATE ADULTHOOD

One of the alternatives to satisfaction and happiness is despair, the possibility of which looms ever larger with the progressive shortening of our spans.

Integrity Versus Despair: Erikson

The fundamental conflict between despair and a sense of integrity, a conviction that life has been useful and worthwhile, is the essence of Erikson's final stage of the life cycle: **integrity versus despair.** What the elderly need to do, says Erikson, is integrate the experiences of a lifetime, make sense of them, and achieve a feeling of acceptance and contentment. The alternative to a sense of integrity is despair. Feelings of integrity and satisfaction result from a positive evaluation of one's life and an acceptance of its final outcome as natural and inevitable, note Botella and Feixas (1992/1993); in contrast, despair is characterized by regret over the past, by the frustration that accompanies the realization that it is now too late to do anything further, and by fear of aging. As we saw, fear of aging, which can be tapped by various scales (see Lasher & Faulkender, 1993), is not uncommon even among young adults.

■ INTEGRITY STATUS

In the same way as progression through the identity crisis of adolescence can be described in terms of the balance between crisis and commitment, so too can progression through this final developmental stage. Thus, there are those who have achieved a sense of worthwhileness, of purpose and identity **(integrity achieving)**; others find themselves in a state of crisis, struggling against despair, uncertain and ambivalent about the meaningfulness of their lives **(dissonant)**; some carefully avoid a crisis, closing their minds to an examina-

tion of the possibility that their lives might have meant less than they should **(integrity foreclosed)**; and others have struggled to achieve integrity but have failed and given up, and are now sad and depressed **(despairing)**. Walasky, Whitbourne, and Nehrke (1983/1984) developed an interview assessment (the *Ego Integrity Status Interview*) that appears to identify these developmental stages among the elderly. In their study of forty elderly adults, they found, not surprisingly, that the least happy were the *despairing* and the *dissonant.* Both the *integrity achieving* and the *integrity foreclosed* groups were marked by a high degree of satisfaction.

Erikson, still active when more than eighty years old, spoke of two new insights regarding the upper end of the lifespan. The first is his realization that the elderly are far more creative, far more *generative,* than he had thought; the second is the recognition that increased life expectancy may require a reexamination of the entire lifespan, but especially of the upper end of the lifespan (Erikson, Erikson, & Kivnick, 1986).

Peck's Elaboration of Erikson

As we saw in Chapter 16, Peck (1968) believed that Erikson's description of psychosocial conflicts in adulthood did not do justice to the variety of important events that can occur during this period. Accordingly, he describes three stages that span late adulthood. He believes that successful resolution of the conflicts that characterize each is important for adjustment and happiness in old age.

■ EGO DIFFERENTIATION VERSUS WORK-ROLE PREOCCUPATION

According to our current models, development does not end with middle age but continues well into old age. With retirement, for example, it often becomes necessary to develop new interests—to shift one's preoccupations from work and career to other aspects of living. The identity and self-definition, as well as the sense of importance and of being worthwhile that are often one of the rewards of work, must now be abandoned. But they need to be replaced if the individual is to maintain a sense of integrity and worth.

■ BODY TRANSCENDENCE VERSUS BODY PREOCCUPATION

One of the prices we sometimes pay for our longer lives is a longer period during which we suffer aches, pains, and disabilities of greater or lesser severity. As these become more evident, there is a tendency to become preoccupied with affairs of the body. Resolution of the resulting psychosocial conflict requires that the individual's preoccupations transcend the flesh.

■ EGO TRANSCENDENCE VERSUS EGO PREOCCUPATION

In the same way as the aging individual must transcend preoccupation with bodily aches and pains, so there is a need to transcend a preoccupation with the inevitability of death. Those who fear death unduly must also fear life, for one is surely the price we pay for the other.

Fisher's Five Periods of Older Adulthood

To obtain greater insights into the experience of older adulthood, Fisher (1993) conducted detailed interviews with seventy-four people aged sixty or more. Analysis of information from these interviews suggests it might be useful to describe the upper lifespan in terms of five distinct periods.

1. CONTINUITY WITH MIDDLE AGE

For many of Fisher's interviewees, old age and retirement don't bring very sudden or dramatic changes in attitudes, but are marked, instead, by a continuation of many of the preoccupations and behaviors of middle age. This continuity, notes Fisher, may be apparent in that leisure activities (traveling, playing golf, fishing) are now substituted for work activities, and everything else carries on much as it was. It may also be apparent in that the material problems (saving for a trip, buying a new car, paying the rent) and other preoccupations of life continue relatively unchanged for a period of time.

2. EARLY TRANSITION

Often, however, some major event, either voluntary or involuntary, eventually precipitates a transition. Most common among Fisher's interviewees were things like the death of a spouse, an important change in health, or the need to relocate. As an example, for many people, moving from a house to an apartment following retirement is the first step in a major early transition. Early transitions mark a definite break with middle age, notes Fisher, and are often accompanied by a sense of loss and sadness.

3. REVISED LIFESTYLE

The early transitions of the second period require major readjustments and often result in a revision of the person's lifestyle. If, for example, transitions in the second period were precipitated by the death of a spouse with whom the person previously traveled, traveling might now involve organized tours with like-aged people. If the transition were precipitated by ill health, there might be important changes in the person's leisure activities.

For many, adaptations during this period are highly positive; for others, they are less so. The result is typically a relatively stable lifestyle, sometimes marked by highly predictable, effective, and satisfying routines.

4. LATER TRANSITION

In Fisher's sample of seventy-four elderly individuals, later transitions of old age are tied mainly to health losses, often accompanied by loss of mobility and sometimes loss of some independence as well. Understandably, few individuals expect the precipitating event and deliberately prepare for it. That is, the elderly who are financially independent typically don't move into retirement communities or into children's or other relatives' homes until illness and the inability to live independently force them to.

5. FINAL PERIOD

With the fourth period's loss of health, independence, or mobility, and the increased need for assistance, there is a need for new adjustments and a need to develop new goals and activities consistent with the individual's capabilities and interests. With these adjustments, there is a new period of stability. And for many in Fisher's sample, this is a time of new challenges, new interests, and new growth. It is also a time during which the inevitability of death and decline forces a recognition of mortality and leads to a new sense of resignation and acceptance.

Although these five periods, which are summarized in Table 18.1, are sequential, they are clearly tied to major life events rather than to age. Thus, those who continue to be healthy, independent, and active into their eighties and nineties might retain a continuity with middle age far longer than others, and might never be forced to revise their lifestyles in the way that others who suffer serious health losses do. For some in Fisher's group, for example, continuity with middle age extended into the seventies; in contrast, others in their early seventies were already well into the final period. (See Summary Table 18.2.)

TABLE 18.1

Fisher's Five Periods of Older Adulthood

1. Continuity with middle age	Retirement plans pursued.
	Middle-age lifestyle continued.
	Other activities substituted for work.
2. Early transition	Involuntary transitional events.
	Voluntary transitional events.
	End of continuity with middle age.
3. Revised lifestyle	Adaptation to changes of early transition.
	Stable lifestyle appropriate to older adulthood.
	Socialization realized through age-group affiliations.
4. Later transition	Loss of health and mobility.
	Need for assistance and/or care.
	Loss of autonomy.
5. Final period	Adaptation to changes of later transition.
	Stable lifestyle appropriate to level of dependency.
	Sense of finitude, mortality.

Source: Based on Fisher (1993, p. 81).

Stages of Late Adulthood: Three Views

THEORIST	STAGES/DESCRIPTIONS
Erikson (single stage spans adulthood; requires new adjustments and competencies)	■ Integrity versus despair: Conflict between despair (linked with mortality, goals not accomplished, a sense of futility) and a sense of purpose and worthwhileness. Progress of the individual describable in terms of *identity achieving* (crisis resolved, integrity achieved), *dissonant* (in crisis), *foreclosed* (avoiding crisis), and *despairing* (unable to achieve integrity).
Peck (elaborates Erikson's final stage into three late-adulthood psychosocial stages, each marked by a major conflict and challenge)	■ Ego differentiation versus work-role preoccupation (shift from career to self). ■ Body transcendence versus body preoccupation (danger of overconcern with negative physical and mental changes). ■ Ego transcendence versus ego preoccupation (acceptance of mortality).
Fisher (changes determined largely by life events; hence don't occur for all individuals; occur very late for some, much earlier for others)	■ Continuity with middle age (substituting other things for work). ■ Early transition (voluntary and involuntary events mark discontinuity with preoccupations of middle age). ■ Revised lifestyle (different age-group affiliations and concerns). ■ Later transition (loss of health and changes in mobility force transition). ■ Final period (heightened dependence, sense of mortality).

The life review is common among the old. It takes the form of reminiscing about past experiences, evaluating earlier deeds and misdeeds, and resolving or simply accepting old conflicts. The life review is essentially a positive process associated more with a sense of psychological well-being than with despair, frustration, or regret.

One of the functions of these personal narratives, claims Cohler (1982), is to provide us with a sense of stability and consistency—a feeling of continuity that spans the course of our lives. In a sense, it is as though we tell ourselves stories of our lives, giving them beginning, middle, and end, providing them with an orderliness and predictability that real life usually lacks. Through these stories, we come to understand *our* selves in relation to *other* selves (Taylor, 1989).

But we do not simply construct the story of our lives, as though it were ours to invent. Instead, we recall important episodes; we reminisce about them; perhaps we review and evaluate them. These processes, according to a growing number of theorists, are extremely important at all stages of the lifespan, but especially in later adulthood, when the personal narrative often takes the form of a *life review*. An examination of life reviews can provide psychologists with important insights into the lives of the elderly, notes Sokolovsky (1996).

■THE LIFE REVIEW

Resolving the various psychosocial conflicts of old age that Erikson and Peck describe, or adjusting to the transitions of which Fisher speaks, requires less the development of new competencies or new social skills than changes in attitudes. And one of the most important tools in bringing about these changes is what Butler (1963) labels a **life review.**

Personal Narratives

"We tell ourselves stories in order to live," Didion (1979, p. 11) informs us. These stories, called **personal narratives,** are stories about our own lives. They result from our attempts to weave the different events of our lives into a meaningful, sensible story. This story integrates past and present events, and includes a vision of the future. According to McAdams (1984), its principal character is the self and its main themes are love and power.

■ PERSONAL NARRATIVES OF THE ELDERLY

The personal narratives that the elderly construct often take the form of an ongoing review and evaluation of their lives. They involve more reminiscing and more nostalgia than might a story constructed by a younger person. And, not surprisingly, they may not reach as far into the future. When de Vries and Watt (1996) analyzed the personal narratives of younger and older adults, looking primarily at the nature of important life events in these narratives, they found, as expected, that the younger groups identified far more events that were still in the future. Interestingly, both the younger and the older groups tended to identify great clusters of important events as having occurred around adolescence and early adulthood. It seems that even after people live most of an entire lifespan, decisions such as those surrounding careers and marriage or other lifestyles remain the most important events of life.

There is an important difference between **reminiscence** and the life review. Reminiscence is a passive activity, a largely purposeless remembering of the past. The content of reminiscence consists of odd tidbits of nostalgic memories. Reminiscing might be pleasant and distracting, but is not highly purposeful or evaluative, unlike a life review. The old, we are told, are more prone to reminiscing than are the young (Berman, 1992/1993). The *life review*, in contrast, is more active, more dynamic. It, too, is based on the past and makes extensive use of reminiscing. But it goes one step further: Instead of requiring nothing more than simple recall and idle enjoyment of scattered memories, it demands a concerted attempt to analyze and evaluate past experiences. And one of its important features is that it brings to mind unresolved conflicts. A principal purpose of the life review is to resolve these conflicts or to arrive at some acceptance of them.

■ LIFE REVIEW THROUGH THE LIFESPAN

Life reviews can occur throughout the lifespan, note Van Ranst and Marcoen (1997). They are most likely to be triggered by specific crises and events in one's life—for example, the death of a spouse, the loss of employment, or a life-threatening illness. Accordingly, most major transitions in life (such as those described by Levinson and Sheehy) might trigger a life review. Reviewing the past, Webster and Young (1988) argue, provides the substance and the motivation for making changes in the present and ultimately exercising some control over the future.

In late adulthood, conducting a life review is a highly positive event, contrary to the notion that reminiscing and daydreaming by the old might be a sign of withdrawal and might be unhealthy. Haight (1991) reviewed ninety-seven studies of reminiscing published between 1960 and 1990. Of these, only seven reported that reminiscing might be associated with negative outcomes. Similarly, Fry (1991) found that reminiscing among the old is essentially a pleasant and positive activity associated more with a sense of psychological well-being than with negative feelings such as frustration, despair, regret, and loneliness.

With advancing age, the life review becomes more urgent and more universal—perhaps because of the person's need to achieve a sense of meaningfulness and integrity. This feeling of integrity, along with a concomitant conquering of despair, results from a positive evaluation of the past—as well as the future. However, this doesn't mean that all adults engage in a life-review process. Merriam (1993) studied centenarians, eighty-year-olds, and sixty-year-olds. Although the number of individuals who had engaged in a life review increased after age sixty, more than half claimed not to have done so. The sample of 289 is admittedly somewhat biased, however, in that all of these individuals had to be relatively independent (cognitively intact and community dwelling). To the extent that a life review is often precipitated by some important life change, individuals who have lost some degree of independence may be more likely to have conducted a life review (see Figure 18.1).

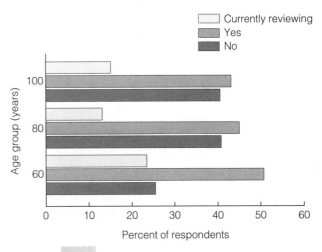

FIGURE 18.1

Percentage of 60-, 80-, and 100-year-olds who have conducted a life review. (Based on Merriam, 1993, p. 170.)

Satisfaction and the Life Review

It is worth emphasizing that the life review is not characteristically negative. For example, McAdams and associates (1997) looked at the life stories of forty highly generative (productive) adults. It is perhaps revealing that the **protagonists** in these stories were strikingly *positive* characters, endowed with important virtues and motives. These were protagonists with close family relationships, a clear personal ideology, sensitivity to the suffering and plights of others, and goals directed squarely at the betterment of society.

Nor does the fact that many older people engage in reminiscing and reviewing their lives mean that they are invariably turned inward and toward the past. In fact, many do not reminisce any more than younger adults, and many are remarkably future oriented. For example, among O'Brien and Conger's (1991) sample of senior athletes, 73 percent of the women and 80 percent of the men claimed that they were indeed very much looking forward to the future. The most common themes among the things to which they looked forward included continuing relationships with family and friends, and doing or seeing new things. Many of them had clear future goals. For men, these often included sports and competition, physical fitness, and traveling and adventuring. For women, hobbies, volunteer work, physical activity, and traveling were all part of future plans.

One of the important features of a life review is evaluation of the rightness of past behaviors, of moral and ethical issues, of the advisability of certain decisions in terms of their implications for the lives of others as well as for the self. Often, as Coleman (1986) notes, behaviors that might have seemed traumatic, immoral, or inadvisable in the context in which they occurred will, in the present context, seem trivial. Thus, the life review gives the older person an opportunity to re-evaluate incidents that might have been a source of guilt and unhappiness; the result might be the elimination of guilt and

CONCEPTS	DEFINITIONS/EXPLANATIONS
Personal narrative	■ Stories we tell ourselves of our lives, with us as the protagonists, giving our lives meaning and continuity.
Reminiscence	■ A largely passive activity; a remembering of past events and experiences; typically not purposeful or evaluative.
Life review	■ An active, purposeful process by which we evaluate our lives; includes elements of the personal narrative and of reminiscing.
	■ Can occur at any stage of life; often precipitated by a crisis, a major change in personal circumstances.
	■ Becomes less future oriented among the elderly; also becomes more urgent and more universal.
	■ Important for resolving crises, for dealing with past issues, for alleviating guilt, and for achieving a sense of integrity, of worthwhileness, and perhaps of satisfaction and happiness.

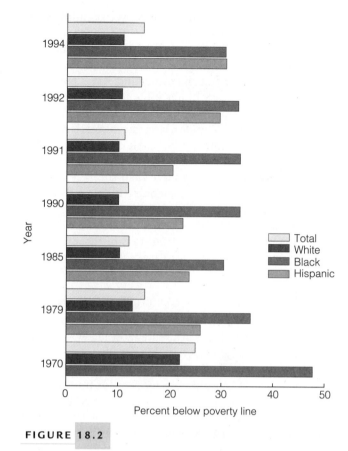

FIGURE 18.2

Percentage of people below the poverty line in the United States. (Based on U.S. Bureau of the Census, 1996, p. 472.)

the restoration of a measure of happiness. And contrary to what we might think, there is little about their past lives that most older adults would change. When DeGenova (1992) asked 122 retired persons what they would do differently if they had their lives to lead over again, the one area in which the largest number of people would have made changes was in education. Men would have spent more time pursuing education, often for career reasons, and women would have spent more time improving their intellects, often for personal reasons. On the whole, however, most of the elderly are happy with their choices—although not all retire gladly from work. (See Summary Table 18.3.)

RETIREMENT AND DISENGAGEMENT

Retirement is a twentieth-century phenomenon, a luxury made possible by a rapidly increasing standard of living, extraordinarily high productivity, and a relatively large surplus of labor. It was not always this way. Before this century, **retirement**, most often defined in terms of leaving full-time work and receiving a pension, was almost unknown. Although people might have stopped working when they were too old or not well enough to continue, there were no pensions (Ransom, Sutch, & Williamson, 1993). Significantly, the number of people below poverty level in the United States is now about half of what it was in 1970 (14.5 percent in 1994; 24.6 percent in 1970) (U.S. Bureau of the Census, 1996; Fig-

ure 18.2). In the United States, however, poverty levels are especially high among elderly blacks and Hispanics.

Our prevailing attitude now is that retirement is everybody's right—that it is not a luxury that should be available only to the select few, but that it is society's duty to look after all who have worked long enough. We earn our pensions and, by gar, we deserve them!

Changing Demographics and Employment Patterns

The next century might bring changes again. For example, there are current signs of changing employment patterns where redundancy or economics force "early" retirement (Coleman, 1992). On the other hand, dramatically declining birthrates, coupled with the fact that the population bulge associated with the last of the big baby booms is rapidly approaching retirement age, mean that ultimately there will be fewer workers and far more retirees—hence fewer people to produce the goods and pay the taxes that maintain complex Western societies. Eventually the shrinking work force will no longer be sufficient to look after both the old and retired as well as the young and not yet employed. Increasingly, argues Canaff (1997), people won't retire at sixty-five;

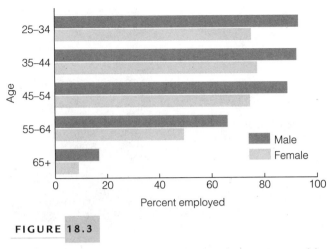

FIGURE 18.3

Participation rates, U.S. labor force, 1995. (Based on U.S. Bureau of the Census, 1996, p. 393.)

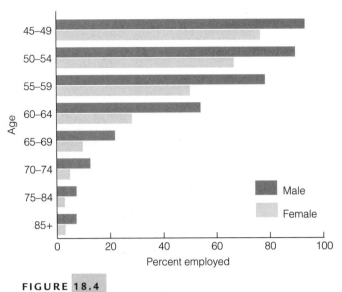

FIGURE 18.4

Participation rates, Canadian work force, 1991. (Based on Elliot, Hunt, & Hutchison, 1996, p. 94.)

if they do, they may be urged back into the work force later. Even now, a significant number of American and Canadian seniors continue to work well beyond age sixty-five (Figures 18.3 and 18.4).

There is a third crucial factor that may bring our dream of the easy and well-fed retirement to its knees: **inflation.** Consider, for example, that if the annual inflation rate were 12 percent, the purchasing power of an unindexed pension would be reduced by approximately 90 percent in a mere twenty years. At lower inflation rates, it simply takes longer. And when pensions are indexed (adjusted yearly according to increases in the cost of living), the amount of money required to maintain them simply increases at the same rate as the purchasing power would otherwise have decreased. The effects of inflation on retired individuals are compounded by the fact that, at retirement, average income drops significantly.

Attitudes Toward Retirement

Atchley's (1989) investigations of retirement suggest that people generally have positive attitudes toward retiring, particularly if they have looked forward to it, have planned it, and expect to have adequate income. Apparently, the higher the person's expected retirement income, the more likely it is that retirement will be viewed positively. Similarly, people with higher levels of education often look forward to retiring. Negative attitudes toward retirement are most common among those who are forced to retire but who would prefer to continue working (Laczko, 1989).

Attitude toward retirement is an important predictor of later satisfaction; so is social support. Robbins, Lee, and Han (1994) report that those whose social networks are most supportive of retirement are more likely to experience high quality of leisure time and more life satisfaction. Nevertheless, as many as one-third of all retirees experience some difficulty in making the postwork transition (Jensen-Scott, 1993). In an

in-depth study of seventeen new retirees, Theriault (1994) found that retirement led to significant increases in measures of anxiety.

In spite of this, and contrary to earlier findings and speculation, the overall effect of retirement on happiness and health is positive. Kelly and Westcott's (1991) case studies of twenty-five recent retirees found the vast majority of these "ordinary" retirees to be happy in their retirement. "On the whole," they write, "retirement is now going as well or better than expected" (p. 84). Retirees especially enjoy their sense of freedom and the time to do what they want.

Atchley (1989) found that retirement is most likely to be a positive experience under four sets of circumstances: (1) retirement is voluntary rather than forced, (2) work is not the only or even the most important thing for the individual, (3) both health and income are adequate to permit the enjoyment of increased leisure, and (4) the retirement has been prepared for and planned.

Phases of Retirement

Atchley (1982, 1985) describes retirement in terms of seven sequential phases, several of which appear to be optional— that is, experienced by some but not all retirees (see Table 18.4). Although these phases are sequential, they cannot, of course, be tied to chronological ages, not only because retirement occurs at different ages for different individuals but also because some will spend more time than others in a given phase. What Atchley's seven phases represent, in effect, are the various processes involved in taking on the role of the retired person, carrying it out, and eventually giving it up. They emphasize strongly that retirement is a process rather than a final state.

TABLE 18.4

*Atchley's Phases of Retirement**

PHASE	MY COUSIN LUKE'S RESPONSE
Preretirement	"It's gonna be great living out there on the coast, fishing, visiting the kids, playing. . . ."
Honeymoon	"Let's go, Elizabeth! We never had time to see much, and now we're gonna cruise right around the old ball. Just got to get me my check cashed. Love it!"
Rest and relaxation	"No meetings for me, no canvassing, no causes. Nosiree, Elizabeth, I'm bloody retired, and I'm gonna put my feet up there next to yours."
Disenchantment	"Sure I think your camp cooking is as good as your mother's was, Elizabeth. But the fishing isn't what it used to be."
Reorientation	"Hey, they've got an opening for a night watchman out there at the underwear factory."
Routine	"What's today? Monday? We always get our groceries on Monday."
Termination	"Enough of this being retired and independent guff, Lizzie. Let's go terrorize our kids."

*These are not always sequential, nor are they universal. Only a small number go through the disenchantment and reorientation phases. Many go directly from the honeymoon to the retirement routine.

A time of intense and joyful activity may occur during the honeymoon stage immediately following retirement. This is when the new retiree finds time and energy to do all those things that couldn't be done before.

PRERETIREMENT

Prior to retirement, the individual begins to consider its occurrence and to prepare for it. As the time of retirement approaches, more time and energy are devoted to elaborating sequences of fantasies about what life will be like after work. People who worry about retirement at this stage are usually concerned more with health and income than with the prospect of abandoning work.

It has become increasingly important for people to prepare for retirement, both economically and psychologically, notes Canaff (1997). It is, after all, a very major life event to which not all individuals will adjust equally well. In Fox's (1997) investigation of retirees, financial status was one of the most important predictors of satisfaction with life. Also important was the extent to which the retiree had a network of close social relationships, and the extent to which the retiree had developed interests that could no longer be pursued. Not surprisingly, poor health is one of the most powerful predictors of dissatisfaction.

HONEYMOON

For the first period following retirement, many individuals go through a time of intense and usually joyful activity. As Long (1989) notes, retirement is not just the end of paid employment and a time to grow old; rather, it is a time for new leisure pursuits. This is the time when retirees do all those things they never had time to do. Many go through this period with newfound vigor and zest. But like most honey-

moons, this one seldom lasts forever. Money, time, energy—all may eventually run out. In addition, as Gibson (1992) points out, married couples often experience new problems following retirement. Some of these may relate to the new roles that each might have to develop with respect to home-related tasks, increased contact, and perhaps uncertainty about how to deal with each other during this transitional period.

REST AND RELAXATION

When the honeymoon is over, it's time to settle down. Atchley (1982) observed that many people go through a period of low activity following retirement. This period is usually temporary and is often followed by a return to higher levels of activity. In this context, activity includes participation in religious and political organizations, community involvements, hobbies, volunteer work, recreational activities, and exercise. For the retirees studied by Kelly and Westcott (1991), family-related activities were highly common. The general picture, claim Kelly and Westcott, is one of continuity—doing the kinds of things that were done before retirement.

DISENCHANTMENT

Among the retirement phases not experienced by the majority of retirees, but still common enough to merit attention, is a period of disenchantment that sometimes follows the honeymoon and settling-down phases. Disenchantment is most common among those who fantasized most unrealistically about what retirement would be like and who were subsequently most disappointed. In addition, poor health and loss of a spouse are the most common causes of dissatisfaction in retirement among those who have adequate income (Richardson & Kilty, 1991).

REORIENTATION

When disenchantment occurs, its resolution generally requires a phase of reorientation, during which the person reexamines life, explores available options, and begins to develop new commitments. Some individuals reorient themselves by going back to work, when that is possible. Others embark on entirely new careers. Eisler (1984) argues that new careers (or the resumption of old ones) for the retired and elderly are important for maintaining their independence and sense of worth. He cautions that we have largely ignored careers in old age because of the tendency to view all people over the age of sixty-five as retired and no longer involved in careers. In fact, however, in many cases retirement is an artifact of the places we work. Self-employed individuals, although they may not be rewarded with gold watches and pensions at the age of sixty or sixty-five, might well continue to work with much of the same commitment and dedication, and perhaps more wisdom and grace, than they did when younger.

ROUTINE

Routines involve predictable, orderly ways of doing things. Many older adults seem to develop an increasing need for routines; many also come to dislike disruptions of routine (Reich & Zautra, 1991). Accordingly, one of the eventual characteristics of most happy retirements is the establishment of routines. This does not mean that the retired life does not allow for change or for excitement, but it does indicate that retirement tends to be stable rather than unpredictable. Atchley (1985) reports that many individuals go directly to this phase from the honeymoon phase. For these individuals, there is no brief period of rest sandwiched between periods of higher activity, no disenchantment requiring reorientation. Instead, the transition from preretirement to the stable and generally satisfying routines of retirement is smooth.

TERMINATION

The retirement role, as described by Atchley, does not invariably continue through the remainder of the lifespan but is sometimes interrupted by illness and perhaps by eventual loss of independence. In these cases, the individual takes on different, more dependent roles (those of the sick or disabled, for example).

These phases should be viewed as broad descriptions of very general patterns through retirement. They provide a useful way of looking at retirement as an active and ongoing process that requires a series of new adjustments and that, like all adjustments, can have happy or less happy outcomes.

Engagement or Disengagement

Day (1991) summarizes a large number of studies that have looked at human aging and that have tried to define what is meant by "successful" aging. She identifies three different groups of variables that these studies have looked at: developmental (such as those described by Erikson, like wisdom and generativity), psychological (like optimism and satisfaction), and environmental (like longevity and continued independence).

In its simplest sense, to age successfully is to age in relative contentment and happiness. That must surely be an almost universal goal. And to age unsuccessfully might be to age in misery and despair—and perhaps alone and in poverty as well. As our sensationalist media often remind us, some of the elderly struggle desperately for survival on meager incomes. And a few do eat foods that the more affluent feed their pets, and do sometimes freeze in unheated dwellings. But that is only a minority, you say. Perhaps. But it is not so small a minority—almost 12 percent of all those aged sixty-five or more, about one-quarter of the elderly who are black or Hispanic, are poor (Figure 18.5). That this minority even exists is a sad reflection on our humanity.

Attempts to understand and explain the lives and the activities of those who appear to age successfully have led to two somewhat different points of view concerning the most likely course for the aged: **disengagement theory** and **activity theory**.

DISENGAGEMENT THEORY

Disengagement theory is based on the notion that as people age, they progressively *disengage,* withdrawing from social, physical, and emotional interaction with the world. And while this process is largely voluntary, it is also two-sided. Not only does the aging person gradually give up active social roles and narrow the sphere of emotional commitment, but society begins to withdraw its engagement with the aging person. This happens in several ways, the most obvious relating to the ways in which society often encourages—or even legislates—retirement from work and sometimes from other commitments as well.

One of the basic premises of disengagement theory is that withdrawal is not only natural but desirable. The predominant argument is that with declining physical and mental powers, the elderly find it increasingly difficult to continue to

FIGURE 18.5

Percent of people over age 64 below the poverty level, by race, 1970 to 1994. (Based on U.S. Bureau of the Census, 1996, p. 473.)

Some of the elderly disengage from social, emotional, and political involvement. Others, like this Delaware grandmother who still cares to tell of the magic of the symbols, remain actively engaged—and perhaps happier.

engage successfully in work-related activities, as well as in social, emotional, or political involvements. Consequently, they look forward to withdrawing and experience greater satisfaction and happiness if they are permitted to do so. Disengagement, notes G. F. Manning (1993), is one of the ways in which the elderly learn to cope with age-related loss.

Much of the research that has looked at disengagement theory has found that disengagement is often an accurate description of what happens in old age. However, disengagement is not often descriptive of the entire period of old age, but usually of the later years (Fry, 1992). And it often involves less disengagement than strict interpretation of the theory might indicate. That is, although most individuals will have withdrawn from work and from many other involvements by the time they are seventy-five or eighty, few will have completely withdrawn from important emotional commitments. Many will continue to fulfill crucial social roles as wives and husbands; some will be actively engaged in productive activities, such as looking after grandchildren or raising geraniums and chickens and growing potatoes; and many will be active in religious, political, and community organizations. We should note, too, that societies that do not have marked discontinuities between adulthood and old age do not require or encourage disengagement.

ACTIVITY THEORY

In fact, these societies encourage continued involvement and activity in all areas; as such, they exemplify *activity theory,* which is, in some important ways, the opposite of disengagement theory. Although it recognizes that a great deal of social and psychological disengagement does occur among older people, activity theory stresses that life satisfaction is highly dependent upon continued active involvement. According to this theory, those who age "best" are those who maintain the highest level of social, emotional, and physical involvement.

Among the variety of studies that have attempted to evaluate these opposing points of view, the majority indicate that continued involvement is often associated with satisfaction in later life. Stevens (1993), for example, questioned 108 older adults and found that continued involvement with the family and with significant others, as well as involvement in the community, produced a sense of usefulness that was highly correlated with satisfaction in later life. Similarly, Myers (1993) reports that the social breakdown and negative adjustment of many older people, especially in institutions, can often be halted and perhaps reversed by *empowering* the elderly—that is, by giving them control over their own lives, by keeping them physically and psychologically well, and by changing attitudes of caregivers who tend to view them as helpless and powerless.

A CONCLUSION

The research seems pretty clear that activity and engagement are positive for most of the elderly. For example, Patterson (1996) found that among a group of elderly widows and widowers, those who continued to be most involved in leisure and in social activities expressed the highest degree of satisfaction with their lives. And in one nursing home for veterans, even the oldest of the residents (up to age ninety-seven at the time of the study) continued to want to feel needed and worthwhile (Ghusn et al., 1996).

It's also clear that some degree of disengagement is usually characteristic of aging. But it isn't as though the elderly must make a choice between full disengagement or full activity. As Fry (1992) points out, disengagement occurs at various levels. Thus, some may disengage socially as a means of finding time for contemplation and personal growth. Others may also turn inward to contemplate and review their lives, but without disengaging the least bit socially. And, of course, the vast majority will eventually disengage economically, but not

TABLE 18.6

Havighurst's Developmental Tasks in Old Age

1. Adjusting to physical changes.
2. Adjusting to retirement and to changes in income.
3. Establishing satisfactory living arrangements.
4. Learning to live with spouse in retirement.
5. Adjusting to death of spouse.
6. Forming affiliations with aging peers.
7. Adopting flexible social roles.

- There has been a recent trend toward earlier retirement; however, demographic trends suggest that in industrialized countries, there will be a progressively shrinking work force looking after increasing numbers of elderly people; there may eventually be an opposite trend toward later retirement.

- Preretirement attitudes are an important predictor of adjustment to retirement; adequate income and, especially, good health are powerful predictors of satisfaction in later life.

- Phases of retirement *might* include *preretirement* (anticipation); *honeymoon* (period of high energy and activity); *rest and relaxation* (temporary period of quiet following hectic days of honeymoon); *disenchantment* (occasional unhappiness and disappointment with current roles); *reorientation* (reappraisal of roles and readjustment); *routine* (establishment of satisfying patterns); *termination* (new roles brought about by changes in life circumstances).

- Aging is often characterized by varying degrees of disengagement from social, physical, and emotional roles *(disengagement theory)*; research suggests that continued high involvement is positively related with happiness and adjustment *(activity theory)*.

necessarily socially, or in terms of their interest in and concern about the larger community.

There are some, like my grandmother, who crave involvement, responsibility, and activity; there are others, like Old Man Boutin, who prefer the contentment of solitary rocking chairs. (See Summary Table 18.5.)

▌SOCIAL RELATIONSHIPS IN LATE ADULTHOOD

It is important to stress once more that the age span with which we deal in this chapter stretches across many years and is marked by tremendous variation in abilities, interests, activities, and family relationships. Any generalizations that we might make must always be tempered by the awareness that the average older adult, to whom our generalizations are meant to apply, is probably even scarcer than the average child. The life circumstances of older adults vary tremendously from one individual to another. In addition, these circumstances often change, sometimes dramatically, from the beginning to the end of this possibly lengthy period. As a result, the combination of family relationships, living arrangements, financial strength, health, and involvement of an older person might be quite unique to that person.

Still, we cannot say very much about unique individuals in a text such as this; we can only speak generally. (See Table 18.6 for a general description of developmental tasks of late adulthood.)

Common sense and research both agree that, in general, family relationships are usually the most important of all so-

cial relationships throughout the entire lifespan; they continue to be tremendously important to the very end.

▌Relationships with Children

Following a survey of the literature, Phillipson (1997) reports that one of the clearest findings is that, other than their own marital relationship, the most important social relationships for the vast majority of these couples are with their children. Almost half of all elderly people who have children talk to them or see them at least once a week. And even in highly mobile, industrialized societies such as those in North America, the vast majority of children live within a half hour of their elderly parents. Still, about one-quarter of parents would like to live closer to their children and would like to see them more often (Elliot, Hunt, & Hutchison, 1996). Being closer would make visiting easier and perhaps more frequent. (See "At a Glance: Contact Between Elderly Parents and Their Children" and Figures 18.6 and 18.7.)

It is highly revealing, too, that whereas fewer than 5 percent of the very old live in institutions, far more live with their children. Gibson (1992), for example, reports a British study in which 3.7 percent of the elderly lived in institutions but a full 42 percent lived with their children. Another 40 percent lived less than a half hour away. Kelly and Westcott (1991) found that retirees plan much of their lives around trips to visit children and other family. For those with children, the immediate family is usually the center of their social world.

Manifestations of the complex of relationships that exist between older parents and their children include such things as the exchange of gifts, services (mowing lawns, doing tax returns), advice, and financial help. These, of course, do not always flow in only one direction, particularly if the parents are not yet very old. As Roberto and Stroes (1995) found, for example, grandmothers are sometimes an important source of child-rearing advice for mothers.

As parents age, relationships with their children also change. One of the outcomes of increased longevity is a larger population of very old people who suffer from a variety of

Contact Between Elderly Parents and Their Children

The most important relationships for most older people, other than those they might have with a spouse, are those with their children. In the United States and Canada, more than half of those age sixty-five or older live within a half hour of their children; almost half see or talk to their children every week. As they age, elderly parents tend to move *closer* to, rather than farther from, their children. In one British survey, 42 percent of older adults who had children lived with them.

FIGURE 18.6

A *Frequency of contact and* B *proximity between persons age 65 and older and their children, by age. (From U.S. Bureau of the Census, 1988, p. 36.)*

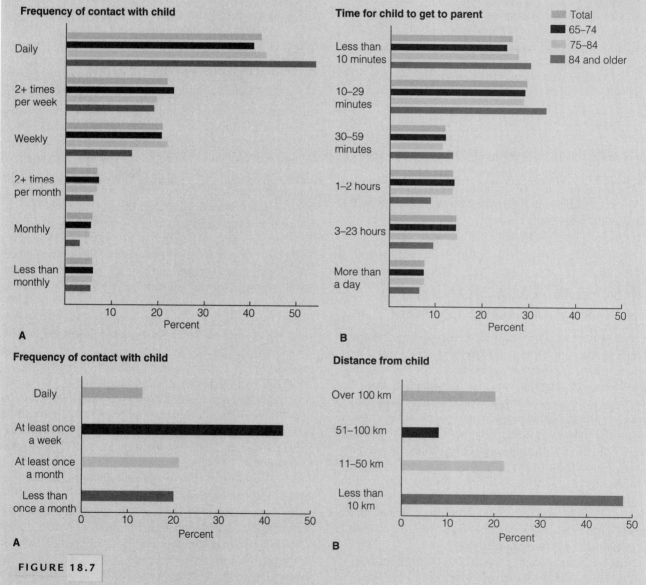

FIGURE 18.7

Frequency of contact between those in Canada aged 65+ and their children, and proximity of most often visited child. (From Elliot, Hunt, & Hutchison, 1996, pp. 34, 36.)

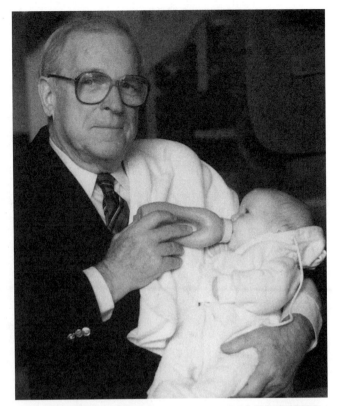

The most important relationships for the very old are those with their spouses and other partners—if they are still alive. Second are their relationships with their children and grandchildren.

The most common role of grandparents vis-à-vis their grandchildren is a formal role where there is no involvement in parenting but nevertheless emotional involvement; others, like the grandfather shown here, gladly accept the role of surrogate parent while the grandchild's parents work.

physical and mental disorders, and who require increasing care. When Silver (1993) analyzed the life reviews of twenty elderly women, she found that three themes recurred repeatedly in these personal narratives: one, dealing with loss and fear of dying, she labeled *mourning;* a second dealt with the *integrity* issues we discussed earlier (the conflict between despair and a sense that life has been worthwhile); the third dealt with "caring and being cared for."

As children are increasingly being called upon to provide assistance to their frail parents—what we spoke of in Chapter 16 as **role-reversal**—important adjustments are often called for, explains Silver (1993). For both parents and children, it is often a struggle to balance "caring for" and "being cared for." The burden of care, especially of aging mothers, most often falls on their daughters. In Malonebeach and Zarit's (1991) words, this is an undertaking that can be "expensive to the caregiver socially, psychologically, physically, and financially" (p. 103).

Relationships with Grandchildren

Clearly, however, only a small percentage of late adults are very old and in need of special care. In fact, late adults are often the ones who care for their grandchildren. For many children, their grandparents' home is a special and very safe place, almost like another home, and grandparents are a

source of love and support—a little like another set of parents. Some grandparents take their grandchildren in regularly, or go to their homes, so that their daughters or daughters-in-law can work. Strom and Strom (1995) report that under these circumstances, children respond to grandparents very much as they would to their parents. This is what Neugarten and Weinstein (1964) term the **surrogate-parent role,** one of five distinct styles of grandparenting. Others are the **fun-seeking grandparent role** (indulgent playmate), the **grandparent-as-distant-figure role** (benevolent but uninvolved), the **reservoir-of-family-wisdom role** (important, traditional source of advice), and the **formal grandparenting style** (interested, emotionally attached, but not directly involved).

The formal style appears to be the most common style of grandparenting in North America. It's an approach that pays strict attention to the widely accepted rule that grandparents should not interfere in the upbringing of their grandchildren, that they should be very careful not to offer advice or criticism. The formal grandparenting role permits buying presents on suitable occasions (birthdays and Christmas) and infrequent and irregular babysitting or holiday visits. It also permits the establishment of very warm, loving relationships between grandparents and grandchildren. But it does not permit the type of control, guidance, or decision making that parents are called upon to make. In this model, parents do all the parenting; grandparents do the

Grandparenting Styles

The roles of grandparents are not clearly defined in North American society and may take a variety of styles. These grandparenting styles are influenced by the grandparents' personalities, as well as by geography, health, finances, personalities of the grandchildren, and the ages of both grandchildren and grandparents. Per-haps the most important influence in determining the nature of grandparent-ing styles is the explicit or implicit wishes of the parents. Grandparenting roles are complex and dy-namic, and they change with circumstances.

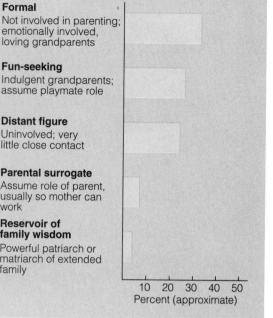

Formal
Not involved in parenting; emotionally involved, loving grandparents

Fun-seeking
Indulgent grandparents; assume playmate role

Distant figure
Uninvolved; very little close contact

Parental surrogate
Assume role of parent, usually so mother can work

Reservoir of family wisdom
Powerful patriarch or matriarch of extended family

10 20 30 40 50
Percent (approximate)

FIGURE 18.8

Styles of grandparenting as identified by Neugarten and Weinstein (1964).

grandparenting. (See "At a Glance: Grandparenting Styles" and Figure 18.8.)

Studies of the relationship between children and their grandparents typically reveal very close ties. For example, following a telephone survey of more than 200 randomly selected adult grandchildren, Hodgson (1995) reports that the vast majority of these grandchildren have frequent con-tact with their grandparents. In fact, 40 percent of them inter-act with their grandparents at least once a week, and only 1.5 percent claim to have no contact with them at all. Similarly, Langer (1995) found that most of the adult grandchildren in her study of 118 grandparents and their grandchildren felt they had very close relationships with their grandparents. Many felt what might be termed **grandfilial responsibility**—a sense that grandparents should rely on them if they were in need. For their part, many grandparents also felt very close to their grandchildren. And the majority thought they received more than they gave.

Relationships between elderly grandparents and their grandchildren can be both a source of happiness and a source of problems for grandparents. As Gibson (1992) points out, grandparents strongly attached to their grandchildren may experience distress at not being granted sufficient contact with them. This is especially true in situations in which par-ents divorce and custody of the children remains with the unrelated parent. Increasingly, however, various jurisdictions have begun to grant grandparents the right to petition the courts for legal access to their grandchildren following di-vorce or separation (Stewart, 1997).

Relationship with Spouse

One of the clearest predictors of satisfaction and happiness in old age is a life that includes a spouse or, in an increasing number of cases, cohabitation with an intimate friend. As we saw in Chapter 16, marital satisfaction begins to increase at around the empty nest phase; it apparently continues to do so into old age. When the elderly are asked whether they think their marital relationship is equitable and fair, the vast ma-jority say yes (Keith, Schafer, & Wacker, 1995). And when they are asked about their marital satisfaction, their happi-ness with their marriages, as many as 91 percent claim to be *happy, very happy,* or *extremely happy* (Lauer, Lauer, & Kerr, 1995). In a general way, the pattern of rising and falling mar-ital happiness, notes Cox (1988), conforms with a couple's opportunity for shared time—which is often curvilinear. Thus, spouses tend to spend a great deal of time doing things together early in the marriage, share less time alone with the advent of children and increasing work pressures, and again begin to share more activities as children leave home and one or both partners retire. Not surprisingly, a large num-ber of studies report that the relationship between marital happiness and length of marriage is best expressed as a U-shaped curve. Highest happiness scores are typically evident early and late in the marriage (Peterson, 1995).

This doesn't mean, of course, that there is never strife in the marriages of the elderly. In fact, as Qualls (1995) reports, even long-term, highly stable marriages may be subject to

One of the best predictors of happiness and satisfaction in old age is a life that includes a spouse or some other intimate cohabiting friend. Not surprisingly, as increasing numbers of the very old remain independent for longer periods of time, more are getting remarried at later ages, often following the death of a spouse.

major crises. Often these are precipitated by major life events such as departure of children, physical illness, and problems with older children. Ultimately, too, there is often the need for one of the spouses to adjust to the death of the other. Subsequently, there may also be a remarriage or the establishment of an intimate, cohabiting relationship. As we noted in Chapter 16, remarriages after the death of a spouse sometimes require difficult adjustments as well.

Sexual activity typically continues to be an important part of a couple's relationship through the older years (Gibson, 1992). Among elderly people who do not continue to engage in sex, the most important reason is simply lack of a partner, a situation that is far more common among women than men. Remarriage and cohabitation in old age have become more frequent in recent years, partly explaining the fact that fewer older persons now live with their children (Cox, 1988).

Relationships with Friends

Contrary to our popular stereotype of the elderly person as often lonely, most older people have one or more close friends and do not consider themselves very lonely. In one survey, 35 percent of males over sixty-five and 26 percent of females claimed to have more than ten friends. Still, in this survey, 18 percent of males and 14 percent of females had *no*

friends (Elliot, Hunt, & Hutchison, 1996). And the loneliest among the elderly, report Mullins, Elston, and Gutkowski (1996), are those with no children and no friends. In their study of more than 1,000 elderly people, they also found that those who thought themselves in poor health and those who considered their finances to be inadequate also reported more loneliness. Also highly important to the older adult's social relationships is degree of mobility. Not surprisingly, those who cannot easily get out to visit friends and family, and those confined largely to their rooms or to wheelchairs, are more lonely (Mollenkopf et al., 1997). Related to this, Potts (1997) found that having friends *outside* a retirement community is especially important for the well-being of those who live in retirement homes or in care facilities.

Friends satisfy many needs in late adulthood. In some ways, reports O'Connor (1995), relationships with friends may be more important for general life satisfaction than relationships with children. Most important is not so much the number of friends as the quality of the relationship. Close friendships might provide intimacy, an opportunity for shared leisure activity, or cognitive stimulation. They can be a source of excitement and joy. They can be important confidants and serve to help control and relieve the tensions and stresses of everyday life.

Although the elderly do not ordinarily make many new friends, relationships with existing friends become more rather than less important with the passage of time. Even among a sample of adults aged eighty-five or more, the majority continued to be in very close contact with their friends (Johnson & Troll, 1994). And when Flanagan (1982) asked seventy-year-olds to list things that most contributed to an "excellent" quality of life, friends, spouse, and children were almost always at the top of the list.

In an intergenerational study that looked at young adult women, their mothers, and their grandmothers, social support for all three groups came from friends as well as close family members (Levitt, Weber, & Guacci, 1993). Interestingly, however, the older generation tended to include more family members among their sources of social support than did the younger generation.

Friendships among the elderly are especially important for women, because they are far more likely than men to lose their spouses. Whereas about 80 percent of all men aged sixty-five or more are still married, only about half of the women are; above age seventy-four, almost three-quarters of men are still married, but only about one-quarter of women are (U.S. Bureau of the Census, 1996; Statistics Canada, 1996).

Widowhood

The much higher percentage of **widows** than **widowers** is due to the greater fragility of the male and a life expectancy that, at present, is about eight years shorter. As a result, by age sixty-five, there are already about 50 percent more women than men—and the ratio becomes increasingly unbalanced at higher age levels (U.S. Bureau of the Census, 1996). In

The Widowed Elderly

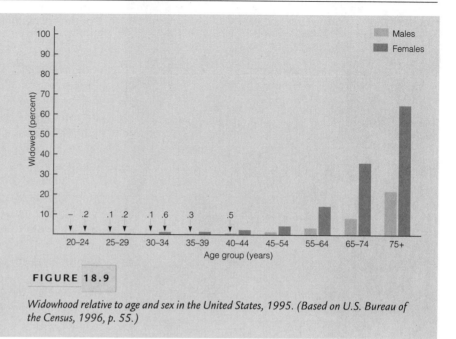

In 1995, 62.7 percent of the total male population were married, 2.5 percent were widowed, and 8 percent were divorced. Among females, 59.2 percent were married, 11.1 percent widowed, and 10.3 percent divorced. Given the longer life expectancies of women, the number of widows increases far more dramatically with age than does the number of widowers. In 1995, 21.6 percent of men over the age of seventy-five were widowed, while 64.9 percent of women in the same age bracket were widows.

FIGURE 18.9

Widowhood relative to age and sex in the United States, 1995. (Based on U.S. Bureau of the Census, 1996, p. 55.)

Barer's (1994) sample of 150 very old community-dwelling men and women (average ages 88.1 for the men, 89.2 for the women), more than half the men were still married and living with their spouse. In contrast, only 10 percent of the women were still married.

In 1995, there were 8.6 million widows above age sixty-four in the United States but only some 1.8 million widowers in the same age range. The chance of a woman being a widow, and therefore involuntarily single, at the age of sixty-five is almost one in two; by age eighty-five, it is more than three in four (U.S. Bureau of the Census, 1996). (See "At a Glance: The Widowed Elderly" and Figure 18.9.)

Society does not prepare us well for widowhood; we don't often speak openly of the possible deaths of those near to us. Some research indicates that the impact of the death of a spouse is more severe for younger than older survivors, perhaps because with age we are exposed to increasing numbers of people who are widowed—and perhaps also because as we grow older, we are more likely to confront the possibility, at least privately, and to begin to prepare for it (DiGiulio, 1992). Research indicates that the impact is, in fact, sufficiently severe that it may reduce the life expectancy of the surviving spouse, especially for men (Gibson, 1992). That being prepared for the death of a spouse is important is evident in the observation that increased risk of mortality is greater when the spouse dies suddenly than when the spouse dies after a long illness (Smith & Zick, 1996).

One of the relatively common outcomes of loss of a spouse is depression that is serious enough to require treatment and sometimes hospitalization. In a longitudinal study of widows (average age seventy-five), Bennett (1996) found significant changes in mental health and in morale following death of the spouse. However, in the majority of cases, the depression is of relatively short duration.

Even in the absence of serious depression, after the initial period of mourning that follows the death of a spouse, there are often periods of loneliness and sorrow that can sometimes last for a very long time. One of the problems often associated with widowhood, apart from the resulting grief and loneliness, is the need to redefine the self. This is especially true for widows whose identity has centered on being a wife. Resolution of the resulting conflicts often takes the form of investing more energy in work or in social organizations, or becoming more involved with friends and family (Pellman, 1992). For women who do not have many friends before widowhood and who are not involved in outside work, these transitions are often difficult.

Not surprisingly, studies of satisfaction and happiness often report less positive emotions among the widowed. But with the passage of time, many widows and widowers adjust quite happily to their new circumstances. And for some, remarriage is sometimes the solution (Owen, 1996). Unfortunately, given the far greater number of women than men who are widowed, the option of remarriage is not available to many women. In fact, among women aged sixty-five or more, there are more widowed than married women; in contrast, married men outnumber widowers by more than five to one. (See Figures 18.10 and 18.11.) (See Summary Table 18.7.)

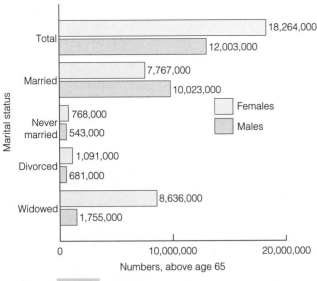

FIGURE 18.10

Marital status of the U.S. population age 65 or older, 1995. (Based on U.S. Bureau of the Census, 1996, p. 55.)

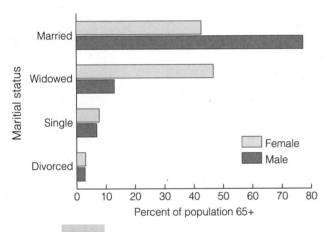

FIGURE 18.11

Marital status of the Canadian population age 65 and older, 1995. (Based on Elliot, Hunt, & Hutchison, 1996, p. 18.)

RELATIONSHIP	IMPORTANCE AND CHARACTERISTICS
With children	■ Extremely important; more than half of the elderly see or talk to their children at least every week; more than half live within 30 minutes of them. ■ With advancing age, there is often a reversal of caregiving roles, and sometimes some difficult adjustments between caring for and being cared for.
With grandchildren	■ Generally very warm, close, and reciprocal; feelings of grandfilial responsibility among some grandchildren. ■ Five common grandparenting roles: 1. Formal (most common; emotionally involved; no parenting involvement). 2. Fun-seeking (indulgent grandparents). 3. Distant figure (little involvement or contact). 4. Parental surrogate (assume parenting role, usually temporarily). 5. Reservoir of family wisdom (patriarchal or matriarchal roles).
With spouse	■ Relationship with spouse one of best predictors of satisfaction and happiness among the elderly; very high percentage report high happiness with marriage. ■ Possibility of strife precipitated by major life changes.
With friends	■ Most of the elderly have one or many friends; others are very lonely. ■ Important functions include those of confidant, of sharing leisure, of intimacy and stress release.
Widowhood	■ At age 65 or more, more women are widowed than married; about 5 times more men are married than are widowers. ■ Widowhood sometimes has negative consequences on physical and mental well-being, including a slightly higher risk of death.

CARE OF THE VERY OLD

One of the fears of many elderly married women, notes Gibson (1992), is that they will be left alone in their later years. The fear is not unfounded given the rate at which men die. In 1995, for example, there were about 5 million more women than men above age sixty-five in the United States. The picture is similar in Canada, where almost 80 percent of men above age sixty-five are still married, but fewer than half of women are (Figures 18.10 and 18.11).

Family Care

Most elderly adults in North America live in their homes and care for themselves. And, not surprisingly, older adults who continue to live independently and to care for themselves have higher self-esteem and a higher sense of satisfaction with life (Bunce & Harrison, 1991). Most are anxious not to become dependent (O'Bryant, 1991).

In shared households, the majority of which consist of husband and wife, it is not uncommon that one partner will

The majority of elderly adults in North America live in their own homes or apartments and care for themselves. A small percentage of the elderly live in special care facilities of various kinds. And some, like this grandmother, live with their children and grandchildren—a situation that has become rarer with the increasing mobility of the family and with governments and employers accepting more responsibility for financial and social assistance to the elderly.

assume most of the caregiving functions. Contrary to our popular stereotype, which holds that caregiving is undertaken almost exclusively by females, in about one quarter of all cases the caregivers are male—usually the husband, but sometimes a son or other relative. Arber and Gilbert (1989) note that female caregivers often assume their responsibilities as a result of a deliberate decision, perhaps motivated by social expectations (for example, a daughter looking after aging parents). In contrast, men usually come into the caregiving role by virtue of living arrangements rather than as a result of a deliberate decision (for example, a husband looking after an ailing wife, or an unmarried son who has not left the parental home gradually assuming a caregiving role). Other things being equal, there is a slightly greater tendency for children to care for the like-sexed parent (Lee et al., 1993).

In many cultures (such as the Chinese or Japanese), notions of **filial responsibility** (or filial piety) dictate that children will look after their parents in their old age (Yamamoto & Wallhagen, 1997). Even in Western cultures, there is a strong social expectation that offspring will make every effort to meet their parents' needs. And, in fact, that is generally what

occurs (Pruchno, Burant, & Peters, 1997). Specific manifestations of filial responsibility might take the form of shopping with (or for) parents, escorting them to various events, helping them with daily tasks, perhaps sharing living arrangements with them, and caring for them or making arrangements for their care when necessary.

Although adult children continue to provide primary support for aging parents, certain contemporary trends have made this more difficult and perhaps less likely in some cases. Pensions and other forms of social assistance for the elderly constitute one such trend; increasing urbanization and increasing family mobility are others. As governments and other institutions accept more responsibility for the financial well-being of the aged, children's financial responsibilities for their parents are increasingly becoming the exception rather than the rule. In addition, many families are so widely scattered that adult children are quite incapable of assuming day-to-day filial responsibilities. Moreover, even when geography is not a problem, many adult children are physically, emotionally, or economically unable to provide long-term care for their parents. This is especially true in families where both spouses work (Stephens, Franks, & Atienza, 1997).

Care Facilities for the Elderly

There is a hierarchy of support available for most of the elderly, note Hogan and Eggebeen (1995). First in line are spouses; next are children, siblings, other kin, and various nonkin, each of whom can help with different crises and problems. But when the elderly are no longer able to care for themselves and the burden of their care has become too overwhelming for their spouse, children, or friends, they may be cared for in one of a number of **care facilities for the elderly.** There are a number of such facilities, the most common being hospitals and nursing homes. In general, only the very old live permanently in these facilities. The majority are there because of physical or mental impairments. In spite of this, in many cases the institutionalized person feels abandoned and alone, and the family suffers from feelings of guilt.

There is some evidence of **"excess institutionalization"**— that is, individuals who are inappropriately given over to the permanent care of a facility. Large-scale surveys, based on the functional capabilities of the institutionalized elderly, suggest that this might occur in 10 to 18 percent of cases (Lawton, 1981). This is less likely to happen for individuals who have a spouse or children.

■ ELDER ABUSE

There is also some evidence of **elder abuse** in some care facilities. Abuse of the elderly, like child abuse, may be physical or emotional, and often involves *neglect* as well as overt actions (Shiferaw, Mittelmark, & Hofford, 1994). Godkin, Wolf, and Pillemer (1995) describe various forms of elder abuse: *physical,* including the inflicting of pain or injury, as well as sexual abuse; *psychological,* including producing mental anguish, perhaps by calling names, humiliating, or fright-

69-year-old great grandmother, too frightened to allow her real name to be used, is recovering in hospital following a violent mugging as she was walking home from a bus stop on Saturday night. Her assailant not only stole her purse, which contained only $30, but subsequently stabbed her twice in the abdomen. She was the second victim of violent attacks against elderly women in as many nights. On Friday night, a 75-year-old woman was beaten for $10. Police have not ruled out the possibility that the same attacker might have been involved in both cases. In response to the suggestion that the elderly should learn new ways of protecting themselves, an older spokeslady bristled that the elderly are fed up with trying to learn how to defend themselves against mean youngsters. "Educate the youth, the bullies who pick on the old who can't fight back," she retorted.

1. Bradley, K. (1997, Nov. 10). Punk stabs senior for $30. *Edmonton Sun,* News 3.

To Research

Using library resources, find data that might allow you to assess the extent of violence against the elderly and to determine whether or not it is increasing.

On the Net

For information about crime rates, the application of justice, and other topics related to violence, see the following Bureau of Justice page:

http://www.ojp.usdoj.gov/bjs/welcome.html

ening; and *material* (exploitation, taking advantage of, illegal use of funds and resources). In addition, he describes two kinds of *neglect* to which the elderly are sometimes subject: *active* (refusal to fulfill a caretaking obligation, with the conscious intention of inflicting harm or distress) and *passive* (refusal to fulfill a caretaking obligation without the conscious intention of causing harm or distress).

The extent of adult abuse isn't at all clear, partly because it often goes unreported. And when it is reported, it tends to be dealt with within the institution rather than by outside agencies (such as the police) who would be more likely to keep records (Hall, 1995). Adult abuse often reflects a form of ageism in which the very old are seen as helpless and burdensome. Pietrukowicz and Johnson (1991) suggest that mistreatment of the elderly in care facilities is often linked to the impersonal and largely negative view that caregivers might have of their elderly residents—a condition that is worse in commercial care facilities where resident-to-staff ratios are high. They report that something as simple as including a brief life biography in each resident's medical chart can contribute significantly to staffs' positive perceptions of the elderly in their care.

Other Alternatives

In recent years, the provision of alternatives to institutional care for the elderly has been emphasized. These alternatives include providing community-based assistance for the elderly in private homes. Such assistance might take the form of home visitations by personnel with expertise in the care of the old, or perhaps the delivery of hot meals on a regular basis. It might also include visits by community volunteers, who sometimes simply talk with the elderly but who might also assist them with chores such as shopping and might occasionally take them outside the home to various athletic and cultural events.

The variety of other alternatives to institutionalization includes the many housing projects that are designed specifically for the elderly. Some of these are government assisted; others are private. They include apartment- or motel-type projects as well as single-unit, detached dwellings. Some are designed to provide a wide range of services, including residential medical care, much as a nursing home might; others do little more than bring elderly people together, where they can live independently but in close community. One of the things that is especially important to the elderly, both in their own homes and in other alternatives, is security. (See "In the News and on the Net: Violence Against the Elderly.") Also important for many is access to nature (Talbot & Kaplan, 1991).

Numerous studies have been designed to assess whether communities designed specifically for the elderly are as satisfactory for them as simply living in a "normal" community, which is where more than 90 percent of those over age sixty-five live. These studies have typically presented a relatively positive picture in terms of the degree to which residents feel satisfied with their housing, with the social interaction available to them, and with their participation in various activities (Lawton, 1981). Among the advantages of retirement communities is that they increase the availability and proximity of peers, thereby providing opportunities for new friendships to develop. In addition, they tend to increase social participation and delay disengagement.

Although most of the elderly would prefer to remain independent, or to move in with relatives if they cannot remain independent, the need for other alternatives is increasing rapidly. This demand is occurring not only because the absolute number of elderly people is increasing dramatically, but also because of medical advances that now make it possible for individuals to live longer following the onset of a variety of chronic disorders. Many of these alternatives can perhaps fill the gap between independence and institutionalization and, in the process, make the lives of the very old far happier.

HAPPINESS IN OLD AGE

Early in this chapter, we looked at two theories of aging: *Disengagement* theory describes a process of gradual withdrawal from active involvement and a transition to the passive existence exemplified perhaps by the rocking chair; *activity* theory describes continued involvement in social, economic, political, religious, or other areas, and might be exemplified by the life of the older person who writes a personal narrative or who chases fish with a grandchild. And who will be happier? The old person in the solitary rocking chair or the one writing biographies or catching fish?

Either one might be happy, or both might be unhappy, suggests research. It may be a platitude, but it is no less true to say that it depends very much on the individual and on that person's dreams and accomplishments. Some people seek rocking chairs in old age because they are satisfied that they have done their life's work and they wish to rest; others want to remain active, and do so. And both might be very content.

But there are also those who find themselves in their rocking chairs not by choice but because age has put them there, and they now lack the abilities or the strength required to continue their activities. And there are those who remain active but who labor with a sense of frustration, not only because of the insufficient time they have left but also because they recognize the meaninglessness of their lives. Both of these might be unhappy.

Factors Linked to Happiness

At all stages of the life cycle, health is closely associated with happiness. It becomes an even more critical factor with the physical decline and increased susceptibility to disease of old age. Not surprisingly, health is often the single most important determinant of adjustment and happiness, or depression, in old age (Fox, 1997). (See "Across Cultures: Mrs. Smith and Mrs. Crawford.")

Income is also related to a sense of well-being in old age, perhaps partly because of the feeling of security that comes with having enough money and partly because those who are healthy and who have sufficient money are more easily

Happiness in very old age, psychology tells us, is linked with good health, income, educational level, emotional stability, and close friendships. And a good joke now and again doesn't hurt either.

Mrs. Smith and Mrs. Crawford

rs. Smith, age eighty-four, is a widow who lives alone in a rented set of rooms. She sleeps not in a bedroom, but on a davenport in the main room. With an income below $5,000 per year, she is one of America's poor—the one out of every ten people above age sixty-five who lives below the poverty level (for blacks and Hispanics, the proportion is closer to one in four; U.S. Bureau of the Census, 1996). Not only is she poor, but she is also abandoned, isolated, in poor health, depressed, and highly dependent on others for shopping, meals, laundry, housework, managing her finances, and so on. When asked what she does, she answered, "I don't do anything" (Day, 1991, p. 247). Her eyesight is too poor to allow her to do any of the things she likes. In the past year, she has visited no one, gone nowhere, and had no friends or relatives visit. Asked what she expects of the future, she replied, "I don't think I'll be here in a couple of years. I hope I am not" (p. 247).

Mrs. Crawford, age eighty-eight, is confined to a wheelchair and is entirely dependent on her husband for household chores and cooking, as well as for personal care. In spite of this, she is profoundly contented. Her kitchen is filled with her books and music, and

she banters lightheartedly and pleasantly with her husband. She is happy and optimistic about the future (Day, 1991).

To Think About

Both Mrs. Crawford and Mrs. Smith are very dependent on others for their care. But one is highly satisfied, and the other is defeated and unhappy. Their situations underline, once more, how poorly our generalizations apply to individuals identified only on the basis of age. One reason why Mrs. Crawford and Mrs. Smith have such different evaluations of their lives, explains Day (1991), relates to the social supports that Mrs. Crawford has and that Mrs. Smith lacks. Can you think of any other con-

textual reasons for contentment or discontentment in old age? Can you think of noncontextual reasons (for example, personality variables)?

---

able to remain actively involved (Kelly & Westcott, 1991; Fox, 1997).

Another factor that appears to be related to happiness is educational level (Dillard, Campbell, & Chisolm, 1984). Again, this may be related to the opportunities that education provides for continued involvement in interesting activities, such as reading or doing crossword puzzles, sometimes well beyond the time that physical strength, energy, or general well-being allows more physical involvements. It is noteworthy that in DeGenova's (1992) study, in response to the question "What would you do differently if...?" participants most regretted not having spent more time on education and intellectual self-improvement.

As we saw, relationships with spouse, children, siblings, and other relatives are also very closely related to happiness (O'Connor, 1995). So, too, are positive life events and the absence of negative life events. Stallings and associates (1997) found that life events such as divorces, death, health declines, and hospitalizations tended to have negative effects on measures of well-being. Effects were most pronounced when these events were unexpected.

There are several personality characteristics that also appear to contribute to happiness. Costa and McCrae (1984), in a longitudinal investigation of psychological well-being, identified three such characteristics: emotional stability, objectivity, and friendliness. Those high on measures of emotional stability are, by definition, less likely to suffer serious depression. Those who are characterized by objectivity rather than subjectivity are less concerned with internal states, perhaps less preoccupied with declining capacities, and, by the same token, more likely to be involved in external activities. And those high on friendliness are more likely to have more friends and to satisfy continuing needs for intimacy. The presence of close friends can be tremendously important in maintaining happiness, even in the face of serious and tragic events such as the death of a spouse or serious illness.

In conclusion, we cannot easily say that old age is a happier or a sadder time than any other in the lifespan. For some, it may indeed be happier, or at least as happy; for others, it might be much sadder. But whether it brings sorrow, joy, or simple resignation, it will also bring new roles and new problems, and it requires a whole new set of adjustments.

▲ SUMMARY TABLE 18.8

Care and Well-Being of the Elderly:
Summary Concepts

- The majority of those 65+ live at home; adult children frequently look after aging parents (role-reversal), sometimes in the parents' home, sometimes in their own home.

- The 5 percent or so who live in care facilities like nursing homes and hospitals are primarily the oldest-old and those with health problems.

- Increasing numbers of elder adults live in retirement communities.

- Happiness in old age is positively associated with good health; presence of a spouse; presence of children, grandchildren, and other social relationships; adequate finances; absence of unexpected negative life events; and personality characteristics such as extraversion (sociability) and emotional stability.

Perhaps none of these adjustments is more difficult or painful than the need to face the certainty of death. We look at this topic in Chapter 19. (See Summary Table 18.8.)

FOCUS QUESTIONS:
SUMMARY ANSWERS

1. What is a life review? How does it relate to the personal narrative and to reminiscing?

   ▪ Personal narratives are sensible stories of our lives that give them continuity and purpose. Reminiscing is a passive, purposeless recollection of memories. The life review is an active process by which we evaluate our lives using personal narratives and reminiscences. It is one means of resolving old conflicts and coming to terms with the finality of life.

2. Is successful, well-adjusted aging most likely to be associated with continued social, emotional, and community involvement following retirement? Or is it more likely to come to those who have disengaged?

   ▪ Retirement is a twentieth-century phenomenon made possible by a high standard of living, high worker productivity, and a surplus of labor. Atchley's seven phases of retirement are as follows: *preretirement* (fantasies about retirement), *honeymoon* (vigorous doing

of things not done before), *rest and relaxation* (a quiet period), *disenchantment* (a relatively rare period of disillusionment), *reorientation* (coming to terms with disenchantment), *routine* (establishing satisfying routines), and *termination* (withdrawal from the retirement role). Disengagement theory suggests that, with failing physical and mental capabilities, the elderly seek to withdraw from active social roles and that they should be allowed, perhaps encouraged, to do so. Activity theory argues that continued social, physical, and emotional involvement is important to physical and emotional well-being.

3. How important are family relationships? What are the roles of grandparents?

   ▪ Family relationships are ordinarily the most important of all social relationships throughout the entire lifespan—and other than that with a spouse, the most important are with children. Grandparents can play different roles: *surrogate parent* (caring for children), *fun-seeking* (indulgent playmate), *distant figure* (occasional gifts), *reservoir-of-family-wisdom* (patriarch or matriarch of extended family), and *formal* (nonintrusive but emotionally involved).

4. What factors are most closely linked with happiness in old age?

   ▪ Both disengagement and continued activity may be associated with happiness or unhappiness. Health, income, presence of a spouse or intimate friend, friendships, and personality variables appear to be important factors for happiness in late adulthood.

STUDY
TERMS

activity theory, 523

care facilities for the elderly, 532

despairing, 516

disengagement theory, 523

dissonant, 516

ego transcendence versus ego preoccupation, 516

elder abuse, 532

excess institutionalization, 532

filial responsibility, 532

formal grandparenting style, 527

fun-seeking grandparent role, 527

grandfilial responsibility, 528

grandparent-as-distant-figure role, 527

inflation, 521

integrity achieving, 516

integrity foreclosed, 516

integrity versus despair, 516

life review, 518

personal narratives, 518

protagonists, 519

reminiscence, 519

reservoir-of-family-wisdom role, 527

retirement, 520

FURTHER READINGS

The following is a highly readable collection of short research articles dealing with important social relationships in later life.

Hendricks, J. (Ed.). (1995). *The ties of later life*. Amityville, NY: Baywood.

In the following book, Gibson provides a clear and candid look at sexuality in the lives of older adults. The book also deals with family relationships, health, and social problems of aging:

Gibson, H. B. (1992). *The emotional and sexual lives of older people: A manual for professionals*. New York: Chapman and Hall.

Bengtson's collection looks at change and stability among the elderly in a wide range of areas:

Bengtson, V. L. (Ed.). (1996). *Adulthood and aging: Research on continuities and discontinuities*. New York: Springer.

The first of the following two books presents insights into the lives of widows; the second deals with a topic considered less often, *widowers:*

Owen, M. (1996). *A world of widows*. Atlantic Highlands, NJ: Zed.

Campbell, S., & Silverman, P. R. (1996). *Widower: When men are left alone*. Amityville, NY: Baywood.

PART NINE

The End

"People can't die, along the coast," said Mr. Peggotty, "except when the tide's pretty nigh out. They can't be born, unless it's pretty nigh in—not properly born, till flood. He's a going out with the tide."

CHARLES DICKENS
David Copperfield

book is a little like a life: It has a beginning, a middle, and an end. And sometimes it seems to have a willfulness, a vitality, that are reminiscent of life. ¶ But if it has life, then it must also have death. Because one is surely the price to be paid for the other. Much as we would like not to think so, they are two sides of the same coin, are they not? Is there ever one without the other? ¶ Sadly, the tide is nigh out for this book. There remains only one last chapter in this, the final section. ¶ Throughout this book, the coin of life has lain faceup on the table of our reason. Now, in this final chapter, we must pick it up, turn it, and look at the other side.

CHAPTER 19   Dying

FOCUS QUESTIONS

1. What do children understand of death? What do adolescents understand? And you?

2. What are some possible stages of dying?

3. What is euthanasia? Is it legal?

4. How inevitable is grief following bereavement? Is it important to grieve?

Dying

Do not go gentle into that good night,
Old age should burn and rave at close of day;
Rage, rage against the dying of the light.

DYLAN THOMAS
"Do Not Go Gentle"

Old man! 'Tis not so difficult to die.

LORD BYRON
Manfred

t's late summer and Mouche, Marc Voisin's dirty-yellow dog, has cornered a bear in the raspberries and foolishly insists on snarling at its heels. We watch from the other side of the fence, close enough to the barn that we can run for it if we have to. Finally annoyed, the bear turns suddenly and clouts Mouche up the side of the head. Then, as if bewildered by what he's done, or maybe simply no longer hungry for raspberries, he trundles off across the pasture and into the trees. The boss cow, the one we call Imelda, stares balefully at the bear as he waddles past.* ¶ We find Mouche lying there among the raspberry canes. "I think he's dead," Marc announces gravely. ¶ "How can you tell?" I ask. ¶ "My dad showed me," he answers. "Wait here." And off he runs, leaving me alone among the raspberry canes. I wait a long time, looking at Mouche but not quite daring to touch him; I'm not absolutely certain that death isn't catching, it being my first close experience with the phenomenon. ¶ When Marc comes back, he's carrying a small mirror, which he holds in front of the dog's nostrils. "If he's still alive, it'll cloud over," Marc says. "That's what my dad showed me." ¶ Mouche is dead, which we now prove. Then we prove we're still alive by repeatedly clouding the mirror. And for a few months after that, I always carry a small mirror around with me in case I should ever need it—until the day Robert Gaudry trips me and I fall into the river and break my mirror and maybe almost drown and die, but I wouldn't have had my mirror anymore to prove it. ¶

---

*Parts of Imelda's story are told in G. R. Lefrançois, *Psychology for teaching: A bear is politically correct,* 9th ed., 1997. Belmont, CA: Wadsworth.

cience doesn't need a mirror to prove death (although it might sometimes be useful to prove life); it has other ways.

Science's understanding of death and dying is the subject of this chapter. It looks at what death is and at how medicine and common sense define it. It examines developmental changes in our beliefs about dying. It traces the stages that death may take. And it deals with the effects of death on those who are left to mourn.

And in the end, the chapter turns and looks once more at the themes that were presented at the very beginning of the text—themes that underlie our study and understanding of development throughout the lifespan.

UNDERSTANDING AND FEAR OF DEATH

Dying is a highly personal thing. For some, perhaps it is not so difficult a thing, but there are many who burn and rave and rage at its coming. My grandfather tried to go more gently and with a little humor. Having probably read a translation of Viscount Henry John Temple Palmerston's famous last words,* he paraphrased them for my grandmother: "Die?" he is reported to have said, "That's the last thing I'm gonna do!" Which he then did.

That, of course, is the problem with dying. Once we have done it, we can no longer write textbooks about it—although there are those who argue that one of the reasons we write

---

*Viscount Palmerston's last words were, allegedly, "Die, my dear Doctor, that's the last thing I shall do!"

books and do other creative things *before* we die is precisely because we fear our own mortality. Death and fear of dying, says Abra (1995), is one of the goads that prods us to be creative, as though by so being, we in some way defeat our own mortality. It is perhaps that we know so well that when death does come, we will create no more—that we will be forced to take death's secrets silently to our graves.

But science has ways to pry the dusty grave, ways to define, analyze, and measure even this most private, unique, and ultimate of all events.

Some Definitions

Not very many years ago, if someone stopped breathing, or the heart stopped beating, everybody agreed that that person was dead. Doctors noted, as well, that the pupils dilated when someone died, that being the reason, in so many movies, that the possibly dead person's eyelids are lifted by someone who then peers intently at the eyeball. Other changes that characterize death include eventual **rigor mortis** (stiffening of the corpse) and relaxation of the sphincter muscle.

Now, however, there is a new concept of **death** in the medical professions: that of neurological, or brain, death. When the dying person's heart and lungs stop functioning, the brain is quickly deprived of oxygen, and electrical activity of the brain, detected by means of an **electroencephalogram (EEG)**, eventually stops. Death is said to have occurred following complete cessation of brain activity for a certain period of time. However, recent medical advances now make it possible to restart heart and lung action or to substitute for their normal functioning by means of life-sustaining equipment. In fact, it is now possible to keep some people alive in the physiological sense—that is, their bodies consume and

Fear of dying, of no longer existing, is expressed in a search for immortality. To this end, the ancient Egyptians built pyramids and invented mummification. Now we resort to lines carved in stone to preserve a memory of the dead.

process nutrients and oxygen, and eliminate wastes—even though they have suffered irreparable brain damage as a result of temporary cessation of heart and lung activity. Defining death in such circumstances presents serious medical and ethical problems.

Bereavement is the term used to describe the loss suffered by those who are friends and relatives of the person who has died. The bereaved are those left behind—those from whom something has been taken. Bereavement is typically accompanied by **grief**—the bereaved person's emotional reaction to the loss. Grief reactions may include feelings of anger, guilt, anxiety, depression, or preoccupation with thoughts of the deceased. In addition, grief reactions sometimes include physical components such as shortness of breath, dizziness, heart palpitations, loss of appetite, and sighing. As we saw in Chapter 18, there is also a slight reduction in life expectancy for the widowed person for a few years immediately following death of the spouse (we look at grief in more detail later in this chapter). The term **mourning,** which describes external manifestations of grief, is often used to indicate a period of time during which the bereaved person grieves.

Distancing and Denying Death

Throughout many of the world's cultures, the most common attitudes toward death are fear and denial (Davies, 1996). We do not resign ourselves easily to the inevitability of our ends.

We deny death in countless ways. We seldom speak seriously about it—and we speak of it in a personal way even less often. Nor are we willing to admit our fear of dying, says Belsky (1990); somehow, it embarrasses us. When death does come, we often pretend that it is an accident—especially if it came before the end of what we expect will be a normal lifespan. We use expressions such as *untimely* or *sudden* or *unexpected* to describe it. And we invent euphemisms to replace the harsh reality of the words *dead* or *died*: "Passed away," we say, or "dearly departed," or "departed loved ones," or "gone beyond," or "passed on."

Contemporary society distances itself from death not only in its language, but also in the way funerals are generally handled. For example, it has become rare for the deceased to be kept at home, or even in churches, for a brief period of mourning. In North America, the vast majority of funerals now occur in funeral parlors, with brief periods of visitation by family members and friends.

Our denial of death is evident as well in the limited training that many medical schools provide physicians and other health personnel with respect to death and dying. For example, when Rappaport and Witzke (1993) questioned 106 medical students whose practical training had required them to care for a terminally ill patient, they found that most considered themselves poorly prepared for the undertaking. In addition, 41 percent had never been present when a physician had attended a dying patient, 35 percent had never discussed attending a dying patient with a physician, 73 per-

cent had never witnessed hospital staff advising relatives regarding negative outcomes of surgery, and 85 percent had never been present when family members were advised of a patient's death. As Gloth (1994) notes, the medical profession pays relatively little formal attention to the process of dying and to how to care for terminally ill patients.

The process of dying, itself, is often very private. Many hospitals go to great lengths to isolate patients who are expected to die, and then remove the bodies as unobtrusively as possible. Unless we have been in wars, or have witnessed automobile accidents or other similar events, most of us have not had a great deal of exposure to human death and dying. For many, all there has been is a brief glimpse of the deceased in a well-lined casket. Ironically, under these circumstances, the dead are carefully arranged to look as lifelike as possible.

Given our society's widespread denial and avoidance of death, what do children—to say nothing of adolescents and adults at all stages of adulthood—know of dying?

Children's Understanding of Death

Many children's first real exposure to death comes when a family pet dies. But for most, there is a great deal of second-hand exposure to death and dying in the media. Television is especially prone to presenting vivid and dramatic portrayals of death—especially of violent death. Its depictions of grief and remorse are considerably more rare.

Do children, as a result of personal and vicarious experience, understand death?

Early research and theorizing indicated that they typically know very little. Very young children (ages three to four), reported Nagy (1948), don't understand the finality of death. And older children (ages five to nine), tend to *personify* it, turning death into a "bogeyman," a "witch," or some other wicked something that is capable of taking people away. Only after age ten or so do children begin to understand that the end of life is a biological process, that its cause lies within the body rather than with some outside force.

Perhaps because of widespread media exposure to dying, even very young children now seem to have a somewhat clearer understanding of the nature of death. Still, report Pettle and Britten (1995), many children under five don't understand the finality of death. They may ask, for example, when the dead person will return. Between ages five and ten, children come to understand the irreversible and universal nature of dying. And with adolescence, explain Pettle and Britten, may come increasing fears of dying and increasing efforts to keep death at a distance.

The fact that some young children's answers to questions about death and dying reveal a limited awareness of what dying is does not mean that they do not understand or respond to loss. The ability to verbalize an understanding of death presupposes some relatively advanced cognitive and language skills. Perhaps because infants and young children do not yet possess these skills, their cognitive understanding of death seems undeveloped. In fact, their distress at losing a parent, for example, provides overwhelming behavioral evidence indicating that loss does have profound meaning for them (Aspinall, 1996).

As children become older and more sophisticated intellectually, their verbalized understanding of death becomes progressively more adult. But for most of them, thoughts of death are remote and abstract. There is little reason to be concerned with dying when the future stretches ahead seemingly forever.

Kastenbaum (1985) suggests that people's understandings of death at any age may have as much, or more, to do with their life experiences than with their age. Thus, although active, healthy children do not ordinarily think very much about death, and do not necessarily develop very sophisticated notions of what it means, those who are terminally ill seem to have an understanding of dying that goes well beyond their years. Ball, Bignold, and Cribb (1996) report that terminally ill children understand the inevitability and the absolute finality of death even in early childhood. The time orientation of these children changes dramatically. As death nears, conversations about the distant future disappear from their speech. Now the future that concerns them is very immediate—the next birthday, Christmas, Easter. Some children pay a lot of attention to these upcoming events, almost as though trying to rush them, to make them more real and immediate by talking about them.

Adolescents' Notions of Death

Adolescents understand clearly the finality, the inevitability, and the unpredictability of death. Following a series of interviews with adolescents, Morin and Welsh (1996) report that these understandings are relatively well developed by age nine or ten. Still, adolescents' views are often colored by the personal fables they have developed. These fables stress adolescents' specialness, the concern others have for them, and their invulnerability. It might follow from this that they would not be very concerned about dying. Yet some evidence indicates that thoughts of dying and accompanying fears are common in adolescence. This may be at least partly due to the fact that violent and unexpected deaths occur quite frequently in adolescence, especially among males.

Kastenbaum (1985) notes that some studies have reported little concern about death among adolescents, whereas others have suggested that adolescents are extremely preoccupied with and worried about death. The contradiction may be at least partly due to the reluctance of adolescents (and others) to talk about dying. Talking about death in a personal way, admitting fears and concerns, requires, in a very real sense, an admission of what we are socialized to deny at every turn. We do not easily admit that death is something that might happen to us personally—either in adolescence or later; for most, the thought is very frightening. So we repress it and tell each other that it is wise to smell the roses.

Deep down, that, too, may be an admission of fear of death.

Notions of Death in Early and Middle Adulthood

Through adulthood, many events generally conspire to emphasize the transitory nature of living. These include the sometimes painful observation that with every passing decade, more and more of our friends, acquaintances, and relatives die. In addition, many adults experience the loss of their parents or observe signs of aging and impending loss. Because we all know that parents are supposed to die before children, we perhaps fear death less while our parents still live—and more after they die.

With passing years, the inevitability of death becomes clearer, and we begin to think in terms of the number of years we have yet to live rather than of the time we have lived (Neugarten, 1990). This change in time orientation is one aspect of the midlife crisis described in Chapter 16.

Views of Death in Late Adulthood

How do old people feel about dying? Reassuringly, they often report less fear of death than at earlier ages. At the same time, they are less likely to deny their fear of dying (see Neimeyer, 1994). This might be partly because the elderly have usually had far more experience with death than younger people, and many of these experiences have involved close friends, relatives, perhaps even a spouse. They have therefore been repeatedly compelled to think about death. In addition, progressive changes in their own bodies, often accompanied by one or more diseases, continue to emphasize that their own end is imminent, forcing them to adjust gradually to thoughts of dying. "Whereas death is accidental in other stages," notes Assmann (1994), "it becomes existential in old age" (p. 215).

Our knowledge of what normal life expectancy is has led us to accept a lifespan of seventy or so years as one over which we have few legitimate complaints. But if we should live so long, then life expectancy tables tell us we can expect to live another 14.0 years (U.S. Bureau of the Census, 1996; see "At a Glance: Age-Based Life Expectancies" and Figure 19.1).

■ FEAR OF DYING

It would be misleading to imply that fear of dying gradually diminishes and finally vanishes altogether in old age. In fact, among some individuals, fear of dying is sufficiently severe that it manifests itself as one of the symptoms of emotional disturbances such as **panic disorder** (Shioiri et al., 1996).

Although the majority of adults do not report a pathological fear of death, **death anxiety** is found at all age levels including late adulthood (Seigle, 1993). We no longer believe in the **bogeyman** that we invented in our childish minds, the one we feared might come one dark night and get our parents—or, worse yet, us. Yet, if we think about it, the bogeyman still lurks there in the shadows, and deep down we know that we are never completely safe.

AT A GLANCE — Age-Based Life Expectancies

I n 1994, the average life expectancy in the United States for all races and sexes combined was 75.7 years—a full 12.9 years longer than in 1940 (U.S. Bureau of the Census, 1996). In Canada in 1993, life expectancy at birth was 77.8 years (Statistics Canada, 1996). When we are young, Neugarten says, we think in terms of how old we are—how long we have lived. But starting in midlife, we begin to think more about how long we have left to live. Reassuringly, the longer we have lived, the longer we can expect to live—up to a point. Thus, although our life expectancy at birth might be 75, if we actually reach the age of 75, we can reasonably expect to live 10.9 more years (12.0 if we are white and female, 9.5 if white and male. Corresponding life expectancies for 75-year-old black females and males are 11.1 and 8.7, respectively).

FIGURE 19.1

Average life expectancy in the United States, 1993, for individuals of given age. (Based on U.S. Bureau of the Census, 1996, p. 89.)

It is not a happy thought. Say what we will, few of us are not afraid of dying; few of us can remain perfectly calm at the thought of the bogeyman—which is why we keep him in the shadows.

There are at least seven reasons why we might fear death, claim Schultz and Ewen (1988):

- Fear of physical suffering and pain
- Fear of the impact of death on those left behind
- Fear of the deaths of those we love
- Fear of eternal punishment
- Fear of not achieving important goals
- Fear of humiliation and cowardice
- Fear of not existing

This last source of fear, fear of not existing, may be what has driven so many to search for some form of immortality. Arnett (1991) describes how the kings of ancient Assyria tried to achieve a form of immortality by emphasizing the continuity and importance of the family tree, and especially of the males in this line. Each king took great pains to remember the achievements and glories of past kings, to praise their names—expecting, in turn, that succeeding kings would do the same for them. Thus could kings buy a hint of immortality in the memories of generations to come.

The elderly spend more time thinking about dying than do those who are younger. But they also report less fear of death—perhaps because they have seen more of it, and maybe because their declining physical powers have led them to confront their own mortality and they have succeeded in overcoming the despair that can result.

▲ SUMMARY TABLE 19.1
Understanding and Fear of Death

SUMMARY TABLE 19.1
Understanding and Fear of Death

CONCEPTS	SIGNIFICANCE/OBSERVATIONS
Death	■ Cessation of vital activity; medically, cessation of brain activity.
Bereavement	■ The taking away of something important; describes loss suffered by those close to one who dies.
Grief	■ Emotional reaction to bereavement.
Mourning	■ Manifestations of grief; period of time during which grieving occurs.
Evidence of death denial	■ We seldom speak of death or dying; when we do, we often use euphemisms; we provide little training in dealing with death, even among medical practitioners; we have formalized, distanced, and made a professional industry of looking after the disposition of those who have died.
Understandings of death through the lifespan	■ Before age 5, vague and incomplete understanding of the biological finality of death. ■ By age 10, relatively clear understanding of the irreversible and universal nature of dying. ■ Increasing fear of death in adolescence. ■ Increasing personal exposure to death through adulthood; increasing recognition of personal mortality. ■ Less reported fear of death among the elderly.

■ EGO INTEGRITY

Freud is said to have become increasingly preoccupied with dying in his later years. "On March 13 of this year," he writes, "I quite suddenly took a step into real old age. Since then the thought of death has not left me. Sometimes I have the impression that seven of my internal organs are fighting to have the honor of bringing my life to an end" (quoted in Jones, 1957, p. 78). In spite of his constant thoughts of death, however, Freud was reportedly not overwhelmed or depressed at the prospect of dying. "Still, I have not succumbed to this hypochondria," he continues, "but view it quite coolly…" (p. 79).

Our reactions to dying, says Bromley (1990), are highly individual. They include calm acceptance, grim determination to fight, or profound depression. One of the important developmental tasks of late adulthood, according to Erikson, is to confront our mortality while still maintaining a sense of integrity, a feeling that life has been worthwhile. Those who have truly achieved integrity do not fear death.

Not everyone resolves the crisis in the same way, or equally effectively. To realize the inevitability of our ends is not necessarily to become reconciled to death. There are some who, in Dylan Thomas's words, "Do not go gentle into that good night" but instead "Rage, rage against the dying of the light." (See Summary Table 19.1.)

DYING

Psychologists have divided much of our lifespans into stages. There is nothing magical about these stages, nor is there anything intrinsically correct about them. They are simply inventions that simplify our understanding and that sometimes lead to important theoretical and practical insights.

Stages of Dying

Must we also die in stages? Some theorists suggest that this might sometimes be the case. Clearly, we need not resort to stages to understand the immediate and senseless finality of a gun, a bomb, or a plane crash. But perhaps a stage approach might be useful for understanding the process of dying when the person knows that death is near. (See "At a Glance: Common Causes of Death" and Figures 19.2, 19.3, and 19.4.)

Common Causes of Death

n 1993 almost 90 percent of all deaths in the United States and Canada were assigned to ten leading causes. Of these, heart disease remains the most common killer, espe-cially among men; cancer (malignant neoplasms) is second. For many of these diseases, there is some indication of reduced death rates in recent years. For example, deaths from atheroscle-rosis, heart disease, and liver disease have been declining. However, between 1985 and 1993, there were increases in deaths from AIDS and pulmonary diseases.

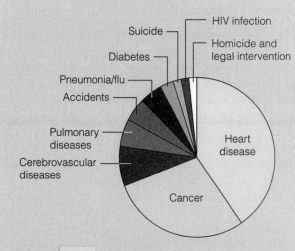

FIGURE 19.2

Leading causes of death, U.S., 1993, both sexes. (Based on U.S. Bureau of the Census, 1996, p. 96.)

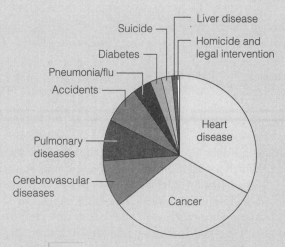

FIGURE 19.3

Leading causes of death, Canada, 1991, both sexes. (Based on Statistics Canada, 1996, p. 114.)

FIGURE 19.4

Heart disease, age, and sex: Death rate from heart disease per 100,000 population. (Based on U.S. Bureau of the Census, 1996, p. 97.)

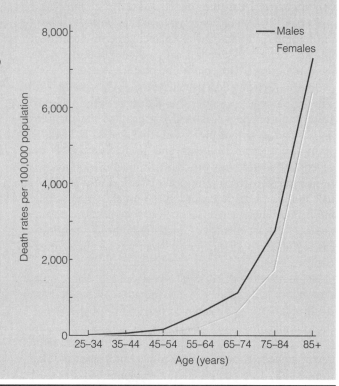

TABLE 19.2

Kübler-Ross's Sequential Stages of Dying

STAGE	ILLUSTRATION
Denial	"Not me! I don't believe it! There must be a mistake!"
Anger	"Why me? Lots of people smoked more than I did, and look at them! It isn't fair!"
Bargaining	"Okay, I might die. Just let me live a little longer so I can wrap up the business and see my new grandson."
Depression	"Yes, it's happening. There's nothing I can do. I wish I had died a long time ago."
Acceptance	"Let it happen. It's OK. I'm not interested in anything anymore. I'm not unhappy, just tired."

Elisabeth Kübler-Ross (1969, 1974) describes five stages through which a patient progresses after learning of a terminal illness. In the first, **denial,** the patient often rejects the diagnosis and its implications: "This can't happen to me. There must be some mistake." Denial is sometimes followed by **anger:** "Why me? It shouldn't be me." The third stage, **bargaining,** is characterized by the patient's attempts to look after unfinished business (with God, for example), promising to do well in exchange for a longer life or less suffering. The fourth stage, **depression,** frequently follows. Finally, the patient may arrive at an **acceptance** of death. (See Table 19.2.)

Kübler-Ross's main concerns have been with the needs of the dying and with those who are left to mourn. Accordingly, much of her work deals less with a description of stages of dying than with advice concerning practical questions related to dying: When should a patient be told? Who should do the telling? How can we reduce fear of death? Nevertheless, her description of the stages of dying has had a tremendous impact on the various professions that deal with death. For example, Holleman, Holleman, and Gershenhorn (1994) surveyed 101 senior class presidents in medical schools with respect to their training in dealing with death. More than half had received 3 hours or less of formal training—which most considered inadequate in preparing them to care effectively for dying patients. Significantly, in the vast majority of cases, Kübler-Ross's stages were what was taught in those 3 hours or less.

Some have criticized Kübler-Ross's stages, claiming that they are a highly subjective interpretation of the process of dying and that many people do not pass through these five stages in the order prescribed (Doka, 1995). Some alternate between different stages, vacillating between acceptance and denial, sometimes depressed and other times resigned. Moreover, Kübler-Ross's stages do not recognize that one of the recurring emotions characterizing many of the terminally ill is *hope.* There is a need, argues Doka (1995), to recognize the individuality and complexity of people's responses to immi-

nent death. Still, Kübler-Ross's description provides a useful way of looking at dying. Claxton (1993) notes that many terminally ill cancer patients do appear to go through emotional stages very much like those described by Kübler-Ross, and suggests that health care workers' knowledge of these stages might enable them to help patients express their emotions and achieve some degree of acceptance.

Life's Trajectories

Kübler-Ross's stages are one way of understanding the process of dying; trajectories are a second. A **life trajectory** implies something quite different from a stage. Stages are like steps, small plateaus that must be successively scaled. They imply a marked degree of discontinuity. Hence, each stage can be labeled differently, and each can be compared and contrasted with preceding and succeeding stages. One of the main values of stages is that they tell us very specific and sometimes very important things about people at each plateau or level. And sometimes they tell us things about the process of getting from one stage to another as well.

A trajectory is a continuous path. It has a beginning and an end, and it can usually be described as ascending or descending (or sometimes both). But it is not described in steps or stages. A missile's path or the flight of a baseball represent trajectories; a journey from my basement to my kitchen represents stages.

Our lives, as we have seen repeatedly throughout this book, can be conceived of in terms of stages, as can our dying. They can also be thought of in terms of trajectories. These are, after all, only metaphors. Neither conception need be evaluated in terms of correctness; it need only provide insight.

Rutter (1996) describes the *life trajectory* as a description of the course of a human life in terms of its major turning points. It is our life's trajectory about which we construct personal narratives and in which we are the incomparable heroes. And it is also our life's trajectory about which we reminisce, analyze, and evaluate when, in old age, we conduct our life review.

▮ DYING TRAJECTORIES

When, either in old age or sometime earlier, something happens that informs us that the end of our span is imminent, our life trajectory becomes a **dying trajectory.** The phrase *dying trajectory* is used in medicine and psychology to refer to the speed of dying. For example, *expected swift death* describes a trajectory often found in emergency wards; *expected temporary recovery* is another possible trajectory. *Expected lingering while dying* describes a trajectory that is sometimes characteristic of diseases such as cancer. Ball, Bignold, and Cribb (1996) also describe the trajectory associated with many cancers as a *trajectory of uncertainty.* Such trajectories, note Muzzin and colleagues (1994), often span many years (half of those with cancer survive more than five years) and present serious adjustment problems for the individuals concerned. Many of these relate to how relationships with others are negatively affected by a dying trajectory.

Belsky (1990) points out that misdiagnosed trajectories or trajectories that change during the patient's illness can have serious implications for both the patient and his or her relatives. Patients who linger far longer than expected might occasionally be given less care than required because they have been expected to die. And going from an "expected to die within weeks" to "in temporary remission" complicates the process of accepting death as well as that of advance grieving undertaken by survivors.

Like stages, trajectories do not describe patterns or movements that are common to everyone. Dying is a highly individualistic process.

So is living.

Terminal Care

In much the same way that most people try to avoid thinking about their personal deaths, so too do most try to avoid the death of others. In fact, even those in the medical professions are sometimes guilty of trying to distance themselves from death. Not only does medical training often pay little attention to death and dying, but the care afforded those who are most likely to die is often inferior to that afforded others. Mills, Davies, and Macrae (1994) analyzed the care given fifty dying patients in thirteen wards of four large teaching hospitals. Among other things, they found that often little effort was made to provide for patient comfort (providing water, encouraging them to eat, brushing their teeth). In addition, contact between nursing staff and dying patients tended to be minimal, and the patient's isolation tended to increase as death became more imminent.

PALLIATIVE CARE AND HOSPICES

Palliative care, a medical specialization concerned specifically with the needs of the terminally ill, is aimed toward easing the physical and psychological distress of those who are dying. Thus, palliative care is concerned in part with the psychological well-being of the dying as well as with the control of physical pain (McQuillan et al., 1996).

Palliative care units are often found in conventional hospitals but may also be found in facilities set up specifically to care for those who are dying. The palliative care and hospice movement, notes Dudgeon (1994), arose specifically because the needs of terminal patients were not being met by the established health care system.

A **hospice** might be a medical or housing facility specifically dedicated to the care of the terminally ill, or it might be the terminally ill patient's own home. In the past ten years, notes Hohl (1994), home health care has grown dramatically. This is partly because of a rapidly aging population, and also because of an overburdened and expensive medical system. Home health care now includes such elements of care as IV (intravenous) therapy, changing dressings, and physical therapy. When the home is used as a hospice—that is, as a place to die in dignity—hospice workers, who are trained medical personnel, usually visit the home daily—as might psychological, occupational, physical, and other therapists (Smith & Yuen, 1994).

Palliative care in out-of-home hospices reflects a new sensitivity to death and dying. It is a movement that is characterized by a "hands-on" type of care, very similar to that which a terminally ill person might receive in a private home. Such care is intended only for short-term patients with *expected-to-die-soon* trajectories. In one survey of 405 hospice patients, average survival time following admission was 29 days (Christakis, 1994).

When dying patients are brought into a separate hospice facility, members of their families are ordinarily expected to provide much of the needed care, sometimes being required to remain in the hospice with the terminally ill person on a full-time basis. As a result, about half of all hospice patients are male, although they make up a much smaller proportion of the elderly population. Also, because of the cost, hospice care is available to only a small proportion of the terminally ill. Hospices provide medical attention, including pain-relieving drugs, but they do not ordinarily use any life-prolonging measures. Their goals are not only to ease the process of dying for the person involved but also to ease the process for friends and relatives. As a result, many of them also include elements of spirituality, and sometimes of religion as well.

The hospice movement is not without critics. Because it shifts the burden of medical care for the terminally ill from hospital facilities, where care is very expensive, to the home, where care is relatively inexpensive, there is a danger that hospices may become dumping grounds for certain patients who require a lot of medically uncomplicated care. However, the fact that hospice care is restricted to those diagnosed as terminally ill reduces this risk somewhat. By the same token, restricting hospices in this way makes them inappropriate for many of the dying. Only if both the patient and the patient's family have completely accepted the inevitability of death is the patient eligible for hospice care. Accordingly, entering a hospice requires giving up whatever vestige of hope might have been left. And even at the very end—even after complete acceptance of the inevitability of imminent death—there is always room for a little hope.

We can always hope for a miracle, for those who believe in such things; or for a happy day or a happy hour; or maybe for just one last sniff of the rose.

Euthanasia

Popularly referred to as *mercy killing,* **euthanasia** encompasses a complicated and controversial collection of issues, which are presented here starkly, with little evaluative comment; our consciences make their own comments.

n November 1994, Robert Latimer was convicted of second-degree murder for killing his twelve-year-old daughter, a severely disabled girl who had cerebral palsy. In November 1997, he lost his appeal. The jury in this case had no choice but to find him guilty after he admitted that yes, he had placed his daughter in the truck and run a hose from the exhaust into the passenger compartment. He argued that she was in pain, that she looked forward to nothing but a life of surgery and suffering, and that he had acted solely out of compassion. The jury was visibly moved. Although the minimum sentence mandated by law is twenty-five years with no possibility of parole for ten years, they recommended a one-year sentence. Judge Ted Noble agreed and, for the first time in Canadian history, waived the minimum penalty, instead sentencing Latimer to one year less a day in jail (experts say he will be released in a few months) followed by one year of voluntary custody at his farm. Reaction to the sentencing is extreme. On one hand are those who are outraged at the court's leniency and who fear "open season" on the disabled, excusable on grounds of compassion. Others are equally upset that Robert Latimer should be punished at all. As of this writing, there is a possibility of an appeal by the prosecution.

In some ways, the Latimer case is similar to that of the Rambergs, who, fifty years earlier, killed their two-year-old son, Victor. Victor was suffering from terminal, inoperable cancer, and screamed in pain, day and night. In the end, the parents ran a hose from the automobile exhaust into Victor's room. Although they described clearly what they had done, the jury refused to convict them (Toneguzzi, 1994).

1. Law waived for Latimer. (1997, Dec. 2). *Edmonton Sun,* p. News 3.

A Challenge

Can you present a balanced, reasoned, scientifically based evaluation of the issues involved?

On the Net

For more detailed (and recent) information on this case, go to

http://www.canoe.ca/Canoe/home.html

and do a search of news archives using Robert Latimer as the initial search term.

■ DEFINITIONS

The term euthanasia is of Greek origin and means, literally, "good death." A distinction is often made between *passive* and *active* euthanasia. *Active euthanasia* involves deliberately doing certain things to shorten life, such as administering a lethal injection or removing a patient from life-support systems. *Passive euthanasia* involves not doing certain things that might have prolonged life and is illustrated in those instances in which heart surgery is not performed or blood transfusions are not given.

Holland is one of the few countries in the world that fully accepts euthanasia. A number of U.S. states—for example, Oregon—also permit what is sometimes termed *physician-assisted suicide* under certain prescribed conditions (Ganzini et al., 1996). Some, like Michigan, specifically prohibit it. As Pappas (1996) notes, the legal situation remains highly controversial and changes almost weekly.

In Holland, certain guidelines govern the use of euthanasia. Most important is that two conditions be met: The patient must be terminally ill, suffering hopelessly, and with no possibility of a cure; and there must be repeated requests for assisted suicide. Euthanasia has now been practiced in Holland for more than ten years, but still remains highly controversial.

■ THE CONTROVERSY

Some physicians, for example, absolutely refuse to perform euthanasia under any circumstance (often for religious reasons) (Harvey, 1994). A survey of Oregon psychiatrists following passage of the ballot legalizing physician-assisted suicide revealed that one-third of them opposed this initiative (Ganzini et al., 1996). Some medical practitioners believe flatly that assisted suicide is never defensible (Lester & Leenaars, 1996). Some fear that legalizing voluntary euthanasia may quickly lead to *involuntary* euthanasia. There are apparently several hundred cases in Holland every year in which the conditions for euthanasia have not been clearly met but in which the patient's life is ended in any case (Saunders, 1994). Others caution that terminally ill patients' spoken thoughts about dying, and even their requests for assistance in so doing, do not necessarily reflect a sustained desire for assisted suicide or euthanasia (Block & Billings, 1994). Depression, note Peruzzi, Canapary, and Bongar (1996), is a very common outcome of imminent death, and suicidal thoughts often accompany depression. Hence, it isn't highly surprising that many of those who are dying should occasionally express a desire to have life end prematurely. But in the absence of careful psychiatric examination, it might be premature to conclude that this request is being made *while in full possession of one's faculties.*

The palliative care community has also expressed strong objections to the legalization of physician-assisted suicide (Uzych, 1996; Cherny, 1996). One of the arguments is that there are often a variety of measures that can be taken to alleviate pain and suffering. The trend toward euthanasia, they insist, has not looked carefully enough at these alternatives.

Interestingly, after a review of the situation in Holland, the Board of Trustees of the American Medical Association strongly recommended that euthanasia and physician-assisted suicide be rejected by the American Medical Association (Anonymous, 1994).

On the other hand, there are others who argue that terminally ill patients have a right to refuse medical care and that their decisions should be respected and supported (Cain et al., 1990). In one study, 141 critical care nurses (out of 1,600) had received requests from patients or family members to assist in suicide. A full 129 of these admitted anonymously that they had participated in such actions (Asch, 1996).

Suicide is very common among the elderly, notes Carpenter (1993), in spite of the fact that public opinion is predominantly negative. He argues that the elderly have a right to what he labels "ethical" suicide, unobstructed suicide following a rational decision based on the "wisdom" of old age. Similarly, Humphry (1992) argues that although "old age" should never be sufficient grounds for legal suicide, the presence of an irreversible, pain-causing, terminal illness should be. (See "In the News and on the Net: Compassionate Murder?")

■ THE LIVING WILL

Do we have a moral or a legal right to decide when we, or others, shall die? Do conditions such as severe and irreversible pain, coupled with inevitable and imminent death, justify euthanasia? Is passive euthanasia less objectionable than active euthanasia? Are there significant ethical or biological issues that clearly separate suicide, euthanasia, and perhaps even abortion?

These questions are far easier to ask than to answer. But for those whose answers are clear and who believe they would want to choose death under certain circumstances, the Euthanasia Education Council provides a document that can be used to formalize these wishes. It is called a **living will** and is reproduced in Figure 19.5. This is merely a sample form. State-specific forms are available, free of charge, from Choice in Dying.

FIGURE 19.5

A living will. (Reprinted with permission from Choice in Dying, 200 Varick Street, New York, NY 10014.)

ADVANCE DIRECTIVE
Living Will and Health Care Proxy

Death is a part of life. It is a reality like birth, growth and aging. I am using this advance directive to convey my wishes about medical care to my doctors and other people looking after me at the end of my life. It is called an advance directive because it gives instructions in advance about what I want to happen to me in the future. It expresses my wishes about medical treatment that might keep me alive. I want this to be legally binding.

If I cannot make or communicate decisions about my medical care, those around me should rely on this document for instructions about measures that could keep me alive.

I do not want medical treatment (including feeding and water by tube) that will keep me alive if:
• I am unconscious and there is no reasonable prospect that I will ever be conscious again (even if I am not going to die soon in my medical condition), or
• I am near death from an illness or injury with no reasonable prospect of recovery.

I do want medicine and other care to make me more comfortable and to take care of pain and suffering. I want this even if the pain medicine makes me die sooner.

I want to give some extra instructions: *[Here list any special instructions, e.g., some people fear being kept alive after a debilitating stroke. If you have wishes about this, or any other conditions, please write them here.]*

The legal language in the box that follows is a health care proxy.
It gives another person the power to make medical decisions for me.

I name _____, who lives at _____
_____, phone number _____
to make medical decisions for me if I cannot make them myself. This person is called a health care "surrogate," "agent," "proxy," or "attorney in fact." This power of attorney shall become effective when I become incapable of making or communicating decisions about my medical care. This means that this document stays legal when and if I lose the power to speak for myself, for instance, if I am in a coma or have Alzheimer's disease.

My health care proxy has power to tell others what my advance directive means. This person also has power to make decisions for me, based either on what I would have wanted, or, if this is not known, on what he or she thinks is best for me.

If my first choice health care proxy cannot or decides not to act for me, I name _____
_____, address _____
phone number _____, as my second choice.

(over, please)

LWGEN

I have discussed my wishes with my health care proxy, and with my second choice if I have chosen to appoint a second person. My proxy(ies) has(have) agreed to act for me.

I have thought about this advance directive carefully. I know what it means and want to sign it. I have chosen two witnesses, neither of whom is a member of my family, nor will inherit from me when I die. My witnesses are not the same people as those I named as my health care proxies. I understand that this form should be notarized if I use the box to name (a) health care proxy(ies).

Signature _____
Date _____
Address _____

Witness' signature _____
Witness' printed name _____
Address _____

Witness' signature _____
Witness' printed name _____
Address _____

Notary [to be used if proxy is appointed] _____

Drafted and Distributed by Choice In Dying, Inc.—the National Council for the right to Die. Choice In Dying is a National not-for-profit organization which works for the rights of patients at the end of life. In addition to this generic advance directive, Choice In Dying distributes advance directives that conform to each state's specific legal requirements and maintains a national Living Will Registry for completed documents.

CHOICE IN DYING INC.—
the national council for the right to die
(formerly Concern for Dying/Society for the Right to Die)
200 Varick Street, New York, NY 10014 (212) 366-5540

5/92

When Hozumi, a Japanese nobleman, saw Shakespeare's *Hamlet* for the first time, he was somewhat taken aback at Hamlet's reaction of fear when faced with his father's ghost, victim of a "foul and most unnatural murder." "Ghost scenes are not uncommon in Japanese theatres," he writes, "and when the ghost appears to the parents, sons, daughters, friends or lovers, those who meet never show signs of dread, but those of joy for the meeting" (quoted in Hamabata, 1990, p. 54).

In Japan, explains Hamabata, the dead and their ancestors are as much a part of the household, of the *ie*, as the living. And although the dead are transformed, through stages observed by regular and formal ritual, from spirits of the newly deceased *(shiryoo)* to new-buddhas *(nii-botoke)*, then to buddhas *(hotoke)*, and finally to ancestors-cum-gods *(senzo)*, they are not forgotten. Among the many ceremonies that remember the dead is the *obon,* an annual four-day series of rituals during which the spirits of the dead are welcomed back to their households. On the first day of the *obon,* the living of the family go to the temple graveyard, clean the tombstones, offer flowers and food, and, in the evening, lead the spirits of the dead back to their homes with a lantern bearing the family's crest. And, four days later, they lead them back to the temple, or they light a fire to guide them on their journey from the living to the dead.

This, the *obon,* is only one of many rituals involving care of the dead. Makoto Moriuchi, for example, has a cabinet in a corner of his large dining room. In the cabinet is a photograph of Mr. Moriuchi, his dead father. Also there are candles and flowers and other objects such as a brass container with cooked rice in it, a dish of fruit, and a miniature bottle of Johnnie Walker Black Label scotch. "Father likes to drink," explained Makoto, after he had introduced his guest to his father—always speaking in the present tense (Hamabata, 1990, p. 61).

Forty-nine days after Mr. Moriuchi's death, a special traditional ceremony took place wherein his remains were placed in the household tomb. This marked the transformation of his spirit from the world of the newly dead to that of the new-buddha. And it also marked a change in the relationship between members of the family and Mr. Moriuchi. In Hamabata's (1990) words, these ceremonies "did not eliminate Mr. Moriuchi from their lives. Instead, they opened the way for Mr. Moriuchi's continued presence in the household" (p. 67). The ghost of Mr. Moriuchi lives.

To Think About

These few short paragraphs cannot do justice to the richness and meaning of these ceremonies and beliefs. But they outline attitudes and customs very different from those prevalent in North America, where quickly forgetting the dead is often seen as a mark of strength and adjustment. What advantages (if any) do you think one system might have over the other? How might these different attitudes and beliefs be reflected in our attitudes toward our own dying, as well as toward the death of others?

BEREAVEMENT AND GRIEVING

Bereavement, as we saw earlier, is the loss of something or someone important. *Grief* is an intense emotional reaction to bereavement. Mourning is what is done as a result of grief—for example, crying, praying, or, as at some Irish wakes, singing and drinking, and perhaps even fighting and dancing, in addition to crying and praying.

In some cultures and in some religions, length of mourning is predetermined. Often, too, certain ritual behaviors are undertaken by the bereaved. Some of these behaviors, like wearing the black colors of "widow's weeds" or sprinkling ashes on one's head, may serve as external symbols of loss. They are also a sign of homage for the deceased. But perhaps even more importantly, they provide a ritualized and acceptable way of displaying grief, and they may accelerate the eventual acceptance of the loss. (See "Across Cultures: Makoto Moriuchi's Father's Ghost.")

Effects of Bereavement

Bereavement appears to have both long-term and relatively short-term effects.

SHORT-TERM EFFECTS

There is considerable variation in the ways in which different people express grief, as well as in the length of time required for recovery. However, there are a number of symptoms and behaviors that appear to be quite general following the death of someone close. Among these are physiological signs of distress such as crying, eating and sleeping disturbances, and other physical symptoms such as constriction of the throat, heart palpitations, trembling, and sighing. Also, many who are recently bereaved are constantly preoccupied with the image of the dead person, almost as though it were a hallucination. Some hear the dead person's voice, or think they have caught glimpses of the deceased among crowds. This, Sormanti and August (1997) report, is highly common among parents who have recently lost a child. In one study of 312 adults, almost half reported continued contact with the deceased (Frantz, Trolley, & Johll, 1996). Many reported feeling a sort of presence; some feared that they were losing their minds. Still others become obsessed with details of the dead person's last days or hours. In addition, there may be feelings of guilt about things that were done or not done for the deceased.

LONG-TERM EFFECTS

Most of the short-term effects of bereavement disappear slowly and are typically gone within the first year. However, Byrne and Raphael (1994) found that about 50 percent of a sample of widowed, elderly men continued to manifest recurring symptoms of severe grief thirteen months after their bereavement. Among possible long-term effects of bereavement are physical complaints and sometimes even decreased life expectancy (Gibson, 1992). Other studies suggest that severe depression requiring medical or psychiatric attention is more common following bereavement (Horowitz et al., 1997). Depression after bereavement, however, is not ordinarily as severe as depression resulting from other causes, and usually responds to treatment. And five years following bereavement, there is no longer higher incidence of illness or of mortality.

The long-term effects of bereavement vary considerably from one person to another, depending partly on individual personality characteristics and partly on the nature of the bereavement. Loss of a child is especially difficult for parents (Shapiro, 1996). In contrast, loss of an elderly parent is more easily accepted.

ANTICIPATORY GRIEF

In addition, there is some evidence that loss that is anticipated may lead to less severe and shorter-duration grief reactions, a fact sometimes attributed to what is termed **anticipatory grief** (Byrne & Raphael, 1994). Anticipatory grief relates to the grief reactions that people experience in the time between learning that someone is terminally ill and the actual death. Anticipatory grief can be very profound and is often accompanied by many of the physiological and psychological symptoms that follow actual bereavement. It

Intense numbness and confusion, followed by deep sadness, are common reactions to bereavement. Recovery from bereavement is sometimes faster among those who mourn openly than among those who deny and hide their grief.

would seem to make sense that this period of *anticipatory grief* would be reflected in less grief and easier adjustment following death. But the evidence is mixed and contradictory. In one study of thirty-four bereaved men and women, those who had anticipated the death of their loved one and who had therefore had an opportunity for anticipatory grief did not experience a shorter or easier grieving period after the death (Hogan, Morse, & Tason, 1996). Also, Ponder and Pomeroy (1996) found that anticipatory grief waxes and wanes while the dying person remains alive, but that it does not abate with time.

STAGES OF GRIEF

Grieving following bereavement is sometimes described in terms of three stages (Parkes, 1987; Worden, 1982). Clearly, however, not all individuals experience grief in the same way. Still, knowledge of these common patterns of grief can be very useful, and sometimes highly reassuring, for those in the process of grieving, as well as for mental health practitioners.

■ *Phase 1: Numbness and Shock.* The first few weeks following the loss, notes Worden (1982), are marked by incredulity, shock, disbelief, numbness. Those grieving often feel numb and confused. In addition, many experience physiological symptoms such as shortness of breath, dizziness, palpitations, and tightness in the chest. Many fear they are losing their sanity. Jenike (1997) cautions that the bereaved may be highly vulnerable to alcohol or drug abuse during this period, and that health care practitioners need to be especially vigilant with those who are most vulnerable (those with mental disorders or a tendency toward alcoholism, and those who lack social support).

■ *Phase 2: Preoccupation and Deep Sadness.* During much of the next year, the bereaved may continue to be preoccupied with thoughts of the dead person. Intense sorrow and prolonged weeping are not uncommon—as, too, are a range of emotions such as guilt and anger. It is during this period that the bereaved may sense the presence of the dead person, often in dreams as well as while awake. With time, the intensity of grief diminishes and thoughts of the dead person become less frequent and less obsessive.

- *Phase 3: Recovery.* The third phase begins when the bereaved has regained interest in life. This, notes Parkes (1987), usually begins by about a year following the loss—although it may take considerably longer or may occur much sooner. By this time, appetite and sleep patterns have generally returned to normal, and thoughts of the deceased aren't accompanied by the intensity of emotions that marked the beginning of the second phase. Many of the bereaved are now ready to begin new relationships and to continue with their lives.

GOOD GRIEF

Some theorists believe that working through grief (often referred to as *grief work* or **good grief**) is extremely important to recovering from bereavement and to subsequent happiness and well-being. *Good grief* is a label sometimes used to reflect the assumption that people need to *work through* their grief, that doing so is *good,* that the result of grieving is adjustment, and that absence of expected grieving is basically unhealthy. This, says Lieberman (1996), is the illness model of grief. It maintains that a bereaved person must recognize, explore, and feel his or her grief, and that this will eventually restore the person to a level of functioning comparable to that which existed prior to the loss. The model also assumes that failure to recover is largely a function of not having grieved sufficiently or properly, and that not to grieve insufficiently or inappropriately can result in psychological and physical illness.

The "good grief" model, argues Hewson (1997), has no empirical support. It has not been established that a certain amount or manner of grieving is essential for timely adjustment to a loss through death. Death, and widowhood, should be viewed as a fundamental part of life, says Lieberman (1996). Grieving is only one of the challenges facing widows, and each might react in highly individualistic ways.

SUMMARY TABLE 19.3
Dying and Grieving

CONCEPTS AND ISSUES	SIGNIFICANCE/OBSERVATIONS
Kübler-Ross: stages of dying	- (For those who know death is imminent): denial ("not me"), anger ("why me?"), bargaining ("let me suffer less and I will . . ."), depression, and acceptance. - These are a *description* of possible reactions—not a *prescription* meant to illustrate how people *should* react.
Life trajectory	- Description of the course of a human life in terms of its major turning points; the gist of our personal narratives.
Dying trajectory	- Description of the course of human life when death is expected (for example, *expected swift death, expected lingering while dying*).
Palliative care	- Medical specialization concerned with the needs of the terminally ill; emphasis is often on psychological and physical pain relief; palliative care often occurs in *hospices*.
Euthanasia	- Passive: Where something *is not* done to preserve life. - Active: Where something *is* done to end life. - May take the form of physician-assisted suicide. - Highly controversial; legal in some jurisdictions, illegal in others. - The *living will* can be used to formalize wishes regarding nature of terminal care desired under certain circumstances.
Bereavement and grieving	- Short-term effects might include crying, sleep disturbances, eating disturbances, preoccupation with thoughts of the dead person, and other physical and psychological symptoms. - Long-term effects might include recurring symptoms of grief, decreased life expectancy, and depression.
Anticipatory grief	- Grief that occurs prior to the terminally ill person's death. - Some evidence suggests that anticipatory grief might lessen the severity and length of grieving after death; other evidence suggests that anticipatory grief often has no effect on subsequent grieving. - Theorists describe three possible stages of grief: numbness and disbelief (first few weeks); preoccupation and deep sadness (perhaps one year); recovery (by the beginning of year 2).
Good grief	- Reflects old *illness* model, which assumes that people need to *work through* their grief, that doing so is *good,* that the result of grieving is adjustment, and that the absence of expected grieving is basically unhealthy. - Current lifespan model suggests that grieving is highly individualistic and that the absence of prolonged grief is not a sign of maladjustment or a signal that professional help is required.

Nor is the absence of prolonged grief a sign of maladjustment, or a signal that professional help is required.

Unfortunately, there are no easy recipes for alleviating the pain and anguish of the bereaved. And although formal periods of mourning that are dictated and sanctioned by society sometimes appear helpful, for some individuals, grief work may not be very important for adjustment to death. (See Summary Table 19.3.)

FINAL THEMES

Dying and grieving are not happy notes upon which to end a chapter—or a book; birth would have been happier. Unfortunately, however, the chronology of our lives inevitably runs in a womb-to-tomb direction. And *The Lifespan* has been structured along that same chronology.

But this isn't real life; it's just a book. We can end where and how we please. If we wanted to, we could slap a birth right onto the tail end of this tale, pretend life is a huge cycle, and start all over again, full of joy and hope.

Instead, we end not with a new birth but with a brief summary of the most important themes that have run through this book, giving it continuity. These themes, which define the lifespan perspective, are presented as an introduction in Chapter 1. Here, they are a summary.

- *Development is continuous.* It isn't something that happens only to infants, children, and perhaps adolescents, and then ceases with adulthood. There are important positive changes throughout the entire lifespan. Sadly, there are negative changes, too.

- *Maturity is relative.* Human development does not eventually culminate in a predetermined, final state of maturity. Hence, the developmental psychologist is interested as much in the *processes* of development as in states of competence. Our competencies are relative; they do not always endure. A mature and fully competent two-year-old can pull my baseball cap over her ears, but cannot tie her shoes; a mature ten-year-old can tie his shoes, but cannot solve an abstract problem of Boolean algebra; a mature sixty-five-year-old may solve the problem in Boolean algebra, but will be hard-pressed to explain the final and absolute meaning of existence.

- *Development is contextual.* What we become and how we think, feel, and act are bound to the contexts from which we have emerged and in which we continue to interact. The conclusions of developmental psychology need to be interpreted in light of what we know of the lives and the cultures of those whose behaviors led to the conclusions. Intelligence in North America presupposes the ability to acquire high levels of facility with symbolic systems such as written language; elsewhere, intelligence might be more closely related to the ability to recognize the marks of a slug's passing in the sand.

- *Developmental influences are bidirectional.* We are part of our contexts; we carry them around with us. They shape us; we shape them. Jessica's parents bought her a set of encyclopedias—which helped her prove to them (and others) that she was as intelligent as they suspected. That they suspected she was intelligent influenced them to buy the books in the first place. Her behavior influenced their suspicions, which influenced their behavior, which influenced her....

- *Heredity and environment interact throughout the lifespan.* Gene–environment interactions affect all aspects of human functioning: physical, social, and intellectual. Alone, neither explains very much at all.

- *There is no average person.* Each of us is unique, very special, quite wonderful.

And perhaps even after our mirrors no longer cloud over, we may still continue to be very special and wonderful.

Perhaps God's great black oxen will not trample our bones after all. Maybe when they reach us, they will pause for a moment so that we might scramble onto their broad backs. And then they will carry us through eternity, stopping as often as we wish so that we can smell the new roses.

FOCUS QUESTIONS: SUMMARY ANSWERS

1. What do children understand of death? What do adolescents understand? And you?

- Neurological, or brain, death signifies cessation of electrical activity in the brain. Our culture tends to distance and deny death (through euphemisms and avoidance of contact or care). Very young children often do not completely understand the finality of death, although media exposure has made them considerably more sophisticated. With advancing age, declining health and other events conspire to make us more conscious of our mortality. Fear of death appears at all stages of life.

2. What are some possible stages of dying?

- Kübler-Ross describes five possible stages of dying (for those who know death is imminent): denial ("not me"), anger ("why me?"), bargaining ("let me suffer less and I will..."), depression, and acceptance. Not all people go through these stages and in this order.

3. What is euthanasia? Is it legal?

■ *Euthanasia*, popularly called mercy killing, is a controversial procedure that can be either passive (not doing something that would prolong life) or active (deliberately doing something to shorten life). It can take the form of *physician-assisted suicide*. In certain jurisdictions, it is legal; in others, it is not.

4. How inevitable is grief following bereavement? Is it important to grieve?

■ Grief can result in a wide range of short-term symptoms and behaviors (appetite loss, sleep disturbances, crying); longer-term effects of bereavement can include psychological and physical problems, sometimes evident in serious depression. Some theorists describe three stages of grief: *numbness and shock* (first few weeks), *preoccupation and deep sadness* (perhaps one year), and *recovery*. The illness model assumes that experiencing grief (*good grief* or *grief work*) is necessary for adjustment to bereavement and that not doing so is unhealthy. The lifespan model suggests that grieving is highly individualistic and that not everyone needs to *work* through his or her grief.

STUDY TERMS

FURTHER READINGS

A classic layperson's book on death and dying is the one by Kübler-Ross:

Kübler-Ross, E. (1969). *On death and dying*. New York: Macmillan.

In the first of the following two books, Irish provides an enlightening look at how different cultures react to bereavement; the second looks at how Western cultures deny death and distance themselves from it:

Irish, D. P. (1993). *Ethnic variations in dying, death, and grief: Diversity in universality*. Washington, DC: Hemisphere.

Howarth, G., & Jupp, P. C. (Eds.). *Contemporary issues in the sociology of death, dying and disposal*. New York: St. Martin's.

The following are two useful guides intended specifically for those involved in helping children cope with death and dying:

Ward, B. (1993). *Good grief: Exploring feelings, loss, and death with under elevens: A holistic approach*. Bristol, PA: Jessica Kingsley.

Pennells, M., & Smith, S. C. (1995). *The forgotten mourners: Guidelines for working with bereaved children*. Bristol, PA: Jessica Kingsley.

References

AAMD Ad Hoc Committee on Terminology and Classification. (1992). *Mental retardation: Definition, classification, and systems of support* (9th ed.). Washington, DC: American Association on Mental Retardation.

Abra, J. (1995). Do the muses dwell in Elysium? Death as a motive for creativity. *Creativity Research Journal, 8,* 205–217.

Abramsky, L. (1994). Counselling prior to prenatal testing. In L. Abramsky & J. Chapple (Eds.), *Prenatal diagnosis: The human side.* New York: Chapman and Hall.

Abramsky, L., & Chapple, J. (Eds.). (1994). *Prenatal diagnosis: The human side.* New York: Chapman and Hall.

Abramson, L. (1991). Facial expressivity in failure to thrive and normal infants: Implications for their capacity to engage in the world. *Merrill–Palmer Quarterly, 37,* 159–182.

Adams, G. R., Gullotta, T. P., & Montemayor, R. (Eds.). (1992). *Adolescent identity formation* (Vol. 4). Newbury Park, CA: Sage.

Adams, R. E., Jr., & Passman, R. H. (1981). The effects of preparing two-year-olds for brief separations from their mothers. *Child Development, 52,* 1068–1070.

Adams, R. E., Jr., & Passman, R. H. (1983). Explaining to young children about an upcoming separation from their mother: When do I tell them? *Journal of Applied Developmental Psychology, 4,* 35–42.

Adegoke, A. A. (1993). The experience of spermarche (the age of onset of sperm emission) among selected adolescent boys in Nigeria. *Journal of Youth and Adolescence, 22,* 201–209.

Adler, P. A., Kless, S. J., & Adler, P. (1992). Socialization to gender roles: Popularity among elementary school boys and girls. *Sociology of Education, 65,* 169–187.

Agras, W. S., Rossiter, E. M., Arnow, B., Schneider, J. A., Telch, C. F., Raeburn, S. D., Bruce, B., Perl, M., & Koran, L. M. (1994). Pharmacologic and cognitive–behavioral treatment for bulimia nervosa: A controlled comparison. *American Journal of Psychiatry, 149,* 82–87.

AIDS will kill 4M women by 2000: WHO. (1993, Sept. 8). *Edmonton Journal,* p. A12.

The AIDS threat: Who's at risk? (1988, March 14). *Newsweek,* pp. 42–52.

Ainsworth, M. D. S., Blehar, M. C., Waters, E., & Wall, S. (1978). *Patterns of attachment.* Hillsdale, NJ: Erlbaum.

Albert, R. S., & Runco, M. A. (1986). The achievement of eminence: A model based on a longitudinal study of exceptionally gifted boys and their families. In R. J. Sternberg & J. E. Davidson (Eds.), *Conceptions of giftedness.* New York: Cambridge University Press.

Alcamo, I. E. (1993). A vaccine for AIDS. *American Biology Teacher, 55,* 198–202.

Alcock, J. (1984). *Animal behavior: An evolutionary approach* (3rd ed.). Sunderland, MA: Sinauer.

Allen, K. R. (1993). The dispassionate discourse of children's adjustment to divorce. *Journal of Marriage and the Family, 55,* 46–50.

Allen, M. C., & Alexander, G. R. (1997). Using motor milestones as a multistep process to screen preterm infants for cerebral palsy. *Developmental Medicine and Child Neurology, 39,* 12–16.

Alpert, E. J., Cohen, S., & Sege, R. D. (1997). Family violence: An overview. *Academic Medicine, 72,* S3–S6.

Alvy, K. T. (1987). *Parent training: A social necessity.* Studio City, CA: Center for the Improvement of Child Caring.

Alwin, D. F. (1994). Aging, personality, and social change: The stability of individual differences over the adult life span. In D. L. Featherman, R. M. Lerner, & M. Perlmutter (Eds.), *Lifespan development and behavior* (Vol. 12). Hillsdale, NJ: Erlbaum.

Amato, P. R. (1993). Children's adjustment to divorce: Theories, hypotheses, and empirical support. *Journal of Marriage and the Family, 55,* 23–38.

Amato, P. R., & Keith, B. (1991). Parental divorce and the well-being of children: A meta-analysis. *Psychological Bulletin, 110,* 26–46.

Ambert, A. M. (1992). *The effect of children on parents.* New York: Haworth.

American Psychiatric Association. (1987). *Diagnostic and statistical manual of mental disorders* (3rd ed.). Washington, DC: Author.

American Psychiatric Association. (1994). *Diagnostic and statistical manual of mental disorders* (4th ed.). Washington, DC: Author.

Ames, C. (1992). Classrooms: Goals, structures, and student motivation. *Journal of Educational Psychology, 84,* 261–271.

Ammerman, R. T. (1990). Predisposing child factors. In R. T. Ammerman & M. Hersen (Eds.), *Children at risk: An evaluation of factors contributing to child abuse and neglect.* New York: Plenum.

Amponsah, B., & Krekling, S. (1997). Sex differences in visual–spatial performance among Ghanaian and Norwegian adults. *Journal of Cross-Cultural Psychology, 28,* 81–92.

Anderson, J. (1996). Gynecological and obstetrical issues for HIV-infected women. In R. R. Faden & N. E. Kass (Eds.), *HIV, AIDS and childbearing.* New York: Oxford University Press.

Anderson, J. R. (1980). *Cognitive psychology and its applications*. San Francisco: Freeman.

Anisfeld, M. (1991). Review: Neonatal imitation. *Developmental Review, 11,* 60–97.

Anonymous. (1994). Report of the Board of Trustees of the American Medical Association. Euthanasia/physician-assisted suicide: Lessons in the Dutch experience. *Issues in Law and Medicine, 10,* 81–90.

Anonymous. (1996). Positioning and sudden infant death syndrome (SIDS): Update. American Academy of Pediatrics Task Force on Infant Positioning and SIDS. *Pediatrics, 98,* 1216–1218.

Anonymous. (1997). Does bed sharing affect the risk of SIDS? American Academy of Pediatrics. Task Force on Infant Positioning and SIDS. *Pediatrics, 100,* 272.

Anthony, E. J. (Ed.). (1975). *Exploration in child psychiatry*. New York: Plenum.

Antonarakis, S. E. (1991). Parental origin of the extra chromosome in trisomy 21 as indicated by analysis of DNA polymorphisms. Down Syndrome Collaborative Group. *New England Journal of Medicine, 324,* 872–876.

Aquilino, W. S. (1990). The likelihood of parent–adult child coresidence: Effects of family structure and parental characteristics. *Journal of Marriage and the Family, 52,* 405–419.

Arber, S., & Gilbert, G. N. (1989). Transitions in caring: Gender, life course and the care of the elderly. In B. Bytheway, T. Keil, P. Allatt, & A. Bryman (Eds.), *Becoming and being old: Sociological approaches to later life*. London: Sage.

Arditti, J. A., & Michaelena, K. (1994). Fathers' perspectives of their co-parental relationships postdivorce: Implications for family practice and legal reform. *Family Relations, 43,* 61–67.

Ariès, P. (1962). *Centuries of childhood: A social history of family life* (R. Baldick, Trans.). New York: Knopf. (Originally published 1960.)

Armen, J. C. (1974). *Gazelle boy*. New York: Universe Books. (Translated by S. Hardman from *L'enfant sauvage du grand désert*. Neuchâtel: Delachaux & Niestlé.)

Arnett, J. (1992). Reckless behavior in adolescence: A developmental perspective. *Developmental Review, 12,* 339–373.

Arnett, W. S. (1991). Growing old in the cradle: Old age and immortality among the kings of ancient Assyria. *International Journal of Aging and Human Development, 32,* 135–141.

Asch, D. A. (1996). The role of critical care nurses in euthanasia and assisted suicide. *New England Journal of Medicine, 334,* 1374–1379.

Aslin, R. N. (1987). Visual and auditory development in infancy. In J. D. Osofsky (Ed.), *Handbook of infant development*. New York: John Wiley.

Aslin, R. N., Pisoni, D. P., & Jusczyk, P. W. (1983). Auditory development and speech perception in infancy. In M. H. Haith & J. J. Campos (Eds.), *Handbook of child psychology* (Vol. 2): *Infancy and developmental psychology*. New York: John Wiley.

Aslin, R. N., & Smith, L. B. (1988). Perceptual development. *Annual Review of Psychology, 39,* 435–473.

Asp, E., & Garbarino, J. (1988). Integrative processes at school and in the community. In T. D. Yawkey & J. E. Johnson (Eds.), *Integrative processes and socialization: Early to middle childhood*. Hillsdale, NJ: Erlbaum.

Aspinall, S. Y. (1996). Educating children to cope with death: A preventive model. *Psychology in the Schools, 33,* 341–349.

Assmann, A. (1994). Wholesome knowledge: Concepts of wisdom in a historical and cross-cultural perspective. In D. L. Featherman, R. M. Lerner, & M. Perlmutter (Eds.), *Life-span development and behavior* (Vol. 12). Hillsdale, NJ: Erlbaum.

Astington, J. W. (1991). Intention in the child's theory of mind. In D. Frye & C. Moore (Eds.), *Children's theories of mind: Mental states and social understanding*. Hillsdale, NJ: Erlbaum.

Astroth, K. A. (1993). Are youth at risk? Reevaluating the deficit model of youth development. *Journal of Extension, 31,* 22–25.

Atchley, R. C. (1982). Retirement: Leaving the world of work. *Annals of the American Academy of Political and Social Sciences, 464,* 120–131.

Atchley, R. C. (1985). *Social forces and aging: An introduction to social gerontology* (4th ed.). Belmont, CA: Wadsworth.

Atchley, R. C. (1989). A continuity theory of aging. *Gerontologist, 29,* 183–190.

Atkinson, R. C., & Shiffrin, R. M. (1971). The control of short-term memory. *Scientific American, 225,* 82–90.

Aubrey, C. (1993). An investigation of the mathematical knowledge and competencies which young children bring into school. *British Educational Research Journal, 19,* 27–41.

Babies without dads: Single women turning to artificial insemination. (1992, Jan. 16). *Edmonton Journal*, p. B9.

Bader, J. E. (1994). Essential lessons of gerontology and geriatrics. *Journal of the American Optometric Association, 65,* 58–62.

Baer, D. M., & Pinkston, E. M. (1997). *Environment and behavior*. Boulder, CO: Westview.

Bagley, C., Bolitho, F., & Bertrand, L. (1997). Sexual assault in school, mental health, and suicidal behaviors in adolescent women in Canada. *Adolescence, 32,* 361–394.

Bahrick, H. P., Bahrick, P. O., & Wittlinger, R. P. (1975). Fifty years of memory for names and faces: A cross-sectional approach. *Journal of Experimental Psychology: General, 104,* 54–75.

Bailey, T. (1991). Jobs of the future and the education they will require: Evidence from occupational forecasts. *Educational Researcher, 20,* 11–20.

Baillargeon, R. (1987). Object permanence in 3 1/2- and 4 1/2-month-old infants. *Developmental Psychology, 23,* 655–664.

Baillargeon, R. (1992). The object concept revisited. In *Visual perception and cognition in infancy: Carnegie-Mellon symposia on cognition* (Vol. 23). Hillsdale, NJ: Erlbaum.

Baird sounds off at Snell. (1994, Oct. 20). *Gateway,* p. 3.

Bajaj, J. S., Misra, A., Rajalakshmi, M., & Madan, R. (1993). Environmental release of chemicals and reproductive ecology. *Environmental Health Perspectives, 2,* 125–130.

Baker, D. P. (1993). Compared to Japan, the U.S. is a low achiever…really: New evidence and comment on Westbury. *Educational Researcher, 22,* 18–20.

Bakwin, H. (1949). Psychologic aspects of pediatrics. *Journal of Pediatrics, 35,* 512–521.

Ball, S. J., Bignold, S., & Cribb, A. (1996). Death and the disease: Inside the culture of childhood cancer. In G. Howarth & P. C. Jupp (Eds.), *Contemporary issues in the sociology of death, dying and disposal.* New York: St. Martin's.

Baltes, M. M., & Silverberg, S. B. (1994). The dynamics between dependency and autonomy: Illustrations across the lifespan. In D. L. Featherman, R. M. Lerner, & M. Perlmutter (Eds.), *Life-span development and behavior* (Vol. 12). Hillsdale, NJ: Erlbaum.

Baltes, P. B., & Staudinger, U. M. (1996). *Interactive minds: Lifespan perspectives on the social foundation of cognition.* New York: Cambridge University Press.

Banaji, M. R., & Prentice, D. A. (1994). The self in adolescence. *Annual Review of Psychology, 45,* 297–332.

Bandura, A. (1969). *Principles of behavior modification.* New York: Holt, Rinehart & Winston.

Bandura, A. (1977). *Social learning theory.* Englewood Cliffs, NJ: Prentice-Hall.

Bandura, A. (1981). Self-referent thought: A developmental analysis of self-efficacy. In J. H. Flavell & L. Ross (Eds.), *Social cognitive development: Frontiers and possible futures.* Cambridge: Cambridge University Press.

Bandura, A. (1986). *Social foundations of thought and action: A social cognitive theory.* Englewood Cliffs, NJ: Prentice-Hall.

Bandura, A. (1993). Perceived self-efficacy in cognitive development and functioning. *Educational Psychologist, 28,* 117–148.

Bandura, A. (Ed.). (1995). *Self-efficacy in changing societies.* New York: Cambridge University Press.

Bandura, A., Ross, D., & Ross, S. A. (1963). Vicarious reinforcement and imitative learning. *Journal of Abnormal and Social Psychology, 67,* 601–607.

Bandura, A., & Walters, R. (1963). *Social learning and personality development.* New York: Holt, Rinehart & Winston.

Banerjee, M. (1997). Hidden emotions: Preschoolers' knowledge of appearance-reality and emotion display rules. *Social Cognition, 15,* 107–132.

Banks, M. S. (1980). The development of visual accommodation during early infancy. *Child Development, 51,* 646–666.

Baran, S. I., Chase, L. I., & Courtright, J. A. (1979). Television drama as a facilitator of prosocial behavior: "The Waltons." *Journal of Broadcasting, 23,* 277–285.

Baranowski, T., Smith, M., Hearn, M. D., Lin, L. S., Baranowski, J., Doyle, C., Resnicow, K., & Wang, D. T. (1997). Patterns in children's fruit and vegetable consumption by meal and day of the week. *Journal of the American College of Nutrition, 16,* 216–223.

Barer, B. M. (1994). Men and women aging differently. *International Journal of Aging and Human Development, 38,* 29–40.

Baris, M. A., & Garrity, C. B. (1997). Co-parenting post-divorce: Helping parents negotiate and maintain low-conflict separations. In W. K. Halford & H. J. Markman (Eds.), *Clinical handbook of marriage and couples interventions.* Chichester, England: John Wiley.

Barnett, W. S. (1992). Benefits of compensatory preschool education. *Journal of Human Resources, 27,* 279–312.

Barnett, W. S. (1993). Benefit–cost analysis of preschool education: Findings from a 25-year follow-up. *American Journal of Orthopsychiatry, 63,* 500–508.

Barrett, G. V., & Depinet, R. L. (1991). A reconsideration of testing for competence rather than for intelligence. *American Psychologist, 46,* 1012–1024.

Bartoshuk, L. M., & Beauchamp, G. K. (1994). Chemical senses. *Annual Review of Psychology, 45,* 419–449.

Bascom-Slack, C. A., Ross, L. O., & Dawson, D. S. (1997). Chiasmata, crossovers, and meiotic chromosome segregation. In J. C. Hall & J. C. Dunlap (Eds.), *Advances in genetics: Incorporating molecular genetic medicine.* San Diego, CA: Academic Press.

Basseches, M. (1984). *Dialectical thinking and adult development.* Norwood, NJ: Ablex.

Basseches, M. (1986). Comments on social cognition in adulthood: A dialectical perspective. *Educational Gerontology, 12,* 327–334.

Bates, E., Thal, D., Whitesell, K., Fenson, L., & Oakes, L. (1989). Integrating language and gesture in infancy. *Developmental Psychology, 25,* 1004–1019.

Bates, J. E. (1989). Concepts and measures of temperament. In G. A. Kohnstamm, J. E. Bates, & M. K. Rothbart (Eds.), *Temperament in Childhood.* New York: John Wiley.

Battistich, V., Watson, M., Solomon, D. I., Schaps, E., & Solomon, J. (1991). The child development project:

A comprehensive program for the development of prosocial character. In W. M. Kurtines & J. L. Gewirtz (Eds.), *Handbook of moral behavior and development* (Vol. 3: Application). Hillsdale, NJ: Erlbaum.

Baum, C. G., & Forehand, R. (1984). Social factors associated with adolescent obesity. *Journal of Pediatric Psychology, 9,* 293–302.

Baumrind, D. (1967). Child care practices anteceding three patterns of pre-school behavior. *Genetic Psychology Monographs, 75,* 43–88.

Baumrind, D. (1977). Some thoughts about child rearing. In S. Cohen & T. J. Comiskey (Eds.), *Child development: Contemporary perspectives.* Itasca, IL: F. E. Peacock.

Baumrind, D. (1989). Rearing competent children. In W. Damon (Ed.), *Child development today and tomorrow.* San Francisco: Jossey-Bass.

Baumrind, D. (1993). The average expectable environment is not good enough: A response to Scarr. *Child Development, 64,* 1299–1317.

Bayer, L. M., Whissell-Buechy, D., & Honzik, M. P. (1981). Health in the middle years. In D. H. Eichorn, J. A. Clausen, N. Haan, M. P. Honzik, & P. H. Mussen (Eds.), *Present and past in middle life.* New York: Academic Press.

Bayley, N. (1969). *Bayley scales of infant development.* New York: The Psychological Corporation.

Beach, S. R. H., & O'Leary, K. D. (1993). Dysphoria and marital discord: Are dysphoric individuals at risk for marital maladjustment? *Journal of Marital and Family Therapy, 19,* 355–368.

Beatty, P. (1991). Foreword. *The Journal of Drug Issues, 21,* 1–7.

Beauchamp, G. K., Cowart, B. J., & Schmidt, H. J. (1991). Development of chemosensory sensitivity and preference. In T. V. Getchell, R. L. Doty, J. B. Snow, & L. M. Bartoshuk (Eds.), *Smell and taste in health and disease.* New York: Raven.

Beck, C. T. (1996). A meta-analysis of the relationship between postpartum depression and infant temperament. *Nursing Research, 45,* 225–230.

Beckwith, L., & Rodning, C. (1991). Intellectual functioning in children born preterm: Recent research. In L. Okagaki & R. J. Sternberg (Eds.), *Directors of development: Influences on the development of children's thinking.* Hillsdale, NJ: Erlbaum.

Beckwith, R. T. (1991). The language of emotion, the emotions, and nominalist bootstrapping. In D. Frye & C. Moore (Eds.), *Children's theories of mind: Mental states and social understanding.* Hillsdale, NJ: Erlbaum.

Bell, A., & Weinberg, M. (1978). *Homosexuality: A study of diversity among men and women.* New York: Simon & Schuster.

Bellamy, C. (1996). *The state of the world's children: 1996.* New York: Oxford University Press.

Bellamy, C. (1997). *The state of the world's children: 1997.* New York: Oxford University Press.

Bellantoni, M. F., & Blackman, M. R. (1996). Menopause and its consequences. In E. L. Schneider & J. W. Rowe (Eds.), *Handbook of the biology of aging.* New York: Academic Press.

Bellow, S. (1982). *The dean's December.* New York: Harper & Row.

Belmont, J. M. (1989). Cognitive strategies and strategic learning: The socio-instructional approach. *American Psychologist, 44,* 142–148.

Belsky, J. (1981). Early human experience: A family perspective. *Developmental Psychology, 17,* 3–23.

Belsky, J. K. (1990). *The psychology of aging: Theory, research, and interventions* (2nd ed.). Pacific Grove, CA: Brooks/Cole.

Belsky, J., Lerner, R. M., & Spanier, G. B. (1984). *The child in the family.* Reading, MA: Addison-Wesley.

Belsky, J., & Rovine, M. (1990). Patterns of marital change across the transition to parenthood: Pregnancy to three years postpartum. *Journal of Marriage and the Family, 52,* 5–20.

Bem, S. (1981). Gender schema theory: A cognitive account of sex typing. *Psychological Review, 88,* 354–364.

Bem, S. L. (1974). The measurement of psychological androgyny. *Journal of Consulting and Clinical Psychology, 42,* 155–162.

Bem, S. L. (1989). Genital knowledge and gender constancy in preschool children. *Child Development, 60,* 649–662.

Benasich, A. A., & Brooks-Gunn, J. (1996). Maternal attitudes and knowledge of child-rearing: Associations with family and child outcomes. *Child Development, 67,* 1186–1205.

Benasich, A. A., Curtiss, S., & Tallal, P. (1993). Language, learning, and behavioral disturbances in childhood: A longitudinal perspective. *Journal of the American Academy of Child and Adolescent Psychiatry, 32,* 585–594.

Benet, S. (1976). *How to live to be 100.* New York: Dial.

Bengtson, V. L. (Ed.). (1996). *Adulthood and aging: Research on continuities and discontinuities.* New York: Springer.

Bennett, K. M. (1996). A longitudinal study of wellbeing in widowed women. *International Journal of Geriatric Psychiatry, 11,* 1005–1010.

Benson-von der Ohe, E. (1984). First and second marriages: The first three years of married life. In S. A. Mednick, M. Harway, & K. M. Finello (Eds.), *Handbook of longitudinal research* (Vol. 2): *Teenage and adult cohorts.* New York: Praeger.

Benthin, A., Slovic, P., & Severson, H. (1993). A psychometric study of adolescent risk perception. *Journal of Adolescence, 16,* 153–168.

Bentley, K. S., & Fox, R. A. (1991). Mothers and fathers of young children: Comparison of parenting styles. *Psychological Reports, 69,* 320–322.

Berg, B., & Turner, D. (1993). MTV unleashed: Sixth graders create music videos based on works of art. *Techtrends, 38,* 28–31.

Berg, S. (1996). Aging, behavior, and terminal decline. In J. E. Birren, K. W. Schaie, R. P. Abeles, M. Gatz, & T. A. Salthouse (Eds.), *Handbook of the psychology of aging* (4th ed.). San Diego, CA: Academic Press.

Berg, W. K., & Berg, K. M. (1987). Psychophysiological development in infancy: State, startle, and attention. In J. D. Osofsky (Ed.), *Handbook of infant development* (2nd ed.). New York: John Wiley.

Bergman, L. R. (1996). Measurement and data quality in longitudinal research. *European Child and Adolescent Psychiatry, 5,* 28–32.

Berkman, C. S., & Zinberg, G. (1997). Homophobia and heterosexism in social workers. *Social Work, 42,* 319–332.

Berko-Gleason, J. (Ed.). (1993). *The development of language* (3rd ed.). Columbus, OH: Merrill.

Berkovic, S. F., & Scheffer, I. E. (1997). Genetics of human partial epilepsy. *Current Opinion in Neurology, 10,* 110–114.

Berland, M. (1991). Genital herpes and childbirth. *Revue Francaise de Gynécologie et D'Obstétrique, 86,* 639–643.

Berman, H. J. (1992/1993). Joyce Carol Oates's "A theory of Knowledge." *International Journal of Aging and Human Development, 36,* 293–302.

Bernal, G., Bonilla, J., & Bellido, C. (1995). Ecological validity and cultural sensitivity for outcome research: Issues for the cultural adaptation and development of psychosocial treatments with Hispanics. Special Issue: Psychosocial treatment research. *Journal of Abnormal Child Psychology, 23,* 67–82.

Berndt, T. J. (1979). Developmental changes in conformity to peers and parents. *Developmental Psychology, 15,* 608–616.

Berndt, T. J. (1988). The nature and significance of children's relationships. In R. Vasta (Ed.), *Annals of child development* (Vol. 5). Greenwich, CT: JAI Press.

Berndt, T. J. (1989). Friendships in childhood and adolescence. In W. Damon (Ed.), *Child development today and tomorrow.* San Francisco: Jossey-Bass.

Berndt, T. J., Cheung, P. C., Lau, S., Hau, K. T., & Lew, W. J. F. (1993). Perceptions of parenting in Mainland China, Taiwan, and Hong Kong: Sex differences and societal differences. *Developmental Psychology, 29,* 156–164.

Berner, R. T. (1992). *Parents whose parents were divorced.* New York: Haworth.

Bertenthal, B. I., & Campos, J. J. (1990). A systems approach to the organizing effects of self-produced locomotion during infancy. In C. Rovee-Collier & L. P. Lipsitt (Eds.), *Advances in infancy research* (Vol. 6). Norwood, NJ: Ablex.

Berthier, M., Oriot, D., Bonneau, D., Chevrel, J., Magnin, G., & Garnier, P. (1993). Failure to prevent physical child abuse despite detection of risk factors at birth and social work follow-up. *Child Abuse and Neglect, 17,* 691–692.

Betz, P., Puschel, K., Miltner, E., Lignitz, E., & Eisenmenger, W. (1996). Morphometrical analysis of retinal hemorrhages in the shaken baby syndrome. *Forensic Science International, 78,* 71–80.

Beunen, G., & Malina, R. M. (1988). Growth and physical performance relative to the timing of the adolescent spurt. *Exercise and Sport Sciences Review, 16,* 503–540.

Beyene, Y. (1989). *From menarche to menopause: Reproductive lives of peasant women in two cultures.* New York: State University of New York Press.

Beyth-Marom, R., Austin, L., Fischhoff, B., Palmgren, C., & Jacobs-Quadrel, M. (1993). Perceived consequences of risky behaviors: Adults and adolescents. *Developmental Psychology, 29,* 549–563.

Bibby, R. W., & Posterski, D. C. (1985). *The emerging generation: An inside look at Canada's teenagers.* Toronto: Irwin.

Bibby, R. W., & Posterski, D. C. (1992). *Teen trends: A nation in motion.* Toronto: Stoddart Publishing.

Bijou, S. W. (1989). Psychological linguistics: Implications for a theory of initial development and a method for research. In H. W. Reese (Ed.), *Advances in child development and behavior.* New York: Academic Press.

Binder, A. (1988). Juvenile delinquency. *Annual Review of Psychology, 39,* 253–282.

Bjorklund, D. F. (1997a). In search of a metatheory for cognitive development (or, Piaget is dead and I don't feel so good myself). *Child Development, 68,* 144–148.

Bjorklund, D. F. (1997b). The role of immaturity in human development. *Psychological Bulletin, 122,* 153–169.

Black, C., & DeBlassie, R. R. (1985). Adolescent pregnancy: Contributing factors, consequences, treatment, and plausible solutions. *Adolescence, 78,* 281–290.

Blake, J., & de Boysson-Bardies, B. (1992). Patterns in babbling: A cross-linguistic study. *Journal of Child Language, 19,* 51–74.

Blau, G. M., Whewell, M. C., Gullotta, T. P., & Bloom, M. (1994). The prevention and treatment of child abuse in households of substance abusers: A research demonstration progress report. *Child Welfare, 73,* 83–94.

Bleeker, S. (1970). *The Zulu of South Africa: Cattlemen, farmers, and warriors.* New York: Morrow.

Bloch, D. P. (1996). Career development and workforce preparation: Educational policy versus school practice. *Career Development Quarterly, 45,* 20–40.

Bloch, H. A., & Niederhoffer, A. (1958). *The gang: A study of adolescent behavior.* New York: Philosophical Library.

Block, J., & Robins, R. W. (1993). A longitudinal study of consistency and change in self-esteem from early adolescence to early adulthood. *Child Development, 64,* 909–923.

Block, S. D., & Billings, J. A. (1994). Patient requests to hasten death. Evaluation and management in terminal care. *Archives of Internal Medicine, 154,* 2039–2047.

Blood, R. O. (1967). *Love match and arranged marriage: A Tokyo–Detroit comparison.* New York: The Free Press.

Bloom, H. G. (1996). Geriatric nutrition. *Journal of Long Term Home Health Care, 15,* 8–23.

Bloom, L., Margulis, C., Tinker, E., & Fujita, N. (1996). Early conversations and word learning: Contributions from child and adult. *Child Development, 67,* 3154–3175.

Blum, K., Noble, E. P., Sheridan, P. J., Montgomery, A., Ritchie, T., Jagadeeswaran, P., Nogami, H., Briggs, A. H., & Cohn, J. B. (1990). Allelic association of human dopamine D$_2$ receptor gene in alcoholism. *Journal of the American Medical Association, 263,* 2055–2060.

Blumenthal, J. A., Sanders Williams, R., Needels, T. L., & Wallace, A. G. (1982). Psychological changes accompany aerobic exercise in healthy middle-aged adults. *Psychosomatic Medicine, 44,* 529–536.

Blustein, D. L. (1997). The role of work in adolescent development. *Career Development Quarterly, 45,* 381–389.

Bodmer, W., & McKie, R. (1995). *The book of man: The Human Genome Project and the quest to discover our genetic heritage.* New York: Scribner.

Bogolub, E. B. (1991). Women and mid-life divorce: Some practical issues. *Social Work, 36,* 428–433.

Boldizar, J. P. (1991). Assessing sex typing and androgyny in children: The Children's Sex Role Inventory. *Developmental Psychology, 27,* 505–515.

Bonen, A. (1994). Exercise-induced menstrual cycle changes. A functional, temporary adaptation to metabolic stress. *Sports Medicine, 17,* 373–392.

Bonta, B. D. (1997). Cooperation and competition in peaceful societies. *Psychological Bulletin, 121,* 299–320.

Boodman, S. (1994, Oct. 8). "Miracle" babies face physical, intellectual disabilities—study. *Edmonton Journal,* p. E2.

Booth, F. W., Weeden, S. H., & Tseng, B. S. (1994). Effect of aging on human skeletal muscle and motor function. *Medicine and Science in Sports and Exercise, 26,* 556–560.

Boring, E. G. (1923). Intelligence as the tests test it. *New Republic, 35,* 35–37.

Bornstein, M. H., & Marks, L. E. (1982, January). Color revisionism. *Psychology Today, 16,* pp. 64–72.

Botella, L., & Feixas, G. (1992/1993). The autobiographical group: A tool for the reconstruction of past life experience with the aged. *International Journal of Aging and Human Development, 36,* 303–319.

Bottoms, B. L., Shaver, P. R., Goodman, G. S., & Qin, J. (1995). In the name of God: A profile of religion-related child abuse. *Journal of Social Issues, 51,* 85–111.

Botwin, M. D., Buss, D. M., & Shackelford, T. K. (1997). Personality and mate preferences: Five factors in mate selection and marital satisfaction. *Journal of Personality, 65,* 107–136.

Botwinick, J. (1984). *Aging and behavior* (3rd ed.). New York: Springer-Verlag.

Bouchard, C., Shephard, R. J., Stephens, T., Sutton, J. R., & McPherson, B. D. (Eds). (1990). *Exercise, fitness, and health: A consensus of current knowledge.* Champaign, IL: Human Kinetics Books.

Bouchard, T. J., Jr., & McGue, M. (1981). Familial studies of intelligence: A review. *Science, 212,* 1055–1059.

Boulton, M. J. (1993). Proximate causes of aggressive fighting in middle-school children. *British Journal of Educational Psychology, 63,* 231–244.

Boulton, M. J. (1996). A comparison of 8– and 11–year-old girls' and boys' participation in specific types of rough-and-tumble play and aggressive fighting: Implications for functional hypotheses. *Aggressive Behavior, 22,* 271–287.

Bower, T. G. R. (1989). *The rational infant: Learning in infancy.* New York: W. H. Freeman.

Bowlby, J. (1958). The nature of the child's tie to his mother. *International Journal of Psychoanalysis, 39,* 350–373.

Bowlby, J. (1969). *Attachment and loss* (Vol. 1): *Attachment.* New York: Basic Books.

Bowlby, J. (1979). *The making and breaking of affectional bonds.* London: Tavistock.

Bowlby, J. (1980). *Attachment and loss* (Vol. 3): *Loss, sadness and depression.* New York: Basic Books.

Bowlby, J. (1982). *Attachment and loss* (Vol. 1): *Attachment* (2nd ed.). London: Hogarth.

Bowman, B. (1993). Early childhood education. In L. Darling-Hammond (Ed.), *Review of Research in Education* (Vol. 19). Washington, DC: American Educational Research Association.

Bowman, J. M. (1990). Maternal blood group immunization. In R. D. Eden, F. H. Boehm, & M. Haire (Eds.), *Assessment and care of the fetus: Physiological, clinical, and medicolegal principles.* Norwalk, CT: Appleton & Lange.

Boyatzis, C. J., Chazan, E., & Ting, C. Z. (1993). Preschool children's decoding of facial emotions. *Journal of Genetic Psychology, 154,* 375–382.

Boyd, G. A. (1976). *Developmental processes in the child's acquisition of syntax: Linguistics in the elementary school.* Itasca, IL: F. E. Peacock.

Boyles, M., & Tilman, R. (1993). Thorstein Veblen, Edward O. Wilson, and sociobiology: An interpretation. *Journal of Economic Issues, 27,* 1195–1218.

Bradley, K. (1997, Nov. 10). Punk stabs senior for $30. *Edmonton Sun,* News 3.

Bradshaw, G. L., & Anderson, J. R. (1982). Elaborative encoding as an explanation of levels of processing. *Journal of Verbal Learning and Verbal Behavior, 21,* 165–174.

Braet, C., Mervielde, I., & Vandereycken, W. (1997). Psychological aspects of childhood obesity: A controlled study in a clinical and nonclinical sample. *Journal of Pediatric Psychology, 22,* 59–71.

Braine, L. G., Pomerantz, E., Lorber, D., & Krantz, D. H. (1991). Conflicts with authority: Children's feelings, actions, and justifications. *Developmental Psychology, 27,* 829–840.

Bramham, D. (1994, April 16). Putting pain in punishment. *Edmonton Journal,* p. G3.

Brannen, J. (1996). Discourses of adolescence: Young people's independence and autonomy within families. In J. Brannen & M. O'Brien (Eds.), *Children in families: Research and policy.* Washington, DC: Falmer.

Brannen, J., & O'Brien, M. (Eds.). (1996). *Children in families: Research and policy.* Washington, DC: Falmer.

Brazelton, T. B. (1973). *Neonatal behavior assessment scale.* Philadelphia: Lippincott.

Brazelton, T. B. (1990). Saving the bathwater. *Child Development, 61,* 1661–1671.

Brazelton, T. B., Nugent, J. K., & Lester, B. M. (1987). Neonatal behavioral assessment scale. In J. D. Osofsky (Ed.), *Handbook of infant development.* New York: John Wiley.

Brecher, E. M., and the editors of Consumer Reports books. (1984). *Love, sex and aging: A Consumers Union Report.* Boston: Little, Brown.

Brendt, R. L., & Beckman, D. A. (1990). Teratology. In R. D. Eden, F. H. Boehm, & M. Haire (Eds.), *Assessment and care of the fetus: Physiological, clinical, and medicolegal principles.* Norwalk, CT: Appleton & Lange.

Brenner, J., & Mueller, E. (1982). Shared meaning in boy toddler's peer relations. *Child Development, 53,* 380–391.

Bretherton, I. (1991). Intentional communication and the development of an understanding of mind. In D. Frye & C. Moore (Eds.), *Children's theories of mind: Mental states and social understanding.* Hillsdale, NJ: Erlbaum.

Brick, P., & Roffman, D. M. (1993). "Abstinence, no buts" is simplistic. *Educational Leadership, 51,* 90–92.

Bridges, L. J., Connell, J. P., & Belsky, J. (1988). Similarities and differences in infant–mother and infant–father interaction in the strange situation: A component process analysis. *Developmental Psychology, 24,* 92–100.

Brisk, M. E. (1991). Toward multilingual and multicultural mainstream education. *Journal of Education, 173,* 114–129.

Britner, P. A., & Phillips, D. A. (1995). Predictors of parent and provider satisfaction with child day care dimensions: A comparison of center-based and family child day care. *Child Welfare, 74,* 1135–1168.

Brodaty, H., & Moore, C. M. (1997). The Clock Drawing Test for dementia of the Alzheimer's type: A comparison of three scoring methods in a memory disorders clinic. *International Journal of Geriatric Psychiatry, 12,* 619–627.

Brodigan, D. E. (1992). Osteoporosis. The effects of exercise variables. *Melpomene Journal, 11,* 16–22.

Bromley, D. B. (1990). *Behavioural gerontology: Central issues in the psychology of ageing.* New York: John Wiley.

Bronfenbrenner, U. (1979). *The ecology of human development.* Cambridge, MA: Harvard University Press.

Bronfenbrenner, U. (1989). Ecological systems theory. In R. Vasta (Ed.), *Annals of child development* (Vol. 6). Greenwich, CT: JAI Press.

Bronfenbrenner, U:, Belsky, J., & Steinberg, L. (1977). Daycare in context: An ecological perspective on research and public policy. In *Policy issues in daycare.* Washington, DC: U.S. Department of Health & Human Services.

Bronson, G. W. (1972). Infants' reactions to unfamiliar persons and novel objects. *Monographs of the Society for Research in Child Development, 37*(3).

Bronstein, P., Clauson, J., Stoll, M. F., & Abrams, C. L. (1993). Parenting behavior and children's social, psychological, and academic adjustment in diverse family structures. *Family Relations, 42,* 268–276.

Brookins, C. C. (1996). Exploring psychosocial task resolution and self-concept among African-American adolescents. *Perceptual and Motor Skills, 82,* 803–810.

Brooks, J. B. (1981). *The process of parenting.* Palo Alto, CA: Mayfield.

Brooks-Gunn, J. (1988). Antecedents and consequences of variations in girls' maturational timing. *Journal of Adolescent Health Care, 9,* 365–373.

Brooks-Gunn, J., & Furstenberg, F. F., Jr. (1989). Adolescent sexual behavior. *American Psychologist, 44,* 249–257.

Brouwer, A. (1990). The nature of ageing. In M. A. Horan & A. Brouwer (Eds.), *Gerontology: Approaches to biomedical and clinical research.* London: Edward Arnold.

Brouwers, M., & Wiggum, C. D. (1993). Bulimia and perfectionism: Developing the courage to be imperfect. *Journal of Mental Health Counseling, 15,* 141–149.

Brown, B. B., Mounts, N., Lamborn, S. D., & Steinberg, L. (1993). Parenting practices and peer group affiliation in adolescence. *Child Development, 64,* 467–482.

Brown, J., & Finn, P. (1982). Drinking to get drunk: Findings of a survey of junior and senior high school students. *Journal of Alcohol and Drug Education, 27,* 13–25.

Brown, J. L. (1964). States in newborn infants. *Merrill–Palmer Quarterly, 10,* 313–327.

Brown, K., Covell, K., & Abramovitch, R. (1991). Time course and control of emotion: Age differences in understanding and recognition. *Merrill–Palmer Quarterly, 37,* 273–287.

Brown, M. H. (1991). Innovations in the treatment of bulimia: Transpersonal psychology, relaxation, imagination, hypnosis, myth, and ritual. *Journal of Humanistic Education and Development, 30,* 50–60.

Brown, R. (1973). *A first language: The early stages.* Cambridge, MA: Harvard University Press.

Brownell, K. D., & Wadden, T. A. (1992). Etiology and treatment of obesity: Understanding a serious, prevalent, and refractory disorder. *Journal of Consulting and Clinical Psychology, 60,* 505–517.

Bruner, J. S. (1978, September). Learning the mother tongue. *Human Nature,* pp. 43–49.

Bruner, J. S. (1983). *Child's talk.* New York: Norton.

Bruner, J. S. (1986). *Actual minds, possible worlds.* Cambridge, MA: Harvard University Press.

Bryant, B. K. (1992). Conflict resolution strategies in relation to children's peer relations. *Journal of Applied Developmental Psychology, 13,* 35–50.

Buchanan, C. M., Eccles, J. S., & Becker, J. B. (1992). Are adolescents the victims of raging hormones: Evidence for activational effects of hormones on moods and behavior at adolescence. *Psychological Bulletin, 111,* 62–107.

Buchholz, E. S., & Korn-Bursztyn, C. (1993). Children of adolescent mothers: Are they at risk for abuse? *Adolescence, 28,* 361–382.

Bullies drive teen to suicide. (1994, Dec. 6). *Edmonton Sun,* p. 24.

Bullinger, A. (1985). The sensorimotor nature of the infant visual system: Cognitive problems. In V. L. Shulman, L. C. R. Restaino-Baumann, & L. Butler (Eds.), *The future of Piagetian theory: The neo-Piagetians* (pp. 19–32). New York: Plenum.

Bullock, J. R. (1993). Children's loneliness and their relationships with family and peers. *Family Relations, 42,* 46–49.

Bullock, J. R. (1994). Children without friends: Who are they and how can teachers help? *Childhood Education, 69,* 92–96.

Bullock, M. (1985). Animism in childhood thinking: A new look at an old question. *Developmental Psychology, 21,* 217–225.

Bullough, V. L., & Bullough, B. (1997). The history of the science of sexual orientation 1880–1980: An overview. *Journal of Psychology and Human Sexuality, 9,* 1–16.

Bunce, V. L., & Harrison, D. W. (1991). Child- or adult-directed speech and esteem: Effects on performance and arousal in elderly adults. *International Journal of Aging and Human Development, 32,* 125–134.

Burgard, D. (1993). Psychological theory seeks to define obesity. *Obesity and Health, 7,* 25–27, 37.

Burkam, D. T., Lee, V. E., & Smerdon, B. A. (1997). Gender and science learning early in high school: Subject matter and laboratory experiences. *American Educational Research Journal, 34,* 297–331.

Burke, J. (1991). Teenagers, clothes, and gang violence. *Educational Leadership, 49,* 11–13.

Burleson, B. R., Kunkel, A. W., & Szolwinski, J. B. (1997). Similarity in cognitive complexity and attraction to friends and lovers: Experimental and correlational studies. *Journal of Constructivist Psychology, 10,* 221–248.

Burnett, B. B. (1993). The psychological abuse of latency age children: A survey. *Child Abuse and Neglect: The International Journal, 17,* 441–454.

Burns, A., Dunlop, R., & Taylor, A. (1997). Children and parental divorce: The meaning of small effects. *Australian Psychologist, 32,* 136–138.

Burr, D. C., Morrone, M. C., & Fiorentini, A. (1996). Spatial and temporal properties of infant colour vision. In F. Vital-Durand, J. Atkinson, & O. J. Braddick (Eds.), *Infant vision.* New York: Oxford University Press.

Burton, E. (1993). *Eating disorders: Personal construct therapy and change.* New York: John Wiley.

Bush calls for unprecedented increase in Head Start program. (1992, Jan. 22). *Monterey Herald,* p. A3.

Bushnell, E. W., & Boudreau, J. P. (1993). Motor development and the mind: The potential role of motor abilities as a determinant of aspects of perceptual development. *Child Development, 64,* 1005–1021.

Buss, A. H., & Plomin, R. (1985). *Temperament: Early developing personality traits.* Hillsdale, NJ: Erlbaum.

Bussey, K. (1992). Lying and truthfulness: Children's definitions, standards, and evaluative reactions. *Child Development, 63,* 129–137.

Butler, E. R. (1993). Alcohol use by college students: A rites of passage ritual. *Naspa Journal, 31,* 48–55.

Butler, J. R., & Burton, L. M. (1990). Rethinking teenage childbearing: Is sexual abuse a missing link? *Family Relations, 39,* 73–80.

Butler, R. N. (1963). The life review: An interpretation of reminiscence in the aged. *Psychiatry, 26,* 65–76.

Butler, R. N. (1989). Productive aging. In V. L. Bengtson & K. W. Schaie (Eds.), *The course of later life: Research and reflections.* New York: Springer.

Buzzelli, C. A. (1992). Young children's moral understanding: Learning about right and wrong. *Young Children, 47,* 48–53.

Byczkowski, J. Z., Gearhart, J. M., & Fisher, J. W. (1994). "Occupational" exposure of infants to toxic chemicals via breast milk. *Nutrition, 10,* 43–48.

Bynner, J. M. (1997). Basic skills in adolescents' occupational preparation. *Career Development Quarterly, 45*, 304–321.

Byrne, B. M., & Shavelson, R. J. (1987). Adolescent self-concept: Testing the assumption of equivalent structure across gender. *American Educational Research Journal, 24*, 365–385.

Byrne, G. J., & Raphael, B. (1994). A longitudinal study of bereavement phenomena in recently widowed elderly men. *Psychological Medicine, 24*, 411–421.

Cain, J., Stacy, L., Jusenius, K., & Figge, D. (1990). The quality of dying: Financial, psychological, and ethical dilemmas. *Obstetrics and Gynecology, 76*, 149–152.

Cairns, R. B., Gariépy, J. L., & Hood, K. E. (1990). Development, microevolution, and social behavior. *Psychological Review, 97*, 49–65.

Caldwell, B. (1991). Educare: New product, new future. *Journal of Developmental and Behavioral Pediatrics, 12*, 199–205.

Caldwell, B. M. (1989). Achieving rights for children: Role of the early childhood profession. *Childhood Education, 66*, 4–7.

Calgarian, 101, on the road again. (1997, Oct. 4). *Edmonton Journal*, p. A11.

Camp, B. W. (1995). Maternal characteristics of adolescent mothers and older mothers of infants. *Psychological Reports, 77*, 1152–1154.

Campbell, A. (1981). *The sense of well-being in America: Recent patterns and trends.* New York: McGraw-Hill.

Campbell, A., Converse, P. E., & Rodgers, W. L. (1976). *The quality of American life: Perceptions, evaluations, and satisfactions.* New York: Russell Sage.

Campbell, F. A., & Ramey, C. T. (1990). The relationship between Piagetian cognitive development, mental test performance, and academic achievement in high-risk students with and without early educational intervention. *Intelligence, 14*, 293–308.

Campbell, S., & Silverman, P. R. (1996). *Widower: When men are left alone.* Amityville, NY: Baywood.

Campbell, S. B., & Cohn, J. F. (1991). Prevalence and correlates of postpartum depression in first-time mothers. *Journal of Abnormal Psychology, 100*, 594–599.

Canada Yearbook 1997. Ottawa, Ontario: Minister of Industry, Communications Division, Statistics Canada, 1996.

Canaff, A. L. (1997). Later life career planning: A new challenge for career counselors. *Journal of Employment Counseling, 34*, 85–93.

Canning, P. M., & Lyon, M. E. (1991). Misconceptions about early child care, education and intervention. *Journal of Child and Youth Care, 5*, 1–10.

Cantor, C. H., Leenaars, A. A., Lester, D., Slater, P. J., et al. (1996). Suicide trends in eight predominantly English-speaking countries, 1960–1989. *Social Psychiatry and Psychiatric Epidemiology, 31*, 363–373.

Carey, W. B. (1989). Introduction: Basic issues. In W. B. Carey & S. C. McDevitt (Eds.), *Clinical and educational applications of temperament research.* Berwyn, PA: Swets North America.

Carey, W. B., & McDevitt, S. C. (Eds.). (1989). *Clinical and educational applications of temperament research.* Berwyn, PA: Swets North America.

Carpenter, B. D. (1993). A review and new look at ethical suicide in advanced age. *Gerontologist, 33*, 359–365.

Carroll, J. C., & Rest, J. R. (1982). Moral development. In B. B. Wolman et al. (Eds.), *Handbook of developmental psychology.* Englewood Cliffs, NJ: Prentice-Hall.

Case, R., Hayward, S., Lewis, M., & Hurst, P. (1988). Toward a neo-Piagetian theory of cognitive and emotional development. *Developmental Review, 8*, 1–51.

Caspi, A., Lynam, D., Moffitt, T. E., & Silva, P. A. (1993). Unraveling girls' delinquency: Biological, dispositional, and contextual contributions to adolescent misbehavior. *Developmental Psychology, 29*, 19–30.

Cattell, R. B. (1971). *Abilities: Their structure, growth, and action.* Boston: Houghton Mifflin.

Caughy, M. O., DiPietro, J. A., & Strobino, D. M. (1994). Day care participation as a protective factor in the cognitive development of low-income children. *Child Development, 65*, 457–471.

Ceci, S. J. (1991). How much does schooling influence general intelligence and its cognitive components? A reassessment of the evidence. *Developmental Psychology, 27*, 703–722.

Celiberti, D. A., Bobo, H. E., Kelly, K. S., Harris, S. L., & Handleman, J. S. (1997). The differential and temporal effects of antecedent exercise on the self-stimulatory behavior of a child with autism. *Research in Developmental Disabilities, 18*, 139–150.

Center for Disease Control. (1992). Vigorous physical activity among high school students—United States, 1990. *Morbidity and Mortality Weekly Report, 41*, 33–36.

Chapman, P., Toma, R. B., Tuveson, R. V., & Jacob, M. (1997). Nutrition knowledge among adolescent high school female athletes. *Adolescence, 32*, 437–446.

Chappell, P. A., & Steitz, J. A. (1993). Young children's human figure drawings and cognitive development. *Perceptual and Motor Skills, 76*, 611–617.

Charlesworth, W. R. (1995). An evolutionary approach to cognition and learning. In C. A. Nelson (Ed.), *Basic and applied perspectives on learning, cognition, and development: The Minnesota Symposia on Child Psychology* (Vol. 28). Mahwah, NJ: Erlbaum.

Charlesworth, W. R. (1996). Co-operation and competition: Contributions to an evolutionary and developmental model. *International Journal of Behavioral Development, 19,* 25–38.

Chase-Lansdale, P. L., & Brooks-Gunn, J. (1994). Correlates of adolescent pregnancy and parenthood. In C. B. Fisher & R. M. Lerner (Eds.), *Applied developmental psychology.* New York: McGraw-Hill.

Cheng, Pui-wan. (1993). Metacognition and giftedness. *Gifted Child Quarterly, 37,* 105–112.

Cherian, V. I. (1990). Academic achievement of children from monogamous and polygynous families. *Journal of Social Psychology, 130,* 117–119.

Cherny, N. I. (1996). The problem of inadequately relieved suffering. *Journal of Social Issues, 52,* 13–30.

Chester, R. D. (1992). Views from the mainstream: Learning disabled students as perceived by regular education classroom teachers and by non-learning disabled secondary students. *Canadian Journal of School Psychology, 8,* 93–102.

Cheung, R. T. F., & Hachinski, V. (1997). Vascular factors in cognitive decline. In H. M. Fillit & R. N. Butler (Eds.), *Cognitive decline: Strategies for prevention.* London: Greenwich Medical Media.

Cheung, Y. W., Erickson, P. G., & Landau, T. C. (1991). Experience of crack use: Findings from a community-based sample in Toronto. *Journal of Drug Issues, 21,* 121–140.

Chez, R. A., & Chervenak, J. L. (1990). Nutrition in pregnancy. In R. D. Eden, F. H. Boehm, & M. Haire (Eds.), *Assessment and care of the fetus: Physiological, clinical, and medicolegal principles.* Norwalk, CT: Appleton & Lange.

Childhood Obesity. KRON-TV, September 24, 1997.

Children's Defense Fund (CDF). (1996). *The state of America's children: Yearbook 1996.* Washington, DC: Author.

Chiocca, E. M. (1995). Shaken baby syndrome: A nursing perspective. *Pediatric Nursing, 21,* 33–38.

Chipman, S. F. (1988). Far too sexy a topic. *Educational Researcher, 17,* 46–49.

Chiriboga, D. A. (1996). In search of continuities and discontinuities across time and culture. In V. L. Bengtson (Ed.), *Adulthood and aging: Research on continuities and discontinuities.* New York: Springer.

Chodzko-Zajko, W. J. (1997). The Heidelberg Guidelines for Promoting Physical Activity Among Older Persons. *Journal of Aging and Physical Activity, 5,* 2–8.

Chomsky, N. (1957). *Syntactic structures.* The Hague: Mouton.

Chomsky, N. (1965). *Aspects of the theory of syntax.* Cambridge, MA: MIT Press.

Chrisman, A. B. (1968). *Shen of the sea: Chinese stories for children.* New York: Dutton.

Christakis, N. A. (1994). Timing of referral of terminally ill patients to an outpatient hospice. *Journal of General Internal Medicine, 9,* 314–320.

Christensen, H., Henderson, A. S., Griffiths, K., & Levings, C. (1997). Does ageing inevitably lead to declines in cognitive performance: A longitudinal study of elite academics. *Personality and Individual Differences, 23,* 67–78.

Christian, L., & Morgan, G. H. (1993). Roses are red, violets are blue, my child is gifted and my family's a zoo. *Gifted Child Today, 16,* 14–17.

Christie, N. G., & Dinham, S. M. (1991). Institutional and external influences on social integration in the freshman year. *Journal of Higher Education, 62,* 412–436.

Christopher, F. S., & Roosa, M. W. (1990). An evaluation of an adolescent pregnancy prevention program: Is "Just say no" enough? *Family Relations, 39,* 68–72.

Christopherson, V. A. (1988). The family as a socialization context. In T. D. Yawkey & J. E. Johnson (Eds.), *Integrative processes and socialization: Early to middle childhood.* Hillsdale, NJ: Erlbaum.

Ciesielski, K. T., & Knight, J. E. (1994). Cerebellar abnormality in autism: A nonspecific effect of early brain damage? *Acta Neurobiologiae Experimentalis, 54,* 151–154.

Claes, M., & Simard, R. (1992). Friendship characteristics of delinquent adolescents. *International Journal of Adolescence and Youth, 3,* 287–301.

Clark, M. L., & Bittle, M. L. (1992). Friendship expectations and the evaluation of present friendships in middle childhood and early adolescence. *Child Study Journal, 22,* 115–135.

Clarke-Stewart, K. A., Gruber, C. P., & Fitzgerald, L. M. (1994). *Children at home and in day care.* Hillsdale, NJ: Erlbaum.

Clausen, S. E. (1996). Parenting styles and adolescent drug use behaviours. *Childhood, 3,* 403–414.

Claxton, J. W. (1993). Paving the way to acceptance. Psychological adaptation to death and dying in cancer. *Professional Nurse, 8,* 206–211.

Clayton, V. P., & Birren, J. E. (1980). The development of wisdom across the life span: A reexamination of an ancient topic. In P. B. Baltes & O. G. Brim, Jr. (Eds.), *Life-span development and behavior* (Vol. 3). New York: Academic Press.

Clerici, M., Carta, I., & Cazzullo, C. L. (1994). Drug addiction behaviors, attempted suicide and adolescent crisis. *Psychologie Medicale, 26,* 33–36.

Clifford, B. R., Gunter, B., & McAleer, J. (1995). *Television and children: Program evaluation, comprehension, and impact.* Hillsdale, NJ: Erlbaum.

Cobb, P. (1994). Constructivism in mathematics and science education. *Educational Researcher, 23,* 4.

Cohen, S. (1993/1994). Television in the lives of children and their families. *Childhood Education, 70,* 103–104.

Cohler, B. J. (1982). Personal narrative and lifecourse. In P. B. Baltes & O. G. Brim, Jr. (Eds.), *Life-span development and behavior* (Vol. 4, pp. 205–241). New York: Academic Press.

Cohler, B. J., & Grunebaum, H. V. (1981). *Mothers, grandmothers and daughters: Personality and childcare in three-generation families.* New York: John Wiley.

Colborn, T., vom Saal, F. S., & Soto, A. M. (1993). Developmental effects of endocrine-disrupting chemicals in wildlife and humans. *Environmental Health Perspectives, 101,* 378–384.

Colby, A., & Damon, W. (1995). The development of extraordinary moral commitment. In M. Killen & D. Hart (Eds.), *Morality in everyday life: Developmental perspectives.* New York: Cambridge University Press.

Colby, A., & Kohlberg, L. (1984). Invariant sequence and internal consistency in moral judgment stages. In W. M. Kertines & J. L. Gewirtz (Eds.), *Morality, moral behavior, and moral development* (pp. 41–51). New York: John Wiley.

Cole, P. G. (1993). A critical analysis of Siegel's case for revision of the learning disability construct. *International Journal of Disability, Development and Education, 40,* 5–21.

Cole, P. M., Usher, B. A., & Cargo, A. P. (1993). Cognitive risk and its association with risk for disruptive behavior disorder in preschoolers. *Journal of Clinical Child Psychology, 22,* 154–164.

Coleman, A. (1992). Coping with change: Focus on "retirement." *International Review of Education, 38,* 438–443.

Coleman, J. S. (1974). *Youth: Transition to adulthood.* Chicago: University of Chicago Press.

Coleman, P. G. (1986). *Aging and reminiscence processes: Social and clinical implications.* New York: John Wiley.

Coleman, P. M. (1993). Depression during the female climacteric period. *Journal of Advanced Nursing, 18,* 1540–1546.

Collett, J., & Serrano, B. (1992). Stirring it up: The inclusive classroom. *New Directions for Teaching and Learning, 49,* 35–48.

Collins, A., Brown, J. S., & Newman, S. E. (1989). Cognitive apprenticeship: Teaching the craft of reading, writing, and mathematics. In L. B. Resnick (Ed.), *Knowing, learning, and instruction: Essays in honor of Robert Glaser.* Hillsdale, NJ: Erlbaum.

Collins, C., Stommel, M., Wang, S., & Given, C. W. (1994). Caregiving transitions: Changes in depression among family caregivers of relatives with dementia. *Nursing Research, 43,* 220–225.

Collins, N. L., Dunkel-Schetter, C., Lobel, M., & Scrimshaw, S. C. (1993). Social support in pregnancy: Psychosocial correlates of birth outcomes and postpartum depression. *Journal of Personality and Social Psychology, 65,* 1243–1258.

Collins, W. A., & Gunnar, M. R. (1990). Social and personality development. *Annual Review of Psychology, 41,* 387–416.

Collins, W. A., & Russell, G. (1991). Mother–child and father–child relationships in middle childhood and adolescence: A developmental analysis. *Developmental Review, 11,* 99–136.

Committee on Drugs, American Academy of Pedriatrics. (1994). The transfer of drugs and other chemicals into human milk. *Pediatrics, 93,* 135–150.

Connidis, I. A., & McMullin, J. A. (1993). To have or have not: Parent status and the subjective well-being of older men and women. *Gerontologist, 33,* 630–636.

Cooke, B. (1991). Family life education. *Family Relations, 40,* 3–13.

Cooksey, E. C., Rindfuss, R. R., & Guilkey, D. K. (1996). The initiation of adolescent sexual and contraceptive behavior during changing times. *Journal of Health and Social Behavior, 37,* 59–74.

Cookson, C., & Green, D. (1997, Nov. 5). Genetic research gathers steam. *Financial Times,* p. 60.

Cooley, C. H. (1902). *Human nature and the social order.* New York: Scribner's.

Coombs, R. H. (1991). Marital status and personal well-being: A literature review. *Family Relations, 40,* 97–102.

Cooney, T. M., & Uhlenberg, P. (1992). Support from parents over the life course: The adult child's perspective. *Social Forces, 71,* 63–84.

Corbin, C. B., & Pangrazi, R. P. (1992). Are American children and youth fit? *Research Quarterly for Exercise and Sport, 62,* 96–106.

Corlett, E. S., & Millner, N. B. (1993). *Navigating midlife: Using typology as a guide.* Palo Alto, CA: CPP Books.

Correy, J. F., Newman, N. M., Collins, J. A., Burrows, E. A., Burrows, R. F., & Curran, J. T. (1992). Use of prescription drugs in the first trimester and congenital malformations. *Australian & New Zealand Journal of Obstetrics & Gynaecology, 31,* 340–344.

Costa, P. T., Jr., & McCrae, R. R. (1978). Objective personality assessment. In M. Storandt, I. C. Siegler, & M. F. Elias (Eds.), *The clinical psychology of aging.* New York: Plenum.

Costa, P. T., Jr., & McCrae, R. R. (1980). Still stable after all these years: Personality as a key to some issues in aging. In P. B. Baltes & O. G. Brim (Eds.), *Life-span development and behavior* (Vol. 3). New York: Academic Press.

Costa, P. T., Jr., & McCrae, R. R. (1984). Personality as a lifelong determinant of well being. In C. Z. Malatesta & C. E. Izard (Eds.), *Emotion in adult development* (pp. 141–158). Beverly Hills, CA: Sage.

Costa, P. T., Jr., & McCrae, R. R. (1994). Set like plaster? Evidence for the stability of adult personality. In T. F. Heatherton & J. L. Weinberger (Eds.), *Can personality change?* Washington, DC: American Psychological Association.

Costa, P. T., Jr., McCrae, R. R., & Arenberg, D. (1983). Recent longitudinal research on personality and aging. In K. W. Schaie (Ed.), *Longitudinal studies of adult psychological development* (pp. 222–265). New York: Guilford.

Côté, J. E., & Levine, C. (1988). A critical examination of the ego identity status paradigm. *Developmental Review, 8,* 147–184.

Côté, J. E., & Levine, C. G. (1992). The genesis of the humanistic academic: A second test of Erikson's theory of ego identity formation. *Youth and Society, 23,* 387–410.

Coulter, D. L. (1993). Epilepsy and mental retardation: An overview. *American Journal on Mental Retardation, 98,* 1–11.

Court to decide right of surrogate mother. (1992, Jan. 24). *Monterey Herald,* p. A8.

Coustan, D. R. (1990). Diabetes mellitus. In R. D. Eden, F. H. Boehm, & M. Haire (Eds.), *Assessment and care of the fetus: Physiological, clinical, and medicolegal principles.* Norwalk, CT: Appleton & Lange.

Coward, R. T., Hogan, T. L., Duncan, R. P., & Horne, C. H. (1995). Job satisfaction of nurses employed in rural and urban long-term care facilities. *Research in Nursing and Health, 18,* 271–284.

Cowen, E. L., Work, W. C., Hightower, A. D., Wyman, P. A., Parker, G. R., & Lotyczewski, B. S. (1991). Toward the development of a measure of perceived self-efficacy in children. *Journal of Clinical Child Psychology, 20,* 169–178.

Cox, H. G. (1988). *Later life: The realities of aging* (2nd ed.). Englewood Cliffs, NJ: Prentice-Hall.

Cox, T. C., Jacobs, M. R., Leblanc, A. E., & Marshman, J. A. (1983). *Drugs and drug abuse: A reference test.* Toronto: Addiction Research Foundation.

Craig, O. (1997, Dec. 2). Surrogate pregnant with dead woman's frozen embryo. *Edmonton Journal,* p. A7.

Craik, F. I. M., & Jacoby, L. L. (1996). Aging and memory: Implications for skilled performance. In W. A. Rogers, A. D. Fisk, & N. Walker (Eds.), *Aging and skilled performance: Advances in theory and applications.* Mahwah, NJ: Erlbaum.

Crawford, M. A. (1993). The role of essential fatty acids in neural development: Implications for perinatal nutrition. *American Journal of Clinical Nutrition, 57,* 703s–709s.

Crawford, M. A., Doyle, W., Leaf, A., Leighfield, M., Ghebremeskel, K., & Phylactos, A. (1993). Nutrition and neurodevelopmental disorders. *Nutrition and Health, 9,* 81–97.

Crawford, P. B., & Shapiro, L. R. (1991). How obesity develops: A new look at nature and nurture. *Obesity and Health, 5,* 40–41.

Creasy, R. K. (1990). Preterm labor. In R. D. Eden, F. H. Boehm, & M. Haire (Eds.), *Assessment and care of the fetus: Physiological, clinical, and medicolegal principles.* Norwalk, CT: Appleton & Lange.

Crick, N. R. (1996). The role of relational aggression, overt aggression, and prosocial behavior in the prediction of children's future social adjustment. *Child Development, 67,* 2317–2327.

Crick, N. R., Casas, J. F., & Mosher, M. (1997). Relational and overt aggression in preschool. *Developmental Psychology, 33,* 579–588.

Crick, N. R., & Ladd, G. W. (1993). Children's perceptions of their peer experiences: Attributions, loneliness, social anxiety, and social avoidance. *Developmental Psychology, 29,* 244–254.

Crockett, L. J., & Petersen, A. C. (1987). Pubertal status and psychosocial development: Findings from the early adolescence study. In R. M. Lerner & T. T. Foch (Eds.), *Biological–psychosocial interactions in early adolescence: A life-span perspective.* Hillsdale, NJ: Erlbaum.

Crosbie-Burnett, M., & Helmbrecht, L. (1993). A descriptive empirical study of gay male stepfamilies. *Family Relations, 42,* 256–262.

Crouter, A. C., Mchale, S. M., & Bartko, W. T. (1993). Gender as an organizing feature in parent–child relationships. In R. A. Pierce & M. A. Black (Eds.), *Life-span development: A diversity reader.* Dubuque, IA: Kendall/Hunt.

Crowell, J. A., & Feldman, S. S. (1991). Mothers' working models of attachment relationships and mother and child behavior during separation and reunion. *Developmental Psychology, 27,* 597–605.

Crystal, D. S., Watanabe, H., & Chin, W. (1997). Intolerance of human differences: A cross-cultural and developmental study of American, Japanese, and Chinese children. *Journal of Applied Developmental Psychology, 18,* 149–167.

Cummins, J., & Swain, M. (1986). *Bilingualism in education: Aspects of theory, research and practice.* London: Taylor & Fry.

Cunningham, H. (1996). The history of childhood. In C. P. Hwang, M. E. Lamb, & I. E. Sigel (Eds.), *Images of Childhood.* Mahwah, NJ: Erlbaum.

Curcio, C. A., Millican, C. L., Allen, K. A., & Kalina, R. E. (1994). Aging of the human photoreceptor mosaic: Evidence for selective vulnerability of rods in central retina. *Investigative Ophthalmology and Visual Science, 34,* 3278–3296.

Curtiss, S. (1977). *Genie: A psycholinguistic study of a modern-day wild child.* New York: Academic Press.

Curtius, H. C., Endres, W., & Blau, N. (1994). Effect of high-protein meal plus aspartame ingestion on plasma phenylalanine concentrations in obligate heterozygotes for phenylketonuria. *Metabolism: Clinical and Experimental, 43,* 413–416.

Cutright, M. C. (1992). Self-esteem: The key to a child's success and happiness. *PTA Today, 17,* 5–6.

Cziko, G. A. (1992). The evaluation of bilingual education. *Educational Researcher, 21,* 10–15.

Dalton, K. (1980). *Depression after childbirth.* Oxford: Oxford University Press.

Dalton, T. C., & Bergenn, V. W. (1995). Reconsidering McGraw's contribution to developmental psychology. In T. C. Dalton & V. W. Bergenn (Eds.), *Beyond heredity and environment: Myrtle McGraw and the maturation controversy.* Boulder, CO: Westview.

Damon, W., & Colby, A. (1987). Social influence and moral change. In W. M. Kurtines & J. L. Gewirtz (Eds.), *Moral development through social interaction.* New York: John Wiley.

Darley, J. M., & Shultz, T. R. (1990). Moral rules: Their content and acquisition. *Annual Review of Psychology, 41,* 525–556.

Darling, C. A., Kallen, D. J., & Van Dusen, J. E. (1984). Sex in transition, 1900–1980. *Journal of Youth and Adolescence, 13,* 385–394.

Darwin, C. (1877). A biographical sketch of an infant. *Mind, 2,* 285–294.

Das, J. P. (1995). Some thoughts on two aspects of Vygotsky's work. *Educational Psychologist, 30,* 93–97.

Datan, N., Rodeheaver, D., & Hughes, F. (1987). Adult development and aging. *Annual Review of Psychology, 38,* 153–180.

D'Augelli, A. R. (1993). Lesbian and gay male undergraduates' experiences of harassment and fear on campus. In R. A. Pierce & M. A. Black (Eds.), *Life-span development: A diversity reader.* Dubuque, IA: Kendall/Hunt.

Davidson, J. K., Sr., & Darling, C. A. (1988). Changing autoerotic attitudes and practices among college females: A two-year follow-up study. *Adolescence, 23,* 773–792.

Davies, C. (1996). Dirt, death, decay, and dissolution: American denial and British avoidance. In G. Howarth & P. C. Jupp (Eds.), *Contemporary issues in the sociology of death, dying and disposal.* New York: St. Martin's.

Davies, G. M. (1993). Children's memory for other people: An integrative review. In C. A. Nelson (Ed.), *Memory and affect in development: The Minnesota Symposia on Child Psychology* (Vol. 26). Hillsdale, NJ: Erlbaum.

Davies, I. (1990). A physiological approach to ageing. In M. A. Horan & A. Brouwer (Eds.), *Gerontology: Approaches to biomedical and clinical research.* London: Edward Arnold.

Davis, D. W. (1997). Review of cerebral palsy, Part I: Description, incidence, and etiology. *Neonatal Network, 16,* 7–12.

Dawis, R. V. (1992). The individual differences tradition in counseling psychology. *Journal of Counseling Psychology, 39,* 7–19.

Dawkins, M. P. (1997). Drug use and violent crime among adolescents. *Adolescence, 32,* 395–405.

Day, A. T. (1991). *Remarkable survivors: Insights into successful aging among women.* Washington, DC: Urban Institute Press.

Deal, L. V., & Haas, W. H. (1996). Hearing and the development of language and speech. *Folia Phoniatrtica et Logopedica, 48,* 111–116.

Deary, I. J., Fowkes, F. G., Donnan, P. T., & Housley, E. (1994). Hostile personality and risks of peripheral arterial disease in the general population. *Psychosomatic Medicine, 56,* 197–202.

Deater-Deckard, K., & Scarr, S. (1996). Parenting stress among dual-earner mothers and fathers: Are there gender differences? *Journal of Family Psychology, 10,* 45–59.

DeCasper, A. J., & Fifer, W. P. (1980). Of human bonding: Newborns prefer their mother's voices. *Science, 208,* 1174–1176.

DeGenova, M. K. (1992). If you had your life to live over again: What would you do differently? *International Journal of Aging and Human Development, 34,* 135–143.

de Haan, M., & Nelson, C. A. (1997). Recognition of the mother's face by six-month-old infants: A neurobehavioral study. *Child Development, 68,* 187–210.

de Jonge, J. (1995). The theological roots of violence in families. *Journal of Psychology and Christianity, 14,* 26–37.

Dekle, D. J., Beal, C. R., Elliott, R., & Huneycutt, D. (1996). Children as witnesses: A comparison of lineup versus showup identification methods. *Applied Cognitive Psychology, 10,* 1–12.

Dekovic, M., & Janssens, J. M. (1992). Parents' child-rearing style and child's sociometric status. *Developmental Psychology, 28,* 925–932.

DeLong, G. R. (1993). Effects of nutrition on brain development in humans. *American Journal of Clinical Nutrition, 57,* 286s–290s.

Demaris, A., & MacDonald, W. (1993). Premarital cohabitation and marital instability: A test of the unconventionality hypothesis. *Journal of Marriage and the Family, 55,* 399–407.

DeMause, L. (1974). The evolution of childhood. In L. DeMause (Ed.), *The History of Childhood.* New York: Psychohistory Press.

DeMeis, D. K., & Perkins, H. W. (1996). "Supermoms" of the nineties: Homemaker and employed mothers' performance and perceptions of the motherhood role. *Journal of Family Issues, 17,* 776–792.

Demetriou, A., Efklides, A., & Papadaki, M. (1993). Structure and development of causal-experimental thought: From early adolescence to youth. *Developmental Psychology, 29,* 480–497.

Demo, D. H. (1993). The relentless search for effects of divorce: Forging new trails or tumbling down the beaten path. *Journal of Marriage and the Family, 55,* 42–45.

Demo, D. H., & Acock, A. C. (1993). Family diversity and the division of domestic labor: How much have things really changed? *Family Relations, 42,* 323–331.

Denham, S. A. (1993). Maternal emotional responsiveness and toddlers' social–emotional competence. *Journal of Child Psychology and Psychiatry and Allied Disciplines, 34,* 715–728.

Denham, S. A. (1997). "When I have a bad dream mommy holds me": Preschoolers' conceptions of emotions, parental socialisation, and emotional competence. *International Journal of Behavioral Development, 20,* 301–319.

Denham, S. A., & Holt, R. W. (1993). Preschooler's likability as cause or consequence of their social behavior. *Developmental Psychology, 29,* 271–275.

Dennis, W. (1951). A further analysis of reports of wild children. *Child Development, 22,* 153–158.

Dennis, W. (1966). Creative productivity between the ages of 20 and 80. *Journal of Gerontology, 21,* 1–18.

Derby, S. E. (1991). Ageism in cancer care of the elderly. *Oncology Nursing Forum, 18,* 921–926.

Deuel, R. K. (1992). Motor skill disorders. In S. R. Hooper, G. W. Hynd, & R. E. Mattison (Eds.), *Developmental disorders: Diagnostic criteria and clinical assessment.* Hillsdale, NJ: Erlbaum.

Devine, M. (1991). *Baby talk: The art of communicating with infants and toddlers.* New York: Plenum.

de Vries, B., & Watt, D. (1996). A lifetime of events: Age and gender variations in the life story. *International Journal of Aging and Human Development, 42,* 81–102.

deVries, M. W. (1989). Difficult temperament: A universal and culturally embedded concept. In W. B. Carey & S. C. McDevitt (Eds.), *Clinical and educational applications of temperament research.* Berwyn, PA: Swets North America.

deVries, M. W., & Sameroff, A. J. (1984). Culture and temperament: Influences on infant temperament in three East African societies. *American Journal of Orthopsychiatry, 54,* 83–96.

DeVries, R. (1997). Piaget's social theory. *Educational Researcher, 26,* 4–18.

Dewey, D. (1993). Error analysis of limb and orofacial praxis in children with developmental motor deficits. *Brain and Cognition, 23,* 203–221.

Diamond, A. M. (1986). The life-cycle research productivity of mathematicians and scientists. *Journal of Gerontology, 41,* 520–525.

Diamond, M. (1996). Prenatal predisposition and the clinical management of some pediatric conditions. *Journal of Sex and Marital Therapy, 22,* 139–147.

Diaz, R. M. (1983). Thought and two languages: The impact of bilingualism on cognitive development. In E. W. Gordon (Ed.), *Review of research in education* (Vol. 10). Washington, DC: American Educational Research Association.

Dick-Read, G. (1972). *Childbirth without fear: The original approach to natural childbirth* (4th ed.). (H. Wessel & H. F. Ellis, Eds.). New York: Harper & Row.

Didion, J. (1979). *The white album.* New York: Simon & Schuster.

Diefenbach, D. L. (1997). The portrayal of mental illness on prime-time television. *Journal of Community Psychology, 25,* 289–302.

Diener, C. I., & Dweck, C. S. (1980). An analysis of learned helplessness: II. The processing of success. *Journal of Personality and Social Psychology, 39,* 940–952.

Dietz-Omar, M. (1991). Couple adaptation in stepfamilies and traditional nuclear families during pregnancy. *Nursing Practice, 4,* 6–10.

DiGiulio, J. F. (1992). Early widowhood: An atypical transition. *Journal of Mental Health Counseling, 14,* 97–109.

Dill, F., & McGillivray, B. (1992). Chromosome anomolies. In J. M. Friedman, F. J. Dill, M. R. Hayden, & B. C. McGillivray (Eds.), *Genetics.* Baltimore: Williams & Wilkins.

Dillard, J. M., Campbell, N. J., & Chisolm, G. B. (1984). Correlates of life satisfaction of aged persons. *Psychological Reports, 54,* 977–978.

Dimmock, B. (1992). Stepfamilies. "A child of our own." *Health Visitor, 65,* 368–370.

Dinges, M. M., & Oetting, E. R. (1993). Similarity in drug use patterns between adolescents and their friends. *Adolescence, 28,* 253–266.

DiPietro, J. A., Hodgson, D. M., Costigan, K. A., & Johnson, T. R. (1996). Fetal antecedents of infant temperament. *Child Development, 67,* 2568–2583.

Dittmann-Kohli, F., & Baltes, P. B. (1986). Towards a neofunctionalist conception of adult intellectual development: Wisdom as a prototypical case of intellectual growth. In C. Alexander & E. Langer (Eds.), *Beyond formal operations: Alternative endpoints to human development.* New York: Oxford University Press.

Division of STD Prevention. (1995) *Sexually Transmitted Disease Surveillance, 1994.* U.S. Department of Health and Human Services, Public Health Service. Atlanta: Centers for Disease Control and Prevention, September 1995.

Doka, K. J. (1995). Coping with life-threatening illness: A task model. *Omega—Journal of Death and Dying, 32,* 111–122.

Doman, G. J. (1984). *How to multiply your baby's intelligence.* Garden City, NY: Doubleday.

Donaldson, M. (1978). *Children's minds.* London: Fontana/Croom Helm.

Donate-Bartfield, E., & Passman, R. H. (1985). Attentiveness of mothers and fathers to their baby's cries. *Infant Behavior and Development, 8,* 385–393.

Donders, G. G., Desmyter, J., De Wet, D. H., & Van Assche, F. A. (1993). The association of gonorrhoea and syphilis with premature birth and low birthweight. *Genitourinary Medicine, 69,* 98–101.

Donnay, D. A. C. (1997). E. K. Strong's legacy and beyond: 70 years of the Strong Interest Inventory. *Career Development Quarterly, 46,* 2–22.

Donnelly, B. W., & Voydanoff, P. (1991). Factors associated with releasing for adoption among adolescent mothers. *Family Relations, 40,* 404–410.

Dorius, G. L., Heaton, T. B., & Steffan, P. (1993). Adolescent life events and their association with the onset of sexual intercourse. *Youth and Society, 25,* 3–23.

Dowell, H. H. (1997). The Ausubelian Preschool Program: Balancing child-directed and teacher-directed approaches. *Early Childhood News, 9,* 12–17.

Drebing, C. E., & Gooden, W. E. (1991). The impact of the dream on mental health functioning in the male midlife transition. *International Journal of Aging and Human Development, 32,* 277–287.

Dreyer, P. H. (1982). Sexuality during adolescence. In B. B. Wolman (Ed.), *Handbook of developmental psychology.* Englewood Cliffs, NJ: Prentice-Hall.

Driver, R., Asoko, H., Leach, J., Mortimer, E., & Scott, P. (1994). Constructing scientific knowledge in the classroom. *Educational Researcher, 23,* 5–12.

Drummond, R. J., & Ryan, C. W. (1995). *Career counseling: A developmental approach.* Englewood Cliffs, NJ: Prentice-Hall.

Drummond, W. J. (1991). Adolescent relationships in a period of change: A New Zealand perspective. *International Journal of Adolescence and Youth, 2,* 275–286.

Dubas, J. S., & Petersen, A. C. (1993). Female pubertal development. In M. Sugar (Ed.), *Female adolescent development.* New York: Brunner/Mazel.

Dubowitz, H., Black, M., & Harrington, D. (1993). A follow-up study of behavior problems associated with child sexual abuse. *Child Abuse and Neglect: The International Journal, 17,* 743–754.

Dudgeon, D. J. (1994). Physician/nursing roles and perspectives in relationship to delivery of palliative care. *Annals of the Academy of Medicine, Singapore, 23,* 249–251.

Durkin, K., & Howarth, N. (1997). Mugged by the facts? Children's ability to distinguish their own and witnesses' perspectives on televised crime events. *Journal of Applied Developmental Psychology, 18,* 245–256.

Duvall, E. M. (1977). *Marriage and family development* (5th ed.). New York: Harper & Row.

Dweck, C. S. (1975). The role of expectations and attributions in the alleviation of learned helplessness. *Journal of Personality and Social Psychology, 31,* 674–685.

Dweck, C. S. (1986). Motivational processes affecting learning. *American Psychologist, 41,* 1040–1048.

Echenne, B., Humbertclaude, V., Rivier, F., Malafosse, A., & Cheminal, R. (1994). Benign infantile epilepsy with autosomal dominant inheritance. *Brain and Development, 16,* 108–111.

Eden, R. D., Blanco, J. D., Tomasi, A., & Gall, S. A. (1990). Maternal–fetal infection. In R. D. Eden, F. H. Boehm, & M. Haire (Eds.), *Assessment and care of the fetus: Physiological, clinical, and medicolegal principles.* Norwalk, CT: Appleton & Lange.

Eilers, R. E., & Oller, D. K. (1988). Precursors to speech. In R. Vasta (Ed.), *Annals of child development* (Vol. 5). Greenwich, CT: JAI Press.

Eisenberg, N., Fabes, R. A., Carlo, G., Speer, A. L., Switzer, G., Karbon, M., & Troyer, D. (1993). The relations of empathy-related emotions and maternal practices to children's comforting behavior. *Journal of Experimental Child Psychology, 55,* 131–150.

Eisenberg, N., Guthrie, I. K., Fabes, R. A., Reiser, M., Murphy, B. C., Holgren, R., Maszk, P., & Losoya, S. (1997). The relations of regulation and emotionality to resiliency and competent social functioning in elementary school children. *Child Development, 68,* 295–311.

Eisenberg, N., Miller, P. A., & Shell, R. (1991). Prosocial development in adolescence: A longitudinal study. *Developmental Psychology, 27,* 849–858.

Eisenberg, N., Miller, P. A., Shell, R., McNalley, S., & Shea, C. (1991). Prosocial development in adolescence: A longitudinal study. *Developmental Psychology, 27,* 849–857.

Eisler, D. (1997). A cautionary tale. *Maclean's,* Feb. 10.

Eisler, T. A. (1984). Career impact on independence of the elderly. In W. H. Quinn & G. A. Hughston (Eds.), *Independent aging: Family and social systems perspectives* (pp. 256–264). Rockville, MD: Aspen.

Elder, G. H., Jr. (1979). Historical change in life patterns and personality. In P. B. Baltes & O. G. Brim, Jr. (Eds.), *Life-span development and behavior* (Vol. 2). New York: Academic Press.

Elder, G. H., Jr., Nguyen, T. Van, & Caspi, A. (1985). Linking family hardship to children's lives. *Child Development, 56,* 361–375.

Elias, G., & Broerse, J. (1996). Developmental changes in the incidence and likelihood of simultaneous talk during the first two years: A question of function. *Journal of Child Language, 23,* 201–217.

Elkind, D. (1967). Egocentrism in adolescence. *Child Development, 38,* 1025–1034.

Elkind, D. (1981a). *The hurried child: Growing up too fast too soon.* Reading, MA: Addison-Wesley.

Elkind, D. (1981b). Understanding the young adolescent. In L. D. Steinberg (Ed.), *The life cycle: Readings in human development.* New York: Columbia University Press.

Elkind, D. (1987). *Miseducation: Preschoolers at risk.* New York: Knopf.

Elkind, D., & Bowen, R. (1979). Imaginary audience behavior in children and adolescents. *Developmental Psychology, 15*(1), 38–44.

Elliot, G., Hunt, M., & Hutchison, K. (Eds.). (1996). *Facts on aging in Canada*. Hamilton, Ontario: Office of Gerontological Studies, McMaster University.

Ellman, J. P. (1996). Analyst and patient at midlife. *Psychoanalytic Quarterly, 65*, 353–371.

Emery, A. E., & Mueller, R. F. (1992). *Elements of medical genetics* (8th ed.). Edinburgh & London: Churchill-Livingstone.

Emery, R. E. (1989). Family violence. *American Psychologist, 44*, 321–328.

Endsley, R. C., & Bradbard, M. R. (1981). *Quality day care: A handbook of choices for parents and caregivers*. Englewood Cliffs, NJ: Prentice-Hall.

Enright, R., Shukla, D., & Lapsley, D. (1980). Adolescent egocentrism–sociocentrism in early and late adolescence. *Adolescence, 14*, 687–695.

Erdley, C. A., & Dweck, C. S. (1993). Children's implicit personality theories as predictors of their social judgments. *Child Development, 64*, 863–878.

Erickson, M. T. (1992). *Behavior disorders of children and adolescents* (2nd ed.). Englewood Cliffs, NJ: Prentice-Hall.

Erikson, E. H. (1956). The problems of ego identity. *Journal of the American Psychoanalytic Association, 4*, 56–121.

Erikson, E. H. (1959). Identity and the life cycle: Selected papers. *Psychological Issue Monograph Series, I* (No. 1). New York: International Universities Press.

Erikson, E. H. (1961). The roots of virtue. In J. Huxley (Ed.), *The humanist frame*. New York: Harper & Row.

Erikson, E. H. (1968). *Identity, youth and crisis*. New York: Norton.

Erikson, E. H. (1980). *Themes of work and love in adulthood*. Cambridge, MA: Harvard University Press.

Erikson, E. H. (1987). *A way of looking at things: Selected papers from 1930 to 1980*. New York: Norton.

Erikson, E. H., Erikson, J. M., & Kivnick, H. G. (1986). *Vital involvement in old age*. New York: Norton.

Erikson, E., & Hall, E. A. (1983, June). A conversation with Erik Erikson. *Psychology Today, 17*, pp. 22–30.

Ernst, C., & Angst, J. (1983). *Birth order: Its influence on personality*. New York: Springer-Verlag.

Ernst, C., Foldenyi, M., & Angst, J. (1993). The Zurich Study: XXI. Sexual dysfunctions and disturbances in young adults. Data of a longitudinal epidemiological study. *European Archives of Psychiatry and Clinical Neuroscience, 243*, 179–188.

Erwin, P. (1993). *Friendship and peer relationships in children*. New York: John Wiley.

Ethical standards for research with children. (1973). *SRCD Newsletter*, Winter, 3–4.

Etnier, J. L., & Landers, D. M. (1997). The influence of age and fitness on performance and learning. *Journal of Aging and Physical Activity, 5*, 175–189.

Euromac Project Group. (1992). Euromac: A European concerted action: Maternal alcohol consumption and its relation to the outcome of pregnancy and child development at 18 months. *International Journal of Epidemiology, 21*, S1–S87.

Evans, R. I. (1989). *Albert Bandura: The man and his ideas—a dialogue*. New York: Praeger.

Evra, J. V. (1990). *Television and child development*. Hillsdale, NJ: Erlbaum.

Eysenck, H. J., & Kamin, L. (1981). *Intelligence: The battle for the mind*. London: Macmillan.

Fabricius, W. V., & Wellman, H. M. (1993). Two roads diverged: Young children's ability to judge distance. *Child Development, 64*, 399–419.

Faden, R. R., & Kass, N. E. (Eds.). (1996). *HIV, AIDS and childbearing*. New York: Oxford University Press.

Fantz, R. L. (1963). Pattern vision in newborn infants. *Science, 140*, 269–297.

Farbman, A. I. (1994). The cellular basis of olfaction. *Endeavour, 18*, 2–8.

Farmer, A. E. (1996). The genetics of depressive disorders. *International Review of Psychiatry, 8*, 369–372.

Fasick, F. A. (1988). Patterns of formal education in high school as rites de passage. *Adolescence, 23*, 457–471.

Fassati, A., Murphy, S., & Dickson, G. (1997). Gene therapy of Duchenne muscular dystrophy. In J. C. Hall & J. C. Dunlap (Eds.), *Advances in genetics: Incorporating molecular genetic medicine*. San Diego, CA: Academic Press.

Feagans, L. V., & Proctor, A. (1994). The effects of mild illness in infancy on later development: The sample case of the effects of otitis media (middle ear effusion). In C. B. Fisher & R. M. Lerner (Eds.), *Applied developmental psychology*. New York: McGraw-Hill.

Fiebert, M. S., & Meyer, M. W. (1997). Gender stereotypes: A bias against men. *Journal of Psychology, 131*, 407–410.

Filiano, J. J., & Kinney, H. C. (1994). A perspective on neuropathologic findings in victims of the sudden infant death syndrome: The triple-risk model. *Biology of the Neonate, 65*, 194–197.

Filkins, D. (1997, Oct. 27). India's marriage pipeline to the Mideast. *Los Angeles Times*, p. 1.

Fillit, H. (1997). The clinical significance of normal cognitive decline in late life. In H. M. Fillit & R. N. Butler (Eds.), *Cognitive decline: Strategies for prevention*. London: Greenwich Medical Media.

Fillit, H. M., & Butler, R. N. (Eds.). (1997). *Cognitive decline: Strategies for prevention*. London: Greenwich Medical Media.

Fine, M. A. (1993). Current approaches to understanding family diversity: An overview of the special issue. *Family Relations, 42*, 235–237.

Fine, M. A., & Fine, D. R. (1992). Recent changes in laws affecting stepfamilies: Suggestions for legal reform. *Family Relations, 41,* 334–340.

Finkelhor, D., et al. (1986). *A sourcebook on child sexual abuse.* Beverly Hills, CA: Sage.

Finley, C., & Corty, E. (1993). Rape on campus: The prevalence of sexual assault while enrolled in college. *Journal of College Student Development, 34,* 113–117.

Fisher, E. M. C. (1997). The contribution of the mouse to advances in human genetics. In J. C. Hall and J. C. Dunlap (Eds.), *Advances in genetics: Incorporating molecular genetic medicine.* San Diego, CA: Academic Press.

Fisher, J. C. (1993). A framework for describing developmental change among older adults. *Adult Education Quarterly, 43,* 76–89.

Fisher-Thompson, D., Sausa, A. D., & Wright, T. F. (1995). Toy selection for children: Personality and toy request influence. *Sex Roles, 33,* 239–255.

Fiske, S. T. (1993). Social cognition and social perception. *Annual Review of Psychology, 44,* 155–194.

Flanagan, J. C. (1982). *New insights to improve the quality of life at age 70.* Palo Alto, CA: American Institutes for Research.

Flavell, J. H. (1985). *Cognitive development* (2nd ed.). Englewood Cliffs, NJ: Prentice-Hall.

Flavell, J. H., Green, F. L., Flavell, E. R., & Grossman, J. B. (1997). The development of children's knowledge about inner speech. *Child Development, 68,* 39–47.

Fleischhacker, W. W., Meise, U., Gunther, V., & Kurz, M. (1994). Compliance with antipsychotic drug treatment: Influence of side effects. *Acta Psychiatrica Scandinavica, Supplementum, 382,* 11–15.

Fleming, P. J. (1994). Understanding and preventing sudden infant death syndrome. *Current Opinion in Pediatrics, 6,* 158–162.

Flin, R., Kearney, B., & Murray, K. (1996). Children's evidence: Scottish research and law. *Criminal Justice and Behavior, 23,* 358–376.

Flynn, J. R. (1987). Massive IQ gains in 14 nations: What IQ tests really measure. *Psychological Bulletin, 17,* 171–191.

Fogel, A., Toda, S., & Kawai, M. (1988). Mother–infant face-to-face interaction in Japan and the United States: A laboratory comparison using 3-month-old infants. *Developmental Psychology, 3,* 398–406.

Fontes, L. A. (Ed.). (1995). *Sexual abuse in nine North American cultures: Treatment and prevention.* Thousand Oaks, CA: Sage.

Food and Nutrition Board. (1990). *Nutrition during pregnancy.* Washington, DC: National Academy Press.

Food and Nutrition Board. (1992). *Nutrition during pregnancy.* Washington, DC: National Academy Press.

Food and Nutrition Board, Subcommittee on the Tenth Edition of the RDAs. (1989). *Recommended dietary allowances* (10th ed.). Washington, DC: National Academy Press.

Fouts, R. S. (1987). Chimpanzee signing and emergent levels. In G. Greenberg & E. Tobach (Eds.), *Cognition, language and consciousness: Integrative levels.* Hillsdale, NJ: Erlbaum.

Fox, N. A., Kimmerly, N. L., & Schafer, W. D. (1991). Attachment to mother/attachment to father: A meta-analysis. *Child Development, 62,* 210–225.

Fox, R. A. (1990). *Assessing parenting of young children.* Bethesda, MD: National Center for Nursing Research of the National Institutes of Health. (Contract 1 RO1 NRO160901A1.)

Fox, S. L. (1997). Correlates of successful retirement and aging. Dissertation submitted to the University of Alberta, Edmonton, Alberta, in partial fulfilment of the requirements for the degree of Masters of Education.

Franco, F., & Butterworth, G. (1996). Pointing and social awareness: Declaring and requesting in the second year. *Journal of Child Language, 23,* 307–336.

Frankenburg, W. K., & Dodds, J. B. (1992). *Denver II* (2nd ed.). *Training Manual.* Denver: Denver Developmental Materials.

Frankenburg, W. K., Fandal, A. W., Sciarillo, W., & Burgess, D. (1981). The newly abbreviated and revised Denver Developmental Screening Test. *Journal of Pediatrics, 99,* 995–999.

Frantz, T. T., Trolley, B. C., & Johll, M. P. (1996). Religious aspects of bereavement. *Pastoral Psychology, 44,* 151–163.

Franzen, U., & Gerlinghoff, M. (1997). Parenting by patients with eating disorders: Experiences with a mother–child group. *Eating Disorders: The Journal of Treatment and Prevention, 5,* 5–14.

Freeman, S. C. (1993). Donald Super: A perspective on career development. *Journal of Career Development, 19,* 255–264.

Freud, S. (1935). *A general introduction to psychoanalysis* (rev. ed.). (J. Riviere, Trans.). New York: Liveright.

Freud, S. (1963). *The sexual enlightenment of children.* New York: Collier.

Fridell, S. R., Zucker, K. J., Bradley, S. J., & Maing, D. M. (1996). Physical attractiveness of girls with gender identity disorder. *Archives of Sexual Behavior, 25,* 17–31.

Fried, P. A. (1993). Prenatal exposure to tobacco and marijuana: Effects during pregnancy, infancy, and early childhood. *Clinical Obstetrics and Gynecology, 36,* 319–337.

Fried, P. A. (1996). Behavioral outcomes in preschool and school-age children exposed prenatally to marijuana: A review and speculative interpretation. In C. L. Wetherington, V. L. Smeriglio, & L. P. Finnegan (Eds.), *Behavioral studies of drug-exposed offspring: Methodological issues in human and animal research.* NIDA Research Monograph 164, 1996. Rockville, MD: U.S. Department of Health and Human Services.

Friedman, H. S., Tucker, J. S., Schwartz, J. E., & Tomlinson, K. S. (1995). Psychosocial and behavioral predictors of longevity: The aging and death of the "Termites." *American Psychologist, 50,* 69–78.

Friedman, J. M. (1992). Teratogenesis and mutagenesis. In J. M. Friedman, F. J. Dill, M. R. Hayden, & B. C. McGillivray (Eds.), *Genetics.* Baltimore: Williams & Wilkins.

Friedman, J. M., Dill, F. J., Hayden, M. R., & McGillivray, B. C. (Eds.). (1992). *Genetics.* Baltimore: Williams & Wilkins.

Friedman, J. M., & McGillivray, B. (1992). Genetic paradigms in human disease. In J. M. Friedman, F. J. Dill, M. R. Hayden, & B. C. McGillivray (Eds.), *Genetics.* Baltimore: Williams & Wilkins.

Friedman, J. M., & Polifka, J. E. (1996). *The effects of drugs on the fetus and nursing infant.* Baltimore, MD: Johns Hopkins University Press.

Friedman, M., & Rosenman, R. H. (1974). *Type A behavior and your heart.* Greenwich, CT: Fawcett.

Frieman, B. B. (1993). Separation and divorce: Children want their teachers to know—meeting the needs of preschool and primary school children. *Young Children, 48,* 58–63.

Friendly, D. S. (1993). Development of vision in infants and young children. *Pediatric Clinics of North America, 40,* 693–703.

Frozen life: Will Julie become a mother from beyond the grave? (1997, Oct. 19). *Edmonton Journal,* p. B3.

Fry, P. S. (1991). Individual differences in reminiscence among older adults: Predictors of frequency and pleasantness ratings of reminiscence activity. *International Journal of Aging and Human Development, 33,* 311–326.

Fry, P. S. (1992). Major social theories of aging and their implications for counseling concepts and practice: A critical review. *Counseling Psychologist, 20,* 246–329.

Frydenberg, E. (1997). *Adolescent coping: Theoretical and research perspectives.* New York: Routledge.

Frye, D. (1991). The origins of intention in infancy. In D. Frye & C. Moore (Eds.), *Children's theories of mind: Mental states and social understanding.* Hillsdale, NJ: Erlbaum.

Frye, D., & Moore, C. (Eds.). (1991). *Children's theories of mind: Mental states and social understanding.* Hillsdale, NJ: Erlbaum.

Fuligni, A. J., & Eccles, J. S. (1993). Perceived parent–child relationships and early adolescents' orientation toward peers. *Developmental Psychology, 29,* 622–632.

Fundaro, C., Solinas, A., Martino, A. M., Genovese, O., Noia, G., Conte, G. L., & Segni, G. (1994). Neonatal abstinence syndrome and maternal toxicological profile. *Minerva Pediatrica, 46,* 83–88.

Furstenberg, F. F., Jr. (1987). The new extended family: The experience of children and parents after remarriage. In K. Pasley and M. Ihinger-Tallman (Eds.), *Remarriage and stepparenting: Current research and theory.* New York: Guilford.

Furstenberg, F. F., Jr., Brooks-Gunn, J., & Chase-Lansdale, L. (1989). Teenaged pregnancy and childbearing. *American Psychologist, 44,* 313–320.

Furstenberg, F. F., Jr., & Spanier, G. B. (1984). *Recycling the family: Remarriage after divorce.* Beverly Hills, CA: Sage.

Furth, H. G. (1980). Piagetian perspectives. In J. Sants (Ed.), *Developmental psychology and society.* London: Macmillan.

Gage, M. G., & Hendrickson Christenson, D. (1991). Parental role socialization and the transition to parenthood. *Family Relations, 40,* 332–337.

Galef, B. G., Jr. (1991). A contrarian view of the wisdom of the body as it relates to dietary self-selection. *Psychological Review, 98,* 218–223.

Galen, B. R., & Underwood, M. K. (1997). A developmental investigation of social aggression among children. *Developmental Psychology, 33,* 589–600.

Galton, F. (1896). *Hereditary genius: An enquiry into its law and consequences.* London: Macmillan.

Gamble, T. J., & Zigler, E. (1986). Effects of infant day care: Another look at the evidence. *American Journal of Orthopsychiatry, 56,* 26–42.

Ganzini, L., Fenn, D. S., Lee, M. A., Heintz, R. T., et al. (1996). Attitudes of Oregon psychiatrists toward physician-assisted suicide. *American Journal of Psychiatry, 153,* 1469–1475.

Garcia, E. E. (1993). Language, culture, and education. In L. Darling-Hammond (Ed.), *Review of Research in Education* (Vol. 19). Washington, DC: American Educational Research Association.

Gardner, H. (1983). *Frames of mind: The theory of multiple intelligences.* New York: Basic Books.

Gardner, H. (1993). Educating for understanding. *American School Board Journal, 180,* 20–24.

Gardner, H., & Hatch, T. (1989). Multiple intelligences go to school: Educational implications of the theory of multiple intelligences. *Educational Researcher, 18,* 4–10.

Garnier, H. E., Stein, J. A., & Jacobs, J. K. (1997). The process of dropping out of high school: A 19-year perspective. *American Educational Research Journal, 34,* 395–419.

Garrett, C., & Carlton, L. (1994). Difficult decisions in prenatal diagnosis. In L. Abramsky & J. Chapple (Eds.), *Prenatal diagnosis: The human side.* New York: Chapman and Hall.

Garvey, C. (1977). *Play.* Cambridge, MA: Harvard University Press.

Gathercole, S. E., Adams, A. M., & Hitch, G. J. (1994). Do young children rehearse? An individual-difference analysis. *Memory and Cognition, 22,* 201–207.

Gaudin, J. M., Jr. (1993). *Child neglect: A guide for intervention. The User Manual Series.* National Center on Child Abuse and Neglect. Washington, DC: Westover Consultants.

Gauvain, M., & Cole, M. (Eds.). (1993). *Readings on the development of children.* New York: W. H. Freeman.

Gayford, J. J. (1978). Battered wives. In J. P. Martin (Ed.), *Violence and the family.* New York: John Wiley.

Gaynor, J. L. R., & Runco, M. A. (1992). Family size, birth-order, age-interval, and the creativity of children. *Journal of Creative Behavior, 26,* 108–118.

Geiger, B. (1996). *Fathers as primary caregivers.* Westport, CT: Greenwood.

Geiger, S., & Newhagen, J. (1993). Revealing the black box: Information processing and media effects. *Journal of Communication, 43,* 42–50.

Geller, J., Johnson, C., & Madsen, K. (1997). The role of shape and weight in self-concept: The Shape and Weight Based Self-Esteem Inventory. *Cognitive Therapy & Research, 21,* 5–24.

Gelles, R. J. (1978). Violence in the American family. In J. P. Martin (Ed.), *Violence and the family.* New York: John Wiley.

Gelles, R. J. (1997). *Intimate violence in families* (3rd ed.). Thousand Oaks, CA: Sage.

Gelman, R. (1982). Basic numerical abilities. In R. J. Sternberg (Ed.), *Advances in the psychology of human intelligence* (Vol. 1). Hillsdale, NJ: Erlbaum.

Gelman, R., & Gallistel, C. R. (1978). *The young child's understanding of number.* Cambridge, MA: Harvard University Press.

Genovese, R. G. (1997). *Americans at midlife: Caught between generations.* Westport, CT: Bergin & Garvey.

"Gentle giant" stabs boy for taunts. (1994, Dec. 6). *Edmonton Sun,* p. 24.

Gerson, R. (1995). The family life cycle: Phases, stages, and crises. In R. H. Mikesell, D. D. Lusterman, & S. H. McDaniel (Eds.), *Integrating family therapy: Handbook of family psychology and systems theory.* Washington, DC: American Psychological Association.

Gesell, A. (1925). *The mental growth of the preschool child.* New York: Macmillan.

Gewirtz, J. L. (1965). The course of infant smiling in four child-rearing environments in Israel. In B. M. Foss (Ed.), *Determinants of infant behavior III.* London: Methuen.

Ghusn, H. F., Hyde, D., Stevens, E. S., & Hyde, M. (1996). Enhancing satisfaction in later life: What makes a difference for nursing home residents? *Journal of Gerontological Social Work, 26,* 27–47.

Gianino, A., & Tronick, E. Z. (1988). The mutual regulation model: The infant's self and interactive regulation coping and defense. In T. Field, P. McCabe, & N. Schneiderman (Eds.), *Stress and coping.* Hillsdale, NJ: Erlbaum.

Gibbs, J. C. (1987). Social processes in delinquency: The need to facilitate empathy as well as socio-moral reasoning. In W. M. Kurtines & J. L. Gewirtz (Eds.), *Moral development through social interaction.* New York: John Wiley.

Gibson, E. J., & Walk, R. D. (1960). The "visual cliff." *Scientific American, 202,* 64–71.

Gibson, H. B. (1992). *The emotional and sexual lives of older people: A manual for professionals.* New York: Chapman and Hall.

Gibson, K. (1996). The ontogeny and evolution of the brain, cognition, and language. In A. Lock & C. R. Peters (Eds.), *Handbook of human symbolic evolution.* Oxford, England: Clarendon Press/Oxford University Press.

Gibson-Cline, J. (Ed.). (1996). *Adolescence: From crisis to coping: A thirteen nation study.* Boston: Butterworth/Heinemann.

Giles, H., Coupland, N., Coupland, J., Williams, A., & Nussbaum, J. (1992). Intergenerational talk and communication with older people. *International Journal of Aging and Human Development, 34,* 271–297.

Gill, W. (1992). Helping African American males: The cure. *Negro Educational Review, 43,* 31–36.

Gillespie, D., & Hillman, S. B. (1993). *Impact of self-efficacy expectations on adolescent career choice.* Paper presented at the Annual Meeting of the American Psychological Association, Toronto, August 20–24, 1993.

Gilligan, C. (1982). *In a different voice: Psychological theory and women's development.* Cambridge, MA: Harvard University Press.

Ginzberg, E. (1972). Toward a theory of occupational choice: A restatement. *Vocational Guidance Quarterly, 20,* 169–176.

Glasgow, K. L., Dornbusch, S. M., Troyer, L., Steinberg, L., & Ritter, P. L. (1997). Parenting styles, adolescents' attributions, and educational outcomes in nine heterogeneous high schools. *Child Development, 68,* 507–529.

Glenmark, B., Hedberg, G., Kaijser, L., & Jansson, E. (1994). Muscle strength from adolescence to adulthood—relationship to muscle fibre types. *European Journal of Applied Physiology and Occupational Physiology, 68,* 9–19.

Gloth, F. M. III. (1994). Hospice: The most important thing you didn't learn in medical school. *Maryland Medical Journal, 43,* 511–513.

Glueck, S., & Glueck, E. (1950). *Unravelling juvenile delinquency.* New York: Commonwealth Fund.

Godkin, M. A., Wolf, R. S., & Pillemer, K. A. (1995). A case-comparison analysis of elder abuse and neglect.

In J. Hendricks (Ed.), *The ties of later life*. Amityville, NY: Baywood.

Goetting, A. (1994). Do Americans really like children? Hartman National Conference: Children and Their Families (1993, New London, Connecticut). *Journal of Primary Prevention, 15*, 81–92.

Gold, M. S. (1989). *Drugs of abuse: A comprehensive series for clinicians* (Vol. 1) *Marijuana*. New York: Plenum.

Goldberg, S. (1983). Parent–infant bonding: Another look. *Child Development, 54*, 1355–1382.

Goldfield, B. A., & Reznick, J. S. (1996). Measuring the vocabulary spurt: A reply to Mervis and Bertrand. *Journal of Child Language, 23*, 241–246.

Goldsmith, J. (1990). *Childbirth wisdom: From the world's oldest societies*. Brookline, MA: East West Health Books.

Goncu, A. (1993). Development of intersubjectivity in the dyadic play of preschoolers. *Early Childhood Research Quarterly, 8*, 99–116.

Goode, E. T. (1985). Medical aspects of the bulimic syndrome and bulimarexia. *Transactional Analysis Journal, 15*, 4–11.

Gooden, W., & Toye, R. (1984). Occupational dream, relation to parents and depression in the early adult transition. *Journal of Clinical Psychology, 4*, 945–954.

Goodenough, F. (1926). *Measurement of intelligence by drawings*. New York: Harcourt.

Goodman, J., & Blum, T. C. (1996). Assessing the non-random sampling effects of subject attrition in longitudinal research. *Journal of Management, 22*, 627–652.

Gordon, C. P. (1996). Adolescent decision making: A broadly based theory and its application to the prevention of early pregnancy. *Adolescence, 31*, 561–584.

Gorman, C. (1994, Nov. 12). An eye on Alzheimer's. *Time, 144*, p. 71.

Gorsky, R. D., Koplan, J. P., Peterson, H. B., & Thacker, S. B. (1994). Relative risks and benefits of long-term estrogen replacement therapy: A decision analysis. *Obstetrics and Gynecology, 83*, 161–166.

Gottesman, I. I. (1974). Developmental genetics and ontogenetic psychology: Overdue detente and propositions from a matchmaker. In A. Pick (Ed.), *Minnesota Symposia on Psychology* (Vol. 12) (pp. 55–180).

Gottesman, I. I., & Shields, J. (1982). *The schizophrenic puzzle*. New York: Cambridge University Press.

Gottlieb, G. (1992). *Individual development and evolution: The genesis of novel behavior*. Oxford: Oxford University Press.

Gottman, J. M. (1977). Toward a definition of social isolation in children. *Child Development, 48*, 513–517.

Goudsmit, E., Neijmeijer-Leloux, A., & Swaab, D. F. (1992). The human hypothalamo-neurohypophyseal system in relation to development, aging and Alzheimer's disease. *Progress in Brain Research, 93*, 237–247.

Gould, R. L. (1972). The phases of adult life: A study in developmental psychology. *American Journal of Psychiatry, 129*, 521–531.

Gould, R. L. (1978). *Transformations: Growth and change in adult life*. New York: Simon & Schuster.

Gould, R. L. (1990). Clinical lessons from adult development theory. In R. A. Nemiroff & C. A. Colarusso (Eds.), *New dimensions in adult development*. New York: Basic Books.

Gould, S. J. (1981). *The mismeasure of man*. New York: Norton.

Graham, M. V. (1993). Parental sensitivity to infant cues: Similarities and differences between mothers and fathers. *Journal of Pediatric Nursing, 8*, 376–384.

Grant, J. P. (1992). *The state of the world's children: 1992*. New York: Oxford University Press.

Grant, J. P. (1993). *The state of the world's children: 1993*. New York: Oxford University Press.

Grant, L. D. (1996). Effects of ageism on individual and health care providers' responses to healthy aging. *Health and Social Work, 21*, 9–15.

Grattan, M. P., DeVos, E., Levy, J., & McClintock, M. K. (1992). Asymmetric action in the human newborn: Sex differences in patterns of organization. *Child Development, 63*, 273–289.

Gray, P., & Feldman, J. (1997). Patterns of age mixing and gender mixing among children and adolescents at an ungraded democratic school. *Merrill–Palmer Quarterly, 43*, 67–86.

Green, J. M. (1994). Women's experiences of prenatal screening and diagnosis. In L. Abramsky & J. Chapple (Eds.), *Prenatal diagnosis: The human side*. New York: Chapman and Hall.

Green, V., Johnson, S. A., & Kaplan, D. (1992). Predictors of adolescent female decision making regarding contraceptive usage. *Adolescence, 27*, 613–632.

Greenberg, B. S., & Brand, J. E. (1993). Television news and advertising in schools: The "Channel One" controversy. *Journal of Communication, 43*, 143–151.

Greene, K., Rubin, D. L., Hale, J. L., & Walters, L. H. (1996). The utility of understanding adolescent egocentrism in designing health promotion messages. *Health Communication, 8*, 131–152.

Greenfield, P. M., & Savage-Rumbaugh, E. S. (1993). Comparing communicative competence in child and chimp: The pragmatics of repetition. *Journal of Child Language, 20*, 1–26.

Grieser, D. L., & Kuhl, P. K. (1988). Maternal speech to infants in a tonal language: Support for universal prosodic features in motherese. *Developmental Psychology, 24*, 14–20.

Griffiths, M. D. (1991). Amusement machine playing in childhood and adolescence: A comparative analysis of video games and fruit machines. *Journal of Adolescence, 14*, 53–73.

Groome, L. J., Swiber, M. J., Atterbury, J. L., Bentz, L. S., & Holland, S. B. (1997). Similarities and differences in behavioral state organization during sleep periods in the perinatal infant before and after birth. *Child Development, 68*, 1–11.

Grossman, H. (1995). *Special education in a diverse society.* Boston: Allyn & Bacon.

Grotevant, H. D. (1994). Assessment of parent–adolescent relationships. In C. B. Fisher & R. M. Lerner (Eds.), *Applied developmental psychology.* New York: McGraw-Hill.

Grotpeter, J. K., & Crick, N. R. (1996). Relational aggression, overt aggression, and friendship. *Child Development, 67*, 2328–2338.

Grunebaum, H. (1997). Thinking about romantic/erotic love. *Journal of Marital and Family Therapy, 23*, 295–307.

Guilford, J. P. (1950). Creativity. *American Psychologist, 5*, 444–454.

The guinea pigs. (1997, Oct. 19). *Edmonton Journal*, p. F3.

Gullette, M. M. (1997). *Declining to decline: Cultural combat and the politics of the midlife.* Charlottesville: University Press of Virginia.

Gullone, E., & King, N. J. (1997). Three-year follow-up of normal fear in children and adolescents aged 7 to 18 years. *British Journal of Developmental Psychology, 15*, 97–111.

Gunnar, M. R., Larson, M. C., Hertsgaard, L., Harris, M. L., & Brodersen, L. (1992). The stressfulness of separation among nine-month-old infants: Effects of social context variables and infant temperament. *Child Development, 63*, 290–303.

Gunter, B., & McAleer, J. L. (1990). *Children and television. The one-eyed monster?* New York: Routledge.

Guntheroth, W. G. (1995). *Crib death: The sudden infant death syndrome* (3rd ed.). Armonk, NY: Futura.

Gustafson, G. E., & Harris, K. L. (1990). Women's responses to young infants' cries. *Developmental Psychology, 26*, 144–152.

Gustafsson, J. E., & Undheim, J. O. (1992). Stability and change in broad and narrow factors of intelligence from ages 12 to 15. *Journal of Educational Psychology, 84*, 141–149.

Gutierrez, P., King, C. A., & Ghaziuddin, N. (1996). Adolescent attitudes about death in relation to suicidality. *Suicide and Life-Threatening Behavior, 26*, 8–18.

Gutmann, D. (1990). Psychological development and pathology in later adulthood. In R. A. Nemiroff & C. A. Colarusso (Eds.), *New dimensions in adult development.* New York: Basic Books.

Guttman, H. A. (1991). Parental death as a precipitant of marital conflict in middle age. *Journal of Marital and Family Therapy, 17*, 81–87.

Hack, M., Breslau, N., Aram, D., Weissman, B., Klein, N., & Borawski-Clark, E. (1992). The effect of very low birth weight and social risk on neurocognitive abilities at school age. *Journal of Developmental and Behavioral Pediatrics, 13*, 412–420.

Hack, M., Weissman, B., Breslau, N., Klein, N., Borawski-Clark, E., & Fanaroff, A. A. (1993). Health of very low birth weight children during their first eight years. *Journal of Pediatrics, 122*, 887–892.

Hadeed, A., & Siegel, S. (1993). Newborn cardiac arrhythmias associated with maternal caffeine use during pregnancy. *Clinical Pediatrics, 32*, 45–47.

Hagborg, W. J. (1993). The Rosenberg Self-Esteem Scale and Harter's Self-Perception Profile for Adolescents: A concurrent validity study. *Psychology in the Schools, 30*, 132–136.

Hagopian, L. P., Fisher, W. W., & Legacy, S. M. (1994). Schedule effects of noncontingent reinforcement on attention-maintained destructive behavior in identical quadruplets. *Journal of Applied Behavior Analysis*, 317–325.

Hague, W. J. (1991). Kohlberg's legacy—more than ideas: An essay review. *The Alberta Journal of Educational Research, 37*, 277–294.

Haight, B. K. (1991). Reminiscing: The state of the art as a basis for practice. *International Journal of Aging and Human Development, 33*, 1–32.

Haines, C. J., Chung, T. K., & Leung, D. H. (1994). A prospective study of the frequency of acute menopausal symptoms in Hong Kong Chinese women. *Maturitas, 18*, 175–181.

Haith, M. M. (1980). *Rules that babies look by: The organization of newborn visual activity.* Hillsdale, NJ: Erlbaum.

Haith, M. M. (1991). *Setting a path for the '90s: Some goals and challenges. Infant sensory and perceptual development.* Paper presented at the Biennial Meeting of the Society for Research in Child Development, Seattle, April 18–20.

Hakuta, K., & D'Andrea, D. (1992). Some properties of bilingual maintenance and loss in Mexican background high-school students. *Applied Linguistics, 13*, 72–99.

Hakuta, K., & Garcia, E. E. (1989). Bilingualism and education. *American Psychologist, 44*, 374–379.

Halasz, G. (1996). The rights of the child in psychotherapy. *American Journal of Psychotherapy, 50*, 285–297.

Haldeman, D. C. (1994). The practice and ethics of sexual orientation conversion therapy. *Journal of Consulting and Clinical Psychology, 62*, 221–227.

Hall, A. S., & Meei-Ju, L. (1995). Theory and practice of children's rights: Implications for mental health counselors. *Journal of Mental Health Counseling, 17*, 63–80.

Hall, D. R. (1996). Marriage as a pure relationship: Exploring the link between premarital cohabitation and divorce in Canada. *Journal of Comparative Family Studies, 27,* 1–12.

Hall, G. S. (1891). The contents of children's minds on entering school. *Pediatric Seminars, 1,* 139–173.

Hall, G. S. (1916). *Adolescence* (2 vols.). New York: Appleton-Century-Crofts.

Hall, G. S. (1922). *Senescence: The last half of life.* New York: Appleton-Century-Crofts.

Hall, J. C., & Dunlap, J. C. (Eds.). (1997). *Advances in genetics: Incorporating molecular genetic medicine.* San Diego, CA: Academic Press.

Hall, P. A. (1995). Elder maltreatment items, subgroups, and types: Policy and practice implications. In J. Hendricks (Ed.), *The ties of later life.* Amityville, NY: Baywood.

Hallahan, D. P., & Kauffman, J. M. (1991). *Exceptional children: Introduction to special education.* Englewood Cliffs, NJ: Prentice Hall.

Halle, P. A., de Boysson-Bardies, B., & Vihman, M. M. (1991). Beginnings of prosodic organization: Intonation and duration patterns of disyllables produced by Japanese and French infants. *Language and Speech, 34,* 299–318.

Halpern, J. (1994). The sandwich generation: Conflicts between adult children and their aging parents. In D. D. Cahn (Ed.), *Conflict in personal relationships.* Mahwah, NJ: Erlbaum.

Hamabata, M. M. (1990). *Crested kimono: Power and love in the Japanese business family.* Ithaca, NY: Cornell University Press.

Hamilton, B. (1996). Ethnicity and the family life cycle: The Chinese-American family. *Family Therapy, 23,* 199–212.

Hammill, D. D. (1993). A brief look at the learning disabilities movement in the United States. *Journal of Learning Disabilities, 26,* 295–310.

Hampson, J., & Nelson, K. (1993). The relation of maternal language to variation in rate and style of language acquisition. *Journal of Child Language, 20,* 313–342.

Handyside, A. H. (1991). Preimplantation diagnosis by DNA amplification. In M. Chapman, G. Grudzinskas, & T. Chard (Eds.), *The embryo: Normal and abnormal development and growth.* New York: Springer-Verlag.

Hanna, E., & Meltzoff, A. N. (1993). Peer imitation by toddlers in laboratory, home, and day-care contexts: Implications for social learning and memory. *Developmental Psychology, 29,* 701–710.

Hansen, L. S. (1993). Career development trends and issues in the United States. *Journal of Career Development, 20,* 7–24.

Hargarten, K. M. (1994). Menopause. How exercise mitigates symptoms. *Physician and Sports Medicine, 22,* 48–50, 53–56.

Harkness, S., & Super, C. M. (1993). East Africa. In R. A. Pierce & M. A. Black (Eds.), *Life-span development: A diversity reader.* Dubuque, IA: Kendall/Hunt.

Harlow, H. F. (1959). Love in infant monkeys. *Scientific American, 200,* 68–74.

Harman, D. (1993). Free radical involvement in aging. Pathophysiology and therapeutic implications. *Drugs and Aging, 3,* 60–80.

Harmon, B. V., & Allan, D. J. (1997). Apoptosis. In J. C. Hall & J. C. Dunlap (Eds.), *Advances in genetics: Incorporating molecular genetic medicine.* San Diego, CA: Academic Press.

Harris, D. (1963). *Children's drawings as measures of intellectual maturity.* New York: Harcourt.

Harris, J. A., et al. (1930). *The measurement of man.* Bloomington: University of Minnesota Press.

Harris, Y. R., & Hamidullah, J. (1993). Maternal and child utilization of memory strategies. *Current Psychology: Research and Reviews, 12,* 81–94.

Harrison, L. (1985). Effects of early supplemental stimulation programs for premature infants: Review of the literature. *Maternal–Child Nursing Journal, 14,* 69–90.

Harry, J. (1983). Gay male and lesbian relationships. In E. D. Macklin & R. H. Rubin (Eds.), *Contemporary families and alternative lifestyles: Handbook on research and theory* (pp. 216–233). Beverly Hills, CA: Sage.

Hart, D., & Yates, M. (1996). The interrelation of self and identity in adolescence: A developmental account. In *Annals of Child Development, 12,* 207–242.

Harter, S. (1983). Developmental perspectives on the self-system. In P. H. Mussen (Ed.), *Handbook of child psychology* (4th ed.) (Vol. 4): *Socialization, personality, and social development* (E. M. Hetherington, Ed.). New York: John Wiley.

Harter, S. (1987). The determinants and mediational role of global self-worth in children. In N. Eisenberg (Ed.), *Contemporary topics in developmental psychology.* New York: John Wiley.

Harter, S. (1988). Developmental processes in the construction of self. In T. D. Yawkey & J. E. Johnson (Eds.), *Integrative processes and socialization: Early to middle childhood.* Hillsdale, NJ: Erlbaum.

Harter, S. (1990). Processes underlying adolescent self-concept formation. In R. Montemayor, G. R. Adams, & T. P. Gullotta (Eds.), *From childhood to adolescence: A transitional period?* (*Advances in adolescent development,* Vol. 2). Newbury Park, CA: Sage.

Hartup, W. W. (1983). Peer relations. In P. H. Mussen (Ed.), *Handbook of child psychology* (4th ed.) (Vol. 4): *Socialization, personality, and social development* (pp. 103–196). (E. M. Hetherington, Ed.). New York: John Wiley.

Harvey, B. (1994, Nov. 20). Mercy Killing. *Edmonton Journal,* p. C1.

Hashimoto, N. (1991). Memory development in early childhood: Encoding process in a spatial task. *Journal of Genetic Psychology, 152,* 101–117.

Haskins, R. (1989). Beyond metaphor: The efficacy of early childhood education. *American Psychologist, 44,* 274–282.

Hatch, R. G. (1995). *Aging and cohabitation.* New York: Garland.

Havighurst, R. J. (1972). *Developmental tasks and education.* New York: D. McKay.

Havighurst, R. J. (1979). *Developmental tasks and education* (4th ed.). New York: D. McKay.

Hawkins, A. J., & Dollahite, D. C. (Eds.). (1997). *Generative fathering: Beyond deficit perspectives.* Current issues in the family series, Vol. 3. Thousand Oaks, CA: Sage.

Hawley, T. L., Halle, T. G., Drasin, R. E., & Thomas, N. G. (1995). Children of addicted mothers: Effects of "crack epidemic" on the caregiving environment and the development of preschoolers. *American Journal of Orthopsychiatry, 65,* 364–379.

Hay, D. F., Stimson, C. A., & Castle, J. (1991). A meeting of minds in infancy: Imitation and desire. In D. Frye & C. Moore (Eds.), *Children's theories of mind: Mental states and social understanding.* Hillsdale, NJ: Erlbaum.

Hayes, B. K., & Delamothe, K. (1997). Cognitive interviewing procedures and suggestibility in children's recall. *Journal of Applied Psychology, 82,* 562–577.

Hayes, C. D., Palmer, J. L., & Zaslow, M. J. (Eds.). (1990). *Who cares for America's children? Child care policy for the 1990's.* Washington, DC: National Academy Press.

Hayes, D. S., & Casey, D. M. (1992). Young children and television: The retention of emotional reactions. *Child Development, 63,* 1423–1436.

Hayes, K. J., & Hayes, C. (1951). Intellectual development of a home-raised chimpanzee. *Proceedings of the American Philosophical Society, 95,* 105–109.

Hayflick, L. (1975, September). Why grow old? *Stanford Magazine,* pp. 36–43.

Haynes, N. M. (1993). Reducing the risk of teen parenthood: An approach that works. *Nassp Bulletin, 77,* 36–40.

Hazelwood, M. E., Brown, J. K., Rowe, P. J., & Salter, P. M. (1994). The use of therapeutic electrical stimulation in the treatment of hemiplegic cerebral palsy. *Developmental Medicine and Child Neurology, 36,* 661–673.

Hazen, N. L., & Lockman, J. J. (1989). Skill and context. In J. J. Lockman & N. L. Hazen (Eds.), *Action in social context: Perspectives on early development.* New York: Plenum.

Health Guide: Pregnancy: Pregnancy Tests. (1997, Oct. 21). Internet: http://healthguide.com/VBeAMothr/tests.stm

Hebb, D. O. (1966). *A textbook of psychology* (2nd ed.). Philadelphia: Saunders.

Hedges, L. V., & Friedman, L. (1993). Gender differences in variability in intellectual abilities: A reanalysis of Feingold's results. *Review of Educational Research, 63,* 94–105.

Heinzen, T. E. (1991). A paradigm for research in creativity. *The Creative Child and Adult Quarterly, 16,* 164–174.

Heisel, B. E., & Ritter, K. (1981). Young children's storage behavior in a memory for location task. *Journal of Experimental Child Psychology, 31,* 250–364.

Helson, R., & Wink, P. (1992). Personality change in women from the early 40's to the early 50's. *Psychology and Aging, 7,* 46–55.

Helwig, A. A., & Myrin, M. D. (1997). Ten year stability of Holland codes within one family. *Career Development Quarterly, 46,* 62–71.

Hendricks, J. (Ed.). (1995). *The ties of later life.* Amityville, NY: Baywood.

Henker, B., & Whalen, C. K. (1989). Hyperactivity and attention deficits. *American Psychologist, 44,* 216–223.

Henry, C. S., Stephenson, A. L., Hanson, M. F., & Hargett, W. (1993). Adolescent suicide and families: An ecological approach. *Adolescence, 28,* 291–308.

Henshaw, A., Kelly, J., & Gratton, C. (1992). Skipping's for girls: Children's perceptions of gender roles and gender preferences. *Educational Research, 34,* 229–235.

Hernandez, D. J. (1997). Child development and the social demography of childhood. *Child Development, 68,* 149–169.

Hernandez, D. J., & Myers, D. E. (1993). *America's children: Resources from family, government, and the economy.* New York: Russell Sage.

Herr, E. L. (1997). Super's life-span, life-space approach and its outlook for refinement. *Career Development Quarterly, 45,* 238–246.

Hertz, R. (1986). *More equal than others: Women and men in dual-career marriages.* Berkeley: University of California Press.

Hess, G. C. (1990). Sexual abstinence, a revived option for teenagers. *Modern Psychology, 1,* 19–21.

Hewson, D. (1997). Coping with loss of ability: "Good grief" or episodic stress response. *Social Science and Medicine, 44,* 1129–1139.

Hildebrand, H. P. (1990). The other side of the wall: A psychoanalytic study of creativity in later life. In R. A. Nemiroff & C. A. Colarusso (Eds.), *New dimensions in adult development.* New York: Basic Books.

Hill, M. S. (1992). The role of economic resources and remarriage in financial assistance for children of divorce. *Journal of Family Issues, 13,* 158–178.

Hillman, L. S. (1991). Theories and research. In C. A. Corr, H. Fuller, C. A. Barnickol, & D. M. Corr (Eds.), *Sudden Infant Death Syndrome: Who can help and how.* New York: Springer.

Hinago, T. (1979). What are the characteristics of the method of early childhood education and care in Japan? In Early Childhood Education Association of Japan (Ed.), *Early childhood education and care in Japan.* Tokyo, Japan: Child Honsha.

Hinchcliffe, V. (1996). Fairy stories and children's developing theories of mind. *International Journal of Early Years Education, 4,* 35–46.

Hinde, R. A. (1983). Ethology and child development. In P. H. Mussen (Ed.), *Handbook of child psychology* (4th ed.) (Vol. 2): *Infancy and developmental psychobiology* (pp. 27–94) (M. M. Haith & J. J. Campos, Eds.). New York: John Wiley.

Hirsch, B. J., & Dubois, D. L. (1991). Self-esteem in early adolescence: The identification and prediction of contrasting longitudinal trajectories. *Journal of Youth and Adolescence, 20,* 53–72.

Ho, D. (1983). Asian concepts in behavioral science. *Bulletin of the Hong Kong Psychological Society, 10,* 41–49.

Ho, D. Y. F. (1987). Fatherhood in Chinese culture. In M. E. Lamb (Ed.), *The father's role: Cross-cultural perspectives.* Hillsdale, NJ: Erlbaum.

Hodapp, R. M., & Mueller, E. (1982). Early social development. In B. B. Wolman et al. (Eds.), *Handbook of developmental psychology.* Englewood Cliffs, NJ: Prentice-Hall.

Hodgson, L. G. (1995). Adult grandchildren and their grandparents: The enduring bond. In J. Hendricks (Ed.), *The ties of later life.* Amityville, NY: Baywood.

Hofer, M. A. (1981). *The roots of human behavior: An introduction to the psychobiology of early development.* San Francisco: Freeman.

Hofferth, S. L. (1992). The demand for and supply of child care in the 1990s. In A. Booth (Ed.), *Child care in the 1990's: Trends and consequences.* Hillsdale, NJ: Erlbaum.

Hoffman, L. W. (1991). The influence of the family environment on personality: Accounting for sibling differences. *Psychological Bulletin, 110,* 187–203.

Hoffman, L. W., & Kloska, D. D. (1995). Parents' gender-based attitudes toward marital roles and child rearing: Development and validation of new measures. *Sex Roles, 32,* 273–295.

Hoffman, M. L. (1979). Development of moral thought, feeling, and behavior. *American Psychologist, 34,* 958–966.

Hogan, D. P., & Eggebeen, D. J. (1995). Sources of emergency help and routine assistance in old age. *Social Forces, 73,* 917–936.

Hogan, N., Morse, J. M., & Tason, M. C. (1996). Toward an Experiential Theory of Bereavement. *Omega—Journal of Death and Dying, 33,* 43–65.

Hoge, R. D., & Renzulli, J. S. (1993). Exploring the link between giftedness and self-concept. *Review of Educational Research, 63,* 449–465.

Hohl, D. (1994). Patient satisfaction in home care/hospice. *Nursing Management, 25,* 52–54.

Holahan, C. K. (1996). Lifetime achievement among the Terman gifted women. *Gifted and Talented International, 11,* 65–71.

Holbrook, R. H., Jr., Laros, R. K., Jr., & Creasy, R. K. (1988). Evaluation of a risk-scoring system for prediction of preterm labor. *American Journal of Perinatology 6,* 62.

Holland, J. L. (1992). *Making vocational choices* (2nd ed.). Odessa, FL: Psychological Assessment Resources.

Holland, J. L. (1994). Separate but unequal is better. In M. L. Savikas & R. W. Lent (Eds.), *Convergence in career development theories.* Palo Alto, CA: CPP Books.

Holleman, W. L., Holleman, M. C., & Gershenhorn, S. (1994). Death education curricula in U.S. medical schools. *Teaching and Learning in Medicine, 6,* 260–263.

Holloway, S. D., Rambaud, M. F., Bruce, F., & Eggers-Pierola, C. (1995). What is "appropriate practice" at home and in child care? Low-income mothers' views on preparing their children for school. *Early Childhood Research Quarterly, 10,* 451–473.

Holmes, T. H., & Rahe, R. H. (1967). The social readjustment rating scale. *Journal of Psychosomatic Research, 11,* 213–218.

Holzapfel, S. (1993). Sexual medicine in family practice, Part 2: Treating sexual dysfunction. *Canadian Family Physician, 39,* 618–620.

Honig, A. S. (1993). Mental health for babies: What do theory and research teach us? *Young Children, 48,* 69–76.

Honzik, M. P. (1984). Life-span development. *Annual Review of Psychology, 35,* 309–331.

Hooker, K., & Kaus, C. R. (1994). Health-related possible selves in young and middle adulthood. *Psychology and Aging, 9,* 126–133.

Hooper, S. R. (1992). The classification of developmental disorders: An overview. In S. R. Hooper, G. W. Hynd, & R. E. Mattison (Eds.), *Developmental disorders: Diagnostic criteria and clinical assessment.* Hillsdale, NJ: Erlbaum.

Hooper, S. R., Hynd, G. W., & Mattison, R. E. (Eds.). (1992). *Developmental disorders: Diagnostic criteria and clinical assessment.* Hillsdale, NJ: Erlbaum.

Hopper, C. A., Munoz, K. D., Gruber, M. B., MacConnie, S., et al. (1996). A school-based cardiovascular exercise and nutrition program with parent participation: An evaluation study. *Children's Health Care, 25,* 221–235.

Hopper, J. L., & Seeman, E. (1994). The bone density of female twins discordant for tobacco use. *New England Journal of Medicine, 330,* 387–392.

Horiuchi, Y. (1979). What kind of accomplishments do Japanese children have? In Early Childhood Education Association of Japan (Ed.), *Early childhood education and care in Japan.* Tokyo, Japan: Child Honsha.

Horn, J. L., & Donaldson, G. (1980). Cognitive development in adulthood. In O. G. Brim, Jr., & J. Kagan (Eds.), *Constancy and change in human development.* Cambridge, MA: Harvard University Press.

Horn, J. M. (1983). The Texas adoption project. *Child Development, 54,* 268–275.

Horowitz, M. J., Siegel, B., Holen, A., & Bonanno, G. A. (1997). Diagnostic criteria for complicated grief disorder. *American Journal of Psychiatry, 154,* 904–910.

Hough, K. J., & Erwin, P. G. (1997). Children's attitudes toward violence on television. *Journal of Psychology, 131,* 411–415.

Howarth, G., & Jupp, P. C. (Eds.). *Contemporary issues in the sociology of death, dying and disposal.* New York: St. Martin's.

Howe, M. L., & Courage, M. L. (1993). On resolving the enigma of infantile amnesia. *Psychological Bulletin, 113,* 305–326.

Howes, C., & Segal, J. (1993). Children's relationships with alternative caregivers: The special case of maltreated children removed from their homes. *Journal of Applied Developmental Psychology, 14,* 71–81.

Hucyk, M. H. (1996). Continuities and discontinuities in gender identity. In V. L. Bengtson (Ed.), *Adulthood and aging: Research on continuities and discontinuities.* New York: Springer.

Huesmann, L. R., & Eron, L. D. (1986). The development of aggression in children of different cultures: Psychological processes and exposure to violence. In L. R. Huesmann & L. D. Eron (Eds.), *Television and the aggressive child: A cross-national comparison.* Hillsdale, NJ: Erlbaum.

Hughes, F. P. (1990). *Children, play, and development.* Boston: Allyn & Bacon.

Humphry, D. (1992). Rational suicide among the elderly. *Suicide and Life-Threatening Behavior, 22,* 125–129.

Hunt, C. E. (1991). Sudden infant death syndrome: The neurobehavioral perspective. *Journal of Applied Developmental Psychology, 12,* 185–188.

Hunt, E., & Agnoli, F. (1991). The Whorfian hypothesis: A cognitive psychology perspective. *Psychological Review, 98,* 377–389.

Huntington, D. D., & Bender, W. N. (1993). Adolescents with learning disabilities at risk? Emotional well-being, depression, suicide. *Journal of Learning Disabilities, 26,* 159–166.

Hurrelmann, K. (1990). Parents, peers, teachers and other significant partners in adolescence. *International Journal of Adolescence and Youth, 2,* 211–236.

Husén, T., & Tuijnman, A. (1991). The contribution of formal schooling to the increase in intellectual capital. *Educational Researcher, 20,* 17–25.

Huston, A. C., Wright, J. C., Rice, M. L., Kerkman, D., & St. Peters, M. (1990). Development of television viewing patterns in early childhood: A longitudinal investigation. *Developmental Psychology, 26,* 409–420.

Hutchinson, J. (1991). What crack does to babies. *American Educator, 15,* 31–32.

Hutton, N. (1996). Health prospects for children born to HIV-infected women. In R. R. Faden & N. E. Kass (Eds.), *HIV, AIDS and childbearing.* New York: Oxford University Press.

Hwang, C. P., Lamb, M. E., & Sigel, I. E. (Eds.). (1996). *Images of childhood.* Mahwah, NJ: Erlbaum.

Hyde, J. S., Fennema, E., & Lamon, S. J. (1990). Gender differences in mathematics performance: A meta-analysis. *Psychological Bulletin, 107,* 139–155.

Hyde, J. S., Krajnik, M., & Skuldt-Niederberger, K. (1991). Androgyny across the life span: A replication and longitudinal follow-up. *Developmental Psychology, 27,* 516–519.

Iffy, L., Apuzzio, J. J., Mitra, S., Evans, H., Ganesh, V., & Zentay, Z. (1994). Rates of cesarean section and perinatal outcome. Perinatal mortality. *Acta Obstetricia et Gynecologica Scandinavica, 73,* 225–230.

Ijzendoorn, M. H. Van (1993). Intergenerational transmission of parenting: A review of studies in nonclinical populations. *Developmental Review, 12,* 76–99.

ILO. (1992). *World Labour Report 1992.* Geneva, Switzerland: Author.

Infusino, P., Mercurio, M., Galasso, M. A., Filardi, A., et al. (1996). Multidimensional evaluation in a group of centenarians. *Archives of Gerontology and Geriatrics, Supplement 5,* 377–380.

Ingram, D. (1991). A historical observation on "Why 'Mama' and 'Papa'?" *Journal of Child Language, 18,* 711–713.

Inhelder, B., & Piaget, J. (1958). *The growth of logical thinking from childhood to adolescence.* New York: Basic Books.

Intons-Peterson, M. J. (1988). *Gender concepts of Swedish and American youth.* Hillsdale, NJ: Erlbaum.

Irish, D. P. (1993). *Ethnic variations in dying, death, and grief: Diversity in universality.* Washington, DC: Hemisphere.

Isabell, B. J., & McKee, L. (1980). Society's cradle: An anthropological perspective on the socialization of cognition. In J. Sants (Ed.), *Developmental psychology and society.* London: Macmillan.

Izard, C. E., & Malatesta, C. Z. (1987). Perspectives on emotional development I: Differential emotions theory of early emotional development. In J. D. Osofsky (Ed.), *Handbook of infant development* (2nd ed.). New York: John Wiley.

Jacklin, C. N. (1989). Female and male: Issues of gender. *American Psychologist, 44,* 127–133.

Jacobs, R. H. (1979). *Life after youth.* Boston: Beacon.

Jacobson, D., & Melvin, N. (1995). A comparison of temperament and maternal bother in infants with and without colic. *Journal of Pediatric Nursing, 10,* 181–188.

Jacobson, J. L., & Jacobson, S. W. (1990). Methodological issues in human behavioral teratology. In C. Rovee-Collier & L. P. Lipsitt (Eds.), *Advances in infancy research* (Vol. 6). Norwood, NJ: Ablex.

Jacobson, J. L., & Wille, D. E. (1984). Influence of attachment and separation experience on separation distress at 18 months. *Developmental Psychology, 20,* 477–484.

Jacobson, S. W., Fein, G. G., Jacobson, J. L., Schwartz, P. M., & Dowler, J. K. (1985). Neonatal correlates of exposure to smoking, caffeine, and alcohol. *Infant and Behavior Development, 7,* 253–265.

Jacobvitz, R. S., Wood, M. R., & Albin, K. (1991). Cognitive skills and young children's comprehension of television. *Journal of Applied Developmental Psychology, 12,* 219–235.

Jacopini, G. A., D'Amico, R., Frontali, M., & Vivona, G. (1992). Attitudes of persons at risk and their partners toward predictive testing. In G. Evers-Kiebooms, J. P. Fryns, J. J. Cassiman, & H. Van den Berghe (Eds.), *Psychosocial aspects of genetic counseling.* New York: John Wiley.

Jaffke, F. (1996). *Work and play in early childhood.* Edinburgh, Scotland: Floris.

Jahnke, H. C., & Blanchard-Fields, F. (1993). A test of two models of adolescent egocentrism. *Journal of Youth and Adolescence, 22,* 313–326.

James, W. (1890). *The principles of psychology.* New York: Henry Holt.

James, W. (1892). *Psychology: The briefer course.* New York: Henry Holt.

Janus, M., & Goldberg, S. (1997). Factors influencing family participation in a longitudinal study: Comparison of pediatric and healthy samples. *Journal of Pediatric Psychology, 22,* 245–262.

Janus, S., & Janus, C. (1993). *The Janus report on sexual behavior.* New York: John Wiley.

Jarow, J. P. (1994). Life-threatening conditions associated with male infertility. *Urologic Clinics of North America, 21,* 409–415.

Jean-Gilles, M., & Crittenden, P. M. (1990). Maltreating families: A look at siblings. *Family Relations, 39,* 323–329.

Jenike, M. A. (1997). Topics in geriatrics. *Journal of Geriatric Psychiatry and Neurology, 10,* 47–48.

Jenkins, C. D., Zyzanski, S. J., & Rosenman, R. H. (1971). Progress toward validation of a computer-scored test of the type A coronary-prone behavior pattern. *Psychosomatic Medicine, 33,* 192–202.

Jenkins, R. (1995). Midwifery—a matter of politics. In T. Murphy-Black (Ed.), *Issues in midwifery.* New York: Churchill-Livingstone.

Jensen, W. A., Heinrich, B., Wake, D. B., Wake, M. H., & Wolfe, S. L. (1979). *Biology.* Belmont, CA: Wadsworth.

Jensen-Scott, R. L. (1993). Counseling to promote retirement adjustment. *Career Development Quarterly, 41,* 257–267.

Jimenez, M. (1997, Nov. 25). "Worst nightmare" for slain girl's parents. *Edmonton Journal,* p. A3.

Johnson, B. D., Badr, M. S., & Dempsey, J. A. (1994). Impact of the aging pulmonary system on the response to exercise. *Clinics in Chest Medicine, 15,* 229–246.

Johnson, C. L., & Troll, L. E. (1994). Constraints and facilitators to friendships in late late life. *Gerontologist, 34,* 79–87.

Johnson, D. W., & Johnson, R. T. (1994). *Learning together and alone: Cooperative, competitive, and individualistic learning* (4th ed.). Boston: Allyn & Bacon.

Johnson, J. H. (1986). *Life events as stressors in childhood and adolescence.* Beverly Hills, CA: Sage.

Johnson, M. K., Bransford, J. D., & Solomon, S. (1973). Memory for tacit implications of sentences. *Journal of Experimental Psychology, 98,* 203–205.

Johnson, S. A., & Green, V. (1993). Female adolescent contraceptive decision making and risk taking. *Adolescence, 28,* 81–96.

Johnston, W. B., & Packer, A. B. (1987). *Workforce 2000: Work and workers for the 21st century.* Indianapolis, IN: Hudson Institute.

Jones, C. J., & Meredith, W. (1996). Patterns of personality change across the life span. *Psychology and Aging, 11,* 57–65.

Jones, J. (1995). Institutional abuse: Understanding domination from the inside looking out. *Early Child Development and Care, 113,* 85–92.

Jones, M. C. (1957). The later careers of boys who are early- or late-maturing. *Child Development, 28,* 113–128.

Jones, W. H. (1979). Grief and involuntary career change: Its implications for counseling. *Vocational Guidance Quarterly, 27,* 196–201.

Jopling, D. A. (1996). "Take away the life-lie /p./p./p.": Positive illusions and creative self-deception. *Philosophical Psychology, 9,* 525–544.

Jordan, N. H. (1993). Sexual abuse prevention programs in early childhood education: A caveat. *Young Children, 48,* 76–79.

Jorgensen, S. R. (1991). Project Taking Charge: An evaluation of an adolescent pregnancy prevention program. *Family Relations, 40,* 373–380.

Joshi, H., & Davies, H. (1992). Day care in Europe and mothers' foregone earnings. *International Labor Review, 131,* 561–579.

Joy, L. A., Kimball, M., & Zabrack, M. L. (1977, June). *Television exposure and children's aggressive behavior.* Paper presented at the annual meeting of the Canadian Psychological Association, Vancouver.

Julian, F. H. (1993). Date and acquaintance rape: The legal point of view. Part 2: Reform of rape laws and alternatives to criminal prosecution. *College Student Affairs Journal, 12,* 9–17.

Juvonen, J. (1991). Deviance, perceived responsibility, and negative peer reactions. *Developmental Psychology, 27,* 672–681.

Kagan, J. (1992). Yesterday's premises, tomorrow's promises. *Developmental Psychology, 28,* 990–997.

Kagan, J. (1997). Temperament and the reactions to unfamiliarity. *Child Development, 68,* 139–143.

Kagan, J., & Snidman, N. (1991). Temperamental factors in human development. *American Psychologist, 46,* 856–862.

Kahne, J. (1996). The politics of self-esteem. *American Educational Research Journal, 33,* 3–22.

Kaiser, P. (1996). Relationships in the extended family and diverse family forms. In A. E. Auhagen & M. von Salisch (Eds.), *The diversity of human relationships.* New York: Cambridge University Press.

Kaiser-Messmer, G. (1993). Results of an empirical study into gender differences in attitudes towards mathematics. *Educational Studies in Mathematics, 25,* 209–233.

Kaitz, M., Meschulach-Sarfaty, O., Auerbach, J., & Eidelman, A. (1988). A reexamination of newborns' ability to imitate facial expressions. *Developmental Psychology, 24,* 3–7.

Kalanin, J., Takarada, Y., Kagawa, S., Yamashita, K., Ohtsuka, N., & Matsuoka, A. (1994). Gypsy phenylketonuria: A point mutation of the phenylalanine hydroxylase gene in Gypsy families from Slovakia. *American Journal of Medical Genetics, 49,* 235–239.

Kandall, S. R., Gaines, J., Habel, L., et al. (1993). Relationship of maternal substance abuse to subsequent sudden infant death syndrome in offspring. *Journal of Pediatrics, 123,* 120–126.

Kant, I. (1977). *Die metaphysic der sitten.* Frankfurt: Suhrkamp. (Originally published in 1797.)

Kanter, R. M. (1981). *Men and women of the corporation.* New York: Basic Books.

Kaplan, L. J. (1984). *Adolescence: The farewell to childhood.* New York: Simon & Schuster.

Kaplan, P. S., Fox, K. B., & Huckeby, E. R. (1992). Faces as reinforcers: Effects of pairing condition and facial expression. *Developmental Psychobiology, 25,* 299–312.

Karacostas, D. D., & Fisher, G. L. (1993). Chemical dependency in students with and without learning disabilities. *Journal of Learning Disabilities, 26,* 491–495.

Karges-Bone, L. (1993). Parenting the gifted young scientist: Mrs. Wizard at home. *Gifted Child Today, 16,* 55–59.

Kasof, J. (1993). Sex bias in the naming of stimulus persons. *Psychological Bulletin, 113,* 140–163.

Kastenbaum, R. (1985). Dying and death: A lifespan approach. In J. E. Birren & K. W. Schaie (Eds.), *Handbook of the psychology of aging* (2nd ed.). New York: Van Nostrand Reinhold.

Katz, L. F., & Gottman, J. M. (1997). Buffering children from marital conflict and dissolution. *Journal of Clinical Child Psychology, 26,* 157–171.

Katz, R. C., Frazer, N., & Wilson, L. (1993). Sexual fears are increasing. *Psychological Reports, 73,* 476–478.

Kaufman, A. S., Kaufman, J. C., Chen, T.H., & Kaufman, N. L. (1996). Differences on six Horn abilities for 14 age groups between 15–16 and 75–94 years. *Psychological Assessment, 8,* 161–171.

Kaufman, H. H., Bodensteiner, J., Burkart, B., Gutmann, L., Kopitnik, T., Hochberg, V., Loy, N., Cox-Ganser, J., & Hobbs, G. (1994). Treatment of spastic gait in cerebral palsy. *West Virginia Medical Journal, 90,* 190–192.

Kavale, K. A. (1993). How many learning disabilities are there? A commentary on Stanovich's "Dysrationalia: A new specific learning disability." *Journal of Learning Disabilities, 26,* 520–523.

Kayser, K. (1996). The marital disaffection scale: An inventory for assessing emotional estrangement in marriage. *American Journal of Family Therapy, 24,* 83–88.

Kazdin, A. E. (1989). Developmental psychopathology: Current research, issues, and directions. *American Psychologist, 44,* 180–187.

Kazdin, A. E. (1995). *Conduct disorders in childhood and adolescence* (2nd ed.). Thousand Oaks, CA: Sage.

Keel, P. K., Fulkerson, J. A., & Leon, G. R. (1997). Disordered eating precursors in pre- and early adolescent girls and boys. *Journal of Youth and Adolescence, 26,* 203–217.

Kegan, R. (1982). *The evolving self: Problem and process in human development.* Cambridge, MA: Harvard University Press.

Keith, P. M., Schafer, R. B., & Wacker, R. (1995). Outcomes of equity/inequity among older spouses. In J. Hendricks (Ed.), *The ties of later life.* Amityville, NY: Baywood.

Kelly, J. R., & Westcott, G. (1991). Ordinary retirement: Commonalities and continuity. *International Journal of Aging and Human Development, 32,* 81–89.

Kelly, K. R. (1993). The relation of gender and academic achievement to career self-efficacy and interests. *Gifted Child Quarterly, 37,* 59–64.

Kendall-Tackett, K. A., Williams, L. M., & Finkelhor, D. (1993). Impact of sexual abuse on children: A review and synthesis of recent empirical studies. *Psychological Bulletin, 113,* 164–180.

Kennedy, G. J., Haque, M., & Zarankow, B. (1997). Human sexuality in late life. *International Journal of Mental Health, 26,* 35–46.

Kessen, W. (1965). *The child.* New York: John Wiley.

Kett, J. F. (1977). *Rites of passage: Adolescence in America, 1790 to the present.* New York: Basic Books.

Kiley, D. (1983). *The Peter Pan Syndrome: Men who have never grown up.* New York: Dodd, Mead.

Killen, M., & Hart, D. (Eds.). (1995). *Morality in everyday life: Developmental perspectives.* New York: Cambridge University Press.

Kindermann, J., & Valsiner, J. (1995). *Development of person–context relations.* Hillsdale, NJ: Erlbaum.

Kinsey, A. C., Pomeroy, W. B., & Martin, C. E. (1948). *Sexual behavior in the human male.* Philadelphia: W. B. Saunders.

Kinsey, A. C, Pomeroy, W. B., Martin, C. E., & Gebhard, P. H. (1953). *Sexual behavior in the human female.* Philadelphia: W. B. Saunders.

Klaus, M., & Kennell, J. (1976). *Maternal–infant bonding.* St. Louis: C. V. Mosby.

Klaus, M., & Kennell, J. (1983). *Bonding: The beginnings of parent–infant attachment* (rev. ed.). St. Louis: C. V. Mosby. (Originally published as *Maternal–infant bonding.*)

Klaus, M., Kreger, N., McAlpine, W., Steffa, M., & Kennell, J. (1972). Maternal attachment: Importance of the first post-partum days. *New England Journal of Medicine, 286,* 460–463.

Kleemeier, R. (1962). Intellectual changes in the senium. *Proceedings of the Social Section of the American Statistical Association, 1,* 290–295.

Klein, K., Forehand, R., Armistead, L., & Long, P. (1997). Delinquency during the transition to early adulthood: Family and parenting predictors from early adolescence. *Adolescence, 32,* 61–80.

Kloza, E. M. (1990). Low MSAFP and new biochemical markers for Down syndrome: Implications for genetic counselors. In B. A. Fine, E. Gettig, K. Greendale, B. Leopold, & N .W. Paul (Eds.), *Strategies in genetic counseling: Reproductive genetics and new technologies.* White Plains, NY: March of Dimes Birth Defects Foundation.

Knoblauch, K., Bieber, M., & Werner, J. S. (1996). Assessing dimensionality in infant colour vision. In F. Vital-Durand, J. Atkinson, & O. J. Braddick (Eds.), *Infant vision.* New York: Oxford Univeristy Press.

Knox, G. W., Laske, D. L., & Tromanhauser, E. D. (1992). *Schools under siege.* Dubuque, IA: Kendall/Hunt.

Knuppel, R. A., & Angel, J. L. (1990). Diagnosis of fetal–maternal hemorrhage. In R. D. Eden, F. H. Boehm, & M. Haire (Eds.), *Assessment and care of the fetus: Physiological, clinical, and medicolegal principles.* Norwalk, CT: Appleton & Lange.

Kochanska, G. (1997). Mutually responsive orientation between mothers and their young children: Implications for early socialization. *Child Development, 68,* 94–112.

Kochanska, G., Clark, L. A., & Goldman, M. A. (1997). Implications of mothers' personality for their parenting and their young children's development outcomes. *Journal of Personality, 65,* 387–420.

Kochanska, G., Murray, K., & Coy, K. C. (1997). Inhibitory control as a contributor to conscience in childhood: From toddler to early school age. *Child Development, 68,* 263–277.

Kohlberg, L. A. (1964). Development of moral character and moral ideology. In M. L. Hoffman & L. W. Hoffman (Eds.), *Review of child development research* (Vol. 1). New York: Russell Sage.

Kohlberg, L. A. (1966). Cognitive–development analysis of children's sex-role concepts and attitudes. In E. Maccoby (Ed.), *The development of sex differences.* Stanford, CA: Stanford University Press.

Kohlberg, L. A. (1969). Stage and sequence: The cognitive developmental approach to socialization. In D. Gosslin (Ed.), *Handbook of socialization theory and research.* Chicago: Rand McNally.

Kohlberg, L. A. (1980). *The meaning and measurement of moral development.* Worcester, MA: Clark University Press.

Koli, K., & Keski-Oja, J. (1992). Cellular senescence. *Annals of Medicine, 24,* 313–318.

Kondro, W. (1992). Canada: Controversy over Royal Commission on Reproductive Technologies. *Lancet, 310,* 1214–1215.

Konner, M. (1982). Biological aspects of the mother–infant bond. In C. Parks & J. Stevenson-Hinde (Eds.), *The place of attachment in human behavior.* New York: Basic Books.

Kopp, N., Denoroy, L., Eymin, C., Gay, N., Richard, F., Awano, K., Gilly, R., & Jordan, D. (1994). Studies of neuroregulators in the brain stem of SIDS. *Biology of the Neonate, 65,* 189–193.

Kopp, R. G., & Ruzicka, M. F. (1993). Women's multiple roles and psychological well-being. *Psychological Reports, 72,* 1351–1354.

Kopper, B. A. (1996). Gender, gender identity, rape myth acceptance, and time of initial resistance on the perception of acquaintance rape blame and avoidability. *Sex Roles, 34,* 81–93.

Korten, A. E., Henderson, A. S., Christensen, H., Jorm, A. F., et al. (1997). A prospective study of cognitive function in the elderly. *Psychological Medicine, 27,* 919–930.

Koss, M. (1988). Hidden rape: Sexual aggression and victimization in a national sample of students in higher education. In A. Burgess (Ed.), *Rape and sexual assault* (Vol. 2). New York: Garland.

Kotch, J. B. (1993). Morbidity and death due to child abuse in New Zealand. *Child Abuse and Neglect: The International Journal, 17,* 233–247.

Koutsouvanou, E. (1993). Television and child language development. *International Journal of Early Childhood, 25,* 27–32.

Kovacs, M. (1989). Affective disorders in children and adolescents. *American Psychologist, 44,* 209–215.

Kozulin, A. (1990). *Vygotsky's psychology: A biography of ideas.* New York: Harvester Wheatsheaf.

Kracke, B. (1997). Parental behaviors and adolescents' career exploration. *Career Development Quarterly, 45,* 341–350.

Krampen, G. (1997). Promotion of creativity (divergent productions) and convergent productions by systematic-relaxation exercises: Empirical evidence from five experimental studies with children, young adults, and elderly. *European Journal of Personality, 11,* 83–99.

Kroger, J. (1993). Ego identity: An overview. In J. Kroger (Ed.), *Discussions on ego identity.* Hillsdale, NJ: Erlbaum.

Kroupa, S. E. (1988). Perceived parental acceptance and female juvenile delinquency. *Adolescence, 23,* 143–155.

Krucoff, C. (1997, Oct. 27). More folks improving step by step. *Los Angeles Times,* p. S3.

Kruse, A., Lindenberger, U., & Baltes, P. B. (1993). Longitudinal research on human aging: The power of combining real-time, microgenetic, and simulation approaches. In D. Magnusson & P. Casaer (Eds.), *Longitudinal research on individual development: Present status and future perspectives.* Cambridge: Cambridge University Press.

Kruyer, H., Miranda, M., Volpini, V., & Estivill, X. (1994). Carrier detection and microsatellite analysis of Duchenne and Becker muscular dystrophy in Spanish families. *Prenatal Diagnosis, 14,* 123–130.

Kübler-Ross, E. (1969). *On death and dying.* New York: Macmillan.

Kübler-Ross, E. (1974). *Questions and answers on death and dying.* New York: Macmillan.

Kuczynski, L., & Kochanska, G. (1995). Function and content of maternal demands: Developmental significance of early demands for competent action. *Child Development, 66,* 616–628.

Kuder, F. (1977). *Activity, interests, and occupational choice.* Chicago: Science Research Associates.

Kuhn, D. (1984). Cognitive development. In M. H. Bornstein & M. E. Lamb (Eds.), *Developmental psychology: An advanced textbook* (pp. 133–180). Hillsdale, NJ: Erlbaum.

Kuhn, T. S. (1970). *The structure of scientific revolutions* (2nd ed., enl.). Chicago: University of Chicago Press.

Kumari, R. (1989). *Brides are not for burning: Dowry victims in India.* Kalkaji, New Delhi: Radiant.

Kumin, L. (1994). Intelligibility of speech in children with Down syndrome in natural settings: Parents' perspective. *Perceptual and Motor Skills, 78,* 307–313.

Kupetz, B. N. (1993). Reducing stress in your child's life. *PTA Today, 18,* 10–12.

Kurdek, L. A. (1993). Issues in proposing a general model of the effects of divorce on children. *Journal of Marriage and the Family, 55,* 39–41.

Kurita, H. (1996). Specificity and developmental consequences of speech loss in children with pervasive developmental disorders. *Psychiatry and Clinical Neurosciences, 50,* 181–184.

Kurtines, W. M., & Gewirtz, J. L. (Eds.). (1995). *Moral development: An introduction.* Boston: Allyn & Bacon.

Kuzyk, B. (1993, Sept. 2). Breast-feeding is best for babies. *Edmonton Sun,* p. 38.

Kwok, S. K., Ho, P. C. P., Chan, A. K. H., Ghandi, S. R., et al. (1996). Ocular defects in children and adolescents with severe mental deficiency. *Journal of Intellectual Disability Research, 40,* 330–335.

Labouvie, E. W. (1990). Personality and alcohol and marijuana use: Patterns of convergence in young adulthood. *International Journal of Addictions, 25,* 237–252.

Labouvie-Vief, G. (1980). Beyond formal operations: Uses and limits of pure logic in life-span development. *Human Development, 23,* 141–161.

Labouvie-Vief, G. (1986). Modes of knowledge and the organization of development. In M. L. Commons, L. Kohlberg, F. A. Richards, & J. Sinnott (Eds.), *Beyond formal operations 3: Models and methods in the study of adult and adolescent thought.* New York: Praeger.

Labouvie-Vief, G., & Lawrence, R. (1985). Object knowledge, personal knowledge, and processes of equilibration in adult cognition. *Human Development, 28,* 25–39.

Lachenmeyer, J. R., & Muni-Brander, P. (1988). Eating disorders in a nonclinical adolescent population: Implications for treatment. *Adolescence, 23*(90), 303–312.

Lachman, M. E., & James, J. B. (Eds.). (1997). *Multiple paths of midlife development.* Chicago: University of Chicago Press.

Laczko, F. (1989). Between work and retirement: Becoming "old" in the 1980's. In B. Bytheway, T. Keil, P. Allatt, & A. Bryman (Eds.), *Becoming and being old: Sociological approaches to later life.* London: Sage.

La Greca, A. M., & Stone, W. L. (1993). Social anxiety scale for children revised: Factor structure and concurrent validity. *Journal of Clinical Child Psychology, 22,* 17–27.

Lal, S. R., Lal, D., & Achilles, C. M. (1993). *Handbook on gangs in schools: Strategies to reduce gang-related activities.* Thousand Oaks, CA: Corwin.

Lally, K. (1997, Oct. 22). Poll: Russian kids aim to be lawyers, killers. *Seattle Times.*

Lam, T. C. L. (1992). Review of practices and problems in the evaluation of bilingual education. *Review of Educational Research, 62,* 181–203.

Lamanna, M. A., & Riedmann, A. (1988). *Marriages and families: Making choices and facing change* (3rd ed.). Belmont, CA: Wadsworth.

Lamb, M. E. (1980). The development of parent–infant attachment in the first two years of life. In F. A. Pedersen (Ed.), *The father–infant relationship: Observational studies in the family setting.* New York: Holt, Rinehart & Winston.

Lamb, M. E. (Ed.). (1987). *The father's role: Cross-cultural perspectives.* Hillsdale, NJ: Erlbaum.

Lamb, S., & Coakley, M. (1993). "Normal" childhood sexual play and games: Differentiating play from abuse. *Child Abuse and Neglect: The International Journal, 17,* 515–526.

Lambert, W. E. (1975). Culture and language as factors in learning and education. In A. Wolfgang (Ed.), *Education of immigrant students.* Toronto: Ontario Institute for Studies in Education.

Lamport, L. L., & Andre, T. (1993). AIDS knowledge and sexual responsibility. *Youth and Society, 25,* 38–61.

Landerman, R., George, L. K., & Blazer, D. G. (1991). Adult vulnerability for psychiatric disorders: Interactive effects of negative childhood experiences and recent stress. *Journal of Nervous and Mental Disease, 179,* 656–663.

Landreth, G. L. (1993). Child-centered play therapy. *Elementary School Guidance and Counseling, 28,* 17–29.

Lane, H. (1977). *The wild boy of Aveyron.* London: Allen & Unwin.

Langer, L. M., & Tubman, J. G. (1997). Risky sexual behavior among substance-abusing adolescents: Psychosocial and contextual factors. *American Journal of Orthopsychiatry, 67,* 315–322.

Langer, N. (1995). Grandparents and adult grandchildren: What do they do for one another? In J. Hendricks (Ed.), *The ties of later life.* Amityville, NY: Baywood.

Langlois, J. H., Ritter, J. M., Roggman, L. A., & Vaughn, L. S. (1991). Facial diversity and infant preferences for attractive faces. *Developmental Psychology, 27,* 79–84.

Langlois, J. H., & Roggman, L. A. (1990). Attractive faces are only average. *Psychological Science, 1,* 115–121.

Langlois, J. H., Roggman, L. A., & Rieser-Danner, L. A. (1990). Infants' differential social responses to attractive and unattractive faces. *Developmental Psychology, 26,* 153–159.

Langs, R., Badalamenti, A. F., & Savage-Rumbaugh, S. (1996). Two mathematically defined expressive language structures in humans and chimpanzees. *Behavioral Science, 41,* 124–135.

Langton, J. (1997, Dec. 1). American doctors selling made-to-order embryos. *Daily Telegraph (London),* p. 6.

Lapierre, S., Bouffard, L., & Bastin, E. (1992/1993). Motivational goal objects in later life. *International Journal of Aging and Human Development, 36,* 279–292.

Lapsley, D. K. (1990). Continuity and discontinuity in adolescent social cognitive development. In R. Montemayor, G. R. Adams, & T. P. Gullotta (Eds.), *From childhood to adolescence: A transitional period?* (*Advances in Adolescent Development,* Vol. 2). Newbury Park, CA: Sage.

Larson, R., & Ham, M. (1993). Stress and "storm and stress" in early adolescence: The relationship of negative events with dysphoric affect. *Developmental Psychology, 29,* 130–140.

Larson, R. W. (1997). The emergence of solitude as a constructive domain of experience in early adolescence. *Child Development, 68,* 80–93.

Lasher, K. P., & Faulkender, P. J. (1993). Measurement of aging anxiety: Development of the Anxiety about Aging Scale. *International Journal of Aging and Human Development, 37,* 247–259.

Lasley, J. R. (1992). Age, social context, and street gang membership: Are "youth" gangs becoming "adult" gangs? *Youth and Society, 23,* 434–451.

Latané, R., & Darley, J. M. (1970). *The unresponsive bystander: Why doesn't he help?* New York: Appleton-Century-Crofts.

Lauer, R. H., Lauer, J. C., & Kerr, S. T. (1995). The long-term marriage: Perceptions of stability and satisfaction. In J. Hendricks (Ed.), *The ties of later life.* Amityville, NY: Baywood.

Lauter, D. (1997, Oct. 28). Man infects 9 with AIDS virus in semirural NY. *Los Angeles Times,* p. 1.

Lavee, Y., & Olson, D. H. (1993). Seven types of marriage: Empirical typology based on ENRICH. *Journal of Marital and Family Therapy, 19,* 325–340.

Lavery, B., Siegel, A. W., Cousins, J. H., & Rubovits, D. S. (1993). Adolescent risk-taking: An analysis of problem behaviors in problem children. *Journal of Experimental Child Psychology, 55,* 277–294.

Law waived for Latimer. (1997, Dec. 2). *Edmonton Sun,* p. News 3.

Lawton, M. P. (1981). Community supports for the aged. *Journal of Social Issues, 37,* 102–115.

Lazarus, R. S. (1993). From psychological stress to the emotions: A history of changing outlooks. *Annual Review of Psychology, 44,* 1–21.

Leaf, A. (1973, September). Getting old. *Scientific American, 299,* 44–53.

Leboyer, F. (1975). *Birth without violence.* New York: Random House.

Ledoux, S., Choquet, M., & Manfredi, R. (1993). Associated factors for self-reported binge eating among male and female adolescents. *Journal of Adolescence, 16,* 75–91.

Lee, C. (1990). *The growth and development of children* (4th ed.). New York: Longman.

Lee, G. R., Dwyer, J. W., & Coward, R. T. (1993). Gender differences in parent care: Demographic factors and same-gender preferences. *Journal of Gerontology, 48,* S9–S16.

Lee, K. (1992). Pattern of night waking and crying of Korean infants from 3 months to 2 years old and its relation with various factors. *Journal of Developmental and Behavioral Pediatrics, 13,* 326–330.

Lee, M. K., et al. (1997). Hyperaccumulation of FAD-linked presenilin 1 variants in vivo. *Nature Medicine, 3,* 756–760.

Lee, V. E., Brooks-Gunn, J., & Schnur, E. (1988). Does Head Start work? A 1-year follow-up comparison of disadvantaged children attending Head Start, no preschool, and other preschool programs. *Developmental Psychology, 24,* 210–222.

Lee, V. E., Croninger, R. G., Linn, E., & Chen, X. (1996). The culture of sexual harassment in secondary schools. *American Educational Research Journal, 33,* 383–417.

Lefrançois, G. R. (1973). *Of children.* Belmont, CA: Wadsworth.

Lefrançois, G. R. (1995). *Theories of Learning: Kro's Report* (3rd ed.). Pacific Grove, CA: Brooks/Cole.

Lefrançois, G. R. (1997). *Psychology for Teaching* (9th ed.). Belmont, CA: Wadsworth.

Legerstee, M. (1991). Changes in the quality of infant sounds as a function of social and nonsocial stimulation. *First Language, 11,* 327–343.

Lehman, A. B. (1996). Nutrition and health: What is new? *Reviews in Clinical Gerontology, 6,* 147–168.

Lehman, H. C. (1953). *Age and achievement.* Princeton, NJ: Princeton University Press.

Leidy, N. K., & Darling-Fischer, C. S. (1995). Reliability and validity of the Modified Erikson Psychosocial Stage Inventory in diverse samples. *Western Journal of Nursing Research, 17,* 168–187.

Leiter, J., & Johnsen, M. C. (1997). Child maltreatment and school performance declines: An event–history analysis. *American Educational Research Journal, 34,* 563–589.

Lemerise, E. A. (1997). Patterns of peer acceptance, social status, and social reputation in mixed-age preschool and primary classrooms. *Merrill–Palmer Quarterly, 43,* 199–218.

Lemme, B. H. (1995). *Development in adulthood.* Boston: Allyn & Bacon.

Lenneberg, E. H. (1969). On explaining language. *Science, 164,* 635–643.

Lent, R. W. (1996). Career counseling, science, and policy: Revitalizing our paradigms and roles. *Career Development Quarterly, 45,* 58–64.

Leon, M. (1992). The neurobiology of learning. *Annual Review of Psychology, 43,* 377–398.

Lerner, J. V., & Abrams, L. A. (1994). Developmental correlates of maternal employment influences on children. In C. B. Fisher & R. M. Lerner (Eds.), *Applied developmental psychology.* New York: McGraw-Hill.

Lerner, R. M. (1991). Changing organism–context relations as the basic process of development: A developmental

contextual perspective. *Developmental Psychology, 27,* 27–32.

Lerner, R. M. (1993). The demise of the nature–nurture dichotomy. *Human Development, 36,* 119–124.

Lerner, R. M., Lerner, J. V., Winelle, M., Hooker, K., Lenez, K., et al. (1986). Children and adolescents in their contexts: Tests of the goodness of fit model. In R. Plomin & J. Dunn (Eds.), *The study of temperament: Changes, continuities and challenges.* Hillsdale, NJ: Erlbaum.

Lerner, R. M., Miller, J. R., Knott, J. H., Kenneth, E. C., Bynum, T. S., Hoopfer, L. C., McKinney, M. H., Abrams, A., Hula, R. C., & Terry, P. A. (1992). Integrating scholarship and outreach in human development research, policy, and service: A developmental contextual perspective. In D. L. Featherman, R. M. Lerner, & M. Perlmutter (Eds.), *Lifespan development and behavior* (Vol. 12). Hillsdale, NJ: Erlbaum.

Leslie, A. M. (1988). Some implications of pretense for mechanisms underlying the child's theory of mind. In J. W. Astington, P. L. Harris, & D. R. Olson (Eds.), *Developing theories of mind.* New York: Cambridge University Press.

Lester, B. M., LaGasse, L., Freier, K., & Brunner, S. (1996). Studies of cocaine-exposed human infants. In C. L. Wetherington, V. L. Smeriglio, & L. P. Finnegan (Eds.), *Behavioral studies of drug-exposed offspring: Methodological issues in human and animal research.* NIDA Research Monograph 164, 1996. Rockville, MD: U.S. Department of Health and Human Services.

Lester, D. (1995). Why are some nations experiencing an increase in youth suicide rates? *Homeostasis in Health and Disease, 36,* 232–233.

Lester, D., & Leenaars, A. A. (1996). The ethics of suicide and suicide prevention. *Death Studies, 20,* 163–184.

Leventhal, E. A., Levanthal, H., & Shacham, S. (1989). Active coping reduces reports of pain from childbirth. *Journal of Consulting and Clinical Psychology, 57,* 365–371.

Levine, J. M., Resnick, L. B., & Higgins, E. T. (1993). Social foundations of cognition. *Annual Review of Psychology, 44,* 585–612.

Levine, M. P., Smolak, L., & Schermer, F. (1996). Media analysis and resistance by elementary school children in the primary prevention of eating problems. *Eating Disorders: The Journal of Treatment and Prevention, 4,* 310–322.

Levine, R. A. (1987). Women's schooling, patterns of fertility, and child survival. *Educational Researcher, 16,* 21–27.

Levinson, D. (1990). *The seasons of a woman's life: Implications for women and men.* Paper presented at the Annual Meeting of the American Psychological Association, Boston.

Levinson, D. J. (1978). *The seasons of a man's life.* New York: Knopf.

Levinson, D. J. (1981). The midlife transition: A period in adult psychosocial development. In L. D. Steinberg

(Ed.), *The life cycle: Readings in human development.* New York: Columbia University Press.

Levinson, D. J. (1996). *The seasons of a woman's life.* New York: Knopf.

Levitt, A. G., & Utman, J. G. (1992). From babbling towards the sound systems of English and French: A longitudinal two-case study. *Journal of Child Language, 19,* 19–49.

Levitt, M. J., Weber, R. A., & Guacci, N. (1993). Convoys of social support: An intergenerational analysis. *Psychology and Aging, 8,* 323–326.

Levy, G. D. (1993). Introduction: An integrated collection on early gender-role development. *Developmental Review, 13,* 123–125.

Lewis, C. A., Lanigan, C., Joseph, S., & de Fockert, J. (1997). Religiosity and happiness: No evidence for an association among undergraduates. *Personality and Individual Differences, 22,* 119–121.

Lewis, K. G., & Moon, S. (1997). Always single and single again women: A qualitative study. *Journal of Marital and Family Therapy, 23,* 115–134.

Liben, L. (1975, April). *Perspective-taking skills in young children: Seeing the world through rose-colored glasses.* Paper presented at the meeting of the Society for Research in Child Development, Denver.

Liddell, D. L., & Douvanis, C. J. (1994). The social and legal status of gay and lesbian students: An update for colleges and universities. *Naspa Journal, 31,* 121–129.

Lieberman, A. B. (1987). *Giving birth.* New York: St. Martin's.

Lieberman, M. A. (1996). Perspective on adult life crises. In V. L. Bengtson (Ed.), *Adulthood and aging: Research on continuities and discontinuities.* New York: Springer.

Liggins, G. C. (1988). The onset of labor: An historical review. In C. T. Jones (Ed.), *Research in perinatal medicine (VII): Fetal and neonatal development.* Ithaca, NY: Perinatology Press.

Lindstrom, P. (1996). Family interaction, neighbourhood context and deviant behaviour: A research note. *Studies on Crime and Crime Prevention, 5,* 113–119.

Linn, M. C., & Hyde, J. S. (1989). Gender, mathematics, and science. *Educational Researcher, 18,* 17–27.

Linn, R. (1995). "Thirty nothing": What do counsellors know about mature single women who wish for a child and a family? *International Journal for the Advancement of Counselling, 18,* 69–84.

Livesey, D. J., & Intili, D. (1996). A gender difference in visual–spatial ability in 4-year-old children: Effects on performance of a kinesthetic acuity task. *Journal of Experimental Child Psychology, 63,* 436–446.

Lobel, T. E., Agami-Rozenblat, O., & Bempechat, J. (1993). Personality correlates of career choice in the kibbutz: A comparison between career and noncareer women. *Sex Roles: A Journal of Research, 29,* 359–370.

Locke, J. (1699). *Some thoughts concerning education* (4th ed.). London: A. & J. Churchills.

Locke, J. L. (1992). Thirty years of research on developmental neurolinguistics. *Pediatric Neurology, 8,* 245–250.

Lockhart, A. S. (1980). Motor learning and motor development during infancy and childhood. In C. B. Corbin (Ed.), *A textbook of motor development.* Dubuque, IA: Brown.

Loehlin, J. C., Horn, J. M., & Willerman, L. (1994). Differential inheritance of mental abilities in the Texas Adoption Project. *Intelligence, 19,* 325–336.

Loehlin, J. C., Horn, J. M., & Willerman, L. (1997). Heredity, environment and IQ in the Texas Adoption Project. In R. J. Sternberg & E. L. Grigorenko (Eds.), *Intelligence, heredity, and environment.* New York: Cambridge University Press.

Logli, P. A. (1994). We must criminalize fetal neglect. In G. E. McCuen (Ed.), *Born hooked: Poisoned in the womb* (2nd ed.). Hudson, WI: Gary McCuen Publications.

Long, J. (1989). A part to play: Men experiencing leisure through retirement. In B. Bytheway, T. Keil, P. Allatt, & A. Bryman (Eds.), *Becoming and being old: Sociological approaches to later life.* London: Sage.

Long, J., & Porter, K. L. (1984). Multiple roles of midlife women: A case for new directions in theory, research, and policy. In G. Baruch & J. Brooks-Gunn (Eds.), *Women in midlife.* New York: Plenum.

Long, V. O. (1991). Gender role conditioning and women's self-concept. *Journal of Humanistic Education and Development, 30,* 19–29.

Longstreth, G. F., & Wolde-Tsadik, G. (1993). Irritable bowel-type symptoms in HMO examinees. Prevalence, demographics, and clinical correlates. *Digestive Diseases and Sciences, 38,* 1581–1589.

Lonsway, K. A. (1996). Preventing acquaintance rape through education: What do we know? *Psychology of Women Quarterly, 20,* 229–265.

Lookabaugh, S. L., & Fu, V. R. (1992). Children's use of inanimate transitional objects in coping with hassles. *Journal of Genetic Psychology, 153,* 37–46.

Looney, M. A., & Plowman, S. A. (1990). Passing rates of American children and youth on the FITNESS-GRAM criterion-referenced physical fitness standards. *Research Quarterly for Exercise and Sport, 61,* 215–223.

Lorenz, K. (1952). *King Solomon's ring.* London: Methuen.

Los, M., & Chamard, S. E. (1997). Selling newspapers or educating the public? Sexual violence in the media. *Canadian Journal of Criminology, 39,* 294–328.

Lourenco, O., & Machado, A. (1996). In defense of Piaget's theory: A reply to 10 common criticisms. *Psychological Review, 10,* 143–164.

Lu, L., & Argyle, M. (1993). TV watching, soap opera and happiness. *Kaohsiung Journal of Medical Sciences, 9,* 501–507.

Lu, L., & Argyle, M. (1994). Leisure satisfaction and happiness as a function of leisure activity. *Kaohsiung Journal of Medical Sciences, 10,* 89–96.

Lu, L., & Shih, J. B. (1997). Personality and happiness: Is mental health a mediator? *Personality and Individual Differences, 22,* 249–256.

Luke, C. (1988). *Television and your child: A guide for concerned parents.* Toronto: Kagan & Woo.

Lupart, J. L., & Pyryt, M. C. (1996). "Hidden gifted" students: Underachiever prevalence and profile. *Journal for the Education of the Gifted, 20,* 36–53.

Luqmani, R., Gordon, C., & Bacon, P. (1994). Clinical pharmacology and modification of autoimmunity and inflammation in rheumatoid disease. *Drugs, 47,* 259–285.

Luthar, S. S., & Cushing, G. (1997). Substance use and personal adjustment among disadvantaged teenagers: A six-month prospective study. *Journal of Youth and Adolescence, 26,* 353–372.

Luyendijk, W., & Treffers, P. D. (1992). The smile in anencephalic infants. *Clinical Neurology and Neurosurgery,* 1994 Supplement, S113–S117.

Lye, D. N., & Biblarz, T. J. (1993). The effects of attitudes toward family life and gender roles on marital satisfaction. *Journal of Family Issues, 14,* 157–188.

Lyne, J., & Howe, H. F. (1990). The rhetoric of expertise: E. O. Wilson and sociobiology. *Quarterly Journal of Speech, 76,* 134–152.

Lyon, M., Chatoor, I., Atkins, D., Silber, T., Mosimann, J., & Gray, J. (1997). Testing the hypothesis of the multidimensional model of anorexia nervosa in adolescents. *Adolescence, 32,* 101–113.

Maccoby, E. E., & Jacklin, C. N. (1974). *The psychology of sex differences.* Stanford, CA: Stanford University Press.

Maccoby, E. E., & Jacklin, C. N. (1980). Sex differences in aggression: A rejoinder and reprise. *Child Development, 51,* 964–980.

Mack, J. (1980). *Zulus.* London: Macdonald Educational.

MacNeal, J. U. (1992). *Kids as customers.* New York: Lexington.

Macrae, J. H. (1991). Presbycusis and noise-induced permanent threshold shift. *Journal of the Acoustical Society of America, 90,* 2513–2516.

Madak, P. R., & Berg, D. H. (1992). The prevention of sexual abuse: An evaluation of "Talking about Touching." *Canadian Journal of Counselling, 26,* 29–40.

Madonna, P. G., Van Scoyk, S., & Jones, D. P. (1991). Family interactions within incest and nonincest families. *American Journal of Psychiatry, 148,* 46–49.

Madsen, M. C. (1971). Developmental and cross-cultural differences in the cooperation and competitive behavior of young children. *Journal of Cross-Cultural Psychology, 2,* 365–371.

Madsen, M. C., & Lancy, D. F. (1981). Cooperative and competitive behavior: Experiments related to ethnic identity and urbanization in Papua New Guinea. *Journal of Cross-Cultural Psychology, 12,* 389–409.

Mahoney, M. J. (1991). *Human change processes: The scientific foundations of psychotherapy.* New York: Basic Books.

Main, M., & Cassidy, J. (1988). Categories of response to reunion with the parent at age 6: Predictable from infant attachment classifications and stable over a 1-month period. *Developmental Psychology, 24,* 415–426.

Males, M. (1993a). Schools, society, and "teen" pregnancy. *Phi Delta Kappan, 74,* 566–568.

Males, M. (1993b). School-age pregnancy: Why hasn't prevention worked? *Journal of School Health, 63,* 429–432.

Malina, R. M. (1990). Physical growth and performance during the transitional years (9 to 16). In R. Montemayor, G. R. Adams, & T. P. Gullotta (Eds.), *From childhood to adolescence: A transitional period?* (*Advances in Adolescent Development,* Vol. 2). Newbury Park, CA: Sage.

Malina, R. M., & Bouchard, C. (1991). *Growth, maturation, and physical activity.* Champaign, IL: Human Kinetics Books.

Malina, R. M., Bouchard, C., & Beunen, G. (1988). Human growth: Selected aspects of current research on well-nourished children. *Annual Review of Anthropology, 17,* 187–219.

Malonebeach, E. E., & Zarit, S. H. (1991). Current research issues in caregiving to the elderly. *International Journal of Aging and Human Development, 32,* 103–114.

Maltas, C. (1992). Trouble in paradise: Marital crises of midlife. *Psychiatry, 55,* 122–131.

Mandel, M. (1997, Nov. 2). Terror comes to town. *Edmonton Sun,* p. News 10.

Mandich, M., Simons, C. J., Ritchie, S., Schmidt, D., & Mullett, M. (1994). Motor development, infantile reactions and postural responses of preterm, at-risk infants. *Developmental Medicine and Child Neurology, 36,* 397–405.

Manning, A. (1997, Sept. 11). AIDS death rate continues to decline. *USA Today.*

Manning, G. F. (1993). Loss and renewal in old age: Some literary models. *Canadian Journal on Aging, 12,* 469–484.

Manning, W. D. (1993). Marriage and cohabitation following premarital conception. *Journal of Marriage and the Family, 55,* 839–850.

Marcia, J. E. (1966). Development and validation of ego-identity status. *Journal of Personality and Social Psychology, 3,* 551–558.

Marcia, J. E. (1980). Identity in adolescence. In J. Adelson (Ed.), *Handbook of adolescent psychology.* New York: John Wiley.

Marcia, J. E. (1993). The relational roots of identity. In J. Kroger (Ed.), *Discussions on ego identity.* Hillsdale, NJ: Erlbaum.

Marcon, R. A. (1993). Socioemotional versus academic emphasis: Impact on kindergartners' development and achievement. *Early Child Development and Care, 96,* 81–91.

Marjoribanks, K. (1997). Ordinal position, family environment, and status attainment among Australian young adults. *Journal of Social Psychology, 137,* 398–399.

Markides, K., & Martin, H. (1979). A causal model of life satisfaction among the elderly. *Journal of Gerontology, 34,* 86–93.

Marks, M. N. (1996). Characteristics and causes of infanticide in Britain. *International Review of Psychiatry, 8,* 99–106.

Marlatt, G. A., Baer, J. S., Donovan, D. M., & Kivlahan, D. R. (1988). Addictive behaviors: Etiology and treatment. *Annual Review of Psychology, 39,* 223–252.

Marsiglio, W. (1986). Teenage fatherhood: High school accreditation and educational attainment. In A. B. Elster & M. E. Lamb (Eds.), *Adolescent fatherhood.* Hillsdale, NJ: Erlbaum.

Martin, C. L., & Halverson, C. F. (1987). The role of cognition in sex role acquisition. In D. B. Carter (Ed.), *Current conceptions of sex roles and sex typing: Theory and research.* New York: Praeger.

Martin, M. E. (1993). Prevalence of eating disorders such as anorexia and bulimia nervosa among the college population. *College Student Affairs Journal, 12,* 77–80.

Martin, N., & Jardine, R. (1986). Eysenck's contributions to behaviour genetics. In S. Modgil & C. Modgil (Eds.), *Hans Eysenck: Consensus and controversy.* Philadelphia: Falmer.

Martin, P. (1991/1992). Zapping those zits: Helping teens handle acne. *PTA Today, 17,* 20–21.

Maslow, A. H. (1970). *Motivation and personality* (2nd ed.). New York: Harper & Row.

Mason, M. A., & Mauldon, J. (1996). The new stepfamily requires a new public policy. *Journal of Social Issues, 52,* 11–27.

Masters, W. H., & Johnson, V. E. (1966). *Human sexual response.* London: Churchill.

Masur, E. F. (1993). Transitions in representational ability: Infants' verbal, vocal, and action imitation during the second year. *Merrill–Palmer Quarterly, 39,* 437–455.

Mathews, A., & MacLeod, C. (1994). Cognitive approaches to emotion and emotional disorders. *Annual Review of Psychology, 45,* 25–50.

Mathieu, P. S., Sowa, C. J., & Niles, S. G. (1993). Differences in career self-efficacy among women. *Journal of Career Development, 19,* 187–196.

Matthews, G. P., & Das, A. (1996). Dense vitreous hemorrhages predict poor visual and neurological prognosis in infants with shaken baby syndrome. *Journal of Pediatric Ophthalmology and Strabismus, 33,* 260–265.

Maxim, G. W. (1993). *The very young* (4th ed.). Columbus, OH: Merrill.

Mayberry, L. J., & Affonso, D. D. (1993). Infant temperament and postpartum depression: A review. *Health Care for Women International, 14,* 201–211.

Mayer, N. K., & Tronick, E. Z. (1985). Mother's turn-giving signals and infant turn-taking in mother–infant interaction. In T. M. Field & N. A. Fox (Eds.), *Social perception in infants.* Norwood, NJ: Ablex.

Mayo, K. E. (1993). Learning strategy instruction: Exploring the potential of metacognition. *Reading Improvement, 30,* 130–133.

McAdams, D. P. (1984). Love, power, and images of the self. In C. Z. Malatesta & C. E. Izard (Eds.), *Emotion in adult development* (pp. 159–174). Beverly Hills, CA: Sage.

McAdams, D. P., Diamond, A., de St. Aubin, E., & Mansfield, E. (1997). Stories of commitment: The psychosocial construction of generative lives. *Journal of Personality and Social Psychology, 72,* 678–694.

McAdams, D. P., St. Aubin, E. D., & Logan, R. L. (1993). Generativity among young, midlife, and older adults. *Psychology and Aging, 8,* 221–230.

McBride, B. A., & Darragh, J. (1995). Interpreting the data on father involvement: Implications for parenting programs for men. *Families in Society, 76,* 490–497

McCartney, K., Bernieri, F., & Harris, M. J. (1990). Growing up and growing apart: A developmental meta-analysis of twin studies. *Psychological Bulletin, 107,* 226–237.

McCartney, K., & Howley, E. (1992). Parents as instruments of intervention in home-based preschool programs. In L. Okagaki & R. J. Sternberg (Eds.), *Directors of development: Influences on the development of children's thinking.* Hillsdale, NJ: Erlbaum.

McCartney, K., & Jordan, E. (1990). Parallels between research on child care and research on school effects. *Educational Researcher, 19,* 21–27.

McClelland, D. C. (1973). Testing for competence rather than for "intelligence." *American Psychologist, 28,* 1–14.

McClure, F. H., & Teyber, E. (1996). Attention-deficit/hyperactivity disorder: Case illustration of Timmy: An 8-year-old biracial child. In H. McClure & E. Teyber (Eds.), *Child and adolescent therapy: A multicultural–relational approach.* Ft. Worth, TX: Harcourt.

McCord, J. (Ed.). *Coercion and punishment in long-term perspectives.* New York: Cambridge University Press.

McCormick, L. H. (1997). Treatment with buspirone in a patient with autism. *Archives of Family Medicine, 6,* 368–370.

McCrae, R. R., & Costa, P. T. (1984). *Emerging lives: Enduring predispositions.* Boston: Little, Brown.

McCune, L. (1993). The development of play as the development of consciousness. *New Directions for Child Development, 59,* 67–79.

McCurdy, H. G. (in collaboration with Helen Follett). (Eds.). (1966). *Barbara: The unconscious autobiography of a child genius.* Chapel Hill, NC: University of North Carolina Press.

McKay, A. (1996). Rural parents' attitudes toward school-based sexual health education. *Canadian Journal of Human Sexuality, 5,* 15–23.

McKay, M. M. (1994). The link between domestic violence and child abuse: Assessment and treatment considerations. *Child Welfare, 73,* 29–39.

McKusick, V. A. (1992). *Mendelian inheritance in man* (10th ed.). Baltimore: Johns Hopkins University Press.

McLaughlin, C. R., Hull, J. G., Edwards, W. H., Cramer, C. P., & Dewey, W. L. (1993). Neonatal pain: A comprehensive survey of attitudes and practices. *Journal of Pain and Symptom Management, 8,* 7–16.

McQuillan, R., Finlay, K. L., Branch, C., Roberts, D., et al. (1996). Improving analgesic prescribing in a general teaching hospital. *Journal of Pain and Symptom Management, 11,* 172–180.

Mead, M. (1935). *Sex and temperament in three primitive societies.* New York: New American Library.

Mead, M. (1970). Marriage in two steps. In H. A. Otto (Ed.), *The family in search of a future.* New York: Appleton-Century-Crofts.

Medoff-Cooper, B., Carey, W. B., & McDevitt, S. C. (1993). The Early Infancy Temperament Questionnaire. *Journal of Developmental and Behavioral Pediatrics, 14,* 230–235.

Meeus, W., Dekovic, M., & Ledema, J. (1997). Unemployment and identity in adolescence; A social comparison perspective. *Career Development Quarterly, 45,* 368–380.

Meltzoff, A. N., & Moore, M. K. (1989). Imitation in newborn infants: Exploring the range of gestures imitated and the underlying mechanisms. *Developmental Psychology, 25,* 954–962.

Meneese, W. B., Yutrzenka, B. A., & Vitale, P. (1992). An analysis of adolescent suicidal ideation. *Current Psychology: Research & Reviews, 11,* 51–58.

Mengel, M. H., Marcus, D. B., & Dunkle, R. E. (1996). "What will happen to my child when I'm gone?" A support and education group for aging parents as caregivers. *Gerontologist, 36,* 816–820.

Mercer, C. D. (1990). Learning disabilities. In N. G. Haring & L. McCormick (Eds.), *Exceptional children and youth* (5th ed.). Columbus, OH: Merrill.

Merriam, S. B. (1993). Butler's life review: How universal is it? *International Journal of Aging and Human Development, 37,* 163–175.

Mesibov, G. B., & Van Bourgondien, M. E. (1992). Autism. In S. R. Hooper, G. W. Hynd, & R. E. Mattison (Eds.), *Developmental disorders: Diagnostic criteria and clinical assessment.* Hillsdale, NJ: Erlbaum.

Meyer, W. J. (1985). Summary, integration, and prospective. In J. B. Dusek (Ed.), *Teacher expectancies.* Hillsdale, NJ: Erlbaum.

Michael, R. T., Gagnon, J. H., Laumann, E. O., & Kolata, G. (1994). *Sex in America: A definitive survey.* New York: Little, Brown.

Miles, H. L. (1997). Anthropomorphism, apes, and language. In R. W. Mitchell, N. S. Thompson, & H. L. Miles (Eds.), *Anthropomorphism, anecdotes, and animals.* SUNY Series in Philosophy and Biology. Albany, NY: State University of New York Press.

Millen, B. E., Quatromoni, P. A., Gagnon, D. R., Cupples, L. A., et al. (1996). Dietary patterns of men and women suggest targets for health promotion: The Framingham nutrition studies. *American Journal of Health Promotion, 11,* 42–52.

Miller, B. D. (1981). *The endangered sex: Neglect of female children in rural North India.* Ithaca, NY: Cornell University Press.

Miller, C. E., Edwards, J. G., Shipley, C. F., & Best, R. B. (1990). Assessment of routine amniocentesis for unexplained maternal serum alpha-fetoprotein elevations. In B. A. Fine, E. Getting, K. Greendale, B. Leopold, & N. W. Paul (Eds.), *Strategies in genetic counseling: Reproductive genetics and new technologies.* White Plains, NY: March of Dimes Birth Defects Foundation.

Miller, C. T., Clarke, R. T., & Malcarno, V. L. (1991). Expectations and social interactions of children with and without mental retardation. *Journal of Special Education, 24,* 54–72.

Miller, D. A., McCluskey-Fawcett, K., & Irving, L. M. (1993). The relationship between childhood sexual abuse and subsequent onset of bulimia nervosa. *Child Abuse & Neglect: The International Journal, 17,* 305–314.

Miller, G. A. (1956). The magical number seven, plus or minus two: Some limits on our capacity for processing information. *Psychological Review, 63,* 81–97.

Miller, J. B., & Lane, M. (1991). Relations between young adults and their parents. *Journal of Adolescence, 14,* 179–194.

Miller, L. B., & Bizzell, R. P. (1983). Long-term effects of four preschool programs: sixth, seventh, and eighth grades. *Child Development, 54,* 727–741.

Miller, P. H. (1993). *Theories of developmental psychology* (3rd ed.). New York: W. H. Freeman.

Mills, M., Davies, H. T., & Macrae, W. A. (1994). Care of dying patients in hospital. *British Medical Journal, 309,* 583–586.

Miyawaki, K., Strange, W., Verbrugge, K., Liberman, A. M., Jenkins, J. J., & Fujimura, O. (1975). An effect of linguistic experience: The discrimination of [r] and [l] by native speakers of Japanese and English. *Perception & Psychophysics, 18,* 331–340.

Mobley, C. E. (1996). Assessment of health knowledge in preschoolers. *Children's Health Care, 25,* 11–18.

Moerk, E. L. (1991). Positive evidence for negative evidence. *First Language, 11,* 219–251.

Moffatt, S. (1991). Becoming bilingual in the classroom: Code choice in school. *Language and Education: An International Journal, 5,* 55–71.

Moffitt, A. R. (1971). Consonant cue perception by 20–24 week old infants. *Child Development, 42,* 717–731.

Molfese, V. J., DiLalla, L. F., & Bunce, D. (1997). Prediction of the intelligence test scores of 3- to 8-year-old children by home environment, socioeconomic status, and biomedical risks. *Merrill–Palmer Quarterly, 43,* 219–234.

Mollenkopf, H., Marcellini, F., Ruoppila, I., & Flaschenstrager, P. (1997). Outdoor mobility and social relationships of elderly people. *Archives of Gerontology and Geriatrics, 24,* 295–310.

Mom, 60, delivers healthy girl. (1994, Feb. 22, Jerusalem, AP). *Edmonton Sun,* p. 18.

Monroe, S. M., Roberts, J. E., Kupfer, D. J., & Frank, E. (1996). Life stress and treatment course of recurrent depression: II. Postrecovery associations with attrition, symptom course, and recurrence over 3 years. *Journal of Abnormal Psychology, 105,* 313–328.

Montemayor, R., & Flannery, D. J. (1990). Making the transition from childhood to early adolescence. In R. Montemayor, G. R. Adams, & T. P. Gullotta (Eds.), *From childhood to adolescence: A transitional period? (Advances in Adolescent Development,* Vol. 2). Newbury Park, CA: Sage.

Montessori, M. (1912). *The Montessori method.* New York: Frederick A. Stokes.

Montgomery, R. L., Haemmerlie, F. M., & Zoellner, S. (1996). The "imaginary audience," self-handicapping, and drinking patterns among college students. *Psychological Reports, 79,* 783–786.

Moore, C., & Frye, D. (1991). The acquisition and utility of theories of mind. In D. Frye & C. Moore (Eds.), *Children's theories of mind: Mental states and social understanding.* Hillsdale, NJ: Erlbaum.

Moore, R. C. (1986). *Childhood's domain: Play and place in child development.* London: Croom Helm.

Morelock, M. J. (1996). On the nature of giftedness and talent: Imposing order on chaos. *Roeper Review, 19,* 4–12.

Morgane, P. J., Austin-LaFrance, R., Bronzino, J., Tonkiss, J., Diaz-Cintra, S., Cintra, L., Kemper, T., & Galler, J. R. (1993). Prenatal malnutrition and development of the brain. *Neuroscience & Biobehavioral Reviews, 17,* 91–128.

Morganti, J. B., Nehrke, M. F., Hulicka, I. M., & Cataldo, J. R. (1988). Life-span differences in life satisfaction, self-concept, and locus of control. *International Journal of Aging and Human Development, 26,* 45–56.

Moriarty, A. (1990). Deterring the molester and abuser. Pre-employment testing for child and youth care workers. *Child and Youth Care Quarterly, 18,* 59–65.

Morin, S. M., & Welsh, L. A. (1996). Adolescents' perceptions and experiences of death and grieving. *Adolescence, 31,* 585–595.

Morinaga, Y., Frieze, I., & Ferligoj, A. (1993). Career plans and gender-role attitudes of college students in the United States, Japan, and Slovenia. *Sex Roles: A Journal of Research, 29,* 317–334.

Morioka, I., Shiraishi, T., Nishimura, K., Kuroda, M., Kuriyama, Y., Matsui, K., Matsumoto, K., & Takeda, S. (1990). Age variation in the upper limit of hearing and amplitude of eye accommodation in childhood and adolescence. *Annals of Human Biology, 17,* 235–243.

Morrill, C. M., Leach, J. N., Shreeve, W. C., Radenaugh, M. R., & Linder, K. (1991). Teenage obesity. An academic issue. *International Journal of Adolescence and Youth, 2,* 245–250.

Morris, A. M., Williams, J. M., Atwater, A. E., & Wilmore, J. H. (1982). Age and sex differences in motor performance of 3 through 6 year old children. *Research Quarterly for Exercise and Sport, 534,* 214–221.

Morrison, K., & Rosales-Ruiz, J. (1997). The effect of object preferences on task performance and stereotypy in a child with autism. *Research in Developmental Disabilities, 18,* 127–137.

Morrison, T. G., McLeod, L. D., Morrison, M. A., Anderson, D., et al. (1997). Gender stereotyping, homonegativity, and misconceptions about sexually coercive behavior among adolescents. *Youth and Society, 28,* 351–382.

Mortensen, E. L., & Kleven, M. (1993). A WAIS longitudinal study of cognitive development during the life span from ages 50 to 70. *Developmental Neuropsychology, 9,* 115–130.

Morton, J., & Johnson, M. H. (1991). CONSPEC and CONLERN: A two-process theory of infant face recognition. *Psychological Review, 98,* 164–181.

Moseley, M. J. (1990). Mother–child interaction with preschool language-delayed children: Structuring conversations. *Journal of Communication Disorders, 23,* 187–203.

Mosley, W. H. (1994). Population change, health planning and human resource development in the health sector. *World Health Statistics Quarter—Rapport Trimestriel de Statistiques Sanitaires Mondiales, 47,* 26–30.

Moss, M. S., & Moss, S. Z. (1996). Remarriage of widowed persons: A triadic relationship. In D. Klass, P. R. Silverman, & S. L. Nickman (Eds.), *Continuing bonds: New understandings of grief. Series in death education, aging, and health care.* Washington, DC: Taylor & Francis.

Moss, M. S., Moss, S. Z., & Rubinstein, R. (1993). Impact of elderly mother's death on middle age daughters. *International Journal of Aging and Human Development, 37,* 1–22.

Mowat, F. (1952). *People of the deer.* Boston: Little, Brown.

Moynahan, E. D. (1973). The development of knowledge concerning the effect of categorization upon free recall. *Child Development, 44,* 238–245.

Muecke, L., Simons-Morton, B., & Huang, I. W. (1992). Is childhood obesity associated with high-fat foods and low physical activity? *Journal of School Health, 62,* 19–23.

Mulcahy, B. F. (1991). Developing autonomous learners. *Alberta Journal of Educational Research, 37,* 385–397.

Mullin, J. B. (1992). Children prenatally exposed to cocaine and crack: Implications for schools. *B.C. Journal of Special Education, 16,* 282–289.

Mullins, L. C., Elston, C. H., & Gutkowski, S. M. (1996). Social determinants of loneliness among older Americans. *Genetic, Social, and General Psychology Monographs, 122,* 453–473.

Mullis, R. L., Youngs, G. A., Jr., Mullis, A. K., & Rathge, R. W. (1993). Adolescent stress: Issues of measurement. *Adolescence, 28,* 280–290.

Murdock, G. P. (1957). World ethnographic sample. *American Anthropologist, 59,* 676–688.

Murphy, B. C., & Eisenburg, N. (1996). Provoked by a peer: Children's anger-related responses and their relations to social functioning. *Merrill–Palmer Quarterly, 42,* 103–124.

Murphy, C., Cain, W. S., Gilmore, M. M., & Skinner, R. B. (1991). Sensory and semantic factors in recognition memory for odors and graphic stimuli: Elderly versus young persons. *American Journal of Psychology, 104,* 161–192.

Murphy-Berman, V., Levesque, H. L., & Berman, J. J. (1996). U.N. Convention on the Rights of the Child: A cross-cultural view. *American Psychologist, 51,* 1257–1261.

Murray, J., Henjum, R., & Freeze, R. (1992). Analysis of male and female experiences with abuse in family of origin. *Canadian Journal of Special Education, 8,* 90–100.

Muss, R. E. (1988). Carol Gilligan's theory of sex differences in the development of moral reasoning during adolescence. *Adolescence, 23,* 229–243.

Mussen, P. H., Honzik, M. P., & Eichorn, D. H. (1982). Early adult antecedents of life satisfaction at age 70. *Journal of Gerontology, 37,* 316–322.

Muzzin, L. J., Anderson, N. J., Figueredo, A. T., & Gudelis, S. O. (1994). The experience of cancer. *Social Science and Medicine, 38,* 1201–1208.

Myers, J. E. (1993). Personal empowerment. *Aging International, 20,* 3–4, 6–8.

Nadelson, C. C., & Nadelson, T. (1980). Dual-career marriages: Benefits and costs. In F. Pepitone-Rockwell (Ed.), *Dual-career couples.* Beverly Hills, CA: Sage.

Naglieri, J. A. (1988). *DAP; draw a person: A quantitative scoring system.* New York: Harcourt.

Nagy, M. H. (1948). The child's theories concerning death. *Journal of Genetic Psychology, 73,* 3–27.

Nanpon, H. (1991). Les âges de la vie: La représentation des âges de l'existence par un groupe de jeunes étudiants. *Enfance, 45,* 205–219.

Narváez, D., & Rest, J. (1995). The four components of acting morally. In W. M. Kurtines & J. L. Gewirtz (Eds.), *Moral development: An introduction.* Boston: Allyn & Bacon.

Nashelsky, M. B., & Dix, J. D. (1995). The time interval between lethal infant shaking and onset of symptoms. A review of the shaken baby syndrome literature. *American Journal of Forensic Medicine and Pathology, 16,* 154–157.

Naylor, F. D., Elsworth, G. R., Care, A. E., & Harvey-Beavis, A. (1997). Sex, status, and generic interests in fields of work, parents and offspring, and fields of study. *Australian Psychologist, 32,* 14–20.

Nazzari, M. (1991). *Disappearance of the dowry: Women, families, and social change in São Paulo, Brazil (1600–1900).* Stanford, CA: Stanford University Press.

Nehlig, A., & Debry, G. (1994). Consequences on the newborn of chronic maternal consumption of coffee during gestation and lactation: A review. *Journal of the American College of Nutrition, 13,* 6–21.

Neimeyer, R. A. (Ed.). (1994). *Death anxiety handbook: Research, instrumentation, and application.* Washington, DC: Taylor & Francis.

Nelson, C. A. (Ed.). (1993). *Memory and affect in development: The Minnesota Symposia on Child Psychology* (Vol. 26). Hillsdale, NJ: Erlbaum.

Nelson, K. (1993). Events, narratives, memory: What develops? In C. A. Nelson (Ed.), *Memory and affect in development: The Minnesota Symposia on Child Psychology* (Vol. 26). Hillsdale, NJ: Erlbaum.

Nelson, K. (1996). *Language in cognitive development: Emergence of the mediated mind.* New York: Cambridge University Press.

Nelson, M. (1992). Cable TV: The re-regulation, re-wiring, and re-education of America. *Computers in Libraries, 12,* 40–42.

Nettelbeck, T., & Rabbitt, P. M. A. (1992). Aging, cognitive performance, and mental speed. *Intelligence, 16,* 189–205.

Neugarten, B. L. (1964). *Personality in middle and late life.* New York: Lieber-Atherton.

Neugarten, B. L. (Ed.). (1968). *Middle age and aging: A reader in social psychology.* Chicago: University of Chicago Press.

Neugarten, B. L. (1990). Social and psychological characteristics of older persons. In C. K. Cassel, D. E. Riesenberg, L. B. Sorenson, & J. R. Walsh (Eds.), *Geriatric medicine* (2nd ed.). New York: Springer-Verlag.

Neugarten, B. L., & Datan, N. (1981). The subjective experience of middle age. In L. D. Steinberg (Ed.), *The life cycle: Readings in human development.* New York: Columbia University Press.

Neugarten, B. L., & Weinstein, K. K. (1964). The changing American grandparents. *Journal of Marriage and the Family, 26,* 199–204.

Neugarten, D. A. (Ed.). (1996). *The meanings of age: Selected papers of Bernice L. Neugarten.* Chicago: University of Chicago Press.

Neugebauer, R. (1994). Impressive growth projected for centers into the 21st century. *Child Care Information Exchange, 95,* 80–87.

Neuman, S. B. (1991). *Literacy in the television age: The myth of the TV effect.* Norwood, NJ: Ablex.

Newcomb, A. F., Bukowski, W. M., & Pattee, L. (1993). Children's peer relations: A meta-analytic review of popular, rejected, neglected, controversial, and average sociometric status. *Psychological Bulletin, 113,* 99–128.

Newcomb, M. D., & Bentler, P. M. (1988). *Consequences of adolescent drug use: Impact on the lives of young adults.* Newbury Park, CA: Sage.

Newcomb, M. D., & Bentler, P. M. (1989). Substance use and abuse among children and teenagers. *American Psychologist, 44,* 242–248.

Newcombe, N., & Fox, N. A. (1994). Infantile amnesia: Through a glass darkly. *Child Development, 65,* 31–40.

Newman, L. F., & Buka, S. L. (1991). Clipped wings: The fullest look yet at how prenatal exposure to drugs, alcohol, and nicotine hobbles children's learning. *American Educator, 15,* 27–30, 33, 42.

Ng, S. H., Giles, H., & Moody, J. (1991). Information-seeking triggered by age. *International Journal of Aging and Human Development, 33,* 269–277.

Ngubane, H. (1986). *Zulus of southern Africa.* East Sussex, England: Wayland.

Nicolopoulou, A. (1993). Play, cognitive development, and the social world: Piaget, Vygotsky, and beyond. *Human Development, 36,* 1–23.

Nieman, D. C., & Henson, D. A. (1994). Role of endurance exercise in immune senescence. *Medicine and Science in Sports and Exercise, 26,* 172–181.

Nightingale, E. O., & Wolverton, L. (1993). Adolescent rolelessness in modern society. *Teacher's College Record, 94,* 472–486.

1997 Canadian Sourcebook. (1997). Toronto, Ontario: Southam.

Nock, S. L. (1979). The family life cycle: Empirical or conceptual tool? *Journal of Marriage and the Family, 41,* 15–26.

Novak, L. (1972). Aging, total body potassium, fat-free mass, and cell mass in males and females between ages 18 and 85 years. *Journal of Gerontology, 27,* 438–443.

Noyes, J., Stebbens, V., Sobhan, G., Samuels, M., & Southall, D. (1996). Home monitoring of infants at increased risk of sudden death. *Journal of Clinical Nursing, 5,* 297–306.

Nozza, R. J., Miller, S. L., Rossman, R. N., & Bond, L. C. (1990a). Reliability and validity of infant speech–sound discrimination-in-noise thresholds. *Journal of Speech and Hearing Research, 34,* 643–650.

Nozza, R. J., Rossman, R. N., Bond, L. C., & Miller, S. L. (1990b). Infant speech–sound discrimination in noise. *Journal of the Acoustical Society of America, 87,* 339–350.

Nucci, L., Guerra, N., & Lee, J. (1991). Adolescent judgments of the personal, prudential, and normative aspects of drug use. *Developmental Psychology, 27,* 841–848.

Nunner-Winkler, G. (1984). Two moralities? A critical discussion of an ethic of care and responsibility versus an ethic of rights and justice. In W. M. Kurtines & J. L. Gewirtz (Eds.), *Morality, moral behavior, and moral development.* New York: John Wiley.

Nurmi, J. E. (1991). How do adolescents see their future? A review of the development of future orientation and planning. *Developmental Review, 11,* 1–59.

Oatley, K., & Jenkins, J. M. (1992). Human emotions: Function and dysfunction. *Annual Review of Psychology, 32,* 55–85.

Oberg, C. N., Bryant, N. A., & Bach, M. L. (1995). A portrait of America's children: The impact of poverty and a call to action. *Journal of Social Distress and the Homeless, 4,* 43–56.

Oberklaid, F., Sanson, A., Pedlow, R., & Prior, M. (1993). Predicting preschool behavior problems from temperament and other variables in infancy. *Pediatrics, 91,* 113–120.

O'Brien, M. (1996). Child-rearing difficulties reported by parents of infants and toddlers. *Journal of Pediatric Psychology, 21,* 433–446.

O'Brien, S. J., & Conger, P. R. (1991). No time to look back: Approaching the finish line of life's course. *International Journal of Aging and Human Development, 33,* 75–87.

O'Bryant, S. L. (1991). Older widows and independent lifestyles. *International Journal of Aging and Human Development, 32,* 41–51.

O'Connor, B. P. (1995). Family and friend relationships among older and younger adults: Interaction motivation, mood, and quality. *International Journal of Aging and Human Development, 40,* 9–29.

Oden, M. (1968). The fulfillment of promise: 40-year follow-up of the Terman gifted group. In R. S. Albert (Ed.) (1983), *Genius and eminence: The social psychology of creativity and exceptional achievement.* New York: Oxford University Press.

Offer, D. O., Ostrov, E., & Howard, K. (1981). *The adolescent: A psychological self-portrait.* New York: Basic Books.

Offer, D. O., Ostrov, E., & Howard, K. (1984). *Patterns of adolescent self-image.* San Francisco: Jossey-Bass.

Offer, D. O., Ostrov, E., Howard, H., & Atkinson, R. (1988). *The teenage world: Adolescents' self-image in ten countries.* New York: Plenum.

Offner, S. (1992). A plain English map of the human chromosomes. *American Biology Teacher, 54,* 87.

Offner, S. (1993). A revised map of the human chromosomes. *American Biology Teacher, 55,* 406–410.

O'Hagan, H. (1979). Tay John. In D. Gutteridge (Ed.), *Rites of passage*. Toronto: McClelland & Stewart.

Ohba, M. (1979). What are the characteristics of the way of living in Japan? In Early Childhood Education Association of Japan (Ed.), *Early childhood education and care in Japan*. Tokyo, Japan: Child Honsha.

O'Koon, J. (1997). Attachment to parents and peers in late adolescence and their relationship with self-image. *Adolescence, 32,* 471–482.

O'Leary, K. D., & Smith, D. A. (1991). Marital interactions. *Annual Review of Psychology, 42,* 191–212.

Ollendick, T. H., Weist, M. D., & Borden, M. C. (1992). Sociometric status and academic, behavioral, and psychological adjustment: A five-year longitudinal study. *Journal of Consulting and Clinical Psychology, 60,* 80–87.

Ondis, G. W., Gibson-Cline, J., Dragoon, M., & Jones, C. (1996). Continental United States. In J. Gibson-Cline (Ed.), *Adolescence: From crisis to coping: A thirteen nation study*. Boston: Butterworth/Heinemann.

O'Reilly, A. W., & Bornstein, M. H. (1993). Caregiver–child interaction in play. *New Directions for Child Development, 59,* 55–66.

Ornstein, P. A., Baker-Ward, L., & Naus, M. J. (1988). The development of mnemonic skill. In F. E. Weinert & M. Perlmutter (Eds.), *Memory development: Universal changes and individual differences*. Hillsdale, NJ: Erlbaum.

Osterling, J., & Dawson, G. (1994). Early recognition of children with autism: A study of first birthday home videotapes. *Journal of Autism and Developmental Disorders, 24,* 247–257.

Ovcharchyn, C. A., Johnson, H. H., & Petzel, T. P. (1981). Type A behavior, academic aspirations, and academic success. *Journal of Personality, 49,* 248–256.

Owen, M. (1996). *A world of widows*. Atlantic Highlands, NJ: Zed.

Ozar, L. A. (1994). Diverse assessment—key to richer learning. *Momentum, 25,* 53–56.

Ozturk, M., & Ozturk, O. M. (1990). Thumbsucking and falling asleep. *Turkish Journal of Pediatrics, 32,* 161–174.

Packard, V. (1968). *The sexual wilderness*. New York: Pocket Books.

Paikoff, R. L., & Brooks-Gunn, J. (1991). Do parent–child relationships change during puberty? *Psychological Bulletin, 110,* 47–66.

Painter, K. (1997a, Sept. 9). A brief history of the AIDS epidemic. *USA Today*.

Painter, K. (1997b, Sept. 9). AZT slashes HIV rates in newborns. *USA Today*.

Pajares, F. (1996). Self-efficacy beliefs in academic settings. *Review of Educational Research, 66,* 543–578.

Paley, V. G. (1984). *Boys and girls: Superheroes in the doll corner*. Chicago: University of Chicago Press.

Paley, V. G. (1986). *Mollie is three: Growing up in school*. Chicago: University of Chicago Press.

Palmlund, I., Apfel, R., Buitendijk, S., Cabau, A., & Forsberg, J. G. (1993). Effects of diethylstilbestrol (DES) medication during pregnancy: From a symposium at the 10th International Congress of ISPOG. *Journal of Psychosomatic Obstetrics and Gynecology, 14,* 71–89.

Palo, P., & Erkkola, R. (1993). Risk factors and deliveries associated with preterm, severely small for gestational age fetuses. *American Journal of Perinatology, 10,* 88–91.

Pandey, H. (1991). Impact of preschool education component in Integrated Child Development Services programme on the cognitive development of children. *Journal of Tropical Pediatrics, 37,* 235–239.

Pangrazi, R. P., & Corbin, C. B. (1993). Physical fitness: Questions teachers ask. *Journal of Physical Education, Recreation & Dance, 64,* 14–19.

Pape, K. E., Kirsch, S. E., Galil, A., White, M. A., & Chipman, M. (1994). Neuromuscular approach to the motor deficits of cerebral palsy: A pilot study. *Journal of Pediatric Orthopaedics, 13,* 628–633.

Papert, S. (1993). *The children's machine: Rethinking school in the age of the computer*. New York: Basic Books.

Pappas, D. M. (1996). Euthanasia and assisted suicide: Are doctors' duties when following patients' orders a bitter pill to swallow? In G. Howarth & P. C. Jupp (Eds.), *Contemporary issues in the sociology of death, dying and disposal*. New York: St. Martin's.

Paris, S. G., & Lindauer, B. K. (1976). The role of inference in children's comprehension and memory for sentences. *Cognitive Psychology, 8,* 217–227.

Paris, S. G., & Lindauer, B. K. (1982). Cognitive development in infancy. In B. B. Wolman et al. (Eds.), *Handbook of developmental psychology*. Englewood Cliffs, NJ: Prentice-Hall.

Park, K. A., Lay, K. L., & Ramsay, L. (1993). Individual differences and developmental changes in preschoolers' friendships. *Developmental Psychology, 29,* 264–270.

Parke, R. D. (1994). Progress, paradigms, and unresolved problems: A commentary on recent advances in our understanding of children's emotions. *Merrill–Palmer Quarterly, 40,* 157–169.

Parker, J. G., & Asher, S. R. (1993). Friendship and friendship quality in middle childhood: Links with peer group acceptance and feelings of loneliness and social dissatisfaction. *Developmental Psychology, 29,* 611–621.

Parkes, C. M. (1987). *Bereavement: Studies of grief in adult life* (2nd ed.). Madison, CT: International Universities Press.

Parkhurst, J. T., & Asher, S. R. (1992). Rejection in middle school: Subgroup differences in behavior, loneliness, and interpersonal concerns. *Developmental Psychology, 28,* 231–241.

Parten, M. B. (1932). Social participation among pre-school children. *Journal of Abnormal Social Psychology, 27*, 243–270.

Pasley, K., Dollahite, D. C., & Ihinger-Tallman, M. (1993). Bridging the gap: Clinical applications of research findings on the spouse and stepparent roles in remarriage. *Family Relations, 42*, 315–322.

Pasley, K., Rhoden, L., Visher, E. B., & Visher, J. S. (1996). Successful stepfamily therapy: Clients' perspectives. *Journal of Marital and Family Therapy, 22*, 343–357.

Passino, A. W., Whitman, T. L., Borkowski, J. G., Schellenbach, C. J., Maxwell, S. E., Keogh, D., & Rellinger, E. (1993). Personal adjustment during pregnancy and adolescent parenting. *Adolescence, 28*, 67–79.

Passman, R. H. (1987). Attachments to inanimate objects: Are children who have security blankets insecure? *Journal of Consulting and Clinical Psychology, 55*, 825–830.

Passman, R. H., & Adams, R. E. (1982). Preferences for mothers and security blankets and their effectiveness as reinforcers for young children's behaviors. *Journal of Child Psychology and Psychiatry, 23*, 223–236.

Passman, R. H., & Halonen, J. S. (1979). A developmental survey of young children's attachments to inanimate objects. *Journal of Genetic Psychology, 134*, 165–178.

Passman, R. H., & Weisberg, P. (1975). Mothers and blankets as agents for promoting play and exploration by young children in a novel environment: The effects of social and nonsocial attachment objects. *Developmental Psychology, 11*, 170–177.

Patel, B. D. (1994). The fragile X syndrome. *British Journal of Clinical Practice, 48*, 42–44.

Patel, J., & Edwards, A. D. (1997). Prediction of outcome after perinatal asphyxia. *Current Opinion in Pediatrics, 9*, 128–132.

Patterson, C. J. (1997). Children of lesbian and gay parents. *Advances in Clinical Child Psychology, 19*, 235–282.

Patterson, I. (1996). Participation in leisure activities by older adults after a stressful life event: The loss of a spouse. *International Journal of Aging and Human Development, 42*, 123–142.

Patton, J. M., Prillaman, D., & Tassel-Baska, J. V. (1990). The nature and extent of programs for the disadvantaged gifted in the United States and territories. *Gifted Child Quarterly, 34*, 94–96.

Patton, J. R., & Polloway, E. A. (1990). Mild mental retardation. In N. G. Haring & L. McCormick (Eds.), *Exceptional children and youth* (5th ed.). Columbus, OH: Charles E. Merrill.

Paul, R., & Alforde, S. (1993). Grammatical morpheme acquisition in 4-year-olds with normal, impaired, and late-developing language. *Journal of Speech and Hearing Research, 36*, 1271–1275.

Pavlov, I. P. (1927). *Conditional reflexes.* London: Oxford University Press.

Pearce, J. C. (1977). *Magical child: Rediscovering nature's plan for our children.* New York: Bantam.

Pearl, R., Bryan, T., & Herzog, A. (1990). Resisting or acquiescing to peer pressure to engage in misconduct: Adolescents' expectations of probable consequences. *Journal of Youth and Adolescence, 19*, 43–55.

Pearson, J. C. (1996). Forty-forever years? Primary relationships and senior citizens. In N. Vanzetti & S. Duck (Eds.), *A lifetime of relationships.* Pacific Grove, CA: Brooks/Cole.

Pease-Alvarez, L., & Hakuta, K. (1992). Enriching our views of bilingualism and bilingual education. *Educational Researcher, 2*, 4–6.

Peck, R. C. (1968). Psychological developments in the second half of life. In B. L. Neugarten (Ed.), *Middle age and aging.* Chicago: University of Chicago Press.

Peiser, N. C., & Heaven, P. C. L. (1996). Family influences on self-reported delinquency among high school students. *Journal of Adolescence, 19*, 557–568.

Pelaez-Nogueras, M., & Gewirtz, J. L. (1993). *Mothers' contingent imitation increases infant vocalizations.* Paper presented at the Biennial Meeting of the Society for Research in Child Development, New Orleans, March 25–28.

Pelham, W. E., Jr., Carlson, C., Sams, S. E., Vallano, G., Dixon, M. J., & Hoza, B. (1993). Separate and combined effects of methylphenidate and behavior modification on boys with attention deficit-hyperactivity disorder in the classroom. *Journal of Consulting & Clinical Psychology, 61*, 506–515.

Pellman, J. (1992). Widowhood in elderly women: Exploring its relationship to community integration, hassles, stress, social support, and social support seeking. *International Journal of Aging and Human Development, 35*, 253–264.

Pendergast, D. R., Fisher, N. M., & Calkins, E. (1993). Cardiovascular, neuromuscular, and metabolic alterations with age leading to frailty. *Journal of Gerontology, 48*, 61–67.

Pennells, M., & Smith, S. C. (1995). *The forgotten mourners: Guidelines for working with bereaved children.* Bristol, PA: Jessica Kingsley.

Penner, L. A., Thompson, J. K., & Coovert, D. L. (1991). Size overestimation among anorexics: Much ado about very little? *Journal of Abnormal Psychology, 100*, 90–93.

Pentz, M. A. (1994). Primary prevention of adolescent drug abuse. In C. B. Fisher & R. M. Lerner (Eds.), *Applied developmental psychology.* New York: McGraw-Hill.

Peplau, L. A. (1981). What homosexuals want in relationships. *Psychology Today, 15*, pp. 28–38.

Pergament, E. (1990). Reproductive genetics in the 21st century: Fact and fantasy. In B. A. Fine, E. Getting,

K. Greendale, B. Leopold, & N. W. Paul (Eds.), *Strategies in genetic counseling: Reproductive genetics and new technologies.* White Plains, NY: March of Dimes Birth Defects Foundation.

Perkins, D., Jay, E., & Tishman, S. (1993). Introduction: New conceptions of thinking. *Educational Psychologist, 28,* 1–5.

Perlmutter, M. (1980). Development of memory in the preschool years. In R. Greene & T. D. Yawkey (Eds.), *Childhood development.* Westport, CT: Technomic.

Perlmutter, M. (1988). Cognitive potential throughout life. In J. E. Birren & V. L. Bengtson (Eds.), *Emergent theories of aging.* New York: Springer.

Perlmutter, M. (1994). Cognitive skills within the context of adult development and old age. In C. B. Fisher & R. M. Lerner (Eds.), *Applied developmental psychology.* New York: McGraw-Hill.

Perner, J. (1991). On representing that: The asymmetry between belief and desire in children's theory of mind. In D. Frye & C. Moore (Eds.), *Children's theories of mind: Mental states and social understanding.* Hillsdale, NJ: Erlbaum.

Perry, P., Pasnak, R., & Holt, R. W. (1992). Instruction on concrete operations for children who are mildly mentally retarded. *Education and Training in Mental Retardation, 27,* 273–281.

Peruzzi, N., Canapary, A., & Bongar, B. (1996). Physician-assisted suicide: The role of mental health professionals. *Ethics and Behavior, 6,* 353–366.

Peters, H., & Theorell, C. J. (1991). Fetal and neonatal effects of maternal cocaine use. *Journal of Obstetric, Gynecologic, and Neonatal Nursing, 20,* 121–126.

Petersen, A. C. (1988). Adolescent development. *Annual Review of Psychology, 39,* 583–607.

Peterson, C. C. (1995). Husbands' and wives' perceptions of marital fairness across the family life cycle. In J. Hendricks (Ed.), *The ties of later life.* Amityville, NY: Baywood.

Peterson, G. W., Leigh, G. K, & Day, R. D. (1984). Family stress theory and the impact of divorce on children. *Journal of Divorce, 7,* 1–20.

Peterson, K. L., & Roscoe, B. (1991). Imaginary audience behavior in older adolescent females. *Adolescence, 26,* 195–200.

Pettle, S. A., & Britten, C. M. (1995). Talking with children about death and dying. *Child: Care, Health, and Development, 21,* 395–404.

Peverly, S. T. (1991). Problems with the knowledge-based explanation of memory and development. *Review of Educational Research, 61,* 71–93.

Phares, V. (1992). Where's poppa? The relative lack of attention to the role of fathers in child and adolescent psychopathology. *American Psychologist, 47,* 656–664.

Phillips, S. (1997). Toward an expanded definition of adaptive decision making. *Career Development Quarterly, 45,* 275–287.

Phillipson, C. (1997). Social relationships in later life: A review of the research literature. *International Journal of Geriatric Psychiatry, 12,* 505–512.

Philps, A. (1997, Oct. 6). Russian kids prefer life of crime, not final frontier. *Edmonton Journal,* p. A2.

Piaget, J. (1923). *Le langage et la pensée chez l'enfant.* London: Kegan Paul.

Piaget, J. (1932). *The moral judgment of the child.* London: Routledge & Kegan Paul.

Piaget, J. (1951). *Play, dreams and imitation in childhood.* New York: Norton.

Piaget, J. (1954). *The construction of reality in the child.* New York: Basic Books.

Piaget, J. (1960). *The child's conception of the world.* London: Routledge.

Piaget, J. (1961). The genetic approach to the psychology of thought. *Journal of Educational Psychology, 52,* 275–281.

Piaget, J., & Garcia, R. (1991). *Toward a logic of meanings.* Hillsdale, NJ: Erlbaum.

Pianta, R. C., & Ball, R. M. (1993). Maternal social support as a predictor of child adjustment in kindergarten. *Journal of Applied Developmental Psychology, 14,* 107–120.

Piattelli-Palmarini, M. (1994). Ever since language and learning: Afterthoughts on Piaget–Chomsky debate. *Cognition, 50,* 315–346.

Pierce, E. F., Butterworth, S. W., Lynn, T. D., O'Shea, J., & Hammer, W. G. (1992). Fitness profiles and activity patterns of entering college students. *Journal of American College Health, 41,* 59–62.

Pietrukowicz, M. E., & Johnson, M. M. S. (1991). Using life histories to individualize nursing home staff attitudes toward residents. *Gerontologist, 31,* 102–106.

Pilkington, L. R., White, J., & Matheny, K. B. (1997). Perceived coping resources and psychological birth order in school-aged children. *Individual Psychology: Journal of Adlerian Theory, Research and Practice, 53,* 42–57.

Pill, C. J. (1990). Stepfamilies: Redefining the family. *Family Relations, 39,* 186–193.

Pina, D. L., & Bengtson, V. L. (1993). The division of household labor and wives' happiness: Ideology, employment, and perceptions of support. *Journal of Marriage and the Family, 55,* 901–912.

Pinchbeck, I., & Hewitt, M. (1973). *Children in English society* (Vol. 1). London: Routledge & Kegan Paul.

Pines, M. (1966). *Revolution in learning: The years from birth to six.* New York: Harper & Row.

Pinyerd, B. J. (1994). Infant cries: Physiology and assessment. *Neonatal Network, 13,* 15–20.

Plomin, R. (1987). Developmental behavioral genetics and infancy. In J. D. Osofsky (Ed.), *Handbook of infant development* (2nd ed.). New York: John Wiley.

Plomin, R. (1989). Environment and genes: Determinants of behavior. *American Psychologist, 44,* 105–111.

Plotnick, R. D. (1992). The effects of attitudes on teenage premarital pregnancy and its resolution. *American Sociological Review, 57,* 800–811.

Pogrebin, L. C. (1980). *Growing up free: Raising your child in the 80's.* New York: McGraw-Hill.

Pogue-Geile, M. F., & Rose, R. J. (1985). Developmental genetic studies of adult personality. *Developmental Psychology, 21,* 547–557.

Polson, B., & Newton, M. (1984). *Not my kid: A family's guide to kids and drugs.* New York: Arbor House.

Ponder, R. J., & Pomeroy, E. C. (1996). The grief of caregivers: How pervasive is it? *Journal of Gerontological Social Work, 27,* 3–21.

Poon, L. W. (1985). Differences in human memory with aging: Nature, causes, and clinical implications. In J. E. Birren & K. W. Schaie (Eds.), *Handbook of the psychology of aging* (2nd ed.). New York: Van Nostrand Reinhold.

Poon, L. W., Messner, S., Martin, P., Noble, C. A., Clayton, G. M., & Johnson, M. A. (1992). The influences of cognitive resources on adaptation and old age. *International Journal of Aging and Human Development, 34,* 31–46.

Pope, A. W., Bierman, K. L., & Mumma, G. H. (1991). Aggression, hyperactivity, and inattention–immaturity: Behavior dimensions associated with peer rejection in elementary school boys. *Developmental Psychology, 27,* 663–671.

Porath, M. (1996). Affective and motivational considerations in the assessment of gifted learners. *Roeper Review, 19,* 13–17.

Porcile, A., Gallardo, E., Onetto, P., & Schachter, D. (1994). Very low estrogen–desogestrel contraceptive in perimenopausal hormonal replacement. *Maturitas, 18,* 93–103.

Porter, R. H., Makin, J. W., Davis, L. B., & Christensen, K. M. (1991). An assessment of the salient olfactory environment of formula-fed infants. *Physiology and Behavior, 50,* 907–911.

Post, S. G. (1994). Genetics, ethics, and Alzheimer disease. *Journal of the American Geriatrics Society, 42,* 782–786.

Potts, M. K. (1997). Social support and depression among older adults living alone: The importance of friends within and outside of a retirement community. *Social Work, 42,* 348–362.

Potts, R., & Henderson, J. (1991). The dangerous world of television: A content analysis of physical injuries in children's television programming. *Children's Environments Quarterly, 8,* 7–14.

Powell, L. A., Branco, K. J., & Williamson, J. B. (1996). *The senior rights movement: Framing the policy debate in America.* New York: Twayne.

Powell, M. B. (1991). Investigating and reporting child sexual abuse: Review and recommendations for clinical practice. *Australian Psychologist, 26,* 77–83.

Preemies' diet seen key to progress. (1988, Feb. 1). *Edmonton Journal,* p. C1.

Preyer, W. (1888/1889). *The mind of the child* (2 vols.). New York: Appleton-Century-Crofts. (First published in German, 1882.)

Pruchno, R. A., Burant, C. J., & Peters, N. D. (1997). Typologies of caregiving families: Family congruence and individual well-being. *Gerontologist, 37,* 157–167.

Puretz, S. L., Haas, A., & Meltzer, D. (1996). Profile of exercising women. *Perceptual and Motor Skills, 82,* 890.

Pyryt, M. C. (1993). The three faces of creativity revisited: Intimacy, passion, and commitment. *Gifted Education International, 9,* 22–23.

Quaid, K. A., & Morris, M. (1993). Reluctance to undergo predictive testing: The case of Huntington disease. *American Journal of Medical Genetics, 45,* 41–45.

Qualls, S. H. (1995). Marital therapy with later life couples. *Journal of Geriatric Psychiatry, 28,* 139–163.

Quan, M. (1994). Pelvic inflammatory disease: Diagnosis and management. *Journal of the American Board of Family Practice, 7,* 110–123.

Quay, H. C. (1987). Intelligence. In H. C. Quay (Ed.), *Handbook of juvenile delinquency* (pp. 106–117). New York: John Wiley.

Rabiner, D. L., Keane, S. P., & Mackinnon-Lewis, C. (1993). Children's beliefs about familiar and unfamiliar peers in relation to their sociometric status. *Developmental Psychology, 29,* 236–243.

Rahe, R. H. (1972). Subjects' recent life changes and their near-future illness susceptibility. In Z. J. Lipowski (Ed.), *Advances in psychosomatic medicine* (Vol. 8): *Psychosocial aspects of physical illness.* Basel, Switzerland: S. Karger.

Raley, R. K. (1996). A shortage of marriageable men? A note on the role of cohabitation in black–white differences in marriage rates. *American Sociological Review, 61,* 973–983.

Rand, D. C. (1997). The spectrum of parental alienation syndrome (Part I). *American Journal of Forensic Psychology, 15,* 23–52.

Randall, V. (1997). Gifted girls: What challenges do they face: A summary of the research. *Gifted Child Today, 20,* 42–50.

Rankin-Esquer, L. A., Burnett, C. K., Baucom, D. H., & Epstein, N. (1997). Autonomy and relatedness in marital functioning. *Journal of Marital and Family Therapy, 23,* 175–190.

Ransom, R. L., Sutch, R., & Williamson, S. H. (1993). Inventing pensions: The origins of the company-provided pension in the United States, 1900–1940. In K. W. Schaie & W. A. Achenbaum (Eds.), *Societal impact on aging: Historical perspectives.* New York: Springer.

Rappaport, W., & Witzke, D. (1993). Education about death and dying during the clinical years of medical school. *Surgery, 113,* 163–165.

Ratner, H. H., Padgett, R. J., & Bushey, N. (1988). Old and young adults' recall of events. *Developmental Psychology, 24,* 664–671.

Ray, W. J. (1993). *Methods toward a science of behavior and experience* (4th ed.). Pacific Grove, CA: Brooks/Cole.

Rayna, S., Sinclair, H., & Stambak, M. (1989). Infants and physics. In H. Sinclair, M. Stambak, I. Lézine, S. Rayna, & M. Verba (Eds.), *Infants and objects: The creativity of cognitive development.* New York: Academic Press.

Read, B. K. (1994). Motivation factors in technical college women's selection of nontraditional careers. *Journal of Career Development, 20,* 239–258.

Recommended dietary allowances (9th ed.). (1980). Washington, DC: National Academy of Sciences.

Redding, N. P., & Dowling, W. D. (1992). Rites of passage among women reentering higher education. *Adult Education Quarterly, 42,* 221–236.

Reich, J. W., & Zautra, A. J. (1991). Analyzing the trait of routinization in older adults. *International Journal of Aging and Human Development, 32,* 161–180.

Reid, L. D., & Carpenter, D. J. (1990). Alcohol-abuse and alcoholism. In L. D. Reid (Ed.), *Opioids, bulimia, and alcohol abuse & alcoholism.* New York: Springer-Verlag.

Reissland, N. (1988). Neonatal imitation in the first hour of life: Observations in rural Nepal. *Developmental Psychology, 24,* 464–469.

Reschly, D. J. (1990). Adaptive behavior. In A. Thomas & J. Grimes (Eds.), *Best practices in school psychology* (2nd ed.). Washington, DC: National Association of School Psychologists.

Reschly, D. J. (1992). Mental retardation: Conceptual foundations, definitional criteria, and diagnostic operations. In S. R. Hooper, G. W. Hynd, & R. E. Mattison (Eds.), *Developmental disorders: Diagnostic criteria and clinical assessment.* Hillsdale, NJ: Erlbaum.

Rescorla, L. (1991). Early academics: Introduction to the debate. *New Directions for Child Development, 53,* 5–11.

Resnick, H. S., Kilpatrick, D. G., & Dansky, B. S. (1993). Prevalence of civilian trauma and posttraumatic stress disorder in a representative national sample of women. *Journal of Consulting and Clinical Psychology, 61,* 984–991.

Reuters. (1997, Nov. 27). Slovak regional mafia boss shot dead. *Bratislava.*

Reyna, V. F. (1996). Conceptions of memory development with implications for reasoning and decision making. *Annals of Child Development, 12,* 49–86.

Rheingold, H. L. (1985). Development as the acquisition of familiarity. *Annual Review of Psychology, 36,* 1–17.

Ricciardelli, L. A. (1992). Bilingualism and cognitive development in relation to threshold theory. *Journal of Psycholinguistic Research, 21,* 301–316.

Ricciuti, H. N. (1991). Malnutrition and cognitive development: Research-policy linkages and current research directions. In L. Okagaki & R. J. Sternberg (Eds.), *Directors of development: Influences on the development of children's thinking.* Hillsdale, NJ: Erlbaum.

Ricco, R. B. (1993). Revising the logic of operations as a relevance logic: From hypothesis testing to explanation. *Human Development, 36,* 125–146.

Rice, B. (1982, February). The Hawthorne defect: Persistence of a flawed theory. *Psychology Today,* pp. 71–74.

Rice, E. (1972). *Mother India's children.* New York: Friendship Press.

Rice, M. L. (1989). Children's language acquisition. *American Psychologist, 44,* 149–156.

Richards, L. N., & Schmeige, C. J. (1993). Problems and strengths of single-parent families: Implications for practice and policy. *Family Relations, 42,* 277–285.

Richardson, V., & Kilty, K. M. (1991). Adjustment to retirement: Continuity vs. discontinuity. *International Journal of Aging and Human Development, 33,* 151–169.

Ridgeway, C. L. (1997). Interaction and the conservation of gender inequality: Considering employment. *American Sociological Review, 62,* 218–235.

Ridley, D. R., & Harrison, B. S. (1996). Comments on "Sense of humor and longevity" by Yoder and Haude. *Psychological Reports, 78,* 254.

Ridley-Johnson, R., Surdy, T., & O'Laughlin, E. (1991). Parent survey on television violence viewing: Fear, aggression, and sex differences. *Journal of Applied Developmental Psychology, 12,* 63–71.

Riegel, K. F. (1970). The language acquisition process: A reinterpretation of selected research findings. In L. R. Goulet & P. B. Baltes (Eds.), *Life-span developmental psychology: Research and theory.* New York: Academic Press.

Riegel, K. F. (1972). Influence of economic and political ideologies on the development of developmental psychology. *Psychological Bulletin, 78,* 129–141.

Riegel, K. F. (1973a). Dialectic operations: The final period of cognitive development. *Human Development, 16,* 346–370.

Riegel, K. F. (1973b). Language and cognition: Some life-span developmental issues. *Gerontologist, 13,* 478–482.

Riegel, K. F. (1976). The dialectics of human development. *American Psychologist, 31,* 689–700.

Ringwalt, C. L., & Palmer, J. H. (1989). Cocaine and crack users compared. *Adolescence, 24,* 851–859.

Ritts, V., Patterson, M. L., & Tubbs, M. E. (1992). Expectations, impressions, and judgments of physically attractive students: A review. *Review of Educational Research, 62,* 413–426.

Rizzo, T. A., Metzger, B. E., Dooley, S. L., & Cho, N. H. (1997). Early malnutrition and child neurobehavioral development: Insights from the study of children of diabetic mothers. *Child Development, 68,* 26–38.

Robbins, S. B., Lee, R. M., & Han, T. T. M. (1994). Goal continuity as a mediator of early retirement adjustment: Testing a multidimensional model. *Journal of Counseling Psychology, 41,* 18–26.

Roberto, K. A., & Stroes, J. (1995). Grandchildren and grandparents: Roles, influences, and relationships. In J. Hendricks (Ed.), *The ties of later life.* Amityville, NY: Baywood.

Roberts, B. W. (1997). Plaster or plasticity: Are adult work experiences associated with personality change in women? *Journal of Personality, 65,* 205–232.

Roberts, D. (1997, Nov. 13). Abortion link pursued in shooting. *Toronto Globe and Mail,* p. A1.

Roberts, J. (1995). The role of graduate education in midwifery in the USA. In Murphy-Black, T. (Ed.), *Issues in midwifery.* New York: Churchill-Livingstone.

Roberts, P., & Newton, P. (1990). Levinsonian studies of women's adult development. *Psychology and Aging, 2,* 154–163.

Roberts, R. B. (1996). *Sexually transmitted diseases.* Internet: http://edcenter.med.cornell.edu/Pathophysiology_Cases /STDs/STD_04.html

Robertson, S. S. (1993a). Mechanism and function of cyclicity in spontaneous movement. In W. P. Smotherman & S. R. Robinson (Eds.), *Behavior of the fetus.* Caldwell, NJ: Telford.

Robertson, S. S. (1993b). Oscillation and complexity in early infant behavior. *Child Development, 64,* 1022–1035.

Robinshaw, H. M. (1996). The pattern of development from non-communicative behaviour to language by hearing impaired and hearing infants. *British Journal of Audiology, 30,* 177–198.

Robinson, N. M., Abbott, R. D., Berninger, V. W., & Busse, J. (1996). Structure of abilities in math-precocious young children: Gender similarities and differences. *Journal of Educational Psychology, 88,* 341–352.

Robinson, S. (1989). Caring for childbearing women: The interrelationship between midwifery and medical responsibilities. In S. Robinson & A. M. Thomson (Eds.), *Midwives, research and childbirth* (Vol. 1). New York: Chapman & Hall.

Roche, J. (1996). The politics of children's rights. In J. Brannen & M. O'Brien (Eds.), *Children in families: Research and policy.* Washington, DC: Falmer.

Roche, J. P., & Ramsbey, T. W. (1993). Premarital sexuality: A five-year follow-up study of attitudes and behavior by dating stage. *Adolescence, 28,* 67–80.

Rodgers, B. (1996). Social and psychological wellbeing of children from divorced families: Australian research findings. *Australian Psychologist, 31,* 174–182.

Rodgers, B. (1997). Children and parental divorce: The meaning of small effects—a reply. *Australian Psychologist, 32,* 139–142.

Roethlisberger, S. J., & Dickson, W. J. (1939). *Management and the worker.* Cambridge, MA: Harvard University Press.

Rogers, C. R. (1951). *Client-centered therapy: Its current practice, its implications, and theory.* Boston: Houghton Mifflin.

Rogers, M. A., & Evans, W. J. (1993). Changes in skeletal muscle with aging: Effects of exercise training. *Exercise and Sport Sciences Reviews, 21,* 65–102.

Rogers, M. N. (1993). Are we on equal terms yet? Subject headings concerning women in "LCSH," 1975–1991. *Library Resources and Technical Services, 37,* 181–196.

Rogers, W. A., Fisk, A. D., & Walker, N. (1997). *Aging and skilled performance: Advances in theory and applications.* Mahwah, NJ: Erlbaum.

Rollins, B. C., & Feldman, H. (1981). Marital satisfaction over the family life cycle. In L. D. Steinberg (Ed.), *The life cycle: Readings in human development.* New York: Columbia University Press.

Romanin, S., & Over, R. (1993). Australian academics: Career patterns, work roles, and family life-cycle commitments of men and women. *Higher Education, 26,* 411–429.

Romig, C. A., & Bakken, L. (1990). Teens at risk for pregnancy: The role of ego development and family processes. *Journal of Adolescence, 13,* 195–199.

Rontoyannis, G. P. (1992). Sixty-three years of competitive sport activity. Case study. *Journal of Sports Medicine and Physical Fitness, 32,* 332–339.

Roopnarine, J. L., Johnson, J. E., & Hooper, F. H. (Eds.). (1994). *Children's play in diverse cultures.* Albany: State University of New York Press.

Roosa, M. W. (1991). Adolescent pregnancy programs collection: An introduction. *Family Relations, 40,* 370–372.

Rose, N. C., Palomaki, G. E., Haddow, J. E., Goodman, D. B., & Mennuti, M. T. (1994). Maternal serum alpha-fetoprotein screening for chromosomal abnormalities: A prospective study in women aged 35 and older. *American Journal of Obstetrics and Gynecology, 170,* 1073–1078.

Rosen, M. (1995). Gender differences in structure, means and variances of hierarchically ordered ability dimensions. *Learning and Instruction, 5,* 37–62.

Rosenak, D., Diamant, Y. Z., Yaffe, H., & Hornstein, E. (1990). Cocaine: Maternal use during pregnancy and its effect on the mother, the fetus, and the infant. *Obstetrical and Gynecological Survey, 45,* 348–357.

Rosenberg, H. (1995). The elderly and the use of illicit drugs: Sociological and epidemiological considerations. *International Journal of Addictions, 30,* 1925–1951.

Rosengren, K. E., & Windahl, S. (1989). *Media matter: TV use in childhood and adolescence.* Norwood, NJ: Ablex.

Rosenkoetter, L. I., Huston, A. C., & Wright, J. C. (1990). Television and the moral judgment of the young child. *Journal of Applied Developmental Psychology, 11,* 123–137.

Rosenthal, E. R. (Ed.). (1990). *Women, aging, and ageism.* New York: Harrington Park Press.

Rosenthal, R., & Jacobson, L. (1968a). *Pygmalion in the classroom: Teacher expectations and pupils' intellectual development.* New York: Holt, Rinehart & Winston.

Rosenthal, R., & Jacobson, L. (1968b). Teacher expectations for the disadvantaged. *Scientific American, 218,* 19–23.

Ross, A. O. (1980). *Psychological disorders of children: A behavioral approach to theory, research, and therapy* (2nd ed.). New York: McGraw-Hill.

Ross, G., Lipper, E. G., & Auld, P. A. (1991). Educational status and school-related abilities of very low birth weight premature children. *Pediatrics, 88,* 1125–1134.

Rossing, B. E. (1991). Patterns of informal incidental learning: Insights from community action. *International Journal of Lifelong Education, 10,* 45–60.

Rothbart, M. K., & Ahadi, S. A. (1994). Temperament and the development of personality. *Journal of Abnormal Psychology, 103,* 55–66.

Rothstein, E. (1980, Oct. 9). The scar of Sigmund Freud. *New York Review of Books,* pp. 14–20.

Rousseau, J. J. (1911). *Emile, or on education* (B. Foxley, Trans.). London: Dent. (Originally published 1762.)

Rovee-Collier, C. (1996). Shifting the focus from what to why. *Infant Behavior and Development, 19,* 385–400.

Rovee-Collier, C. K. (1987). Learning and memory in infancy. In J. D. Osofsky (Ed.), *Handbook of infant development.* New York: John Wiley.

Rowan, A. B., Foy, D. W., & Rodriguez, N. (1994). Post-traumatic Stress Disorder in a clinical sample of adults sexually abused as children. *Child Abuse and Neglect: The International Journal, 18,* 151–161.

Royal College of Psychiatrists (1987). *Drug scenes: A report on drugs and drug dependence by the Royal College of Psychiatrists.* London: Gaskell.

Royer, J. M., Cisero, C. A., & Carlo, M. S. (1993). Techniques and procedures for assessing cognitive skills. *Review of Educational Research, 63,* 201–243.

Ruben, R. J. (1993). Communication disorders in children: A challenge for health care. *Preventive Medicine, 22,* 585–588.

Rubin, J. D., Ferencz, C., & Loffredo, C. (1993). Use of prescription and non-prescription drugs in pregnancy. The Baltimore–Washington Infant Study Group. *Journal of Clinical Epidemiology, 46,* 581–589.

Rubin, J. Z., Provenzano, J. J., & Luria, Z. (1974). The eye of the beholder: Parents' views on sex of newborns. *American Journal of Orthopsychiatry, 44,* 512–519.

Rubin, Z. (1970). Measurement of romantic love. *Journal of Personality and Social Psychology, 16,* 265–273.

Rubin, Z. (1980). *Children's friendships.* Cambridge, MA: Harvard University Press.

Ruff, H. A., & Saltarelli, L. M. (1993). Exploratory play with objects: Basic cognitive processes and individual differences. *New Directions for Child Development, 59,* 5–16.

Ruffman, T., Olson, D. R., Ash, T., & Keenan, T. (1993). The ABCs of deception: Do young children understand deception in the same way as adults? *Developmental Psychology, 29,* 74–87.

Rumbaugh, D. M., & Savage-Rumbaugh, E. S. (1996). Biobehavioral roots of language: Words, apes, and a child. In B. M. Velichkovsky & D. M. Rumbaugh (Eds.), *Communicating meaning: The evolution and development of language.* Mahwah, NJ: Erlbaum.

Runco, M. A. (1986a). Flexibility and originality in children's divergent thinking. *Journal of Psychology, 120,* 345–352.

Runco, M. A. (1986b). Maximal performance on divergent thinking tests by gifted, talented, and nongifted children. *Psychology in the Schools, 23,* 308–315.

Runco, M. A. (1996). Personal creativity: Definition and developmental issues. *New Directions for Child Development, 72,* 3–27.

Rushforth, J. A., & Levene, M. I. (1994). Behavioural response to pain in healthy neonates. *Archives of Disease in Childhood, 70,* F174–F176.

Russ, S. W. (1996). Development of creative processes in children. *New Directions for Child Development, 72,* 31–42.

Russel, G. (1983). *The changing role of fathers.* Milton Keynes, Australia: Open University Press.

Rutter, M. (1996). Transitions and turning points in developmental psychopathology: As applied to the age span between childhood and mid-adulthood. *International Journal of Behavioral Development, 19,* 603–626.

Rymer, R. (1993). *Genie: A scientific tragedy.* New York: Harper Perennial.

Rys, G. S., & Bear, G. G. (1997). Relational aggression and peer relations: Gender and developmental issues. *Merrill–Palmer Quarterly, 43,* 87–106.

Saarnio, D. A. (1993). Scene memory in young children. *Merrill–Palmer Quarterly, 39,* 196–212.

Sadowski, P. M., & Loesch, L. C. (1993). Using children's drawings to detect potential child sexual abuse. *Elementary School Guidance and Counseling, 28,* 115–123.

Sagan, C. (1977). *The dragons of Eden.* New York: Ballantine.

Sagi, A., Ijzendoorn, M. H. Van, & Koren-Karie, N. (1991). Primary appraisal of the strange situation: A cross-cultural analysis of preseparation episodes. *Developmental Psychology, 27,* 587–596.

Saidla, D. D. (1992). Children's rights regarding physical abuse. *Journal of Humanistic Education and Development, 31,* 73–83.

Salomon, G., Perkins, D. N., & Globerson, T. (1991). Partners in cognition: Extending human intelligence with intelligent technologies. *Educational Researcher, 20,* 2–9.

Salzinger, S., Feldman, R. S., & Hammer, M. (1993). The effects of physical abuse on children's social relationships. *Child Development, 64,* 169–187.

Sambrook, P., Kelly, P., & Eisman, J. (1993). Bone mass and ageing. *Baillieres Clinical Rheumatology, 7,* 445–457.

Sampson, J. P., Jr., & Reardon, R. C. (1990). Evaluating computer-assisted career guidance systems: Synthesis and implications. *Journal of Career Development, 17,* 143–149.

Sampson, J. P., Jr., Reardon, R. C., & Lenz, J. G. (1991). Computer-assisted career guidance: Improving the design and use of systems. *Journal of Career Development, 17,* 185–190.

Sanders, M. R., Nicholson, J. M., & Floyd, F. J. (1997). Couples' relationships and children. In W. K. Halford & H. J. Markman (Eds.), *Clinical handbook of marriage and couples interventions.* Chichester, England: John Wiley.

Sarantokos, S. (1996). Same-sex couples: Problems and prospects. *Journal of Family Studies, 2,* 147–163.

Sarna, S., Sahi, T., Koskenvuo, M., & Kaprio, J. (1993). Increased life expectancy of world class male athletes. *Medicine and Science in Sports and Exercise, 25,* 237–244.

Sas, L. D., Wolfe, D. A., & Gowdey, D. A. (1996). Children and the courts in Canada. *Criminal Justice and Behavior, 23,* 338–357.

Sasser-Coen, J. R. (1993). Qualitative changes in creativity in the second half of life: A life-span developmental perspective. *Journal of Creative Behavior, 27,* 18–27.

Saudi woman gives birth to septuplets. (1997, Sept. 26). *Arabic News,* p. 1.

Saunders, C. (1994). Euthanasia—definition, dangers and alternatives. *Annals of the Academy of Medicine, Singapore, 23,* 300–303.

Savage-Rumbaugh, E. S., Murphy, J., Sevcik, R. A., Brakke, K. E., Williams, S. L., & Rumbaugh, D. M. (1993). Language comprehension in ape and child. *Monographs of the Society for Research in Child Development, 58,* 1–222.

Savickas, M. L. (1997). Career adaptability: An integrative construct for life-span, life-space theory. *Career Development Quarterly, 45,* 247–259.

Savickas, M. L., & Lent, R. W. (Eds.). (1994). *Convergence in career development theories.* Palo Alto, CA: CPP Books.

Savin-Williams, R. C., & Small, S. A. (1986). The timing of puberty and its relationship to adolescent and parent perceptions of family interactions. *Developmental Psychology, 22,* 342–347.

Sawyer, R. K. (1997). *Pretend play as improvisation: Conversation in the preschool classroom.* Mahwah, NJ: Erlbaum.

The "Scene" and the Skinheads. (1990, Nov. 18). *Edmonton Journal,* p. E1.

Schaeffer, A. M., & Nelson, E. S. (1993). Rape-supportive attitudes: Effects of on-campus residence and education. *Journal of College Student Development, 34,* 175–179.

Schaffer, H. R. (1984). *The child's entry into a social world.* New York: Academic Press.

Schaie, K. W. (1965). A general model for the study of developmental problems. *Psychological Bulletin, 64,* 92–107.

Schaie, K. W. (1977/1978). Toward a stage theory of adult cognitive development. *International Journal of Aging and Human Development, 8,* 129–136.

Schaie, K. W. (Ed.). (1983a). *Longitudinal studies of adult psychological development.* New York: Guilford.

Schaie, K. W. (1983b). What can we learn from the longitudinal study of adult psychological development? In K. W. Schaie (Ed.), *Longitudinal studies of adult psychological development* (pp. 1–19). New York: Guilford.

Schaie, K. W. (1986, December). *Variability in cognitive function in the elderly: Implications for social participation.* Paper presented at the Symposium on Phenotypic Variation in Populations: Relevance to Risk Assessment. Brookhaven National Laboratory, Upton, New York.

Schaie, K. W. (1993). The Seattle Longitudinal Study: A thirty-five-year inquiry of adult intellectual development. *Zeitschrift fur Gerontologie, 26,* 129–137.

Schaie, K. W. (1994). The course of adult intellectual development. *American Psychologist, 49,* 304–313.

Schaie, K. W. (1996). *Intellectual development in adulthood.* New York: Cambridge University Press.

Schaie, K. W. (1997). Normal cognitive development in adulthood. In H. M. Fillit & R. N. Butler (Eds.), *Cognitive decline: Strategies for prevention.* London: Greenwich Medical Media.

Schiff, I. (1996). *Menopause.* New York: Random House.

Schlegel, A., & Barry, H., III. (1991). *Adolescence: An anthropological inquiry.* New York: The Free Press.

Schlesinger, B. (1996). The sexless years of sex rediscovered. *Journal of Gerontological Social Work, 26,* 117–131.

Schmidt, M. (1995). Anglo Americans and sexual child abuse. In L. A. Fontes (Ed.), *Sexual abuse in nine North*

American cultures: Treatment and prevention. Thousand Oaks, CA: Sage.

Schneider, D. S., Sledge, P. A., Shuchter, S. R., & Zisook, S. (1996). Dating and remarriage over the first two years of widowhood. *Annals of Clinical Psychiatry, 8,* 51–57.

Schneider, E. L., & Rowe, J. W. (Eds.). (1996). *Handbook of the biology of aging.* New York: Academic Press.

Schneider-Rosen, K., Braunwald, K. G., Carlson, V., & Cicchetti, D. (1985). Current perspectives in attachment theory: Illustration from the study of maltreated infants. In I. Bretherton & E. Waters (Eds.), *Growing points of attachment theory and research* (*Monographs of the Society for Research in Child Development, 50,* No. 209).

Schoen, R., & Weinick, R. M. (1993). Partner choice in marriages and cohabitations. *Journal of Marriage and the Family, 55,* 404–414.

Schultz, R., & Ewen, R. B. (1988). *Adult development and aging: Myths and emerging realities.* New York: Macmillan.

Schwartzman, H. B. (1987). A cross-cultural perspective on child-structured play activities and materials. In A. W. Gottfried & C. C. Brown (Eds.), *Play interactions: The contribution of play materials and parental involvement to children's development.* Lexington, MA: Heath.

Scragg, R. K., Mitchell, E. A., Stewart, A. W., Ford, R. P., Taylor, B. J., Hassall, I. B., Williams, S. M., & Thompson, J. M. (1996). Infant room-sharing and prone sleep position in sudden infant death syndrome. New Zealand Cot Death Study Group. *Lancet, 347,* 7–12.

Seals, D. R., Taylor, J. A., Ng, A. V., & Esler, M. D. (1994). Exercise and aging: Autonomic control of the circulation. *Medicine and Science in Sports and Exercise, 26,* 568–576.

Sears, P. S., & Barbee, A. H. (1977). Care and life satisfactions among Terman's gifted women. In J. C. Stanley, W. C. George, and C. H. Solano (Eds.), *The gifted and the creative: A fifty-year perspective.* Baltimore: Johns Hopkins University Press.

Sears, W. (1995). *SIDS: A parent's guide to understanding and preventing Sudden Infant Death Syndrome.* Boston: Little, Brown.

Segal, B. (1997). The inhalant dilemma: A theoretical perspective. *Drugs and Society, 10,* 79–102.

Segal, N. L., Connelly, S. L., & Topoloski, T. D. (1996). Twin children with unfamiliar partners: Genotypic and gender influences on cooperation. *Journal of Child Psychology and Psychiatry and Allied Disciplines, 37,* 731–735.

Segal, U. A. (1995). Child abuse by the middle class? A study of professionals in India. *Child Abuse and Neglect, 19,* 217–231.

Seigle, S. P. (1993). On death and dying. *Connecticut Medicine, 57,* 69–71.

Selman, P., & Glendinning, C. (1996). Teenage pregnancy: Do social policies make a difference? In J. Brannen & M. O'Brien (Eds.), *Children in families: Research and policy.* Washington, DC: Falmer.

Selman, R. L. (1980). *The growth of interpersonal understanding.* New York: Academic Press.

Selman, R. L. (1981). The child as friendship philosopher. In S. R. Asher & J. M. Gottman (Eds.), *The development of children's friendships.* New York: Cambridge University Press.

Seltzer, B., Vasterling, J. J., Yoder, J., & Thompson, K. (1997). Awareness of deficit in Alzheimer's disease: Relation to caregiver burden. *Educational Research, 37,* 20–24.

Seltzer, M. M., & Ryff, C. D. (1994). Parenting across the life-span: The normative and nonnormative cases. In D. L. Featherman, R. M. Lerner, & M. Perlmutter (Eds.), *Lifespan development and behavior* (Vol. 12). Hillsdale, NJ: Erlbaum.

Semrud-Clikeman, M., & Hynd, G. W. (1992). Developmental arithmetic disorder. In S. R. Hooper, G. W. Hynd, & R. E. Mattison (Eds.), *Developmental disorders: Diagnostic criteria and clinical assessment.* Hillsdale, NJ: Erlbaum.

Serafini, S. (1991). Multiculturalism in the schools of Canada: Presentation to the fourth conference of CCMIE. *Multiculturalism, 14,* 12–14.

Serbin, L. A., Powlishta, K. K., & Gulko, J. (1993). The development of sex typing in middle childhood. *Monographs of the Society for Research in Child Development, 58,* No. 2.

Shanklin, D. R., & Hodin, J. (1979). *Maternal nutrition and child health.* Springfield, IL: Charles C Thomas.

Shanley, L. K. (1994). *Unassisted childbirth.* Westport, CT: Berfin & Garvey.

Shapiro, E. R. (1996). Family bereavement and cultural diversity: A social developmental perspective. *Family Process, 35,* 313–332.

Shaw, D. S., Owens, E. B., Vondra, J. I., & Keenan, K. (1996). Early risk factors and pathways in the development of early disruptive behavior problems. *Development and Psychopathology, 8,* 679–699.

Shaw, M. P., & Runco, M. A. (Eds.). (1994). *Creativity and affect.* Norwood, NJ: Ablex.

Sheard, N. F. (1994). Iron deficiency and infant development. *Nutrition Reviews, 52,* 137–140.

Shedler, J., & Block, J. (1990). Adolescent drug use and psychological health: A longitudinal inquiry. *American Psychologist, 45,* 612–630.

Sheehy, G. (1976). *Passages: Predictable crises of adult life.* New York: Dutton.

Sheehy, G. (1981). *Pathfinders.* New York: Morrow.

Sheepish about human genes. (1997). Reuters. Internet: abcnews.com/sections/sci.tech/rt-polly724

Shek, D. T. L. (1996). Midlife crisis in Chinese men and women. *Journal of Psychology, 130,* 109–119.

Shepherd-Look, D. L. (1982). Sex differentiation and the development of sex roles. In B. B. Wolman et al. (Eds.), *Handbook of developmental psychology.* Englewood Cliffs, NJ: Prentice-Hall.

Sheppard, H. (1976). Work and retirement. In R. Binstock & E. Shanas (Eds.), *Handbook of aging and the social sciences.* New York: Van Nostrand Reinhold.

Sherman, M., & Key, C. B. (1932). The intelligence of isolated mountain children. *Child Development, 3,* 279–290.

Sherrell, K., & Newton, N. (1996). Parent care as a developmental task. *Families in Society, 77,* 174–181.

Sherrod, L. R. (1996). Leaving home: The role of individual and familial factors. *New Directions for Child Development, 71,* 111–119.

Shiferaw, B., Mittelmark, M. B., & Hofford, J. L. (1994). The investigation and outcome of reported cases of elder abuse: The Forsyth County Aging Study. *Gerontologist, 34,* 123–125.

Shimonaka, Y., Nakazato, K., & Homma, A. (1996). Personality, longevity, and successful aging among Tokyo metropolitan centenarians. *International Journal of Aging and Human Development, 42,* 173–187.

Shioiri, T., Someya, T., Murashita, J., & Takahashi, S. (1996). The symptom structure of panic disorder: A trial using factor and cluster analysis. *Acta Psychiatrica Scandinavica, 93,* 80–86.

Shisslak, C. M., Crago, M., & Estes, L. S. (1995). The spectrum of eating disturbances. *International Journal of Eating Disorders, 18,* 201–219.

Short, E. J., Schatschneider, C. W., & Friebert, S. E. (1993). Relationship Between Memory and Metamemory Performance: A Comparison of Specific and General Strategy Knowledge. *Journal of Educational Psychology, 85,* 412–423.

Shortening the time between the bench and the bedside. (1993, Nov. 21). *University of Alberta Folio,* p. 4.

Shreeve, D. F. (1991). Elective mutism: Origins of stranger anxiety and selective attention. *Bulletin of the Menninger Clinic, 55,* 491–504.

Shreve, B. W., & Kunkel, M. A. (1991). Self-psychology, shame, and adolescent suicide: Theoretical and practical considerations. *Journal of Counseling and Development, 69,* 305–311.

Siegel, A. W., & White, S. H. (1982). The child study movement: Early growth and development of the symbolized child. In H. W. Reese (Ed.), *Advances in child development and behavior* (Vol. 17). New York: Academic Press.

Siegler, R. S. (1989). Mechanisms of cognitive development. *Annual Review of Psychology, 40,* 353–379.

Siegler, R. S., & Ellis, S. (1996). Piaget on childhood. *Psychological Science, 7,* 211–215.

Sigel, I. E. (1987). Does hothousing rob children of their childhood? *Early Childhood Research Quarterly, 2,* 211–225.

Silver, M. H. (1993). Balancing "caring and being cared for" in old age: The development of mutual parenting. In J. Demick, K. Bursik, & R. Dibiase (Eds.), *Parental development.* Hillsdale, NJ: Erlbaum.

Silverstein, F. S., & Johnston, M. V. (1990). Neurological assessment of children: The damaged child. In R. D. Eden, F. H. Boehm, & M. Haire (Eds.), *Assessment and care of the fetus: Physiological, clinical, and medicolegal principles.* Norwalk, CT: Appleton & Lange.

Silverstein, L. B. (1991). Transforming the debate about child care and maternal employment. *American Psychologist, 46,* 1025–1032.

Silvestri, G. T., & Lukasiewicz, J. M. (1989). Projections of occupational employment: 1988–2000. *Monthly Labor Review, 112,* 42–65.

Silvestri, L., Dantonio, M., & Eason, S. (1994). Enhancement of self-esteem in at-risk elementary students. *Journal of Health Education, 25,* 30–36.

Simic, M. G. (1992). The rate of DNA damage and aging. *EXS, 62,* 20–30.

Simmons, L. (1960). Aging in preindustrial societies. In C. Tibbitts (Ed.), *Handbook of social gerontology.* Chicago: University of Chicago Press.

Simmons, R. G., & Blyth, D. (1987). *Moving into adolescence: The impact of pubertal change and school context.* New York: Aldine & Gruyter.

Simon, L. (1992). Mainstreaming: Is it in the best interests of all children? *B.C. Journal of Special Education, 16,* 131–138.

Simpson, J. L. (1991). Aetiology of pregnancy failure. In M. Chapman, G. Grudzinskas, & T. Chard (Eds.), *The embryo: Normal and abnormal development and growth.* New York: Springer-Verlag.

Singer, D. G., & Singer, J. L. (1990). *The house of make-believe: Children's play and developing imagination.* Cambridge, MA: Harvard University Press.

Singh, J. A., & Zingg, R. N. (1942). *Wolf-children and feral man.* New York: Harper & Row.

Sivan, Y., Kornecki, A., Baharav, A., Glaser, N., & Spicer, Z. (1997). Home monitoring for infants at high risk for the sudden infant death syndrome. *Israel Journal of Medical Sciences, 33,* 45–49.

Sizer, F. S., & Whitney, E. N. (1997). *Nutrition: Concepts and controversies* (7th ed.). Belmont, CA: West/Wadsworth.

Skinner, B. F. (1953). *Science and human behavior.* New York: Macmillan.

Skinner, B. F. (1957). *Verbal behavior.* Englewood Cliffs, NJ: Prentice-Hall.

Skinner, B. F. (1961). *Cumulative record* (rev. ed.). New York: Appleton-Century-Crofts.

Skinner, E. A., & Wellborn, J. G. (1994). Coping during childhood and adolescence: A motivational perspective. In D. L. Featherman, R. M. Lerner, & M. Perlmutter (Eds.), *Lifespan development and behavior* (Vol. 12). Hillsdale, NJ: Erlbaum.

Skolnick, A. (1978, February). The myth of the vulnerable child. *Psychology Today*, pp. 56–60, 65.

Skolnick, A. (1981). Married lives: Longitudinal perspectives on marriage. In D. H. Eichorn, J. A. Clausen, N. Haan, M. P. Honzik, & P. H. Mussen (Eds.), *Present and past in middle life*. New York: Academic Press.

Slater, A. (1996). The organization of visual perception in early infancy. In F. Vital-Durand, J. Atkinson, & O. J. Braddick (Eds.), *Infant vision*. New York: Oxford University Press.

Sleeping with the enemy. (1991, Dec. 9). *Newsweek*, 58–59.

Slobodian, L. (1997, Nov. 16). Sudan's ugliest secret. *Edmonton Sun*, Sunday Express, p. 15.

Small, S. A., & Eastman, G. (1991). Rearing adolescents in contemporary society: A conceptual framework for understanding the responsibilities and needs of parents. *Family Relations, 40*, 455–462.

Smetana, J. G. (1995). Context, conflict, and constraint in adolescent–parenting authority relationships. In M. Killen & D. Hart (Eds.), *Morality in everyday life: Developmental perspectives*. New York: Cambridge University Press.

Smith, C. (1996). The link between childhood maltreatment and teenage pregnancy. *Social Work Research, 20*, 131–141.

Smith, C. A. (1997). Factors associated with early sexual activity among urban adolescents. *Social Work, 42*, 334–346.

Smith, C. I., & Notarangelo, L. D. (1997). Molecular basis for X-linked immunodeficiencies. In J. C. Hall & J. C. Dunlap (Eds.), *Advances in genetics: Incorporating molecular genetic medicine*. San Diego, CA: Academic Press.

Smith, C. L. (1979). Children's understanding of natural language hierarchies. *Journal of Experimental Child Psychology, 27*, 437–458.

Smith, C. V., Satt, B., Phelan, J. P., & Paul, R. H. (1990). Intrauterine sound levels: Intrapartum assessment with an intrauterine microphone. *American Journal of Perinatology, 7*, 312–315.

Smith, D. F. (1994). Type A personalities tend to have low platelet monoamine oxidase activity. *Acta Psychiatrica Scandinavica, 89*, 88–91.

Smith, G. E., Wong, J. S., Ivnik, R. J., & Malec, J. F. (1997). Mayo's Older American Normative Studies: Separate norms for WMS-R logical memory stories. *Assessment, 4*, 79–86.

Smith, J., Berthelsen, D., & O'Connor, I. (1997). Child adjustment in high conflict families. *Child: Care, Health, and Development, 23*, 113–133.

Smith, K. R., & Zick, C. D. (1996). Risk of mortality following widowhood: Age and sex differences by mode of death. *Social Biology, 43*, 59–71.

Smith, L. (1993). *Necessary knowledge: Piagetian perspectives on constructivism*. Hillsdale, NJ: Erlbaum.

Smith, L. B. (1995). Self-organizing processes in learning to learn words: Development is not induction. In C. A. Nelson (Ed.), *Basic and applied perspectives on learning, cognition, and development: The Minnesota Symposia on Child Psychology*, Vol. 28. Mahwah, NJ: Erlbaum.

Smith, M., & Yuen, K. (1994). Palliative care in the home. The GP/home hospice team. *Australian Family Physician, 23*, 1260–1265.

Smith, M. A. B. (1994). Teen incentives program: Evaluation of a health promotion model for adolescent pregnancy prevention. *Journal of Health Education, 25*, 24–29.

Smolak, L., Levine, M. P., & Gralen, S. (1993). The impact of puberty and dating on eating problems among middle school girls. *Journal of Youth and Adolescence, 22*, 355–368.

Smoll, F. L., & Schutz, R. W. (1990). Quantifying gender differences in physical performance: A developmental perspective. *Developmental Psychology, 26*, 360–369.

Snarey, J. (1993). *How fathers care for the next generation: A four-decade study*. Cambridge, MA: Harvard University Press.

Snyder, J., Horsch, E., & Childs, J. (1997). Peer relationships of young children: Affiliative choices and the shaping of aggressive behavior. *Journal of Clinical Child Psychology, 26*, 145–156.

Snyderman, M., & Rothman, S. (1987). Survey of expert opinion on intelligence and aptitude testing. *American Psychologist, 42*, 137–144.

Sobsey, D. (1993). Integration outcomes: Theoretical models and empirical investigations. *Developmental Disabilities Bulletin, 21*, 1–14.

Sokolovsky, M. (1996). Case study as a research method to study life histories of elderly people: Some ideas and a case study of a case study. *Journal of Aging Studies, 10*, 281–294.

Solnick, R. E., & Corby, N. (1983). Human sexuality and aging. In D. S. Woodruff & J. E. Birren (Eds.), *Aging: Scientific perspectives and social issues* (2nd ed.) (pp. 202–224). Pacific Grove, CA: Brooks/Cole.

Solstad, K., & Garde, K. (1992). Middle-aged Danish men's ideas of a male climacteric—and of the female climacteric. *Maturitas, 15*, 7–16.

Somers, M. D. (1993). A comparison of voluntarily child-free adults and parents. *Journal of Marriage and the Family, 55*, 643–650.

Sophian, C. (1996). Young children's numerical cognition: What develops? *Annals of Child Development, 12*, 49–86.

Sormanti, M., & August, J. (1997). Parental bereavement: Spiritual connections with deceased children. *American Journal of Orthopsychiatry, 67,* 460–469.

South, S. J. (1991). Sociodemographic differentials in mate selection preferences. *Journal of Marriage and the Family, 53,* 928–940.

Soutter, A. (1996). A longitudinal study of three cases of gender identity disorder of childhood successfully resolved in the school setting. *School Psychology International, 17,* 49–57.

Sparks, S. P., Jovanovic-Peterson, L., & Peterson, C. M. (1993). Blood glucose rise following prenatal vitamins in gestational diabetes. *Journal of the American College of Nutrition, 12,* 543–546.

Spellacy, W. N., Miller, S. J., & Winegar, A. (1986). Pregnancy after 40 years of age. *Obstetrics and Gynecology, 68,* 452–454.

Spence, A. P. (1989). *Biology of human aging.* Englewood Cliffs, NJ: Prentice-Hall.

Sperling, L. S., Henriksen, T. B., Ulrichsen, H. J., Hedegard, M., Moller, H., Hansen, V., Ovlisen, B., & Secher, N. J. (1994). Indications for cesarean section in singleton pregnancies in two Danish counties with different cesarean section rates. *Acta Obstetricia et Gynecologica Scandinavica, 73,* 129–135.

Spieker, M. R., & Brannen, S. J. (1996). Supine infant sleep: What do family physicians recommend? *Journal of the American Board of Family Practice, 9,* 319–323.

Spinillo, A., Capuzzo, E., Orcesi, S., Stronati, M., DiMario, M., & Fazzi, E. (1997). Antenatal and delivery risk factors simultaneously associated with neonatal death and cerebral palsy in preterm infants. *Early Human Development, 48,* 81–91.

Springer, C., & Wallerstein, J. S. (1983). Young adolescents' responses to their parents' divorces. In L. A. Kurdek (Ed.), *Children and divorce: New directions for child development* (pp. 15–28). San Francisco: Jossey-Bass.

Squire, L. R., Knowlton, B., & Musen, G. (1993). The structure and organization of memory. *Annual Review of Psychology, 44,* 453–495.

Sroufe, L. A. (1996). *Emotional development: The organization of emotional life in the early years.* New York: Cambridge University Press.

St. C. Levy, K. (1997). Multifactorial self-concept and delinquency in Australian adolescents. *Journal of Social Psychology, 137,* 277–283.

Stack, S. (1993). The media and suicide: A nonadditive model, 1968–1980. *Suicide and Life-Threatening Behavior, 23,* 63–66.

Stall, R. D., Coates, T. J., & Hoff, C. (1988). Behavioral risk reduction for HIV infection among gay and bisexual men. *American Psychologist, 43,* 878–885.

Stallings, M. C., Dunham, C. C., Gatz, M., Baker, L. A., et al. (1997). Relationships among life events and psychological well-being: More evidence for a two-factor theory of well-being. *Journal of Applied Gerontology, 16,* 104–119.

Stambak, M., Sinclair, H., Verba, M., Moreno, L., & Rayna, S. (1989). Infants and logic. In H. Sinclair, M. Stambak, I. Lézine, S. Rayna, & M. Verba (Eds.), *Infants and objects: The creativity of cognitive development.* New York: Academic Press.

Stander, V., & Jensen, L. (1993). The relationship of value orientation to moral cognition: Gender and cultural differences in the United States and China explored. *Journal of Cross-Cultural Psychology, 24,* 42–52.

Stanford, L. D., & Hynd, G. W. (1994). Congruence of behavioral symptomatology in children with ADD/H, ADD/WO, and learning disabilities. *Journal of Learning Disabilities, 27,* 243–253.

Stanovich, K. E. (1992). Developmental reading disorder. In S. R. Hooper, G. W. Hynd, & R. E. Mattison (Eds.), *Developmental disorders: Diagnostic criteria and clinical assessment.* Hillsdale, NJ: Erlbaum.

Stanovich, K. E. (1993). Dysrationalia: A new specific learning disability. *Journal of Learning Disabilities, 26,* 501–515.

Stanton, W. R. (1993). A cognitive developmental framework. *Current Psychology: Research and Reviews, 12,* 26–45.

Starling, S. P., Holden, J. R., & Jenny, C. (1995). Abusive head trauma: The relationship of perpetrators to their victims. *Pediatrics, 95,* 259–262.

Statistics Canada. (1995). *Market Research Handbook, 1995.* Ottawa: Minister of Industry, Science, and Technology.

Statistics Canada. (1996). *The 1997 Canada Yearbook.* Ottawa: Minister of Industry.

Stattin, H., & Klackenberg-Larsson, I. (1993). Early language and intelligence development and their relationship to future criminal behavior. *Journal of Abnormal Psychology, 102,* 369–378.

Stattin, H., & Magnusson, D. (1990). *Pubertal maturation in female development.* Hillsdale, NJ: Erlbaum.

Stephens, M. A. P., Franks, M. M., & Atienza, A. (1997). Where two roles intersect: Spillover between parent care and employment. *Psychology and Aging, 12,* 30–37.

Stephens, R. S., Roffman, R. A., & Simpson, E. E. (1993). Adult marijuana users seeking treatment. *Journal of Consulting and Clinical Psychology, 61,* 1100–1104.

Stern, C. (1956). Hereditary factors affecting adoption. In *A Study of Adoption Practices* (Vol. 2). New York: Child Welfare League of America.

Sternberg, R. J. (1984). A contextualist view of the nature of intelligence. *International Journal of Psychology, 19,* 307–334.

Sternberg, R. J. (1985). *Beyond IQ: A triarchic theory of human intelligence.* New York: Cambridge University Press.

Sternberg, R. J. (1986). A triangular theory of love. *Psychological Review, 93,* 119–135.

Sternberg, R. J. (1991). Directors of development: A play in an unknown number of acts. In L. Okagaki & R. J. Sternberg (Eds.), *Directors of development: Influences on the development of children's thinking.* Hillsdale, NJ: Erlbaum.

Stets, J. E. (1990). Verbal and physical aggression in marriage. *Journal of Marriage and the Family, 52,* 501–514.

Stets, J. E. (1993). The link between past and present intimate relationships. *Journal of Family Issues, 14,* 236–260.

Stevens, E. S. (1993). Making sense of usefulness: An avenue toward satisfaction in later life. *International Journal of Aging and Human Development, 37,* 315–325.

Stevens-Long, J. (1990). Adult development: Theories past and future. In R. A. Nemiroff & C. A. Colarusso (Eds.), *New dimensions in adult development.* New York: Basic Books.

Stevenson, H. W., Chen, C., Lee, S. Y., & Fuligni, A. J. (1991). Schooling, culture, and cognitive development. In L. Okagaki & R. J. Sternberg (Eds.), *Directors of development: Influences on the development of children's thinking.* Hillsdale, NJ: Erlbaum.

Stewart, M. (1997, Oct. 1). Grandparents' visits now protected by law. *Edmonton Journal,* p. A3.

Stier, D. M., Leventhal, J. M., Berg, A. T., Johnson, L., & Mezger, J. (1993). Are children born to young mothers at increased risk of maltreatment? *Pediatrics, 91,* 642–648.

Stifter, C. A., & Fox, N. A. (1990). Infant reactivity: Physiological correlates of newborn and 5–month temperament. *Developmental Psychology, 26,* 582–588.

Stifter, C. A., & Jain, A. (1996). Psychophysiological correlates of infant temperament: Stability of behavior and autonomic patterning from 5 to 18 months. *Developmental Psychobiology 29,* 379–391.

Stimpson, D., Neff, W., Jensen, L. C., & Newby, T. (1991). The caring morality and gender differences. *Psychological Reports, 69,* 407–414.

Stockman, J. A., III. (1990). Fetal hematology. In R. D. Eden, F. H. Boehm, & M. Haire (Eds.), *Assessment and care of the fetus: Physiological, clinical, and medicolegal principles.* Norwalk, CT: Appleton & Lange.

Stoll, S. K., & Beller, J. M. (1993). *The effect of a longitudinal teaching methodology and classroom environment on both cognitive and behavioral moral development.* Paper presented at the Annual Meeting of the American Alliance for Health, Physical Education, Recreation and Dance, Washington, DC, March 24–28.

Stoltz-Loike, M. (1996). Annual review: Practice and research in career development and counseling—1995. *Career Development Quarterly, 45,* 98–140.

Stormo, K. J., Lang, A. R., & Stritzke, W. G. K. (1997). Attributions about acquaintance rape: The role of alcohol and individual differences. *Journal of Applied Social Psychology, 27,* 279–305.

Stormont-Spurgin, M., & Zentall, S. (1996). Child-rearing practices associated with aggression in youth with and without ADHD: An exploratory study. *International Journal of Disability, Development and Education, 43,* 135–146.

Story, M. (1997). Promoting healthy eating and ensuring adequate weight gain in pregnant adolescents: Issues and strategies. *Annals of the New York Academy of Sciences, 817,* 321–333.

Stoutjesdyk, D., & Jevne, R. (1993). Eating disorders among high performance athletes. *Journal of Youth and Adolescence, 22,* 271–279.

Straus, M. A. (1980a). The marriage license as a hitting license: Evidence from popular culture, law, and social science. In M. A. Straus & G. T. Hotaling (Eds.), *The social causes of husband–wife violence.* Minneapolis: University of Minnesota Press.

Straus, M. A. (1980b). Wife-beating: How common and why? In M. A. Straus & G. T. Hotaling (Eds.), *The social causes of husband–wife violence.* Minneapolis: University of Minnesota Press.

Straus, M. A., & Gelles, R. (1986). Societal change and change in family violence from 1975 to 1985 as revealed by two national surveys. *Journal of Marriage and the Family, 48,* 465–479.

Straus, M. A., & Kurz, D. (1997). Domestic violence: Are women as likely as men to initiate physical assaults in partner relationships? In M. R. Walsh (Ed.), *Women, men, and gender: Ongoing debates.* New Haven, CT: Yale University Press.

Streissguth, A. P., Landesman-Dwyer, S., Martin, J. C., & Smith, D. W. (1980). Teratogen effects of alcohol in humans and laboratory animals. *Science, 209,* 353–361.

Strelau, J. (1989). Temperament risk factors in children and adolescents as studied in Eastern Europe. In W. B. Carey & S. C. McDevitt (Eds.), *Clinical and educational applications of temperament research.* Berwyn, PA: Swets North America.

Strom, R., & Strom, S. (1995). Raising expectations for grandparents: A three generational study. In J. Hendricks (Ed.), *The ties of later life.* Amityville, NY: Baywood.

Sugar, M. (Ed.). (1993). *Female adolescent development.* New York: Brunner/Mazel.

Sullivan, C. M., Rumptz, M. H., Campbell, R., Eby, K., et al. (1996). Retaining participants in longitudinal community research: A comprehensive protocol. *Journal of Applied Behavioral Science, 32,* 262–276.

Sullivan, R. M., Taborsky-Barba, S., Mendoza, R., Itano, A., Leon, M., Cotman, C. W., Payne, T. F., & Lott, I. (1991). Olfactory classical conditioning in neonates. *Pediatrics, 87,* 511–518.

Super, D. (1990). A life-span life-space approach to career development. In D. Brown & L. Brooks (Eds.), *Career choice and development* (2nd ed.). San Francisco: Jossey-Bass.

Super, D. (1994). A life span, life space perspective on convergence. In M. L. Savikas & R. W. Lent (Eds.), *Convergence in career development theories.* Palo Alto, CA: CPP Books.

Super, D. E., Savickas, M. L., & Super, C. M. (1996). The life-span, life-space approach to careers. In D. Brown, L. Brooks, et al. (Eds.), *Career choice and development* (3rd ed.). San Francisco: Jossey-Bass.

Suzuki, K. (1994). Molecular genetics of Tay–Sachs and related disorders: A personal account. *Journal of Neuropathology & Experimental Neurology, 53,* 344–350.

Swaim, R. C., Oetting, E. R., Thurman, P. J., Beauvais, F., & Edwards, R. W. (1993). American Indian adolescent drug use and socialization characteristics: A cross-cultural comparison. *Journal of Cross-Cultural Psychology, 24,* 53–70.

Swain, I. U., Zelazo, P. R., & Clifton, R. K. (1993). Newborn infants' memory for speech sounds retained over 24 hours. *Developmental Psychology, 29,* 312–323.

Swan, G. E., & Carmelli, D. (1996). Curiosity and mortality in aging adults: A 5-year follow-up of the Western Collaborative Group Study. *Psychology and Aging, 11,* 449–453.

Swanson, H. L. (1992). The relationship between metacognition and problem solving in gifted children. *Roeper Review, 15,* 43–48.

Swanson, H. L. (1993). Working memory in learning disability subgroups. *Journal of Experimental Child Psychology, 56,* 87–114.

Swanson, H. L., & Hill, G. (1993). Metacognitive aspects of moral reasoning and behavior. *Adolescence, 28,* 711–736.

Swanson, J. M., Cantwell, D., Lerner, M., McBurnett, K., & Hanna, G. (1991). Effects of stimulant medication on learning in children with ADHD. *Journal of Learning Disabilities, 24,* 219–230.

Szymborska, W. (1995). *View with a grain of sand: Selected poems.* New York: Harcourt.

Talbot, J. F., & Kaplan, R. (1991). The benefits of nearby nature for elderly apartment residents. *International Journal of Aging and Human Development, 33,* 119–130.

Tamir, L. (1982). *Men in their forties: The transition to middle age.* New York: Springer.

Tamis-LeMonda, C. S., & Bornstein, M. H. (1993). Play and its relations to other mental functions in the child. *New Directions in Child Development, 59,* 17–28.

Tang, S. (1997). The timing of home leaving: A comparison of early, on-time, and late home leavers. *Journal of Youth and Adolescence, 26,* 13–23.

Tanner, J. M., Whitehouse, R. H., & Takaishi, M. (1966). Standards from birth to maturity for height, weight, height velocity, and weight velocity: British Children 1965—I. *Archives of Disease in Childhood, 41,* 454–471.

Tappan, M. B. (1997). Language, culture, and moral development: A Vygotskian perspective. *Developmental Review, 17,* 78–100.

Tattum, D., & Herbert, G. (1993). *Countering bullying: Initiatives by schools and local authorities.* Stoke-on-Trent, England: Trentham.

Tavris, C., & Baumgartner, A. I. (1983, February). How would your life be different if you'd been born a boy? *Redbook,* p. 99.

Taylor, A. R. (1996). Conditions for American children, youth, and families: Are we "world class"? *Educational Researcher, 25,* 10–12.

Taylor, C. (1989). *Sources of the self.* Cambridge, MA: Harvard University Press.

Taylor, M., & Carlson, M. (1997). The relation between individual differences in fantasy and theory of mind. *Child Development, 68,* 436–455.

Taylor, M., Cartwright, B. S., & Carlson, S. M. (1993). A developmental investigation of children's imaginary companions. *Developmental Psychology, 29,* 276–285.

Television and your children. (1985). Ontario, Canada: TV Ontario, the Ontario Educational Communications Authority.

Tennyson, S. A., Pereyra, P. M., & Becker, L. E. (1994). The development of the diaphragm in infants with sudden infant death syndrome. *Early Human Development, 37,* 1–8.

Terkel, S. (1972). *Working.* New York: Random House.

Terman, L. M., assisted by B. T. Baldwin et al. (1925). *Genetic studies of genius* (Vol. 1). Stanford, CA: Stanford University Press.

Termine, N. T., & Izard, C. E. (1988). Infants' responses to their mothers' expressions of joy and sadness. *Developmental Psychology, 24,* 223–229.

Terrace, H. S. (1985). In the beginning was the "Name." *American Psychologist, 40,* 1011–1028.

Theriault, J. (1994). Retirement as a psychosocial transition: Process of adaptation to change. *International Journal of Aging and Human Development, 38,* 153–170.

Thinner Michelin Man. (1997, Dec. 4). *Edmonton Sun,* p. 2.

Thoma, S. J. (1993). The relationship between political preference and moral judgment development in late adolescence. *Merrill–Palmer Quarterly, 39,* 359–374.

Thomas, A., & Chess, S. (1977). *Temperament and development.* New York: Brunner/Mazel.

Thomas, A., & Chess, S. (1981). The role of temperament in the contribution of individuals to their development. In R. M. Lerner & N. A. Busch-Rossnagel (Eds.), *Individuals as producers of their development*. New York: Academic Press.

Thomas, A., Chess, S., & Birch, H. G. (1968). *Temperament and behavior disorders in children*. New York: New York University Press.

Thomas, A., Chess, S., & Birch, H. G. (1970). The origin of personality. *Scientific American, 223*, 102–109.

Thomas, A., Chess, S., & Korn, S. J. (1982). The reality of difficult temperament. *Merrill–Palmer Quarterly, 28*, 1–20.

Thomas, H., & Lohaus, A. (1993). Modeling growth and individual differences in spatial tasks. *Monographs of the Society for Research in Child Development, 58* (237, 9).

Thomas, R. M. (1996). *Comparing theories of child development* (4th ed.). Pacific Grove, CA: Brooks/Cole.

Thompson, R. J., Jr., Gil, K. M., & Abrams, M. R. (1992). Stress, coping, and psychological adjustment of adults with sickle cell disease. *Journal of Consulting & Clinical Psychology, 60*, 33–40.

Thompson, R. W., Grow, C. R., & Ruma, P. R. (1993). Evaluation of a practical parenting program with middle- and low-income families. *Family Relations, 42*, 21–25.

Thomson, E., & Colella, U. (1992). Cohabitation and marital stability: Quality or commitment. *Journal of Marriage and the Family, 54*, 259–267.

Thorp, J. A., Meyer, B. A., Cohen, G. R., Yeast, Y. D., & Hu, D. (1994). Epidural analgesia in labor and cesarean delivery for dystocia. *Obstetrical and Gynecological Survey, 49*, 362–369.

Thorpe, W. H. (1963). *Learning and instinct in animals* (2nd ed.). London: Methuen.

Tierney, J. (1988). Not to worry. *Hippocrates*, January/February, pp. 29–36.

Tisak, M. S. (1993). Preschool children's judgments of moral and personal events involving physical harm and property damage. *Merrill–Palmer Quarterly, 39*, 375–390.

Tite, R. (1993). How teachers define and respond to child abuse: The distinction between theoretical and reportable cases. *Child Abuse and Neglect: The International Journal, 17*, 591–603.

Tobin, J. J., Wu, D. Y. H., & Davidson, D. H. (1989). *Preschool in three cultures: Japan, China, and the United States*. New Haven, CT: Yale University Press.

Tomporowski, P. D. (1997). The effects of physical and mental training on the mental abilities of older adults. *Journal of Aging and Physical Activity, 5*, 9–26.

Toneguzzi, M. (1994, Nov. 20). Jury refused to convict couple who killed son. *Edmonton Journal*, p. C2.

Toray, T., Coughlin, C., Vuchinich, S., & Patricelli, P. (1991). Gender differences associated with adolescent substance abuse: Comparisons and implications for treatment. *Family Relations, 40*, 338–344.

Tot gnawed on his thumb during five days alone: cops. (1997, Nov. 20). *Edmonton Sun*, p. 43.

Tough curbs urged for reproductive medicine. (1993, Nov. 30). *Edmonton Journal*, p. A1.

Tranel, D., Benton, A., & Olson, K. (1997). A 10-year longitudinal study of cognitive changes in elderly persons. *Developmental Neuropsychology, 13*, 87–96.

Trehub, S. E., Schneider, B. A., Thorpe, L. A., & Judge, P. (1991). Observational measures of auditory sensitivity in early infancy. *Developmental Psychology, 27*, 40–49.

Trickett, P. K., Aber, J. L., Carlson, V., & Cicchetti, D. (1991). Relationship of socioeconomic status to the etiology and developmental sequelae of physical child abuse. *Developmental Psychology, 27*, 148–158.

Trickett, P. K., & Susman, E. J. (1988). Parental perceptions of child-rearing practices in physically abusive and nonabusive families. *Developmental Psychology, 24*, 270–276.

Tronick, E. Z. (1989). Emotions and emotional communication in infants. *American Psychologist, 44*, 112–119.

Trotter, A. (1991). Rites of passage. *Executive Educator, 13*, 48–49.

Trudel, G., Landry, L., & Larose, Y. (1997). Low sexual desire: The role of anxiety, depression and marital adjustment. *Sexual and Marital Therapy, 12*, 95–99.

Trudel, G., Ravart, M., & Matte, B. (1993). The use of the multiaxial diagnostic system for sexual dysfunctions in the assessment of hypoactive sexual desire. *Journal of Sex and Marital Therapy, 19*, 123–130.

Tryon, R. C. (1940). Genetic differences in maze learning in rats. *Yearbook of the National Society for Studies in Education, 39*, 111–119.

Tsuchiyama, B. (1992). Philippines OMEP kindergartens for poor children. *International Journal of Early Childhood Education, 24*, 56–64.

Tubman, J. G. (1993). Family risk factors, parental alcohol use, and problem behaviors among school-age children. *Family Relations, 42*, 81–86.

Tucker, J. S., Friedman, H. S., Schwartz, J. E., Criqui, M. H., et al. (1997). Parental divorce: Effects on individual behavior and longevity. *Journal of Personality and Social Psychology, 73*, 381–391.

Tucker, J. S., Friedman, H. S., Wingard, D. L., & Schwartz, J. E. (1996). Marital history at midlife as a predictor of longevity: Alternative explanations to the protective effect of marriage. *Health Psychology, 15*, 94–101.

Tudge, J., Shanahan, M. J., & Valsiner, J. (Eds.). (1997). *Comparisons in human development: Understanding time and context*. New York: Cambridge University Press.

Tudge, J. R. H., & Winterhoff, P. A. (1993). Vygotsky, Piaget, and Bandura: Perspectives on the relations between the social world and cognitive development. *Human Development, 36*, 61–81.

Tulving, E. (1991). Concepts in human memory. In L. R. Squire, N. M. Weinberger, G. Lynch, & J. L. McGaugh (Eds.), *Memory: Organization and locus of change*. New York: Oxford University Press.

Tuma, J. M. (1989). Mental health services for children. *American Psychologist, 44*, 188–195.

Turkey baster used to help make baby. (1993, April 21). *Edmonton Sun*, p. 28.

Turkheimer, E. (1991). Individual and group differences in adoption studies of IQ. *Psychological Bulletin, 110*, 392–405.

Tye, L. (1997, Dec. 1). Septuplets still face challenges ahead. *Boston Globe*, p. C11.

Uchiyama, A. (1994). An analysis of characteristics of child abuse cases. *Reports of National Research Institute of Police Science, 35*, 177–187.

Udani, P. M. (1992). Protein energy malnutrition (PEM), brain and various facets of child development. *Indian Journal of Pediatrics, 59*, 165–186.

U.S. Bureau of the Census. (1988). *Statistical abstracts of the United States, 1987* (108th ed.). Washington, DC: U.S. Government Printing Office.

U.S. Bureau of the Census. (1991). *Statistical abstracts of the United States, 1991* (111th ed.). Washington, DC: U.S. Government Printing Office.

U.S. Bureau of the Census. (1992). *Statistical abstracts of the United States, 1992* (112th ed.). Washington, DC: U.S. Government Printing Office.

U.S. Bureau of the Census. (1993). *Statistical abstracts of the United States, 1993* (113th ed.). Washington, DC: U.S. Government Printing Office.

U.S. Bureau of the Census. (1994). *Statistical abstracts of the United States, 1994* (114th ed.). Washington, DC: U.S. Government Printing Office.

U.S. Bureau of the Census. (1996). *Statistical abstracts of the United States, 1996* (116th ed.). Washington, DC: U.S. Government Printing Office.

U.S. Department of Education. (1991). *Twelfth annual report to Congress on the implementation of PL 94–142: The Education for All Handicapped Children Act*. Washington, DC: U.S. Government Printing Office.

U.S. English Press Releases and Newsletters. (1997). Internet: http://www.us-english.org/pressrel.htm

U.S. parents kept girl, 7, in dog cage, say police. (1997, Nov. 20). *Edmonton Sun*, p. 43.

Uzych, L. (1996). Euthanasia. *Canadian Journal of Psychiatry, 41*, 315.

Vaillant, C. O., & Vaillant, G. E. (1993). Is the U-Curve of marital satisfaction an illusion? A 40-year study of marriage. *Journal of Marriage and the Family, 55*, 230–239.

Vaillant, G. E., & Milofsky, E. (1980). Natural history of male psychological health: IX. Empirical evidence for Erikson's model of the life cycle. *American Journal of Psychiatry, 137*, 1348–1359.

Valdes-Dapena, M. A. (1991). The phenomenon of sudden infant death syndrome and its challenges. In C. A. Corr, H. Fuller, C. A. Barnickol, & D. M. Corr (Eds.), *Sudden infant death syndrome: Who can help and how*. New York: Springer.

Valsiner, J. (1987). *Culture and the development of children's action: A cultural–historical theory of developmental psychology*. New York: John Wiley.

Vandell, D. L., & Ramanan, J. (1991). Children of the National Longitudinal Survey of Youth: Choices in after-school care and child development. *Developmental Psychology, 27*, 637–643.

Vandell, D. L., Wilson, K. S., & Buchanan, N. R. (1980). Peer interaction in the first year of life: An examination of its structure, content, and sensitivity to toys. *Child Development, 51*, 481–488.

Van Ranst, N., & Marcoen, A. (1997). Meaning in life of young and elderly adults: An examination of the factorial validity and invariance of the Life Regard Index. *Personality and Individual Differences, 22*, 877–884.

Vartanian, L. R., & Powlishta, K. K. (1996). A longitudinal examination of the social–cognitive foundations of adolescent egocentrism. *Journal of Early Adolescence, 16*, 157–178.

Vicary, J. R., Klingaman, L. R., & Harkness, W. L. (1995). Risk factors associated with date rape and sexual assault of adolescent girls. *Journal of Adolescence, 18*, 289–306.

Vikan, A., & Clausen, S. E. (1993). Freud, Piaget, or neither? Beliefs in controlling others by wishful thinking and magical behavior in young children. *Journal of Genetic Psychology, 154*, 297–314.

Vining, E. P., Freeman, J. M., Pillas, D. J., Uematsu, S., Carson, B. S., Brandt, J., Boatman, D., Pulsifer, M. B., & Zuckerberg, A. (1997). Why would you remove half a brain? The outcome of 58 children after hemispherectomy—the Johns Hopkins experience: 1968 to 1996. *Pediatrics, 100*, 163–171.

Visher, E. B., & Visher, J. S. (1996). *Therapy with stepfamilies*. New York: Brunner/Mazel.

Vitaro, F., Tremblay, R. E., & Gagnon, C. (1992). Peer rejection from kindergarten to grade 2: Outcomes, correlates, and prediction. *Merrill–Palmer Quarterly, 38*, 382–400.

Volling, B. L., & Belsky, J. (1993). Maternal employment: Parent, infant, and contextual characteristics related to maternal employment decisions in the first year of infancy. *Family Relations, 42*, 4–12.

Voorrips, L. E., Lemmink, K. A., van Heuvelen, M. J., Bult, P., & van Staveren, W. A. (1993). The physical condition of elderly women differing in habitual physical activity.

Medicine and Science in Sports and Exercise, 25, 1152–1157.

Voss, S. (1992). The usage of pregnancy tests in one health district. *British Journal of Obstetrics and Gynaecology, 99,* 1000–1003.

Vostanis, P., Harrington, R., Prendergast, M., & Farndon, P. (1994). Case reports of autism with interstitial deletion of chromosome 17 (p11.2 p11.2) and monosomy of chromosome 5 (5pter | 5p15.3). *Psychiatric Genetics, 4,* 109–111.

Vuchinich, S., Vuchinich, R., & Wood, B. (1993). The interparental relationship and family problem solving with preadolescent males. *Child Development, 64,* 1389–1400.

Vygotsky, L. S. (1977). *Mind in society: The development of higher psychological processes.* Cambridge, MA: Harvard University Press.

Vygotsky, L. S. (1986). *Thought and language* (translated and revised by A. Kozulin). Cambridge, MA: MIT Press.

Wachs, T. D., McCabe, G., Moussa, W., Yunis, F., et al. (1996). Cognitive performance of Egyptian adults as a function of nutritional intake and sociodemographic factors. *Intelligence, 22,* 129–154.

Waddington, C. H. (1975). *The evolution of an evolutionist.* Edinburgh, Scotland: Edinburgh University Press.

Wadsworth, B. J. (1996). *Piaget's theory of cognitive and affective development* (5th ed.). New York: Longman.

Walasky, M., Whitbourne, S. K., & Nehrke, M. F. (1983/1984). Construction and validation of an ego integrity status interview. *International Journal of Aging and Human Development, 18,* 61–72.

Walker, L. J., Pitts, R. C., Hennig, K. H., & Matsuba, M. K. (1995). Reasoning about morality and real-life moral problems. In M. Killen & D. Hart (Eds.), *Morality in everyday life: Developmental perspectives.* New York: Cambridge University Press.

Wallace, J. E. (1995). Corporatist control and organizational commitment among professionals: The case of lawyers working in law firms. *Social Forces, 73,* 811–840.

Wallach, M. A., & Kogan, N. (1965). *Modes of thinking in young children: A study of the creativity–intelligence distinction.* New York: Holt, Rinehart & Winston.

Wallerstein, J. S. (1989, Jan. 23). Children after divorce: Wounds that don't heal. *New York Times Magazine,* pp. 19–21, 41–44.

Wallerstein, J. S., & Kelly, J. B. (1976). The effects of parental divorce: Experiences of the child in later latency. *American Journal of Orthopsychiatry, 46,* 256–269.

Wallerstein, J. S., & Kelly, J. B. (1980). *Surviving the breakup: How children and parents cope with divorce.* London: Grant McIntyre.

Walma van der Molen, J. H., & van der Voort, T. H. A. (1997). Children's recall of television and print news: A media comparison study. *Journal of Educational Psychology, 39,* 82–91.

Walton, S. J. (1994). Date rape: New liability for colleges and universities. *Naspa Journal, 31,* 195–200.

Wang, I. Y., & Fraser, I. S. (1994). Reproductive function and contraception in the postpartum period. *Obstetrical and Gynecological Survey, 49,* 56–63.

Wang, M. C., Haertel, G. D., & Walberg, H. J. (1993). Toward a knowledge base for school learning. *Review of Educational Research, 63,* 249–294.

War Crimes. (1994, Feb. 13). *Edmonton Sun,* p. 13.

Warah, A. (1993). Overactivity and boundary setting in anorexia nervosa: An existential perspective. *Journal of Adolescence, 16,* 93–100.

Ward, B. (1993). *Good grief: Exploring feelings, loss, and death with under elevens: A holistic approach.* Bristol, PA: Jessica Kingsley.

Ward, J. (1994). Exercise and the older person. *Australian Family Physician, 23,* 642–645.

Ward, R. A. (1993). Marital happiness and household equity in later life. *Journal of Marriage and the Family, 55,* 427–438.

Ward, S. K., Chapman, K., Cohn, E., White, S., & Williams, K. (1991). Acquaintance rape and the college social scene. *Family Relations, 40,* 65–71.

Warfield-Coppock, N. (1992). The rites of passage movement: A resurgence of African-centered practices for socializing African American youth. *Journal of Negro Education, 61,* 471–482.

Warner, J. E., & Hansen, D. J. (1994). The identification and reporting of physical abuse by physicians: A review and implications for research. *Child Abuse and Neglect: The International Journal, 18,* 11–25.

Warren, S. L., Huston, L., Egeland, B., & Sroufe, L. A. (1997). Child and adolescent anxiety disorders and early attachment. *Journal of the American Academy of Child and Adolescent Psychiatry, 36,* 637–644.

Washton, A. M. (1989). *Cocaine addiction: Treatment, recovery, and relapse prevention.* New York: Norton.

Waskel, S. A. (1995). Temperament types: Midlife death concerns, demographics, and intensity of crisis. *Journal of Psychology, 129,* 221–233.

Waskel, S. A., & Phelps, L. H. (1995). Women ages 30–60 and their crisis events. *Psychological Reports, 77,* 1211–1217.

Waters, E., Hay, D., & Richters, J. (1986). Infant–parent attachment and the origins of prosocial and antisocial behavior. In D. Olweus, J. Block, & M. Radke-Yarrow (Eds.), *Development of antisocial and prosocial behavior: Research, theories, and issues.* New York: Academic Press.

Watson, J. B. (1914). *Behavior: An introduction to comparative psychology.* New York: Holt, Rinehart & Winston.

Watson, J. B. (1930). *Behaviorism* (2nd ed.). Chicago: University of Chicago Press.

Watson, J. B., & Rayner, R. (1920). Conditioned emotional reactions. *Journal of Experimental Psychology, 3,* 1–14.

Watson, P. (1994, Dec. 14). Somali crowd cheers each stone as Islamic justice dispatches rapist. *Edmonton Journal,* p. A1, A16.

Wattam-Bell, J. R. B. (1996). Development of visual motion processing. In F. Vital-Durand, J. Atkinson, & O. J. Braddick (Eds.), *Infant vision.* New York: Oxford University Press.

Watts, W. D., & Wright, L. S. (1990). The relationship of alcohol, tobacco, marijuana, and other illegal drug use to delinquency among Mexican-American, black, and white adolescent males. *Adolescence, 25,* 171–181.

Weber, K. S., Frankenberg, W., & Heilman, K. (1992). The effects of Ritalin on the academic achievement of children diagnosed with attention-deficit hyperactivity disorder. *Developmental Disabilities Bulletin, 20,* 49–68.

Webster, J. D., & Young, R. A. (1988). Process variables of the life review: Counseling implications. *International Journal of Aging and Human Development, 26,* 315–323.

Weinberg, R. (1989). Intelligence and IQ. *American Psychologist, 44,* 98–104.

Weiner, B. (1980). *Human motivation.* New York: Holt, Rinehart & Winston.

Weiner, B. (1994). Integrating social and personal theories of achievement striving. *Review of Educational Research, 64,* 557–573.

Weis, D. L. (1983). "Open" marriage and multilateral relationships: The emergence of nonexclusive models of the marital relationship. In E. D. Macklin and R. H. Rubin (Eds.), *Contemporary Families and Alternative Lifestyles: Handbook on Research and Theory.* Beverly Hills, CA: Sage.

Weisfeld, G. E. (1982). The nature–nurture issue and the integrating concept of function. In B. B. Wolman et al. (Eds.), *Handbook of developmental psychology.* Englewood Cliffs, NJ: Prentice-Hall.

Weiss, L. H., & Schwarz, J. C. (1996). The relationship between parenting types and older adolescents' personality, academic achievement, adjustment, and substance use. *Child Development, 67,* 2101–2114.

Weisskopf, M. (1987). Lead astray: The poisoning of America. *Discovery, 8,* 76–77.

Wellman, H. M. (1988). The early development of memory strategies. In F. E. Weinert & M. Perlmutter (Eds.), *Memory development: Universal changes and individual differences.* Hillsdale, NJ: Erlbaum.

Wellman, H. M. (1990). *The child's theory of mind.* Cambridge, MA: MIT Press.

Wellman, H. M., & Gelman, S. A. (1992). Cognitive development: Foundational theories of core domains. *Annual Review of Psychology, 43,* 337–375.

Wellman, M. M. (1993). Child sexual abuse and gender differences: Attitudes and prevalence. *Child Abuse and Neglect: The International Journal, 17,* 539–547.

Wells, G. (1985). *Language development in the pre-school years.* Cambridge: Cambridge University Press.

Werner, E. E. (1993). Children of the garden island. In M. Gauvain & M. Cole (Eds.), *Readings on the development of children.* New York: W. H. Freeman.

Westbury, I. (1992). Comparing American and Japanese achievement: Is the United States really a low achiever? *Educational Researcher, 21,* 18–24.

Westbury, I., Ethington, C., Sosniak, L., & Baker, D. (Eds.). (1993). *In search of more effective mathematics education: Examining data from the IEA Second International Mathematics Study.* Norwood, NJ: Ablex.

Westman, J. C. (1991). Introduction. In J. C. Westman (Ed.), *Who speaks for the children?* Sarasota, FL: Professional Resource Exchange.

Westoff, L. A., & Westoff, C. L. (1971). *From now to zero.* Boston: Little, Brown.

Westrom, L. V. (1994). Sexually transmitted diseases and infertility. *Sexually Transmitted Diseases, 21,* S32–S37.

Wetzler, S., Asnis, G. M., Hyman, R. B., Virtue, C., et al. (1996). Characteristics of suicidality among adolescents. *Suicide and Life-Threatening Behavior, 26,* 37–45.

Whaley, D. E., & Ebbeck, V. (1997). Older adults' constraints to participation in structured exercise classes. *Journal of Aging and Physical Activity, 5,* 190–212.

Whiffen, V. E., & Gotlib, I. H. (1993). Comparison of postpartum and nonpostpartum depression: Clinical presentation, psychiatric history, and psychosocial functioning. *Journal of Personality and Social Psychology, 61,* 485–494.

Whitaker, L. C., & Slimak, R. E. (Eds.). (1990). *College student suicide.* New York: Haworth.

White, B. L. (1985). *The first three years of life* (rev. ed.). Englewood Cliffs, NJ: Prentice-Hall.

White, D., & Woollett, A. (1992). *Families: A context for development.* New York: Falmer.

White, J., Campbell, L., Steward, A., Davies, M., et al. (1997). The relationships of psychological birth order to career interests. *Individual Psychology: Journal of Adlerian Theory, Research and Practice, 53,* 89–104.

White, K. R., Taylor, M. J., & Moss, V. D. (1992). Does research support claims about the benefits of involving parents in early intervention programs? *Review of Educational Research, 62,* 91–125.

Whitney, E. N., & Hamilton, E. M. N. (1984). *Understanding nutrition* (3rd ed.). St. Paul, MN: West.

Whorf, B. L. (1956). *Language, thought and reality.* New York: John Wiley.

Widiger, T. A., & Smith, G. T. (1994). Substance use disorder: Abuse, dependence and dyscontrol. *Addiction, 89,* 267–282.

Widstrom, A. M., & Thingstrom-Paulsson, J. (1993). The position of the tongue during rooting reflexes elicited in newborn infants before the first suckle. *Acta Paediatrica, 82,* 281–283.

Wiebe, E., & Wiebe, A. (1994). Fragile X syndrome. *Canadian Family Physician, 40,* 290–295.

Wigfield, R., Gilbert, R., & Fleming, P. J. (1994). SIDS: Risk reduction measures. Conference on Ethnicity and the Sudden Infant Death Syndrome (1993, Cardiff, Wales). *Early Human Development, 38,* 161–164.

Wiggins, J. S., & Pincus, A. L. (1992). Personality: Structure and assessment. *Annual Review of Psychology, 43,* 473–504.

Wilbush, J. (1994). Confrontation in the climacteric. *Journal of the Royal Society of Medicine, 87,* 342–347.

Wilcox, B. L., Robbennolt, J. K., O'Keeffe, J. E., & Pynchon, M. E. (1996). Teen nonmarital childbearing and welfare: The gap between research and political discourse. *Journal of Social Issues, 52,* 71–90.

Wiley, D. C., Gay, J., Jordon-Belver, C., Furney, S., et al. (1996). Assessing the health behaviors of Texas college students. *Journal of American College Health, 44,* 167–172.

Wilfley, D. E., Agras, W. S., Telch, C. F., Rossiter, E. M., Schneider, J. A., Cole, A. G., Sifford, L. A., & Raeburn, S. D. (1993). Group cognitive–behavioral therapy and group interpersonal psychotherapy for the nonpurging bulimic individual: A controlled comparison. *Journal of Consulting & Clinical Psychology, 61,* 296–305.

Wilk, C. A. (1986). *Career women and childbearing: A psychological analysis of the decision process.* New York: Van Nostrand Reinhold.

Williams, K., Haywood, K., & Vansant, A. (1991). Throwing patterns of older adults: A follow-up investigation. *International Journal of Aging and Human Development, 33,* 279–294.

Williams, T. H., & Handford, A. G. (1986). Television and other leisure activities. In T. H. Williams (Ed.), *The impact of television: A natural experiment in three communities.* Orlando, FL: Academic Press.

Willis, S. L. (1997). Intervening in age-related cognitive decline in late life. In H. M. Fillit & R. N. Butler (Eds.), *Cognitive decline: Strategies for prevention.* London: Greenwich Medical Media.

Willis, S. L., & Schaie, K. W. (1994). Assessing everyday competence in the elderly. In C. B. Fisher & R. M. Lerner (Eds.), *Applied developmental psychology.* New York: McGraw-Hill.

Willoughby, D. S., Roozen, M., & Barnes, R. (1997). Effects of aerobic exercise on the functional capacity and cardiovascular efficiency of elderly post–CABG patients. *Journal of Aging and Physical Activity, 5,* 87–97.

Wilmoth, T. A., & Elder, J. P. (1995). An assessment of research on breast-feeding promotion strategies in developing countries. *Social Science and Medicine, 41,* 579–594.

Wilson, A. L. (1997). State of South Dakota's child: 1996. *South Dakota Journal of Medicine, 50,* 11–16.

Wilson, D. S. (1994). Adaptive genetic variation and human evolutionary psychology. *Ethology and Sociobiology, 15,* 219–225.

Wilson, E. O. (1975). *Sociobiology: The new synthesis.* Cambridge, MA: Belknap.

Wilson, E. O. (1976). Academic vigilantism and the political significance of sociobiology. *Bio-science, 183,* 187–190.

Wilson, G. T. (1994). Behavioral treatment of obesity: Thirty years and counting. *Advances in Behavior Research and Therapy, 16,* 31–75.

Wilson, G. T., & Fairburn, C. G. (1993). Cognitive treatments for eating disorders. *Journal of Consulting and Clinical Psychology, 61,* 261–269.

Wilson, M. E., Hall, E. O., & White, M. A. (1994). Family dynamics and infant temperament in Danish families. *Scandinavian Journal of Caring Sciences, 8,* 9–15.

Windle, R. C., & Windle, M. (1995). Longitudinal patterns of physical aggression: Associations with adult social, psychiatric, and personality functioning and testosterone levels. *Development and Psychopathology, 7,* 563–585.

Winer, G. A., & McGlone, C. (1993). On the uncertainty of conservation: Responses to misleading conservation questions. *Developmental Psychology, 29,* 760–769.

Wink, P. (1996). Transition from the early 40s to the early 50s in self-directed women. *Journal of Personality, 64,* 49–69.

Winnicott, D. W. (1971). *Playing and reality.* New York: Basic Books.

Wisniewski, H. M., Silverman, W., & Wegiel, J. (1994). Ageing, Alzheimer disease and mental retardation. *Journal of Intellectual Disability Research, 38,* 233–239.

Witt, S. D. (1997). Parental influence on children's socialization to gender roles. *Adolescence, 32,* 253–259.

Wolff, P. H. (1963). Observations of the early development of smiling. In B. M. Foss (Ed.), *Determinants of infant behavior 2.* London: Methuen.

Wolff, P. H. (1966). The causes, controls, and organization of behavior in the neonate. *Psychological Issues, 5(1)* (Whole No. 17), 1–105.

Wolff, P. H. (1969). The natural history of crying and other vocalizations in early infancy. In B. Foss (Ed.), *Determinants of infant behavior 4.* London: Methuen.

Wolke, D., Gray, P., & Meyer, R. (1994). Excessive infant crying: A controlled study of mothers helping mothers. *Pediatrics, 94,* 322–333.

Wolman, W. L., Chalmers, B., Hofmeyr, F. J., & Nikodem, V. C. (1993). Postpartum depression and companionship in the clinical birth environment. *American Journal of Obstetrics & Gynecology, 168,* 1388–1393.

Wong, J. S., Wong, P. K., & Yech, R. L. (1995). Ocular manifestations in shaken baby syndrome. *Singapore Medical Journal, 36,* 391–392.

Wood, B. S. (1981). *Children and communication: Verbal and nonverbal language development.* (2nd ed.). Englewood Cliffs, NJ: Prentice-Hall.

Worden, W. (1982). *Grief counseling and grief therapy: A handbook for the mental health practitioner.* New York: Springer.

Workman, J. E., & Orr, R. L. (1996). Clothing, sex of subject, and rape myth acceptance as factors affecting attributions about an incident of acquaintance rape. *Clothing and Textiles Research Journal, 14,* 276–284.

Wright, H. F. (1960). Observational child study. In P. H. Mussen (Ed.), *Handbook of research methods in child development.* New York: John Wiley.

Wu, D. Y. H. (1981). Child abuse in Taiwan. In J. E. Korbin (Ed.), *Child abuse and neglect: Cross-cultural perspectives.* Berkeley: University of California Press.

Wyrwicka, W. (1996). *Imitation in human and animal behavior.* New Brunswick, NJ: Transaction.

Yamamoto, N., & Wallhagen, M. I. (1997). The continuation of family caregiving in Japan. *Journal of Health and Social Behavior, 38,* 164–176.

Yarrow, I. J., & Goodwin, M. S. (1973). The immediate impact of separation: Reactions of infants to a change in mother figures. In L. J. Stone, H. T. Smith, & L. B. Murphy (Eds.), *The competent infant: Research and commentary.* New York: Basic Books.

Yoshida, K., & Kumar, R. (1996). Breast feeding and psychotropic drugs. *International Review of Psychiatry, 8,* 117–124.

Zajonc, R. B. (1976). Family configuration and intelligence. *Science, 192,* 227–236.

Zajonc, R. B., & Mullally, P. R. (1997). Birth order: Reconciling conflicting effects. *American Psychologist, 52,* 685–699.

Zani, B. (1991). Male and female patterns in the discovery of sexuality during adolescence. *Journal of Adolescence, 14,* 163–178.

Zentall, S. S. (1993). Research on the educational implications of attention deficit hyperactivity disorder. *Exceptional Children, 60,* 143–153.

Zigler, E. (1994). Reshaping early childhood intervention to be a more effective weapon against poverty. *American Journal of Community Psychology, 22,* 37–47.

Zigler, E., & Freedman, J. (1987). Early experience, malleability, and Head Start. In J. J. Gallagher & C. T. Ramey (Eds.), *The malleability of children.* Baltimore: Brookes.

Zigler, E., & Hodapp, R. M. (1991). Behavioral functioning in individuals with mental retardation. *Annual Review of Psychology, 42,* 29–50.

Zigler, E. F., Kagan, S. L., & Hall, N. W. (Eds.). (1996). *Children, families, and government: Preparing for the twenty-first century.* New York: Cambridge University Press.

Zigler, E. F., & Styfco, S. (1996). Head Start and early childhood intervention: The changing course of social science and social policy. In E. F. Zigler, S. L. Kagan, & N. W. Hall (Eds.), *Children, families, and government: Preparing for the twenty-first century.* New York: Cambridge University Press.

Zimmerman, M. A., Copeland, L. A., & Shope, J. T. (1997). A longitudinal study of self-esteem: Implications for adolescent development. *Journal of Youth and Adolescence, 26,* 117–141.

Zuckerman, B., & Bresnahan, K. (1991). Developmental and behavioral consequences of prenatal drug and alcohol exposure. *Pediatric Clinics of North America, 38,* 1387–1406.

Glossary

This glossary defines the most important terms and expressions used in this text. They are boldfaced throughout the text, and most are listed as study terms at the end of each chapter. In each case, the meaning given corresponds to the text usage. (The number after each definition indicates the page (or pages) on which the term is discussed.) For more complete definitions, consult a standard psychological dictionary.

Acceptance   The fifth stage in Kübler-Ross's description of dying, marked by resignation. 548

Accommodation   The modification of an activity or an ability that the child already has in order to conform to environmental demands. Piaget's description of development holds that assimilation and accommodation are the means by which an individual interacts with and adapts to the world. 46, 141

Achieving stage   A Schaie early-adulthood stage of cognitive development during which the individual becomes increasingly concerned with learning things that will be useful in achieving goals (such as career goals). (See *acquisition stage; responsibility stage; executive stage; reintegration stage.*) 399

Acquaintance rape   Forcible sexual intercourse where the victim and the perpetrator are at least acquaintances. Also labeled *date rape.* 432

Acquired immune deficiency syndrome (AIDS)   An incurable and fatal disease, transmitted through the exchange of body fluids. 102, 360

Acquisition stage   The first of Schaie's stages of adult cognitive development, spanning childhood and adolescence, and marked by the acquisition of information without much regard for its long-term importance. (See *achieving stage; responsibility stage; executive stage; reintegration stage.*) 399

Active vocabulary   Consists of words the child actually uses. (See *passive vocabulary.*) 147

Activity theory   A theory of aging based on the belief that successful aging is more likely among those who remain most involved in world and community affairs. (See *disengagement theory.*) 523

Acute brain syndrome   A transient (as opposed to recurring) condition that may be characterized by confusion, speech disturbances, hysteria, paranoia, or other symptoms of mental disturbance. Often seen in the elderly, and often associated with drug overdoses. 499

Acute pelvic inflammatory disease   A sexually transmitted disease that frequently results from other STDs such as gonorrhea. Also termed salpingitis or endometritis, pelvic inflammatory disease affects about 1 million women a year and is often associated with infertility and tubal pregnancies. 361

Adaptation   Changes in an organism in response to the environment. Such changes are assumed to facilitate interaction with the environment. Adaptation plays a central role in Piaget's theory. 46, 141

Additive bilingualism   Phrase used to describe situations in which learning a second language has a positive effect on the first, as well as on general psychological functioning. (See *subtractive bilingualism.*) 207

Adolescence   A general term for the period from the onset of puberty to adulthood and typically including the teenage years. 312

Adolescent egocentrism   A cognitive and emotional self-centeredness characteristic of the adolescent, resulting from a confusion of the thoughts of the self with those of others. Evident in the imaginary audience and the personal fable. (See *imaginary audience* and *personal fable.*) 327

Adolescent moratorium   Erikson's term for the social function of the hiatus between childhood and adulthood. The adolescent period is a moratorium in that it provides the child with a period of time during which to experiment with various identities. 344

Adrenal glands   Part of the endocrine gland system. A pair of ductless glands near the kidneys, the main function of which is to produce epinephrine (adrenaline) and certain steroids. Also produce a small amount of estrogen and other sex hormones. 446

Adultery   Voluntary sexual intercourse, while married, with someone other than the spouse. Extramarital sex. 419

Affiliation   A positive emotional relationship. Affiliative behavior is evident in behavior designed to make friends and includes talking, smiling, and playing with others. Affiliation implies a weaker relationship than does attachment.

Affiliative behaviors   Behaviors that indicate wanting to interact with or do things with someone—for example, smiling, looking at, laughing, and giving things to. Contrasted with attachment, a more powerful emotional bond evident in seeking to be close, clinging, wanting to be picked up, putting the head in the lap, snuggling, and so on. 170

AFP test   A screening test designed to detect the likelihood of a fetal neural tube defect by revealing the presence of alphafetoprotein in the mother's blood. 82

Afterbirth   The placenta and other membranes that are expelled from the uterus following childbirth. 111

Ageism   Negative stereotyped prejudice based on age; common with respect to the elderly. 488

Aggression   Actions intended to dominate, to control, to frighten, to humiliate. May take the form of overt or social aggression. (See *overt aggression; social aggression; violence.*)

Alzheimer's disease   A disease associated with old age (but also occurring as young as forty), marked by progressive loss of memory, loss of brain function, and eventual death. 499

Amenorrhea   Cessation of menstruation, or failure to begin—as opposed to normal termination following menopause. (See *menopause.*) 105

Amniocentesis   A procedure in which amniotic fluid is removed by a hollow needle from around the fetus in a pregnant woman. Subsequent analysis of this fluid may reveal chromosomal aberrations (Down syndrome, for example) and other fetal problems. 84

Amniotic fluid   A clear or straw-colored fluid in which the fetus develops in the uterus. 84

Amniotic sac   The sac, filled with amniotic fluid, in which the fetus develops in the uterus. 109

Anal stage   The second of Freud's psychosexual stages of development, beginning at approximately eight months and lasting until around eighteen months. It is characterized by the child's preoccupation with physical anal activities. 33

Androgynous   Characterized by a balance of masculine and feminine characteristics. 225, 351, 469

Anencephalic   A condition involving missing parts or all of the brain. 162

Anger   The second stage in Kübler-Ross's description of dying, marked by resentment at being singled out to die. 548

Animistic thinking   Attributing lifelike qualities to inanimate objects. In Piaget's theory, young preschoolers are sometimes described as using animistic thinking. 193

Anorexia nervosa   A medical condition not due to any detectable illness, primarily affecting adolescent girls, and involving a loss of 15 to 25 percent of ideal body weight and subsequent refusal or inability to eat normally. 304, 320

Anoxia   A condition in which there is an insufficient supply of oxygen to the brain. 115

Anticipatory grief   Refers to the grief reactions that people experience in the time between learning that someone is terminally ill and the actual death. 553

Anxiety   An unpleasant emotional reaction whose most identifiable characteristic is fear. Anxiety can vary from mild trepidation to severe panic, and appears to be implicated in many mental disorders. 386

Apgar scale   Widely used standardized evaluation procedure for newborns that looks at their heart rate, respiration, muscle tone, color, and reflexive responses. 113

Apnea   Cessation of breathing during sleep, often accompanied or caused by a temporary collapse or paralysis of throat muscles. Severe cases can be fatal. Sometimes associated with SIDS. (See *SIDS.*) 129

Arousal   A term with both physiological and psychological meaning. Physiologically, arousal refers to changes in heart rate, respiration, brain activity, and so on. Psychologically, it refers to corresponding changes in alertness or vigilance. 45

Arteriosclerosis   Thickening and hardening of artery walls; associated with aging. (See *atherosclerosis.*) 443, 497

Artificial insemination   A breeding procedure often used in animal husbandry and sometimes with humans. The procedure eliminates the need for a physical union between male and female. 66, 92

Assimilation   The act of incorporating objects or aspects of objects to previously learned activities. To assimilate is, in a sense, to ingest or to use something that is previously learned; more simply, it is the exercise of previously learned responses. 46, 141

Association   Relates to associationism, a term employed almost synonymously with stimulus–response learning. Associationism refers to the formation of associations or links between stimuli, between responses, or between stimuli and responses. 38

Associative play   A sort of parallel play where two children play independently sharing toys or even activities, but not sharing rules or goals. (See *cooperative play; parallel play; onlooker play; primitive social play; solitary play.*) 223

Atherosclerosis   The gradual accumulation of plaque (fatty deposits) on the insides of blood vessels. (See *arteriosclerosis.*) 443

Attachment   A powerful emotional bond. Parent–infant attachment is important for healthy infant development. 164, 165

Attention deficit disorder (ADD)   A disorder primarily characteristic of childhood, marked by consistent problems in paying attention. More common among boys than girls. When accompanied by serious *hyperactivity,* labeled *attention deficit hyperactivity disorder (ADHD)*. (See *attention deficit hyperactivity disorder [ADHD]*.) 302

Attention deficit hyperactivity disorder (ADHD)   A disorder marked by excessive general activity relative to the child's age, attention problems, high impulsivity, and low frustration tolerance. 302

Attention span   In one sense, equivalent to short-term memory, hence the amount of information that can be held in immediate consciousness. Thought to be limited to seven plus or minus two items. More colloquially, refers to the amount of time during which an individual is able (or willing) to persist at a given task. 257

Attribution   An assignment of cause or blame for the outcomes of our behaviors. Our attributions are important influences on our behavior. 290

Authoritarian parenting   A highly controlling, dogmatic, obedience-oriented parenting style in which there is little recourse to reasoning and no acceptance of the child's autonomy. 229

Authoritative parenting   A moderately controlling parenting style in which value is placed on independence and reasoning, but in which parents impose some regulations and controls. 230

Autism   A serious childhood mental disorder that is usually apparent by age three and that is characterized by social unresponsiveness, poor or nonexistent communication skills, and bizarre behavior. 178

Autoimmunity   A malfunction in the body's disease-fighting capabilities whereby the body's own benign cells are identified as harmful and thus attacked. Autoimmunity is thought to be involved in some age-related diseases. 494

Automatic responding   Behaviors that can be performed with little or no conscious attention. Well-practiced, habitual responses. 505

Autonomy   Piaget's label for the second stage of moral development, marked by a reliance on internal standards as guides for behaving and for judging morality. (See *heteronomy*.) 332

Autonomy versus shame and doubt   The second Erikson stage, about ages eighteen months to two or three years, when the preschooler faces the challenge of developing a sense of mastery and control (autonomy) and giving up some of the security of relying on parents. 35, 216

Autosome   Any chromosome in mature sperm and ova other than the sex chromosome. Each of these cells therefore contains twenty-two autosomes. 68

Average-for-gestational age (AGA)   Infants weighing between the tenth and the ninetieth percentile with respect to average weight of infants of their gestational age. (See *large-for-gestational age; small-for-gestational age*.) 112

Axillary hair   Armpit hair. 315

Babbling   The relatively meaningless sounds that young infants make or repeat.

Babinski reflex   A reflex present in the newborn child but disappearing later in life. When infants' feet are tickled in the center of their soles, the toes fan outward. Normal adults curl their toes inward. 95, 131

Baby tossing   The medieval practice of tossing infants from one player to another in a bizarre game; the object was to throw accurately and not drop the baby. Someone usually lost. 12

Balanced bilinguals   People who are equally proficient in two languages—that is, for whom neither language is clearly dominant or preferred. 207

Bargaining   The third stage in Kübler-Ross's description of dying, characterized by the patient's attempts to look after unfinished business. 548

Basic gender understanding   An early stage in the development of gender awareness where the infant recognizes that there are two different genders and that he is a boy or she is a girl. 225

Basic need   An unlearned physiological requirement of the human organism. Specifically, the need for food, drink, and sex. 56

Behavior modification   A general term for the application of behavioristic principles (primarily those of operant conditioning) in systematic and deliberate attempts to change behavior. 40

Behaviorism   A general term used to describe approaches to learning and development that are concerned primarily with the observable, objective components of behavior (such as stimuli and responses). 37

Behavioristic theory   A general term for those theories of learning that are primarily concerned with the observable components of behavior (stimuli and responses). Such theories are labeled S–R learning theories and are exemplified in classical and operant conditioning. 37

Bereavement   A term used to describe the loss suffered by friends and relatives of a person who has died. 543

Bidirectionality   Describes the reciprocal effects on one another of people or people and their environment. 5

Bigamy   Legal term for the crime of marrying someone while still legally married to someone else. 419

Bilingual   Proficient in two languages, as opposed to *monolingual* (only one language) or *trilingual* (three languages) or *multilingual* (many languages). 207

Birth order   The position that a child occupies in a family (for example, first-, second-, or third-born). 232

Body Mass Index (BMI)   The ratio of height to weight, computed by dividing weight in kilograms by the square of height in meters. Normal BMI is between about 20 and 27 (somewhat higher with increasing age). Indexes above and below these cutoffs indicate that one is obese or underweight. 319, 384

Bogeyman A childish invention that personifies the source of bad things. Death is sometimes attributed to the *bogeyman*. 544

Brazelton Neonatal Behavioral Assessment Scale (NBAS) A wide-ranging assessment scale for newborns that looks at a large number of different reflexes and several dozen different types of behaviors. 113

Breech birth An abnormal presentation of the fetus at birth with the buttocks first rather than the head first. 110

Bulimia nervosa Significant overconcern over body shape and weight, manifested in recurrent episodes of binge eating often accompanied by self-induced vomiting, use of laxatives or diuretics, strict fasting, or vigorous exercise. 322

Burnout A general term used to describe the effects of stress associated with job overload. Often expressed in a feeling of not being able to cope. 457

Bystander apathy The well-researched tendency of many people not to intervene even when they witness some horrendous act being perpetrated. 330

Canalization Waddington's term to describe the extent to which genetically determined characteristics are resistant to environmental influences. A highly canalized trait (such as hair color) remains unchanged in the face of most environmental influences; less canalized characteristics (such as manifested intelligence) are highly influenced by the environment. 70

Cardinal properties With respect to number, the fact that they represent a collection of specified magnitude (that is, one, two, or what have you items). (See *ordinal properties*.) 256

Care facilities for the elderly Any of a number of different facilities dedicated to the care of the elderly ranging from homes where residents are highly independent and self-sufficient to facilities where care is provided on a full-time basis. 532

Career A broad term including a range of related occupations or jobs that often span an entire working lifetime. (See *job; work; occupation*.) 391

Career self-efficacy The individual's expectations of success and competence in a career. Closely tied to sex, previous achievement, interests, and experience. 396, 458

Case study A research technique in the social sciences where investigators do an in-depth analysis of an individual participant or of a small number of participants. 248

Cataracts A clouding of the eye caused by fibrous growth over the eyeball. Associated with aging and surgically correctable. 442

Cell error theory A theory of aging based on the notion that with the passage of time, certain changes occur in DNA material causing the cell to malfunction or to cease functioning. 494

Centenarians People who live to be 100 or more years old. 496

Cephalocaudal Referring to the direction of development, beginning with the head and proceeding outward toward the tail. Early infant development is cephalocaudal because children acquire control over their heads before gaining control over their limbs. 96, 134

Cerebral palsy Label for a collection of congenital motor problems associated with brain damage and manifested in motor problems of varying severity, and occasionally in other problems such as convulsions or behavior disorders. (See *significant developmental motor disability*.) 127, 176

Cervix The small circular opening to the womb (uterus) that dilates considerably during birth to allow passage of the child. 109

Cesarean delivery A common surgical procedure in which the fetus is delivered by means of an incision in the mother's abdomen and uterus. 111

Child maltreatment Any of a number of possible abusive actions taken with respect to someone under eighteen. Can take the form of neglect, physical abuse, sexual abuse, emotional maltreatment, or medical maltreatment. 295

Chlamydia A highly common STD, especially among women, often asymptotic (without apparent symptoms), especially in its early stages, and therefore often undetected and unreported. A common cause of infertility among women. 360

Chorion Part of the placenta, the flat membrane on the inside of the uterus, to which the umbilical cord is attached. (See *chorion villus sampling; placenta*.) 85

Chorion biopsy A procedure in which samples of the membrane lining the uterus are used to permit prenatal diagnosis of potential birth defects. 85

Chromosomal disorders Abnormalities, inconsistencies, or deformities in chromosomes, sometimes involving absent or extra chromosomes. 82

Chromosome A microscopic body in the nucleus of all human and plant cells containing genes—the carriers of heredity. Each mature human sex cell (sperm or ovum) contains twenty-three chromosomes, each containing countless numbers of genes.

Chunking A type of memory strategy (cognitive strategy) whereby related items are grouped into more easily remembered "chunks" (for example, a prefix and four digits for a phone number rather than seven unrelated numbers). 258

Cirrhosis A degenerative disease of the liver, often associated with excessive alcohol consumption. A common cause of death. 369

Class In logic, an abstraction signifying a collection of items (for example, people, ideas, things) that share one or more identifiable characteristics (for example, the class of blue things, or the class of blue things that are also round). 255

Classical conditioning   Also called learning through stimulus substitution, it involves the repeated pairing of two stimuli so that a previously neutral (conditioned) stimulus eventually elicits the same (conditioned) response that was previously evoked by the first (unconditioned) stimulus. Pavlov was the first to describe this type of conditioning. 38

Climacteric   Popularly called the "change of life" that accompanies middle age. It involves reduced reproductive capabilities in both men and women and culminates in menopause for women. (See *menopause*.) 445, 502

Climacteric syndrome   Medical label for symptoms that sometimes accompany the climacteric. Might include dizziness, hot flashes, headaches, mood fluctuations, and general weakness. 446

Clock Drawing Test   A cognitive screening test that can be used to assess memory loss. Requires drawing and identifying basic components of a clock face. 500

Clone   A genetically identical copy. Typically applied not to identical twins but to identical individuals produced through genetic manipulation. 67

Cocaine   A stimulant drug, ordinarily inhaled as a white powder, the primary effects of which are feelings of euphoria. 369

Cognition   To cognize is to know. Hence, cognition refers to knowing, understanding, problem solving, and related intellectual processes. 45

Cognitive   Descriptive of mental processes such as thinking, knowing, and remembering. Cognitive theories attempt to explain intellectual development and functioning. 40, 45

Cognitive–behavior therapy   A therapeutic approach that combines the use of reinforcement and/or punishment (behavioristic techniques) with more reason-based approaches. 323

Cognitive strategies   Procedures, knowledge, and information that relate to the processes involved in learning and remembering rather than to the content of what is learned. Cognitive strategies are used to identify problems, select approaches to their solution, monitor progress, and use feedback. Cognitive strategies are closely related to metacognition and metamemory. 257, 325

Cohabitation   Living together without being married. (See *common-law marriages*.) 414

Cohort   A group of individuals born within the same specific period of time. For example, the 1920s cohort includes those born between 1920 and 1929. 20, 449

Colic   Infant disorder characterized by excessive crying, often following feeding. More precisely, intense abdominal pain resulting from muscular spasms. 160

Commitment   The decision-making aspect of Sternberg's theory of love. Involves deciding that one is in love and deciding what to do as a consequence. (See *passion; intimacy; triangular theory of love*.) 411

Common-law marriages   Couple relationships established without a formal legal or religious marriage ceremony. In many jurisdictions, such unions nevertheless have legal status. 414, 415

Common sense   That which we use to bolster our arguments when we lack the support of either theory or data. Ironically, in spite of the fact that common sense is allegedly *common,* we often have a hard time deciding what is actually common sense and what is just plain stupid. 350

Commune   A community. A group of individuals joined by common beliefs and purpose. May take just about as many forms as there are different beliefs and purposes. 418

Communication   The transmission of messages. Communication does not require language, although it is greatly facilitated by it. Nonhuman animals communicate even though they do not possess language. 145

Compensation   A logical rule stating that certain changes can compensate for opposing changes, thereby negating their effects. For example, as a square object becomes thinner, it also becomes longer; increases in length compensate for decreases in width. These changes combine to negate any actual changes in the object's mass. 254

Compensatory preschool programs   Preschool education programs whose purpose is to make up for early disadvantages in the lives of some children. The best known of these programs in the United States is Project Head Start. (See *Project Head Start*.) 200

Competition   The process of contending with others with a view to obtaining a goal that cannot be shared by all competitors. (See *cooperation*.) 217

Concept   A collection of perceptual experiences or ideas related by virtue of their common properties. 192

Conception   The beginning of human and other animal life. Also called *fertilization,* conception occurs with the union of a sperm cell with an egg cell. 66, 92

Conceptualization   The forming of concepts (ideas or meanings). An intellectual process leading to thinking and understanding. 134

Concrete operations   The third of Piaget's four major stages, lasting from age seven or eight to approximately eleven or twelve, and characterized primarily by the child's ability to deal with concrete problems and objects, or objects and problems easily imagined in a concrete sense. 47, 252

Conditioned response   A response that is elicited by a conditioned stimulus. In some obvious ways, a conditioned response resembles its corresponding unconditioned response, although they are not identical. 39

Conditioned stimulus   A stimulus that either does not elicit any response or initially elicits a global orienting response. As a result of being paired with an unconditioned stimulus and its response, the conditioned stimulus comes to elicit the same response. For example, a stimulus that is always present at the time of a fear reaction may become a conditioned stimulus for fear. 39

Conditioning   A term that describes a simple type of learning. (See also *classical conditioning; operant conditioning*.) 38

Confluence model   Zajonc's term for the hypothesis that various factors such as family size, birth order, and family spacing interact to determine the intellectual climate of the home, and have a profound influence on the intellectual development of children. (See *birth order; family spacing; intellectual climate*.) 232

Congenital   Present at birth, although not necessarily inherited. For example, a birth defect would be *congenital* if it is due to the influence of drugs, and *genetic* if it is a condition determined by genetic makeup. 100, 176

Conscience   An internalized set of rules governing an individual's behavior. 32

Conservation   A Piagetian term implying that certain quantitative attributes of objects remain unchanged unless something is added to or taken away from them. Mass, number, area, and volume are capable of being conserved. 191, 253

Constructivism   A psychological–philosophical orientation that views the central problem in explaining cognitive development as one of understanding how the mind succeeds in inventing (constructing) relationships among objects and events. 48

Consummate love   According to Sternberg, love that is marked by a high degree of intimacy, passion, and commitment. Similar to what is sometimes labeled *romantic/ erotic love*. (See *romantic/erotic love*.) 412

Contextual model   A developmental model that emphasizes the importance of environmental variables such as culture, cohort, family, and historical events. This model maintains that in order to explain and understand human development, the context in which development occurs must be considered. 156

Contextual theory of intelligence   The label for Sternberg's belief that intelligence involves adaptation in real-life contexts (in contrast with the view that intelligence is best measured by means of abstract timed questions and problems). 263

Continuous society   A society that does not clearly mark passage from one period of life to another. (See *discontinuous society*.) 312

Control group   A group of subjects who are not experimented with but who are used as comparisons to an experimental group to ascertain whether an experimental procedure affected the experimental group. 17

Conventional   Kohlberg's second level of morality, reflecting a desire to establish and maintain good relations with others (law and order, obedience). 333

Convergent thinking   Guilford's expression for thinking that leads to a unique, correct solution, in contrast with *divergent thinking*, which leads to the production of a wide variety of different solutions. 272

Cooley's approach to self-worth   The belief that evaluation of self is a direct function of perceived notion of others' evaluation of the self. (See *James's approach to self-worth*.) 282

Cooperation   The process of working with others toward a shared goal. (See *competition*.) 217

Cooperative play   Where children play together, helping each other (cooperating) in the attainment of shared goals. (See *associative play; parallel play; onlooker play; primitive social play; solitary play*.) 223

Correlational fallacy   The apparently logical but often false assumption that if two events are related (correlated), one causes the other. 17

Correlational study   A study that looks at the relationship (correlation) between two or more variables— for example, home background and delinquency, or achievement and intelligence. 17

Crack   Name given to the drug that results when cocaine is "cooked down" with bicarbonate of soda to produce freebase cocaine (also called *rock*). It is usually smoked rather than snorted and produces a much stronger and more immediate rush than cocaine. 369

Creativity   Generally refers to the capacity of individuals to produce novel or original answers or products. The term *creative* is an adjective that may be used to describe people, products, or processes. 271

Cretinism   Congenital (present at birth) condition associated with thyroid deficiency; marked by retarded physical development, thyroidism, and mental retardation. 127

Critical period   The period during which an appropriate stimulus must be presented to an organism for imprinting to occur. 49, 165

Cross-linking theory   Describes an aging process whereby unexpected bonds form between body cells, altering the functioning of the cells. 494

Cross-sectional study   A technique in the investigation of human development that involves observing and comparing different subjects at different age levels. For example, a cross-sectional study might compare four- and six-year-olds by observing two different groups of children at the same time, one group consisting of four-year-old children and the other of six-year-old children. A longitudinal study would require that the same children be examined at age four and again at age six. 18, 449

Crystallized abilities Cattell's term for intellectual abilities that are highly dependent on experience (verbal and computational skills and general information, for example). These abilities may continue to improve well into old age. (See also *fluid abilities*.) 263, 450, 505

Culture fair A general label for intelligence tests that are less heavily biased in favor of the cultural groups for which the tests were initially designed and on which they have been normed—in other words, tests that are more fair to certain cultures. 000

Cyclic movements Expression used to describe the infant's spontaneous, regularly recurring, motor movements. 132

Cytomegalovirus A human herpes virus that is a major medical problem in individuals with immune system problems (such as HIV). One of the main infectious causes of mental retardation. 102

Daydreaming Engaging in waking dreams or reveries. Unlike sleeping dreams, daydreams are mainly under the dreamer's control. Daydreaming is a common form of children's imaginative play. It is also very common among adults, in spite of their grandmothers' repeated admonitions that they should "quit daydreaming and get to work." 222

Dead enders Kanter's term for those who don't reach very lofty heights in their career paths, either because they are in *low-ceiling* employment, where there are no opportunities for advancement, or because they take the wrong paths in *high-ceiling* employment. 398

Deadline decade Sheehy's term for the midlife transition. 469

Deafness The inability to hear sounds clearly enough for the ordinary purposes of life—as opposed to the *hard of hearing*. (See *hard of hearing*.) 251

Death Cessation of vital functioning. Medically, death is usually defined in terms of cessation of brain activity. 542

Death anxiety Fear of dying. A highly common human fear. In severe cases, may be pathological and interfere with the enjoyment of life. 544

Declarative memory Explicit, conscious long-term memory, in contrast with implicit (or nondeclarative) memory. Declarative memory may be either semantic or episodic. (See *semantic memory; episodic memory*.) 259, 503

Defense mechanism A relatively irrational and sometimes unhealthy method used by people to compensate for their inability to satisfy basic desires and to overcome the anxiety accompanying this inability. 34

Deferred imitation Imitating people or events in their absence. Deferred imitation is assumed by Piaget to be critical to developing language.

Delinquency A legal category defined by the apprehension and conviction of a juvenile for transgression of some law. 362

Dementia Term used to describe deterioration in mental functioning due to physiological causes. For example, dementia is often associated with Alzheimer's disease.

Denial The first stage in Kübler-Ross's description of the stages of dying, marked by an initial rejection of the diagnosis and its implications. 548

Denver II A developmental screening test that provides age norms corresponding to the levels at which 25, 50, 75, and 90 percent of children are expected to demonstrate a given capability (language, personal–social, fine motor, and gross motor). 187

Dependent variable The variable that may or may not be affected by manipulations of the independent variable in an experimental situation. 16

Depression The fourth stage in Kübler-Ross's description of dying, marked by intense sadness. 548

Despairing In Erikson's system, describes those who *have* struggled to achieve integrity but have failed and are now sad and depressed. (See *integrity achieving; dissonant; integrity foreclosed*.) 516

Development The total process whereby individuals adapt to their environment. Development includes growth, maturation, and learning. 6

Developmental arithmetic disorder A learning disability evident in specific problems in developing arithmetic skills in the absence of other problems such as mental retardation. 270

Developmental career model An approach to career guidance that attempts to prepare individuals for career choice by facilitating a sequence of decisions and personal preparations related to a career. (See *job–person matching*.) 392

Developmental coordination disorder A childhood motor skills disorder not associated with brain damage or cerebral palsy, often evident in difficulties in learning or in carrying out motor tasks. 177

Developmental psychology The study of changes in the behavior and thinking of human beings over time. 4

Developmental reading disorder A learning disability manifested in reading problems of varying severity—sometimes evident in spelling difficulties. Also labeled "dyslexia" or "specific reading disability." 270

Developmental task A social, cultural, or physical milestone that requires the development of new capabilities or the assumption of new responsibilities at a given developmental stage. Accomplishing a developmental task leads to adjustment and happiness; failure to do so may lead to unhappiness and difficulty with later tasks. 378, 440

Developmental theory A body of psychological theories concerned with the development of children from birth to maturity. 37

Developmental timetable A list of observable developmental achievements with information concerning the average ages at which populations of children normally attain these achievements. Such timetables are often used as instruments to assess the relative development of individual children. 187

Diabetes Disease associated with deficient secretion of insulin, resulting in abnormally high sugar levels in the blood and urine. 102

Dialectical schemata Basseches's expression for ways of thinking dialectically. For example, dialectical schemata might focus attention on relationships, on moral questions, on sources of conflict and agreement. Dialectical schemata are geared toward the recognition and resolution of conflict. (See *dialectical thinking*.) 452

Dialectical thinking According to Riegel, thinking that recognizes, accepts, and attempts to resolve conflicts. Dialectical thinking is thought to be more characteristic of adults than of children or adolescents. 400

Diary description As a method of child study, it involves recording sequential descriptions of a child's behavior at predetermined intervals (daily or weekly, for example). Sometimes useful for arriving at a better understanding of general developmental patterns. 17

Difficult infants A type of temperament characterized by irregularity with respect to things like eating, sleeping, and toilet functions; withdrawal from unfamiliar situations; slow adaptation to change; and intense as well as negative moods. 159

Dilation and curettage (D & C) A surgical procedure that involves scraping the walls of the uterus. It is occasionally necessary after birth if all of the placenta has not been expelled. 111

Discontinuous society A society that clearly marks passage from one developmental stage to another. Many nonindustrialized societies are labeled "discontinuous" because of their childhood-to-adulthood rites of passage. (See *continuous society*.) 312

Disengagement theory A theory of aging that holds that it is normal and useful for the elderly to disengage themselves from community and other involvements. (See *activity theory*.) 523

Disinhibitory effect See *inhibitory–disinhibitory effect*. 42, 217

Disorganized/disoriented Describes infants whose attachment behaviors toward caregivers are confused, unclear, and sometimes contradictory. 166

Dissonant Describes those among the elderly in crisis who are still struggling against despair, trying to achieve a sense of the meaningfulness of their lives. (See *integrity achieving; integrity foreclosed; despairing*.) 516

Dizygotic Resulting from two separate eggs and forming fraternal (nonidentical) twins. 75

D-lysergic acid diethylamide tartrate See *LSD*. 368

DNA (deoxyribonucleic acid) A substance assumed to be the basis of all life, consisting of four chemical bases arranged in an extremely large number of combinations. The two strands of the DNA molecule that compose genes are arranged in the form of a double spiral (helix). These double strands are capable of replicating themselves as well as crossing over from one strand of the spiral to the other and forming new combinations of their genetic material. The nuclei of all cells contain DNA molecules. 67

Dominant gene The gene (carrier of heredity) that takes precedence over all other related genes in genetically determined traits. Because all genes in the fertilized egg occur in pairs (one from the male and one from the female), a dominant gene as one member of the pair of genes means that the related hereditary characteristic will be present in the individual. 69

Double-blind procedure An experimental method in which experimenters collecting or analyzing data do not know which subjects are members of experimental or control groups. Double-blind procedures are used as a safeguard against experimenter bias. 23

Double career Expression that describes a situation in which the individual assumes responsibility for two careers simultaneously. Common among mothers who have both an out-of-home and a family-based career. (See *dual-career family*.) 457

Double helix The natural state of DNA molecules. Essentially, two spiraling, intertwining chains of corresponding molecules. 68

Down syndrome The most common chromosomal birth defect, related to the presence of an extra twenty-first chromosome (technically labeled Trisomy 21) and sometimes evident in mild to severe mental retardation. 82

Drug abuse The recreational use of drugs. The APA considers drug abuse a disorder when it impairs functioning. 365

Drug dependence A strong, sometimes overwhelming desire to continue taking a drug. (See also *physiological dependence; psychological dependence*.) 365

Drug tolerance A change resulting from drug use in which the user requires more frequent or stronger doses of the drug to maintain its initial effects. 365

Drugs Chemical substances that have marked physiological effects on living organisms. 365

Dual-career family A family in which both husband and wife develop separate, equally important careers, neither being sacrificed for the other—or for the family. (See *double career*.) 456

Dyadic interaction An interaction involving two principals. For example, mother–infant interaction. 156

Dying trajectories An expression used in reference to the process of dying. Dying trajectories are temporal—that is, described in terms of time (for example, expected swift death, expected lingering while dying, or expected temporary recovery). See *life trajectory.* 548

Dyslexia A form of learning disability manifested in reading problems of varying severity. Dyslexia may be evident in spelling errors that are erratic rather than consistent. 270

Dysphoria A general unhappiness. The opposite of *euphoria.* 422

Early adulthood A developmental period that spans the ages of twenty to forty or forty-five. 378

Early home leaver For research purposes, often defined as someone who leaves home before age eighteen (the typical age of high school graduation). 348

Easy infants A temperament type marked by high regularity in eating, sleeping, and so on; high interest in novel situations; high adaptability to change; and a preponderance of positive moods, as well as low or moderate intensity of reaction. 159

Ecological systems theory Label for Bronfenbrenner's theory, which is based on the notion that understanding human development requires understanding the interactions that occur between individuals and their contexts (their ecologies). 53

Ecological validity The extent to which conclusions and generalizations are applicable in different contexts. 23

Ecology The study of the interrelationships between organisms and their environment. In developmental psychology, ecology relates to the social context in which behavior and development occur. 5

Educable mentally retarded (EMR) Alternate label for those who are *mildly* retarded—approximately between IQ 50 and 70. 269

Egg cell See *ovum.* 66, 269

Ego The second stage of the human personality, according to Freud. It is the rational, reality-oriented level of human personality that develops as the child becomes aware of what the environment makes possible and impossible, thereby serving as a damper to the id. The id tends toward immediate gratification of impulses as they are felt, whereas the ego imposes restrictions that are based on environmental reality. 32

Ego transcendence vs. ego preoccupation An Eriksonian developmental stage described by Peck, characteristic of very late adulthood, marked by the need to accept the inevitability of dying without becoming preoccupied with it. 516

Egocentric Adjective based on Latin words for *self* (ego) and *center.* Literally, it describes a self-centered behavior, attitude, or personality characteristic. Although egocentrism often has negative connotations of selfishness, it is simply descriptive when applied to the child's perception of the world. For example, egocentric perception is characterized by an inability to assume an objective point of view. 194, 327

Egocentric speech Vygotsky's intermediate stage of language development, common between ages three and seven, during which children often talk to themselves in an apparent effort to control their own behavior. (See *inner speech; social speech.*) 52

Elaborating A long-term memory process involving changing or adding to material, or making associations to make remembering easier. (See *organizing; rehearsing.*) 140, 260

Elder abuse The maltreatment of the elderly. May be physical or emotional, and often involves neglect as well as overt actions. 532

Electra complex A Freudian development stage during which a girl's unconscious sexual feelings toward her father lead to jealousy of her mother. (See *Oedipus complex.*) 33

Electroencephalogram (EEG) A graphlike recording of the strength and nature of electrical activity in the brain. 542

Elicited response A response brought about by a stimulus. This expression is synonymous with the term *respondent.* 39

Eliciting effect That type of imitative behavior in which the observer does not copy the model's responses but simply behaves in a related manner. 43, 217

Embryo stage The second stage of prenatal development, lasting from the end of the second through the eighth week after conception. 93

Emitted response A response not elicited by a known stimulus but simply by the organism. An emitted response is an *operant.* 40

Emotional abuse Child maltreatment that causes emotional and psychological rather than physical harm (for example, shaming, ridiculing, ignoring, or humiliating children). A form of "mental cruelty" to children. 298

Emotional disorder (also termed *behavior disorder*) A classification used to include a wide range of nonphysical exceptionalities ranging from relatively minor behavior problems to serious mental disorders such as autism or schizophrenia. 301

Emotional display rules Implicit, socially accepted rules that tell us when it is appropriate to display emotion, how it should be displayed, and what other people's emotional displays mean. 220

Empowered A somewhat jargonistic term denoting a sense of personal power, a sense of control and responsibility over decisions that are personally important. 398

Empty nest phase The seventh stage in Duvall's family life cycle, beginning when the last child leaves home and lasting about fifteen years. 472

Endocrine glands   Ductless glands, such as the pituitary, the adrenals, and the gonads, that secrete hormones directly into the bloodstream. Centrally involved in regulating growth as well as sexual maturation and sexual behavior. 314

English Only   Highly vocal U.S. lobby group whose mission is to crusade for the establishment of English as the only official U.S. language. 209

English Plus   A U.S. lobby group that, in contrast to *English Only* and *U.S. English,* advocates publicly funded and expanded bilingual programs in U.S. schools. 209

Environment   The significant aspects of an individual's surroundings. Includes all experiences and events that influence the child's development. 64

Epidural analgesia   Injection of anesthetic commonly used to relieve childbirth pain. 111

Epigenesis   The developmental unfolding of genetically influenced characteristics. 71

Epigenetic landscape   Waddington's graphic analogy used to clarify the relationship between genetic forces and environmental forces. 71

Epilepsy   A seizure disorder, sometimes genetic in origin, varying in severity, often treatable or controllable with drugs. 177

Episiotomy   A small cut made in the vagina to facilitate the birth of a child. An episiotomy prevents the tearing of membranes and ensures that once the cut has been sutured, healing will be rapid and complete. 110

Episodic memory   A type of declarative, autobiographical (conscious, long-term) memory consisting of knowledge about personal experiences, tied to specific times and places. (See *semantic memory.*) 260, 503

Equilibration   A Piagetian term for the process by which we maintain a balance between assimilation (using old learning) and accommodation (changing behavior, learning new things). Equilibration is essential for adaptation and cognitive growth. 141

Erectile dysfunction   A male sexual disfunction, also termed *impotence.* The inability to achieve or maintain an erection. 389

Erikson Psychosocial Stage Inventory   An inventory (test questionnaire), the responses to which indicate generally the extent to which the individual has accomplished progressive psychosocial tasks that define Erikson's theory. 409

ESL   Acronym for *English as a second language.* Used as a label for educational programs designed to teach English to nonnative English speakers. 409

Estrogen   A female sex hormone. No longer produced after menopause. 446

Estrogen replacement therapy (ERT)   A medical treatment in which women whose production of hormones has declined or ceased—often because of menopause or surgical removal of the ovaries—are given estrogen. ERT has been found to reduce risk of osteoporosis but remains controversial given a possible link with cancer. 447

Ethologists   Scientists who study the behavior of animals in their natural habitats. 49, 165

Eugenics   A form of genetic engineering that selects specific individuals for reproduction. Although widely accepted and practiced with animals, as applied to humans, the concept raises many serious moral and ethical questions. 73

Euthanasia   Deliberate ending of another's life for reasons of compassion. Also called *mercy killing* or *assisted suicide.* 549

Event sampling   A method of child study in which specific behaviors are observed and recorded and unrelated behaviors are ignored. 16

Exceptionality   A category used to describe physical, social, or intellectual abilities and performance that are significantly above or below average. 175

Excess institutionalization   Phrase used to describe the inappropriate placement of the elderly in institutions. 532

Excitement   Part of the normal human sexual response, a preparatory phase marked by the signs of sexual arousal (for example, erection in males, vaginal lubrication in females). (See *plateau; orgasm; resolution.*) 387

Executive stage   A middle childhood stage of cognitive development in Schaie's system; part of the *responsibility stage,* reflected in the individual's increasing responsiveness to political, social, and religious responsibilities. (See *acquisition stage; responsibility stage; achievement stage; reintegration stage.*) 399

Exosystem   Interactions between a system in which the child is involved (microsystem) and another system that does not ordinarily include the child (father's relationships with employers, for example). 54

Experiment   A procedure for scientific investigation that requires manipulation of some aspects of the environment to determine the effects of this manipulation. 16

Experimental group   A group of subjects who undergo experimental manipulation. The group to which something is done in order to observe its effects. 16

Explicit memory   See *declarative memory.* 16, 259

Extended family   A large family group consisting of parents, children, grandparents, and sometimes uncles, aunts, cousins, and so on. 228, 425

External orientation   A tendency to attribute the outcomes of behavior to factors outside the individual, hence not under the individual's control (such as luck or the difficulty of a task). (See *attribution; internal orientation; locus of control; mastery orientation; learned helplessness.*) 290

External speech   Another label for what Vygotsky calls *social speech.* (See *social speech.*) 52

Extraversion   A personality type described by McCrae, characterized by traits such as those sometimes labeled "sensation seeking" (adventurousness), "activity," and "sociability." (See *neuroticism; openness; NEO typology*.) 476

Failure to thrive (FTT)   (also called *maternal deprivation syndrome* or *growth failure*) A medical condition where an apparently normal infant fails to gain weight (below the third percentile for weight). Often associated with listlessness, loss of appetite, illness, and sometimes death. 165

Fallopian tube   One of two tubes that link the ovaries and the uterus. Fertilization (conception) ordinarily occurs in the Fallopian tubes. From there, the fertilized egg cell moves into the uterus and attaches to the uterine wall. 93

Family household   According to the U.S. Census definition, a family where there is at least one parent or caregiver and at least one child under eighteen. 228

Family life cycle   A sociological term referring to the stages through which typical families progress (for example, early marriage, raising children, raising adolescents, postchildren, and dissolution). 425

Family spacing   Distance between successive siblings. A closely spaced family has many siblings born very close together. According to Zajonc's *confluence model*, family spacing is an important variable in determining the intellectual climate of the home. (See *confluence model; intellectual climate*.) 233

Fast trackers   Kanter's term for those who progress extraordinarily rapidly through the promotional rungs of their careers. (See *dead enders*.) 398

Fat-free mass   The major constituent of the human body, consisting largely of organs, muscles, and bone (which, in turn, consist primarily of water). 246, 314

Fat mass   Made up mostly of white adipose tissue (fat cells). Accounts for an average of about 30 percent of body weight in adult females and about 15 percent in adult males. 246, 314

Feral children   Those raised by animals in the wild and away from human contact. 64

Fertilized ovum   The first stage of prenatal development, beginning at fertilization and ending at the end of the second week. 93

Fetal alcohol syndrome (FAS)   A pattern of birth defects associated with alcohol consumption by pregnant women. FAS symptoms include mental retardation, retarded physical growth, and facial and cranial deformities. 99

Fetal erythroblastosis   A medical condition in the newborn marked by lack of red blood cells. If sufficiently serious and not attended to in time, can be fatal. 106

Fetoscopy   A surgical procedure that allows the physician to see the fetus while obtaining tissue samples to determine its status. 85

Fetus stage   The final stage of prenatal development, which begins at the end of the eighth week after conception and lasts until the baby's birth. 93

Filial piety   A fundamental virtue in many oriental cultures. Says, in effect, that people should always, under all circumstances and at all ages, display the highest devotion and complete obedience to their parents, that the welfare of parents always comes first. My kids are occidental. 333

Filial responsibility   Responsibility that children bear for the care of their parents. A highly valued concept in many Eastern societies. 532

Flexibility   A factor tapped by production measures of divergent thinking (of creativity). Evident in the ability or propensity to switch from one class of responses or solutions to another. (See *fluency; originality*.) 272

Flexibility   A measure of range of joint motion. Without training or practice, flexibility begins to decline at about age twelve. 382

Fluency   A factor thought to be involved in creativity, evident in the production of a large number of responses or solutions in a problem situation. (See *flexibility; originality*.) 272

Fluid abilities   Cattell's term for intellectual abilities that seem to underlie much of our intelligent behavior and that are not highly affected by experience (general reasoning, attention span, memory for numbers). Fluid abilities are more likely to decline in old age than are crystallized abilities. (See also *crystallized abilities*.) 263, 450, 505

Food Guide Pyramid   A pyramidal structure designed to represent recommended nutritional balance among five essential food groups, plus a sixth (sugars, fats, and oils) that is to be used sparingly. 383, 445

Forceps   Clamplike instruments that may sometimes be used in a baby's delivery. 115

Foreclosure   Marcia's term for the adoption of a ready-made identity. 345

Formal grandparenting style   The most common grandparenting style in North America. Marked by a close relationship with grandchildren but no direct involvement in or advice about childrearing. 527

Formal operations   The last of Piaget's four major stages, beginning around the age of eleven or twelve and lasting until about fourteen or fifteen. It is characterized by the child's increasing ability to use logical thought processes. 47, 323

Fragile X syndrome   A sex-linked, primarily male disorder that is often manifested in mental retardation. Susceptibility increases with the mother's age. 83

Fraternal twins   Twins whose genetic origins are two separate eggs. Such twins are as genetically dissimilar as average siblings. (See also *dizygotic*.) 64, 75

Free-radical theory   Argues that portions of cells sometimes become detached, becoming "free radicals" that significantly affect the cell's ability to function normally and that account for some of the components of aging. 494

Free recall   Describes memory tasks where participants are asked to generate a correct recollection from memory—as opposed to *recognizing* it. (See *recognition recall*.) 504

Freestyle fifties   Sheehy's label for the developmental period spanning the 50's. 469

Fun-seeking grandparent role   A grandparenting style marked by high indulgence of grandchildren. 527

Galvanic skin response (GSR)   A measure of the skin's electrical conductivity. With increases in emotional reaction (arousal), conductivity increases; hence, GSR measures may be considered indexes of arousal or emotion. 131

Gametes   Mature sex cells. In humans, the egg cell (ovum) and the sperm cell. 67

Gang   A small group that interacts frequently face-to-face and that defines itself through conflict—sometimes with other gangs, sometimes with established authority, often with both. 364

Gateway drug-use theory   The observation that certain drugs such as tobacco, alcohol, and marijuana are typically used first (usually in the order mentioned) before other "stronger" drugs, in a sense serving as a gateway to use of other drugs. 367

Gender   The characteristics typically associated with biological sex. Thus, there are two genders, masculine and feminine, corresponding with the two sexes, male and female. 351

Gender constancy   Refers to the developing child's realization that gender is permanent and unchangeable. 225

Gender identity disorder   Label for the relatively rare condition where individuals don't feel comfortable with their anatomical sex—where they feel themselves to *be* the other sex, and have strong preferences for that alternative. 226

Gender roles   Attitudes, personality characteristics, behavior, and other qualities associated with being male or female in a specific culture. Gender roles are the groupings of qualities that define masculine and feminine. Because they are largely culturally defined, gender roles may be quite different in different cultures. 175, 224, 351

Gender schema theory   A cognitive gender typing theory that recognizes that elements of both cognitive explanations (the child's growing understanding of the nature and meaning of gender) and social learning explanations (the influence of models and reinforcements) are useful to account for the shaping of gender roles. 226

Gender schemas   Notions of what males and females should be. 225

Gender-splitting   Levinson's expression for gender differences in important developmental areas—such as in the nature of the *dream* that shapes many people's lives and against which success can be measured. 468

Gender typing   Learning behavior appropriate to the sex of the individual. The term refers specifically to the acquisition of masculine behavior by a boy or feminine behavior by a girl. 175, 224, 351

Gene   A carrier of heredity. Each of the twenty-three chromosomes contributed by the sperm cell and the ovum at conception is believed to contain 50,0 to 100,0 genes. 69

General factor theory   A theory of intelligence based on the assumption that there is a basic underlying quality of intellectual functioning that determines intelligence in all areas. This quality is sometimes termed *g*. 263

Generalizability   The extent to which conclusions can be applied (generalized) from one situation to others: the generality of conclusions. 22

Generativity   A seventh, adult, stage added to Erikson's theory by Vaillant and Milofsky, reflecting the extent to which the individual has assumed responsibility for others (for example, involvement with raising children and with the community). 409

Generativity versus self-absorption   Erikson's label for a psychosocial stage spanning middle adulthood, marked by a need to be productive (generative)—that is, to engage in tasks beneficial to society—as opposed to being self-absorbed (concerned mainly with the self). 465

Genetic–congenital   Label for one possible source of causes for various mental disorders as well as other conditions. Inherited or at least present at birth. Genetic–congenital causes include chromosomal and genetic problems as well as the effects of maternal malnutrition or birth injury. (See *social–psychological*.) 302

Genetic theory of aging   Holds that the biological limits of life are programmed into cells and that, once they have reproduced a predetermined number of times, they die. 494

Genetics   The science that studies heredity. 67

Genital herpes   A viral STD evident in lesions on the genitals (like tiny cold sores). 360

Genitalia   A general term referring to sex organs.

Genital stage   The last of Freud's stages of psychosexual development, beginning around age eleven and lasting until around eighteen. It is characterized by involvement with normal adult modes of sexual gratification. 33

Genome   One set of single chromosomes with the genes they contain; considered an organism's genetic map.

Genotype   Genetic makeup. Can sometimes be inferred from phenotype. (See *phenotype*.) 69

Germinal stage   Another label for the prenatal developmental period of the fertilized ovum, the first stage of intrauterine growth. (See *fertilized ovum*.) 93

Gestation period   The time between conception and birth (typically 266 days for humans). 92

Gist memory   Describes the remembering of main ideas, of central themes, rather than of details. Much of our memory appears to be gist memory. We remember the gist of something and generate the details. 258

Glaucoma   A medical condition defined in terms of increased pressure in the eye that is associated with age; if untreated, glaucoma can damage vision and even lead to blindness. 442

Gonads   Sexual endocrine glands: testes in the male, ovaries in the female. 315

Gonorrhea   A relatively common STD, most strains of which are easily treated with antibiotics. Common symptoms in the male include a discharge from the penis, and painful urination. Symptoms in women are more subtle. 115, 360

Goodenough–Harris Drawing Test   A simple intelligence test that asks children to draw the very best person (man or woman) they can. Drawings are scored on the basis of detail, completeness, and quality, using strict guidelines and norming tables, and yield a score comparable to more sophisticated measures of IQ. 188

Good grief   Label which reflects the assumption that people need to *work through* their grief, that doing so is *good*, that the end result of grieving is adjustment, and absence of expected grieving is basically unhealthy. 554

Grandfilial responsibility   A grandchild's feeling that he or she bears some responsibility for the well-being of a grandparent—that the grandparent should rely on him or her when in need. 528

Grand mal   Label sometimes used for the more severe forms of epilepsy. Sometimes also used to refer specifically to the seizures that accompany this form of epilepsy. (See *petit mal*.) 177

Grandparent-as-distant-figure role   Grandparenting style where grandparents are seen as benevolent but distant and uninvolved. 527

Grief   An emotional reaction to loss. Grief reactions are sometimes accompanied by both physical and psychological symptoms (shortness of breath, heart palpitations, sighing, loss of appetite, and so on, as well as anxiety, depression, anger, and guilt). 543

Group intelligence test   An intelligence test, generally of the paper-and-pencil variety, that can be administered to large groups of individuals at a time. 265

Growth   In the study of children, a term that ordinarily refers to physical changes that are primarily quantitative because they involve addition rather than transformation. 5

Growth deceleration   Reduction in the rate at which physical growth (e.g., increases in height and weight) occurs. Growth deceleration occurs through the first and second year of life, and again after the growth spurt of pubescence. 184

Growth spurt   Sudden acceleration of physical growth, dramatically evident in early adolescence. 313

Habituate   Become accustomed to. In psychological research, habituation is said to have occurred when the organism no longer responds as it would to a novel stimulus. 140

Happiness   A personal, highly subjective feeling of well-being, of contentment. The term has shorter-term connotations than *satisfaction* and is more subject to mood. (See *satisfaction*.) 479

Hard of hearing   Those who suffer from some hearing loss but who can function with a hearing aid and sometimes without. (See *deafness*.) 251

Head-turning reflex   A reflex elicited in infants by stroking the cheek or the corner of the mouth. Infants turn their heads toward the side being stimulated. 131

Hedonistic   Relating to the pain–pleasure principle—to the tendency to seek pleasure and avoid pain. 333

Hemispherectomy   Surgical procedure involving ablation (removal) of part of the brain. Often used in an attempt to control epileptic seizures. 177

Heredity   The transmission of physical and personality characteristics and predispositions from parent to offspring. 64

Heteronomy   Piaget's label for the first stage of moral development, marked by reliance on outside authority. (See *autonomy*.) 332

Heterozygous   Refers to the presence of different genes with respect to a single trait. One of these genes is dominant, and the other is recessive. 80

Heuristic value   *Heuristic* is from a Greek word meaning "to find out." Something is said to have heuristic value if it aids or guides the discovery of truth.

Holland Vocational Preference Inventory   An instrument that attempts to sort individuals into one of six categories reflecting their main "coping styles" (realistic, intellectual, artistic, social, enterprising, or conventional), and uses this information in career guidance. 393

Holophrase   Term used to describe a single word in early infant speech, the meaning of which is global and imprecise, including a wide range of actions, objects, or events. 151

Homophobia   Fear of homosexuality, often expressed in harassment, fear, distrust, or loathing relative to known or suspected homosexuals. 415

Homozygous   Refers to an individual's genetic makeup. Individuals are homozygous with respect to a particular trait if they possess identical genes for that trait. 80

Hormone   Substance secreted by an endocrine gland (such as testosterone or estrogen) into the bloodstream and carried to some part of the body where it has a specific effect. 314

Hormone replacement therapy (HRT)   Therapeutic treatment mainly of women, often following menopause, with hormones designed to replace those no longer produced by the ovaries (primarily estrogen). 443

Hospice   A facility established to provide care for the terminally ill. May be part of a hospital, in a private home, or a separate institution. (See *palliative care*.) 549

Hot flashes   Sensations of intense bodily heat, often accompanied by perspiration and other physical symptoms, sometimes characteristic of the post menopausal years. 446

Human chorionic gonadotropin (HCG)   Hormone released in a pregnant woman's bloodstream and detectable as well in her urine. (See *pregnancy hormone*.) 92

Human immunodeficiency virus (HIV)   The presumed cause of *acquired immune deficiency syndrome (AIDS)*, a virus that appears to be able to mutate rapidly and whose control has proven difficult. (See *acquired immune deficiency syndrome [AIDS]*.) 360

Humanism   A philosophical and psychological orientation primarily concerned with the worth of humans as individuals and with processes that augment their human qualities. (See *self-actualization*.) 55

Huntington's disease   An inherited neurological disorder characterized by neural degeneration typically beginning between the ages of twenty and forty, and usually leading to death. 79

Hurried child   Expression coined by Elkind for children whose parents are so eager for them to learn and to accomplish that they "rush" them through childhood, dragging them from one lesson or school to another, scarcely giving them time to pause and play and just be children. 200

Hydration   Water intake. 499

Hyperactivity   See *attention deficit hyperactivity disorder (ADHD)*. 302

Hypoactive sexual desire   A sexual dysfunction evident in a lower than normal interest in sexual activity. 389

Hypothesis   A prediction based on partial evidence of some effect, process, or phenomenon that must be experimentally verified. 16

Id   One of the three levels of the human personality, according to Freudian theory. The id is defined as all the instinctual urges to which humans are heir; it is the level of personality that contains human motives. A newborn child's personality, according to Freud, is all id. 32

Identical twins   Twins whose genetic origin is a single egg. Such twins are genetically identical. (See *monozygotic*.) 64, 75

Identification   A general term referring to the process of assuming the goals, ambitions, mannerisms, and so on of another person—of identifying with that person. (See *imitation*.) 33, 217

Identity   A term with several meanings. (1) A logical rule specifying that certain activities leave objects or situations unchanged. (2) In Erikson's theory, a term closely related to self. To achieve identity is to arrive at a clear notion of who one is. It includes the goals, values, and beliefs to which the individual is committed. (3) Often used synonymously with the term *self, identity* refers to the individual's self-definition, a personal sense of who and what one is. One of the important tasks of adolescence is to select and develop a strong sense of identity. 35, 254, 340

Identity achieved   Marcia's term for individuals who have experienced a crisis and made a commitment, thus achieving a sense of identity. 345

Identity diffusion   Marcia's term for an adolescent state devoid of commitment or identity crisis; common in early adolescence. 345

Identity versus identity diffusion   An Erikson developmental stage spanning adolescence. 36

Identity versus role diffusion   Erikson's description of the adolescent's basic conflict between finding and developing an identity and experimenting with various conflicting identities. 344

Imaginary audience   One manifestation of adolescent egocentrism. A reflection of the adolescent belief that a wide range of individuals are always aware of the adolescent's behavior and are very concerned about it. 327

Imaginary Audience Scale   A scale developed by Elkind and Bowen to assess the extent to which the individual is responsive to the assumed interest and judgments of others. Provides an indirect measure of adolescent egocentrism. (See *adolescent egocentrism; personal fable; imaginary audience*.) 328

Imaginary playmate   My imaginary playmate is my best friend and goes everywhere with me and likes a lot of the same things I do and gets upset if I don't say hello and other stuff. . . . 222

Imaginative play   Activities that include make-believe games; these are particularly prevalent during the preschool years. 221

Imitation   The complex process of learning through observation of a model. 42, 217

Immature birth   A miscarriage occurring sometime between the twentieth and twenty-eighth weeks of pregnancy and resulting in the birth of a fetus weighing between one and two pounds. 112

Implicit memory   See *nondeclarative memory*. 49, 259

Imprinting An instinctlike type of learning that occurs shortly after birth in certain species and that is seen in the "following" behavior of young ducks and geese. 49

In utero A Latin term meaning "inside the uterus." 138

Incidental mnemonics The young preschooler's accidental rather than deliberate and systematic memory aids. Includes such things as paying attention and repeated exposure. 190

Incongruity hypothesis The supposition that infant fear reactions result from a discrepancy between reality and what the infant has learned to expect. 170

Independent variable The variable in an experiment that can be manipulated to observe its effects on other variables. 16

Individual intelligence test An intelligence test, like the Wechsler or the Stanford–Binet, that can be administered to only one individual at a time. 265

Induction As an aspect of rites of passage, acceptance into adult status. 312

Industry vs. inferiority Erikson's label for a developmental period spanning middle childhood, characterized by emphasis on interaction with peers. 36

Infancy A period of development that begins a few weeks after birth and lasts until approximately the age of two. 157

Infantile amnesia A generally unexplained but apparently universal human phenomenon evident in the fact that most people do not remember events of infancy or of the early preschool period. 190

Infant state An expression used to describe the general, current condition of an infant—for example, sleeping, crying, drowsy, or alert. 157

Infertility The inability to conceive a child. 390

Inflation An unstable, unpredictable price increase, reflected in an increasing cost of living and declining value of monetary units. 521

Information-processing approach A psychological orientation that attempts to explain cognitive processes such as remembering, decision making, or problem solving. This orientation is primarily concerned with how information is acquired and stored (acquisition of a knowledge base), as well as the development of both cognitive strategies and notions of the self as a processor of information (metacognition). 256, 325

Inhibitory–disinhibitory effect Imitative behavior that results in either the suppression (inhibition) or appearance (disinhibition) of previously acquired deviant behavior. 42

Inhibitory effect Bandura's description of how punishing a model can sometimes serve to inhibit deviant behavior in observers. 217

Initiation Ceremonies and rituals that, in some societies, mark entry into adulthood. 312

Initiative versus guilt The third of Erikson's stages (two or three to six years), marked by a developing sense of self and of responsibility, and a greater independence from parents. 36, 216

Inner speech Vygotsky's final stage in the development of speech, attained at around age seven, and characterized by silent "self-talk," the stream-of-consciousness flow of verbalizations that gives direction and substance to our thinking and behavior. Inner speech is involved in all higher mental functioning. (See *egocentric speech; social speech.*) 52

Insecure–ambivalent Describes infants who are profoundly upset when the principal caregiver leaves and who often display anger when that person returns. 166

Insecure–avoidant Describes infants who are anxiously attached to a caregiver, who show little signs of distress when that person leaves, and who initially avoid reestablishing contact when the person returns. 166

Integrity achieving A division of Erikson's final developmental stage, descriptive of individuals successful in achieving integrity and overcoming despair. (See *dissonant; integrity foreclosed; despairing.*) 516

Integrity foreclosed Describes those among the elderly who avoid an integrity-versus-despair crisis. (See *integrity achieving; dissonant; despairing.*) 516

Integrity vs. despair The final developmental stage described by Erikson, marked by the need to integrate the experiences of a lifetime, to make sense of them, and to overcome the despair that sometimes characterizes old age. 516

Intellectual climate Phrase used by Zajonc to describe the *confluence* of home-based factors that affect the intellectual development of the child—mainly, measurable factors such as family size, birth order, and family spacing. (See *confluence model; birth order; family spacing.*) 232

Intelligence quotient (IQ) A measure of intelligence. Initially, the ratio of mental to chronological age, multiplied by 100. Average IQ is therefore 100, and is based on a comparison between an individual's performance and that of comparable others on tasks that presumably require intelligence. 265, 448

Internal orientation A tendency to attribute the outcomes of behavior to factors within the individual's control (such as effort or ability). (See *locus of control; external orientation; mastery orientation; learned helplessness.*) 290

Interpersonal attraction A degree of liking, often preliminary to strong liking or loving. Appears to require some degree of similarity and physical attraction, as well as proximity. 413

Interspousal violence Extreme forms of aggression among spouses. 430

Intimacy In Sternberg's theory of love, refers to emotions that lead two people to want to share things, perhaps to

disclose personal, private things. (See *passion; commitment; triangular theory of love*.) 411

Intimacy vs. isolation   Erikson's label for a developmental period spanning young adulthood, marked by the need to develop close relationships with others. 465

Introjection   Freudian term for the unconscious process of adopting as part of one's own belief system the inferred attitudes, beliefs, desires, and so on of significant other persons. 225

Intuitive   A substage of Piaget's preoperational period, lasting from age four to about seven or eight, marked by problem solutions more intuitive than logical, and characterized by excessive reliance on perception. 192

Invulnerable   Label used to describe highly resilient children—children who, although they are at high risk for problems, cope and adjust exceptionally well. 305

James's approach to self-worth   The belief that notions of self-esteem are a direct function of the difference between perceived self and self-ideal. (See *Cooley's approach to self-worth*.) 282

Job   Specific task or duty associated with one's work or employment. (See *career; occupation*.) 391

Job–person matching   Theories of career choice that advocate matching a person with a career on the basis of the person's characteristics and interests and the principal requirements of the job. (See *developmental career model*.) 392

Kindergarten   Preschool that typically takes in children in their last year prior to entry into first grade. In many jurisdictions, kindergartens have prescribed curricula; in some, attendance is mandatory. 198

Klinefelter's syndrome   Disorder caused by the presence of an extra X chromosome in a male child, marked by the presence of both male and female secondary sexual characteristics. 83

Knowledge acquisition components   One of Sternberg's three components of intelligence. Refers to processes used in acquiring information, such as separating the important from the unimportant, organizing, and comparing new with old information. (See *metacomponents; performance components*.) 264

Knowledge base   All that is in memory. Information-processing approaches to learning and development look at the nature of the knowledge base, its creation, strategies for adding material to, or retrieving from, the knowledge base, and the knower's awareness of self as knower. 257, 325

Labor   The process during which the fetus, placenta, and other membranes are separated from the mother's body and expelled. The termination of labor usually is birth. 108

Lactation   The production of milk. 125

Lamaze method   A method of natural childbirth based on a variety of breathing and relaxation exercises designed to remove, or at least reduce, the need for anesthetics and other medical intervention. 114

Language   Complex arrangements of arbitrary sounds that have accepted referents and can therefore be used for communication among humans. 146, 202

Language acquisition device (LAD)   A label used by Chomsky to describe the neurological something that corresponds to grammar and which children are assumed to have in their brains as they learn language. 204

Language acquisition support system (LASS)   Bruner's label for the series of interactions between caregiver and infant that are fundamental to the learning of language. So labeled partly as a response to Chomsky's *language acquisition device (LAD)*. (See *language acquisition device [LAD]*.) 147

Lanugo   Downy, soft hair that covers the fetus. Lanugo grows over most of the child's body sometime after the fifth month of pregnancy and is usually shed during the seventh month. However, some lanugo is often present at birth, especially on the infant's back. 96

Large-for-gestational age (LGA)   Infants weighing more than 90 percent of what average newborns of the same gestational age weigh. (See *average-for-gestational age; small-for-gestational age*.) 112

Latchkey children   Label for children who return (from schools, playground, gym, or wherever) to caretakerless homes. So-called because parents sometimes hang their house keys around children's necks so that they are less likely to lose them. 240

Late home leaver   For research purposes, someone who leaves home after the age of twenty-four. 348

Latency stage   The fourth of Freud's stages of psychosexual development, characterized by both the development of the superego (conscience) and loss of interest in sexual gratification. This stage is assumed to last from ages six to eleven. 33

Later adulthood   The final developmental period, beginning at around ages 65–70 onward. 378

Launching phase   The sixth of Duvall's eight stages of the family life cycle, spanning the years from the leaving of the first child to the leaving of the last. 472

Learned helplessness   Personality characteristic evident in a tendency to attribute outcomes to causes over which the person has no control. (See *mastery-oriented*.) 44, 290

Learning   Changes in behavior resulting from experience rather than from the maturational process. 6

Learning disability   Significant impairment in a specific skill or ability in the absence of mental retardation (a general depression in ability to learn). 269

Leboyer method   A method of prepared childbirth emphasizing birthing conditions rather than preparation of the mother (for example, birth occurs in a softly lit room; the infant is immersed in a lukewarm bath and later placed directly on the mother's abdomen). 114

Leisure   Freedom from the demands of work. Discretionary time. Time for enjoyment, relaxation, recreation. 459

Levinson's dream   In Levinson's description, a sort of fantasy developed in early adulthood, including the individual's goals and aspirations. Successes and failures are later measured against the dream. 467

Libido   A general Freudian term denoting sexual urges. The libido is assumed to be the source of energy for sexual urges. Freud considered these urges the most important force in human motivation. 32

Life-career rainbow   Super's phrase for a graphic representation of the longitudinal nature of the many roles that individuals might play in the course of their lives. Each band of the rainbow's arc represents a different role; each goes from the beginning to the end, gaining in importance during different phases; and, taken all together, they paint the colors of our lives. 395

Life crisis   An identifiable, discrete change or life event that entails some degree of distress, challenge, or hazard, often requiring major readjustments. 470

Life expectancy   The expected duration of a human life. An average of the ages at which individuals die. 494

Life review   A dynamic process whereby an individual remembers, analyzes, and evaluates past experiences in an effort to resolve and accept personal conflicts. The life review is common in late adulthood but may occur throughout life. (See *personal narrative*.) 399, 518

Lifespan   The total length of an individual life; not an expectancy, but the maximum attainable in the absence of accident and disease. 494

Lifespan developmental psychology   The area of psychology concerned with the development of individuals from conception to death—that is, with the entire lifespan. 4

Life-span, life-space approach   Label for Super's developmental guidance model—so-called because it extends over most of the lifespan and takes into consideration the possibility of starting a new career at any point in life. 392

Life trajectory   A description of the course of a human life in terms of its major turning points. (See *dying trajectory*.) 548

Little's disease   One of the first labels for *cerebral palsy*. (See *cerebral palsy*.) 176

Living will   A document that can be used to formalize one's wishes regarding the use of heroic resuscitation or life-preserving measures under prescribed circumstances. 551

Locomotor abilities   Abilities involved in self-propelled motion, hence essential for moving oneself from one position or location to another (crawling or walking, for example). 168

Locus of control   An aspect of personality evident in the individual's consistent tendency to attribute behavioral outcomes to a specific class of causes—causes over which the individual does, or does not, have control. (See *internal orientation; external orientation; mastery orientation; learned helplessness*.) 290

Logic of propositions   Piaget's phrase for the kind of logic that is *potentially* available with the advent of formal operations. It is an abstract form of reasoning that allows for the logical manipulation of *propositions*. (See *proposition*.) 324

Longevity   Length of life. Average expected longevity is *life expectancy*. Actual longevity is defined by the time span between birth and death. 495

Longitudinal study   A research technique in the study of child development that observes the same subjects over a period of time. 18, 449

Long-term memory   A type of memory whereby with continued rehearsal and recoding of sensory input (processing in terms of meaning, for example), material will be available for recall over a longer period of time (minutes to years). 258, 503

Love   The poets may grasp this one more clearly than the scientists. A strong, interpersonal attraction, says science. A combination of passion, intimacy, and commitment. 411

LSD-25 (d-lysergic acid diethylamide tartrate)   A particularly powerful hallucinogenic drug, this inexpensive, easily made synthetic chemical can sometimes have profound influences on human perception. In everyday parlance, it is often called *acid*. 368

Lunar month   The length of a complete moon cycle (twenty-eight days)—from full moon to full moon, for example. 92

Lymphoid system   Includes all lymph tissues in the body (for example, in lymph glands, the tonsils, the thymus, the intestine). These produce a yellowish liquid, lymph, involved in the individual's immunological system. 126

Macrosystem   All interactive social systems that define a culture or subculture. 54

Mainstreaming   The practice of placing students in need of special services in regular classrooms rather than segregating them. Also called *inclusive education*. 251, 274

Major gene determination   The determination of genetically based characteristics as a function of the relative dominance or recessiveness of a single pair of genes. (See *dominant gene; recessive gene; polygenetic determination*.) 69

Marker genes   A length of DNA material that seems to be identical in all individuals with a specific characteristic. 71

Mastery-oriented   A personality characteristic marked by a tendency to attribute the outcomes of behavior to factors under personal control. (See *learned helplessness*.) 44, 290

Masturbation   The self-stimulation of one's genitals for sexual gratification. 356

Maturation   A term used to describe changes in human development that are relatively independent of the environment. 6, 141

Mature birth   The birth of an infant between the thirty-seventh and forty-second weeks of pregnancy. 112

Mechanistic model   A model of human development based on the belief that it is useful to view human beings in terms of their reactive, machinelike characteristics. 38

Medical neglect   Child maltreatment where caregivers fail to provide adequate medical care to children in need—sometimes through carelessness, sometimes for religious reasons. 298

Meiosis   The division of a single sex cell into two separate cells, each consisting of twenty-three chromosomes rather than twenty-three pairs of chromosomes. Meiosis therefore results in cells that are completely different, whereas mitosis results in identical cells. 68

Memory   Ability to recognize or to recollect previous experiences. (See *short-term memory; long-term memory; declarative memory; semantic memory; episodic memory; nondeclarative memory*.) 503

Memory strategies   Systematic plans or procedures designed to improve the likelihood of remembering. The most common adult memory strategies are *organization, grouping, rehearsing,* and *elaboration.* (See *organization; grouping; rehearsing; elaboration*.) 190

Menarche   A girl's first menstrual period, an event that transpires during pubescence. 23, 315, 316

Mendelian genetics   The study of heredity through an examination of the characteristics of parents and offspring. (See *molecular genetics*.) 71

Menopause   The cessation of menstruation in women. Menopause may begin in the early forties or late thirties and usually is complete around age fifty. (See *climacteric*.) 66, 445

Menses   A monthly discharge of blood and tissue from the womb of a mature female. The term refers to menstruation. 92

Mental retardation   A global term referring to the mental state of individuals whose intellectual development is significantly slower than that of normal individuals and whose ability to adapt to their environment is therefore limited. 268

Mentor   An especially influential model who also serves directly as an informal guide or tutor, often on a one-to-one basis. Mentors and their "clients" engage in a one-to-one teaching/learning relationship where teachers serve not only as a source of information, but also as important models with respect to values, beliefs, philosophies, and attitudes. 262, 468

Mesosystem   Interactions among two or more microsystems (for example, family and school). 54

Meta-analysis   A research technique that involves the careful, systematic analysis of all or most of the relevant studies that have looked at a research question, in an attempt to arrive at conclusions that are far more general and reliable than those that might be based on the results of a single study. 234

Metacognition   Knowledge about knowing. As we grow and learn, we develop notions about ourselves as learners. Accordingly, we develop strategies that recognize our limitations and that allow us to monitor our progress and take advantage of our efforts. 222, 257, 262, 325

Metacomponents   One of Sternberg's three components of human intelligence. Include skills involved in planning, monitoring, and evaluating cognitive performance (cognitive strategies). (See *performance components; knowledge acquisition components*.) 264

Metamemory   The knowledge that we develop about our own memory processes—knowledge about how to remember rather than simply about our memories. 192, 262

Metaneed   Maslow's term for a "higher" need. In contrast to a basic need, a metaneed is concerned not with physiological but with psychological functions. It includes the need to know truth, beauty, justice, and to self-actualize. 56

Methylmercury   Mercury compound that tends to accumulate in fatty tissue and that is associated with birth deformities and malformations in offspring. 98

Microcephaly   A birth condition characterized by an abnormally small head. 101

Microsystem   Defined by immediate, face-to-face interactions, where everybody affects everybody (for example, child and parent). 54

Middle adulthood   The midlife developmental period, generally considered to span ages 40–45 to 65–70. 378, 440

Middle childhood   An arbitrary division in the sequence of development beginning somewhere around age six and ending at approximately twelve. 246

Midlife crisis   A popular expression for the potential emotional turmoil that sometimes occurs in middle age with the individual's growing recognition of mortality and with the realization that the dreams of younger years may never be achieved. 464, 467, 470

Midwife   In many jurisdictions, a licensed professional, generally female but occasionally male, who assists in childbirth—but who is generally neither a doctor nor a nurse. 114

Mild retardation   A classification of mental retardation identified by degree and usually defined in terms of an

IQ range between 50 and about 70. Also termed "educable," children with mild retardation are capable of achievement at about the sixth-grade level, and of adequate social adaptation. 268

Minimata disease   Disease linked with the presence of methylmercury. Affects prenatal development, typically causing severe deformations, mental retardation, blindness, and even death. 98

Mitosis   The division of a cell into two identical cells. Mitosis occurs in body cells rather than in sex cells. 68

Model   A pattern for behavior that can be copied by someone else. (See also *symbolic models.*) Alternatively, a model is a representation, usually abstract, of some phenomenon or system. Thus, we might have a model of the universe or a model of some aspects of behavior. 42

Modeling effect   Imitative behavior involving the learning of a novel response. 42, 217

Moderate retardation   A degree of mental retardation defined in terms of an IQ range between 35 or 40 and 50 or 55. Individuals at this level can achieve at about the second-grade level and can profit from training in social and occupational skills. 269

Molecular genetics   The study of genetics based on the structure of chromosomes. (See *Mendelian genetics.*) 71

Monogamy   The practice of being married to one person at a time. (See *polygamy.*) 419

Monolingual   Proficient in a single language (as opposed to bilingual). 207

Monozygotic   Twins resulting from the division of a single fertilized egg. The process results in identical twins. 75

Montessori method   A compensatory preschool education program developed for use with children with mental handicaps but also adapted for use with normal children both at the preschool and post-preschool level. Makes extensive use of specially prepared materials designed to train the senses. 201

Morality   The ethical aspect of human behavior. Morality is intimately bound to the development of an awareness of acceptable and unacceptable behaviors. It is therefore linked to what is often called conscience. (See *conscience.*) 330

Moro reflex   The generalized startle reaction of a newborn infant. It characteristically involves throwing out the arms and feet symmetrically and then bringing them back in toward the center of the body. 131

Morpheme   Combination of phonemes that make up the meaningful units of a language. 147, 203

Motherese   Term for changes in a caregiver's language when interacting with a child. 205

Mother–infant bond   Expression for a biological and physiological process involved in the very early formation of emotional links between mother and infant. 164

Mourning   The external manifestations of grief. Many cultures and religions have prescribed periods of mourn-

ing—periods during which the bereaved are expected to show their grief. 543

Muscular dystrophy (MD)   A degenerative muscular disorder, most forms of which are genetic, usually manifested in an inability to walk and sometimes fatal. 81

Mutagen   Substance capable of causing changes in genetic material. (See *teratogen.*) 96

Mythos   Labouvie-Vief's label for the mythical (as opposed to logical) thinking of old age. Thinking that is subjective, personal, pragmatic, and intuitive. 507

Naive theory   A general term for folk beliefs in psychology. Also referred to as *commonsense* or *implicit* theories, naive theories typically have no scientific basis. 30

Natural childbirth   Also called *prepared childbirth,* refers to the process of giving birth without anesthetics. 114

Naturalistic   Investigations where observations are made in natural rather than in more contrived situations (such as in laboratories or in experimental situations). 16

Nature–nurture controversy   A long-standing psychological argument over whether genetics (nature) or environment (nurture) is more responsible for determining development. 15

Negative identities   Erikson's expression for the rebellious, nonconformist, anti-establishment roles with which adolescents sometimes experiment. 344

Negative reinforcement   A stimulus that increases the probability of a response when the stimulus is removed from the situation. A negative reinforcer is usually an unpleasant or noxious stimulus that is removed when the desired response occurs. 40

Neonatal abstinence syndrome   Neonatal symptoms associated with narcotics use by the mother that has resulted in the newborn also being addicted. Severe cases may be fatal. 100

Neonate   A newborn infant. Newborns typically lose weight immediately after birth, but regain it within two weeks. The neonate period terminates when birth weight is regained. 111, 124

NEO typology   Costa and McCrae's analysis of personality into three types: neuroticism (anxiety, depression), extraversion (sensation seeking, adventurousness), and openness (dogmatism, rigidity, authoritarianism). 476

Neural tube defects   Spinal cord defects often linked with recessive genes, sometimes evident in failure of the spine to close (spina bifida), or in absence of portions of the brain. 82

Neuroticism   A personality type described by McCrae, characterized by traits such as anxiety, depression, and excessive emotionality. (See *extraversion; openness; NEO typology.*) 476

Nominal fallacy   The assumption that naming something explains it. 30

Nondeclarative memory   Also termed *implicit* or *procedural* memory, refers to unconscious, nonverbalizable effects of experience such as might be manifested in acquired motor skills or in classical conditioning. (See *declarative memory; semantic memory; episodic memory.*) 259, 503

Norm   An average or standard way of behaving. Cultural norms, for example, refer to the behaviors expected of individuals who are members of that culture.

Normal cognitive decline   Age-related decrements in cognitive functioning associated with changes in neurological and physiological functioning that are a normal consequence of aging. (See *pathological cognitive decline.*) 451

Normal curve   A mathematical function represented in the form of a symmetrical, bell-shaped curve that illustrates how a large number of naturally occurring or chance events are distributed. 70

Nuclear family   A family consisting of a mother, a father, and their offspring. 228, 425

Nursery schools   Preschool child-care facilities that typically take in very young children (say, ages two or three to five) and that emphasize play and social development. 198

Obesity   A medical condition where the individual's weight is at least 20 percent more than average for one's height, age, and sex. 247, 320, 384

Object concept   The realization that objects have a permanence and identity of their own, that they continue to exist even when they are not being perceived. 142

Observational learning   Learning through imitation. 42

Occupation   A relatively broad employment classification such as secretary or accountant. (See *job; work; career.*) 391

Oedipus complex   A Freudian stage of development during which a boy unconsciously has sexual desires for his mother and a consequent resentment of his father. (See *Electra complex.*) 33

Old-old   A Neugarten classification of the elderly, including those roughly between seventy-five and eighty-five, less active physically, but often still highly involved in various activities. (See *young-old; oldest-old.*) 488

Oldest-old   In Neugarten's classification of the elderly, those above eighty-five, still a highly heterogeneous group. (See *young-old; old-old.*) 488

Onlooker play   Play that is social only in the sense that it involves a player *watching* others play while not participating. (See *cooperative play; associative play; parallel play; primitive social play; solitary play.*) 223

Ontogeny   Systematic changes that occur in the lives of individuals. Changes that define lifespan development. (See *phylogeny.*) 15

Openness   A personality type described by McCrae, characterized by traits such as receptivity to new experiences and flexibility rather than rigidity. (See *extraversion; neuroticism; NEO typology.*) 476

Open systems   Describes interactive systems where the outcome depends on complex interactions and is never entirely predictable—hence is open rather than closed. 53

Operant   The label used by Skinner to describe a response not elicited by any known or obvious stimulus. Most significant human behaviors appear to be operant. Such behaviors as writing a letter or going for a walk are operants if no known specific stimulus elicits them. 40

Operant conditioning   A type of learning involving an increased probability of a response occurring as a result of reinforcement. Much of B. F. Skinner's experimental work investigates the principles of operant conditioning. 38

Operation   Piaget's term for mental activity. An operation is a thought process characterized by certain rules of logic. Preoperations are more intuitive and egocentric and less logical. 47, 192, 253

Oppositional defiant disorder   An American Psychiatric Association diagnostic category characterized by extreme noncompliance (disobedience, rebelliousness). 304

Oral stage   Freud's first stage of psychosexual development, lasting from birth to approximately eight months of age. The oral stage is characterized by preoccupation with the immediate gratification of desires. This is accomplished primarily with the mouth, by sucking, biting, swallowing, playing with the lips, and so on. 33

Ordinal properties   With respect to number, their ordered sequence (first, second, third, . . .). (See *cardinal properties.*) 256

Organismic model   This model in human development assumes that it is useful to view people as active rather than simply reactive, as more like biological organisms than machines.

Organizing   A memory strategy involving grouping and relating material to maintain it in long-term memory. (See *elaborating; rehearsing.*) 140, 260

Orgasm   Phase of sexual release involving contractions and spasms in the women, seminal emission in the man. (See *excitement; plateau; resolution.*) 388

Orienting response   The initial response of humans and other animals to novel stimulation. Also called the *orienting reflex* or *orientation reaction*. Components of the orienting response include changes in EEG patterns, respiration rate, heart rate, and conductivity of the skin to electricity. 131

Originality   A measure of creativity evident in the production of novel (unexpected or statistically rare) responses or solutions in a problem situation. (See *flexibility; fluency.*) 272

Osteoporosis   A thinning and weakening of the bones, often associated with aging, and more common in women than in men. 272, 443, 497

Other-directed regulatory behaviors Means of controlling emotional reaction that involves affecting or controlling the external situation (for example, running away when frightened or indicating through body language that a parent is to stop some annoying behavior). (See *self-directed regulatory behavior.*) 163

Otitis media A highly common childhood disease of the middle ear, sometimes accompanied by prolonged hearing loss, the main medical symptom of which is fluid in the middle ear. May be associated with language problems. 251

Ovary A female organ (most women have two) that produces ova (egg cells). 93, 315

Overt aggression Visible, outwardly manifested form of aggression that includes a range of possible forceful human actions intended to dominate, to frighten, perhaps even to hurt physically. One extreme form of overt aggression is violence. (See *social aggression; aggression; violence.*) 292, 353

Ovulation The release of a mature egg by the ovaries. In normal, mature women (between puberty and menopause), ovulation occurs approximately once every twenty-eight days, somewhere around the middle of the menstrual cycle. 92

Ovum (plural *ova*) The sex cell produced by a mature female approximately once every twenty-eight days. When mature, it consists of twenty-three chromosomes as opposed to all other human body cells (somatoplasm), which consist of twenty-three pairs of chromosomes. It is often referred to as an *egg cell.* 66

Palliative care Care of the terminally ill, designed primarily to ease their physical and psychological distress. Specifically, the kind of care provided in hospices. (See *hospice.*) 549

Palmar reflex The grasping reflex that a newborn infant exhibits when an object is placed in its hand. 131

Panic disorder A psychiatric disturbance marked by any of a variety of occasional transient symptoms such as sensations of choking, sweating, nausea, flushes, dizziness, palpitations, trembling, agoraphobia (fear in unfamiliar surroundings), fear of dying, fear of going crazy, and chest pains. 544

Parallel play Situation where two players play side by side but not together, sharing neither toys nor rules. (See *cooperative play; associative play; onlooker play; primitive social play; solitary play.*) 223

Parent alienation syndrome (PAS) Label for condition where child becomes alienated from one or both parents. Sometimes a consequence of a high-stress, high-conflict divorce, where child forms an alliance with one parent in opposition to the other. May have serious long-term consequences for happiness and adjustment. 236

Parental disengagement Phrase used to describe the degree to which the parents' relationship is discordant or ruptured (disengaged). Ranges from varying levels of marital discord through temporary separation, long-term separation, divorce, and death. Degree of parental disengagement may affect children's social competence. 237

Parkinson's disease Generally a disease of the elderly, although it sometimes presents in middle age. Linked to a dopamine deficiency and is evident in tremors, weakness, and sleep disturbances. 499

Partial syndrome eating disorder A highly common form of eating disorder where only some of the symptoms of conventional eating disorders such as anorexia or bulimia are present, or where the eating disorder is periodic rather than constant. 320

Passages Sheehy's term for major developmental milestones during adulthood, used in place of *crisis,* which hints too strongly of calamity; used, as well, to emphasize how each stage serves as a preparation, a passage, into the next. 469

Passion In Sternberg's theory of love, a strong, often sexual, sometimes almost overwhelming desire to be with another person. (See *commitment; intimacy; triangular theory of love.*) 411

Passive vocabulary Consists of all the words the child understands. Not all of these words will actually be used in the child's speech. (See *active vocabulary.*) 147

Pathological cognitive decline A manifestation of age-related cognitive decline where the decline is associated with various conditions such as illness, trauma, or disease that are not inevitable and irreversible consequences of aging. (See *normal cognitive decline.*) 451

Peak height velocity Period during which stature (height) is increasing at the highest rate. Occurs during the adolescent growth spurt and coincides, approximately, with sexual maturation. 247

Peak physical performance Point at which the individual's combination of strength, stamina, agility, and practiced skill permits the highest lifetime level of physical or athletic performance. Occurs in the mid-twenties to mid-thirties for most sports. 381

Peer group A group of equals. Peer groups may be social groups, age groups, intellectual groups, or work groups. When the term applies to young children, it typically refers to age and grade mates. 286

Peers Equals. 188

Perception Reaction to and interpretation of physical stimulation (sensation). A conceptual process, dependent on the activity of the brain. 134

Performance components One of Sternberg's three components of intelligence. Performance components relate to actually doing (reasoning, rehearsing, encoding, analyzing, remembering). (See *metacomponents; knowledge acquisition components.*) 264

Perinatal asphyxia Shortage of oxygen at birth, often caused by a prolapsed umbilical cord. 176

Permissive parenting A parenting style that may be characterized as laissez-faire. Permissive parents are nonpunitive and undemanding. Their children are autonomous rather than obedient, and thus are responsible for their own decisions and actions. 229

Personal fable The belief that we are unique, special, and right. This belief is sometimes exaggerated in adolescence as a function of adolescent egocentrism. 328

Personal narrative The stories we tell ourselves of our own lives that give them a sense of stability and continuity. Includes reminiscences as well as goals. In later life, personal narratives may become more evaluative, taking the form of a life review. (See *life review*.) 518

Personality The set of characteristics that we typically manifest in our interactions with others. It includes all the abilities, predispositions, habits, and other qualities that make each of us different. 158, 476

Pervasive developmental disorder A disorder first manifested in infancy or childhood, evident in delayed or abnormal development especially in social skills, communication, and emotional maturity. May take the form of autism or childhood schizophrenia. 178

Peter Pan syndrome Label for an unwillingness to grow up as adults, evident in a reluctance to accept the responsibilities that normally come with increasing age. 378

Petit mal Label for the milder forms of epilepsy, not characterized by major seizures, and often controllable with drugs. (See *grand mal*.) 177

Phallic stage The third stage in Freud's theory of psychosexual development, beginning at eighteen months and lasting to approximately six years of age. During this stage, children become concerned with their genitals and may show evidence of the much-discussed Oedipus and Electra complexes. 33

Phenomenology An approach concerned primarily with how individuals view their own world. Its basic assumption is that each individual perceives and reacts to the world in a unique manner, and that it is this phenomenological world view that is important in understanding the individual's behavior. 55

Phenotype Manifested characteristics. (See *genotype*.) 69

Phenylketonuria (PKU) A genetic disorder associated with the presence of two recessive genes. 81

Phoneme The simplest unit of language, consisting of a single sound, such as a vowel. 146

Phonology One of the four major components of language. Phonology has to do with the sounds (phonemes) of a language. 146

Phylogeny Changes that occur in a species over generations. Evolutionary changes. (See *ontogeny*.) 15

Physical abuse The main criterion of physical abuse is physical injury, as might result from excessive beating or "shaken baby syndrome." 297

Physical neglect Child maltreatment involving acts of omission rather than commission (failure to provide nourishment, shelter, and/or clothing). Makes up almost half of reported abuse cases. 298

Physiological dependence Also known as *addiction*. The desire to continue using a drug for organic or physiological reasons, and involving unpleasant reactions when the drug is not taken. 365

Placenta A flat, thick membrane attached to the inside of the uterus and to the developing fetus during pregnancy. The placenta connects the mother and the fetus by the umbilical cord. 94

Plateau Continuing sexual arousal following initial excitement, but preceding orgasm. (See *excitement; orgasm; resolution*.) 388

Play May be defined as activities that have no goal other than the enjoyment derived from them. 220

Polyandry Where a wife is permitted more than one husband. (See *bigamy; polygyny; polygamy*.) 419

Polychlorinated biphenyls (PCBs) Group of chemicals, such as dioxin, that may be associated with miscarriage and deformities in offspring. 98

Polygamy Forms of marriage that permit a husband to have more than one wife (polygyny) or a wife to have more than one husband (polyandry) at the same time. (See *bigamy; polygyny; polyandry*.) 419

Polygenetic determination The determination of genetically based characteristics as a function of the interaction of groups of genes. (See *major gene determination*.) 69

Polygyny Where a man is permitted to have more than one wife. (See *bigamy; polygamy; polyandry*.) 419

Population Collections of individuals (or objects or situations) with similar characteristics—for example, the population of all adults above age eighty in institutional care in North America. (See *sample*.) 22

Positive reinforcement A stimulus that increases the probability of a response recurring as a result of being added to a situation after the response has occurred. It usually takes the form of a pleasant stimulus (reward) that results from a specific response. 40

Postconventional Kohlberg's third level of morality, reflecting an understanding of social contract and more individualistic principles of morality. 333

Postmature birth The birth of an infant after the forty-second week of pregnancy. 112

Postpartum depression A form of depression that affects about 10 percent of all women beginning shortly after childbirth. In some cases, postpartum depression can be serious and dangerous, but usually ameliorates and disappears with time. 115

Posttraumatic stress disorder A mental disorder that may not manifest until a considerable period of time following a particularly stressful experience such as being in war, being tortured, or being sexually abused.

Possible symptoms include fatigue, depression, loss of appetite, and obsessive thoughts. 300

Practice play   See *sensorimotor play*. 221

Pragmatics   One of four components of language, relating to the practical aspects of language. Pragmatics includes all the implicit rules that govern when and how speakers interact in conversation, as well as the subtle rules of intonation, accent, emphasis, and other variations that give rise to different meanings. 147

Preconcept   The label given to the preconceptual child's incomplete understanding of concept, resulting from an inability to classify. 192

Preconceptual   Piaget's label for the first subphase of the preoperational period, spanning ages two to four, characterized by an excessive reliance on perception and egocentricity. 192

Preconventional   The first of Kohlberg's three stages of moral development, based on hedonistic or obedience-oriented judgments. 332

Pregnancy   The condition of a woman who has had an ovum (egg cell) fertilized and who, nature willing, will eventually give birth. 92

Pregnancy hormone   Specifically, human chorionic gonadotropin (HCG), a hormone detectable in a pregnant woman's urine and blood. Its presence is the basis for most home pregnancy detection kits. 92

Preimplantation diagnosis   A fetal diagnostic technique in which fertilization typically occurs *in vitro* and a cell from the fertilized ovum is removed and examined for abnormalities prior to implantation in the mother. 85

Premature birth   The birth of a baby between the twenty-ninth and thirty-sixth weeks of pregnancy. A premature baby weighs between 2 and 5½ pounds (1,0 to 2,499 grams). 112

Premature ejaculation   A male sexual dysfunction marked by an inability to control ejaculation. 389

Prenatal development   The period of development beginning at conception and ending at birth. That period lasts approximately nine calendar months in the human female (266 days). Chickens develop considerably faster. 92

Preoperation   Piaget's label for a thought that is not limited by ordinary rules of logic. Preoperations tend to be unstable, idiosyncratic, perception dominated, and egocentric. 253

Preoperational   Piaget's general label for the period that precedes the development of thought processes governed by clear rules of logic (approximately up to age 6 or 7). Also used to describe thinking that is egocentric and perception bound. 192

Preoperational thought   The second of Piaget's four major stages, lasting from about two to seven or eight years. It consists of two substages: intuitive thinking and preconceptual thinking. 47

Presbycusis   Most common cause of hearing loss with age, associated with degeneration of auditory system. Most evident in loss of ability to hear higher tones. 442, 496

Presbyopia   A form of farsightedness due primarily to loss of elasticity of the lens, making it difficult to accommodate vision for close distances. Common with increasing age. 500

Pretend play   See *imaginative play*. 221

Primary aging   Nearly universal changes associated with advancing age, such as loss or atrophy of brain cells or loss of bone calcium. 497

Primary circular reaction   An expression used by Piaget to describe a simple reflex activity such as thumb-sucking. 143

Primary sexual characteristics   Sexual characteristics directly associated with reproduction (for example, ovaries and testes). 315

Primitive social play   Precursor to true social play, in which player (typically an infant) interacts with another, but without any clear notion of shared rules (as in an infant's *peek-a-boo* game). (See *cooperative play*; *associative play*; *parallel play*; *onlooker play*; *solitary play*.) 223

Process disorders   A type of learning disability that involves a deficit in a basic psychological process such as perceiving, remembering, or paying attention. In practice, process disorders are difficult to separate from other specific learning disabilities such as developmental reading or arithmetic disorder. (See *developmental reading disorder*; *developmental arithmetic disorder*.) 270

Profound retardation   A degree of mental retardation defined in terms of a measured IQ below 20 or 25 and marked by limited motor development and a need for nursing care. 269

Project Head Start   A large-scale, federally funded preschool program in the United States conceived as part of the war on poverty. It is designed to overcome some of the disadvantages associated with economic and social deprivation in early life and, in a sense, to give children a head start. 200

Prolapsed cord   A condition that sometimes occurs during birth when the umbilical cord becomes constricted. The effect may be brain damage, the severity of which relates to the length of time during which oxygen supply is cut off or reduced. 115

Prone   On the belly. A sleep position. 129

Propinquity   Nearness in place or time. Social psychology's term for physical proximity—clearly essential for interpersonal attraction and love. 413

Proposition   In my grandmother's lexicon, something that comes on the heels of a dishonorable impulse. In logic, a statement or declaration presented for discussion or proof. A statement that is capable of being true or false. 324

Protagonist The lead character. The one who plays the main part. Generally, the "good" person (as opposed to the *antagonist*). We are our own protagonists in our personal narratives. 519

Proteins Molecules made up of chains of one or more amino acids. In a sense, proteins are the basis of organic life. 67

Proud-to-be-eighties Sheehy's label for the development period that spans the 80's. 469

Proximodistal Literally, from near to far. Refers to a developmental progression in which central organs develop before external limbs, and the infant acquires control over muscles close to the center of the body before acquiring control over those that are more peripheral. 96, 134

Psychoanalytic General label for Freudian theory. Also used to describe clinical or therapeutic procedures based on Freudian ideas, and especially on ideas related to the subconscious. 31

Psycholinguists Those who study the relationship between language (linguistics) and development, thinking, learning, and behaving (psychology). 146

Psychological dependence Drug dependence in which the desire to continue taking a drug is related primarily to its psychological rather than its physical effects (for example, a strong sense of well-being). 365

Psychology The science that examines human behavior (and that of animals as well). 4

Psychosexual A term used to describe psychological phenomena based on sexuality. Freud's theories are psychosexual in that they attribute development to sexually based forces and motives. 33

Psychosocial Pertaining to events or behaviors that relate to the social aspects of development. Erikson's theory is psychosocial in that it deals with the resolution of social crises and the development of social competencies (independence or identity, for example). 35, 216, 408, 464

Puberty Sexual maturity following pubescence. 66, 313

Pubescence Changes that occur in late childhood or early adolescence and that result in sexual maturity. In boys, these changes include enlargement of the testes, growth of axillary hair, deepening of the voice, and the ability to ejaculate semen. In girls, pubescence is characterized by rapid physical growth, occurrence of the first menstrual period (menarche), a slight lowering of the voice, and enlargement and development of the breasts. 313

Punishment Involves either the presentation of an unpleasant stimulus (punishment I or castigation) or the withdrawal of a pleasant stimulus (punishment II or penalty) as a consequence of behavior. Punishment should not be confused with negative reinforcement because punishment does not increase the probability of a response occurring; rather, it is intended to have the opposite result. 40

Pupillary reflex An involuntary change in the size of the pupil as a function of brightness; it is present in the neonate. 135

Quickening The name given to the first movements of the fetus in utero. Quickening does not occur until after the fifth month of pregnancy. 92

Rape Forcible sexual intercourse. In some legal jurisdictions, the definition would specify *with someone other than a spouse*. 431

Rape myth Any of a large number of widely held, culturally based fictions about male and female sexuality used primarily by males to downplay the significance of sexual harassment and acquaintance rape. Most of these myths view the woman as at least partly to blame for unwanted sexual activity. 433

Rape shield law Legislation which prohibits that the victim's sexual history or possibly promiscuous behaviors be used against her. 433

Rapid eye movement (REM) sleep A stage of sleep characterized by rapid eye movements. Most of our dreaming occurs during REM sleep, which accounts for approximately 25 percent of an adult's sleep time and as much as 50 percent of an infant's. 157

Reaction range All the possible outcomes for a particular characteristic given variations in the nature and timing of environmental influences. 71

Recessive gene A gene whose characteristics are not manifest in the offspring unless it is paired with another recessive gene. When a recessive gene is paired with a dominant gene, the characteristics of the dominant gene will be manifest. 69

Reciprocal determinism Bandura's expression for the notion that not only does the social context affect the individual, but the individual also affects the context. This idea is also a fundamental aspect of Bronfenbrenner's position. 53

Recognition recall Describes memory tasks that require participants simply to recognize familiar experiences. (See *free recall.*) 504

Reflex(es) Simple, unlearned, genetically based, unconscious, and largely unavoidable reactions to specific stimuli—such as blinking the eye in response to a puff of air. 124, 131

Reflex smiling Also termed *spontaneous smiling*, the earliest form of infant smile, reflecting bursts of cortical activity rather than contentment or social reactivity. (See *social smiling; selective social smiling.*) 162

Rehearsing A memory process involving repetition, important in maintaining information in short-term memory and in transferring it to long-term memory. (See *elaborating; organizing.*) 140, 260

Reinforcement The effect of a reinforcer. Specifically, to increase the probability of a response recurring. 40

Reinforcer   A reinforcing stimulus. A consequence, such as a reward, that increases the probability of a behavior recurring. 40

Reintegration stage   The last of Schaie's stages of adult cognitive development, beginning at about the time of retirement from career as well as from child-rearing and other social, political, or religious responsibilities. Marked by a reexamination of goals and of life. (See *acquisition stage; responsibility stage; executive stage; achievement stage.*) 399

Relational aggression   See *social aggression.* 292

Releaser   A biological term for the stimulus that first gives rise to instinct-like behaviors such as the "following" behavior of newly hatched chicks. In this case, the *releaser* is generally the mother hen. 49

Reliable   A measure is reliable to the extent that it measures accurately whatever it measures. 263

Reminiscence   A largely passive activity defined mainly in terms of scattered recollections of past events and experiences. Typically not purposeful or evaluative as might be a *life review.* (See *life review.*) 519

Reservoir-of-family-wisdom role   A grandparenting role where grandparents are seen as an important source of wisdom and advice. 527

Resolution   A rapid return to a preexcitement phase in the normal cycle of human sexual responding. (See *excitement; orgasm; plateau.*) 388

Respondent   A response elicited by a specific known stimulus, used by Skinner to contrast with *operant.* 40, 388

Response   Any organic, muscular, glandular, or psychic reaction resulting from stimulation. 38

Responsibility stage   The middle adulthood stage of cognitive development in Schaie's proposal, marked by the reevaluation of goals and behaviors in response primarily to social and family responsibilities. (See *acquisition stage; achieving stage; executive stage; reintegration stage.*) 399

Restriction fragment length polymorphisms   Abbreviated RFLPs (pronounced "rifflips"), describes the results of a scientific procedure in molecular genetics whereby enzymes cause pieces of chromosome to break up into fragments of different lengths when their genetic structure is different. Used to identify marker genes associated with various defects and other characteristics. (See *marker genes.*) 71

Retarded ejaculation   A male sexual dysfunction in which the man is occasionally incapable of achieving an orgasm during intercourse. 389

Retirement   Permanent leaving of full-time work, often with a pension, and sometimes mandatory at a given age. 520

Retrospective studies   A research procedure where investigators try to gather information about subjects' histories in an attempt to explain current outcomes. 230

Reversibility   A logical property manifested in the ability to reverse or undo activity in either an empirical or conceptual sense. An idea is said to be reversible when a child can unthink it and realizes that certain logical consequences follow from doing so. 192, 254

Reward   An object, stimulus, event, or outcome that is perceived as pleasant and may therefore be reinforcing. 38

Rh factor   A blood protein found in some individuals but not in others. When present in the fetus's blood but not in the mother, can cause birth complications. 106

Rhogam   (Rh Immune Globulin or RhIG). Substance used to inoculate Rh(D) negative mothers to prevent the formation of Rh antibodies. Rhogam is blood that already contains passive antibodies. 106

Rigor mortis   Literally, the "stiffness of death." Refers to the characteristic rigidity of the human body shortly after death. 542

Ritalin   A stimulant drug of the amphetamine family whose effect is to sedate rather than stimulate children diagnosed with hyperactivity. Also a relatively common street drug that is combined with the drug Talwin to produce what is sometimes known as "poor man's heroin." 303

Rites de passage   A collective term for the ceremonies and rites that accompany transition from one stage to another within a culture. The most dramatic examples of rites de passage include the initiation or puberty rites of some "primitive" cultures. 312

Role-reversal   The reversal of traditional roles—as, for example, when children are called upon to care for their aging parents. 527

Romantic/erotic love   Love that is distinct from mother/infant or sibling love, for example. Love marked by strong feelings of longing, a desire to be intimate, a preoccupation and overvaluation of the loved one, and a belief that the other is necessary for one's happiness. In Sternberg's theory of love, equivalent to *consummate love.* (See *consummate love.*) 411

Rooting reflex   A neonatal reflex manifested, for example, in the infant's attempts to find a breast. 131

Rubber band hypothesis   Stern's comparison of human intelligence to a rubber band, the original length of which is genetically determined but the final length of which is affected by the environmental forces that stretch it. 78

Sample   A subset of a population. A representative selection of individuals with similar characteristics drawn from a larger group—for example, a sample comprising one-third of adults above age eighty in institutional care facilities in one city. (See *population.*) 22

Satisfaction   A relatively stable dimension related to the fulfillment of one's expectations or aspirations or to a resignation to the way things are. (See *happiness*.) 479

Scarification   The formation of scars. Often a deliberate part of primitive passage rites. 312

Scheme   (also *schema* or *schemata*) The label used by Piaget to describe a unit in cognitive structure. In one sense, a scheme is an activity together with its structural connotations. In another sense, a scheme may be thought of as an idea or a concept. It usually labels a specific activity: the looking scheme, the grasping scheme, the sucking scheme. 46, 141

Script   A term used to describe our knowledge of what goes with what and in what sequence. Scripts are a part of cognitive structure that deals with the routine and the predictable. 258

Secondary circular reaction   Infant responses that are circular in the sense that the response serves as a stimulus for its own repetition and secondary because the responses do not center on the child's body, as do primary circular reactions. 143

Secondary sexual characteristics   Sex-linked features not directly linked with reproduction (for example, facial hair or breast development). 315

Securely attached   Describes infants who are strongly and positively attached to a caregiver, who are distressed when that person leaves, and who quickly reestablish contact when the person returns. 166

Selective sixties   Sheehy's label for the decade of the 60's. 469

Selective social smile   Smiling in response to social stimuli that the infant can identify as familiar. (See *reflex smiling; social smiling*.) 162

Self   The concept that an individual has of himself or herself. Notions of the self are often closely allied with individuals' beliefs about how others perceive them. 282, 340

Self-actualization   The process or act of becoming oneself, developing one's potential, achieving an awareness of one's identity, fulfilling oneself. The term *actualization* is central to humanistic psychology. 56

Self-concept   The concept that an individual has of him- or herself. Notions of the self are often closely allied with individuals' beliefs about how others perceive them. 282

Self-directed regulatory behaviors   Means of controlling emotional reaction that focus on the infant's body (for example, thumb-sucking or closing one's eyes so as not to be frightened). (See *other-directed regulatory behavior*.) 163

Self-efficacy   Personal estimates of our effectiveness in dealing with the world. 44, 396

Self-esteem   See *self-worth*. 282, 340

Self-image   Expression often used interchangeably with self concept. Literally, how people view themselves. 342

Self-referent   Pertaining to the self. Self-referent thought is thought that concerns our own mental processes (for example, thoughts that evaluate our abilities or that monitor our progress in solving problems). 44

Self-worth   The desire to be held in high esteem by others and to maintain a high opinion of one's own behavior and person. 282

Semantic memory   A type of declarative (conscious, long-term) memory consisting of stable knowledge about the world, principles, rules and procedures, and other verbalizable aspects of knowledge, including language. (See *episodic memory*.) 260, 503

Semantics   The component of language that relates to meaning or significance of sounds. 147

Seminal emission   Ejaculation. The emission of semen, a liquid containing sperm, by the male. 388

Senescence   Technically, the period in later adulthood marked by physical and cognitive decline. It begins at different ages for different individuals and is not always characterized by very dramatic changes. 497

Sensation   The physical effect of stimulation. A physiological process dependent on activity of the senses. 134

Sensation-seeking   A personality trait reflected in a willingness, and a desire, to take risks for the sensations involved. A high sensation-seeking drive might be evident in activities such as driving motorcycles, automobile racing, ice-climbing, or using drugs. 330

Sensitive period   A period during which specific experiences have their most pronounced effects—for example, the first six months of life, during which the infant forms strong attachment bonds to the mother or caregiver. 50

Sensory motor   See sensorimotor period. 132

Sensorimotor period   The first stage of development in Piaget's classification. It lasts from birth to approximately age two and is so-called because children understand their world primarily through their activities toward it and sensations of it. 47, 143

Sensorimotor play (also called *practice play*)   Activity involving the manipulation of objects or execution of activities simply for the sensations that are produced. (See *play*.) 221

Sensory memory   The simple sensory recognition of stimuli (also called *short-term sensory memory*). Sensory memory requires no cognitive processing and does not involve conscious awareness or attention. 257

Separation protest   Label used to describe the infant or young child's reaction to short-term separation from a primary caregiver. 170

Sequential designs   Research strategies that involve taking a sequence of samples at different times of measurement in order to reduce or eliminate biases that may result from confounding the effects of the age of subjects, the time of testing, and the cohort to which subjects belong. 21, 450

Seriation   The ordering of objects according to one or more empirical properties. To seriate is essentially to place in order. 256

Severe retardation   A level of mental retardation defined in terms of an IQ range between 20 or 25 and 35 or 40. Individuals at this level can learn to communicate and, with systematic training, to take care of simple hygiene. 269

Sex cells   Technically, *gametes*. Sperm and ovum. Mature sex cells each contain twenty-three chromosomes rather than twenty-three pairs, and are different from each other. (See *somatic cells; gametes*.) 68

Sex chromosome   A chromosome contained in sperm cells and ova that is responsible for determining the sex of offspring. Sex chromosomes produced by the female are of one variety (X); those produced by the male are either X or Y. At fertilization (the union of sperm and ovum), an XX pairing will result in a girl, and an XY pairing will result in a boy. The sperm cell is essentially responsible for determining the offspring's sex. 68

Sex roles   See *gender roles*. 175

Sexual abuse   A form of maltreatment in which the victim is forced—physically or by virtue of the abuser's status and power—to submit to sexual behaviors (ranging from talking, looking, or touching to actual intercourse or other sexual acts). Children are often victims of sexual abuse. 298

Sexual assault   Covers a wide variety of unwanted sexual behaviors, including sexual innuendo, unwanted suggestions, and forcible rape. (See *sexual harassment*.) 431

Sexual double standard   An unwritten, culturally based understanding that certain sexual behaviors are permissible for one sex (male) but not the other. In some industrialized countries, the double standard has been torn to shreds; in many parts of the world, it still flies. 354

Sexual dysfunction   Impediments to participation in or enjoyment of sexual intercourse. Includes impotence, premature ejaculation, and vaginismus (painful contractions of the vagina). 389

Sexual harassment   Generally used to describe the milder forms of sexual assault, short of forcible sexual intercourse (rape). 431

Sexual stereotype   A preconceived belief about gender differences and gender roles. 351

Sexually transmitted diseases (STDs)   Diseases transmitted solely or primarily through sexual activity. The most common STDs are chlamydia, gonorrhea, and herpes; less common are syphilis and AIDS. 360

Shaken baby syndrome   The effects of violent shaking of an infant. Essentially a whiplash-related brain injury, typically with retinal damage sometimes leading to blindness. Fatal or permanently harmful in a large percentage of cases. 297

Short-term memory   A type of memory in which material is available for recall for a matter of seconds. Short-term memory primarily involves rehearsal rather than more in-depth processing. It defines our immediate consciousness or awareness. 257, 503

Siblings   Offspring whose parents are the same; brothers and sisters. 75

Sickle-cell anemia   A blood-cell disorder associated with a recessive gene, far more common among blacks than whites. 80

SIDS home monitors   Cardiorespiratory sensors sometimes used by parents to monitor the breathing and pulse of their sleeping, at-risk infants. 130

Significant developmental motor disability   A collection of symptoms manifested early in life, evident primarily in motor problems, associated with brain damage, and commonly labeled "cerebral palsy." Can vary in severity from barely detectable to severe paralysis. (See *cerebral palsy*.) 176

Slow-to-warm-up infants   An infant temperament type marked by low activity level, high initial withdrawal from the unfamiliar, slow adaptation to change, and a somewhat negative mood, with moderate or low intensity of reaction. 159

Small-for-gestational age (SGA)   Infants who weigh less than 90 percent of average weight of newborns of the same gestational age. (See *large-for-gestational age; average-for-gestational age*.) 112

Social aggression   A form of aggression that seeks to harm someone by disrupting his or her social relations (also called *relational aggression*). The methods of relational aggression are ridicule, social exclusion, rumor mongering, malicious teasing, contempt, and disdain. (See *aggression; violence; overt aggression*.) 292, 353

Social cognition   The realization that others have feelings, motives, intentions, and so on; knowledge of the emotions of others. 280

Social isolates   Those who interact very little with others. Some social isolates are socially rejected (not well liked); others are well liked, but still don't interact very much socially. 287

Social learning theory   Theory that looks at the acquisition of socially acceptable behavior. Alternatively, theory that explains learning on the basis of observation. 225

Social play   Activity that involves interaction between two or more children and frequently takes the form of games with more or less precisely defined rules. 222

Social–psychological   Label for causes of disorders that are not genetic–congenital. Might include factors such as neglect, maltreatment, malnutrition, head injuries, and diseases and illnesses, as well as conditions within the family, like stress associated with conflict. (See *genetic–congenital*.) 302

Social readjustment rating scale   A scale that attempts to measure stress by looking at recent changes in an individual's life. 386

Social referencing   The act of looking at how others respond to a social situation as a guide for one's own reactions. 219

Social smiling   The second phase in the development of smiling, initially occurring in response to auditory and visual stimuli that are social in nature, like the caregiver's voice. (See *reflex smiling; selective social smiling.*) 162

Social speech   In Vygotsky's theorizing, the most primitive stage of language development, evident before age three, during which the child expresses simple thoughts and emotions out loud. The function of social speech is to control the behavior of others. (See *egocentric speech; inner speech.*) 52

Socialization   The complex process of learning those behaviors that are appropriate within a given culture as well as those that are less appropriate. The primary agents of socialization are home, school, and peer groups. 216, 219

Sociobiology   The systematic study of the biological basis of all social behavior. 50

Sociogram   A pictorial or graphic representation of the social structure of a group. 287

Sociometric status   A description of how wll a person is accepted and liked by members of a peer group. 287

Sociometry   A measurement procedure used extensively in sociological studies. It attempts to determine patterns of likes and dislikes in groups; it also plots group structure. 287

Solitary play   Play involving a single child. Contrasted with *social play.* (See *social play.*) 223

Solitude   A state forced on those who have no friends and who cannot, or will not, buy companionship. Also, a state chosen by those who simply prefer to be alone (at least part of the time). 350

Somatic cells   Also called *body cells,* all cells in our body other than sex cells. Normal somatic cells each contain twenty-three pairs of chromosomes. All our body cells normally contain identical genetic information. (See *sex cells.*) 68

Special abilities theory   A theory of intelligence based on the assumption that intelligence consists of several separate factors (for example, numerical, verbal, memory) rather than a single underlying factor common to performance in all areas. (See *general factor theory.*) 263

Special needs   Global term that includes all who need special training, equipment, or services to reach their full human potential. What is often termed *special education* is also *special needs education* or education for those with *special needs.* 251

Specimen description   As a method of child study, it involves recording detailed, specific instances of a child's behavior. Useful for in-depth studies of individual children. 16

Sperm cell   The sex cell produced by a mature male. Like egg cells (ova), sperm cells consist of twenty-three chromosomes rather than twenty-three pairs of chromosomes. 66

Spermarche   A boy's first ejaculation. Often a nocturnal event. (See *menarche.*) 316, 356

Spontaneous abortion   A miscarriage occurring usually before the twentieth week of pregnancy when the fetus normally weighs less than one pound. 112

Stage   An identifiable phase in the development of human beings. Developmental theories such as Piaget's are referred to as *stage theories* because they describe behavior at different developmental levels. 15

Standard deviation   A mathematical measure of the distribution of scores around their mean (average). In a *normal distribution,* about 68 percent of all scores fall within one standard deviation of the mean; 95 percent fall within two standard deviations of the mean. 246

Stereotype   Denotes a fixed, firm, relatively unexamined belief typically generalized to a class of superficially similar situations or individuals. 225

Stethoscope   A medical instrument that amplifies the sound of a heartbeat. 92

Stimulus   (plural *stimuli*) Any change in the physical environment capable of exciting a sense organ. 38

Strange Situation   Label for Ainsworth's widely used approach for investigating infant–caregiver attachment, based on the infant's reaction to separation and reunion with the caregiver. (See *securely attached.*) 166

Stress   A force exerted on an individual often related to change or to high environmental demands; sometimes associated with high arousal. 304, 344, 386

Strong Interest Inventory   A well-known, highly respected instrument used primarily to measure vocational interest. 392

Stunting   Severe growth retardation, defined as more than 2 sandard deviations below average height relative to normal children of the same age. (See *wasting.*) 246

Sturm und drang   Literally, "storm and stress" (German). G. Stanley Hall's expression to describe what he thought was the confusion, the turmoil, the stresses, the difficulties of the adolescent period. 312, 343

Subtractive bilingualism   Phrase used to describe a situation where learning a second language has a generally negative effect often evident in lower proficiency in both languages. (See *additive bilingualism.*) 207

Sucking reflex   The automatic sucking response of a newborn child when the mouth is stimulated. Nipples are particularly appropriate for eliciting the sucking reflex. 95, 131

Sudden infant death syndrome (SIDS)   Unexplained and unexpected infant death. The leading cause of infant death between ages one month and one year. (Not really a cause, because it is unknown; SIDS is simply a label.) 100, 128

Superego   The third level of personality, according to Freud. It defines the moral or ethical aspects of personality and, like the ego, is in constant conflict with the id. 32

Supermale syndrome   A chromosomal disorder affecting males with 2 Y chromosomes (hency XYY), sometimes linked with greater than average height, lower intelligence, higher impulsivity, and, tentatively, higher criminality. 83

Supine   On the back. A sleep position. 130

Surrogate parent role   A grandparenting style where grandparents assume the childcaring roles of parents, acting as substitute parents. 527

Symbolic   The final stage in the development of a child's representation of the world. The term may also be used to describe a representation of the world through arbitrary symbols. Symbolic representation includes language, as well as theoretical or hypothetical systems.

Symbolic models   Nonhuman models such as movies, television programs, verbal and written instructions, and religious, literary, musical, and folk heroes. 42, 219

Syncretic reasoning   A type of semilogical reasoning characteristic of the classification behavior of the very young preschooler. In syncretic reasoning, objects are grouped according to egocentric criteria. These criteria change from object to object. In other words, children do not classify on the basis of a single dimension but change dimensions as they classify. 193

Syntax   Part of the grammar of a language that consists of the set of implicit or explicit rules that govern the combination of words that compose a language. 147

Taboo   A prohibition imposed by social custom or as a protective measure. 312

Tay–Sachs disease   A fatal genetic enzyme disorder that can be detected before birth, but that cannot yet be prevented or cured. 81

Temperament   The biological basis of personality—its hereditary components. 158

Teratogen   An external influence (as opposed to an inherited genetic influence) such as a virus or a drug that is capable of producing defects in a fetus. 96

Terman studies   An ongoing, long-term, longitudinal investigation initially designed to study the development and correlates of high intelligence in children (initially called the Terman Studies of Genius). The Terman studies have provided data relevant to a large number of lifespan developmental issues. 234

Terminal drop   A label for the observed decline in measured intelligence that sometimes occurs a year or two before a person's death. 506

Tertiary circular reaction   An infant's response that is circular in the sense that the response serves as the stimulus for its own repetition, although the repeated response is not identical to the first response. This last characteristic, the altered response, distinguishes a tertiary from a secondary circular reaction. 144

Testes   Organs, of which there are two, that produce sperm in males. 315

Testosterone   Important male sex hormone, produced by the testes. Associated with sex drive, as well as with aggression. 353

Tests of divergent thinking   Creativity tests. Usually open-ended *production* tests designed to measure factors such as fluency, flexibility, and originality. 272

Tetrahydrocannabinol (THC)   The active ingredient in marijuana and related substances (hashish, bhang). 367

Theory   In its simplest sense, an explanation of observations. Theories emphasize which facts (observations) are important for understanding and which relationships among facts are most important. 30

Theory of immune system malfunction   A theory of aging that reflects the idea that with advancing age, the immune system weakens and is less able to protect us from disease and infection, and that it sometimes makes errors that define *autoimmunity*. (See *autoimmunity*.) 494

Theory of mind   The child's loosely organized notions about the nature of thinking, imagining, remembering, learning, and other mental processes. The child's understanding of the "mind" and of mental states, and the realization that these exist in both self and others. 222, 280

Theory of multiple intelligences   Howard Gardner's belief that human intelligence consists of seven distinct and largely unrelated areas of talent or capability: logical–mathematical, linguistic, musical, spatial, bodily–kinesthetic, interpersonal, and intrapersonal. 265

Thoughtful seventies   Sheehy's label for the developmental period spanning ages 70 to 79. 469

Time-lag study   A research design in which subjects of the same age but belonging to different cohorts are compared (for example, forty-year-olds in 1985 are compared with other cohorts of forty-year-olds in 1990 and 1995). 21

Time sampling   A method of child observation in which behavior is observed during specific time intervals, frequently with the aim of recording instances or frequency of specific behaviors. 16

Toxin theory of cell malfunction   Recognizes that a gradual buildup of foreign material in body cells may eventually lead to their death and is one of the explanations for aging. 494

Trait   Any distinct, consistent quality in which one person can be different from another. (See *types*.) 476

Transductive reasoning   The type of semilogical reasoning that proceeds from particular to particular rather than from particular to general or from general to particular. One example of transductive reasoning is the following: (1) Cows give milk; (2) goats give milk; (3) therefore, goats are cows. 193

Transgenics   Term used to describe a genetic engineering procedure that combines gene material from different species. 67

Transitional bilingualism   Describes a situation in which a minority language is gradually replaced by the dominant language, essentially disappearing within a few generations. 207

Transitional objects   A general term for objects such as blankets and bears that are temporary objects of attachment and affection for some children while they are in transition between high dependence on parents and growing personal independence. 171

Transplacental hemorrhage   The transmission of blood from mother to fetus via the placenta. Occurs in approximately 50 percent of all pregnancies. 106

Transverse presentation   A crosswise presentation of the fetus at birth. 110

Triangular theory of love   Sternberg's notion that love consists of a particular combination of passion, commitment, and intimacy, and can take a variety of different forms depending on the presence or absence of each of these. (See *commitment; intimacy; passion.*) 411

Triarchic theory of intelligence   Sternberg's notion that intelligence can usefully be viewed in terms of three parts (three arches): the contextual (intelligence defined in terms of its immediate context), the componential (meta-, performance, and knowledge-acquisition components of intelligent behavior), and the experiential (a practical, experienced-based intelligence). 000

Trisomy 21   The medical label for *Down syndrome.* (See *Down syndrome.*) 82

Trust versus mistrust   The first of Erikson's stages (to age two), marked by a conflict between the infant's need to develop trust and an urge to remain dependent. 35, 216

Turner's syndrome   A chromosomal abnormality in which a female child is born with a missing sex chromosome, characterized by underdeveloped secondary sexual characteristics that can sometimes be improved with injections of estrogen before puberty. 83

Type A individuals   A personality type descriptive of individuals who are hard-driving, aggressive, ambitious, impatient, and competitive. (See *Type B individuals.*) 386

Type B individuals   A personality type defined in terms of individuals who are relaxed, easygoing, and noncompetitive. (See *Type A individuals.*) 386

Types   Any of several clusterings of personality traits. *Extraversion,* for example, is a personality type that includes traits such as boldness, outgoingness, assertiveness, and sociability. (See *trait.*) 158, 476

Ultrasound   A diagnostic technique in medicine whereby high-frequency sound waves are used to provide images of internal body structures. Ultrasound recordings are used extensively to evaluate the condition of the fetus. 85

Umbilical cord   A long, thick cord attached to what will be the child's navel at one end and to the placenta at the other. It transmits nourishment and oxygen to the growing fetus from the mother and carries away waste material from the fetus. 94

Unconditioned response   A response elicited by an unconditioned stimulus. 39

Unconditioned stimulus   A stimulus that elicits a response prior to learning. All stimuli capable of eliciting reflexive behaviors are examples of unconditioned stimuli. For example, food is an unconditioned stimulus for the response of salivation. 39

U.S. English   One of several highly organized lobby groups dedicated to the promotion of English as the sole language in U.S. schools and governments. 209

Uterus   The organ in which the embryo or fetus is contained and nourished during pregnancy; also called the *womb.* 93

Vaginismus   A female sexual dysfunction marked by involuntary contractions of the vagina that make intercourse painful or impossible. 389

Valid   A measure is said to be valid to the extent that it measures what it is intended to measure. (See *reliable.*) 263

Variable   A property, measurement, or characteristic that is susceptible to variation. In psychological experimentation, qualities of human beings such as intelligence and creativity are referred to as variables. (See *dependent variable; independent variable.*) 16

Vegetative reflex   A reflex pertaining to the intake of food (for example, swallowing and sucking). 131

Venereal diseases   Infrequently used expression for *sexually transmitted diseases (STDs).* (See *sexually transmitted diseases [STDs].*) 360

Version   Turning the fetus manually to assist delivery. 110

Villi   Tiny, tentacle-like growths emanating from the fertilized egg, allowing it to attach itself to the uterine wall, to what will become the placenta. 94

Violence   An extreme form of aggressiveness, implying physical action and real or possible physical harm to people or objects. (See *aggression.*) 292

Visually impaired   Technically, those who, with corrected vision in their best eye, can see at 20 feet what normal people see at 200 feet—which level of sight defines *legal blindness.* 251

Vocation   Refers to a "calling" and is usually restricted to a religious occupation, although it is also sometimes used to refer to certain white-collar careers such as law or medicine. (See *work; job; occupation; career.*) 391

Wasting Defined as more than 2 standard deviations below normal weight for average children of that age—that is, in the bottom 2.27 percent of a comparable population. (See *stunting*.) 246

Whorfian hypothesis In its extreme form, the belief that language is essential for thinking, that thinking does not occur in its absence. In its more moderate form, the belief that language *influences* thinking. 210

Widowers Men whose wives are dead and who have not remarried. 529

Widows Women whose husbands have died and who are not remarried. 529

Wisdom A quality of human personality and behavior reflected in knowledge that is wide-ranging and deep, not easily accessible, and directed toward goodness. Often associated with old age. 508

Work Activities engaged in for gain rather than primarily for the pleasure derived from them. A general term that includes jobs, occupations, and careers. 391

Young-old A Neugarten classification of the elderly, roughly between ages fifty-five and seventy-five, often still marked by high activity levels and productive use of time. 488

Youth A general term for young people, often loosely defined. In this text, it spans the period from age fourteen to age twenty-four—because nobody can be called an adult prior to the age of fourteen and nobody can still be classed as a child after the age of twenty-four. 378

Zone of proximal development Vygotsky's phrase for the individual's current potential for further intellectual development—a capacity not ordinarily measured by conventional intelligence tests. Vygotsky suggests that hints and questions might help in assessing this zone. 53

Zygote A fertilized egg cell (ovum), formed from the union of sperm and egg cells, and normally containing a full complement of twenty-three pairs of chromosomes. 83, 93

Photo Credits

p. 2 MHH/Stock, Boston; p. 6 Mary Cassat, *Women Admiring a Child*, pastel, 1897, Gift of Edward Chandler Walker, © 1987 The Detroit Institute of Arts; p. 7 Courtesy of the Huntington Library; p. 8 (below) Corbis-Bettmann; p. 8 (above) UPI/Corbis-Bettmann; p. 14 Robert Brenner/PhotoEdit; p. 11 Reuters/Corbis-Bettmann; p. 12 SuperStock; p. 18 (all 5) Courtesy of the Herman Friedman estate; p. 19 © Jean Claude Lejeune/Stock, Boston; p. 24 John Bergez; p. 28 Gale S. Zucker/Stock, Boston; p. 31 Wide World Photos; p. 32 Marti Wall; p. 35 Tekla Weber; p. 42 Jim Mahoney/The Image Works; p. 43 Reuters/Corbis-Bettmann; p. 47 Karen Garrison; p. 52 Nita Winter; p. 50 © Eric Neurath/Stock, Boston; p. 56 AP/Wide World Photos; p. 62 UPI/Corbis-Bettmann; p. 64 Corbis-Bettmann; p. 67 Corbis-Bettmann; p. 69 Catherine Linberg; p. 70 Ann Butler; p. 82 Susan Walters; p. 75 Ira Berger/Woodfin Camp & Associates; p. 81 The National Foundation for the March of Dimes; p. 90 Stock, Boston; p. 93 © Omikron/Photo Researchers, Inc.; p. 94 Carnegie Institute of Washington, Department of Embryology, Davis Division; p. 99 Elizabeth Crews; p. 101 Peter Hendrie/The Image Bank; p. 104 Alon Reininger/Woodfin Camp & Associates; p. 108 Brandon Carson; p. 111 Patricia Waldo; p. 114 Elizabeth Crews/Stock, Boston; p. 117 Bill Aron/Jeroboam; p. 122 Marvin E. Newman/The Image Bank; p. 126 & 127 Tekla Weber; p. 130 © Nubar Alexanain/Stock, Boston; p. 133 (clockwise) Elizabeth Crews, Michael Weisbrot/Stock, Boston, Elizabeth Crews/Stock, Boston, Elizabeth Crews/Stock, Boston; p. 134 Hickman Archives; p. 137 Lucy T. Howat Archives; p. 139 Julie Davis; p. 142 Brandon Carson; p. 144 © Suzanne Szasz/Photo Researchers, Inc.; p. 148 Rohn Engh/

The Image Works; p. 135 Both photos courtesy William Vandivert, *Scientific American*, April 1960; p. 154 J. Du Boisberran/The Image Bank; p. 156 © Michael Weisbrot/The Image Works; p. 158 (above) Karen Garrison; p. 158 (below) Guy Lefrançois; p. 162 Cecilia Mantecon; p. 167 Harlow Primate Laboratory, University of Wisconsin; p. 164 D. Ogust/The Image Works; p. 168 Roberta Broyer; p. 170 Elizabeth Crews/Stock, Boston; p. 173 (above) Jill Jacobson; p. 173 (below) Robert Kauser; p. 174 Angela Mann; p. 187 B. Wells/The Image Works; p. 179 © Alan Carey/The Image Works; p. 182 © Michael Weisbrot/The Image Works; p. 186 © Camille Tokerud/Photo Researchers, Inc.; p. 187 Angela Mann; p. 191 JRH/Stock, Boston; p. 193 Stephen Rapley; p. 196 Matthew Lyle; p. 198 Nita Winter; p. 199 Peter Menzel; p. 200 © Jon Burbank/The Image Works; p. 202 Patricia Waldo; p. 206 Antman/The Image Works; p. 207 Roberta Broyer; p. 208 Elizabeth Crews/The Image Works; p. 209 © Shirley Z./Photo Researchers, Inc.; p. 214 Corbis-Bettmann; p. 216 Michael Blanpied; p. 217 Cecilia Mantecon; p. 223 Elizabeth Crews; p. 225 SuperStock; p. 229 (above) Jane Scherr/Jeroboam; p. 229 (below) SuperStock; p. 233 AP/Wide World Photos; p. 235 Patricia Hollander Gross/Stock, Boston; p. 239 Diana Tejo; p. 244 © Danny Brass/Photo Researchers, Inc.; p. 249 AP/Wide World Photos; p. 250 Christopher Brown/Stock, Boston; p. 248 Patricia Waldo; p. 253 Nita Winter; p. 259 & 264 Roberta Broyer; p. 271 Alan Venable; p. 278 Giuliano Colliva/The Image Bank; p. 282 Roger Holden/Photophile; p. 285 © James Carroll/Stock, Boston; p. 287 SuperStock; p. 290 AP/Wide World Photos; p. 293 (left) © Erika Stone/Photo Researchers, Inc.; p. 293 (right) © James Carroll Stock, Boston; p. 298 © Suzanne Arms/The Image Works; p. 299 © Ed Lettao/Photo Researchers, Inc.; p. 303 Adriane Bosworth; p. 310 Corbis-Bettmann; p. 313 Carol Carreon; p. 314 Carolyn Deacy; p. 315 Jean Claude Lejeune/Stock, Boston; p. 317 Cleo Photography/PhotoEdit; p. 322 Tony Freeman/PhotoEdit; p. 324 Margrete Lyons; p. 326 Laurie Campbell; p. 327 Margrete Lyons; p. 329 Alan Carey/The Image Works; p. 331 (above) Peter Menzel/Stock, Boston; p. 331 (below) Margrete Lyons; p. 336 AP/Wide World Photos; p. 338 © Bob Daemmrich/The Image Works; p. 341 Nita Winter; p. 344 Karen Garrison; p. 347 Michael Weisbrot/Stock, Boston; p. 350 MLW/Stock, Boston; p. 352 Robert Ginn/Photophile; p. 354 © Ursula Markas/Photo Researchers, Inc.; p. 359 Robert Ginn/Photophile; p. 361 AP/Wide World Photos; p. 364 Alon Reininger/Woodfin

Camp & Associates; p. 368 Suzanne Astier; p. 371 Jim Mahoney/The Image Works; p. 376 © T. Arruza/The Image Works; p. 378 Carol Carreon; p. 380 Joel Gordon; p. 381 John Maher/Stock, Boston; p. 384 AP/Wide World Photos; p. 385 © Network Prod./The Image Works; p. 394 Brandon Carson; p. 393 © Bachmann/The Image Works; p. 397 Stephen Wilkes/The Image Bank; p. 398 Catherine Linberg; p. 400 Victor Poznanski; p. 401 Karen Garrison; p. 406 Reuters/Corbis-Bettmann; p. 409 Victor Poznanski; p. 410 Robert Kauser; p. 413 Sabra Horne; p. 414 SuperStock; p. 420 Nancy Spellman; p. 428 (above) UPI/Corbis-Bettmann; p. 428 (below) Martha Branch; p. 432 © Lichtenstein/The Image Works; p. 434 Angela Mann; p. 438 AP/Wide World Photos; p. 442 Kent Reno/Jeroboam; p. 443 Jerilyn Emori; p. 446 © B. Daemmrich/The Image Works; p. 449 Tom Tracy/Photophile; p. 453 © B. Daemmrich/Stock, Boston; p. 454 Alex Webb/Magnum Photos; p. 456 UPI/Corbis-Bettmann; p. 468 (above) Bill Ralph; p. 458 (below) Photo Researchers, Inc.; p. 459 © McLaughlin/The Image Works; p. 462 Giraudon/Art Resource, NY; p. 464 SuperStock; p. 465 AP/Wide World Photos; p. 472 Lionel J-M Delevingne/ Stock, Boston; p. 473 Roberta Broyer; p. 475 courtesy of Jean Freeman Deacy; p. 474 Sandra Craig; p. 479 Randy Matusow; p. 486 Bill Gallery /Stock, Boston; p. 491 Super-Stock; p. 493 Karen Garrison; p. 495 AP/Wide World Photos; p. 497 Arthur Grace/Stock, Boston; p. 498 AP/Wide World Photos; p. 500 Patricia Waldo; p. 501 SuperStock; p. 502 & 508 J. Berndt/Stock, Boston; p. 509 California Institute of Technology Archives; p. 510 Patti McConville/ The Image Bank; p. 514 SuperStock; p. 518 © K. Denny MR/PhotoEdit; p. 522 SuperStock; p. 524 Carol Carreon; p. 526 Elizabeth Crews; p. 527 (l) Lucy T. Howat Archives; p. 527 (r) Patricia Waldo; p. 529 Nancy Spellman; p. 532 Karen Hunt; p. 533 Michael Weisbrot/Stock, Boston; p. 535 UPI/Corbis-Bettmann; p. 534 Amy Yates; p. 540 Greenberg/PhotoEdit; p. 542 Bill Ralph; p. 545 Michael Grecco/ Stock, Boston; p. 546 Norman Transcript; p. 550 AP/Wide World Photos; p. 552 Jim Anderson/Woodfin Camp & Associates, Inc.; p. 553 Richard J. Balzen/Stock, Boston; **First Color Section**—clockwise: p. 1 (top) CC Studio/ Science Photo Library; p. 1 (middle) courtesy of Catherine Linberg; p. 1 (bottom) courtesy of Detta Penna; p. 2 (top) Richard Frieman/Photo Researchers, Inc.; p. 2 (middle) Myrleen Ferguson Cate/PhotoEdit; p. 2 (bottom) courtesy of Naomi Angoff Chedd; p. 3 (top) courtesy of Gary M. LaFata; p. 3 (middle) courtesy of Luz Johnston; p. 3 (bottom) Elizabeth Crews; p. 4 (top) courtesy of Michael Blanpied; p. 4

(middle r)courtesy of the Gilbert family; p. 4 (bottom l) courtesy of Catherine Linberg; p. 5 (top) courtesy of Luz Johnston; p. 5 (bottom l) courtesy of Luz Johnston; p. 5 (bottom r) Joseph Schuyler/Stock, Boston; p. 6 (top) courtesy of Jennie Redwitz; p. 6 (middle) courtesy of Jennifer Lee; p. 6 (bottom) courtesy of Yanna Walters; p. 7 (top) SuperStock; p. 7 (middle l) Yva Momatiuk & John Eastcott/The Image Works; p. 7 (bottom r) SuperStock; p. 8 (top) David Young-Wolff/PhotoEdit; p. 8 (middle) courtesy of Catherine Linberg; p. 8 (bottom) PhotoEdit; **Second Color Section**— clockwise: p. 9 (top) Bob Daemmrich/ The Image Works; p. 9 (middle) Myrleen Ferguson Cate/ PhotoEdit; p. 9 (bottom) Tony Freeman/PhotoEdit; p. 10 (top) Elizabeth Crews; p. 10 (middle r) John Boykin/ PhotoEdit; p. 10 (bottom l) David Wells/Stock, Boston; p. 11 (top l) Tony Freeman/PhotoEdit; p. 11 (middle r) Super-Stock; p. 11 (bottom) courtesy of Pat Waldo; p. 12 (top l) SuperStock; p. 12 (top r) SuperStock; p. 12 (bottom) David Young-Wolff/PhotoEdit; p. 13 (top) Shamsi-Basha/The Image Works; p. 13 (middle) courtesy of Jennie Redwitz; p. 13 (bottom) SuperStock; p. 14 (top l) Dana White/ PhotoEdit; p. 14 (middle r) courtesy of Jennie Redwitz; p. 14 (bottom) Barbara Stitzer/PhotoEdit; p. 15 (top) Bob Daemmrich/The Image Works; p. 15 (middle) John Cole/ Stock, Boston; p. 15 (bottom) David Young-Wolff/PhotoEdit; p. 16 (top) courtesy of Thomas O'Neill; p. 16 (bottom l) courtesy of Thomas and Barbara O'Neill; p. 16 (bottom r) Bonnie Kamin/PhotoEdit; **Third Color Section**—clockwise: p. 17 (top) Bonnie Kamin/PhotoEdit; p. 17 (middle) David Young-Wolff/PhotoEdit; p. 17 (bottom) Susan Mary Friedman Fitzer; p. 18 (top l) courtesy of Jennie Redwitz; p. 18 (top r) Doug Menuez/Stock, Boston; p. 18 (bottom) Bob Daemmrich/The Image Works; p. 19 (top) Bob Daemmrich/The Image Works; p. 19 (middle) Frank Siteman/ Stock, Boston; p. 19 (bottom) R. Lord/The Image Works; p. 20 (top) David Young-Wolff/PhotoEdit; p. 20 (middle) courtesy of Detta Penna; p. 20 (bottom) courtesy of Detta Penna; p. 21 (top) Spelvin Archives; p. 21 (middle) courtesy of Susan Friedman; p. 21 (below) Elizabeth Crews/The Image Works; p. 22 (top) Lawrence Migdale/ Stock, Boston; p. 22 (middle) courtesy of Detta Penna; p. 22 (bottom) Barbara Alper/Stock, Boston; p. 23 (top) Bill Aron/PhotoEdit; p. 23 (middle) courtesy of Gloria Leithold; p. 23 (below) Billy E. Barnes/PhotoEdit; p. 24 (top) David Sams/Stock, Boston; p. 24 (middle) SuperStock; p. 24 (bottom) Jerry Howard/Stock, Boston.

Subject and Author Index

Bolitho, F., 371
Bonanno, G. A., 553
Bond, L. C., 149
Bonding, 50, 51t. *See also* Attachment
Bonen, A., 390
Bongar, B., 550
Bonilla, J., 23
Bonneau, D., 300, 301
Bonta, B. D., 218, 219
Boodman, S., 117
Booth, F. W., 497, 498
Borawski-Clark, E., 117
Borden, M. C., 289
Boring, E. G., 262
Borkowski, J. G., 359
Bornstein, M. H., 135, 221, 224
Botella, L., 516
Bottoms, B. L., 297, 298
Botwin, M. D., 424, 480
Botwinick, J., 501
Bouchard, C., 125, 247, 248, 249, 314, 315,
    320, 441
Bouchard, T. J., Jr., 76
Boudreau, J. P., 132, 188
Bouffard, L., 506
Boulton, M. J., 249, 250, 295
Bowen, R., 328
Bower, T. G. R., 138, 142
Bowlby, J., 50, 165, 168
Bowman, B., 172, 224, 240
Bowman, J. M., 106
Boyatzis, C. J., 220
Boyd, G. A., 150
Boyles, M., 51
Bradbard, M. R., 240
Bradley, S. J., 226
Bradshaw, G. L., 260
Braet, C., 247
Braine, L. G., 286
Brakke, K. E., 202
Bramham, D., 43
Branch, C., 549
Branco, K. J., 491
Brand, J. E., 294
Brandt, J., 177
Brannen, J., 347
Brannen, S. J., 129
Bransford, J. D., 258
Braunwald, K. G., 168
Brazelton, T. B., 113, 115
Brazelton Neonatal Behavioral Assessment Scale
    (NBAS), 113
Breastfeeding, 124–125
    changing patterns in, 126
    pros and cons of, 128t
Brecher, E. M., 502
Brendt, R. L., 100
Brenner, J., 223
Breslau, N., 117
Bresnahan, K., 100
Bretherton, I., 149
Brick, P., 359
Bridges, L. J., 170
Briggs, A. H., 77
Brisk, M. E., 209
Britner, P. A., 240
Britten, C. M., 543
Brodaty, H., 500
Brodersen, L., 171
Brodigan, D. E., 443
Broerse, J., 148
Bromley, D. B., 451, 506, 507, 546
Bronfenbrenner, U., 51, 240
    ecological systems theory of, 53–55
Bronson, G. W., 163
Bronstein, P., 231, 234

Bronzino, J., 96, 105
Brookins, C. C., 410
Brooks, J. B., 232
Brooks-Gunn, J., 200, 230, 316, 348, 355, 358,
    359, 363
Brouwer, A., 494
Brown, B. B., 348, 349, 350
Brown, J., 369
Brown, J. K., 176
Brown, J. L., 157
Brown, J. S., 262
Brown, K., 220
Brown, R., 146, 203
Brownell, K. D., 320
Bruce, B., 323
Bruce, F., 240
Bruner, J. S., 55, 147, 205
Brunner, S., 100
Bryan, T., 367
Bryant, B. K., 288
Bryant, N. A., 11
Buchanan, C. M., 343
Buchanan, N. R., 223
Buchholz, E. S., 105
Buitendijk, S., 97
Buka, S. L., 99, 100
Bukowski, W. M., 288
Bulimia nervosa, 322–323, 323t
    medical consequences of, 322t
    prevalence rates of, 321f
Bullinger, A., 48
Bullock, J. R., 11, 285, 286
Bullock, M., 194
Bullough, B., 415
Bullough, V. L., 415
Bullying, 279, 336
Bult, P., 498
Bunce, D., 75
Bunce, V. L., 492, 531
Burant, C. J., 532
Burgard, D., 320
Burgess, D., 187
Burkam, D. T., 353
Burkart, B., 176
Burke, J., 364
Burleson, B. R., 413
Burnett, B. B., 298
Burnett, C. K., 424
Burns, A., 234, 236, 237
Burr, D. C., 135
Burrows, E. A., 97
Burrows, R. F., 97
Burton, L. M., 299
Bushey, N., 505
Bushnell, E. W., 132, 188
Buss, A. H., 158, 159
Buss, D. M., 424, 480
Busse, J., 353
Bussey, K., 334
Butler, E. R., 313
Butler, J. R., 299
Butler, R. N., 499, 518
Butterworth, G., 149
Butterworth, S. W., 381
Buzzelli, C. A., 334
Byczkowski, J. Z., 125
Bynner, J. M., 396
Bynum, T.S., 5
Byrne, B. M., 340
Byrne, G. J., 553
Bystander apathy, 330–331

Cabau, A., 97
Caffeine, fetal effects of, 99
Cain, J., 551
Cain, W. S., 501

Cairns, R. B., 73
Caldwell, B., 13, 199
Calkins, E., 498, 499
Camp, B. W., 359
Campbell, A., 418, 479, 480
Campbell, F. A., 255
Campbell, L., 232
Campbell, N. J., 535
Campbell, R., 19
Campbell, S. B., 115
Campos, J. J., 135
Canada
    age distribution in, 14f
    AIDS cases in, 103f
    birth rates in, 107, 108f, 426f
    demographic changes in, 489f, 490f
    fertility rates in, 108f
    single-parent households in, 228
    women in work force, 454f
Canada Yearbook, 108, 228, 330, 392, 414,
    416–417
Canadian Sourcebook, 229, 236, 421
Canaff, A. L., 520, 522
Canalization, 70–71, 72t
Canapary, A., 550
Canning, P. M., 197
Cantor, C. H., 370
Cantwell, D., 303
Capuzzo, E., 176
Cardinal properties of numbers, 256
Care
    of children. *See* Day care
    of elderly, 531–534
    of premature infants, 118
    of terminally ill, 549
Care, A. E., 396
Career(s)
    and childbearing decisions, 427
    definition of, 391
    double, 457
    dual, 456–457
Career change(s)
    in late adulthood, 508, 523
    in midlife, 457–459
Career preparation, 390–398, 399t
    developmental models, 394–396
    factors influencing, 396
    and identity formation, 345–346
    job-person matching, 392–394, 394t
    life-span, life-space theory of, 395t, 395–396
Caregivers, nonparental, 239–241
Carey, W. B., 159, 160
Cargo, A. P., 302
Carlo, G., 219
Carlo, M. S., 262
Carlson, C., 303
Carlson, M., 280
Carlson, S. M., 222
Carlson, V., 168, 300
Carlton, L., 85
Carmelli, D., 495
Carpenter, B. D., 551
Carpenter, D. J., 368
Carroll, J. C., 330, 331
Carson, B. S., 177
Carta, I., 371
Cartwright, B. S., 222
Casas, J. F., 292
Case, R., 258
Casey, D. M., 292
Caspi, A., 77, 78, 364
Cassidy, J., 168
Castigation, 40, 41t
Castle, J., 145
Cataldo, J. R., 480, 481
Cattell, R. B., 263

Caughy, M. O., 240
Causation, versus correlation, 18
Cazzullo, C. L., 371
CDF. See Children's Defense Fund
Ceci, S. J., 289
Celiberti, D. A., 178
Cell division, 68, 72t
Cell error theory, 494
Center for Disease Control, 250
Cephalocaudal development, 134
Cerebral palsy, 176, 177t, 178t
    causes of, 127
    genetic transmission of, 86t
CERs. See Conditioned emotional reactions
Cesarean delivery, 111, 112f
Chalmers, B., 115
Chamard, S. E., 433
Chan, A. K. H., 251
Change
    and continuity, 1
    human development and, 5
    intraindividual, longitudinal studies and, 18, 19
Chapman, K., 432
Chapman, P., 319
Chappell, P. A., 188
Charlesworth, W. R., 77, 219
Chase, L. I., 294
Chase-Lansdale, P. L., 355, 358, 359, 363
Chatoor, I., 321
Chazan, E., 220
Chemicals, prenatal effects of, 98–99, 102t
Cheminal, R., 177
Chen, C., 289
Chen, T. H., 263, 451
Cheng, Pui-wan, 273
Cherian, V. I., 419
Cherny, N. I., 551
Chervenak, J. L., 105
Chess, S., 158, 159, 160
Chester, R. D., 274
Cheung, P. C., 174
Cheung, R. T. F., 505, 506
Cheung, Y. W., 369
Chevrel, J., 300, 301
Chez, R. A., 105
Child(ren)
    abandoned. See Abandoned children
    adopted, studies of, 77, 77t
    demographic changes and, 11–12
    in developing countries, 8, 9–10
    feral (wild), 63, 64–65
    historical trends in treatment of, 6–12, 12t
    of homosexual parents, 416
    in industrialized countries, 10
    lifespan perspective on, 5
    maltreatment of, 7, 295–301
    in medieval Europe, 6–7
    in nineteenth century, 7–9
    research with, ethical issues in, 24
    rights of, 12–13, 13t
    scientific study of, roots of, 6
    understanding of death by, 543–544
    war and, 10, 11
    See also Early childhood; Middle childhood; Infant(s)
Child care. See Day care
Child labor, 7–9, 10
Child rearing, 427–429
Childbearing decisions, 426–427, 427f
Childbirth. See Birth(s)
Child-directed speech, 205–206
    toward elderly, 491–492
Children's Defense Fund (CDF), 11
Childs, J., 285
Chin, W., 288

China
    birth rates in, 107
    filial piety in, 333, 463–464
Chiocca, E. M., 297
Chipman, M., 176
Chipman, S. F., 353
Chiriboga, D. A., 478
Chisolm, G. B., 535
Chlamydia, 360
Cho, N. H., 105
Chodzko-Zajko, W. J., 498
Chomsky, N., 204
Choquet, M., 322
Chorionic villus biopsy (CVS), 85, 87t
Chrisman, A. B., 464
Christakis, N. A., 549
Christensen, H., 505
Christensen, K. M., 138
Christian, L., 274
Christie, N. G., 313
Christopher, F. S., 359
Christopherson, V. A., 231
Chromosomal disorders, 82–84, 84t
    parental age and, 83, 83f
Chromosomes, 68, 72t
    sex, 68, 72t
Chung, T. K., 447
Cicchetti, D., 168, 300
Ciesielski, K. T., 178
Cintra, L., 96, 105
Circular reactions, in infants, 143, 144, 146t
Cisero, C. A., 262
Claes, M., 363
Clark, L. A., 231
Clark, M. L., 286
Clarke, R. T., 290
Clarke-Stewart, K. A., 172, 239, 240
Classes, children's understanding of, 255, 257t
Classical conditioning, 38–39, 39f
Classification problems, preschoolers and, 194
Clausen, S. E., 184, 366
Clauson, J., 231, 234
Claxton, J. W., 548
Clayton, G. M., 505, 506, 507
Clayton, V. P., 509
Cleft palate, genetic transmission of, 86t
Clerici, M., 371
Clifford, B. R., 294
Clifton, R. K., 140
Climacteric, 445–447, 448t
Cloning, 67
Club foot, genetic transmission of, 86t
Coakley, M., 299
Coates, T. J., 361
Cobb, P., 48
Cocaine, 369
    intoxication among breast-feeding infants, 125
    prenatal effects of, 100–101
Cognitive decline, normal versus pathological, 451
Cognitive development
    in adolescence, 323–326, 327t
    in adulthood
        early, 398–402, 402t
        late, 503–508, 508t
        middle, 447–453, 453t
    in childhood
        early, 189–197
        middle, 252–275
    in infancy, 138–145, 152t
        factors shaping, 141, 141t
    information-processing approach to, 256–257, 263t, 325–326, 327t
    motor development and, 188

Piaget's theory of, 45–49, 48t
Cognitive strategies
    in adolescence, 326
    teaching, 262
Cognitive-behavior therapy, 323
Cohabitation, 414–415
Cohen, G. R., 111
Cohen, S., 291, 294, 295, 430
Cohler, B. J., 473, 518
Cohn, E., 432
Cohn, J. B., 77
Cohn, J. F., 115
Cohort
    versus age, separating effect of, 20
    definition of, 20
Colborn, T., 98
Colby, A., 334, 335
Cole, A. G., 323
Cole, P. G., 269
Cole, P. M., 302
Colella, U., 415
Coleman, A., 520
Coleman, J. S., 378, 379
    transitional tasks of, 379t, 379–380
Coleman, P. G., 519
Coleman, P. M., 446
Colic, 160
Collett, J., 209
Collins, A., 262
Collins, C., 474
Collins, J. A., 97
Collins, N. L., 115
Collins, W. A., 170, 174
Commitment, 412
Committee on Drugs, American Academy of Pediatrics, 125
Common-law marriage, 414, 415
Communes, 418
Communication, without language, 145
Compensatory preschool programs, 200–202, 202t
Competition, versus cooperation, 217–219, 219t
Conception, 66–67, 72t
Conceptualization, 134
Concrete operational thinking, 47, 48t, 252–256, 257t
Conditioned emotional reactions (CERs), 39
Conditioned response (CR), 39
Conditioned stimulus (CS), 39
Conditioning, 38
    classical, 38–39, 39f
    operant (instrumental), 39–41, 40f
Conflict(s)
    and dialectical thinking, 400
    life review and resolution of, 519
    marital, 422–423
        versus divorce, 238
        divorce and, 236–237
    in middle years, 474
    parent-adolescent, 348, 351t
    and psychosocial development, 408
Confluence Model, 232
Congenital heart disease, genetic transmission, 86t
Conger, P. R., 498, 519
Connell, J. P., 170
Connelly, S. L., 219
Connidis, I. A., 473
Conservation problems, mastery of
    in early childhood, 194
    in middle childhood, 253–255, 257t
    tests of, 254f
Constructivism, 48
Consummate love, 412, 412t
Conte, G. L., 100

Context
  average, 25
  developmental, 5
  levels of, in Bronfenbrenner's theory, 54, 54t
Contextual theory of intelligence, 263–264,
  264f
Continuous societies, 312, 319t, 347
Control, personal, development of, 45
Control group, 17
Convergent thinking, 272
Conversation, language and, 211, 212t
Converse, P. E., 479
Cooke, B., 230
Cooksey, E. C., 355
Cooley, C. H., theory of self-esteem, 282, 283t
Coombs, R. H., 423
Cooney, T. M., 472
Cooper, Anthony Ashley, 8
Cooperation, versus competition, 217–219,
  219t
Cooperation board, four-person, 217–218, 218f
Cooperative play, 223–224, 224t
Coovert, D. L., 321
Copeland, L. A., 341
Corbin, C. B., 250
Corby, N., 424
Corlett, E. S., 468
Correlational fallacy, 17–18
Correlational studies, 17–18, 22t
Correy, J. F., 97
Corty, E., 432
Costa, P. T., Jr., 471, 476, 477, 478, 535
Costigan, K. A., 158
Côté, J. E., 345, 408
Cotman, C. W., 140
Coughlin, C., 366
Coulter, D. L., 268
Coupland, J., 492
Coupland, N., 492
Courage, M. L., 190
Courtright, J. A., 294
Courts, children and, 7, 261–262
Cousins, J. H., 329, 330
Coustan, D. R., 101
Covell, K., 220
Coward, R. T., 397, 432, 474, 532
Cowart, B. J., 138
Cowen, E. L., 44
Cox, H. G., 528, 529
Cox, T. C., 368
Cox-Ganser, J., 176
Coy, K. C., 335
CR. See Conditioned response
Crack, 369
Crago, M., 320, 321
Craik, F. I. M., 504, 505
Cramer, C. P., 138
Crawford, M. A., 126
Crawford, P. B., 320
Creasy, R. K., 115
Creativity
  adult, 452t, 452–453
  child, 271–274
  elements of, 412
  tests of, 272, 272t
Cretinism, 101, 127
Cribb, A., 544, 548
Crick, N. R., 288, 292
Crime, international comparisons, 43, 295
Criqui, M. H., 235
Crisis, midlife, 467, 470–471
Critical period
  in imprinting, 49–50, 51t
  in language development, 204
  in mother-infant bonding, 165
Crittenden, P. M., 300

Crockett, L. J., 316
Crosbie-Burnett, M., 416
Cross-linking theory of cell malfunction, 494
Cross-sectional study, 16, 18
  advantages and disadvantages of, 20, 22t
Crouter, A. C., 225
Crowell, J. A., 171
Crying, infant, 161–162, 164t
Crystal, D. S., 288
Crystallized intelligence, 263, 450–451, 451f
  age and changes in, 505, 506f
CS. See Conditioned stimulus
Cultural-historical theory, Vygotsky's, 51–53, 53t
  critique of, 55
Culture(s)
  and aging, 495, 496
  and child abuse, 297
  and competition versus cooperation, 218
  and gender roles, 175
  and human development
    Bronfenbrenner's view of, 53
    Vygotsky's view of, 51–52, 53t
  and infant attachment, 169
  and infant temperament, 160–161
  and intelligence tests, 267
  and moral development, 333
  and parenting, 174
  and play, 224
  and self, 343
  studies across, ecological validity of, 22–23
Cunningham, H., 7
Cupples, L. A., 384, 445
Curcio, C. A., 442
Curran, J. T., 97
Curtiss, S., 65, 205, 210
Curtius, H. C., 81
Cushing, G., 366
Cutright, M. C., 284
CVS. See Chorionic villus biopsy
Cyclic movements, infant, 132, 165
Cytomegalovirus, fetal effects of, 102
Cziko, G. A., 209

Dalton, K., 115
Dalton, T. C., 65
D'Amico, R., 80
Damon, W., 335
D'Andrea, D., 207
Dansky, B. S., 430
Dantonio, M., 284
Darley, J. M., 330, 333
Darling, C. A., 355, 356
Darling-Fischer, C. S., 409
Darragh, J., 169
Darwin, Charles, 15, 16t
Das, A., 297
Das, J. P., 52
Datan, N., 447, 477, 507
Dating behavior, in adolescence, 356t, 356f
D'Augelli, A. R., 415
Davidson, D. H., 200
Davidson, J. K., Sr., 356
Davies, C., 543
Davies, G. M., 261, 262
Davies, H., 457, 549
Davies, I., 494
Davies, M., 232
Davis, D. W., 176
Davis, L. B., 138
Dawis, R. V., 397
Dawkins, M. P., 367
Dawson, D. S., 68
Dawson, G., 178
Day, A. T., 523, 535
Day, R. D., 237
Day care, 199, 239–241

effects of, 172–173, 240
high-quality, characteristics of, 240–241, 241t
Daydreaming, 222
de Boysson-Bardies, B., 149
de Fockert, J., 480
de Haan, M., 136
de Jonge, J., 295
de St. Aubin, E., 519
de Vries, B., 518
De Wet, D. H., 115
Deafness, 251
  genetic transmission of, 86t
Deal, L. V., 149
Deary, I. J., 386
Deater-Deckard, K., 457
Death and dying, 541–556, 554t
  adolescents' understanding of, 544
  adult notions of, 544–545
  bereavement and grief following, 552–555
  in childbirth, 109
  children's understanding of, 543–544
  defining, 542–543
  denial of, 543, 548
  fear of, 542, 544–545
  intelligence drop prior to, 506
  leading causes of, 383–384, 547f
  parental, impact of, 474
  of spouse, 530
  stages of, 546–548, 548t
  theoretical explanations for, 494
  trajectories of, 548–549
DeBlassie, R. R., 358
Debry, G., 99
DeCasper, A. J., 138
Deception, and theory of mind, 280
Declarative memory, 259–260, 263t
Deductive reasoning, 193
Defense mechanisms, Freudian, 34t
Deficiency needs, 56, 56f, 57t
DeGenova, M. K., 520, 535
Dekle, D. J., 261
Dekovic, M., 287, 345, 346
Delamothe, K., 261
Delinquency, 362–364, 372t
Delivery, 110, 110f
DeLong, G. R., 127
Demaris, A., 414, 415
DeMause, L., 12
DeMeis, D. K., 457
Demetriou, A., 326
Demo, D. H., 237, 457
Demographic changes
  effect on children, 11–12
  longevity and, 488–489, 489f, 490f
  in U.S., 207, 208, 489f, 490f
Dempsey, J. A., 443
Denham, S. A., 219, 220, 223
Denial, as defense mechanism, 34t
Dennis, W., 65, 452, 511
Denoroy, L., 129
Denver Developmental Screening Test, 187,
  187t
Deoxyribonucleic acid. See DNA
Dependent variables, 16
Depinet, R. L., 267
Depression
  postpartum, 115
  and infant temperament, 160, 161
  and suicide, 371, 550
Derby, S. E., 491
DES. See Diethylstilbestrol
Desmyter, J., 115
Despair, versus integrity, 36t, 37, 516
Determinism, reciprocal, 53–54
Deuel, R. K., 177
Developing countries

Levings, C., 505
Levinson, D. J., 457
   seasons of man's life, 466–468, 467*f*
Levitt, A. G., 149
Levitt, M. J., 529
Levy, G. D., 225
Levy, J., 132
Lew, W. J. F., 174
Lewis, C. A., 480
Lewis, K. G., 416
Lewis, M., 258
Liben, L., 195
Liberman, A. M., 149
Libido, 32
Liddell, D. L., 415
Lieberman, A. B., 111
Lieberman, M. A., 470, 554
Life expectancy, 14, 492–496, 493*t*
   age-based, 544, 545*f*
   versus lifespan, 494
Life review, 399–400, 518–520, 520*t*
Life trajectories, 548–549
Life-cycle approach to family, 425*f*, 425–429
Lifespan, 494
   factors influencing, 495–496
Life-span, life-space career development model, 395*t*, 395–396
Lifespan developmental psychology, 4
   roots of, 6
   themes of, 4–5, 6*t*
Lifestyle(s)
   alternative nonexclusive, 420*t*
   choices of, 413–418, 418*t*
   old age and revision of, 517
Liggins, G. C., 107
Lignitz, E., 297
Lin, L. S., 319
Lindauer, B. K., 259, 261
Lindenberger, U., 507
Linder, K., 320
Lindstrom, P., 363
Linn, M. C., 353
Linn, R., 416
Lipper, E. G., 117
Little Albert, 39
Little's disease, 176
Livesey, D. J., 353
Living will, 551*f*
Lobel, M., 115
Lobel, T. E., 396
Locke, J. L., 149
Locke, John, 13–14, 16*t*
Lockhart, A. S., 249
Lockman, J. J., 131
Loehlin, J. C., 77
Loesch, L. C., 299
Loffredo, C., 97
Logan, R. L., 466
Logic
   adolescents and, 324–325
   rules of, 253–255
Logli, P. A., 101
Lohaus, A., 253
Loneliness
   among adolescents, 350–351, 351*t*
   among elderly, 529
Long, J., 471, 522
Long, P., 363
Long, V. O., 351
Longevity, 495–496
Longitudinal study, 15–16, 18
   advantages and disadvantages of, 19–20, 22*t*
Longstreth, G. F., 386
Long-term memory, 258*f*, 258–259, 259*t*
   in late adulthood, 503–504, 505

types of, 259–260, 260*f*, 263*t*
Lonsway, K. A., 433
Lookabaugh, S. L., 171
Looking-glass self, 282, 283*t*
Looney, M. A., 247, 250
Lorber, D., 286
Lorenz, K., 49
Los, M., 433
Losoya, S., 220
Loss of subjects, in longitudinal study, 19
Lott, I., 140
Lotyczewski, B. S., 44
Lourenco, O., 196
Love, 408, 411–413, 418*t*
   beginning of, 413
   categories of, 412*t*
   in Maslow's hierarchy of needs, 56*f*
   measuring, 411, 411*t*
   triangular theory of, 411–412, 412*f*
Loy, N., 176
LSD, 368
Lu, L., 459, 480, 481
Lukasiewicz, J. M., 391
Luke, C., 294
Lupart, J. L., 273
Luqmani, R., 494
Luria, Z., 175
Luthar, S. S., 366
Luyendijk, W., 162
Lye, D. N., 422
Lymphoid system, development in infants, 126, 127*f*
Lynam, D., 364
Lyne, J., 50
Lynn, T. D., 381
Lyon, M., 321
Lyon, M. E., 197

Maccoby, E. E., 227, 353
MacConnie, S., 248
MacDonald, W., 414, 415
Machado, A., 196
Mack, J., 124
Mackinnon-Lewis, C., 288
MacLeod, C., 220
MacNeal, J. U., 294
Macrae, J. H., 501
Macrae, W. A., 549
Macrosystem, in Bronfenbrenner's theory, 54, 54*t*
Madak, P. R., 301
Madan, R., 98
Madonna, P. G., 300
Madsen, K., 434
Madsen, M. C., 217, 218, 219
Maes, B., 83
Magnin, G., 300, 301
Magnusson, D., 316
Mahoney, M. J., 57
Main, M., 168
Maing, D. M., 226
Mainstreaming, 251, 274
Major gene determination, 69, 72*t*
Makin, J. W., 138
Malafosse, A., 177
Malatesta, C. Z., 161
Malaysia, crime and punishment in, 43
Malcarno, V. L., 290
Malec, J. F., 505
Males, M., 104, 357, 358, 359, 360
Malina, R. M., 125, 247, 248, 249, 314, 315, 316, 320, 441
Malnutrition
   in developing countries, 246, 246*f*, 247
   during pregnancy, fetal effects of, 96, 126–127

Malonebeach, E. E., 527
Maltas, C., 474
Maltreatment, child, 295–301, 301*t*
   consequences of, 299–301
   nature of, 296–299
   prevalence of, 295–296
   and school performance, 18–19
Mandich, M., 131
Manfredi, R., 322
Manic-depressive psychosis, 86*t*
Manning, A., 102
Manning, G. F., 524
Manning, W. D., 414
Mansfield, E., 519
Marcellini, F., 529
Marcia, J. E., 344, 345
Marcoen, A., 519
Marcon, R. A., 199
Marcus, D. B., 472
Margulis, C., 151
Marijuana, 367–368
   fetal effects of, 100
Marital conflict(s), 422–423
   versus divorce, 238
   divorce and, 236–237
   in middle years, 474
Marjoribanks, K., 232, 233
Marker genes, 71, 72*t*
Markides, K., 481
Marks, L. E., 135
Marks, M. N., 7
Marlatt, G. A., 367
Marriage(s), 419–424, 424*t*
   child's influence on, 156
   cohabitation and, 415
   common-law, 414, 415
   first, median age of, 419*f*
   and happiness, 423*f*, 423–424, 480–481
   in Japan, 456
   median duration of, 420*f*
   in middle age, 474–476
   in old age, 528–529, 531*f*
   types of, 421–424, 422*f*
Marshman, J. A., 368
Marsiglio, W., 359
Martin, Anne, 7
Martin, C. E., 354
Martin, C. L., 226
Martin, H., 481
Martin, J. C., 100
Martin, M. E., 320
Martin, N., 76
Martin, P., 317, 505, 506, 507
Martino, A. M., 100
Maslow, Abraham, humanistic theory of, 56–57, 57*t*
Mason, M. A., 238
Masters, W. H., 387
Mastery-oriented people, 44, 290–291
Masturbation, in adolescence, 356
Masur, E. F., 145, 148, 151
Maszk, P., 220
Mate selection, 413–414
Mathematics achievement, cultural comparison, 22
Matheny, K. B., 232, 233
Mathews, A., 220
Mathieu, P. S., 458
Matsuba, M. K., 333
Matsui, K., 382
Matsumoto, K., 382
Matsuoka, A., 81
Matte, B., 389
Matthews, G. P., 297
Maturation, 141, 141*t*

Onetto, P., 446, 447
Onlooker play, 223, 224t
Ontogeny, and phylogeny, 15
Open systems, 53
Operant conditioning, 39–41, 40f
Oppositional defiant disorder, 304
Oral rehydration therapy (ORT), 10
Oral stage, in psychosexual development, 33, 34t
Orcesi, S., 176
Ordinal properties of numbers, 256
O'Reilly, A. W., 224
Organizing, and remembering, 260–261
Orgasm, 388
Orienting response, in newborn, 131, 139
Oriot, D., 300, 301
Ornstein, P. A., 191
Orr, R. L., 433
ORT. *See* Oral rehydration therapy
O'Shea, J., 381
Osteoporosis, 499
Osterling, J., 178
Ostrov, E., 342, 343–344, 362
Other-directed regulatory behaviors, 163–164, 164t
Otitis media, 251
Ovcharchyn, C. A., 387
Over, R., 427
Ovlisen, B., 111
Ovum, 66–67
    division of, 68
    fertilized, 93f, 93–94
Owen, M., 530
Owens, E. B., 168
Ozar, L. A., 290
Ozturk, M., 171
Ozturk, O. M., 171

Packard, V., 355
Packer, A. B., 391
Padgett, R. J., 505
Paikoff, R. L., 348
Pain, newborn's sensitivity to, 138
Pain cry, 162, 164t
Painter, K., 102, 103
Pajares, F., 44
Paley, V. G., 221, 227
Palliative care, 549
Palmar reflex, 131, 132t
Palmer, J. H., 369
Palmgren, C., 329
Palmlund, I., 97
Palo, P., 113
Palomaki, G. E., 85
Pandey, H., 197
Pangrazi, R. P., 250
Papadaki, M., 326
Pape, K. E., 176
Pappas, D. M., 550
Parallel play, 223, 224t
Parent(s)
    abusive, characteristics of, 300
    aging, relations with, 473–474
    and juvenile delinquency, 363
    versus peers, conformity to, 286–287, 287f
    teenage, 104–105, 358–359, 362t
    See also Parent-child relations; Parenting
Parental alienation syndrome (PAS), 236
Parental disengagement, and child's social competence, 237
Parent-child relations
    in adolescence, 346–348, 350, 351t
    in adulthood
        early, 409
        late, 525–527
        middle, 472–473

in infancy. *See* Parent-infant attachment
    interactive (bidirectional) influences in, 156, 160, 205
Parent-infant attachment, 50, 164–170
    child care and, 172
    stages of, 166–168, 169t
    studying, 165–166
    types of, 166, 167t
Parenting
    of adolescents, 347–348, 351t, 472
    effects on children, 230–231, 232t
    effects on parents, 427–429
    of infants, 174–175
    information on, sources of, 231–232, 232t
    of preschoolers, 228–230
    and self-esteem, development of, 284
    styles of, 228–230, 230t, 232t
        intergenerational transmission of, 231
        and morality development, 335
        and peer relationships, 287
    temperament of child and, 160
Paris, S. G., 259, 261
Park, K. A., 221, 223, 285
Parke, R. D., 219
Parker, G. R., 44
Parker, J. G., 289
Parkes, C. M., 553, 554
Parkhurst, J. T., 288
Parkinson's disease, 499
Parnell, 13
Parten, M. B., 223
PAS. *See* Parental alienation syndrome
Pasley, K., 239, 476
Pasnak, R., 255
Passino, A. W., 359
Passion, 412
Passman, R. H., 162, 171
Patel, B. D., 83
Patel, J., 176
Patricelli, P., 366
Pattee, L., 288
Patterson, C. J., 416
Patterson, I., 524
Patterson, M. L., 78
Patton, J. M., 271
Patton, J. R., 268
Paul, R., 137, 138, 203
Pavlov, Ivan, 38
Payne, T. F., 140
PCBs. *See* Polychlorinated biphenyls
Pearce, J. C., 184, 274
Pearl, R., 367
Pearson, J. C., 474
Pease-Alvarez, L., 207, 208
Peck, R. C., 509
    on developmental tasks, 465–466, 466f, 516–517
Pedlow, R., 160
Peer group(s), 286
    acceptance by, 287–288
        consequences of, 288–289
    in adolescence, 348–350, 351t
    in childhood, 286–287, 287f
    and delinquency, 363
Peiser, N. C., 363
Pelaez-Nogueras, M., 206
Pelham, W. E., Jr., 303
Pellman, J., 530
Pelvic inflammatory disease (PID), 361
Penalty, 40–41, 41t
Pendergast, D. R., 498, 499
Penner, L. A., 321
Pentz, M. A., 367
Peplau, L. A., 416
Perception, definition of, 134
Pereyra, P. M., 129

Pergament, E., 87, 88
Perkins, D., 262, 267
Perkins, H. W., 457
Perl, M., 323
Perlmutter, M., 140, 500, 501, 503, 504, 505, 508
Permissive parenting, 229, 230t
Perner, J., 280
Perry, P., 255
Personal fable, 328, 330t
Personal narratives, 518–519
Personality
    age and changes in, 477–478
    and delinquency, 363
    genes and, 69
    genetic versus context influences on, 76–77
    of gifted children, 272–273
    and happiness, 480, 535
    levels of, in Freud's theory, 32, 33f
    and marital satisfaction, 423–424
    versus temperament, 158
    types of, 476–477
Persuasion, and self-efficacy judgments, 44, 46t
Peruzzi, N., 550
Peter Pan syndrome, 377, 378
Peters, H., 100
Peters, N. D., 532
Petersen, A. C., 315, 316
Peterson, C. C., 528
Peterson, C. M., 102
Peterson, G. W., 237
Peterson, H. B., 443
Peterson, K. L., 328
Pettle, S. A., 543
Petzel, T. P., 387
Phallic stage, in psychosexual development, 33, 34t
Phares, V., 170
Phelan, J. P., 137, 138
Phelps, L. H., 471
Phenomenology, 55, 57t
Phenotype, 69–70, 70f, 72t
Phenylketonuria (PKU), 81, 84t
Phillips, D. A., 240
Phillips, S., 396
Phillipson, C., 525
Philps, A., 439
Phonemes, 146
Phylactos, A., 126
Phylogeny, ontogeny and, 15
Physical abuse, of children, 297–298
Physical appearance
    concerns in adolescence, 317
    infant preferences for, 136
    late adulthood and changes in, 497
    middle adulthood and changes in, 440–442
    and self-worth, 283, 284t
Physical development
    in adolescence, 313–318
    in adulthood
        early, 380–383, 388t
        late, 497–503, 503t
        middle, 440–447, 448t
    in childhood
        early, 183–189, 189t
        middle, 246–252
    in infancy, 125–128, 127f, 128t
Physical growth. *See* Growth
Physical neglect, 298
Piaget, Jean, 48, 323, 331
    basic ideas of, 140–141
    cognitive development theory of, 45–49, 48t
    concept of childhood, 14
    on language development, 204
    on language-thought interactions, 210
    on moral development, 331–332

Topical Arrangement of Contents